LICENSING OF INTELLECTUAL PROPERTY AND OTHER INFORMATION ASSETS

LICENSING OF INTELLECTUAL PROPERTY AND OTHER INFORMATION ASSETS

RAYMOND T. NIMMER
Leonard H. Childs Professor of Law
Co-Director, Intellectual Property and Information Law Institute
University of Houston Law Center

 LexisNexis

Library of Congress Cataloging-in-Publication Data

Nimmer, Raymond T., 1944—

Licensing of intellectual property and other information assets / Raymond T. Nimmer.
    p. cm.
    Includes index.
    ISBN 1-4224-1765-4 (hardbound)
    1. Intellectual property—United States. 2. License agreements—United States.
    3. Copyright and electronic data processing—United States. I. Title
                                          2007935887

NOTE TO USERS
**To ensure that you are using the latest materials available in this area,
please be sure to periodically check the LexisNexis Law School web site
for downloadable updates and supplements at www.lexisnexis.com/
lawschool**

Editorial Offices
744 Broad Street, Newark, NJ 07102 (973) 820-2000
201 Mission St., San Francisco, CA 94105-1831 (415) 908-3200
701 East Water Street, Charlottesville, VA 22902-7587 (434) 972-7600
www.lexis.com

(Pub. 3202)

PREFACE

This is a book about licensing law. The fact that licensing of intellectual property and other information assets has become a focus for law school discussion and for treatment in many courts and legislatures testifies to the power of the information economy which has transformed how we think about economic value, commercial and mass-market transactions, and the nature of law.

For many, these materials and the course in which they are used will be seen as an extension of intellectual property law. Indeed, many contractual licenses relate to intellectual property assets and, in that sense, this subject matter is the transactional manifestation of the intellectual property field. For the intellectual property lawyer, whether focused on copyright, patent, trademark or other similar law, a license is one of the primary means by which those assets are commercially exploited. Although, several generations ago, most lawyers and many companies engaged in practice and commerce without ever encountering a license transaction, that is no longer true. As a flexible transaction to grant and allocate rights in informational subject matter, licenses have become an integral and widespread part of modern commerce. These materials address many of the transactional issues that these transactions entail.

For others, these materials and this course can be viewed as an advanced contract law course. Indeed, licenses are contracts and the issues we discuss here often entail advanced applications of contract law principles. Licensing law is a form of commercial contract law, and the issues these transactions present are increasingly important to the practice and the theory of contract law. Reflecting this aspect of the subject matter, in this book, you will encounter ordinary case law material, but also a number of problems that point toward the role of law here in relation to transactions and commercial practice.

For still others, these materials provide insight to law and practices associated with transactions in the digital industries in online commerce.

In sum, for licensing law, as for other important areas of law, the issues here touch on many aspects of society and commerce. As happens often in our society, sea changes in commerce work important changes and adaptations in law and legal practice. The topics addressed here go to the essence of the new economy, and their treatment in law and practice will shape the future.

October 4, 2004
Raymond T. Nimmer

TABLE OF CONTENTS

Part I: GENERAL ISSUES

Chapter 1

NATURE OF A LICENSE AND APPLICABLE LAW

I. WHAT IS A LICENSE?

A license is a contract.

A license contract deals with rights, permissions and restrictions related to the use of information assets and intellectual property and with contractual and other obligations associated with the exchange in which these rights, permissions or restrictions are transferred. The contract is distinguished from other types of contracts by its primary subject matter (e.g. information, access to information, intellectual property rights, etc.) and by how it deals with that subject matter. In this book, we take a close look at the law and practice of licensing information.

Licenses of information are a centerpiece of the modern economy. A license, however, is only one of a number of contractual and other relationships that can be, and are, used to distribute information and intellectual property rights. In practice, of course, a good deal of information is given away or freely disseminated. But most licenses are part of a commercial transaction where the person transferring the information, access, or rights places limitations on its use and retains rights in the information or the system to which access is permitted. As one court observed, "a license . . . is a transfer of limited rights, less than the whole interest which might have been transferred." *Exxon Corp. v. Oxxford Clothes, Inc.*, 109 F.3d 1070, 1076 (5th Cir. 1997).

Licensing of informational assets is an old practice. In the mid-1800s, for example, licenses between Dun and Bradstreet and its clients limited the client's use of the business data transferred to it. But today, licensing is a significant aspect of virtually all areas of commerce that deal with information or information services. Licensing practice has been introduced to ordinary citizens in the licensing of software, telecommunications services, online resources, and other ordinary facets of the digital age. The practice of licensing information and informational rights is central not only in commercial practice between two or more businesses, but also in the modern mass retail market.

Licenses are often contrasted with assignments of rights in information. The novice can think of an "assignment" as the equivalent of a sale of all rights in the intangible subject matter and not be far wrong. Commercial practice, however, frequently blurs the line between a license and an assignment. The fundamental difference between a license and an assignment is that, while licenses and assignments both focus on rights in, or use of information, in an assignment the original rights owner tends to divest itself of rights in the subject matter, while in a license the transferor ("licensor") retains more rights in the subject matter of the license. It can do this not only because the parties have agreed to a transaction that enables a split of ownership and use rights in the information, but because unlike hard goods, information can be both transferred and retained. Raymond T. Nimmer, *Licensing in the Contemporary Information Economy*, 8 WASH. U. J.L. & POLICY 99 (2002). If that is confusing, simply think of your most recent final exam. Your exam communicated (transferred) information to the professor, but at least for a time, you also retained that same information.

There are numerous subcategories of licenses that provide relevant benchmarks for understanding the law of licensing. One traditional distinction is between an "exclusive" and a "non-exclusive" license. The difference between these two lies in the language of the contract, and that language varies. In general, however, an exclusive license gives the licensee some "exclusive" rights in reference to the licensed subject matter and contains a promise (express or implied), that the licensor will not make another license covering the same subject matter, scope and rights as that given to this licensee. UCITA § 307 (2000 Official Text). There will be more to say about "exclusive licenses" in Chapter 4. For now, it is enough to say that licenses of this type often resemble assignments and, indeed, may be treated as if they were assignments for some purposes in law.

A "non-exclusive" license conveys no commitment to exclusivity. Form 1.1 illustrates a non-exclusive patent license:

FORM 1.1
NON-EXCLUSIVE LICENSE
Dated: ----------

1. Parties

This agreement is between Big Company [hereafter "Big"], a Texas corporation having a place of business at _____, and Small Company [hereinafter "Small"], a California Corporation having a place of business at _____.

2. Grant

Small grants Big a non-exclusive license to use the technology covered by the following patents within the United States:

U.S. Patent No. 5,325,320, issued 4/11/2006, with an effective U.S. application date of 6/15/2005

U.S. Patent No. 6,100,000, issued 6/30/2004, with an effective U.S. application date of 7/1/2003

3. Duration

This license shall continue with respect to each patent until the patent term expires or unless the license is previously canceled for breach by either party.

4. Royalty and Other Payments

4.1. Big will pay to Small $100,000 U.S. on the effective date of this agreement.

4.2. Big will pay to Small a royalty equal to 3% of the gross receipts from the sale of products manufactured by or for Big in whole or in part by use of the technology described in paragraph 2 with no deduction for returns or other adjustments. Payment shall be due sixty days after the last day of each calendar year during the term of this license for products sold during that calendar year. Small shall have the right to demand an audit of all records of Big relating to the computation of this royalty within thirty days after receipt of any royalty payment. The audit shall be conducted by -----.

4.3 In the event that either patent referred to in Paragraph 2 expires or is declared invalid by a final judgment in a U.S. court of appropriate jurisdiction, as of the date that the patent expires or the judgment becomes final, the royalty in paragraph 4.2 shall be reduced by fifty percent and applied to only those products manufactured by use of the patent that remains in effect and has not been declared invalid. In the event of the expiration or a judicial determination of invalidity in a final judgment by a U.S. court of appropriate jurisdiction of both patents in Paragraph 2, no further royalties shall be payable for products manufactured using either technology following the date of expiration of the last effective patent or the date that a judgment declaring the last effective patent invalid becomes final.

5. Ownership

Small warrants that it is the sole owner of all right, title and interest in and to the patents described in Paragraph 2.

6. Effective Dates

The "Effective Date" of this agreement is the date on which this writing has been signed by an authorized representative of each party to the agreement; provided, however, that the license in Paragraph 2 does not become effective until Small receives the payment described in Paragraph 4.1.

7. Breach and Cancellation

In the event of breach, the non-breaching party shall be entitled to all remedies available under a simple contract and under applicable intellectual property law. In addition, in the event of material breach of this agreement by either party, the non-breaching party may cancel this license, thereby ending all future rights and obligations under the license. A breach is material if 1) it is material under ordinarily applicable legal standards, or 2) if, within sixty calendar days after receipt of a written demand for cure, the party in breach fails to fully cure the breach by tender of a conforming performance.

8. No Other Agreements

This writing contains the full and complete agreement of the parties and supersedes any and all other representations, promises or statements is relying on any other representation or understanding not expressed in this writing.

Signed:

_____, President and CEO, Big Corporation

_____, President and CEO, Small Corporation

Form 1.1 is a non-exclusive patent license. The licensed patents apparently relate to technology that can be used in the manufacture of products.

In dealing with information assets, property and other rights come from laws that are not the same as those applicable to goods or real estate. In the foregoing license, the source is federal patent law. For students who have not been exposed to patent law, patents in the United States are issued (or rejected) by the U.S. Patent Office after a process of application by the claimed inventor, and review by the Patent Office. In part because of this, all patents in this country can be identified by a unique patent number, a fact that impacts licensing practice.[1] A patent is valid from the time it is issued by the Office for a period of twenty years from the date that the application for the patent was filed, unless it is declared to be invalid by a court or other entity of appropriate jurisdiction. 35 U.S.C. § 154(a). The details of patent law (or other bodies of intellectual property law) are not our concern. Under U.S. law, however, a patent gives patent owner rights that, in relevant part, are described in the following terms in the statute:

> [Whoever] without authority makes, uses, offers to sell, or sells any patented invention, within the United States or imports into the United States any patented invention during the term of the patent . . . infringes the patent.

35 U.S.C. § 271(a). Perhaps the most important feature of this statutory rule is what it does not say. The rights involve the ability to prevent another from making, using, selling or the other listed activities by suing for infringement. There is no affirmative right to use the patented technology or invention.

Take a close look at Form 1.1. How many of these rights did Small grant to Big in that license?

PROBLEM 1.1

Consider the relationship between the language of the license in Form 1.1, the property rights created under patent law, and the following events:

---

[1] The same cannot be said for copyrights, trade secrets, or trademarks, the other three "traditional" intellectual property laws. While some trademarks and copyrights are registered, there is no comprehensive registration scheme.

a. Shortly after the license to Big, a potential licensee willing to pay $500,000 plus 6% royalties for use of the two patents contacts Small. Can Small grant that license without breaching the Big license?

b. What result if Big did not pay the $100,000 fee, but began using the patents?

c. What result if, after paying the fee and beginning to use the technology, Big discovers that it is inappropriate for the manufacturing that Big had in mind and, indeed, for any task, because the technology is twice as expensive as other existing, non-patented technology? Can Big sue for breach?

Other sources of property law yield rights different from those in the patent statute and, as we will see in this book, this can influence how licenses are structured and what issues the parties deal with in the license. Copyright law describes the rights held by the owner of a copyright in a copyrighted work in the following terms:

> . . . the owner of copyright . . . has the exclusive rights to do and to authorize any of the following:
>
> (1) to reproduce the copyrighted work in copies or phonorecords;
>
> (2) to prepare derivative works based on the copyrighted work;
>
> (3) to distribute copies or phonorecords of the copyrighted work to the public by sale or other transfer of ownership, or by rental, lease or lending;
>
> (4) . . . to perform the copyrighted work publicly;
>
> (5) . . . to display the copyrighted work publicly and
>
> (6) in the case of sound recording, to perform the copyrighted work publicly by means of a digital audio transmission.

17 U.S.C. §106. Unlike in patent law, rights under copyright law exist as soon as the copyrightable work is created, although registration in the federal Copyright Office may be important for various reasons, including as a precondition for the right to sue for infringement of a work of U.S. origin. The statute provides that copyright cannot create exclusive rights in facts, methods or operation (processes), or ideas. 17 U.S.C. §102(b). As might be expected, these exclusions are the grist for extensive litigation. They may also affect the rationale for, and effect of licensing.

PROBLEM 1.2

Assume that the technology that Big Company desired to license in Form 1.1 was copyrighted computer software. How would you rewrite the "grant" portion of the license in Form 1.1?

SPINDELFABRIK SUESSEN-SCHURR STAHLECKER & GRILL v. SCHUBERT & SALZER MASCHINENFABRIK AKTIENGESELLSCHAFT
829 F.2d 1075 (Fed. Cir. 1987)

BALDWIN, SENIOR CIRCUIT JUDGE.

This is a consolidation of appeals from two judgments of the United States District Court . . . (1) declaring U.S. Patent No. 4,059,946 (the '946 patent) and U.S. Patent No. 4,175,370 (the '370 patent) valid and infringed and awarding increased damages and attorney fees based on a finding of willful infringement of the '946 patent and (2) granting a motion to enjoin subsequent infringement by a redesign of the accused device. [We affirm.]

Background

In 1983, the three appellees, Hans Stahlecker, Fritz Stahlecker, and Spindelfabrik Suessen-Schurr, Stahlecker and Grill GmbH (collectively and individually "Suessen"), brought an action in the district court for infringement of two patents relating to improvements in the technology of open-end spinning devices, the '946 patent and the '370 patent. It was charged that an open-end spinning device, the Spincomat, produced and marketed by appellants, Schubert and Salzer Maschinenfabrik Aktiengesellschaft and Schubert and Salzer Machine Works, Inc. (collectively and individually "Schubert"), infringes claim 18 of the '946 patent and infringes claims 1-7, 9-13, and 17-20 of the '370 patent. The district court rejected the Schubert defenses of invalidity, unenforceability, non-infringement, and implied license. . . . Six weeks later, on October 28, 1985, the district court issued an order declaring that, despite Schubert's efforts to produce a non-infringing modification, the redesigned version of the Spincomat also infringes the '946 patent. . . .

The Implied License Defense

Schubert argues that it has an implied license under the '946 patent. Its argument involves two agreements.

The first was a license agreement entered in 1982 between Schubert and Murata Machinery, Ltd. (Murata). That agreement, entered into before the filing of this suit in 1983, in pertinent part reads:

> Murata hereby grants to Licensee [Schubert] a non-exclusive world-wide license under the Patents to make, use and sell the patented device only as part of the open end spinning machines of the License. The License hereby granted is a limited license, and Murata reserves all rights not expressly granted.

The "Patents" were defined [to] include U.S. Patent No. 4,022,011 ('011 patent) and other patents belonging to Murata in the name of Hironorai Hirai. Schubert asserts that, notwithstanding any infringement of '946, its accused infringement is merely a practicing of the '011 invention, which it is licensed to do under the 1982 agreement.

The second agreement, entered in 1984 after this lawsuit began, involved Suessen's purchase of the '011 and [other] patents from Murata. The agreement reads, in pertinent part:

> Suessen has been advised by Murata that a non-exclusive license of the patents and patent applications mentioned under 1. above had been granted by Murata to Messrs. Schubert & Salzer AG, Ingolstadt, F.R. Germany (hereinafter called the Licensee). Suessen hereby agrees to purchase the patents and patent applications mentioned under 1 above together with the License Agreement as of 23rd/28th July, 1982, with the said Licensee and agrees that you and your business/license concerns will maintain the licensed rights of the Licensee under the License Agreement as stipulated during the life of the patents and patent applications mentioned under 1. above.

Schubert asserts that, per the 1984 agreement, Suessen "stepped in the shoes of Murata" [and] cannot — just as Murata cannot — sue under the '946 or any other patent for infringement based on practicing the '011 invention. To allow such a suit, Schubert argues, would unfairly take away what it paid for in 1982. Schubert labels its argument one of "legal estoppel."

The district court concluded that Schubert in 1982 could not have acquired from Murata any rights greater than those which Murata had the right to grant and that Murata had nothing more than a right to exclude others from using the Hirai patents. It then concluded, regarding the 1984 agreement:

> There is nothing whatsoever in this agreement about the '946 patent, any patent corresponding to the '946 patent, or any technology specifically covered by those patents. Nor is there any language in the agreement that can be construed as a grant by Suessen of any right to practice any particular technology which might be covered by other Suessen patent rights. All this agreement does is to convey to Suessen the entire right, title and interest in all of the Hirai patents, with the express reservation to the effect that a nonexclusive license under these Hirai patents had already been granted by Murata to [Schubert], and with the express acknowledgment by Suessen that it would continue to recognize the existence of that license under the Hirai patents. While this latter acknowledgment might seem redundant from the viewpoint of the law in this country (whereby a patent assignee under normal circumstances would be bound as a matter of law by its assignor's prior grant of a license to a third party), it served a clear purpose under German law since . . . the German High Court had recently handed down a ruling, the effect of which was that an existing nonexclusive right under a German patent could be defeated by an assignment of the patent by the owner to a third party.

The net effect of the 1984 agreement, said the district court, was that Schubert is "the beneficiary of a guarantee by Suessen that the nonexclusive rights under the Hirai patents granted to [Schubert] by Murata in 1982 could not be taken away by the new patent owner, Suessen" and that the enforcement of the '946 patent against Schubert in this litigation "in no way affects that guarantee."

The district court then added:

> Beyond these two agreements, defendants offered no further evidence in
> support of the existence of any implied license — not even the testimony
> of defendants to the effect that they ever even thought they might have
> an implied license or that they were led to take or ever took any action
> upon reliance that they had rights under the '946 patents.

[The] district court concluded that equitable estoppel could not be a basis for
implied license in this case.

Discussion

[Schubert] asserts an implied license based on its theory of legal estoppel.
Though we recognize that theory in appropriate circumstances, it does not
work for Schubert here. Legal estoppel "is merely shorthand for saying that a
grantor of a property right or interest cannot derogate from the right granted
by his own subsequent acts." *AMP v. United States,* 389 F.2d at 453. The rationale for that is to estop the grantor from taking back that for which he received
consideration. Here, however, we have a suit by a third party, Suessen, under
a patent owned by Suessen. The license by the grantor, Murata, did not
purport to, and indeed could not, protect Schubert from a suit by Suessen
under '946. Hence, Suessen, by filing in 1983 and now maintaining its suit
under '946, does not derogate from the right given by Murata in the 1982
license agreement.

Schubert nevertheless urges this three prong argument: (1) "legal estoppel"
would prevent *Murata* from suing under the '946 patent if it were to acquire
it; (2) Suessen "stepped into" Murata's shoes in 1984 when Suessen acquired
the Hirai patents and committed to maintain Schubert's licensed rights; and
hence, (3) just as Murata could not, Suessen cannot sue under the '946 patent.
We reject that argument.

As a threshold matter, a patent license agreement is in essence nothing
more than a promise by the licensor not to sue the licensee. Even if couched in
terms of "[l]icensee is given the right to make, use, or sell X," the agreement
cannot convey that absolute right because not even the patentee of X is given
that right. His right is merely one to exclude others from making, using or
selling X, 35 U.S.C. § 154. Indeed, the patentee of X and his licensee, when
making, using, or selling X, can be subject to suit under other patents. In any
event, patent license agreements can be written to convey different scopes of
promises not to sue, *e.g.,* a promise not to sue under a specific patent or, more
broadly, a promise not to sue under any patent the licensor now has or may
acquire in the future.

As stated previously, the first prong of Schubert's three part "stepping in the
shoes" argument is that legal estoppel would prevent Murata from suing
Schubert under the '946 patent if Murata were to acquire that patent.
However, even assuming, *arguendo,* that such estoppel against Murata exists,
the final two prongs of Schubert's "stepping in the shoes" argument would fail.
Given the assumption of estoppel against Murata, the 1982 license agreement
would necessarily be a promise by Murata not to sue under any patent, includ-

ing those acquired by Murata in the future. In the 1984 agreement, Suessen incurred what Murata promised in 1982. Thus, Suessen would be committed to forebear from suit under (1) the transferred patents and (2) any of Murata's nontransferred patents (future and present). That commitment does not include a promise not to sue under Suessen's own '946 patent.

Schubert's "standing in the shoes" argument, however, would add to Suessen's commitment a promise not to sue under Suessen's separate patents that Murata never owned. On the facts of this case, we cannot interpret the 1984 agreement so broadly, at least not with respect to the '946 patent.

The district court correctly determined that there is nothing in the 1984 agreement about the '946 or other Suessen patent rights. Schubert points to no extraneous evidence tending to show any understanding on the part of either contracting party that Suessen was to forego rights under the '946 or any other patent then owned by Suessen. To the contrary, that a lawsuit under '946 was ongoing but not mentioned in the 1984 agreement indicates strongly that there was no intent by the parties to have Suessen forfeit its rights under '946. Furthermore, an implied promise by Suessen to forego its '946 suit is inconsistent not only with Suessen maintaining its lawsuit after the 1984 agreement but, also, with the course of events leading up to the 1984 contract. In sum, we agree with the district court's conclusion that the 1984 agreement did not impose on Suessen any obligation to stop its ongoing suit under the '946 patent.

Schubert argues that not implying a license in this case is unfair because Schubert paid valuable consideration for the right to practice the '011 invention but is in danger of losing that right as a result of doing no more than that for which it paid. We disagree. The right Schubert paid for in the 1982 agreement was freedom from suit by Murata, not Suessen. Indeed, when Schubert signed the 1982 agreement, it was aware of possible suit by Suessen, who had previously denied Schubert a license under the '946 patent. Moreover, Schubert has not shown us that it has lost any obligation Murata may still owe it under the 1982 license agreement, *e.g.,* not to sue under any patents Murata still has or may acquire. To rule that the Suessen acquisition of the '011 patent somehow bestows on Schubert an absolute defense to a suit already filed by Suessen under '946, would result in an unintended windfall to Schubert that makes no sense under the facts of this case. . . .

AFFIRMED

We return to "estoppel" and "implied licenses" in Chapter 7. For present purposes, the important point is how the court addresses the character of the license. The idea that a license is a mere covenant to not sue states a very limited, passive view of the transaction involved — in effect, the licensor is presumed to have said: "I will not sue you if you stay within the terms of the license, but beyond that and what I have expressly promised in our written contract, I am giving you no further assurances about anything." Notice that the court suggests that this limited view governs even if the license is "couched in terms of '[l]icensee is given the right to make, use, or sell X.'" Yet, a license agreement can expand on the rights given. What language do you think would be sufficient to do so? What language would be sufficient in the non-exclusive license in Form 1.1? Why would a court suggest that such unusually express language would be required?

The description of a license as a mere covenant not to sue is common in the case law approaching license issues from an intellectual property law perspective. *See General Talking Pictures Corp. v. Western Electric Co.*, 304 U.S. 175, 181 (1938) (patent license "a mere waiver of the right to sue."); *Cohen v. Paramount Pictures Corp.*, 845 F.2d 851 (9th Cir 1988); *Wang Laboratories, Inc. v. Mitsubishi Electronics*, 103 F.3d 1571, 1580 (Fed. Cir. 1997) ("an implied license merely signifies a patentee's waiver of the statutory right to exclude others from making, using or selling a patented invention"); *Harris v. Emus Records Corp.*, 734 F.2d 1329 (9th Cir. 1984) ("a license has been characterized as an agreement not to sue the licensee for infringement. [We] hold therefore that [a] license is not an interest in a copyright.").

While this view is widespread, it is not the only view of licensing and, for some types of licensing, it is not the dominant view. To begin to understand alternative approaches, consider what the defendant in *Spindelfabrik* was arguing. On what basis did it suggest that allowing suit on a different patent would not be fair? What right or expectation would be unfairly taken away from the defendant if the lawsuit were allowed?

License transactions are treated as more than mere passive grants in transactions governed by Uniform Commercial Code (UCC) Article 2 or by the Uniform Computer Information Transaction Act (UCITA). Under either statute, in the absence of disclaimers, there are likely to be implied warranties of quality and non-infringement that give the licensee some assurance of the usability of the subject matter.

Of course, Article 2 applies to relatively few licenses, and UCITA is currently law in only two states. Thus, one is often left with the question of when more than a mere covenant to not sue is involved, even though the parties did not expressly so state. Should a court look to ordinary trade expectations in similar transactions, to the underlying property rights, to some policy of fairness, or to other factors?

PROBLEM 1.3

Coast Oil Company trades oil futures and oil contracts. In its industry, contracts for delivery of shipments of oil from the Middle East are often traded ten or more times among companies while the oil itself is in transit by tanker. Licensor operates an online price-tracking site that records and makes available in real time the price for all grades of oil delivered at all major United States ports. There are several other companies in licensor's business. One guarantees the accuracy of its data, but the others do not. The license between Licensor and Coast to access and use the site is silent on the issue. The cost for use of the site is $500,000 per month. One day, the data are inaccurate and Coast loses a large amount of money. It sues. Based solely on what you have read so far, how can it best argue its case for liability?

PROBLEM 1.4

Cargill Industries is the owner and user of a trademark ("Corison") used in relation to its plastic cookware products. Cargill grants Jean Co. a non-exclusive license to use the mark in connection with a line of consumer electronics products to be distributed in ten southwestern states. Consumer electronics is an entirely new area of commerce for the mark. Assume that trademark law provides that the owner of a mark that has become associated with its products or services may prevent use of the mark in a way that is likely to cause consumer confusion. This means that uses of the mark for entirely different types of products may not infringe if the difference and the nature of the use avoid the risk of confusing sponsorship of one product with that of the other.

Consider the following: 1) how should this license be characterized in terms of whether it is a mere covenant not to sue, 2) should the licensee assume that Cargill has given it assurance of the right to use the mark as against other companies who may have similar brand names and marks in the consumer electronic field, and 3) what cause of action may Cargill pursue if Jean uses the mark outside the designated states?

While many licenses involve information that has intellectual property associated with it, many significant licensing frameworks involve subject matter outside the scope of intellectual property law. Digital information and communications systems, along with the increased value of information in modern commerce, have enhanced the importance of non-intellectual-property licensing. In reading the following case, note that neither copyright nor patent law creates property rights in factual data such as names and addresses. This means that, as to those bodies of law, the data can be freely copied and distributed. Given that result, what is the basis for the contract and enforcement discussed in the case? Is the transaction properly described as a license and, if so, what does this suggest about the nature of a license in modern practice?

SIEDLE v. NATIONAL ASSOCIATION OF SECURITIES DEALERS, INC.
248 F. Supp. 2d 1140 (M.D. Fla. 2003)

BUCKLEW, DISTRICT JUDGE.

This case was brought by Plaintiff Edward A. Siedle, a former Securities and Exchange Commission attorney and a former associate counsel and director of compliance for a "major money management company." Siedle further states that he is president of Benchmark Financial Services, Inc., which is a broker-dealer registered with the National Association of Securities Dealers, Inc., and that he published *The Siedle Directory Securities Dealers* ("*The Siedle Directory*") up until May 30, 2002. . . .

The Siedle Directory contains material copied from the Central Registration Depository ("CRD"). Plaintiffs allege that the NASD and/or its affiliates maintain and include the CRD as part of the NASD's Public Disclosure

Program ("PDP"), which is made available through a web site operated by NASD and/or its affiliates (the "PDP web site"). Plaintiffs further allege that NASD and others administer the CRD under the oversight of the United States Securities and Exchange Commission and that the PDP was created pursuant to the statutory mandate of 15 U.S.C. § 78o-3(i).

[The] PDP web site includes a "click agreement" to which users must agree in order to request and obtain CRD information. Plaintiffs attach a copy of the "original click agreement" as Exhibit B to the Amended Complaint (the "First Click Agreement"). The First Click Agreement addresses restrictions on the commercial use of the contents of the PDP web site.

In December 2001, Plaintiff Siedle hired a computer programmer to create a program so that he could download the content found on the PDP web site in its entirety, and, in February 2002, the programmer copied content from the PDP web site for the purpose of Plaintiffs' reproduction and commercialization of that content in *The Siedle Directory*. Plaintiffs sell hard copies of *The Siedle Directory* for approximately $850 per copy.

[NASD] revised its click agreement on or about March 12, 2002. . . . The Second Click Agreement also addresses restrictions on the commercial use of the contents of the PDP web site.

Plaintiffs seek a declaration that they are entitled under the First Click Agreement to publish and sell *The Siedle Directory,* which admittedly contains content copied from the PDP web site without interference from NASD. Count I, Amended Complaint. Plaintiffs likewise seek a declaration that they are entitled to copy and republish the PDP web site content for commercial resale under the Second Click Agreement. Count II, Amended Complaint. In Counts III and IV, Plaintiffs seek orders from this Court temporarily and permanently enjoining NASD from interfering with their continued copying of PDP web site content, their reproduction of that content in *The Siedle Directory,* and their commercial sale of *The Siedle Directory*.

Defendant now moves to dismiss the Amended Complaint . . . arguing that each of Plaintiffs' claims fails as a matter of law because Plaintiffs have agreed and must agree to comply with the First and Second Click Agreements, which prohibit the copying and republication of the PDP web site content for com- mercial sale. Plaintiffs contend that click agreements should be held unen- forceable and, if held enforceable, the First Click Agreement on its face does not limit the Plaintiffs' access and use of the PDP information. Plaintiffs also argue that even if the First Click Agreement and the Second Click Agreement could be construed as valid, they are unenforceable because they are against public policy and violate the NASD's federal mandate. . . .

This Court must first address the Plaintiffs' argument that the validity of click agreements is a matter of first impression in Florida and that they should not be enforced in this case. This Court is unpersuaded by Plaintiffs' argument against the validity of click agreements. There are any number of cases from other state and federal courts expressly and implicitly approving the validity of click agreements. In addition, although there may be no Florida case law directly on point, the Plaintiffs were unable to cite the Court to any case law,

Florida or otherwise, holding a click agreement unenforceable or invalid. Accordingly, this Court finds no reason to hold that the click agreements in this case are unenforceable or invalid.

Having found the click agreements enforceable, this Court next addresses Defendant's argument that Count I fails to state a claim because the First Click Agreement expressly prohibits commercial exploitation of content downloaded from the PDP web site. [Plaintiffs] argue that the language of the First Click Agreement clearly allows their commercial use under subparagraph (a). The First Click Agreement provides, in relevant part, that:

1. Information provided through the Public Disclosure Program shall be used ONLY:

> a. to assist in determining whether to conduct or continue to conduct securities or commodities business with NASD Member Firms or Associated Persons;

> b. in judicial proceedings or arbitration proceedings relating to securities or commodities transactions; or

> c. for other non-commercial purposes consistent with the promotion of just and equitable principles of trade and the protection of investors and the public interest.

Plaintiffs contend that subparagraph (c) of paragraph 1 does not modify subparagraphs (a) and (b) of paragraph 1 because of the use of the disjunctive "or" and that, therefore, commercial use of the content is permitted so long as the use is for purposes identified in subparagraphs (a) and (b).

It is well settled that contract interpretation is a question of law. Questions of fact arise only when an ambiguity in a contract forces the court to examine extrinsic evidence of the parties' intent. Under the ordinary rules of contract construction, a court first examines the "natural and plain meaning" of the contract, and "ambiguity does not exist simply because a contract requires interpretation or fails to define a term. . . ." In this case, the terms of the First Click Agreement are clear and unambiguous.

To adopt the Plaintiffs' reading of the contract, the word "other" in subparagraph (c) would be completely superfluous. The word "other" must be read to refer to the prohibition on commercial use even for purposes identified in subparagraphs (a) and (b). The law compels that a contract should not be interpreted in a manner that would render a word, or term, extraneous. *See Restatement (Second) of Contracts* §203(a) (1981) ("[A]n interpretation which gives a reasonable, lawful, and effective meaning to all the terms is preferred to an interpretation which leaves a part unreasonable, unlawful, or of no effect.").

Individual terms must not be considered in isolation when interpreting a contract, but rather must be interpreted as a whole and in relation to one another. Accordingly, the word "or" is properly read as connecting a series of non-commercial uses; not demarcating between commercial use and non-commercial use, as argued by the Plaintiffs.

The terms of paragraph 1 of the First Click Agreement soundly support the conclusion that the First Click Agreement prohibits Plaintiffs' copying of the

PDP web site content and from republishing that content for their own commercial purposes. Taken as a whole, the agreement clearly permits access to and use of the PDP web site content solely for an individual's or his advisor's use in deciding with whom to conduct securities or commodities business, for use in legal proceedings, or otherwise for the protection of investors and not for commercial purposes. As a result, Count I and the related claims for injunctive relief fail as a matter of law. . . .

Plaintiffs do not argue that the Second Click Agreement can be interpreted to allow commercial use of the PDP web site content, but alternatively argue that if the First and Second Click Agreements are construed as valid, they are still unenforceable because they are against the policy of public disclosure and violate NASD's federal mandate. This argument rings hollow as Plaintiffs fail to cite to any authority in support of their argument. Indeed, the federal statute which requires the NASD to provide requested PDP information through its web site or otherwise does not address commercial use of the information.

Pursuant to the SEC's mandate delegated to NASD under 15 U.S.C. § 78o-3(i), NASD must:

> (1) establish and maintain a toll-free telephone listing to receive inquiries regarding disciplinary actions involving its members and their associated persons, and (2) promptly respond to such inquiries in writing. Such association may charge persons, other than individual investors, reasonable fees for written responses to such inquiries. . . .

The prohibitions in the First and Second Click Agreements against commercial use of the PDP web site content are not inconsistent with the goal of making information public and aiding investors. The PDP web site is available to individual investors and their advisors to provide them with the information to be used in selecting an NASD member firm or associated person, for use in judicial proceedings, or for other non-commercial purposes to protect investors. . . . Accordingly, Count II and the related claims for injunctive relief are dismissed without leave to amend. . . .

Defendant's Motion to Dismiss is GRANTED. . . .

NOTES

1. What was licensed in *Siedle*? Assuming that the CRD data are not subject to copyright protection, why did Siedle agree to the license? For a similar outcome, see *Register.com v. Verio, Inc.*, 356 F.3d 393 (2d Cir. 2004) (data on domain name registrants). Some argue that contracts such as in *Siedle* and *Register.com* limiting use of data creates a risk that contract will be used to circumvent policies of intellectual property law and that the contracts should be precluded or at least closely constrained. But the reported cases and the common nature of the practice in commerce suggest otherwise. Is contract inconsistent with property rights law, or is it simply a different species of relationship justified by considerations of open markets and enforceable assent independent of property rights concerns? *See ProCD, Inc. v. Zeidenberg*, 86 F.3d 1447 (7th Cir. 1996) (enforcing contract that limits use of factual database).

2. As *Siedle* suggests, an infrequently used contract law doctrine precludes enforcement of terms that conflict with fundamental public policy even if the statute or regulation establishing the policy does not directly invalidate the contract. Reflecting the value placed on contract enforcement, the *Restatement (Second) of Contracts* §178 (1981) states: "(1) A promise or other term of an agreement is unenforceable on grounds of public policy if legislation provides that it is unenforceable or the interest in its enforcement is clearly outweighed in the circumstances by a public policy against the enforcement of such terms." UCITA states a similar principle: "If a term of a contract violates a fundamental public policy, the court may refuse to enforce the contract, enforce the remainder of the contract without the impermissible term, or limit the application of the impermissible term so as to avoid a result contrary to public policy, in each case to the extent that the interest in enforcement is clearly outweighed by a public policy against enforcement of the term." UCITA §105(b) (2000 Official Text). Why did the court in *Siedle* reject the public policy argument?

3. Policy arguments aside, one clear difference exists between an intellectual property license and a license not grounded in a property right. The difference surfaces by asking a simple question: what remedies are available to a licensor if 1) a licensee breaches a license by making copies of a copyrighted work beyond those permitted by the license, or 2) if the licensee makes copies of non-copyrighted information?

II.   WHAT LAW APPLIES: FEDERAL PROPERTY RULES — A FIRST LOOK

Asking "what law applies" commonly leads to a discussion of the law that governs choice of what state's (or country's) law applies to a transaction or a dispute. That topic, while important, is best left to a course on the arcane rules of conflicts of law. We focus on two different questions. First, to what extent are license agreements governed by state or by federal law? Second, to the extent that state law applies, which law within a state governs license contracts? These issues will recur throughout the course, and are merely introduced here.

The property rights that underlie many licenses come from a variety of sources. Some are grounded in federal law, while others are not. Copyright and patent laws, for example, are entirely federal law in the United States. Trademark law, on the other hand, is both federal and state law, although the federal Lanham Act is the dominant influence. Trade secret law is state law, as are many other emerging rights. The licensor of an online system can turn to federal or state law to control access to and use of its system.

In licensing, most issues of federal-state interaction relate to copyright or patent law. Here, federal law dominates property rights issues, but state law dominates the contract law side of the equation. Yet, the relationship is more complex than simply saying one or the other dominates — the rules interact.

Federal law can preempt state law, but it often does not. Determining whether a particular federal rule preempts a state law requires analysis of (1) the characteristics of the relevant federal rule, (2) the overall body of law to which it relates, and (3) its interaction with the particular state rule for which preemption is claimed. Three types of preemption that emerge from such analyses:

1. *Express preemption:* Federal law expressly provides for preemption.

2. *Field preemption:* Federal law entirely and exclusively occupies a field.

3. *Conflict preemption:* State law is inconsistent with and impedes the achievement of federal policy in federal statute or regulation.

See, e.g., Saridakis v. United Airlines, 166 F.3d 1272, 1276 (9th Cir. 1999). Federal patent law has no express statutory rule on preemption, although a Supreme Court decision in the 1960s held that federal policy in the Patent Act preempted a particular state contract law default rule. *See Lear, Inc. v. Adkins,* 395 U.S. 653 (1969). We discuss *Lear* later.

The Copyright Act does contain preemptive language. Section 301 states:

> [All] legal and equitable rights that are equivalent to any of the exclusive rights within the general scope of copyright . . . in works of authorship that are fixed in a tangible medium of expression and come within the subject matter of copyright . . . are governed exclusively by [the Copyright Act]. [But nothing] in this title annuls or limits any rights or remedies under the . . . law . . . of any state with respect to . . . activities violating legal or equitable rights that are not equivalent to any of the exclusive rights within the general scope of copyright.

17 U.S.C. § 301.

ProCD, INC. v. ZEIDENBERG
86 F.3d 1447 (7th Cir. 1996)

EASTERBROOK, CIRCUIT JUDGE.

Must buyers of computer software obey the terms of shrinkwrap licenses? The district court held not, for two reasons: first, they are not contracts because the licenses are inside the box rather than printed on the outside; second, federal law forbids enforcement even if the licenses are contracts. The parties and numerous amici curiae have briefed many other issues, but these are the only two that matter — and we disagree with the district judge's conclusion on each. Shrinkwrap licenses are enforceable unless their terms are objectionable on grounds applicable to contracts in general (for example, if they violate a rule of positive law, or if they are unconscionable). . . .

I

ProCD, the plaintiff, has compiled information from more than 3,000 telephone directories into a computer database. We may assume that this database cannot be copyrighted, although it is more complex, contains more information (nine- digit zip codes and census industrial codes), is organized differently, and therefore is more original than the single alphabetical directory at issue in *Feist*

Publications, Inc. v. Rural Telephone Service Co., 499 U.S. 340 (1991). ProCD sells a version of the database, called SelectPhone, on CD-ROM discs. (CD-ROM means "compact disc — read only memory." The "shrinkwrap license" gets its name from the fact that retail software packages are covered in plastic or cellophane "shrinkwrap," and some vendors, though not ProCD, have written licenses that become effective as soon as the customer tears the wrapping from the package. Vendors prefer "end user license," but we use the more common term.) A proprietary method of compressing the data serves as effective encryption too. Customers decrypt and use the data with the aid of an application program that ProCD has written. This program, which is copyrighted, searches the database in response to users' criteria (such as "find all people named Tatum in Tennessee, plus all firms with 'Door Systems' in the corporate name"). The resulting lists (or, as ProCD prefers, "listings") can be read and manipulated by other software, such as word processing programs.

The database in SelectPhone costs more than $10 million to compile and is expensive to keep current. It is much more valuable to some users than to others. The combination of names, addresses, and SIC codes enables manufacturers to compile lists of potential customers. Manufacturers and retailers pay high prices to specialized information intermediaries for such mailing lists; ProCD offers a potentially cheaper alternative. People with nothing to sell could use the database as a substitute for calling long distance information, or as a way to look up old friends who have moved to unknown towns, or just as an electronic substitute for the local phone book. ProCD decided to engage in price discrimination, selling its database to the general public for personal use at a low price (approximately $150 for the set of five discs) while selling information to the trade for a higher price. It has adopted some intermediate strategies too: access to the SelectPhone (trademark) database is available via the America Online service for the price America Online charges to its clients (approximately $3 per hour), but this service has been tailored to be useful only to the general public.

If ProCD had to recover all of its costs and make a profit by charging a single price — that is, if it could not charge more to commercial users than to the general public — it would have to raise the price substantially over $150. The ensuing reduction in sales would harm consumers who value the information at, say, $200. They get consumer surplus of $50 under the current arrangement but would cease to buy if the price rose substantially. If because of high elasticity of demand in the consumer segment of the market the only way to make a profit turned out to be a price attractive to commercial users alone, then all consumers would lose out — and so would the commercial clients, who would have to pay more for the listings because ProCD could not obtain any contribution toward costs from the consumer market.

To make price discrimination work, however, the seller must be able to control arbitrage. An air carrier sells tickets for less to vacationers than to business travelers, using advance purchase and Saturday-night-stay requirements to distinguish the categories. A producer of movies segments the market by time, releasing first to theaters, then to pay-per-view services, next to the videotape and laserdisc market, and finally to cable and commercial tv. Vendors of computer software have a harder task. Anyone can walk into a retail store and buy a box. Customers do not wear tags saying "commercial user" or "consumer user." Anyway, even a commercial-user-detector at the door would not work, because a consumer could buy the software and resell to a commercial user. That arbitrage would break down the price discrimination and drive up the minimum price at which ProCD would sell to anyone.

Instead of tinkering with the product and letting users sort themselves — for example, furnishing current data at a high price that would be attractive only to commercial customers, and two-year-old data at a low price — ProCD turned to the institution of contract. Every box containing its consumer product declares that the software comes with restrictions stated in an enclosed license. This license, which is encoded on the CD-ROM disks as well as printed in the manual, and which appears on a user's screen every time the software runs, limits use of the application program and listings to non-commercial purposes.

Matthew Zeidenberg bought a consumer package of SelectPhone (trademark) in 1994 from a retail outlet in Madison, Wisconsin, but decided to ignore the license. He formed Silken Mountain Web Services, Inc., to resell the information in the SelectPhone (trademark) database. The corporation makes the database available on the Internet to anyone willing to pay its price — which, needless to say, is less than ProCD charges its commercial customers. Zeidenberg has purchased two additional SelectPhone (trademark) packages, each with an updated version of the database, and made the latest information available over the World Wide Web, for a price, through his corporation. ProCD filed this suit seeking an injunction against further dissemination that exceeds the rights specified in the licenses (identical in each of the three packages Zeidenberg purchased). The district court held the licenses ineffectual because their terms do not appear on the outside of the packages. The court added that the second and third licenses stand no different from the first, even though they are identical, because they *might* have been different, and a purchaser does not agree to — and cannot be bound by — terms that were secret at the time of purchase.

II

[The court held that the shrinkwrap license created a contract enforceable under state law.]

III

The district court held that, even if Wisconsin treats shrinkwrap licenses as contracts, §301(a) of the Copyright Act, 17 U.S.C. §301(a), prevents their enforcement. 908 F. Supp. at 656-59. The relevant part of §301(a) preempts any "legal or equitable rights [under state law] that are equivalent to any of the exclusive rights within the general scope of copyright as specified by section 106 in works of authorship that are fixed in a tangible medium of expression and come within the subject matter of copyright as specified by sections 102 and 103." ProCD's software and data are "fixed in a tangible medium of expression," and the district judge held that they are "within the subject matter of copyright." The latter conclusion is plainly right for the copyrighted application program, and the judge thought that the data likewise are "within the subject matter of copyright" even if, after *Feist*, they are not sufficiently original to be copyrighted. One function of §301(a) is to prevent states from giving special protection to works of authorship that Congress has decided should be in the public domain, which it can accomplish only if "subject matter of copyright" includes all works of a *type* covered by sections 102 and 103, even if federal law does not afford protection to them.

But are rights created by contract "equivalent to any of the exclusive rights within the general scope of copyright"? Three courts of appeals have answered "no." *National Car Rental System, Inc. v. Computer Associates International, Inc.*, 991 F.2d 426, 433 (8th Cir.1993); *Taquino v. Teledyne Monarch Rubber*, 893 F.2d 1488, 1501 (5th Cir.1990); *Acorn Structures, Inc. v. Swantz*, 846 F.2d 923, 926 (4th Cir.1988). The district court disagreed with these decisions, but we think them sound. Rights "equivalent to any of the exclusive rights within the general scope of copyright" are rights established *by law* — rights that restrict the options of persons who are strangers to the author. Copyright law forbids duplication, public performance, and so on, unless the person wishing to copy or perform the work gets permission; silence means a ban on copying. A copyright is a right against the world. Contracts, by contrast, generally affect only their parties; strangers may do as they please, so contracts do not create "exclusive rights." Someone who found a copy of SelectPhone (trademark) on the street would not be affected by the shrinkwrap license — though the federal copyright laws of their own force would limit the finder's ability to copy or transmit the application program.

Think for a moment about trade secrets. One common trade secret is a customer list. After *Feist,* a simple alphabetical list of a firm's customers, with address and telephone numbers, could not be protected by copyright. Yet *Kewanee Oil Co. v. Bicron Corp.,* 416 U.S. 470 (1974), holds that contracts about trade secrets may be enforced — precisely because they do not affect strangers' ability to discover and use the information independently. If the amendment of §301(a) in 1976 overruled *Kewanee* and abolished consensual protection of those trade secrets that cannot be copyrighted, no one has noticed — though abolition is a logical consequence of the district court's approach. Think, too, about everyday transactions in intellectual property. A customer visits a video store and rents a copy of *Night of the Lepus.* The customer's contract with the store limits use of the tape to home viewing and requires its return in two days. May the customer keep the tape, on the ground that §301(a) makes the promise unenforceable?

A law student uses the LEXIS database, containing public-domain documents, under a contract limiting the results to educational endeavors; may the student resell his access to this database to a law firm from which LEXIS seeks to collect a much higher hourly rate? Suppose ProCD hires a firm to scour the nation for telephone directories, promising to pay $100 for each that ProCD does not already have. The firm locates 100 new directories, which it sends to ProCD with an invoice for $10,000. ProCD incorporates the directories into its database; does it have to pay the bill? Surely yes; *Aronson v. Quick Point Pencil Co.,* 440 U.S. 257 (1979), holds that promises to pay for intellectual property may be enforced even though federal law (in *Aronson,* the patent law) offers no protection against third-party uses of that property. But these illustrations are what our case is about. ProCD offers software and data for two prices: one for personal use, a higher price for commercial use. Zeidenberg wants to use the data without paying the seller's price; if the law student and Quick Point Pencil Co. could not do that, neither can Zeidenberg.

Although Congress possesses power to preempt even the enforcement of contracts about intellectual property . . . courts usually read preemption clauses to leave private contracts unaffected. *American Airlines, Inc. v. Wolens,* 513 U.S. 219 (1995), provides a nice illustration. A federal statute preempts any state "law, rule, regulation, standard, or other provision . . . relating to rates, routes, or services of any air carrier." Does such a law preempt the law of contracts — so that, for example, an air carrier need not honor a quoted price (or a contract to reduce the price by the value of frequent flyer miles)? The Court allowed that it is possible to read the statute that broadly but thought such an interpretation would make little sense. Terms and conditions offered by contract reflect private ordering, essential to the efficient functioning of markets. Although some principles that carry the name of contract law are designed to defeat rather than implement consensual transactions, the rules that respect private choice are not preempted by a clause such as § 1305(a)(1). Section 301(a) plays a role similar to § 1301(a)(1): it prevents states from substituting their own regulatory systems for those of the national government. Just as § 301(a) does not itself interfere with private transactions in intellectual property, so it does not prevent states from respecting those transactions. Like the Supreme Court in *Wolens,* we think it prudent to refrain from adopting a rule that anything with the label "contract" is necessarily outside the preemption clause: the variations and possibilities are too numerous to foresee. *National Car Rental* likewise recognizes the possibility that some applications of the law of contract could interfere with the attainment of national objectives and therefore come within the domain of § 301(a). But general enforcement of shrinkwrap licenses of the kind before us does not create such interference.

Aronson emphasized that enforcement of the contract between Aronson and Quick Point Pencil Company would not withdraw any information from the public domain. That is equally true of the contract between ProCD and Zeidenberg. Everyone remains free to copy and disseminate all 3,000 telephone books that have been incorporated into ProCD's database. Anyone can add SIC codes and zip codes. ProCD's rivals have done so. Enforcement of the shrinkwrap license may even make information more readily available, by reducing the price ProCD charges to consumer buyers. To the extent licenses facilitate distribution of object code while concealing the source code (the point of a clause forbidding disassembly), they serve the same procompetitive functions as does the law of trade secrets. Licenses may have other benefits for consumers: many licenses permit users to make extra copies, to use the software on multiple computers, even to incorporate the software into the user's products. But whether a particular license is generous or restrictive, a simple two-party contract is not "equivalent to any of the exclusive rights within the general scope of copyright" and therefore may be enforced.

REVERSED AND REMANDED.

NOTES

1. Most courts that have reviewed application of Section 301 to state law claims adopt what has been described as the "extra-element" test. Under this approach, a state law claim is not preempted if it requires proof of a qualitatively extra or different element from that required to prove infringement. *Zeidenberg*, and a number of other decisions, stand for the proposition that a contract claim involves that extra element. How would you describe the "extra element" that is involved?

2. Judge Easterbrook suggests that some contract claims might be within copyright preemption. What type of claim would that be? For example, if a licensee breaches a contract covering a copyrighted work by making an unauthorized copy of the work, is the breach of contract claim preempted? What must be equivalent — the act involved or the basis for the right?

3. As in *Zeidenberg,* in the absence of misuse or over-reaching, courts have enforced standard form contracts even if the contract terms create rights or obligations that would not be present if the case were presented solely under copyright, patent or other property rights law. The contract creates an element that is not present in a pure property rights claim; in many cases, the contract creates (or precludes) a relationship on which property rights might hinge. Some, however, have argued that a standard form, non-negotiated contract should not be allowed to alter the rights or privileges created by property law, especially where the terms are used in reference to widely distributed information products. There are few modern decisions that apply this reasoning, but its tone is suggested by the dissenting opinion of Judge Dyk in *Bowers v. Baystate Technologies, Inc.*, 320 F.3d 1317 (Fed. Cir. 2003), a case that held that a shrinkwrap license precluding reverse engineering of software was not preempted. In dissent, the judge commented:

> A state is not free to eliminate the fair use defense. Enforcement of a total ban on reverse engineering would conflict with the Copyright Act itself by protecting otherwise unprotectable material. If state law provided that a copyright holder could bar fair use of the copyrighted material by placing a black dot on each copy of the work offered for sale, there would be no question but that the state law would be preempted. A state law that allowed a copyright holder to simply label its products so as to eliminate a fair use defense would "substantially impede" the public's right to fair use and allow the copyright holder, through state law, to protect material that the Congress has determined must be free to all under the Copyright Act. I nonetheless agree with the majority opinion that a state can permit parties to contract away a fair use defense or to agree not to engage in uses of copyrighted material that are permitted by the copyright law, if the contract is freely negotiated. A freely negotiated agreement represents the "extra element" that prevents preemption of a state law claim that would otherwise be identical to the infringement claim barred by the fair use defense of reverse engineering. However, state law giving effect to shrinkwrap licenses is no different in substance from a hypothetical black dot law. Like any other contract of adhesion, the only choice offered to the purchaser is to avoid making the purchase in the first

place. State law thus gives the copyright holder the ability to eliminate the fair use defense in each and every instance at its option.

Bowers v. Baystate Technologies, Inc., 320 F.3d 1317, 1336-37.

Is the distinction between "freely negotiated" and "adhesion" contracts viable for this issue? If I am willing to sell my car only under stated terms that I will not negotiate, is there a contract if you agree to those terms? On the other hand, if I am not a party to a contract by which you obtained a copy of a motion picture, when I make a fair use of that copy that would have been prohibited by the contract, am I liable to the copyright owner simply because there may be a breach of your contract?

LASERCOMB v. REYNOLDS
911 F.2d 970 (4th Cir. 1990)

SPROUSE, CIRCUIT JUDGE:

Appellants and defendants below are Larry Holliday, president and sole shareholder of Holiday Steel Rule Die Corporation (Holiday Steel), and Job Reynolds, a computer programmer for that company. Appellee is Lasercomb America, Inc. (Lasercomb), the plaintiff below. Holiday Steel and Lasercomb were competitors in the manufacture of steel rule dies that are used to cut and score paper and cardboard for folding into boxes and cartons. Lasercomb developed a software program, Interact, which is the object of the dispute between the parties. Using this program, a designer creates a template of a cardboard cutout on a computer screen and the software directs the mechanized creation of the conforming steel rule die.

In 1983, before Lasercomb was ready to market its Interact program generally, it licensed four prerelease copies to Holiday Steel which paid $35,000 for the first copy, $17,500 each for the next two copies, and $2,000 for the fourth copy. Lasercomb informed Holiday Steel that it would charge $2,000 for each additional copy Holiday Steel cared to purchase. Apparently ambitious to create for itself an even better deal, Holiday Steel circumvented the protective devices Lasercomb had provided with the software and made three unauthorized copies of Interact which it used on its computer systems. Perhaps buoyed by its success in copying, Holiday Steel then created a software program called "PDS-1000," which was almost entirely a direct copy of Interact, and marketed it as its own CAD/CAM die-making software. These infringing activities were accomplished by Job Reynolds at the direction of Larry Holliday.

There is no question that defendants engaged in unauthorized copying, and the purposefulness of their unlawful action is manifest from their deceptive practices. . . . When Lasercomb discovered Holiday Steel's activities, it registered its copyright in Interact and filed this action against Holiday Steel, Holliday, and Reynolds on March 7, 1986. Lasercomb claimed copyright infringement, breach of contract, misappropriation of trade secret, false designation of origin, unfair competition, and fraud. Defendants filed a number of counterclaims. On March 24, 1986, the district court entered a preliminary injunction, enjoining defendants from marketing the PDS-1000 software.

Holliday and Reynolds [do] not dispute that they copied Interact, but they contend that Lasercomb is barred from recovery for infringement by its concomitant culpability. They assert that, assuming Lasercomb had a perfected copyright, it impermissibly abused it. This assertion of the "misuse of copyright" defense is based on language in Lasercomb's standard licensing agreement, restricting licensees from creating any of their own CAD/CAM die-making software. . . .

Misuse of Copyright Defense

A successful defense of misuse of copyright bars a culpable plaintiff from prevailing on an action for infringement of the misused copyright. Here, appellants claim Lasercomb has misused its copyright by including in its standard licensing agreement clauses which prevent the licensee from participating in any manner in the creation of computer-assisted die-making software. The offending paragraphs read:

> D. Licensee agrees during the term of this Agreement that it will not permit or suffer its directors, officers and employees, directly or indirectly, to write, develop, produce or sell computer assisted die making software.

> E. Licensee agrees during the term of this Agreement and for one (1) year after the termination of this Agreement, that it will not write, develop, produce or sell or assist others in the writing, developing, producing or selling computer assisted die making software, directly or indirectly without Lasercomb's prior written consent. Any such activity undertaken without Lasercomb's written consent shall nullify any warranties or agreements of Lasercomb set forth herein.

The "term of this Agreement" referred to in these clauses is ninety-nine years.

Defendants were not themselves bound by the standard licensing agreement. Lasercomb had sent the agreement to Holiday Steel with a request that it be signed and returned. Larry Holliday, however, decided not to sign the document, and Lasercomb apparently overlooked the fact that the document had not been returned. Although defendants were not party to the restrictions of which they complain, they proved at trial that at least one Interact licensee had entered into the standard agreement, including the anticompetitive language.

The district court rejected the copyright misuse defense for three reasons. First, it noted that defendants had not explicitly agreed to the contract clauses alleged to constitute copyright misuse. Second, it found "such a clause is reasonable in light of the delicate and sensitive area of computer software." And, third, it questioned whether such a defense exists. We consider the district court's reasoning in reverse order.

A. *Does a "Misuse of Copyright" Defense Exist?*

We agree with the district court that much uncertainty engulfs the "misuse of copyright" defense. We are persuaded, however, that a misuse of copyright defense is inherent in the law of copyright just as a misuse of patent defense is inherent in patent law.

The misuse of a patent is a potential defense to suit for its infringement, and both the existence and parameters of that body of law are well established. Although there is little case law on the subject, courts from time to time have intimated that the similarity of rationales underlying the law of patents and the law of copyrights argues for a defense to an infringement of copyright based on misuse of the copyright. The origins of patent and copyright law in England, the treatment of these two aspects of intellectual property by the framers of our Constitution, and the later statutory and judicial development of patent and copyright law in this country persuade us that parallel public policies underlie the protection of both types of intellectual property rights. We think these parallel policies call for application of the misuse defense to copyright as well as patent law.

1. Overview

Because of the paucity of precedent in the copyright misuse area, some historical perspective of the elements underlying intellectual property law is helpful to our inquiry. Fortunately, respected treatise authors have captured well the essence of the relevant historical perspective.

During the sixteenth century, it became common for the English Crown to grant "letters patent" which gave individuals exclusive rights to produce, import and/or sell given items within the kingdom. 1 *Walker on Patents* §§ 1:1-1:2. These monopolies were granted for such commonplace items as salt, vinegar, and calfskins, to name but a few. The practice of granting monopolies led to widespread abuses, such as shortages and inflated prices for items that would otherwise be easily and cheaply available. Consequently, Parliament passed the Statute of Monopolies (1623-24), prohibiting the creation of such monopolies by the Crown. An exception was made, however, to permit a patent to be granted for a period of fourteen years to the creator of a new invention.

The rationale for allowing patents for new inventions was and is to encourage their creation for the benefit of society. 1 *Walker on Patents* § 1:6. The monopolies granted by the Crown had been odious because they restrained trade in articles that had previously been a part of the public domain. An invention, however, does not withdraw anything from public traffic; rather, it introduces something new. To encourage and reward inventors for increasing the inventory of useful objects, the government grants them, for a limited time, the right to exclude others from making and selling their inventions.

The development of copyright law in England likewise grew out of a differentiation by Parliament between a monopoly that restricts publication of works and a limited copyright that encourages the efforts of authors. In sixteenth-century England, the Crown granted to the Stationers' Company the exclusive right to publish and print all published works (apparently to enable censorship of Protestant materials). In the early 1700s, the Stationer's Company petitioned Parliament to recognize that these rights inured to it in perpetuity. Instead, Parliament passed the Statute of Anne (1709-10), the first known copyright legislation. That statute gave authors the sole right of publication for up to twenty-eight years. Thus, the English statutory treatment of copyright was similar to that of patent in that it granted the creator a monopoly for a limited time only.

It is significant, we think, that the framers of our Constitution continued the English development of intellectual property law and considered in tandem those property rights protectable by copyrights and those protectable by patents. In giving Congress the power to create copyright and patent laws, the framers combined the two concepts in one clause, stating a unitary purpose — to promote progress. Article I, section 8, clause 8 of the United States Constitution provides:

> [The Congress shall have power] To promote the Progress of Science and useful Arts, by securing for limited Times to Authors and Inventors the exclusive Right to their respective Writings and Discoveries.

This clause was adopted without debate, and material explaining the intention of the framers is limited. However, a comment in *The Federalist* papers indicates the public policy behind the grant of copyright and patent powers is essentially the same:

> The utility of this power will scarcely be questioned. The copyright of authors has been solemnly adjudged, in Great Britain, to be a right of common law. The right to useful inventions seems with equal reason to belong to the inventors. The public good fully coincides in both cases with the claims of individuals.

The Federalist, No. 43 at 279 (J. Madison) (Mod. Lib. ed. 1941).

Supreme Court comment has likewise equated the public policies of copyright and patent. For example, in *Mazer v. Stein,* 347 U.S. 201, 219 (1953), the Supreme Court stated:

> The economic philosophy behind the clause empowering Congress to grant *patents and copyrights* is the conviction that encouragement of individual effort by personal gain is the best way to advance public welfare through the talents of authors and inventors in "Science and useful Arts." Sacrificial days devoted to such creative activities deserve rewards commensurate with the services rendered.

(Emphasis added.) *See also Loew's,* 371 U.S. [38,] at 44-51 [(1962)]; *Paramount Pictures,* 334 U.S. [131,] at 154-59 [(1948)]. The philosophy behind copyright, parallel to that discussed above for patent, is that the public benefits from the efforts of authors to introduce new ideas and knowledge into the public domain. To encourage such efforts, society grants authors exclusive rights in their works for a limited time.

2. The Misuse of Patent Defense

Although a patent misuse defense was recognized by the courts as early as 1917, most commentators point to *Morton Salt Co. v. G.S. Suppiger,* 314 U.S. 488 (1942), as the foundational patent misuse case. In that case, the plaintiff Morton Salt brought suit on the basis that the defendant had infringed Morton's patent in a salt-depositing machine. The salt tablets were not themselves a patented item, but Morton's patent license required that licensees use only salt tablets produced by Morton. Morton was thereby using its patent to restrain competition in the sale of an item which was not within the scope of the patent's privilege. The Supreme Court held that, as a court of equity, it would not aid Morton in protecting its patent when Morton was using that patent in a manner contrary to public policy. The Court stated:

> The grant to the inventor of the special privilege of a patent monopoly carries out a public policy adopted by the Constitution and laws of the United States, "to promote the Progress of Science and useful Arts, by securing for limited Times to . . . Inventors the exclusive Right . . ." to their "new and useful" inventions. United States Constitution, Art. I, §8, cl. 8, 35 U.S.C. §31. But the public policy which includes inventions within the granted monopoly excludes from it all that is not embraced in the invention. It equally forbids the use of the patent to secure an exclusive right or limited monopoly not granted by the Patent Office and which it is contrary to public policy to grant.

Id. at 492. Thus, the Supreme Court endorsed "misuse of patent" as an equitable defense to a suit for infringement of that patent.

Since *Morton Salt,* the courts have recognized patent misuse as a valid defense and have applied it in a number of cases in which patent owners have attempted to use their patents for price fixing, tie-ins, territorial restrictions, and so forth. The patent misuse defense also has been acknowledged by Congress in the 1988 Patent Misuse Reform Act (codified at 35 U.S.C. §271(d)(4) & (5)), which limited but did not eliminate the defense.

3. The "Misuse of Copyright" Defense

Although the patent misuse defense has been generally recognized since *Morton Salt,* it has been much less certain whether an analogous copyright misuse defense exists. This uncertainty persists because no United States Supreme Court decision has firmly established a copyright misuse defense in a manner analogous to the establishment of the patent misuse defense by *Morton Salt.* The few courts considering the issue have split on whether the defense should be recognized, and we have discovered only one case which has actually applied copyright misuse to bar an action for infringement.

We are of the view, however, that since copyright and patent law serve parallel public interests, a "misuse" defense should apply to infringement actions brought to vindicate either right. As discussed above, the similarity of the policies underlying patent and copyright is great and historically has been consistently recognized. Both patent law and copyright law seek to increase the store of human knowledge and arts by rewarding inventors and authors with the exclusive rights to their works for a limited time. At the same time, the granted monopoly power does not extend to property not covered by the patent or copyright.

Thus, we are persuaded that the rationale of *Morton Salt* in establishing the misuse defense applies to copyrights. In the passage from *Morton Salt* quoted above, the phraseology adapts easily to a copyright context:

> The grant to the [author] of the special privilege of a [copyright] carries out a public policy adopted by the Constitution and laws of the United States, "to promote the Progress of Science and useful Arts, by securing for limited Times to [Authors] . . . the exclusive Right . . ." to their ["original" works]. United States Constitution, Art. I, §8, cl. 8,

[17 U.S.C. § 102]. But the public policy which includes [original works] within the granted monopoly excludes from it all that is not embraced in the [original expression]. It equally forbids the use of the [copyright] to secure an exclusive right or limited monopoly not granted by the [Copyright] Office and which it is contrary to public policy to grant.

Having determined that "misuse of copyright" is a valid defense, analogous to the misuse of patent defense, our next task is to determine whether the defense should have been applied by the district court to bar Lasercomb's infringement action against the defendants in this case.

B. The . . . Finding that the Anticompetitive Clauses Are Reasonable

In declining to recognize a misuse of copyright defense, the district court found "reasonable" Lasercomb's attempt to protect its software copyright by using anticompetitive clauses in their licensing agreement. In briefly expressing its reasoning, the court referred to the "delicate and sensitive" nature of software. It also observed that Lasercomb's president had testified that the noncompete language was negotiable.

If, as it appears, the district court analogized from the "rule of reason" concept of antitrust law, we think its reliance on that principle was misplaced. Such reliance is, however, understandable. Both the presentation by appellants and the literature tend to intermingle antitrust and misuse defenses. A patent or copyright is often regarded as a limited monopoly — an exception to the general public policy against restraints of trade. Since antitrust law is the statutory embodiment of that public policy, there is an understandable association of antitrust law with the misuse defense. Certainly, an entity which uses its patent as the means of violating antitrust law is subject to a misuse of patent defense. However, *Morton Salt* held that it is not necessary to prove an antitrust violation in order to successfully assert patent misuse:

> It is unnecessary to decide whether respondent has violated the Clayton Act, for we conclude that in any event the maintenance of the present suit to restrain petitioner's manufacture or sale of the alleged infringing machines is contrary to public policy and that the district court rightly dismissed the complaint for want of equity.

So while it is true that the attempted use of a copyright to violate antitrust law probably would give rise to a misuse of copyright defense, the converse is not necessarily true — a misuse need not be a violation of antitrust law in order to comprise an equitable defense to an infringement action. The question is not whether the copyright is being used in a manner violative of antitrust law (such as whether the licensing agreement is "reasonable"), but whether the copyright is being used in a manner violative of the public policy embodied in the grant of a copyright.

Lasercomb undoubtedly has the right to protect against copying of the Interact code. Its standard licensing agreement, however, goes much further and essentially attempts to suppress any attempt by the licensee to independently implement the idea which Interact expresses. The agreement forbids the licensee to develop or assist in developing *any* kind of computer-assisted die-making software. If the licensee is a business, it is to prevent all its directors, officers and employees from assisting in any manner to develop computer-assisted die-making software. Although one or another licensee might succeed in negotiating out the noncompete provisions, this does not negate the fact that Lasercomb is attempting to use its copyright in a manner adverse to the public policy embodied in copyright law, and that it has succeeded in doing so with at least one licensee.

The language employed in the Lasercomb agreement is extremely broad. Each time Lasercomb sells its Interact program to a company and obtains that company's agreement to the noncompete language, the company is required to forego utilization of the creative abilities of all its officers, directors and employees in the area of CAD/CAM die-making software. Of yet greater concern, these creative abilities are withdrawn from the public. The period for which this anticompetitive restraint exists is ninety-nine years, which could be longer than the life of the copyright itself.

We previously have considered the effect of anticompetitive language in a licensing agreement in the context of patent misuse. *Compton v. Metal Products, Inc.,* 453 F.2d 38 (4th Cir.1971), *cert. denied,* 406 U.S. 968 (1972). Compton had invented and patented coal auguring equipment. He granted an exclusive license in the patents to Joy Manufacturing, and the license agreement included a provision that Compton would not "engage in any business or activity relating to the manufacture or sale of equipment of the type licensed hereunder" for as long as he was due royalties under the patents. Suit for infringement of the Compton patents was brought against Metal Products, and the district court granted injunctive relief and damages. On appeal we held that relief for the infringement was barred by the misuse defense, stating:

> The need of Joy to protect its investment does not outweigh the public's right under our system to expect competition and the benefits which flow therefrom, and the total withdrawal of Compton from the mining machine business ·. . . everywhere in the world for a period of 20 years unreasonably lessens the competition which the public has a right to expect, and constitutes misuse of the patents.

Id. at 45.

We think the anticompetitive language in Lasercomb's licensing agreement is at least as egregious as that which led us to bar the infringement action in *Compton,* and therefore amounts to misuse of its copyright. Again, the analysis necessary to a finding of misuse is similar to but separate from the analysis necessary to a finding of antitrust violation. The misuse arises from Lasercomb's attempt to use its copyright in a particular expression, the Interact software, to control competition in an area outside the copyright, *i.e.,* the idea of computer-assisted die manufacture, regardless of whether such conduct amounts to an antitrust violation.

C. The Effect of Appellants Not Being Party to the Anticompetitive Contract

In its rejection of the copyright misuse defense, the district court emphasized that Holiday Steel was not explicitly party to a licensing agreement containing the offending language. However, again analogizing to patent misuse, the defense of copyright misuse is available even if the defendants themselves have not been injured by the misuse. In *Morton Salt,* the defendant was not a party to the license requirement that only Morton-produced salt tablets be used with Morton's salt-depositing machine. Nevertheless, suit against defendant for infringement of Morton's patent was barred on public policy grounds. Similarly, in *Compton,* even though the defendant Metal Products was not a party to the license agreement that restrained competition by Compton, suit against Metal Products was barred because of the public interest in free competition.

Therefore, the fact that appellants here were not parties to one of Lasercomb's standard license agreements is inapposite to their copyright misuse defense. The question is whether Lasercomb is using its copyright in a manner contrary to public policy, which question we have answered in the affirmative.

NOTES

1. Doctrines of patent misuse and copyright misuse are distinctive features of licensing law. Patent misuse doctrine flourished as a restraint on licensing during the 1960s and through part of the 1970s as an active distrust of intellectual property characterized many court and some regulatory decisions. The frequency of successful misuse claims has greatly diminished because judicial attitude and agency policy changed. The Patent Misuse Reform Act of 1988 added clauses (4) and (5) to Section 271(d) of the Patent Act which provide:

> No patent owner otherwise entitled to relief for infringement or contributory infringement of a patent shall be denied relief or deemed guilty of misuse or illegal extension of the patent right by reason of his having done one or more of the following: . . . (4) refused to license or use any rights to the patent; or (5) conditioned the license of any rights to the patent or the sale of the patented product on the acquisition of a license to rights in another patent or purchase of a separate product, unless, in view of the circumstances, the patent owner has market power in the relevant market for the patent or patented product on which the license or sale is conditioned.

After the Reform Act, patent misuse doctrine has seen no expansion and infrequent application. We introduce the concept here. It resurfaces later in these materials in context of several licensing practices that may present misuse concerns.

2. While copyright misuse doctrine has been around for many years, *Lasercomb* reintroduced it in the modern era. What policy dictates a misuse defense as described by *Lasercomb*? It is easy to argue that the non-competition terms were aggressive and potentially over-reaching, but how did those terms relate to the intellectual property right? Was the copyright wrongfully leveraged to suppress competition?

3. The theory that an intellectual property right creates risk of wrongful leveraging to control conduct outside the scope of the property right is a common theme in patent misuse decisions. *See Zenith Radio Corporation v. Hazeltine Research, Inc.,* 395 U.S. 100, 114-125 (1969). *Lasercomb* rejected the idea that proof of market power sufficient for an antitrust violation was necessary to show misuse. In the absence of market power, however, how can there be wrongful leveraging? If the licensee had other options but chose to accept a license, why is the exercise of choice not sufficient to quell any misuse claim?

Other courts require a closer connection between antitrust violations and misuse doctrine. In *Mallinckrodt, Inc. v. Medipart, Inc.*, 976 F.2d 700 (Fed. Cir. 1992), the Federal Circuit held that even if the restrictions or conditions placed on the sale of patented goods "went well beyond" the subject matter within the scope of the patent, they would be tested "according with the rule of reason" unless they were *per se* violations of antitrust laws or existing misuse principles.

4. In 2006, the Supreme Court revisited the issue of market power being presumed from the mere existence of an intellectual property right. *Illinois Tool Works, Inc. v. Independent Ink, Inc.*, 126 S.Ct. 1281 (2006) dealt with that issue in context of an antitrust claim involving a patent license. The Court noted that the presumption of market power arose from misuse law, rather than antitrust law, and that the presumption had been extensively criticized. Indeed, Congress specifically rejected the presumption in its origins (misuse law) under the Misuse Reform Act. The Court concluded that, while some "arrangements are still unlawful, such as those that are the product of a true monopoly or a marketwide conspiracy, that conclusion must be supported by proof of power in the relevant market rather than by a mere presumption thereof." Does this analysis undermine the continued viability of the court's reasoning in *Lasercomb*?

5. Independent of misuse arguments, in employee contracts, non-competition clauses have been routinely subjected to scrutiny of their reasonableness under state law and invalidated (or rewritten by a court) if found to be unreasonable in duration, scope or other elements. Could *Lasercomb* have taken that approach?

PROBLEM 1.5

You represent the company in *Lasercomb*. Shortly after the decision becomes final, your client asks you to redraft the license to avoid results such as in this case. You are aware that, if the company cures (purges) the misuse, the effect of the *Lasercomb* ruling on the company will be eliminated. The company informs you, however, that maintaining some protection against competition is important. How would you recommend redrafting the contract? What additional information would you need to make your recommendation?

III. WHAT LAW APPLIES WITHIN A STATE

In 1934, Llewellyn commented: "'One system of precedent' we may have, but it works in forty different ways." Karl Llewellyn, *On Philosophy in American Law*, 82 U. PA. L. REV. 205, 205 n.178 (1934). That observation is even more accurate today as regulatory statutes and newly emerging areas of commerce have even further fragmented contract law in the various states.

To persons who view contract law as essentially having two categories — Uniform Commercial Code contracts and common law contracts represented by the *Restatement (Second) of Contracts* — the issue of what law within a state applies might seem to be a narrow one, choosing between two relatively standardized bodies of law. But that is not the case, and there is significantly greater diversity. The *Restatement* states one group's view of what the general common law should be, but does not purport to be uniformly applicable across all subject matter or all states. It does not account for variations in, for example, franchise law, consumer protection rules, services contract doctrines, products liability considerations, and the myriad other different sources of focus for common law, more accurately, non-UCC law.

That being said, we can nonetheless learn a lot about variations in local state laws by looking at the interaction between UCC Article 2 (and now Article 2A) on the one hand, and the common law on the other. In most licensing cases, whether Article 2 applies is resolved without any debate — Article 2 does not apply. The subject matter of Article 2 (and Article 2A) is goods, defined as things that are "movable" at the time of their identification to the contract, while the subject matter of licensing is information or other intangibles even though the information may sometimes be delivered in a book, a paper-based report, or a diskette, CD, DVD or other medium. *See* U.C.C. §2-105; UCITA §102(a). Furthermore, even if Article 2 were to apply to a licensing transaction, it would most often have nothing to say about the issues that most often frame disputes — e.g., the scope of a license, application to future technologies, exclusivity, competition, etc. *See* Raymond T. Nimmer, *Through the Looking Glass: What Courts and UCITA have to say About the Scope of Contract Law in the Information Age*, 38 DUQUESNE L. REV. 1 (2000).

ZAPATHA v. DAIRY MART, INC.
381 Mass. 284, 408 N.E.2d 1370 (Mass. 1980)

WILKINS, JUSTICE.

We are concerned here with the question whether Dairy Mart, Inc. (Dairy Mart), lawfully undertook to terminate a franchise agreement under which the Zapathas operated a Dairy Mart store on Wilbraham Road in Springfield. The Zapathas brought this action seeking to enjoin the termination of the agreement, alleging that the contract provision purporting to authorize the termination of the franchise agreement without cause was unconscionable and that Dairy Mart's conduct was an unfair and deceptive act or practice in violation of G.L. c. 93A. The judge ruled that Dairy Mart did not act in good faith, that the termination provision was unconscionable. . . . We reverse the judgments.

Mr. Zapatha is a high school graduate who had attended college for one year and had also taken college evening courses in business administration and business law. From 1952 to May, 1973, he was employed by a company engaged in the business of electroplating. He rose through the ranks to foreman and then to the position of operations manager, at one time being in charge of all metal finishing in the plant with 150 people working under him. In May, 1973, he was discharged and began looking for other opportunities, in particular a business of his own. Several months later he met with a representative of Dairy Mart. Dairy Mart operates a chain of franchised "convenience" stores. The Dairy Mart representative told Mr. Zapatha that working for Dairy Mart was being in business for one's self and that such a business was very stable and secure. Mr. Zapatha signed an application to be considered for a franchise. In addition, he was presented with a brochure entitled "Here's a Chance," which made certain representations concerning the status of a franchise holder.

Dairy Mart approved Mr. Zapatha's application and offered him a store in Agawam. On November 8, 1973, a representative of Dairy Mart showed him a form of franchise agreement, entitled Limited Franchise and License Agreement, asked him to read it, and explained that his wife would have to sign the agreement as well.

Under the terms of the agreement, Dairy Mart would license the Zapathas to operate a Dairy Mart store, using the Dairy Mart trademark and associated insignia, and utilizing Dairy Mart's "confidential" merchandising methods. Dairy Mart would furnish the store and the equipment and would pay rent and gas and electric bills as well as certain other costs of doing business. In return Dairy Mart would receive a franchise fee, computed as a percentage of the store's gross sales. The Zapathas would have to pay for the starting inventory, and maintain a minimum stock of saleable merchandise thereafter. They were also responsible for wages of employees, related taxes, and any sales taxes. The termination provision . . . allowed either party, after twelve months, to terminate the agreement without cause on ninety days' written notice. In the event of termination initiated by it without cause, Dairy Mart agreed to repurchase the saleable merchandise inventory at retail prices, less 20%.

The Dairy Mart representative read and explained the termination provision to Mr. Zapatha. Mr. Zapatha later testified that, while he understood every word in the provision, he had interpreted it to mean that Dairy Mart could terminate the agreement only for cause. . . . In 1974, another store became available on Wilbraham Road in Springfield, and the Zapathas elected to surrender the Agawam store. They executed a new franchise agreement, on an identical printed form, relating to the new location.

In November, 1977, Dairy Mart presented a new and more detailed form of "Independent Operator's Agreement" to the Zapathas for execution. Some of the terms were less favorable to the store operator than those of the earlier form of agreement. Mr. Zapatha told representatives of Dairy Mart that he was content with the existing contract and had decided not to sign the new agreement. On January 20, 1978, Dairy Mart gave written notice to the Zapathas that their contract was being terminated effective in ninety days. The termination notice stated that Dairy Mart "remains available to enter into discussions with you with respect to entering into a new Independent Operator's Agreement; however, there is no assurance that Dairy Mart will enter into a new Agreement with you, or even if entered into, what terms such Agreement will contain." The notice also indicated that Dairy Mart was prepared to purchase the Zapathas' saleable inventory. . . .

1. We consider first the question whether the franchise agreement involves a "transaction in goods" within the meaning of those words in article two of the Uniform Commercial Code . . . and that consequently the provisions of the sales articles of the Uniform Commercial Code govern the relationship between the parties. The Zapathas point specifically to the authority of a court to refuse to enforce "any clause of the contract" that the court finds "to have been unconscionable at the time it was made." [UCC § 2-302]. They point additionally to the obligation of good faith in the performance and enforcement of a contract [and] to the specialized definition of "good faith" in the sales article as meaning "in the case of a merchant . . . honesty in fact and the observance of reasonable commercial standards of fair dealing in the trade." [UCC § 2-103(1)(b)].

We need not pause long over the question whether the franchise agreement and the relationship of the parties involved a transaction in goods. Certainly, the agreement required the plaintiffs to purchase goods from Dairy Mart. "Goods" for the purpose of the sales article means generally "all things . . . which are movable." [UCC § 2-105(1)]. However, the franchise agreement dealt with many subjects unrelated to the sale of goods by Dairy Mart. About 70% of the goods the plaintiffs sold were not purchased from Dairy Mart. Dairy Mart's profit was intended to come from the franchise fee and not from the sale of items to its franchisees. Thus, the sale of goods by Dairy Mart to the Zapathas was, in a commercial sense, a minor aspect of the entire relationship. We would be disinclined to import automatically all the provisions of the sales article into a relationship involving a variety of subjects other than the sale of goods, merely because the contract dealt in part with the sale of goods. Similarly, we would not be inclined to apply the sales article only to aspects of the agreement that concerned goods. Different principles of law might then govern separate portions of the same agreement with possibly inconsistent and unsatisfactory consequences.

[However, we] view the legislative statements of policy concerning good faith and unconscionability as fairly applicable to all aspects of the franchise agreement, not by subjecting the franchise relationship to the provisions of the sales article but rather by applying the stated principles by analogy. This basic common law approach, applied to statutory statements of policy, permits a selective application of those principles expressed in a statute that reasonably should govern situations to which the statute does not apply explicitly.

[We] consider first the plaintiffs' argument that the termination clause of the franchise agreement, authorizing Dairy Mart to terminate the agreement without cause, on ninety days' notice, was unconscionable by the standards expressed in [Article 2]. The same standards are set forth in *Restatement (Second) of Contracts* § 234. The issue is one of law for the court, and the test is to be made as of the time the contract was made. In measuring the unconscionability of the termination provision, the fact that the law imposes an obligation of good faith on Dairy Mart in its performance under the agreement should be weighed.

[The] official comment to § 2-302 states that "[t]he basic test is whether, in the light of the general commercial background and the commercial needs of the particular trade or case, the clauses involved are so one-sided as to be unconscionable under the circumstances existing at the time of the making of the contract. [The] principle is one of prevention of oppression and unfair surprise [and] not of disturbance of allocation of risks because of superior bargaining power." Official Comment 1 to U.C.C. § 2-302. . . .

We start with a recognition that the Uniform Commercial Code itself implies that a contract provision allowing termination without cause is not per se unconscionable. Section 2-309(3) provides that "[t]ermination of a contract by one party except on the happening of an agreed event requires that reasonable notification be received by the other party and an agreement dispensing with notification is invalid if its operation would be unconscionable." [UCC § 2-309.] This language implies that termination of a sales contract without agreed "cause" is authorized by the Code, provided reasonable notice is given. There is no suggestion that the ninety days' notice provided in the Dairy Mart franchise agreement was unreasonable.

We find no potential for unfair surprise to the Zapathas in the provision allowing termination without cause. We view the question of unfair surprise as focused on the circumstances under which the agreement was entered into. The termination provision was neither obscurely worded, nor buried in fine print in the contract. The provision was specifically pointed out to Mr. Zapatha before it was signed; Mr. Zapatha testified that he thought the provision was "straightforward," and he declined the opportunity to take the agreement to a lawyer for advice. The Zapathas had ample opportunity to consider the agreement before they signed it. . . . We conclude that a person of Mr. Zapatha's business experience and education should not have been surprised by the termination provision and, if in fact he was, there was no element of unfairness in the inclusion of that provision in the agreement.

We further conclude that there was no oppression in the inclusion of a termination clause in the franchise agreement. We view the question of oppression as directed to the substantive fairness to the parties of permitting the termination provisions to operate as written. The Zapathas took over a going business on premises provided by Dairy Mart, using equipment furnished by Dairy Mart. As an investment, the Zapathas had only to purchase the inventory of goods to be sold but, as Dairy Mart concedes, on termination by it without cause Dairy Mart was obliged to repurchase all the Zapathas' saleable merchandise inventory, including items not purchased from Dairy Mart, at 80% of its retail value. There was no potential for forfeiture or loss of investment. There is no question here of a need for a reasonable time to recoup the franchisees' initial investment. The Zapathas were entitled to their net profits through the entire term of the agreement. They failed to sustain their burden of showing that the agreement allocated the risks and benefits connected with termination in an unreasonably disproportionate way and that the termination provision was not reasonably related to legitimate commercial needs of Dairy Mart. To find the termination clause oppressive merely because it did not require cause for termination would be to establish an unwarranted barrier to the use of termination at will clauses in contracts in this Commonwealth, where each party received the anticipated and bargained for consideration during the full term of the agreement.

We see no basis on the record for concluding that Dairy Mart did not act in good faith. [The] judge concluded that the absence of any commercial purpose for the termination other than the Zapathas' refusal to sign a new franchise agreement violated Dairy Mart's obligation of good faith. Dairy Mart's right to terminate was clear, and it exercised that right for a reason it openly disclosed. The sole test of "honesty in fact" is whether the person was honest. We think that, whether or not termination according to the terms of the franchise agreement may have been arbitrary, it was not dishonest. . . .

REVERSED

NOTES

1. *Zapatha* illustrates two ways that Article 2 might be brought to bear on a license arrangement. The court rejected one (e.g., transfer of goods as the predominant purpose of the license), but accepted the other. Standards of good faith and unconscionability are the most common Article 2 rules that have been applied by analogy to non-UCC transactions. Indeed, unlike at the time of *Zapatha*, they are now part of the common law of most states. Why would these rules be primary targets of reasoning by analogy?

2. A number of state and federal franchise laws restrict the right of a franchisor to terminate a franchise, and regulate the content of franchise disclosures. When applicable, these rules supersede general good faith or unconscionability arguments.

3. Before its analysis by analogy, the court applied the predominant purpose test and held that the license elements of the transaction predominated over the goods elements. What was the basis for this decision? Was the decision based on the relative dollar value attributed of the goods and the license, or on another analysis? If the agreement was not in Article 2, what law applies to determine if the inventory purchased by Zapatha came with an implied warranty of merchantability that is in Article 2, but not common law?

4. *Zapatha* recognizes that "intangibles" such as a trademark license do not constitute goods and should be separately considered in a predominant purpose analysis. *See also Stewart v. Lucero*, 121 N.M. 722, 918 P.2d 1 (N.M. 1996). The predominant purpose test is commonly applied to distinguish between goods and services contracts. Would it ever be appropriate to apply Article 2 implied warranties to an intellectual property right in a license simply because the predominant purpose of the transaction was to obtain the goods?

PROBLEM 1.6

Client owns a catalog business that it plans to sell to Buyer as a going business. Client operates the business under a ten-year trademark license with Seers Corp., a national retail company. The license calls for monthly fees of 10% of net sales during the month. The business name is "Seers Consumer Shop." Client has a contract with each of the goods manufacturers whose goods it sells that requires the manufacturers to supply goods as needed by Client. Client maintains an inventory of goods worth approximately $2,500,000, but for most sales, it orders the goods from the manufacturer when it receives an order from the customer. Monthly sales average $2 million. Seers agreed to the transfer of the license, and the sale to the Buyer will also include all of the inventory and the contracts with manufacturers. The purchase price is $10 million cash. Is this transaction governed by Article 2?

PROBLEM 1.7

Client intends to sell the assets of its advertising division to Buyer. These assets consist of 1) computers, office furnishings and the like (valued at $1.5 million), 2) a non-competition agreement with the former chairman of the division which has five years remaining (valued at $800,000 by the parties), and 3) various designs and drawings on paper and on digital CDs that are used in the business (valued at $900,000). There is to be no transfer of any trademark or other asset. Is this transaction governed by Article 2?

GILMER v. BUENA VISTA HOME VIDEO
939 F. Supp. 665 (W.D. Ark. 1996)

H. FRANKLIN WATERS, CHIEF JUDGE.

These consolidated cases are currently before the court on the defendants' motion to dismiss and the plaintiff's response thereto. These putative class action cases were filed by Janet Gilmer on behalf of herself and all other similarly situated individuals throughout the United States who have purchased certain home videos, namely "The Lion King," "The Fox and the Hound," and "Little Mermaid."

The plaintiff claims that the video cassettes or the plastic video cassette case of these three Disney films contain drawings and animated scenes depicting sexual messages or other sexually related material unsuitable for young children and/or family viewing. Specifically, plaintiff alleges that the front cover of the plastic case in which "The Little Mermaid" was distributed in 1989 & 1990 contains a depiction of an erect penis on one of the spires of the castle drawn between the two main characters. With respect to "The Fox and the Hound" distributed in 1994, plaintiff contends that one scene contains a subliminal message consisting of the widow in the film "giving the finger" to the camera after picking up Tod, the fox. With respect to "The Lion King" distributed in 1995, plaintiff alleges it contains a subliminal scene where a cloud of milk-weed particles form the word "Sex" in the sky above one of the main characters in the movie.

The amended complaint . . . asserts the following causes of action: (1) invasion of privacy; (2) common law fraud; (3) breach of warranties both express and implied; and (4) negligence. Defendants, Buena Vista Home Video, Inc. (BVHV), and Walt Disney Pictures and Television (WDP), have now moved for dismissal of the complaint on a number of grounds. . . .

[The court initially held that, while motion pictures are a form of speech, subliminal messages contained in them may not be subject to as full of protection as other types of speech and, thus, there would be no dismissal of the claims based on First Amendment grounds.]

[Breach of Warranty].

Plaintiff asserts breaches of express warranties and breaches of the implied warranties of merchantability and fitness for a particular purpose. Defendants do not separately address each type of warranty. Instead, defendants concentrate on the asserted breach of an implied warranty of merchantability.

To recover for breach of an implied warranty of merchantability, the plaintiffs must prove: (1) that they sustained damages; (2) that the goods sold to them were not merchantable, *i.e.,* fit for the ordinary purpose for which such goods are used; (3) that the unmerchantable condition was a proximate cause of the plaintiffs' damages; and (4) that the plaintiffs were persons whom the defendants might reasonably expect to use or be affected by the goods.

In defendants' view, plaintiff's breach of warranty claims boil down to the allegation that BVHV should be liable for promoting the videos as suitable for young children even though they allegedly contain subliminal sexual messages. In determining whether a breach of warranty exists, defendant contends the court must distinguish between the tangible properties of the goods sold and the thoughts or ideas conveyed thereby. They contend the implied warranty from a merchant who regularly sells video cassette is limited to the physical properties of such cassettes and does not extend to their content. BVHV relies, *inter alia,* on *Winter v. G.P. Putnam's Sons,* 938 F.2d 1033 (9th Cir.1991) and *Cardozo v. True,* 342 So.2d 1053 (Fla.Dist.Ct.App.1977), *cert. denied,* 353 So.2d 674 (Fla.1977). Both cases hold that a book publisher warrants only the tangible, physical properties of a book and makes no warranty regarding the content of the book communicated by the book's author or publisher.

Plaintiff contends these cases are easily distinguished. Here, the video cassettes are sold as a package which consists of the tape itself and the cover. These items together, according to plaintiff, constitute goods within the meaning of the Uniform Commercial Code as adopted in Arkansas. In the cases cited by defendants, the plaintiff contends the courts refused to impose liability because there was nothing whatsoever wrong with the books *i.e.,* the books said exactly what they were supposed to say. Thus, any cause of action which proceeded on a theory that the ideas conveyed in the books were harmful to the people was inappropriate.

Here, plaintiff argues the "tangible properties" do not conform to the defendants' warranties and the plaintiff's complaint is about the tangible properties of the product itself — not just the ideas conveyed by the offensive materials. As examples, plaintiff points to the cover of "The Little Mermaid" and the still photograph from "The Fox and the Hound."

We disagree with plaintiff's characterization. Plaintiff does not complain in any respect about the physical properties of the film or the covers as opposed to the ideas, thoughts, or images contained thereon. There is no allegation that the videos contained physical defects. Rather, plaintiff's complaint is that the videos and/or the covers contain offensive or morally unfit images or messages.

However, plaintiff does allege that BVHV, in promoting and marketing the videos, warranted that they were suitable for viewing by children despite its knowledge at the time of marketing that the videos contained subliminal messages. These allegations are sufficient to withstand a motion to dismiss even under the cases relied on by defendants. Whether plaintiff can withstand a properly supported summary judgment motion will be determined at a later point in time.

Conclusion.

[Defendants'] motion to dismiss will be granted in part and denied in part.

NOTES

1. Did the court hold that Article 2 applied or not? Did the court use a predominant purpose test or was it using a different type of analysis? The result in *Gilmer* as to information content is widely followed. What is the policy rationale for excluding information content from Article 2 implied warranty law?

2. The court in *Cardozo v. True*, 342 So. 2d 1053, 1057 (Fla. Dist. Ct. App. 1977), cited by the *Gilmer* court, commented: "[W]e hold that absent allegations that a book seller knew that there was reason to warn the public as to the contents of a book, the implied warranty in respect to sale of books by a merchant who regularly sells them is limited to a warranty of the physical properties of such books and does not extend to the material communicated by the book's author or publisher."

3. UCITA defines subject matter like that addressed in *Gilmer* as "informational content" and provides that there is generally no implied warranty with respect to the quality such content, although the parties may create express warranties by agreement. UCITA § 404 (2000 Official Text).

PROBLEM 1.8

Client has developed software that enables homebuilders to create self-operating homes — houses that monitor all utilities and optimize their use. Client will license that software to builders and to homeowners. It asks you to develop a relevant contract. Before doing so, you must determine what law applies. What is your answer? What would be your answer if Client was distributing copies of digital e-books (texts in digital form that include text and software to allow the user to search for specific entries and background material on aspects of the book)?

ADVENT SYSTEMS LTD. v. UNISYS CORP.
925 F.2d 670 (3d Cir. 1991)

WEIS, CIRCUIT JUDGE.

Plaintiff, Advent Systems Limited, is engaged primarily in the production of software for computers. As a result of its research and development efforts, by 1986 the company had developed an electronic document management system

(EDMS), a process for transforming engineering drawings and similar documents into a computer database.

Unisys Corporation manufactures a variety of computers. As a result of information gained by its wholly-owned United Kingdom subsidiary during 1986, Unisys decided to market the document management system in the United States. In June 1987 Advent and Unisys signed two documents, one labeled "Heads of Agreement" (in British parlance "an outline of agreement") and, the other "Distribution Agreement."

In these documents, Advent agreed to provide the software and hardware making up the document systems to be sold by Unisys in the United States. Advent was obligated to provide sales and marketing material and manpower as well as technical personnel to work with Unisys employees in building and installing the document systems. The agreement was to continue for two years, subject to automatic renewal or termination on notice.

During the summer of 1987, Unisys attempted to sell the document system to Arco, a large oil company, but was unsuccessful. Nevertheless, progress on the sales and training programs in the United States was satisfactory, and negotiations for a contract between Unisys (UK) and Advent were underway. The relationship, however, soon came to an end. Unisys, in the throes of restructuring, decided it would be better served by developing its own document system and in December 1987 told Advent their arrangement had ended. Unisys also advised its UK subsidiary of those developments and, as a result, negotiations there were terminated.

Advent filed a complaint in the district court alleging, inter alia, breach of contract, fraud, and tortious interference with contractual relations. The district court ruled at pretrial that the Uniform Commercial Code did not apply because although goods were to be sold, the services aspect of the contract predominated.

Software and the Uniform Commercial Code

The district court ruled that as a matter of law the arrangement between the two parties was not within the Uniform Commercial Code and, consequently, the statute of frauds was not applicable. As the district court appraised the transaction, provisions for services outweighed those for products and, consequently, the arrangement was not predominantly one for the sale of goods.

In the "Heads of Agreement" Advent and Unisys purported to enter into a "joint business collaboration." Advent was to modify its software and hardware interfaces to run initially on equipment not manufactured by Unisys but eventually on Unisys hardware. It was Advent's responsibility to purchase the necessary hardware. "[I]n so far as Advent has successfully completed [some of the processing] of software and hardware interfaces," Unisys promised to reimburse Advent to the extent of $150,000 derived from a "surcharge" on products purchased. Advent agreed to provide twelve man-weeks of marketing manpower, but with Unisys bearing certain expenses. Advent also undertook to furnish an experienced systems builder to work with Unisys personnel at

Advent's prevailing rates, and to provide sales and support training for Unisys staff as well as its customers.

The Distribution Agreement begins with the statement, "Unisys desires to purchase, and Advent desires to sell, on a non-exclusive basis, certain of Advent hardware products and software licenses for resale worldwide." Following a heading "Subject Matter of Sales," appears this sentence, "(a) Advent agrees to sell hardware and license software to Unisys, and Unisys agrees to buy from Advent the products listed in Schedule A." Schedule A lists twenty products, such as computer cards, plotters, imagers, scanners and designer systems.

Advent was to invoice Unisys for each product purchased upon shipment, but to issue separate invoices for maintenance fees. The cost of the "support services" was set at 3% "per annum of the prevailing Advent user list price of each software module for which Unisys is receiving revenue from a customer." Services included field technical bulletins, enhancement and maintenance releases, telephone consultation, and software patches, among others. At no charge to Unisys, Advent was to provide publications such as installation manuals, servicing and adjustment manuals, diagnostic operation and test procedures, sales materials, product brochures and similar items. In turn, Unisys was to "employ resources in performing marketing efforts" and develop "the technical ability to be thoroughly familiar" with the products.

In support of the district court's ruling that the U.C.C. did not apply, Advent contends that the agreement's requirement of furnishing services did not come within the Code. Moreover, the argument continues, the "software" referred to in the agreement as a "product" was not a "good" but intellectual property outside the ambit of the Uniform Commercial Code.

Because software was a major portion of the "products" described in the agreement, this matter requires some discussion. Computer systems consist of "hardware" and "software." Hardware is the computer machinery, its electronic circuitry and peripheral items such as keyboards, readers, scanners and printers. Software is a more elusive concept. Generally speaking, "software" refers to the medium that stores input and output data as well as computer programs. The medium includes hard disks, floppy disks, and magnetic tapes.

In simplistic terms, programs are codes prepared by a programmer that instruct the computer to perform certain functions. When the program is transposed onto a medium compatible with the computer's needs, it becomes software. . . . The increasing frequency of computer products as subjects of commercial litigation has led to controversy over whether software is a "good" or intellectual property. The Code does not specifically mention software.

In the absence of express legislative guidance, courts interpret the Code in light of commercial and technological developments. The Code is designed "[t]o simplify, clarify and modernize the law governing commercial transactions" and "[t]o permit the continued expansion of commercial practices." As the Official Commentary makes clear:

> This Act is drawn to provide flexibility so that, since it is intended to
> be a semi-permanent piece of legislation, it will provide its own

machinery for expansion of commercial practices. It is intended to make it possible for the law embodied in this Act to be developed by the courts in the light of unforeseen and new circumstances and practices.

The Code "applies to transactions in goods." Goods are defined as "all things (including specially manufactured goods) which are moveable at the time of the identification for sale." The Pennsylvania courts have recognized that " 'goods' has a very extensive meaning" under the U.C.C. Our Court has addressed computer package sales in other cases, but has not been required to consider whether the U.C.C. applied to software per se. Other Courts of Appeals have also discussed transactions of this nature. *RRX Industries, Inc. v. Lab-Con, Inc.*, 772 F.2d 543 (9th Cir.1985) (goods aspects of transaction predominated in a sale of a software system); *Triangle Underwriters, Inc. v. Honeywell, Inc.*, 604 F.2d 737, 742-43 (2d Cir.1979) (in sale of computer hardware, software, and customized software, goods aspects predominated; services were incidental).

Computer programs are the product of an intellectual process, but once implanted in a medium are widely distributed to computer owners. An analogy can be drawn to a compact disc recording of an orchestral rendition. The music is produced by the artistry of musicians and in itself is not a "good," but when transferred to a laser-readable disc becomes a readily merchantable commodity. Similarly, when a professor delivers a lecture, it is not a good, but, when transcribed as a book, it becomes a good.

That a computer program may be copyrightable as intellectual property does not alter the fact that once in the form of a floppy disc or other medium, the program is tangible, moveable and available in the marketplace. The fact that some programs may be tailored for specific purposes need not alter their status as "goods" because the Code definition includes "specially manufactured goods."

The topic has stimulated academic commentary with the majority espousing the view that software fits within the definition of a "good" in the U.C.C. Applying the U.C.C. to computer software transactions offers substantial benefits to litigants and the courts. The Code offers a uniform body of law on a wide range of questions likely to arise in computer software disputes: implied warranties, consequential damages, disclaimers of liability, the statute of limitations, to name a few.

The importance of software to the commercial world and the advantages to be gained by the uniformity inherent in the U.C.C. are strong policy arguments favoring inclusion. The contrary arguments are not persuasive, and we hold that software is a "good" within the definition in the Code.

The relationship at issue here is a typical mixed goods and services arrangement. The services are not substantially different from those generally accompanying package sales of computer systems consisting of hardware and software. Although determining the applicability of the U.C.C. to a contract by examining the predominance of goods or services has been criticized, we see no reason to depart from that practice here. As we pointed out in *De Filippo v. Ford Motor Co.*, 516 F.2d 1313, 1323 (3d Cir.), *cert. denied*, 423 U.S. 912

(1975), segregating goods from non-goods and insisting "that the Statute of Frauds apply only to a portion of the contract, would be to make the contract divisible and impossible of performance within the intention of the parties."

We consider the purpose or essence of the contract. Comparing the relative costs of the materials supplied with the costs of the labor may be helpful in this analysis, but not dispositive. In this case the contract's main objective was to transfer "products." The specific provisions for training of Unisys personnel by Advent were but a small part of the parties' contemplated relationship.

The compensation structure of the agreement also focuses on "goods." The projected sales figures introduced during the trial demonstrate that in the contemplation of the parties the sale of goods clearly predominated. The payment provision of $150,000 for developmental work which Advent had previously completed, was to be made through individual purchases of software and hardware rather than through the fees for services and is further evidence that the intellectual work was to be subsumed into tangible items for sale.

We are persuaded that the transaction at issue here was within the scope of the Uniform Commercial Code and, therefore, the judgment in favor of the plaintiff must be reversed. . . .

[The court held that the Article 2 statute of frauds did not preclude enforcement of this contract, despite the absence of an express quantity term in the agreement, in part because Section 2-306 recognizes exclusive dealing agreements and imposes a duty of good faith that satisfies the requirement of a stated quantity.]

NOTES

1. As the court notes, many cases hold that transactions in computer software are within the scope of Article 2. Many of these involved contracts in which the software was delivered with hardware during a time when hardware was expensive and software was not; the courts used a predominant purpose test. Some cases, however, focused on the fact that the software was delivered on a diskette (a tangible item). Are such deliveries distinguishable from the delivery of a blueprint on paper from an architect, a final draft of a will from a lawyer, a book, or a DVD of a motion picture? Would or should these be considered transactions in goods?

2. Many courts discussing distribution contracts for software have declined to apply Article 2. Consider the comment of the court in *Architectronics, Inc. v. Control Sys., Inc.*, 935 F. Supp. 425 (S.D.N.Y. 1996):

> The [agreement] provided for two licenses. Under the first license, Architectronics granted CSI the right to use its DynaMenu software prototypes for joint venture-related purposes only. That license gave CSI a tool necessary for the development of the "Derivative Work," a new display driver. Under the second license, CSI granted Architectronics and CADSource the right to use, copy, and distribute the "Derivative Work." That license was the centerpiece of the transaction, because it provided Architectronics and CADSource with the

valuable right to manufacture the new display driver and sell it to the public. Architectronics and CADSource bargained primarily for the right to mass market the product, not for the right to install single copies of the display driver onto their own PCs. CSI's upside in the deal also was linked to the rights to reproduce and distribute: the parties anticipated thousands of sales of the new product, and Architectronics and CADSource promised to pay CSI a $20-per-copy royalty on those sales. CSI stood to gain in royalties a sum that would dwarf the $2,000 development fee. Because the predominant feature of the SDLA was a transfer of intellectual property rights, the agreement is not subject to Article Two of the UCC.

3. The appropriate treatment of software has been controversial and led to uniform legislation addressing the question. In 1999, the National Conference of Commissioners on Uniform State Laws (NCCUSL) promulgated UCITA, which treats software (and other computer information transactions) under a uniform law separate from Article 2, but modeled in part after Article 2 rules. UCITA has been adopted in two states and referred to by a number of courts by analogy. Around the same time, revised Article 9 was promulgated and adopted in all fifty states. Article 9, which deals with secured financing, excludes most computer software from the definition of "goods." It states:

> "Goods" means all things that are movable when a security interest attaches. The term includes . . . A computer program embedded in goods and any supporting information provided in connection with a transaction relating to the program if (i) the program is associated with the goods in such a manner that it customarily is considered part of the goods, or (ii) by becoming the owner of the goods, a person acquires a right to use the program in connection with the goods. The term does not include a computer program embedded in goods that consist solely of the medium in which the program is embedded. The term also does not include accounts, chattel paper, commercial tort claims, deposit accounts, documents, general intangibles. . . .

UCC § 9-102(a)(44). The term "general intangibles" includes "software."

After over 12 years of debate, amendments to Article 2 were promulgated by NCCUSL and the American Law Institute in 2003. The amendments define goods to mean "all things that are movable at the time of identification to a contract for sale. . . . The term does not include information. . . ." The comments to this section state:

> The definition of "goods" in this article has been amended to exclude information not associated with goods. Thus, this article does not directly apply to an electronic transfer of information, such as the transaction involved in *Specht v. Netscape*, 150 F. Supp. 2d 585 (S. D.N.Y. 2001). However, transactions often include both goods and information: some are transactions in goods as that term is used in Section 2-102, and some are not. For example, the sale of "smart goods" such as an automobile is a transaction in goods fully within this article even though the automobile contains many computer programs. On the other hand, an architect's provision of architectural plans on a

computer disk would not be a transaction in goods. When a transaction includes both the sale of goods and the transfer of rights in information, it is up to the courts to determine whether the transaction is entirely within or outside of this article, or whether or to what extent this article should be applied to a portion of the transaction. While this article may apply to a transaction including information, nothing in this Article alters, creates, or diminishes intellectual property rights.

UCC § 2-103, cmt. 7 (2003 Official Text).

While Article 2 does not define "information," two other NCCUSL Uniform Laws promulgated during the late 1990s do. The Uniform Electronic Transactions Act (UETA), which has been adopted in over forty states, defines "information" as "data, text, images, sounds, codes, computer programs, software, databases, or the like." UETA § 2(10). There is case law to a similar effect under federal law. *Green v. America Online*, 318 F.3d 465 (3d Cir. 2003), held that under the Communications Decency Act, Section 230, a computer program was within the definition of "information" for purposes of Section 230.

4. Reported cases split on whether Article 2 applies to software or other development contracts. The issue in such cases is often described as determining whether the contract predominantly involves the development services, or whether it is a contract for goods (e.g., the end product delivered). The answer may turn on issues such as how is the developer paid, what is defined as successful completion of the contract, and what language does the agreement use. *See Micro-Managers, Inc. v. Gregory*, 434 N.W.2d 97 (Wisc. App. 1988); *Data Processing v. L.H. Smith Oil Corp.*, 493 N.E.2d 1272 (Ind. App. 1986) ("DPS was to act with specific regard to Smith's need. Smith bargained for DPS's skill in developing a system to meet its specific needs."). *Compare USM Corp. v. Arthur D. Little Systems, Inc.*, 546 N.E.2d 888 (Mass. App. 1989); *Micro Data Base Sys., Inc. v. Dharma Systems, Inc.*, 148 F.3d 649 (7th Cir. 1998).

PROBLEM 1.9

Micro licenses Packard to distribute copies of the Micro operating system software in the computers it sells. The agreement calls for a royalty of $80 for each copy distributed and limits the right to distribute copies to copies embedded in Packard computers. When sold to customers, the customer pays $1,500 for the Packard computer, but cannot use the software unless it agrees to a click wrap license provided within the software by Micro. If the customer does not agree, Packard takes the computer back and refunds the price. The retail price of Micro operating system is $200. Consider the following:

a. Is the Packard-Micro contract a transaction in goods if each software copy is provided on a CD to Packard by Micro? What result if Micro delivers a single, master copy to Packard and the license allows it to make and distribute copies as needed?

b. Is the transaction with the end user a transaction in goods?

c. Would the result differ if the subject matter of the transaction was not operating system software, but a video game?

MICROSOFT CORP. v. AT&T CORP.
127 S. CT. 1746; 167 L. ED. 2D 737 (U.S. 2007)

GINSBURG, J

It is the general rule under United States patent law that no infringement occurs when a patented product is made and sold in another country. There is an exception. Section 271(f) of the Patent Act, adopted in 1984, provides that infringement does occur when one "supplies . . . from the United States," for "combination" abroad, a patented invention's "components." This case concerns the applicability of §271(F) to computer software first sent from the United States to a foreign manufacturer on a master disk, or by electronic transmission, then copied by the foreign recipient for installation on computers made and sold abroad.

AT&T holds a patent on an apparatus for digitally encoding and compressing recorded speech. Microsoft's Windows operating system, it is conceded, has the potential to infringe AT&T's patent, because Windows incorporates software code that, when installed, enables a computer to process speech in the manner claimed by that patent. It bears emphasis, however, that uninstalled Windows software does not infringe AT&T's patent any more than a computer standing alone does; instead, the patent is infringed only when a computer is loaded with Windows and is thereby rendered capable of performing as the patented speech processor. The question before us: Does Microsoft's liability extend to computers made in another country when loaded with Windows software copied abroad from a master disk or electronic transmission dispatched by Microsoft from the United States? Our answer is "No."

The master disk or electronic transmission Microsoft sends from the United States is never installed on any of the foreign-made computers in question. Instead, copies made abroad are used for installation. Because Microsoft does not export from the United States the copies actually installed, it does not "suppl[y] . . . from the United States" "components" of the relevant computers, and therefore is not liable under §271(f) as currently written.

Plausible arguments can be made for and against extending §271(f) to the conduct charged in this case as infringing AT&T's patent. Recognizing that §271(f) is an exception to the general rule that our patent law does not apply extraterritorially, we resist giving the language in which Congress cast §271(f) an expansive interpretation. Our decision leaves to Congress' informed judgment any adjustment of §271(f) it deems necessary or proper.

I

Our decision some 35 years ago in *Deepsouth Packing Co. v. Laitram Corp.,* 406 U.S. 518 (1972), a case about a shrimp deveining machine, led Congress to enact §271(f). In that case, Laitram, holder of a patent on the time-and-expense-saving machine, sued Deepsouth, manufacturer of an infringing deveiner. Deepsouth conceded that the Patent Act barred it from making and selling its deveining machine in the United States, but sought to salvage a portion of its business: Nothing in United States patent law, Deepsouth urged, stopped it from making in the United States the *parts* of its deveiner, as opposed to the machine itself, and selling those *parts* to foreign buyers for assembly and use abroad. We agreed.

Interpreting our patent law as then written, we reiterated in *Deepsouth* that it was "not an infringement to make or use a patented product outside of the United States." Deepsouth's foreign buyers did not infringe Laitram's patent, we held, because they assembled and used the deveining machines outside the United States. Deepsouth, we therefore concluded, could not be charged with inducing or contributing to an infringement. Nor could Deepsouth be held liable as a direct infringer, for it did not make, sell, or use the patented invention-the fully assembled deveining machine-within the United States. The parts of the machine were not themselves patented, we noted, hence export of those parts, unassembled, did not rank as an infringement of Laitram's patent.

Laitram had argued in *Deepsouth* that resistance to extension of the patent privilege to cover exported parts "derived from too narrow and technical an interpretation of the [Patent Act]." *Id.*, at 529, 92 S.Ct. 1700. Rejecting that argument, we referred to prior decisions holding that "a combination patent protects only against the operable assembly of the whole and not the manufacture of its parts." *Id.*, at 528, 92 S.Ct. 1700. Congress' codification of patent law, we said, signaled no intention to broaden the scope of the privilege. And we again emphasized that "[o]ur patent system makes no claim to extraterritorial effect; these acts of Congress do not, and were not intended to, operate beyond the limits of the United States; and we correspondingly reject the claims of others to such control over our markets."

Absent "a clear congressional indication of intent," we stated, courts had no warrant to stop the manufacture and sale of the parts of patented inventions for assembly and use abroad.

Focusing its attention on *Deepsouth,* Congress enacted § 271(f). The provision expands the definition of infringement to include supplying from the United States a patented invention's components:

> (1) Whoever without authority supplies or causes to be supplied in or from the United States all or a substantial portion of the components of a patented invention, where such components are uncombined in whole or in part, in such manner as to actively induce the combination of such components outside of the United States in a manner that would infringe the patent if such combination occurred within the United States, shall be liable as an infringer.

> (2) Whoever without authority supplies or causes to be supplied in or from the United States any component of a patented invention that is especially made or especially adapted for use in the invention and not a staple article or commodity of commerce suitable for substantial noninfringing use, where such component is uncombined in whole or in part, knowing that such component is so made or adapted and intending that such component will be combined outside of the United States in a manner that would infringe the patent if such combination occurred within the United States, shall be liable as an infringer.

II

Windows is designed, authored, and tested at Microsoft's Redmond, Washington, headquarters. Microsoft sells Windows to end users and computer manufacturers, both foreign and domestic. Purchasing manufacturers install the software onto the computers they sell. Microsoft sends to each of the foreign manufacturers a master version of Windows, either on a disk or via encrypted electronic transmission. The manufacturer uses the master version to generate copies. Those copies, not the master sent by Microsoft, are installed on the foreign manufacturer's computers. Once assembly is complete, the foreign-made computers are sold to users abroad.

AT&T's patent ('580 patent) is for an apparatus (as relevant here, a computer) capable of digitally encoding and compressing recorded speech. Windows, the parties agree, contains software that enables a computer to process speech in the manner claimed by the '580 patent. In 2001, AT&T filed an infringement suit in the United States District Court for the Southern District of New York, charging Microsoft with liability for domestic and foreign installations of Windows.

Neither Windows software (*e.g.,* in a box on the shelf) nor a computer standing alone (*i.e.,* without Windows installed) infringes AT&T's patent. Infringement occurs only when Windows is installed on a computer, thereby rendering it capable of performing as the patented speech processor. Microsoft stipulated that by installing Windows on its own computers during the software development process, it directly infringed the '580 patent. Microsoft further acknowledged that by licensing copies of Windows to manufacturers of computers sold in the United States, it induced infringement of AT&T's patent. . . .

III

A

This case poses two questions: First, when, or in what form, does software qualify as a "component" under §271(f)? Second, were "components" of the foreign-made computers involved in this case "supplie[d]" by Microsoft "from the United States"?

As to the first question, no one in this litigation argues that software can *never* rank as a "component". . . . The parties disagree, however, over the stage at which software becomes a component. Software, the "set of instructions, known as code, that directs a computer to perform specified functions or operations," can be conceptualized in (at least) two ways. One can speak of software in the abstract: the instructions themselves detached from any medium. (An analogy: The notes of Beethoven's Ninth Symphony.) One can alternatively envision a tangible "copy" of software, the instructions encoded on a medium such as a CD-ROM. (Sheet music for Beethoven's Ninth.) AT&T argues that software in the abstract, not simply a particular copy of software, qualifies as a "component" under §271. Microsoft and the United States argue that only a copy of software, not software in the abstract, can be a component.

The significance of these diverse views becomes apparent when we turn to the second question: Were components of the foreign-made computers involved in this case "supplie[d]" by Microsoft "from the United States"? If the relevant components are the copies of Windows actually installed on the foreign computers, AT&T could not persuasively argue that those components, though generated abroad, were "supplie[d] . . . from the United States" as § 271(f) requires for liability to attach. If, on the other hand, Windows in the abstract qualifies as a component within § 271(f)'s compass, it would not matter that the master copies of Windows software dispatched from the United States were not themselves installed abroad as working parts of the foreign computers.

With this explanation of the relationship between the two questions in view, we further consider the twin inquiries.

B

First, when, or in what form, does software become a "component" under § 271(f)? We construe § 271(f)'s terms "in accordance with [their] ordinary or natural meaning." Section 271(f) applies to the supply abroad of the "components of a patented invention, where *such components* are uncombined in whole or in part, in such manner as to actively induce the combination of *such components.*" The provision thus applies only to "such components" as are combined to form the "patented invention" at issue. The patented invention here is AT&T's speech-processing computer.

Until it is expressed as a computer-readable "copy," *e.g.,* on a CD-ROM, Windows software-indeed any software detached from an activating medium-remains uncombinable. It cannot be inserted into a CD-ROM drive or downloaded from the Internet; it cannot be installed or executed on a computer. Abstract software code is an idea without physical embodiment, and as such, it does not match § 271(f)'s categorization: "components" amenable to "combination." Windows abstracted from a tangible copy no doubt is information — a detailed set of instructions — and thus might be compared to a blueprint (or anything containing design information, *e.g.,* a schematic, template, or prototype). A blueprint may contain precise instructions for the construction and combination of the components of a patented device, but it is not itself a combinable component of that device. AT&T and its *amici* do not suggest otherwise.

AT&T urges that software, at least when expressed as machine-readable object code, is distinguishable from design information presented in a blueprint. Software, unlike a blueprint, is "modular"; it is a stand-alone product developed and marketed "for use on many different types of computer hardware and in conjunction with many other types of software." Software's modularity persists even after installation; it can be updated or removed (deleted) without affecting the hardware on which it is installed. Software, unlike a blueprint, is also "dynamic." After a device has been built according to a blueprint's instructions, the blueprint's work is done (as AT&T puts it, the blueprint's instructions have been "exhausted." Software's instructions, in contrast, are contained in and continuously performed by a computer.

The distinctions advanced by AT&T do not persuade us to characterize software, uncoupled from a medium, as a combinable component. Blueprints too, or any design information for that matter, can be independently developed, bought, and sold. If the point of AT&T's argument is that we do not see blueprints lining stores' shelves, the same observation may be made about software in the abstract: What retailers sell, and consumers buy, are *copies* of software. Likewise, before software can be contained in and continuously performed by a computer, before it can be updated or deleted, an actual, physical copy of the software must be delivered by CD-ROM or some other means capable of interfacing with the computer.

Because it is so easy to encode software's instructions onto a medium that can be read by a computer, AT&T intimates, that extra step should not play a decisive role under § 271(f). But the extra step is what renders the software a usable, combinable part of a computer; easy or not, the copy-producing step is essential. Moreover, many tools may be used easily and inexpensively to generate the parts of a device. A machine for making sprockets might be used by a manufacturer to produce tens of thousands of sprockets an hour. That does not make the machine a "component" of the tens of thousands of devices in which the sprockets are incorporated, at least not under any ordinary understanding of the term "component." Congress, of course, might have included within § 271(f)'s compass, for example, not only combinable "components" of a patented invention, but also "information, instructions, or tools from which those components readily may be generated." It did not. In sum, a copy of Windows, not Windows in the abstract, qualifies as a "component"

C

The next question, has Microsoft "supplie[d] . . . from the United States" components of the computers here involved? Under a conventional reading of § 271(f)'s text, the answer would be "No," for the foreign-made copies of Windows actually installed on the computers were "supplie[d]" from places outside the United States. The Federal Circuit majority concluded, however, that "for software 'components,' the act of copying is subsumed in the act of 'supplying.'" A master sent abroad, the majority observed, differs not at all from the exact copies, easily, inexpensively, and swiftly generated from the master; hence "sending a single copy abroad with the intent that it be replicated invokes § 271(f) liability for th[e] foreign-made copies."

Judge Rader, dissenting, noted that "supplying" is ordinarily understood to mean an activity separate and distinct from any subsequent "copying, replicating, or reproducing-in effect manufacturing." He further observed: "The only true difference between making and supplying software components and physical components [of other patented inventions] is that copies of software components are easier to make and transport." But nothing in § 271(f)'s text, Judge Rader maintained, renders ease of copying a relevant, no less decisive, factor in triggering liability for infringement. We agree.

Section 271(f) prohibits the supply of components "from the United States . . . in such manner as to actively induce the combination of *such components*." Under this formulation, the very components supplied from the United States, and not copies thereof, trigger § 271(f) liability when combined abroad to form the patented invention at issue. Here, as we have repeatedly noted, the copies of Windows actually installed on the foreign computers were not themselves supplied from the United States.[2] Indeed, those copies did not exist until they were generated by third parties outside the United States.[3] Copying software abroad, all might agree, is indeed easy and inexpensive. But the same could be said of other items: "Keys or machine parts might be copied from a master; chemical or biological substances might be created by reproduction; and paper products might be made by electronic copying and printing." Section 271(f) contains no instruction to gauge when duplication is easy and cheap enough to deem a copy in fact made abroad nevertheless "supplie[d] . . . from the United States." The absence of anything addressing copying in the statutory text weighs against a judicial determination that replication abroad of a master dispatched from the United States "supplies" the foreign-made copies from the United States within the *intendment* of § 271(f)

. . . .

IV

AT&T urges that reading § 271(f) to cover only those copies of software actually dispatched from the United States creates a "loophole" for software makers. Liability for infringing a United States patent could be avoided, as Microsoft's practice shows, by an easily arranged circumvention: Instead of making installation copies of software in the United States, the copies can be made abroad, swiftly and at small cost, by generating them from a master supplied from the United States. The Federal Circuit majority found AT&T's plea compelling:

> Were we to hold that Microsoft's supply by exportation of the master versions of the Windows & reg; software-specifically for the purpose of foreign replication-avoids infringement, we would be subverting the remedial nature of § 271(f), permitting a technical avoidance of the statute by ignoring the advances in a field of technology-and its associated industry practices-that developed after the enactment of § 271(f) . . . . Section § 271(f), if it is to remain effective, must therefore be interpreted in a manner that is appropriate to the nature of the technology at issue.

While the majority's concern is understandable, we are not persuaded that dynamic judicial interpretation of § 271(f) is in order. The "loophole," in our judgment, is properly left for Congress to consider, and to close if it finds such action warranted.

---

[2] [FN14] In a footnote, Microsoft suggests that even a disk shipped from the United States, and used to install Windows directly on a foreign computer, would not give rise to liability under § 271(f) if the disk were removed after installation. See Brief for Petitioner 37, n. 11; cf. *post*, at - -- - ----2-4 (ALITO, J., concurring). We need not and do not reach that issue here.

[3] [FN15] The dissent analogizes Microsoft's supply of master versions of Windows abroad to "the export of an inventory of . . . knives to be warehoused until used to complete the assembly of an infringing machine." But as we have underscored, foreign-made copies of Windows, not the masters Microsoft dispatched from the United States, were installed on the computers here involved. A more apt analogy, therefore, would be the export of knives for *copying* abroad, with the foreign-made *copies* "warehoused until used to complete the assembly of an infringing machine." Without stretching § 271(f) beyond the text Congress composed, a copy made entirely abroad does not fit the description "supplie[d] . . . from the United States."

There is no dispute, we note again, that §271(f) is inapplicable to the export of design tools-blueprints, schematics, templates, and prototypes-all of which may provide the information required to construct and combine overseas the components of inventions patented under United States law. We have no license to attribute to Congress an unstated intention to place the information Microsoft dispatched from the United States in a separate category.

Section 271(f) was a direct response to a gap in our patent law revealed by this Court's *Deepsouth* decision. The facts of that case were undeniably at the fore when §271(f) was in the congressional hopper. In *Deepsouth,* the items exported were kits containing all the physical, readily assemblable parts of a shrimp deveining machine (not an intangible set of instructions), and those parts themselves (not foreign-made copies of them) would be combined abroad by foreign buyers. Having attended to the gap made evident in *Deepsouth,* Congress did not address other arguable gaps: Section 271(f) does not identify as an infringing act conduct in the United States that facilitates making a component of a patented invention outside the United States; nor does the provision check "suppl[ying] . . . from the United States" information, instructions, or other materials needed to make copies abroad. Given that Congress did not home in on the loophole AT&T describes, and in view of the expanded extraterritorial thrust AT&T's reading of §271(f) entails, our precedent leads us to leave in Congress' court the patent-protective determination AT&T seeks.

Congress is doubtless aware of the ease with which software (and other electronic media) can be copied, and has not left the matter untouched. In 1998, Congress addressed "the ease with which pirates could copy and distribute a copyrightable work in digital form." The resulting measure, the Digital Millennium Copyright Act, "backed with legal sanctions the efforts of copyright owners to protect their works from piracy behind digital walls such as encryption codes or password protections." *Universal City Studios,* 273 F.3d, at 435. If the patent law is to be adjusted better "to account for the realities of software distribution," 414 F.3d, at 1370, the alteration should be made after focused legislative consideration, and not by the Judiciary forecasting Congress' likely disposition.

* * *

For the reasons stated, the judgment of the Court of Appeals for the Federal Circuit is

Reversed.

JUSTICE ALITO, with whom Justice THOMAS and Justice BREYER join, concurring as to all but footnote 14.

I agree with the Court that no "component[s]" of the foreign-made computers involved in this case were "supplie[d]" by Microsoft "from the United States." 35 U.S.C. §271(f)(1). I write separately because I reach this conclusion through somewhat different reasoning.

I

Computer programmers typically write programs in a "human readable" programming language. This "'source code'" is then generally converted by the computer into a "machine readable code" or "machine language" expressed in a binary format. During the Windows writing process, the program exists in the form of machine readable code on the magnetic tape fields of Microsoft's computers' hard drives.

When Microsoft finishes writing its Windows program in the United States, it encodes Windows onto CD-ROMs known as "'golden masters'" in the form of machine readable code. This is done by engraving each disk in a specific way such that another computer can read the engravings, understand what they mean, and write the code onto the magnetic fields of its hard drive.

Microsoft ships these disks (or sends the code via electronic transmission) abroad, where the code is copied onto other disks that are then placed into foreign-made computers for purposes of installing the Windows program. No physical aspect of a Windows CD-ROM-original disk or copy-is ever incorporated into the computer itself. The intact CD-ROM is then removed and may be discarded without affecting the computer's implementation of the code. The parties agree for purposes of this litigation that a foreign-made computer containing the Windows code would violate AT&T's patent if present in the United States.

II

A

I agree with the Court that a component of a machine, whether a shrimp deveiner or a personal computer, must be something physical. This is because the word "component," when concerning a physical device, is most naturally read to mean a physical part of the device. See Webster's Third New International Dictionary 466 (1976) (component is a "constituent part: Ingredient"); Random House Dictionary of the English Language 301 (1967) (component is a "a component part; constituent"). Furthermore, § 271(f) requires that the component be "combined" with other components to form the infringing device, meaning that the component must remain a part of any. Webster's, *supra,* at 452 (combine means "to join in physical or chemical union"; "to become one"; "to unite into a chemical compound"); Random House, *supra,* at 293 (combine means "to bring or join into a close union or whole"). For these reasons, I agree with the Court that a set of instructions on how to build an infringing device, or even a template of the device, does not qualify as a component.

B

As the parties agree, an inventor can patent a machine that carries out a certain process, and a computer may constitute such a machine when it executes commands-given to it by code-that allow it to carry out that process. Such a computer would not become an infringing device until enough of the code is installed on the computer to allow it to execute the process in question. The computer would not be an infringing device prior to the installation, or even during the installation. And the computer remains an infringing device after the installation process because, even though the original installation device (such as a CD-ROM) has been removed from the computer, the code remains on the hard drive.

III

Here, Windows software originating in the United States was sent abroad, whether on a master disk or by means of an electronic transmission, and eventually copied onto the hard drives of the foreign-made computers. Once the copying process was completed, the Windows program was recorded in a physical form, *i.e.,* in magnetic fields on the computers' hard drives. See Brief for Respondent 5. The physical form of the Windows program on the master disk, *i.e.,* the engravings on the CD-ROM, remained on the disk in a form unchanged by the copying process. See Brief for Petitioner 4, n. 2 (citing White, How Computers Work, at 144-145, 172-173). There is nothing in the record to suggest that any physical part of the disk became a physical part of the foreign-made computer, and such an occurrence would be contrary to the general workings of computers.

Because no physical object originating in the United States was combined with these computers, there was no violation of § 271(f). Accordingly, it is irrelevant that the Windows software was not copied onto the foreign-made computers *directly* from the master disk or from an electronic transmission that originated in the United States. To be sure, if these computers could not run Windows without inserting and keeping a CD-ROM in the appropriate drive, then the CD-ROMs might be components of the computer. But that is not the case here.

* * *

Because the physical incarnation of code on the Windows CD-ROM supplied from the United States is not a "component" of an infringing device under § 271(f), it logically follows that a copy of such a CD-ROM also is not a component. For this reason, I join the Court's opinion, except for footnote 14.

Chapter 2

CONTRACT FORMATION ISSUES

I. NATURE OF THE TOPIC

In principle, contract formation issues for licenses are governed by the same rules that govern other agreements.

That premise, however, masks a vivid diversity of law. While themes introduced by UCC Article 2 that define rules for sales of goods have also altered common law in many respects, there remain significant differences between the flexible contract formation rules of UCC Article 2 and the rules contemplated by "common law." Additionally, within the common law, there are significant variations among the states and there are various types of subject matter and industry practice that present unique issues of contract formation.

In any context, however, proving an enforceable contract requires establishing an objective manifestation of assent or indicia of agreement under circumstances that satisfy applicable formalities. Article 2, for example, states its concept about forming a contract in the following way:

> (1) A contract for the sale of goods may be made in any manner sufficient to show agreement, including conduct by both parties which recognizes the existence of such a contract.

> (2) An agreement sufficient to constitute a contract for sale may be found even though the moment of its making is undetermined.

> (3) Even though one or more terms are left open a contract for sale does not fail for indefiniteness if the parties have intended to make a contract and there is a reasonably certain basis for giving an appropriate remedy.

UCC § 2-204 (1998 Official Text). The Article 2 approach allows the finding of a contract despite substantial uncertainty in terms or timing. All that is required is a manifestation of agreement by both parties and a "reasonably certain" basis for giving an appropriate *remedy*. UCITA follows a similar formulation as does the *Restatement (Second) of Contracts* § 19(1) ("The manifestation of assent may be made wholly or partly by written or spoken words or by other acts or by failure to act.").

Common law, while sometimes consistent with these standards, more often enforces more demanding standards of clarity and completeness, and in some cases statutes, regulations, or common law traditions require substantial detail to form particular types of contracts.

Under any approach, however, some transactions concerning informational assets present special issues associated with the subject matter or with industry practices. One involves situations in which one party discloses information to the other before the creation of a formal license. The issue concerns under what circumstances the disclosure imposes obligations on the party receiving it and whether that obligation is treated as a contract or a quasi-contractual one. A second concerns contract formation issues in two types of modern licensing practice — online agreements and so-called shrinkwrap contracts.

II. PRETRANSACTION DISCLOSURE AND IDEA SUBMISSION

We all freely give and receive information throughout every day. Against this background, one function of contract law lies in identifying when an exchange or release of information crosses a line that separates simple gifts or unqualified releases from relationships that create obligations enforceable in law.

Vast numbers of cases do not cross that line.

Consider Richard and his friend Jane. Over cocktails, Richard says: "Wow, do I have interesting information about Sam. If I tell it to you, will you promise to not tell anyone else?" Jane says "sure" and Richard reveals the information. Jane later discloses the information to Bill, who publishes it in a local newspaper. Should Jane be called into court for breach of her promise? While her conduct might affect her friendship with Richard (and Bill) most of us will agree that Richard should have no claim. To explain that result, we will most likely say that there was no contract and no implied legal obligation to not disclose, but this is simply to conclude that law should not intrude into such ordinary social interactions. Whether Sam should have a claim for breach of privacy is a topic for a different course. But you should consider this simple case in terms of what is or should be the presumption in law about obligations relating to information disclosed from one person to another. Would the case change if Richard asked for and was paid ten dollars before disclosing the information?

While many disclosures do not create enforceable obligations, others do. Sometimes this occurs automatically because of property law (e.g., a copyright or patent). In other cases, the source is contract law.

Enforceable rights might exist if the disclosure involves confidential information that may be a trade secret or if the disclosure invokes what is often described as the law of idea submissions. In each of these, there are at least two competing interests. The first centers on the person contemplating the disclosure and involves determining how or whether that person should be protected against loss of value in the information that may enrich the other party. The second concerns the recipient's interest. The disclosures may not be valuable, enriching, or sought by the recipient; there is an interest in protecting that person against unwarranted claims or liability.

PROBLEM 2.1

Richard approaches his friend, Jane, in her office. Richard tells Jane that he knows the secret of his employer's successful ice cream formula. He will reveal the secret to Jane for $50 in cash, the current price for one shot of the latest street drug in the city, if Jane agrees to not disclose the information to others. Jane agrees and pays the $50, but Richard never discloses the information.

a. Assuming that this is not an illegal transaction, what result when Jane sues Richard?

b. Assuming that this is not an illegal transaction, what result if after Richard reveals the information to Jane, he sues because Jane discloses the formula to others?

A. Trade Secrets and Disclosure

The Supreme Court has held that a trade secret constitutes a form of "property." But that property right is conditioned on the information being retained in at least relative secrecy and on the right of the "owner" to enforce confidentiality restrictions against other parties. There are three different sources of trade secret doctrine in this country — the *Restatement (First) of Torts,* the Uniform Trade Secrets Act (UTSA), and the *Restatement (Third) of Unfair Competition* (the most recent formulation). While these differ in detail, they all point in the same direction as to the nature of the rights involved. The *Restatement (First) of Torts* contains the traditional common law definition:

> [A trade secret consists of] information which is used in one's business and which gives him an opportunity to obtain an advantage over competitors who do not know or use it. . . . A substantial element of secrecy must exist, so that, except by use of improper means, there would be difficulties in acquiring the information. . . . Protection is not based on a policy of rewarding or otherwise encouraging the development of secret processes or devices. The protection is merely against breach of faith and reprehensible means of learning another's secret.

Restatement of Torts § 757, cmt. b (1977). Common law misappropriation of a trade secret is a cause of action in *tort* in most states. The UTSA states:

> "Trade secret" means information, including a formula, pattern, compilation, program, device, method, technique or process, that:
>
>> 1. Derives independent economic value, actual or potential, from not being generally known to, and not being readily ascertainable by proper means by other persons who can obtain economic value from its disclosure, and
>
>> 2. Is the subject of efforts that are reasonable under the circumstance to maintain its secrecy.

UTSA § 1(3).

Because of the nature of the property and the commercial value involved, trade secret licenses are essentially conditional disclosures of confidential information in a manner that places sufficient restrictions on the transferee's use to retain the confidential, relatively secret nature of the information. But many transferees desire to review and evaluate the information before committing to a full license. Therein lies the pre-transaction disclosure problem.

An unrestricted, non-confidential disclosure may relinquish the underlying property right, but a refusal to provide for a preliminary examination of the information may prevent the transaction from ever occurring.

EXPANSION PLUS INC. v. BROWN-FOREMAN CORP.
132 F.3d 1083 (5th Cir. 1998)

HIGGENBOTHAM, CIRCUIT JUDGE:

This case requires us to determine the obligations of the parties not to disclose information about the subject matter of their agreement. Based on our examination of the parties' negotiations and the documents evidencing their agreement, we hold that at the relevant time, Brown-Forman did not owe EPI a duty not to disclose. The judgment of the district court is AFFIRMED.

I

Expansion Plus, Inc. developed a credit card "data capture" and "paper processing" program. After implementing the Program on a small scale, EPI sought a national expansion. EPI contacted Brown-Forman about working together to promote the Program. The two companies conducted negotiations during which EPI disclosed confidential information to Brown-Forman. Both parties recognized the confidential nature of the information disclosed. These initial negotiations led to a Master Agreement, executed in 1987. The Master Agreement contained a non-disclosure provision under which Brown-Forman agreed not to disclose any information relating to the Program and to advise its employees of the nondisclosure obligation it owed EPI. This provision expressly stated that the obligation not to disclose was to remain in effect until three years after the termination or expiration of the agreement for any reason whatsoever.

In 1988, the parties executed a new contract. Under the 1988 Agreement, EPI transferred and assigned to Brown-Forman "all of its rights, title and interest in and to the Program" and Brown-Forman agreed "to accept the right to control, implement, and promote the Program." The 1988 Agreement expressly stated that it was for a term of five years. It also contained an integration clause stating "[t]his agreement contains the entire agreement of the parties relating to the subject matter hereof and supersedes any prior agreements and representations relating to such subject matter that are not set forth herein." The 1988 Agreement did not contain any non-disclosure provisions. EPI received up front a $225,000 consulting fee and approximately $1.8 million over the term of the contract from its percentage of the transaction fees that Brown-Forman received from the Program.

In September 1993, the 1988 Agreement expired by its own terms and Brown-Forman sold the Program to NaBanco Merchant Services Corporation, First Financial Bank, and National Bancard Corporation for more than $31 million. At the time of the sale, EPI was a shell company with few assets. More than six months after the sale to NaBanco, EPI wrote Brown-Forman contending for the first time that the 1988 Agreement was a marketing and consulting contract; that it did not transfer ownership of the Program from EPI to Brown-

Forman. After receiving this letter, Brown-Forman filed suit in the Western District of Kentucky seeking a declaration of the parties' rights under the 1988 Agreement. EPI then filed suit in a Texas state court alleging that by the sale to NaBanco, Brown-Forman converted EPI's property, misappropriated its trade secrets, breached their confidential relationship, and tortiously interfered with EPI's contracts. EPI abjured any claim for breach of contract. . . .

[The] district court [granted] summary judgment against EPI on its breach [of] misappropriation of trade secrets claims. EPI appeals. . . .

II

Though the parties and the trial court have devoted much attention to whether EPI's claims sound in contract or tort, we need not enter this fray. At oral argument, EPI conceded, and properly so, that for any of its claims to prevail, Brown-Forman must have owed it a duty not to disclose confidential information at the time Brown-Forman sold the Program to NaBanco. We turn first to this issue. . . .

A confidential relationship may arise "'where one person trusts in and relies upon another, whether the relation is a moral, social, domestic, or merely personal one.'" *Crim Truck & Tractor v. Navistar Int'l Transp. Corp.,* 823 S.W.2d 591, 594 (Tex. 1992). Trusting another or enjoying a cordial relationship of long duration is not enough to establish a confidential relationship. In order to determine the nature of the relationship between EPI and Brown-Forman at the time of sale, we look to the contracts they executed in the course of their dealings with each other.

Their agreements convince us that at the time of the sale to NaBanco, Brown-Forman had no duty not to disclose information about the Program. The 1988 Agreement manifested their entire agreement and terminated the 1987 Master Agreement. The absence of a nondisclosure provision in the 1988 Agreement is significant. In 1987, the parties bargained for confidentiality to last for three years after their agreement was terminated for any reason. The 1988 Agreement addressed nothing on this score. Assuming the 1988 Agreement did not abrogate the nondisclosure provision of the 1987 Agreement, the best case for EPI, the nondisclosure obligation remained in effect only until 1991, three years after its termination. In 1993, Brown-Forman was free to sell the Program as it did not owe EPI any duty of confidentiality at that time.

EPI's assertions to the contrary are unpersuasive. EPI places great weight on the fact that during their negotiations Brown-Forman recognized the confidential nature of the information surrounding the Program. This observation is of no moment. We agree that at one time Brown-Forman owed EPI a duty of confidentiality. The parties defined that duty by their contract and it expired prior to 1993. The suggestion that a common law duty of confidentiality with open-ended limits of duration and scope was untouched by the written agreements of the parties makes no sense. It would cut the heart from the carefully crafted bargain.

Similarly, Brown-Forman's treatment of the Program as confidential after the 1988 Agreement does not affect our conclusion. First, Brown-Forman was arguably bound by the confidentiality provision in the 1987 Master Agreement.

That provision precluded Brown-Forman from disclosing information about the Program until 1991 and required it to advise its employees about the confidential obligation it owed EPI. Second, any representations Brown-Forman made to third parties about the confidential nature of the Program did not affect its nondisclosure obligation. There is no evidence in the record that Brown-Forman's performance demonstrated its intent to alter the deal struck in 1988. Any subjective trust of EPI that Brown-Forman would not disclose the Program after 1991 is not enough to create a confidential relationship. "The objective intent of the parties controls, and absent an allegation of ambiguity in the contract's language, the contract alone will generally be deemed to express the intent of the parties."

[The] trial court here examined the prior agreements between EPI and Brown-Forman to determine the nature of their relationship. The parties' bargained for the terms of a confidential relationship and that bargain provided that it expired no later than 1991.

The judgment of the district court is AFFIRMED.

NOTE

Does the court elevate form over substance or did it correctly determine the scope and duration of the confidentiality obligation? What would be the consequence of a ruling that the earlier agreement on confidentiality carried forward for purposes of trade secret law beyond the term of the agreement? In the case as presented to the court, could the transferor have sued for breach of contract? Should the court have implied a confidentiality term in the last agreement based on the fact that the parties had previously included one in their prior agreements if the parties had simply not discussed the issue in reaching the last agreement?

CELERITAS TECHNOLOGIES, LTD. v. ROCKWELL INTERNATIONAL CORP.
150 F.3d 1354 (Fed. Cir. 1998)

LOURIE, CIRCUIT JUDGE.

Rockwell International Corporation appeals from the decision of the United States District Court for the Central District of California denying Rockwell's motions for judgment as a matter of law and for a new trial following a jury verdict that Rockwell willfully infringed Celeritas Technologies, Ltd.'s patent, misappropriated its trade secrets, and breached a non-disclosure agreement relating to the protected subject matter. [We affirm.]

BACKGROUND

On July 28, 1993, Michael Dolan filed a patent application for an apparatus for increasing the rate of data transmission over analog cellular telephone networks. The resulting patent, U.S. Patent 5,386,590, assigned to Celeritas, was issued on

January 31, 1995 with two claims. As described in the patent, a conventional analog cellular communications system suffers from noise that the listener hears as a high frequency hiss. Analog cellular networks combat this noise by boosting the high frequency components of the transmitted signal (typically a speaker's voice) and then decreasing these components at the receiving end. . . . The claimed invention overcomes the problem of distortion induced by the pre-emphasis and limiter circuits found in conventional analog cellular communications systems.

[In] September 1993, Dolan and other officials of Celeritas met with representatives from Rockwell to demonstrate their proprietary de-emphasis technology. Rockwell is the leading manufacturer of modem "chip sets" which contain the core functions of commercial modems, including the modulation function where de-emphasis is performed. The parties entered into a non-disclosure agreement (NDA), which covered the subject matter of the meeting and provided in pertinent part that Rockwell "shall not disclose or use any Proprietary Information (or any derivative thereof) except for the purpose of evaluating the prospective business arrangements between Celeritas and Rockwell."

The agreement provided that proprietary information "shall not include information which . . . was in the public domain on the date hereof or comes into the public domain other than through the fault or negligence of [Rockwell]." [In] March 1994, AT&T Paradyne began to sell a modem that incorporated de-emphasis technology. In that same month, Rockwell informed Celeritas that it would not license the use of Celeritas's proprietary technology, and concurrently began a development project to incorporate de-emphasis technology into its modem chip sets. Significantly, Rockwell did not independently develop its own de-emphasis technology, but instead assigned the same engineers who had learned of Celeritas's technology under the NDA to work on the de-emphasis development project. In January 1995, Rockwell began shipping its first prototype chip sets that contained de-emphasis technology. By the time of trial in 1997, Rockwell's sales were surpassing its projections.

On September 22, 1995, Celeritas sued Rockwell, alleging breach of contract, misappropriation of trade secrets, and patent infringement. In order to simplify the trial and avoid a duplicative recovery, Celeritas stipulated that it would accept the highest award under the three independent theories. The jury returned a verdict for Celeritas on each of the three theories, awarding Celeritas $57,658,000 each on the patent infringement and breach of contract claims, and $26,850,000 each in compensatory and exemplary damages on the trade secret misappropriation claim. The contract and patent infringement damages were based on a hypothetical lump-sum paid-up license for the use of the proprietary technology in Rockwell's products. The misappropriation damages were based on a finding that Celeritas's proprietary technology gave Rockwell a twenty-one month "head start" in its product development. [Rockwell] moved for JMOL on liability and for a new trial on damages. . . .

Discussion

A. *Breach of the NDA*

Rockwell first argues that the district court erred by denying its motion for JMOL on the breach of contract claim. Citing the prior art submitted to the

United States Patent and Trademark Office (PTO) by Celeritas, Rockwell argues that the evidence at trial clearly demonstrates that the de-emphasis technology disclosed to Rockwell was already in the public domain. Even if the technology were proprietary at the time of disclosure, Rockwell argues, the technology had entered the public domain before Rockwell used it, concededly no later than March 1994. Specifically, Rockwell asserts that AT&T Paradyne had already placed the technology in the public domain through the sale of a modem incorporating de-emphasis technology ("the modem"). Rockwell asserts that the technology was "readily ascertainable" because any competent engineer could have reverse engineered the modem. Rockwell further argues that any confidentiality obligation under the NDA regarding de-emphasis technology was extinguished once the '590 patent issued in January 1995.

Celeritas responds that substantial evidence supports the jury's verdict that Rockwell used its proprietary information. Celeritas argues that in order for a trade secret to enter the public domain in California, it must actually have been ascertained by proper means, and not merely have been ascertainable. Celeritas maintains that, in any event, the only evidence at trial supports the jury's implicit finding that the information was not readily ascertainable from inspection of the modem. Celeritas also argues that the issuance of its patent in 1995 is immaterial because Rockwell had already breached the agreement by using its proprietary information in 1994.

We agree with Celeritas that substantial evidence supports the jury's conclusion that Rockwell breached the NDA. The jury implicitly found that the information given to Rockwell by Celeritas was proprietary. Unrebutted testimony established that Celeritas disclosed to Rockwell implementation details and techniques that went beyond the information disclosed in the patent. Thus, even if every detail disclosed in the patent were in the prior art, a fact never alleged by Rockwell, that fact would not undermine the jury's conclusion that Celeritas revealed proprietary information to Rockwell which it then used in developing its modem chip sets. Accordingly, Rockwell's reliance on the prosecution history of the '590 patent and the prior art submitted to the PTO is misplaced.

The jury also implicitly found that the technology had not been placed in the public domain by the sale of the modem. California law appears somewhat unsettled regarding whether a trade secret enters the public domain when it is "readily ascertainable" or whether it must also be "actually ascertained" by the public. Because the judgment is supportable under either standard, we need not attempt to resolve this issue of state law. Suffice it to say that substantial evidence supports a finding that the technology implementing the de-emphasis function in the modem was not "readily ascertainable." In fact, Dolan's testimony, the only evidence cited by Rockwell, belies its contentions. [Dolan] stated that (1) a spectrum analyzer would be needed to discover the de-emphasis technology, (2) most engineers that he talked to did not have spectrum analyzers, and (3) only if an engineer had a spectrum analyzer and knew what to look for could the engineer discover that the modem had de-emphasis technology. His express caveat that the use of de-emphasis could have been discovered if it was being affirmatively pursued is not an admission that the technology would be "readily ascertainable." Because substantial evidence supports the conclusion that the information disclosed to Rockwell had not entered the public domain before its unauthorized use by Rockwell, the court did not err in denying Rockwell's motion for JMOL regarding its breach of the NDA.

B. *Damages for Breach of the NDA*

Rockwell argues that the jury's damage award is not sustainable under California contract law [because] (1) the contract expressly excludes damages based on a royalty bearing agreement, (2) the damage award is not directly related to any harm caused by the breach, and (3) Rockwell's liability for breach ended once the information entered the public domain.

Rockwell's first argument is without merit. The contract expressly provides that because damages *may be difficult to calculate,* injunctive relief is available. It does not preclude an award of damages. The clause providing for injunctive relief in fact clearly and unambiguously provides for an injunction "in addition to any other relief to which it may be entitled." The standard remedy for breach of contract is, of course, damages. Rockwell also relies on the contract definition of "proprietary information" which specifically excludes information that comes into the public domain. This contract provision clearly allows Rockwell to use information that is proprietary at the time of contracting only after it enters the public domain. It cannot be reasonably construed as relieving Rockwell of liability for use made of proprietary information before it enters the public domain.

Rockwell's second argument is also without merit. Celeritas was undoubtedly harmed. It is in the business of licensing its technology. Celeritas entered into the NDA with Rockwell with the reasonable expectation that Rockwell would compensate it for any use made of the disclosed information. This expectation was the motivating factor for Celeritas to share its knowledge with Rockwell. After Celeritas disclosed its proprietary technology to Rockwell, Rockwell was faced with two legitimate choices: it could have used the technology and entered into a licensing agreement with Celeritas or it could have refrained from using the technology. It chose instead to use the technology without compensating Celeritas. To compensate Celeritas for the breach, the jury properly determined the license fee Rockwell would have paid had it not breached the agreement.

As to quantum, the amount of the damage award is far from speculative. The evidence established that lump-sum paid-up licenses based on projected royalties were common in the industry. Celeritas's damages expert testified as to a reasonable royalty rate based on the past licensing practices of Celeritas, Rockwell, and others in the modem business. The expert then determined the lump-sum amount Rockwell would have paid by multiplying the royalty rate by Rockwell's 1994 sales projections for the accused devices and then discounting the total to net present value. By adopting this lump-sum amount as the proper measure of damages, the jury implicitly accepted the expert's methodology.

Rockwell's third argument confuses the remedy for breach of contract with California's statutory remedies for misappropriation of trade secrets. It may be true that in the absence of a contract, liability for Rockwell's misappropriation of Celeritas's trade secrets may be statutorily limited to the "head start" period. However, liability for breach of contract is not so limited.

Celeritas's damages may include that which Rockwell might have paid for use of the technology at the time of the breach in 1994 if it had chosen not to breach the contract. . . .

C. *Patent Validity*

[The court held that the patent was invalid because it was anticipated (e.g., the technology was described in a prior article).]

CONCLUSION

The jury's verdict awarding Celeritas damages for breach of contract was supported by substantial evidence and the theory under which damages were awarded was not legally unsound. Thus, the district court did not err in denying Rockwell's motion for JMOL on liability and for a new trial on damages. Pursuant to Celeritas's stipulation, the district court properly awarded Celeritas damages only on its breach of contract claim. . . .

NOTES

1. *Celeritas* upheld a claim based on breach of contract (a license), but did not consider the claim of misappropriation of a trade secret because of the stipulation by the parties. Had the court addressed whether misappropriation had been proven, what result would have been appropriate? Is there a different legal basis for a contract breach claim and for misappropriation?

2. It is generally assumed that a trade secret misappropriation claim will not exist for information that is already widely known. To understand why, consider the definition of a "trade secret." Is the same true for a breach of contract claim? In contract law doctrine, what consideration exists for disclosure of information that is already available in the public domain?

3. In *Celeritas*, the contract stated that covered information "shall not include information which [was] in the public domain on the date hereof or comes into the public domain other than through the fault or negligence of [Rockwell]." What is the purpose of such a provision? In light of the outcome in *Celeritas*, would you modify the language for future transactions? What language would you propose?

4. In *Berkla v. Corel Corp.,* 66 F. Supp. 2d 1129 (E.D. Cal. 1999), Berkla submitted to Corel various electronic images of leaves, blades of grass, flowers, pinecones and the like which could be digitally sprayed with colors to create realistic images. Corel rejected the submission, but a later release of its own software included images similar to Berkla's. Corel had signed a nondisclosure agreement that excluded information in the *public domain* at the time of the disclosure to it or that subsequently entered the *public domain* without breach of any confidentiality obligation. Corel admitted that it used Berkla's information, but argued that the information was within the exclusion. The court agreed: "Borrowing the statutory canon of construction, *noscitur a sociis* (a word is known by the company it keeps), the term public domain should be interpreted in the same sense as the other modifiers of confidential information — not available to the public. [This] interpretation dovetails with the common law meaning of public domain under California law. . . . The images became publicly available no later than the commercial release of software containing the images, but the over-distribution [of the images beyond the terms of the agreement] within Corel [before] that date [was] not protected by the contract exclusion."

PROBLEM 2.2

Client is involved in development of dietary and performance enhancing drugs. It has over five hundred ongoing research projects and several hundred drugs that it distributes commercially. While many of the projects involve patented technology, others do not. Client is negotiating with RI to obtain RI's data on several drug development projects. RI is willing to disclose the data under a license calling for a royalty of 3% of the gross proceeds from commercial sales by Client of any drugs developed using its data and precluding Client's disclosure of the data to any other company or entity not required by law. Not having seen the data or conclusions of RI's studies, Client asks what terms it should seek as part of the deal to avoid the risk of its other projects being tainted by the royalty terms or of the data simply repeating studies already published by academic researchers. How do you respond and what is RI's likely reaction to your proposal? What language would protect both parties and allow the transaction to proceed?

PROBLEM 2.3

Register is a company that registers Internet domain names. It has a database of the names of registrants, which it combines with similar databases from other registrars. It offers the combined list to third parties under a license that charges 1) $50,000 for the list to be used solely for informational purposes and not for commercial solicitation, and 2) an additional $10,000 per year for annual updates to the list. Similar lists can be obtained from other sources or could be compiled by obtaining lists from ten other registrars and combining them. Dominic Enterprises purchases a copy of the list, promising to pay the $50,000. When the bill becomes due, Dominic refuses to pay, claiming that the data are in the public domain. What result?

B. Idea Submissions

NADEL v. PLAY-BY-PLAY TOYS & NOVELTIES, INC.
208 F.3d 368 (2d Cir. 1999)

SOTOMAYOR, CIRCUIT JUDGE

Craig P. Nadel (Nadel) brought this action against Play-By-Play Toys & Novelties, Inc. (Play-By-Play) for breach of contract, quasi contract, and unfair competition. . . .

Background

Nadel is a toy idea man. Toy companies regularly do business with independent inventors such as Nadel in order to develop and market new toy concepts as quickly as possible. To facilitate the exchange of ideas, the standard custom and practice in the toy industry calls for companies to treat the submission of an idea as confidential. If the company subsequently uses the disclosed idea, industry custom provides that the company shall compensate the inventor, unless, of course, the disclosed idea was already known to the company.

In 1996, Nadel developed the toy concept at issue in this case. He transplanted the "eccentric mechanism"[1] found in several hanging Halloween toys then on the market [and] placed the mechanism inside of a plush toy monkey skin to develop the prototype for a new table-top monkey toy. This plush toy figure sat upright, emitted sound, and spun when placed on a flat surface.

In October 1996, Nadel met with Neil Wasserman, an executive at Play-By-Play who was responsible for the development of its plush toy line. According to Nadel, he showed his prototype monkey toy to Wasserman, who expressed interest in adapting the concept to a non-moving, plush Tazmanian Devil toy that Play-By-Play was already producing under license from Warner Bros. Nadel contends that, consistent with industry custom, any ideas that he disclosed to Wasserman during their October 1996 meeting were subject to an agreement by Play-By-Play to keep such ideas confidential and to compensate Nadel in the event of their use.

Nadel claims that he sent his prototype monkey toy to Wasserman as a sample and awaited the "Taz skin" and voice tape, which Wasserman allegedly said he would send, so that Nadel could make a sample spinning/laughing Tazmanian Devil toy for Play-By-Play. Wasserman never provided Nadel with the Taz skin and voice tape, however, and denies ever having received the prototype monkey toy from Nadel.

Notwithstanding Wasserman's denial, his secretary, Melissa Rodriguez, testified that Nadel's prototype monkey toy remained in Wasserman's office for several months. According to Ms. Rodriguez, the monkey toy was usually kept in a glass cabinet behind Wasserman's desk, but she remembered that on one occasion she had seen it on a table in Wasserman's office. Despite Nadel's multiple requests, Wasserman did not return Nadel's prototype monkey toy until February 1997, after Play-by-Play introduced its "Tornado Taz" product at the New York Toy Fair.

The parties do not dispute that "Tornado Taz" has the same general characteristics as Nadel's prototype monkey [toy]. Nadel claims that, in violation of their alleged agreement, Play-By-Play used his idea without paying him compensation. Play-By-Play contends, however, that it independently developed the Tornado Taz product concept and that Nadel is therefore not entitled to any compensation. Specifically, Play-By-Play maintains that, as early as June or July of 1996, two of its officers — Wasserman and Slattery — met in Hong

---

[1] [FN 1] An eccentric mechanism typically consists of a housing containing a motor with an eccentric weight attached to the motor shaft. When the motor is activated, the motor rotates the weight centrifugally, causing the housing to shake or spin.

Kong and began discussing ways to create a spinning or vibrating Tazmanian Devil, including the possible use of an eccentric mechanism. Furthermore, Play-By-Play claims that in late September or early October 1996, it commissioned an outside manufacturing agent — Barter Trading of Hong Kong — to begin developing Tornado Taz.

Play-By-Play also argues that, even if it did use Nadel's idea to develop Tornado Taz, Nadel is not entitled to compensation because Nadel's concept was unoriginal and non-novel to the toy industry in October 1996. . . .

I. Nadel's Claims

On January 21, 1999, the district court granted Play-By-Play's motion for summary judgment dismissing Nadel's claims for breach of contract, quasi contract, and unfair competition. Interpreting New York law, the district court stated that "a party is not entitled to recover for theft of an idea unless the idea is novel or original." Applying that principle to Nadel's claims, the district court concluded that, even if the spinning toy concept were novel to Play-By-Play at the time Nadel made the disclosure to Wasserman in October 1996, Nadel's claims must nonetheless fail for lack of novelty or originality because "numerous toys containing the characteristics of [Nadel's] monkey were in existence prior to October 1996." . . .

A. *Submission-of-Idea Cases Under New York Law*

Our analysis begins with the New York Court of Appeals' most recent discussion of the law governing idea submission cases, *Apfel v. Prudential-Bache Securities, Inc.*, 616 N.E.2d 1095 (1993). In *Apfel*, the Court of Appeals discussed the type of novelty an idea must have in order to sustain a contract-based or property-based claim for its uncompensated use. Specifically, Apfel clarified an important distinction between the requirement of "novelty to the buyer" for contract claims, on the one hand, and "originality" (or novelty generally) for misappropriation claims, on the other hand.

Under the facts of *Apfel*, the plaintiff disclosed his idea to the defendant pursuant to a confidentiality agreement and, subsequent to disclosure, entered into another agreement wherein the defendant agreed to pay a stipulated price for the idea's use. The defendant used the idea but refused to pay plaintiff pursuant to the post-disclosure agreement on the asserted ground that "no contract existed between the parties because the sale agreement lacked consideration." The defendant argued that an idea could not constitute legally sufficient consideration unless it was original or novel generally and that, because plaintiff's idea was not original or novel generally (it had been in the public domain at the time of the post-disclosure agreement), the idea provided insufficient consideration to support the parties' post-disclosure contract.

In rejecting defendant's argument, the Court of Appeals held that there was sufficient consideration to support plaintiff's contract claim because the idea at issue had value to the defendant at the time the parties concluded their post-disclosure agreement. The *Apfel* court noted that "traditional principles of contract law" provide that parties "are free to make their bargain, even if the consideration exchanged is grossly unequal or of dubious value," and that, so long as the "defendant received something of value" under the contract, the contract would not be void for lack of consideration. *See also id.* ("[T]he buyer knows what he or she is buying and has agreed that the idea has value, and the Court will not ordinarily go behind that determination.").

The *Apfel* court explicitly rejected defendant's contention that the court should carve out "an exception to traditional principles of contract law" for submission-of-idea cases by requiring that an idea must ꜜalso be original or novel generally in order to constitute valid consideration. In essence, the defendant sought to impose a requirement that an idea be novel in absolute terms, as opposed to only the defendant buyer, in order to constitute valid consideration for the bargain. In rejecting this argument, the *Apfel* court clarified the standards for both contract-based and property-based claims in submission-of-idea cases. That analysis guides our decision here.

The *Apfel* court first noted that "novelty as an element of an idea seller's claim" is a distinct element of proof with respect to both (1) "a claim based on a property theory" and (2) "a claim based on a contract theory." The court then proceeded to discuss how the leading submission-of-idea case — *Downey v. General Foods Corp.*, 286 N.E.2d 257 (1972) — treated novelty with respect to property-based and contract-based claims. First, the *Apfel* court explained that the plaintiff's property-based claims for misappropriation were dismissed in *Downey* because "the elements of novelty and originality [were] absent," i.e., the ideas were so common as to be unoriginal and known generally. Second, the *Apfel* court explained that the plaintiff's contract claims in *Downey* had been dismissed on the separate ground that the "defendant possessed plaintiff's ideas prior to plaintiff's disclosure [and thus], the ideas could have no value to defendant and could not supply consideration for any agreement between the parties."

By distinguishing between the two types of claims addressed in *Downey* and the different bases for rejecting each claim, the New York Court of Appeals clarified that the novelty requirement in submission-of-idea cases is different for misappropriation of property and breach of contract claims. . . .

Thus, the *Apfel* court refused to read *Downey* and "similar decisions" as requiring originality or novelty generally in all cases involving disclosure of ideas. Rather, the *Apfel* court clarified that the longstanding requirement that an idea have originality or general novelty in order to support a misappropriation claim does not apply to contract claims. For contract-based claims in submission-of-idea cases, a showing of novelty to the buyer will supply sufficient consideration to support a contract.

Moreover, *Apfel* made clear that the "novelty to the buyer" standard is not limited to cases involving an express post-disclosure contract for payment based on an idea's use. The *Apfel* court explicitly discussed the pre-disclosure contract scenario present in the instant case, where "the buyer and seller contract for disclosure of the idea with payment based on use, but no separate postdisclosure contract for the use of the idea has been made." In such a scenario, a seller might, as Nadel did here, bring an action against a buyer who allegedly used his ideas without payment, claiming both misappropriation of property and breach of an express or implied-in-fact contract. The *Apfel* court recognized that these cases present courts with the difficult problem of determining "whether the idea the buyer was using was, in fact, the seller's." Specifically, the court noted that, with respect to a misappropriation of property claim, it is difficult to "prove that the buyer obtained the idea from [the seller] and nowhere else." With respect to a breach of contract claim, the court noted that it would be inequitable to enforce a contract if "it turns out upon disclosure that the buyer already possessed the idea." The court then concluded that, with respect to these cases, "[a] showing of novelty, at least novelty as to the buyer" should address these problems.

We note, moreover, that the "novelty to the buyer" standard comports with traditional principles of contract law. While an idea may be unoriginal or non-novel in a general sense, it may have substantial value to a particular buyer who is unaware of it and therefore willing to enter into contract to acquire and exploit it. In fact, the notion that an unoriginal idea may still be novel (and valuable) to a particular buyer is not itself a novel proposition. . . . In contrast to contract-based claims, a misappropriation claim can only arise from the taking of an idea that is original or novel in absolute terms, because the law of property does not protect against the misappropriation or theft of that which is free and available to all. . . .

Finally, although the legal requirements for contract-based claims and property-based claims are well-defined, we note that the determination of novelty in a given case is not always clear. The determination of whether an idea is original or novel depends upon several factors, including, inter alia, the idea's specificity or generality (is it a generic concept or one of specific application?), its commonality (how many people know of this idea?), its uniqueness (how different is this idea from generally known ideas?), and its commercial availability (how widespread is the idea's use in the industry?).

Moreover, in assessing the interrelationship between originality and novelty to the buyer, we note that in some cases an idea may be so unoriginal or lacking in novelty that its obviousness bespeaks widespread and public knowledge of the idea, and such knowledge is therefore imputed to the buyer. In such cases, a court may conclude, as a matter of law, that the idea lacks both the originality necessary to support a misappropriation claim and the novelty to the buyer necessary to support a contract claim.

While we find New York case law in this area to be relatively clear when viewed through the prism of *Apfel*, we nonetheless recognize some post-*Apfel* confusion among the courts. Accordingly, we discuss briefly the post-*Apfel* decisions in New York in an effort to address any lingering uncertainty.

In the first of two post-*Apfel* decisions in New York — *Oasis Music, Inc. v. 900 U.S.A., Inc.*, 614 N.Y.S.2d 878 (1994) — the plaintiff alleged that the defendant misappropriated its ideas for an interactive telephone game in violation of a pre-disclosure confidentiality agreement. The *Oasis Music* court correctly began its contract analysis by reciting *Apfel*'s "novelty as to the buyer" standard. But after concluding that the various aspects of plaintiff's ideas already existed in the public domain, the court appeared to dismiss plaintiff's claims for lack of novelty generally. In light of *Apfel*, we read the *Oasis Music* opinion to hold that, because plaintiff's ideas had such a high degree of commonality, the ideas were so unoriginal that, as a matter of law, they were non-novel to the buyer. . . .

In sum, we find that New York law in submission-of-idea cases is governed by the following principles: Contract-based claims require only a showing that the disclosed idea was novel to the buyer in order to find consideration. Such claims involve a fact-specific inquiry that focuses on the perspective of the particular buyer. By contrast, misappropriation claims require that the idea at issue be original and novel in absolute terms. This is so because unoriginal, known ideas have no value as property and the law does not protect against the use of that which is free and available to all. Finally, an idea may be so unoriginal or lacking in novelty generally that, as a matter of law, the buyer is deemed to have knowledge of the idea. In such cases, neither a property-based nor a contract-based claim for uncompensated use of the idea may lie.

In light of New York's law governing submission-of-idea cases, we next consider whether Nadel's toy idea was original or novel in absolute terms so as to support his misappropriation claim and whether his idea was novel as to Play-By-Play so as to support his contract claims.

B. *Nadel's Misappropriation Claim*

[In] this case, the district court did not decide whether Nadel's idea — a plush toy that sits upright, emits sounds, and spins on a flat surface by means of an internal eccentric motor — was inherently lacking in originality. We therefore remand this issue to the district court to determine whether Nadel's idea exhibited "genuine novelty or invention" or whether it was "a merely clever or useful adaptation of existing knowledge."

Moreover, insofar as the district court found that Nadel's idea lacked originality and novelty generally because similar toys were commercially available prior to October 1996, we believe that there remains a genuine issue of material fact on this point. While the record contains testimony of Play-By-Play's toy expert — Bert Reiner — in support of the finding that Nadel's product concept was already used in more than a dozen different plush toys prior to October 1996, the district court cited the "Giggle Bunny" toy as the only such example. Nadel disputes Reiner's contention and claims, furthermore, that the district court erroneously relied on an undated video depiction of the Giggle Bunny toy to conclude that upright, sound-emitting, spinning plush toys were commercially available prior to October 1996.

With respect to the Giggle Bunny evidence, we agree with Nadel that the Giggle Bunny model depicted in the undated video exhibit is physically different from the earlier Giggle Bunny model known to be commercially available in 1994. Drawing all factual inferences in Nadel's favor, we cannot conclude as a matter of law that the upright, sound-emitting, spinning plush Giggle Bunny shown in the video exhibit was commercially available prior to October 1996, and we certainly cannot conclude based on this one exhibit that similar toys were in the public domain at that time.

Moreover, although we find highly probative Mr. Reiner's testimony that numerous toys with the same general characteristics of Nadel's toy idea were commercially available prior to October 1996, his testimony and related evidence are too ambiguous and incomplete to support a finding of unoriginality as a matter of law. Mr. Reiner's testimony fails to specify precisely which (if any) of the enumerated plush toys were designed to (1) sit upright, (2) on a flat surface, (3) emit sounds, and (4) spin or rotate (rather than simply vibrate like "Tickle Me Elmo," for example). Without this information, a reasonable finder of fact could discount Mr. Reiner's testimony as vague and inconclusive.

On remand, the district court is free to consider whether further discovery is warranted to determine whether Nadel's product concept was inherently original or whether it was novel to the industry prior to October 1996. A finding of unoriginality or lack of general novelty would, of course, preclude Nadel from bringing a misappropriation claim against Play-By-Play. Moreover, in evaluating the originality or general novelty of Nadel's idea in connection with his misappropriation claim, the district may consider whether the idea is so unoriginal that Play-By-Play should, as a matter of law, be deemed to have already possessed the idea, and dismiss Nadel's contract claims on that ground.

C. *Nadel's Contract Claims*

Mindful that, under New York law, a finding of novelty as to Play-By-Play will provide sufficient consideration to support Nadel's contract claims. [Reading the] record in a light most favorable to Nadel, we conclude that there exists a genuine issue of material fact as to whether Nadel's idea was, at the time he disclosed it to Wasserman in early October 1996, novel to Play-By-Play. Notably, the timing of Play-By-Play's development and release of Tornado Taz in relation to Nadel's October 1996 disclosure is, taken alone, highly probative. Moreover, although custom in the toy industry provides that a company shall promptly return all samples if it already possesses (or does not want to use) a disclosed idea, Play-By-Play in this case failed to return Nadel's prototype monkey toy for several months, despite Nadel's multiple requests for its return. According to Wasserman's secretary, Melissa Rodriguez, Nadel's sample was not returned until after the unveiling of "Tornado Taz" at the New York Toy Fair in February 1997. Ms. Rodriguez testified that from October 1996 through February 1997, Nadel's sample was usually kept in a glass cabinet behind Wasserman's desk, and on one occasion, she remembered seeing it on a table in Wasserman's office. These facts give rise to the reasonable inference that Play-By-Play may have used Nadel's prototype as a model for the development of Tornado Taz.

None of the evidence adduced by Play-By-Play compels a finding to the contrary on summary judgment. With regard to the discussions that Play-By-Play purportedly had in June or July of 1996 about possible ways to create a vibrating or spinning Tazmanian Devil toy, those conversations only lasted, according to Mr. Slattery, "a matter of five minutes." Play-By-Play may have "discussed the concept," as Mr. Slattery testified, but the record provides no evidence suggesting that, in June or July of 1996, Play-By-Play understood exactly how it could apply eccentric motor technology to make its Tazmanian Devil toy spin rather than, say, vibrate like Tickle Me Elmo. Similarly, although Play-By-Play asserts that it commissioned an outside manufacturing agent — Barter Trading of Hong Kong — to begin developing Tornado Taz in late September or early October of 1996, Play-By-Play admits that it can only "guess" the exact date. Play-By-Play cannot confirm that its commission of Barter Trading pre-dated Nadel's alleged disclosure to Wasserman on or about October 9, 1996. Nor has Play-By-Play produced any documents, technical or otherwise, relating to its purported business venture with Barter Trading or its independent development of a spinning Tornado Taz prior to October 1996. Based on this evidence, a jury could reasonably infer that Play-By-Play actually contacted Barter Trading, if at all, after learning of Nadel's product concept, and that Play-By-Play's development of Tornado Taz is attributable to Nadel's disclosure.

We therefore conclude that there exists a genuine issue of material fact as to whether Nadel's idea was, at the time he disclosed it to Wasserman in early October 1996, novel to Play-By-Play. As to whether the other elements necessary to find a valid express or implied-in-fact contract are present here, e.g., mutual assent, legal capacity, legal subject matter, we leave that determination to the district court to address, if necessary, on remand. . . .

Conclusion

For the foregoing reasons, we affirm that part of the district court's judgment dismissing Play-By-Play's counterclaims. We vacate that part of the district court's judgment granting Play-By-Play's motion for summary judgment and dismissing Nadel's complaint and remand for further proceedings consistent with this opinion.

NOTES

1. What is the difference between an "idea submission" case and a case involving disclosure of a trade secret? Should they be governed by the same rules as to when a contract exists?

2. In a footnote, the *Nadel* court described what it considered to be the distinction between an "express contract" and an "implied in fact" contract. It stated:

> Where the pre-disclosure agreement is not an express contract to pay for the disclosed idea, an idea seller may argue in the alternative, that the parties entered into an agreement implied-in-fact. Unlike an express contract, an implied-in-fact contract arises "when the agreement and promise have simply not been expressed in words," but "a court may justifiably infer that the promise would have been explicitly made, had attention been drawn to it." Of course, the mere disclosure of an unoriginal idea to a defendant, to whom the idea is novel, will not automatically entitle a plaintiff to compensation upon the defendant's subsequent use of the idea. An implied-in-fact contract "requires such elements as consideration, mutual assent, legal capacity and legal subject matter." The existence of novelty to the buyer only addresses the element of consideration necessary for the formation of the contract. Thus, apart from consideration, the formation of a contract implied-in-fact will depend on the presence of the other elements. The element of mutual assent, for example, must be inferred from the facts

and circumstances of each case, including such factors as the specific conduct of the parties, industry custom, and course of dealing.

Is the difference material to the outcome of a contract claim? Consider:

Company A enters a written agreement to disclose to Company B an idea that pertains to methods of irrigating rice fields. B promises to pay $100,000 for the disclosure, plus 5% of any net profits from the sale or use of irrigation systems based on the idea. When the information is disclosed, it turns out that B already had a development project ongoing based on the same idea. What result when Company A sues for its $100,000?

3. Most reported idea submission cases come from New York or California. *Nadel* is a federal court interpreting New York law. A California decision, *Desny v. Wilder*, 299 P.2d 257 (Cal. 1956), set out the premise that, while ideas do not constitute property, an enforceable contract may arise. The contract can arise either by virtue of an express agreement or by a contract arising from conduct of the parties. The court observed: "If the idea purveyor has clearly conditioned his offer to convey the idea upon an obligation to pay for it if it is used by the offeree and the offeree, knowing the condition before he knows the idea, voluntarily accepts its disclosure and finds it valuable and uses it, the law will either apply the objective test and hold that the parties have made an express (sometimes called implied-in-fact) contract, or under those circumstances . . . the law itself, to prevent fraud and unjust enrichment, will imply a promise to compensate." *Id.* at 268. The court also emphasized that, to form a contract, the recipient must be aware of the terms of the submission and have an opportunity to refuse them.

4. The *Nadel* court refers to trade practices in the toy industry. Why are those practices relevant? Consider the definition of "agreement" set out in the UCC, UCITA and the *Restatement of Contracts*:

"Agreement" means the bargain of the parties in fact as found in their language or by implication from other circumstances including course of dealing or usage of trade or course of performance. . . . Whether an agreement has legal consequence is determined by . . . the law of contracts.

UCC § 1-201(a)(3) (1998 Official Text). Is a decision like that in *Nadel* an intellectual property law decision or a contract law decision? Should it matter?

5. Many companies operate online sites where they invite users of their products to post comments and suggestions. Do idea submission cases present any reason to be concerned about that practice? Consider the following language from the "legal terms" of the IBM website:

IBM does not want to receive confidential or proprietary information from you through our Web site. Please note that any information or material sent to IBM will be deemed NOT to be confidential. By sending IBM any information or material, you grant IBM an unrestricted, irrevocable license to use, reproduce, display, perform, modify, transmit and distribute those materials or information, and you also agree that IBM is free to use any ideas, concepts, know-how or techniques that you send us for any purpose. However, we will not release your name or otherwise publicize the fact that you submitted materials or other information to us unless: (a) we obtain your permission to use your name; or (b) we first notify you that the materials or other information you submit to a particular part of this site will be published or otherwise used with your name on it; or (c) we are required to do so by law.[2]

6. UCITA § 216 (2000 Official Text) states:

(a) The following rules apply to a submission of an idea or information for the creation, development, or enhancement of computer information which is not made pursuant to an existing agreement requiring the submission: . . .

(3) If the recipient seasonably notifies the person making the submission that the recipient maintains a procedure to receive and review submissions, a contract is formed only if:

(A) the submission is made and a contract accepted pursuant to that procedure; or

(B) the recipient expressly agrees to terms concerning the submission.

(b) An agreement to disclose an idea creates a contract enforceable against the receiving party only if the idea as disclosed is confidential, concrete, and novel to the business, trade, or industry or the party receiving the disclosure otherwise expressly agreed.

PROBLEM 2.4

Company A agrees to disclose to Company B an idea about methods of irrigating rice fields. B promises to pay $100,000 for the disclosure, plus 5% of net profits from the sale or use of irrigation systems based on the idea. When the information is disclosed, it turns out that B already had a development project ongoing based on the same idea. What result under *Nadel* or *Desney* if Company A sues for its $100,000? If the contract also required Company B to keep the idea confidential, can Company A recover for breach of that obligation when Company B discloses the idea to the rice-producing world?

PROBLEM 2.5

During a cocktail party celebrating the opening of the MM Studio's most recent motion picture, Bob (an executive with the studio) has a long conversation with Fran, an aspiring screenwriter. Fran describes her idea for a motion picture dealing with the conflict between a tribe of hunter-gatherers in a remote jungle island and a group of animals over the use of a particular part of the island. The story is told from the perspective of the animals. Because of

---

[2] *Available at <www.ibm.com/legal/us/> last visited 9/3/2004.

the heady success of the new motion picture, Bob stays in this conversation far longer than he would ordinarily do so. One year after the cocktail party, MM Studio announces the impending production of a new motion picture portraying the conflict between man and animal over land, as told from the perspective of the animals. The screenplay is being written by William Gold, a famous writer. Fran sues MM. Fran can prove that development of the motion picture did not begin until after her conversation with Bob. MM can prove that Fran has discussed the idea with several hundred people at various parties and the like. Gold claims that the idea for the production was his, but there is evidence that the studio suggested the general outlines to him. What result? What further information would you need?

WRENCH LLC v. TACO BELL
256 F.3d 446 (6th Cir. 2001)

This case raises a question of first impression in this circuit regarding the extent to which the Copyright Act preempts state law claims based on breach of an implied-in-fact contract. Plaintiffs-Appellants Wrench LLC, Joseph Shields, and Thomas Rinks brought this diversity action against Defendant-Appellee Taco Bell Corporation ("Taco Bell"), claiming breach of implied contract and various torts related to Taco Bell's alleged use of appellants' ideas.

I. Background

Appellants Thomas Rinks and Joseph Shields are creators of the "Psycho Chihuahua" cartoon character which they promote, market, and license through their wholly-owned Michigan limited liability company, Wrench LLC. The parties have described Psycho Chihuahua as a clever, feisty dog with an attitude; a self-confident, edgy, cool dog who knows what he wants and will not back down.

In June 1996, Shields and Rinks attended a licensing trade show in New York City, where they were approached by two Taco Bell employees, Rudy Pollak, a vice president, and Ed Alfaro, a creative services manager. Pollak and Alfaro expressed interest in the Psycho Chihuahua character, which they thought would appeal to Taco Bell's core consumers, males aged eighteen to twenty-four. Pollak and Alfaro obtained some Psycho Chihuahua materials to take with them back to Taco Bell's headquarters in California.

Upon returning to California, Alfaro began promoting the Psycho Chihuahua idea within Taco Bell. [After] several meetings with non-marketing executives, Alfaro showed the Psycho Chihuahua materials to Vada Hill, Taco Bell's vice president of brand management, as well as to Taco Bell's then-outside advertising agency, Bozell Worldwide. Alfaro also tested the Psycho Chihuahua marketing concept with focus groups to gauge consumer reaction to the designs submitted by Rinks and Shields.

During this time period, Rinks told Alfaro that instead of using the cartoon version of Psycho Chihuahua in its television advertisements, Taco Bell should use a live dog, manipulated by computer graphic imaging, with the personality of Psycho Chihuahua and a love for Taco Bell food. Rinks and Alfaro also discussed what it was going to cost for Taco Bell to use appellants' character, and although no specific numbers were mentioned, Alfaro understood that if Taco Bell used the Psycho Chihuahua concept, it would have to pay appellants.

In September 1996, Rinks and Shields hired Strategy Licensing ("Strategy"), a licensing agent, to represent Wrench in its dealings with Taco Bell. [On] November 18, 1996, Strategy representatives forwarded a licensing proposal to Alfaro. [Taco Bell] did not accept this proposal, although it did not explicitly reject it or indicate that it was ceasing further discussions with Wrench.

On December 5, 1996, Alfaro met with Hill, who had been promoted to the position of chief marketing officer, and others, to present various licensing ideas, including Psycho Chihuahua. On February 6, 1997, Alfaro again met with appellants and representatives of Strategy to review and finalize a formal presentation featuring Psycho Chihuahua that was to be given to Taco Bell's marketing department in early March 1997. At this meeting, appellants exhibited examples of possible Psycho Chihuahua promotional materials and also orally presented specific ideas for television commercials featuring a live dog manipulated by computer graphics imaging. These ideas included a commercial in which a male dog passed up a female dog in order to get to Taco Bell food.

While Alfaro was meeting with appellants, another marketing firm, TLP Partnership ("TLP"), was also promoting appellants' Psycho Chihuahua to Taco Bell marketing executives. TLP presented several ideas, including the Psycho Chihuahua concept, to Taco Bell in anticipation of an upcoming summer promotion. TLP had discovered Psycho Chihuahua at a trade show in New York and had received Strategy's consent to use the image in its presentation. [But] Taco Bell decided not to use any of TLP's ideas.

Alfaro was unable to arrange a meeting with the marketing department during March 1997 to present the Psycho Chihuahua materials. On April 4, 1997, however, Strategy made a formal presentation to Alfaro and his group using samples of uniform designs, T-shirts, food wrappers, posters, and cup designs based on the ideas discussed during the February 6, 1997, meeting. Alfaro and his group were impressed with Strategy's presentation.

On March 18, 1997, Taco Bell hired a new advertising agency, TBWA Chiat/Day ("Chiat/Day"). Taco Bell advised Chiat/Day that it wanted a campaign ready to launch by July 1997 that would reconnect Taco Bell with its core group of consumers. Chuck Bennett and Clay Williams were designated as the creative directors of Taco Bell's account.

On June 2, 1997, Bennett and Williams proposed a commercial to Taco Bell in which a male Chihuahua would pass up a female Chihuahua to get to a person seated on a bench eating Taco Bell food. Bennett and Williams say that they conceived of the idea for this commercial one day as they were eating Mexican food at a sidewalk cafe and saw a Chihuahua trotting down the street, with no master or human intervention, "on a mission." Bennett and Williams contend that this image caused them jointly to conceive of the idea of using a Chihuahua as a way of personifying the intense desire for Taco Bell food. Williams subsequently wrote an advertisement script using a Chihuahua, which Taco Bell decided to produce as a television commercial.

When, in June 1997, Alfaro learned that Chiat/Day was planning to use a Chihuahua in a commercial, he contacted Hill again about the possibility of using Psycho Chihuahua. Hill passed Alfaro on to Chris Miller, a Taco Bell advertising manager and the liaison between Taco Bell's marketing department and Chiat/Day. On June 27, 1997, Alfaro gave Psycho Chihuahua materials to Miller along with a note suggesting that Taco Bell consider using Psycho Chihuahua as an icon and as a character in its advertising. Miller sent these materials to Chiat/Day, which received them sometime between June 28 and July 26.

Taco Bell aired its first Chihuahua commercial in the northeastern United States in July 1997, and received a very positive consumer reaction [and] launched a nationwide advertising campaign featuring Chihuahua commercials in late December 1997.

Appellants brought suit in January 1998, alleging breach of implied-in-fact contract as well as various tort and statutory claims under Michigan and California law. Appellee filed a motion to dismiss, which the district court granted in part and denied in part. . . .

II. Discussion

[Under] Section 301 of the Copyright Act [a] state common law or statutory claim is preempted if: (1) the work is within the scope of the "subject matter of copyright," as specified in 17 U.S.C. §§ 102, 103; and, (2) the rights granted under state law are equivalent to any exclusive rights within the scope of federal copyright as set out in 17 U.S.C. § 106. Courts and commentators have described this preemption analysis as encompassing a "subject matter requirement" and a "general scope" or "equivalency" requirement.

1. Subject Matter Requirement

Appellants contend that the district court erred in finding that their claims fell within the subject matter provisions of the Copyright Act. Appellants argue that their state law claims are based on ideas and concepts that were conveyed to Taco Bell in both *tangible* and *intangible* form. They conclude that their claims do not come within the subject matter of copyright, and are thus not preempted, because § 102(b) expressly excludes intangible ideas and concepts from the subject matter of copyright.

In *Wrench I,* the district court found that appellants' claims fell within the subject matter of copyright "because they are premised upon ideas and concepts fixed in a tangible medium of expression, namely, 'storyboards' and 'presentation materials' furnished by Plaintiffs." The district court reasoned that appellants' state law claims depended substantially upon works subject to the copyright protection, and did not arise solely out of intangible concepts that were orally conveyed to Taco Bell.

In reaching this conclusion, the district court relied on the Fourth Circuit's decision in [*United States ex. rel.*] *Berge* [*v. Board of Trustees of the Univ. of Ala.,* 104 F.3d 1453 (4th Cir. 1997),] in which a plaintiff brought a state law conversion action claiming that defendants had used ideas and methods contained in plaintiff's dissertation without her permission. The plaintiff contended that because ideas and methods are excluded from copyright protection under § 102, her state law claims could not be preempted under § 301. The court rejected this argument on the ground that the scope of protection afforded under copyright law is not the same as the scope of preemption. Rather, the court concluded that "the shadow actually cast by the [Copyright] Act's preemption is notably broader than the wing of its protection."

Appellants urge this court to reject this conclusion for the same reason urged by the plaintiff in *Berge*. Specifically, appellants argue that *Berge* does not comport with a literal reading of § 102(b), which expressly excludes ideas and other intangible forms of expression from copyright protection. Appellants rely on several district court cases which have held that because ideas and concepts are not afforded copyright protection, they are not within the subject matter of copyright.

The appellate courts that have addressed this question have disagreed with the reasoning of the decisions cited by appellants, however. The Second, Fourth, and Seventh Circuits have held that the scope of the Copyright Act's subject matter extends beyond the tangible expressions that can be protected under the Act to elements of expression which themselves cannot be protected. . . .

We join our sister circuits in holding that the scope of the Copyright Act's subject matter is broader than the scope of the Act's protections. The record demonstrates that appellants expended considerable effort preparing and presenting tangible expressions of their Psycho Chihuahua concept for appellee, which expressions included storyboards, scripts, drawings, clothing designs, and packaging. The position now urged by appellants would require us to separate out appellants' intangible ideas from these tangible expressions, and would afford appellants a state law claim in the face of clear congressional intent to preempt such action. As the Seventh Circuit has noted, "[o]ne function of § 301(a) is to prevent states from giving special protection to works of authorship that Congress has decided should be in the public domain, which it can accomplish only if 'subject matter of copyright' includes all works of a type covered by sections 102 and 103, even if federal law does not afford protection to them." Thus, we conclude that the district court did not err with respect to the subject matter prong of its preemption analysis.

2. Equivalency Requirement

The second prong of the preemption analysis — the so-called "equivalency" or "general scope" requirement — augments the subject matter inquiry by asking whether the state common law or statutory action at issue asserts rights that are the same as those protected under § 106 of the Copyright Act. Under § 301(a), even if appellants' state law claims concern works within the subject matter of copyright, such claims will only be preempted if they assert rights that are "equivalent to any of the exclusive rights within the general scope of copyright as specified by section 106[.]" 17 U.S.C. § 301(a).

Equivalency exists if the right defined by state law may be abridged by an act which in and of itself would infringe one of the exclusive rights. Conversely, if an extra element is required instead of or in addition to the acts of reproduction, performance, distribution or display in order to constitute a state-created cause of action, there is no preemption, provided that the extra element changes the nature of the action so that it is qualitatively different from a copyright infringement claim. We find that appellants' state law implied-in-fact contract claim survives preemption under these rules.

Under Michigan law, "[a]n implied contract, like other contracts, requires mutual assent and consideration." Michigan draws a clear distinction between contracts implied in fact and contracts implied in law:

> The first does not exist, unless the minds of the parties meet, by reason of words or conduct. The second is quasi or constructive, and does not require a meeting of minds, but is imposed by fiction of law[.]

Cascaden v. Magryta, 247 Mich. 267, 225 N.W. 511, 512 (1929).

The gist of appellants' state law implied-in-fact contract claim is breach of an actual promise to pay for appellants' creative work. It is not the use of the work alone but the failure to pay for it that violates the contract and gives rise to the right to recover damages. Thus, the state law right is not abridged by an act which in and of itself would infringe one of the exclusive rights granted by § 106, since the right to be paid for the use of the work is not one of those rights.

An extra element is required instead of or in addition to the acts of reproduction, performance, distribution or display, in order to constitute the state-created cause of action. The extra element is the promise to pay. This extra element does change the nature of the action so that it is qualitatively different from a copyright infringement claim. The qualitative difference includes the requirement of proof of an enforceable promise and a breach thereof which requires, *inter alia,* proof of mutual assent and consideration, as well as proof of the value of the work and appellee's use thereof.

This qualitative difference is further reflected by the difference in the remedy afforded by the state law claim. Under Michigan law, a plaintiff's remedy for breach of an implied-in-fact contract includes recovery of the reasonable value of the services rendered, considering factors such as the general practice of the industry.

Under the Copyright Act, remedies for infringement are limited to injunctions; impounding and destruction of infringing articles; recovery of the copyright owner's actual damages and any additional profits of the infringer or statutory damages; and costs and attorneys fees. The remedies available under copyright law do not include damages for the reasonable value of the defendants' use of the work.

The proposition that a state law breach of contract claim based upon a promise to pay for the use of the work is not preempted is supported by an eminent authority on copyright law. *See* 1 *Nimmer on Copyright* § 1.01[B][1][a] at 1-15 to 1-16, which states:

> Adverting first to contract rights, an author's right to royalties under a publication contract may be conditioned upon the publisher's acts of reproduction and distribution of copies of the work, but there is

also another crucial act that stands as a condition to the publisher's liability: the publisher's promise to pay the stated royalty. Without a promise there is no contract, while a promise on the part of one who engages in unlicensed reproduction or distribution is not required in order to constitute him a copyright infringer. Certainly, pre-emption should be denied, to the extent that a breach of contract cause of action alleges more than reproduction, adaptation, etc. *simplicter* of a copyrighted work.

Here, as in the example given in *Nimmer on Copyright,* there is another crucial act that stands as a condition to the appellee's liability, to wit: its promise to pay for the use of the work. Thus, this is a case in which the breach of contract cause of action alleges more than reproduction, adaptation, etc., *simplicter.*

In finding that appellants' state law contract claim is not preempted, we do not embrace the proposition that all state law contract claims survive preemption simply because they involve the additional element of promise. Under that rationale, a contract which consisted only of a promise not to reproduce the copyrighted work would survive preemption even though it was limited to one of the exclusive rights enumerated in 17 U.S.C. § 106. If the promise amounts only to a promise to refrain from reproducing, performing, distributing or displaying the work, then the contract claim is preempted. The contrary result would clearly violate the rule that state law rights are preempted when they would be abridged by an act which in and of itself would infringe one of the exclusive rights of § 106. As the authors note in 1 *Nimmer on Copyright* § 1.01[B][1][a] at 1-22: "Although the vast majority of contract claims will presumably survive scrutiny . . . nonetheless preemption should continue to strike down claims that, though denominated 'contract,' nonetheless complain directly about the reproduction of expressive materials." . . .

For the purpose of the preemption analysis, there is a crucial difference between a claim based on *quasi*-contract, *i.e.,* a contract implied in law, and a claim based upon a contract implied in fact. In the former, the action depends on nothing more than the unauthorized use of the work. Thus, an action based on a contract implied in law requires no extra element in addition to an act of reproduction, performance, distribution or display, whereas an action based on a contract implied in fact requires the extra element of a promise to pay for the use of the work which is implied from the conduct of the parties. . . .

Here, appellants' implied-in-fact contract claim contains the essential element of expectation of compensation which is an element not envisioned by § 106.

We conclude that the district court erred with respect to the equivalency prong of the preemption analysis and find that appellants' state law implied-in-fact contract claim is not preempted by the Copyright Act.

B. Independent Creation

Appellee argues on appeal that summary judgment should have been granted on the alternate ground that it has shown that the idea to use a live Chihuahua in Taco Bell advertising was independently created by Williams and Bennett at Chiat/Day. Appellee points to *Kienzle v. Capital Cities/Am. Broad. Co.,* 774 F. Supp. 432, 436 (E.D. Mich. 1991), for the proposition that appellee may rebut a prima facie case of improper use of appellants' ideas by showing that the ideas were independently created. Appellants disagree, and contend that they have presented strong circumstantial evidence proving that appellee used appellants' Psycho Chihuahua concept. The district court did not agree with appellants that Taco Bell's Chihuahua strongly resembled Psycho Chihuahua, but nevertheless found that Taco Bell was not entitled to summary judgment on the basis of its affirmative defense of independent creation. *See Wrench III,* 51 F. Supp. 2d at 855-56. Specifically, the district court found that testimony from Taco Bell's interested witnesses on the question of independent creation, by itself, was insufficient to support summary judgment. *Id.*

We agree with the district court's conclusion that the issue of independent creation presents genuine issues of material fact.

C. Novelty

Appellants assert that the district court erred in determining that novelty was required to sustain their contract claim. The district court found that Michigan law required appellants to prove the originality or novelty of their ideas in order to maintain their claims, concluding that appellants' ideas were not novel because they "merely combined themes and executions that had been used many times in a variety of commercials for different products." The district court thus granted summary judgment in favor of appellee on this alternative basis. We conclude that the district court erred in finding that Michigan law requires novelty in a contract-based claim.

. . . The district court seems to have assumed, without further discussion, that if the novelty requirement applied to appellants' conversion and misappropriation claims, it would also apply to appellants' implied-in-fact contract claim.

Conversion is based on property law principles. Courts have usually refused to protect ideas on a property theory, but when they have, it has generally been subject to the requirements of novelty and concreteness. . . . Most courts apply a different rule to contract claims, modifying the requirement of novelty in some circumstances and dispensing with it altogether in others. The reason for the distinction is this: property rights are rights against the world and courts are generally unwilling to accord that kind of protection to ideas; contract rights on the other hand are limited to the contracting parties and it should be for them to decide if an idea is sufficiently valuable to be purchased.

Nevertheless, many courts do require novelty in an action based upon an implied contract theory on the ground that there can be no consideration for an implied promise to pay if the idea does not constitute "property." *See* 4 *Nimmer on Copyright* § 16.08[B] at 16-60, 16-62. The authors of *Nimmer on Copyright* have criticized this view. Referring specifically to the dissenting opinion of former California Chief Justice Traynor in *Stanley v. Columbia Broad. Sys.,* 35 Cal.2d 653, 221 P.2d 73, 84 (1950), the authors of *Nimmer on Copyright* state:

If, as suggested above, an implied contract is regarded as an agreement to pay for the disclosure of an idea, rather than for the idea itself, Chief Justice Traynor's . . . remarks lose much of their persuasiveness. It would seem to be a perfectly reasonable assumption that one would obligate himself to pay for the disclosure of an idea that he would otherwise be *legally* free to use, but that in fact he would be unable to use without such disclosure. Some subsequent decisions in California and elsewhere have recognized that the novelty requirement should not be injected by the court in implied contract actions.

4 *Nimmer on Copyright* § 16.08[B] at 16-62. (footnotes omitted).

Sarver v. Detroit Edison Co., 51 N.W.2d 759 (Mich. App. 1997), tells us where Michigan likely stands on this issue. In *Sarver,* plaintiff brought an action against her employer seeking damages for conversion and breach of contract based on the allegation that defendant appropriated an idea which she submitted through an employee suggestion program. The court rejected plaintiff's conversion cause of action finding that plaintiff's idea "was neither novel nor unique" and "did not constitute property subject to a conversion cause of action." The *Sarver* court went on to hold, however, that plaintiff had stated a breach of contract claim, stating "to the extent that plaintiff seeks compensation for formulating, drafting, and submitting her idea pursuant to defendant's employee suggestion program, rather than for the idea itself, she has stated a breach of contract claim." The *Sarver* court did *not* impose a requirement of novelty on plaintiff's contract claim.

[The] *Sarver* court quoted with approval the decision of the Supreme Court of Alaska in *Reeves v. Alyeska Pipeline Service Co.* In *Reeves,* plaintiff had proposed the idea of creating a visitor center at a location where visitors could view the Alaska oil pipeline. He brought an action alleging tort and contract claims against the pipeline servicing company, which subsequently established such a visitor center. The Supreme Court of Alaska held that the element of novelty was not required for plaintiff's implied contract claim:

> Relying largely on cases from New York, Alyeska argues that novelty and originality should be required in an implied-in-fact claim. Reeves responds that we should follow California's example and not require novelty as an essential element of this sort of claim. Idea-based claims arise most frequently in the entertainment centers of New York and California, but New York requires novelty, whereas California does not. We prefer the California approach. An idea may be valuable to the recipient merely because of its timing or the manner in which it is presented. . . . Implied in fact contracts are closely related to express contracts. Each requires the parties to form an intent to enter into a contract. It is ordinarily not the court's role to evaluate the adequacy of the consideration agreed upon by the parties. The bargain should be left in the hands of the parties. If parties voluntarily choose to bargain for an individual's services in disclosing or developing a non-novel or unoriginal idea, they have the power to do so.

Reeves, 926 P.2d at 1130, 1141-1142. Since the Michigan court in *Sarver* quoted *Reeves* on the requirement of novelty in an action based on conversion and went on to hold that the plaintiff's contract claim survived notwithstanding lack of novelty, we conclude that Michigan follows *Reeves* and the California cases which dispense with the requirement of novelty in actions based on implied-in-fact contracts. . . .

While we conclude that Michigan would not impose a requirement of novelty in an action based upon a contract implied in fact, it does not appear that the result of this case would change even if Michigan were to follow the New York view, which requires only novelty to the defendant. Here, Taco Bell does not claim that it was aware of appellants' ideas prior to disclosure. Accordingly, we find that the district court erred in granting summary judgment to the appellee on the ground that appellants failed to show that their ideas were novel or original.

The judgment of the district court is REVERSED. . . .

NOTES

1. What is the distinction between contracts implied in fact (e.g., actual contracts), and unjust enrichment or similar claims that are described as "implied in law" or "quasi-contract." For implied in fact claims, what takes the claim out from under arguable preemption?

2. *Foad Consulting Group, Inc. v. Musil Govan Azzalino*, 270 F.3d 821 (9th Cir. 2001), provides further insight. There, the court commented:

> In this copyright case, we must decide [which] law, state or federal, governs the creation of an implied, nonexclusive copyright license? We conclude that while federal law answers the threshold question of whether an implied, nonexclusive copyright license can be granted (it can), state law determines the contract question: whether a copyright holder has, in fact, granted such a license. . . . As a general matter, we rely on state law to fill in the gaps Congress leaves in federal statutes. . . . Thus, where the Copyright Act does not address an issue, we turn to state law . . . so long as state law does not otherwise conflict with the Copyright Act. . . . There is no reason we should treat implied copyright licenses any differently. . . . Thus, [we must ask] whether California's parol evidence rule conflicts with federal copyright law or policy. The principle effect of the California parol evidence rule is to lessen the importance of written contracts. It does so because the rule requires courts to consider extrinsic evidence of possible ambiguity even where the terms of the contract appear unequivocal. . . . The Copyright Act places great emphasis on the necessity of writings to grant exclusive licenses, but not when it comes to granting nonexclusive licenses. . . . [We] conclude that application of California's parol evidence rule in interpreting a contract that a party purports to have granted an implied copyright license does not conflict with the Act or its underlying policies.

3. The Patent Act does not contain express preemption language. But some decisions hold that preemption exists where a state-law right conflicts with federal policies regarding information in the public domain. *Bonito Boats, Inc. v. Thunder Craft Boats, Inc.,* 489 U.S. 141 (1989). In *Waner v. Ford Motor Co.,* 331 F.3d 851 (Fed. Cir. 2003), the Court of Appeals for the Federal Circuit held that an unjust enrichment claim was preempted by patent law. The plaintiff had designed and manufactured a fender liner for trucks. It sold the product to a Ford dealer. It then sought an agreement for licensing the design of the liner with Ford Motor Company, but Ford elected to use the idea without payment or permission because it could discern the entire design from the product that had been sold. The court concluded that a suit for unjust enrichment seeking compensation for Ford's use of the idea before issuance of a patent was preempted because it purported to "create a collateral set of rights [under state law] available as an adjunct or expansion to patent rights." This was not proper absent an element of secrecy or confidentiality such as exists in trade secret law.

4. Would copyright preemption bar the misappropriation claim discussed in the *Nadel* case? If not, what is the extra or different element in such a case that takes it outside the scope of copyright preemption?

PROBLEM 2.6

Jane is an unemployed engineer. She has an idea for a method of measuring electron flow diverted to a particular target by an advanced electron channeling device that is already in existence. Jane can describe her idea orally, but she also has a number of drawings and detailed outlines of it. She approaches Pruit, a major company, describing her idea in a two-page letter to Smith, a senior research person at Pruit whose name she obtained from the Pruit website's listing of research personnel at the company. The letter generally describes the idea and offers to provide more information if Pruit is interested. Consider the outcome in each of the following cases:

a. Smith writes to Jane: "Pruit has no interest in pursuing your idea at present." Several months later, however, Smith sees the importance of such measurements and develops (over a period of months) a system that follows an idea similar to Jane's idea. Jane sues.

b. Assume the same facts, but that Smith's letter also stated: "Pruit's standing policy, as described in the attached memorandum which is also posted on our website, is that all ideas submitted to it become Pruit's property and that Pruit will accept no obligations with respect to any submissions made to it unless the submission was requested in writing by a Pruit representative." What result when Jane sues?

c. Would the result in "a" or "b" change if Pruit can prove that Smith was engaged in a research project based on the same idea that Jane had, but which began five months before Jane submitted her idea?

d. Would the result in "a" or "b" change if Jane's initial letter included her drawings and detailed outlines and, when Smith undertook the research a few months later, he referred to, but did not copy these drawings and outlines?

PROBLEM 2.7

MS Technologies is a provider of consumer electronics. It operates a website at which, among other things, it has a chatroom at which product owners can exchange information about MS products, and an idea board at which the users can make suggestions to MS for modifications of existing products or for new products. It asks your advice on two issues: 1) in some cases, the ideas turn out to be valuable and MS uses them, and 2) in other cases the comments parallel research or product development that is already going on in the company. What risk does it have and what do you advise? Draft any relevant language that you might suggest that MS use.

PROBLEM 2.8

After weeks of discussion, Acme Tool and Jason Devices are comfortable that the technology generally described by Jason to Acme could be valuable for Acme. If the technology is as described, Acme would pay a license royalty of 5% of its annual income from retail sales of drills (the product to which the technology relates) for ten years. These sales have ranged between $15 and $20 million. If the technology is less than described, of course, Acme would pay less, or simply not acquire a license for it. The parties conducted their initial negotiations under an agreement that "neither party will disclose information related to [Jason Technology] or [Acme Technology] disclosed to it during negotiation of this Agreement to any other person for a period of five years, except with respect to information that enters the public domain during that time." They have agreed on twenty ordinary terms (e.g., warranties, method of royalty calculation), but before the deal goes through, Acme must review the research results of Jason's research and conduct tests evaluating the performance of the technology. This requires a new agreement.

Focusing on the issues raised in this chapter, what issues should Acme consider in the agreement? What should Jason require? How should the language be drafted? Does Jason have a risk that Acme may refuse the license and disclose or use the technology?

III. SHRINKWRAP LICENSES — CONTRACT FORMATION

Information has long been distributed even in the mass market in ways that entail conditions on access to it, or on its use, retention, or redistribution, whether formally described as a license or other type of contract. The computer software industry, however, brought the idea of licensing explicitly into the mass market under a format that came to be described as "shrinkwrap" licensing because license terms were presented to the end user as part of a package containing a copy of the software and assent was registered by opening the product. The practices have evolved. More importantly, the shrinkwrap framework and variations on it have been adopted by other industries in both mass-market and commercial marketplaces.

Widespread use of this licensing framework testifies to its commercial value and efficiency, especially for industries where a digital or other product can be tailored to market demands and variegated pricing by the terms of a contract. This form of licensing, however, has been controversial. The issues have centered on two very different issues. The first concerns the enforceability of the terms as a matter of contract law: does a shrinkwrap framework establish assent to the terms of the license as a matter of contract law? We focus on that issue here. The second concerns the relationship between terms of a shrinkwrap (or similar license) and intellectual property doctrines that limit property rights protection, such as concepts of "first sale," "patent exhaustion" and "fair use." We have seen one aspect of this in the *ProCD, Inc. v. Zeidenberg* case in Chapter 1, and will return to the issue later.

M.A. MORTENSON COMPANY, INC. v. TIMBERLINE SOFTWARE CORP.
998 P.2d 305 (Wash. 2000)

JOHNSON, J.

Mortenson is a nationwide construction contractor. . . . Respondent Timberline is a software developer located in Beaverton, Oregon. Respondent Softworks, an authorized dealer for Timberline, is located in Kirkland, Washington and provides computer-related services to contractors such as Mortenson.

Since at least 1990, Mortenson has used Timberline's Bid Analysis software to assist with its preparation of bids. Mortenson had used Medallion, an earlier version of Bid Analysis, at its Minnesota headquarters and its regional offices. In early 1993, Mortenson installed a new computer network operating system at its Bellevue office and contacted Mark Reich (Reich), president of Softworks, to reinstall Medallion. Reich discovered, however, that the Medallion software was incompatible with Mortenson's new operating system. Reich informed Mortenson that Precision, a newer version of Bid Analysis, was compatible with its new operating system.

Mortenson wanted multiple copies of the new software for its offices, including copies for its corporate headquarters in Minnesota and its northwest regional office in Bellevue. Reich informed Mortenson he would place an order with Timberline and would deliver eight copies of the Precision software to the Bellevue office, after which Mortenson could distribute the copies among its offices.

After Reich provided Mortenson with a price quote, Mortenson issued a purchase order dated July 12, 1993, confirming the agreed upon purchase price, set up fee, delivery charges, and sales tax for eight copies of the software. The purchase order indicated that Softworks, on behalf of Timberline, would "[f]urnish current versions of Timberline Precision Bid Analysis Program Software and Keys" and "[p]rovide assistance in installation and system configuration for Mortenson's Bellevue Office." The purchase order also contained the following notations:

Provide software support in converting Mortenson's existing Bid Day
Master Files to a format accepted by the newly purchased Bid Day
software. This work shall be accomplished on a time and material
basis of $85.00 per hour. Format information of conversion of existing
D-Base Files to be shared to assist Mortenson Mid-West programmers
in file conversion.

— System software support and upgrades to be available from
Timberline for newly purchased versions of Bid Day Multi-User.

— At some future date should Timberline upgrade "Bid Day" to a
windows version, M.A. Mortenson would be able to upgrade to this
system with Timberline crediting existing software purchase toward
that upgrade on a pro-rated basis to be determined later.

Below the signature line the following was stated: "ADVISE PURCHASING
PROMPTLY IF UNABLE TO SHIP AS REQUIRED. EACH SHIPMENT MUST
INCLUDE A PACKING LIST. SUBSTITUTIONS OF GOODS OR CHANGES
IN COSTS REQUIRE OUR PRIOR APPROVAL." The purchase order did not
contain an integration clause.

Reich signed the purchase order and ordered the requested software from
Timberline. When Reich received the software, he opened the three large shipping boxes and checked the contents against the packing invoice. Contained
inside the shipping boxes were several smaller boxes, containing program diskettes in plastic pouches, installation instructions, and user manuals. One of
the larger boxes also contained the sealed protection devices for the software.

All Timberline software is distributed to its users under license. Both
Medallion and Precision Bid Analysis are licensed Timberline products. In the
case of the Mortenson shipment, the full text of Timberline's license agreement was set forth on the outside of each diskette pouch and the inside cover
of the instruction manuals. The first screen that appears each time the program is used also references the license and states, "[t]his software is licensed
for exclusive use by: Timberline Use Only." Further, a license to use the protection device was wrapped around each of the devices shipped to Mortenson.
The following warning preceded the terms of the license agreement:

CAREFULLY READ THE FOLLOWING TERMS AND CONDITIONS
BEFORE USING THE PROGRAMS. USE OF THE PROGRAMS
INDICATES YOUR ACKNOWLEDGEMENT THAT YOU HAVE
READ THIS LICENSE, UNDERSTAND IT, AND AGREE TO BE
BOUND BY ITS TERMS AND CONDITIONS. IF YOU DO NOT
AGREE TO THESE TERMS AND CONDITIONS, PROMPTLY
RETURN THE PROGRAMS AND USER MANUALS TO THE PLACE
OF PURCHASE AND YOUR PURCHASE PRICE WILL BE
REFUNDED. YOU AGREE THAT YOUR USE OF THE PROGRAM
ACKNOWLEDGES THAT YOU HAVE READ THIS LICENSE,
UNDERSTAND IT, AND AGREE TO BE BOUND BY ITS TERMS
AND CONDITIONS.

Under a separate subheading, the license agreement limited Mortenson's
remedies and provided:

LIMITATION OF REMEDIES AND LIABILITY

NEITHER TIMBERLINE NOR ANYONE ELSE WHO HAS BEEN INVOLVED IN THE CREATION, PRODUCTION OR DELIVERY OF THE PROGRAMS OR USER MANUALS SHALL BE LIABLE TO YOU FOR ANY DAMAGES OF ANY TYPE, INCLUDING BUT NOT LIMITED TO, ANY LOST PROFITS, LOST SAVINGS, LOSS OF ANTICIPATED BENEFITS, OR OTHER INCIDENTAL, OR CONSEQUENTIAL DAMAGES ARISING OUT OF THE USE OR INABILITY TO USE SUCH PROGRAMS, WHETHER ARISING OUT OF CONTRACT, NEGLIGENCE, STRICT TORT, OR UNDER ANY WARRANTY, OR OTHERWISE, EVEN IF TIMBERLINE HAS BEEN ADVISED OF THE POSSIBILITY OF SUCH DAMAGES OR FOR ANY OTHER CLAIM BY ANY OTHER PARTY. TIMBERLINE'S LIABILITY FOR DAMAGES IN NO EVENT SHALL EXCEED THE LICENSE FEE PAID FOR THE RIGHT TO USE THE PROGRAMS.

Reich personally delivered the software to Mortenson's Bellevue office, and was asked to return at a later date for installation. The parties dispute what happened next. According to Neal Ruud (Ruud), Mortenson's chief estimator at its Bellevue office, when Reich arrived to install the software Reich personally opened the smaller product boxes contained within the large shipping boxes and also opened the diskette packaging. Reich inserted the diskettes into the computer, initiated the program, contacted Timberline to receive the activation codes, and wrote down the codes for Mortenson. Reich then started the programs and determined to the best of his knowledge they were operating properly. Ruud states that Mortenson never saw any of the licensing information described above, or any of the manuals that accompanied the software. Ruud adds that copies of the programs purchased for other Mortenson offices were forwarded to those offices.

Reich claims when he arrived at Mortenson's Bellevue office he noticed the software had been opened and had been placed on a desk, along with a manual and a protection device. Reich states he told Mortenson he would install the program at a single workstation and "then they would do the rest." Reich proceeded to install the software and a Mortenson employee attached the protection device. Reich claims he initiated and ran the program, and then observed as a Mortenson employee repeated the installation process on a second computer. An employee then told Reich that Mortenson would install the software at the remaining stations.

In December 1993, Mortenson utilized the Precision Bid Analysis software to prepare a bid for a project at Harborview Medical Center in Seattle. On the day of the bid, the software allegedly malfunctioned multiple times and gave the following message: "Abort: Cannot find alternate." Clerk's Papers at 60. Mortenson received this message 19 times that day. Nevertheless, Mortenson submitted a bid generated by the software. After Mortenson was awarded the Harborview Medical Center project, it learned its bid was approximately $1.95 million lower than intended.

Mortenson filed an action in King County Superior Court against Timberline and Softworks alleging breach of express and implied warranties. . . . Timberline moved for summary judgment of dismissal in July 1997, arguing the limitation on consequential damages in the licensing agreement barred

Mortenson's recovery. Mortenson countered that its entire contract with Timberline consisted of the purchase order and it never saw or agreed to the provisions in the licensing agreement. . . .

ANALYSIS

Applicable Law

Article 2 of the Uniform Commercial Code (U.C.C.), chapter 62A RCW, applies to transactions in goods. The parties agree in their briefing that Article 2 applies to the licensing of software, and we accept this proposition. . . .

Terms of the Contract

Mortenson [argues that] even if the purchase order was not an integrated contract, Timberline's delivery of the license terms merely constituted a request to add additional or different terms, which were never agreed upon by the parties. Mortenson claims under RCW 62A.2-207 the additional terms did not become part of the contract because they were material alterations. Timberline responds that the terms of the license were not a request to add additional terms, but part of the contract between the parties. Timberline further argues that so-called "shrinkwrap" software licenses have been found enforceable by other courts, and that both trade usage and course of dealing support enforcement in the present case. For its section 2-207 analysis, Mortenson relies on *Step-Saver Data Sys., Inc. v. Wyse Tech.,* 939 F.2d 91 (3d Cir.1991). . . . Mortenson claims *Step-Saver* is controlling, as "virtually every element of the transaction in the present case is mirrored in *Step-Saver.*" We disagree.

First, *Step-Saver* did not involve the enforceability of a standard license agreement against an *end user* of the software, but instead involved its applicability to a value added retailer who simply included the software in an integrated system sold to the end user. In fact, in *Step-Saver* the party contesting applicability of the licensing agreement had been assured the license did not apply to it at all. Such is not the case here, as Mortenson was the end user of the Bid Analysis software and was never told the license agreement did not apply.

Further, in *Step-Saver* the seller of the program twice asked the buyer to sign an agreement comparable to their disputed license agreement. Both times the buyer refused, but the seller continued to make the software available. In contrast, Mortenson and Timberline had utilized a license agreement throughout Mortenson's use of the Medallion and Precision Bid Analysis software. Given these distinctions, we find *Step-Saver* to be inapplicable to the present case. We conclude this is a case about contract formation, not contract alteration. As such, RCW 62A.2-204, and not RCW 62A.2-207, provides the proper framework for our analysis.

RCW 62A.2-204 states:

> (1) A contract for sale of goods may be made *in any manner sufficient to show agreement,* including conduct by both parties which recognizes the existence of such a contract.
>
> (2) An agreement sufficient to constitute a contract for sale may be found *even though the moment of its making is undetermined.*

(3) Even though one or more terms are left open a contract for sale does not fail for indefiniteness if the parties have intended to make a contract and there is a reasonably certain basis for giving an appropriate remedy.

(Emphasis added.) Although no Washington case specifically addresses the type of contract formation at issue in this case, a series of recent cases from other jurisdictions have analyzed shrinkwrap licenses under analogous statutes. *See Brower v. Gateway 2000, Inc.,* 246 A.D.2d 246, 250-51, 676 N.Y.S.2d 569 (1998); *Hill v. Gateway 2000, Inc.,* 105 F.3d 1147 (7th Cir.), *cert. denied,* 522 U.S. 808, 118 S.Ct. 47, 139 L.Ed.2d 13 (1997); *ProCD, Inc. v. Zeidenberg,* 86 F.3d 1447 (7th Cir.1996).

In *ProCD,* which involved a retail purchase of software, the Seventh Circuit held software shrinkwrap license agreements are a valid form of contracting under Wisconsin's version of U.C.C. section 2-204, and such agreements are enforceable unless objectionable under general contract law such as the law of unconscionability. The court stated, "[n]otice on the outside, terms on the inside, and a right to return the software for a refund if the terms are unacceptable (a right that the license expressly extends), may be a means of doing business valuable to buyers and sellers alike."

In *Hill,* the customer ordered a computer over the telephone and received the computer in the mail, accompanied by a list of terms to govern if the customer did not return the product within 30 days. Relying in part on *ProCD,* the court held the terms of the "accept-or-return" agreement were effective, stating, "[c]ompetent adults are bound by such documents, *read or unread."* Elaborating on its holding in *ProCD,* the court continued:

> The question in *ProCD* was not whether terms were added to a contract after its formation, but how and when the contract was formed — in particular, whether a vendor may propose that a contract of sale be formed, not in the store (or over the phone) with the payment of money or a general "send me the product," but after the customer has had a chance to inspect both the item and the terms. *ProCD answers "yes," for merchants and consumers alike.*

Hill, 105 F.3d at 1150 (emphasis added). Interpreting the same licensing agreement at issue in *Hill,* the New York Supreme Court, Appellate Division concluded shrinkwrap license terms delivered following a mail order purchase were not proposed additions to the contract, but part of the original agreement between the parties. The court held U.C.C. section 2-207 did not apply because the contract was not formed until after the period to return the merchandise.

We find the approach of the *ProCD, Hill,* and *Brower* courts persuasive and adopt it to guide our analysis under RCW 62A.2-204. We conclude because RCW 62A.2-204 allows a contract to be formed "in any manner sufficient to show agreement . . . even though the moment of its making is undetermined," it allows the formation of "layered contracts" similar to those envisioned by *ProCD, Hill,* and *Brower.* We, therefore, hold under RCW 62A.2-204 the terms of the license were part of the contract between Mortenson and Timberline, and Mortenson's use of the software constituted its assent to the agreement, including the license terms.

The terms of Timberline's license were either set forth explicitly or referenced in numerous locations. The terms were included within the shrinkwrap packaging of each copy of Precision Bid Analysis; they were present in the manuals accompanying the software; they were included with the protection devices for the software, without which the software could not be used. The fact the software was licensed was also noted on the introductory screen each time the software was used. Even accepting Mortenson's contention it never saw the terms of the license, . . . it was not necessary for Mortenson to actually read the agreement in order to be bound by it.

Furthermore, the U.C.C. defines an "agreement" as "the bargain of the parties in fact as found in their language *or by implication from other circumstances including course of dealing or usage of trade* or course of performance. . . ." Mortenson and Timberline had a course of dealing; Mortenson had purchased licensed software from Timberline for years prior to its upgrade to Precision Bid Analysis. All Timberline software, including the prior version of Bid Analysis used by Mortenson since at least 1990, is distributed under license. Moreover, extensive testimony and exhibits before the trial court demonstrate an unquestioned use of such license agreements throughout the software industry. Although Mortenson questioned the relevance of this evidence, there is no evidence in the record to contradict it. While trade usage is a question of fact, *undisputed* evidence of trade usage may be considered on summary judgment.

As the license was part of the contract between Mortenson and Timberline, its terms are enforceable unless "objectionable on grounds applicable to contracts in general. . . ."

Enforceability of Limitation of Remedies Clause

Mortenson contends even if the limitation of remedies clause is part of its contract with Timberline, the clause is unconscionable and, therefore, unenforceable.

Limitations on consequential damages are generally valid under the U.C.C. unless they are unconscionable. . . . Unconscionability "was never intended as a vortex for elements of fairness specifically embodied in other Code provisions." We find Mortenson's unconscionability claim unpersuasive and, therefore, find the limitation of remedies clause to be enforceable.

Conclusion

Mortenson has failed to set forth any material issues of fact on the issue of contract formation, and has also failed to make a threshold showing of unconscionability sufficient to avoid summary judgment. We affirm the Court of Appeals, upholding the trial court's order of summary judgment of dismissal and denial of the motions to vacate and amend.

NOTES

1. The case law overwhelmingly supports the enforceability of shrinkwrap terms when the terms are properly made available to the end user for assent, even if this does not occur until after the product is brought home or to the end user's office. *Mortenson* suggests one way to explain this result. Another way of describing the assent was suggested by the court in *Pro-CD, Inc. v. Zeidenberg*, 86 F.3d 1447, 1450-51 (7th Cir. 1996):

> Zeidenberg does argue, and the district court held, that placing the package of software on the shelf is an "offer," which the customer "accepts" by paying the asking price and leaving the store with the goods. In Wisconsin, as elsewhere, a contract includes only the terms on which the parties have agreed. One cannot agree to hidden terms, the [trial court] judge concluded. So far, so good — but one of the terms to which Zeidenberg agreed by purchasing the software is that the transaction was subject to a license. Zeidenberg's position therefore must be that the printed terms on the outside of a box are the parties' contract — except for printed terms that refer to or incorporate other terms. But why would Wisconsin fetter the parties' choice in this way? Vendors can put the entire terms of a contract on the outside of a box only by using microscopic type, removing other information that buyers might find more useful (such as what the software does, and on which computers it works), or both. The "Read Me" file included with most software, describing system requirements and potential incompatibilities, may be equivalent to ten pages of type; warranties and license restrictions take still more space. Notice on the outside, terms on the inside, and a right to return the software for a refund if the terms are unacceptable (a right that the license expressly extends), may be a means of doing business valuable to buyers and sellers alike. *See Restatement (2d) of Contracts* § 211 comment a (1981) ("Standardization of agreements serves many of the same functions as standardization of goods and services; both are essential to a system of mass production and distribution. Scarce and costly time and skill can be devoted to a class of transactions rather than the details of individual transactions.").

The quoted portion of *Zeidenberg* hinges on the existence of notice or reason to know that the purchase would be subject to a license. UCITA makes this requirement explicit. UCITA § 208(2) (2000 Official Text). In addition it provides that the license terms are not enforceable unless 1) the licensee manifests assent to the license, 2) after having had an opportunity to review its terms, and 3) where the terms are first available after an initial agreement, the licensee had the option of refusing them and returning the licensed subject matter for a refund.

2. In the few cases that decline to enforce shrinkwrap terms, the analysis typically focuses on a failure of the general condition of assent or on other procedural factors, rather than a rejection of the contracting approach in general. The leading case is *Step-Saver Data Sys., Inc. v. Wyse Technology*, 939 F.2d 91, 102-03 (3d Cir. 1991). *Wyse* was a battle of forms case under UCC § 2-207. In that case, one of the arguments by the licensor was that its license was a counter-offer and its willingness to enter the contract was expressly conditional on assent to the terms of that counteroffer. The court held that, under UCC § 2-207, this would require a clear showing beyond the terms of the standard form that the licensor was willing to forgo the transaction unless terms were accepted. The court viewed the issue as close:

[We adopt an approach that] requires the offeree to demonstrate an unwillingness to proceed with the transaction unless the additional or different terms are included in the contract. . . . Using this test, it is apparent that the integration clause and the "consent by opening" language is not sufficient to render TSL's acceptance conditional. [This] type of language provides no real indication that the party is willing to forego the transaction if the additional language is not included in the contract.

The second provision provides a more substantial indication that TSL was willing to forego the contract if the terms of the box-top license were not accepted by Step-Saver. On its face, the box-top license states that TSL will refund the purchase price if the purchaser does not agree to the terms of the license. Even with such a refund term, however, the offeree/counterofferor may be relying on the purchaser's investment in time and energy in reaching this point in the transaction to prevent the purchaser from returning the item. Because a purchaser has made a decision to buy a particular product and has actually obtained the product, the purchaser may use it despite the refund offer, regardless of the additional terms specified after the contract formed. But we need not decide whether such a refund offer could ever amount to a conditional acceptance; the undisputed evidence in this case demonstrates that the terms of the license were not sufficiently important that TSL would forego its sales to Step-Saver if TSL could not obtain Step-Saver's consent to those terms. As discussed, Mr. Greebel testified that TSL assured him that the box-top license did not apply to Step-Saver, as Step-Saver was not the end user of the Multilink Advanced program. Supporting this testimony, TSL on two occasions asked Step-Saver to sign agreements that . . . contained warranty disclaimer and limitation of remedy terms similar to those contained in the box-top license. Step-Saver refused to sign the agreements; nevertheless, TSL continued to sell copies of Multilink Advanced to Step-Saver.

3. Contracting by use of forms supplied for assent after a preliminary agreement has been made is not confined to the software industry, but is increasingly used in other contexts. In *Greenfield v. Twin Vision Graphics, Inc.,* 268 F. Supp. 2d 358 (D.N.J. 2003), for example, the court enforced a use restriction relating to a commercial photograph where the use restriction was contained in the invoice sent by the photograph along with a copy of the photo. The court distinguished the *Step-Saver* analysis based on the fact that the licensor there continued to provide the software even after the transferee had explicitly refused to enter into a contract with the contested term. Here, there was no such discussion or rejection of the terms. In *Puget Sound Financial, LLC v. Unisearch, Inc.,* 47 P.3d 940 (Wash. 2002), the court upheld a damages limitation contained in the invoice provided by a public records search firm. The court affirmed the concept of "layered contracting," but also held that a damage limitation clause became part of a contract whether or not there was effective agreement to the invoice containing the terms because the limitation was common in the trade (trade usage) and routinely used in contracts between the two parties (course of dealing).

4. Especially when the contested terms pertain to the scope of permitted use of the information product, it is relevant to ask what would be the result if the license terms were unenforceable? In such cases, for example, what rights would a licensee of a copyrighted work have to copy or distribute the work? Also, since use terms tend to define the product provided to the transferee and the price that is set, if the terms did not become part of the contract, should there be a contract at all?

5. One basis of the hostility of some toward shrinkwrap licenses lies in an uneasiness about the enforceability of standard forms where no explicit bargaining over terms occurs. Despite some hostility to standard form contracts, contract law in the United States has generally accepted that they are enforceable, but allows courts to monitor terms of the contract to prevent cases of serious abuse and over-reaching. *See, e.g.,* Robert A. Hillman & Jeffrey J. Rachlinski, *Standard-Form Contracting in the Electronic Age,* 77 N.Y.U. L. REV. 429 (2002). The doctrine most often associated with this monitoring is the doctrine of unconscionability. The *Restatement (Second) of Contracts* § 208, for example, states:

> If a contract or term thereof is unconscionable at the time the contract is made a court may refuse to enforce the contract, or may enforce the remainder of the contract without the unconscionable term, or may so limit the application of any unconscionable term as to avoid any unconscionable result.

> Comment:

> . . . Like the obligation of good faith and fair dealing . . . the policy against unconscionable contracts or terms applies to a wide variety of types of conduct. The determination that a contract or term is or is not unconscionable is made in the light of its setting, purpose and effect. Relevant factors include weaknesses in the contracting process like those involved in more specific rules as to contractual capacity, fraud, and other invalidating causes; the policy also overlaps with rules which render particular bargains or terms unenforceable on grounds of public policy. Policing against unconscionable contracts or terms has sometimes been accomplished "by adverse construction of language, by manipulation of the rules of offer and acceptance or by determinations that the clause is contrary to public policy or to the dominant purpose of the contract." Uniform Commercial Code § 2-302 Comment 1. Particularly in the case of standardized agreements, the rule of this Section permits the court to pass directly on the unconscionability of the contract or clause rather than to avoid unconscionable results by interpretation.

PROBLEM 2.9

Recording Studio distributes its copyrighted products in digital form. Last year, the company elected to initiate a new format in which individual disks would be limited in use to designated digital systems. Specifically, ordinary disks can be used in any digital system not linked to the Internet or a computer network. A standard price is charged for this product. A higher price is charged for disks that are authorized for use in computer networks.

There is no technological distinction between the two products. The ordinary disk, however, comes with a contract in the box containing the disk that states that it is to be used only in "non-networked digital systems." The higher price option contains a contract in the box that allows use in networks. The contracts state that using the disk constitutes acceptance of the contract terms.

a. User acquires a copy of the latest rock hit under the ordinary disk product. User copies the music onto its home network, which consists of five machines linked to the Internet. Assume that this would be fair use without the presence of the license. Recording Studio sues. What result?

b. Recording Studio asks how it can restructure its business approach and contract terms to minimize legal problems in the future. What do you advise?

IV. ONLINE LICENSES — FORMATION ISSUES

The Internet introduced a new method of distributing information. Many Internet sites that make information commercially available do so pursuant contractual terms. These are licenses. They provide conditions under which a licensee is permitted access to and use of the online site. Also, in many cases, the licenses set terms under which the licensee can use the information obtained from the site.

SPECHT v. NETSCAPE COMUNICATIONS, INC.
306 F.3d 17 (2d Cir. 2002)

SOTOMAYOR, CIRCUIT JUDGE.

This is an appeal from a judgment of the Southern District of New York denying a motion by defendants-appellants Netscape Communications Corporation and its corporate parent, America Online, Inc. (collectively, "defendants" or "Netscape"), to compel arbitration and to stay court proceedings. In order to resolve the central question of arbitrability presented here, we must address issues of contract formation in cyberspace. Principally, we are asked to determine whether plaintiffs-appellees ("plaintiffs"), by acting upon defendants' invitation to download free software made available on defendants' webpage, agreed to be bound by the software's license terms (which included the arbitration clause at issue), even though plaintiffs could not have learned of the existence of those terms unless, prior to executing the download, they had scrolled down the webpage to a screen located below the download button. We agree with the district court that a reasonably prudent Internet user in circumstances such as these would not have known or learned of the existence of the license terms before responding to defendants' invitation to download the free software, and that defendants therefore did not provide reasonable notice of the license terms. In consequence, plaintiffs' bare act of downloading the software did not unambiguously manifest assent to the arbitration provision contained in the license terms.

We also agree with the district court that plaintiffs' claims relating to the software at issue — a "plug-in" program entitled SmartDownload ("SmartDownload" or "the plug-in program"), offered by Netscape to enhance the functioning of the separate browser program called Netscape Communicator ("Communicator" or "the browser program") — are not subject to an arbitration agreement contained in the license terms governing the use of Communicator. . . . We therefore affirm the district court's denial of defendants' motion to compel arbitration and to stay court proceedings.

Background

I. Facts

In three related putative class actions, plaintiffs alleged that, unknown to them, their use of SmartDownload transmitted to defendants private information about plaintiffs' downloading of files from the Internet, thereby effecting an electronic surveillance of their online activities in violation of two federal statutes, the Electronic Communications Privacy Act, 18 U.S.C. §§ 2510 *et seq.,* and the Computer Fraud and Abuse Act, 18 U.S.C. § 1030. . . .

In the time period relevant to this litigation, Netscape offered on its website various software programs, including Communicator and SmartDownload, which visitors to the site were invited to obtain free of charge. It is undisputed that five of the six named plaintiffs — Michael Fagan, John Gibson, Mark Gruber, Sean Kelly, and Sherry Weindorf — downloaded Communicator from the Netscape website. These plaintiffs acknowledge that when they proceeded to initiate installation of Communicator, they were automatically shown a scrollable text of that program's license agreement and were not permitted to complete the installation until they had clicked on a "Yes" button to indicate that they accepted all the license terms. If a user attempted to install Communicator without clicking "Yes," the installation would be aborted. All five named user plaintiffs expressly agreed to Communicator's license terms by clicking "Yes." The Communicator license agreement that these plaintiffs saw made no mention of SmartDownload or other plug-in programs, and stated that "[t]hese terms apply to Netscape Communicator and Netscape Navigator" and that "all disputes relating to this Agreement (excepting any dispute relating to intellectual property rights)" are subject to "binding arbitration in Santa Clara County, California."

Although Communicator could be obtained independently of SmartDownload, all the named user plaintiffs, except Fagan, downloaded and installed Communicator in connection with downloading SmartDownload. Each of these plaintiffs allegedly arrived at a Netscape webpage captioned "SmartDownload Communicator" that urged them to "Download With Confidence Using SmartDownload!" At or near the bottom of the screen facing plaintiffs was the prompt "Start Download" and a tinted button labeled "Download." By clicking on the button, plaintiffs initiated the download of SmartDownload. Once that process was complete, SmartDownload, as its first plug-in task, permitted plaintiffs to proceed with downloading and installing Communicator, an operation that was accompanied by the clickwrap display of Communicator's license terms described above.

The signal difference between downloading Communicator and downloading SmartDownload was that no clickwrap presentation accompanied the latter operation. Instead, once plaintiffs Gibson, Gruber, Kelly, and Weindorf had clicked on the "Download" button located at or near the bottom of their screen, and the downloading of SmartDownload was complete, these plaintiffs encountered no further information about the plug-in program or the existence of license terms governing its use. The sole reference to SmartDownload's license terms on the "SmartDownload Communicator" webpage was located in text that would have become visible to plaintiffs only if they had scrolled down to the next screen.

Had plaintiffs scrolled down instead of acting on defendants' invitation to click on the "Download" button, they would have encountered the following invitation: "Please review and agree to the terms of the *Netscape SmartDownload software license agreement* before downloading and using the software." Plaintiffs Gibson, Gruber, Kelly, and Weindorf averred in their affidavits that they never saw this reference to the SmartDownload license agreement when they clicked on the "Download" button. They also testified during depositions that they saw no reference to license terms when they clicked to download SmartDownload, although under questioning by defendants' counsel, some plaintiffs added that they could not "remember" or be "sure" whether the screen shots of the SmartDownload page attached to their affidavits reflected precisely what they had seen on their computer screens when they downloaded SmartDownload.

In sum, plaintiffs Gibson, Gruber, Kelly, and Weindorf allege that the process of obtaining SmartDownload contrasted sharply with that of obtaining Communicator. Having selected SmartDownload, they were required neither to express unambiguous assent to that program's license agreement nor even to view the license terms or become aware of their existence before proceeding with the invited download of the free plug-in program. Moreover, once these plaintiffs had initiated the download, the existence of SmartDownload's license terms was not mentioned while the software was running or at any later point in plaintiffs' experience of the product.

Even for a user who, unlike plaintiffs, did happen to scroll down past the download button, SmartDownload's license terms would not have been immediately displayed in the manner of Communicator's clickwrapped terms. Instead, if such a user had seen the notice of SmartDownload's terms and then clicked on the underlined invitation to review and agree to the terms, a hypertext link would have taken the user to a separate webpage entitled "License & Support Agreements." The first paragraph on this page read, in pertinent part:

> The use of each Netscape software product is governed by a license agreement. You must read and agree to the license agreement terms BEFORE acquiring a product. Please click on the appropriate link below to review the current license agreement for the product of interest to you before acquisition. For products available for download, you must read and agree to the license agreement terms BEFORE you install the software. If you do not agree to the license terms, do not download, install or use the software.

Below this paragraph appeared a list of license agreements, the first of which was *"License Agreement for Netscape Navigator and Netscape Communicator Product Family* (Netscape Navigator, Netscape Communicator and Netscape SmartDownload)." If the user clicked on that link, he or she would be taken to yet another webpage that contained the full text of a license agreement that was identical in every respect to the Communicator license agreement except that it stated that its "terms apply to Netscape Communicator, Netscape Navigator, and Netscape SmartDownload." The license agreement granted the user a nonexclusive license to use and reproduce the software, subject to certain terms:

> BY CLICKING THE ACCEPTANCE BUTTON OR INSTALLING OR USING NETSCAPE COMMUNICATOR, NETSCAPE NAVIGATOR, OR NETSCAPE SMARTDOWNLOAD SOFTWARE (THE "PRODUCT"), THE INDIVIDUAL OR ENTITY LICENSING THE PRODUCT ("LICENSEE") IS CONSENTING TO BE BOUND BY AND IS BECOMING A PARTY TO THIS AGREEMENT. IF LICENSEE DOES NOT AGREE TO ALL OF THE TERMS OF THIS AGREEMENT, THE BUTTON INDICATING NON-ACCEPTANCE MUST BE SELECTED, AND LICENSEE MUST NOT INSTALL OR USE THE SOFTWARE.

Among the license terms was a provision requiring virtually all disputes relating to the agreement to be submitted to arbitration:

> Unless otherwise agreed in writing, all disputes relating to this Agreement (excepting any dispute relating to intellectual property rights) shall be subject to final and binding arbitration in Santa Clara County, California, under the auspices of JAMS/EndDispute, with the losing party paying all costs of arbitration.

Unlike the four named user plaintiffs who downloaded SmartDownload from the Netscape website, the fifth named plaintiff, Michael Fagan, claims to have downloaded the plug-in program from a "shareware" website operated by ZDNet, an entity unrelated to Netscape. Shareware sites are websites, maintained by companies or individuals, that contain libraries of free, publicly available software. The pages that a user would have seen while downloading SmartDownload from ZDNet differed from those that he or she would have encountered while downloading SmartDownload from the Netscape website. Notably, instead of any kind of notice of the SmartDownload license agreement, the ZDNet pages offered only a hypertext link to "more information" about SmartDownload, which, if clicked on, took the user to a Netscape webpage that, in turn, contained a link to the license agreement. Thus, a visitor to the ZDNet website could have obtained SmartDownload, as Fagan avers he did, without ever seeing a reference to that program's license terms, even if he or she had scrolled through all of ZDNet's webpages. . . .

Discussion

Defendants argue on appeal that the district court erred in deciding the question of contract formation as a matter of law. A central issue in dispute, according to defendants, is whether the user plaintiffs actually saw the notice of SmartDownload's license terms when they downloaded the plug-in program. Although plaintiffs in their affidavits and depositions generally swore that they never saw the notice of terms on Netscape's webpage, defendants point to deposition testimony in which some plaintiffs, under repeated questioning by defendants' counsel, responded that they could not "remember" or be entirely "sure" whether the link to SmartDownload's license terms was visible on their computer screens. Defendants argue that on some computers, depending on the configuration of the monitor and browser, SmartDownload's license link "appears on the first screen, without any need for the user to scroll at all." Thus, according to defendants, "a trial on the factual issues that Defendants raised about each and every Plaintiffs' [*sic*] downloading experience" is required on remand to remedy the district court's "error" in denying defendants' motion as a matter of law.

Section 4 of the FAA provides, in relevant part, that "[i]f the making of the arbitration agreement . . . be in issue, the court shall proceed summarily to the trial thereof." 9 U.S.C. § 4. We conclude for two reasons, however, that defendants are not entitled to a remand for a full trial. First, during oral argument in the district court on the arbitrability of the five user plaintiffs' claims, defendants' counsel repeatedly insisted that the district court could decide "as a matter of law based on the uncontroverted facts in this case" whether "a reasonably prudent person could or should have known of the [license] terms by which acceptance would be signified." "I don't want you to try the facts," defendants' counsel told the court. "I think that the evidence in this case upon which this court can make a determination [of whether a contract existed] as a matter of law is uncontroverted." Accordingly, the district court decided the issue of reasonable notice and objective manifestation of assent as a matter of law. "[I]t is a well-established general rule that an appellate court will not consider an issue raised for the first time on appeal." Nor would it cause injustice in this case for us to decline to accept defendants' invitation to consider an issue that defendants did not advance below.

Second, after conducting weeks of discovery on defendants' motion to compel arbitration, the parties placed before the district court an ample record consisting of affidavits and extensive deposition testimony by each named plaintiff; numerous declarations by counsel and witnesses for the parties; dozens of exhibits, including computer screen shots and other visual evidence concerning the user plaintiffs' experience of the Netscape webpage; oral argument supplemented by a computer demonstration; and additional briefs following oral argument. This well-developed record contrasts sharply with the meager records that on occasion have caused this Court to remand for trial on the issue of contract formation pursuant to 9 U.S.C. § 4. *See, e.g., Interbras Cayman Co. v. Orient Victory Shipping Co., S.A.,* 663 F.2d 4, 5 (2d Cir.1981) (record consisted of affidavits and other papers); *Interocean Shipping,* 462 F.2d at 676 (record consisted of pleadings, affidavits, and documentary attachments). We are satisfied that the unusually full record before the district court in this case constituted "a hearing where evidence is received." *Interocean Shipping,* 462 F.2d at 677. Moreover, upon the record assembled, a fact-finder could not reasonably find that defendants prevailed in showing that any of the user plaintiffs had entered into an agreement on defendants' license terms.

In sum, we conclude that the district court properly decided the question of reasonable notice and objective manifestation of assent as a matter of law on the record before it, and we decline defendants' request to remand for a full trial on that question.

III. Whether the User Plaintiffs Had Reasonable Notice of and Manifested Assent to the SmartDownload License Agreement

Whether governed by the common law or by Article 2 of the Uniform Commercial Code ("UCC"), a transaction, in order to be a contract, requires a manifestation of agreement between the parties. Mutual manifestation of assent, whether by written or spoken word or by conduct, is the touchstone of contract. *Binder v. Aetna Life Ins. Co.,* 75 Cal. App. 4th 832, 848, 89 Cal. Rptr. 2d 540, 551 (1999); *cf. Restatement (Second) of Contracts* § 19(2) (1981) ("The conduct of a party is not effective as a manifestation of his assent unless he intends to engage in the conduct and knows or has reason to know that the other party may infer from his conduct that he assents."). Although an onlooker observing the disputed transactions in this case would have seen each of the user plaintiffs click on the SmartDownload "Download" button, a consumer's clicking on a download button does not communicate assent to contractual terms if the offer did not make clear to the consumer that clicking on the download button would signify assent to those terms. California's common law is clear that "an offeree, regardless of apparent manifestation of his consent, is not bound by inconspicuous contractual provisions of which he is unaware, contained in a document whose contractual nature is not obvious."

Arbitration agreements are no exception to the requirement of manifestation of assent. "This principle of knowing consent applies with particular force to provisions for arbitration." Clarity and conspicuousness of arbitration terms are important in securing informed assent. "If a party wishes to bind in writing another to an agreement to arbitrate future disputes, such purpose should be accomplished in a way that each party to the arrangement will fully and clearly comprehend that the agreement to arbitrate exists and binds the parties thereto." Thus, California contract law measures assent by an objective standard that takes into account both what the offeree said, wrote, or did and the transactional context in which the offeree verbalized or acted.

A. The Reasonably Prudent Offeree of Downloadable Software

Defendants argue that plaintiffs must be held to a standard of reasonable prudence and that, because notice of the existence of SmartDownload license terms was on the next scrollable screen, plaintiffs were on "inquiry notice" of those terms. We disagree with the proposition that a reasonably prudent offeree in plaintiffs' position would necessarily have known or learned of the existence of the SmartDownload license agreement prior to acting, so that plaintiffs may be held to have assented to that agreement with constructive notice of its terms. *See* Cal. Civ.Code § 1589 ("A voluntary acceptance of the benefit of a transaction is equivalent to a consent to all the obligations arising from it, so far as the facts are known, or ought to be known, to the person accepting."). It is true that "[a] party cannot avoid the terms of a contract on the ground that he or she failed to read it before signing." *Marin Storage & Trucking,* 89 Cal. App. 4th at 1049, 107 Cal. Rptr. 2d at 651. But courts are quick to add: "An exception to this general rule exists when the writing does not appear to be a contract and the terms are not called to the attention of the recipient. In such a case, no contract is formed with respect to the undisclosed term."

Most of the cases cited by defendants in support of their inquiry-notice argument are drawn from the world of paper contracting. *See, e.g., Taussig v. Bode & Haslett,* 134 Cal. 260, 66 P. 259 (1901) (where party had opportunity to read leakage disclaimer printed on warehouse receipt, he had duty to do so); *In re First Capital Life Ins. Co.,* 34 Cal. App. 4th 1283, 1288, 40 Cal. Rptr. 2d 816, 820 (1995) (purchase of insurance policy after opportunity to read and understand policy terms creates binding agreement); *King v. Larsen Realty, Inc.,* 121 Cal. App. 3d 349, 356, 175 Cal. Rptr. 226, 231 (1981) (where realtors' board manual specifying that party was required to arbitrate was "readily available," party was "on notice" that he was agreeing to mandatory arbitration); *Cal. State Auto. Ass'n Inter-Ins. Bureau v. Barrett Garages, Inc.,* 257 Cal. App. 2d 71, 76, 64 Cal. Rptr. 699, 703 (1967) (recipient of airport parking claim check was bound by terms printed on claim check, because a "ordinarily prudent" person would have been alerted to the terms); *Larrus v. First Nat'l Bank,* 122 Cal.App.2d 884, 888, 266 P. 2d 143, 147 (1954) ("clearly printed" statement on bank card stating that depositor agreed to bank's regulations provided sufficient notice to create agreement, where party had opportunity to view statement and to ask for full text of regulations, but did not do so); *see also Hux v. Butler,* 339 F. 2d 696, 700 (6th Cir.1964) (constructive notice found where "slightest inquiry" would have disclosed relevant facts to offeree); *Walker v. Carnival Cruise Lines,* 63 F. Supp. 2d 1083, 1089 (N.D. Cal. 1999) (under California and federal law, "conspicuous notice" directing the attention of parties to existence of contract terms renders terms binding) (quotation marks omitted); *Shacket v. Roger Smith Aircraft Sales, Inc.,* 651 F. Supp. 675, 691 (N.D. Ill.1986) (constructive notice found where "minimal investigation" would have revealed facts to offeree).

As the foregoing cases suggest, receipt of a physical document containing contract terms or notice thereof is frequently deemed, in the world of paper transactions, a sufficient circumstance to place the offeree on inquiry notice of those terms. "Every person who has actual notice of circumstances sufficient to put a prudent man upon inquiry as to a particular fact, has constructive notice of the fact itself in all cases in which, by prosecuting such inquiry, he might have learned such fact." Cal. Civ.Code § 19. These principles apply equally to the emergent world of online product delivery, pop-up screens, hyperlinked pages, clickwrap licensing, scrollable documents, and urgent admonitions to "Download Now!" What plaintiffs saw when they were being invited by defendants to download this fast, free plug-in called SmartDownload was a screen containing praise for the product and, at the very bottom of the screen, a "Download" button. Defendants argue that under the principles set forth in the cases cited above, a "fair and prudent person using ordinary care" would have been on inquiry notice of SmartDownload's license terms.

We are not persuaded that a reasonably prudent offeree in these circumstances would have known of the existence of license terms. Plaintiffs were responding to an offer that did not carry an immediately visible notice of the existence of license terms or require unambiguous manifestation of assent to those terms. Thus, plaintiffs' "apparent manifestation of . . . consent" was to terms "contained in a document whose contractual nature [was] not obvious." *Windsor Mills,* 25 Cal. App. 3d at 992, 101 Cal. Rptr. at 351. Moreover, the fact that, given the position of the scroll bar on their computer screens, plaintiffs may have been aware that an unexplored portion of the Netscape webpage remained below the download button does not mean that they reasonably should have concluded that this portion contained a notice of license terms. In their deposition testimony, plaintiffs variously stated that they used the scroll bar "[o]nly if there is something that I feel I need to see that is on — that is off the page," or that the elevated position of the scroll bar suggested the presence of "mere[ ] formalities, standard lower banner links" or "that the page is bigger than what I can see." Plaintiffs testified, and defendants did not refute, that plaintiffs were in fact unaware that defendants intended to attach license terms to the use of SmartDownload.

We conclude that in circumstances such as these, where consumers are urged to download free software at the immediate click of a button, a reference to the existence of license terms on a submerged screen is not sufficient to place consumers on inquiry or constructive notice of those terms. The SmartDownload webpage screen was "printed in such a manner that it tended to conceal the fact that it was an express acceptance of [Netscape's] rules and regulations." Internet users may have, as defendants put it, "as much time as they need[ ]" to scroll through multiple screens on a webpage, but there is no reason to assume that viewers will scroll down to subsequent screens simply because screens are there. When products are "free" and users are invited to download them in the absence of reasonably conspicuous notice that they are about to bind themselves to contract terms, the transactional circumstances cannot be fully analogized to those in the paper world of arm's-length bargaining. In the next two sections, we discuss case law and other legal authorities that have addressed the circumstances of computer sales, software licensing, and online transacting. Those authorities tend strongly to support our conclusion that plaintiffs did not manifest assent to SmartDownload's license terms.

B. Shrinkwrap Licensing and Related Practices

Defendants cite certain well-known cases involving shrinkwrap licensing and related commercial practices in support of their contention that plaintiffs became bound by the SmartDownload license terms by virtue of inquiry notice. For example, in *Hill v. Gateway 2000, Inc.,* 105 F.3d 1147 (7th Cir. 1997), the Seventh Circuit held that where a purchaser had ordered a computer over the telephone, received the order in a shipped box containing the computer along with printed contract terms, and did not return the computer within the thirty days required by the terms, the purchaser was bound by the contract. In *ProCD, Inc. v. Zeidenberg,* the same court held that where an individual purchased software in a box containing license terms which were displayed on the computer screen every time the user executed the software program, the user had sufficient opportunity to review the terms and to return the software, and so was contractually bound after retaining the product. *ProCD*, 86 F.3d at 1452; *cf. Moore v. Microsoft Corp.*, 293 A.D.2d 587, 587, 741 N.Y.S.2d 91, 92 (2d Dep't 2002) (software user was bound by license agreement where terms were prominently displayed on computer screen before software could be installed and where user was required to indicate assent by clicking "I agree"); *Brower v. Gateway 2000, Inc.*, 246 A.D.2d 246, 251, 676 N.Y.S.2d 569, 572 (1st Dep't 1998) (buyer assented to arbitration clause shipped inside box with computer and software by retaining items beyond date specified by license terms); *M.A. Mortenson Co. v. Timberline Software Corp.*, 93 Wash. App. 819, 970 P.2d 803, 809 (1999) (buyer manifested assent to software license terms by installing and using software), *aff'd*, 140 Wash.2d 568, 998 P.2d 305 (2000); *see also I.Lan Sys.*, 183 F.Supp.2d at 338 (business entity "explicitly accepted the clickwrap license agreement [contained in purchased software] when it clicked on the box stating 'I agree'").

These cases do not help defendants. To the extent that they hold that the purchaser of a computer or tangible software is contractually bound after failing to object to printed license terms provided with the product, *Hill* and *Brower* do not differ markedly from the cases involving traditional paper contracting discussed in the previous section. Insofar as the purchaser in *ProCD* was confronted with conspicuous, mandatory license terms every time he ran the software on his computer, that case actually undermines defendants' contention that downloading in the absence of conspicuous terms is an act that binds plaintiffs to those terms. In *Mortenson*, the full text of license terms was printed on each sealed diskette envelope inside the software box, printed again on the inside cover of the user manual, and notice of the terms appeared on the computer screen every time the purchaser executed the program. In sum, the foregoing cases are clearly distinguishable from the facts of the present action.

C. Online Transactions

Cases in which courts have found contracts arising from Internet use do not assist defendants, because in those circumstances there was much clearer notice than in the present case that a user's act would manifest assent to contract terms. *See, e.g., Hotmail Corp. v. Van$ Money Pie Inc.*, 47 U.S.P.Q.2d 1020, 1025 (N.D. Cal. 1998) (granting preliminary injunction based in part on breach of "Terms of Service" agreement, to which defendants had assented); *America Online, Inc. v. Booker*, 781 So.2d 423, 425 (Fla. Dist. Ct. App. 2001) (upholding forum selection clause in "freely negotiated agreement" contained in online terms of service); *Caspi v. Microsoft Network, L.L.C.*, 323 N.J.Super. 118, 732 A.2d 528, 530, 532-33 (N.J. Super. Ct. App. Div. 1999) (upholding forum selection clause where subscribers to online software were required to review license terms in scrollable window and to click "I Agree" or "I Don't Agree"); *Barnett v. Network Solutions, Inc.*, 38 S.W.3d 200, 203-04 (Tex. App. 2001) (upholding forum selection clause in online contract for registering Internet domain names that required users to scroll through terms before accepting or rejecting them); *cf. Pollstar v. Gigmania, Ltd.*, 170 F. Supp. 2d 974, 981-82 (E.D.Cal.2000) (expressing concern that notice of license terms had appeared in small, gray text on a gray background on a linked webpage, but concluding that it was too early in the case to order dismissal).[3]

After reviewing the California common law and other relevant legal authority, we conclude that under the circumstances here, plaintiffs' downloading of SmartDownload did not constitute acceptance of defendants' license terms. Reasonably conspicuous notice of the existence of contract terms and unambiguous manifestation of assent to those terms by consumers are essential if electronic bargaining is to have integrity and credibility. We hold that a reasonably prudent offeree in plaintiffs' position would not have known or learned, prior to acting on the invitation to download, of the reference to SmartDownload's license terms hidden below the "Download" button on the next screen. We affirm the district court's conclusion that the user plaintiffs, including Fagan, are not bound by the arbitration clause contained in those terms. . . .

For the foregoing reasons, we affirm the district court's denial of defendants' motion to compel arbitration and to stay court proceedings.

---

[3] [FN:17] In addition, the model code, UCITA, . . . generally recognizes the importance of conspicuous notice and unambiguous manifestation of assent in online sales and licensing of computer information. For example, § 112, which addresses manifestation of assent, provides that a user's opportunity to review online contract terms exists if a "record" (or electronic writing) of the contract terms is "made available in a manner that ought to call it to the attention of a reasonable person and permit review." UCITA, § 112(e)(1) (rev. ed. Aug. 23, 2001). Section 112 also provides, in pertinent part, that "[a] person manifests assent to a record or term if the person, acting with knowledge of, or after having an opportunity to review the record or term or a copy of it . . . intentionally engages in conduct or makes statements with reason to know that the other party or its electronic agent may infer from the conduct or statement that the person assents to the record or term." *Id.* § 112(a)(2). In the case of a "mass-market license," a party adopts the terms of the license only by manifesting assent "before or during the party's initial performance or use of or access to the information." *Id.* § 209(a). UCITA § 211 sets forth a number of guidelines for "internet-type" transactions involving the supply of information or software. For example, a licensor should make standard terms "available for review" prior to delivery or obligation to pay (1) by "displaying prominently and in close proximity to a description of the computer information, or to instructions or steps for acquiring it, the standard terms or a reference to an electronic location from which they can be readily obtained," or (2) by "disclosing the availability of the standard terms in a prominent place on the site from which the computer information is offered and promptly furnishing a copy of the standard terms on request before the transfer of the computer information." *Id.* § 211(1)(A-B). The commentary to § 211 adds: "The intent of the close proximity standard is that the terms or the reference to them would be called to the attention of an ordinary reasonable person." *Id.* § 211 cmt. 3. The commentary also approves of prominent hypertext links that draw attention to the existence of a standard agreement and allow users to view the terms of the license. *Id.*

We hasten to point out that UCITA . . . does not govern the parties' transactions in the present case, but we nevertheless find that UCITA's provisions offer insight into the evolving online "circumstances" that defendants argue placed plaintiffs on inquiry notice of the existence of the SmartDownload license terms. UCITA has been controversial as a result of the perceived breadth of some of its provisions. Nonetheless, UCITA's notice and assent provisions seem to be consistent with well-established principles governing contract formation and enforcement. *See* Robert A. Hillman & Jeffrey J. Rachlinski, *Standard-Form Contracting in the Electronic Age*, 77 N.Y.U. L.REV. 429, 491 (2002) ("[W]e contend that UCITA maintains the contextual, balanced approach to standard terms that can be found in the paper world.").

NOTE

Two years after *Specht*, the Second Circuit held that an online contract had been created even though the licensee was not asked to click on any icon indicating agreement to contract terms. Mere downloading of factual data from the site was sufficient to indicate assent. In *Register.com v. Verio, Inc.*, 356 F.3d 393 (2d Cir. 2004), the data consisted of factual information relating to Internet domain name registrants (the "Whois" database). The contract terms limited the user's right to use this factual data. A person making a Whois query through Register's site would receive a reply furnishing the requested Whois information, captioned by a legend stating that: "By submitting a Whois query, you agree that you will use this data only for lawful purposes and that under no circumstances will you use this data to . . . support the transmission of mass unsolicited, commercial advertising or solicitation via email." The court commented:

> Verio contends that in no instance did it receive legally enforceable notice of the conditions Register intended to impose. . . . If Verio had submitted only one query, or even if it had submitted only a few sporadic queries, that would give considerable force to its contention that it obtained the WHOIS data without being conscious that Register intended to impose conditions, and without being deemed to have accepted Register's conditions. But Verio was daily submitting numerous queries, each of which resulted in its receiving notice of the terms Register exacted. Furthermore, Verio admits that it knew perfectly well what terms Register demanded. Verio's argument fails. The situation might be compared to one in which plaintiff P maintains a roadside fruit stand displaying bins of apples. A visitor, defendant D, takes an apple and bites into it. As D turns to leave, D sees a sign, visible only as one turns to exit, which says "Apples — 50 cents apiece." D does not pay for the apple. . . . Thereafter, each day, several times a day, D revisits the stand, takes an apple, and eats it. D never leaves money. . . . In our view, however, D cannot continue on a daily basis to take apples for free, knowing full well that P is offering them only in exchange for 50 cents in compensation. . . . Verio's circumstance is effectively the same. Each day Verio repeatedly enters Register's computers and takes that day's new WHOIS data. Each day upon receiving the requested data, Verio receives Register's notice of the terms on which it makes the data available — that the data not be used for mass solicitation via direct mail, email, or telephone. Verio acknowledges that it continued drawing the data from Register's computers with full knowledge that Register offered access subject to these restrictions. Verio is no more free to take Register's data without being bound by the terms on which Register offers it, than D was free, in the example, once he became aware of the terms of P's offer. . . . We recognize that contract offers on the Internet often require the offeree to click on an "I agree" icon. And no doubt, in many circumstances, such a statement of agreement by the offeree is essential to the formation of a contract. But not in all circumstances. [It] is standard contract doctrine that when a benefit is offered subject to stated conditions, and

the offeree makes a decision to take the benefit with knowledge of the terms of the offer, the taking constitutes an acceptance of the terms, which accordingly become binding on the offeree.

Do you agree with this analysis? Is a similar analysis applicable to shrinkwrap licenses?

Chapter 3

STATUTE OF FRAUDS, WRITINGS AND ELECTRONIC LICENSING

I. FORMALITIES AND DISCLOSURES

Statutes of frauds are requirements in common law and statutory law that to be enforceable particular types of transactions must be in writing accompanied by appropriate signatures and, often, other formalities. As all first year law students learn, statutes of frauds are grounded in early English law and have been the subject of frequent scholarly and judicial criticism. *See, e.g., C.R. Klewin, Inc. v. Flagship Properties, Inc.*, 220 Conn. 569, 600 A.2d 772 (1991) (discussion of the objections to the statute of frauds); 2 CORBIN ON CONTRACTS § 275. Despite the criticism, there remain many settings where a statute or common law rule requires a signed writing (or equivalent) in order to enforce a contract. Even more important are the many situations in which modern law requires disclosures in writing or that particular terms must be signed.

From one perspective, a rule requiring written documentation serves salutary purposes in preventing fraud, giving effective notice, signaling the legal significance of a promise, and providing a record of the terms of the agreement. From another perspective, a writing or signature requirement enhances the risk of fraud (allowing a fraudulent person to make and then avoid a promise), brings unnecessary formality to the process, and imposes a formal requirement where ordinary jury or fact-finding processes would suffice to determine the actual terms of an agreement. Requirements of a written disclosure or of a record of a contract have also met objections based on their alleged incompatibility with modern, electronic means of doing business, a topic we discuss later.

Much might be said about writing or signature requirements, but we are concerned only with their relationship to licensing and related digital information transactions. A primary issue of interest lies in determining when a statute of frauds rule applies and what is the nature of that rule. As is common in licensing practice, the answer can lie in any of several bodies of law.

A. FEDERAL LAW

Let's start with federal law. Federal copyright, patent and trademark law all contain statute of frauds rules. They are as follows:

Copyright Act (17 U.S.C. § 204):

(a) A transfer of copyright ownership, other than by operation of law, is not valid unless an instrument of conveyance, or a note or memorandum of the transfer, is in writing and signed by the owner of the rights conveyed or such owner's duly authorized agent.

(b) A certificate of acknowledgement is not required for the validity of a transfer, but is prima facie evidence of the execution of the transfer if —

(1) in the case of a transfer executed in the United States, the certificate is issued by a person authorized to administer oaths within the United States; or

(2) in the case of a transfer executed in a foreign country, the certificate is issued by a diplomatic or consular officer of the United States, or by a person authorized to administer oaths whose authority is proved by a certificate of such an officer.

Patent Act (35 U.S.C. § 261):

Applications for patent, patents, or any interest therein, shall be assignable in law by an instrument in writing. . . . A certificate of acknowledgment [under conditions stated in the statute] . . . shall be prima facie evidence of the execution of an assignment, grant or conveyance of a patent or application for patent.

Trademark Act (15 U.S.C. § 1060):

(a)(1) A registered mark or a mark for which an application to register has been filed shall be assignable with the good will of the business. . . . Notwithstanding the preceding sentence, no application to register a mark under section 1(b) shall be assignable [until conditions stated in the statute are met], except for an assignment to a successor to the business of the applicant, or portion thereof, to which the mark pertains, if that business is ongoing and existing.

. . . .

(3) Assignments shall be by instruments in writing duly executed. Acknowledgment shall be prima facie evidence of the execution of an assignment, and when the prescribed information reporting the assignment is recorded in the United States Patent and Trademark Office, the record shall be prima facie evidence of execution.

These statutes do not apply to all transactions involving intellectual property. The Copyright Act rule, for example, applies only to a "transfer of copyright ownership." The Act defines this term in the following manner:

A "transfer of copyright ownership" is an assignment, mortgage, exclusive license, or any other conveyance, alienation, or hypothecation of a copyright or of any of the exclusive rights comprised in a copyright, whether or not it is limited in time or place of effect, but not including a nonexclusive license.

17 U.S.C. § 101. Why are "non-exclusive licenses" excluded?

The trademark and patent statutes refer to "assignments" of the applicable rights, but neither statute defines the term "assignment." As will be seen in a subsequent chapter, the meaning of this term has been extensively litigated in respect to exclusive licenses and standing to sue for patent infringement. Without having studied that case law, what would you describe as the difference between an assignment of a trademark and a license of a trademark?

PROBLEM 3.1

Which of the following are governed by a federal statute of frauds?

a. A "License" in which Picture Studio grants Bell Theaters the exclusive right to publicly display and perform the motion picture "Hairs Breath" in theaters in Chicago for six weeks, and promises to not grant a license to any other theater in Chicago during that period?

b. A transaction in which Word Perfect licenses Cooper Industries to use the Word Perfect software for ten years on the Cooper internal network.

c. A transaction in which Patent Owner grants Licensee an exclusive right to use the patented technology in ten states during the remaining life of the patent.

B. State Law

State law rules vary, but the structure can be seen by comparing so-called "common law" and the statute of frauds rules in codified contract law (UCC, UCITA). "Common law" statutes of frauds are actually in statutory form in most states. The statutes derive from old English law, but vary in detail and construction. The *Restatement (Second) of Contracts* § 110 summarizes the law as follows:

> (1) The following classes of contracts are subject to a statute, commonly called the Statute of Frauds, forbidding enforcement unless there is a written memorandum or an applicable exception:
>
>> (a) a contract of an executor or administrator to answer for a duty of his decedent (the executor-administrator provision);
>>
>> (b) a contract to answer for the duty of another (the suretyship provision);
>>
>> (c) a contract made upon consideration of marriage (the marriage provision);
>>
>> (d) a contract for the sale of an interest in land (the land contract provision);
>>
>> (e) a contract that is not to be performed within one year from the making thereof (the one-year provision).
>
> (2) The following classes of contracts, which were traditionally subject to the Statute of Frauds, are now governed by Statute of Frauds provisions of the Uniform Commercial Code:
>
>> (a) a contract for the sale of goods for the price of $500 or more (Uniform Commercial Code § 2-201);
>>
>> (b) a contract for the sale of securities . . .;
>>
>> (c) a contract for the sale of personal property not otherwise covered, to the extent of enforcement by way of action or defense beyond

$5,000 in amount or value of remedy (Uniform Commercial Code § 1-206). . . .

(5) In many states other classes of contracts are subject to a requirement of a writing.

The category of one-year contracts has the greatest significance for licensing. Item 2(c) in this list has been deleted in the pending revisions of UCC Article 1, which has been enacted in some, but not all states.

COMMONWEALTH FILM PROCESSING, INC. v. COURTAULDS UNITED STATES, INC.
717 F. Supp. 1157 (W.D. Va. 1989)

TURK, CHIEF JUDGE.

The material facts on the statute of frauds issue are undisputed. Representatives from Courtaulds United States, Inc. ("Courtaulds") and Commonwealth Film Processing, Inc. ("Commonwealth") met on March 25, 1988 at National Airport for the purpose of discussing possible settlement of the patent case. Martin Processing, plaintiff in the patent case, is the wholly-owned subsidiary of Courtaulds. No attorneys were present at the meeting. It is undisputed that certain basic understandings were reached on issues relevant to a possible license agreement between Courtaulds and Commonwealth which it was believed would settle the patent litigation. It is also undisputed that the oral license agreement which Commonwealth alleges was reached on March 25 was not reduced to writing and signed by Courtaulds. . . .

The rule in the Fourth Circuit is that federal law governs issues regarding the enforceability of settlements and releases in pending federal litigation. To determine the appropriate federal rule, the Court should review "the best-reasoned decisions in the general common law development of the subject." In this case, the alleged agreement is much more than a mere agreement to settle pending litigation. The agreement alleged by Commonwealth is instead a complete, fairly complicated license agreement. Having reviewed the federal case law in the subject area of license agreements in patent cases, the Court finds that the federal rule is, and indeed has been since at least 1867, that such agreements which cannot be fully performed within one year are subject to the statute of frauds. The Court also finds that this long-standing rule is not changed by the fact that the license agreement might be intended to settle pending federal patent litigation. Additionally, [this] this Court has looked to the *Restatement (Second) of Contracts* for guidance and has found further support for its opinion on this issue. The *Restatement*, at § 110 and § 130, provides that any contract which cannot be fully performed within one year is within the statute of frauds and cannot be enforced unless its essential terms are reduced to writing and signed by the party to be charged. Consequently, federal law would require that the alleged license agreement at issue in this case be subject to the statute of frauds if it is incapable of full performance within one year.

The issue of whether an alleged agreement is unenforceable under the statute of frauds is a question of law for the Court. It is clear from the allegations in Commonwealth's complaint that the license agreement they contend was reached cannot be fully performed within one year. In paragraph 11a of the complaint, Commonwealth alleges that the license agreement would be "continuous." Paragraph 11b states that the alleged agreement contained a provision for royalty payments which were to continue for five years. Consequently, the license agreement which is alleged by Commonwealth falls squarely within the statute of frauds and is unenforceable unless saved by a recognized exception to the statute.

Part Performance Exception

Commonwealth asserts that its part performance under the alleged license agreement removes this case from the statute of frauds. To prevail on this argument, Commonwealth must meet each of the following requirements: (1) the oral agreement must be certain and definite in its terms; (2) the acts undertaken must be attributable solely to the contract in question; and (3) the agreement must have been so far executed that a refusal of full execution would operate a fraud upon Commonwealth. Commonwealth has failed to meet any of the three requirements.

It is abundantly clear from the April 7, 1988 letter from counsel for Commonwealth to the Court that the alleged license agreement is uncertain and indefinite. In that letter, counsel for Commonwealth candidly stated that "considerable negotiation over the terms and conditions" was anticipated. The letter went on to state that renewed discovery would be necessary if the parties were unable to "execute mutually agreeable documents." The various drafts of the alleged agreement and considerable correspondence reveals that major terms and conditions considered important by each party, particularly whether the license would be exclusive, were and continue to be disputed. A letter from counsel for Commonwealth dated January 16, 1989 sets forth 41 separate areas of disagreement. The alleged agreement falls woefully short of the requirement that it be clear, definite and unequivocal in all its terms.

Commonwealth also fails to carry its burden of establishing the second requirement — that the acts allegedly undertaken be attributable solely to the contract in question. Most of the acts which Commonwealth alleges in support of its part performance argument are equally or more consistent with a desire to make their business profitable, to provide security for its allegedly unlawful use of the Courtaulds/Martin technology, and to maximize its use of the patent at issue in the case than it is with having entered into a license agreement with Courtaulds. Commonwealth's reliance on its unsupported statement that it has been placing royalties in escrow is also unavailing. Initially, the Court notes that placing royalties in escrow is not attributable to the alleged license agreement, for Commonwealth states that the agreement requires *payment* of royalties to Courtaulds. Secondly, the correspondence indicates that Commonwealth did not attempt to escrow any royalty payments in accordance with the time schedule in the alleged agreement. Finally, any placement of funds into escrow during litigation could clearly be attributable to a party's recognition of potential liability and its desire to maintain reserves for the satisfaction of any resulting judgment.

The Court also finds no basis for Commonwealth's argument that the alleged license agreement has been so far executed that a denial of specific performance would operate as a fraud upon it. Commonwealth has been unable to identify any aspects of the alleged agreement which have been executed, other than its continued use of the patent which is the basis for the underlying patent litigation. Commonwealth's assertion that Martin has ceased prosecuting the patent action and has acquiesced in Commonwealth's use of Martin's technology is unpersuasive both legally and factually. The court record reflects that Martin has consistently prosecuted its case. More importantly, there is no authority that interrupting active litigation to discuss settlement possibilities is an indication that the litigation has been settled and prosecution abandoned.

Having failed to establish any of the requirements of the part performance exception, Commonwealth is unable to avoid the statute of frauds on that basis. . . .

NOTE

The one-year rule is criticized in *C.R. Klewin, Inc. v. Flagship Properties, Inc.*, 220 Conn. 569, 600 A.2d 772 (1991). In that case, Justice Peters argues that the rule implements none of the purported policies that underlie the statute. She comments: "In any case, the one-year rule no longer seems to serve any purpose very well, and today its only remaining effect is arbitrarily to forestall adjudication of possible meritorious claims." Her opinion adopts the rule, widely followed, that a contract is not within the one-year rule unless it cannot be performed within one year under any circumstances. Under this rule, the fact that a given contract is not likely to be performed in one year in fact is not enough.

PROBLEM 3.2

Licensee claims that ABC Corp. granted it a non-exclusive license to use certain trade secret technology for a period of five years. The agreement involved a single, upfront payment of $10,000 and contained no restrictions on Licensee's use of the information, except that it would not disclose the information to others. Is proving this agreement barred by the statute of frauds?

PROBLEM 3.3

Marks Corporation claims that ABC granted it a non-exclusive license to use ABC's patented technology for the full remaining term of the patent for a payment of $100,000. There were no restrictions on Marks' use of the patent. Is this alleged contract within the statute of frauds?

GRAPPO v. ALITALIA LINEE AEREE ITALIANE, S.P.A.
56 F.3d 427 (2d Cir. 1995)

McLAUGHLIN, CIRCUIT JUDGE:

Gary Joseph Grappo filed suit in the United States District Court . . . against his employer, Alitalia Linee Aeree Italiane, S.p.A., an airline owned by the Republic of Italy. Grappo alleged that Alitalia breached its agreement to buy his copyrighted customer service training program. He sued for breach of contract and quantum meruit. . . . The district court granted summary judgment to Alitalia. [We reverse.]

BACKGROUND

[According to Grappo], Alitalia hired him in March, 1992 to work in its New York office implementing a customer service program that it intended to buy from Systema Corporation, a consulting firm specializing in employee training. The cost of the program was at least $250,000. Bianchi was to supervise Grappo in this endeavor.

Coincidentally, Grappo happened to be the author and copyright holder of his own customer service training program registered under the names "Guest*Star" and "People Come First" (hereinafter "Guest*Star"). Like Systema Corporation's program, Grappo's program [sought] to teach employees how to offer better service to customers. Grappo had begun licensing his program to various corporations in 1988.

Alitalia concluded that the Systema program was too expensive, and rejected it. Bianchi then approached Grappo about his own training program. Encouraged by what he heard, Bianchi arranged for Grappo to present his program in Rome to senior Alitalia officials. Based on this presentation, Alitalia decided to purchase from Grappo a non-exclusive license to use the Guest*Star program to train its employees. Although never reduced to a writing, a firm agreement between Bianchi, representing Alitalia, and Grappo took shape over the following months. . . . Although Alitalia distributed the training manuals to its managers, it never implemented Grappo's program. Instead, it used a training program written by Irene Dinola, Alitalia's Training Director, whose office is in Rome. At Bianchi's instruction, Grappo had provided Dinola with copies of his program while he was customizing it for Alitalia. Dinola's program was based, without credit, on Grappo's work. In fact, at Bianchi's direction, Grappo reviewed Dinola's work to verify that it embodied all his ideas. Grappo resigned from Alitalia in July, 1993.

Of course, Alitalia has a different version of these events. It maintains that there was never any agreement, "written or oral," for Alitalia to purchase Guest*Star. Instead, it contends that its negotiations with Grappo involved only "preliminary approval for the possible use" of Guest*Star. . . . In the end, according to Alitalia, it simply decided to reject Grappo's proposal in favor of the program developed independently by Dinola.

Grappo sued Alitalia [for] breach of its agreement "to purchase a non-exclusive license to use Guest*Star." [The] district court granted Alitalia's motion for summary judgment, holding that, because the alleged agreement was not in writing, Grappo's contract claims were barred by the Statute of Frauds contained in § 1-206 of the New York Uniform Commercial Code. . . .

I. *Contract claims*

[Section 1-206(1)] of the New York Uniform Commercial Code provides that

> a contract for the sale of personal property is not enforceable by way of action or defense beyond five thousand dollars in amount or value of remedy unless there is some writing which indicates that a contract for sale has been made between the parties at a defined or stated price, reasonably identifies the subject matter, and is signed by the party against whom enforcement is sought or by his authorized agent.

The accompanying Official Comment indicates that § 1-206 applies to the sale of "general intangibles" as defined in § 9-106. The term "general intangibles" includes "literary rights, copyrights, trademarks, [and] patents." Thus, § 1-206 governs the contract between Grappo and Alitalia.

Because there was no writing between Grappo and Alitalia, Grappo's contract claims are unenforceable under § 1-206 "beyond five thousand dollars." The question remains, however, whether Grappo's claims are enforceable *up to* five thousand dollars, or whether § 1-206 renders an oral contract over $5,000 totally unenforceable.

The district court apparently took the latter view, since it dismissed both of Grappo's contract claims in their entirety. We believe that the plain words of § 1-206 — "a contract for the sale of personal property is not enforceable . . . beyond five thousand dollars . . . unless there is some writing" — permit the plaintiff to recover up to $5,000 on an oral contract. If the thrust of the statute was to bar recovery *in toto,* then the phrase, "beyond five thousand dollars" should immediately follow the words "a contract for the sale of personal property." As drafted, the statute permits a plaintiff to recover up to $5,000 on an oral contract that should have been in writing.

The only New York authority we have been able to locate agrees. [Of course,] under elementary res judicata principles, plaintiff's contract claims would merge in his $5,000 judgment, and he would be barred from recovering the balance. Grappo struggles to avoid this result by recasting his agreement with Alitalia as something other than a contract for the sale of personal property. We turn to these arguments, assuming, without deciding, that the district court retains jurisdiction over Grappo's contract claims, notwithstanding that we have limited them to $5,000.

Relying on *Schenectady Steel Co. v. Bruno Trimpoli General Construction Co.,* 43 A.D.2d 234, 350 N.Y.S.2d 920 (3d Dept.), *aff'd,* 34 N.Y.2d 939, 316 N. E.2d 875, 359 N.Y.S.2d 560 (1974), Grappo first argues that the contract was principally one for services (tailoring Guest*Star), not for the sale of personal property, and thus not subject to the Uniform Commercial Code at all. In *Schenectady Steel,* the court held that an agreement by a contractor to "furnish and erect the structural steel" for a bridge was a contract for services not subject to the Code. The court reached that conclusion because the buyer "was not contracting simply for the steel beams but in essence for their erection and installation with the transfer of the title to the steel a mere incident of the overall transaction, a mere accessory to the work and labor to be performed."

Here, "title" to Guest*Star was hardly "a mere incident" of Grappo's contract with Alitalia; it was its heart and soul. Without a license to use Guest*Star, the contract would have been useless to Alitalia. While Grappo may have tailored the program to Alitalia's needs, those efforts were plainly secondary to the contract. As Grappo himself states in his complaint, the contract was for a non-exclusive license to use Guest*Star. Indeed, the $50,000 invoice Grappo sent to Alitalia specified that Alitalia had been granted a "non-exclusive, unlimited license" for "Customers Come First," the customized version of Guest*Star.

Alternatively, Grappo argues that the contract was not for the sale of personal property (governed by §1-206) but for the sale of "goods" (training manuals and materials) under §2-201, and the invoice he sent Alitalia satisfies the requirement of a writing between merchants. *See* §2-201(2). We reject this argument for the same reason that we reject the proposition that the alleged contract was one for services: the sale of a non-exclusive license for copyrighted material was the core of the contract. The manuals would have been useless to Alitalia absent a legal right to use them. . . .

Finally, Grappo argues that Alitalia should be estopped from relying on the Statute of Frauds. Estoppel has been recognized in a "limited class of cases" where application of the Statute of Frauds would be unconscionable. *Philo Smith & Co. v. USLIFE Corp.,* 554 F.2d 34, 36 (2d Cir. 1977) (applying New York law). "The strongly held public policy reflected in New York's Statute of Frauds would be severely undermined," however, "if a party could be estopped from asserting it every time a court found that some unfairness would otherwise result." *Id.* On the facts alleged by Grappo, we see no indication that Alitalia caused him "to irremediably alter his situation" such that "the interposition of the statute against performance [would constitute] a fraud." *Woolley v. Stewart,* 118 N.E. 847, 848, 222 N.Y. 347, 350-51 (1918).

II. *Quantum meruit*

Grappo's third claim seeks $200,000 in quantum meruit "as the reasonable value of his work and services." The district court dismissed the claim because "under New York law the person who is disappointed for lack of a memorandum can't come in the back door and claim more than the contract price as quantum meruit." We disagree.

It is true, under New York law, that a plaintiff may not escape the Statute of Frauds by simply affixing the label "quantum meruit" to the very contract claim that is barred. A cause of action does exist, however, where the plaintiff "merely seeks to recover for the value of the work performed," as distinct from the contract price. This is because the cause of action does not depend upon an unenforceable promise; rather, it "is in disaffirmance of the void contract." *Id.* The nomenclature is not dispositive. Because Grappo's third cause of action seeks compensation for "the reasonable value of his work and services" — and not the benefit of his bargain — the claim is distinct from his claims under the contract, and should not have been dismissed.

Alitalia appears to argue that a plaintiff who is barred by the Statute of Frauds from enforcing an alleged contract may never seek recovery in quantum meruit. Alitalia relies on *Martin H. Bauman Associates, Inc. v. H & M International Transport, Inc.,* 171 A.D.2d 479, 567 N.Y.S.2d 404 (1st Dep't 1991). Its reliance is misplaced. In *Bauman,* the court rejected the plaintiff's quantum meruit claim because the plaintiff failed to specify the expenditures it made in reliance upon the defendant's representations, as well as the reasonable value of the services performed. Instead, the plaintiff "merely assert[ed] in a conclusory, non-specific manner" that it had performed services for the defendant, and demanded the *contract price.* Understandably, the court found the plaintiff's quantum meruit claim "indistinguishable" from its breach of contract claim. It did not hold, however, that recovery in quantum meruit is never available to a plaintiff who is barred by the Statute of Frauds from enforcing an alleged contract.

Alitalia also argues that Grappo, as an employee of Alitalia, has already been compensated for the time he spent revising Guest*Star, since he performed most of the project during his work day. At least one New York court has rejected that argument, holding that an employee may seek recovery against his employer, notwithstanding that the employee's "invention" took shape on company time. The purpose of permitting recovery is to prevent unjust enrichment. . . .

Conclusion

[We] reverse the district court's dismissal of Grappo's contract claims under New York Uniform Commercial Code § 1-206. . . .

NOTES

1. The court in *Grappo* treated the transaction as if it were a sale. Was that conclusion sound? What was being sold? In most cases, a sale entails a transfer of title to the property. Was title to be transferred in any property in *Grappo?*

2. The David Nimmer treatise on copyright law criticized *Grappo* because "contract rules established under state law can not invalidate any aspect of federal copyright law. Given that the statute of frauds at issue in *Grappo* subjected non-exclusive licenses — which may be oral under federal law regardless of value — to a selective writing requirement under state law, would appear suspect." 3 MELVILLE NIMMER & DAVID NIMMER, NIMMER ON COPYRIGHT, §10.03[A][8] (1999). In contrast, Professor Goldstein commented: "It is not clear whether Congress's decision to omit non-exclusive licenses from § 204(a)'s coverage preempts state statute of frauds provisions requiring that non-exclusive licenses be in writing." 1 GOLDSTEIN, COPYRIGHT § 4.5.1.b (2d ed. 1999).

3. Promulgated revisions of Article 1 delete the statute of frauds discussed in *Grappo* and thus limit the scope of UCC statute of frauds to transactions that are within the scope of other articles of the UCC that have their own statute of frauds.

4. UCC Article 2 has been held to apply to some licenses. UCC § 2-201 as currently enacted, applies to sales of goods for over $500, requiring a signed writing that indicates the existence of the contract. The contract is not enforceable beyond the quantity of goods mentioned in the writing. The statute, however, provides for partial performance as an alternative to a signed writing. Are there any difficulties in applying this rule to a license? For example, what is the relevance of the reference to "quantity" of goods? Proposed 2003 amendments would increase the price amount to $5,000 and deal with electronic records, but make no other relevant changes. The 2003 amendments remain unenacted in any state as of the completion of the writing of this book.

PROBLEM 3.4

You are asked to draft a statute of frauds applicable to non-exclusive licenses of patents and copyrights. Prepare a draft and describe the reasoning behind your draft.

II. ELECTRONIC RECORDS AND SIGNATURES

Digital technology presents unique issues of electronic contracting — creating and recording contracts via digital or similar media. One topic concerns whether electronic records can satisfy writing and signature requirements in law. This has lead to federal legislation, a uniform state law enacted in over forty states, and to a variety of other state and federal actions. Taken together, these create a complex framework of rules that have direct bearing on licensing and other transactions in digital industries.

As we look at several of the themes that have arisen, keep in mind the fundamental question: why do some laws require writings or signatures and how do those reasons translate into digital venues? Is there, for example, a difference between a rule requiring that a contract be in writing (e.g., a statute of frauds) and a rule that certain information must be disclosed in writing to a consumer? Is a digital record more or less susceptible to fraudulent changes than a written record? Should the difference matter? *See generally* RAYMOND T. NIMMER & HOLLY K. TOWLE, THE LAW OF ELECTRONIC COMMERCIAL TRANSACTIONS, ch. 4 (2007 A.S. Pratt).

A. Writings and Signatures: The Basic Issue

Prior to the mid to late 1990s, federal law and the law of all states set out numerous circumstances in which a contract, a disclosure, a contract term, or other legally significant event was required to be in "writing" and, in many cases, accompanied by a "signature." The statutes or regulations number in the thousands in individual states. The number in federal law is unknown, but very large.

As digital commerce began to emerge on the Internet, a concern was whether the two terms (writing, signature) could be transitioned from their paper origins into digital contexts. The fear that electronic records might not satisfy writing and signature requirements was grounded in the risk that courts or regulators might adopt a narrow reading of the writing or signature requirement and conclude that a digital file could not be either.

PARMA TILE MOSAIC & MARBLE v. SHORT
663 N.E.2d 633 (N.Y. 1996)

SMITH, JUDGE.

The issue presented on this appeal is whether the automatic imprinting, by a fax machine, of the sender's name at the top of each page transmitted, satisfies the requirement that a writing be subscribed under New York State's general Statute of Frauds (General Obligations Law § 5-701). We reverse the order of the Appellate Division because we conclude that a subscription requires an act to authenticate the writing. . . . Defendant did not so subscribe to the writing in this case.

In September 1989, Sime Construction Co. (Sime), a subcontractor, sought to purchase from plaintiff a large quantity of ceramic tile for use in a construction project. When plaintiff expressed reluctance to enter into such a large contract without a guaranty, Sime suggested that plaintiff approach MRLS Construction Corporation (MRLS), the general contractor on the project, for a guaranty of payment. Plaintiff contacted MRLS and after several discussions, MRLS faxed a document to plaintiff which plaintiff asserts is a guaranty. MRLS contends that it merely transmitted an unsubscribed proposal for a guaranty by fax.

Plaintiff's copy of the document bore a heading at the top of each page which indicated the name "MRLS Construction," a telephone number, the date and time, an unidentified number and a page number. It is undisputed that sometime before sending the document at issue, MRLS had programmed its fax machine to automatically imprint this information on every transmitted page. By this method, the heading would appear only on the recipient's faxed copy, not on the originating document. The two-page fax document in issue was not preceded by a cover letter or any other identifying document.

After the facsimile transmission, plaintiff began furnishing Sime with quantities of ceramic tile. When Fred Short, the principal of Sime, died in April 1990, plaintiff sought payment for Sime's outstanding invoices from MRLS. MRLS refused to make payment on the ground that the document was not an enforceable guaranty.

Plaintiff commenced this action against MRLS and Sime (sued as the estate of Fred Short herein) to recover the outstanding balances for the ceramic tiles furnished to Sime. After issue was joined, plaintiff and MRLS moved for summary judgment, and the trial court [granted] plaintiff's motion on the third cause of action, which alleged a guaranty of payment, severed the third cause of action from the rest of plaintiff's complaint, and directed entry of judgment against MRLS.

In granting summary judgment to plaintiff, the trial court rejected MRLS' contention that the fax document had not been subscribed as required by the Statute of Frauds. The court held that the heading automatically imprinted by the fax machine on plaintiff's copy of the document satisfied the subscription requirement because an intent to be bound had been demonstrated. MRLS appealed the judgment, and the Appellate Division affirmed the trial court. We granted leave to appeal.

> "Every agreement, promise or undertaking is void, unless it or some note or memorandum thereof be in writing, and subscribed by the party to be charged therewith, or by his lawful agent if such agreement, promise or undertaking . . . [i]s a special promise to answer for the debt, default or miscarriage of another person" . . . .

Plaintiff has failed to demonstrate that MRLS affixed its "signature" to the document sent by facsimile machine sufficient to fulfill the subscription requirement. As former Chief Judge Cardozo has observed, a signature for Statute of Frauds purposes may be "a name, written or printed, [but] is not to be reckoned as a signature unless inserted or adopted with an intent, actual or apparent, to authenticate a writing." Plaintiff contends that we may infer satisfaction of this requirement because the fax machine had been programmed by MRLS to identify each page of the document with "MRLS Construction."

The act of identifying and sending a document to a particular destination does not, by itself, constitute a signing authenticating the contents of the document for Statute of Frauds purposes, and we reject plaintiff's argument that such an inference is warranted here. It is undisputed that MRLS' fax machine, after being programmed to do so, automatically imprinted "MRLS Construction" on every page transmitted, without regard to the applicability of the Statute of Frauds to a particular document. We also reject plaintiff's contention that the intentional act of programming a fax machine, by itself, sufficiently demonstrates to the recipient the sender's apparent intention to authenticate every document subsequently faxed. The intent to authenticate the particular writing at issue must be demonstrated.

The argument that the Statute of Frauds was not meant to permit parties to evade an obligation otherwise incurred begs the question of whether this writing satisfied the statutory requirement. "The purpose of Statutes of Frauds is to avoid fraud by preventing the enforcement of contracts that were never in fact made." To this end, General Obligations Law § 5-701(a) contains two threshold requirements for proving the existence of a binding agreement, promise or undertaking: a writing, and a subscription of the writing by the party to be charged therewith. Since the Legislature selected these objective elements to determine, in the first instance, the existence of an enforceable agreement, promise or undertaking, the absence of a writing or a subscription cannot be remedied by arguing that obligations were nevertheless incurred.

Accordingly, the order of the Appellate Division should be reversed, with costs. . . .

NOTES

1. In *Cloud Corp. v. Hasbro, Inc.*, 314 F.3d 289 (7th Cir. 2002), the issue was whether e-mails sent by a representative of Hasbro satisfied the Article 2 statute of frauds as to the enforceability of an alleged modification of a ongoing contract. Judge Posner concluded that an e-mail was sufficient, commenting:

> The quantity term in a contract for the sale of goods for more than $500 must be memorialized in a writing signed by the party sought to be held to that term, UCC § 2-201(1), and so, therefore, must a modification of that term. UCC § 2-209(3). . . . But what shall we make of the fact that Kathy Esposito's e-mails contained no signature? . . . Neither the common law nor the UCC requires a *handwritten* signature, even though such a signature is better evidence of identity than a typed one. It is not customary, though it is possible, to include an electronic copy of a handwritten signature in an e-mail, and therefore its absence does not create a suspicion of forgery or other fraud — and anyway an electronic copy of a signature could *be* a forgery.

> The purpose of the statute of frauds is to prevent a contracting party from creating a triable issue concerning the terms of the contract — or for that matter concerning whether a contract even exists — on the basis of his say-so alone. That purpose does not require a handwritten signature, especially in a case such as this in which there is other evidence, and not merely say-so evidence, of the existence of the contract (more precisely, the contract modification) besides the writings. The fact that Cloud produced the additional quantity is pretty powerful evidence of a contract, as it would have been taking a terrible risk in doing so had it thought it would have no right to be paid if Hasbro refused to accept delivery but would instead be stuck with a huge quantity of a product that had no salvage value. . . .

> The background to the modification — the fact that the parties had dealt informally with each other (as shown by their disregard of the form contracts), and above all that Hasbro plainly wanted more product and wanted it fast — is further evidence that had Cloud asked for a written purchase order in June 1996 for the additional quantity, Hasbro would have given it, especially since Cloud was offering a lower price. . . .

> So Hasbro's statute of frauds defense fails on a number of independent grounds.

2. Can the two decisions be reconciled? What was lacking in *Parma*? Was that factor present in *Cloud*? UCC § 1-201, which applied background definitions applicable to *Cloud*, contained the following definitions:

> "Signed" includes any symbol executed or adopted by a party with present intention to authenticate a writing.

> "Written" or "writing" includes printing, typewriting or any other intentional reduction to tangible form.

What part of these definitions would prevent a court from holding that e-mails are signed writings regardless of the surrounding evidence? Would these definitions change the result in *Parma*?

3. A number of decisions have held that a name typed onto an e-mail satisfies a signature requirement. Do you agree?

B. Modern Substantive Reforms

Since the mid-1990s, many new laws that require signatures or "writings" directly address the adequacy of electronics to satisfy these requirements. UCITA and Revised Article 9, for example, replace the word "writing" with "record." Thus, the UCITA statute of frauds requires a "record" of the contract:

> "Record" means information that is inscribed on a tangible medium or that is stored in an electronic or other medium and is retrievable in perceivable form.

UCITA § 102(a)(55) (2000 Official Text). This includes electronic records as well as paper records.

UCITA and Article 9 also replace the term "signature" or "signed," substituting the word "authenticate." The Article 9 definition is as follows:

> "Authenticate" means:
>
> (A) to sign; or
>
> (B) to execute or otherwise adopt a symbol, or encrypt or similarly process a record in whole or in part, with the present intent of the authenticating person to identify the person and adopt or accept a record.

U.C.C. § 9-102(a)(7) (2000 Official Text). This definition, which is also in UCITA in slightly different form, incorporates symbols adopted in an electronic medium, but also recognizes that encrypting or "processing" a record with appropriate intent satisfies the statutory standard.

Amendments proposed to Article 2 in 2003 also deal with electronic records and signatures. These amendments, which are controversial for other reasons and have not been enacted in any state as of this publication, adopt the convention of replacing "writing" with "record," but do not directly adopt the concept of "authenticate." Instead, the amendments would alter the definition of "sign" to mean:

> (p) "Sign" means, with present intent to authenticate or adopt a record,
>
> (i) to execute or adopt a tangible symbol; or
>
> (ii) to attach to or logically associate with the record an electronic sound, symbol, or process.

UCC § 2-103(1)(p) (2003 Official Text).

C. "Procedural" Reforms: E-Sign and UETA

While the direct tailoring of individual statutes or regulations is the preferable approach, the sheer number of statutes and regulations that would need to be separately considered and individually amended led many to believe that general legislation was more efficient to set a legal framework for electronic commerce. Two statutes of national importance resulted. The first is the federal "Electronic Signatures in Global and National Commerce Act," better known as "E-Sign," 15 U.S.C. § 7001. The core provision of E-Sign reads:

(a) IN GENERAL. Notwithstanding any statute, regulation, or other rule of law (other than this title and title II), with respect to any transaction in or affecting interstate or foreign commerce:

(1) a signature, contract, or other record relating to such transaction may not be denied legal effect, validity, or enforceability solely because it is in electronic form; and

(2) a contract relating to such transaction may not be denied legal effect, validity, or enforceability solely because an electronic signature or electronic record was used in its formation.

(b) PRESERVATION OF RIGHTS AND OBLIGATIONS. — This title does not —

(1) limit, alter, or otherwise affect any requirement imposed by a statute, regulation, or rule of law relating to the rights and obligations of persons . . . other than a requirement that contracts or other records be written, signed, or in nonelectronic form; or

(2) require any person to agree to use or accept electronic records or electronic signatures, other than a governmental agency with respect to a record other than a contract to which it is a party.

This establishes a rule of equivalence. The rule applies to any law (federal or state) affecting interstate or foreign commerce. With an important exception noted below, E-Sign is preemptive of state law as to the rules in subsection (a).

A similar rule was created under the Uniform Electronic Transactions Act (UETA), which has been adopted as *state law* in over forty states, albeit not always in uniform terms. UETA, however, entails a predicate for establishing a rule of equivalence. The relevant sections read as follows:

Section 5:

. . . .

(b) This [Act] applies only to transactions between parties each of which has agreed to conduct transactions by electronic means. Whether the parties agree to conduct a transaction by electronic means is determined from the context and surrounding circumstances, including the parties' conduct.

(c) A party that agrees to conduct a transaction by electronic means may refuse to conduct other transactions by electronic means. The right granted by this subsection may not be waived by agreement.

Section 7:

(a) A record or signature may not be denied legal effect or enforceability solely because it is in electronic form.

(b) A contract may not be denied legal effect or enforceability solely because an electronic record was used in its formation.

(c) If a law requires a record to be in writing, an electronic record satisfies the law.

(d) If a law requires a signature, an electronic signature satisfies the law.

UETA §§ 5, 7 (1999 Official Text).

The equivalence language in UETA applies only if both parties "agree" to conduct transactions by electronic means. In considering this pre-condition, it is relevant to distinguish between cases in which the applicable rule is a statute of frauds and cases in which the applicable rule requires one party to make a written disclosure to the other party. Are the reasons for requiring prior mutual agreement different in the two cases?

UETA applies to a "transaction" only if each party "has agreed to conduct transactions by electronic means." The meaning of "agreement" here has not yet been explored by the cases. UETA proposes a definition of "agreement" found in the UCC: "'Agreement' means the bargain of the parties in fact, as found in their language or inferred from other circumstances and from rules, regulations, and procedures given the effect of agreements under laws otherwise applicable to a particular transaction." This requires a bargain between the parties, but that is not what the Official Comments to UETA suggest. Official Comments 4 and 5 to the UETA scope section state:

> 4. . . . . Examples of circumstances from which it may be found that parties have reached an agreement to conduct transactions electronically include the following: . . .
>
> B. Joe gives out his business card with his business e-mail address. It may be reasonable, under the circumstances, for a recipient of the card to infer that Joe has agreed to communicate electronically for business purposes. However, in the absence of additional facts, it would not necessarily be reasonable to infer Joe's agreement to communicate electronically for purposes outside the scope of the business indicated by use of the business card.
>
> C. Sally may have several e-mail addresses — home, main office, office of a non-profit organization on whose board Sally sits. In each case, it may be reasonable to infer that Sally is willing to communicate electronically with respect to business related to the business/ purpose associated with the respective e-mail addresses. However,

depending on the circumstances, it may not be reasonable to communicate with Sally for purposes other than those related to the purpose for which she maintained a particular e-mail account.

. . . The examples noted above are intended to focus the inquiry on the party's agreement to conduct a transaction electronically. Similarly, if two people are at a meeting and one tells the other to send an e-mail to confirm a transaction — the requisite agreement under subsection (b) would exist. In each case, the use of a business card, statement at a meeting, or other evidence of willingness to conduct a transaction electronically must be viewed in light of all the surrounding circumstances with a view toward broad validation of electronic transactions.

5. Just as circumstances may indicate the existence of agreement, express or implied from surrounding circumstances, circumstances may also demonstrate the absence of true agreement. For example:

A. If Automaker, Inc. were to issue a recall of automobiles via its Internet website, it would not be able to rely on this Act to validate that notice in the case of a person who never logged on to the website, or indeed, had no ability to do so, notwithstanding a clause in a paper purchase contract by which the buyer agreed to receive such notices in such a manner.

B. Buyer executes a standard form contract in which an agreement to receive all notices electronically is set forth on page 3 in the midst of other fine print. Buyer has never communicated with Seller electronically, and has not provided any other information in the contract to suggest a willingness to deal electronically. Not only is it unlikely that any but the most formalistic of agreements may be found, but nothing in this Act prevents courts from policing such form contracts under common law doctrines relating to contract formation, unconscionability and the like.

UETA § 5, cmts 4, 5 (1999 Official Text).

NOTE

What is the relationship between E-Sign, UETA and other law? Clearly, E-Sign, rather than UETA, applies to federal law and regulations. As to state laws, the situation is more complex. Beyond questions about the scope of E-Sign and the meaning of "agreement" under UETA, E-Sign contains a unique provision that, despite the generally preemptive scope of it primary rules, allows some state laws to retake (or "back in" to) state law control. This rule, designed to protect federalism concerns and entitled "exemption to preemption," states:

(a) IN GENERAL. — A State statute, regulation, or other rule of law may modify, limit, or supersede the provisions of section 101 with respect to State law only if such statute, regulation, or rule of law —

(1) constitutes an enactment or adoption of the Uniform Electronic Transactions Act as approved and recommended for enactment in all the States by the National Conference of Commissioners on Uniform State Laws in 1999, except that any exception to the scope of such Act enacted by a State . . . shall be preempted to the extent such exception is inconsistent with this title . . . or would not be permitted under paragraph (2)(A)(ii) of this subsection; or

(2)(A) specifies the alternative procedures or requirements for the use or acceptance (or both) of electronic records or electronic signatures to establish the legal effect, validity, or enforceability of contracts or other records, if —

> (i) such alternative procedures or requirements are consistent with this title and title II; and

> (ii) such alternative procedures or requirements do not require, or accord greater legal status or effect to, the implementation or application of a specific technology or technical specification . . .; and

(B) if enacted or adopted after the date of the enactment of this Act, makes specific reference to this Act.

For transactions within the scope of E-Sign, the applicability of the state UETA is determined by whether the statute conforms to UETA as approved in 1999 by the National Conference. Survival of state law enactments that deviate from that model is not clear.

PROBLEM 3.5

ABC Corporation opens an online service under which customers purchase access to ABC's database of sports statistics. The system requires the customer to agree to a contract that obligates it to pay a monthly charge for the duration of the contract. The system offers contract terms of one month, one year, two years, and five years, with the price being discounted based on the length of the contract, ranging to a minimum of $100 per month. The customer elects the contract term by clicking in a box on the screen. Payment can be either by direct credit card billing or by monthly paper billing. If the customer elects the latter, it must enter its name and street as well as e-mail address. At the end, the customer clicks on an "I Agree" button to initiate the service.

Assume that Party A agreed to a six-month service and Party B selected a five-year service. Both later refuse to pay. When ABC sues, they defend based on the statute of frauds, claiming that there is no signed writing. What result?

PROBLEM 3.6

Through several telephone calls, Sam and Jane negotiate a purchase price for Jane's purchase of Sam's inventory of ancient coins. At the end of this negotiation, Jane sends Sam an email stating: "I agree to purchase your inventory at the price you offered in our discussions ($500,000), cash to be paid within 90 days from today." Before the 90 days expire, however, Jane calls Sam and says that she has had second thoughts and will not complete the purchase. Sam sues and Jane defends based on the statute of frauds. What result if the transaction is governed by UETA? What result if the transaction is governed by E-Sign? Should either result change if Jane remains willing to proceed on the transaction, but Sam withdraws?

PROBLEM 3.7

Jane manages the "character licensing" division of Des Corporation, a company that owns copyright and other rights in a wide variety of popular images and characters. Jane's division handles licensing of those characters to third parties. Her employees have frequent e-mail and telephone contact with agents, companies, and individuals throughout the country about licensing arrangements. Under applicable law, Jane has not been concerned about the risk of a bad, oral license, because the statute of frauds limits the length and terms of what such oral licenses may entail. She has established a policy that precludes the sending of letters of agreement to third parties unless the terms are reviewed by a Des supervisor. Jane asks your advice about what she should do about e-mails in light of E-Sign and adoption of UETA in her state. What do you advise?

D. Disclosure and Consumer Rules

Assume that a state law requires disclosure to a prospective franchisee in writing of the terms and economic risk of entering into a franchise agreement with a franchisor prior to signing the franchise agreement. Can this disclosure be made in an e-mail, or otherwise by electronic means? Should the result be different for a rule that requires disclosure to a consumer of the rate of interest in a particular, written form, prior to entering a contract?

The answers to these questions lie in complex statutory provisions. In cases covered by E-Sign, there are no special provisions for the franchisee, but there is a rule applicable to consumers. 15 U.S.C. § 7001(c) provides for a several step process to be implemented before the electronic disclosure is made:

(1) CONSENT TO ELECTRONIC RECORDS. — Notwithstanding subsection (a), if a statute, regulation, or other rule of law requires that information relating to a transaction or transactions in or affecting interstate or foreign commerce be provided or made available to a consumer in writing, the use of an electronic record to provide or make available (whichever is required) such information satisfies the requirement that such information be in writing if —

(A) the consumer has affirmatively consented to such use and has not withdrawn such consent;

(B) the consumer, prior to consenting, is provided with a clear and conspicuous statement —

(i) informing the consumer of (I) any right or option of the consumer to have the record provided or made available on paper or in nonelectronic form, and (II) the right of the consumer to withdraw the consent to have the record provided or made available in an electronic form and of any conditions, consequences (which may include termination of the parties' relationship), or fees in the event of such withdrawal;

(ii) informing the consumer of whether the consent applies (I) only to the particular transaction which gave rise to the obligation to provide the record, or (II) to identified categories of records that may be provided or made available during the course of the parties' relationship;

(iii) describing the procedures the consumer must use to withdraw consent as provided in clause (i) and to update information needed to contact the consumer electronically; and

(iv)informing the consumer (I) how, after the consent, the consumer may, upon request, obtain a paper copy of an electronic record, and (II) whether any fee will be charged for such copy;

(C) the consumer —

(i) prior to consenting, is provided with a statement of the hardware and software requirements for access to and retention of the electronic records; and

(ii) consents electronically, or confirms his or her consent electronically, in a manner that reasonably demonstrates that the consumer can access information in the electronic form that will be used to provide the information that is the subject of the consent; and

(D) after the consent of a consumer in accordance with subparagraph (A), if a change in the hardware or software requirements needed to access or retain electronic records creates a material risk that the consumer will not be able to access or retain a subsequent electronic record that was the subject of the consent, the person providing the electronic record —

(i) provides the consumer with a statement of (I) the revised hardware and software requirements for access to and retention of the electronic records, and (II) the right to withdraw consent without the imposition of any fees for such withdrawal and without the imposition of any condition or consequence that was not disclosed under subparagraph (B)(i); and

(ii) again complies with subparagraph (C).

As this indicates, E-Sign incorporates a policy decision that consumer disclosure rules should trigger further protection of the consumer before electronic disclosures can meet a disclosure requirement. Beyond creating problems in working through the language of Section 7001(c)(1), this raises the underlying question of why such protection was thought necessary. Some argue that it protects against the risk that a consumer unable to actually receive electronic records might nevertheless be faced with a claim that an e-mail disclosure (to an unrelated e-mail address?) satisfied the statutory disclosure rule. Is that claim likely to have passed muster with a court?

In any event, subsection (c) is in place for federal disclosure rules and some state laws, subject in the federal context to the ability of regulators to make adjustments consistent with the statute. But what is the result of non-compliance? E-Sign states: "The legal effectiveness, validity, or enforceability of any contract executed by a consumer shall not be denied solely because of the failure to obtain electronic consent or confirmation of consent by that consumer in accordance with paragraph (1)(C)(ii)." That relates to the contract. What about the disclosure?

UETA handles the issues differently. It does not single out consumers for special protection, but does incorporate a number of rules that reflect consumer law policy choices. UETA, of course, requires a prior agreement of the parties to use electronics. Thus, while elaborate procedural limitations are not present, some prior indication of agreement to use electronics must be present for any electronic disclosure.

UETA Section 8 provides:

(a) If parties have agreed to conduct a transaction by electronic means and a law requires a person to provide, send, or deliver information in writing to another person, the requirement is satisfied if the information is provided, sent, or delivered, as the case may be, in an electronic record capable of retention by the recipient at the time of receipt. An electronic record is not capable of retention by the recipient if the sender or its information processing system inhibits the ability of the recipient to print or store the electronic record.

(b) If a law other than this [Act] requires a record (i) to be posted or displayed in a certain manner, (ii) to be sent, communicated, or transmitted by a specified method, or (iii) to contain information that is formatted in a certain manner, the following rules apply:

(1) The record must be posted or displayed in the manner specified in the other law.

(2) Except as otherwise provided in subsection (d)(2), the record must be sent, communicated, or transmitted by the method specified in the other law.

(3) The record must contain the information formatted in the manner specified in the other law.

(c) If a sender inhibits the ability of a recipient to store or print an electronic record, the electronic record is not enforceable against the recipient.

(d) The requirements of this section may not be varied by agreement, but

. . . .

(2) a requirement under a law other than this [Act] to send, communicate, or transmit a record by [first-class mail, postage prepaid] [regular United States mail], may be varied by agreement to the extent permitted by the other law.

Section 8 illustrates how narrowly protective of electronic commerce are the provisions of UETA. The core concept is that the equivalence of electronics should not alter other policy choices made about substantive terms of a disclosure or statute of frauds rule. Section 8 reflects this attitude. Consider, for example, the proper treatment of a state law consumer rule that requires a vendor to "mail a monthly" statement to a consumer relating to the current status of the licensee's account? Can the disclosure be sent by e-mail or by posting on the online site?

PROBLEM 3.8

Assume that a state law applicable to your client's online service requires that online providers supply customers with a written copy of their privacy and security policies prior to entering into a contract, and that they mail copies of any "material" changes in those policies no more than ninety days after the change becomes effective. Customers of your client's service are required to agree online to Client's service contract for access to its system. The contract provides that privacy and security policies may be changed without notice and that the change becomes effective when posted at "[a designated location on Client's site]." What steps must Client take to comply with the privacy law? To what extent can it continue to comply by electronic notices and the like?

E. Attribution of Signatures and Records

One Treatise describes attribution issues as follows:

The Achilles heel of e-commerce is attribution. The problem that is highlighted by the attribution concept lies in proving:

- That the person you are dealing with really is the person with whom you believe you are contracting, or,

- At least, proving that the person or entity you believe should be involved has legal responsibility for the transaction of conduct involved.

Stated simply: when can electronic conduct or operations, such as a clicking "I agree," be attributed to a particular person in law or fact?

RAYMOND T. NIMMER & HOLLY K. TOWLE, THE LAW OF ELECTRONIC COMMERCIAL TRANSACTIONS ¶ 6.01 (2007). Although it deals with a deceptive practices claim, the following case demonstrates the problem.

FTC v. VERITY INTERNATIONAL
124 F. Supp. 2d 193 (S.D.N.Y. 2000)

KAPLAN, DISTRICT JUDGE.

Defendants operate a billing service for Internet pornographers. Web sites containing what defendants euphemistically refer to as adult content ascertain the telephone numbers from which visitors to the sites accessed the Internet through a system known as Automatic Number Identification ("ANI"). Defendants then bill the subscribers of those telephone numbers — who may or may not be the same persons who accessed the web sites — for access to the pornographic materials, although most of the bills here at issue described the services for which the bills were rendered as telephone calls to Madagascar. Defendants insist upon payment by line subscribers irrespective of whether the line subscribers used or authorized the use of their telephone lines to access the web sites of defendants' clients.

The Federal Trade Commission ("FTC" or "Commission") contends principally that defendants' insistence that line subscribers are legally obligated to pay for access to their clients' web sites, even where the line subscribers neither used them nor authorized such use, violates Section 5(a) of the Federal Trade Commission Act (the "Act"). The matter now is before the Court on the FTC's motion for a preliminary injunction. . . .

The FTC received 548 complaints about Verity in the period September 18 through September 22, 2000. The complaints were variations on a theme. Line subscribers said they had neither made nor authorized the calls: the computer at issue was in the line subscriber's possession and switched off at the time the calls allegedly were made; a minor child in the household downloaded the program without authorization; the line subscriber billed had both a 900 block and an international-call block on the line; or the computer at issue was online with another web-based program at the time the call purportedly was made. The FTC has submitted in support of this motion 81 declarations from recipients of these bills who assert that they did not access or authorize anyone to use their telephones to access the services for which Verity billed them.

Notwithstanding this evidence, the Verity defendants stoutly argue that every call for which they billed in fact was made from the line subscriber's [line]. The record at this point is insufficient to determine whether this is so, but in large measure the argument is beside the point. The record is more than sufficient to establish, and the Court finds, that a significant number of line subscribers to whom Verity sent bills did not themselves use, or authorize others to use, their lines to access the services of Verity's clients, even assuming that someone else used their lines to do so. And that is the critical factual premise of the FTC's position — that these defendants have engaged in unfair and deceptive practices by billing and insisting upon payment by line subscribers even where the line subscribers did not themselves agree to pay. . . .

Discussion

[As noted,] the FTC alleges that defendants violated and continue to violate FTC Act Section 5(a) by making the false and deceptive representation that line subscribers are legally obliged to pay for web-site access and by unfairly billing line subscribers even if those subscribers did not access the site, download the dialing program, or authorize either action. Based on the evidence now before it, the Court finds that the FTC is likely to succeed in showing that these practices are deceptive and unfair.

A. False and Deceptive Representations

To establish that defendants violated FTC Act Section 5(a) by engaging in unfair or deceptive acts or practices in or affecting commerce, the FTC ultimately must demonstrate a material representation, omission, or practice that is likely to mislead consumers acting reasonably in the circumstances.

1. Legal Obligation to Pay

To prevail on its first claim for relief, the FTC must establish that (1) Verity's bills represented that line subscribers are legally obligated to pay irrespective of whether they used or authorized use of the services of defendants' clients, and (2) the representation was materially false or deceptive.

Although Verity's bills include the "Total Amount Due" and instruct consumers to detach and return a portion of the bill with payment, they do not state in so many words that the addressees are legally obligated to pay the sum claimed. Nevertheless, courts may not blind themselves to the common understandings of our society. One who tenders a bill thereby renders a statement of account. The bill is a representation that the sum claimed in fact is due and owing and that the addressee is obliged to pay. Certainly recipients of bills ordinarily so understand, and the Court infers for purposes of this motion that this understanding is reasonable. Moreover, it is difficult to imagine a representation that would be more material, as the very point of a bill is to induce the recipient to rely on it and therefore to send defendants the money claimed. The only question of substance in this connection is whether defendants' bills, to the extent that they are sent to line subscribers who neither used nor authorized use of their lines to access the services of defendants' clients, are legally obligated to pay. If they are not, then the bills contained materially false representations.

Of course, many are familiar with the proposition that the subscriber to a telephone line is legally obligated to pay the telephone company and long distance carrier for any calls made on that line. The source of that obligation, however, is not as well known. Typically, the relationship between the line subscriber and the telephone company and long distance carrier is governed by tariffs filed with the Federal Communications Commission ("FCC"). Such tariffs "conclusively and exclusively enumerate the rights and liabilities of the contracting parties." They not only govern a carrier's rates to various destinations, but also set forth customers' obligations and carriers' duties. Customers are presumed conclusively to have knowledge of these filed rates and obligations and courts therefore consistently have held that line subscribers are obliged to pay for telephone calls they never authorized. These principles are known as the filed rate doctrine.

Drawing implicitly on the filed rate doctrine, defendants argue that Verity is merely using ANI-based billing in a way that is common practice in the telecommunications industry. Defendants meet each of the FTC's consumer complaints and bills with a matching Sprint electronic code meant to demonstrate that the call indeed was placed as indicated on the bill. But the argument skips over a critical point.

The Court assumes *arguendo* that the calls, in all or most cases, in fact were placed from the line subscribers' telephones. But the filed rate doctrine would make the line subscribers responsible for those calls only if a filed tariff covering the particular line subscriber so provided. The FTC is likely to establish that this simply is not so.

The FCC long has distinguished between basic telecommunications carriage — principally ordinary telephone and long distance service — and enhanced services such as those offered by Verity's clients. In *Amendment of Section 64.702 of the Commission's Rules and Regulations ("Computer II")*, for example, the FCC declined to institute comprehensive regulation for enhanced services and found that vendors of enhanced services, defined as anything more than basic transmission service, were not engaged in common carrier activity. The Telecommunications Act of 1996 likewise distinguishes between telecommunications services and information services, stating that "a telecommunications carrier shall be treated as a common carrier under this chapter only to the extent that it is engaged in providing telecommunications services." While basic communications services long have been covered by filed tariffs, enhanced and information services have not. Thus, there appear to be no tariffs governing the rates or the terms and conditions upon which these services are offered. At any rate, defendants have pointed to none. In consequence, there appears to be no legal basis for defendants' contention that telephone line subscribers are legally obligated to pay charges for enhanced services accessed over their subscribed lines where the subscribers neither have accessed nor authorized access to those services. Indeed, the FCC has made clear that it is improper to rely solely on ANI as a basis for holding a line subscriber liable for information purchases made from his or her telephone line.

In the absence of a legal obligation to pay based on the filed rate doctrine, the next question is whether a contract exists between the line subscriber and defendants. Assuming *arguendo* that clicking on "I accept" on the disclaimer screens forms a valid contract between the person who clicks and defendants or their clients, it suffices at this stage to note that basic contract principles provide that an offer and acceptance create a contract only between the offeror and the offeree. Indeed, where the person who accepts the offer is incompetent or a minor, the contract is voidable. Accordingly, unless the line subscriber is the person who accepts the offer by clicking on the "I accept" box, there is no contract between the defendants or their clients, on the one hand, and the line subscriber, on the other.

The bills sent out in early September in substance represented that line subscribers were obliged to pay for services accessed over their lines without regard to whether the line subscribers accessed or authorized access to the services. Insofar as these bills were sent to line subscribers who did not access or authorize access to the services for which payment was sought, the FTC is likely to establish that the bills made false and deceptive representations of material fact in suggesting that the line subscribers were obliged to pay the bills.

B. Unfair Practices Claim

The second count of the FTC's amended complaint challenges the ANI-based billing, as applied to line subscribers who have not used or authorized the use of the services offered by Verity's clients, as an unfair trade practice, also in violation of Section 5(a) of the Act. An act or practice is unfair if it "causes or is likely to cause substantial injury to consumers which is not reasonably avoidable by consumers themselves and not outweighed by countervailing benefits to consumers or to competition."

The FTC has established that it likely will prove at trial that a significant number of line subscribers already have been billed without having made or authorized the calls, a substantial injury to these consumers. Defendants nevertheless contend that there has been no unfair trade practice because line subscribers reasonably may protect themselves against such injury by controlling access to the telephone lines over which their clients have been accessed. But the Court is not prepared to accept that assertion, at least at this point. For one thing, there is credible evidence that at least some line subscribers who have 900 number or long-distance blocks on their telephone lines nevertheless have been billed by defendants, thus suggesting that such blocking measures are imperfect. Further, at least at this preliminary stage, this Court finds that the Commission is likely to establish that avoiding misuse of their telephones by children of line subscribers and others with access to their lines imposes an unreasonable burden on many consumers, especially in comparison with the easy alternative sought by the Commission — a bar on imposing liability on line subscribers absent a verifiable agreement to be responsible for the charges.

The defendants argue also that consumers benefit from having an alternative to disclosing credit card information on the Internet. As a broad proposition, that probably is so. Nevertheless, it does not carry the day, at least at this stage. Surely the availability of this alternative does not benefit line subscribers who do not use the service in the first place. On the contrary, they are victimized by the creation of a means that permits unauthorized users to shift costs from themselves to the line subscribers whose lines they abuse. Moreover, while the Court recognizes that defendants would be harmed by an order that effectively would require them to make pre-subscription agreements with line subscribers before charging them for their clients' services on an ANI-based basis, that harm is insufficient to tip the scales. The practical reality here is that many consumers who receive bills simply pay them. Others are not willing to engage in extended debates with billers, as they lack the time or energy or simply are fearful that an alleged creditor will damage their credit ratings and thus limit their access to credit unless they pay as demanded. The harm of which defendants complain would be the product of preventing defendants from capitalizing on the inattention and fear of consumers or on the disparity of power between them and the persons they bill to extract payments which, in many cases, probably are not rightfully theirs.

Defendants contend, finally, that they have an enormous universe of happy customers, claiming that during the period in which they billed through AT&T

they had uncollectible charges of less than three percent. But the evidence submitted by AT&T demonstrates that more than 35 percent of defendants' charges from January 1999 through September 2000 were uncollected, a figure far in excess of the charge back levels experienced by online retailers and credit card companies. This certainly suggests that there was dissatisfaction with defendants' activities even during the period when their charges misleadingly appeared on bills as fees for fictional telephone calls to Madagascar.

In all the circumstances, the Court holds that the Commission is likely to establish that defendants' ANI-based billing of line subscribers who have not themselves used or authorized use of defendants' clients' services is an unfair trade practice. . . .

Accordingly, the FTC's motion for a preliminary injunction barring ANI-based billing is granted to the extent that defendants will be enjoined from engaging in ANI-based billing of any line subscriber unless (a) the line subscriber previously entered into an express verifiable agreement authorizing such billing, or (b) the bill conspicuously contains an express statement that the line subscriber is not obliged to pay the bill unless he or she personally agreed or authorized another to agree to pay for the services for which the bill is rendered and provides a convenient method by which a line subscriber who claims not to have done so may have the bill canceled. The precise details, including the layout and typography of an approved form of bill, will be worked out in the settlement of the preliminary injunction.

What choices exist for determining with whom you are dealing in a business context? In ordinary transactions, there are many answers to this, including that in some cases you have previously dealt with the person across from you or that the letter or other writing you received contains information that only the purported sender would have known. In electronic commerce, the difference in context alters the information sources. Focusing on electronic commerce, one regulatory agency compiled this list, which is not exhaustive:

- Knowledge based authentication, or shared secrets, such as PINs and passwords;

- Biometrics, such as fingerprint, voice, and eye characteristics;

- Secure tokens, such as smart cards;

- Cryptography, including digital signatures, challenge-response protocols (e.g., the "handshake" protocol in Secure Sockets Layer), and message authentication codes;

- Digitized signatures, including digital images of handwritten signatures; and

- Signature dynamics (i.e., measurements of the direction, pressure, speed, and other attributes of a handwritten signature).

Department of the Treasury, "Electronic Authentication Policy," 66 Fed. Reg. No. 2, 394-397 (1/3/2001) at 395, 396.

As this list indicates, while the technological context may create new problems about attribution, it also offers new means for dealing with them. Indeed, some would argue that systems such as digital signatures and other electronic identifiers might more accurately indicate who has sent a message or executed a signature than old-fashioned writings and handwritten signatures.

While the ordinary person might view the question of "attribution" as simply dealing with the question of with whom are you dealing, the issue has a different connotation in law. It asks, instead, who can be held responsible or bound in law by the signature of record that is involved? Attribution as a legal issue involves determining who can be held responsible. UETA's basic attribution rule is in Section 9(a):

> An electronic record or electronic signature is attributable to a person if it was the act of the person. The act of the person may be shown in any manner, including a showing of the efficacy of any security procedure applied to determine the person to which the electronic record or electronic signature was attributable.

In one sense, this is singularly unhelpful because it says I will be deemed to have done something if I did it. But if I did it, no one needs to deem me to have done anything.

UCITA § 213 (2000 Official Text):

> An electronic authentication, display, message, record, or performance is attributed to a person if it was the act of the person or its electronic agent, or if the person is bound by it under agency or other law. The party relying on attribution of an electronic authentication, display, message, record, or performance to another person has the burden of establishing attribution.

In other words, an act will be attributed to me if I did it or my agent, including my electronic agent, did it; or if agency law says that someone else's act is really my act, or if other law says that I am bound by the act.

Both formulations take a passive approach to the role of electronic transaction rules in establishing attribution, leaving the issue to other law. Other laws, such as UCC Article 4A, federal credit card and electronic funds transfer rules are more proactive. Indeed, UCITA, E-Sign and UETA were developed during a period of debate about whether states should adopt so-called digital signature statutes that give enhanced benefits in terms of attribution issues to the use of specific types of encryption systems to verify content and source of a message. A number of states have done so.

Attribution rules under digital signature laws vary. The Utah Digital Signature Act (Signature Act), 46 Utah Code Ann. ch. 3; Utah Admin. Code RI 54-2-101 et seq., was the first such statute. It has subsequently been repealed largely because it attracted little or no commercial use. It set out a system for certification authorities and public key encryption designed to encourage use of digital signatures involving enhanced security and authenticity attributes. In contrast, several of the other statutes permit state governments to set out a process by which individuals can submit signatures to government agencies via electronic means, while others mandate agencies to develop procedures and rules for the use of digital signatures.

The Utah statute did not require public key encryption, but enabled parties to adopt this system and, if they did, delineated some of the legal consequences. The payoff for complying with encryption consisted of two elements. One was the practical reality of actual security and authentication. While not the only means of reliable authentication, the public key system is relatively effective. The payoff in terms of legal consequences involved a set of per se legal rules regarding both the signature and the writing. Use of a digital signature coupled with the use of a licensed certification authority to issue and control security of the keys, typically meant that the resulting signature and text of an electronic message constituted:

- A signature under applicable law

- A writing under applicable law

- An original of the document under applicable law

- An acknowledged writing or signature under applicable law

Signature Act §§ 401-405. The Act buttressed these effects with a set of presumptions about the accuracy and other relevant attributes of the signature and the document. These included:

> In adjudicating a dispute involving a digital signature, a court of this state shall presume that:
>
> . . . .
>
> (3) if a digital signature is verified by the public key listed in a valid certificate issued by a licensed certification authority:
>
> > (a) that the digital signature is the digital signature of the subscriber listed in that certificate;
> >
> > (b) that the digital signature was affixed by the signer with the intention of signing the message; and
> >
> > (c) the recipient of that digital signature has no knowledge or notice that the signer:
> >
> > > (i) breached a duty as a subscriber; or
> > >
> > > (ii) does not rightfully hold the private key used to affix the digital signature. . . .

Signature Act § 406. The Utah statute provided a further rule to account for cases where the party receiving the document that was digitally signed knows or should know that it cannot rely on the record it received:

> Unless otherwise provided by law or contract, the recipient of a digital signature assumes the risk that a digital signature is forged, if reliance on the digital signature is not reasonable under the circumstance. If the recipient determines not to rely on a digital signature pursuant to this section, the recipient shall promptly notify the signer of its determination not to rely on the digital signature.

Utah Signature Act § 402.

NOTES

1. Given the choice, when would you as a licensor opt for coverage under a digital signature law or prefer coverage under the general rules of UETA and UCITA? Would the analysis change if you were a licensee?

2. Are digital signature laws preempted by E-Sign? E-Sign contains the previously discussed back-in language, which allows states some latitude in dealing with electronic equivalence, so long as they do not contradict the core purposes of E-Sign. In relevant part, that language is:

> A State statute, regulation, or other rule of law may modify, limit, or supersede the provisions of section 101 with respect to State law only if such statute, regulation, or rule of law . . . specifies the alternative procedures or requirements for the use or acceptance (or both) of electronic records or electronic signatures to establish the legal effect, validity, or enforceability of contracts or other records, if —

> (i) such alternative procedures or requirements are consistent with this title and title II; and

> (ii) such alternative procedures or requirements do not require, or accord greater legal status or effect to, the implementation or application of a specific technology or technical specification

While the last portion of this language would seem to preclude a statute or regulation that gives preference to one designated technology, this is "back-in" language and refers only to superseding the preemptive effect of E-Sign that requires merely that state laws cannot deny legal enforceability to electronics simply because they are electronic, rather than in writing.

3. What is the relationship between a digital signature statute and UETA? The Prefatory Note to UETA states: "It is important to understand that the purpose of the UETA is to remove barriers to electronic commerce by validating and effectuating electronic records and signatures. It is NOT a general contracting statute — the substantive rules of contracts remain unaffected by UETA. Nor is it a digital signature statute. To the extent that a State has a Digital Signature Law, the UETA is designed to support and compliment that statute." UETA Prefatory Note (1999 Official Text). PROBLEM 3.9

Motion Picture Studio receives an e-mail from Party B ordering a copy of the latest motion picture release for showing in B's theater during a five week period starting two days from the date of the e-mail "under usual terms." Studio has dealt with B before and has B's information on file. The e-mail has *B*'s name and address typed at the bottom. The issue is whether Studio should ship the copy. Since it does business by e-mail with thousands of theaters across the world, should Studio consider any steps to deal with the risk of fraud or the risk of the contract being unenforceable?

Chapter 4

EXCLUSIVE LICENSES

I. NATURE OF THE TRANSACTION

Transactions in information or informational rights generally fall into one of four categories: assignments, exclusive licenses, non-exclusive licenses, and unrestricted sales or leases of copies or products. The format used by the parties affects the rights and privileges conveyed, the obligations of the transferor and transferee, and often the treatment of the transaction under competition and related law.

In this chapter we focus on "exclusive" licenses. While a non-exclusive license is treated as a very limited transfer, "exclusive" licenses often partake of the attributes of an actual sale or transfer of ownership. If one were to line-up the primary formats, running from the least to the most extensive in terms of rights conveyed, the arrangement most would expect would be that indicated in Figure 4.1:

Figure 4.1

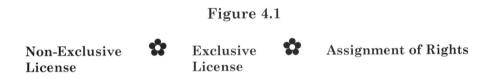

Non-Exclusive License   **Exclusive License**   **Assignment of Rights**

While this relationship often holds true, a wide variety exists within all categories and substantial overlapping occurs in fact. Some "exclusive licenses" give fewer rights than some non-exclusive licenses, while some exclusive licenses are indistinguishable from assignments. As a leading treatise comments that: "[e]ven though a contract states that it is a 'license,' a court will not be governed by form, and the contract will be upheld as an assignment of trademark rights if that is its actual legal effect." J. THOMAS MCCARTHY, MCCARTHY ON TRADEMARKS § 18:5 (4th ed. 2002).

The term "assignment" ordinarily refers to an absolute conveyance of full rights. The transferor retains no current rights in the information, although many assignments include rights of reversion in the event of a breach (say, as to an obligation to pay a royalty) or other specified event. RAYMOND T. NIMMER & JEFF DODD, MODERN LICENSING LAW § 5:3 (2007). In an exclusive license, on the other hand, the licensor at least nominally retains ownership of the intellectual property rights. Given that commercial practice regarding assignments and exclusive licenses often involves carefully tailored relationships, the difference between an assignment and a comprehensive, exclusive license is often difficult to discern.

On the other hand, a fundamental difference between an exclusive and a non-exclusive license resides in the extent to which the licensor is contractually permitted to grant licenses to other persons covering the same scope and conditions that exist in the original license. An exclusive licensor cedes that right, while a non-exclusive licensor retains it.

That being said, definitions must be understood in terms of their purpose and effect. In determining what an exclusive license "is," one must consider the consequences of the answer and the reason for asking the question. One treatise summarizes four possible effects of characterizing a license as "exclusive":

- it affects what obligations the licensor owes to the licensee,

- it affects what obligations the licensee owes to the licensor,

- it affects what rights, powers, and privileges the licensee has vis-à-vis third parties (e.g., standing to pursue infringement claims), and

- it affects whether the transaction must be registered for purposes of enforceability or priority.

RAYMOND T. NIMMER & JEFF DODD, MODERN LICENSING LAW § 5:6 (West 2007).

RITE-HITE CORP. v. KELLY COMPANY, INC.
56 F.3d 1538 (Fed. Cir. 1995)

LOURIE, CIRCUIT JUDGE.

Kelley Company appeals from [a decision] awarding damages for the infringement of U.S. Patent 4,373,847, owned by Rite-Hite Corporation. The district court determined, *inter alia,* that Rite-Hite was entitled to lost profits for lost sales of its devices that were in direct competition with the infringing devices, but which themselves were not covered by the patent in suit. [We] affirm in part, vacate in part, and remand.

BACKGROUND

On March 22, 1983, Rite-Hite sued Kelley, alleging that Kelley's "Truk Stop" vehicle restraint infringed Rite-Hite's U.S. Patent 4,373,847 ("the '847 patent"). The '847 patent, issued February 15, 1983, is directed to a device for securing a vehicle to a loading dock to prevent the vehicle from separating from the dock during loading or unloading. Any such separation would create a gap between the vehicle and dock and create a danger for a forklift operator.

Rite-Hite distributed all its products through its wholly-owned and operated sales organizations and through independent sales organizations (ISOs). During the period of infringement, the Rite-Hite sales organizations accounted for approximately 30 percent of the retail dollar sales of Rite-Hite products, and the ISOs accounted for the remaining 70 percent. Rite-Hite sued for its lost profits at the wholesale level and for the lost retail profits of its own sales organizations. Shortly after this action was filed, several ISOs moved to intervene, contending that they were "exclusive licensees" of the '847 patent by virtue of "Sales Representative Agreements" and "Dok-Lok Supplement" agreements between themselves and Rite-Hite. The court determined that the ISOs were exclusive licensees and accordingly, on August 31, 1984, permitted them to intervene. The ISOs sued for their lost retail profits.

The district court bifurcated the liability and damage phases of the [trial]. The judgment of liability was affirmed by this court. [The] damage issues were tried to the court. Rite-Hite sought damages calculated as lost profits for two types of vehicle restraints that it made and sold: the "Manual Dok-Lok" model 55 (MDL-55), which incorporated the invention covered by the '847 patent, and the "Automatic Dok-Lok" model 100 (ADL-100), which was not covered by the patent in suit. The ADL-100 was the first vehicle restraint Rite-Hite put on the market and it was covered by one or more patents other than the patent in suit. The Kelley Truk Stop restraint was designed to compete primarily with Rite-Hite's ADL-100. Both employed an electric motor and functioned automatically, and each sold for $1,000-$1,500 at the wholesale level, in contrast to the MDL-55, which sold for one-third to one-half the price of the motorized devices. Rite-Hite does not assert that Kelley's Truk Stop restraint infringed the patents covering the ADL-100.

Of the 3,825 infringing Truk Stop devices sold by Kelley, the district court found that, "but for" Kelley's infringement, Rite-Hite would have made 80 more sales of its MDL-55; 3,243 more sales of its ADL-100; and 1,692 more sales of dock levelers, a bridging platform sold with the restraints and used to bridge the edges of a vehicle and dock. The court awarded Rite-Hite as a manufacturer the wholesale profits that it lost on lost sales of the ADL-100 restraints, MDL-55 restraints, and restraint-leveler packages. It also awarded to Rite-Hite as a retailer and to the ISOs reasonable royalty damages on lost ADL-100, MDL-55, and restraint-leveler sales caused by Kelley's infringing sales. . . .

On appeal, Kelley contends that the district court erred as a matter of law in its determination of damages. Kelley does not contest the award of damages for lost sales of the MDL-55 restraints; however, Kelley argues that (1) the patent statute does not provide for damages based on Rite-Hite's lost profits on ADL-100 restraints because the ADL-100s are not covered by the patent in suit; (2) lost profits on unpatented dock levelers are not attributable to demand for the '847 invention and, therefore, are not recoverable losses; (3) the ISOs have no standing to sue for patent infringement damages.

[We affirm the damage award] with respect to Rite-Hite's lost profits as a manufacturer on its ADL-100 restraint sales [and] vacate the damage award with respect to the ISOs because they lack standing. . . .

Discussion

Recovery for lost sales of a device not covered by the patent in suit is not . . . expressly provided for by the patent statute. Express language is not required, however. Statutes speak in general terms rather than specifically expressing every detail. Under the patent statute, damages should be awarded "where necessary to afford the plaintiff full compensation for the infringement." Thus, to refuse to award reasonably foreseeable damages necessary to make Rite-Hite whole would be inconsistent with the meaning of §284.

Kelley asserts that to allow recovery for the ADL-100 would contravene the policy reason for which patents are granted: "[T]o promote the progress of . . . the useful arts." U.S. Const., art. I, §8, cl. 8. Because an inventor is only entitled to exclusivity to the extent he or she has invented and disclosed a novel, nonobvious, and useful device, Kelley argues, a patent may never be used to restrict competition in the sale of products not covered by the patent in suit. In support, Kelley cites antitrust case law condemning the use of a patent as a means to obtain a "monopoly" on unpatented material.

These cases are inapposite to the issue raised here. The present case does not involve expanding the limits of the patent grant in violation of the antitrust laws; it simply asks, once infringement of a valid patent is found, what compensable injuries result from that infringement, *i.e.,* how may the patentee be made whole. Rite-Hite is not attempting to exclude its competitors from making, using, or selling a product not within the scope of its patent. The Truk Stop restraint was found to infringe the '847 patent, and Rite-Hite is simply seeking adequate compensation for that infringement; this is not an antitrust issue. Allowing compensation for such damage will "promote the Progress of . . . the useful Arts" by providing a stimulus to the development of new products and [industries].

Standing of the ISOs

The ISOs asserted claims for patent infringement under 35 U.S.C. §281 as co-plaintiffs with Rite-Hite and were awarded damages calculated on the basis of a reasonable royalty at the retail level on both restraints and dock levelers, based on the number of sales each asserted it lost to Kelley. Kelley challenges any award of damages to the ISOs on the ground that the ISOs had no standing to seek recovery for patent infringement. The ISOs argue that the exclusivity of their sales territories gave them standing as "exclusive licensees." The question of standing to sue is a jurisdictional one, which we review *de novo.* We agree with Kelley that the ISOs must be dismissed for lack of standing.

The right of a patentee to a remedy for patent infringement is created by the statute, which provides that a "patentee" shall have remedy by civil action for infringement of his or her patent, 35 U.S.C. §281 (1988). The term "patentee" includes "not only the patentee to whom the patent was issued but also the successors in title to the patentee." 35 U.S.C. §100(d) (1988).

Generally, one seeking money damages for patent infringement must have held legal title to the patent at the time of the infringement. A conveyance of legal title by the patentee can be made only of the entire patent, an undivided part or share of the entire patent, or all rights under the patent in a specified geographical region of the United States. A transfer of any of these is an assignment and vests the assignee with title in the patent, and a right to sue infringers. A transfer of less than one of these three interests is a license, not an assignment of legal title, and it gives the licensee no right to sue for infringement at law in the licensee's own name.

Under certain circumstances, a licensee may possess sufficient interest in the patent to have standing to sue as a co-plaintiff with the patentee. Such a licensee is usually an "exclusive licensee." To be an exclusive licensee for standing purposes, a party must have received, not only the right to practice the invention within a given territory, but also the patentee's express or implied promise that others shall be excluded from practicing the invention within that territory as well. If the party has not received an express or implied promise of exclusivity under the patent, *i.e.,* the right to exclude others from making, using, or selling the patented invention, the party has a "bare license," and has received only the patentee's promise that that party will not be sued for infringement.

The ISOs maintain that they are allowed to join as co-plaintiffs because each claims it has a virtually exclusive license to sell products made by Rite-Hite to particular customers in an exclusive sales territory. To determine whether the ISOs have standing to be co-plaintiffs, we look to their contracts with Rite-Hite.

The typical original ISO contract provided in pertinent part:

> Representative's right to solicit sales of the Company's products in the Territory shall be exclusive in that the Company will not appoint any other sales representative in the territory so long as, in Company's good faith judgment, Representative is doing an adequate job in the entire Territory for all listed products. [If not,] Company shall have the right to reduce the Territory, if it gives Representative notice of the change. Company shall in no event be liable for any violation or infringement of Representative's territorial rights hereunder except such as are committed directly by Company. Company also reserves the non-exclusive right to make sales of its products within the Territory directly to the motor freight industry, governmental agencies, government contractors, and any other purchasers which, in Company's judgment, can be served best by direct sales.

The subject products are "All Rite-Hite Mechanical and Hydraulic Dock Levelers and Related Equipment." The word "patent" appears nowhere in this document, although, just prior to their intervention as plaintiffs, many of the ISOs executed supplements to their contracts which specified that the "products" of the Sales Representative Agreement include "products *manufactured and sold by [Rite-Hite]*" that embody "any of the claims set forth in Rite-Hite patents relating to 'Dok-Lok' devices, *including (but not by any way of limitation) U.S. Patent No. 4,373,847.*" The agreement also provided that each ISO had, in addition to the right to solicit sales for Rite-Hite, the right to sell products made by Rite-Hite. Rite-Hite reserved the right to sell its products to the motor freight industry.

In the original agreement, Rite-Hite itself expressly retained substantial rights to sell within the assigned territories to specific classes of purchases and to "any other purchasers which, in Company's judgement, can be served best by direct sales." The last minute modifications on the eve of litigation included for the first time products covered by the patent in the definition of the range of products covered by the agreement, and reduced the retained rights of Rite-Hite to sell within the assigned territories. Neither the original agreements nor the modifications granted the ISOs any right to exclude others under the patent.

We agree with Kelley that the district court's conclusion that these contracts conveyed a "sufficient, legally recognized interest in the rights secured by the

['847] patent" to confer standing on the ISOs was erroneous as a matter of law. The contracts in this case were not exclusive patent licenses. As noted, they did not mention the word "patent" until the eve of this lawsuit. The ISO contracts permitted the ISOs only to solicit and make sales of products made by Rite-Hite in a particular "exclusive" sales territory. While the agreements conveyed the right to sell restraints covered by the patent, any "exclusivity" related only to sales territories, not to patent rights. Even this sales exclusivity was conditional on Rite-Hite's judgment that the ISOs were doing an "adequate job."

Most particularly, the ISOs had no right under the agreements to exclude anyone from making, using, or selling the claimed invention. The ISOs could not exclude from their respective territories other ISOs, third parties, or even Rite-Hite itself. Any remedy an ISO might have had for violation of its rights would lie in a breach of contract action against Rite-Hite, if the agreement was breached, not in a patent infringement action against infringers. Rite-Hite had no obligation to file infringement suits at the request of an ISO and the ISOs had no right to share in any recovery from litigation. Moreover, appellees have not contended that such obligations and rights are to be implied. Nor do appellees even argue that the ISOs had the right under their contracts to bring suit for infringement against another ISO or a third party, making Rite-Hite an involuntary plaintiff. To the contrary, under their agreement, if an ISO sold in another's territory, the profits were shared according to Rite-Hite's "split commission" rules. While the patentee and the ISOs have cooperated in this litigation, that fact alone does not establish their right to sue.

Weinar v. Rollform, 744 F.2d 797 (Fed.Cir.1984), *cert. denied,* 470 U.S. 1084 (1985), which is cited by Rite-Hite in support of the ISOs' position, is not to the contrary. In that case, a damage award was upheld to a licensee with the exclusive right to sell in the entire United States. However, the exclusive licensee in *Weinar* was found to have received more than a "bare" license from the patentee. The exclusive licensee and the patentee "shar[ed] the property rights represented by a patent." That is not the case here. The ISOs were not licensees under the patent, except perhaps as non-exclusive licensees by implication. They were not granted any right to exclude others under the patent. They do not accordingly "share" with the patentee the property rights represented by the patent so as to have standing to sue as a co-plaintiff with the patentee.

These agreements were simply sales contracts between Rite-Hite and its independent distributors. They did not transfer any proprietary interest in the '847 patent and they did not give the ISOs the right to sue. If the ISOs lack a remedy in this case, it is because their agreements with Rite-Hite failed to make provisions for the contingency that the granted sales exclusivity would not be maintained. The ISOs could have required Rite-Hite to sue infringers and arrangements could have been agreed upon concerning splitting any damage award. Apparently, this was not done.

The grant of a bare license to sell an invention in a specified territory, even if it is the only license granted by the patentee, does not provide standing without the grant of a right to exclude others. The ISOs are legally no different from the individual salespersons whom the district court earlier refused to allow to join the suit. They are not proper parties to this suit, and their claims must be dismissed. . . .

Conclusion

[We] remand for the court to dismiss the ISOs as plaintiffs and recalculate damages to Rite-Hite.

. . . .

PAULINE NEWMAN, CIRCUIT JUDGE, with whom CIRCUIT JUDGE RADER joins, concurring in part and dissenting in part.

The court today takes an important step toward preserving damages as an effective remedy for patent infringement. Patent infringement is a commercial tort, and the remedy should compensate for the actual financial injury that was caused by the tort. Thus I concur in the majority's result with respect to entitlement to damages for lost sales of the ADL-100. . . .

Twenty-six of the plaintiffs are small businesses or individuals who were directly injured by the infringement. Some of these plaintiffs had previously brought a separate action against Kelley, the district court consolidating these actions. The district court's award of damages to these plaintiffs has not been shown to be clearly erroneous, and I would affirm it.

A. The Position of the ISOs

Adam Smith observed that people work most effectively when they have a personal stake in the fruits of their labor. That is apparently how Rite-Hite structured its business. The ISOs were not "employees," but independent entities. They were responsible for 70% of Rite-Hite's sales. They were not distributors, and most of them were not resellers. They were part of the make/sell activity that was conducted before, not after, the first sale. The issue of their entitlement to the damages that they proved requires objective evaluation, not summary pigeonholing.

Indeed, the ISOs' portion of the injury caused by the infringement is recoverable even on the majority's view of the position of the ISOs in the "original ISO contract," which granted the ISOs the right "to solicit sales in the [exclusive] Territory." The majority states that this commercial relationship was unchanged in any substantive way by the new agreement whereby Rite-Hite designated the ISOs as exclusive sales "licensees." It is not necessary to decide the nuances of this contractual relationship, for the losses experienced at the sales level are compensable. If the ISOs were simply sales agents, as Kelley argues, then Rite-Hite is the seller of the goods. If these plaintiffs do not have "standing," as the majority states, because the lost sales were made by Rite-Hite, not the ISOs, then Rite-Hite is entitled to these damages. Thus, if compensation is not owed to the ISOs, it is owed to Rite-Hite.

Witnesses at the damages trial explained that the profits from Rite-Hite's manufacture and sale of truck restraints were calculated at both the manufacturing level and the sales level. Rite-Hite made about 30% of its sales through its own sales organizations, and 70% of its sales through the ISOs, which were assigned geographically exclusive territories. The district court awarded damages in accordance with which plaintiffs bore the losses, at the manufacturing and the sales levels. The majority apparently recognizes the recovery by Rite-Hite for the sales it made through its own selling arms, but not for those obtained by the ISOs.

The majority may have misunderstood the commercial structure, for it continues the loose reference to Rite-Hite's manufacturing-level price as a "wholesale" price, although the lost sales to the customer — the price at which Kelley and Rite-Hite competed — was not at this manufacturing level of $1,000-1,500, but in the $2,500-3,000 range for the ADL-100. This price included both the manufacturing-level costs and profit and the sales-level costs and profit. Indeed, the district court drew this distinction, although not for the purpose of excluding recovery of sales-level losses, but for the purpose of distinguishing the profits lost at each level. Analyzing the evidence, the district court limited the recovery at the sales level to one third of that claimed, disallowing claims for individual salesmen's commissions.

The trial court has substantial discretion in determining damages. In *State Industries, Inc. v. Mor-Flo Industries, Inc.*, 883 F.2d 1573 (Fed.Cir.1989), *cert. denied*, 493 U.S. 1022 (1990), this court recognized that

> the only limit on [the district court's] discretion in selecting a remedy is that it be adequate to compensate for the damages suffered as a result of the infringement.

This deference that the judicial process accords to the trial court's assessment of damages recognizes the fact-dependency of just compensation. In *Perkins v. Standard Oil Co.*, 395 U.S. 642 (1969), the Court looked at the chain of causation and observed that "Perkins was no mere innocent bystander; he was the principal victim of the price discrimination." So too were the ISOs a principal victim of the infringement, for they and Rite-Hite sold the goods whose sales were lost due to the infringement.

B. The ISOs as Sales Agents

The purpose of legal remedy is the recovery of damages by those injured by the tortious acts of another, provided of course that policy-based criteria are met. [Analogous] to the Seventh Circuit's explanation in *Nelson v. Monroe Regional Medical Center*, 925 F.2d 1555, 1563 (7th Cir.), *cert. dismissed*, 502 U.S. 903 (1991), that standing in antitrust cases follows the causation requirement of common law torts, standing in patent infringement cases follows the same extensive jurisprudence.

Kelley argued at trial, as it does here, that the ISOs can not recover damages because they were not exclusive patent licensees. The district court thoroughly explored the relationships between Rite-Hite and the ISOs. The ISOs were sales agents with certain exclusive rights and exclusive territories, with some exceptions for direct sales by Rite-Hite. Since they are not suing independently of the patentee, there is no relevance to those cases which hold that a non-exclusive licensee can not sue in its own name. When the patentee is joined as a party, as Rite-Hite is here, and the licensee has an exclusive right to make, use, or sell, the licensee has standing to recover for its own injury. In *Western Elec. Co. v. Pacent Reproducer Corp.*, 42 F.2d 116, 119, 5 USPQ 105,

106 (2d Cir.), *cert. denied,* 282 U.S. 873 (1930), the court explained that a less than fully exclusive licensee must join the patentee in any suit for infringement, while a fully exclusive licensee, like an assignee, can sue in its own name (citing *Waterman v. Mackenzie,* 138 U.S. 252, 256 (1891)). In this case the patentee is a party to the suit, thus removing the risk of multiple suits, of which Kelley makes much. In *Weinar v. Rollform, Inc.,* 744 F.2d 797, 807, 223 USPQ 369, 374-75 (Fed. Cir.1984), this court stated that "two parties sharing the property rights represented by a patent may have their respective property rights protected by injunction and each, when properly joined in a suit, may be entitled to damages." In *Innis, Speiden & Co. v. Food Machinery Corp.,* 2 F.R.D. 261, 265, 53 USPQ 330, 334 (D.Del.1942), the court explained that when a licensee is granted an exclusive right to some part of the patent grant, in that case the geographically exclusive right to sell the patented product in Florida, the licensee must be permitted to exclude others from trespassing upon his right, lest he "be in the position of one who has an exclusive easement across Blackacre but could not enjoin trespassers who persisted in impairing his easement."

Thus if the ISOs are viewed as sales agents instead of licensees, either their sales exclusivity suffices to permit them to join with Rite-Hite in this suit, or Rite-Hite as principal can recover on their behalf.

C. General Damages Theory

The jurisprudence of tort damages illustrates myriad relationships between the wrongdoer and the injured party, from which there have evolved general criteria that apply damages law and policy. Precedent deals with the criteria of directness of the injury, foreseeability, and duty, derived from policy considerations whereby the public interest in remedying wrong is balanced with the public interest in placing reasonable limits on liability. Applying these rules, the ISOs were a direct and foreseeable victim of the infringement. Their recovery is not barred by statute or policy. Their entitlement is a question of fact and proof, applying the law and policy of damages. . . .

NOTES

1. The *Rite-Hite* decision is best known in patent law for its holding (omitted here) that damages for infringement of a patent can include losses associated with products that are not covered by the patent. Our concern is with the licensing law issue. As we discuss further in this chapter, standing to sue for infringement is the most litigated issue on which the presence or absence of an exclusive license is relevant. As the court recognizes, the terms of the contract control. What, specifically, was lacking in the ISO contracts that made them something other than an exclusive license of a patent?

2. Assuming that the infringing conduct caused the ISOs to lose sales, what recourse do they have after the decision in *Rite-Hite*? If you were redrafting the ISO agreements from the perspective of the ISOs, what terms would you include to protect them against the type of loss that was incurred in this case? Under what circumstances, if any, should such protection be implied in the absence of express terms? In *Martin v. New Trinidad Lake Asphalt Co.*, 255 F. 93 (D.N.J. 1919), the licensor granted a license to a licensee, but allegedly failed to prevent others from infringing the patents. The court observed: "The license agreement [contains] no provision that the licensor would protect the licensee from infringements by others. In the absence of such a provision, there was no obligation upon the part of the [licensor] to do so." *Id.* at 96-97.

3. In general, in terms of an exclusive or a non-exclusive licensee, what is the appropriate classification of a person who buys a copy of a book containing a copyrighted work or buys a patented product? In answering this question, consider the fact that the owner of a copy of a copyrighted work has the right to distribute that copy under 17 U.S.C. § 109(a), but generally receives no other rights. Patent law, as we shall see, has a concept of "patent exhaustion" that gives the buyer of a patented article limited rights to act with respect to the particular machine.

PROBLEM 4.1

Patent Corporation, the owner of a patent relating to a particular machine, named the "Turf Blaster," delivers a prototype version of the machine to Transferee, in return for payment of a specified purchase price. The contract provides: "Patent transfers to Transferee all its right, title and interest in Turf Blaster." What is Transferee's status with respect to the patent? If the parties intended to create an exclusive license or an assignment of the patent, how would you draft the relevant terms of the contract?

PROBLEM 4.2

Developer agrees to create and deliver software to Client that will control Client's manufacturing plant. This program does not constitute a "work for hire." The contract provides that Developer transfers "all rights to the completed program with no further licensing or royalty fees due." What is Client's status with respect to the copyright in the program?

II. LICENSEE'S OBLIGATIONS AND RIGHTS

A. Obligation to Exploit the Subject Matter

Depending on the terms of the license, its scope and payment obligations, an exclusive license may place the transferor in a position of substantial reliance on the licensee to provide the licensor with a viable commercial return from its property. In such cases, if the parties do not provide performance or revenue standards, a court may provide implied terms to protect the commercial integrity of the transaction. The language and scope of the implied terms vary.

One way of organizing the cases on this issue is to distinguish between an implied obligation of "good faith" and an obligation of the licensee to use "best efforts." But the cases actually use much more varied language. The first question, however, is whether the licensee owes any obligation at all to do anything with the licensed subject matter.

PERMANENCE CORP. v. KENNAMETAL, INC.
725 F. Supp. 907 (E.D. Mich. 1989)

FREEMAN, J.

Before the court is defendant's motion for summary judgment. . . . In this diversity action, plaintiff seeks damages for the breach of an implied obligation of a licensing agreement. [Defendant, Kennametal, Inc. obtained a non-exclusive license to manufacture and sell products "made from and pursuant to" certain listed patents. Two years later, Kennametal exercised a contractual option to convert the license to an exclusive license to manufacture and sell. Plaintiff alleges that Defendant Kennametal] breached and continues to breach to date, its obligations under the aforementioned written agreement between the parties [to exercise its best efforts]. Defendant argues that "[a] best efforts clause will not be implied in a patent license agreement where (i) the agreement is adequately supported by consideration, (ii) the plaintiff was represented by counsel, and (iii) the agreement is expressly an integrated agreement." . . .

In *Vacuum Concrete Corp v. American Machine & Foundry Co.*, 321 F. Supp. 771, 772-73 (S.D.N.Y. 1971), the court adequately summarized the competing interests in determining whether to infer an obligation of best efforts:

> It is settled law that the court will imply a duty on the part of an exclusive licensee to exploit the subject matter of the license with due diligence, where such a covenant is essential as a matter of equity to give meaning and effect to the contract as a whole.

The reasoning [is that] it would be unfair to place the productiveness of the licensed property solely within the control of the licensee, thereby putting the licensor at his mercy, without imposing an obligation to exploit upon the licensee. In effect the court is merely enforcing an obligation which the parties overlooked expressing in their contract or which they considered unnecessary to be expressed. In such circumstances the implied obligation "must conform to what the court may assume would have been the agreement of the parties, if the situation had been anticipated and provided for. Thus whatever obligation is sought to be raised by legal implication, must be of such a character as the court will assume would have been made by the parties if their attention had been called to the subject, and their conduct inspired by principles of justice."

A typical example of an implied covenant to exploit is found in a leading case in New York on the subject, *Wood v. Lucy, Lady Duff-Gordon.* . . . There the defendant, a fashion designer, gave the plaintiff the exclusive privilege of marketing defendant's design. Although the plaintiff did not expressly agree to exploit the design, the court implied such an obligation, since defendant's sole revenue was to be derived from plaintiff's sale of clothes designed by defendant and defendant was thus at the plaintiff's mercy. In this and in similar cases the circumstances revealed that such an obligation was essential to give effect to the contract between the parties and was in accord with their intent. On the other hand, where the parties have considered the matter and deliberately omitted any such obligation, or where it is unnecessary to imply such an obligation in order to give effect to the terms of their contract, it will not be implied.

[Our] starting point, of course, must be the terms of the written contract between the parties. Although the Agreement purported to grant an exclusive license to AMF, obligating it to pay royalties to Vacuum, it is readily apparent that Vacuum, unlike the licensors in those cases where an obligation to exploit has been implied, did not depend for its revenue solely upon sales of the licensed devices (Octopus Lifters) by AMF. In the first place according to the terms of the Agreement Vacuum retained the right itself to manufacture and sell up to $300,000 annually of Octopus Lifters within the licensed territory. The significance of this reservation as a factor negating an implied covenant to exploit is apparent from the undisputed fact that up to the date of the Agreement between the parties Vacuum's maximum gross annual income from sales or licensing of the lifting device in the licensed territory (U.S.) was $63,771 received in 1964, of which $47,939 represented income from the sale of a total of eight machines, parts, and services.

The decision in each case in which a party asserts an implied obligation of best efforts turns upon the circumstances of each case, although certain factors can be distilled from an evaluation of the reported cases. In the *Wood* case, for example, the most important factor in the decision was that the fashion designer would not receive any revenue unless the plaintiff sold the designer's clothes. As a matter of equity, Justice Cardozo held that the contract was "instinct with obligation" on the plaintiff to use reasonable efforts to sell the clothes.

In *Havel v. Kelsey-Hayes Co.*, 83 A.D.2d 380, 445 N.Y.S.2d 333 (App. Div. 1981), the agreement in issue provided as follows:

> By agreement dated January 30, 1973, plaintiff granted to defendant an exclusive license for the use and dissemination of the patented process. Defendant agreed to pay plaintiff a percentage of the cost of super alloy powders used in the process and further agreed that plaintiff would receive 25% of all lump sum payments and 40% of all royalties paid to defendant by sublicensees. The agreement also provided for payment by defendant of minimum royalties of $20,000 per year. The minimum payment was not guaranteed, however, because plaintiff's sole right was to terminate the license on defendant's failure to make up the deficiency if plaintiff's share of the lump sum payments and royalties did not amount to $20,000 in any calendar year.

The court held that the contract, when read as a whole, was instinct with an obligation to use reasonable efforts to exploit the process. Of primary importance to the court was the provision for an exclusive license; of further importance was that the minimum royalty provision was not guaranteed and that public policy supports the use of patents, not their suppression.

In *Willis Bros., Inc. v. Ocean Scallops, Inc.*, 356 F. Supp. 1151 (E.D.N.C. 1972), the license agreement granted to the defendant, an exclusive, world wide right for the life of the patent to manufacture, use and sell a certain scallop shucking process on which plaintiffs had pending an application for letters patent. The plaintiffs agreed not to manufacture, use, or sell the equipment except as to commitments made prior to the agreement. In consideration for this exclusive licensing, the defendant agreed to pay plaintiffs an amount determined on a basis of three cents per net pound of product processed by use of the equipment and/or the processes. There is no minimum royalty provision in the contract. Although the Agency Agreement provides that Willis Brothers will serve as a nonexclusive agent for the defendant in the sale of scallop meat, there is no reservation of rights in the License Agreement permitting the plaintiffs to compete with the license. The Employment Contract provided that Willis was to receive consultant's fees. This agreement was cancelled by the defendant after one year. In order to enable the plaintiffs to pay the debts incurred by the development of the patent, the defendant loaned Willis Brothers seventy thousand dollars. Prepayment of the loan was to be made by application to the principal the royalties under the License Agreement and percentages of the amount payable to Willis Brothers under the Agency Agreement. The prepayment provision providing for payment of the loan from the royalties indicates that a "best efforts" provision is essential to give effect to the agreements between the parties.

Of importance to the court was that the agreement was for an exclusive license to work the patent and that the defendant must use due diligence in working the patent to allow plaintiff to repay the loan defendant made to it as part of the agreement.

In *Bellows v. E.R. Squibb & Sons, Inc.*, 184 U.S.P.Q. 473 (N.D.Ill. 1974), the agreement in issue provided in pertinent part:

4.01 Concurrently with the execution of this Agreement [Squibb] shall pay to [Bellows] the sum of . . . ($50,000.00), which shall represent a credit against future royalties, but shall not be refundable in whole or part in the event no royalties acrue [sic] to Bellows. . . .

8.02 [Squibb] may terminate this Agreement in its entirety . . . by giving [Bellows] written notice at least six (6) months prior to such termination.

8.03 In the event of any of the following, [Bellows] may, at his option, terminate this Agreement:

a) [Squibb] elects not to exploit the license granted hereunder, . . . and [Squibb] shall have so notified [Bellows]. . . .

d) [Squibb] . . . has failed to market the Licensed Product . . . within eighteen (18) months of the date of this Agreement.

e) [Squibb] does not pay to [Bellows] a minimum royalty of ($50,000) for each year after 1974 and during the life of this Agreement.

The court held as a matter of law that there could be no implied duty of best efforts in the exploitation of the invention. The crucial factors in the case are that the agreement specifically recognized that Squibb might decide not to exploit the patent and provided for that contingency. The court also noted that the agreement was the result of arm's length bargaining with both parties assisted by counsel and that "no obligation should be implied to merely cure an unsatisfactory bargain."

Looking at the agreement in this case, the court notes several important factors. First, the defendant exercised its option to obtain the exclusive rights to exploit plaintiff's patents. . . .

Second, plaintiff could only terminate the agreement upon a breach of the agreement by defendant; defendant, however, could terminate the agreement upon 90 days notice provided that it pay the royalties due up to the effective date of the cancellation. Unlike *Bellows*, this agreement does not contain any provision allowing plaintiff to terminate the agreement if best efforts were not used or if certain minimum royalties were not paid. This factor further supports plaintiff's position.

Third, the agreement contained an integration clause:

> This Agreement supersedes all other agreements, oral or written, heretofore made with respect to the subject matter hereof and the transactions contemplated hereby and contains the entire agreement of the parties.

See para. 10.4. Defendant relies upon this provision in arguing against any implied obligation of best efforts. In *Vacuum Concrete Corp.*, 321 F. Supp. at 773-74, the court stated:

> Other provisions of the Agreement which militate against implying a covenant to exploit with due diligence are . . . the stipulation that the Agreement constituted "the entire agreement between the parties." . . . For instance, the merger or integration clause . . . , by emphasizing that the formal contract, which contained no undertaking by AMF to exploit the device, constituted the "entire" Agreement between the parties, negates the thought that they intended to impose such a duty upon AMF.

Fourth, the parties have submitted contradictory affidavits regarding the drafting of the agreement and what was negotiated. *See* McKenna Affidavit para. 9 ("Kennametal responded in a letter dated March 11, 1985, pointing out that Permanence and Kennametal had discussed 'best efforts' during the negotiation and that the parties had agreed to prepaid royalties instead. . . ."); Krass Affidavit para. 4 ("Neither the completed agreement nor any of the draft agreements contained a 'best efforts' clause and, to the best of my knowledge, there were not negotiations with respect to the inclusion of such a clause").

Fifth, on February 8, 1979, defendant pursuant to the agreement paid to plaintiff $250,000, $100,000 of which was an advance payment of royalties. On February 5, 1981, defendant paid plaintiff a second up-front fee of $250,000, $100,000 of which was an advance payment of royalties. The agreement also contained royalty rates on the net sales price of products made by defendant using processes that fall under valid claims of the patents. This factor sways decidedly in defendant's favor.

Finally, there is no dispute that the agreement has no express reference to "best efforts" with regard to the use of the patent, although the court notes that in another portion of the agreement the parties agreed that "Kennametal shall use reasonable efforts to guard against the unauthorized use or disclosure of such technology and technical assistance." The inclusion of the phrase "reasonable efforts" in paragraph 6.4 and the absence of that phrase in any other section of the agreement militates against inferring an implied promise to use best efforts to exploit the patents. This agreement was negotiated at arm's length by competent counsel.

After considering these factors, the court holds that there is no implied obligation of best efforts. Of primary importance is that the defendant paid up-front over $500,000 in fees and advance royalties. Thus, unlike the seminal *Wood* case, plaintiff's sole revenue was not subject to the whim of defendant in exploiting the patents — plaintiff had money in hand and was to receive further royalties under the agreement. While the *Masco* case upon which defendant relies can be distinguished because it involved a nonexclusive license, the Michigan Court of Appeals in that case stated:

> There is no showing by the parties that Masco Corporation ordinarily supplied best effort clauses to licensing agreements. The circumstances surrounding this agreement also do not support the contention that the best efforts clause was so clearly within the contemplation of the parties that they deemed it unnecessary to expressly stipulate it. The record discloses a dispute between the parties as to whether a best efforts clause was considered during negotiation of this agreement. This is not a dispute of fact which would preclude summary judgment. This dispute shows that the parties did not feel that a best efforts clause was so clearly implied that it was unnecessary to include it in the contract.

Masco, slip op. at 4. Similarly, in the instant case, the only disputed factual issue is what occurred during the negotiation of the agreement. The court has carefully read the agreement and holds that no best efforts clause can be implied to it. . . .

NOTES

1. The court commented that the opinion in *Vacuum Concrete* "adequately summarized" the law regarding "best efforts," but in the part of the opinion it cited, the *Vacuum Concrete* court referred to a duty of diligence, not best efforts. Are the standards different? As previously mentioned, the case law is rife with different statements of the implied obligation that might arise in an exclusive license. Some courts refer to "use reasonable efforts," "best efforts for a reasonable time," "good faith effort," "active exploitation in good faith," etc. What is the core issue here? For example, in *Permanence*, if there is no "best efforts" obligation to be implied, by what standard if any would a court measure the licensee's performance under the agreement?

2. For a case consistent with *Permanence*, see *Paradata Computer Networks, Inc. v. Telebit Corp.*, 830 F. Supp. 1001 (E.D. Mich. 1993) (no best effort obligation where defendant paid $1 million up front).

3. There are different ways to define the obligation of good faith. For example, UCC §1-201(a) (1998 Official Text) ("honesty in fact"); UCC §2-103(b) (1998 Official Text) (honesty in fact *and* conformance to commercial standards of fair dealing); UCITA §102(a)(32) ("honesty in fact and the observance of reasonable commercial standards of fair dealing") (2000 Official Text). However, good faith is not a negligence or reasonable care standard. "Observance of reasonable commercial standards of fair dealing" is concerned with the fairness of the conduct rather than the care with which an act is performed. Both fair dealing and ordinary reasonable care are judged in light of reasonable commercial standards, but those standards in each case are directed to different aspects of commercial conduct.

4. What does "best efforts" mean? Presumably, it requires more than "mere" good faith, but how much more? Cases routinely hold that it does not require efforts that are completely unreasonable and destructive in context. The court's analysis in *Perma Research & Dev. Co. v. Singer Co.*, 402 F. Supp. 881, 896, *aff'd*, 542 F.2d 111, 113 (2d Cir. 1976), however, suggests that some effort is necessary. The transferee was required to "use its best efforts for a reasonable time . . . to perfect the product." The court held that the device could have been perfected and made marketable without unreasonable effort and that the assignee had breached its obligation. The required efforts extended to research and development necessary to bring the product to the marketplace. There are no cases, even under a "best effort" rule, that require a licensee to incur disproportionate losses in order to protect the licensor. Indeed, the cases protect a reasoned business decision not to market a product based on the circumstances, including market conditions, performance, and the like.

PROBLEM 4.3

Wills Corp. obtained an exclusive license from Ocean covering all rights under Ocean's patented process for the remaining term of the patent (ten years). The license required an initial royalty payment of $50,000, plus royalties of 10% on 1) any license fees that Wills obtains from licensing the process to others, and 2) net profits at Wills' restaurants that use the process. After four months, Wills concludes that the process is too costly to continue to use it. Wills discontinues use and has made no effort to market the process to others because it believes that the cost involved in using the process makes it unmarketable. One year later, after many complaints to Wills, Ocean sues to cancel the license and to recover royalties lost because of Wills' inaction. What result?

MECHANICAL ICE TRAY
CORP. v. GENERAL MOTORS CORP.
144 F.2d 720 (2d Cir. 1944)

CHASE, CIRCUIT JUDGE.

Mechanical Ice Tray Corporation and I.C.E. Corporation brought this suit against General Motors [for] an accounting and to recover royalties alleged to be due the plaintiffs for ice trays manufactured and sold by the defendant since April 1, 1940, under the terms of a license agreement the parties had made covering the manufacture, use and sale of ice trays for mechanical refrigerators under certain U.S. patents owned by Mechanical Ice Tray Corporation. [Plaintiffs] alleged that the license was an exclusive one and that the defendant had failed in violation of its implied obligation so to do, to exploit the licensed inventions in good faith and to refrain from adopting commercially equivalent devices outside the scope of the claims of the patents included in the license agreement. . . .

The trial court found that the defendant had not manufactured and sold any ice trays which were within the scope of the licensed patents without paying royalties to the plaintiffs. It did, however, find that the defendant had manufactured and sold an ice tray, known as type 4, which was a breach of its implied obligation to exploit the patents and awarded damages computed on the basis of the royalties agreed upon by the parties to the license. Both parties have appealed from the decree. . . .

A license was originally granted to the defendant by I.C.E. Corporation on August 21, 1934. Thereafter Mechanical Ice Tray Corporation, which claimed to own an interest in the patents, became a party to it. That agreement is the one on which this suit is based. It is dated April 1, 1936, and provides, so far as need now be stated, that the defendant was exclusively licensed under the patents within the United States, except in the County of Roscommon, Mich., with the sole exception of a non-exclusive license which had been granted to Westinghouse Electric & Manufacturing Company. It was agreed that if the Westinghouse license should be terminated the defendant should become the sole licensee. A minimum royalty of $5000 a year was payable to the plaintiffs and unit royalties were payable in amounts varying in accordance with the kind and number of ice trays sold each year.

Mechanical agreed to sue infringers upon the written request of the defendant and if it failed to do so within thirty days the defendant was given the right to prosecute infringers in its own name and at its own expense. [The] license could be cancelled by the defendant upon ninety days' notice to the plaintiffs at any time after December 31, 1938, and the plaintiffs could cancel in the same way for any material breach by the defendant but during the notice period the defendant might repair the breach and thereby keep the license in effect. The defendant also was given the right to surrender the exclusive license at the end of any calendar year and retain a non-exclusive license. If it did so it was no longer bound to make the guaranteed minimum royalty payments.

At the request of the defendant four suits were brought against alleged infringers. Three of them were settled before trial. The fourth was against Abraham & Straus [and resulted in a judgment holding the patent claims valid but not infringed as they were then construed].

Paragraph Eleventh (b) of the license agreement provides in part as follows: "It is understood and agreed that in the event any of the claims of any of said patents are construed or held invalid by a decision of a court of competent and final jurisdiction, or by an inferior court from whose decree no appeal is taken within the time required by law, then the requirement to pay royalties under this license with respect to any such claim or claims shall be interpreted in conformity with the court's decision as to the scope or validity of such claims of said patents so that no royalty shall be payable under such claims after the date of such decision upon any ice tray which has heretofore been deemed made under such claims of any such patents and hence subject to royalties hereunder solely because they fell within the claims so held invalid or construed. . . ."

After April 1, 1940, following this decision, the defendant stopped paying royalties on the trays, type 2 and 3, which it continued to manufacture without change in construction. It also changed the construction of other trays it made to what was essentially that of type 2 and 3 but was called type 4 and paid no royalties on [that product].

The second cause of action is based on the duty of an exclusive licensee on the unit royalty basis to exploit in good faith, and its alleged breach. The theory of that cause of action is that the productiveness of the licensor's property having been placed solely within the control of the licensee, a covenant on its part to work the patent in good faith to make it produce royalty income will be implied.

The principle is well established with respect to a wide variety of contracts in which the consideration for a grant of property lies wholly in the payment of "sums of money based upon the earnings of property transferred." *In re Waterson, Berlin & Snyder Co.*, 2 Cir., 48 F.2d 704, 709. It has been applied in [diverse transactions]. It has been held that such a contract includes an implied negative covenant that "neither party shall do anything which will have the effect of destroying or injuring the right of the other party to receive the fruits of the contract."

In a number of cases an express covenant to exploit a patent has been enforced against an exclusive licensee.

We think this license made the defendant an exclusive licensee though it is true that the non-exclusive license to Westinghouse remained in effect. The argument that the Westinghouse license prevented the defendant from becoming an exclusive licensee does not take wholly into account the legal meaning of that term. As this court explained in *Western Electric Co. v. Pacent Reproducer Corp.*, 2 Cir., 42 F.2d 116, it is not the equivalent of "sole licensee." A license can have the attributes which make it exclusive in the legal sense though it is not the only license. There may be one or more previous licenses which are non-exclusive and by contrast with the exclusive license are called bare. When this is so the exclusive license does not, of course, cover the entire field but it binds the licensor not to enlarge thereafter the scope of other licenses already granted or increase the number of licenses. It is plain that these parties intended that the defendant should to that extent be free from competition in the manufacture and sale of trays made under the licensed patents and it is equally plain that they expected the defendant to make and sell trays on which royalties would become due and not merely to pay a guaranteed minimum royalty. The license provided that, "All guaranteed minimum royalties paid [shall] be considered as advance royalty payments and shall be credited against royalties earned under Article Sixth hereof, regardless of when said royalties are earned."

[The] rule of implied covenant of an exclusive licensee to exploit the licensed device in good faith rests, as the doctrine always has rested, upon the ground that not to hold the licensee to that standard of conduct would be unfair and inequitable as between the parties to the license.

There is one well recognized exception to the doctrine as it has previously been applied. That is where there is outside competition which the exclusive licensee cannot meet with reasonable chance of success with the licensed article. If such competition comes from something not commercially better than the licensed device he must meet it by means of the latter. If he sees fit to overcome the competition by purchasing the right to make the competing article, he cannot substitute the latter for the licensed device without thereby violating his covenant to exploit so long as he retains an exclusive license. But if the competition comes from a better article than the one licensed, he is under no obligation to try with no hope of success to meet it with the licensed device. Faced with such a business situation he may, if he can, obtain and exercise the right to make or use the competing article without violating any obligation to exploit under his exclusive license.

Paragraph Eleventh (b) of the license shows that the parties contemplated that their construction of the patent claims might be narrowed by court decision and that, if they were so narrowed, devices which the defendant had made and on which it had paid running royalties could thereafter be manufactured and sold royalty-free. The trays of type 2 and 3 were in this category. The continued manufacture, use and sale of them without payment of running royalties was, therefore, permissible in accordance with the express provisions of the license and no obligation to the contrary can be implied.

Otherwise, however, any obligation to exploit in good faith remained unaffected, for there was no competition to justify a failure by the defendant to do so. The court below found in accordance with sufficient evidence that "Defendant's type 7 tray did not differ materially from and was the commercial equivalent of its type 4 tray. The only reason defendant began manufacturing the type 4 tray in October 1940 was to avoid the payment of royalties to plaintiffs on the type 7 tray under the April 1, 1936, agreement. To accomplish this purpose the lever of the type 4 tray was so shaped and positioned as not to fulcrum on the flange of the tray but on the longitudinal member of the grid. The action of the defendant in making this change was not attributable to any competition." It was in view of this action of the defendant so motivated that the trial judge held that there had been a breach of an implied covenant to exploit.

Assuming, arguendo, that there was an implied covenant not to compete with the licensed trays except to meet outside competition, this manufacture and sale of the type 4 tray was not a breach of it provided the parties had agreed that the defendant might make and sell that tray royalty free. The exercise of good faith in exploiting the licensed patents did not require the defendant to refrain from doing whatever the plaintiffs had expressly agreed that it might do. No obligation not to manufacture and sell whatever kind of trays the license gave the defendant the right so to manufacture and sell can be implied and of course there can be no breach of a non-existent obligation.

Although the type 4 tray was correctly found to be a modification of the type 7 tray, it was in fact also no more than a modification of the type 2 and type 3 trays. The court found that "Type 4 embodies the moveable transverse sections of types 2 and 3 and the two-part structure of the longitudinal member of the grid of type 3. In structure and mode of operation to effect the release of ice blocks from the grid it is quite similar to types 2 and 3." The similarity in operation just mentioned is so close that it is identical. The only mechanical difference is that already mentioned which is the attachment of the lever of type 4 to the grid near one end instead of nearer the center as in the 2 and 3 types. Mechanically the three types, 2, 3 and 4 are equivalent.

There was no covenant, express or implied, limiting the number of types 2 and 3 trays which the defendant could manufacture and sell after the *Abraham & Straus* decision. As type 4 was mechanically, structurally, and commercially the equivalent of types 2 and 3 the manufacture and sale of it was included in the permission to manufacture and sell such trays without limitation.

It should be noticed that the defendant is not charged with having failed to manufacture and sell any trays under the [license]. The record shows that it did continue to sell type 7 trays and sold 1,440,000 on which it paid royalties between April 1, 1940 and December 1, 1942. The second cause of action was therefore not proved and the judgment thereon must be reversed.

Judgment [reversed as to this cause of action].

NOTE

The theme that a "good faith" obligation cannot over-ride express terms is common in licensing and other contract law cases. In the absence of an express clause, how should a court handle a case where the parties were aware of the licensee's involvement in multiple, overlapping products and the licensee must make choices based on its market judgment, relative cost, or other ordinary business considerations? Cases where such choices must be made are common in patent and copyright licensing. In literary fields, the implied obligation is sometimes described as an obligation to "use reasonable efforts to make the work as productive as the circumstances warrant." DAVID NIMMER & MELVILLE NIMMER, NIMMER ON COPYRIGHT § 10.11. What is the substantive content of such an obligation? Under what circumstances is the obligation breached?

PROBLEM 4.4

Studio is a producer and distributor of motion pictures. It has an "inventory" of five thousand motion picture scripts. Many were written by independent authors. Studio holds rights to these under "perpetual," exclusive licenses. Sam is one of the authors. For the past seven years, Sam has been seething with indignation about the fact that no motion picture has been made from the script. The contract with Studio gave Sam an initial payment of $5,000 and a royalty of 5% from the net profits of any motion picture made by Studio based on his script. During these several years, Studio has produced at least ten other motion pictures that have stories similar to Sam's. Several were success-ful, but others were not. Sam, however, does not claim that these other motion pictures infringe the copyright on the script.

a. Sam sues to break the contract. Studio proves that it decided not to pro-duce a picture based on the script because in its judgment the script was not sufficiently exciting for the market. It nevertheless refuses to release its exclu-sive license. What result?

b. As counsel for the Studio, how would you draft the licenses to avoid the risk of losing to people such as Sam?

B. Standing to Sue for Infringement

The most litigated issue involving rights or obligations in an exclusive license concerns the right of an exclusive licensee to sue a third party (or the licensor) for infringement of the licensed subject matter. We previously dis-cussed one case dealing with this issue in a patent infringement context, the *Rite-Hite* case. The following cases expand on that discussion and point to potentially important differences in standing to sue among the different types of intellectual property.

TEXTILE PRODUCTIONS, INC. v. MEAD CORPORATION
134 F.3d 1481 (Fed. Cir. 1998)

RADER, CIRCUIT JUDGE.

The United States District Court for the Eastern District of Michigan dis-missed Textile Production, Inc.'s (Textile's) complaint with prejudice in favor of The Mead Corporation (Mead) and Fiber Trim Sewing Company (Fiber Trim). Because Textile is not an exclusive licensee and therefore has no stand-ing to sue for patent infringement, this court affirms the district court's dis-missal of Textile's infringement claim. However, because Textile may have also asserted a claim for breach of contract against Mead, this court vacates the district court's dismissal of the complaint and remands with instructions.

I.

During the late 1980s, employees of Mead and Textile collaborated on solv-ing a problem for Ford Motor Company, one of Mead's customers. . . . In October 1989, Textile filed a United States patent application on behalf of the inventors of the harness. In February 1990, while the patent application was still pending, Textile and Mead executed a General Agreement and a Purchase Agreement. Under the General Agreement, the parties agreed to split the costs of prosecuting the application and to concurrently execute the Purchase Agreement. The General Agreement also contained two other rele-vant provisions:

> 5. Upon conclusion of the examination of the PATENT APPLICATION, [Textile] shall assign its entire interest in and to any and all patents derived therefrom to [Mead].

6. Should any aforesaid assigned patent be proposed by [Mead] for reissue or reexamination, or become the subject of litigation, [Mead] shall give reasonable notice to [Textile] and shall allow [Textile] to participate, through its . . . counsel, in any such proceeding on any reasonable basis directed to protecting [Textile's] interests therein and in this Agreement. . . .

The Purchase Agreement provided that Mead would "purchase" and Textile would "manufacture and supply" 100% of Mead's "requirements" for the wire harness sock product. Textile was to be Mead's "exclusive source" and Mead was to be Textile's "sole customer" for the "PRODUCT." The Purchase Agreement defined the "PRODUCT" as anything "covered within the literal description found in any then currently existing claim" of the pending U.S. patent application "or any U.S. patent which may be granted thereon." The Purchase Agreement also had a "second source contingency" provision. This provision provided:

16. Second Source Contingency.

(a) If [Textile] cannot or shall not meet [Mead's] reasonable delivery requirements for the PRODUCT, then [Mead] shall have the right to obtain elsewhere (for the duration of [Textile's] failure to supply) the PRODUCT in the amount of any shortfall. . . .

(b) In the event that a customer of [Mead] requires a second source of supply of the PRODUCT, [Mead] has the right to grant the necessary licenses so that the customer shall have the right to obtain the PRODUCT from a source other than [Textile] and [Mead] shall split with [Textile] any royalty fees received from such other source by [Mead]. . . .

The Purchase Agreement set its own term as the greater of (1) three years, (2) the pendency of the U.S. patent application, or (3) the term of any last-to-expire U.S. patent that issued.

On May 21, 1991, the application issued as U.S. Patent No. 5,016,859 ("the '859 patent"). Under the General Agreement, Textile assigned the patent to Mead. . . . In March 1995, without notifying Textile, Mead contacted Fiber Trim about manufacturing harnesses. Mead purchased part of its requirements from Fiber Trim until September 1995. At that point, Textile discovered that Fiber Trim was manufacturing the harnesses. In the ensuing dispute, Mead notified Textile that it was suspending performance under the Purchase Agreement.

Textile filed suit against Mead and Fiber Trim, alleging that Textile was an exclusive licensee of the '859 patent with an exclusive nationwide license to make the invention and that Mead and Fiber Trim had infringed this right. . . . Mead and Fiber Trim filed a motion for summary judgment challenging Textile's standing to assert patent infringement. The district court found that Textile did not have standing to sue for patent infringement as an exclusive licensee. . . . Textile appeals.

II.

[Only] a patentee may bring an action for patent infringement. Title 35 defines "patentee" as the party to whom the patent issued or any successors in title to the patent. *See* 35 U.S.C. § 100(d) (1994). A licensee is not entitled to bring suit in its own name as a patentee, unless the licensee holds "all substantial rights" under the patent. Such a licensee is in effect an "assignee" and therefore a patentee.

Thus, although a patentee has standing to sue in its own name, an exclusive licensee that does not have all substantial rights has standing to sue third parties only as a co-plaintiff with the patentee. At least one exception to that rule exists, however: an exclusive licensee that does not have all substantial rights does have standing to sue in his own name when "necessary to prevent an absolute failure of justice, as where the patentee is the infringer, and cannot sue himself." *Waterman v. Mackenzie*, 138 U.S. 252, 255, 34 L. Ed. 923, 11 S. Ct. 334 (1891); *Ortho Pharm. Corp. v. Genetics Inst., Inc.*, 52 F.3d 1026, 1030 (Fed. Cir. 1995). On the other hand, a bare licensee has no standing at all.

Determining whether a licensee is an exclusive licensee or a bare licensee is a question of ascertaining the intent of the parties to the license as manifested by the terms of their agreement and examining the substance of the grant. The use of the word "exclusive" is not controlling; what matters is the substance of the arrangement. Because patent rights are rights to "exclude others," a licensee is an exclusive licensee only if the patentee has promised, expressly or impliedly, that "others shall be excluded from practicing the invention" within the field covered by the license. Put another way, an exclusive license is "a license to practice the invention . . . accompanied by the patent owner's promise that others shall be excluded from practicing it within the field of use wherein the licensee is given leave." Thus, if a patentee-licensor is free to grant licenses to others, licensees under that patent are not exclusive licensees.

III.

In this case, Textile asserts that it is an exclusive licensee — not an assignee — yet it seeks to bring an infringement action in its own name. Normally, this alone would be sufficient grounds to dismiss Textile's infringement claim. However, Textile invokes the exception outlined above, claiming that although Mead is the patentee, it is also "liable as an infringer." *See* 35 U.S.C. § 271(b).

However, only an exclusive licensee has standing to sue for infringement, even under the exception outlined above. The task before this court, therefore, is to determine whether Textile is actually an exclusive licensee or is simply a bare licensee.

This case presents the question of whether a requirements contract for a patented product automatically converts the exclusive supplier into an exclusive licensee of the patent. The contractual manufacturing rights of a party do not alone, however, confer a right to exclude all others from making an invention. To qualify as an exclusive license, an agreement must clearly manifest the patentee's promise to refrain from granting to anyone else a license in the area of exclusivity. The agreement between Mead and Textile does not clearly manifest a promise by Mead to do so.

The terms of paragraphs (a) and (b) of the "second source contingency" provision, however, in combination with Mead's covenant to purchase all its requirements from Textile, do restrict Mead's ability to license third parties to some extent. Mead's express covenant to purchase all its requirements from Textile prevents Mead from licensing others to make the invention for Mead. Although paragraph (a) makes it clear that the restriction is not absolute, any right Mead has to license others to supply its own requirements arises only on the occurrence of conditions precedent. These conditions require a shortfall in Textile's performance and an opportunity to meet Mead's demands.

Similarly, paragraph (b) of the "second source contingency" provision, as properly construed, contains an implied promise that Mead will not license others to make the invention for Mead's customers. Again, although the paragraph expressly demonstrates that Mead has the right to do so, this right arises only on occurrence of a condition precedent, namely, that a Mead customer "requires" it.

However, both Agreements are silent about Mead's ability to grant licenses to suppliers for non-Mead customers or to those who wish to make the invention for their own use. In the face of Textile's promise to "assign its entire interest in and to any and all patents derived therefrom to [Mead]," this court must assume that Mead retained such rights. Thus, Mead did not promise that all others (beyond Textile) "shall be excluded from [making the invention]." Mead retained the right to license third parties to manufacture the harness for their own use or for sale to others. In sum, Mead did not grant Textile the rights of an exclusive licensee, but retained for itself important rights to license the invention to others.

In an effort to show that the Agreements result in more than just a requirements contract coupled with a bare license, Textile points to three other aspects of the Agreements. First, Textile asserts that because the term of the Purchase Agreement is coextensive with the term of the '859 patent, it shows the parties intended to grant an exclusive license under the patent. Yet, this provision of the Agreement is just as consistent with a bare license as it is with an exclusive license. Second, Textile points to the requirement that Mead split any royalty with Textile if paragraph (b) of the "second source contingency" provision is ever invoked. Although this is not a provision ordinarily found in a bare license agreement, it is not inconsistent with a bare license. More importantly, it does not evidence a covenant by Mead to not permit others to make the invention. Finally, Textile points to the General Agreement's "participation in litigation" provision. Again, however, this provision does not show that Mead gave Textile an exclusive right to make the invention. The right to participate in litigation does not necessarily encompass the right to participate as a party. Even if this provision were read broadly to give Textile an independent right to sue in Mead's name, such a provision would be ineffectual of its own force. A "right to sue" provision within a license cannot, of its own force, confer standing on a bare licensee. Accordingly, the district court correctly determined that Textile was not an exclusive licensee of the '859 patent and had no standing to assert patent infringement.

IV.

[Accordingly,] this court affirms the district court's dismissal of Textile's infringement claim, vacates the district court's dismissal of the complaint, and remands with instructions.

INTELLECTUAL PROPERTY DEVELOPMENT, INC. v. TCI CABLEVISION OF CALIFORNIA, INC.
248 F.3d 1333 (Fed. Cir. 2001)

Gajarsa, Circuit Judge.

TCI Cablevision of California, Inc. ("TCI-California") appeals the January 27, 2000 order of the United States District Court for the Central District of California, No. 99-CV-2982 (C.D. Cal. Jan. 27, 2000). The district court granted the motion filed by Intellectual Property Development, Inc. ("IPD") and Communications Patents Ltd. ("CPL") to dismiss its complaint against TCI-California with [prejudice]. We affirm.

Background

CPL . . . is the assignee of United States Patent No. 4,135,202 ("the '202 patent"), which issued in 1979. The '202 patent covers certain wired broadcasting systems. CPL entered liquidation on May 12, 1993. On June 30, 1993, acting through a liquidator, CPL and IPD entered into an agreement that granted IPD numerous rights in the '202 patent. The agreement accords IPD "an exclusive license, to make, use, and sell the inventions, the right to grant sublicenses, the right to collect monies, damages and/or royalties for past infringement and the right to bring legal action to collect the same." Further, the agreement provides:

> [IPD] shall be entitled to take action under the ['202 patent] in [IPD's] own name to prevent infringement, or to collect damages for past infringement, or to defend proceedings for revocation in circumstances where [CPL] is not a necessary party to that action (a "Sole Action") provided that [IPD] notifies [CPL] in writing. . . . [IPD] shall keep [CPL] fully informed and consult with [CPL] about the conduct of the Sole Action. [IPD] shall not without the prior written consent of [CPL], which shall not be unreasonably withheld, settle or agree to any compromise. . . . In the event that [CPL] may be a necessary party to any litigation or legal action under the ['202 patent] (a "Joint Action") [IPD] shall not proceed with the Joint Action without the prior written consent of [CPL]. [CPL] reserves the right to withdraw consent to the Joint Action proceeding at any time up to termination of the Joint Action. . . . [IPD] further agrees to pay [CPL] fifty percent (50%) of the net profit of [IPD] derived from . . . realisations [sic] realised [sic]: such as but not limited to litigation.

The rights CPL granted to IPD are subject to a nonexclusive license in the '202 patent that CPL previously granted to [Cabletime Limited]. Additionally, the agreement provides that CPL maintains the right to "assign all [of its] rights and obligations" under the agreement and further allows CPL to prevent IPD from assigning its benefits under the agreement to a third party without prior written consent from CPL.

On September 1, 1994, IPD filed a suit against UA-Columbia Cablevision of Westchester, Inc. ("UA-Westchester") and Tele Communications, Inc. ("TCI") in the United States District Court for the Southern District of New York (the "New York case"). IPD asserted that UA Westchester and TCI infringed the '202 patent prior to its expiration on January 16, 1996. . . . On May 15, 1995, TCI filed a motion to dismiss the New York case on the grounds that IPD lacked standing, or alternatively, because CPL was an indispensable party. Subsequently, by letter, CPL agreed to be bound by any judgment in the New York case. On September 8, 1995, the judge in the New York case determined that IPD maintained standing to bring the suit in its own name. . . .

On April 6, 1999, IPD filed a motion with the Judicial Panel for Multi-District Litigation ("JPML") to consolidate the 1999 cases and the New York case. On April 19, 1999, while the motion to consolidate was pending before the JPML, TCI-California moved to dismiss [for] lack of subject matter jurisdiction, or alternatively, based on IPD's failure to join an indispensable party — CPL. [On] May 26, 1999, the district court issued an order (the "May 26, 1999 order") in which it granted TCI California's motion to dismiss for "lack of standing." The court, however, delayed signing the order to allow IPD to amend its complaint to add CPL as a party plaintiff and thereby rectify its "lack of standing." . . . Thereafter, IPD amended its complaint to add CPL as a party on June 21, 1999.

The district court, on June 28, 1999, denied TCI-California's motion for reconsideration and also clarified its May 26, 1999 order. The court stated that in the May 26, 1999 order, it had not held "that [IPD] lacked any element of constitutional standing so as to deprive the [c]ourt of jurisdiction over this case." It explained that "IPD made an adequate showing on the three elements required by the Constitution for standing to exist". . . . The court also indicated that it "found IPD to be an exclusive licensee that alleged a legally cognizable injury" and therefore noted that "[t]he [c]ourt's use of the words 'lack of standing' in the May 26[, 1999] Order referred to a prudential limitation on IPD's right to bring suit without joining the patentee." That is, the court determined that the rights retained by the patent owner, CPL, are "of the type that make a patent owner who granted an exclusive license a necessary party to an infringement action brought by the licensee." Therefore, the court concluded by indicating that in its May 26, 1999 order it recognized that as an exclusive licensee, IPD did not have standing to sue in its own name and consequently the court required joinder of the patent owner, CPL. . . .

On August 19, 1999, the JPML consolidated the 1999 cases and the New York case and transferred them to the United States District Court for the Central District of California, where this case was pending, for joint pretrial proceedings. IPD subsequently entered into tolling agreements with several TCI subsidiaries, which resulted in the stipulated dismissal of all of the 1999 cases other than the case at bar.

[On] January 27, 2000, the district court granted IPD and CPL's motion for voluntary dismissal, which effected the dismissal of its complaint with prejudice and the dismissal of TCI-California's counterclaims for lack of subject matter jurisdiction without prejudice. TCI-California appeals the district court's failure to dismiss the initial complaint — filed solely by IPD — for lack of standing and its subsequent grant of the motion for voluntary dismissal. . . .

[D. IPD's Standing in the District Court]

1. Rights Transferred from CPL to IPD

A patent is "a bundle of rights which may be divided and assigned, or retained in whole or in part." To determine whether a patent transfer agreement conveys all substantial rights under a patent to a transferee or fewer than all of those rights, a court must assess the substance of the rights transferred and the intention of the parties involved.

In making such a determination, it is helpful to consider rights retained by the grantor in addition to rights transferred to the grantee. In the case at issue, under the CPL-IPD agreement, while IPD possesses an "exclusive license to make, use, and sell" the invention claimed in the '202 patent, CPL retains: (1) the right in certain circumstances (when CPL is a "necessary" party) to require IPD to obtain its consent to proceed with litigation (which can be withdrawn "at any time" until termination of the litigation); (2) the right in other circumstances (when CPL is not a "necessary" party) to be fully informed and to be consulted with regard to litigation; (3) the right to assign "all [of its] rights and obligations" under the agreement; (4) the right to prevent IPD from assigning its benefit under the agreement to a third party without prior written consent from CPL; (5) the right to require its consent to settlements (which shall not be "unreasonably withheld"); and (6) the right to collect fifty percent of profits realized from litigation.

This court has addressed the issue of whether an agreement transfers all or fewer than all substantial patent rights on several occasions. In *Abbott Laboratories v. Diamedix Corp.*, 47 F.3d 1128, 33 USPQ2d 1771 (Fed.Cir.1995), this court determined that a transfer of certain, but not all, patent rights from Diamedix to Abbott constituted an exclusive license of fewer than all substantial patent rights rather than an assignment of all such rights. In that case, Diamedix retained the right to make and use the products claimed in the patents for its own benefit and the right to sell those products to parties with whom Diamedix maintained pre-existing contracts and licenses. While Abbott was given the right of first refusal to sue alleged infringers, Diamedix retained the right to bring its own infringement actions. That is, although Abbott possessed the right to initiate suit for infringement, it could not "indulge" or permit an infringement, which the *Abbott* court indicated normally accompanies a complete conveyance of the right to sue. Diamedix also retained the right to prevent Abbott from assigning its rights under the license to any party other than a successor in business. Finally, the *Abbott* court noted that it appeared that Diamedix retained the right to participate in a suit brought by Abbott because the agreement provided that Diamedix is "entitled to be represented therein by counsel of its own selection at its own expense." For these reasons, the *Abbott* court held that Abbott was granted fewer than all substantial rights under the patents.

Conversely, in *Vaupel* [*Textilmaschinen KG v. Meccanica Euro Italia S.P.S.*, 944 F.2d 870, 873, 20 U.S.P.Q.2D (BNA) 1045, 1047 (Fed. Cir. 1991)], this court determined that an agreement transferring certain patent rights from Markowsky to Vaupel constituted an assignment of all substantial rights in the patent at issue. Markowsky retained: (1) a veto right on sublicensing by Vaupel; (2) the right to obtain patents on the invention in other countries; (3) a reversionary right to the patent in the event of bankruptcy or termination of production by Vaupel; and (4) a right to receive infringement damages. The *Vaupel* court stated that it found "particularly dispositive" the agreement provision that transferred the right to sue for infringement of the patent at issue subject only to the obligation to *inform* Markowsky.

This court recently determined in *Speedplay, Inc. v. Bebop, Inc.*, 211 F.3d 1245, 53 USPQ2d 1984 (Fed.Cir.2000), that an agreement transferring certain patent rights constituted an assignment of all substantial rights in the patents at issue. The agreement in *Speedplay* effected a transfer from Bryne and Zoumaras to Speedplay of the exclusive right to manufacture, have manufactured, distribute, market, use and sell products covered by the patents at issue. Bryne and Zoumaras, however, retained the option to initiate legal action against an alleged infringer in their own name, but only if Speedplay failed to bring such a suit within three months. Yet, the agreement at issue in *Speedplay* did not grant Bryne and Zoumaras the right to participate in an infringement action brought by Speedplay, nor did it limit Speedplay's management of any such action. This court determined that Bryne and Zoumaras's right to sue an infringer was illusory because Speedplay could render that right nugatory by granting the alleged infringer a royalty-free sublicense. Indeed, the *Speedplay* court concluded, "Speedplay . . . controls enforcement of [the patent at issue] for all practical purposes." Finally, while Speedplay could not assign its interest without consent from Bryne and Zoumaras, the agreement provided that such consent "shall not be withheld unreasonably." The court deemed this provision not significantly restrictive of the scope of Speedplay's patent rights.

Guided by the aforementioned jurisprudence, we must assess the agreement at issue in this case, weighing the rights in the '202 patent transferred to IPD against those retained by CPL, to determine whether CPL assigned all substantial rights in the '202 patent to IPD or conveyed fewer than all such rights. The title of the agreement at issue, which uses the term "license" rather than the term "assignment," is not determinative of the nature of the rights transferred under the agreement; actual consideration of the rights transferred is the linchpin of such a determination.

Under the agreement at issue, IPD is granted the right to "make, use, and sell" the invention claimed in the '202 patent. The agreement fails to suggest that CPL continues to possess similar rights as this court found salient in *Abbott*. While this right transferred to IPD is substantial, every other pertinent factor weighs in favor of finding that the agreement is an exclusive license of fewer than all substantial rights in the '202 patent.

In both *Vaupel* and *Speedplay,* contrary to *Abbott,* the transferees effectively obtained the sole right to sue other parties for infringement. The right to sue in *Vaupel,* which was deemed "particularly dispositive," was only subject to an obligation to *inform* the transferor of any impending litigation. In *Speedplay,* this court determined that the transferors' right to sue an infringer was illusory. Further, in *Mentor H/S, Inc. v. Medical Device Alliance,* 240 F.3d 1016, 1018, 57 USPQ2d 1819, 1820 (Fed.Cir.2001), this court deemed the transferee of patent rights to be an exclusive licensee of fewer than all substantial rights rather than an assignee of all of those rights in large part because the transferor retained the first opportunity to sue alleged infringers; that is, the transferee could only file such suits if the transferor failed to file a suit.

Pursuant to the agreement in the case at bar, CPL retains differing rights depending on whether it is a "necessary" party. The agreement fails to elucidate cogently the definition of "necessary." Yet, it suffices to recognize that in certain circumstances — when CPL is a "necessary" party — CPL must consent to litigation and can withdraw that consent at any time. That is, CPL can permit infringement when it is a "necessary" party, which is relevant to a finding that CPL granted IPD fewer than all substantial rights in the '202 patent. Indeed, a transferee that receives all substantial patent rights from a transferor would never need consent from the transferor to file suit because such an assignment essentially transfers title in the patent to the transferee. 35 U.S.C. § 100(d) (1994). Further, even if CPL is not a "necessary party" to a suit, IPD must keep CPL fully informed, and consult with CPL, as to any litigation pertaining to the patents at issue in the agreement.[1]

CPL also retains the right to prevent IPD from assigning its benefits to a third party without first receiving CPL's consent. The *Abbott* court indicated that limits on a transferee's assignment rights weigh in favor of finding that an agreement constitutes a transfer of fewer than all substantial rights in a patent. Similarly, while the *Vaupel* court found that the agreement at issue in that case constituted an assignment of all substantial patent rights, it nevertheless recognized that a restriction on a transferee's right to assign is a substantial right reserved by the transferor. We also recognize that limits on the assignment of rights are a factor weighing in favor of finding a transfer of fewer than all substantial rights in the '202 patent.

In light of CPL's right to permit infringement in certain cases, the requirement that CPL consent to certain actions and be consulted in others, and the limits on IPD's right to assign its interests in the '202 patent, we find that the CPL IPD agreement at issue transfers fewer than all substantial rights in the '202 patent from CPL to IPD.

2. Article III and Prudential Standing Requirements

Standing in a patent infringement case is derived from the Patent Act, which provides: "A patentee shall have remedy by civil action for infringement of his patent." 35 U.S.C. § 281 (1994). The term "patentee" comprises "not only

---

[1] [FN 21] While CPL must consent to settlement of a litigation by IPD, that consent cannot be "unreasonably withheld." In Speedplay, a consent requirement pertaining to assignment of rights that could not be "unreasonably withheld" was deemed not significantly restrictive of the scope of Speedplay's patent rights. Therefore, we find this factor to be neutral.

the patentee to whom the patent was issued but also the successors in title to the patentee." 35 U.S.C. § 100(d) (1994).

A grant of all substantial rights in a patent amounts to an assignment — that is, a transfer of title in the patent — which confers constitutional standing on the assignee to sue another for patent infringement in its own name. Conversely, a nonexclusive license or "bare" license — a covenant by the patent owner not to sue the licensee for making, using, or selling the patented invention and under which the patent owner reserves the right to grant similar licenses to other entities — confers no constitutional standing on the licensee under the Patent Act to bring suit or even to join a suit with the patentee because a nonexclusive (or "bare") licensee suffers no legal injury from infringement. It is clear that IPD is an exclusive licensee rather than a non-exclusive or "bare" licensee. An exclusive licensee receives more substantial rights in a patent than a nonexclusive licensee, but receives fewer rights than an assignee of all substantial patent rights. For example, an exclusive licensee could receive the exclusive right to practice an invention within a given limited territory.

As stated earlier, IPD is an exclusive licensee that has some, but fewer than all, substantial rights in the '202 patent. TCI-California argues that CPL should have been a required party to the district court suit at the outset of the litigation. That is, TCI-California contends that as an exclusive licensee having fewer than all substantial rights in the '202 patent, IPD lacked Article III standing to bring suit in its own name and could not create standing, and thus jurisdiction, by simply joining CPL rather than by dismissing the case and refiling jointly with CPL. Therefore, TCI-California asserts that the district court judge improperly allowed IPD to amend its complaint to add CPL as a party plaintiff.

TCI-California points out that the Supreme Court has stated: "The actual or threatened injury required by Article III may exist solely by virtue of 'statutes creating legal rights, the invasion of which creates standing. . . .'" *Warth v. Seldin,* 422 U.S. 490, 500, 95 S.Ct. 2197, 45 L.Ed.2d 343 (1975) (quoting *Linda R.S. v. Richard D.,* 410 U.S. 614, 617 n. 3, 93 S.Ct. 1146, 35 L.Ed.2d 536 (1973)). Because the Patent Act creates the sole remedy for infringement of a patent and because the Patent Act indicates that only "patentees" and "assignees" shall have a remedy for patent infringement, *see* 35 U.S.C. §§ 281 and 100(d), TCI-California contends that, under *Warth,* only a "patentee" or an "assignee" (and not an "exclusive licensee" having fewer than all substantial patent rights) possesses Article III standing to bring a patent infringement suit. Further, TCI-California cites a footnote in *Lujan v. Defenders of Wildlife,* 504 U.S. 555, 571 n. 4, 112 S.Ct. 2130, 119 L.Ed.2d 351 (1992), for the proposition that a constitutional standing defect cannot be cured by joinder. That is, TCI-California asserts that federal jurisdiction must exist at the time an action is filed.

Article III standing requires a party invoking federal jurisdiction to establish three elements. First, the plaintiff "must have suffered an injury in fact — an invasion of a legally protected interest which is (a) concrete and particularized and (b) 'actual or imminent, not conjectural or hypothetical.'" Second, "there must be a causal connection between the injury and the conduct complained of-the injury has to be 'fairly . . . trace[able] to the challenged action of the defendant and not . . . th[e] result [of] the independent action of some third party not before the court.'" *Id.* (citations omitted). Third, "it must be 'likely,' as opposed to merely 'speculative,' that the injury will be 'redressed by a favorable decision.'"

TCI-California is correct in its assertion that Article III standing to sue in this case derives solely from the Patent Act. Section 281 of title 35 of the United States Code provides: "A patentee shall have remedy by civil action for infringement of his patent." A "patentee" includes "not only the patentee to whom the patent was issued but also the successors in title [assignees] to the patentee." 35 U.S.C. § 100(d). This statutory language, however, fails to limit Article III standing to patentees and assignees. As discussed above, IPD is an exclusive licensee having fewer than all substantial rights in the '202 patent. To determine whether IPD possesses constitutional standing, we must consider whether IPD meets each *Lujan* factor.

A party such as IPD that has the right to exclude others from making, using, and selling an invention described in the claims of a patent is constitutionally injured by another entity that makes, uses, or sells the invention. Indeed, the Supreme Court has stated that a patent owner that grants "the exclusive right to make, use, or vend [a patented invention], which does not constitute a statutory assignment . . . must allow the use of his name as plaintiff in any action brought by the licensee . . . to obtain damages for the *injury to his exclusive right.*"

Further, IPD's injury is directly related to the allegedly infringing conduct of TCI-California. This relationship meets the "fairly traceable" standard for causation described in *Lujan*. Finally, IPD's injury is redressable because, if successful in an infringement suit against TCI-California, IPD could recover damages pursuant to 35 U.S.C. § 284 and could prohibit TCI-California from further making, using and selling its allegedly infringing products under 35 U.S.C. § 283. Indeed, this court has awarded damages to exclusive licensees as compensation for patent infringement injuries. *Weinar v. Rollform, Inc.,* 744 F.2d 797, 807-08, 223 USPQ 369, 374-75 (Fed.Cir.1984). In sum, IPD meets the three-pronged *Lujan* test for Article III standing.

Moreover, it was proper for IPD, as an exclusive licensee of fewer than all substantial rights in the '202 patent, to add CPL as a party plaintiff. The Supreme Court addressed the right to sue for patent infringement under a predecessor patent statute in *Independent Wireless* [*Tel. Co. v. Radio Corp. of Am.,* 269 U.S. 459, 468-69 (1926)], a case involving an exclusive licensee (as distinguished from an assignee) that sought to obtain an injunction and damages against an alleged patent infringer without joining the patent owner to the suit. The Court stated:

> The presence of the owner of the patent as a party is indispensable, not only to give jurisdiction under patent laws, but also in most cases to enable the alleged infringer to respond in one action to all claims of infringement for his act, and thus either to defeat all claims in the one action, or by satisfying one adverse decree to bar all subsequent actions.

Id. at 468, 46 S.Ct. 166.

The *Independent Wireless* Court recognized an exception to this rule in circumstances where a patent owner refuses, or is unable, to be joined as a co-plaintiff with an exclusive licensee. In such cases, "the licensee may make [the patent owner] a party defendant by process [that is, involuntarily], and he will be lined up by the court in the party character he should assume."

The *Independent Wireless* Court then explained that:

> [T]he owner of a patent, who grants to another the exclusive right to make, use, or vend the invention, which does not constitute a statutory assignment, holds title to the patent in trust for such licensee, to the extent that he must allow the use of his name as plaintiff in any action brought at the instance of the licensee in law or in equity to obtain damages for the injury to his exclusive right by an infringer, or to enjoin infringement of it.

Id. at 469, 46 S.Ct. 166.

As a general rule, in accordance with *Independent Wireless,* this court adheres to the principle that a patent owner should be joined, either voluntarily or involuntarily, in any patent infringement suit brought by an exclusive licensee having fewer than all substantial patent rights. That is, unlike an assignee that may sue in its own name, an exclusive licensee having fewer than all substantial patent rights (that is not subject to an exception) that seeks to enforce its rights in a patent generally must sue jointly with the patent owner.

The general principle set forth in *Independent Wireless* requiring that a patent owner be joined, either voluntarily or involuntarily, in any infringement suit brought by an exclusive licensee having fewer than all substantial rights is prudential rather than constitutional. In addition to the three-prong Article III standing test delineated in *Lujan,* standing doctrine embraces judicially self-imposed limits, known as prudential limits, on the exercise of jurisdiction.

As a prudential principle, an exclusive licensee having fewer than all substantial patent rights possesses standing under the Patent Act as long as it sues in the name of, and jointly with, the patent owner and meets the *Lujan* requirements. This principle holds true except in extraordinary circumstances, such as where the infringer is the patentee and cannot sue itself. Indeed, the Supreme Court in *Independent Wireless* recognized that when an exclusive licensee files a patent infringement suit, "the presence of the owner of a patent as a party is indispensable . . . to give jurisdiction under the patent laws. . . ."

3. IPD's Joinder of CPL

TCI-California argues that because IPD, an exclusive licensee having fewer than all substantial rights in the '202 patent, initially filed this suit in its own name, the district court lacked jurisdiction and therefore could not grant IPD leave to amend its complaint to add CPL as a party. However, this court has recognized the principle that a patent owner may be joined by an exclusive licensee. For example, in *Abbott,* an exclusive licensee having fewer than all substantial patent rights brought a patent infringement suit in its own name. Thereafter, the patent owner filed a motion to intervene. This court determined that the patent owner's "joinder [was] required as a matter of statutory standing." Yet, the court did not dismiss the case for lack of jurisdiction and require that the patent owner and exclusive licensee jointly refile. Rather, the court reversed the district court's denial of the motion to intervene.

TCI-California cites footnote four of the Supreme Court's *Lujan* decision for the proposition that a standing defect cannot be cured by joinder of a party to a suit. TCI-California's reliance on this footnote is misplaced. In *Lujan,* the Supreme Court determined that the plaintiffs lacked constitutional standing because they failed to assert a sufficiently imminent injury and because their claimed injury was not redressable. As discussed above, IPD met the constitutional requirements for standing from the outset of its suit. Therefore, the cited portion of *Lujan* is inapposite.

Conclusion

For the reasons set forth in this opinion, we affirm the district court's order, which effected dismissal of the complaint filed by IPD and CPL with prejudice and dismissal of TCI-California's counterclaims without prejudice.

Affirmed.

NOTES

1. Under *TCI*, what contractual terms alter the status of an "exclusive license" for purposes of standing? Does the absence of a contractual grant to the licensee to bring infringement claims mean that the licensee is a bare licensee? What about the right to collect and control infringement settlements? The right to transfer its rights?

2. We have three categories in reference to patent infringement claims: 1) exclusive with standing to sue in its own name, 2) exclusive with right to sue by joining the patent owner, 3) not exclusive and, therefore, no right to sue at all. To what extent are these categories mandated by constitutional concerns? Statutory concerns?

ICEE DISTRIBUTORS, INC. v. J&J SNACK FOODS CORP.
325 F.3d 586 (5th Cir. 2003)

PATRICK E. HIGGENBOTHAM, CIRCUIT JUDGE:

These appeals concern a disagreement between two ICEE distributors as to whether one, J&J Snack Foods, can distribute frozen ICEE squeeze-up tubes of various flavors in the same territory that the other, ICEE Distributors, distributes ICEEs in a cup. After a jury trial, the district court entered a permanent injunction barring J&J and Wal-Mart Stores, which sold J&J's squeeze-up tubes within the territory, from continuing to distribute the tubes. We affirm.

I

In the 1960s, the John E. Mitchell Company ("Mitchell Company") developed the ICEE, a semi-frozen beverage consisting of carbonated water and syrup mixed together that stands up when poured into a cup. Through its subsidiary, ICEEQUIP, the Mitchell Company owned the trademark rights to the ICEE name on products such as the cups for holding the frozen carbonated beverage, the machines for making the beverage, and the beverage itself. ICEEQUIP entered into several trademark licensing agreements with ICEE distributors in different parts of the country. The plaintiff-appellee, ICEE Distributors, Inc. ("Distributors"), by virtue of its purchase of several regional distributorships that had each entered into these licensing agreements, is a party to these identically-worded agreements for its various distribution territories. . . .

In the 1980s, the Mitchell Company went out of business. [The] regional licensees, including Distributors and The ICEE Company, a subsidiary of J&J, formed ICEE of America ("IOA"). IOA acquired the ownership rights and interests in the trademarks previously held by ICEEQUIP. Both Distributors and The ICEE Company own stock in IOA, with The ICEE Company being the largest shareholder and Distributors the second largest.

In 1999, J&J began manufacturing frozen squeeze-up tubes under the name "ICEE" on a nationwide basis. Appellant Wal-Mart sold these tubes in its Sam's Club stores. Although J&J requested permission from Distributors to sell the tubes in its territory, Distributors refused. J&J sold the tubes in Distributors' territory nonetheless. Distributors filed this suit in May 1999 against J&J and Wal-Mart for trademark infringement and dilution.

After the case was filed, J&J attempted unsuccessfully to register [a trademark] for the use of the ICEE name on the tubes. The PTO rejected the application on the basis that the proposed trademark would likely be confused with IOA's trademarks on the ICEE beverage, cups, and beverage machine. J&J then assigned the trademark application to IOA, which successfully registered the trademark. . . . The district court granted summary judgment in the defendants' favor on the trademark infringement claim, but held a trial on the trademark dilution and breach of contract claims, bifurcating the liability and damages stages. After the liability stage of the trial, the jury found J&J and Wal-Mart liable for willful trademark dilution and IOA liable for breach of contract.

Based on the jury verdict, the trial court subsequently entered a permanent injunction against J&J and Wal-Mart. . . . [Defendants appeal.]

IV

A

The district court rested the injunction on the jury's findings regarding both breach of contract and trademark dilution. J&J and Wal-Mart urge that the trademark dilution would not support injunctive relief because IOA, rather than Distributors, owns the ICEE trademarks and therefore Distributors could not sue under the Federal Trademark Dilution Act. The [Act provides] that

> [t]he *owner* of a famous mark shall be entitled, subject to the principles of equity and upon such terms as the court deems reasonable, to an injunction against another person's commercial use in commerce of a mark or trade name, if such use begins after the mark has become famous and causes dilution of the distinctive quality of the mark. . . .

15 U.S.C. § 1125(c) (emphasis added).

Appellants assert that since the federal trademark registrations show that IOA owns the trademarks, Distributors has no standing to sue under the Act. Distributors counters that the jury weighed the evidence and found that Distributors owned the ICEE trademarks with respect to its distribution territory. . . . It points to language in *Quabaug Rubber Co. v. Fabiano Shoe Co.,* [567 F.2d 154, 159 (1st Cir. 1977),] in which the First Circuit explained,

> [some courts] have permitted trademark infringement suits to be maintained by exclusive distributors and sellers of trademarked goods, i.e., "exclusive licensees" who had a right by agreement with the owner of the trademark to exclude even him from selling in their territory.

It further relies upon the principle that "[e]ven though a contract states that it is a 'license,' a court will not be governed by form, and the contract will be upheld as an assignment of trademark rights if that is its actual legal effect." . . .

Appellants reply that under the contract IOA retained ownership rights to the trademarks. . . .

B

"[A] license to use a mark . . . is a transfer of limited rights, less than the whole interest which might have been transferred." As one court has explained,

> One of the ways that the law extends the benefits of trademarks and protects incentives to develop them is by allowing trademark owners to license the use of their marks to distributors and franchisees. Such licensing allows more information to be conveyed to more consumers *without the licensor having to risk losing title to its mark.*

TMT North America, Inc. v. Magic Touch GmbH, 124 F.3d 876, 882 (7th Cir. 1997) (emphasis added).

It would be antithetical to the basic principles of trademark law to extend to a licensee the rights of an assignee without caution, since deeming a licensee an assignee would allow the assignee to hold the registered trademark owner liable under trademark law, rather than simply under contract law, for diluting the mark by utilizing a similar trademark in the assignee's area.

Although "a truly exclusive licensee, one who has the right even to exclude his licensor from using the mark" might be considered an assignee since no right to use the mark is reserved to the licensor, an agreement that sets forth "many duties and rights between the parties that are inconsistent with an assignment, such as geographic limitations on the licensee's territory, does not constitute an assignment." The contract at issue here does not explicitly exclude IOA itself from using the marks in Distributors' territory. Moreover, the agreements with Distributors contain strict geographic limitations, and reserves to ICEEQUIP certain rights indicative of ownership, such as IOA's ability to monitor the quality control of Distributors' product and its responsibility to renew the trademark registrations. Taken together, the contractual provisions cited by appellants convince us that the contract is an exclusive license arrangement only, with ultimate control and ownership of the trademarks resting with IOA.

This conclusion is borne out by the testimony of one of IOA's other regional distributors. As part of its case-in-chief, Distributors called Nate Parish, owner of Middle Tennessee ICEE, Inc. He testified that IOA "is the holder of the 'ICEE' trademark, the look, the block letters, and it's their job to police the trademark in respects to, I guess I'd say the entire country." Parish further explained that at the 1999 IOA board of directors meeting, he made a motion to allow J&J to make the ICEE squeeze tubes and distribute the tubes in J&J's own territory, not nationally. In explaining why a motion was necessary to allow J&J to distribute the tubes even in its own area, the witness stated, "If I was to produce an ICEE cup with the Tennessee Titans, the bear with the Tennessee Titans uniform on, I have to get permission from ICEE of America for that to take place."

This exchange between Distributors and their own witness indicates that IOA must give specific permission for regional distributors to either use a trademarked term such as "ICEE" on a different product or alter a trademark. IOA's powers of oversight are inconsistent with the notion that each regional distributor owns the trademarks in their respective territories.[2] Instead, as an umbrella organization for all of the distributors, IOA serves the purpose of "policing the trademarks" within each distributors' individual region to assure that the marks are not being used in an undesirable fashion.

In conclusion, this evidence indicates that the district court clearly erred in determining that Distributors, not IOA, was the owner of the ICEE registrations. Because Distributors is not the owner of the marks, but merely an exclusive licensee, it has no standing to sue under the Dilution Act, and the district court abused its discretion in basing its injunction in part on the jury's verdict on the dilution claim.[3] However, we will not reverse the trial court's grant of injunction because it is independently sustainable as a proper remedy for the breach of contract. AFFIRMED.

GRUEN MARKETING CORP. v. BENRUS WATCH COMPANY, INC.
955 F. Supp. 979 (N.D. Ill. 1997)

HART, DISTRICT JUDGE.

Gruen Marketing Corporation ("Gruen") brings this action against defendants Benrus Watch Company, Inc. ("Benrus"), Hampden Watch Co., Inc. ("Hampden"), Irving Wein, Joseph Wein and Jim Herbert. [Defendants] move to dismiss Gruen's complaint.

---

[2] [FN 45] Along these lines, appellants persuasively argue that ICEEQUIP executed identical exclusive licensing agreements with several regional distributors, and it would be illogical to hold that these many agreements create a "patchwork of trademark owners," because "[s]uch divided national ownership would jeopardize the goodwill associated with the [t]rademarks, create customer confusion, and diminish the trademarks' value of indicating a single source and quality of ICEE [products]."

[3] [FN 46] We note that, although the licensing contracts between Distributors and IOA give Distributors the power to bring trademark infringement actions in its territory, they do not provide that Distributors may bring trademark dilution claims in its area.

I. Alleged Factual Background

Gruen, a Delaware corporation, is in the business of merchandising various products, such as watches, to major retailers and others. Benrus, a Delaware corporation, also sells watches and is the registrant for the trademark BENRUS. Hampden, a U.S. Virgin Islands corporation, assembles and sells watches for Benrus. Irving Wein controls Hampden and his son, Joseph Wein is a shareholder and officer of Benrus. Jim Herbert is a former Benrus employee.

Until June 1995, Benrus had sold its watches both with and without the BENRUS trademark. The watches not bearing the BENRUS trademark were sold as either personalized watches or private label watches. Personalized watches are sold by retailers with custom changes to the watch dial. Private label watches bear trademarks or logos of third parties, such as retailers.

In June 1995, Gruen and Benrus entered into three agreements, a License Agreement, Purchase Agreement and a Letter Agreement, each relating to Benrus' BENRUS line of watches. Pursuant to these agreements, Gruen acquired Benrus' business in BENRUS watches, including a master customer list, inventory, components and raw materials, intellectual property and a sales force to carry on the business. The License Agreement granted an exclusive license to Gruen for all uses of the BENRUS mark worldwide, except in Japan. Under the License Agreement, Benrus was not permitted to use the BENRUS mark without the prior written consent of Gruen. In addition, defendants Joseph Wein and Jim Herbert became Gruen sales agents. Gruen has paid $722,727.30 to Benrus under the License Agreement. Pursuant to the Purchase Agreement, Gruen paid $4,360,000 for all of Benrus' inventory, components and raw materials.

Despite its contractual obligations, Benrus did not discontinue using the BENRUS mark. Benrus and Irving Wein continued to use the BENRUS mark on Benrus letterhead and in other written materials. Benrus has sold watches bearing the BENRUS mark after the effective date of the License Agreement. The inventory delivered to Gruen pursuant to the Purchase Agreement was not of merchantable quality or salable in the ordinary course of business, despite Benrus' express representations and warranties to the contrary in the Purchase Agreement.

At a watch industry trade show in Hong Kong in September 1996, Joseph Wein stated to vendors and actual and potential customers of Gruen that Gruen was insolvent and unable to fulfill orders for BENRUS watches. Irving Wein has also made these representations, as well as stated that, in the future, Benrus will continue to sell BENRUS watches. In fact, Gruen is not insolvent and has substantial financial backing. Gruen's representatives have spent considerable time and effort to correct Irving and Joseph Wein's representations. In October 1996, Benrus diverted a shipment of watch cases from Gruen to itself. Benrus was able accomplish the diversion by using information learned as a result of its position as licensor of the BENRUS mark.

Irving Wein and Jim Herbert are former Benrus employees who became Gruen sales agents after the execution of the agreements between Benrus and

Gruen. Benrus owed one of its customers a credit for returned BENRUS watches sold prior to the execution of the agreements. Joseph Wein directed the customer to apply the credit against invoices for watches purchased from Gruen. Jim Herbert persuaded certain Gruen customers to purchase Benrus' private label watches, although Herbert was working for Gruen at the time.

On November 12, 1996, Gruen filed its seven-count complaint. . . .

II. Discussion

On a motion to dismiss, plaintiff's well-pleaded allegations of fact are taken as true and all reasonable inferences must be drawn in plaintiff's favor. . . .

A. Count I — Trademark Infringement

In Count I, Gruen alleges that defendants are liable for trademark infringement because they used the BENRUS mark after the effective date of the License Agreement. Defendants argue that Gruen, as a licensee of Benrus, lacks standing to assert a claim under the Lanham Act. Gruen responds that it has standing because the License Agreement assigned, rather than merely licensed, the BENRUS trademark to Gruen.

Section 32 of the Lanham Act, 15 U.S.C. § 1114(1), grants standing to assert a claim for trademark infringement only to the "registrant" of the trademark. The term "registrant" includes the registrant and its "legal representatives, predecessors, successors and assigns." Several courts have held that a licensee has no right to sue a licensor under the Lanham Act, even where the licensee has been granted an exclusive right to use the trademark. Gruen, therefore, has standing to assert a trademark infringement claim only if the rights granted to Gruen by the License Agreement amount to an assignment, as contemplated by the statute. An "assignment" of a mark is "an outright sale of all rights in that mark," whereas a license is "a limited permit to another to use the mark."

Gruen asserts that it should be deemed an assignee because its allegation in its complaint that the BENRUS mark was assigned to it is sufficient to survive a motion to dismiss. Standing, however, is a jurisdictional question. In considering jurisdictional questions, factual disputes may be resolved and facts outside those alleged in the complaint may be considered. However, where the jurisdictional issue involves factual disputes requiring discovery or is intertwined with the merits of the case, it is sometimes appropriate to postpone to the time of trial resolution of the jurisdictional issue.

Benrus argues that the terms of the License Agreement demonstrate that Gruen is a licensee and not an assignee of the BENRUS mark. Benrus asserts that the License Agreement unequivocally reserved numerous rights in the BENRUS mark indicating that the BENRUS mark was not assigned to Gruen. For example, the License Agreement excludes Gruen from using the BENRUS mark in Japan and requires Gruen to obtain Benrus' approval for certain uses of the mark, such as advertising. In addition, Benrus reserved the right to sell BENRUS-marked goods to Jan Bell Marketing, Inc. and to use the mark on certain products sold through catalogs and direct mailings. Gruen was required to obtain Benrus' approval before assigning Gruen's rights under the License Agreement. Finally, the License Agreement contained the following provision:

> [Gruen] acknowledges that, as between [Gruen] and [Benrus], [Benrus] is the owner of all right, title and interest in and to the Licensed Mark in any form or embodiment thereof.

For its part, Gruen argues that it was assigned the BENRUS mark because "[n]otwithstanding the use of the term 'license' in an agreement, if a contract gives a party an exclusive license to use a trademark and otherwise discloses a purpose to transfer the rights in the trademark, the transfer is an assignment for purposes of the federal trademark laws." Gruen asserts that this is the case since it received the exclusive right to exploit the BENRUS mark, the right to sue for infringement, and the executory right to secure permanent transfer of the mark to Gruen. Gruen argues that its agreements with Benrus were akin to a mortgage or installment sale where Gruen's rights did not become final until future payment of funds.

Gruen's argument, however, does not overcome the express language of the License Agreement that Benrus retained ownership of the BENRUS mark. A licensee lacks standing where the agreement indicates that the licensor retains exclusive ownership of the mark. Other provisions of the agreement also support the conclusion that Gruen received only a license to use the BENRUS mark. For example, the License Agreement provides that Benrus "grants an exclusive license" to Gruen. Gruen was obligated to make royalty payments to Benrus and failure to do so terminated the license. Benrus retained the power to assure that Gruen maintained the quality of the BENRUS mark, a requirement consistent with a trademark license but not an assignment. That the License Agreement contemplated that Gruen one day would have the right to acquire title in the BENRUS mark does not mean Gruen was assigned the mark from the outset of the parties' relationship. Thus, title in the BENRUS mark did not pass to Gruen and Gruen does not have standing under 15 U.S.C. § 1114.

B. Count II — Section 43(a) of the Lanham Act

Benrus moves to dismiss Count II, Gruen's Section 43(a) claim, on the same standing grounds as Gruen's trademark infringement claim. Under Section 43(a), however, a plaintiff need not be the owner of a registered trademark in order to have standing to sue. Although a few cases have treated standing under Section 43(a) as interchangeable with standing under 15 U.S.C. § 1114, the better rule is that a licensee may assert a Section 43(a) claim against its licensor and third parties. Section 43(a) states that a person who violates its prohibitions shall be liable in a civil action "by any person who believes that he or she is likely to be damaged" by a prohibited act. 15 U.S.C. § 1125(a). This language is broader than the language of 15 U.S.C. § 1114(1), which states that trademark infringers "shall be liable in a civil action by the registrant." Consistent with the language of the statute, a plaintiff will be required to show "the proof of ownership of a proprietary right" or that it has "a reasonable interest to protect, which some courts have characterized as a commercial interest." CHARLES E. MCKENNEY & GEORGE F. LONG III, FEDERAL UNFAIR COMPETITION: LANHAM ACT § 43(a), § 9.03[1] at 11-12. (Release # 7, 5/96). Because Gruen possesses a license to use the BENRUS mark, Gruen has standing under Section 43(a) to bring an action against Benrus and the other defendants.

Benrus contends, however, that even if Gruen has standing to raise a Section 43(a) claim, Gruen has failed state a claim beyond a breach by Benrus of the License Agreement. Because this argument is not a jurisdictional challenge, the allegations of the complaint will be taken as true and all disputed facts will be resolved in favor of the plaintiff. In Count II, Gruen alleges that Benrus' use of the BENRUS trademark constitutes false designation of origin and constitutes "passing off" of its watches as Gruen's BENRUS watches. In order to prove a claim pursuant to Section 43(a), a plaintiff must show "(1) that its trademark may be protected and (2) that the relevant group of buyers is likely to confuse the alleged infringer's products or services with those of plaintiff."

Gruen's right to relief hinges on its ability to enforce the exclusivity provision of the License Agreement. Gruen has not alleged anything beyond Benrus' alleged breach of the License Agreement. As one court has noted in considering an exclusive licensee's claim against its licensor for unfair infringement:

> [T]his case is essentially a contract dispute between an exclusive licensee and a licensor over the right to use the trademark MEAT LOAF. Silverstar's dispute should be determined by the principles of contract law, as it is the contract that defines the parties' relationship and provides mechanisms to redress alleged breaches thereto. The Lanham Act, in contrast, establishes marketplace rules governing the conduct of parties not otherwise limited. This is not a case of either the licensee or licensor attempting to protect a trademark from unscrupulous use in the marketplace by third parties. Rather, this case involves the alleged breach of a license agreement.

Silverstar [Enterprises, Inc. v. Aday], 537 F.Supp. at 242 [(S.D.N.Y. 1982),]. *Silverstar*'s reasoning applies in this case. Moreover, the principle that a contractual dispute concerning a license will not give rise to a federal cause of action has been recognized in this circuit. Contract law, not the Lanham Act, governs the parties' dispute. Count II will be dismissed. . . .

NOTES

1. Is the difference in treatment of trademark and patent claims justifiable as a matter of policy?

2. In both *ICEE* and *Gruen*, claims were brought against the exclusive licensor. As the cases indicate, when the defendant is the licensor, one must distinguish between breach of contract and infringement claims. How would you describe the circumstances in which a Lanham Act claim against a licensor is appropriate, when a contract breach claim is appropriate, and when both might be appropriate?

3. Copyright law introduces another approach to standing. The Copyright Act provides: "The legal or beneficial owner of an exclusive right under copyright is entitled . . . to institute an action for any infringement of that particular right committed while he or she is the owner of it. . . . The court may require the joinder, and shall permit the intervention, of any person having or claiming an interest in the copyright." 17 U.S.C. § 501(b). The Act also defines a "transfer of copyright ownership" in the following way:

> A "transfer of copyright ownership" is an assignment, mortgage, exclusive license, or any other conveyance, alienation, or hypothecation of a copyright or of any of the exclusive rights comprised in a copyright, whether or not it is limited in time or place of effect, but not including a nonexclusive license.

17 U.S.C. § 101. Under this language, should the licensee of an exclusive license to "publicly perform a [named motion picture] in the city of Chicago during the period of June 1 through June 15" have standing to sue for infringement of the copyright during that period of time?

4. Trade secret law is grounded in state tort law and in protecting against misappropriation of information whose value derives from being at least relatively secret. As we have seen, a trade secret license is essentially a conditional, confidential disclosure of this information. What about an exclusive license of a trade secret? Who owns the right to sue for misappropriation if the information is wrongfully acquired and disclosed?

PROBLEM 4.5

Publisher obtains an exclusive license to make and distribute copies in hardcover form in the United States of the original novel "Bilked at Dawn," written by Jason Jones. Jones, however, subsequently grants Distributor a license to distribute the novel in paperback and hardcover form in the state of New York. Publisher sues Distributor for infringement when the hardcover books begin to appear on the market. What result? Can Publisher sue Jones? On what basis?

III. LICENSOR OBLIGATIONS IN AN EXCLUSIVE LICENSE

While the terms of the actual agreements vary widely, the defining feature of an exclusive license is a commitment by the licensor that it will not grant further licenses covering the same subject matter and scope. There are, however, potentially significant drafting and policy issues present in applying this concept of exclusivity to the licensor's conduct.

DONALD F. DUNCAN, INC. v. ROYAL TOPS MANUFACTURING CO., INC.
343 F.2d 655 (7th Cir. 1965)

MAJOR, CIRCUIT JUDGE.

This action was brought by plaintiff (appellee) against defendants[4] for alleged trademark infringement of its registered trademarks, "Yo-Yo," "Genuine

---

[4] [FN 1] Defendant Royal Tops Manufacturing Co., Inc. will be referred to as "Royal," and defendant Randy Brown as "Brown." Where both defendants are referred to, it will be as "defendants."

Duncan Yo-Yo" and "Butterfly," unfair competition, false representation of goods and unauthorized use of plaintiff's trademarks. Defendants by answer denied all allegations of the complaint relevant to plaintiff's claim for relief.

Following a lengthy trial, the District Court entered its findings of fact, conclusions of law and a judgment order in favor of plaintiff, from which defendants appeal. . . .

On July 23, 1948, plaintiff's predecessor (a co-partnership) entered into an agreement with Louis Marx & Company, Inc. and Charmore Company, whereby the licensor granted them a license to use the trademark "Yo-Yo." The agreement provided that "should Marx abandon the manufacture or/and sale of the bandalore types of toy spinning tops, manufactured and sold by it, then Duncan shall have the right to cancel the license granted herein upon thirty (30) days' notice in writing given to Marx."

In 1951, Royal's predecessor brought an action for declaratory judgment in the District Court for the Northern District of Illinois, by which it sought a cancellation of plaintiff's registration, "Yo-Yo," on the ground that it was the generic or a descriptive name of the article upon which it was used. Brown was not a party to this action.

On September 14, 1955, plaintiff entered into a license agreement with Royal by which it granted to Royal "an exclusive and non-transferable right to use Licensor's trade-mark, 'Yo-Yo,' on or upon or in association with bandalore tops." This agreement provided, "The parties hereto agree that they will enter into appropriate papers in the United States District Court in the aforesaid litigation (referring to the action for declaratory judgment) wherein said trade-marks shall be held to be valid and existing."

On November 21, 1955, a consent judgment was entered which found plaintiff to be the owner of the trademark registrations for "Yo-Yo" and for "Genuine Duncan Yo-Yo." The judgment recited, "Each of the above trademarks is applied and used in connection with a disc-shaped top manipulated up and down on a string, more commonly known as a bandalore top or quiz." The judgment determined that the trademarks "are valid."

On September 6, 1961, plaintiff's attorney directed a letter of cancellation to the Marx and Charmore Companies, the licensees named in the 1948 license agreement stating, "Please consider this letter as the thirty-days' written notice." This notice was given as required by a provision contained in that agreement.

We need not cite or discuss cases which support the general rule that a trademark licensee is estopped to dispute validity or that a consent decree, the same as any other decree, is binding on the parties. Royal contends that these rules are not applicable because plaintiff, as an inducement for the 1955 license agreement, fraudulently represented that there was no outstanding license agreement when as a matter of fact it knew or should have known the 1948 agreement with Louis Marx & Company, Inc. and Charmore Company was in force and effect. In any event, Royal argues that the license agreement was invalid because of a mutual mistake as to a material fact and that the consent decree was entered as a result of and as provided for in the license agreement and was, therefore, tainted with the same fraud or mutual mistake.

Plaintiff's response to these contentions is based upon a finding by the District Court. "This license (referring to the 1948 license to Marx and Charmore) was cancelled by mutual agreement in 1952," and "Correspondence between Marx and plaintiff indicates an acknowledgment of the cancellation of 1952." In our judgment, these findings as well as the argument predicated thereon are clearly erroneous and must be rejected.

Plaintiff in support of its cancellation theory relies upon the testimony of Donald Duncan, Sr., that the license was cancelled in 1952 by mutual agreement in a conversation with Marx. Admittedly he gave no thirty-day written notice of cancellation as required by the Duncan-Marx agreement. Nor was such a notice given until 1961, when it was given by plaintiff's attorney. Plaintiff attempts to bolster its contention on this score by inferences drawn from correspondence between Duncan and Marx following the alleged oral cancellation. An examination of this correspondence as a whole completely negates the inferences which plaintiff professes to discern. For instance, on July 14, 1961, the attorneys for Marx wrote plaintiff, stating, "Our client is licensed by you to use the name 'Yo-Yo' as provided in the 1948 agreement." On July 26, 1961, Marx wrote plaintiff, "We have an agreement to that effect (our right to use the name 'Yo-Yo') giving us full permission to use it." (This is the same Marx with whom Duncan claimed to have had the oral agreement of cancellation in 1952.)

Even after plaintiff's counsel gave written notice of cancellation in his letter of September 6, 1961, Marx was still contending that its 1948 agreement with plaintiff was in effect. In response to the written notice of cancellation, the attorneys for Marx wrote that they ". . . consider this attempted cancellation to be without validity or effect." It may be that when plaintiff's counsel gave written notice of cancellation in 1961, he was without knowledge of the alleged oral cancellation in 1952, or if he had such knowledge, recognized it as futile. In this connection it is pertinent to note that Donald F. Duncan, Jr., plaintiff's president, testified that to his knowledge the 1948 agreement with Marx and Charmore had not been cancelled and was still in full force and effect in 1955, when the license agreement was entered into between plaintiff and Royal.

Thus, the conclusion is inescapable that the 1948 license agreement between plaintiff and Marx and Charmore was in full force and effect at the time plaintiff entered into a license agreement with Royal and granted to it "an exclusive" right. Royal's president, Joseph T. Radovan, testified that he would not have settled Royal's suit against plaintiff for declaratory judgment if he had known there was an outstanding license agreement with some other company. The most charitable characterization which can be made of plaintiff's misrepresentation is that it was a mutual mistake, relied upon by Royal to its prejudice. The license agreement relied on is, therefore, invalid. . . .

NOTES

1. Compare the instant case and *San Juan Products, Inc. v. San Juan Pools of Kansas, Inc.*, 849 F.2d 468 (10th Cir. 1988) (license agreement purporting to give exclusive right to sell fiberglass swimming pools in a state was void from onset or voidable at dealer's insistence due to mistake of fact and the fact that manufacturer had already given third party exclusive rights in the state), with *Mechanical Ice Tray Corp. v. General Motors Corp.*, 144 F.2d 720 (2d Cir. 1944) (license treated as exclusive and enforceable even with prior licenses in existence).

2. Misrepresentation enables invalidation of the agreement only if the misrepresentation concerns a material fact. Are there circumstances in which the existence of a prior license, even if not disclosed, might not be a material fact?

3. The court in *Duncan* refers to licensee estoppel. We will have more to say about this doctrine in a later chapter. In *Duncan*, however, the ruling on fraud or mutual mistake allowed the court to avoid the question of whether an existing license precluded a challenge to a trademark. If we reverse the issue, what is the effect of a finding that the underlying rights are invalid on the enforceability of an existing license by the licensor? The court in *Drackett Chemical Co. v. Chamberlain Co.*, 63 F.2d 853, 854-55 (6th Cir. 1933), commented:

> [W]here the monopoly . . . apparently created by the grant of a patent . . . has been destroyed by a decree of invalidity in a court of competent jurisdiction . . . there has been a complete failure of consideration — an eviction — which should justify a termination of the contract. Prior to such eviction, the mere invalidity of the patent is properly held not to be a sufficient defense, because the licensee may still continue to enjoy all of the benefits of a valid patent. It may be respected, and the licensee would then have just what he bargained for. It is only when, by judicial decree or otherwise, it is published to the world that the monopoly is destroyed, that the licensee can claim corresponding release from his obligation to pay royalties. . . . Licenses may be exclusive, partially exclusive, or nonexclusive. The principles which we have stated apply with equal force to all of these types.

PROBLEM 4.6

Inventor Corp. grants Manufacturer an "exclusive license to make, offer to sell, and sell machines" covered by Inventor's patent. The license covers the entire U.S. and lasts for "so long as the patent remains valid and in force." Manufacturer agrees to pay royalties of 20% of the sale price of all machines it sells. There is no upfront royalty payment. Several months after the license, Manufacturer discovers that Inventor had previously given a non-exclusive license to Maine Corp. to make, offer to sell, and sell the same machines in the state of Maine. Maine sells approximately 200 machines per year.

a. What remedy, if any, does Manufacturer have?

b. What result if, one year after the license to Manufacturer, Maine expands its sales force and begins to sell machines throughout New England, increasing its sales to over 1,000 per year. Inventor refuses to sue for infringement because it has a long-term relationship with Maine.

KEPNER-TREGOE, INC. v. VROOM
186 F.3d 283 (2d Cir. 1999)

MOTLEY, DISTRICT JUDGE:

This is an appeal of a civil judgment against Professor Victor H. Vroom for breach of contract and copyright infringement relating to an exclusive licensing agreement between Dr. Vroom and Kepner-Tregoe, Inc. (K-T). The licensing agreement provided K-T with the exclusive use of executive leadership training materials co-authored by Dr. Vroom in return for the payment of royalties to Dr. Vroom. The two issues presented by this appeal are (1) whether the district court's finding of liability against Dr. Vroom for intentional copyright infringement and breach of contract should be upheld, and (2) whether the district court properly assessed damages in the amount of $219,855.21 plus attorneys' fees. For the reasons discussed below, the decision of the district court is affirmed.

BACKGROUND

In 1972, Dr. Vroom, a professor at Yale University's School of Organization and Management, entered into a licensing agreement with K-T, an international management training company. This agreement granted K-T the exclusive worldwide rights to specific copyrighted materials co-authored by Dr. Vroom. These materials, known as the Vroom-Yetton model, were used to teach managers how to make better decisions. In return, K-T agreed to pay Dr. Vroom and his co-author, Dr. Philip W. Yetton, royalties based on its exclusive use of the licensed materials. The licensing agreement also included a teaching clause that allowed Dr. Vroom to retain non-assignable rights to use the licensed materials for his "own teaching and private consultation work."

In the mid-1980s, Dr. Vroom created a more sophisticated software program, entitled "Managing Participation in Organizations" (MPO), which partially overlapped with the materials licensed to K-T. Dr. Vroom used the MPO program to conduct management training seminars for corporate executives at Yale University and other college campuses. Upon learning of Dr. Vroom's use of the copyrighted materials, K-T initiated this lawsuit in 1989.

K-T alleges that Dr. Vroom's use of the MPO program in his teaching of executives in the university setting infringes on its copyrights and constitutes a breach of the licensing agreement. It further alleges that Dr. Vroom breached the licensing agreement by assigning the rights to the MPO program, which infringed K-T's licensed materials, to Leadership Software Inc. (LSI), a Texas company founded by Dr. Vroom and his colleague, Dr. Arthur Jago. LSI was created to market the MPO program.

In 1990, K-T initiated a separate lawsuit against LSI and Dr. Jago in federal district court in Texas. Dr. Vroom was not a defendant in the suit because personal jurisdiction was unavailable. In that case, K-T alleged copyright infringement based on LSI's sales of the MPO program, which contained substantial similarities to the Vroom-Yetton model, the copyrighted materials exclusively licensed to K-T. The Texas district court found in favor of K-T and awarded it $46,000 in actual damages as well as injunctive relief. The Fifth

Circuit modified the injunction entered by the district court, but affirmed its finding of liability.

After a five-day bench trial in April 1997, the district court in the present action held that Dr. Vroom's use of the licensed materials, including the infringing MPO program, in his teaching of executives in the university setting was not permitted under the teaching clause of the licensing agreement. The trial court found that the teaching clause was ambiguous as written and looked to other contemporaneous documentary evidence for clarification of the parties' intentions. The lower court interpreted the teaching clause to mean that Dr. Vroom was only allowed to use the copyrighted materials for his teaching of bona fide enrolled graduate and undergraduate students. Moreover, the district court found that Dr. Vroom willfully infringed the copyrighted material licensed to K-T and breached his contract with K-T when he taught the exclusively licensed materials to large groups of executives in the university setting. The court below also found that Dr. Vroom violated the licensing agreement when he assigned his rights to the licensed materials to LSI.

Awarding K-T the maximum statutory damages of $100,000, the district court found that Dr. Vroom's continued use of the MPO program in his executive training seminars, despite his knowledge of two federal court decisions in Texas that held the MPO program infringed K-T's copyrights, constituted willful infringement. The district court further held that K-T was entitled to attorneys' fees and costs under the Copyright Act, 17 U.S.C. § 505. The trial court issued an injunction prohibiting Dr. Vroom from using the MPO program or other materials exclusively licensed to K-T in any proscribed manner. The lower court also awarded K-T $119,855.21 in compensatory damages on its breach of contract claim. The contractual damage award reflected the costs K-T incurred in litigating the Texas suit, which the district court found to be a direct consequence of Dr. Vroom's breach of the licensing agreement.

Discussion

There is no dispute between the parties that the MPO program contains elements of the materials exclusively licensed to K-T. Rather, the only issues on appeal are (1) whether Dr. Vroom's use of the MPO program and other licensed materials in his executive training workshops on campus falls within the teaching clause of the licensing agreement, and (2) whether the district court properly assessed damages. Dr. Vroom contends that the district court erred in rejecting his acquiescence and public domain defenses to the copyright infringement claim. He further argues that the damage award constitutes a double recovery for a single injury. We will address the issue of copyright infringement before turning to Dr. Vroom's appeal of the damage award.

I. Copyright Infringement & Breach of Contract Claims

The central issue in this case involves the proper interpretation of the teaching clause of the licensing agreement, which allows Dr. Vroom to use the licensed materials in the course of his "own teaching and private consultation work." We find that the district court did not err in finding the teaching clause ambiguous. It properly looked to prior negotiations between the parties to determine the parties' intentions regarding the interpretation of the clause.

Furthermore, credible evidence was presented at trial that supported the lower court's interpretation of the teaching clause so as to limit Dr. Vroom's teaching to only bona fide enrolled undergraduate and graduate students.

A. *Interpretation of Teaching Clause*

Dr. Vroom argues that the district court effectively rewrote the clear and unambiguous language of the licensing agreement by restricting his teaching of the licensed materials to only students. Dr. Vroom contends that the parties intended to allow him to retain broad and unlimited rights to use the licensed materials in his teaching, including his teaching of executives in the university setting. Dr. Vroom also claims that the trial court's decision will virtually deprive him of his right to earn a living because he is enjoined from using the MPO program in his courses for executives at Yale and other colleges.

We review the district court's construction of the text of the licensing contract *de novo*. To begin with, we agree with the district court that the teaching clause was ambiguous. K-T contends that this clause was only intended to allow the teaching of undergraduate and graduate students; Dr. Vroom argues that this clause, which also allowed "private consulting," also permitted him to teach classes to large groups of executives. We hold, as did the district court, that in the context of the agreement the word "teaching" was susceptible to the interpretation advanced by either Dr. Vroom or K-T. Accordingly, the district court was entitled to consider extrinsic evidence to interpret the contractual language.

We also affirm the district court's holding limiting the clause to the teaching of enrolled graduate and undergraduate students. The communications of the parties during the negotiation of the licensing agreement support this interpretation. K-T wrote a memorandum to Dr. Vroom in January of 1972, stating that it wanted to prevent "mass" teaching of the materials. Dr. Vroom produced no evidence at trial that he ever contradicted K-T's interpretation of the teaching clause in any communications with K-T throughout the remainder of the negotiations. The district court properly relied on this evidence to conclude that the teaching clause did not extend beyond the teaching of enrolled graduate and undergraduate students.

B. *Acquiescence*

Contrary to Dr. Vroom's contention, the district court materially addressed the acquiescence argument in the context of its discussion of breach of contract and the proper interpretation of the teaching clause. We find that the district court properly rejected this defense, for which Dr. Vroom bore the burden of proof. Dr. Vroom presented no evidence that K-T knew he was using licensed materials in his executive training seminars. K-T only knew Dr. Vroom was teaching executive seminars on campus. Since Dr. Vroom presented no evidence that suggested that K-T had knowledge that he was using the copyrighted materials and failed to object, we hold that the district court did not err in rejecting Dr. Vroom's acquiescence defense. . . .

II. *Damages*

[The court affirmed the award of enhanced damages for willful infringement.]

Dr. Vroom further contends that the district court erred in awarding a double recovery to K-T. Dr. Vroom argues that K-T is being compensated twice for the same alleged injury under two legal theories, copyright infringement and breach of contract. K-T objects to this ground for appeal, claiming that Dr. Vroom did not raise this issue in the district court.

The district court's damage award does not represent a double recovery. The fact that Dr. Vroom did not raise this issue in his Post-Trial Memorandum does not preclude this court from addressing the issue. Dr. Vroom cannot be said to have reasonably anticipated that the lower court would make an allegedly double damage award. However, this court finds that the district court did not award K-T double damages as Dr. Vroom contends. The approximately $120,000 in contract damages represents the cost of litigating the Texas suit, which was found to be a direct consequence of Dr. Vroom's breach of the licensing agreement. Such damages are permissible under *Ingersoll Milling Mach. Co. v. M/V Bodena*, 829 F.2d 293, 309 (2d Cir.1987), which allowed for the recovery of counsel fees and other litigation expenses incurred in a prior suit to enforce contract rights against a third party.

Thus, there are two distinct categories of damages based on two separate acts. The $100,000 statutory damage award stems from Dr. Vroom's willful acts of copyright infringement after the Texas court enjoined the sale or use of the infringing MPO program. The approximately $120,000 contractual damage award represents K-T's consequential damages of having to litigate a suit in Texas to enforce its copyright rights stemming from Dr. Vroom's breach of the licensing agreement when he assigned the rights to the MPO to a third party. Thus, the two elements of the district court's damage award are permissible and do not constitute a double recovery.

Conclusion

[The] decision of the district court is affirmed.

NOTES

1. As indicated by the court, in a separate proceeding, the Fifth Circuit held that the computer program developed by the professor infringed the copyright of the work licensed to the company. The court there only briefly referred to the terms of the license, commenting: "When Vroom and Yetton sold K-T an exclusive license to copyrighted materials, which included the V-Y Model, they signed away the right to copy, at least for commercial purposes, protectable elements of the V-Y Model. LSI may not now incorporate substantially similar expression into computer programs for commercial sale: it was precisely the right to make such commercial use of the V-Y Model that Vroom and Yetton sold to K-T for hundreds of thousands of dollars." *Kepner-Tregoe, Inc. v. Leadership Software, Inc.*, 12 F.3d 527 (5th Cir. 1994). In light of these decisions, who is the owner of the copyright in the "leadership model"?

2. In *CRC Press, LLC v. Wolfram Research, Inc.*, 57 U.S.P.Q.2d 1220 (C.D. Ill. 2001), the court granted a preliminary injunction against the author of a mathematics encyclopedia from continuing to publish a web site containing substantially the same material as the encyclopedia. The author had contracted to write the print publication, conveying ownership of the copyright in the work to the publisher. Later, a second agreement established the right of the publisher to do a CD Rom version of the encyclopedia. The web site was already in existence. The court held that there was a likelihood of success on the publisher's claim that the contractual transfer covered the web site materials and that, therefore, continued use was infringement. Here, the two forms of text were virtually identical and, unless the publisher controlled both, it was difficult to see what value it had received under the contract.

3. UCITA Section 307 provides that:

A grant of an "exclusive license," or a grant in similar terms, means that:

(A) for the duration of the license, the licensor will not exercise, and will not grant to any other person, rights in the same information or informational rights within the scope of the exclusive grant; and

(B) the licensor affirms that it has not previously granted those rights in a contract in effect when the licensee's rights may be exercised.

UCITA § 307(f)(2) (2000 Official Text). This is a default rule subject to contrary agreement by the parties.

PROBLEM 4.7

Developer agrees to create a software program for Client to operate Client's accounts. Client expects to obtain ownership of the program. Developer will use prior templates from programs it has created for other clients, but will add approximately 30% new lines of code (out of about 10 million lines). Two of the processes implemented by the code are covered by patents owned by Developer and have been used in work with prior clients. Developer asks your advice about what language should be included in the exclusive license it plans to grant to the Client. What do you suggest?

Part II: TERMS OF A LICENSE

Chapter 5

INTERPRETATION AND THE GRANT CLAUSE

I. NATURE OF INTERPRETATION ISSUES

Since licensing law is primarily contract law, the terms of the agreement generally control the obligations and rights created. In this context, significant portions of licensing law and many reported cases are primarily concerned with interpreting that agreement.

The questions that arise in contract interpretation deal with two fundamentally different topics: 1) how to give meaning to the actual language of the agreement, and 2) what background rules apply when the agreement does not deal with the topic of the dispute? Implicit in both is the policy that, unless an over-riding reason exists to the contrary, contract law enforces the choices of the parties.

As a general principle, a license is "governed by ordinary principles of state contract law." *Power Lift, Inc. v. Weatherford Nipple-Up Sys., Inc.*, 871 F.2d 1082 (Fed. Cir. 1989). This means that many of the general tools and issues of contract interpretation also apply specifically to interpretation of licenses. Thus, in this book, we encounter the parol evidence rule, trade use and other sources of practical construction, and application of the rules of interpretation or construction that courts frequently cite and often rely on to resolve questions about the meaning of ambiguous contract language. It also means that decisions on these issues often reflect a particular court's preferred approach to the particular contract law theory, rather than a fundamental choice applicable primarily to licensing cases. For example, how courts apply the parol evidence rule varies among the states, with some courts routinely allowing parties to introduce extrinsic evidence to interpret a contract, while others routinely require a showing that the writing was not fully integrated and that the terms are ambiguous before extrinsic evidence will be permitted. These differences are important, but they are not directly related to licensing law, as compared to differences in approach to contract law in general.

This does not mean that license contract interpretation law is subsumed entirely within these broader themes. Quite the opposite is true. We will see many situations in which the decisions are grounded in the special language, expectations, background and property law context of licensing practice.

NOTE ON RULES OF INTERPRETATION

The *Restatement (Second) of Contracts* distinguishes between "interpretation" and "construction" of a contract. *See Restatement (Second) of Contracts* § 200. While some courts and commentators observe this distinction, many do not. In brief, the distinction lies in the fact that "interpretation" focuses on determining the meaning of the contract, while "construction" pertains to determining the legal effect of the agreement. *See Restatement (Second) of Contracts* § 200 cmt. c.

This book treats both as rules of interpretation. A "rule of interpretation" is a principle or approach that guides a court in understanding the meaning of *express* language in a contract. Rules of interpretation arise in litigation, but they also have a role in drafting. They create one source of information about how to craft an effective contract.

Some question whether rules of interpretation provide actual guidance, or are merely used to justify a decision reached by the court on other grounds. These "rules" are subject to the primary rule that the terms of the agreement control; they are, in that sense, typical contract law rules. They also frequently state commonsense or obvious principles in understanding a written text. On the other hand, in some circumstances, although a court refers to a rule of interpretation to support its conclusion, a legal realist might conclude that other factors truly explain the result.

Most likely, the role of these rules varies — in some cases, they lead a court to a conclusion, while in others they are make-weights or rationalizations. Whether persuasive, suggestive, or mere off-the-shelf explanations for a result, however, courts frequently refer to interpretation rules in licensing cases. The *Restatement* lists more than fourteen rules or themes associated with interpretation of a contract. Various authors identify lists of differing numbers and courts sometimes state a principle axiom that does not appear on any list. A flavor for these rules is seen in the following list:

- Give words their *plain* and *ordinary* meaning.

- Construe ambiguities against the drafter.

- Interpret words to carry out the agreement's purpose.

- Express terms control over trade use and course of dealing.

- Specific terms control the meaning of general terms.

- Handwritten terms prevail over printed or typewritten terms.

- Interpret to achieve internal consistency if possible.

- Interpret to give effect to each part of contract if possible.

- Express conveyance of one excludes conveyance of others.

- Correct obvious grammar or typographical mistakes.

- Construe agreements to make them valid rather than void.

- Technical terms and words of art receive their technical meaning.

- Interpret in the light of commercial circumstances.

- Interpret to avoid absurd results.

See generally Restatement (Second) of Contracts §§ 201-208; RAYMOND T. NIMMER & JEFF C. DODD, MODERN LICENSING LAW ch. 4 (2007); James P. Nehf, *Writing Contracts in the Client's Interest*, 51 S.C. L. REV. 153 (1999).

PROBLEM 5.1

A franchise agreement for a fast food restaurant drafted by Franchisor provides that the "franchise and related licenses may be transferred by the franchisee with the prior consent of the Franchisor." Smith, a franchisee, proposes to transfer the franchise to Jones. Jones meets all economic and other conditions for a franchise. Franchisor agrees to the transfer, but demands payment of $500,000, which is one-half the fee it charges to new franchisees. Franchisor allows the transfer to occur, reserving its rights to be paid.

In the subsequent litigation, Franchisor cites trade practices in the franchise industry that either preclude transfer of a license, or allow transfer on the payment of a new fee. Smith cites the fact that the agreement is silent on the issue of transfer fee. The agreement contains no other relevant language, except that it does provide that the franchisee can acquire additional franchises when available for an additional $500,000 fee, if it is not in default at the time. The parties did not discuss the issue of transfer fee in negotiating the contract.

What result on the claim for $500,000?

PROBLEM 5.2

ABCO granted a license to DBD Truck Company to "make and use the item of manufacture described in ABCO's patent #5,443,456." This covers an apparatus that, when attached to the cab of a truck better ensures that movement of the truck's trailer will not cause it to go out of control. DBD operates a fleet of 1,000 trucks, but also manufactures and sells truck cabs. The parties are disputing whether this license gives DBD the right to sell the appliance as part of the truck cabs that it manufactures. There is evidence that the parties had discussed this before agreeing on the license and that ABCO had indicated in a letter that this would be permitted. The license makes no reference to sales of the item and contains a "merger" clause stating that the writing contains the entire agreement of the parties and supersedes any prior representations or agreements. What result? Recall that a patent gives the patent owner the right to preclude others from making, using, selling or offering to sell the patented subject matter.

PROBLEM 5.3

Draken, an Internet search company that competes with Google and whose name is famous, grants a license to Flight Corporation to use the "Draken" trademark. Flight plans to begin a new online business. The license gives Flight the right to "use the Draken trademark as part of the name of a new company it plans to start and as part of the domain name for that company and in accordance with the terms and conditions of the license." Flight creates the new company and domain name, and uses the Draken name on the first page of the website. Draken sues for trademark infringement. Is this use licensed by the agreement?

II. GRANTING CLAUSES: DEFINING THE SUBJECT MATTER

Whether express or implied, the terms of a license contract can be broken down into three categories: 1) terms that define the license rights granted or agreed to, and the subject matter to which they pertain, 2) terms that relate to various collateral promises by either or both parties regarding topics such as payment, royalties, warranties, choice of law, marketing standards, transferability, and the like, and 3) terms defining breach and remedies for breach. Each category presents potentially unique issues.

We begin with the license grant. The grant terms define the subject matter of the transaction. In this respect, granting clauses present issues far different from subject-matter descriptions in many other agreements. In many commercial transactions, the subject matter is self-defining. That is less likely to be true in a license.

Consider, for example, a transaction in which the vendor agrees to sell a specific car to a purchaser. The contract need spend little time describing the subject matter and rights involved. The idea of "sale" has clear connotations (e.g., a transfer of title), while the car itself is a self-defining subject matter, defined by the physical item itself. It might well be sufficient for purposes of the grant to simply state: "Vendor sells his Mercedes SL 600 to Purchaser." While that language leaves open many questions such as warranties, time of delivery, and price, the subject matter is quite clear.

Now consider the following contracts:

"Licensor grants Purchaser a license in its copyrighted software, 'Wordiness' "

"Licensor grants Purchaser a license in Patent #6,000,111"

"Licensor grants Purchaser a license in Licensor's trademark 'Hot Reds.' "

While each grant describes a transaction, each leaves many issues uncertain. Is the software license a license to make and distribute copies of the software (if so, how many), to use the software in a single machine (if so, which one), to install the software in a network, to modify and distribute modified copies of the software, etc.? Is the patent license a license to "make," "use" or "sell" the patented subject matter?

In a license, the grant and subject matter are not self-defining. As a result, the language in a granting clause or elsewhere in the agreement must define the subject matter. One article describes this by observing that the license is the "product," whereas in the sale of the Mercedes the product is the car. Gomulkiewicz & Williamson, *A Brief Defense of Mass Market Software License Agreements,* 22 RUTGERS COMPUTER & TECH. L.J. 335 (1996). The options in how to tailor the grant are potentially infinite. This means that the background of property rights and the terms of the license are critical; they often produce litigation. As you consider the following two cases, both of which involved large and well-counseled companies, keep in mind the difference in function between a granting clause in a license and the more simple task of the subject matter clause in a sale of goods.

CYRIX CORP. v. INTEL CORP.
77 F.3d 1381 (Fed. Cir. 1996)

LOURIE, CIRCUIT JUDGE.

Intel Corporation appeals from the decision of the United States District Court for the Eastern District of Texas entering judgment in favor of Cyrix Corporation, SGS-Thomson Microelectronics, Inc. (ST), and International Business Machines Corporation (IBM), and holding that IBM and ST acted within the scope of their respective patent license agreements with Intel when IBM made, and ST had made, products for Cyrix. [We] affirm.

BACKGROUND

Cyrix designed and sold microprocessors. Since it did not have its own facility for manufacturing the microprocessors it designed, it contracted with other companies to act as its foundries. Under such an arrangement, Cyrix provided the foundries with its microprocessor designs, and the foundries manufactured integrated circuit chips containing those microprocessors and sold them to Cyrix. Cyrix then sold the microprocessors in the marketplace under its own brand name.

It was Cyrix's practice to use manufacturing facilities of companies that were licensed under Intel's patents. IBM was such a company; it had obtained a license to Intel's patents in a patent license agreement dated October 1, 1989. The granting clause of the IBM-Intel agreement provided as follows:

> 2.2 Subject to the provisions of Sections 2.7 and 3.3, INTEL, on behalf of itself and its Subsidiaries, hereby grants to IBM a worldwide, royalty-free, nonexclusive license under the INTEL Licensed Patents:

> 2.2.1 to make, use, lease, sell and otherwise transfer IBM Licensed Products and to practice any method or process involved in the manufacture or use thereof;

> 2.2.2 to have made and/or have designed Semiconductor Apparatus;

> 2.2.3 to have made IBM Licensed Products (other than Semiconductor Apparatus) by another manufacturer for the use, lease, sale or other transfer by IBM. . . .

The agreement defined "IBM Licensed Products" as follows:

> 1.23 "IBM Licensed Products" shall mean IHS Products, IHS Complexes, IHS Programs, Supplies and any combination of any, some or all of the foregoing and, also, Semiconductor Apparatus. Any such combination shall be considered an IBM Licensed Product even though its elements are leased, sold or otherwise transferred at different times.

Cyrix also used ST as a foundry. Initially, ST manufactured the chips, but when ST was unable to meet Cyrix's demands, ST requested its affiliate in Italy, SGS-Thomson Microelectronics S.r.L. (ST-Italy), to manufacture the needed chips, which ST then sold to Cyrix.

ST was operating under a license agreement between Mostek and Intel, which ST acquired by assignment. The agreement contains the following granting clause:

> INTEL grants and agrees to grant to MOSTEK non-exclusive, non-transferrable, world-wide licenses under INTEL PATENTS and INTEL PATENT APPLICATIONS to make, to have made, to use, to sell (either directly or indirectly), to lease and to otherwise dispose of LICENSED PRODUCTS.

The agreement defined "LICENSED PRODUCTS" as follows:

> "LICENSED PRODUCTS" shall mean any product manufactured, used or sold by either party covered by patents of the other party.

It is undisputed that ST-Italy is legally not a "subsidiary" of ST and is thus not licensed under the ST-Intel agreement. ST therefore relied upon its "have made" rights to obtain products from ST-Italy, which it then sold to Cyrix to fulfill its contractual obligation.

Cyrix filed a declaratory judgment action against Intel, alleging a "reasonable apprehension" that it would be sued for patent infringement. Cyrix sought a declaration that it did not infringe the Intel patents, claiming immunity on the ground that IBM and ST were both licensed under the patents. Cyrix's view was that because IBM and ST acted within the scope of their respective licenses from Intel, its sales of microprocessors were shielded from any holding of infringement, the microprocessors having been obtained from authorized licensees. *See Unidisco, Inc. v. Schattner,* 824 F.2d 965, 968, 3 USPQ2d 1439, 1441 (Fed.Cir.1987) ("Resale of the product by Unidisco could not infringe the patent if Unidisco purchased the product from an authorized seller.").

IBM and ST intervened, seeking an adjudication of their rights under their respective agreements with Intel. On motions for summary judgment by Intel, IBM, and ST, the district court granted summary judgment for IBM and ST, and denied summary judgment for Intel. The district court also entered judgment for Cyrix.

The district court held that IBM had a right to act as a foundry in supplying microprocessors to Cyrix. It found that the definition of "IBM Licensed Products" in the IBM-Intel agreement did not limit the products it was licensed to sell to those designed by IBM. The district court distinguished *Intel Corp. v. U.S. Int'l Trade Comm'n,* 946 F.2d 821, 828, 20 USPQ2d 1161, 1167-68 (Fed.Cir.1991) ("*Atmel*") (construing the term "Sanyo . . . products" in a license agreement as limiting the grant of rights to Sanyo-designed and Sanyo-manufactured products). The district court concluded that, unlike the situation in *Atmel,* an internal conflict in the IBM-Intel agreement was not created by construing the license grant to cover products other than IBM-designed products. The court considered the facts to be more analogous to those in *ULSI,* rather than to those in *Atmel. See Intel Corp. v. ULSI Sys. Technology, Inc.,* 995 F.2d 1566, 27 USPQ2d 1136 (Fed.Cir.1993).

The district court also held that ST had the right to have microprocessors made for it by any third party, including ST-Italy, and the right to sell those microprocessors to Cyrix. The district court found that the microprocessors were made for ST, not Cyrix, and that the supply agreement between ST and ST-Italy was not a sublicense that exceeded ST's rights under the ST-Intel agreement. The district court thus distinguished the case that Intel cited in support of its position, *E.I. du Pont de Nemours and Co. v. Shell Oil Co.*, 498 A.2d 1108, 1114-15 (Del. 1985) (holding that a third-party's manufacturing of a product for itself under a licensee's "have made" rights was a prohibited sublicense). This appeal followed.

Discussion

A. *IBM-Intel Agreement*

Intel argues that the IBM-Intel agreement does not support a grant of foundry rights. Intel relies upon the word "IBM" as modifying the term "licensed products" in arguing that this modifier is a so-called "Sanyo limitation," limiting the scope of the products licensed and indicating that the parties did not intend to provide foundry rights. Intel also asserts that the "have designed" provision in the license does not provide IBM with the right to act as a foundry in manufacturing products designed by Cyrix.

Cyrix and IBM argue that the plain language of the IBM-Intel agreement grants to IBM the right to make and sell to Cyrix microprocessors that Cyrix designed. They argue that the "IBM" modifier in section 2.2.1 of the agreement was intended to distinguish "IBM Licensed Products" from "Intel Licensed Products," and that "IBM Licensed Products" as defined in the agreement are not limited to those products specifically designed by IBM and made for itself. They argue that the term "IBM" used in the term "IBM Licensed Products" is not a "Sanyo limitation."

We agree with the district court. . . . The agreement granted IBM the right to make and sell "IBM Licensed Products," which are defined elsewhere in the agreement and are not limited to products designed by IBM. Sections 2.2.1, which grants a license to sell "IBM Licensed Products," and 1.23, which defines "IBM Licensed Products," must be read together. When this is done, the granting provision essentially reads as follows:

> 2.2.1 to make, use, lease, sell and otherwise transfer *IHS Products, IHS Complexes, IHS Programs, Supplies and any combination of any, some or all of the foregoing and, also, Semiconductor Apparatus* and to practice any method or process involved in the manufacture or use thereof;

The products so defined are not limited to IBM-designed products. They include categories of products defined without the IBM prefix. The agreement defined these items as follows:

> 1.1 "Information Handling System" shall mean any instrumentality or aggregate of instrumentalities primarily designed to compute, classify, process, transmit, receive, retrieve, originate, switch, store, display, manifest, measure, detect, record, reproduce, handle or utilize any form of information, intelligence or data for business, scientific,

control or other purposes.

1.2 "IHS Product" shall mean an Information Handling System or any instrumentality or aggregate of instrumentalities (including, without limitation, any component or subassembly) designed for incorporation in an Information Handling System; *provided, however,* that a Manufacturing Apparatus shall not be considered to be an IHS Product.

1.3 "IHS Program" shall mean a plurality of instructions capable of being executed by an IHS Product or Complex, whether or not such instructions are in a machine-readable form.

1.4 "Supply" shall mean, as to each party hereto, any article or matter designed for use in or by, and adapted to be effectively consumed in the course of operation of an IHS Product licensed herein to that party.

. . . .

1.22 "Semiconductor Apparatus" shall mean any Semiconductor Material, Semiconductor Device, Semiconductor Memory and/or Integrated Circuit.

Accordingly, we conclude that the district court correctly held that "IBM Licensed Products" are not limited to products designed by IBM.

We also do not agree with Intel that the "IBM" modifier is analogous to the "Sanyo limitation" in *Atmel.* The agreement in *Atmel* contained the following provision:

Intel hereby grants and will grant to Sanyo an [sic] non-exclusive, world-wide royalty-free license without the right to sublicense except to its Subsidiaries, under Intel Patents which read on any *Sanyo* Semiconductor Material, Semiconductor Device, Magnetic Bubble Memory Device, Integrated Circuit and Electronic Circuit products, for the lives of such patents, to make, use and sell *such products.*

We construed the term "Sanyo" to limit the products listed after that term. Such a construction was required because it gave meaning to the term "Sanyo" which was consistent with other provisions of the contract. Otherwise, the term "Sanyo" would have lacked meaning, and a contract must be construed if possible to give meaning to all its provisions. In contrast, the term "IBM Licensed Products" is thoroughly defined in the IBM-Intel agreement to provide no Sanyo-type limitation. Moreover, as argued by IBM, the "IBM" modifier is readily explained by its being distinguished from "Intel Licensed Products."

This case is more analogous to *ULSI* than *Atmel.* In *ULSI,* Hewlett-Packard Company (HP) acted as a foundry to make and sell math coprocessor chips to ULSI. HP obtained a license to Intel's patents under an agreement in which "each granted to the other an 'irrevocable, retroactive, nonexclusive, world-wide, royalty-free license.'" ULSI sought to be shielded from infringement of Intel's patents by purchasing the math coprocessor chips from HP, which was acting as an authorized seller. In concluding that HP's agreement with Intel provided HP with the right to act as a foundry for ULSI, we stated that, in contrast to the "Sanyo limitation" discussed in *Atmel,* "the licensing agreement between Intel and HP here contains no restriction on HP's right to sell or serve as a foundry." There was no "Sanyo limitation" in *ULSI*. The products that were licensed were defined broadly. Notwithstanding the presence of the modifier "IBM," the same is true here.

Intel also argues that the "have designed" provision of section 2.2.2 limits the products IBM is entitled to make to those designed for IBM, presumably meaning for IBM's sole use. We find no such limitation in the agreement. Section 2.2.2 by its plain terms granted IBM the right "to have made and/or have designed Semiconductor Apparatus[,]" defined in the agreement as "any Semiconductor Material, Semiconductor Device, Semiconductor Memory and/or Integrated Circuit." The microprocessors in question surely meet the definition of "Semiconductor Apparatus." This provision contains no limitation to the designs of any particular entity. Therefore, the right to have designed, make, and sell Semiconductor Apparatus clearly entitled IBM to act as a foundry for Cyrix by making a product designed by Cyrix.

Intel also argues that section 2.2.3, providing a right to "have made" products only when the designs are furnished by IBM, limits IBM's right to have products designed by Cyrix. IBM did not have the products made for it, and thus this provision does not limit its rights to make and have designed the products it sold to Cyrix. Moreover, 2.2.3 relates to products "other than Semiconductor Apparatus." We do not accept Intel's argument that section 2.2.3's limitations with respect to other products somehow cut back on unambiguous rights granted in sections 2.2.1 and 2.2.2 regarding the products in question. In summary, IBM properly made and sold microprocessors under section 2.2.1; IBM properly had microprocessors designed under section 2.2.2; and IBM did not "have made" microprocessors under the more limited section 2.2.3. Thus, IBM did not act outside the terms of the Intel agreement. . . .

Intel also makes a policy argument premised on a preamble clause in its agreement with IBM in which the parties stated that "each expects to continue a research and development effort which will produce further patents and each may require a nonexclusive license under such patents of the other." Intel argues that interpreting the agreement in favor of IBM would discourage the research the agreement was intended to foster. That argument totally misses the mark. The meaning of that clause is simply that the parties were entering into the agreement to facilitate their future research, *i.e.,* to provide themselves with patent freedom for the future. Even if Intel never intended IBM to act as a foundry, this vague preamble cannot be interpreted to give effect to that intention if doing so would override clear operative language in the agreement. This agreement clearly gave IBM the right to make and sell to Cyrix microprocessors designed by Cyrix.

B. ST-Intel Agreement

Intel argues that the arrangement between ST and ST-Italy is in effect a sublicense, which it is clear is not permissible under the ST-Intel agreement. In particular, it argues that under ST's "have made" rights, ST is only permitted to have products made for itself. Intel posits that the arrangement among ST, ST-Italy, and Cyrix was a mere paper transaction, *i.e.,* a "sham." *See E.I. du Pont,* 498 A.2d at 1116 (holding that a third party made a product for itself, not for a licensee, when it made a product and sold it to the licensee, who simultaneously sold it back to the third party).

ST and Cyrix argue that ST was acting within the scope of its "have made" rights. ST denies that its arrangement with ST-Italy was a "sham" and claims that it was using ST-Italy to manufacture products for it in order to meet its obligation to supply microprocessors to Cyrix. They distinguish *du Pont* on its facts, noting that in *du Pont* the party manufacturing under the "have made" right was also using the product itself, whereas here the product made under the "have made" right was sent to and eventually sold by the licensee.

We start with the clear proposition that, under its agreement, ST had the right to have the product made for it and to sell that product to third parties. It relied upon that right to have the product made by ST-Italy and to sell it to Cyrix. The district court found that the arrangement was distinguishable from that in *du Pont*. In *du Pont,* Carbide sought a license under du Pont's patent to manufacture a product known as methomyl, but du Pont refused to grant Carbide a license. Carbide then entered into an agreement with Shell, du Pont's licensee, whereby Carbide would manufacture methomyl for Shell under Shell's "have made" rights and Shell would sell it back to Carbide. Carbide would then use it (or sell it) as it wished. The Supreme Court of Delaware, whose law governed that agreement, concluded that the two agreements, one to enable Carbide to manufacture methomyl for Shell and the other whereby Shell sold it back to Carbide, were two halves of a single business transaction. The net result was that they enabled Carbide to make and use the patented product. The court held that that was in effect a sublicense, which was prohibited under the Shell-du Pont agreement.

The district court identified several important differences between the situation in *du Pont* and the arrangement among ST, ST-Italy, and Cyrix, and concluded in its Memorandum Opinion and Order as follows:

> The substance of the arrangement between Cyrix and ST and ST and ST-Italy is that when Cyrix needs wafers, it issues a purchase order to ST. ST then either manufactures the wafers itself at its Carrollton, Texas, facility or arranges for ST-Italy to manufacture the wafers at its Italian facility. ST is selling wafers. It is not selling or receiving payment for the use of its license from Intel. It has not authorized ST-Italy to make the wafers for or sell them to anyone other than ST. The production of the wafers is for the use of ST, the original licensee, and not for the use of ST-Italy. This is a valid exercise of the have-made rights granted under the License Agreement and does not constitute a sublicense.

Cyrix Corp. v. Intel Corp., 879 F.Supp. 666, 671 (E.D.Tex.1995).

We agree with the district court that the facts here are thoroughly distinguishable from those in *du Pont*. In *du Pont,* the arrangement was a sham. The third-party (Carbide) acting under Shell's "have made" rights was manufacturing and selling the product to Shell and then buying it back in what was only a set of paper transactions. Here, however, the third-party (ST-Italy) properly manufactured microprocessors under ST's "have made" rights, and

ST then properly sold the products to a different entity, Cyrix. The two agreements, one permitting ST-Italy to manufacture microprocessors for ST and the other providing for ST's sale of microprocessors to Cyrix, were separate business transactions. As the district court found, ST was using both its own facility and ST-Italy's to satisfy its obligation to provide microprocessors to Cyrix. The products manufactured by ST-Italy were made for ST. If the facts in this case had been that Cyrix made the product for ST under ST's "have made" rights and then ST sold the product back to Cyrix, then they would have been analogous to those in *du Pont,* but those are not our facts. We accordingly conclude that the district court did not err in holding that the arrangements among ST, ST-Italy, and Cyrix were a valid exercise of ST's "have made" rights under its agreement with Intel. The district court thus did not err in granting a declaratory judgment of noninfringement in favor of Cyrix and ST.

AFFIRMED.

NOTES

1. To understand the difficulties of drafting a license in the environment discussed by this court, you might want to copy out and place side-by-side the license grants discussed in this case. The differences in language are not large, but are significant. Why was Intel concerned about the so-called "foundry" use by Cyrix? Would this problem be solved by a "Sanyo limitation"? What is a "Sanyo limitation"?

2. Does this case and the cases discussed in it give an answer to what is the default rule with respect to the permitted purposes of a licensee's use of a licensed patent? Would IBM be entitled to use the patents to make products for third parties if the license had stated merely: "Intel grants to IBM a worldwide, royalty-free, nonexclusive license under the Intel Licensed Patents: to make, use, lease, sell and otherwise transfer products and to practice any method or process involved in the manufacture or use thereof"?

3. Consider the so-called "have-made" right. In the hypothetical version of the license quoted in Note 2, would IBM have the right to have products made for it by a third party? Will your answer to that question depend on the view of a license that you bring to the analysis? For example, what result if a license is nothing more that a mere covenant not to sue the particular licensee? Is a different result suggested if we view a license as a more affirmative, commercial grant and the licensor knew at the time of the transaction that most of the licensee's manufacturing was done in plants owned by third parties? We discuss transferability of a license in a later chapter. For now however, what would you describe as the difference between a "have made" grant and a grant of a right to sublicense?

PROBLEM 5.4

Draft a grant clause for a license that allows Licensee, a manufacturer, to create products using a process patented by your Client, where the only thing that Licensee may do is make the products and sell them to your client for distribution under Client's name. After you draft that clause, consider whether the Licensee has the right to make modifications in the product? If licensee insists on such right, how would you rewrite the grant?

PROBLEM 5.5

Client intends to grant a manufacturing and sale license to Small Company with respect to several of Client's patents. It is concerned about the risk that the license will create competition between it and third parties using its own technology. How can it prevent that in the grant clause?

PROBLEM 5.6

A license provides: "3. The licensor hereby grants to the licensee a nonexclusive nontransferable license to manufacture the Apparatus and to sell the apparatus of the licensee's manufacture, as follows: (a) To radio amateurs for use in radio amateur stations; (b) To radio experimenters and scientific schools or universities, for use in experimental and scientific school or university radio stations." "Apparatus" is defined to include products containing the circuits covered by the licensed patent. Does this license allow the licensee to have the products manufactured by third parties? Does it allow the licensee to sell the apparatus to dealers for experimental use by those dealers?

APPLE COMPUTER, INC. v. MICROSOFT CORP.
35 F.3d 1435 (9th Cir. 1994)

RYMER, CIRCUIT JUDGE:

Lisa and Macintosh are Apple computers. Each has a graphical user interface ("GUI") which Apple Computer, Inc. registered for copyright as an audiovisual work. Both GUIs were developed as a user-friendly way for ordinary mortals to communicate with the Apple computer; the Lisa Desktop and the Macintosh Finder are based on a desktop metaphor with windows, icons and pull-down menus which can be manipulated on the screen with a hand-held device called a mouse. When Microsoft Corporation released Windows 1.0, having a similar GUI, Apple complained. As a result, the two agreed to a license giving Microsoft the right to use and sublicense derivative works generated by Windows 1.0 in present and future products. Microsoft released Windows 2.03 and later, Windows 3.0; its licensee, Hewlett-Packard Company (HP), introduced NewWave 1.0 and later, NewWave 3.0, which run in conjunction with Windows to make IBM-compatible computers easier to use. Apple believed that these versions exceed the license, make Windows more "Mac-like," and infringe its copyright. This action followed.

In a series of published rulings, the district court construed the agreement to license visual displays in the Windows 1.0 interface, not the interface itself; determined that all visual displays in Windows 2.03 and 3.0 were in Windows 1.0 except for the use of overlapping windows and some changes in the appearance and manipulation of icons; dissected the Macintosh, Windows and NewWave interfaces based on a list of similarities submitted by Apple to decide which are protectable; and applied the limiting doctrines of originality, functionality, standardization, *scenes a faire* and merger to find no copying of protectable elements in Windows 2.03 or 3.0, and to limit the scope of copyright protection to a handful of individual elements in NewWave. The court then held that those elements in NewWave would be compared with their equivalent Apple elements for substantial similarity, and that the NewWave and Windows 2.03 and 3.0 works as a whole would be compared with Apple's works for virtual identity. When Apple declined to oppose motions for summary judgment of noninfringement for lack of virtual identity, however, judgments in favor of Microsoft and HP were entered.

Apple asks us to reverse because of two fundamental errors in the district court's reasoning. First, Apple argues that the court should not have allowed the license for Windows 1.0 to serve as a partial defense. Second, Apple contends that the court went astray by dissecting Apple's works so as to eliminate unprotectable and licensed elements from comparison with Windows 2.03, 3.0 and NewWave as a whole, incorrectly leading it to adopt a standard of virtual identity instead of substantial similarity. We disagree.

The district court's approach was on target. In so holding, we readily acknowledge how much more complex and difficult its task was than ours. . . . From this vantage point, it is clear that treatment of Apple's GUIs, whose visual displays are licensed to a great degree and which are a tool for the user to access various functions of a computer in an aesthetically and ergonomically pleasing way, follows naturally from a long line of copyright decisions which recognizes that works cannot be substantially similar where analytic dissection demonstrates that similarities in expression are either authorized, or arise from the use of common ideas or their logical extensions. . . .

Analysis of Apple's infringement claims must start with an agreement signed in 1985 by Apple and Microsoft, which resolved a dispute about visual displays generated by Microsoft software products. The 1985 Agreement licensed the right to use the visual displays generated by Apple's Lisa and Macintosh graphic user interface programs which appeared as derivative works in Windows 1.0. [Ed: relevant portions of the agreement follow this opinion.] As a result, to the extent that later versions of Windows and NewWave use the visual displays in Windows 1.0 (which came from Apple), that use is authorized.

Apple's appeal turns on whether the Agreement, properly construed, gives Microsoft the right to transfer individual elements or design features used in Windows 1.0. Apple [objects] to any interpretation that would permit later Windows products to look more like the Macintosh than Windows 1.0 looked.

The plain language of the Agreement disposes of Apple's argument. It licenses Microsoft to use "these derivative works." "These derivative works" can only refer to Microsoft's acknowledgment that the "visual displays" generated by Windows 1.0 "are derivative works of the visual displays generated by Apple's Lisa and Macintosh graphic user interface programs." As the district court explained:

> Had it been the parties' intent to limit the license to the Windows 1.0 interface, they would have known how to say so. Instead, the "derivative works" covered by the license are identified as the "visual displays" in the Windows 1.0 interface, not the interface itself. And there is nothing in the 1985 Agreement that indicates that it was intended as a product license restricting Microsoft and its licensees to the use of the Windows 1.0 interface as a whole.

Apple II, [*Apple Computer, Inc. v. Microsoft Corp.,*] 717 F.Supp. [1428] at 1430-31 [(N.D. Cal. 1989)].

Apple contends that the term "visual displays" is ambiguous and can reasonably be construed (against Microsoft, as drafter) to distinguish audiovisual copyrights protecting visual works from literary copyrights protecting programs, and to cover use of so much of Apple's visual copyrights as were used in Windows 1.0 but no more. This argument fails because Apple tried to limit Microsoft's license to Windows 1.0 as a whole — but did not succeed. Apple's first draft included language providing that "at no time shall this grant extend to any appearance, look, feel, visual feature or operation other than that incorporated in Microsoft Windows." Microsoft, however, rejected this limitation. Thus, the parties had already staked out their positions by the time Microsoft produced the final draft. Accordingly, there is no basis for construing the Agreement to grant the narrow license Apple bargained for but gave up.

Apple relies on statements by various Microsoft employees in support of its ambiguity argument. These are unavailing because the Agreement has an integration clause which precludes contradicting its terms by collateral understandings. In any event, testimony by the two employees who opined that the phrase "visual displays" is ambiguous lacks force because both are engineers who took no part in negotiating the 1985 Agreement. Likewise, an internal Microsoft memorandum by Bill Gates, which states that Microsoft must "be careful not to take additional things from apple screens when we make enhancements — everything we do today is fine," raises no triable issue as it is consistent with Gates' understanding that the license was for individual displays, not the interface as a whole, and with testimony by Apple's chief negotiator that Apple's license from Microsoft gave Apple the right to incorporate into the Macintosh interface any "new visual feature" developed by Microsoft for Windows.

Apple's further contention that the district court's interpretation of the Agreement must be wrong because it would be unreasonable to suppose that Apple knowingly gave away its most valuable technological asset ignores the fact that Apple itself received valuable consideration under the Agreement: the right to use and license any new displays created by Microsoft within five years, together with Microsoft's promises to delay release of an IBM-compatible version of Excel and to release an improved version of Microsoft Word for the Macintosh. Under these circumstances, the district court properly concluded that the Agreement is not reasonably susceptible to Apple's interpretation. . . .

Apple raises one additional point. . . . The argument is that even if the 1985 Agreement does confer a partial license to use visual displays, Microsoft and HP exceeded its scope and therefore infringed Apple's copyrights. The cases on which Apple relies, however, merely establish that the breach of a prohibition in the license agreement can lead to a finding of infringement. Finally, contrary to Apple's suggestion, by concluding that the 1985 Agreement provides a partial defense, the district court did not preclude Apple from prevailing on its infringement claims; the court merely required Apple to prove that Microsoft and HP copied unlicensed, *protected* expression. We see no error in the court's ruling.

[The court held that there was no infringement by Microsoft under a standard that compared the two works excluding, among other things, those aspects of the Microsoft product that were licensed to it by Apple and then requiring proof of virtual identity between the two works.]

AFFIRMED IN PART. . . .

The Apple-Microsoft agreement, remarkable for its brevity in light of the huge economic consequences that it had, read in relevant part as follows:

AGREEMENT

This Agreement is entered into on this 22nd day of November, 1985, by and between Apple Computer, Inc. . . . and Microsoft Corporation. . . .

The parties have a long history of cooperation and trust and wish to maintain that mutually beneficial relationship. However, a dispute has arisen concerning the ownership of and possible copyright infringement as to certain visual displays generated by several Microsoft software products. These products are Microsoft's operating environment program, "Microsoft Windows Version 1.0," the three Microsoft applications programs developed under the January 22, 1982, agreement between Microsoft and Apple for use on Apple's MacIntosh Computers: an electronic spread sheet program ("Microsoft Multiplan"), a business graphics program ("Microsoft Chart") and a database program ("Microsoft File"), and two other Microsoft application programs: an integrated electronic spread sheet program ("Microsoft Excel") and a word processing program ("Microsoft Word").

By means of this Agreement the parties intend to resolve the dispute and each acknowledges that the valuable consideration underlying this Agreement consists of the resolution of the dispute and the several undertakings and accommodations of the respective parties described below. Accordingly, the parties agree as follows:

1. Acknowledgement. For purposes of resolving this dispute and in consideration of the license grant from Apple described in section 2 below, Microsoft acknowledges that the visual displays in the above-listed Microsoft programs are derivative works of the visual displays generated by Apple's Lisa and Macintosh graphic user interface programs.

2. Visual Copyright License from Apple.

A. Grant. Apple hereby grants to Microsoft a non-exclusive, worldwide, royalty-free, perpetual, non-transferable license to use these derivative works in present and future software programs and to license them to and through third parties for use in their software programs. This license shall not include new software programs written by Microsoft which are similar in function to Microsoft Excel and are offered to the public prior to October 1, 1986. As a condition to this license, Microsoft shall cause its visual copyright notice to appear in its products which use visual displays licensed hereunder.

B. Warranty. Apple hereby warrants that neither Apple nor any of its agents, representatives or attorneys knows of any patent, copyright, trade secret or any other right or claim of or by any third party to these licensed visual copyrights in the Lisa and Macintosh graphic user interface programs. Each party shall notify the other promptly of any such claim and will cooperate fully in the defense of such a claim. Apple shall indemnify and hold Microsoft harmless from any such claim of which it had such knowledge and any damages and reasonable expenses arising therefrom.

. . . .

4. Release. Apple hereby waives any other copyright, patent, trade secret or other claim or right it may have as to Microsoft Windows Version 1.0.

5. Visual Copyright License from Microsoft. Microsoft hereby grants to Apple a nonexclusive, worldwide, royalty-free, perpetual, nontransferable license to use any new visual displays created by Microsoft during a period of its Microsoft Windows retail software product in software programs and to license them to and through third parties for use in their software programs. As a condition to this license, Apple shall cause its visual copyright notice to appear in its products which use such Microsoft visual displays.

6. Revision of Microsoft Word. Microsoft shall revise Microsoft Word which operates on the Apple Macintosh computer by enhancing and improving the program as specified in Exhibit A to this Agreement. Microsoft shall use its best efforts to complete the revision by July 31, 1986.

7. General Provisions.

. . . .

E. Assignment. Except in the case of the sale of substantially all of the assets of controlling stock, this Agreement may not be assigned, nor the rights granted hereunder (other than the sublicensing rights contained in paragraph 2) transferred by either party without the prior written consent of the other party.

. . . .

G. Entire Agreement. This Agreement constitutes the entire agreement between the parties with respect to the subject matter treated herein. This Agreement shall not be amended except by a written agreement signed by both parties.

PROBLEM 5.7

Redraft the Apple-Microsoft license from the Apple perspective to avoid the problems Apple encountered.

A. Scope as Compared to Covenant

SUN MICROSYSTEMS, INC. v. MICROSOFT CORP.
188 F.3d 1115 (9th Cir. 1999)

SCHROEDER, CIRCUIT JUDGE:

This case illustrates how fast technology can outdistance the capacity of contract drafters to provide for the ramifications of a computer software licensing arrangement. The license in question runs from plaintiff-appellee Sun Microsystems to defendant-appellant Microsoft. It involves Java, a computer programming language Sun developed to enable the writing of programs that work on any computer operating system. The license agreement was negotiated on a rushed basis in 1996, and by 1997 both Microsoft and Sun had developed what they believed to be significant improvements to Java.

Sun filed this suit for copyright infringement, claiming that Microsoft had exceeded the scope of its license by creating an enhanced version of Java that was fully operable only on Microsoft's operating system, and further, by not adapting its implementation of Java to be compatible with Sun's addition to Java of a component known as the "Java Native Interface" ("JNI"). Sun sought an injunction barring Microsoft from including incompatible Java technology in its products. The district court granted a preliminary injunction to Sun, and Microsoft appeals. The underlying facts, the details of the negotiations, and the nature of the software involved are all more fully described in the district court's detailed opinion.

Before the district court, the parties bitterly contested the proper interpretation of the terms of the license agreement. Microsoft maintained that the agreement fully authorized all of the conduct that Sun challenged as infringing. Sun's interpretation was, of course, to the contrary. After a careful analysis of the parties' contentions, the district court held that Sun was likely to prevail on the merits of its claim that Microsoft had violated the license agreement.

The parties also disputed whether Sun's suit was properly considered as one for copyright infringement, as Sun contended, or as one for breach of contract, as Microsoft contended. The district court concluded that the claim was properly considered as an infringement action, thereby entitling Sun to a presumption of irreparable harm. The district court did not elaborate on why the case was a copyright infringement rather than a contract interpretation dispute, and it is on this point that Microsoft expends most of its ammunition on this appeal. It contends that the disputed compatibility requirements of the license agreement are affirmative covenants rather than limitations on the scope of the license, and that accordingly contractual rather than copyright remedies are appropriate if there has been any breach. The district court apparently did not expressly rule on this issue.

[We] agree with Sun that significant evidence supports the district court's holding that Sun is likely to prevail on its interpretation of the language of the agreement and to prove that Microsoft's conduct violated it. We agree with Microsoft, however, that the district court should not have invoked the presumption of irreparable harm applicable to copyright infringement claims before it determined that the compatibility requirements were a limit on the scope of the license rather than independent contractual covenants. We therefore vacate the preliminary injunction and remand for further proceedings.

There is also a claim of unfair competition under California law. The district court entered an injunction on that claim solely on the basis of past conduct. Microsoft correctly contends that under California law an injunction must be based on the prospect of future conduct. We therefore also vacate the injunction insofar as it relates to the unfair competition claim and remand for consideration of that issue.

Factual Background

In March 1996, Microsoft and Sun entered into a "Technology License and Distribution Agreement" ("TLDA") for Java. Microsoft agreed to pay Sun $3.75 million a year for broad rights to use the language. In exchange, Sun granted Microsoft a non-exclusive license to "make, access, use, copy, view, display, modify, adapt, and create Derivative Works of the Technology in Source Code form" and to "make, use, import, reproduce, license, rent, lease, offer to sell, sell or otherwise distribute to end users as part of a Product . . . the Technology and Derivative Works thereof in binary form."

Sun had created Java so that programmers could write a single program that would work on any operating system. Because Sun wanted Java to remain cross-platform compatible, the TLDA includes compatibility requirements. Section 2.6(a)(iv) requires Microsoft to produce a compatible implementation of Java within six months of the date that Sun creates a "significant upgrade" to Java. Section 2.6(a)(vi) provides that Microsoft shall make available only products that are compatible implementations. Section 2.6(b)(iv) contains the compatibility requirements for compilers. It provides that Microsoft's Java compilers "shall include a mode which a Tool Customer may use to permit such Product to pass the Java Language Test Suite that accompanies" any upgrades of Java that Sun creates. To determine compatibility, the TLDA refers to a set of mostly automated tests that Sun had developed.

In late 1997, Sun became concerned that Microsoft was distributing a "polluted" version of Java that Microsoft had modified in ways that made it incompatible with Sun's standards. Sun filed suit against Microsoft on October 7,

1997, alleging, among other things, trademark infringement, unfair competition, and breach of contract. In November 1997, Sun moved for a preliminary injunction barring Microsoft from using Sun's "Java Compatible" logo on products that failed Sun's compatibility tests. On March 24, 1998, the district court entered a preliminary injunction. Microsoft did not appeal this injunction.

Sun then amended its complaint to add a claim for copyright infringement and filed motions for a preliminary injunction under 17 U.S.C. § 502 for copyright infringement and under California Business & Professions Code § 17200 for unfair competition. The copyright infringement motion sought an order immediately enjoining Microsoft from distributing its development kit for Java programmers, and enjoining it from distributing Internet Explorer or Windows98 unless it could show within ninety days that those products passed Sun's compatibility tests. . . .

[The district Court granted the injunction and Microsoft appealed.]

Analysis

I. The Copyright Infringement Claim

The standard for a preliminary injunction balances the plaintiff's likelihood of success against the relative hardships to the parties. To receive a preliminary injunction, Sun was required to show "either a likelihood of success on the merits and the possibility of irreparable injury, or that serious questions going to the merits were raised and the balance of hardships tips sharply in its favor." . . . Under federal copyright law, however, a plaintiff that demonstrates a likelihood of success on the merits of a copyright infringement claim is entitled to a presumption of irreparable harm. . . .

The district court found that Sun was likely to succeed on its contentions that Microsoft had violated the terms of the TLDA by failing to support JNI and by extending the Java language and modifying the compiler. It therefore held that Sun was entitled to a presumption of irreparable harm. The district court did not make any finding on whether there would be irreparable harm absent the copyright presumption. Finally, the district court briefly addressed hardship, stating that the potential harm to Microsoft was not "unduly burdensome" and that the requested relief would not harm the interests of third parties. It did not discuss the likely extent of harm to Sun if a preliminary injunction were not entered.

We address in turn the likelihood of success on the merits and the applicability of a presumption of irreparable harm. With regard to the likelihood of success, the issue is whether there is sufficient evidence to support the district court's conclusion that Sun was likely to prove that Microsoft's conduct violated the terms of the TLDA. We conclude that there is such evidence. With regard to the applicability of a presumption of irreparable harm, we agree with Microsoft that the issue turns upon whether the terms Microsoft allegedly breached were limitations on the scope of the license, which would mean that Microsoft had infringed the copyright by acting outside the scope of the license; or whether the terms were merely separate contractual covenants, which would make this a contract dispute in which the copyright presumption of irreparable harm has no application. We conclude that the district court must decide this latter issue before it decides whether Sun is entitled to a presumption of irreparable harm, and so we vacate the injunction and remand the case.

A. Likelihood of Success

The district court held that Sun had shown that it was likely to prove that Microsoft had violated the TLDA in two ways: by adding new features to its compiler that caused it to fail Sun's compatibility tests referenced in the TLDA and by failing to support Sun's "Java Native Interface" ("JNI"), a tool for integrating platform-specific (or "native") code into a Java program.

There is significant evidence to support the district court's holding that Sun has a reasonable likelihood of proving that Microsoft's Java compiler violated the compatibility provisions of the TLDA. The TLDA generally permits Microsoft to modify its compiler, for section 2.1(a) allows Microsoft to "modify" the "Java Technology," and section 1.25 defines the Java "Technology" to include the "Java Compiler." Microsoft modified the Java compiler by adding an extended mode that includes two keyword extensions and three compiler directives that enable programmers to use some Windows features and to program more efficiently in the Windows environment. The district court found that the use of Microsoft's additional compiler directives and keyword extensions can result in programs that fail Sun's compatibility tests.

Microsoft's compiler, however, contains a mode that disables the compiler directives and keyword extensions; when the compiler is operated in that mode, there are no compatibility problems. Microsoft argues that because of the inclusion of this mode, TLDA § 2.6(b)(iv) permits the compiler modifications. That section provides that any new Java compilers that Microsoft makes commercially available "shall include a mode which a Tool Customer may use to permit such Product to pass the Java Language Test Suite that accompanied the Significant Upgrade." Section 2.6(b)(iv), however, says only that the compiler must have the described mode; it does not say that any compiler that includes the described mode is allowable. The disputed issue is whether the *extended* mode of Microsoft's compiler, which the district court concluded causes the compiler to fail the Java Language Test Suite, violates the TLDA.

Considerable evidence supports the district court's conclusion that Microsoft's extended compiler mode is impermissible. Microsoft's extended compiler fails a requirement, contained in the documentation to the Java Language Test Suite, that "the output from your Java compiler implementation (if applicable) must execute properly with a JavaSoft Virtual Machine of the same version as the Java Compatibility Kit you are using." Moreover, the Java Language Specification implicitly prohibits the addition of keywords by defining a complete list of keywords and then reserving only two words for later inclusion. This reading of the specification is buttressed by the preface, which states that the specification is meant to ensure that "the behavior of every language construct [be] specified, so that all implementations of Java will accept the same programs."

There is also evidence to support the district court's holding that Sun has a reasonable likelihood of proving that the TLDA obligates Microsoft to support

JNI. In the district court, the parties disputed whether JNI is part of the AAPI (the "Applet Application Programming Interface"), with which Microsoft's products must comply under sections 1.15 and 2.6(a)(vi) of the TLDA. Section 1.1(a) of the TLDA defines the AAPI in relevant part as "the public application programming interface to the Java Applet Environment." The issues before the district court thus reduced to whether JNI is a "public application programming interface," a term the TLDA does not define, and whether it is an interface to the Java Applet Environment. Although Microsoft's experts testified to the contrary, there is substantial evidence in the record from Sun's experts that JNI is a "public application programming interface." According to section 2.9(e) of the TLDA, moreover, native code interfaces, such as JNI, are interfaces to the Java Reference Implementation virtual machine. Because section 1.25 of the TLDA states that the virtual machine is part of the Java Applet Environment, JNI appears to be an interface to the Java Applet Environment. There is thus considerable evidence that JNI falls within Microsoft's compliance obligations.

Microsoft nevertheless stresses that the district court erred in holding that the TLDA requires Microsoft to support JNI because JNI did not even exist at the time the parties signed the TLDA. The district court concluded that the addition of JNI was a permissible upgrade to Java under section 1.1(a) of the TLDA. That section defines the AAPI, of which JNI is a part, as "(a) the public application programming interface to the Java Applet Environment . . . and (d) the OEM Java API Specification, as modified by SUN during the term of this agreement." The district court did not err in adopting the grammatically plausible reading that the "as modified" language refers not only to section 1.1(d), but to section 1.1(a) as well, and thus allows the AAPI to be modified to include JNI. We therefore hold that sufficient evidence supports the district court's finding that Sun demonstrated a probability of success on the merits of its claim that Microsoft's modifications of Java violated the TLDA.

B. Presumption of Irreparable Harm

Federal copyright law presumes irreparable harm from the infringement of a copyright. The district court held that this case is a copyright infringement case and not a contract case and therefore presumed irreparable harm. It is not clear, however, how the district court reached its decision that this case should be analyzed under the copyright infringement standard. It stated only that "Microsoft's argument that . . . Sun does not enjoy a presumption of irreparable harm merely rehashes its argument, which the court has rejected, that Sun's claims arise out of breach of contract rather than copyright infringement." We were unable to determine, and the parties were unable to inform us at oral argument, where in the record before us the district court had previously addressed this issue.

Whether this is a copyright or a contract case turns on whether the compatibility provisions help define the scope of the license. Generally, a "copyright owner who grants a nonexclusive license to use his copyrighted material waives his right to sue the licensee for copyright infringement" and can sue only for breach of contract. *Graham v. James,* 144 F.3d 229, 236 (2d Cir. 1998). If, however, a license is limited in scope and the licensee acts outside the scope, the licensor can bring an action for copyright infringement. *See S.O.S.,*

Inc. v. Payday, Inc., 886 F.2d 1081, 1087 (9th Cir. 1989); NIMMER ON COPYRIGHT, § 1015[A] (1999).

Microsoft argues, more strongly on appeal than before the district court, that the compatibility provisions on which Sun relies are contractual covenants that do not limit the scope of the license. Microsoft asserts that the broad grants of section 2.2 of the TLDA allow it an unrestricted right to modify Sun's source code and create derivative works, and that it made a separate contractual promise in section 2.6 to honor the compatibility requirements. Sun argues that the granting language of section 2.2 and the compatibility terms of section 2.6 must be read together to create a license that grants Microsoft only the right to make *compatible* modifications and derivative works. The district court did not address these arguments in its opinion. It is thus not clear whether it agreed with Sun that the compatibility terms in question are limitations on the scope of the license or whether it believed the distinction between affirmative covenants and limitations on scope to be immaterial.

The enforcement of a copyright license raises issues that lie at the intersection of copyright and contract law, an area of law that is not yet well developed. We must decide an issue of first impression: whether, where two sophisticated parties have negotiated a copyright license and dispute its scope, the copyright holder who has demonstrated likely success on the merits is entitled to a presumption of irreparable harm. We hold that it is, but only after the copyright holder has established that the disputed terms are limitations on the scope of the license rather than independent contractual covenants. In other words, before Sun can gain the benefits of copyright enforcement, it must definitively establish that the rights it claims were violated are copyright, not contractual, rights.

In reaching this result, we find considerable support in *Video Trip Corp. v. Lightning Video, Inc.,* 866 F.2d 50 (2d Cir. 1989), in which the Second Circuit held that preliminary contractual issues, such as the ownership of the copyright, must be resolved before the copyright presumption of irreparable harm applies. . . . As here, the parties disputed what preliminary injunction standard should apply. The Second Circuit stated: "It is understandable why a party claiming copyright protection would prefer to ignore the contract dispute and assume the validity of the ownership of the copyright. The rules for obtaining a preliminary injunction are less onerous than in other cases." *Id. at 52.* The court held that "since the issue as to the ownership of the copyright is still to be determined, we review the order of the court below in denying the application for a preliminary injunction in light of the rule applicable in any contract case." *Id.*

The determination of whether the compatibility terms in the TLDA are covenants or limitations on the scope of the license is likewise a contractual issue, for it requires us to construe the license. We recognized this in *S.O.S., Inc. v. Payday, Inc.,* 886 F.2d 1081 (9th Cir. 1989). In *S.O.S.,* the plaintiff, which held a copyright in a computer program, had granted the defendant a license to "use" the software and had explicitly reserved all other rights. The plaintiff claimed that by modifying the software the defendant had exceeded the scope of the license and therefore infringed the copyright. The district court, using California contract law to construe the license, applied the rule that contracts should be construed against the drafter and held that the license therefore permitted any uses not explicitly forbidden. On appeal, we agreed that we should "rely on state law to provide the canons of contractual construction" provided that "such rules do not interfere with federal copyright law or policy."

The principles illustrated by *Video Trip* and *S.O.S.* indicate that the disputed question in this case, whether the compatibility terms in the TLDA are license restrictions or separate covenants, is a preliminary contractual issue that must be resolved under California law favorably to Sun before Sun is entitled to the copyright presumption of irreparable harm. The district court did not decide this issue. . . . We therefore vacate the preliminary injunction and remand the case. Because we vacate the injunction, we also leave it to the district court to consider in the first instance Microsoft's argument that, under the district court's prior interpretation of the TLDA, an injunction may be granted only if Microsoft intentionally and willfully violated the TLDA's compatibility requirements. . . .

II. The Unfair Competition Claim

We also vacate the portion of the district court's preliminary injunction that is based on the California Unfair Business Practices Act. . . . The injunction is VACATED and the case REMANDED to the district court for further proceedings.

The District Court, on remand, held that the claims were contractual in nature, rather than a copyright claim. It commented:

> The rules of contract construction embodied in California law control the interpretation of the TLDA to the extent that such rules are consistent with federal copyright law and policy. Therefore, the court must review the entire TLDA and effect the mutual intention of the parties "as gathered from the four corners of the instrument." . . . [S]ee also Cal. Civ.Code § 1641 ("the whole of a contract is to be taken together, so as to give effect to every part, if reasonably practicable, each clause helping to interpret the other.").

> The language and structure of the TLDA suggest that the compatibility obligations are separate covenants and not conditions of, or restrictions on, the license grants. The license grants in sections 2.1 ("Source Code and Development License to Technology") and 2.2 ("Distribution License to Technology") allow Microsoft to distribute the Technology and Derivative Works of the Technology as part of a Product but say nothing about the license grants being subject to, conditional on, or limited by compliance with the compatibility obligations set forth in Section 2.6 ("Compatibility"). In contrast, the language used in the Trademark License incorporated into the TLDA expressly limits Microsoft's license to use Sun's Compatibility Logo to those Products that have passed the Java Test Suites. . . . Similarly, in setting forth Microsoft's rights with respect to Surviving Products following expiration of the TLDA or a termination of the TLDA for a willful breach, the parties state that Microsoft's rights are "subject to its continued compliance with the Test Suites current at the time of expira-

tion or termination. . . ." TLDA § 11.3. The contrast in language between that used for the license grants in sections 2.1 and 2.2 with that used in the Trademark License and for Surviving Products supports the conclusion that the parties regarded the compatibility provisions of section 2.6 as separate covenants rather than limitations on the scope of the licenses.

Sun Microsystems, Inc. v. Microsoft Corp., 81 F. Supp. 2d 1026 (N.D. Cal. 2000). Subsequently, however, the court held that a preliminary injunction would be sustained under California law of unfair competition. *Sun Microsystems, Inc. v. Microsoft Corp.*, 87 F. Supp. 2d 992 (N.D. Cal. 2000).

NOTES

1. If Microsoft was in breach of the compatibility provisions of the license, why does its conduct not justify an immediate claim for copyright infringement for making and distributing non-compliant copies? The answer lies in the distinction between scope provisions and covenants. What is the justification for making that distinction?

Scope terms define the subject matter of a license and the range within which the licensee's conduct is covered by the license. Conduct that falls within the scope of an existing license is not infringement. What about conduct that is outside the scope?

Covenants, on the other hand, are mere promises. Consider the following license:

> 1.0 Licensor grants licensee the right to make and distribute up to 50,000 copies of the Licensed Work.

> 1.1 Licensee promises to pay Licensor $10 for each copy it makes.

Which of these terms defines scope and which is a covenant? In this hypothetical, if a failure to make a timely payment would not mean that copies made after this failure are infringement, what is the remedy if non-payment continues for an extended period?

2. What substantive provisions define of the scope of the license? There is no single answer. The licensed scope is often stated in the granting clause, but that is not always true. The District Court in *Sun Microsystems* suggested that the following terms of a trademark license that was not at issue in the case were part of the scope even though not in the grant of a right to distribute software with the Java certification trademark: "This License applies only to versions of Licensee's Products that have successfully passed the Java Test Suites made available by SUN pursuant to the TLDA, and which otherwise fully comply with all other compatibility and certification requirements of the TLDA." Why is this a scope provision and the compatibility language in the main case a mere covenant?

3. If the parties agree that products covered by the licensor's intellectual property can be sold under a license, but that the products should be of a certain (defined) minimum quality, what determines whether that latter condition should be part of the scope of the license or a covenant? Which party benefits from treating the quality issue as a covenant?

PROBLEM 5.8

You are asked to draft a license with compatibility provisions that Sun can use in future agreements, but that will avoid the litigation it experienced with Microsoft by making compatibility part of the license scope. In relevant part, the following are the terms of the original agreement. How would you modify them?

> § 2.1(a) Sun grants to Licensee a perpetual non-exclusive develop-ment license under the Intellectual Property Rights of Sun to make, access, use, copy, distribute, view, display, modify, adapt, and create Derivative Works of the Technology and resulting Products.

> § 2.6(a)(vi) Licensee agrees that any new version of a Product that Licensee makes commercially available to the public after the most recent Compatibility Date shall only include the corresponding Compatible Implementation.

Assume that the terms that begin with capital letters are all appropriately defined in the agreement. A "Product" is any software including Java, and "Compatible Implementation" refers to compliance with all compatibility standards set by Sun.

PROBLEM 5.9

As an associate of Big Law Firm, you receive a terms list to which ABC (your client) and Thomas, the proposed licensee, have agreed:

> Use Rights: Make, have made and sell circuits covered by patent #5,432,776

> License duration: ten years

> Location of use: Thomas' New York plant

> Purpose of use: resale to manufacturers of computers

> Payment: 10% of sale price for all circuit boards sold

You are asked to reduce these terms to a draft to be given to the parties for their approval. It is not necessary to deal with other provisions. However, your senior partner wants two drafts. In one, the terms should all be part of the scope of the license, while in the other the only scope provision should be the first term on the list. Respond.

B. Language and Rights

There are virtually an infinite number of potential variations in language used to describe the subject matter of a license and the rights granted. Practices differ widely. In industries where patent or copyright interests are dominant and the rights under those laws are considered adequate for flexibility in licensing, the granting clauses are often couched in terms of the subject matter and enumerated rights in those statutes. Thus, licenses of the following type are common:

> "Licensor grants licensee a nonexclusive right to make and distribute copies of the Licensed Work for a period of ten years."

> "Licensor grants Licensee the non-exclusive right to *make and sell* the machine covered by Patent No. ____."

The two hypothetical grants illustrate one difference between the two fields. While many copyrights are registered and the relevant works might then be identified by registration number, that does not occur for all copyrighted subject matter. In contrast, in a patent license not involving related know how, trade secrets or other information, an ordinary practice is to identify the subject matter by number and the rights by reference to the statutory rights set out in the Patent Act.

As licensing moves away from this structured environment, it is more difficult to identify either the subject matter or the rights granted. This is ultimately a drafting problem, but there are recurring, conceptually important circumstances. For example, in *Behr Venture Partners, Ltd. v. Bedford Computer Corp.*, 62 B.R. 555 (Bankr. D.N.H. 1986), the agreement provided that a financing entity would obtain ownership of new software developed by the debtor using funds from the venture financing. The agreement, however, provided no means to distinguish between old and "new" software, and the practices of the developer did not provide a factual basis to make the distinction. Not surprisingly, the court held that the ownership claim failed. The issue in *Bedford* arises commonly where the task is to select out of a mass of not clearly identifiable subject matter. The issue in *Bedford* does not arise when the intent is to license or transfer all of a particular type of asset.

The software and other digital industries frequently rely on licenses that do not use language from the copyright statute, even though for most software, the primary intellectual property rights are in copyright law. Instead of referring to the designated rights in the statute, many licenses grant the licensee a right to "use" the licensed software. Similarly, many online access licenses refer to rights to "use" or "access" the online site.

What does a right to "use" mean in a license that is not premised on patent rights? The answer lies in the commercial context and what the licensee anticipates under the license. The court in *SOS, Inc. v. Payday, Inc.*, 886 F.2d 1081 (9th Cir. 1989), dealt with a software license and this language. The issue was whether a license that granted Payday the right to use copyrighted software in its business of supplying reports to third parties, covered Payday when it made a copy of the program and modified it for its use. The court recognized the uneasy fit between this common language and the copyright statutory scheme. It commented:

> The contract between S.O.S. and Payday states, "This series of programs is the property of SOS, and PAYDAY is acquiring the right of use, SOS retains all rights of ownership." This language is unambiguous. Payday acquired the right to use the software, but S.O.S. retained

all ownership rights. In the context of the parties' entire agreement, it is clear that the "right of use" was not intended to refer to copyright use. The contract does not refer explicitly to copyright or to any of the copyright owner's exclusive rights. Payday clearly was concerned solely with obtaining output in the form of processing payroll information for its customers. The provisions stating that Payday would lease the disk drive and other hardware necessary to run the program, and that the equipment would be kept in the office of a third party (and later at S.O.S.'s office), demonstrate that neither party expected Payday to be able to gain access to the source code itself, as opposed to putting in its customers' data and receiving output.

Compare this analysis with the following case that did not deal with software.

KENNEDY v. NATIONAL JUVENILE DETENTION ASSOCIATION
187 F.3d 690 (7th Cir. 1999)

BAUER, CIRCUIT JUDGE.

Edwin Kennedy appeals the district court's decision to dismiss his copyright infringement claim pursuant to Federal Rule of Civil Procedure 12(b)(6) for failure to state a claim upon which relief can be granted. Kennedy claims that this decision was in error because the consulting agreement he entered into with the National Juvenile Detention Association ("NJDA") did not grant either the NJDA or the Illinois Juvenile Justice Commission ("IJJC") the right to produce derivative works from his report. For the reasons set forth below, we affirm the district court's decision.

I. Background

The facts of the case, predominantly taken from Kennedy's first amended complaint, are regarded as true for the purposes of this appeal. On October 30, 1995, Kennedy and the NJDA entered into an agreement for Kennedy to provide consulting services, to conduct a study of the juvenile justice requirements of the Seventh Judicial Circuit of Illinois (the "circuit"), and to submit a written report of his findings. The study was funded by the IJJC. The goals of the study were to collect data regarding current juvenile detention practices, to recommend improvements in the juvenile detention process, and to estimate future juvenile detention requirements within the circuit. The contract was to run until September 30, 1996.

On September 20, 1996, Kennedy submitted a draft of his report to the NJDA. At the behest of the NJDA and IJJC, Kennedy made minor revisions to his report for no additional compensation. A few months later, the NJDA requested that Kennedy, in exchange for an additional $10,000, make more revisions to his report because the original changes were not as extensive as they had hoped. Kennedy refused to make the revisions because he was concerned about compromising the integrity of his work, and he subsequently applied to register a copyright in his work. The copyright was effectively registered on January 13, 1997. In the meantime, the NJDA requested that

Kennedy provide a disk with his copy of the final report. Thinking this was a condition for payment according to the agreement, Kennedy supplied the NJDA with the disk. When the contract had expired and Kennedy had refused to make further revisions to his report, the NJDA hired Craig Boersema to supervise the completion of the report. Kennedy was fully compensated for his completed work.

On January 17, 1997, Anne Studzinski, administrator of the IJJC, hosted a meeting in Chicago, attended by the NJDA's Executive Director Earl Dunlap, and Boersema, for the purpose of altering Kennedy's report; Kennedy neither knew of nor assented to the revision. Studzinski defended her revision of the report based on a clause in the contract which states:

> Where activities supported by this contract produce original computer programs (the term computer programs includes executable computer programs and supporting data in any form), writing, sound recordings, pictorial reproductions, drawing or other graphical representations and works of any similar nature, the government has the right to use, duplicate and disclose, in whole or in part, such materials in any manner for any purpose whatsoever and have others do so. If the material is copyrightable, Edwin Kennedy may copyright such, but the government reserves a royalty-free non-exclusive and irreversible license to reproduce, publish, and use such materials in whole or in part and to authorize others to do so.

In March of 1997, Kennedy released his version of the report, and on April 1, 1997, Dunlap issued a press release discrediting Kennedy and his work in order to promote the revised version of the work. The NJDA published the official report in August of 1997.

Kennedy filed suit against the NJDA and IJJC for copyright infringement. . . . The NJDA and IJJC filed motions to dismiss the claim based on lack of subject matter jurisdiction, lack of personal jurisdiction, improper venue, and failure to state a claim. . . . The district court [granted] defendants' motions to dismiss for failure to state a claim, rejecting the other theories as well as the request for sanctions. [Kennedy appeals.] The NJDA re-asserts its contention that it had the right to produce derivative works from Kennedy's report or, in the alternative, that it had a right, as a joint author of the study, to publish its version of the report.

II. Analysis

Kennedy concedes that the contractual agreement conferred upon the NJDA the right to reproduce and publish his report, however he argues that it did not grant either the NJDA or IJJC the right to create derivative works from it. . . .

Normal rules of contract construction are generally applied in construing copyright agreements. Under Wisconsin law, contracts are to be construed as they are written. [The] district court found, and we agree, that the consulting agreement granted the NJDA a nonexclusive license to reproduce, publish, and use Kennedy's copyrighted report. The court also found that the term "use" must give the defendants rights beyond those of reproduction and publication. Moreover, it found that, considering the broad, comprehensive grant of authority given to the NJDA and IJJC, it was irrelevant that the agreement did not specifically refer to the defendants' right to create derivative works from Kennedy's copyrighted materials. Therefore, the district court found that the agreement gave the defendants permission to alter Kennedy's report and create a derivative work from it.

The NJDA suggests in its brief that the word "use" in this case is synonymous with "prepare derivative works." While we will not go so far as to agree with this interpretation, in the context of the consulting agreement between Kennedy and the NJDA, the term "use" does encompass the act of creating derivative works. As stated above, the agreement gave the defendants "the right to use, duplicate and disclose, in whole or in part, such materials in any manner *for any purpose whatsoever*." (emphasis added). This phrase grants considerable latitude to the defendants to use Kennedy's report. Additionally, it gives the defendants the right to "reproduce, publish, *and use*" any copyrighted material (emphasis added). Kennedy argues that the defendants' rights are limited to those of reproduction and publication of his works. In accordance with general contract construction, however, we agree with the district court that this contract granted rights beyond those of reproduction and publication. In the context of copyright law, one of those other rights is the right to prepare derivative works. To read the agreement any other way would render the term "use" superfluous.

Kennedy also argues that the district court erred by construing ambiguous language of the consulting agreement in favor of the drafting party, the NJDA. This argument is without merit. The district court did not find, nor do we, that the language in the agreement is ambiguous. Accordingly, we construe the contract as it stands. And as the contract stands, it grants the defendants the right to use Kennedy's report for any purpose whatsoever.

Because we have decided that the language of the consulting agreement granted the NJDA and the IJJC the right to produce derivative works, we need not decide whether the NJDA and Kennedy are joint authors of the report. Such a decision would be necessary should the NJDA try to copyright the report, but we are not faced with that issue. . . .

[AFFIRMED.]

. . . .

MANION, CIRCUIT JUDGE, concurring in part and dissenting in part.

The court accurately sets out the law governing copyright law but I respectfully dissent from the court's application of that law. In all other respects I concur.

At this point in the litigation, the defendants do not dispute that Kennedy has a valid copyright interest in his report. As copyright holder, Kennedy has three exclusive rights that are relevant here: the right "to reproduce the copyrighted work," 17 U.S.C. § 106(1); the right "to prepare derivative works based upon the copyrighted work," § 106(2); and the right "to distribute copies . . . of the copyrighted work," § 106(3). Kennedy alleges, and the defendants do not dispute, that the report the defendants prepared is a derivative work based upon his report. The issue before us, then, is whether the defendants had a license to make this derivative work.

As the court notes, the contract between the parties contained two separate clauses granting the defendants rights in works created as part of the study: one clause applied (presumably to non-copyrightable materials) generally, and the other applied to copyrightable works. The general clause stated: "the government has the right to use, duplicate and disclose, in whole or in part, such materials in any manner or for any purpose whatsoever." The clause for copyrightable works was similar, but different in important respects: "the government reserves a royalty-free non-exclusive and irreversible license to reproduce, publish, and use such materials in whole or in part." First, the clause governing copyrightable materials does not include the phrase from the general clause "in any manner or for any purpose whatsoever," so it apparently grants somewhat more limited rights than does the general clause. Second, two of the three verbs describing the rights granted are different. Although the words used in the general clause, "duplicate" and "disclose," are very similar in meaning to the ones used in the copyrightable clause, "reproduce" and "publish," the latter two are terms of art taken from the Copyright Act while the former are not. As noted above, a copyright holder has the right to "reproduce" and "distribute" the copyrighted work, and under the Act "publish" means the same as "distribute," *see* 17 U.S.C. § 101 (defines "publication" using same language that § 106(3) uses to describe "distribute"). There is no dispute then that the contract unambiguously grants the defendants two of Kennedy's exclusive statutory rights. But those two don't include the third, the right to make derivative works, the right at issue here.

So the issue is whether "use," the third verb in the clause, unambiguously grants to the defendants the right to prepare derivative works. The other two verbs in this clause are unambiguous because they are statutory terms of art. But the drafters of the contract (the defendants) chose not to use the third term of art — "prepare derivative works." Instead they used the vague term "use." This suggests that the parties intended "use" to mean something other than simply "prepare derivative works." They may have intended it to mean something more than prepare derivative works or perhaps something less. It is very possible that they intended it to mean only prepare derivative works. But their intention is not clear from the contract's text, and so this term is "ambiguous." Thus the parties should be given the opportunity to create a record to show what meaning was intended, and doubts should be construed against the drafters to the extent doing so does not otherwise frustrate the intentions of the parties. Thus I would reverse the district court's dismissal. . . .

NOTES

1. What, indeed, does the word "use" mean? More importantly, what references should be relied on ("used"?) to determine the meaning? Two dictionary definitions of "use" are:

- "The application or employment of something" BLACK'S LAW DICTIONARY (8th ed. 2004).

- "legal enjoyment of property that consists in its employment, occupation, exercise or practice" WEBSTER'S NEW COLLEGIATE DICTIONARY.

Should a dictionary be the primary reference or should one look elsewhere? For example, is the relevant approach to ask what practices in the trade, if any, establish as the meaning of the word "use"?

2. In light of *Kennedy*, if you were drafting the grant clause of an end user license for word processing software that previously referred to a "right to use" the software, would you change the language? Before answering this, consider that case law routinely holds that loading software into a computer makes a copy and that automatically copying parts of the software into different parts of memory may also make a copy of the work.

3. Terms of art are particularly prone to interpretation disputes when used in a license. For example, in *Computer Associates, Inc. v. State Street Bank*, 789 F. Supp. 470 (D. Mass. 1992), the issue was whether a software license involving multi-user rights covered use by the licensee to provide services of a particular type to customers. The court was asked to interpret terminology, such as "timesharing" and "service bureau," that at the time had widespread use in the industry. There were conflicts, however, in the various definitions used in the trade, and the license seemed to treat otherwise includable uses as outside these terms. The court held that none of the trade uses clearly controlled. What should be the court's next step in its analysis?

PROBLEM 5.10

Your Client licenses its database software under a license that provides that "Licensor grants Licensee a perpetual right to use the database software in return for payment of $100,000." The software is used in bank processing of financial data. Every three or four months, Client makes upgrades of the software available; these consist of the original software changed to improve its performance or add functions. The changes would be derivative works under copyright law. The software is copyrighted; the process it creates is covered by a patent. Client is concerned that some banks, using their own programmers, have modified the software to more closely fit their own needs and that the market for its upgrades and new versions is being reduced.

a. What advice do you give the client? Would you propose a change in the language of the license?

b. Would your advice change if the software was provided for remote access and use at the Client's home computer, but no copies were ever delivered to the licensee?

PROBLEM 5.11

You are drafting terms for a standard form license that will give the licensee access to an online database containing reported case law, statutes, regulations and other materials related to labor law. Client will price discriminate — charging a lower price for uses that are non-commercial or educational in nature, than for commercial uses of the data and the access. Draft the respective grant provisions of the license.

III. CHANGING TECHNOLOGY AND CONTEXT

STATE CONTRACTING & ENGINEERING CORP. v. FLORIDA
258 F.3d 1329 (Fed. Cir. 2001)

DYK, CIRCUIT JUDGE.

State Contracting & Engineering Corporation ("State Contracting") and State Paving Corporation ("State Paving") (collectively "plaintiffs") appeal the decision of the United States District Court for the Southern District of Florida granting summary judgment in favor of the defendants. We affirm [in part and reverse in part].

BACKGROUND

In 1989, State Paving Corporation, a highway construction company, successfully bid on a State of Florida Department of Transportation ("FDOT" or "State of Florida") project for construction of sound barrier walls. The original agreement was reduced to writing and expressly incorporated the FDOT Standard Specifications for Road and Bridge Construction ("Standard Specifications"). During the course of the construction, State Paving submitted a Value Engineering Change Proposal ("VECP") proposing to use a new design for sound walls that would reduce costs. The new sound wall design described in the VECP allegedly included the use of a post (column) positioned in a cement-filled pile using a new method devised by State Paving which was particularly suitable for use in sandy soil. FDOT accepted the VECP on July 5, 1990, agreeing to change the specifications of the contract to include the use of the sound wall design described in the VECP. The "Supplemental Agreement" signed by the parties stated that the contract adjustment and sum agreed to "constitutes a full and complete settlement" and that State Paving "accepts the terms of this Supplemental Agreement as full compensation for all costs of equipment, manpower, materials, overhead, profit and delay damages and for all their costs, whether direct or indirect, or whether incurred now or in the future, related to the issues set forth in this Agreement." Pursuant to the contract and "Supplemental Agreement," the State of Florida paid State Paving fifty percent of the cost savings realized by the VECP.

On June 29, 1990, State Paving filed a patent application with the United States Patent and Trademark Office for a structure and method using the technology described in the VECP. The application matured into two U.S. patents. . . . FDOT began using data from the VECP in subsequent requests for bids. State Paving learned about one of these instances in September 1992 and sent a letter to potential bidders, advising them of the pending patent application and seeking a patent royalty. State Paving also sought additional payments under the contract for its use of the VECP data in other contracts to which State Paving was not a party.

[In] August 1997 State Paving and State Contracting (collectively "State Contracting" or "plaintiffs") brought the present lawsuit against the State of Florida and seven private contractors in the United States District Court for the Southern District of Florida. The plaintiffs filed a seven-count amended complaint on June 5, 1998. . . . In the final order of March 2, 2000, the district court . . . granted summary judgment . . . on counts III and VII (patent infringement) to the private contractors on the ground that the contract with the State created a license to practice the patent. . . . State Contracting appealed to this court.

Discussion

[The] district court reasoned that the patent infringement claims against the private contractors (counts III and VII) were barred because State Contracting had agreed to license the State of Florida under its patents. We conclude that the district court erred as to these claims.

The contract in question was drafted by the State of Florida, and was lengthy. It incorporated what are known as value engineering provisions — designed to encourage contractors to develop better methods of doing the job. As noted above, the contract provided for additional payments to the contractor if it developed such methods and allowed the state to use these methods on the contract and on option contracts free of charge.

The relevant portion of the contract, section 4-3.5.8 of the FDOT Standard Specifications, entitled "Department's Future Rights to a VECP," provided:

> In the event of acceptance of a VECP, the Contractor hereby grants to the Department *all rights to use, duplicate or disclose,* in whole or in part, in any manner and for any purpose whatsoever, and to have or to permit others to do so, *data* reasonably necessary to fully utilize such proposal *on this and any other Department contract.*

(emphases added). These provisions were not limited to the contract in question, but extended to all future State of Florida use. The district court found this language to be unambiguous and held that "Plaintiffs agreed in the VECP to allow FDOT to utilize their then unpatented data, without any agreement to compensate Plaintiffs for future use, beyond the instant contract savings and any optional work included in the original contract." While we agree with the district court that this language is unambiguous, we disagree with the district court's interpretation of this language. We conclude that the contract does not provide a license for patent rights to the private contractors.

"Whether express or implied, a license is a contract 'governed by ordinary principles of state contract law.' " Although we apply Florida law in construing the contract, it is significant that the Supreme Court has recognized that patent rights and trade secret rights are quite distinct, and that a contract may provide for different treatment of the two. For example, in *Aronson v. Quick Point Pencil Co.,* 440 U.S. 257 (1979), the Supreme Court held that even though a patent application had not issued, the parties' agreement for the payment of a royalty for the use of proprietary technology was valid, because "[s]tate law is not displaced merely because the contract relates to intellectual property which may or may not be patentable." So too in *Kewanee Oil Co. v.*

Bicron Corp., 416 U.S. 470, 474, 491-93 (1974), the Supreme Court held that Ohio's law protecting trade secrets was not preempted by the federal patent laws because the trade secret law did not clash with the objectives of the federal patent law.

The right to use State Contracting's proprietary technology on the original contract was covered by the supplemental VECP agreement itself as discussed above. The only rights that the state acquired for future contracts were by virtue of section 4-3.5.8. To be sure, the provision apparently contemplated that State Contracting's "proposal" would be used on "other Department contract[s]." But that section only conveyed rights to use "data" in future contracts, and did not in terms convey the right to manufacture the sound barriers using plaintiffs' design or to use plaintiffs' manufacturing method. Most significantly the section did not explicitly convey any patent rights, require the contractor to surrender its rights to the technology, or bar the contractor from securing a patent on the invention.

The contract's failure to explicitly provide for the licensing of patent rights is a glaring omission, particularly where, as here, the contracting parties clearly contemplated that there might be relevant patents. Section 7- 3 of the FDOT Standard Specifications, entitled "Patented Devices, Materials and Processes," provides: "It is agreed that, without exception, contract prices are to include all royalties and costs arising from patents, trademarks, and copyrights, in any way involved in the work." The provision for licensing of patents is limited to work under the contract and does not convey any license to future use of the patented technology. The existence of this provision shows that, if the parties had intended to convey other patent rights, they would have done so explicitly.

Under these circumstances we think it clear that the contract did not in fact provide a license for patent rights to the private contractors under future contracts. The State of Florida drafted the contract, and Florida law requires that it be construed against the drafter. Therefore, we vacate the district court's grant of summary judgment to the private contractors on the patent infringement counts (counts III and VII), and remand for proceedings consistent with this opinion. . . .

BOOSEY & HAWKES MUSIC PUBLISHERS, LTD. v. THE WALT DISNEY CO.
145 F.3d 481 (2d Cir. 1998)

Leval, Circuit Judge:

Boosey & Hawkes Music Publishers Ltd., an English corporation and the assignee of Igor Stravinsky's copyrights for "The Rite of Spring," brought this action alleging that the Walt Disney Company's foreign distribution in video cassette and laser disc format ("video format") of the film "Fantasia," featuring Stravinsky's work, infringed Boosey's rights. In 1939 Stravinsky licensed Disney's distribution of The Rite of Spring in the motion picture. Boosey, which acquired Stravinsky's copyright in 1947, contends that the license does not authorize distribution in video format. . . . We hold that summary judgment was properly granted to Disney with respect to Boosey's Lanham Act claims, but that material issues of fact barred the other grants of summary judgment. [We] remand all but the Lanham Act claim for trial.

I. Background

During 1938, Disney sought Stravinsky's authorization to use The Rite of Spring (sometimes referred to as the "work" or the "composition") throughout the world in a motion picture. Because under United States law the work was in the public domain, Disney needed no authorization to record or distribute it in this country, but permission was required for distribution in countries where Stravinsky enjoyed copyright protection. In January 1939 the parties executed an agreement (the "1939 Agreement") giving Disney rights to use the work in a motion picture in consideration of a fee to Stravinsky of $6000.

The 1939 Agreement provided that:

> In consideration of the sum of Six Thousand ($6,000.) Dollars, receipt of which is hereby acknowledged, [Stravinsky] does hereby give and grant unto Walt Disney Enterprises, a California corporation . . . the nonexclusive, irrevocable right, license, privilege and authority to record in any manner, medium or form, and to license the performance of, the musical composition hereinbelow set out. . . .

Under "type of use" in ¶ 3, the Agreement specified that

> The music of said musical composition may be used in one motion picture throughout the length thereof or through such portion or portions thereof as the Purchaser shall desire. The said music may be used in whole or in part and may be adapted, changed, added to or subtracted from, all as shall appear desirable to the Purchaser in its uncontrolled discretion. . . . The title "Rites of Spring" or "Le Sacre de Printemps," or any other title, may be used as the title of said motion picture and the name of [Stravinsky] may be announced in or in connection with said motion picture.

The Agreement went on to specify in ¶ 4 that Disney's license to the work "is limited to the use of the musical composition in synchronism or timed-relation with the motion picture." Paragraph Five of the Agreement provided that

> The right to record the musical composition as covered by this agreement is conditioned upon the performance of the musical work in theatres having valid licenses from the American Society of Composers, Authors and Publishers, or any other performing rights society having jurisdiction in the territory in which the said musical composition is performed.

We refer to this clause, which is of importance to the litigation, as "the ASCAP Condition."

Finally, ¶ 7 of the Agreement provided that "the licensor reserves to himself all rights and uses in and to the said musical composition not herein specifically granted" (the "reservation clause").

Disney released Fantasia, starring Mickey Mouse, in 1940. The film contains no dialogue. It matches a pantomime of animated beasts and fantastic creatures to passages of great classical music, creating what critics celebrated as a "partnership between fine music and animated film." The soundtrack uses compositions of Bach, Beethoven, Dukas, Schubert, Tchaikovsky, and Stravinsky, all performed by the Philadelphia Orchestra under the direction of Leopold Stokowski. As it appears in the film soundtrack, The Rite of Spring was shortened from its original 34 minutes to about 22.5; sections of the score were cut, while other sections were reordered. For more than five decades Disney exhibited The Rite of Spring in Fantasia under the 1939 license. The film has been re-released for theatrical distribution at least seven times since 1940, and although Fantasia has never appeared on television in its entirety, excerpts including portions of The Rite of Spring have been televised occasionally over the years. Neither Stravinsky nor Boosey has ever previously objected to any of the distributions.

In 1991 Disney first released Fantasia in video format. The video has been sold in foreign countries, as well as in the United States. To date, the Fantasia video release has generated more than $360 million in gross revenue for Disney.

Boosey brought this action in February 1993. [On] cross-motions for summary judgment [in] determining that the license did not cover the distribution of a video format, the district court found that while the broad language of the license gave Disney "the right to record [the work] on video tape and laser disc," the ASCAP Condition "prevents Disney from distributing video tapes or laser discs directly to consumers." The court therefore concluded that Disney's video format sales exceeded the scope of the license. . . .

II. Discussion

[Disney] challenges the summary judgment which declared that the 1939 Agreement does not authorize video distribution of The Rite of Spring. . . .

A. Declaratory Judgment on the Scope of the License.

Boosey's request for declaratory judgment raises two issues of contract interpretation: whether the general grant of permission under the 1939 Agreement licensed Disney to use The Rite of Spring in the video format version of Fantasia (on which the district court found in Disney's favor); and, if so, whether the ASCAP Condition barred Disney from exploiting the work through video format (on which the district court found for Boosey).

1. *Whether the "motion picture" license covers video format.*

Boosey contends that the license to use Stravinsky's work in a "motion picture" did not authorize distribution of the motion picture in video format, especially in view of the absence of an express provision for "future technologies" and Stravinsky's reservation of all rights not granted in the Agreement. Disputes about whether licensees may exploit licensed works through new marketing channels made possible by technologies developed after the licensing contract — often called "new-use" problems — have vexed courts since at least the advent of the motion picture. *See* 3 MELVILLE B. NIMMER AND DAVID NIMMER, NIMMER ON COPYRIGHT, § 10.10[A] at 10-86 (hereinafter "NIMMER"); *Kirke La Shelle Co. v. Paul Armstrong Co.*, 263 N.Y. 79, 188 N.E. 163 (1938) (deciding whether a license for a stage production also conveyed rights in sound motion pictures).

In *Bartsch v. Metro-Goldwyn-Mayer, Inc.*, [391 F.2d 150 (2d Cir.1968),] we held that "licensees may properly pursue any uses which may reasonably be said to fall within the medium as described in the license." 391 F.2d 150, 155 (2d Cir. 1968). We held in *Bartsch* that a license of motion picture rights to a play included the right to telecast the motion picture. We observed that "if the words are broad enough to cover the new use, it seems fairer that the burden of framing and negotiating an exception should fall on the grantor," at least when the new medium is not completely unknown at the time of contracting.

The 1939 Agreement conveys the right "to record [the composition] in any manner, medium or form" for use "in [a] motion picture." We believe this language is broad enough to include distribution of the motion picture in video format. At a minimum, *Bartsch* holds that when a license includes a grant of rights that is reasonably read to cover a new use (at least where the new use was foreseeable at the time of contracting), the burden of excluding the right to the new use will rest on the grantor. *See also Bloom v. Hearst Entertainment Inc.*, 33 F.3d 518, 524-25 (5th Cir. 1994) (applying *Bartsch* to hold that a grant of movie and television rights to a book encompassed video rights as well). The license "to record in any manner, medium or form" doubtless extends to videocassette recording and we can see no reason why the grant of "motion picture" reproduction rights should not include the video format, absent any indication in the Agreement to the contrary. *See Bourne v. Walt Disney Co.*, 68 F.3d 621, 630 (2d Cir. 1995). If a new-use license hinges on the foreseeability of the new channels of distribution at the time of contracting — a question left open in *Bartsch* — Disney has proffered unrefuted evidence that a nascent market for home viewing of feature films existed by 1939. The *Bartsch* analysis thus compels the conclusion that the license for motion picture rights extends to video format distribution.

We recognize that courts and scholars are not in complete accord on the capacity of a broad license to cover future developed markets resulting from new technologies. The NIMMER treatise describes two principal approaches to the problem. According to the first view, advocated here by Boosey, "a license of rights in a given medium (e.g., 'motion picture rights') includes only such uses as fall within the unambiguous core meaning of the term (e.g., exhibition of motion picture film in motion picture theaters) and exclude any uses that lie within the ambiguous penumbra (e.g., exhibition of motion picture on television)." Under this approach, a license given in 1939 to "motion picture" rights would include only the core uses of "motion picture" as understood in 1939 — presumably theatrical distribution — and would not include subsequently developed methods of distribution of a motion picture such as television videocassettes or laser discs.

The second position described by NIMMER is "that the licensee may properly pursue any uses that may reasonably be said to fall within the medium as described in the license." NIMMER expresses clear preferences for the latter approach on the ground that it is "less likely to prove unjust." As Judge Friendly noted in *Bartsch*, "So do we."

We acknowledge that a result which deprives the author-licensor of participation in the profits of new unforeseen channels of distribution is not an altogether happy solution. Nonetheless, we think it more fair and sensible than a
result that would deprive a contracting party of the rights reasonably found in
the terms of the contract it negotiates. This issue is too often, and improperly,
framed as one of favoritism as between licensors and licensees. Because licensors are often authors — whose creativity the copyright laws intend to nurture
— and are often impecunious, while licensees are often large business organizations, there is sometimes a tendency in copyright scholarship and adjudication to seek solutions that favor licensors over licensees. Thus in *Cohen* [*v.
Paramount Pictures, Inc.*], 845 F.2d [851] at 854 [(9th Cir. 1988)], the Ninth
Circuit wrote that a "license must be construed in accordance with the purpose
underlying federal copyright law," which the court construed as the granting
of valuable, enforceable rights to authors and the encouragement of the production of literary works. Asserting that copyright law "is enacted for the
benefit of the composer," the court concluded that it would "frustrate the purposes of the [copyright] Act" to construe the license as encompassing video
technology, which did not exist when the license was granted. [S]*ee also*
WILLIAM F. PATRY, 1 COPYRIGHT LAW AND PRACTICE 392 (1994) (arguing that
"agreements should, wherever possible, be construed in favor of the copyright
transferor," to reflect Congress's "policy judgment that copyright owners
should retain all rights unless specifically transferred").

In our view, new-use analysis should rely on neutral principles of contract
interpretation rather than solicitude for either party. Although *Bartsch* speaks
of placing the "burden of framing and negotiating an exception . . . on the
grantor," it should not be understood to adopt a default rule in favor of copyright licensees or any default rule whatsoever.[1] What governs under *Bartsch* is
the language of the contract. If the contract is more reasonably read to convey
one meaning, the party benefited by that reading should be able to rely on it;
the party seeking exception or deviation from the meaning reasonably conveyed
by the words of the contract should bear the burden of negotiating for language
that would express the limitation or deviation. This principle favors neither
licensors nor licensees. It follows simply from the words of the contract.

The words of Disney's license are more reasonably read to include than to
exclude a motion picture distributed in video format. Thus, we conclude that
the burden fell on Stravinsky, if he wished to exclude new markets arising
from subsequently developed motion picture technology, to insert such language of limitation in the license, rather than on Disney to add language that
reiterated what the license already stated.

Other significant jurisprudential and policy considerations confirm our
approach to new-use problems. We think that our view is more consistent with

---

[1][FN3]We note that commentators and courts have misinterpreted *Bartsch* in just this way.
See, e.g., Film Video Releasing Corp. v. Hastings, 426 F. Supp. 690, 695 (S.D.N.Y. 1976) (interpreting
Bartsch to mean that "the words of the grant are to be construed against the grantor"); James W.
Dabney, *Licenses and New Technology: Apportioning and Benefits*, C674 ALI-ABA 85, 89, 96 (characterizing *Bartsch* as a "pro-licensee" decision that articulates a rule of contract construction favoring licensees in new-use cases). We emphasize that *Bartsch* favors neither party and announces no
special rule of contract interpretation for the new-use context. Rather, it instructs courts to rely on
the language of the license contract and basic principles of interpretation.

the law of contract than the view that would exclude new technologies even when they reasonably fall within the description of what is licensed. Although contract interpretation normally requires inquiry into the intent of the contracting parties, intent is not likely to be helpful when the subject of the inquiry is something the parties were not thinking about. *See* NIMMER, § 10.10[B] at 10-90 (noting that usually "there simply was no intent at all at the time of execution with respect to . . . whether the grant includes a new use developed at a later time"). Nor is extrinsic evidence such as past dealings or industry custom likely to illuminate the intent of the parties, because the use in question was, by hypothesis, new, and could not have been the subject of prior negotiations or established practice. Moreover, many years after formation of the contract, it may well be impossible to consult the principals or retrieve documentary evidence to ascertain the parties' intent, if any, with respect to new uses. On the other hand, the parties or assignees of the contract should be entitled to rely on the words of the contract. Especially where, as here, evidence probative of intent is likely to be both scant and unreliable, the burden of justifying a departure from the most reasonable reading of the contract should fall on the party advocating the departure.

Nor do we believe that our approach disadvantages licensors. By holding contracting parties accountable to the reasonable interpretation of their agreements, we encourage licensors and licensees to anticipate and bargain for the full value of potential future uses. Licensors reluctant to anticipate future developments remain free to negotiate language that clearly reserves the rights to future uses. But the creation of exceptional principles of contract construction that places doubt on the capacity of a license to transfer new technologies is likely to harm licensors together with licensees, by placing a significant percentage of the profits they might have shared in the hands of lawyers instead.

Neither the absence of a future technologies clause in the Agreement nor the presence of the reservation clause alters that analysis. The reservation clause stands for no more than the truism that Stravinsky retained whatever he had not granted. It contributes nothing to the definition of the boundaries of the license. And irrespective of the presence or absence of a clause expressly confirming a license over future technologies, the burden still falls on the party advancing a deviation from the most reasonable reading of the license to insure that the desired deviation is reflected in the final terms of the contract. As we have already stated, if the broad terms of the license are more reasonably read to include the particular future technology in question, then the licensee may rely on that language.

Bartsch therefore continues to articulate our "preferred" approach to new-use questions, NIMMER, § 10.10[B] at 10-91, and we hold that the district court properly applied it to find that the basic terms of Disney's license included the right to record and distribute Fantasia in video format.

2.*The ASCAP Condition.*

Boosey further contends that distribution of Fantasia in video format violated the ASCAP Condition. The district court agreed. It granted summary judgment to Boosey declaring that the ASCAP Condition "prevents Disney from distributing video tapes and laser discs directly to consumers." We disagree with the district court's analysis.

The ASCAP Condition provides that:

> The right to record the musical composition as covered by this agree-
> ment is conditioned upon the performance of the musical work in the-
> aters having valid licenses from the American Society of Composers,
> Authors and Publishers, or any other performing rights society having
> jurisdiction in the territory in which the said musical composition is
> performed.

The court apparently believed, as Boosey argues, that the ASCAP Condition
unambiguously limited Disney's exploitation of its motion picture to theaters
operating under a license from ASCAP or similar performing rights society.
This interpretation treats the clause as if it stated explicitly either that the
license extends only to performances in theaters licensed by ASCAP, or that
Disney commits itself to exploit the license only in such theaters. But that is
not what the clause says.

The terms of the provision condition Disney's right to record the work only
"upon the performance of the . . . work in theaters" having ASCAP (or similar)
licenses. Read literally, this language requires no more of Disney than that it
expose the motion picture in two or more ASCAP-certified theaters, a condition
surely long ago satisfied. Whatever may have been the intention, the ASCAP
Condition does not unambiguously prohibit Disney from exhibiting the composition in non-ASCAP theaters, or from distributing the film directly to consumers.

Apart from the fact that the language of the Condition does not compel
Boosey's interpretation, there is also good reason to regard that construction
as improbable. Because the work was in the public domain in the United
States, the license pertained only to foreign rights, which the contract
described as world wide. Construing the Condition as Boosey argues would
mean that the film could not be shown at all in any country where the work
was protected and theaters did not employ ASCAP-type licenses.

Furthermore, we learn from a leading treatise on music licensing that this
very clause was industry boilerplate that appeared in "countless synchronization licenses" for U.S. films. AL KOHN & BOB KOHN, KOHN ON MUSIC LICENSING,
838-40, 857-58 (2d ed. 1996). If the clause meant what Boosey contends, studios whose films included copyrighted works licensed with this boilerplate
provision would be completely prohibited from showing their films at all in the
United States in the event that U.S. movie theaters ceased to employ ASCAP
licenses. It seems highly unlikely that the film industry entered into contracts
that would place it at the mercy of its licensors, in the event that ASCAP
licensing was for whatever reason abandoned.

Indeed, ASCAP licenses did disappear from U.S. theaters as a result of an
antitrust ruling in 1948. Under Boosey's reading, "countless" movies containing copyrighted works licensed with the ASCAP Condition were thereafter
barred from U.S. theatrical release. If Boosey's interpretation of the Condition
was widely shared, frequent litigation to sort out the rights of licensors and
licensees after the demise of ASCAP theater licensing would have been inevitable. That Boosey has not cited a single court decision confirming its view of
the ASCAP Condition strongly suggests that its view of the provision was not,
in fact, widely held.

KOHN appears to indicate, moreover, that the ASCAP Condition remained industry boilerplate until sometime in the 1950s. If this is true, Boosey's view of the Condition requires us to believe that studios agreed to limit distribution of movies containing licensed works to ASCAP-licensed theaters even after ASCAP licensing of theaters had been declared unlawful. Not only would it would be nonsensical for moviemakers to predicate their license to copyrighted works on a condition that could not lawfully be satisfied, but it is unimaginable that they would produce films whose distribution to the domestic market hinged on subsequent permission, or quiescence, of licensors.

We find that neither party's interpretation is compelled by the plain terms of the provision. The Condition is sufficiently unclear on its face to justify consideration of extrinsic evidence.

Boosey argues that any ambiguity regarding the meaning of the ASCAP Provision is dissipated by extrinsic evidence showing Disney knew that the 1939 Agreement permitted use of the composition only in ASCAP-licensed motion picture theaters. We do not find this evidence persuasive.

Boosey first points to the parties' limited post-contract course of dealing. In 1941, Boosey notes, Disney acknowledged that the Agreement did not license use of The Rite of Spring on radio. In 1969, Disney negotiated and paid for the right to release the soundtrack recording of "The Rite of Spring" as part of a complete Fantasia album. And in 1990, Disney unsuccessfully sought Boosey's permission to use sections of the composition "in a new performance by ... Pink Floyd to be filmed at the Great Pyramid of Giza, while imagery from 'Fantasia' is projected across the entire face of the Pyramid." Boosey would have us infer that these requests for permission demonstrate Disney's awareness that its right to the composition was limited to exploitation in licensed motion picture theaters.

However, those exploitations of the composition seem clearly beyond the scope of the 1939 Agreement. None of the proposed uses involved "the use of the musical composition in synchronism or timed-relation" with Fantasia, as required by ¶ 4 of the Agreement; the 1941 and 1969 requests did not even envision use of the composition in a motion picture, as required by ¶ 3 of the Agreement. Because the Agreement could not reasonably be interpreted to cover these uses, Disney's decision to seek supplemental permission for them reveals nothing regarding its view as to whether it was authorized to license Fantasia otherwise than in theaters with ASCAP licenses.

Indeed, there is course of dealing evidence that supports the opposite conclusion — that Disney did not view the license as restricted to performance in ASCAP-licensed theaters. Without seeking Boosey's permission, Disney appears to have sold Fantasia directly to consumers in at least two foreign markets and telecast the composition in excerpts from "Fantasia" several times. That Disney sought permission for uses of the composition not involving the motion picture Fantasia, but did not seek permission for direct distribution of Fantasia in alternative motion picture formats, arguably rebuts Boosey's argument that Disney's conduct shows it agreed with Boosey's interpretation.

Boosey's other extrinsic evidence is no more compelling. Boosey points out that in contracts for other compositions used in Fantasia, negotiated at about the same time as the 1939 Agreement, it was Disney's "right *to license* the performance" that was conditioned on ASCAP performance (emphasis added). In Stravinsky's contract it was the right "to record" that was so conditioned. Because a condition on the "right to record" is more drastic than a limitation on the right to license, Boosey argues that Stravinsky bargained for an enhanced interest in Fantasia's continuing revenue stream.

We find the argument unpersuasive. Even if Disney did agree to a more drastic restriction resulting from its failure to comply with the ASCAP Condition, that sheds no light on what conduct was needed to satisfy the Condition. Furthermore, Boosey's point is illusory. Because The Rite of Spring was in the public domain in the United States — where Disney was making its motion picture — Disney did not need a license from Stravinsky "to record" the composition. It needed Stravinsky's permission only to license performances in countries where Stravinsky's copyright interest was recognized. As a practical matter, therefore, Disney did not place more at stake in agreeing to a condition on its right "to record" than in other contracts where the condition applied to its right "to license." Indeed, it is arguable that because the condition applied only to something Disney had the right to do without Stravinsky's permission, the ASCAP Condition had no functional significance at all.

Neither the plain terms of the 1939 Agreement nor the sparse and contradictory extrinsic evidence require the conclusion that Disney's license is limited to theatrical performance of the composition. Summary judgment is therefore inappropriate. . . .

Conclusion

The grants of summary judgment in Boosey's favor . . . are vacated.

RANDOM HOUSE, INC. v. ROSETTA BOOKS, LLC
150 F. Supp. 2d 613 (S.D.N.Y. 2002), *aff'd*, 283 F.3d 490 (2d Cir. 2002)

BACKGROUND

In the year 2000 and the beginning of 2001, Rosetta Books contracted with several authors to publish certain of their works — including *The Confessions of Nat Turner* and *Sophie's Choice* by William Styron; *Slaughterhouse-Five, Breakfast of Champions, The Sirens of Titan, Cat's Cradle,* and *Player Piano* by Kurt Vonnegut; and *Promised Land* by Robert B. Parker — in digital format over the internet. On February 26, 2001 Rosetta Books launched its ebook business, offering those titles and others for sale in digital format. The next day, Random House filed this complaint accusing Rosetta Books of committing copyright infringement and tortiously interfering with the contracts Random House had with Messrs. Parker, Styron and Vonnegut by selling its ebooks. It simultaneously moved for a preliminary injunction prohibiting Rosetta from infringing plaintiff's copyrights.

A. Ebooks

Ebooks are "digital book[s] that you can read on a computer screen or an electronic device." Ebooks are created by converting digitized text into a format readable by computer software. The text can be viewed on a desktop or laptop computer, personal digital assistant or handheld dedicated ebook reading device. Rosetta's ebooks can only be read after they are downloaded into a computer that contains either Microsoft Reader, Adobe Acrobat Reader, or Adobe Acrobat eBook Reader software.

Included in a Rosetta ebook is a book cover, title page, copyright page and "eforward" all created by Rosetta Books. Although the text of the ebook is exactly the same as the text of the original work, the ebook contains various features that take advantage of its digital format. For example, ebook users can search the work electronically to find specific words and phrases. They can electronically "highlight" and "bookmark" certain text, which can then be automatically indexed and accessed through hyperlinks. They can use hyperlinks in the table of contents to jump to specific chapters.

Users can also type electronic notes which are stored with the related text. These notes can be automatically indexed, sorted and filed. Users can also change the font size and style of the text to accommodate personal preferences; thus, an electronic screen of text may contain more words, fewer words, or the same number of words as a page of the original published book. In addition, users can have displayed the definition of any word in the text. In one version of the software, the word can also be pronounced aloud.

Rosetta's ebooks contain certain security features to prevent users from printing, emailing or otherwise distributing the text. Although it is technologically possible to foil these security features, anyone who does so would be violating the licensing agreement accompanying the software.

B. Random House's Licensing Agreements

While each agreement between the author and Random House differs in some respects, each uses the phrase "print, publish and sell the work in book form" to convey rights from the author to the publisher.

1. Styron Agreements

Forty years ago, in 1961, William Styron granted Random House the right to publish *The Confessions of Nat Turner*. Besides granting Random House an exclusive license to "print, publish and sell the work in book form," Styron also gave it the right to "license publication of the work by book clubs," "license publication of a reprint edition," "license after book publication the publication of the work, in whole or in part, in anthologies, school books," and other shortened forms, "license without charge publication of the work in Braille, or photographing, recording, and microfilming the work for the physically handicapped," and "publish or permit others to publish or broadcast by radio or television . . . selections from the work, for publicity purposes. . . ." Styron demonstrated that he was not granting Random House the rights to license publication in the British Commonwealth or in foreign languages by crossing out these clauses on the form contract supplied by Random House.

The publisher agreed in the contract to "publish the work at its own expense and in such style and manner and at such a price as it deems suitable." The contract also contains a non-compete clause that provides, in relevant part, that "[t]he Author agrees that during the term of this agreement he will not, without the written permission of the Publisher, publish or permit to be published any material in book or pamphlet form, based on the material in the work, or which is reasonably likely to injure its sale." Styron's contract with Random House for the right to publish *Sophie's Choice,* executed in 1977, is virtually identical to his 1961 contract to publish *The Confessions of Nat Turner.*

2. Vonnegut Agreements

Kurt Vonnegut's 1967 contract granting Random House's predecessor-in-interest Dell Publishing Co., Inc. the license to publish *Slaughterhouse-Five* and *Breakfast of Champions* follows a similar structure to the Styron agreements. Paragraph #1 is captioned "grant of rights" and contains those rights the author is granting to the book publisher. Certain rights on the publisher's form contract are crossed out, indicating that the author reserved them for himself. One of the rights granted by the author includes the "[e]xclusive right to publish and to license the Work for publication, after book publication . . . in anthologies, selections, digests, abridgements, magazine condensations, serialization, newspaper syndication, picture book versions, microfilming, Xerox and other forms of copying, either now in use or hereafter developed."

Vonnegut specifically reserved for himself the "dramatic . . . motion picture (silent and sound) . . . radio broadcasting (including mechanical renditions and/or recordings of the text) . . . [and] television" rights. Unlike the Styron agreements, this contract does not contain a non-compete clause.

Vonnegut's 1970 contract granting Dell the license to publish *The Sirens of Titan, Cat's Cradle,* and *Player Piano* contains virtually identical grants and reservations of rights as his 1967 contract. However, it does contain a non-compete clause, which provides that "the Author . . . will not publish or permit to be published any edition, adaptation or abridgment of the Work by any party other than Dell without Dell's prior written consent."

3. Parker Agreement

Robert B. Parker's 1982 contract granting Dell the license to publish *Promised Land* is similar to the 1970 Vonnegut contract. Paragraph #1 contains the "grant of rights," certain of which have been crossed out by the author. The contract does grant Random House the right to "Xerox and other forms of copying of the printed page, either now in use or hereafter developed." Parker also reserved the rights to the "dramatic . . . motion picture (silent and sound) . . . radio broadcasting . . . television . . . mechanical or electronic recordings of the text. . . ." There is also a non-compete clause that provides, in relevant part, that "[t]he Author . . . will not, without the written permission of Dell, publish or permit to be published any material based on the material in the Work, or which is reasonably likely to injure its sale."

Discussion

. . . .

B. Ownership of a Valid Copyright

Two elements must be proven in order to establish a prima facie case of infringement: "(1) ownership of a valid copyright, and (2) copying of constituent elements of the work that are original." In this case, only the first element — ownership of a valid copyright — is at issue, since all parties concede that the text of the ebook is identical to the text of the book published by Random House.

It is well settled that although the authors own the copyrights to their works, "[t]he legal or beneficial owner of an exclusive right under a copyright is entitled . . . to institute an action for any infringement of that particular right committed while he or she is the owner of it." 17 U.S.C. § 501(b); MELVILLE B. NIMMER & DAVID NIMMER, NIMMER ON COPYRIGHT § 12.02[b] at 12-50-51 (May, 2000) ("[A]n exclusive licensee may not sue for infringement of rights as to which he is not licensed, even if the subject matter of the infringement is the work as to which he is a licensee."). The question for resolution, therefore, is whether Random House is the beneficial owner of the right to publish these works as ebooks.

1. . . . Legal Standards

Random House claims to own the rights in question through its licensing agreements with the authors. Interpretation of an agreement purporting to grant a copyright license is a matter of state contract law.

In New York, a written contract is to be interpreted so as to give effect to the intention of the parties as expressed in the contract's language. The court must consider the entire contract and reconcile all parts, if possible, to avoid an inconsistency.

Determining whether a contract provision is ambiguous is a question of law to be decided by the court. Pursuant to New York law, "[c]ontract language is ambiguous if it is capable of more than one meaning when viewed objectively by a reasonably intelligent person who has examined the context of the entire integrated agreement and who is cognizant of the customs, practices, usages and terminology as generally understood in the particular trade or business." "No ambiguity exists when contract language has a 'definite and precise meaning, unattended by danger of misconception in the purport of the [contract] itself, and concerning which there is no reasonable basis for a difference of opinion.' "

If the language of a contract is ambiguous, interpretation of the contract becomes a question of fact for the finder of fact and extrinsic evidence is admissible.

These principles are in accord with the approach the U.S. Court of Appeals for the Second Circuit uses in analyzing contractual language in disputes, such as this one, "about whether licensees may exploit licensed works through new marketing channels made possible by technologies developed after the licensing contract — often called 'new use' problems." *Boosey & Hawkes Music Publishers, Ltd. v. Walt Disney Co.,* 145 F.3d 481, 486 (2d Cir.1998). The two leading cases in this Circuit on how to determine whether "new uses" come within prior grants of rights are *Boosey* and *Bartsch v. Metro-Goldwyn-Mayer, Inc.,* 391 F.2d 150 (2d Cir.1968), decided three decades apart.

In *Bartsch,* the author of the play "Maytime" granted Hans Bartsch in 1930 "the motion picture rights [to 'Maytime'] throughout the world," including the right to "copyright, vend, license and exhibit such motion picture photoplays throughout the world; together with the further sole and exclusive rights by mechanical and/or electrical means to record, reproduce and transmit sound, including spoken words. . . ." He in turn assigned those rights to Warner Bros. Pictures, which transferred them to MGM. In 1958 MGM licensed its motion picture "Maytime" for viewing on television. Bartsch sued, claiming the right to transmit the play over television had not been given to MGM.

Judge Henry Friendly, for the Second Circuit, wrote in 1968 that "any effort to reconstruct what the parties actually intended nearly forty years ago is doomed to failure." He added that the words of the grant by Bartsch "were well designed to give the assignee [i.e., MGM] the broadest rights with respect to its copyrighted property." The words of the grant were broad enough to cover the new use — i.e. viewing on television — and Judge Friendly interpreted them to do so. This interpretation, he wrote, permitted the licensee to "properly pursue any uses which may reasonably be said to fall within the medium as described in the license." That interpretation also avoided the risk "that a deadlock between the grantor and the grantee might prevent the work's being shown over the new medium at all."

In *Boosey,* the plaintiff was the assignee of Igor Stravinsky's copyrights in the musical composition, "The Rite of Spring." In 1939, Stravinsky had licensed Disney's use of "The Rite of Spring" in the motion picture "Fantasia." Fifty-two years later, in 1991, Disney released "Fantasia" in video format and Boosey brought an action seeking, among other relief, a declaration that the grant of rights did not include the right to use the Stravinsky work in video format. In *Boosey,* just as in *Bartsch,* the language of the grant was broad, enabling the licensee "to record in any manner, medium or form, and to license the performance of, the musical composition [for use] in a motion picture."

At the Second Circuit, a unanimous panel focused on "neutral principles of contract interpretation rather than solicitude for either party." "What governs," Judge Pierre Leval wrote, "is the language of the contract. If the contract is more reasonably read to convey one meaning, the party benefited by that reading should be able to rely on it; the party seeking exception or deviation from the meaning reasonably conveyed by the words of the contract should bear the burden of negotiating for language that would express the limitation or deviation. This principle favors neither licensors nor licensees. It follows simply from the words of the contract."

The Second Circuit's neutral approach was specifically influenced by policy considerations on both sides. On the one hand, the approach seeks to encourage licensees — here, the publishers — to develop new technologies that will enable all to enjoy the creative work in a new way. On the other hand, it seeks to fulfill the purpose underlying federal copyright law — to encourage authors to create literary works.

2. Application of Legal Standards

Relying on "the language of the license contract and basic principles of interpretation," as instructed to do so by *Boosey* and *Bartsch,* this Court finds that the most reasonable interpretation of the grant in the contracts at issue to "print, publish and sell the work in book form" does not include the right to publish the work as an ebook. At the outset, the phrase itself distinguishes between the pure content — i.e. "the work" — and the format of display — "in book form." The *Random House Webster's Unabridged Dictionary* defines a "book" as "a written or printed work of fiction or nonfiction, usually on sheets of paper fastened or bound together within covers" and defines "form" as "external appearance of a clearly defined area, as distinguished from color or material; the shape of a thing or person."

Manifestly, paragraph #1 of each contract — entitled either "grant of rights" or "exclusive publication right" — conveys certain rights from the author to the publisher. In that paragraph, separate grant language is used to convey the rights to publish book club editions, reprint editions, abridged forms, and editions in Braille. This language would not be necessary if the phrase "in book form" encompassed all types of books. That paragraph specifies exactly which rights were being granted by the author to the publisher. Indeed, many of the rights set forth in the publisher's form contracts were in fact not granted to the publisher, but rather were reserved by the authors to themselves. For example, each of the authors specifically reserved certain rights for themselves by striking out phrases, sentences, and paragraphs of the publisher's form contract. This evidences an intent by these authors not to grant the publisher the broadest rights in their works.

Random House contends that the phrase "in book form" means to faithfully reproduce the author's text in its complete form as a reading experience and that, since ebooks concededly contain the complete text of the work, Rosetta cannot also possess those rights. While Random House's definition distinguishes "book form" from other formats that require separate contractual language — such as audio books and serialization rights — it does not distinguish other formats specifically mentioned in paragraph #1 of the contracts, such as book club editions and reprint editions. Because the Court must, if possible, give effect to all contractual language in order to "safeguard against adopting an interpretation that would render any individual provision superfluous," Random House's definition cannot be adopted.

Random House points specifically to the clause requiring it to "publish the work at its own expense and in such a style and manner and at such a price as [Random House] deems suitable" as support for its position. However, plaintiff takes this clause out of context. It appears in paragraph #2, captioned "Style, Price and Date of Publication," not paragraph #1, which includes all the grants of rights. In context, the phrase simply means that Random House has control over the appearance of the formats granted to Random House in the first paragraph; i.e., control over the style of the book.

Random House also cites the non-compete clauses as evidence that the authors granted it broad, exclusive rights in their work. Random House reasons that because the authors could not permit any material that would injure the sale of the work to be published without Random House's consent, the authors must have granted the right to publish ebooks to Random House. This reasoning turns the analysis on its head. First, the grant of rights follows from the grant language alone. Second, non- compete clauses must be limited in scope in order to be enforceable in New York. Third, even if the authors did violate this provision of their Random House agreements by contracting with Rosetta Books — a point on which this Court does not opine — the remedy is a breach of contract action against the authors, not a copyright infringement action against Rosetta Books.

The photocopy clause — giving Random House the right to "Xerox and other forms of copying, either now in use or hereafter developed" — similarly does not bolster Random House's position. Although the clause does appear in the grant language paragraph, taken in context, it clearly refers only to new developments in xerography and other forms of photocopying. Stretching it to include new forms of publishing, such as ebooks, would make the rest of the contract superfluous because there would be no reason for authors to reserve rights to forms of publishing "now in use." This interpretation also comports with the publishing industry's trade usage of the phrase.

Not only does the language of the contract itself lead almost ineluctably to the conclusion that Random House does not own the right to publish the works as ebooks, but also a reasonable person "cognizant of the customs, practices, usages and terminology as generally understood in the particular trade or business," would conclude that the grant language does not include ebooks. "To print, publish and sell the work in book form" is understood in the publishing industry to be a "limited" grant.

In *Field v. True Comics*, [89 F. Supp. 611 (S.D.N.Y. 1950),] the court held that "the sole and exclusive right to publish, print and market *in book form*" — especially when the author had specifically reserved rights for himself — was "much more limited" than "the sole and exclusive right to publish, print and market *the book*." In fact, the publishing industry generally interprets the phrase "in book form" as granting the publisher "the exclusive right to publish a hardcover trade book in English for distribution in North America." 1 LINDEY ON ENTERTAINMENT, PUBLISHING AND THE ARTS Form 1.01-1 (2d ed.2000) (using the Random House form contract to explain the meaning of each clause).

3. Comparison to Prior "New Use" Caselaw

The finding that the five licensing agreements at issue do not convey the right to publish the works as ebooks accords with Second Circuit and New York case law. Indeed, the two leading cases limned above that found that a particular new use was included within the grant language can be distinguished from this case on four grounds.

First, the language conveying the rights in *Boosey* and *Bartsch* was far broader than here. Second, the "new use" in those cases — i.e. display of a motion picture on television or videocassette — fell squarely within the same medium as the original grant. . . .

In this case, the "new use" — electronic digital signals sent over the internet — is a separate medium from the original use — printed words on paper. Random House's own expert concludes that the media are distinct because information stored digitally can be manipulated in ways that analog information cannot. Ebooks take advantage of the digital medium's ability to manipulate data by allowing ebook users to electronically search the text for specific words and phrases, change the font size and style, type notes into the text and electronically organize them, highlight and bookmark, hyperlink to specific parts of the text, and, in the future, to other sites on related topics as well, and access a dictionary that pronounces words in the ebook aloud. The need for a software program to interact with the data in order to make it usable, as well as the need for a piece of hardware to enable the reader to view the text, also distinguishes analog formats from digital formats. *See Greenberg v. National Geographic Soc'y,* 244 F.3d 1267, 1273 n. 12 (11th Cir.2001) (Digital format is not analogous to reproducing the magazine in microfilm or microfiche because it "requires the interaction of a computer program in order to accomplish the useful reproduction involved with the new medium.").

Therefore, *Boosey* and *Bartsch,* which apply to new uses within the same medium, do not control this case. *See, e.g., Raine* [*v. CBS, Inc.*], 25 F.Supp.2d 434, 445 (S.D.N.Y.1998) (finding that the right to "television broadcasts" did not include broadcasts on cable television or videocassettes); *Tele-Pac, Inc. v. Grainger,* 168 A.D.2d 11, 570 N.Y.S.2d 521 (1st Dep't 1991) (distinguishing Second Circuit "new use" doctrine by holding that right to "broadcast[ ] by television or any other similar device now known or hereafter to be made known" was so dissimilar from display on videocassette and videodisc "as to preclude consideration of video rights as even falling within the 'ambiguous penumbra' of the terms used in the agreement").

The third significant difference between the licensee in the motion picture cases cited above and the book publisher in this action is that the licensees in the motion picture cases have actually created a new work based on the material from the licensor. Therefore, the right to display that new work — whether on television or video — is derivative of the right to create that work. In the book publishing context, the publishers, although they participate in the editorial process, display the words written by the author, not themselves.

Fourth, the courts in *Boosey* and *Bartsch* were concerned that any approach to new use problems that "tilts against licensees [here, Random House] gives rise to antiprogressive incentives" insofar as licensees "would be reluctant to explore and utilize innovative technologies." However, in this action, the policy rationale of encouraging development in new technology is at least as well served by finding that the licensors — i.e., the authors — retain these rights to their works. In the 21st century, it cannot be said that licensees such as book publishers and movie producers are ipso facto more likely to make advances in digital technology than start-up companies.

Other case law interpreting the scope of book publishing licensing agreements is similarly unhelpful to Random House. In *Dolch v. Garrard Pub. Co.,* 289 F. Supp. 687 (S.D.N.Y.1968), the district court found that a license granting the publisher "the exclusive right of publication of the books" included the right to publish the books in paperback. Besides the obvious distinction that the grant language in *Dolch* is far broader — there is no distinction between "book" and "work" — the *Dolch* Court was applying Illinois contract law — not New York — which is far stricter about the use of parol evidence.

In *Dresser v. William Morrow & Co.,* 278 A.D. 931, 105 N.Y.S.2d 706 (1st Dep't 1951), *aff'd* 304 N.Y. 603, 107 N.E.2d 89 (N.Y. 1952), the issue was whether an author could receive additional payments for reprint editions of his book when his publishing contract only provided for an "outright fixed payment." The *Dresser* court found that, under the terms of the contract, he could not. The court relied on the fact that the contract was "at variance with the usual pattern of contracts between author and publisher." Here, although each contract is slightly different, none varies greatly from the usual pattern of contracts between author and publisher; therefore, there is no reason to depart from the usual meaning of such contracts.

In contrast to *Dresser* and *Dolch,* other federal courts applying New York law have interpreted publishing licensing agreements more narrowly. *See Werbungs Und Commerz Union Austalt v. Collectors' Guild, Ltd.,* 930 F.2d 1021, 1026 (2d Cir. 1991) (finding contract which conveys "right, title and interest in said two editions and all earnings therefrom" ambiguous as to whether it conveyed rights in the illustrations contained in those editions as well); *Field,* 89 F. Supp. at 613 (finding right to "publish, print and market in book form . . . the work" is limited right and does not include publication of cartoon strip in a magazine). . . .

Conclusion

Employing the most important tool in the armamentarium of contract interpretation — the language of the contract itself — this Court has concluded that Random House is not the beneficial owner of the right to publish the eight works at issue as ebooks. This is neither a victory for technophiles nor a defeat for Luddites. It is merely a determination, relying on neutral principles of contract interpretation, that because Random House is not likely to succeed on the merits of its copyright infringement claim and cannot demonstrate irreparable harm, its motion for a preliminary injunction should be denied.

NOTES

1. The Supreme Court in *New York Times Co., Inc. v. Tasini,* 533 U.S. 483 (2001), held that a copyright law rule that gives the author of a compilation the right to make revisions of the compilation does not give it the right to place a print compilation into an Internet environment in which individual, separately copyrighted, articles can be separately accessed. Digital formats substantially affect the market for the individual articles as independent works. Unless the author of the contribution gave the publisher of the compilation a license to do so, the author retains control over Internet and similar uses of its work.

2. The court in *CRC Press, LLC v. Wolfram Research, Inc.,* 149 F. Supp. 2d 500 (C.D. Ill. 2000), granted a preliminary injunction against the author of a mathematics encyclopedia from continuing to publish a web site containing substantially the same material as the encyclopedia. The author had contracted to write the print publication, conveying ownership of the copyright in the work to the publisher, and to do a CD Rom version of the encyclopedia. The web site was previously in existence. The court held that there was a likelihood of success on the publisher's claim that the web site materials infringed. Here, the two forms of text were virtually identical and, unless the publisher controlled both, it was difficult to see what value it had received under the contract.

PROBLEM 5.12

Big Oil and Lankster are companies involved in seismic studies for the purpose of discovering oil. The studies involve creating sound waves in the earth in a given area, recording the return of the sound waves and creating computerized images of the data. In a major breakthrough, Big Oil obtains a patent on a process that allows the computer to create two-dimensional cross-sectional images and place these visually next to each other, creating the image of a three-dimensional underground map. The method for doing this involves use of mathematical cross-correlation, a widely known and widely used mathematics technique. The method is described as "series analysis." Lankster desires a license for this technology, and since it is in the same business, wants the license to cover future developments in this technology. Big Oil is willing to grant the license. Lankster proposes that the grant clause read "a license for use of 'series analysis' and any analysis process for seismic data that evolve from the licensed technology." What do you advise either party about this license grant?

PROBLEM 5.13

Client is a business management professor who has developed a renowned management theory. The theory involves collecting data in a particular way, running it through various statistical tests, and producing guidance for individual financial managers on how to succeed in their work environment. Professor is intending to grant an exclusive license for a course he developed based on the theory. The course, which is for business executives, involves several booklets based on the theory, along with questionnaires and notes for presentations. The licensee will agree to allow the licensor to use any of these materials in "teaching activities" by Client. What risks do you see and how would you respond to them?

Chapter 6

TRANSFER, FIRST SALE, AND EXHAUSTION

I. BASIC FRAMEWORK

This chapter focuses on issues about transferring rights related to a license. While that issue might appear to have limited importance, it in fact is one of the core issues of licensing law and practice, and it is an issue on which the law applicable to license agreements differs remarkably from that applicable to other types of contracts.

Although ancient common law may have assumed the non-transferability of contracts, for many years the modern common law and the commercial code position on transfer of contracts has assumed that a right to transfer exists unless the contract otherwise provides or the circumstances indicate that the transfer will adversely impact the other party to the contract. The *Restatement*, which distinguishes between assignment of "rights" and delegation of "duties," suggests the following:

Restatement (Second) of Contracts § 317(2):

> (2) A contractual right can be assigned unless
>
> > (a) the substitution of a right of the assignee for the right of the assignor would materially change the duty of the obligor, or materially increase the burden or risk imposed on him by his contract, or materially impair his chance of obtaining return performance, or materially reduce its value to him, or
> >
> > (b) the assignment is forbidden by statute or is otherwise inoperative on grounds of public policy, or
> >
> > (c) assignment is validly precluded by contract.

Restatement (Second) of Contracts § 318:

> (1) An obligor can properly delegate the performance of his duty to another unless the delegation is contrary to public policy or the terms of his promise.
>
> (2) Unless otherwise agreed, a promise requires performance by a particular person only to the extent that the obligee has a substantial interest in having that person perform or control the acts promised.
>
> (3) Unless the obligee agrees otherwise, neither delegation of performance nor a contract to assume the duty made with the obligor by the person delegated discharges any duty or liability of the delegating obligor.

The case law does not typically follow the terminology or policy set out in the *Restatement*. The language in the delegation rule (§ 318), for example, is more often described by courts as a rule regarding personal services contracts: if a party contracts for performance by a particular person, that person's duty to perform cannot be delegated to another person.

UCC Article 2 adopts a rule similar to that of the *Restatement*, retaining the language of "rights" and "duties." UCC § 2-210(1) ("A party may perform his duty through a delegate unless otherwise agreed or unless the other party has a substantial interest in having his original promissor perform or control the acts required by the contract.").

UCITA carries these concepts forward in the following terms:

(1) A party's contractual interest may be transferred unless the transfer:

(A) is prohibited by other law; or

(B) except as otherwise provided in paragraph (3), would materially change the duty of the other party, materially increase the burden or risk imposed on the other party, or materially impair the other party's property or its likelihood or expectation of obtaining return performance.

(2) Except as otherwise provided in paragraph (3) [and in this paragraph], a term prohibiting transfer of a party's contractual interest is enforceable, and a transfer made in violation of that term is a breach of contract and is ineffective to create contractual rights in the transferee against the nontransferring party. . . .

(3) A . . . right to payment arising out of the transferor's due performance of its entire obligation may be transferred notwithstanding an agreement otherwise.

UCITA § 503 (2000 Official Text).

Many problems arise in applying the idea of "rights" and "duties" to an ordinary license. For example, how should one treat a license between Party A and Party B, under which Party B pays $1,000 per month for a license to use the subject matter of the license in Georgia? Does B have any "duties" under this contract? Is there a duty to not use the subject matter outside Georgia. Does Party A have any rights or duties under this contract? Is it more productive to speak about transferability in general when dealing with a license?

PROBLEM 6.1

A patent license between Party A and Party B requires that Party B pay $1,000 per month for a license to use the subject matter of the license in Georgia. Under the *Restatement* rule, can Party A assign all its interest in the license to Party C? Can Party B assign its interests in the contract to Party D? Is the result different under Article 2 or UCITA?

EVEREX SYSTEMS, INC. v. CADTRAK CORP.
(In re CFLC, INC.)
89 F.3d 673 (9th Cir. 1996)

PREGERSON, CIRCUIT JUDGE:

Everex Systems, Inc., a buyer of certain of the assets of CFLC, Inc. in a Chapter 11 bankruptcy, appeals [a] court order denying CFLC's motion as debtor to assume and assign to Everex a patent license from Cadtrak Corporation to CFLC. . . .

[Background]

In a 1986 agreement, as modified by a 1989 supplemental agreement, Cadtrak, in return for a one-time $290,000 payment, granted CFLC, a personal computer company, a royalty-free, worldwide, nonexclusive license to use certain computer graphics technology for which Cadtrak holds a patent (the "Cadtrak license"). The license agreement specified, among other things, that the license was non-transferrable, that it extended to any company more than 50% of which was owned by CFLC, that it conferred on CFLC no right to sublicense, that it could be terminated by Cadtrak upon CFLC's bankruptcy, and that it was to be construed according to California law.

On January 4, 1993, CFLC began a Chapter 11 proceeding, in the course of which it sold certain divisions, foreign subsidiaries, and assets for nearly $20 million. It then sought and received approval to sell "substantially all" of its remaining assets to Everex. The sale closed on November 12, 1993; Everex paid approximately $4 million. The agreement provided that the parties would seek the assumption and assignment by CFLC to Everex of certain designated executory [contracts]. On December 8, 1993, Everex designated [the] Cadtrak license. On January 4, 1994, CFLC moved to assume and assign executory contracts, including the Cadtrak license; Cadtrak objected to the assumption and assignment. Bankruptcy Judge Randall J. Newsome . . . denied the motion. . . .

Assumption & Assignment of Executory Contracts in Bankruptcy

Section 365 of the Bankruptcy Code "gives a trustee in bankruptcy the authority either to reject or to assume executory contracts and unexpired leases. Ordinarily, a trustee may take either of these actions without the consent of the other party to the contract or lease and notwithstanding a provision in the applicable agreement that purports to restrict assignment. *See* 11 U. S.C. §§ 365(a) & (f)(1)." Once a contract has been assumed, the trustee can assign it. "The trustee's power, however, is not absolute," and both § 365(a), which authorizes assumption, and § 365(f), which authorizes assignment, are *expressly* subject to an exception provided in § 365(c):

> The trustee may not assume or assign any executory contract or unexpired lease of the debtor, whether or not such contract or lease prohibits or restricts assignment of rights or delegation of duties, if —
>
> > (1)(A) applicable law excuses a party, other than the debtor, to such contract or lease from accepting performance from or rendering performance to an entity other than the debtor or the debtor in possession, whether or not such contract or lease prohibits or restricts assignment of rights or delegation of duties; and
> >
> > > (B) such party does not consent to such assumption or assignment.

The parties agree that if the exception of 365(c) applies to the Cadtrak license, the bankruptcy court was correct in denying the motion to assume and assign that license.

At least two circuits have offered apparently differing views on the scope of §365(c); on the interplay between §365(f), which authorizes the assignment of assumed contracts, and §365(c). . . . [However, because,] as we hold below, a nonexclusive patent license is personal and nondelegable under federal law, §365(c) bars the assumption and assignment of the license in this case under either test and we need not attempt to resolve whatever conflict exists between the two decisions. . . .

Does Federal or State Law Apply?

Whether 365(c) bars assumption and assignment of the Cadtrak license [turns] on whether or not "applicable" law excuses Cadtrak from accepting performance from, or rendering performance to, anyone other than CFLC. The bankruptcy and district courts held that the applicable law is federal law, and that federal common law makes patent licenses nonassignable. Everex argues that the applicable law is California law, and that [it] does not bar the assignment of rights, or delegation of duties, under patent licenses.

The statutes governing patents are basically silent on the issue of licenses. The construction of a patent license is generally a matter of state contract law, except where state law "would be inconsistent with the aims of federal patent policy." Two circuits have found such an inconsistency and expressly held that "[q]uestions with respect to the assignability of a patent license are controlled by federal law." *PPG Industries, Inc. v. Guardian Industries Corp.,* 597 F.2d 1090, 1093 (6th Cir.), *cert. denied,* 444 U.S. 930 (1979); *Unarco Industries, Inc. v. Kelley Co.,* 465 F.2d 1303, 1306 (7th Cir.1972) ("[T]he question of assignability of a patent license is a specific policy of federal patent law dealing with federal patent law. Therefore, we hold federal law applies to the question of the assignability of the patent license in question."), *cert. denied,* 410 U.S. 929 (1973).

Everex argues that these holdings are incorrect in applying federal law. It begins from the premise that "[t]here is no federal general common law." Since the federal patent laws are silent on the question of licenses and their assignability, a federal rule of decision on assignability is possible only if this is an area "in which judicial creation of a special federal rule would be justified."[1] Everex notes that such areas are "few and restricted," and "limited to situations where there is a 'significant conflict between some federal policy or interest and the use of state law,'" and challenges whether the cases holding that federal law governs patent-license assignability meet these criteria.

Unarco expressly considered the issue of whether, in a post-*Erie* world, federal or state law governs the assignability of patent licenses and advanced two reasons for applying federal law. First, it quoted from *Sola Electric Co. v.*

[1] [FN 4] Much of the argument is based on Justice Traynor's opinion for the California Supreme Court in [*Farmland Irrigation Co. v.*] *Dopplmaier,* [48 Cal. 2d 208, 308 P.2d 732 (1957)]. Based on well-established law that a suit to enforce a patent license does not arise under the patent laws so as to confer exclusive jurisdiction on federal courts, Justice Traynor concluded that, under *Erie [R. Co. v. Tompkins,* 304 U.S. 64 (1938)], state law governed patent licenses. He acknowledged that on any particular question, state law would have to give way if federal policy — embodied either in statute or federal common law — required. He then considered the federal cases holding that patent licenses are not assignable — some decided before *Erie* and the others not addressing the question of which law governs — and could discover no federal "policy underlying the federal patent statutes that requires a uniform federal rule of construction of license contracts to determine their assignability."

Jefferson Electric Co., 317 U.S. 173 (1942), in which the Supreme Court held that federal law preempted any state law which would estop a patent licensee from challenging a provision of the license as a violation of the Sherman Act. *Unarco* quoted the *Sola* Court's view that *Erie* does not apply

> to those areas of judicial decision within which the policy of the law is so dominated by the sweep of federal statutes that legal relations which they affect must be deemed governed by federal law having its source in those statutes, rather than by local law. . . . To the federal statute and policy, conflicting state law and policy must yield.

Unarco, 465 F.2d at 1306. Everex argues, with some justification, that *Sola* found that federal law governed in that case because of federal antitrust, rather than patent, policy, which suggests that *Sola* applied federal law to that particular question of licensee estoppel because of the sweep of federal antitrust policy, not federal patent policy. . . .

The second ground offered by *Unarco* in support of applying federal law to the question of assignability of a patent license is also less firm than might be wished. The court noted that a patentee's act in licensing the patent is a use of a monopoly authorized by the Constitution and enacted by Congress. "This monopoly conferred by federal statute as well as the policy perpetuating this monopoly, so affects the licensing of patents, and the policy behind such licensing is so intertwined with the sweep of federal statutes, that *any* question with respect thereto must be governed by federal law." *Unarco,* 465 F.2d at 1306. This conclusion seems insupportably broad given the general rule that most questions with respect to the construction of patent licenses are governed by state law.

Federal patent policy, however, does justify the application of federal law here. The fundamental policy of the patent system is to "encourage the creation and disclosure of new, useful, and non-obvious advances in technology and design" by granting the inventor the reward of "the exclusive right to practice the invention for a period of years." *Bonito Boats, Inc. v. Thunder Craft Boats, Inc.,* 489 U.S. 141, 150-51 (1989). Allowing free assignability — or, more accurately, allowing states to allow free assignability — of nonexclusive patent licenses would undermine the reward that encourages invention because a party seeking to use the patented invention could either seek a license from the patent holder *or* seek an assignment of an existing patent license from a licensee. In essence, every licensee would become a potential competitor with the licensor-patent holder in the market for licenses under the patents. And while the patent holder could presumably control the absolute *number* of licenses in existence under a free-assignability regime, it would lose the very important ability to control the *identity* of its licensees. Thus, any license a patent holder granted — even to the smallest firm in the product market most remote from its own — would be fraught with the danger that the licensee would assign it to the patent holder's most serious competitor, a party whom the patent holder itself might be absolutely unwilling to license. As a practical matter, free assignability of patent licenses might spell the end to paid-up licenses such as the one involved in this case. Few patent holders would be willing to grant a license in return for a one-time lump-sum payment, rather than for per-use royalties, if the license could be assigned to a completely different company which might make far greater use of the patented invention than could the original licensee.

Thus, federal law governs the assignability of patent licenses because of the conflict between federal patent policy and state laws, such as California's, that would allow assignability.

Does Federal Law Bar Assignment of Nonexclusive Patent Licenses?

Federal law holds a nonexclusive patent license to be personal and nonassignable and therefore would excuse Cadtrak from accepting performance from, or rendering it to, anyone other than CFLC. "It is well settled that a non-exclusive licensee of a patent has only a personal and not a property interest in the patent and that this personal right cannot be assigned unless the patent owner authorizes the assignment or the license itself permits assignment." *Gilson v. Republic of Ireland,* 787 F.2d 655, 658 (D.C.Cir.1986) (Friedman, J.). *See also Stenograph Corp. v. Fulkerson,* 972 F.2d 726, 729 n. 2 (7th Cir.1992) ("Patent licenses are *not* assignable in the absence of express language."); *PPG Industries,* 597 F.2d at 1093 ("It has long been held by federal courts that agreements granting patent licenses are personal and not assignable unless expressly made so."); *Unarco,* 465 F.2d at 1306 ("The long standing federal rule of law with respect to the assignability of patent license agreement provides that these agreements are personal to the licensee and not assignable unless expressly made so in the agreement."); *Rock-Ola Manufacturing Corp. v. Filben Manufacturing Co.,* 168 F.2d 919, 922 (8th Cir.), *cert. dismissed,* 335 U.S. 855-6 (1948); *E.I. du Pont de Nemours & Co. v. Shell Oil Co.,* 498 A.2d 1108, 1114 (Del.1985) (rights conveyed by nonexclusive patent license are personal to licensee and not susceptible to sublicensing unless specific permission given).

The only decision cited to the contrary is Justice Traynor's opinion in *Dopplmaier.* While that opinion raises not insignificant questions about the actual holdings, relevance, and continued vitality of the nineteenth-century Supreme Court decisions which are cited for the origins of the federal rule, those questions are not so significant as to compel departure from the uniform rule of modern federal decisions reading those precedents as defining nonexclusive patent licenses as personal and non-assignable.

Conclusion

Because federal law governs the assignability of nonexclusive patent licenses, and because federal law makes such licenses personal and assignable only with the consent of the licensor, the Cadtrak license is not assumable and assignable in bankruptcy under 11 U.S.C. § 365(c). The decision of the district court is therefore AFFIRMED.

NOTES

1. The rule stated in *Everex* is widely followed. Is the risk of harm from transfer of a non-exclusive patent license materially different from the risk of a transfer of a contract to purchase goods?

2. A rule different from *Everex* was adopted by one court in the limited circumstance of a Chapter 11 bankruptcy reorganization where the transfer was to the reorganized debtor — technically a different entity, but functionally the same licensee. *See Institut Pasteur v. Cambridge Biotech Corp.*, 104 F.3d 489 (1st Cir. 1997) (court adopts what it describes as the "actual performance" test, rather that the "hypothetical test" in *Everex*; transfer is barred only if it is to an entity that is actually, rather than hypothetically, different).

3. Should *Everex* apply to transfers by the *licensor*? If not, how should one analyze the right of an inventor to assign (sell) its patent and transfer the right to royalties under the patent license to a third party without obtaining the licensee's consent to the transaction? Is this a transfer of rights, duties, or both?

4. The rule in *Everex* also applies to non-exclusive copyright licenses. In *Harris v. Emus Records Corp.,* 734 F.2d 1329 (9th Cir. 1984), for example, the court commented:

> It has been held that a copyright licensee is a "bare licensee . . . without any right to assign its privilege." Where precedent in copyright cases is lacking, it is appropriate to look for guidance to patent law "because of the historic kinship between patent law and copyright law." . . . A patent license has been characterized as "a naked license to make and sell the patented improvement as a part of its business, which right, if it existed, was a mere personal one, and not transferable, and was extinguished with the dissolution of the corporation." . . . Such an interpretation of a license accords with the policies underlying enactment of the Copyright Act. The legislative history reveals an acute awareness of the need to delicately balance competing interests. On the one hand, there was a strong reluctance to allow a monopolization of works or compositions; at the same time, there was an awareness of the necessity of preserving the rights of authors and composers in order to stimulate creativity. . . . By licensing rather than assigning his interest in the copyright, the owner reserves certain rights, including that of collecting royalties. His ability to monitor use would be jeopardized by allowing sublicensing without notice. In fact precisely such a scenario underlies this litigation.

The court held that a company that acquired a master copy of a recording from a bankruptcy estate did not thereby acquire a license to mechanically reproduce the copy "[b]ecause a copyright license can not be transferred by the licensee without authorization." *But see* David A. Rice, *Licensing Use of Computer Program Copies and the Copyright Act First Sale Doctrine*, 30 JURIMETRICS J. 157 (1990). *Cf Stenograph Corp. v. Fulkerson*, 972 F.2d 726 (7th Cir. 1992).

5. The federal rule has not generally applied to an exclusive license which is more of a conveyance of patent or copyright ownership, at least in some cases. That view was called into question in *Gardner v. Nike, Inc.*, 279 F.3d 774 (9th Cir. 2002), where the court held that an exclusive copyright license was presumptively non-transferable. *Cf In re Golden Books Family Entertainment, Inc.*, 269 B.R. 311 (Bankr. D. Del. 2001) (disagreeing with *Gardner*; exclusive license could be assigned without licensor's consent).

6. If the federal rule stated in *Everex* did not apply, would a licensee be able to transfer its rights under a non-exclusive license?

PROBLEM 6.2

Software-X grants a license to Smith Corporation, a wholesale distributor of consumer products in Seattle. The license grants Smith the "exclusive right to distribute copies of Software's X-1 Word Processing software to retail stores in the city of Seattle." The license is for ten years at a fixed royalty per copy distributed. During the second year, Smith is contacted by Computer Corporation, a competitor of Software-X. Computer offers Smith $100,000 for its rights under the license. Smith takes the money and assigns its rights to Computer. Computer sets a very high price for Software-X, resulting in few sales and shifting the Seattle market to Computer's own products.

a. Although the license is silent on assignability, Software-X sues to cancel the license and claims that Computer's sales infringe its copyright in X-1. What result?

b. Should the result in (a) change if the assignment were made to Carter, another distributor in Seattle, but not a competitor of Software-X?

PROBLEM 6.3

Texas Inc., a large technology company, grants a non-exclusive license to Phillips to use know-how provided to it by Texas for use in the design of manufacturing systems for manufacturing super-conductive products. Texas delivers the know-how in documentary form, but also provides consulting services during the term of the license. Texas will receive a monthly payment of $500,000 plus 10% of profits made by Phillips on the products. The contract is silent on transferability.

a. Texas plans to assign the license to Hewlett, as part of a transfer of a major division of Texas to Hewlett. Does the transfer require the consent of Phillips?

b. If the transfer to Hewlett did not occur, but Phillips desires to transfer its interest in the license to Carolina in return for $500,000, must it obtain Texas' consent?

c. Would your answers change if the technology was patented by Texas?

TAP PUBLICATIONS, INC. v. CHINESE YELLOWPAGES (NEW YORK), INC.
925 F. Supp. 212 (S.D.N.Y. 1996)

KOELTL, DISTRICT JUDGE:

This case concerns a dispute over the right to use in the New York metropolitan area a trademark consisting of the four Chinese characters pronounced "Hua Shang Nien Chien" ("the mark"). The undisputed owner of the mark, which in English means "Chinese Business Yearbook," is the defendant Asia System Media, Inc. ("ASM"). ASM uses the mark as the title for the numerous Chinese business directories ASM and its licensees publish throughout the United States and Canada. The plaintiff Tap Publications Co. ("Tap") contends that it has the exclusive right to use the mark in the New York metropolitan area pursuant to a 1986 settlement agreement between ASM and Key Publications, Inc. ("Key"), Tap's alleged predecessor corporation, and that ASM violated the terms of this settlement by entering into a licensing agreement with defendant Chinese Yellow Pages (New York), Inc. ("CYPNY").

Tap initiated this action and made claims against both CYPNY and ASM under Section 43(a) of the Lanham Act, 15 U.S.C. §1125(a), for false designation of origin as well as under state trademark law and state law against unfair competition. In addition, Tap alleges that ASM breached the 1986 settlement agreement. . . .

Conclusions of Law

1. The plaintiff Tap first claims that both CYPNY and ASM violated section 43(a) of the Lanham Act, 15 U.S.C. §1125(a)(1)(A). Tap alleges that with ASM's approval CYPNY placed advertisements containing the mark in various Chinese-language publications circulated in several states. Tap argues that by using the mark CYPNY misled the public that its directories were published by or affiliated with Tap.

2. Tap has no standing to assert a claim under the Lanham Act. Even assuming that Tap has the exclusive right to use the mark in the New York area as an assignee of the 1986 settlement agreement, a licensee has no right to sue the licensor under the Lanham Act.

3. Moreover, Tap's claims against ASM are claims for breach of contract rather than Lanham Act claims. Tap concedes that ASM is the owner of the mark at issue in the case. Tap's claim that it has exclusive rights to use the mark in the New York metropolitan region rests solely on its claim that the 1986 settlement agreement gave this right to Key, which Tap alleges is its predecessor. Whether Key obtained this right and had the right to assign it to Tap involve questions of contract interpretation. The mere fact that a trademark was the subject of the contract does not convert a state-law breach of contract issue into a federal Lanham Act claim. [The] "dispute should be determined by the principles of contract law, as it is the contract that defines the parties' relationship and provides mechanisms to address alleged breaches thereto. The Lanham Act, in contrast, establishes marketplace rules governing the conduct of parties not otherwise limited." . . .

5. Tap's breach of contract claim against ASM alleging that ASM violated the 1986 settlement agreement must also be dismissed because Tap has no rights to the mark under the 1986 settlement agreement.

6. It is undisputed that the 1986 settlement agreement did not expressly give Tap any rights in the mark. Indeed, Tap did not even exist in 1986. Tap claims instead that it enjoys the same rights to use the mark as its alleged predecessor Key did under the terms of the 1986 agreement because Key assigned Tap its rights under the agreement.

7. Tap's argument fails for two independent reasons. First, the 1986 settlement agreement did not give Tap the power to assign or transfer its rights in the mark. Second, the February 19, 1992 agreement between Tap and Key did not include any rights in the mark that Key may have had.

8. First, neither the Chinese nor English language settlement papers grant Key the right to assign its rights in the mark at issue: in this regard, the contract language is precise and unambiguous. Even if the contract were ambiguous on this issue, Tap did not present any evidence at trial that the parties intended that Tap would have such a right to assign or transfer. In fact, the settlement agreement granting Key the right to use the mark in the New York area indicates the contrary. Key's continued use of the mark was an express condition of the agreement, which specifically provided that

> as long as Party A [Key] continues to publish Chinese/English telephone directories in the metropolitan New York area, Party B [ASM] agrees not to publish Chinese telephone directories or similar directories in the metropolitan New York area. If Party A ceases to so publish, then Party B shall be permitted to so publish.

Accordingly, it is clear that the rights conferred upon Key to use the mark [were] personal to Key, and that these rights were not assignable or otherwise transferable. Thus, once Key dissolved in 1992, ASM regained the right to use its mark in the New York metropolitan area.

9. Tap's argument that trademark rights are assignable absent express language to the contrary is incorrect. A leading treatise on trademark law addressed the issue of whether a license to use a mark is assignable as follows:

> The right of a licensee to sub-license to others must be determined by whether the license clearly grants such a power. Similarly, the general rule is that unless the license states otherwise, the licensee's right to use the licensed mark is personal and cannot be assigned to another.

2 MCCARTHY ON TRADEMARKS AND UNFAIR COMPETITION § 18.14[2]; 25.07[3] (3d ed. 1996). As the above treatise explains, "since the licensor-trademark owner has the duty to control the quality of goods sold under its mark, it must have the right to pass upon the abilities of new potential licensees."

10. Second, even if Key had the power to assign or transfer its rights in the mark under the 1986 settlement agreement, Key failed to make an effective transfer. Key claims that the February 19, 1992 document transferring Key's right, title, and interest in any copyright for the 1992 edition of its publication effectively transferred its right to the mark as well. This document makes no mention of trademark rights or licenses, however, and does not discuss any editions other than the 1992 edition, and the general recitation ". . . and all other right there in . . ." is insufficient to effect the wholesale transfer Tap now claims. Tap failed to present any evidence that the parties intended this agreement to include the assignment of any rights Key had in the mark pursuant to the 1986 settlement agreement. . . .

NOTES

1. In understanding *Tap*, you should know that a doctrine discussed later in this book creates a risk that a trademark owner will forfeit the trademark if it grants a license without exercising quality control over the licensee's products or services. With that in mind, is the result in *Tap* dictated by federal law, or is it the product of a contract law noted earlier?

2. Contrast *Tap* with *In re Rooster, Inc.,* 100 B.R. 228 (Bankr. E.D. Pa. 1989), where the court held that a trademark license was not a personal services contract and could be assigned to a third party as part of a bankruptcy proceeding. The agreement was for the manufacture and sale of "Bill Blass" neckties. The court focused on the fact that the licensor and the designer of the neck ties retained and exercised control over the product and had a right to veto or alter any product bearing the mark if it did not meet their standards. In effect, the licensee had no relevant discretion other than to select which approved design it would use.

PROBLEM 6.4

McDonald's operates its restaurant business through locations that it owns and through locations that are owned and operated by franchisees. The franchise arrangements allow the owner to use the McDonald's name, logos, and other trademarked materials in return for an upfront fee and a royalty based on the gross sales at the location. The agreements contain twenty pages of detailed description about how the locations are to be operated, maintained and advertised. McDonald's has the right to cancel the franchise agreement for any material breach of the agreement.

a. While such contracts typically contain clauses prohibiting assignment without permission of the franchisor, assume that the McDonald's contract does not. Can a franchisee assign the contract to a third party without McDonald's assent? Would your answer depend on whether the assignee meets McDonald's financial and other eligibility criteria for a franchise?

b. Would your analysis change if, rather than a McDonald's franchise, we are dealing with a contract between Acme (a shoe manufacturer) and Retailer (a retail seller of shoes), and the agreement allows Retailer to use Acme logos in its store from which it also sells Acme shoes?

II. NON-ASSIGNMENT CLAUSES

Many licenses contain clauses that preclude transfer entirely, or that allow transfer only subject to stated conditions. Contract terms regarding transfer can alter application of the underlying presumption about nontransferability. In such cases, the contractual language controls and the issue becomes a matter of contract interpretation.

PPG INDUSTRIES, INC. v. GUARDIAN INDUSTRIES CORP.
597 F.2d 1090 (6th Cir. 1979)

LIVELY, CIRCUIT JUDGE

The question in this case is whether the surviving or resultant corporation in a statutory merger acquires patent license rights of the constituent corporations. . . .

Prior to 1964 both PPG and Permaglass, Inc., were engaged in fabrication of glass products which required that sheets of glass be shaped for particular uses. Independently of each other the two fabricators developed similar processes which involved "floating glass on a bed of gas, while it was being heated and bent." This process is known in the industry as "gas hearth technology" and "air float technology"; the two terms are interchangeable. After a period of negotiations PPG and Permaglass entered into an agreement on January 1, 1964 whereby each granted rights to the other under "gas hearth system" patents already issued and in the process of prosecution. [The license grants read as follows:]

SECTION 3. GRANT FROM PERMAGLASS TO PPG

3.1 Subject to the reservation set forth in Subsection 3.3 below, PERMAGLASS hereby grants to PPG an exclusive license, with right of sublicense, to use PERMAGLASS Technical Data in Gas Hearth Systems throughout the United States of America, its territories and possessions, and all countries of the world foreign thereto.

3.2 Subject to the reservation set forth in Subsection 3.3 below, PERMAGLASS hereby grants to PPG an unlimited exclusive license, with right of sublicense, under PERMAGLASS Patent Rights.

3.3 The licenses granted to PPG under Subsections 3.1 and 3.2 above shall be subject to the reservation of a non-exclusive, non-transferable, royalty-free, world-wide right and license for the benefit and use of PERMAGLASS.

SECTION 4. GRANT FROM PPG TO PERMAGLASS

4.1 PPG hereby grants to PERMAGLASS a non-exclusive, non-transferable, royalty-free right and license to heat, bend, thermally temper and/or anneal glass using Gas Hearth Systems under PPG Patent Rights, excepting in the Dominion of Canada, and to use or sell glass articles produced thereby, but no license, express or implied, is hereby granted to PERMAGLASS under any claim of any PPG patent expressly covering any coating method, coating composition, or coated article.

Assignability of the agreement and of the license granted to Permaglass and termination of the license granted to Permaglass were covered in the following language:

SECTION 9. ASSIGNABILITY

9.1 This Agreement shall be assignable by PPG to any successor of the entire flat glass business of PPG but shall otherwise be non-assignable except with the consent of PERMAGLASS first obtained in writing.

9.2 This Agreement and the license granted by PPG to PERMAGLASS hereunder shall be personal to PERMAGLASS and non-assignable except with the consent of PPG first obtained in writing.

SECTION 11. TERMINATION

11.2 In the event that a majority of the voting stock of PERMAGLASS shall at any time become owned or controlled directly or indirectly by a manufacturer of automobiles or a manufacturer or fabricator of glass other than the present owners, the license granted to PERMAGLASS under Subsection 4.1 shall terminate forthwith.

Eleven patents are involved in this suit. . . . In Section 9.1 and 9.2 assignability was treated somewhat differently as between the parties, and the Section 11.2 provisions with regard to termination apply only to the license granted to Permaglass.

As of December 1969 Permaglass was merged into [Guardian]. Guardian was engaged primarily in the business of fabricating and distributing wind-shields for automobiles and trucks. It had decided to construct a facility to manufacture raw glass and the capacity of that facility would be greater than its own requirements. Permaglass had no glass manufacturing capability and it was contemplated that its operations would utilize a large part of the excess output of the proposed Guardian [facility].

Shortly after the merger was consummated PPG filed the present action, claiming infringement by Guardian in the use of apparatus and processes described and claimed in eleven patents which were identified by number and origin. The eleven patents were covered by the terms of the 1964 agreement. PPG asserted that it became the exclusive licensee of the nine patents which originated with Permaglass under the 1964 agreement and that the rights reserved by Permaglass were personal to it and non-transferable and non-assignable. PPG also claimed that Guardian had no rights with respect to the two patents which had originated with PPG because the license under these patents was personal to Permaglass and non-transferable and non-assignable except with the permission of PPG. In addition it claimed that the license with respect to these two patents had terminated under the provisions of Section 11.2 by reason of the merger.

One of the defenses pled by Guardian [was] that it was a licensee of the patents in suit. It described the merger with Permaglass and claimed it "had succeeded to all rights, powers, ownerships, etc., of Permaglass, and as Permaglass' successor, defendant is legally entitled to operate in place of Permaglass under the January 1, 1964 agreement between Permaglass and plaintiff, free of any claim of infringement of the patents. . . ."

[The] district court concluded that the parties to the 1964 agreement did not intend that the rights reserved by Permaglass in its nine patents or the rights assigned to Permaglass in the two PPG patents would not pass to a successor corporation by way of merger. The court held that there had been no assignment or transfer of the rights by Permaglass, but rather that Guardian acquired these rights by operation of law under the merger statutes of Ohio and Delaware. The provisions of the 1964 agreement making the license rights of Permaglass non-assignable and non-transferable were held not to apply because of the "continuity of interest inherent in a statutory merger that distinguishes it from the ordinary assignment or transfer case." . . .

II

Questions with respect to the assignability of a patent license are controlled by federal law. It has long been held by federal courts that agreements granting patent licenses are personal and not assignable unless expressly made so.

This has been the rule at least since 1852 when the Supreme Court decided *Troy Iron & Nail v. Corning*, 55 U.S. (14 How.) 193, 14 L. Ed. 383 (1852). The district court recognized this rule in the present case, but concluded that where patent licenses are claimed to pass by operation of law to the resultant or surviving corporation in a statutory merger there has been no assignment or transfer.

There appear to be no reported cases where the precise issue in this case has been decided. At least two treatises contain the statement that rights under a patent license owned by a constituent corporation pass to the consolidated corporation in the case of a consolidation, *W. Fletcher, Cyclopedia of the Law of Corporations* § 7089 (revised ed. 1973); and to the new or resultant corporation in the case of a merger, *A. Deller, Walker on Patents* § 409 (2d ed. 1965). However, the cases cited in support of these statements by the commentators do not actually provide such support because their facts take them outside the general rule of non-assignability. Both texts rely on the decision in *Hartford-Empire Co. v. Demuth Glass Works, Inc.*, 19 F. Supp. 626 (E.D.N.Y.1937). The agreement involved in that case specified that the patent license was assignable and its assignability was not an issue. Clearly the statement in the *Hartford-Empire* opinion that the merger conveyed to the new corporation the patent licenses owned by the old corporation results from the fact that the licenses in question were expressly made assignable, not from any general principle that such licenses pass to the resultant corporation where there is a merger. It is also noteworthy that the surviving corporation following the merger in *Hartford-Empire* was the original licensee, whereas in the present case the original licensee was merged into Guardian, which was the survivor. . . .

Guardian relies on two classes of cases where rights of a constituent corporation have been held to pass by merger to the resultant corporation even though such rights are not otherwise assignable or transferable. It points out that the courts have consistently held that "shop rights" do pass in a statutory merger. A shop right is an implied license which accrues to an employer in cases where an employee has perfected a patentable device while working for the employer. Though the employee is the owner of the patent he is estopped from claiming infringement by the employer. This estoppel arises from the fact that the patent work has been done on the employer's time and that the employer has furnished materials for the experiments and financial backing to the employee.

The rule that prevents an employee-inventor from claiming infringement against a successor to the entire business and good will of his employer is but one feature of the broad doctrine of estoppel which underlies the shop right cases. No element of estoppel exists in the present case. The license rights of Permaglass did not arise by implication. They were bargained for at arms length and the agreement which defines the rights of the parties provides that Permaglass received non-transferable, non-assignable personal licenses. We do not believe that the express prohibition against assignment and transfer in a written instrument may be held ineffective by analogy to a rule based on estoppel in situations where there is no written contract and the rights of the parties have arisen by implication because of their past relationship.

The other group of cases which the district court and Guardian found to be analogous hold that the resultant corporation in a merger succeeds to the rights of the constituent corporations under real estate leases. The most obvious difficulty in drawing an analogy between the lease cases and those concerning patent licenses is that a lease is an interest in real property. As such, it is subject to the deep-rooted policy against restraints on alienation. [There] is no similar policy which is offended by the decision of a patent owner to make a license under his patent personal to the licensee, and non-assignable and non-transferable. In fact the law treats a license as if it contained these restrictions in the absence of express provisions to the contrary.

We conclude that the district court misconceived the intent of the parties to the 1964 agreement. We believe the district court put the burden on the wrong party in stating:

> Because the parties failed to provide that Permaglass' rights under the 1964 license agreement would not pass to the corporation surviving a merger, the Court finds that Guardian succeeded to Permaglass' license.

The agreement provides with respect to the license which Permaglass granted to PPG that Permaglass reserved "a non-exclusive, non-transferable, royalty-free, world-wide right and license for the benefit and use of Permaglass." Similarly, with respect to its own two patents, PPG granted to Permaglass "a non-exclusive, non-transferable, royalty-free right and license. . . ." Further, the agreement provides that both it and the license granted to Permaglass "shall be personal to PERMAGLASS and non-assignable except with the consent of PPG first obtained in writing."

The quoted language from Sections 3, 4 and 9 of the 1964 agreement evinces an intent that only Permaglass was to enjoy the privileges of licensee. If the parties had intended an exception in the event of a merger, it would have been a simple matter to have so provided in the agreement. Guardian contends such an exception is not necessary since it is universally recognized that patent licenses pass from a licensee to the resultant corporation in case of a merger. This does not appear to be the case. In *Packard Instrument Co. v. ANS, Inc.*, 416 F.2d 943 (2d Cir. 1969), a license agreement provided that rights thereunder could not be transferred or assigned "except . . . (b) if the entire ownership and business of ANS is transferred by sale, merger, or consolidation. . . ." Similarly, the agreement construed in *Freeman v. Seiberling Rubber Co.*, 72 F.2d 124 (6th Cir. 1934), provided that the license was not assignable except with the entire business and good will of the licensee. We conclude that if the parties had intended an exception in case of a merger to the provisions against assignment and transfer they would have included it in the agreement. It should be noted also that the district court in *Packard, supra*, held that an assignment had taken place when the licensee was merged into another corporation. . . .

Thus, Sections 3, 4 and 9 of the 1964 agreement between PPG and Permaglass show an intent that the licenses held by Permaglass in the eleven patents in suit not be transferable. While this conclusion disposes of the license defense as to all eleven patents, it should be noted that Guardian's claim to licenses under the two patents which originated with PPG is also defeated by Section 11.2 of the 1964 agreement. This section addresses a different concern from that addressed in Sections 3, 4 and 9. The restrictions on transferability and assignability in those sections prevent the patent licenses from becoming the property of third parties. The termination clause, however, provides that Permaglass' license with respect to the two PPG patents will terminate if the ownership of a majority of the voting stock of Permaglass passes from the 1964 stockholders to designated classes of persons, even though the licenses themselves might never have changed hands.

Apparently PPG was willing for Permaglass to continue as licensee under the nine patents even though ownership of its stock might change. These patents originated with Permaglass and so long as Permaglass continued to use the licenses for its own benefit a mere change in ownership of Permaglass stock would not nullify the licenses. Only a transfer or assignment would cause a termination. However, the agreement provides for termination with respect to the two original PPG patents in the event of an indirect takeover of Permaglass by a change in the ownership of a majority of its stock. The fact that PPG sought and obtained a stricter provision with respect to the two patents which it originally owned in no way indicates an intention to permit transfer of licenses under the other nine in case of a merger. None of the eleven licenses was transferable; but two of them, those involving PPG's own development in the field of gas hearth technology, were not to continue even for the benefit of the licensee if it came under the control of a manufacturer of automobiles or a competitor of PPG in the glass industry "other than the present owners" of Permaglass. A consistency among the provisions of the agreement is discernible when the different origins of the various patents are considered. . . .

NOTES

1. Transferability questions are especially important in mergers or sales of corporate enterprises because of the sheer number of license agreements involved in a modern business. Indeed, in one case, a conveyance of the accounts receivable processing system of a mid-size jewelry company involved transfer of over five hundred licenses that comprised the processing system. In all such cases, reviewing the conditions for transfer of the license by the licensee is an important part of modern due diligence in business transactions.

2. Some agreements permit transfer in merger or acquisition contexts. In *Cyrix Corp. v. Intel Corp.*, 803 F. Supp. 1200 (E.D. Tex. 1992), for example, a license for microprocessor technology gave the licensee the right to transfer the license as part of a transfer of all or substantially all of the licensee's assets. The court held that a transfer of most, but not all, of the licensee's assets fell within the meaning of this clause. The court viewed the appropriate standard as coming from corporate law to the effect that a "company sells all or substantially all of its assets when the sale is of assets quantitatively vital to the operation of the corporation and is out of the ordinary and substantially affects the existence and purpose of the corporation." If you were drafting a license in which the parties had agreed to allow transfers as part of a merger, how would you express that intent in the contract?

3. In *PPG*, did violation of the no-assignment rule mean that the transfer was ineffective or simply that the transfer breached the contract, giving the licensor a right to cancel the license for breach? Does the difference matter? Consider the following language from the *Restatement*:

§ 322. Contractual Prohibition of Assignment

(1) Unless the circumstances indicate the contrary, a contract term prohibiting assignment of "the contract" bars only the delegation to an assignee of the performance by the assignor of a duty or condition.

(2) A contract term prohibiting assignment of rights under the contract, unless a different intention is manifested,

(a) does not forbid assignment of a . . . right arising out of the assignor's due performance of his entire obligation;

(b) gives the obligor a right to damages for breach of the terms forbidding assignment but does not render the assignment ineffective;

(c) is for the benefit of the obligor, and does not prevent the assignee from acquiring rights against the assignor or the obligor from discharging his duty as if there were no such prohibition.

Comment c elaborates: "The rules stated in this Section do not exhaust the factors to be taken into account in construing and applying a prohibition against assignment. 'Not transferable' has a clear meaning in a theatre ticket; in a certificate of deposit the same words may refer to negotiability rather than assignability. Where there is a promise not to assign but no provision that an assignment is ineffective, the question whether breach of the promise discharges the obligor's duty depends on all the circumstances."

Is the rule proposed by the *Restatement* preferable, or should the rule be that the prohibition on transfer renders the assignment ineffective as to the other party of the contract? If the *Restatement* rule applied in *PPG*, what would be the result on the infringement claim? UCITA rejected the *Restatement* rule and many courts similarly do not follow it. UCITA § 503(2)(3) (2000 Official Text) states, in relevant part:

(2) [A] term prohibiting transfer of a party's contractual interest is enforceable, and a transfer made in violation of that term is a breach of contract and is ineffective to create contractual rights in the transferee against the nontransferring party, except to the extent that:

(A) the contract is a license for incorporation or use of the licensed information or informational rights with information or informational rights from other sources in a combined work for public distribution or public performance and the transfer is of the completed, combined work; or

(B) the transfer is of a right to payment arising out of the transferor's due performance of less than its entire obligation and the transfer would be enforceable . . . in the absence of the term prohibiting transfer [or]

(3) A right to damages for breach of the whole contract or a right to payment arising out of the transferor's due performance of its entire obligation may be transferred notwithstanding an agreement otherwise.

PROBLEM 6.5

Client will license valuable trademark and copyright rights on a non-exclusive basis to Bobcat, a mid-size manufacturing and retail company doing business in the Midwest. While all other terms of the license are agreed to, it asks you to comment on the following language, which is part of its standard form: "This license is non-transferable and may not be assigned without the consent of Licensor, except that the license may be transferred to the new company as part of the merger of Licensee with another company."

a. Client asks whether this language protects it against a transfer to a competitor, to a company with higher volume use, or a company with a bad reputation. If a non-conforming transfer occurs, can Client prevent use of the trademarks and copyrights by the licensee through a lawsuit for infringement?

b. Client asks that you redraft the clause to deal with these issues. Draft appropriate language.

FIRST NATIONWIDE BANK v. FLORIDA SOFTWARE SERVICES, INC.
770 F. Supp. 1537 (M.D. Fla. 1991)

Kellam, Senior District Judge.

First Nationwide Bank ("FNB") and Pathway Financial, A Federal Association ("Pathway") filed this declaratory judgment action on March 3, 1989 against The Kirchman Corporation ("Kirchman") and Florida Software Services ("FSS"). FNB and Pathway seek a determination by the Court that they are not in breach of antiassignment clauses contained in certain computer software licensing agreements with Kirchman and FSS. . . .

I.

[In] December 1988, the Federal Home Loan Bank Board ("FHLBB") approved the acquisition of two insolvent savings and loan associations by FNB. With federal assistance, FNB purchased substantially all of the assets and liabilities of the insolvent Bloomfield Savings and Loan Association, F.A. ("Bloomfield") from the Federal Savings and Loan Insurance Association ("FSLIC"). Also in December of 1988, pursuant to a federally supervised conversion, First Nationwide Financial Corporation ("FNFC") purchased 100% of the common stock of Pathway, which was also insolvent. . . .

Prior to their acquisition, Pathway and Bloomfield had licensed computer software packages from Kirchman and FSS. The terms of Pathway's basic license agreements were from December 1986 to December 1991; and the term of Bloomfield's was from April 1985 to April 1990. In addition to regular quarterly payments, the license agreements required Pathway to pay Kirchman and FSS $561,995 in license fees upon execution of the license agreements; Bloomfield, in addition to the quarterly payments, was required to pay $200,000 in license fees. The license agreements contained anti-assignment clauses which were substantially identical and stated as follows:

> Customer shall not, without prior written consent of FSS, sell, lease, transfer or assign its interest as Licensee under this Agreement, or sell, lease, assign, transfer, sublicense or permit the duplication, reproduction or copying of the FSS Property (except as a part of standard computer industry backup procedures), or otherwise make available for any purpose, whether gratuitously or for consideration, the FSS Property or any part thereof or any information pertaining thereto, to any person or entity whatsoever [other than (i) employees of the Customer for use by them solely in connection with the performance of data processing services by customer, (ii) independent Certified Public Accountants for auditing purposes, or (iii) for compliance with governmental regulatory authorities]. The transfer of more than sixty percent (60%) of the common stock of Customer, without the prior written consent of FSS, shall be deemed an attempted transfer of this License Agreement and the license granted herein, which is in violation of the prohibitions against transfer contained in this Paragraph. . . . Such consent shall not be unreasonably withheld.

In January 1989, Kirchman and FSS sent letters to FNB and Pathway which asserted that the acquisition by FNB violated the anti-assignment clauses contained in the license agreements. The letters advised that Kirchman and FSS would terminate the license agreements within twenty days, and that the computer system was to be returned within ten days of the Notice of Termination. The letters went on to state that Pathway could continue using the computer system if they executed a new License Agreement and paid a new license fee of $1,187,000; Bloomfield could continue using the system for a new license fee of $754,000. After receiving these letters, Pathway and FNB initiated this action for declaratory relief; Kirchman and FSS filed immediately thereafter.

Regardless of the termination letters, FNB and Pathway continued using the computer software and making the quarterly payments to Kirchman and FSS. At first, Kirchman and FSS continued to accept the quarterly payments under the original license agreements and continued to send software information to Pathway and FNB. Kirchman and FSS subsequently refused to accept the quarterly payments; as a result, FNB and Pathway have continued to deposit the remainder of the quarterly payments into the Court registry. Upon the scheduled termination of Bloomfield's contract in April of 1990, all of the software materials and equipment were returned to FSS.

Although Bloomfield and Pathway never sought the consent of Kirchman or FSS before the acquisitions, the evidence at trial establishes that to do so would have been both improper and futile. Testimony at trial showed that information concerning the acquisitions of the assets and converted stock of said institutions was highly confidential, and any dissemination of that information was strictly regulated: the reason being that if information of the proposed acquisition leaked out, the insolvent institutions' depositors may have become concerned and made a run on the institutions' deposits. Such an occurrence would devastate the value of the institutions. Furthermore, testimony at trial established that even if FNB and Pathway had requested consent prior to the acquisitions, consent still would have been withheld until the payment of the higher license fees.

The evidence further established that no expansion of the software's use occurred and no one gained access to Kirchman and FSS trade secrets other than the parties to the original agreements; this fact is illustrated by Kirchman and FSS's withdrawal of allegations of trade secret violations in their counter-claim. Although Kirchman and FSS received assurances that no unauthorized use of the software would occur, they still refused to consent to the assignment of the license agreements unless FNB and Pathway would agree to pay the increased license fees. Furthermore, the evidence established that Kirchman and FSS suffered no damages. . . .

Kirchman and [FSS] have no cause of action under Florida contract law. In each of the license agreements, the parties stipulated that the agreements would be governed by and construed in accordance with the laws of the state of Florida. Such a forum selection clause is to be specifically enforced unless it is clearly established that enforcement of the clause would be unreasonable and unjust, or that the clause was invalid for such reasons as fraud or over-reaching. Additionally, forum selection clauses have the salutary effect of dispelling any confusion about where suits arising from the contract must be brought and defended, sparing litigants the time and expense of pretrial motions to determine the correct forum, and conserving judicial resources that otherwise would be devoted to deciding those motions. Accordingly, the Court will apply the law of Florida in deciding whether FNB's acquisition of Bloomfield and Pathway constitutes a breach of the license agreements.

Every contract includes not only its written provisions, but also the terms and matters which, though not actually expressed, are implied by law, and these are as binding as the terms which are actually written or spoken. One such implied term of a contract, recognized by Florida law, is the implied covenant of good faith and commercial reasonableness. A party's good faith cooperation is an implied condition precedent to performance of a contract, and where that cooperation is unreasonably withheld, the recalcitrant party is estopped from availing himself of his own wrongdoing.

The *Fernandez* [*v. Vazquez*, 397 So. 2d 1171 (Fla. Dist. Ct. App. 1981),] case provides some persuasive insight to Florida contract law. The issue in the *Fernandez* case was whether a lessor could refuse to consent to the assignment of a commercial lease in order that he may charge a higher rent than originally contracted for. The Court in that case held that a lessor may not arbitrarily refuse consent to an assignment of a commercial lease which provides, even without limiting language, that a lessee shall not assign the lease without the written consent of the lessor. *Fernandez*, 397 So.2d at 1174; *see e.g. Ringwood Associates, Ltd. v. Jack's of Route 23, Inc.,* 153 N.J.Super. 294, 379 A.2d 508, 512 (1977) ("The fact that the lessor could obtain a higher rent under a new lease agreement but not under an assignment of [the tenant's] lease did not justify the lessor's refusal to consent to the assignment."); *Funk v. Funk,* 102 Idaho 521, 633 P.2d 586 (1981) (court will not uphold a landlord's arbitrary refusal of consent where it is apparent that the refusal to consent was withheld for purely financial reasons and that the landlord wanted the lessees to enter into an entirely new lease agreement with substantial increased financial benefits to the landlord.); *Cowan v. Chalamidas,* 98 N.M. 14, 644 P.2d 528 (1982) (a landlord may not unreasonably and arbitrarily withhold consent to a subleasing agreement when the lease agreement merely provides that the tenant must obtain the written consent of the landlord before subleasing). The Court in *Fernandez* went on to state that a withholding of consent to assign a lease, which fails the tests for good faith and commercial reasonableness, constitutes a breach of the lease agreement. The Court held that denying consent solely on the basis of personal taste, convenience or sensibility or in order that the landlord may charge a higher rent than originally contracted for are all arbitrary reasons which fail the tests of good faith and reasonableness under commercial leases.

IV.

In the case at bar, it appears that the sole reason Kirchman and FSS refused to consent to the assignment of the license agreements was the refusal of FNB and Pathway to pay new and substantially increased license fees. Such conduct on the part of Kirchman and FSS is contrary to the general contract principles of good faith and fair dealing. Indeed, such demands for higher license fees and the refusal to provide ongoing customer service and technical support may, themselves, constitute a breach of the license agreements. Florida law is clear — a lessor may not withhold consent to the assignment of a lease in order to charge a higher rent than originally contracted for. Although the case at bar involves a license agreement, the same basic contract principles apply. The license agreement in this case is, for all practical purposes, a commercial lease between a computer software company and a financial institution.

Under the rule set forth in the *Fernandez* case, Kirchman and FSS are bound to act in a commercially reasonable manner under the license agreement. Commercial reasonableness is determined by reference to the provisions negotiated in the original license agreements, and not by reference to what Kirchman and FSS later find most economically advantageous.

In addition to Florida case law, Kirchman and FSS also have a statutory duty of good faith under the [UCC]. Under Florida's version of the UCC there is an "obligation of good faith in a contract's performance or obligation."

The facts of this case are plain and simple: two insolvent financial institutions under the control and supervision of a government agency are acquired by another financial institution in the interests of the public welfare; a computer software company leasing equipment to the insolvent financial institutions which has already been paid its license fees uses the unfortunate circumstances to demand new license fee increases of more than three hundred percent or have the original license agreements terminated; although no unauthorized use of the software occurred, the license agreements, for which the original fees had been paid, were terminated; the president of the software company admits that the license agreements were terminated because the newly acquired institutions would not pay the increased license fees. Such an attempt at extortion is obviously contrary to the spirit of good faith and cooperation implied in the very license agreements which Kirchman and FSS terminated.

Kirchman and FSS now ask this Court to reward their actions by holding that Pathway and Bloomfield breached the license agreements by not obtaining Kirchman and FSS's consent before the acquisitions by FNB. As the evidence established, Pathway and Bloomfield were prohibited, under federal confidentiality rules, from notifying Kirchman or FSS of the proposed acquisition. Even assuming that they had notified Kirchman and FSS, the testimony of Mr. Kirchman established that consent would still have been withheld until the higher fees were paid. Mr. Kirchman also testified that the anti-assignment clauses were designed to protect his company from unauthorized use of the computer software. However, the evidence showed that no trade secret violations occurred as a result of the acquisitions, no unauthorized use of the software took place and Kirchman and FSS continued to receive all payments due under the original contracts.

No desirable public policy is served by allowing Kirchman and FSS to extract an undeserved windfall as a result of the unfortunate circumstances which forced Bloomfield and Pathway into insolvency. It was in the public interest and the best interest of depositors and creditors that FNB's federally-assisted acquisitions of Bloomfield and Pathway were arranged. Ironically, if Bloomfield and Pathway had been liquidated, Kirchman and FSS may have received little, if any, of the monies owed to them by those financial institutions. Instead, as a result of the acquisitions, Kirchman and FSS now have contracts with solvent institutions that have continued to make payments and have promised to protect the software from unauthorized use.

A contract is an agreement whereby each party promises to perform their part of the bargain in good faith, and expects the other party to do the same. Under the contracts in dispute here, Bloomfield and Pathway agreed to pay for the computer software and protect against its unauthorized use. Kirchman and FSS agreed to let Pathway and Bloomfield use the software and promised that they would not unreasonably withhold any consent to an assignment of the contracts. [It] is the opinion of the Court that Kirchman and FSS acted unreasonably by withholding consent to the assignment until FNB and Pathway paid substantially increased license fees.

NOTES

1. "Consent to transfer" clauses are common. Based on *First Nationwide*, what are the risks for a licensor agreeing to the clause? Indeed, why should such clauses ever be included? The parties are free to modify their contract to allow transfer should they choose to do so. That is, a licensor desiring to allow a transfer of the license would not be impeded by a lack of a "consent to transfer" provision. Given that, who benefits from such clauses?

2. Is it preferable to spell out the conditions under which consent will be given or withheld? For example, in the transaction in *First Nationwide*, how would you draft a mutually acceptable clause for the initial agreement that would have taken into account the circumstances that actually occurred in that case?

3. The court in *First Nationwide* commented that no "desirable public policy" would be served by giving force to the licensor's claim to a right to extract a new fee for the transfer. Do you agree? What is the public policy that supports denying effect to a contract term agreed to by two commercial entities?

III.   LICENSE, FIRST SALE, AND PATENT EXHAUSTION

A license is a conditional transaction in which some permission or right to use informational assets is given to the transferee, while other rights are not. Another common form of conditional transaction involves an unconditional sale of a copy of a copyrighted work or a patented machine. In each case, while the buyer is the owner of the copy or machine, many uses of it or of the contents are restricted by copyright, patent or other intellectual property rights of another party.

Patent law, copyright, trademark, and trade secret law all contain doctrines that give the owner of the copy or machine some latitude in dealing with it in a way that would otherwise infringe the intellectual property rights of another party who authorized a sale to the owner of the copy. In copyright law, these tend to be referred to as "first sale" doctrine, while in patent law the concepts are referred to as the doctrine of "patent exhaustion." Both doctrines present questions about what benefits in property law they give to the owner of the copy, and about when they apply. We discuss the issues here because one benefit that the owner of a copy or a machine obtains is the right to distribute or sell that copy without obtaining permission of the rights owner.

A.   Copyright First Sale

Although it originated in case law, the doctrine of "first sale" is now incorporated in two sections of the Copyright Act. Section 109 is the primary section. It now occupies two full pages in a standard statutory codification. Section 117 is a related form of first sale doctrine applicable to owners or copies of a "computer program." It occupies another full page of an ordinary statutory codification.

There are two ways to approach the idea of "first sale" for our purposes. One is to look closely at the statutory terms; what emerges is a complicated set of limited privileges or defenses that, as a matter of property law, flow from an authorized transfer of ownership of a copy of a copyrighted work. Necessarily, this also outlines what copyright rights remain fully enforceable against the owner of a copy. What emerges is a form of statutory license, with conditions and exclusions that apply in property law to the owner of a copy.

The second is to focus on first sale as a policy premise. During the past decade, it is at this level that the idea of "first sale" is at the center of sharp policy debates about intellectual property rights in digital works. In that debate, opponents of rights expansion often treat "first sale" as an expected method of distribution of information, leaving the copy owner largely free to do what it desires with the information so long as its use does not exceed "fair use." *See, e.g.,* Julie E. Cohen, *Copyright and the Jurisprudence of Self-Help,* 13 BERKELEY TECH. L.J. 1089 (1998); Mark Lemley, *Beyond Preemption: The Law and Policy of Intellectual Property Licensing,* 87 CAL. L. REV. 111 (1998). Under this approach, the core of "first sale" doctrine is in an assumption of unconditional sales of copies:

> Notwithstanding the provisions of section 106(3) [right to distribute copies], the owner of a particular copy or phonorecord lawfully made under this title, or any person authorized by such owner, is entitled, without the authority of the copyright owner, to sell or otherwise dispose of the possession of that copy or phonorecord.

17 U.S.C. § 109(a). Facially, this language only applies to a copy owner's right to distribute the copy, but it is in the absence of other controls in an unconditional first sale that the doctrine finds its alleged policy impact, especially when coupled with assumptions about what uses are fair use or permitted by the First Amendment. *See* Holly K. Towle, *The Politics of Licensing Law,* 36 HOUS. L. REV. 121 (1999). The contrasting view, which dominates the case law, is that there is no mandate that precludes transfers other than a sale, that Section 109 does not give rights but only a defense to infringement, and that it does not bar contracts or enforcing contract terms. This is one of many points in law and policy on which there is a modern debate between so-called rights-enhancers and so-called rights restrictors.

In any event, §§ 109 and 117 apply only to owners.

DSC COMMUNICATIONS
CORP. v. PULSE COMMUNICATIONS
170 F.3d 1354 (Fed. Cir. 1999)

BRYSON, CIRCUIT JUDGE.

DSC Communications Corporation (DSC) and Pulse Communications, Inc. (Pulsecom) make products for the telephone industry and compete for the business of the Regional Bell Operating Companies, more commonly known as the "RBOCs." Competition between the two parties led to this litigation over certain products that the two produce for use in commercial telephone systems.

DSC struck first, filing an action in the United States District Court for the Eastern District of Virginia in which it alleged that Pulsecom had committed various federal and state law violations, including (1) contributory infringement of DSC's copyright in certain software used with one of DSC's products; (2) direct infringement of DSC's copyright in that software; (3) misappropriation of DSC's trade secrets; and (4) tortious interference with DSC's business expectancy. Pulsecom then counterclaimed, charging that DSC had infringed Pulsecom's U.S. Patent No. 5,263,081 (the '081 patent).

The parties went to trial on DSC's claims, and at the close of DSC's case-in-chief, Pulsecom moved for judgment as a matter of law. The court granted the motion and dismissed all four of DSC's claims. . . .

I

This case involves certain components of digital loop carrier systems (DLCs), electronic devices that allow telephone companies to serve large numbers of subscribers efficiently. Before the advent of DLCs, telephone companies had to run copper wire from their central offices to the telephones of each of their subscribers. DLCs allow the individual copper lines to be run over much shorter distances, resulting in large savings for telephone companies. Typically, a DLC is placed in a location central to a number of subscribers, and copper lines are run over the relatively short distances from the DLC to the subscribers.

The DLC acts as an analog-to-digital converter and as a signal modulator-demodulator. The electrical signals that travel over the copper lines between the DLC and the subscribers are voice-frequency analog signals, but the signals that travel between the DLC and the central telephone office are digital signals that travel over a high-bandwidth (*e.g.*, fiber optic) digital channel. The DLC converts the various analog signals it receives from individual subscribers to a digital format and modulates those digital signals into a high-bandwidth composite signal that is sent to the central office through the digital channel. The DLC performs the reverse process on signals traveling from the central office to individual subscribers.

The devices at the heart of the dispute in this case are the "Litespan 2000" DLC, which is manufactured by DSC, and the interface cards, which DSC and Pulsecom designed to work with the Litespan. The Litespan has a backplane connecting 500 interface card slots . . . to a microprocessor. The backplane is controlled by [an] integrated circuit that uses a particular signaling protocol. The purpose of the interface cards is to [provide] a particular type of service to subscribers. For example, a single Litespan might have some interface cards providing POTS (plain old telephone service) service and other interface cards providing PBX (private branch exchange) service. The analog signals traveling between the subscribers and the two types of interface cards may be quite different, but the interface cards process the signals so that they are compatible with the Litespan's backplane protocol.

Litespans and individual interface cards each have their own microprocessors and interface circuitry, which require software to operate. Two software packages are at issue here. The first is the Litespan System software, which includes both the Litespan operating system software and various Litespan utility programs. The second is the POTS-DI (download image) software, which DSC developed to operate its POTS interface cards. Both the Litespan System software and the POTS-DI software normally reside in nonvolatile storage within Litespan systems. When a DSC POTS card is inserted into a Litespan and powered up, a copy of the POTS-DI software is downloaded into volatile memory on the POTS card. When the POTS card is powered down, its copy of the POTS-DI software ceases to exist. This design allows changes to be made to the POTS-DI software in a central location (*i.e.,* in the Litespan system) with no need to update software in the individual POTS cards.

DSC designed the Litespan to be used in the telephone networks of the RBOCs, and it transferred the Litespan technology to the RBOCs through a series of comprehensive agreements. The seven agreements at issue here — DSC-Ameritech, DSC-NYNEX, DSC-Bell Atlantic (1993-96 and 1996-99), DSC-U.S. West, DSC-Pacific Bell, and DSC-BellSouth — have generally similar provisions. The agreements all contain provisions that license, under a variety of restrictions, the Litespan System software and POTS-DI software to the RBOCs.

Pulsecom has developed a Litespan-compatible POTS card to compete with DSC's POTS card. Pulsecom decided not to develop the software necessary to operate its POTS card, but rather to design the card so that — like DSC's POTS card — it downloads the POTS-DI software from the host Litespan into its resident memory upon power-up. Pulsecom's design has the obvious advantage of allowing Pulsecom's POTS cards to remain compatible with the Litespan system if DSC modifies its Litespan System software and POTS-DI software.

II

DSC's principal contention on appeal is that the district court improperly granted judgment to Pulsecom on DSC's contributory copyright infringement claim at the close of DSC's case. . . .

DSC's theory of contributory infringement is that each time an RBOC powers up a Pulsecom POTS card in one of its Litespan systems, it directly infringes DSC's POTS-DI software copyright by copying the POTS-DI software from the Litespan into the resident memory of a Pulsecom POTS card. An act of direct infringement is a necessary predicate for any derivative liability on the part of Pulsecom; absent direct infringement, there can be no contributory infringement. The district court disposed of DSC's claim on the ground that DSC had not made a prima facie showing of direct infringement.

Pivotal to the proper resolution of DSC's copyright infringement claim is the interpretation and application of section 117 of the Copyright Act, 17 U.S.C. §117. . . . The district court concluded that making copies of the POTS-DI software (in the resident memory of POTS cards) was an "essential step in the utilization" of the POTS-DI software and that there was no evidence that the RBOCs used the software in any other manner that would constitute infringement. Accordingly, under the district court's theory of the case there was no direct infringement (and thus no contributory infringement) if the RBOCs were section 117 "owners" of copies of the POTS-DI software.

The district court then held that the RBOCs were "owners" of copies of the POTS-DI software because they obtained the software by making a single payment and obtaining a right to possession of the software for an unlimited period. Those attributes of the transaction, the court concluded, made the transaction a "sale."

DSC challenges the district court's conclusion that, based on the terms of the purchase transactions between DSC and the RBOCs, the RBOCs were "owners" of copies of the POTS-DI software. In order to resolve that issue, we must determine what attributes are necessary to constitute ownership of copies of software in this context.

Unfortunately, ownership is an imprecise concept, and the Copyright Act does not define the term. Nor is there much useful guidance to be obtained from either the legislative history of the statute or the cases that have construed it. The National Commission on New Technological Uses of Copyrighted Works ("CONTU") was created by Congress to recommend changes in the Copyright Act to accommodate advances in computer technology. In its final report, CONTU proposed a version of section 117 that is identical to the one that was ultimately enacted, except for a single change. The proposed CONTU version provided that "it is not an infringement for the *rightful possessor of a copy* of a computer program to make or authorize the making of another copy or adaptation of that program." *Final Report of the National Commission on New Technological Uses of Copyrighted Works,* U.S. Dept. of Commerce, PB-282141, at 30 (July 31, 1978) (emphasis added). Congress, however, substituted the words "owner of a copy" in place of the words "rightful possessor of a copy." The legislative history does not explain the reason for the change, but it is clear from the fact of the substitution of the term "owner" for "rightful possessor" that Congress must have meant to require more than "rightful possession" to trigger the section 117 defense.

In the leading case on section 117 ownership, the Ninth Circuit considered an agreement in which MAI, the owner of a software copyright, transferred copies of the copyrighted software to Peak under an agreement that imposed severe restrictions on Peak's rights with respect to those copies. *See MAI Sys. Corp. v. Peak Computer, Inc.,* 991 F.2d 511 (9th Cir.1995). The court held that Peak was not an "owner" of the copies of the software for purposes of section 117 and thus did not enjoy the right to copy conferred on owners by that statute. The Ninth Circuit stated that it reached the conclusion that Peak was not an owner because Peak had licensed the software from MAI. That explanation of the court's decision has been criticized for failing to recognize the distinction between ownership of a copyright, which can be licensed, and ownership of copies of the copyrighted software. Plainly, a party who purchases copies of software from the copyright owner can hold a license under a copyright while still being an "owner" of a copy of the copyrighted software for purposes of section 117. We therefore do not adopt the Ninth Circuit's characterization of all licensees as non-owners. Nonetheless, the *MAI* case is instructive, because the agreement between MAI and Peak, like the agreements at issue in this case, imposed more severe restrictions on Peak's rights with respect to the software than would be imposed on a party who owned copies of software subject only to the rights of the copyright holder under the Copyright Act. And for that reason, it was proper to hold that Peak was not an "owner" of copies of the copyrighted software for purposes of section 117. We therefore turn to the agreements between DSC and the RBOCs to determine whether those agreements establish that the RBOCs are section 117 "owners" of copies of the copyrighted POTS-DI software.

Each of the DSC-RBOC agreements contains a provision that is similar in effect to the following, taken from the DSC-BellSouth agreement: "All rights, title and interest in the Software are and shall remain with seller, subject, however, to a license to Buyer to use the Software solely in conjunction with the Material [*i.e.,* the Litespan-2000 and related equipment] during the useful life of the Material." Two of the agreements also contain clauses that provide for the passage of title to all the material transferred from DSC to the RBOCs, except for the software. The language and the context of those clauses makes it clear that the clauses refer to DSC's rights to the copies of the software in the RBOCs' possession, not DSC's copyright interest in the software. There was no need for a contract clause making clear that DSC was not selling its copyrights in its software to its customers, as it was obvious that DSC did not intend to convey any ownership rights in its copyright as part of the licensing agreements with the RBOCs. The question of ownership of the copies of the software, by contrast, was a matter that needed to be addressed in the contracts.

Not only do the agreements characterize the RBOCs as non-owners of copies of the software, but the restrictions imposed on the RBOCs' rights with respect to the software are consistent with that characterization. In particular, the licensing agreements severely limit the rights of the RBOCs with respect to the POTS-DI software in ways that are inconsistent with the rights normally enjoyed by owners of copies of software.

Section 106 of the Copyright Act, 17 U.S.C. § 106, reserves for a copyright owner the following exclusive rights in the copyrighted work: the right to reproduce the work; the right to prepare derivative works; the right to distribute copies of the work; the right to perform the work publicly; and the right to display the work publicly. Those rights are expressly limited, however, by sections 107 through 120 of the Act. Of particular importance are the limitations of sections 109 and 117. As we have seen, section 117 limits the copyright owner's exclusive rights by allowing an owner of a copy of a computer program to reproduce or adapt the program if reproduction or adaptation is necessary for the program to be used in conjunction with a machine. Section 109, which embodies the "first sale" doctrine, limits the copyright owner's otherwise exclusive right of distribution. . . .

Each of the DSC-RBOC agreements limits the contracting RBOC's right to transfer copies of the POTS-DI software or to disclose the details of the software to third parties. For example, the DSC-Ameritech agreement provides that Ameritech shall "not provide, disclose or make the Software or any portions or aspects thereof available to any person except its employees on a 'need to know' basis without the prior written consent of [DSC]. . . ." Such a restriction is plainly at odds with the section 109 right to transfer owned copies of software to third parties. The agreements also prohibit the RBOCs from using the software on hardware other than that provided by DSC. If the RBOCs were "owners of copies" of the software, section 117 would allow them to use the software on any hardware, regardless of origin. Because the DSC-RBOC agreements substantially limit the rights of the RBOCs compared to the rights they would enjoy as "owners of copies" of the POTS-DI software under the Copyright Act, the contents of the agreements support the characterization of the RBOCs as non-owners of the copies of the POTS-DI software.

In finding that the RBOCs were owners of copies of the POTS-DI software, the district court relied heavily on its finding that the RBOCs obtained their interests in the copies of the software through a single payment and for an unlimited period of time. It is true that the transfer of rights to the POTS-DI software in each of the agreements did not take the form of a lease, and that the transfer in each case was in exchange for a single payment and was for a term that was either unlimited or nearly so. One commentator has argued that when a copy of a software program is transferred for a single payment and for an unlimited term, the transferee should be considered an "owner" of the copy of the software program regardless of other restrictions on his use of the software. That view has not been accepted by other courts, however, and we think it overly simplistic. The concept of ownership of a copy entails a variety of rights and interests. The fact that the right of possession is perpetual, or that the possessor's rights were obtained through a single payment, is certainly relevant to whether the possessor is an owner, but those factors are not necessarily dispositive if the possessor's right to use the software is heavily encumbered by other restrictions that are inconsistent with the status of owner.

In passing, the district court found added support for its ruling on the contributory infringement issue in the "non-exclusive market rights" clause in DSC's contracts with the RBOCs. The court concluded that the market rights clause supported its view that the RBOCs were entitled to use the POTS-DI software in connection with Pulsecom's POTS cards, because otherwise there would be no point in permitting the RBOCs to buy equipment such as POTS cards from another source.

We conclude that the district court read the market rights clause too broadly. The market rights clause gave the RBOCs the right to obtain competing products and software from other sources, but it did not give the RBOCs the right to copy DSC's copyrighted software in the course of using other companies' products. In fact, the contracts specifically prohibited the RBOCs from copying DSC's software except for use with DSC equipment.

In light of the restrictions on the RBOCs' rights in the copies of the POTS-DI software, we hold that it was improper for the court to conclude, as a matter of law, that the RBOCs were "owners" under section 117 of the copies of DSC's software that were in their possession. The court was therefore incorrect to rule, at the close of DSC's case, that section 117 of the Copyright Act gave the RBOCs the right to copy the POTS-DI software when using Pulsecom's POTS cards without violating DSC's copyright in the software. Accordingly, we reverse the district court's order granting judgment for Pulsecom on DSC's contributory infringement claim. . . .

NOTES

1. With few exceptions, courts that address the issue have held that the terms of the agreement determine ownership; a restrictive license leaves the transferee of a copy something other than an owner of that copy. In addition to *MAI* discussed in the *DSC* case, see also *S.O.S., Inc. v. Payday, Inc.*, 886 F.2d 1081, 1087 (9th Cir. 1989).

Bobbs-Merrill Co. v. Straus, 210 U.S. 339 (1908), which established first sale doctrine in a case dealing with the sale of copies of books that contained non-contractual restrictive notices, commented that "[It] is to be remembered that this is purely a question of statutory construction. There is no claim in this case of contract limitation, nor license agreement controlling the subsequent sales of the book." *See also Quality King Distr., Inc. v. L'Anza Research Int'l, Inc.,* 523 U.S. 135, 147 (1998) ("[first-sale doctrine] is available only to the 'owner' of a lawfully made copy . . . the first sale doctrine would not provide a defense to [an] action against any nonowner such as a bailee, a licensee, a consignee, or one whose possession of the copy was unlawful.").

2. The court in *DSC* concluded that in some circumstances a transferee could be both a licensee and the owner of a copy. When would that occur? Would a transferee be the owner of a copy if the license provided: "Licensee is granted the right to make and distribute copies of the work contained on the copy delivered to it in return for payment of a royalty of $1 per copy." Approached from the other perspective, what contractual limitations exclude ownership under *DSC*?

ADOBE SYSTEMS, INC. v. ONE STOP MICRO, INC.
84 F. Supp. 2d 1086 (N.D. Cal. 2000)

WARE, DISTRICT JUDGE.

On February 2, 1999, Defendant One Stop Micro, Inc. ("One Stop") filed a motion for summary judgment and noticed it for hearing on March 8, 1999. [Based] upon all papers filed to date and the oral argument of the parties, the Court denies Defendant's motion for summary judgment and grants in part Plaintiff's motion for partial summary judgment.

Factual Background

Adobe is a software development and publishing company. Adobe's products include "Adobe PageMaker," "Adobe Photoshop," "Adobe Premiere," and "Adobe Illustrator." These programs are among the most successful graphics and desktop publishing software tools on the market. In addition to making full retail versions of its software packages, Adobe also makes educational versions, which are available to students and educators at a significant discount. Unlike the full retail versions of the programs, the educational versions do not include upgrades and technical support. In addition, some educational versions lack certain program features and functions.

Adobe initially distributes the educational versions to an Adobe-authorized educational distributor, who then transfers the software to an Adobe-authorized educational reseller. The educational reseller's relationship with Adobe is governed by the "Off Campus Reseller Agreement" or the "On Campus Reseller Agreement" ("OCRA"). Under the OCRA, an educational reseller is "to make the Educational Software Products available to certain of Reseller's customers who are Educational End Users."

Defendant One Stop buys and sells computer hardware and software on the open market. Adobe alleges that One Stop improperly acquired educational versions, which it then adulterated and sold as full retail versions to non-educational end users. One Stop admits that it adulterated approximately one half of the Adobe educational versions it acquired in 1996 and 1997 by doing the following: (1) cutting open and removing Adobe's shrink-wrap; (2) peeling off and destroying the "EDUCATION VERSION — Academic ID Required" stickers, as well as the UPC bar code label and the serial number label which further identify the packages as educational versions; and (3) re-shrink-wrapping the boxes. One Stop then distributed these adulterated versions.

On October 30, 1997, Adobe filed suit against One Stop. . . .

[In its present motion,] One Stop moves for summary judgment of the copyright infringement claim and the remaining trademark infringement claims on the grounds that they are barred by the first sale doctrine. One Stop argues that the first sale doctrine is applicable because the OCRA constitutes a sales agreement. In its cross motion, Adobe argues that it is entitled to summary adjudication of its copyright infringement claim and the remainder of its federal trademark infringement claim because the OCRA is in fact a licensing agreement. . . .

IV. Discussion

A. The OCRA — Sale or License

Section 106 of the Copyright Act outlines the exclusive rights enjoyed by owners of a copyright, including the exclusive right "to distribute copies or phonorecords of the copyrighted work to the public by sale or other transfer of ownership, or by rental, lease, or lending." Section 109(a), which forms the basis of the first sale doctrine, provides an important exception to § 106(3). . . . Thus, under the first sale doctrine, "a sale of a 'lawfully made' copy terminates a copyright holder's authority to interfere with subsequent sales or distribution of that particular copy." The first sale doctrine is only triggered by an actual sale. Accordingly, a copyright owner does not forfeit his right of distribution by entering into a licensing agreement. *See Microsoft v. Harmony Computers & Electronics,* 846 F.Supp. 208 (E.D.N.Y. 1994).

One Stop asserts the first sale doctrine as a defense to Adobe's copyright infringement claims. One Stop obtained its educational versions of Adobe software from educational resellers, who in turn obtained the software from Adobe through the OCRA. One Stop argues that the OCRA is a sales agreement. Thus, by purchasing copies of "sold" software programs, One Stop's distribution of those programs is protected by the first sale doctrine. Adobe, on the other hand, argues that the first sale doctrine is inapplicable because the OCRA is in fact a licensing agreement.

In interpreting the OCRA, the Court must give effect to the mutual intention of the parties. The parties' intent is inferred exclusively from the language of the contract, assuming the language is "clear and explicit." Under the parol evidence rule the Court is prohibited from considering any extrinsic evidence to vary or add to the terms of a contract. "However, the exception to the parol evidence rule is broad — extrinsic evidence is admissible to demonstrate that there is an ambiguity in an instrument and for the purpose of construing this ambiguity." Among the extrinsic evidence a court may consider are custom and usage of words in a certain trade.

One Stop vigorously argues that the language of the OCRA is clear and explicit and is properly construed without reference to extrinsic evidence. It further contends that the OCRA's unambiguous use of sales terminology such as "purchase" and "own" compels interpretation of the OCRA as a sales agreement. One Stop points to the following language in support of its argument:

> Reseller shall have the right to *purchase* Educational Software Products. . . . OCRA, ¶ 3(a) (emphasis added).

> Reseller shall submit to Adobe within ten (10) days after the effective date of termination a summary of the number of the respective Educational Software Products *owned* by Reseller as of the effective date of the termination. Adobe may, at its option, *repurchase* any or all of such Educational Software Products from Reseller. . . . OCRA, ¶ 11(c)(iv)(A) (emphasis added).

However, the OCRA contains additional language indicating that it only confers a license. For instance, paragraph three of the agreement outlines numerous restrictions imposed upon the reseller regarding distribution of the software.[2] The restriction found in ¶ 3(a)(ii) is particularly compelling: "Reseller distributes only pursuant to the terms and conditions of the then current applicable 'Software Product End-User License Agreement.'" The End-User License Agreement ("EULA") is a shrink-wrap license agreement which accompanies every Adobe software product. The EULA states that "Adobe grants to you a nonexclusive license to use the Software and Documentation," provided the user agrees to certain restrictions. Thus, under the EULA the end user is only granted a license to use the software. Adobe's specific incorporation of the EULA indicates that the reseller obtains a license. It would be incongruous to conclude that educational resellers are owners of the Adobe educational versions, while the end users who the resellers distribute to are granted a mere license.

---

2 [FN 2] The following is language from subpart (a) of ¶ 3. While the remainder of the paragraph contains additional restrictions, the Court finds it sufficient to include the following excerpt as an example:

> (a) *Reseller Rights.* Reseller shall have the right to purchase Educational Software Products from Adobe or authorized Adobe distributors who carry the Educational Software Products and to distribute the Educational Software Products so long as it remains in compliance with all of the following conditions:

> (i) Reseller does not distribute outside the country in which its principal place of business is located.

> (ii) Reseller distributes pursuant to the terms and conditions of the then current applicable Software Product End-User License Agreement ("End User Agreement").

> (iii) Reseller distributes solely to Educational End Users at Reseller's Outlet or through Reseller's direct sales force.

> (iv) Reseller requires each Educational End User to provide identification as follows: (1) in the case of a purchase by an individual, a valid photo ID or such other identification as is used by the educational institution for faculty, staff, or student, or (2) in the case of a purchase by an entity, an official purchase order indicating the name of the entity.

> (v) Reseller distributes the Educational Software Products solely in the form obtained from Adobe.

> (vi) Reseller provides adequate service and support in connection with the distribution of the Educational Software Products.

These numerous restrictions imposed by Adobe indicate a license rather than a sale because they undeniably interfere with the reseller's ability to further distribute the software. . . .

While the above language supports interpretation of the OCRA as a licensing agreement, the Court finds some ambiguity remains about the ultimate interpretation of the agreement due to its use of sales terminology. Based upon this ambiguity, the Court finds it appropriate to rely upon extrinsic evidence. In a declaration submitted by Judi Webster, Adobe's Vice President and General Manager of North America, and the individual responsible for the distribution of all Adobe software products, she states that it is "Adobe's intent in drafting and signing these documents to create a license, rather than a sale of our software." Thus, Adobe's intent is to create a licensing agreement by entering into the OCRA.

There is also evidence from Adobe resellers indicating that they, too, intended to enter into a licensing agreement. Jeffrey Gentile, Vice President of Marketing and Purchasing for Micro Warehouse, Inc., which is an educational reseller and consequently a signatory to the OCRA, states in his declaration that he understands "Adobe's software [to be] distributed under license." [Furthermore,] evidence of trade usage demonstrates that it is commonplace for sales terminology to be used [in] software licensing agreements. . . .

B. Copyright Infringement

As discussed above, 17 U.S.C. § 106(3) grants a copyright holder the exclusive right to distribute its copyrighted work. A common method of distribution is through licensing agreements, which permit the copyright holder to place restrictions upon the distribution of its products. "A licensee infringes the owner's copyright if its use exceeds the scope of its license."

The Court initially notes that while One Stop is not a signatory to an Adobe licensing agreement, it is nevertheless subject to the restrictions of those agreements. In *Microsoft v. Harmony Computers & Electronics,* 846 F.Supp. 208 (E.D.N.Y.1994), the court found that "[t]o the extent that defendants bought their Microsoft Products from authorized Microsoft licensees, they were subject to the same licensing restrictions under which those licensees operated." According to One Stop, its main source for educational versions of Adobe software was Programmers Paradise, an Adobe-authorized educational reseller and consequently a signatory to the OCRA. Thus, by obtaining Adobe software from a party to an Adobe licensing agreement, One Stop was bound by any restrictions imposed by that agreement.

The OCRA specifically permits the reseller to distribute "solely to Educational End Users at Reseller's Outlet or through reseller's direct sales force." In his January 21, 1999 deposition, Lawrence Firestone, the President of One Stop, admits to adulterating educational versions of Adobe software and re-packaging them as full retail versions. In the following portion of his testimony Mr. Firestone unequivocally admits to distributing those mislabeled versions to noneducational end users. . . . One Stop's admitted distribution of educational versions of Adobe software to non-educational end users is manifestly outside the scope of Adobe's license and in violation of its right to distribute under § 106(3). Accordingly, the Court finds that One Stop has committed copyright infringement as a matter of law under § 501(a). . . .

NOTES

1. *Softman Product Co. v. Adobe Systems, Inc.*, 171 F. Supp. 2d 1075 (C.D. Cal. 2001), dealt with a preliminary injunction in a claim against Softman, a company that acquired Adobe software works on CD's that were compilations transferred as a single work. Softman separated out selected CD's and sold them at a higher price. Adobe argued that the redistribution was infringement because it violated the terms of the upstream licenses used by Adobe. The District Court rejected this argument, concluding that the transfer of the software was a first sale.

> [It is] well-settled that in determining whether a transaction is a sale, a lease, or a license, courts look to the economic realities of the exchange. . . . Adobe frames the issue as a dispute about the ownership of intellectual property. In fact, it is a dispute about the ownership of individual pieces of Adobe software. . . . What is at stake here is the right of the purchaser to dispose of that purchaser's particular copy of the software.

> The Court finds that the circumstances surrounding the transaction strongly suggest that the transaction is in fact a sale rather than a license. For example, the purchaser commonly obtains a single copy of the software, with documentation, for a single price, which the purchaser pays at the time of the transaction, and which constitutes the entire payment for the "license." The license runs for an indefinite term without provisions for renewal. . . . The reality of the business environment also suggests that Adobe sells its software to distributors. Adobe transfers large amounts of merchandise to distributors. The distributors pay full value for the merchandise and accept the risk that the software may be damaged or lost. The distributors also accept the risk that they will be unable to resell the product. . . . The secondary market and the ultimate consumer also pay full value for the product, and accept the risk that the product may be lost or damaged. This evidence suggests a transfer of title in the good. . . .

> [Adobe] relies on *Adobe Sys. Inc. v. One Stop Micro, Inc.,* 84 F.Supp.2d 1086, 1093 (N.D.Cal.2000). . . . To the extent that the court in *One Stop* found that the transaction at issue was in fact a license, and not a sale, this Court simply declines to adopt that analysis. In *One Stop,* the court placed great weight on the declarations of Adobe's experts that licensing is the preferred method of distributing software. . . . However, this preference does not alter the Court's analysis that the substance of the transaction at issue here is a sale and not a license.

Id at xxx.

The relatively few cases that adopt this analysis are trial court rulings subsequently withdrawn for other reasons. In its analysis, what led *Softman* to conclude that participants in the distribution chain paid "full value" for the software? If I am distributing copies with significant use restrictions to you, would you expect to pay the same amount as if there were no restrictions? Since all Adobe software is distributed under these license agreements, is it not a reasonable inference that the fee charged reflects the license restrictions, rather than an unconditional sale? *Softman* did not cite *MAI, DSC,* or *SOS v. Payday*. If *DSC* were followed, would the result in *Softman* be different?

2. *One-Stop* suggests that later transferees are "bound" by upstream terms. What does that mean? This issue deals with the effect of a break in the distribution chain by virtue of an unauthorized distribution of a copyrighted work. Is it true that the only way to be affected by upstream terms is to become party to a contract creating them? We will return to that issue later, since it involves juxtaposing licensing law with the ordinary personal property law doctrine of bona fide purchaser.

3. As counsel for Adobe, would you recommend changes in the company's distribution procedures for 1) educational software, or 2) collections of CDs or diskettes distributed as a single work?

PROBLEM 6.6

Your client will distribute software that aids in the design of architectural works, such as homes. Client wishes to distribute the software through several distribution systems: 1) to architectural firms for their business use ($10,000 per copy); 2) to university architecture colleges for use solely in classes ($700 per copy); and 3) to consumers for noncommercial use ($100 per copy). It will supply copies of its works to distributors who will distribute to others. How should it set up its contracts to achieve its desired results?

PROBLEM 6.7

Assuming that Client is the owner of a copy and that no fair use defense or license applies, which of the following would be permitted under Sections 109 and 117 of the Copyright Act?

a. Client lends a copy of a book to a friend.

b. Client makes and distributes a copy of a computer program to a friend.

c. Client engages in a public display of a work to a group of students in a classroom.

d. Client uses a copy of a video game in his restaurant in a manner that constitutes a public performance of it.

e. Client makes copies of computer software available for rent for periods of time of up to one week.

CENTRAL POINT SOFTWARE, INC. v. GLOBAL SOFTWARE & ACCESSORIES, INC.
880 F. Supp. 957 (E.D.N.Y. 1995)

WEXLER, DISTRICT JUDGE.

Plaintiffs [who are] computer software manufacturers and members of the Software Publishers Association ("SPA"), bring this action against defendant Global Software & Accessories, Inc. ("Global") alleging copyright infringement for violations of the Computer Software Rental Amendments Act of 1990 (the

"Rental Amendment"), which amended section 109 of the Copyright Act, 17 U. S.C. § 109. . . . The action was tried without a jury on September 7 and 8, 1994. The following constitutes this Court's findings of fact and conclusions of law.

Findings of Fact

Plaintiffs are in the business of developing and marketing computer programs recorded on the medium of magnetic disks, commonly referred to as "computer software," for use on microcomputers of the type commonly referred to as "personal computers" or "PCs."

[Global] has been engaged in the business of, *inter alia,* renting computer software since 1988. . . .

Plaintiffs claim that Global infringed their copyrights in various computer software programs by renting copies of those programs in violation of the Rental Amendment. The Rental Amendment . . . provides in relevant part:

> [U]nless authorized by the . . . owner of copyright in a computer program (including any tape, disk or other medium embodying such program), . . . [no] person in possession of a particular copy of a computer program (including any tape, disk or other medium embodying such program), may, for the purposes of direct or indirect commercial advantage, dispose of, or authorize the disposal of, the possession of that . . . computer program (including any tape, disk or other medium embodying such program), by rental, lease, or lending, or by any other act or practice in the nature of rental, lease, or lending.

17 U.S.C. § 109(b)(1)(A).

Global's owner and president, William Morales ("Morales"), actively opposed the Rental Amendment. [At] issue is plaintiffs' claim that Global has rented, and continues to rent, copies of plaintiffs' copyrighted computer software. . . .

Global sought to market software . . . through a so-called "Deferred Billing Plan" (the "DBP"), devised by Morales in March or April 1991, without the advice of legal counsel. Global used the DBP exclusively for copies of computer software it acquired on or after December 1, 1990. In short, under the DBP, Global permits its customers to take computer software home and keep it for up to five days for a fee, which Global refers to as a "nonrefundable deposit" or "restocking fee." If the customer returns the software within the five-day period, the customer is not charged the balance of the purchase price.

In practice, Global's rental and DBP transactions are substantially the same. Signs on Global's stores advertise, *inter alia,* computer software rentals. Global's brochures advertise available rental and DBP software. For rental software, these brochures indicate the "rental fee"; for DBP software, certain brochures indicate the nonrefundable deposit and purchase price, but other brochures indicate only the nonrefundable deposit. In the store, rental and DBP software are displayed together. . . .

Under the DBP, only the nonrefundable deposit is charged to the customer's credit card initially, although credit card approval is obtained for the full purchase price. The nonrefundable deposit is only a fraction of the purchase price, typically ranging from $7.50 to $20.00. The customer is given a receipt indicating when the five-day period expires. Global's store policy does not provide for extension of the five-day return period. If the customer returns the software for any reason within the five-day period, Global keeps the nonrefundable deposit and the customer is not charged the balance of the purchase price. On the other hand, if the customer does not return the DBP software within the five-day period, the nonrefundable deposit is applied to the purchase price and the balance of the purchase price is charged to the customer's credit card. Only then is the customer provided the manufacturer's registration card. The manufacturer's registration card allows the owner to register with the manufacturer. Technical support from the software manufacturer is typically available only to registered users. . . .

Global's records indicate that of 448 transactions summarized, approximately 300 were DBP transactions. Of the approximately 300 DBP transactions, the customer returned the software within five days in all but three transactions. . . .

Conclusions of Law

[As] for whether Global's DBP transactions violated the Rental Amendment, this Court's interpretation of the statute starts with its language. The Rental Amendment prohibits not only the rental of computer software, but "any other act or practice in the nature of rental, lease or lending." The statute, however, does not define the quoted phrase, and apparently there are no reported cases interpreting this language in the context of alleged computer software rentals.

Global argues that this Court is required to look to state law to determine whether a transaction is a sale or a rental under the Rental Amendment. In this respect, Global contends that its DBP transactions are not prohibited by the Rental Amendment because a DBP transaction would be considered a "sale on approval" under Article 2 of New York's Uniform Commercial Code. Plaintiffs argue that Global's DBP transactions are, in substance, the rental of computer software in violation of the Rental Amendment, and "sale[s] in name only," as evidenced by the nearly 100% return rate. Global counters that plaintiffs' reliance on the percentage of returns is "flawed and illogical" because there is no basis for comparison with industry-wide statistics, and because "misreliance on statistics creates a situation where transactions may not be classified as sales or rentals until a significant period of time (undefined) has elapsed after the transactions have been completed so that the incidence of returns may be examined." In response, plaintiffs argue that the Rental Amendment's language and legislative history "make clear Congress' intent that enforcement of the rental prohibition not be thwarted by formalistic interpretations of state law."

In deciding whether a transaction is a sale or a rental under the Rental Amendment, this Court must construe the amendment " 'in light of the mischief to be corrected and the end to be attained.'" The Rental Amendment was intended to address the threat rental of computer software posed to the computer software industry. Congress considered the threat posed to the computer software industry by rental of software "even more compelling" than the threat posed by the rental of phonograph records to the record industry. In this respect, Congress recognized that

> [t]he price disparity between the sale and rental prices is greater than
> the case with phonorecords: software selling for $495 has been rented
> for $35. And unlike phonorecords, which are an entertainment prod-
> uct, software is typically a utilitarian product. Short term rental of
> software is, under most circumstances, inconsistent with the purposes
> for which software is intended. Rental of software will, most likely,
> encourage unauthorized copying, deprive copyright owners of a return
> on investment, and thereby discourage creation of new products.

Id. The purpose of the rental ban . . . "was to protect the investment of software
publishers in their copyrighted computer programs by preventing rental,
lending, leasing, or *similar disposal* of copyrighted software for direct or
indirect commercial gain without the copyright holder's permission." Congress
considered then-existing protections afforded copyright holders of computer
software inadequate because of the first sale doctrine, and because "the market
for rental of computer programs exhibits several characteristics that could
facilitate or even promote illegal copying of rented software by lessees." As
Congress recognized:

> Despite the protection of the copyright law, abuses of software copying
> remain. The easy accessibility of computer programs distributed in
> magnetic media format, together with the widespread distribution of
> popular applications programs, has led to persistent illegal copying of
> these programs.

The Record Rental Amendment of 1984, which amended section 109 of the
Copyright Act to prohibit the rental of phonograph records, added the language at issue in this case, *i.e.,* "any other act or practice in the nature of
rental, lease, or lending." The legislative history to that amendment indicates
that Congress intended that language to

> cover transactions which common sense indicates are equivalent to
> rentals, but which may be disguised in an attempt to avoid liability
> under the law. For example, a retailer who "sold" an album to be
> "bought back" a few days later, or a club organized to lend records to
> its members who paid a membership fee rather than a direct rental
> fee, would be performing acts or practices in the nature of rental, lease
> or lending and would be in violation of the law unless permission of the
> copyright owner had been obtained.

See H.Rep. No. 987, 98th Cong., 2d Sess. 4 (1984).

The Act's language and its legislative history demonstrate that Congress
intended to proscribe not only transactions that are called rentals, but also
practices that are in substance rentals. Although, as between transacting
parties (*e.g.,* Global and its customers), whether a transaction is a "sale on
approval" is one of state law, this determination does not control the determination of rights afforded the copyright owner (*e.g.,* plaintiffs) by the federal copyright statute. Where a practice is, in substance, no different from
rental, the practice is prohibited regardless of whether, under state law, the
transaction may be considered a "sale on approval" between buyer and
seller.

Based on the evidence presented, this Court finds that Global's DBP operates as a "practice in the nature of rental" under the Act, and, therefore, is prohibited. A combination of factors indicate that Global is, in substance, engaged in rental of software under the DBP: the nearly 100% return rate; certain DBP brochures advertise only the "nonrefundable deposit," not the purchase price; the "nonrefundable deposits" are comparable to rental fees; the relatively short DBP term is comparable to the rental term, obviously allowing Global to use the same copy of software in another DBP transaction within a short time; and the customer is not given the manufacturer's registration card until the purchase price is paid. Even though it is the customer's choice whether to return the software, given the nearly 100% return rate, Global should have known that its DBP operated substantially the same as its legitimate software rentals.

As for Global's reliance on Intuit's plan or any other manufacturer's marketing plan, Global ignores the obvious: a manufacturer is not barred from renting its own software; the Act expressly recognizes that a manufacturer is free to authorize rental of its copyrighted software. Thus, whether Intuit's plan or any other manufacturer's plan is in substance a sale or a rental is irrelevant, as are any similarities between those plans and Global's DBP.

By its decision, this Court does not construe the Act to prohibit a return policy which allows a customer truly unsatisfied with a particular copy of a computer software program to return the software in exchange for a refund of the purchase price, less a true "restocking fee." Such a business practice, aside from its apparently prudent business implications, appears to fall outside the Act's rental ban. However, these are not the circumstances presented here. . . .

B. Patent Exhaustion

The doctrine of "patent exhaustion" is the patent law counterpart of the "first sale" doctrine. Because the underlying property rights are different, the scope and terms of the concepts are different. Exhaustion cases deal with more than merely the right to distribute the patented subject matter. Taken together, they indicate that the buyer of a patented product obtains the right to use that product, to sell it, and to "repair" the item because the authorized sale exhausts those rights of patent as to that item. We defer discussion of the "repair" right to the chapter on implied licenses. For now, we focus on when "patent exhaustion" occurs.

MALLINCKRODT, INC. v. MEDIPART, INC.
976 F.2d 700 (Fed. Cir. 1992)

Newman, Circuit Judge.

This action for patent infringement and inducement to infringe relates to the use of a patented medical device in violation of a "single use only" notice that accompanied the sale of the device. Mallinckrodt sold its patented device to hospitals, which after initial use of the devices sent them to Medipart for servicing that enabled the hospitals to use the device again. Mallinckrodt claimed that Medipart thus induced infringement by the hospitals and itself infringed the patent.

The district court held that violation of the "single use only" notice cannot be remedied by suit for patent infringement, and granted summary judgment of noninfringement. The district court did not decide whether the form of the "single use only" notice was legally sufficient to constitute a license or condition of sale from Mallinckrodt to the hospitals. Nor did the district court decide whether any deficiencies in the "single use only" notice were cured by Mallinckrodt's attempted subsequent notice, the release of which was enjoined by the district court on the ground that it would harm Medipart's business. Thus there was no ruling on whether, if the initial notice was legally defective as a restrictive notice, such defect was cured in the subsequent notice. The district court also specifically stated that it was not deciding whether Mallinckrodt could enforce this notice under contract law. These aspects are not presented on this appeal, and the factual premises were not explored at the summary judgment proceeding from which this appeal is taken.

Instead, the district court held that no restriction whatsoever could be imposed under the patent law, whether or not the restriction was enforceable under some other law, and whether or not this was a first sale to a purchaser with notice. This ruling is incorrect, for if Mallinckrodt's restriction was a valid condition of the sale, then in accordance with *General Talking Pictures Corp. v. Western Electric Co.*, 304 U.S. 175, *aff'd on reh'g*, 305 U.S. 124 (1938), it was not excluded from enforcement under the patent law.

. . . .

Background

The patented device is an apparatus for delivery of radioactive or therapeutic material in aerosol mist form to the lungs of a patient, for diagnosis and treatment of pulmonary disease. Radioactive material is delivered primarily for image scanning in diagnosis of lung conditions. Therapeutic agents may be administered to patients suffering various lung diseases.

The device is manufactured by Mallinckrodt, who sells it to hospitals as a unitary kit that consists of a "nebulizer" which generates a mist of the radioactive material or the prescribed drug, a "manifold" that directs the flow of oxygen or air and the active material, a filter, tubing, a mouthpiece, and a nose clip. In use, the radioactive material or drug is placed in the nebulizer, is atomized, and the patient inhales and exhales through the closed system. The device traps and retains any radioactive or other toxic material in the exhalate. The device fits into a lead-shielded container that is provided by Mallinckrodt to minimize exposure to radiation and for safe disposal after use.

The device is marked with the appropriate patent numbers, and bears the trademarks "Mallinckrodt" and "UltraVent" and the inscription "Single Use Only." The package insert provided with each unit states "For Single Patient Use Only" and instructs that the entire contaminated apparatus be disposed of in accordance with procedures for the disposal of biohazardous waste. The hospital is instructed to seal the used apparatus in the radiation-shielded container prior to proper disposal. The hospitals whose activities led to this action do not dispose of the UltraVent apparatus, or limit it to a single use.

Instead, the hospitals ship the used manifold/nebulizer assemblies to Medipart, Inc. Medipart in turn packages the assemblies and sends them to Radiation Sterilizers Inc., who exposes the packages to at least 2.5 megarads of gamma radiation, and returns them to Medipart. Medipart personnel then check each assembly for damage and leaks, and place the assembly in a plastic bag together with a new filter, tubing, mouthpiece, and nose clip. The "reconditioned" units, as Medipart calls them, are shipped back to the hospitals from whence they came. Neither Radiation Sterilizers nor Medipart tests the reconditioned units for any residual biological activity or for radioactivity. The assemblies still bear the inscription "Single Use Only" and the trademarks "Mallinckrodt" and "UltraVent."

Mallinckrodt filed suit against Medipart, asserting patent infringement and inducement to infringe. [Both] parties moved for summary judgment on all counts. The district court granted Medipart's motion on the patent infringement counts, holding that the " Single Use Only " restriction could not be enforced by suit for patent infringement. [The] district court also enjoined Mallinckrodt pendente lite from distributing a new notice to its hospital customers. The proposed new notice emphasized the "Single Use Only" restriction and stated that the purpose of this restriction is to protect the hospital and its patients from potential adverse consequences of reconditioning, such as infectious disease transmission, material instability, and/or decreased diagnostic performance; that the UltraVent device is covered by certain patents; that the hospital is licensed under these patents to use the device only once; and that reuse of the device would be deemed infringement of the patents.

Mallinckrodt appeals the grant of summary judgment on the infringement issue, and the grant of the preliminary injunction.

The Restriction on Reuse

Mallinckrodt describes the restriction on reuse as a label license for a specified field of use, wherein the field is single (i.e., disposable) use. On this motion for summary judgment, there was no issue of whether this form of license gave notice of the restriction. Notice was not disputed. Nor was it disputed that sale to the hospitals was the first sale of the patented device. The issue that the district court decided on summary judgment was the enforceability of the restriction by suit for patent infringement. The court's premise was that even if the notice was sufficient to constitute a valid condition of sale, violation of that condition cannot be remedied under the patent law. . . .

The district court described the cases sustaining field of use and other restrictions as "in tension" with the cases prohibiting restrictions such as price-fixing and tying, and with the cases holding that the patent right is exhausted with the first sale. The court stated that policy considerations require that no conditions be imposed on patented goods after their sale and that Mallinckrodt's restriction could not "convert[] what was in substance a sale into a license." As we shall discuss, [the] court erred in its analysis of the law, for not all restrictions on the use of patented goods are unenforceable.

The enforceability of restrictions on the use of patented goods derives from the patent grant, which is in classical terms of property: the right to exclude. . . . This right to exclude may be waived in whole or in part. The conditions of such waiver are subject to patent, contract, anti-trust, and any other applicable law, as well as equitable considerations such as are reflected in the law of patent misuse. As in other areas of commerce, private parties may contract as they choose, provided that no law is violated thereby:

> The rule is, with few exceptions, that any conditions which are not in their very nature illegal with regard to this kind of property, imposed by the patentee and agreed to by the licensee for the right to manufacture or use or sell the [patented] article, will be upheld by the courts.

E. Bement & Sons v. National Harrow Co., 186 U.S. 70, 91 (1902).

The district court's ruling that Mallinckrodt's restriction on reuse was unenforceable was an application of the doctrine of patent misuse, although the court declined to use that designation. The concept of patent misuse arose to restrain practices that did not in themselves violate any law, but that drew anticompetitive strength from the patent right, and thus were deemed to be contrary to public policy. The policy purpose was to prevent a patentee from using the patent to obtain market benefit beyond that which inheres in the statutory patent right. . . .

[The court reviewed a group of cases involving price-fixing and other issues, concluding that they did not preclude the challenged practice under antitrust or related law.]

Restrictions on use are judged in terms of their relation to the patentee's right to exclude from all or part of the patent grant, *see, e.g.*, W.F. Baxter, *The Viability of Vertical Restraints Doctrine*, 75 CALIF. L. REV. 933, 935 (1987) ("historically, legal prohibition began with [resale price control and tie-in agreements] and, with rare exceptions, now continues only with those devices"); and where an anticompetitive effect is asserted, the rule of reason is the basis of determining the legality of the provision. In *Windsurfing International, Inc. v. AMF, Inc.*, 782 F.2d 995, 228 USPQ 562 (Fed. Cir.), *cert. denied*, 477 U.S. 905 (1986), this court stated:

> To sustain a misuse defense involving a licensing arrangement not held to have been per se anticompetitive by the Supreme Court, a factual determination must reveal that the overall effect of the license tends to restrain competition unlawfully in an appropriately defined relevant market.

. . . .

In support of its ruling, the district court also cited a group of cases in which the Court considered and affirmed the basic principles that unconditional sale of a patented device exhausts the patentee's right to control the purchaser's use of the device; and that the sale of patented goods, like other goods, can be conditioned. The principle of exhaustion of the patent right did not turn a conditional sale into an unconditional one. . . .

Adams v. Burke, 84 U.S. (17 Wall.) 453 (1874), dealt with patented coffin-lids that an assignee had the exclusive right to make, use, and sell within a ten-mile radius of Boston. The coffin was "sold [to Burke, an undertaker,] within said circle by said [assignee], without condition or restriction," and used by Burke in the town of Natick, outside of the Boston circle." 84 U.S. (17 Wall.) at 455 (statement of the case). Adams, who owned the patent rights outside of the Boston circle, sued Burke for patent infringement. The Court stated that "when the patentee . . . sells a machine or instrument whose sole value is in its use, he receives the consideration for its use and he parts with the right to restrict that use." The Court remarked that the coffin-lid [patent] "perishes in the first use of it," and that to imply a geographic limitation on the purchaser "would be to engraft a limitation upon the right of use not contemplated by the statute nor within the reason of the contract." This holding is in accord with the other cases of that era, *e.g., Bloomer v. McQuewan,* 55 U.S. (14 How.) 539 (1852), wherein the Court held that when the sale of the patented device was without restriction, the purchaser need not pay an additional sum when the patent term was extended. . . .

In *Keeler v. Standard Folding Bed Co.,* 157 U.S. 659 (1895), the Court restated that the purchaser of a patented machine, without any conditions, may use or resell the device anywhere in the United States, explaining:

> [When a patentee] has himself constructed a machine and sold it *without any conditions,* or authorized another to construct, sell, and deliver it, or to construct, use, and operate it, *without any conditions,* and the consideration has been paid to him for the thing patented, the rule is well established that the patentee must be understood to have parted to that extent with all his exclusive right, and that he ceases to have any interest whatever in the patented machine so sold and delivered or authorized to be constructed and operated.

157 U.S. at 663.[3]

Another relevant early case is *Providence Rubber Co. v. Goodyear,* 76 U.S. (9 Wall.) 788 (1870). Goodyear had granted a restricted license to Chaffee "to make and sell India-rubber cloth, to be used in the place, and for the purposes, of patent or japanned leather." The Court upheld Goodyear's right to sue for patent infringement, when Providence Rubber used the India-rubber cloth in the manufacture of rubber shoes. The Court stated that the license "conveyed authority only to this extent [for the specified use] and nothing more."

---

[3] [FN 6] In *Keeler,* the Court stated that "[w]hether a patentee may protect himself and his assignees by special contracts brought home to the purchasers . . . would arise as a question of contract, and not as one under the inherent meaning and effect of the patent laws." The question of whether a license restriction is binding on the purchaser is indeed one of contract law. However, the remedy for breach of a binding license provision is not exclusively in contract, for a license is simply a promise not to sue for what would otherwise be patent infringement. . . . The district court stated that it intimated no opinion as to whether Mallinckrodt might enforce the restriction on "contract law or property law" or on "equitable grounds." We agree that a patentee may choose among alternate remedies, but to deny a patentee access to statutory remedies is to withhold the protection of the law. Thus whether Mallinckrodt may also have a remedy outside of the patent law is not before us.

In *American Cotton-Tie Co. v. Simmons,* 106 U.S. 89 (1882), metal ties for cotton bales were sold with the notice "Licensed to use once only" stamped on the ties. The Court held that suit for patent infringement could be maintained against persons who refurbished the ties for reuse. The *Cotton-Tie* decision was discussed in *Aro Manufacturing Co. v. Convertible Top Replacement Co.,* 365 U.S. 336, 81 S. Ct. 599 (1961) (*Aro I*), the Court explaining that the "license to be used once only was deemed of importance to the court." *Id.* at 343 n. 9. The Court of Claims, in *General Electric Co. v. United States,* 572 F.2d 745, 215 Ct. Cl. 636, 198 USPQ 65 (1978), referred to *Cotton-Tie* and *Aro I* as supporting the viability of conditions imposed on the sale of patented goods, explaining that absent such conditions the buyer's use is unrestricted:

> Unless there is some definite provision in the sale to the contrary . . . *as explained in Aro I* . . . it can properly be assumed that as part of the bargain the sale of a device incorporating a patented composition (composed, as here, of unpatented elements) authorizes the buyer to continue to use the device so long as the latter can and does use the elements he purchased from the patentee or licensor.

Id.

[It] appears that the Court simply applied, to a variety of factual situations, the rule of contract law that sale may be conditioned. *Adams v. Burke*[, 84 U. S. (17 Wall.) 453 (1874),] and its kindred cases do not stand for the proposition that no restriction or condition may be placed upon the sale of a patented article. It was error for the district court to derive that proposition from the precedent. Unless the condition violates some other law or policy (in the patent field, notably the misuse or antitrust law), private parties retain the freedom to contract concerning conditions of sale. As we have discussed, the district court cited the price-fixing and tying cases as reflecting what the court deemed to be the correct policy, viz., that no condition can be placed on the sale of patented goods, for any reason. However, this is not a price-fixing or tying case, and the per se antitrust and misuse violations found in the *Bauer* trilogy and *Motion Picture Patents* are not here present. The appropriate criterion is whether Mallinckrodt's restriction is reasonably within the patent grant, or whether the patentee has ventured beyond the patent grant and into behavior having an anticompetitive effect not justifiable under the rule of reason.

Should the restriction be found to be reasonably within the patent grant, i.e., that it relates to subject matter within the scope of the patent claims, that ends the inquiry. However, should such inquiry lead to the conclusion that there are anticompetitive effects extending beyond the patentee's statutory right to exclude, these effects do not automatically impeach the restriction. Anticompetitive effects that are not per se violations of law are reviewed in accordance with the rule of reason. Patent owners should not be in a worse position, by virtue of the patent right to exclude, than owners of other property used in trade. . . .

We conclude that the district court erred in holding that the restriction on reuse was, as a matter of law, unenforceable under the patent law. If the sale of the UltraVent was validly conditioned under the applicable law such as the law governing sales and licenses, and if the restriction on reuse was within the scope of the patent grant or otherwise justified, then violation of the restriction may be remedied by action for patent infringement. The grant of summary judgment is reversed, and the cause is remanded.

II

REPAIR AND RECONSTRUCTION

Even an unconditioned sale of a patented device is subject to the prohibition against "reconstruction" of the thing patented. A purchaser's right to use a patented device does not extend to reconstructing it, for reconstruction is deemed analogous to construction of a new device. However, repair is permissible. Although the rule is straightforward its implementation is less so, for it is not always clear where the boundary lies: how much "repair" is fair before the device is deemed reconstructed. [The court vacated the trial court ruling on this issue.]

NOTES

1. The parties, or at least one of them, described the single use restriction as a "label license." This term is used in some areas of patent law practice. Based on the discussion here, how would you define a "label license"? Under what circumstances is such a license enforceable?

2. *Jazz Photo Corp. v. International Trade Commission,* 264 F.3d 1094 (Fed. Cir. 2001), took up where *Mallinckrodt* left off. Fuji distributed disposable cameras for which the package instructions and warnings printed on the covers of the cameras arguable restricted the camera to a single use. The court held that notices and information on the box containing the camera were insufficient, commenting that "a license is governed by the laws of contract, [but that i]t was undisputed [in this case] that no express conditions of sale, license terms or restrictions attended the sale of the cameras."

> "A seller's intent, unless embodied in an enforceable contract, does not create a limitation on the right of the purchaser to use, sell, or modify a patented product as long as a reconstruction of the patented combination is avoided." . . . We do not discern an enforceable restriction on the reuse of these cameras based on the package statements. These statements are instructions and warning of risk, not mutual promises or conditions placed on the sale. . . .

Jazz Photo also involved the question of whether reconditioning the cameras for further use was within the implied right to "repair" a patented product acquired at a valid sale. We discuss that issue in the next chapter of this book.

PROBLEM 6.8

Monster Corp. produces genetically engineered seeds that are covered by a patent that it owns. It sells these seeds to farmers. Under the agreement with the farmers, the farmer is allowed to use the seed for planting a crop, but is prohibited from using the product of the crop to obtain seeds for an additional planting. In essence, this is a single use restriction that allows Monster to sell new seeds each year and to prevent farmers from going into competition with it. One customer, J. Farmer, ignores the restriction and uses the second crop of seeds for its next year planting. Monster sues.

a. What is the proper basis for the lawsuit and what result?

b. Would your answer in (a) change if the limiting terms were stated on the label of the package delivered to the farmer and no written agreement was signed?

INTEL CORP. v. ULSI SYSTEM TECHNOLOGY, INC.
995 F.2d 1566 (Fed. Cir. 1993)

LOURIE, CIRCUIT JUDGE.

ULSI System Technology, Inc. appeals from the order of the United States District Court for the District of Oregon granting Intel Corporation's motion for a preliminary injunction enjoining ULSI from infringing U.S. Patent Re. 33,629. Because the district court clearly erred in concluding that Intel had established a reasonable likelihood of success on the issue of infringement, we reverse.

Background

Intel is the assignee of U.S. Patent Re. 33,629 to John F. Palmer, et al., entitled "Numerical Data Processor." The claims of the '629 patent are directed to the design and operation of a floating-point arithmetic processor capable of mixed precision calculations, mixed mode arithmetic calculations, and rounding operations. Intel has developed a line of math coprocessors covered by the patent, including the Intel 8087, 80287, and 80387 coprocessors.

On January 10, 1983, Intel and the Hewlett-Packard Company (HP) entered into a cross-licensing agreement to "increase their freedom of design by obtaining a license under present and future patents and patent applications owned or controlled by the other." Under that agreement, Intel and HP each granted to the other an "irrevocable, retroactive, nonexclusive, world-wide, royalty-free license" under all patents and patent applications "having an effective filing date prior to January 1, 2000, said license to be effective until the expiration of said patents."

ULSI sells a math coprocessor known as the US83C87 ('C87 coprocessor) which is compatible with the Intel 80386 microprocessor and competes commercially with the Intel 80387 coprocessor. Since September 22, 1989, ULSI has purchased the 'C87 coprocessors from HP under an agreement entered into on August 2, 1988, in which HP agreed to manufacture the coprocessors for ULSI. As is apparently common in such "foundry" arrangements in the semiconductor industry, ULSI supplied HP with proprietary design specifications and HP then manufactured and shipped completed coprocessor chips to ULSI, which resold them as ULSI products.

Intel first became aware of ULSI's 'C87 coprocessor sales on February 4, 1991. On July 29, 1991, Intel brought an action in the U.S. District Court for the District of Oregon alleging infringement of the '629 patent by ULSI's "making and selling, and inducing others to make, sell and use, the 'US83C87' [coprocessor]." . . .

The district court . . . concluded that Intel had established a likelihood of success on the merits with respect to the issues of infringement, validity, and enforceability of the '629 patent. . . . [It] granted Intel's motion.

Discussion

In opposition to the motion [for preliminary injunction], ULSI maintained that HP was permitted under the licensing agreement to act as a foundry for ULSI and that the sale of the coprocessors by HP to ULSI was a "first sale" that extinguished Intel's patent rights with respect to those products. The district court, however, rejected ULSI's argument because it determined that the licensing agreement did not grant HP the "power to sublicense" the '629 patent. On appeal, ULSI claims that the district court erred in concluding that the "patent exhaustion" or "first sale" doctrine did not shield ULSI from Intel's claim of infringement. . . .

The law is well settled that an authorized sale of a patented product places that product beyond the reach of the patent. The patent owner's rights with respect to the product end with its sale, and a purchaser of such a product may use or resell the product free of the patent. This longstanding principle applies similarly to a sale of a patented product manufactured by a licensee acting within the scope of its license.

In the instant case, the issue as to whether ULSI is free from infringement liability turns on whether there was a sale of 'C87 coprocessors by HP to ULSI. Intel argues that the "patent exhaustion" doctrine does not apply because HP never sold a product to ULSI. Although Intel claims, as it must, that the 'C87 coprocessor infringes the '629 patent, it maintains that what was actually sold by HP under the foundry agreement was its fabrication services with an ancillary sale of wafers and chemicals. Intel asserts that HP could not have sold a product covered by the '629 patent because HP never had or retained any ownership rights in the 'C87 coprocessors. Thus, according to Intel, no sale ever took place that could support ULSI's "first sale" defense. That argument is incorrect.

Interpretation of a contract is a question of law which we review de novo. After reviewing the HP-ULSI contract, we cannot accept Intel's characterization of that agreement as one in which HP merely provided fabrication services to ULSI. That agreement, entitled "Terms and Conditions of Sale," is replete with references to the sale of semiconductor wafers (i.e., chips) that incorporate the 'C87 coprocessor design. For example, the section of the agreement headed "Section 2: Production Fabrication" provided that HP "will sell CMOS34 wafers to" ULSI. That section recites prices for the chips and includes a delivery schedule for shipments of the chips to ULSI. Although the agreement also includes a section delineating the "engineering services" to be provided by HP, the agreement clearly involved the sale of chips, not merely the sale of fabrication services.

Nor, as Intel contends, must the licensed seller of a patented product own intellectual property rights to the product in order for there to be a sale. Intel makes much of the fact that the 'C87 chip was based on a design provided by ULSI. Intel confuses the issue of design origin with the issue of sale. Who designed the chip and whether it embodies inventions other than Intel's have no bearing on the controlling issue whether the 'C87 coprocessors were sold by HP to ULSI and thus extinguished Intel's patent rights relating to those products.

That ULSI, rather than HP, might have owned any existing intellectual property rights to the chips was a matter between ULSI and HP, and did not concern Intel. Intel does not dispute that HP was authorized under the broad terms of the licensing agreement to sell the chips at issue. To the extent that Intel had a patent covering the chips, HP's conceded right to sell the chips deprives Intel of any claim of infringement, as long as HP sold the chips. If it had not granted that license or if the license had been limited in some relevant way, that would be a different case from the one before us. Intel might thereby have retained its right to proceed against those who entered into foundry agreements such as the present one. While Intel may not in retrospect be pleased with the deal that it made permitting HP to make unrestricted sales, it nevertheless granted HP that right in 1983, presumably for consideration it believed to be of value at that time. It cannot now renege on that grant to avoid its consequences.

We also reject Intel's contention that the sale of chips by HP to ULSI consti- tuted a "de facto sublicense" prohibited by the licensing agreement. We found a similar argument to be "without merit and specious" in *Lisle Corp. v. Edwards*, 777 F.2d 693, 227 USPQ 894 (Fed. Cir. 1985). In *Lisle*, a licensed manufacturer sold products covered by the licensor's patent to a third party which resold them under its trademark. The licensor brought an infringement action against both the licensee and the third party on the basis that the manufacture of the patented product for the third party constituted a subli- cense. Because such sublicensing was prohibited under the licensing agree- ment, the patent owner claimed that the products were infringing. The court in *Lisle*, however, concluded that the licensee's sales were authorized and that the resale by the third party did not create a sublicense. Similarly, the sale by HP to ULSI here did not create a sublicense. HP did not empower ULSI to make Intel-patented chips or to use or sell any such chips except those law- fully sold to it by HP; these would have been the incidents of a sublicense.

Relatedly, we do not agree with the district court's conclusion that the sale of chips by HP to ULSI was not a "first sale" because HP was not authorized to sublicense ULSI to design products covered by the '629 patent. That HP did not have the authority to sublicense the '629 patent to ULSI is irrelevant. The agreement between HP and ULSI was not a sublicense, but a contract for the manufacture and sale of chips. Thus, HP did not grant a sublicense; it sold a product, albeit one designed by its purchaser. ULSI is immune from infringe- ment, not because it was a sublicensee, which it was not, but because HP was a licensed and therefore legitimate source of the chips. Moreover, ULSI was not required to be sublicensed in order to provide its chip design to HP.

Both parties cite our earlier decision in *Int'l Corp. v. United States Int'l Trade Comm'n*, 946 F.2d 821 (Fed. Cir. 1991) ("*Atmel*"), as supporting author- ity. *Atmel* is similar to, but distinguishable from, the instant case. . . . As an initial matter, the court in *Atmel* expressly recognized the freedom from pat- ent infringement of one purchasing products from a licensed party under a foundry agreement. The court stated that if the Intel/Sanyo agreement permits Sanyo to act as a foundry for another company for products covered by the Intel patents, the purchaser of those licensed products from Sanyo would be free to use and/or resell the products. Such further use and sale is beyond the reach of the patent statutes.

Thus, the court agreed that Atmel would be shielded from Intel's claims of infringement if Atmel could establish that Sanyo was authorized to sell the EPROMs to Atmel.

In determining whether the licensing agreement provided for foundry rights, the court focused on what was meant by the "Sanyo limitation" in the agreement. The court concluded that the limitation precluded Sanyo from serving as a foundry for non-Sanyo EPROMs because Sanyo was only permitted to sell Sanyo products. Sanyo was prohibited from producing and selling EPROMs to Atmel for resale as Atmel products, and the court thus held that Atmel could not rely on the license defense. In contrast, the licensing agreement between Intel and HP here contains no restriction on HP's right to sell or serve as a foundry.

In light of our discussion above, we hold that the 'C87 coprocessors were insulated from Intel's claim of infringement because they were sold to ULSI by HP, which was authorized to do so under its licensing agreement with Intel. Accordingly, we conclude that Intel cannot establish a likelihood of success on the issue of infringement. . . .

REVERSED.

NOTE

What would the result be in *Intel* if the court had concluded that the sale was not an authorized sale under the license?

IV. BONA FIDE PURCHASE, UNAUTHORIZED TRANSFERS

RHONE-POULENC AGRO,
S.A. v. DeKALB GENETICS CORP.
284 F.3d 1323 (Fed. Cir. 2002)

DYK, CIRCUIT JUDGE.

Rhone-Poulenc Agro, S.A. ("RPA") appeals from the decision of the United States District Court for the Middle District of North Carolina granting summary judgment of non-infringement on the ground that Monsanto Co. ("Monsanto") has a valid license to U.S. Patent No. 5,510,471. [The] issue here is whether a sublicensee (Monsanto) that acquired the sublicense from a licensee (DeKalb Genetics Corp. ("DeKalb")), that acquired the original license by fraud, may retain the sublicense by establishing that the sublicensee was a bona fide purchaser for value. [We] hold that the bona fide purchaser defense is governed by federal law and is not available to non-exclusive licensees in the circumstances of this case. Accordingly, we vacate the decision of the district court and remand for further proceedings consistent with this opinion.

BACKGROUND

. . . Briefly the facts are these. From 1991 through 1994, RPA and DeKalb collaborated on the development of biotechnology related to specific genetic materials. During this time, a scientist at RPA, Dr. DeRose, developed an optimized transit peptide ("OTP") with a particular maize gene, which proved useful in growing herbicide resistant corn plants. The OTP is covered by the claims of the 471 patent and is the subject of RPA's patent infringement claim against Monsanto.

In 1994, RPA, DeKalb, and non-party Calgene, Inc. ("Calgene") entered into an agreement (the "1994 Agreement") that provided:

> RPA and CALGENE hereby grant to DEKALB the world-wide, paid-up right to use the RPA/CALGENE Technology and RPA/CALGENE Genetic Material in the field of use of corn. DEKALB shall have the right to grant sublicenses to the aforementioned right to use without further payment being made to RPA or CALGENE.

The RPA/CALGENE Technology and RPA/CALGENE Genetic Material included the invention claimed in the 471 patent. In 1996, DeKalb sublicensed its rights to the RPA/Calgene Technology and Genetic Material to Monsanto. At the same time Monsanto granted to DeKalb licenses to use certain intellectual property related to genetically-engineered corn. Monsanto also acquired a forty percent equity interest in DeKalb, and ten percent of DeKalb Class A (voting) stock.

On October 30, 1997, RPA filed suit against DeKalb and Monsanto, seeking, inter alia, to rescind the 1994 Agreement on the ground that DeKalb had procured the license (the "right to use") by fraud. RPA also alleged that DeKalb and Monsanto were infringing the 471 patent and had misappropriated RPA's trade secrets. . . . The district court ordered rescission of the 1994 Agreement. Nonetheless, Monsanto moved the district court for summary judgment that it had a valid license to the 471 patent and the right to use RPA's trade secrets because under the 1996 Agreement Monsanto was a bona fide purchaser for value of the sublicense to the patent and the trade secrets. The district court orally granted this motion and dismissed the infringement and misappropriation claims against Monsanto. . . .

RPA filed this timely appeal, which concerns only the validity of Monsanto's license to practice the 471 patent. On this appeal, RPA does not challenge the district court's dismissal of RPA's claim for trade secret misappropriation.

Discussion

. . . In *Rhone-Poulenc I*, we affirmed the judgment of the district court, rescinding the 1994 licensing agreement based on a jury verdict finding that DeKalb acquired its patent license by fraud. RPA asserts that it necessarily follows that the Monsanto sublicense to the 471 patent is void, and that Monsanto can be sued for patent infringement. We agree. . . .

Under some circumstances the bona fide purchaser defense in patent cases is governed by a federal statute, 35 U.S.C. § 261. The statute provides that "an assignment, grant or conveyance shall be void as against any subsequent purchaser or mortgagee for a valuable consideration, without notice, unless it is recorded in the Patent and Trademark Office within three months from its date or prior to the date of such subsequent purchase or mortgage."

But this case does not involve a situation covered by § 261. That statute is by its terms limited to situations in which the patent owner makes inconsistent assignments, grants, or conveyances to two entities, and the question is whether the later assignee should prevail. Section 261 provides that a later bona fide purchaser for value without notice (a later assignee) prevails if the earlier assignment was not timely recorded in the patent office. This case, however, involves a different situation — the circumstance in which the interest in the patent held by the grantor is voidable and the question is whether a grantee may retain its interest even if the grantor's interest is voided. Section 261 does not directly govern the resolution of this question.

Since section 261 does not apply directly, we must turn to other provisions of the Patent Act. Section 271 of the Act provides: "whoever without authority makes, uses, offers to sell, or sells any patented invention . . . infringes the patent." We are charged with the task of determining the meaning of the term "without authority." Under this provision, as under other provisions of the Patent Act, the courts have developed a federal rule, where appropriate, and have deferred to state law, where that is appropriate. This issue of whether to apply state or federal law has particular importance in this case because North Carolina state law, the law of the forum state, does not recognize a bona fide purchaser defense unless there has been a title transfer. [Under the law of North Carolina "in the absence of an estoppel, one is not entitled to protection as a bona fide purchaser unless he holds the legal title to the property in dispute."]

In general, the Supreme Court and this court have turned to state law to determine whether there is contractual "authority" to practice the invention of a patent. Thus, the interpretation of contracts for rights under patents is generally governed by state law. Just as the interpretation of patent license contracts is generally governed by state law, so too the consequences of fraud in the negotiation of such contracts is a matter generally governed by state law, as we have recognized in our companion case. It may be argued that the impact of fraud upon the validity of a license as against a bona purchaser defense should also be governed by state law. However, we confront here a unique situation in which a federal patent statute explicitly governs the bona fide purchaser rule in some situations but not in all situations. It would be anomalous for federal law to govern that defense in part and for state law to govern in part. There is quite plainly a need for a uniform body of federal law on the bona fide purchaser defense.

On the related question of the transferability of patent licenses, many courts have concluded that federal law must be applied. In so holding, courts generally have acknowledged the need for a uniform national rule that patent licenses are personal and non-transferable in the absence of an agreement authorizing assignment, contrary to the state common law rule that contractual rights are assignable unless forbidden by an agreement.

So too we have held that the question of whether an invention is the subject of a commercial offer for sale more than one year before a patent is filed is a question of federal rather than state law. . . .

In short, because of the importance of having a uniform national rule, we hold that the bona fide purchaser defense to patent infringement is a matter of federal law. Because such a federal rule implicates an issue of patent law, the law of this circuit governs the rule. Of course, the creation of a federal rule concerning the bona fide purchaser defense is informed by the various state common law bona fide purchaser rules as they are generally understood. . . .

Congress has specifically provided that patents are to be treated as personal property. At common law, a bona fide purchaser (also known as a "good faith buyer") who acquired title to personal property was entitled to retain the property against the real owner who had lost title to the property, for example, by fraud. Generally, a bona fide purchaser is one who purchases legal title to property in good faith for valuable consideration, without notice of any other claim of interest in the property. The bona fide purchaser rule exists to protect innocent purchasers of property from competing equitable interests in the property because "strong as a plaintiff's equity may be, it can in no case be stronger than that of a purchaser, who has put himself in peril by purchasing a title, and paying a valuable consideration, without notice of any defect in it, or adverse claim to it." *Boone v. Chiles*, 35 U.S. 177, 210 (1836).

At common law, however, it was quite clear that one who did not acquire title to the property could not assert the protection of the bona fide purchaser rule. Many courts have held that a party to an executory contract to purchase title, the owner of a lease, or a purchaser from a vendor who did not have title cannot benefit from the bona fide purchaser rule.

It is clear under the law of North Carolina (the state in which RPA filed suit) that "in the absence of an estoppel, one is not entitled to protection as a bona fide purchaser unless he holds the legal title to the property in dispute."

Monsanto urges that the cases requiring that one obtain title to benefit from the bona fide purchaser defense are "antiquated," and the Uniform Commercial Code's ("U.C.C.") modern approach has rejected the requirement of title. In fact, the title rule is recognized in modern property law, and has been confirmed by the U.C.C., Articles 2 and 2B. Under U.C.C. § 2-403, even "[a] person with voidable title has power to transfer a good title to a good faith purchaser for value." Article 2B of the U.C.C. was recently adopted as the Uniform Computer Information Transactions Act ("UCITA"), U.C.I.T.A. (2000) and is relevant to the application of the bona fide purchaser rule to intellectual property. To be sure, the scope of UCITA is limited to "computer information transactions," UCITA § 103(a), and therefore is not applicable to all patent licensing cases. Nevertheless, UCITA (pertaining to the licensing of intangible property) provides guidance on the U.C.C.'s view of the common law.

Official comment 3 to UCITA § 506(b) makes clear that the drafters of the U.C.C. concluded that at common law the bona fide purchaser rule does not apply to the licensing of intellectual property:

Subsection (b) provides that as a general rule, a licensee's transferee acquires only those contractual or other rights that the licensee was authorized to transfer. There is no principle of bona fide purchaser of a mere contract right. Similarly, neither copyright nor patent recognize concepts of protecting a buyer in the ordinary course (or other good faith purchaser) by giving that person greater rights than were authorized to be transferred even if the transfer includes delivery of a copy associated with the contract. Transfers that exceed or are otherwise unlicensed by a patent or copyright owner create no rights of use in the transferee. Indeed, such transfers may in themselves be an infringing act.

Monsanto has been unable to cite a single common law case in which the bona fide purchaser rule was applied to the holder of a mere contract right, such as a license. Monsanto cites *Wilson v. M & W Gear, Inc.*, 110 Ill. App. 3d 538, 442 N.E.2d 670, 672-73, 66 Ill. Dec. 244 (Ill. App. Ct. 1982). The issue in *Wilson* was whether one who contracts to buy goods and pre-pays the purchase price without taking possession of the goods is a "buyer in the ordinary course of business" entitled to protection against a third party holding a security interest in the goods without regard to the existence, identification, or passage of title of the goods. The court held that

> when a person contracts to buy goods and those goods are in the dealer's inventory, awaiting delivery or being prepared for delivery, that purchaser is a buyer in the ordinary course of business within the meaning of [U.C.C.] section 9-307. Title to the goods does not have to pass to the purchaser nor do the goods need to be identified by number before section 9-307 will protect retail purchasers.

442 N.E.2d at 675. In dictum, the court stated: "antiquated concepts of 'title' do not control the resolution of this appeal. [The U.C.C.] has diminished drastically the importance of title. In particular, the question of whether title has passed is immaterial to the protections afforded to a buyer in the ordinary course of business." *Wilson* held that one who had contracted to purchase goods and had "fully performed his part of the contract," need not formally take title to identified goods to benefit from U.C.C. § 9-307 as a buyer in the ordinary course of business. *Wilson* was concerned with a situation in which a retail buyer, acting in the ordinary course of business, had satisfied all but the formalities of acquiring title. Whether or not *Wilson* was correctly decided, it does not purport to protect a mere license holder.

Monsanto also urges, in its opposition to the petition for rehearing, that under the U.C.C. "bona fide purchaser protection . . . applies broadly to anyone who takes 'by sale, discount, negotiation, mortgage, pledge, lien, security interest, issue or re-issue, gift or any other voluntary transaction creating an interest in property.'" (quoting U.C.C. § 1-201 (defining "purchaser")). While Monsanto accurately quotes the U.C.C.'s definition of a "purchaser," it mistakenly concludes that the bona fide purchaser defense is available to anyone who satisfies this definition.

Monsanto also relies on statements from various treatises on patent licensing for the proposition that a sublicense continues, even when the principal license is terminated. But the statements address the situation where the original licensee is terminated as a matter of contract law, e.g., for breach of contract. These treatises do not address the operation of the bona fide purchaser rule with respect to sublicenses and do not state or suggest that a sublicense continues even when the principal license is rescinded because it has been obtained by fraud. Monsanto also relies on the *Restatement (Restitution)* § 13 (1937) that "[a] person who has entered into a transaction with another . . . is not entitled to restitution from a third person who has received title to or legal interest in the subject matter from the other . . . and has given value . . . without notice" for the proposition that the bona fide purchaser rule applies to transfers of less than title, but this reliance is similarly misplaced. The comments and illustrations accompanying section 13 make clear that in general obtaining or perfecting title is an essential element of the bona fide purchaser defense. *See, e.g., id.* at cmt. a ("a person who innocently has acquired the title to something for which he has paid value is under no duty to restore it to one who would be entitled to reclaim it if the one receiving it had not been innocent or had not obtained the title or had not paid value therefore"). The only illustration of section 13 (illustration 2) in which the third party obtains something less than title, involves a bona fide mortgagee, whose legal interest, of course, empowers the mortgagee to perfect title in the transferred property. Moreover, *Restatement (Restitution)* § 172 and cmt. a indicate that the bona fide purchaser rule only applies to one who "acquires title to property." . . .

Even if the general common law extended the protection of the bona fide purchaser rule to holders of non-exclusive licenses, it would not be appropriate for us to extend such protection to non-exclusive licenses as a matter of federal common law. Section 261 of title 35 reflects a determination by Congress that only those who have obtained an "assignment, grant or conveyance" may benefit from the protection of the statute. This provision thus reflects a congressional judgment that the protections of the bona fide purchaser rule extend only to those who have received an "assignment, grant or conveyance." Under such circumstances, the Supreme Court has made clear that we must consider the purposes of federal statutes in framing a rule of federal common law, even if the statutes are not directly applicable. We have specifically held that non-exclusive licensees are not "assignees" under the statute.

. . . Here the license is non-exclusive, and there is no contention that the license agreement transferred "all substantial rights." Thus, an assignment did not occur, and in the absence of an "assignment, grant or conveyance," Congress contemplated that there would be no bona fide purchaser defense.

Conclusion

In sum, the bona fide purchaser defense does not apply to non-exclusive licensees. We accordingly vacate the decision of the district court and remand for further proceedings consistent with this opinion.

NOTES

1. In *Heidelberg Harris, Inc. v. Loebach*, 145 F.3d 1454 (Fed. Cir. 1998), the court held that Harris was a bona fide purchaser whose exclusive license was good against the ownership claim of Loebach. In this case, Harris obtained the license from a third party who had obtained an assignment of rights from Loebach. The assignment, however, was subsequently rescinded because it had been obtained by fraud. "[The] bona fide purchaser for value rule, as applied to patents, provides that one who acquires an interest in a patent for valuable consideration from the legal title holder, 'without notice of an outstanding equitable claim or title,' is entitled to retain the purchased interest, 'free of any equitable encumbrance.'"

2. *Rhone Poulenc* deals with a patent license. Do the themes discussed in the case apply equally to a copyright license? What result in a transaction involving a license of a trade secret?

MICROSOFT CORP. v. HARMONY COMPUTERS & ELECTRONICS, INC.
846 F. Supp. 208 (E.D.N.Y. 1994)

DEARIE, DISTRICT JUDGE.

This is an action for copyright infringement, trademark infringement, and related statutory and common law claims. Plaintiff Microsoft Corporation, a developer, manufacturer, and marketer of computer software programs, seeks declaratory and injunctive relief and treble damages against Harmony Computers & Electronics Inc. ("Harmony") and its president, Stanley Furst (together the "defendants"), for allegedly selling, without license or authorization, copyrighted Microsoft MS-DOS and Microsoft Windows software programs and accompanying materials ("Microsoft Products" or "Products").

BACKGROUND

On January 12, 1994, upon plaintiff's ex parte application and based on plaintiff's evidence that defendants were illegally copying and distributing Microsoft Products in violation of plaintiff's exclusive rights as the copyright holder, the Court ordered the seizure and impoundment of Microsoft Products and related business records at defendants' retail establishment, and temporarily restrained defendants from copying, using, distributing, secreting, or destroying any of plaintiff's copyrighted software.

Pursuant to the Court's Order, United States Marshals seized and impounded 106 pieces of Microsoft software. The Court held an initial hearing on plaintiff's motion for preliminary injunction on January 20, 1994. At that time, the parties did not identify any material facts in dispute and indeed most of the relevant facts are well established. Also at that time, the Court invited the parties to submit any supporting papers. On January 24, 1994, the Court extended the Temporary Restraining Order until February 1, 1994, pending the Court's decision on plaintiff's motion for preliminary injunction.

Plaintiff argues that because defendants are not licensed by Microsoft, they are not legitimately in possession of, and are not entitled to sell, any Microsoft Products, whether counterfeit or not. To the extent that defendants bought their Microsoft Products from legitimate Microsoft licensees, plaintiff argues that defendants violated Microsoft's licensing restrictions by distributing the Products "stand-alone," that is, by themselves rather than bundled with one of the personal computer systems manufactured by Microsoft licensees. Furthermore, plaintiff alleges, and defendants acknowledge, that defendants persisted in their sales of Microsoft Products despite being notified of the alleged illegality of their activity by plaintiff's cease and desist letters of April 19, June 16, July 14, and September 14, 1993. Plaintiff has advised the Court, by the declarations of Robert Wanezek, Program Manager of Microsoft's Replication Group, and of Lee Gates, its Software Design Test Engineer, that twenty-one pieces of the Products seized from defendants' premises were counterfeit.

Defendants do not contest that they sold Microsoft Products, or that they sold such Products stand-alone as well as loaded onto the hard disks of computers. Defendants argue, however, that because the Products they sold were purchased from Microsoft licensees, they are immune from liability for copyright infringement under the first sale doctrine. In response, plaintiff argues that the first sale doctrine does not apply to the present case because Microsoft never sells but rather only licenses its Products. Defendants also deny that any of the Microsoft Products that they sold were counterfeit. Alternatively, defendants argue, even if any of the Products were counterfeit, they bought them from Microsoft licensees under the good faith belief that the Products were genuine. . . . By Order of February 1, 1994, the Court granted plaintiff's motion for preliminary injunction.

Discussion

To establish a prima facie case of copyright infringement, the plaintiff must show that (1) it is the valid owner of a copyright and (2) defendant has engaged in unauthorized "copying," where "copying" "is shorthand for the infringing of any of the copyright owner's five exclusive rights, described at 17 U.S.C. § 106." Section 106 of title 17 of the United States Code provides in relevant part:

> [T]he owner of copyright under this title has the exclusive rights to do and to authorize . . .
>
> (1) to reproduce the copyrighted work in copies
>
>   . . . .
>
> (3) to distribute copies . . . of the copyrighted work to the public by sale or other transfer of ownership, or by rental, lease, or lending. . . .

17 U.S.C. § 106 (1977). Upon establishing a "reasonable likelihood of success on the merits," in an action for copyright infringement, irreparable injury is presumed. . . .

B. Unauthorized Distribution

Defendants are not Microsoft licensees and therefore are not authorized to sell Microsoft Products. Barbara Schmidt, an accounting supervisor for Microsoft's domestic Original Equipment Manufacturer ("OEM") licensing, declares that defendant Harmony was never at any time a Microsoft licensee.

Defendants do not contest this fact. Furthermore, although defendant Stanley Furst was a signatory to a license agreement dated December 2, 1993, between Microsoft and another one of Furst's companies, Everything Computers, Inc., Mr. Furst was not himself a Microsoft licensee. The license held by Everything Computers does not authorize defendants Harmony or Furst to distribute Microsoft Products.

Defendants sold Microsoft Products, as evidenced by the fact that private investigators hired by Microsoft successfully bought various Microsoft Products from defendants, that Harmony advertised the sale of MS-DOS 6.0, and that persons who had bought Microsoft Products from Harmony had called Microsoft's Piracy Hotline to question the legitimacy of their purchases. Defendants do not contest that they sold Microsoft Products, nor do they dispute that such activity would constitute copyright infringement absent the protection of the first sale doctrine. Because defendants are not authorized by Microsoft to distribute Microsoft Products, their distribution of those Products constitutes a prima facie case, that is, a likelihood of success on the merits of plaintiff's copyright infringement claim. Irreparable harm to plaintiff is therefore presumed.

Defendants argue that they in good faith believed that they were buying Products from authorized Microsoft licensees, and that their sales of the Products were therefore lawful. It is unlikely, in this case, that defendants were innocent infringers, as they were notified by Microsoft of the unlawfulness of their activities by letters dated April 19, June 16, July 14, and September 14, of 1993. Moreover, good faith is no defense against liability for copyright infringement. *ISC-Bunker Ramo Corp. v. Altech, Inc.*, 765 F.Supp. 1310, 1331 (N.D.Ill.1990) ("there is no such thing as a bona fide purchase for value in copyright law"). Accordingly, defendants' good faith defense must fail.

Finally, it is undisputed that any sale of counterfeit Microsoft Products by defendants would violate the federal copyright laws. Plaintiff has submitted the declarations of Robert L. Wanezek, Program Manager of Microsoft's Replication Group, and of Lee R. Gates, a Software Design Test Engineer for Microsoft, and samples of seized "counterfeit" Microsoft Products from defendants' premises, to support their claim that defendants sold counterfeit Products. Although defendants deny that any of the Products they sold were counterfeit, they provide no evidence to contradict plaintiff's sworn assertions. In the absence of an evidentiary hearing, and given that plaintiff is likely to succeed on the merits of its copyright infringement claim on the grounds that defendants were not licensees and therefore not authorized to distribute any Microsoft products, counterfeit or not, the Court declines at this juncture to make a finding as to the genuineness of the Microsoft Products sold by defendants.

First Sale Doctrine Does Not Apply

Defendants argue that even though they sold Microsoft Products without a license, they are immune under the first sale doctrine from liability for copyright infringement. Defendants fail to prove that the first sale doctrine applies because they do not trace their purchase of Microsoft Products to a "first sale" by Microsoft or any party authorized by Microsoft to sell the Products.

The first sale doctrine is codified at section 109(a) of title 17 of the United States Code, which provides that:

> (a) Notwithstanding the provisions of section 106(3), the owner of a particular copy . . . lawfully made under this title, or any person authorized by such owner, is entitled, without the authority of the copyright owner, to sell or otherwise dispose of the possession of that copy. . . .

17 U.S.C. § 109(a) (1977). This statute "restates and confirms the principle that, where the copyright owner has transferred ownership of a particular copy . . . of a work, the person to whom the copy . . . is transferred is entitled to dispose of it by sale . . . or any other means." In civil actions for copyright infringement, the defendant has the burden of proving that the particular pieces of the copyrighted work that he sold were lawfully made or acquired.

Defendants argue that a "first sale" occurred when they bought their Microsoft Products from entities whom they believed to be authorized Microsoft licensees. Although a sale of a copyrighted work by a party authorized by the copyright holder may constitute a "first sale" for purposes of the first sale doctrine, defendants have the burden of tracing the chain of title to show that their authority to sell Microsoft Products flows from the copyright holder.

Defendants' only evidence of a chain of title for any of their Products is an invoice of their purchase of several pieces of Microsoft Products from an entity called Innovative Datronics Corp. The fact that defendants bought their Microsoft Products from another party does not by itself establish a first sale. "Even an unwitting purchaser who buys a copy in the secondary market can be held liable for infringement if the copy was not the subject of a first sale by the copyright holder . . . unless title to the copy passes through a first sale by the copyright holder, subsequent sales do not confer good title." *American Int'l Pictures, Inc.* [*v. Foreman*], 576 F.2d [661,] at 664 [(5th Cir. 1978)]. *See also Platt & Munk Co. v. Republic Graphics, Inc.*, 315 F.2d 847 (2d Cir.1963) ("it has been held that sale of a book purchased from a merchant who bought it from an agent of the copyright proprietor, where the agent had been entrusted with possession of the book but not with actual authority to sell it, is infringement"). No evidence has been presented to show that Innovative Datronics or any party in the chain of title was a licensee of Microsoft and authorized to sell the product.

Defendants' failure to trace their Microsoft Products to a "first sale" by the copyright holder is aggravated by the fact that plaintiff has "established a course of conduct . . . consistent with an intention to retain all the rights associated with the grant of copyright" of the Microsoft Products. Plaintiff's counsel declares that Microsoft only licenses and does not sell its Products. Entering a license agreement is not a "sale" for purposes of the first sale doctrine. Moreover, the only chain of distribution that Microsoft authorizes is one in which all possessors of Microsoft Products have only a license to use, rather than actual ownership of the Products.

Defendants' failure to meet their burden of proving a chain of title distinguishes this case from *Burke* [*& Van Heusen, Inc. v. Arrow Drug, Inc.*, 233 F. Supp. 881, 884 (E.D. Pa. 1964),] and precludes the applicability of the first sale doctrine to this case.

Exceeding Scope of License Agreements

Plaintiff is likely to succeed on its claim that defendants are liable for copyright infringement for exceeding the scope of Microsoft's license agreements.

Plaintiff has traced a unit of MS-DOS 6.0 that Harmony had sold to plaintiff's undercover investigators, back to Amax Engineering, a Microsoft licensee that was authorized to distribute MS-DOS 6.0 exclusively with the sale of its personal computer systems. Plaintiff has also traced four of the MS-DOS 6.2 units seized from defendants' premises, back to Arche Technologies, a Microsoft licensee that was authorized to distribute MS-DOS and Windows only with its computer systems. The remainder of the Microsoft software seized from defendants' premises were not traceable to a specific licensee, but plaintiff's counsel affirms that none of the Products was authorized to be sold stand-alone.

To the extent that defendants bought their Microsoft Products from authorized Microsoft licensees, they were subject to the same licensing restrictions under which those licensees operated. Plaintiff's counsel have represented to the Court that every Microsoft license agreement contains the same licensing language, which provides in relevant part, that licensees:

> . . . shall distribute Product(s) only with [licensee's] Customer System(s) . . . for the particular Product(s) and only inside the Customer System package. [The licensee] shall provide a copy of the . . . Product with, and only with, each Customer System on which the corresponding Preinstalled Product Software is distributed.

This restriction requires that Microsoft Products only be sold together with a "Customer System," that is, a "single user computer system" rather than on a stand-alone basis. Indeed, plaintiff's in-house counsel declares that "it is generally known in the computer software industry that except for upgrade products, Microsoft does not authorize anyone to distribute stand-alone MS-DOS product." Plaintiff explains that Products that are sold stand-alone or otherwise outside the scope of Microsoft's license agreements, though identical in exterior appearance to authorized Microsoft Products, do not come with the product support system, warranties, and assured compatibility with their personal computer systems that Microsoft provides for its legitimately distributed Products. Therefore, plaintiff argues, the sale of stand-alone Products irreparably harms Microsoft's goodwill and reputation as a reliable software producer.

Plaintiff's private investigator purchased Microsoft Products from defendants in stand-alone form. Defendants admit that they sold stand-alone Microsoft Products, but allege that they were entitled to do so because Microsoft itself or its licensees sold stand-alone Products. In support of this argument, defendants have submitted invoices which purport to show that Furst's company, Everything Computers, a Microsoft licensee, purchased stand-alone units of Microsoft software from plaintiff.

Defendants' argument is unpersuasive. First, to the extent that defendants' argument invokes the first sale doctrine, it must fail for the reasons stated above. Second, even assuming that Microsoft sells its software to its licensees on a stand-alone basis, this does not change the fact that when the licensees in turn distribute the software, they are restricted by the license agreement in a way that the copyright holder itself is not. *See* Microsoft License Agreement, ¶ 5(a)(i) (restricting Everything Computers to distributing Microsoft Products only together with its computer systems). In fact, plaintiff's in-house counsel affirms that "[a] legitimate retail market for stand-alone MS-DOS does not exist." Third, if defendants purchased their Products from Microsoft licensees who were acting outside the scope of their licenses by selling the Products stand-alone, any distribution of the Products by defendants, whether within the scope of plaintiff's license agreement or not, would constitute copyright infringement.

Chapter 7

IMPLIED LICENSES

I. NATURE OF IMPLIED LICENSE CASE LAW

While courts often refer to the idea of an "implied license" in litigation dealing with intellectual property claims, the content of the doctrine and its scope of application is far from settled and, often, seems far from coherent. One treatise comments:

> [In] many modern implied license cases, courts attempt to describe the doctrine in terms of categories or types of implied licenses. In our view, most of these efforts are incomplete or worse; they create over-lapping categories to the point that the categories confuse, rather than aid in analysis. . . . The fact that the doctrine involves over-lapping, difficult to describe concepts, however, does not mean that implied license cases are random; it means, rather, that so many different concepts are brought into this concept that understanding it as a single theme is difficult. In some cases, ideas of implied license can be associated with contract law doctrines of interpretation and dealing with . . . issues that were not actually addressed by the parties. [In other cases,] implied license terminology applies to situations in which, under modern contract law not tied to licensing traditions, the analysis would simply ask whether the parties' conduct and words indicated that a contract (license) exists under [modern] principles holding that contracts can be formed in any manner, including by conduct of both parties.

> In still other cases, an alleged implied license seems more associated with so-called quasi-contract theories, which are reflections of remedial doctrines that prevent unjust enrichment or the like. [Often,] a court that uses the term "implied license" is simply engaged in the process of contract interpretation related [to] whether a promise exists based on the circumstances, context, conduct, or words even though no express language of promise may have been employed. Sometimes courts describe such terms as being "implied in fact," but terms and promises are also implied to cover the omitted or unforeseen case and to give substance to a bargain on a point that the parties did not address. Others, also said to be implied, are imposed as a matter of law to achieve what the court or the legislature views as rough justice "without regard to expressions of assent by either words or acts" or without regard to legal defenses that would otherwise deny relief to a party.

> Because it is comprised of so many and such diverse facets, it is difficult and perhaps ultimately not useful to attempt to precisely articulate how far concepts of "implied license" reach and how often they affect modern licensing law. [If we focus on] cases in which courts are asked to imply a license or a term of a license that cannot fairly be linked to a statutory mandate or to the expressed intention of the

parties[, the] effective scope of implied license law is relatively narrow; successful claims that an implied license exists are relatively infrequent.

RAYMOND T. NIMMER & JEFF DODD, MODERN LICENSING LAW §§ 4:2-4:3 (2007).

WANG LABORATORIES, INC. v. MITSUBISHI ELECTRONICS AMERICA, INC.
103 F.3d 1571 (Fed. Cir. 1997)

RICH, CIRCUIT JUDGE.

Appellant Wang Laboratories, Inc. sued Mitsubishi Electronics America, Inc. for infringement of two patents. Mitsubishi and its parent, Mitsubishi Electric Corporation, (collectively "Mitsubishi") filed a declaratory judgment action and the cases were consolidated in the United States District Court for the Central District of California. The district court granted Mitsubishi partial summary judgment of non-infringement of one patent. A jury then found both patents not invalid and that Mitsubishi literally infringed the other patent. But the jury concluded that Wang's conduct in dealing with Mitsubishi created an implied license from Wang to Mitsubishi to practice the invention. . . . Wang appeals and Mitsubishi cross-appeals. Since we agree that Mitsubishi was licensed, there was no infringement and we therefore affirm.

Background

The two patents in suit relate to memory modules known as "Single In-line Memory Modules" or SIMMs. . . . James Clayton, the named inventor in the patents in suit, joined Wang Laboratories in the fall of 1982. At the time, computer memory components remained relatively large, expensive, and difficult to upgrade. In the spring of 1983, Clayton developed the SIMM as a smaller, lower cost, replaceable form of computer memory. On September 2, 1983, Clayton, with Wang as assignee, applied for a patent on the SIMM invention, application serial number 528,817. The [application was denied, then modified, and denied again]. Wang submitted a file wrapper continuation application, serial number 873,879, on June 12, 1986, replacing claims 4, 5, and 6 with claim 7. [The] application resulted in patent No. 4,656,605 ('605 patent), issued April 7, 1987. [Wang] filed another application, on February 20, 1987, as a continuation of application number 873,879. This application comprised two claims and led to patent No. 4,727,513 ('513 patent), which issued on February 23, 1988. . . .

A panel of Wang employees, including Clayton, introduced the SIMM technology to members of the computer industry press in June 1983. [Wang] hoped to preempt the anticipated future introduction of 256K chips by Japanese manufacturers in a format known as the Small Outline Integrated Circuit or SOIC. [There was] an expected struggle at the Joint Electronic Device Council ("JEDEC"), a committee of the Electronic Industries Association invested with responsibility for setting industry standards, over which format would become the memory module standard.

Clayton described the period preceding the upcoming JEDEC meetings, with manufacturers awaiting indication of which way the market would go before committing to a module design. He explained Wang's belief that the present introduction of its new package should be the catalyst to sway the industry to its approach. Clayton revealed that Wang would not produce SIMMs. Instead, Wang intended to encourage others to produce the modules and would then buy SIMMs for use in its products. The panel indicated that companies already were preparing to make SIMMs. In response to questions, a panelist stated that Wang was not seeking patent rights in the SIMM, that no licensing agreements were involved for the companies approached by Wang to make SIMMs, and that SIMM makers could sell their products to third parties. Panelist Daniel Devlin summarized Wang's goal: "Hopefully if they sell it, and if they have enough interest, and the market gets big enough, we get the advantage of the cost reduction because of the volumes involved." Numerous trade publications carried SIMM stories in their July or August 1983 issues.

Wang subsequently brought its SIMMs to JEDEC and sought to persuade the group to designate Wang's design a standard. Wang argued for adoption of the SIMM from September 1983 through June 1986, when JEDEC accepted the SIMM as a standard. During that period, Wang did not inform JEDEC of its ongoing pursuit of patent rights in the SIMM. Meanwhile, several manufacturers cooperated with Wang to begin mass-producing and marketing SIMMs. As predicted in the 1983 press presentation, a large market developed for the modules and Wang became a high volume purchaser.

Mitsubishi first met with Wang regarding SIMMs in December 1983. In their meetings, Wang supplied drawings and other details to Mitsubishi and repeatedly requested that Mitsubishi manufacture SIMMs. Mitsubishi researched the possibility of producing SIMMs for Wang, but did not proceed with the project at that time. After Mitsubishi began making 256K memory chips, however, Mitsubishi decided to assemble 256K SIMMs, incorporating the new chips into a SIMM similar to Wang's, for sale to Wang and others. Mitsubishi declined to assess engineering costs to Wang, contrary to its asserted practice when creating a custom product exclusively for a particular purchaser.

In 1985 meetings, in the context of ongoing contacts between the two companies, Mitsubishi and Wang discussed Mitsubishi's new 256K SIMMs. In one meeting, Clayton suggested that Mitsubishi modify its SIMM by placing the decoupling capacitors on the same side of the substrate with the chips, as in the original Wang design. Mitsubishi complied. Mitsubishi went on to mass produce 256K SIMMs; and in 1987, Wang began buying Mitsubishi SIMMs. Wang never informed Mitsubishi of its patent applications, patents, or of any intent to execute a license or receive royalties until a December 22, 1989 letter accusing Mitsubishi of infringing the '605 and '513 patents, which had issued in 1987 and 1988 respectively.

Wang sued Mitsubishi for infringement on June 4, 1992. . . . The relevant question to the jury on the Special Verdict Form read, "Has Mitsubishi proven by a preponderance of the evidence that Wang licensed Mitsubishi to make, use, or sell the subject matter of the '513 patent?" The jury answered "Yes." . . .

Analysis

[Because] the second step of this review will require us to determine whether the factual findings support the conclusion of law, we must first ascertain what facts the jury found relating to Mitsubishi's implied license defense. The Special Verdict Form asked the jury to answer only the ultimate question of whether an implied license exists, so the jury instructions serve as our most direct guide to what the jury decided. In order to arrive at its affirmative answer on the implied license question, the jury necessarily found that (1) a relationship existed between Wang and Mitsubishi, (2) within that relationship, Wang granted to Mitsubishi a right to use its SIMM inventions, (3) Wang received valuable consideration for that grant of right, (4) Wang denied that Mitsubishi had an implied license, and (5) Wang's statements and conduct created the impression that Wang consented to Mitsubishi making, using, or selling Wang's patented inventions, including sales to consumers other than Wang. Separately, the jury found that Mitsubishi made, used, or sold several versions of SIMMs that would infringe the '513 patent but for the license.

[Wang] challenges only the finding of valuable consideration. Before we can apply the substantial evidence test to this finding, however, it becomes necessary to look beyond the jury instructions and verdict to discover what the jury understood to constitute "valuable consideration." The district court's order denying Wang's motion for JMOL identified three benefits conferred on Wang: (1) by agreeing to manufacture and sell SIMMs, Mitsubishi contributed to a "high volume supply and downward pressure on [the] price" of SIMMs, which benefited Wang as a purchaser of SIMMs; (2) Mitsubishi absorbed development and tooling costs; and (3) Mitsubishi redesigned its SIMMs to conform to Wang's preferred design. The district court ruled that each form of consideration was supported by substantial evidence.

[Wang's] own statements show that when the company introduced its SIMM design in June 1983, Wang intended to buy SIMMs from other producers rather than produce SIMMs itself. Eventually, Wang hoped to "get the advantage of the cost reduction because of the volumes involved." The evidence indicates that Wang considered lower prices and a larger market to be of value to it, as they obviously were as a large user of SIMMs. In time, JEDEC adopted Wang's SIMM design as a standard in what became a multi-billion dollar market. The market grew; prices dropped. The record contains evidence that Mitsubishi contributed to this advantageous outcome. Clayton's notes about Mitsubishi, for example, contain references to prices "dropping to mid-teens." Wang introduced evidence that dozens of producers have participated in making the SIMM market, and that Mitsubishi sold $361 million worth of SIMMs between April 1985 and March 1994. A reasonable person could conclude from the evidence that Mitsubishi supplied consideration to Wang by helping Wang achieve the market scenario it sought and valued.

Substantial evidence of the second and third benefits also appears on the record. Mitsubishi personnel testified that they made design changes to accommodate Wang's needs: specifically, moving the capacitors onto the same side of the substrate as the memory chips. Similarly, testimony indicated that Mitsubishi declined to assess development and tooling charges to Wang because it understood Wang was permitting Mitsubishi to sell SIMMs to other customers. Clayton's notes reveal that, from the first meeting onward, he closely followed Mitsubishi's development and tooling of SIMMs with 64K or 256K chips in PLCCs. Clayton clearly wanted Mitsubishi to make 64K SIMMs, which Mitsubishi decided against, but Clayton also sought "to open [communication with] Japan for us on a 256K X9 SIMM." All the while, Wang and Mitsubishi exchanged designs and samples. A reasonable person could conclude that Wang received something it valued because Mitsubishi was persuaded to follow Wang's design suggestions, but was led to believe the resultant SIMMs were not custom products for Wang and did not assess charges. Although Wang points to contrary evidence, we cannot reevaluate credibility or substitute our choices for those of the jury. Therefore, these findings survive the substantial evidence test.

[We] now turn to the legal conclusion that an implied license exists. In patent law, an implied license merely signifies a patentee's waiver of the statutory right to exclude others from making, using, or selling the patented invention. In the words of the Supreme Court,

> No formal granting of a license is necessary in order to give it effect. Any language used by the owner of the patent, or any conduct on his part exhibited to another from which that other may properly infer that the owner consents to his use of the patent in making or using it, or selling it, upon which the other acts, constitutes a license and a defense to an action for a tort.

De Forest Radio Tel. Co. v. United States, 273 U.S. 236, 241 (1927). Since *De Forest*, this court and others have attempted to identify and isolate various avenues to an implied license. As a result, courts and commentators relate that implied licenses arise by acquiescence, by conduct, by equitable estoppel (estoppel in pais), or by legal estoppel. These labels describe not different kinds of licenses, but rather different categories of conduct which lead to the same conclusion: an implied license. The label denotes the rationale for reaching the legal result.

One of our predecessor courts observed that "courts generally have first looked for facts which give rise to an estoppel in the process of concluding that there is an implied license." The opinions that hew most closely to the *De Forest* language and the "entire course of conduct" analysis rely on the doctrine of equitable estoppel, because *De Forest* requires that conduct of the patentee led the other to act. *Bandag, Inc. v. Al Bolser's Tire Stores, Inc.*, 750 F.2d 903, 925-26, 223 USPQ 982, 998-99 (Fed.Cir.1984); *Stickle v. Heublein, Inc.*, 716 F.2d 1550, 1559, 219 USPQ 377, 383 (Fed.Cir.1983). In *Bandag*, we reversed a conclusion of implied license because the infringer failed to show an awareness of the conduct which supposedly created the license. In *Stickle*, we affirmed that no implied license existed absent the required nexus between the patentee's conduct and the infringing actions, given that the course of infringing action only began later and distinct from the cited conduct.

Neither this court nor the Supreme Court, however, has required a formal finding of equitable estoppel as a prerequisite to a legal conclusion of implied license. To do so would remove all distinction between the doctrines. Rather the estoppel doctrines serve as guidelines. The primary difference between the estoppel analysis in implied license cases and the analysis in equitable estoppel cases is that implied license looks for an affirmative grant of consent or permission to make, use, or sell: i.e., a license. Equitable estoppel, on the other hand, focuses on "misleading" conduct suggesting that the patentee will not enforce patent rights. *A.C. Aukerman Co. v. R.L. Chaides Constr. Co.*, 960 F.2d 1020 (Fed.Cir.1992). In *Aukerman*, we described a typical equitable estoppel situation as one in which (1) the infringer knows of the patent, (2) the patentee objects to the infringer's activities, (3) but the patentee does not seek relief until much later, (4) thereby misleading the infringer to believe the patentee will not act. Thus, the two doctrines are not conterminous. Illustratively, both the jury, in its advisory capacity, and the district court decided against Mitsubishi on the defense of equitable estoppel per se, with misleading conduct as a required component of that defense.

Legal estoppel refers to a narrower category of conduct encompassing scenarios where a patentee has licensed or assigned a right, received consideration, and then sought to derogate from the right granted. In *AMP*, [*Inc. v. United States*, 182 Ct. Cl. 86, 389 F.2d 448, 156 U.S.P.Q. (BNA) 647 (Ct. Cl. 1968),] for example, a patentee granted a license to, and received payment from, the United States for use of an "idea" which later became the subject matter of its patent. The patentee then discovered a preexisting patent covering an aspect of the invention. After acquiring the preexisting patent, the patentee sued the government for infringement of the preexisting patent. The Court of Claims held that an implied license barred patentee from using the preexisting-but-after-acquired patent to derogate from the express license negotiated under the other patent.

We review issues of law, like the implied license defense, de novo. . . . Here, we agree with the district court that the factual findings support the jury's legal conclusion on the implied license defense, although we do not necessarily agree with all of the district court's reasoning. The jury's findings may support an implied license in the nature of legal estoppel given the transfer of a right for consideration and the subsequent suit for infringement, but we instead follow the lead of our predecessor, the United States Court of Claims, and focus on an alternative form of estoppel. *See AMP*, 389 F.2d at 452, 156 USPQ at 650 (rejected equitable estoppel and affirmed based on legal estoppel).

Although judicially implied licenses are rare under any doctrine, Mitsubishi proved that the "entire course of conduct" between the parties over a six-year period led Mitsubishi to infer consent to manufacture and sell the patented products. Furthermore, the level of interaction between the parties while Mitsubishi designed and made SIMMs distinguishes this scenario from *Bandag* where the infringer based its failed defense on conduct unknown to the infringer when the infringement occurred. The record shows that Wang tried to coax Mitsubishi into the SIMM market, that Wang provided designs, suggestions, and samples to Mitsubishi, and that Wang eventually purchased SIMMs from Mitsubishi, before accusing Mitsubishi years later of infringement. We hold, as a matter of law, that Mitsubishi properly inferred consent to its use of the invention of Wang's patents.

The findings that Wang bestowed "a right to use the SIMM invention" and that Mitsubishi supplied valuable consideration to Wang, support our holding that Wang's conduct created a license. This falls short of the express licenses or assignments usually discussed in conjunction with legal estoppel, but it constitutes part of a course of conduct that transcends "unilateral expectations . . . of one party." Wang not only led Mitsubishi to infer consent, Wang obtained payment. Wang publicly announced its desired compensation. Wang also manifested this desire in other ways, for example, by Wang's efforts at JEDEC to have its SIMM designated a standard. With the contributions of Mitsubishi and others, Wang received exactly the remuneration it desired: Wang's design is an industry standard, and the benefits of a large market and lower prices for SIMMs redound to this day. In sum, Wang consented to Mitsubishi's use of the invention, granted the right to make, use, or sell the patented SIMMs without interference from Wang, and received consideration. Therefore, we agree with the district court's determination, reiterated in denying Wang's motion to amend the judgment, that Mitsubishi possesses an irrevocable royalty-free license under the '513 patent.

Because the jury's findings of fact are supported by substantial evidence and the jury reached the correct legal conclusion based on its findings, we affirm the judgment regarding Mitsubishi's implied license defense. In reaching this result, we hold that Mitsubishi's implied license is in the nature of equitable rather than legal estoppel, because the license arose from an accord implicit in the entire course of conduct between the parties as discussed in *De Forest* and subsequent cases relying on equitable estoppel as a guideline. . . .

NOTES

1. Is there a practical difference between finding that a license exists because of estoppel and a finding that the conduct of the parties indicates that they agreed to a contractual license, but had not reduced that agreement to writing? Which characterization best describes the circumstances in *Wang*?

2. Modern contract law recognizes the creation of a contract by conduct. What purpose is served by referring to such arrangements as "implied"? If the conduct does not establish a true contract, are there circumstances in which an implied permission to use the subject matter should be found?

3. Several years before *Wang,* the court in *Bandag, Inc. v. Al Bolser's Tire Stores, Inc.,* 750 F.2d 903, 925 (Fed. Cir. 1984), commented:

> The relatively few instances where implied licenses have been found rely on the doctrine of equitable estoppel. One common thread in cases in which equitable estoppel applies is that the actor committed himself to act, and indeed acted, as a direct consequence of another's conduct. Thus, an implied license cannot arise out of the unilateral expectations or even reasonable hopes of one party. One must have been led to take action by the conduct of the other party.

PROBLEM 7.1

Jones is a professional photographer. During a driving trip from Colorado to Florida to participate in a pre-arranged photography session involving a sailboat, Jones stopped off at a retail store in a small town. While there, he struck up a conversation with the owner. During the conversation, Jones said that he would take a picture on the sailboat of a couple simulating a drinking party wearing tee-shirts and caps with the store's logo and that the store owner could use in a new line of tee shirts. The owner gave Jones some merchandise from the store. Jones sent copies of the photographs to the owner with a letter instructing the owner to use Jones' name with printers so the owner would not "'get hassled about copyright.'" The owner had the shirts printed and sent samples of the merchandise to Jones. Jones sues for infringement. What result?

FOAD CONSULTING GROUP
INC. v. MUSIL GOVAN AZZALINO
270 F.3d 821 (9th Cir. 2001)

In this copyright case, we must decide an issue unaddressed by our prior decisions: Which law, state or federal, governs the creation of an implied, non-exclusive copyright license? We conclude that while federal law answers the threshold question of whether an implied, nonexclusive copyright license can be granted (it can), state law determines the contract question: whether a copyright holder has, in fact, granted such a license. Construing California law and applying it to the facts of this case, we conclude that Foad Consulting Group, Inc., gave an implied, nonexclusive license to the predecessor in interest of defendants Canyon Partners, LLC, and Agra, LLC, to reproduce and adapt the revised project plan at issue in this case and to publish the subsequent work, all in conjunction with defendants' development of a shopping center. Because we also conclude that defendants' modification and use of the plans did not exceed the scope of the implied license, we affirm the district court's grant of summary judgment to defendants.

Background

In August 1995, GenCom, Inc., hired the engineering firm Foad Consulting Group, Inc. to create a "preliminary Concept Development Plan" for a 45.5 acre shopping center project (the project) that GenCom intended to build in Arroyo Grande, California (the city). Pursuant to a contract dated August 18, 1995, Foad prepared a preliminary plot plan that showed the "location of the proposed buildings, parking lots, [and] landscape areas." GenCom submitted this plan to the city on January 3, 1996, as part of its application to build the shopping center. GenCom and Foad entered into a second contract, dated February 12, 1996, under which Foad agreed to create "final engineering drawings" for the project, including a revised plot plan, and to "process the [various] plans through the offices of the city of Arroyo Grande." The revised plot plan was subsequently submitted to the city, and the city approved GenCom's application for the project on July 9, 1996.

After it obtained the city's approval, GenCom transferred its rights to develop the project to Claire Enterprises, LLC. In October 1996, Claire hired Hawkeye Investments, LLC, as the project's developer. Hawkeye, in turn, hired the predecessor of Musil Govan Azzalino (MGA), to perform architectural and engineering services. MGA obtained copies of the revised plot plan and other documents from the city; it also obtained copies of various documents relating to the project from Foad. Based on the plot plan approved by the city, and suggestions and requirements of the project owners, the city, and potential tenants, MGA prepared final site plans for the project. In creating the final site plan, MGA copied much of Foad's revised plot plan by tracing from it onto an overlay. The developers wished to substantially revise Foad's plan, but the city was unwilling to allow major deviation from the plan that it had already approved. MGA circulated the final site plans to the city as well as to the shopping center's potential tenants.

Concerned that its copyright was being infringed, Foad sent a letter of admonition to MGA, dated February 3, 1997, informing MGA that Foad's revised plot plan was copyrighted and that Foad would pursue any violation of its copyright in federal court. Foad also obtained a Certificate of Registration for the revised plot plan from the Register of Copyrights, which is also dated February 3, 1997. On August 15, 1997, Foad filed a complaint in federal district court alleging copyright infringement. On April 15, 1998, the district court heard defendants' motion for summary judgment. It granted the motion because it concluded that the merger doctrine applied. On April 17, the court entered final judgment for the defendants. Foad timely appealed.

Discussion

One who owns a copyright in a work has the exclusive right to reproduce, adapt, publish, perform, and display the work. A copyright holder may transfer any or all of these rights, *id.* § 201(d)(2), but in order for the transfer to be valid it must be in writing,

Foad argues that defendants infringed its copyright in the revised plot plan by copying and modifying it and by publishing the resulting work. Defendants also infringed its reproduction rights, Foad contends, by using the revised plot plan without its permission to build the project. They infringed its exclusive right to adapt the revised plot plan by using it as a basis for the final site plan. And by filing the final site plan with the city and circulating it among prospective tenants, defendants infringed Foad's publication rights. There is nothing in either contract between GenCom and Foad which purports to transfer any of Foad's exclusive rights to GenCom, and defendants do not point to any other writing that evidences a transfer of copyright. Thus, we cannot conclude from the writings that Foad transferred to GenCom explicitly its reproduction, adaptation, and publication rights in the revised plot plan. . . .

II.

We have recognized, however, that § 204(a)'s writing requirement applies only to the transfer of exclusive rights; grants of nonexclusive copyright licenses need not be in writing. So we must consider whether Foad granted GenCom a nonexclusive license to copy and modify its revised plot plan and to publish the resulting work. A nonexclusive copyright license may be granted orally or by implication. Defendants argue that Foad granted GenCom an implied license to reproduce, adapt, and publish in the February 1996 contract between the parties. We agree that the contract grants GenCom an implied license to use the revised plot plan to complete development of the project, to hire another firm to create derivative works using the revised plot plan for the purpose of completing the project, and to publish the resulting work.

Foad asks us to consider certain extrinsic evidence in interpreting the contract. The contract was formed in California, concerns work that was done in California, and contains a choice-of-law clause that identifies California law as governing its interpretation. In contrast to many other states, California has a liberal parol evidence rule: It permits consideration of extrinsic evidence to explain the meaning of the terms of a contract even when the meaning appears unambiguous. Thus, if state law determines whether an implied, nonexclusive copyright license has been granted, we should consider whether Foad's extrinsic evidence discloses a latent ambiguity in the contract. If state law does not apply, then we will need to consider whether the extrinsic evidence is admissible under federal common law. Accordingly, before we interpret the contract between Foad and GenCom, we consider whether federal or state law determines whether a copyright holder has granted an implied, nonexclusive copyright license to another.

As a general matter, we rely on state law to fill in the gaps Congress leaves in federal statutes. "The case for adopting state law rules is strongest where Congress legislates interstitially, leaving state law largely undisturbed. Under those circumstances, comity and common sense counsel against exercising the power of federal courts to fashion rules of decision as a matter of federal common law." In enacting the Copyright Act, Congress did not preempt the field. Thus, where the Copyright Act does not address an issue, we turn to state law to resolve the matter, so long as state law does not otherwise conflict with the Copyright Act. . . . There is no reason we should treat implied copyright licenses any differently. Congress did not choose to regulate the conditions under which a copyright holder can grant a nonexclusive copyright license to another. Thus, so long as it does not conflict with the Copyright Act, state law determines whether a copyright holder has granted such a license.

We must ask, then, whether California's parol evidence rule conflicts with federal copyright law or policy. The principle effect of the California parol evidence rule is to lessen the importance of written contracts. It does so because the rule requires courts to consider extrinsic evidence of possible ambiguity even where the terms of the contract appear unequivocal. And if a party's extrinsic evidence creates the possibility of ambiguity, a court may not rely on the text of the contract alone to determine the intent of the parties. The Copyright Act places great emphasis on the necessity of writings to grant exclusive licenses, but not when it comes to granting nonexclusive licenses: As we have noted, nonexclusive licenses may be granted orally. Thus, if a copyright holder and another have a contract that clearly does not grant the other an exclusive copyright license, in a copyright infringement suit the other may nonetheless introduce nonwritten evidence — such as testimony, course of conduct, and custom and practice — to show that the copyright holder orally granted her a nonexclusive license. Since the Copyright Act itself places no particular emphasis on writings in the case of nonexclusive licenses, we conclude that application of California's parol evidence rule in interpreting a contract that a party purports to have granted an implied copyright license does not conflict with the Act or its underlying policies.

III.

We must now determine whether the February 1996 contract between Foad and GenCom granted GenCom an implied copyright license. In this analysis, we consider whether Foad's extrinsic evidence discloses any ambiguities in the contract.

a. License to Reproduce

Foad claims that defendants infringed its reproduction rights to build the project by using the revised plot plan without its permission. We conclude from the terms of the contract that Foad granted GenCom an implied license to do just that. The central purpose of the contract was the production of a set of engineering documents "for 'The Grande Plaza' Commercial Center in the city of Arroyo Grande." Under the contract, Foad agreed to create multiple maps, drawings, and plans for the project and to "process" these documents with the city. For this service, GenCom agreed to pay Foad a fee of $175,000. Given the amount of money GenCom paid for Foad's services and because part of the agreement was for Foad to help GenCom with its application to the city, it would be surprising if the parties had intended for GenCom to seek Foad's permission before using the plans to build the project. Had that been the parties' intention, one would expect to see the requirement spelled out explicitly in the agreement. But nowhere does the contract state that after the city had granted its approval, GenCom would need to obtain Foad's permission before commencing work. We conclude that the contract gives GenCom an implied license to use the revised plot plan to build the project.

As evidence that the contract indicates the parties' intent to restrict GenCom's ability to use the revised plot plan without Foad's approval, Foad asks us to consider a legend that appears on the plan. The legend reads:

> All ideas, designs, arrangements and plans indicated or represented by this drawing are owned by, and the property of Foad Consulting Group, Inc. and were created, evolved and developed for use on, and in connection with the specified project. None of such ideas, designs, arrangements or plans shall be used without written permission of Foad Consulting Group, Inc.

This legend does not divulge a latent ambiguity in the contract, much less show that under the contract Foad's permission was required before GenCom could start work. It is patent that the plans were developed for use on the specific project that was built. Although the legend states that no "plans shall be used without written permission of Foad," it appears on a document that was created after the agreement was made, and presumably was written by Foad or its agent. What's more, the legend would apply, if at all, to projects other than the specified project. Foad offers no explanation of how such a statement calls into question the parties' intent, as manifested by the contract, that GenCom would pay Foad for plans that it could use to develop its property.

b. License to Adapt

Foad next alleges that defendants infringed its adaptation rights by using much of the revised plot plan in creating the final site plan. But the February 1996 contract contains no language prohibiting others from modifying the revised plot plan. Quite the opposite: The contract contains a clause requiring GenCom to indemnify Foad in the event that others modify the plan and the changes lead to some liability. In addition, that clause does not require GenCom to obtain Foad's consent in order to modify the plans; it only requires consent in order to avoid Foad's waiver of liability. The indemnification clause plus the absence of any prohibition against modification by others indicates that the contract granted GenCom an implied license to hire others to create derivative works using the revised plot plan for the purpose of completing the project.

Foad points to paragraph 12 of the contract in support of its argument that it did not grant GenCom a license to hire another company to complete the project using the revised plot plan. Paragraph 12 states:

> All original drawings, plans, documents, other papers and copies thereof prepared in connection with this agreement will remain the property of FOAD CONSULTING GROUP, INC. and may be used without the consent of the client and/or owner(s). [T]he aforementioned papers will be kept on file by FOAD CONSULTING GROUP, INC. and copies will be provided to the client and/or owner(s) at client and/owner(s)'s request, and at client and/owner(s)'s expense.

The paragraph provides Foad no support. It concerns ownership of the original documents and copies prepared by Foad under the agreement. It also makes plain Foad's intention to retain its right to "use" the documents, presumably by reproduction, adaptation, or publication. However, the paragraph is silent about what GenCom may or may not do with the copies prepared for it.

Foad also asks us to consider extrinsic evidence: a declaration from an alleged architectural expert who asserted that, under the custom and practice in the industry, a plan "may not be used to produce a similar plan, without the permission of the original designer." This statement does nothing to undermine our conclusion that the contract grants GenCom an implied license to modify the revised plot plan. The contract protects Foad against any liability that might arise from a plan modified by others while imposing no restriction on such modifications. Even assuming that industry custom and practice requires a client to obtain an engineer's consent before modifying a plan created by the engineer, we conclude that the contract gave GenCom the requisite permission.

c. License to Publish

Finally, Foad contends that defendants infringed its publication rights by filing the final site plan with the city and circulating it among prospective tenants. The conclusion that the February 1996 contract granted GenCom an implied license to file the final site plan with the city and to use the plan to attract potential tenants follows from our previous analysis. The contract granted GenCom a license to reproduce and adapt the revised plot plan for the purpose of developing the project. It would defy common sense to conclude that the contract at the same time withheld permission to publish the resulting work for the same purpose. In the absence of a contractual provision concerning GenCom's right to circulate any derivative works as part of its development of the project, we conclude that GenCom did not infringe Foad's publication rights.

. . . .

Conclusion

The Copyright Act permits copyright holders to grant nonexclusive copyright licenses by implication. But whether a copyright holder has properly granted another a nonexclusive license by implication is a matter of state contract law, provided that the state law does not conflict with the Copyright Act or its underlying policies. In this case, the February 1996 contract granted GenCom an implied license to copy and adapt Foad's revised plot plan and to publish the resulting derivative work in aid of constructing the project for which it was designed. The extrinsic evidence which we consider as required by California law reveals no latent ambiguity in the contract. The defendants did not exceed the scope of the license by using the revised plot plan to create a final site plan, build the project, and publish the final site plan. Finally, the clause in the contract limiting assignments does not affect the validity of GenCom's transfer of its development rights. For these reasons, the district court's grant of summary judgment to defendants is AFFIRMED.

KOZINSKI, J., concurring:

The parties will no doubt be surprised by the majority opinion, as it decides a question they neither briefed nor argued, and that wasn't even raised below. [As] best I can tell, the majority assumes that anything that is called a contract — including an implied contract — must be governed by state law. But not every implied contract is, in fact, a contract. Certainly, some implied contracts are governed by state law. Those contracts really are contracts; they are actual agreements between parties, albeit imperfectly articulated. The cases on which the majority relies all involve this type of contract.

But there is another type of implied contract, one that is "created otherwise than by assent and without any words or conduct that are interpreted as promissory." 3 ARTHUR LINTON CORBIN, CORBIN ON CONTRACTS §561, at 276-77 (1960). Such an implied contract is not a contract at all; it is a legal obligation the law imposes between certain parties where there is no actual agreement between them. If the implied contract that gives rise to the nonexclusive license . . . is this kind of contract, then it has nothing at all to do with contract law. Rather, it is an incident of the copyright and is therefore governed by federal law.

In *Effects Associates*, we imposed a nonexclusive license as an incident of the transfer of the copyrighted work but did not expressly say that it was a creation of federal law. I believe that this was the clear implication of our ruling, but I would leave resolution of the question to a case where the issue is properly raised below and the parties have briefed and argued it before us. In this case, I would decide the question as a matter of federal law, as the parties and district court assumed it is.

Purporting to apply state law, the majority infers "from the terms of the contract" that Foad and GenCom agreed to a nonexclusive license. Yet there is nothing in the written contract between Foad and GenCom that remotely touches upon the plans' copyright. The contract says nothing about whether GenCom had the right to modify or distribute the plans. It says nothing about the circumstances in which GenCom can use the plans to build the project. The parties seem to have negotiated, written and signed the contract without ever discussing (or perhaps being aware of) these copyright issues. . . . Which leads to the question: Exactly which terms of the contract give rise to the license? The majority never says, relying instead on what the contract does not say. . . . In other words, Foad's failure to expressly reserve its rights raises an implication that Foad licensed those rights. This makes intuitive sense but, as we are applying state law, I would have expected to see state caselaw or a state law treatise cited on this point. The majority offers no state law authority to support its conclusion that a court can infer an agreement from the absence of a contrary agreement. . . .

Part III of the opinion devotes considerable effort to figuring out whether the implied copyright license previously found to exist is nonetheless defeated by parol evidence. This makes about as much sense as calculating how high is up.

Parol evidence consists of words or conduct outside the contract that tends to vary or explain the contract's written terms. . . . [Parol] evidence is used to shed light on words actually used in the contract.

The implied copyright license here is not a term in the contract; rather, as the name suggests, it's a term that is implied from the relationship of the parties. In such circumstances, it makes no sense at all to talk about parol evidence, or to consider whether California applies a broad or narrow parol evidence rule. There are no words of the contact that the parol evidence here can be used to interpret or clarify.

Evidence extrinsic to the contract is, of course, not irrelevant. Because the implied license is derived from the relationship of the parties — which may well extend beyond the contract — it is entirely appropriate to look at any words or conduct that bear on whether a copyright license should be implied. But that is not a question of parol evidence; rather, it goes to whether such a license exists in the first place. . . .

NOTES

1. As the Ninth Circuit commented, implied license cases seldom address the issue of what law applies. Did the majority reach the proper result, or are the ideas of Judge Kozinski more appropriate to distinguish between federal and state law coverage? Under the approach of Judge Kozinski, what law applies to an implied license claim based on estoppel theory? What law should govern on the issue of whether the conduct of the parties in fact created a contractual license?

2. What is the scope of an implied license? In *Diggan v. Cycle Sat, Inc.*, 576 N.W.2d 99 (Iowa 1998), Diggan as an independent contractor developed software for Cycle Sat. Shortly thereafter Cycle Sat hired him as a full-time employee to make "modifications and enhancements" to the software. During his employment, Diggan "refused to give Cycle Sat the crucial source code for the program." Diggan was fired. He demanded that Cycle Sat cease using the software he wrote, but the court found that Cycle Sat had an implied license to use the program. The Iowa Supreme Court held that Diggan's cause of action for a breach of an implied contract to pay more for software development than Cycle Sat already had paid was time-barred, but remanded the issue whether Cycle Sat breached the implied license by continuing to use the software after it had terminated Diggan's employment and Diggan had asked for Cycle Sat to cease that use. The terms and scope of permitted use under an implied license, or with an implied-in-fact contract, depend on "the parties' conduct" though the court suggested that the implied license may have terminated with Diggan's employment.

PROBLEM 7.2

SEEQ proposed to the Joint Electronics Device Council (JEDEC), a committee of the Electronic Industries Association charged with setting industry standards, to adopt the patented SEEQ technology described as "Silicon Signature" as an industry standard. JEDEC studied SEEQ's proposal for six months. During this evaluation, SEEQ stated its willingness to grant royalty free licenses for a one-time fee to any manufacturer who requested one and to place the subject matter of a patent that covered part of the technology in the public domain if JEDEC accepted Silicon Signature as a standard. JEDEC decided to recommend use of Silicon Signature technology, but did not actually implement Silicon Signature as a formal standard.

While this was occurring, STT began manufacturing a product that, without its knowledge, infringed the SEEQ patent. SEEQ sues for infringement. Does STT have a successful claim of an implied license?

II. CLIENTS, EMPLOYERS, AND IMPLIED LICENSES

I.A.E., INC. v. SHAVER
74 F.3d 768 (7th Cir. 1996)

RIPPLE, CIRCUIT JUDGE.

Architect Paul D. Shaver appeals the district court's summary judgment ruling that there was no infringement of Mr. Shaver's copyrighted schematic design drawings. The court concluded that Mr. Shaver had granted an implied nonexclusive license to utilize his drawings in the completion of Gary Regional Airport's air cargo building. For the reasons that follow, we [affirm].

I

BACKGROUND

In July 1992, two construction companies formed a joint venture. I.A.E., Inc. and its president Ramamurty Talluri joined with BEMI Construction and its president William Brewer to become the I.A.E./BEMI Joint Venture ("Joint Venture"). On December 21, 1992, the Joint Venture entered into a contract with the Gary Regional Airport Authority ("Airport") to design and to construct an air cargo/hangar building. Under the contract, Joint Venture was to provide all of the civil, structural, mechanical and electrical engineering services and architectural design services needed to construct the air cargo building.

In furtherance of that goal, Joint Venture subcontracted with Paul D. Shaver, an architect with extensive experience in designing airport facilities, to prepare the schematic design drawings for the airport building. The parties agree that there are four phases to the architectural design of a building: schematic design, preliminary design, final design and construction supervision. The schematic design documents are the product of the first phase of designing a building. They outline the scope of the project and are the basis of the owner's approval for the building design. Schematic design documents are often used as a reference base for further design development.

Mr. Shaver's letter of January 14, 1993, to Mr. Talluri, which constitutes the written contract between the architect and Joint Venture, contained Mr. Shaver's agreement to prepare the schematic design drawings for the Airport building: "With the assistance of your office and the [Airport] staff, agreed design parameters can be established initially to permit the Project to proceed in a normal development manner." The contract price for his services was $10,000 plus reimbursable expenses, less deductions for the participation of I.A.E.'s staff. The contract specifically set forth the services Mr. Shaver intended to perform:

> To prepare, with the assistance of your office and BEMI, Inc., staff, standard Design Documents (15%-19% of the total design work), which would describe the agreed scope of the Project, we estimate a 4-5 week period of time including two or three scheduled approval meetings with your office and [Airport] Authority personnel. These documents would consist of the following which are customarily prepared to describe the scope of the Project and also for general reference: Drawings, 5, Title Sheet, Site Plan, Floor Plans, Elevations and Building Sections Preliminary Construction Cost Estimate.

> [W]e are prepared to complete the required Schematic Design Document preparation for $10,000 subject to adjustment with deductions resulting from participation of staff from your office and your Architectural associate.

> . . . .

> . . . Please advise us if you need any additional data concerning our understanding of the scope of work.

Mr. Shaver believed that, once a design had been approved, he would execute further written contracts for the remaining phases of the architectural work.

After Mr. Shaver attended several meetings with the Airport, he prepared his schematic design drawings of the proposed Airport building. He then delivered copies of his schematic drawings to the Airport, Joint Venture, and other parties involved in the Project. These drawings were submitted with a notice of copyright. The copyrights of those drawings, both as technical drawings and as architectural works, were effective June 2, 1993. Their validity has not been challenged. Mr. Shaver and Mr. Talluri later presented to the Airport the completed schematic designs. On February 22, 1993, the Airport approved one of them. Mr. Shaver was paid $5,000 of his fee on that date.

On March 1, 1993, Joint Venture retained H. Seay Cantrell & Associates ("Cantrell") to perform the remaining architectural work for the air cargo building. When Mr. Shaver realized that he and his firm were no longer involved in the Project, he took two actions. On March 3, 1993, Mr. Shaver wrote to the Airport's Executive Director, Levelle Gatewood, acknowledging that he and his staff were, "under the circumstances, no longer in a position to participate or contribute to the development of the east Air Cargo Building Project." The letter, with enclosed copies of Mr. Shaver's schematic design drawings, also stated:

> We trust that our ideas and knowledge exhibited in our work will assist the Airport in realizing a credible and flexible use Cargo/Hangar facility.

Mr. Shaver's second act, one week later, was to seek collection of the amount that Joint Venture still owed him for the services he had rendered and to notify Joint Venture that he intended to enforce his copyrights if necessary. Mr. Shaver, by his attorney, claimed that he was owed an additional $5,000 fee, plus his out-of-pocket expenses ($887.29), plus (a new claim) a $7,000 payment for the purported "assignment" of his copyright on the schematic design documents. The attorney's letter of March 10, 1993 offered Mr. Talluri a settlement of Mr. Shaver's claim against Joint Venture for $12,887.29. Mr. Talluri agreed to pay the contract costs, $5,887.29, as final payment. According to Mr. Talluri, Mr. Shaver "had never previously raised the issue of copyright, copyright infringement or his alleged entitlement to moneys, in addition to the contract amount, for 'assignment' of his copyright on the schematic design drawings."

Once it was clear that Mr. Shaver and Joint Venture would not reach an accord concerning any amount still owing to Mr. Shaver under the contract, on August 5, 1993, I.A.E. and Mr. Talluri filed this action. They sought a declaratory judgment that they did not infringe any copyrights owned by Mr. Shaver and that they had a right to use Mr. Shaver's drawings; they also sought damages. Mr. Shaver counterclaimed against I.A.E. and Mr. Talluri, seeking damages for copyright infringement and breach of contract. He also filed third-party complaints against Cantrell, BEMI and its president Mr. Brewer, and the Airport, alleging that all the named defendants had infringed his copyrights in the schematic design documents or that they had conspired to do so by copying and using elements of his design in the final bid documents for the Airport Project. Joint Venture and the Airport responded that they had used Mr. Shaver's drawings only as Mr. Shaver had intended their use, to build the Airport's air cargo building. All parties then filed cross-motions for summary judgment. . . .

The district court granted summary judgment on the ground that there was no copyright infringement. . . .

A.

Proof of copyright infringement requires two showings: first, that the claimant has a validly owned copyright, and second, that the "constituent elements of the work that are original" were copied. The first element is not in contention; there is no challenge to the validity of Mr. Shaver's copyrights. It is the second prong of infringement that is at issue; Mr. Shaver asserted that his work was copied. The district court determined, however, that the use of his works was permissible because Mr. Shaver had granted an implied nonexclusive license.

A copyright owner may transfer to another person any of the exclusive rights the owner has in the copyright; however, such a transfer must be made in writing. 17 U.S.C. § 204(a). [The] "transfer of copyright ownership" is defined, in the Copyright Act, as an exclusive license or some other instrument of conveyance. The definition expressly excludes a nonexclusive license. Therefore, even though section 204(a) of the Copyright Act invalidates any transfer of copyright ownership that is not in writing, section 101 explicitly removes a nonexclusive license from the section 204(a) writing requirement. We turn, therefore, to the differences between exclusive and nonexclusive licenses.

In an exclusive license, the copyright holder permits the licensee to use the protected material for a specific use and further promises that the same permission will not be given to others. The licensee violates the copyright by exceeding the scope of this license. The writing requirement serves the goal of predictability and certainty of copyright ownership.

By contrast, in the case of an implied nonexclusive license, the licensor-creator of the work, by granting an implied nonexclusive license, does not transfer ownership of the copyright to the licensee. The copyright owner simply permits the use of a copyrighted work in a particular manner. In contrast to an exclusive license, a "nonexclusive license may be granted orally, or may even be implied from conduct." Nimmer explains that a nonexclusive license "is not expressly provided in the statutory text, but is negatively implied from the fact that a 'transfer of copyright ownership,' which by definition does not include nonexclusive licenses (*see* 17 U.S.C. § 101) must be by written instrument." [Melville B. Nimmer & David Nimmer,] 3 *Nimmer* [*on Copyright*] § 10.03[A] at 10-40.1 n.19 [(1995)]. A nonexclusive license is, therefore, an exception to the writing requirement of section 204. In fact, consent given in the form of mere permission or lack of objection is also equivalent to a nonexclusive license and is not required to be in writing. Although a person holding a nonexclusive license has no standing to sue for copyright infringement, the existence of a license, exclusive or nonexclusive, creates an affirmative defense to a claim of copyright infringement. The concept of an implied nonexclusive license has been recognized [by] the courts, including this one, which universally have recognized that a nonexclusive license may be implied from conduct. Indeed, implied licenses are like implied contracts, which are well recognized in the field of architecture. As the district court noted, the Ninth Circuit, in *Effects* [*Associates, Inc. v. Cohen,* 908 F.2d 555 (9th Cir. 1990)], held that an implied nonexclusive license has been granted when (1) a person (the licensee) requests the creation of a work, (2) the creator (the licensor) makes that particular work and delivers it to the licensee who requested it, and (3) the licensor intends that the licensee-requestor copy and distribute his work.

B.

In light of these principles, we now turn to the record before us. In our analysis, we find helpful, as did the district court, the opinion of our colleagues in the Ninth Circuit in *Effects*. In the case before us, [Shaver] maintains that his expectation was that he would be the architect who would be preparing the final drawings, presumably from his own preliminary drawings, to be used for the construction. We therefore must determine whether the record will support a determination that such an interpretation had any objective foundation.

Effects suggests several objective factors to guide the judicial inquiry as to whether an implied license exists: the language of the copyright registration certificate, the letter agreement, and deposition testimony; and the delivery of the copyrighted material without warning that its further use would constitute copyright infringement. When we apply these factors to the circumstances before us, we must conclude that there is no genuine issue of triable fact and that the district court concluded correctly as a matter of law that Mr. Shaver granted an implied nonexclusive license to Joint Venture.

We note first that Mr. Shaver's certificates of registration, entitling the drawings "East Air Cargo Building, Gary Regional Airport, Indiana: Not Yet Constructed," state that copyrighted designs are to be used for the "Airport Facility." We now turn to the language of the contract itself. The contract in this case was a letter written by Mr. Shaver. This letter, apparently in confirmation of an earlier telephone conversation, demonstrates that the relationship of independent contractor for the purpose of creating the preliminary drawings for the Airport Project existed between Mr. Shaver and Joint Venture. It defines his role in the Airport Project and, specifically, his "understanding of the scope of work": preparation of the preliminary schematic design drawings, which were 15-19% of the total design work. Mr. Shaver stated that his drawings are the type "customarily prepared to describe the scope of the project and also for general reference." Mr. Shaver also quoted the consideration for his work, $10,000. Mr. Shaver's statement that "agreed design parameters can be established initially to permit the Project to proceed in a normal development manner," *id.*, certainly suggests that he considered his contribution to be in furtherance of the entire Project. In short, his letter was clear, to-the-point, and unambiguous. No other work is listed; no expectation of a further role in the Project is mentioned in the contract. Therefore, although Mr. Shaver tells us that he anticipated he would be the architect to take the Project to completion, nothing in his contract gives the slightest indication of that belief. Although Indiana law allows contractual terms to be implied from the intent and action of the parties, the "intent relevant in contract matters is not the parties' subjective intent but their outward manifestation of it." Here the contract is clear.

The plain language of the contract is supported by common sense. As we have already pointed out, Mr. Shaver created a work — preliminary architectural drawings — and handed them over to the Joint Venture for use on the Airport Project. For that work the architect received $10,000 compensation. As the Ninth Circuit concluded in *Effects*:

> To hold that Effects did not at the same time convey a license to use the footage in "The Stuff" would mean that plaintiff's contribution to the film was "of minimal value," a conclusion that can't be squared with the fact that Cohen paid Effects almost $56,000 for this footage. Accordingly, we conclude that Effects impliedly granted nonexclusive licenses. . . .

908 F.2d 555, 558. This understanding is reflected throughout the parties' depositions and affidavits. Joint Venture clearly expected to use Mr. Shaver's

drawings for the Project. Mr. Talluri expected that Mr. Shaver's schematic design drawings were to be used in the Airport Project for which they were intended and stated that the drawings were used only in that manner, despite the fact that Mr. Shaver was not the continuing architect.

Not only the language of the copyright registration certificates, the letter contract, and the depositions and common sense support the conclusion of the district court that the defendants had an implied nonexclusive license to use Mr. Shaver's drawings in the Airport Project; Mr. Shaver's actions and subsequent writing also unequivocally support that conclusion. Mr. Shaver delivered his copyrighted designs without any warning that their further use would constitute copyright infringement. In his March 3, 1993 letter, Mr. Shaver acknowledged that he was no longer a contributor to the Project's development, but that he expected "that our ideas and knowledge exhibited in our work will assist the Airport in realizing a credible and flexible use Cargo/Hangar facility." This statement, accompanied by the delivery of copies of his drawings, certainly constitutes a release of those documents to the Airport for its Project and clearly validates a determination that all the objective factors support the existence of an implied license to use Mr. Shaver's drawings in the construction of the air cargo building.

On this record, we cannot conclude that Mr. Shaver has raised a genuine issue of material fact on the issue of the parties' intent. His contention that he never intended to grant a license for the use of his drawings past the drafting stage unless he was the continuing architect is simply not supported by the record.

C.

Mr. Shaver also makes several alternative arguments that accept the existence of a nonexclusive implied license, but suggest that, under the circumstances established by the record, it cannot be enforced. We believe that these arguments cannot be maintained in light of our analysis, but we shall address them briefly for the sake of completeness.

Mr. Shaver submits that, even if there was an implied license for the use of his drawings, the Airport, Cantrell and Joint Venture exceeded the scope of that license by allowing another architect, Cantrell, to use the designs. He relies on *Oddo v. Ries*, 743 F.2d 630 (9th Cir.1984). *Oddo* held that Ries, a publisher, had an implied nonexclusive license to use Oddo's articles to create a particular book. However, Ries exceeded the scope of that implied license when it hired another writer and created a different work, one which included much new material written by the second writer as well as large portions of Oddo's manuscript. By publishing the other writer's book, which was distinct from the plaintiff's manuscript originally licensed for use, the defendant exceeded the scope of the partnership's implied license. In our case, however, the record contains written authorization for the use of Mr. Shaver's copyrighted drawings to "describe the agreed scope of the Project" for Joint Venture and the Airport. The use of his drawings was therefore within the scope of that agreement. Mr. Shaver's assertion that he did not grant the right to further use of his drawings unless he was the architect continuing the Project is simply not supported by the contract. Mr. Shaver's reliance on *Oddo* is therefore of no benefit to him.

Mr. Shaver also asserts that, because only half of the contract sum was paid, the implied license "did not spring into existence." In *Effects*, the Ninth Circuit rejected a virtually identical argument that there could be no implied license until the full payment of the contract price was made. That court recognized that the appellant was treating the complete payment of the contractual consideration as a condition precedent to the use of the copyrighted material. After noting that "conditions precedent are disfavored and will not be read into a contract unless required by plain, unambiguous language," it found nothing in the agreement between the parties indicating such an agreement. Similarly, in the case before us, nothing in the contract or in Mr. Shaver's later letter indicates that full payment was a condition precedent to the use of his drawings. In fact, he first distributed his drawings before any payment was made, and next handed them over to the Airport, with no mention of payment, after half the dollar amount of the contract had been tendered. Clearly at that point a license to use the drawings had impliedly been granted. Mr. Shaver did not state that failure to pay would be viewed as copyright infringement until the March 10, 1993 letter from his attorney.

Conclusion

Mr. Shaver created an implied nonexclusive license to use his schematic design drawings in the Airport Project. Accordingly, there was no infringement of Mr. Shaver's copyrighted works. We conclude that, because there are no genuine issues of material fact before us, we must affirm the judgment of the district court. . . .

NOTES

1. In *Johnson v Jones*, 149 F.3d 494 (6th Cir. 1998), the Sixth Circuit Court of Appeals held that *Shaver* and *Effects* did not apply and that there was no implied license given by an architect for the alteration and use of his drawings. The architect had submitted a draft contract that provided that "The drawings, specifications and other documents furnished by the Design/Builder are instruments of service and shall not become the property of the Owner whether or not the project for which they are made is commenced. Drawings, specifications and other documents shall not be used by the Owner on other projects, additions to this project, or . . . for completion of this Project by others, except by written agreement relating to use, liability and compensation."

Although Johnson began work, the client did not sign the contract. Later, Johnson was terminated and the client retained a different architect to complete the project. The new architect (Tosch) claimed that he had an implied license to use the drawings, citing the *Effects* case. The court commented that

> In *Effects*, defendant, a movie-maker, asked plaintiff, a special effects company, to create footage to enhance action sequences in a film defendant was making. Unhappy with the footage provided by plaintiff, defendant paid only half of the expected amount. . . . Subsequently, defendant incorporated plaintiff's footage into the film and released the film to another company for distribution. The *Effects* court held that plaintiff had granted defendant an implied non-exclusive license to incorporate the footage into the film and then distribute the film.

The circumstances in Effects differ materially from those in the present case. [Here] almost every objective fact in the present case points away from the existence of an implied license. Johnson submitted two AIA contracts, both of which contained express provisions that he would retain ownership of his drawings, and that those drawings would not be used for completion of the Jones house by others, except by written agreement with appropriate compensation. These contractual provisions, although never signed by Jones, speak to Johnson's intent; they demonstrate that Johnson created the drawings with the understanding that he would be the architect in charge of the project. They further demonstrate that Johnson would not have allowed Tosch to finish the project using his drawings without a written agreement, and additional compensation. . . .

PROBLEM 7.3

Munn hired Lindner to photograph mirrored picture frames manufactured and offered for sale by Munn. Lindner photographed approximately 130 different frames. Munn and Lindner understood that the photographs would be used as color slides by Munn's sales agents. The invoice submitted by Lindner specified: "Re: Photography of frames. Usage: For C-Prints to be used by sales people." "C-Prints" is shorthand for negative color prints.

Later, Munn used the photographs in a catalogue, reproduced them in 5,000 brochures, and offered them to clients as magazine "comps" or publicity releases. Defendants also provided Lindner's photographs to Photo-2-Art so they could be scanned into a computer for manipulation and displayed to customers.

Lindner sues for infringement. Munn claims that its uses were licensed. What result?

PROBLEM 7.4

Developer is hired to create custom software for Seers to manage inventory at the four hundred Seers stores nationally. The contract is silent about ownership of the software. Seers pays $300,000 for the program. It makes four hundred copies, installing the program in a local computer at each store. After six months, a change in tax laws means that the program must be adjusted. Seers hires Ajax to make the modifications, which are successfully completed. Six months later, Seers decides to modify the program further, to allow it to also manage the accounts receivables. Seers makes the changes using its own programming staff. After learning of this, Developer sues Seers for infringement. Assume that copyright law holds that Developer owns the copyright to the original program. What result on the infringement claim?

III. IMPLIED LICENSE TO PRESERVE INTENT

HILGRAEVE CORP. v. SYMANTEC CORP.
265 F.3d 1336 (Fed. Cir. 2001)

Dyk, Circuit Judge.

Hilgraeve Corp. ("Hilgraeve") appeals from the decision of the United States District Court for the Eastern District of Michigan granting the motion of

Symantec Corp. ("Symantec") for summary judgment of non-infringement for U.S. Patent No. 5,319,776 (" '776 patent"). Symantec cross-appeals the district court's grant of summary judgment for Hilgraeve that Symantec is not licensed to use the invention claimed in the '776 patent. ("License Defense Order").

We vacate the district court's grant of summary judgment of non-infringement of the '776 patent and generally affirm the district court's grant of summary judgment that Symantec did not license the '776 patent. . . .

Background

Hilgraeve filed suit against Symantec [for] infringement of the '776 patent on September 15, 1997. On the same day, Hilgraeve filed a separate suit against McAfee Associates, Inc. for infringement of the '776 patent, also in the Eastern District of Michigan. The cases were not consolidated. In the McAfee case, the district court's grant of summary judgment of non-infringement, *Hilgraeve Corp. v. McAfee Associates, Inc.*, 70 F.Supp.2d 738 (E.D.Mich.1999) ("*McAfee I*"), was vacated and remanded by this court because, under the agreed claim construction, questions of material fact existed about the operation of the accused device, 224 F.3d 1349, 55 USPQ2d 1656 (Fed.Cir.2000) ("*McAfee II*").

The '776 patent relates to computer virus detection software. The software scans a digital data file for viruses as the file is transferred to a storage medium. If the software detects a virus prior to storing the file, it automatically blocks storage of the file. The software may be used, for example, to scan a file for viruses as the file is transferred from a floppy disk to a hard disk of a computer system, or as the file is transferred over the Internet from one computer system to a storage medium of another computer system. . . .

Hilgraeve contended that several Symantec products, including pcANY-WHERE and Norton Antivirus ("NAV"), infringe the '776 patent. [Symantec] contended that its products do not infringe [and] asserted the affirmative defense [that] it had acquired a license to use the patent under a complex series of transactions involving Delrina Corp. and its subsidiaries. On June 30, 1993, Delrina Corp., Delrina (Delaware) (a subsidiary of Delrina Corp.), and Hilgraeve executed a Technology Transfer Agreement under which Delrina Corp. paid Hilgraeve $1.45 million, and Hilgraeve transferred certain rights to its software, allegedly including the technology at issue in this suit, to Delrina (Delaware). The Technology Transfer Agreement states that it is governed by the laws of the Province of Ontario, Canada. On the same day, Delrina (Canada) (also a subsidiary of Delrina Corp.) and Delrina (Delaware) entered into a Software Development and Cost Sharing Agreement (the "SDCS Agreement") to govern the shared development of software by the parties. In July 1995, Symantec acquired Delrina Corp. On March 30, 1996, Delrina (Canada) licensed its intellectual property to Symantec. On March 2, 1999, Delrina (Delaware) entered into an agreement with Symantec to directly transfer rights to the technology transferred by Hilgraeve to Delrina (Delaware) on June 30, 1993.

The district court granted Hilgraeve's motion for summary judgment that Symantec did not have a license to the '776 patent prior to March 2, 1999, because Symantec had failed to establish that Delrina (Delaware) transferred any rights to the '776 patent to Delrina (Canada) or Delrina Corp., and Symantec therefore failed to show that it acquired any rights to the '776 patent through the 1995 acquisition of Delrina Corp. As to events after March 2, 1999, the district court denied both Hilgraeve's and Symantec's motions for summary judgment regarding Symantec's licensing defense, finding that the March 2, 1999, agreement raised a general issue of material fact as to whether Symantec had acquired a license to the '776 patent through the March 2, 1999 agreement. After granting Symantec's motion for summary judgment of non-infringement, the district court denied all other pending motions in the case without prejudice, and dismissed the case.

Discussion

We review the construction of a license agreement without deference and interpret the licensing agreement under the law governing the agreement, here Ontario law. . . .

The district court held that Symantec had no license defense for the period prior to March 2, 1999, because the purported transfer of patent rights from Delrina (Delaware) to Delrina (Canada) under the June 30, 1993 SDCS agreement was ineffective. While the district court appears to have been correct, we believe that there is a more fundamental defect in Symantec's license defense argument. Delrina (Delaware) itself never acquired a transferable license to practice the '776 patent, and Delrina (Delaware) therefore could not sub-license the '776 patent either before March 2, 1999, or thereafter.

Unless the '776 patent was licensed under the June 30, 1993 Agreement, Symantec agrees that it could not acquire a license. Symantec also admits that there is no express language in the June 30, 1993 Technology Transfer Agreement licensing or transferring rights to the '776 patent or any other Hilgraeve patent. Instead, Symantec points to language in the paragraph 2.1 of the Agreement providing that "HILGRAEVE sells, conveys, assigns and transfers to DELRINA DELAWARE and to HILGRAEVE, as joint tenants and not as tenants in common, all copyright rights in the Software," and that Hilgraeve acknowledged in paragraph 9.1 that as part of the transfer "HILGRAEVE has also agreed to transfer the necessary know-how and technical expertise to DELRINA DELAWARE with respect to the Software." On the basis of this language, Symantec urges us to find that:

> "Software" is more than source code and object code. . . . When read in conjunction with the . . . "know-how" and "technical expertise" transferred to Delrina (Delaware), Delrina (Delaware) essentially acquired Hilgraeve's entire knowledge base with respect to [Hilgraeve's] products. Since the Software included in-transit anti-virus features, Delrina acquired Hilgraeve's knowledge base with respect to those in-transit anti-virus features and could use that knowledge base as it pleased.

In summary, Symantec urges us to find that "the Technology Transfer Agreement covered the technology in this case, which is allegedly covered by the '776 Patent."

Whatever the definition of "knowledge base" proposed by Symantec, we cannot conclude that rights to the '776 patent were transferred by the Technology Transfer Agreement. Under Ontario law, "effect must first be given to the intention of the parties, to be gathered from the words they have used. . . ." When the language of a contract is clear and unambiguous, only the contract is considered for interpretation, not extrinsic evidence. Here, the contract provided for Hilgraeve to transfer "all copyright rights in the Software," but failed to mention the transfer of patent rights. From the terms of the contract we cannot conclude that the parties intended to transfer any patent rights. Symantec relies on *Allan v. Bushnell T.V. Co., Ltd.,* 1 D.L.R. (3d) 534, 539 (Ont. High Ct.1968) for the proposition that "unexpressed term[s] [are implied] to implement [the] parties' presumed intention." *Allan,* however, stated that

> the presumption is against the adding to contracts of terms which the parties have not expressed. The general presumption is that the parties have expressed every material term. . . . But . . . there may be cases where obviously some term must be implied if the intention of the parties is not to be defeated, some term of which it can be predicated that "it goes without saying" some term not expressed but necessary to give to the transaction such business efficacy as the parties must have intended.

Allan was a case involving a contract between a broadcasting company and a news service in which the unexpressed term which was implied in the contract was that the news to be supplied to the company by the service had to be "accurate." Here, we cannot say (and it does not "go without saying") that where the contract provided for the transfer of copyrights in the software, but failed to mention the transfer of patent rights, that we must imply such a term to the contract. The contract has a business efficacy without adding this unexpressed term to it.

Moreover, in the subparagraph immediately following the paragraph 2.1 pertaining to the transfer of copyrights, the contract refers to other intellectual property rights. In paragraph 2.2, the parties agreed that Hilgraeve "shall not assert against DELRINA DELAWARE, any other intellectual property right, including patent rights, it has or may have in the future, with respect to the production, copying, licensing of the Software, or the exercise by DELRINA DELAWARE of any rights transferred hereunder." Since the contract specifically mentions patent rights in paragraph 2.2, we cannot say that the omission of mention of patent rights in paragraph 2.1, which transferred rights to copyrights in the Software, was accidental or that the transfer of patent rights is implicit anywhere the contract.

Symantec also contends that the covenant not to sue for patent infringement in paragraph 2.2 is equivalent to a freely transferable license to the patent. This court has stated that "licenses are considered as nothing more than a promise by the licensor not to sue the licensee." The covenant not to sue in paragraph 2.2 does not grant a *transferable* license to the patent.

Conclusion

Therefore, we vacate the district court's grant of summary judgment of non-infringement, generally affirm the district court's grant of summary judgment that Symantec did not license the '776 patent prior (but without limiting our holding to the period before March 2, 1999), and remand for further proceedings consistent with this opinion.

NOTE

Compare *Hilgraeve* to *Amp Inc. v. United States,* 389 F.2d 448 (Ct. Cl. 1968), where the court found an implied license against a licensor who was attempting to "derogate or detract from" a prior express license. In that case, the licensor granted a license with respect to a wire-splicing tool invention as to which it had a patent. Shortly afterward, the licensor discovered an earlier-filed patent covering the same invention. The licensor acquired the rights to this patent and brought suit against the licensee of the other patent, arguing that the original license only related to the patent it had originally obtained, not the patent it had subsequently acquired. The court rejected the attempt to circumvent the arrangement. It found an implied license in favor of a licensee (or assignee) with respect to all patents that a licensor (or assignor) obtained after the original license (or assignment) that would be infringed by the use of the inventions covered by the original license (or assignment). In other words, a licensor cannot "derogate" from its original grant by "subsequent acts."

JACOBS v. NINTENDO OF AMERICA, INC.
370 F.3d 1097 (Fed. Cir. 2004)

BRYSON, CIRCUIT JUDGE.

Patent owner and appellant Jordan Spencer Jacobs terminated a patent infringement lawsuit against Analog Devices, Inc., by entering into a settlement and licensing agreement with Analog. Jacobs later sued appellee Nintendo of America, Inc., for infringing the same patent. As a defense, Nintendo asserted that the settlement agreement between Jacobs and Analog protected not only Analog, but also Analog's customers, including Nintendo, for making and selling devices that incorporated Analog's components. The district court [entered] summary judgment in Nintendo's favor. We affirm.

I

Jacobs owns U.S. Patent No. 5,059,958 ("the '958 patent"), entitled "Manually Held Tilt Sensitive Non-Joystick Control Box." The invention relates to a video game controller that the operator holds in two hands. The operator tilts the controller to achieve corresponding motion in the video game. Before suing Nintendo, Jacobs sued various hardware manufacturers, including Microsoft and Logitech, alleging that they were directly infringing the '958 patent. In the same action, Jacobs named Analog as a defendant, charging Analog with inducement and contributory infringement. Jacobs alleged that Analog provided tilt-sensitive components called accelerometers to the other defendants. Although Jacobs did not allege that Analog's accelerometers infringed the '958 patent, he alleged that the other defendants used those components in their tilt-sensitive control boxes, which allegedly infringed the '958 patent.

In July 2001, Jacobs's case against Analog was dismissed pursuant to a settlement agreement. Two provisions of the agreement are critical here:

> 3. *License.* Jacobs grants Analog an irrevocable, perpetual, fully paid up license to take any actions set forth in 35 U.S.C. § 271 which would, but for this license, constitute an infringement or violation of Jacobs' patent rights under the '958 patent. Without limiting the foregoing, the license granted hereunder includes the right to make, use, sell, import and export components, including micromachined accelerometers, for use in tilt-sensitive control boxes.
>
> . . . .
>
> 5. *Covenant-not-to-sue.* Jacobs covenants not to sue Analog for any alleged infringement or violation of the '958 patent. This covenant-not-to-sue extends to any cause of action having as an element the infringement of the '958 patent by Analog or any other party, whether occurring in the past, present, or in the future.

After the settlement and dismissal of the litigation against Analog, Jacobs filed a patent infringement action against Nintendo. [The] complaint charged Nintendo with infringing or inducing infringement of the '958 patent by producing the game "Kirby Tilt 'n Tumble" for its hand-held Game Boy video game systems. . . .

Nintendo moved for summary judgment of noninfringement, asserting that it was entitled to practice the '958 patent by virtue of the settlement agreement between Jacobs and Analog, the supplier of the accelerometers for the Kirby game. The district court granted Nintendo's motion and entered judgment of noninfringement for Nintendo. The court held that because the settlement agreement between Jacobs and Analog permitted Analog to sell accelerometers for use in tilt-sensitive control boxes, such as the ones manufactured and sold by Nintendo, the agreement necessarily gave Nintendo an implied license to use the Analog accelerometers in its tilt-sensitive control boxes. For Jacobs to bar Analog's customer, Nintendo, from using Analog's accelerometers in the products expressly referred to in the settlement agreement, the court concluded, would undermine the provision of the agreement permitting the sale of accelerometers "for use in tilt-sensitive control boxes." The court explained that Jacobs should not be permitted to do "through the back door — by suing a customer of Analog — what he cannot do through the front door," i.e., by suing Analog.

II

The agreement between Jacobs and Analog granted Analog two important rights: (1) the right not to be sued for infringement of the '958 patent; and (2) the right to "sell . . . micromachined accelerometers for use in tilt-sensitive control boxes." The first right (granted by paragraph 5 of the agreement) provided "peace" by assuring Analog that it would not face any further claims of infringement of the '958 patent based on any of its past or future conduct, including liability for indirect infringement, i.e., a cause of action "having as an element the infringement of the '958 patent by . . . any other party." The second right (granted by paragraph 3 of the agreement) provided "prosperity" by giving Analog a right to sell its accelerometers for a particular use.

Jacobs argues that the settlement agreement protected Analog against being sued for direct or indirect infringement, but that it did not give Nintendo a general right to use Analog's accelerometers in tilt-sensitive control boxes that infringed the '958 patent. Thus, Jacobs contends that paragraph 3 and paragraph 5 of the agreement both secured Analog against the prospect of suit for any of its conduct or any conduct by Analog's customers, but did not grant similar rights to Analog's customers. Nonetheless, Jacobs does not suggest that Nintendo obtained no rights whatsoever from the agreement between Jacobs and Analog. According to Jacobs, paragraph 3 of the agreement would give Nintendo the right to use Analog's accelerometers in infringing control boxes if it could prove that Analog's accelerometers had no noninfringing uses. In that event, according to Jacobs, the Analog-Jacobs agreement would give Nintendo an implied license to use those accelerometers without liability under the '958 patent, because otherwise the license to sell the accelerometers would be of no commercial benefit to Analog. Jacobs contends, however, that in the absence of proof that the accelerometers had no noninfringing uses, paragraph 3 provides no protection to Nintendo against an action for infringement of the '958 patent based on Nintendo's manufacture and sale of its tilt-sensitive control boxes.

In pressing its argument that Nintendo has an implied license only if it can establish that Analog's accelerometers had no noninfringing uses, Jacobs relies on this court's decision in *Met-Coil Systems Corp. v. Korners Unlimited, Inc.,* 803 F.2d 684, 686 (Fed.Cir.1986). In *Met-Coil,* this court held that a patent owner's sale of a machine useful only in practicing the claimed invention "plainly indicate[d] that the grant of a license [to practice the invention] should be inferred." Because there were no circumstances tending to show the contrary, this court upheld the district court's conclusion that the patent owner's customers enjoyed an implied license under the patent.

The requirement of demonstrating that there is no noninfringing use for the object in question does not apply in the context of this case. The "noninfringing use" doctrine applies when a patentee or its licensee sells an article and the question is whether the sale carries with it a license to engage in conduct that would infringe the patent owner's rights. In that setting, absent an express agreement between the parties, determining whether the sale conveys with it the implied right to use the article in an infringing manner may depend on whether there is any noninfringing use for the article. If there is no noninfringing use, it may be reasonable to infer that there has been "a relinquishment of the patent monopoly with respect to the article sold." *United States v. Univis Lens Co.,* 316 U.S. 241, 249 (1942). In such a case, unless the circumstances of the sale indicate that a grant of a license should not be inferred, the patentee will be barred from asserting its patent rights against a downstream purchaser of the article.

This case is quite different. Here, there is no need to ask whether Analog was authorized to sell its accelerometers to be used in infringing devices, because the Jacobs-Analog agreement must be understood to authorize Analog to sell its accelerometers for such uses.

Jacobs's patent does not, of course, limit anyone's right to make either non-infringing devices or components for noninfringing devices. Therefore, the second sentence of paragraph 3 of the Jacobs-Analog settlement agreement, which authorizes Analog to make and sell accelerometers for use in tilt-sensitive control boxes, makes sense only if it is understood to confer on Analog the right to make and sell accelerometers for use in tilt-sensitive control boxes that would otherwise infringe Jacobs's rights under the '958 patent. For that reason, the question whether there is any noninfringing use for Analog's accelerometers is irrelevant here. The Jacobs-Analog agreement has specifically authorized the sale of those accelerometers for infringing uses. The critical question, then, is whether the clause authorizing that use protects Nintendo against suit based on the use of the accelerometers for the purposes for which Analog was authorized to sell them.

The district court held that the right given to Analog to sell its accelerometers for use in infringing tilt-sensitive control boxes would be meaningless if Jacobs could effectively prevent Analog from making any such sales by suing Analog's customers for putting the accelerometers into infringing control boxes and selling the resulting products. We agree with the district court that the clause granting Analog the right to sell its accelerometers for use in tilt-sensitive control boxes barred Jacobs from interfering with that right by prohibiting Analog's customers from using the accelerometers for that authorized purpose by making, using, and selling control boxes incorporating Analog's devices. That interpretation is in accordance with the basic contract law principle that a party may not assign a right, receive consideration for it, and then take steps that would render the right commercially worthless.

Jacobs urges us to interpret paragraph 3 of the Jacobs-Analog agreement as granting Analog only a bare license, i.e., the right not to be sued for making, using, or selling accelerometers for use in tilt-sensitive control boxes. To interpret paragraph 3 as a bare license, however, would ignore the language of the second sentence of paragraph 3 that goes beyond the creation of a license (conveying the right to make and sell accelerometers "for use in tilt-sensitive control boxes"). In addition, it would make paragraph 3 entirely redundant, because paragraph 5 already ensures Analog freedom from suit "for any alleged infringement or violation of the '958 patent." If all that Jacobs intended to do through the settlement agreement was to free Analog of its liability for infringement, paragraph 5 of the agreement (the covenant not to sue) would have been fully sufficient to serve that purpose. Paragraph 3, however, goes much further by granting Analog an affirmative right to engage in the manufacture and sale of accelerometers to be used in tilt-sensitive control boxes. That grant comes without restriction of any kind.

Jacobs seeks to explain the license granted in paragraph 3 by characterizing it as giving Analog the right to make and sell infringing control boxes on its own or, alternatively, as ensuring that Analog would be free to sell accelerometers to whomever it wanted for use in infringing control boxes, but not protecting Analog's customers from suit for making and selling those boxes. Neither explanation is plausible, however. Jacobs knew that Analog was not in the business of making game controllers, so there is no reason to believe Analog would have bargained for that right. Furthermore, as the district court noted, it is unlikely that Analog would have contracted for the right to manufacture and sell a product knowing that its customers would be unable to use the product that it sold them for the bargained-for purpose. Thus, we agree with the district court that the Jacobs-Analog settlement agreement grants to Analog's customers an implied sublicense to use Analog's accelerometers to make, use, and sell tilt-sensitive control boxes that infringe the '958 patent without interference by Jacobs. The district court therefore properly held that Jacobs was barred from suing Nintendo for infringement of the '958 patent based on Nintendo's manufacture and sale of tilt-sensitive control boxes that incorporated Analog's accelerometers. *AFFIRMED.*

NOTES

1. Although the court refers to an implied license, is its analysis any different from an ordinary contract interpretation analysis — i.e., an analysis designed to interpret the meaning of the express terms of the contract? Is it useful to treat some interpretation questions as implied license issues?

2. Recall Judge Kozinski's discussion in *Foad*. What law governs the implied license analysis in *Jacobs* (state or federal)? Is this a contract law issue of interpreting the parties' intent?

PROBLEM 7.5

Patent Owner grants a license to ABC Corporation to "sell and offer to sell" machines described in Patent Owner's '912 patent. ABC, which is an integrated electronics company that operates manufacturing, wholesale and retail divisions, proceeds to manufacture the machines and to advertise them for sale. Patent Owner sues for infringement. ABC defends based on its license. The evidence relating to the negotiation of the license is unclear about the intended scope of the agreement.

a. What result? Would the result change if the license contained a merger clause indicating that no promises or representations other than those in the written agreement are part of the contract?

b. Would your answers to (a) change if ABC were merely a retail distributor that previously lacked any manufacturing capability?

PROBLEM 7.6

Developer agrees to create software for use by Client Corporation in the large communications systems that it manufactures and sells to third parties. Client will receive an irrevocable license to "copy and distribute the program in its systems" in return for a payment of $1 million. All of Developer's programs are copyrighted. During development of this program, Developer discovers a unique processing approach. It obtains a patent on this discovery after completing the project with Client. Six weeks after the patent is issued, Developer sues Client for patent infringement for selling copies of its patented process. What result?

IV. IMPLIED LICENSES ASSOCIATED WITH SALES

Unless the parties provide otherwise, the purchaser of a patented article has an implied license not only to use and sell it, but also to repair it to enable it to function properly. . . . This implied license covers both the original purchaser of the article and all subsequent purchasers.

Bottom Line Management Inc. v. Pan Man Inc., 228 F.3d 1352, XXXX (Fed. Cir. 2000).

MET-COIL SYSTEMS
CORP. v. KORNERS UNLIMITED, INC.
803 F.2d 684 (Fed. Cir. 1986)

NIES, CIRCUIT JUDGE.

The determinative issue in this appeal is whether a patent owner's unrestricted sale of a machine useful only in practicing the claimed inventions presumptively carries with it an implied license under the patent. The United States District Court for the Western District of Pennsylvania decided that legal issue in the affirmative. We affirm.

I.

Met-Coil Systems Corp. is the assignee of U.S. Patent No. 4,466,641, which claims an apparatus and method for connecting sections of metal ducts of the kind used in heating and air conditioning systems. Under the claimed inventions, the ends of the metal duct sections are bent to form integral flanges, specially shaped corner pieces are snapped in place, and the sections are bolted together. Met-Coil makes and sells roll-forming machines that its customers use to bend integral flanges in the ends of metal ducts so as to practice the claimed inventions. Met-Coil also sells the specially shaped corner pieces for use with the integral flanges. Korners Unlimited, Inc. makes corner pieces for use with Met-Coil's integral flanges and sells them to purchasers of Met-Coil's machines. Met-Coil sued Korners for inducing infringement of claims 1-12, 14-25 of its patent. Korners moved for summary judgment. . . .

The basis of Korners' motion for summary judgment was that Met-Coil, by selling the roll-forming machine, granted an implied license under the patent to its customers. Because of that license, Korners contended, Met-Coil's customers cannot infringe the claims of the patent and, thus, Korners can neither induce infringement nor contributorily infringe. Met-Coil, on the other hand, contended that its sales of the machines do not confer an implied license under the patent upon its customers.

II.

The district court recognized that "the integral flanges are an essential part of Met-Coil's patented duct connecting system" and that the "flanges have no use other than in the practice of the duct connecting system." Applying the holding of *United States v. Univis Lens Co.,* 316 U.S. 241 (1942), to those facts, the court held that purchasers of Met-Coil's machines enjoyed an implied license under the patent.

In *Univis*, the patent covered multifocal eyeglass lenses, and the patent owner sold blank eyeglass lenses to its licensees. The Court held that the sale of the blanks carried a license to complete the lenses:

> But in the case it is plain that where the sale of the blank is by the patentee or his licensee — here the Lens Company — to a finisher, the only use to which it could be put and the only object of the sale is to enable the latter to grind and polish it for use as a lens by the prospective wearer. An incident to the purchase of any article, whether patented or unpatented, is the right to use and sell it, and upon familiar principles the authorized sale of an article which is capable of use only in practicing the patent is a relinquishment of the patent monopoly with respect to the article sold. Sale of a lens blank by the patentee or by his licensee is thus in itself both a complete transfer of ownership of the blank, which is within the protection of the patent law, and a license to practice the final stage of the patent procedure. . . . Where one has sold an uncompleted article which, because it embodies essential features of his patented invention, is within the protection of his patented invention, and has destined the article to be finished by the purchaser in conformity to the patent, he has sold his invention so far as it is or may be embodied in that particular article. The reward he has demanded and received is for the article and the invention which it embodies and which his vendee is to practice upon it.

316 U.S. at 249-51. The trial court recognized that *Univis* was factually distinct from the instant case, but found the distinction to be of no effect:

> It should be noted, however, that unlike *Univis* . . . , the practice of the final stage of Met-Coil's patented system requires not just "finishing" the element sold, i.e. forming the integral flanges, but also the purchase of an additional element of the patented system, i.e. the corner pieces. Met-Coil cites no authority which suggests that this difference takes the present case out of the rule of *Univis*.

628 F. Supp. at 133. Met-Coil appealed the district court's judgment of noninfringement to this court.

III.

On appeal, Met-Coil urges that the district court erred in relying on *Univis*. To support that proposition, Met-Coil cites *Bandag, Inc. v. Al Bolser's Tire Stores, Inc.*, 750 F.2d 903 (Fed. Cir. 1984). In that case, the owner of a patent claiming a method for retreading tires sued a retreader who had purchased retreading equipment from a former licensee of the patent owner. This court set out two requirements for the grant of an implied license by virtue of a sale of nonpatented equipment used to practice a patented invention. First, the equipment involved must have no noninfringing uses. In *Bandag*, the retreading equipment had noninfringing uses, so no license could be implied. To the contrary, Met-Coil's machines have no noninfringing use. Second, the circumstances of the sale must "plainly indicate that the grant of a license should be inferred." The circumstances of the sale in *Bandag*, purchase of the equipment from the former licensee of the patent owner, did not plainly indicate that the grant of a license should be inferred.

Met-Coil contends that this case does not meet the two-part test set out in *Bandag*, that is, although the machines sold have no noninfringing use, the circumstances do not plainly indicate that the grant of a license should be inferred. In this connection Met-Coil introduced certain written notices to customers with respect to the purchase of corner pieces from unlicensed sources. Met-Coil relies on cases holding that no implied license arises where the original sale was accompanied by an express notice negating the grant of an implied license. Those cases, however, are inapposite. Met-Coil does not assert that its customers were notified at the time of the sale of the machine. Rather, the customers were notified after they purchased the machine. The subsequent notices are not a part of the circumstances at the time of the sale, when the implied license would have arisen. After the fact notices are of no use in ascertaining the intent of Met-Coil and its customers at the time of the sales.

Met-Coil urges that, even though it has not shown that the sales were accompanied by an express disclaimer of license, Korners has not met its burden of proof. As the alleged infringer, Korners has the burden of showing the establishment of an implied license. We agree with the district court that Korners met that burden. A patent owner's unrestricted sales of a machine useful only in performing the claimed process and producing the claimed product "plainly indicate that the grant of a license should be inferred." Korners established a prima facie case, thereby shifting the burden of going forward to Met-Coil. Met-Coil offered nothing to carry its burden. Absent any circumstances tending to show the contrary, we see no error in the district court's holding that Met-Coil's customers enjoyed an implied license under the patent.

The sole disputed issue decided by the trial court, the existence of an implied license, is a question of law. The parties raised no genuine issue of material fact. Because of our affirmance of the district court's holding that Met-Coil's customers enjoyed an implied license to practice the inventions claimed in Met-Coil's patent, there can be no direct infringement under the facts of this case. Absent direct infringement of the patent claims, there can be neither contributory infringement nor inducement of infringement. Therefore, Korners was entitled to summary judgment of noninfringement as a matter of law. Accordingly, we affirm the judgment of the district court.

ANTON/BAUER, INC. v. PAG, LTD.
329 F.3d 1343 (Fed. Cir. 2003)

SCHALL, CIRCUIT JUDGE.

On April 10, 2001, Anton/Bauer, Inc. ("Anton/Bauer") filed suit against PAG, Ltd. (PAG) [alleging infringement] of United States Patent No. 4,810,204 entitled "Battery Pack Connection" (the '204 patent). Integral to the combination claimed in the '204 patent are a male and a female plate. . . .

After filing suit, Anton/Bauer moved for a preliminary injunction enjoining PAG from making, offering to sell, and holding itself out as authorized to sell the accused device, the PAG L75 battery pack. On June 12, 2002, the district court granted the motion. . . . PAG now appeals the district court's grant of the preliminary injunction to Anton/Bauer.

We conclude that [the] district court erred as a matter of law when it held that Anton/Bauer had not granted purchasers of its female plate an implied license to practice the invention claimed in the '204 patent. Operating under an implied license, those purchasers could not, as a matter of law, directly infringe the '204 patent. Absent direct infringement, PAG could not be held to have induced infringement under 35 U.S.C. §271(b) or to have contributed to infringement under 35 U.S.C. §271(c). [We] reverse.

I.

Anton/Bauer manufactures and sells a wide variety of batteries and chargers used in video production. The batteries typically require a device that will allow them to be connected mechanically and electrically to a video camera or to a battery charger and then to be released from the camera or charger. Anton/Bauer created various devices that connect batteries to chargers and to video production devices, such as professional video cameras. In March of 1989, Anton/Bauer obtained the '204 patent. The invention claimed in the patent is directed to a battery pack connection that allows a battery pack to be "quickly and efficiently replaced upon discharge of the batteries." Each claim in the '204 patent recites a combination of a female plate and a male plate, where the female plate contains a plurality of keyholes or slots and the male plate contains a plurality of projections that correspond to the female keyholes or slots. Each claim further requires a "releasable locking means." The claimed combination is formed when a female plate and a male plate are fitted together to form a mechanical and an electrical connection. . . . Generally, the claimed connection joins a battery pack to a television camera, where the female plate is attached to the camera or other electrically operated device, such as a battery charger, and the male plate is attached to the housing of a battery pack within which an electrical battery or AC/DC power source is contained. No claim in the '204 patent separately covers the male plate or the female plate.

II.

Anton/Bauer manufactures and sells both female plates and battery packs containing male plates. Instead of selling the combination of female plate and male plate as claimed in the '204 patent, however, it sells its female plates directly to members of the portable television video camera industry. The female plates are, in turn, attached to commercial portable television video cameras manufactured by Sony, Philips, JVC, and other video camera manufacturers. The camera manufacturer then sells the camera, with the female plate incorporated, to the public. Anton/Bauer also sells female plates directly to end-users as an after-market product. Anton/Bauer's female plates are designed exclusively for use in the combination claimed in the '204 patent, and it is undisputed that their use in that combination is their sole use. It is also undisputed that when Anton/Bauer sells its female plate, it does not place any restrictions on the customer's use of the plate.

Anton/Bauer also manufactures and sells battery packs, which have housings that contain Anton/Bauer's male plates. Typically, the male and female plates are not sold together. Although they may, in some instances, be sold at the same time to the same purchaser, they are always sold as separate products.

The PAG L75 battery pack can also be used in combination with Anton/Bauer's female plates. The housing of the PAG L75 battery pack contains a male plate, which allows the battery pack to be connected to the Anton/Bauer female plate. PAG began selling its battery pack in the United States in April of 2000. PAG does not, however, make, use, or sell any female plate in the United States with a "releasable locking means on said female plate," a limitation of the '204 patent claims. . . .

Analysis

We turn first to Anton/Bauer's likelihood of success on the merits of its infringement claims. The district court found that Anton/Bauer would likely succeed in proving inducement of infringement and contributory infringement by PAG and that Anton/Bauer would likely prevail over PAG's defenses. [Anton/Bauer] alleges that PAG actively induces Anton/Bauer's customers to infringe the '204 patent by selling the PAG L75 battery pack for use with Anton/Bauer's female plate and by urging end-users to employ the battery pack with Anton/Bauer's female plate. Anton/Bauer alleges that end-users of PAG's L75 battery pack infringe the '204 patent when they use the battery pack together with Anton/Bauer's female plates, thereby making the combination claimed in the '204 patent.

Under 35 U.S.C. § 271(c):

> Whoever offers to sell or sells within the United States or imports into the United States a component of a patented machine, manufacture, combination or composition, or a material or apparatus for use in practicing a patented process, constituting a material part of the invention, knowing the same to be especially made or especially adapted for use in an infringement of such patent, and not a staple article or commodity of commerce suitable for substantial noninfringing use, shall be liable as a contributory infringer.

35 U.S.C. § 271(c). Anton/Bauer alleges that PAG contributes to the infringement of Anton/Bauer's '204 patent by selling the non-staple PAG L75 battery pack, which it argues is not suitable for any substantial noninfringing uses.

In order to succeed on its claims of inducement of infringement and contributory infringement, Anton/Bauer must prove that its own customers directly infringe the '204 patent when they use PAG's accused PAG L75 battery pack in combination with its female plate. Accordingly, we must determine whether Anton/Bauer's customers directly infringe the '204 patent.

[PAG] does not dispute the scope of the '204 patent's claims; neither does it dispute that its accused PAG L75 battery pack, when used in combination with Anton/Bauer's female plate, results in a connection that literally infringes the '204 patent. Rather, as it did before the district court, PAG argues that Anton/Bauer's customers do not directly infringe the '204 patent because they are protected by the exhaustion doctrine and by an implied license, and, if it applies, by the doctrine of permissible repair. For purposes of this appeal, we assume, without deciding, that Anton/Bauer's customers create a combination encompassed by the '204 patent claims when they place PAG's accused PAG L75 battery pack in combination with Anton/Bauer's female plate.

The exhaustion doctrine is based upon the proposition that "[t]he unrestricted sale of a patented article, by or with the authority of the patentee, 'exhausts' the patentee's right to control further sale and use of that article by enforcing the *patent* under which it was first sold." *Jazz Photo Corp. v. Int'l Trade Comm'n*, 264 F.3d 1094, 1105 (Fed. Cir. 2001). The Supreme Court enunciated this doctrine when it stated that "incident to the purchase of any article, whether patented or unpatented, is the right to use and sell it, and upon familiar principles the authorized sale of an article which is capable of use only in practicing the patent is a relinquishment of the patent monopoly with respect to the article sold." *United States v. Univis Lens Co.*, 316 U.S. 241 (1942). In other words, sale of an unpatented article exhausts the seller's right to control the future sale and use of that article, but only certain circumstances exhaust the seller's patent right and result in an implied license. In *Univis*, which involved a patent covering lens blanks and the process of grinding and polishing them, the Court determined that the "[s]ale of a lens blank by the patentee or by his licensee is thus in itself both a complete transfer of ownership of the blank, which is within the protection of the patent law, and a license to practice the final stage of the patent procedure." The Court's statements in *Univis* demonstrate how closely related the exhaustion doctrine is to the grant of an implied license. Indeed, they suggest that an implied license stems from the exhaustion of a patent right.

At the same time, it is well settled that all or part of a patentee's right to exclude others from making, using, or selling a patented invention may be waived by granting a license, which may be express or implied. A patentee grants an implied license to a purchaser when (1) the patentee sells an article that has no noninfringing uses and (2) the circumstances of the sale plainly indicate that the grant of a license should be inferred. *Met-Coil*, 803 F.3d at 686. An implied license is a defense to patent infringement. Therefore, if Anton/Bauer's customers have an implied license to practice the patented combination, they cannot infringe the '204 patent, and PAG cannot be liable for either inducement of infringement or contributory infringement.

The district court concluded that Anton/Bauer does not grant an implied license to its customers to use the '204 patent's combination. The court based its decision on its finding that the PAG L75 battery pack is not a "replacement" for any component of the mechanical and electrical combination claimed in the '204 patent. The court also found that the circumstances do not indicate that an implied license is granted to Anton/Bauer's customers to practice the '204 patented combination with a male plate from a company other than the patentee. While the court acknowledged that Anton/Bauer does not expressly deny a license, it concluded that Anton/Bauer's actions do not lead a consumer to believe that it may use a non-Anton/Bauer male plate to complete the patented combination.

PAG argues that the district court improperly applied the implied license test laid out in *Met-Coil*. It claims that the court erred by requiring that the accused battery pack be a replacement for an element of the claimed combination and by requiring a showing of affirmative acts on the part of Anton/Bauer that would lead a customer to believe that an implied license had in fact been granted. PAG maintains that the requirements for an implied license are met in this case. Specifically, PAG argues that there are no noninfringing uses for Anton/Bauer's female plate and that the circumstances surrounding sales of the female plate make it clear that an implied license is granted to Anton/Bauer's customers. According to PAG, Anton/Bauer's sales of its female plate are authorized sales of an unpatented part with no express restriction. Pointing out that Anton/Bauer's female plate is useful only in completing the claimed combination, PAG contends that Anton/Bauer exhausts its patent rights with respect to the plates it sells and grants its customers an implied license to practice the combination claimed in the '204 patent. Anton/Bauer responds that an implied license only arises when its female plate and male plate are sold together and that if a consumer buys the PAG L75 battery pack first and then buys a female plate, an implied license does not arise. Anton/Bauer also argues that the patent right cannot be exhausted before the end of the useful life of the components in the combination.

The sale of the unpatented female plate by Anton/Bauer is a complete transfer of the ownership of the plate. In effect, the sale extinguishes Anton/Bauer's right to control the use of the plate, because the plate can only be used in the patented combination and the combination must be completed by the purchaser. "[W]here one has sold an uncompleted article which, because it embodies essential features of his patented invention, is within the protection of his patent, and has destined the article to be finished by the purchaser in conformity to the patent, he has sold his invention so far as it is or may be embodied in that particular article." *Univis,* 316 U.S. at 251.

We must determine whether there are noninfringing uses of the female plate sold by Anton/Bauer and whether circumstances surrounding sales of the plate suggest that a license is implied. PAG and Anton/Bauer agree that there are no noninfringing uses of the female plate sold by Anton/Bauer. Thus, Anton/Bauer places on the market one component of a patented combination that has no other use than to complete the patent combination with a second unpatented component.

With regard to the circumstances of sale, sales of the female plate are authorized sales to Anton/Bauer's customers, and there is no evidence that Anton/Bauer places express restrictions on the use of the female plates it sells or that it requires that manufacturers to whom it sells female plates expressly restrict the grant of a license upon sale of the finished camera product that incorporates the plate. We hold that, by the unrestricted sale of the female plate, Anton/Bauer grants an implied license to its customers to employ the combination claimed in the '204 patent. Accordingly, there is no direct infringement to support a claim of either inducement of infringement or contributory infringement.

We think this case is controlled by *Met-Coil.* There, the patent at issue claimed an apparatus and a method for connecting sections of metal ducts with integral flanges. Met-Coil made and sold roll-forming machines that its customers used to bend integral flanges in the ends of the metal ducts so as to practice the claimed invention. Met-Coil also sold special shaped corner pieces for use with the integral flanges. Met-Coil sued a manufacturer who made and sold to Met-Coil's customers specially shaped corner pieces for use with the integral flanges. The parties agreed that there were no noninfringing uses of the machine sold by Met-Coil. This court held that Met-Coil's unrestricted sales of the machines, useful only in performing the claimed process and producing the claimed apparatus, "plainly indicate that the grant of a license should be inferred." The circumstances present here are similar. Anton/Bauer's unrestricted sale of its female plate, useful only in performing the claimed combination, plainly indicates that the grant of a license to practice the invention should be inferred. If the original purchaser is a manufacturer, then the implied license is passed on to the customer when the customer buys the camera with the female plate from the manufacturer.

Anton/Bauer relies on *Carborundum* [*Co. v. Molten Metal Equip. Innovations, Inc.*, 72 F.3d 872, 876 n.4, 37 USPQ2d 1169, 1177 n.4 (Fed. Cir. 1995),] for the proposition that an implied license only arises when the male plate being replaced has worn out or been broken. We do not think that *Carborundum* helps Anton/Bauer, however. In *Carborundum*, the patentee sold an unpatented pump, whose only use was in the patented combination. We concluded that, under these circumstances, the patentee's customers were free to complete the patented combination with parts obtained from any source because the sale of the pump granted an implied license for the life of the pump. Similarly, absent circumstances indicating otherwise, Anton/Bauer's sale of the female plate grants an implied license to practice the combination claimed in the '204 patent to its customers for the life of the plate. Anton/Bauer confuses the doctrine of implied license with the doctrine of permissible repair. Anton/Bauer's assertion that its male plate will not become worn out during the life of the female plate and that PAG's accused PAG L75 battery pack is not a replacement for any item of the patented combination is immaterial for the purposes of determining whether a license should be implied.

We also are not persuaded by Anton/Bauer's argument that an implied license does not arise if a consumer purchases the PAG L75 battery pack before the consumer obtains Anton/Bauer's female plate. Indisputably, no license is granted to use the patented combination upon purchase of the PAG L75 battery pack and no infringement by PAG occurs due to the sale. However, when a female plate is purchased from Anton/Bauer, the purchaser receives an implied license to practice the claimed invention for the life of the female plate, regardless of when a male plate is acquired. Moreover, the fact that Anton/Bauer sells the second half of the combination, i.e. the male plates, does not, without more, suggest that Anton/Bauer did not intend to grant an implied license. In sum, we conclude that Anton/Bauer's customers have an implied license to practice the patented combination during the life of the female plate purchased from Anton/Bauer. Accordingly, they do not directly infringe the '204 patent, a necessary predicate for Anton/Bauer to establish inducement of infringement and contributory infringement against PAG.

As in *Carborundum*, different facts may have led to a different result. Anton/Bauer could have, if novel, claimed its female plate and male plate individually in the '204 patent in order to improve its protection of its invention. If the male component were patented, PAG would potentially be liable as a direct infringer by manufacturing the part itself, avoiding the question of infringement by the patentee's customers. Moreover, Anton/Bauer had the option of selling its female and male plates together as the patented combination in order to receive compensation for the invention claimed in the patent.

Finally, the determination that an implied license is present here does not, as Anton/Bauer argues, obviate the applicability of contributory infringement in every case. Rather, it merely limits a patentee's ability to assert contributory infringement where the patentee has chosen to sell part, but not all, of its patented combination. It is the involvement of the patentee in this case that saves PAG from being a contributory infringer. We therefore conclude that Anton/Bauer will not likely succeed on the merits of its claims of inducement of infringement or contributory infringement. . . .

The district court erred in its application of the doctrine of implied license, resulting in an erroneous conclusion of a likelihood of success on the merits of infringement. Under these circumstances, the district court abused its discretion in granting a preliminary injunction. The decision of the court is therefore reversed.

NOTES

1. One court described the difference between implied license and patent exhaustion doctrine in the following way:

> The patent exhaustion doctrine (also known as the "first sale rule") is derived from the statutory grant of exclusivity to the patentee. Once a patentee abandons its statutory right to exclusivity through the sale of a patented product or the license of the patent itself, there is no statutory basis for the patentee to impose restrictions or secure royalties on the subsequent use of the invention. . . . When a patentee has sold "the thing patented," he has exhausted his right to exclusivity in the invention. . . . The implied license doctrine, on the other hand, derives not from statute, but from principles of equity. . . . In some circumstances, therefore, although a patent may not be exhausted such that the patentee has abandoned its statutory right to exclude, the patentee may, through its own conduct, grant an implied license to practice the patent to certain downstream purchasers. Principles of equity determine whether the patentee's conduct has created such a license. "A mere sale does not import a license except where the circumstances plainly indicate that the grant of a license should be inferred." . . . In sum, the patent exhaustion doctrine applies when a patentee has, in essence, sold its statutory right to exclusivity through the unrestricted sale or license of the patent. A patentee who has not abandoned its statutory right to exclude others from the use of its patent may nevertheless, through conduct that induces reliance, grant to particular parties an implied license to practice the patent. Although similar in effect, the doctrines require distinct analysis. To determine if a patent was exhausted, the court must assess whether the terms of the patentee's sale remove the invention from the protection of the patent law. The determination of whether an implied license exists, however, is necessarily more fact specific. The court must determine whether the patentee's acts led the accused infringer to believe it had acquired the right to practice the patented invention.

LG Electronics Inc. v. Asustek Computer Inc., 2002 u. s. Dist. Lexis 25956, *8 — 11 (N.D. Cal. 2002).

2. Does the authorized sale of a product that has no use other than in an infringing product or process create patent exhaustion or an implied license? If it is an implied license, what are the preconditions for implying the license? For example, what if a product or part is typically used in connection with a patented machine, but does have a limited number of other uses? Is there still a basis to imply a license? Does it matter whether or not the other uses are commercially viable?

PROBLEM 7.7

Micron holds patents related to a configuration of parts that includes a microprocessor manufactured by Micron. The microprocessor is not itself patented. Micron sells a large quantity of the microprocessors each month. For six months, IBM manufactures its own computers with these microprocessors, using the patented Micron configuration pursuant to a license from Micron. The license expires, but IBM continues to purchase Micron microprocessors and uses them in the patented Micron configuration. Micron sues for patent infringement. What result if the following can be proven:

a. The Micron processors are not used in any other computer in the marketplace because they are specially designed for the Micron configuration.

b. The processors could be modified by a buyer and would then be useful in other, non-patented configurations, but this would increase the cost.

c. The Micron configuration is subject to a U.S. patent, but the processors could be used in other countries as part of the Micron configuration because Micron has no patents outside the U.S.

d. The processors can be used as replacement parts in systems that have the Micron configuration and have previously been sold. Assume that the replacement part use would not infringe the patent.

JAZZ PHOTO CORP. v. INTERNATIONAL TRADE COMMISSION
264 F.3d 1094 (Fed. Cir. 2001)

Newman, J.

In an action brought under section 337 of the Tariff Act of 1930 as amended, Fuji Photo Film Co. charged twenty-seven respondents, including the appellants Jazz Photo Corporation, Dynatec International, Inc., and Opticolor, Inc., with infringement of fifteen patents owned by Fuji. The charge was based on the respondents' importation of used "single-use" cameras called "lens-fitted film packages" (LFFP's), which had been refurbished for reuse in various overseas facilities. Section 337 makes unlawful "[t]he importation into the United States . . . of articles that . . . infringe a valid and enforceable United States patent . . . [or that] are made, produced, processed, . . . under, or by means of, a process covered by the claims of a valid and enforceable United States patent." Eight respondents did not respond to the Commission's complaint, ten more failed to appear before the Commission, and one was dismissed. Eight respondents participated in the hearing, and three have taken this appeal.

The Commission determined that twenty-six respondents, including the appellants, had infringed all or most of the claims in suit of fourteen Fuji United States patents, and issued a General Exclusion Order and Order to Cease and Desist. This court stayed the Commission's orders during this appeal.

The Commission's decision rests on its ruling that the refurbishment of the used cameras is prohibited "reconstruction," as opposed to permissible "repair." On review of the law and its application, we conclude that precedent does not support the Commission's application of the law to the facts that were found. We conclude that for used cameras whose first sale was in the United States with the patentee's authorization, and for which the respondents permitted verification of their representations that their activities were limited to the steps of (1) removing the cardboard cover, (2) cutting open the plastic casing, (3) inserting new film and a container to receive the film, (4) replacing the winding wheel for certain cameras, (5) replacing the battery for flash cameras, (6) resetting the counter, (7) resealing the outer case, and (8) adding a new cardboard cover, the totality of these procedures does not satisfy the standards required by precedent for prohibited reconstruction; precedent requires, as we shall discuss, that the described activities be deemed to be permissible repair.

For those cameras that meet the criteria outlined above, the Commission's ruling of patent infringement is reversed and the Commission's exclusion and cease and desist orders are vacated. For all other cameras, the Commission's orders are affirmed.

The Patented Inventions

The LFFP is a relatively simple camera, whose major elements are an outer plastic casing that holds a shutter, a shutter release button, a lens, a viewfinder, a film advance mechanism, a film counting display, and for some models a flash assembly and battery. The casing also contains a holder for a roll of film, and a container into which the exposed film is wound. At the factory a roll of film is loaded into the camera. The casing is then sealed by ultrasonic welding or light-tight latching, and a cardboard cover is applied to encase the camera.

LFFPs are intended by the patentee to be used only once. After the film is exposed the photo-processor removes the film container by breaking open a pre-weakened portion of the plastic casing which is accessed by removal of the cardboard cover. Discarded LFFPs, subsequently purchased and refurbished by the respondents, are the subject of this action. . . .

The Law of Permissible Repair and Prohibited Reconstruction

The distinction between permitted and prohibited activities, with respect to patented items after they have been placed in commerce by the patentee, has been distilled into the terms "repair" and "reconstruction." The purchaser of a patented article has the rights of any owner of personal property, including the right to use it, repair it, modify it, discard it, or resell it, subject only to overriding conditions of the sale. Thus patented articles when sold "become the private individual property of the purchasers, and are no longer specifically protected by the patent laws." The fact that an article is patented gives the purchaser neither more nor less rights of use and disposition. However, the rights of ownership do not include the right to construct an essentially new article on the template of the original, for the right to make the article remains with the patentee.

While the ownership of a patented article does not include the right to make a substantially new article, it does include the right to preserve the useful life of the original article. It is readily apparent that there is a continuum between these concepts; precedent demonstrates that litigated cases rarely reside at the poles wherein "repair" is readily distinguished from "reconstruction." Thus the law has developed in the body of precedent, illustrating the policy underlying the law as it has been applied in diverse factual contexts.

The principle of the distinction between permissible and prohibited activities was explained in *Wilson v. Simpson*, 50 U.S. (9 How.) 109 (1850), where the Court distinguished the right of a purchaser of a patented planing machine to replace the machine's cutting-knives when they became dull or broken, from the patentee's sole right to make or renew the entire machine. The Court observed that the knives had to be replaced every 60-90 days whereas the machines would last for several years, explaining, "what harm is done to the patentee in the use of his right of invention, when the repair and replacement of a partial injury are confined to the machine which the purchaser has bought?"

This principle underlies the application of the law. It was elaborated by the Court in *Aro Manufacturing Co. v. Convertible Top Replacement Co.*, 365 U.S. 336 (1961), where the patented combination was a fabric convertible top and the associated metal support structure. The Court explained that replacement of the worn fabric top constituted permissible repair of the patented combination, and could not be controlled by the patentee. The Court restated the principles that govern the inquiry as applied to replacement of unpatented parts of a patented article:

> The decisions of this Court require the conclusion that reconstruction of a patented entity, comprised of unpatented elements, is limited to such a true reconstruction of the entity as to "in fact make a new article," after the entity, viewed as a whole, has become spent. In order to call the monopoly, conferred by the patent grant, into play for a second time, it must, indeed, be a second creation of the patented entity. . . . Mere replacement of individual unpatented parts, one at a time, whether of the same part repeatedly or different parts successively, is no more than the lawful right of the owner to repair his property.

365 U.S. at 346.

This right of repair, provided that the activity does not "in fact make a new article," accompanies the article to succeeding owners. In *Wilbur-Ellis Co. v. Kuther*, 377 U.S. 422 (1964), the Court dealt with the refurbishing of patented fish-canning machines by a purchaser of used machines. The Court held that the fairly extensive refurbishment by the new owner, including modification and resizing of six separate parts of the machine, although more than customary repair of spent or broken components, was more like repair than reconstruction, for it extended the useful life of the original machine. *See id.* at 425 ("Petitioners in adapting the old machines to a related use were doing more than repair in the customary sense; but what they did was kin to repair for it bore on the useful capacity of the old combination, on which the royalty had been paid.").

Precedent has classified as repair the disassembly and cleaning of patented articles accompanied by replacement of unpatented parts that had become worn or spent, in order to preserve the utility for which the article was originally intended. In *General Electric Co. v. United States*, 572 F.2d 745 (Ct. Cl. 1978), the court held that the Navy's large scale "overhauling" of patented gun mounts, including disassembly into their component parts and replacement of parts that could not be repaired with parts from other gun mounts or new parts, was permissible repair of the original gun mounts. The court explained that the assembly-line method of reassembly, without regard to where each component had originated, was simply a matter of efficiency and economy, with the same effect as if each gun mount had been refurbished individually by disassembly and reassembly of its original components with replacement of a minor amount of worn elements.

Similarly, in *Dana Corp. v. American Precision Co.*, 827 F.2d 755 (Fed. Cir. 1987), the court held that the "rebuilding" of worn truck clutches, although done on a commercial scale, was permissible repair. The defendants in *Dana Corp.* acquired worn clutches that had been discarded by their original owners, disassembled them, cleaned and sorted the individual parts, replaced worn or defective parts with new or salvaged parts, and reassembled the clutches. Although the patentee stressed that some new parts were used and that the rebuilding was a large scale commercial operation, the activity was held to be repair. The court also observed that in general the new parts were purchased from Dana, the original manufacturer of the patented clutches, and that repair of used clutches was contemplated by the patentee. The court rejected the argument that the complete disassembly and production-line reassembly of the clutches constituted a voluntary destruction followed by a "second creation of the patented entity". . . .

"Reconstruction," precedent shows, requires a more extensive rebuilding of the patented entity than is exemplified in *Aro Manufacturing, Wilbur-Ellis, General Electric*, and *Dana Corp.* . . . In contrast, in *Sandvik Aktiebolag v. E. J. Co.*, 121 F.3d 669, 43 USPQ2d 1620 (Fed. Cir. 1997), reconstruction was held to apply when a patented drill bit was "recreated" by construction of an entirely new cutting tip after the existing cutting tip could no longer be resharpened and reused. The court explained that it was not dispositive that the cutting tip was the "novel feature" of the invention, but that prohibited reconstruction occurred because a "new article" was made after the patented article, "viewed as a whole, has become spent." . . .

Application of the Law

In the Commission's Initial Determination the administrative law judge, applying the four factors discussed in *Sandvik Aktiebolag*, 121 F.3d at 673, held that the remanufacturers had made a new LFFP after the useful life of the original LFFP had been spent. Thus, the ALJ ruled that the remanufacturers were engaged in prohibited reconstruction. The Commission adopted the ALJ's findings and conclusions that the remanufacturers were not simply repairing an article for which either the producer or the purchaser expected a longer useful life, pointing out that the purchaser discarded the camera after use. The Commission ruled that the respondents were not simply repairing the LFFP in order to achieve its intended life span, but created a new single use camera that would again be discarded by its purchaser after use.

Although the Commission's conclusion is supported by its reasoning and reflects concern for the public interest, for there was evidence of imperfections and failures of some refurbished cameras, precedent requires that these cameras be viewed as repaired, not reconstructed. In *Dana Corp.*, for example, the truck clutches had lived their intended lives as originally produced, yet the court ruled that the "rebuilding" of the used clutches was more akin to repair than to reconstruction. The activities of disassembly and rebuilding of the gun mounts of *General Electric* were similarly extensive, yet were deemed to be repair. *Aro Manufacturing* and the other Supreme Court decisions which underlie precedent require that infringing reconstruction be a "second creation" of the patented article. Although the Commission deemed this requirement met by the "remanufactured" LFFPs, precedent places the acts of inserting new film and film container, resetting the film counter, and resealing the broken case — the principal steps performed by the remanufacturers — as more akin to repair.

The Court has cautioned against reliance on any specific set of "factors" in distinguishing permissible from prohibited activities, stating in *Aro Manufacturing* that "While there is language in some lower court opinions indicating that 'repair' or 'reconstruction' depends on a number of factors, it is significant that each of the three cases of this Court, cited for that proposition, holds that a license to use a patented combination includes the right 'to preserve its fitness for use. . . .'" 365 U.S. at 345. Indeed, this criterion is the common thread in precedent, requiring consideration of the remaining useful capacity of the article, and the nature and role of the replaced parts in achieving that useful capacity. The appellants stress that all of the original components of the LFFP except the film and battery have a useful remaining life, and are reused. The appellants state that but for the exposed roll of film and its container, any portion of the case that was broken by the photo processor, and the winding wheel in certain cameras, the refurbished LFFP is substantially the original camera, for which the patent right has been exhausted.

The Commission placed weight on Fuji's intention that the LFFP not be reused. . . . However, the patentee's unilateral intent, without more, does not bar reuse of the patented article, or convert repair into reconstruction. *See Hewlett-Packard*, 123 F.3d at 1453, 43 USPQ2d at 1658 ("a seller's intent, unless embodied in an enforceable contract, does not create a limitation on the right of a purchaser to use, sell, or modify a patented product so long as a reconstruction of the patented combination is avoided"). The appellants state that the film and its removable container are commercial items, and that their replacement in a camera can not be deemed to be reconstruction. As discussed in *Aro Manufacturing*, the replacement of unpatented parts, having a shorter life than is available from the combination as a whole, is characteristic of repair, not reconstruction. On the totality of the circumstances, the changes made by the remanufacturers all relate to the replacement of the film, the LFFP otherwise remaining as originally sold.

License

Fuji alternatively contends that the right to repair the patented cameras is impliedly limited by the circumstances of sale, pointing to the instructions and warnings printed on the covers of the LFFPs, and arguing that these constituted a license limited to a single use. [The court concluded, however, that the notices and warning did not form a contractual license.] These package instructions are not in the form of a contractual agreement by the purchaser to limit reuse of the cameras. There was no showing of a "meeting of the minds" whereby the purchaser, and those obtaining the purchaser's discarded camera, may be deemed to have breached a contract or violated a license limited to a single use of the camera. We conclude that no license limitation may be implied from the circumstances of sale.

V. IMPLIED IN LAW LICENSE

McCOY v. MITSUBOSHI CUTLERY, INC.
67 F.3d 917 (Fed. Cir. 1995)

Rader, Circuit Judge.

BACKGROUND

McCoy owns U.S. Patent No. 4,759,126 on a shrimp knife that peels, deveins, and butterflies in one motion. McCoy arranged for Mitsuboshi, a Japanese knife manufacturer, to produce shrimp knives embodying the patented invention. At McCoy's request, Mitsuboshi stamped the knives with McCoy's registered U.S. Trademarks Nos. 1,687,589 and 1,702,878. From 1988 to 1990, Mitsuboshi manufactured and sold large quantities of these knives to McCoy.

In 1991, McCoy's separate marketing organization, A.T.D. Marketing, Inc. (ATD), ordered 150,000 of the knives from Mitsuboshi. Mitsuboshi produced the knives. When Mitsuboshi timely offered the knives, ATD refused to accept or pay for them. ATD's refusal left Mitsuboshi holding the 150,000 knives in its warehouse in Japan. The record contains no suggestion that the knives were defective.

McCoy acknowledged its responsibility for ATD's refusal to pay. McCoy, however, accepted and paid for only about 20,000 of the 150,000 knives ordered. McCoy refused to pay for the other 130,000 knives. On the basis of these facts, the jury found that McCoy breached its contract with Mitsuboshi. McCoy did not appeal this jury verdict.

Following McCoy's partial payment, Mitsuboshi continued to negotiate for payment and delivery of the remaining 130,000 knives. McCoy, however, remained silent, unable to pay for them. In the face of this silence, Mitsuboshi repeatedly notified McCoy of its intent to resell the knives to mitigate damages. At length, Mitsuboshi sold 6,456 of the knives to Admiral Craft, a mail-order wholesaler of restaurant supplies. Admiral Craft sold 958 of the knives in the United States to restaurants and supply houses in 1993 through its mail catalog.

McCoy sued Mitsuboshi and Admiral Craft for patent and trademark infringement, unfair competition in violation of both federal and Texas law, and several Texas state law torts. Admiral Craft settled, but Mitsuboshi persevered, counterclaiming for breach of contract. At the close of evidence, Mitsuboshi moved for judgment as a matter of law that it was entitled to resell the knives. The trial court denied Mitsuboshi's motion. The jury found against Mitsuboshi on the infringement, unfair competition, and tortious interference counts, and for Mitsuboshi on the breach of contract count. Mitsuboshi then renewed its motion for judgment as a matter of law. The trial court again denied the motion. Mitsuboshi appeals.

Discussion

I.

The jury found, and McCoy does not contest, that McCoy breached its contract with Mitsuboshi. This appeal thus raises the purely legal question of the effect of McCoy's breach on his intellectual property rights in the knives. This court confronts this question for the first time.

A patent confers on its holder the right to exclude others from making, using, or selling what is described in its claims. This court has recognized that these intellectual property rights, like any other property rights, are subject to the contractual obligations of their owner and the applicable law:

> Th[e] right to exclude may be waived in whole or in part. The conditions of such waiver are subject to patent, contract, antitrust, and any other applicable law, as well as equitable considerations such as are reflected in the law of patent misuse. As in other areas of commerce, private parties may contract as they choose, provided that no law is violated thereby. . . .

Mallinckrodt, Inc. v. Medipart, Inc., 976 F.2d 700, 703 (Fed.Cir.1992). Thus, a patent or trademark owner may contract to confer a license on another party. In most instances under contract law, a patent or trademark owner intentionally creates an express license. A licensee, of course, has an affirmative defense to a claim of patent infringement.

In some circumstances, however, the entire course of conduct between a patent or trademark owner and an accused infringer may create an implied license. The Supreme Court stated:

> Any language used by the owner of the patent or any conduct on his part exhibited to another from which that other may properly infer that the owner consents to his use of the patent in making or using it, or selling it, upon which the other acts, constitutes a license and a defense to an action. . . .

De Forest Radio Tel. Co. v. United States, 273 U.S. 236, 241 (1927). When warranted by such a course of conduct, the law implies a license.

Whether express or implied, a license is a contract "governed by ordinary principles of state contract law." Moreover the law may imply licenses "to make effective the contracts of the patentee." An implied license, however, must not exceed the limits necessary to make the contract effective.

To enforce the contracts of the patentee, the law may imply a license where a patent holder sells or authorizes the sale of a patented product — a voluntary sale. Thus, "an authorized sale of a patented product places that product beyond the reach of the patent." Under this implied license, a patent holder receives a reward for inventive work in the first sale of the patented product. As the Supreme Court stated:

> Patentees . . . are entitled to but one royalty for the patented machine, and consequently when a patentee has himself constructed the machine and sold it, or authorized another to construct and sell it, or to construct and use and operate it, and the consideration has been paid to him for the right, he has then to that extent parted with his monopoly, and ceased to have any interest whatever in the machine so sold or so authorized to be constructed and operated.

Bloomer v. Millinger, 68 U.S. (1 Wall.) 340, 350 (1863).

In some cases, the law implies a license where a patent holder does not authorize the sale of a patented product — an involuntary sale. *See, e.g., Wilder v. Kent*, 15 F. 217, 219 (C.C.W.D.Pa.1883). For example, in *Wilder*, the patent holder sued an individual for infringement who purchased a machine at a sheriff's sale. The court dismissed the complaint finding the purchaser had acquired the right to use the patented machine through the purchase at the sheriff's sale. The court reasoned: "To deny to the sheriff's vendee the right to use such machine would in effect prevent its sale upon an execution at law . . . and practically withdraw it from the reach of the owner's execution creditors." While appreciating the unique nature of patent rights, the court noted that "a patented machine is susceptible of manual seizure, and the unrestricted sale thereof does not involve the transfer of any interest in the patent."

Justice Story, sitting on the Massachusetts Circuit Court, recognized a similar principle in denying a patent holder the right to sue a sheriff for infringement for his part in the sale of a patented product at a sheriff's sale. He reasoned that statutes must be construed where possible to avoid introducing "public mischiefs, or manifest incongruities." Justice Story felt a great public mischief would result if courts construed the patent laws to permit an action against a sheriff for selling a patented product at a sheriff's sale.

More recently, in an opinion authored by Judge Friendly, the United States Court of Appeals for the Second Circuit expressly recognized and extended this implied license doctrine to the sale of products by an aggrieved seller to remedy a buyer's breach. *Platt & Munk Co. v. Republic Graphics, Inc.*, 315 F.2d 847 (2d Cir.1963). Platt & Munk owned copyrights on educational toys and contracted with Republic to supply them. After Republic began delivery, Platt & Munk alleged various defects and refused to pay for the balance of the toys. Republic then informed Platt & Munk of its intent to resell the toys to recover its production costs. Platt & Munk responded by seeking an injunction prohibiting Republic from reselling the toys without Platt & Munk's consent. The trial court granted a preliminary injunction without addressing whether the toys were actually defective or whether Platt & Munk had the right to refuse payment. Republic filed an interlocutory appeal.

The Second Circuit remanded to the trial court to determine whether Platt & Munk justifiably refused to pay for the toys. If not, it instructed the trial court to lift the injunction. In other words, if Platt & Munk breached the contract, Republic had a right to resell the toys notwithstanding any copyright protection. The Second Circuit based its holding on New York contract law, which provided a seller of goods the right to mitigate damages for contract breaches. Where Platt & Munk breached, the Second Circuit found that Platt & Munk's copyrights had no effect on Republic's state law right to resell:

> We see no reason why the copyrighted character of the goods should preclude [resale] when — and the qualification is vital — the person for whom the goods were being made unjustifiably refuses to pay the price.

Platt, 315 F.2d at 855.

This ruling extended the implied license doctrine beyond sales under judicial decree to sales under self-help provisions in commercial law. Together, *Wilder*, *Sawin*, and *Platt* demonstrate that the law may create an implied license to enforce the contract obligations of the patent holder and recognize legal rights of aggrieved parties. In the case of the sheriff's sale, the patent holder defaulted on an obligation collateralized by patented merchandise. The creditor can have the property seized by the sheriff and sold. In the case of the self-help sale, the patent holder has defaulted on a contractual obligation based on patented merchandise. Under commercial law, the aggrieved seller can sell the merchandise and recover any losses from the breaching buyer. Absent an implied license in either case, patent holders could frustrate otherwise available commercial remedies.

Here, McCoy and Mitsuboshi had a long-standing business relationship whereby Mitsuboshi manufactured McCoy's patented knives. In 1991, McCoy placed a purchase order for 150,000 knives with Mitsuboshi. Mitsuboshi, in turn, accepted the order and performed its obligations under that agreement. When it tendered the knives to McCoy, McCoy breached the contract by failing to pay. At that point, rather than immediately act, Mitsuboshi continued to negotiate with McCoy in an effort to secure payment and deliver the knives. After repeated failed attempts, Mitsuboshi sold some of the knives to an American company.

The applicable state contract law in this case is Texas's version of the Uniform Commercial Code. Because this case involves the sale of goods, the Texas UCC entitles the seller to resell the goods upon the buyer's wrongful refusal to pay. Consequently, under Texas contract law, when McCoy breached the contract, Mitsuboshi had a right to resell the knives to recoup its losses without McCoy's consent.

As in *Platt*, an implied license properly enforces McCoy's contractual promise to pay for the knives, reflects Mitsuboshi's commercial efforts to resolve the matter, and recognizes Mitsuboshi's rights to mitigate under the Texas UCC. This court, like our sister circuit in *Platt*, sees no reason why the owner of intellectual property rights deserves to evade application of the ordinary contract remedy of resale for an unjustified refusal to pay.

This implied license does not offend the protection afforded patent and trademark rights by federal law. Instead, licenses, like other federal property and contract rights, conform to the applicable state laws. As this court observed in *Power Lift*, the Supreme Court has held that federal patent law does not preempt enforcement of contracts under state law. By the same reasoning, federal trademark law does not preempt contract enforcement either. Intellectual property owners "may contract as they choose," but their intellectual property rights do not entitle them to escape the consequences of dishonoring state contractual obligations.

Mitsuboshi's right to resell under Texas law, furthermore, did not require a prior adjudication that McCoy acted wrongfully in refusing to pay for the knives. Section 2.706(a) of the Texas UCC authorizes a seller to resell without adjudication. . . . In this case, McCoy did not seek nor obtain a preliminary injunction prohibiting Mitsuboshi from reselling the knives, despite McCoy's knowledge that Mitsuboshi intended to resell. Under Texas law, nothing prevented Mitsuboshi from exercising its right to resell in response to McCoy's breach. In sum, Mitsuboshi did not infringe McCoy's patent or trademarks by exercising its Texas law right to resell the knives to mitigate the breach.

Chapter 8

REPRESENTATIONS, WARRANTIES, COVENANTS, AND LIABILITY RISK

I. GENERAL NATURE OF THE ISSUES

This chapter considers issues related to the quality of performance required in a license agreement, including issues about representations and warranties. Unlike with sales of goods, representations and warranties in a license do not run solely in one direction (from the vendor to the transferee). The nature of the transaction dictates that qualitative obligations may run in both directions — from licensor to licensee, and from licensee to licensor. On the other hand, in many licenses, no qualitative obligations exist at all.

There are language issues here. In many contracts express "representations," "warranties" and "covenants" are an important feature of the relationship. These terms are often misused, however. One treatise suggests:

> While many licensing situations provide no opportunity for negotiation of specific terms and conditions, [in other transactions] representations, warranties and covenants made may prove to be critical in resolving any future disputes. [The] terms "representations" and "warranties" are almost invariably linked, and regarded as a single concept. In fact, they are two very different things. A representation is a statement as to the existence or nonexistence of a fact of state of affairs, or state of mind which acts as an inducement to contract. . . . A warranty is a guaranty, an assurance of the existence or future existence of a fact upon which the other party may rely. . . . Finally, covenants are simply contractual promises to do certain acts or to refrain from doing certain acts.

ROGER MILGRIM, MILGRIM ON LICENSING § 23.01. Whether or not one accepts that a distinction exists between "warranty" and "representation" or that the distinction is consistently followed, use of the two words often reflects the confusion that Milgrim describes. But there is other common terminology that bears on qualitative performance considerations. Some contracts refer to "conditions" for performance. For our purposes a "condition" is an event, circumstance, or performance the existence of which determines whether or when performance by the other party is required. Ultimately, the idea of a condition often relates to questions about remedy for breach. Other agreements or court decisions refer to terms that "indemnify" or create "hold harmless" obligations. One treatise comments:

> Once a licensing agreement has been consummated, the licensee would like to have the absolute right to use the licensed intellectual property in accordance with the terms of the agreement. Yet reality may intervene. . . . [A] third party may claim rights in the licensed intellectual property superior to those of licensor or licensee. Based on

that claim, the third party may sue the licensee for infringement solely for exercising [its] purported rights under the licensing agreement. [Licensees] try to protect themselves against the risk of claims of this sort by asking licensors for warranties of noninfringement. They may also ask the licensor to agree, at its expense, to indemnify or defend the licensee against those claims. This sort of warranty or covenant to indemnify or defend is generally enforceable, subject to certain rules of interpretation.

Contractual obligations to defend and indemnify a licensee also may have certain legal consequences. As a matter of . . . substance, the existence of an indemnity may increase the risk of a court finding that infringement was induced or was willful . . . or that the license agreement is an executory contract subject to rejection by a party as debtor in bankruptcy. Thus the mere use of warranties and indemnities against intellectual property infringement entails certain legal risks, wholly apart from the commercial and monetary risk against which they are designed to protect. Yet [these] legal risks seldom influence the decision whether or not to use warranties or indemnities, although they may influence their structuring and drafting.

JAY DRATLER, LICENSING OF INTELLECTUAL PROPERTY § 10.02.(XXXX)

PROBLEM 8.1

You are asked to draft a license for use by Client in transactions with alleged owners of copyrighted photographs. Client will convert the photographs into digital images and make them available to third parties wishing to license their use in various commercial products. Client also plans to include many of the images in a new "clip art" product it licenses to third parties. For each of the obligations or terms mentioned below, consider whether you would treat the obligation as a representation, warranty or covenant, and whether treatment as an indemnity or hold harmless obligation or as a condition would be appropriate. Draft language consistent with your choice on this matter:

a. Licensor has an obligation to act in good faith.

b. Licensee has corporate authority to enter into the contract and is a corporate entity organized under the laws of Washington.

c. The images are copyrighted and do not infringe third party rights.

d. Licensee will not use the images in a work that infringes another person's rights in a way that might cause liability risk to Licensor.

II. INTELLECTUAL PROPERTY RIGHTS

We introduced issues about validity of the rights and the existence of third party claims in connection with exclusive licenses in Chapter 4. Here, we expand that discussion and also look at some express contract terms dealing with infringement, title and related claims.

The risks or issues on which risk might be allocated associated with intellectual property rights in a license include:

- *Public domain and validity issues.* Are there rights recognized in law in the licensed subject matter that give their owner a right to prevent others from using the information without authorization?

- *Authority risk.* Does the licensor control legally recognized rights such that it can grant the license?

- *Co-ownership risk.* Does the licensor have exclusive rights, or do others have co-equal rights relevant to the scope of the license?

- *Exclusivity risk.* Do the licensor or others claiming through the licensor have rights of use within the scope covered by the license after it is granted?

- *Interference risk.* Has the licensor given rights to third parties that would allow it to prevent the licensee's use?

- *Infringement risk.* Does a third party hold intellectual property rights that are infringed when the licensee acts within the scope of the license?

See RAYMOND T. NIMMER, THE LAW OF COMPUTER TECHNOLOGY Ch. 7 (3d ed. 1997).

A. Validity and Non-Infringement: In General

LOEW'S INC. v. WOLFF
101 F. Supp. 981 (S.D. Cal. 1951)

CARTER, DISTRICT JUDGE.

This case raises novel questions concerning literary property and warranties, express and implied, in the sale thereof. . . . On March 21, 1949, defendants, Victoria Wolf and Erich Wolff, sold to the plaintiff, Loew's Inc., a story in manuscript form entitled, "Case History." On that date, a regular form contract used by plaintiff was executed by the defendants. The present action is based upon alleged violations of certain provisions of this contract. . . .

Erich Wolff, a doctor, specializing in cardiology, had met his former wife, Cathy, during chemistry lectures where she was a laboratory assistant at the institute at which he studied. Following their marriage, she later became subject to spells of extreme melancholia and attempted suicide. He investigated shock treatment and radium treatment for ovarian glands. Following her second suicide attempt, she submitted to radium treatment. . . . A third suicide attempt followed and she died on May 22, 1942. A year and a half later, Doctor Wolff read articles in medical journals describing a pre-frontal lobotomy operation for melancholia and the marked change it produced in a patient's personality. [All of these events], as testified to by Dr. Wolff, were factual matters and in the public domain.

Victoria Wolf, a short story writer and novelist met Erich Wolff in 1943. Late that year, he first discussed with her the operation on the brain, known as a prefrontal lobotomy, as the basis of a story. She knew, and Erich Wolff told her of the tragic experiences of Wolff and his former wife. Wolff told her of the lobotomy operation; its cure of melancholia, and its transformation of the character of the patient. Due to other commitments, [however,] Victoria Wolf was unable to write the story for Erich Wolff at that time.

After his discussion with Victoria Wolf, he then contacted Elsie Foulstone, also a writer, and discussed the possibility of her aiding him in preparing a draft of the story for motion picture purpose. He told her of the facts above and she wrote a synopsis of a story entitled, "Swear Not by the Moon," based on those facts, plus additional fictional matter. The end product did not please Erich Wolff and he relieved her of any further duties.

Nothing further was done about the story until some time in 1945, when Erich Wolff again contacted Victoria Wolf and prevailed upon her to work on the story. In that year Victoria Wolf wrote a synopsis of a story entitled, "Through Narrow Streets," which was based upon the doctor's former wife's experiences, the doctor's description of a lobotomy operation and her own research concerning it, and additional fictional matter. Dissatisfied, she next wrote a revision entitled, "Brain Storm" and late in 1948 or early 1949, wrote a second revision entitled, "Case History," the story in suit. It was a combination of fact and fiction. As stated above, this story was sold to the plaintiff in March 1949 for $15,000.

The document executed by the parties was entitled "Assignment of All Rights." By its language (Sec. 1), defendants Erich Wolff and Victoria Wolf transferred and sold to plaintiff all rights of every kind in and to the story and "the complete, unconditional and unencumbered title" thereto. Section 4 of the assignment provided that defendants represented and warranted that each was the "sole author and owner of said work, together with the title thereof"; and "the sole owner of all rights of any and all kinds whatsoever in and to said work, throughout the world"; that each had "the sole and exclusive right to dispose of each and every right herein granted"; that "neither said work nor any part thereof is in the public domain"; that "said work is original with me in all respects"; that "no incident therein contained and no part thereof is taken from or based upon any other literary or dramatic work or any photoplay, or in any way infringes upon the copyright or any other right of any individual, firm, person or corporation." . . .

By Section 6, the defendants guarantee and warrant that they will "indemnify, make good, and hold harmless the purchaser of, from and against any and all loss, damage, costs, charges, legal fees, recoveries, judgments, penalties, and expenses which may be obtained against, imposed upon or suffered by the purchaser by reason of any infringement or violation or alleged violation of any copyright or any other right of any person, firm or corporation, or by reason of or from any use which may be made of said work by the purchaser, or by reason of any term, covenant, representation, or warranty herein contained, or by reason of anything whatsoever which might prejudice the securing to the purchaser of the full benefit of the rights herein granted and/or purported to be granted."

Section 7 provides that the sellers "agree duly to execute, acknowledge and deliver, and/or to procure the due execution, acknowledgment and delivery to the purchaser of any and all further assignments and/or other instruments which in the sole judgment and discretion of the purchaser may be deemed necessary or expedient to carry out or effectuate the purposes or intent of these present instruments."

About three months after the execution of this instrument and the sale, Elsie Foulstone discovered that Erich Wolff had sold his story, and on July 1, 1949, plaintiff was notified that she claimed a portion of the proceeds of the sale because of the work she had done in 1944. On that same day plaintiff notified defendants' agent of the Foulstone claim. On July 30, 1949, plaintiff made a demand on defendants that they obtain a quitclaim and release from Foulstone within a reasonable time or they would be compelled to rescind their agreement of March 21st. On September 21, 1949, Elsie Foulstone filed action in the Superior Court of the State of California, County of Los Angeles, naming Erich Wolff, Victoria Wolf and Meto-Goldwyn-Mayer Pictures as defendants. . . .

On September 30, 1949, the plaintiff served defendant Erich Wolff with a notice of rescission. [On] February 28, 1950, the Superior Court rendered a judgment in favor of defendants finding that Elsie Foulstone had no valid claim or interest in or to the story, "Case History" which was sold to the plaintiff. The present action was filed on November 2, 1949, prior to the above mentioned judgment. . . .

At the conclusion of the trial, the court found:

1. That "Case History" was a different story from "Swear Not By the Moon," and that the only points of similarity were factual matters from the public domain.

2. That Erich Wolff collaborated with Elsie Foulstone on the story, "Swear Not By the Moon."

3. That there had been proved no fraud or fraudulent representations on the part of the defendants, Erich Wolff and Victoria Wolf.

The court now finds:

1. That defendants owned the complete, unconditional and unencumbered title to the story, "Case History."

2. That defendants were the sole owners and authors of said story.

3. That defendants had the sole and exclusive rights to said story.

4. That defendants did not cause the rights assigned to be impaired.

5. That the story was original with defendants.

6. That the use of the story by plaintiff would not violate any rights of Miss Foulstone.

7. That there was no fraudulent concealment of material facts.

The second cause of action, in addition to setting forth express warranties which we have found were not breached rests on plaintiff's claim to a "marketable and perfect" title, free from reasonable doubt. This raises the question of the existence and validity of what will hereafter be referred to as "implied warranties."

I.

There Was No Warranty . . . of "Marketable and Perfect Title" . . . .

A. There was no express warranty.

The plaintiff argues that an express warranty of "marketable and perfect" title, free from reasonable doubt, arose by the use of the words, "complete, unconditional and unencumbered title"; "sole author and owner of said work"; "sole owner of all rights of any and all kinds whatsoever in and to said work, throughout the world"; and "I have the sole and exclusive right to dispose of each and every right herein granted." Nowhere in this most comprehensive instrument can be found the words "marketable, perfect or free from reasonable doubt." Thus, in order to find such an express warranty it must be found that the words actually used in the "Assignment of Rights" were or are synonymous with "marketable and perfect" title.

No case has been cited by counsel nor can any be found by this court which holds that the phrase "complete, unconditional and unencumbered title" is synonymous with "marketable and perfect" title. The common meaning of the word "complete" is "Filled up, with no part, item, or element lacking." It means that the "whole" title has been given and that no part or portion of it has been kept by the seller or sold to any other person. In two cases involving the sale of real estate, the words "complete title" were found to mean the instruments which constitute the evidence of title, and not to mean the estate or interest conveyed.

The warranty of "marketability of title" is a warranty found almost exclusively in connection with the sale of real property. Such words as "merchantable title," "clear title," "good title" and "perfect title" have been held in cases involving the sale of land to mean the same as "marketable title." None of these words can be found in the present instrument. As used in this assignment the word "complete" was not meant to be synonymous with the word "marketable or perfect." It was used to mean just what the word indicated, i.e. "whole title," that is, that no other person owned any interest in the property nor was any kept by the sellers. In this respect, the plaintiffs got what they bargained for. It seems evident that the remaining words used in the assignment are not synonymous with "marketable or perfect" title.

B. There was no implied warranty.

Plaintiff argues that the law implies the warranty of marketable title in the sale of literary property. In doing so, plaintiff wishes to have this court apply a well established doctrine used exclusively in the sale of real property to the sale of personal property. To support its contention, plaintiff cites the case of *Hollywood Plays, Inc. v. Columbia Pictures Corp.*, 299 N.Y. 61, 85 N.E.2d 865, 10 A.L.R.2d 728. In this case, the plaintiffs sought damages for breach of a contract to purchase the motion picture, television, and radio rights to a play. The plaintiffs had purchased an interest in these rights from the trustee of one

Woods, who had originally received 50 per cent of these rights by license from the proprietors of the copyright. In Woods' schedules in bankruptcy, he had listed his ownership as 25 percent. There was no question but that Woods had owned 50 per cent up to two years before his adjudication in bankruptcy, and the plaintiffs contended that the insertion in his schedules of the lesser figure had been due to a mere error. No other explanation was forthcoming, and the plaintiffs relied on the fact that all of Woods' property had in fact, passed to his trustee, and had been included in the sale and assignment by the trustee to the plaintiffs. The New York court in reversing the lower courts, held that "the defendant was excused from performance because of a defect in plaintiffs' title." The court avoided the finding by the trial court that plaintiffs had actual title, and in our opinion erroneously declared the issue to be whether or not plaintiffs had an "unclouded title."

There are more than mere historical reasons for concluding that the doctrine of "marketable title" should be limited to cases involving the sale of real property. This doctrine has a basis in the traditional concepts of judicial fair play. Briefly, the doctrine developed because the courts at common law believed, and rightly so, that since the law required there be a recorded title in the sale of real estate, then that record title should be clear and free from reasonable doubt. A buyer, desiring to purchase the seller's land, would request that the seller deliver to him a "marketable" record of title to the property. If by searching the record, the title was free from reasonable doubt, it was proclaimed that the buyer had a "marketable" title and could not avoid the enforcement of the contract. If on the other hand, a defect appeared in the record title, then the common law courts felt that justice demanded that the seller either clear the record title or they would allow the buyer to avoid the contract. But the doctrine was not applied to the sale of personal property. At common law and with few exceptions the law as it exists today, there was no requirement that the sale of personal property be recorded. The doctrine of caveat emptor therefore prevailed. Without the application of this latter doctrine, it is highly doubtful that any sale of personal property would ever become final. There are no records to search. There is no way to ascertain that a cloud exists on the title. It is not a requirement that a record title be produced before a purchaser will buy the article in question. Thus, because of these differences between the sale of real and personal property, the courts neither then nor now could imply by law into a contract of sale of personal property the doctrine of "marketable" title. If they did so, then there would be no case in which the seller could rest in ease, for if any third person asserted a claim to the property the courts would be compelled to avoid the contract between the parties. To do this would be to place upon the seller an unsurmountable burden, and would leave the door open to allow a discontented purchaser to avoid any contract involving the sale of personal property.

For these reasons, in adopting the Uniform Sales Act the warranty of "marketable" title was conspicuously excluded. [It] is obvious that sales involving literary property are different in some respects from the sale of ordinary goods. The sale of literary property is more analogous to the sale of patents and patent rights. Both literary properties and patents are products of the mind, plus skill. Both utilize matters in the public domain. A review of patent cases confirms the position taken by this court.

In *Consumers' Gas Co. v. American Electric Construction Co.*, 3 Cir., 1892, 50 F. 778, 780, the action was by an electric construction company against a gas company to recover the price of installing an electric plant. The gas company set up by affidavit of defense that a certain patentee had threatened it with a claim for damages for infringement of patent rights if it used the machinery installed by the plaintiff, and that by such use the defendant would also be liable to another patentee. The court held that these facts were no defense, declaring: "A purchaser of property, who has had the full use and enjoyment of same, and is in the undisturbed possession thereof, in the absence of fraud, cannot withhold the purchase price because a third person claims to have a superior title thereto, or an adverse right therein, and threatens to bring suit to enforce the same, or because of an alleged liability on the part of the purchaser to a patentee for an infringement of letters patent, by reason of the use of the property."

It has also been held that the vendee of patent rights cannot maintain, as against an action for the price, the defense that he rescinded because he had been notified by a third party that the patent was an infringement and that he would be held liable therefore. In *Tinsman v. Independent Harvester Co.*, 1917, 205 Ill.App. 239, it was held that the vendee must show the actual invalidity of the patent, or at least that he had been enjoined after reasonable defense.

The rule has been well put in the case of *Computing Scales Co. v. Long*, 66 S.C. 379. There the court said: "If, however, the vendor at the time of the sale knew of a valid outstanding title or encumbrance, and failed to give notice to the vendee, the element of fraud is introduced, and the vendee may rescind without waiting for actual loss to come to him. . . . But mere dispute about the title, or the contingency of future loss, does not warrant a rescission, and, where the buyer returns the goods, and refuses to pay the purchase money, it is incumbent on him to show that there is a valid adverse claim, from which loss to him would inevitably occur. . . . The application of the rule may sometimes result in hardship, but to adopt any other would make it possible for a purchaser to escape from his contract upon any claim coming to his notice, however, baseless or absurd it might be."

The above rules should be even more strictly applied in the sale of literary property. [In] *Golding v. R.K.O. Pictures, Inc.*, 1950, 35 Cal.2d 690, 710, 221 P.2d 95, Justice Schauer of the Supreme Court of California refers to the fact that there are approximately thirty-six basic plots in all writing. Consequently, assertions of similarity and of plagiarism are practically a concomitant of all story writing. To establish then, a rule permitting the purchaser of literary property to return the property and demand back the purchase price upon a mere assertion of similarity or plagiarism is to create a right without the support of reason or principle, the exercise of which would result in untold hardship. There can be no other conclusion but that the law will not imply a warranty of "marketable" title in the sale of literary property.

Since it is the opinion of this court that there was neither an express nor implied warranty of "marketability of title," the second cause of action is accordingly disposed of. Consequently, the third and fifth causes of action which are predicated upon there being a warranty of "marketable" title must likewise fail. . . .

NOTES

1. Under *Wolff*, are there any circumstances where a licensee would have recourse under a warranty against the licensor even though the licensee was successful in defending against a claim that another person owns all or part of the subject matter or that there is an infringement of the third party's rights? What injury might a transferee suffer in such cases? As counsel for a transferee, how would you recommend approaching this issue in an agreement?

2. UCC Article 2A, which deals with leases of goods, provides the following warranty: "(a) There is in a lease contract a warranty that for the lease term no person holds a claim to or interest in the goods that arose from an act or omission of the lessor other than a claim by way of infringement or the like, which will interfere with the lessee's enjoyment of its leasehold interest." UCC § 2A-211(a) (1998 Official Text). Is the concept of this warranty consistent with the result in *Wolff*?

3. A leading treatise on copyright law argued that all licenses or assignments of copyright contain an implicit representation that the subject matter does not entirely fall within the public domain and that a failure of this implied representation not only violates a warranty, but also yields a complete failure of consideration. MELVILLE NIMMER & DAVID NIMMER, NIMMER ON COPYRIGHT § 10.02[A] (1992). In a subsequent edition, the author opines that "even without . . . an express warranty, there may well be an implied warranty of title and of fitness for intended use, under an analogy to the law of sales." MELIVILLE NIMMER & DAVID NIMMER, NIMMER ON COPYRIGHT § 10.13[A] (2003).

4. In *Prudential Insurance Co. of America v. Premit Group*, 704 N.Y.S.2d 253 (App. Div. 2000), the license contained an express warranty of "sole ownership" of a patent. The court held that a judgment determining that two

> individuals had contributed to the invention and were co-owners of the patent was "an incurable material breach of defendants' warranty of sole ownership of the patent under the license agreement, and released plaintiff from any obligation to make further royalty payments thereunder. Under applicable Federal law, the issuance of the patent gave rise to an equitable ownership interest therein of co-inventors not named therein, carrying with it the right of such co-inventors to license others to use the patent without the consent of other co-owners. The existence of such equitable co-owners of the subject patent as of the date of the license agreement was inconsistent with the unambiguous meaning of the licensor's warranty. . . ."

5. What result if the licensor is aware that the patent will most likely be held to be invalid if challenged or that a third-party co-owner may exist? *Schlaifer Nance & Company v. Estate of Andy Warhol*, 119 F.3d 91 (2d Cir. 1997), involved a license from the Andy Warhol estate with respect to photographs and other works. The license to SNC contained a warranty that

> (ii) the Artist is the sole creator and the Estate is the sole owner of the copyrights . . . although certain elements of the Existing Artworks may involve or incorporate concepts in the public domain;

. . . .

(iv) except with respect to Celebrity Works [and] except as noted on Exhibit, the Estate has and will continue to have the sole and exclusive right to transfer to [SNC] all rights to the Existing Artworks and the Works and the Copyrights, Trademarks and New Trademarks granted hereunder;

(v) neither the Existing Artworks, the Trademarks nor the Works infringe the rights of any third parties;

(vi) neither the Artist nor the Estate has granted and the Estate will not grant any right, license or privilege for Licensed Products with respect to the Trademarks, New Trademarks, Copyrights, or the Works or any portion thereof to any person or entity other than [SNC].

Id. at XX

The exhibit referenced no exceptions. Shortly after the license, problems emerged in the estate's title and control over many of the works, but the court rejected a claim of fraud. It held that the circumstances of the transaction would have left any reasonable person with no doubt that title in many of the works was murky.

6. If there is no warranty of validity or of non-infringement, what is the nature of the transaction — what is the licensor giving to the licensee? One view is that a transfer of "all my right, title and interest" in a patent is equivalent to the granting of a quit-claim deed for real property, and carries no express or implied warranty of title. Whether a warranty of title exists depends on whether the licensor purports to sell a definite right or merely the rights that he owns.

PROBLEM 8.2

Carter Systems plans to acquire rights in a software system created by Plans Unlimited. It asks you to draft reasonable scope terms and terms for warranties to be given by Plans relating to title and similar risks. Suggest appropriate language under the following circumstances:

a. Carter intends to modify the software slightly and then distribute it in the mass market for home interior decorating.

b. Carter intends to use the software in its own business and expects significant competitive benefits from the fact that the software is highly efficient.

B. Non-Infringement: UCC and UCITA

CHEMTRON v. AQUA PRODUCTS
830 F. Supp. 314 (E.D. Va. 1993)

HILTON, DISTRICT JUDGE.

On April 23, 1993, plaintiff Chemtron, Inc. filed a complaint for patent infringement against defendant/third party plaintiff Aqua Products, Inc. The action is based upon U.S. patent No. 5,007,559 by Young for a Method and Apparatus for Dispensing a Particulate Material ("the '559 patent"). This device includes a detergent dispenser, detergent container with a screen cap, and a method for dispensing detergent into a dishwashing machine. Aqua alleges that it installs detergent dispensers and distributes detergent-filled containers to restaurants and restaurant service corporations, for use in dishwashers. Third party defendant Viking manufactures detergent dispensers and disposable plastic caps for placement on disposable detergent containers for use with Viking's detergent dispensers. Viking sells component parts such as the detergent dispensers and plastic caps to Aqua.

Aqua filed a third party complaint against Viking for contribution and indemnification, based upon "including without limitation" the Uniform Commercial Code (UCC) warranty against infringement, § 2-312. Aqua asserts that the UCC warranty is applicable due to Viking's sale of "certain dispenser goods including without limitation solid bowls for powdered detergent containers."

In lieu of filing an answer, Viking filed this motion to dismiss. . . . For the reasons stated below, this motion to dismiss must be [granted].

The Uniform Commercial Code, § 2-312, like the other provisions of Article Two of the UCC, applies to the sale of goods. The warranty against infringement, an implied warranty under the UCC, coexists with the UCC's warranties of good title and that the seller's goods are free from liens and encumbrances:

> Unless otherwise agreed a seller who is a merchant regularly dealing in goods of the kind warrants that the goods shall be delivered free of the rightful claim of any third person by way of infringement or the like but a buyer who furnishes specifications to the seller must hold the seller harmless against any such claim which arises out of compliance with the specifications.

UCC § 2-312. When the goods are delivered and title is transferred, the warranty against infringement serves to provide assurances that the goods sold to the buyer are not subject to third party claims.

This language, however, should not be construed to mean that the buyer, after receiving a clean title to purchased goods, can subsequently incur a lien or liability on the purchased goods by his own actions, and then impose such liability on the seller. Accordingly, a buyer, such as Aqua, should not be entitled to purchase goods from a seller, such as Viking, which are not subject to any infringement action, use the non-infringing component goods in an infringing device and incur liability to a third party patentee, Chemtron, and then turn around and attempt to impose liability on the original seller of the component parts.

In *Motorola v. Varo, Inc.*, 656 F.Supp. 716 (N.D.Tex.1986), a defendant manufacturer sought damages from one of its suppliers based on theories of contribution and breach of the UCC warranty against infringement, § 2-312. In that case the defendant had used the supplier's products and formed photoresists, which the defendant then used to infringe on the plaintiff's patented semiconductor manufacturing process. After first denying the defendant's claim for contribution from its supplier under federal patent law, the court then found that the warranty extends only to those goods as transferred from the seller/supplier to the buyer. It does not regulate the buyer's conduct after purchase. The court found that the defendant's reading of the UCC would have the seller/supplier warrant that it has not induced the buyer to infringe on a patent, which would be a "warranty as to conduct, not as to goods."

Similarly, Viking manufactured and sold to Aqua detergent dispensers and plastic caps for placement on disposable detergent containers. At the time of sale these dispensers and caps were delivered free from any third party complaints against infringement. Aqua was sued by Chemtron for direct infringement of the '559 patent and for inducement of infringement based upon its infringing apparatus, which was assembled from non-infringing component parts, some of which were obtained from Viking. As in *Motorola*, the UCC's warranty against infringement should not apply in such situation.

[Because] any cause of action under the patent laws is governed by federal law, Aqua's allegations regarding contribution and indemnity also fail to state claims upon which relief can be granted. There is no claim for contribution under the U.S. patent laws, and none may arise under state law as it is pre-empted by federal law. Therefore, Aqua's assertion that Viking is liable for contribution fails to state a claim upon which relief can be granted.

Aqua's claim that Viking is liable to indemnify it and hold it harmless is likewise unfounded, for Aqua has not alleged any grounds in its third party complaint, outside the UCC warranty provisions, upon which such a claim may be based. For the aforementioned reasons third party defendant Viking Injector Co.'s motion to dismiss the third party complaint pursuant to Fed. R.Civ.P. 12(b)(6) should be granted.

NOTES

1. UCITA follows Article 2 on the non-infringement warranty, but also creates an implied warranty of non-interference which was rejected in Article 2. UCITA § 401 (2000 Official Text). UCITA also follows the rule that, in a pure patent license, there is no implied warranty that use of the invention will not infringe the rights of a third party.

2. Article 2 refers to a "rightful" claim of infringement. Like the discussion in *Wolff*, *supra*, one might expect that this requires that the claim be valid — e.g., to be liable for breach of warranty, use of the subject matter that *in fact* infringes. There is little case law on this, but proposed revisions of UCC Article 2 revise the title warranty provisions to include a warranty against the existence of any "colorable" claim. They do not, however, make the same change with respect to the infringement warranty. The proposed revisions to Section 2-312 state:

> (1) Subject to subsection (2), there is in a contract for sale a warranty by the seller that:

>> (a) the title conveyed shall be good and its transfer rightful and shall not unreasonably expose the buyer to litigation because of any colorable claim to or interest in the goods. . . .

(2) Unless otherwise agreed, a seller that is a merchant regularly dealing in goods of the kind warrants that the goods shall be delivered free of the rightful claim of any third person by way of infringement or the like.

UCC § 2-312 (2004 Official Text). This change, if adopted by a state, presents a difficult interpretation issue since it distinguishes between a "colorable claim or interest" in the goods and a "rightful claim" of infringement. What, for example, would be the proper treatment of the claim in *Chemtron* under this new structure? The comments to the revision state:

> The subsection now expressly states what the courts have long recognized; further protection for the buyer is needed when the title is burdened by colorable claims that affect the value of the goods. . . . Therefore, not only is the buyer entitled to a good title, but the buyer is also entitled to a marketable title, and until the colorable claim is resolved the market for the goods is impaired. The justification for this rule is that the buyer of goods that are warranted for title has a right to rely on the fact that there will be no need later to have to contest ownership. The mere casting of a substantial shadow over the buyer's title, regardless of the ultimate outcome, violates the warranty of good title. It should be noted that not any assertion of a claim by a third party will constitute a breach of the warranty of title. The claim must be reasonable and colorable.

UCC § 2-312, cmt. 1 (2004 Official Text).

3. The warranty in Section 2-312 refers to the goods as delivered. This presents a host of issues with respect to intellectual property infringement claims grounded in processes, rather than physical items. *Chemtron* illustrates one approach to answering such questions. The revisions of Article 2 do not address the issue.

4. In an apparent drafting error, current Article 2 does not contain provisions about how to disclaim the warranty of non-infringement. Warranties of title can be disclaimed by clear and specific language, while implied warranties (e.g., merchantability) are subject to disclaimer language stated in UCC § 2-316. But the infringement warranty is neither a title warranty, nor an implied warranty. That being said, most observers assume that a specific disclaimer suffices.

PROBLEM 8.3

Publisher produces a digital version of an encyclopedia, in a product containing sophisticated search capabilities. One way of searching could result in a compilation of entries identical to that used by Author in her separate book on flora and fauna. Author sues College, a customer of Publisher's, who actually used the search material in a way that created an infringing work. If College loses in the infringement suit, can it recover from Publisher? What if, after a lengthy litigation, College defeats the infringement claim and then files a lawsuit for breach of warranty against Publisher?

C. Estoppel and No-Contest Clauses

TROXEL MANUFACTURING
COMPANY v. SCHWINN BICYCLE CO.
465 F.2d 1253 (6th Cir. 1972)

PHILLIPS, CHIEF JUDGE.

This is an appeal from a decision granting summary judgment to a patent licensee in an action for the recovery of royalties paid under the license agreement. The case requires an interpretation of *Lear, Inc. v. Adkins,* 395 U.S. 653 (1969). . . . We reverse.

Schwinn Bicycle Company is the assignee of a design patent for a bicycle seat issued to Frank Brilando in 1966. In mid-1967, following notice of infringement, Schwinn and Troxel Manufacturing Company entered into a nonexclusive license agreement under which Troxel was released from liability for past infringement and was licensed to manufacture and sell bicycle seats embodying the patented invention at an agreed per-unit royalty, payable quarterly. Schwinn obligated itself to enforce the patent against infringers.

Troxel notified Schwinn in August 1967 that Fisher Cycle Company was importing and selling infringing seats. Six months later Schwinn instituted an infringement action [against] Goodyear Tire and Rubber Company, Fisher's vendee. The Brilando patent was held invalid in January 1969, on the grounds of anticipation and obviousness in view of a prior art seat which had been considered by the Patent Office in the course of examination of the Brilando application. Troxel thereupon informed Schwinn that royalties due under the license agreement would be escrowed pending appeal. Schwinn brought suit against Troxel to collect the escrowed royalties. Upon Troxel's payment of overdue royalties and agreement to continue making regular payments, Schwinn dismissed the suit. The decision [on] the issue of obviousness [was affirmed]. Schwinn thereupon notified its licensees that no royalties would be due for seats sold after the date of that decision.

Three months later Troxel filed this [action seeking] recovery of all royalties paid under the agreement, or alternatively, those royalties paid subsequent to the District Court's holding of invalidity, together with interest [and] a declaration that it had no liability for the payments due from sales during the last quarter of 1970. Schwinn counterclaimed for the unpaid final quarterly royalty payments. Troxel's motion for summary judgment [was] granted. Schwinn was ordered to refund all royalties with interest from the date of judgment. This appeal followed.

I.

It has been the established rule in this Circuit for nearly forty years that a final adjudication of invalidity of a licensed patent operates as an eviction from the license, terminating the licensee's obligation to continue making royalty payments after that date but giving no right to recoup royalties already paid. *See Drackett Chem. Co. v. Chamberlain Co.,* 63 F.2d 853 (6th Cir. 1933). In *Drackett* the patent was held invalid in a District Court decision which was not appealed. Absent a showing that Schwinn prosecuted its appeal to the Ninth Circuit in bad faith, the eviction in this case occurred on the date of the decision of the Court of Appeals.

We are called upon in a case of first impression at the appellate level, to consider the effect of the decision in *Lear, Inc. v. Adkins,* on the eviction rule of this Circuit. The precise holding of *Lear* was that a licensee was not estopped to interpose the invalidity of the licensed patent as a defense to an action brought by the licensor to enforce the license agreement. The District Court in the present case found that "the doctrine of *Lear* would . . . be equally applicable" to the case in which a licensee asserted invalidity offensively to recover royalties already paid. We believe this to be an unwarranted extension of *Lear.*

The abrogation of the licensee estoppel doctrine was the "decent public burial" of a "doctrine which [had] been deprived of life." The "clouded history" of the rule is discussed extensively in *Lear* and will not be repeated here. The Court reached its decision through extended consideration of the effect of federal patent-antitrust policy on traditional contract law concepts. The conflicting policies involved were placed in sharp focus:

> On the one hand, the law of contracts forbids a purchaser to repudiate his promises simply because he later becomes dissatisfied with the bargain he has made. On the other hand, federal law requires that all ideas in general circulation be dedicated to the common good unless they are protected by a valid patent.

Id. at 668. Recognizing that it was seeking "an acceptable middle ground" which would "accommodate the competing demands of the common law of contracts and the federal law of patents," the Court found that: "[T]he equities of the licensor do not weigh very heavily when they are balanced against the important public interest in permitting full and free competition in the use of ideas which are in reality a part of the public domain . . . that the technical requirements of contract doctrine must give way before the demands of the public interest in the typical situation involving the negotiation of a license after a patent has issued."

As noted above, in *Lear* the federal policy in conflict with state contract law was "that all ideas in general circulation be dedicated to the common good unless they are protected by a valid patent." . . . As noted by the Court:

> [I]n rewarding useful invention, the "rights and welfare of the community must be fairly dealt with and effectually guarded." To that end the prerequisites to obtaining a patent are strictly observed, and when the patent has issued the limitations on its exercise are equally strictly enforced. To begin with, a genuine "invention" or "discovery" must be demonstrated "lest in the constant demand for new appliances the heavy hand of tribute be laid on each slight technological advance in an art." Once the patent issues, it is strictly construed, it cannot be used to secure any monopoly beyond that contained in the patent, the patentee's control over the product when it leaves his hands is sharply limited, and the patent monopoly may not be used in disregard of the antitrust laws. . . .

Thus the patent system is one in which uniform federal standards are carefully used to promote invention while at the same time preserving free competition.

Id. at 230-231.

This well developed resolution of the tension between the competing public interests reflected in federal antitrust and patent laws could "not be set at nought" by state law which clashed with its objective. Two terms following *Lear*, the traditional procedural "mutuality of estoppel doctrine" . . . gave way to this public interest. In *Blonder-Tongue, Inc. v. University of Illinois Foundation,* 402 U.S. 313 (1971), the Court held that a defendant in a patent infringement action could assert the defense of *res judicata* where the patent in suit had been adjudged invalid in litigation with a third party. The prior adjudication operated as a prima facie bar to recovery with the burden on the patent owner to demonstrate "that he did not have 'a fair opportunity procedurally, substantively and evidentially to pursue his claim the first time.' " The ruling was said to reflect the "consistent view . . . that the holder of a patent should not be insulated from the assertion of defenses."

II.

With this background we turn to the question of whether a license agreement voidable under *Lear* is void *ab initio*, entitling the licensee to recoup royalties already paid. In *Lear* the respective equities of licensee and licensor were balanced in light of the public interest. As noted by the Court:

Licensees may often be the only individuals with enough economic incentive to challenge the patentability of an inventor's discovery. If they are muzzled, the public may continually be required to pay tribute, to would-be monopolists without need or justification.

A.

A rule that licensees can recover all royalties paid on a patent which later is held to be invalid would do far more than "unmuzzle" licensees. It would give the licensee the advantage of a "heads-I-win, tails-you-lose" option. *Lear* states that it is in the public interest to encourage an early adjudication of invalidity of patents. Application of the holding of the District Court could defeat early adjudication of invalidity and encourage tardy and marginal litigation. If the licensee could recover royalties paid (subject to any statute of limitations) on the basis of an adjudication of invalidity accomplished by another litigant, without incurring the expense or trouble of litigation, there would be less inducement for him to challenge the patent and thus remove an invalid patent from the competitive scene. He would be more likely to wait for somebody else to battle the issue because he would have nothing to lose by the delay.

Rather than stimulating early litigation to test patent validity, such an interpretation of *Lear* would make it advantageous for a licensee to postpone litigation, enjoy the fruits of his licensing agreement, and sue for repayment of royalties near the end of the term of the patent. When a licensed patent is about to expire and the threat of injunction no longer exists, a licensee would have little to lose in bringing an action to recover all the money he has paid in royalties on the ground of the invalidity of the patent. The licensee would have a chance to regain all the royalties paid while never having been subjected to the risk of an injunction. Such an interpretation of *Lear* would defeat one of the expressed purposes of the court in announcing that decision.

B.

Further, the interpretation of *Lear* adopted by the District Court inevitably would discourage the licensing of patents. A patent is a form of intellectual property. The licensing of patents is a business of considerable magnitude.

Under the decision of the District Court, any person who has licensed his invention or patent would have a continuous cloud over any payment of royalties made to him. The cloud might take the form of limiting his credit because of contingent liability. He would be compelled to retain all royalties received in a relatively liquid state until the expiration of the licensed patent, or the running of the applicable statute of limitations. If the licensor should put royalties to work by investing them, a subsequent requirement of repayment could result in the sudden disruption of the investment. The royalties would be taxable to the licensor as ordinary income. Thus royalties from patent licenses, being currently taxable but not distributable as profits or usable to operate or expand a business, could constitute a burden on all except the largest and most wealthy licensors. It is entirely logical to anticipate that the owner of more than one patent would demand higher royalties for each in order to hedge against the possibility that royalties received under one patent might be returned to licensees.

C.

An even more serious consequence of requiring royalty refunds with respect to patents held to be invalid is that it would deter inventors from resorting to the patent system in the first instance. The framers of the Constitution recognized the importance of promoting progress of science and the useful arts. They also recognized that it was important to encourage invention and the public disclosure of inventions to "add to the sum of useful knowledge."

Soon after making a discovery, an inventor must decide whether to protect his invention by a patent or to maintain it as a trade secret. It is public policy to encourage the disclosure and public use of ideas as opposed to the maintenance of trade secrets. The exclusive rights conferred by a patent grant are designed not only to encourage invention, but more importantly, to disclose the invention to the public. It is through disclosure that others will be given the opportunity to improve on the invention. If an inventor must face the possibility of refunding all patent royalties collected by him, he may be encouraged to keep secret an invention which otherwise might have been disclosed through the patent process.

D.

It may be argued that the owner of a valid patent has nothing to fear from the result reached by the District Court — that it is only those whose patents are invalid who will feel the pinch. Unquestionably the public interest demands that developers of unpatentable inventions be deterred from acquiring or enforcing patent protection. However, Judge Learned Hand's observations on patentability should be kept in mind:

> That issue is a fugitive, impalpable, wayward, and vague a phantom as exists in the whole paraphernalia of legal concepts. It involves, or it should involve, as complete a reconstruction of the art that preceded it as is possible. The test of invention is the originality of the discovery, and discovery depends upon the mental act of conceiving the new combination, for substantially every invention is only a combination. Nothing is more illusory, as nothing is more common, than to assume that this can be measured objectively by the magnitude of the physical readjustments required. . . . When all is said, we are called upon imaginatively to project this act of discovery against a hypostatized average practitioner, acquainted with all that has been published and all that has been publicly sold. If there be an issue more troublesome, or more apt for litigation than this, we are not aware of it.

E.

We hold that *Lear* did not overrule *Drackett* and that the rationale of *Drackett* remains the law of this Circuit except insofar as it expresses the licensee estoppel doctrine.

III.

Troxel relies upon the following language of Lear: "For all these reasons, we hold that Lear must be permitted to avoid the payment of all royalties occurring after Adkins' 1960 patent issued if Lear can prove patent invalidity." It is urged by Troxel that Lear said that payment of royalties on an invalid patent could be avoided from the time the patent issued, and not merely from the time the patent was declared to be invalid.

"It is a maxim, not to be disregarded, that general expressions, in every opinion, are to be taken in connection with the case in which these expressions are used." Applying this maxim, we read the above-quoted language in *Lear* in the light of the facts that were before the Court in that case.

Lear had been denying liability for royalties during the entire life of the patent, the license agreement having been entered into before a patent issued. The license agreement called for royalties based upon the use of the alleged invention both before the patent issued and during the life of any patent which might issue. Prior to the issuance of the patent, Lear as licensee notified Adkins as licensor that it had found a patent which it believed fully anticipated Adkins' discovery. Lear terminated all payments under the agreement prior to the issuance of the patent. The patent issued in 1960. No royalties were paid after issuance of the patent. Therefore, the above-quoted language of the Supreme Court must be construed in the light of the issue actually before the court, namely, that of licensee estoppel. We do not construe the decision of the Court, in overruling the doctrine of licensee estoppel, to require that a licensor should be compelled to repay all royalties received from its licensees under a license agreement where the patent subsequently is held to be invalid.

IV.

In reaching its decision, the District Court relied upon principles of equity, saying: "We cannot, however, see why a licensee who has paid royalties should be in a worse position than one who has not. Moreover, the licensor who has to pay back royalties at least has had the use of the licensee's money."

To the contrary we conclude that the decision of the District Court reaches an inequitable result. Absent fraud or misconduct, a patentee should not be held responsible for the issuance of an invalid patent. Patents are creations of Government, issued after examination by the United States Patent Office. This examination includes "a thorough investigation of the available prior art relating to the subject matter sought to be patented" and an evaluation of patentability by the patent examiner. Schwinn's patent was held invalid by the California District Court and by the Court of Appeals for the Ninth Circuit in view of such "available prior art." In these circumstances, once a patent has been declared invalid by a court, we do not consider it equitable to require the disenfranchised patentee to refund to all licensees all royalties that have been collected under licensing agreements prior to the adjudication of invalidity.

We hold that neither equity nor public policy require that Troxel be permitted to recover the royalties it paid to Schwinn. Before entering into the licensing agreement Troxel was provided with a copy of the Schwinn patent and had access to the file history of the prosecution of that patent before the Patent Office. Troxel could have challenged the patent initially instead of taking a license. It could have done so at any time after the license agreement was executed. It failed to take this action. It waited for someone else to challenge the patent. Even after another litigant had undertaken the challenge and had been successful at District Court level, Troxel did not join in that challenge but instead elected to remain a royalty-paying licensee. During all this time it had the benefit of freedom from suit for infringement and agreement of Schwinn to attempt to halt unlicensed infringers. It also enjoyed freedom from liability for past infringement.

Finally, on the licensee's side of the balance, the equities are less compelling than those in *Lear*. Typically, "any royalty payments [are] passed on to the consumers [and] are as a practical matter unrecoverable by those who in fact paid them."

V.

The public interest is protected adequately under *Lear* without imposing on the patent holder the obligation to refund royalties paid under the license of a patent procured and asserted in good faith. A licensee may at any time cease royalty payments, secure in the knowledge that the invalidity of the patent may be urged when the licensor sues for unpaid royalties. If the patent is declared invalid through the efforts and expenditures of another, no further royalties are due under the license agreement. Further, if the evicted licensee is sued as an infringer, the prior adjudication of invalidity enables the licensee to secure pretrial judgment in his favor. To permit a licensee in addition to recoup royalties paid is to extend *Lear* far beyond its rationale. Congress has not seen fit to create an implied warranty of validity in license agreements. We decline to do so by judicial action.

VI.

The sole remaining issue is the disposition of Schwinn's counterclaim for royalties due for goods sold during the last quarter of 1970. *Lear* makes it clear that Troxel may defend against this counterclaim on the ground that the Brilando patent is invalid. Further, the Ninth Circuit ruling of invalidity is "available [as] an estoppel defense that can be pleaded affirmatively and determined on a pretrial motion for judgment on the pleadings or summary judgment."

Reversed and remanded. . . .

NOTES

1. *Lear, Inc. v. Adkins*, 395 U.S. 653 (1969), decided during a period of judicial hostility to intellectual property rights and licensing, held that federal policy preempted a state contract law doctrine of implied licensee estoppel in patent license cases. *Lear* is reproduced in Chapter 14 in connection with preemption and patent misuse doctrine. In *Medimmune, Inc. v. Genentech, Inc.*, 127 S. Ct. 764 (2007), the Court held that a patent licensee can challenge the validity of a licensed patent even though it continues to pay royalties under the license. The challenge was brought as a declaratory judgment action and the Court addressed the case in terms of Article III standing, rather than as an issue of patent or intellectual property law or policy. It held that standing existed in that the continued payment of royalties was "coerced" by the threat of a patent infringement suit and attendant remedies. As a result, there was a sufficient case or controversy between the parties. The Court did not address issues about whether contract doctrines might render this challenge ineffective because a challenging party cannot both accept the benefits of a contract and contest its validity, or whether a promise to not sue for invalidity would be enforceable.

2. In *Studiengesellschaft Kohle m.b.H. v. Shell Oil Co.*, 112 F.3d 1561 (Fed. Cir. 1997), the court held that a licensee could not recover or avoid paying royalties under *Lear* for royalties due prior to the time that the licensee challenged the patent. The court commented that

> With a patent licensing agreement at stake, this court examines the contract for rare, but potential, conflicts between state contract law and federal patent law. For example, in *Lear v. Adkins* . . . the Supreme Court prevented the enforcement of a valid royalty payment agreement to facilitate a determination of patent validity. Specifically, the Supreme Court declined to estop a patent licensee from contesting the validity of the licensed patent. . . . In tones that echo from a past era of skepticism over intellectual property principles, the Court in *Lear* feared that "licensees may often be the only individuals with enough economic incentive to challenge the patentability of an inventor's discovery. If they are muzzled, the public may continually be required to pay tribute to would-be monopolists without need or justification. . . ." As in *Diamond Scientific*, this court detects no significant frustration of federal patent policy by enforcing the 1987 license agreement

between Shell and SGK, to the extent of allowing SGK to recover royalties until the date Shell first challenged the validity of the claims. [As] in *Diamond Scientific*, Shell executed a contractual agreement which produced significant benefits for the corporation and attested to the worth of the patent.

3. Is this concept of eviction the same as saying that a license of a patent carries with it an implied warranty of patent validity? Compare the principal case with the comments of the court in *Drackett Chemical Co. v. Chamberlain*

> *Co.*, 63 F.2d 853, 854-55 (6th Cir. 1933): "[W]here the monopoly . . . apparently created by the grant of a patent . . . has been destroyed by a decree of invalidity in a court of competent jurisdiction . . . there has been a complete failure of consideration — an eviction — which should justify a termination of the contract. Prior to such eviction, the mere invalidity of the patent is properly held not to be a sufficient defense, because the licensee may still continue to enjoy all of the benefits of a valid patent. It may be respected, and the licensee would then have just what he bargained for. It is only when, by judicial decree or otherwise, it is published to the world that the monopoly is destroyed, that the licensee can claim to be correspondingly released from his obligation to pay royalties. . . . Licenses may be exclusive, partially exclusive, or nonexclusive. The principles which we have stated apply with equal force to all of these types."

4. *Diamond Scientific Co. v. Ambico, Inc.*, 848 F.2d 1220 (Fed. Cir. 1988), held that an assignor was estopped from challenging the validity of the

> assigned patent: "To allow the assignor to make that representation [of the worth of the patent] at the time of the assignment (to his advantage) and later to repudiate it (again to his advantage) could work an injustice against the assignee. [Despite] the public policy encouraging people to challenge potentially invalid patents, there are still circumstances in which the equities of the contractual relationships between the parties should deprive one party [of] the right to bring that challenge."

5. Although the licensee estoppel rule in patent cases was struck down in *Lear v. Adkins,* with few exceptions the case law since then has held the *Lear* non-estoppel rule inapplicable in context of ordinary trademark licenses. 3 RUDOLF CALLMANN, UNFAIR COMPETITION, TRADEMARK & MONOPOLIES § 19.48, at 434 (Louis Altman 4th ed. 1998 & 2000 Cum. Supp.) & summarizes the case law:

> The licensee is estopped from claiming any rights against the licensor which are inconsistent with the terms of the license. This is true even after the license expires. He is estopped from contesting the validity of the mark, . . . or challenging the license agreement as void or against public policy, e.g., because it granted a naked license. But he may challenge the licensor's title to the mark based on events which occurred *after* the license expired.

See also J. THOMAS MCCARTHY, TRADEMARKS & UNFAIR COMPETITION § 18:63 (4th ed. 2000).

PROBLEM 8.4

Licensee has a license from Gentech covering use of Gentech's patented wool cleaning process. Licensee is one of several non-exclusive licensees of this process. It has agreed to pay $0.25 per item cleaned using the process, with a minimum annual royalty of $5 million. Clean-it is one of Licensee's competitors in Los Angeles. It has decided to use the Gentech process, but does not seek a license. This gives it a competitive advantage over Licensee, and its market share increases. Genetech, concerned about the validity of its patent, does not sue for infringement.

You represent Licensee, which has six years remaining under the license. Licensee estimates that there is a 30% chance that the patent is invalid and that litigating the issue would take several years. The license provides that Gentech may cancel the license for non-payment of royalties.

What steps would you recommend that Licensee take?

SATURDAY EVENING POST
CO. v. RUMBLESEAT PRESS, INC.
816 F.2d 1191 (7th Cir. 1987)

POSNER, CIRCUIT JUDGE.

In 1979 the Saturday Evening Post Company granted Rumbleseat Press, Inc. an exclusive license to manufacture porcelain dolls derived from certain illustrations done by Norman Rockwell and published in the Saturday Evening Post. Later the Post canceled the license; but, contrary to the terms of the license agreement, Rumbleseat continued making the dolls. This led the Post to sue Rumbleseat. The Post won in the district court. Rumbleseat's appeal raises a variety of jurisdictional and procedural issues, of which the most important are whether the validity of a copyright is arbitrable and whether a provision in a copyright license that forbids the licensee to challenge the validity of the copyright is enforceable. Both are novel issues.

The original term of Rumbleseat's license was three and a half years. Renewal for successive years was automatic, however, unless a party gave notice at least 90 days before the end of the year that it did not want to renew. The license agreement specifies that once the license is canceled Rumbleseat has to stop making or selling the licensed goods, except that it has 275 days after cancellation to liquidate its existing inventory. The agreement also contains a warranty by the Post that it has valid copyright in the Rockwell illustrations. Actually, the Post had copyrighted each of the magazines in which the illustrations appeared but had not copyrighted the illustrations separately, and in the license negotiations Rumbleseat had questioned whether the Post had valid copyrights in the illustrations.

Rumbleseat on its part promised in the agreement to register in the Post's name any copyrights that the Post reasonably deemed necessary to protect its own copyrights. Rumbleseat also agreed that if it acquired any rights in its own name it would transfer them to the Post when the license ended. Works derived from copyrighted material — "derivative works" as they are called —

are copyrightable provided the derivative work has some incremental originality; the copyright in the derivative work is limited to that increment. The
Rockwell illustrations were the original work; the porcelain dolls that the
license authorized Rumbleseat to make and sell were derivative works.

Paragraph 9 of the license agreement provides that Rumbleseat "shall not,
during the Original Term [of the agreement] or any time thereafter dispute or
contest, directly or indirectly, [the] validity of any of the copyrights . . . which
[the Post] may have obtained." This is the no-contest clause. The agreement
also has an arbitration clause: "any controversy or claim arising out of or relating to this contract, or the breach thereof, shall be settled by arbitration in
accordance with the Rules of the American Arbitration Association," and the
arbitrators' judgment "may be entered in any court having jurisdiction
thereof." . . .

[Rumbleseat challenged the validity of the arbitration clause, but the court
held that federal law does not forbid arbitration of the validity of a copyright,
at least where that validity becomes an issue in the arbitration of a contract
dispute.]

Last, we must decide whether a clause in a copyright licensing agreement
forbidding the licensee to contest the validity of the copyright he has licensed
is against public policy, as expressed in the Copyright Act or other possible
sources of federal common law, and is therefore unenforceable. (Rumbleseat's
argument that it is barred by state law requires no extended discussion. The
argument is based on restrictive-covenant cases; they are too remote to be
illuminating.) This is another open question, and again the concern is with
copyright monopolies. Suppose the Rockwell illustrations really were in the
public domain and both the Post and Rumbleseat knew it, but, also knowing
that both would be better off without competition, they agreed to give
Rumbleseat an exclusive license with a no-contest clause, hoping that no other
potential competitor would discover the invalidity of the copyrights and challenge (or defy) them. Somewhat analogous practices involving patents have
been alleged. The danger of this kind of cozy deal would be less if the law forbade the Post to enforce the no-contest clause, so that Rumbleseat, if it
changed its mind about the advantages of mutual forbearance, could go into
competition with the Post notwithstanding the license.

We cannot call this danger nonexistent, although we suspect it is slight
given our earlier remarks about the unlikelihood that a copyright (especially
one that by hypothesis is invalid!) would confer an economically significant
monopoly, one that would raise the price of the monopolized good well above,
and depress its output well below, the competitive level. The danger is not so
great, however, as to justify a rule of federal common law outlawing no-contest
clauses without evidence of any monopolistic danger or effect. Such a clause
serves a useful purpose in most cases. Without it the licensee always has a
club over the licensor's head: the threat that if there is a dispute the licensee
will challenge the copyright's validity. The threat would discourage copyright
licensing and might therefore retard rather than promote the diffusion of copyrighted works. Also, a no-contest clause might actually accelerate rather than
retard challenges to invalid copyrights, by making the would-be licensee think
hard about validity before rather than after he signed the licensing agreement.

Rumbleseat had, in fact, used its expressed doubts of the validity of the Post's copyrights to obtain a lower royalty rate in the negotiations for the license.

What is needed is a balancing of the pros and cons of the clause in each case. That balancing is best done under antitrust law. Section 1 of the Sherman Act, 15 U.S.C. § 1, forbids contracts that restrain trade. If Rumbleseat had wanted, it could have attacked the no-contest clause under that statute. It did not do so. We decline to create a federal common law rule that would jostle uncomfortably with the Sherman Act. Noting the convergence of patent misuse principles with antitrust principles, we said in *USM Corp. v. SPS Technologies, Inc.*, 694 F.2d 505, 512 (7th Cir. 1982): "If misuse claims are not tested by conventional antitrust principles, by what principles shall they be tested? Our law is not rich in alternative concepts of monopolistic abuse; and it is rather late in the date to try to develop one without in the process subjecting the rights of patent holders to debilitating uncertainty." This point applies with even greater force to copyright misuse, where the danger of monopoly is less. We hold that a no-contest clause in a copyright licensing agreement is valid unless shown to violate antitrust law.

This holding is not barred by *Lear v. Adkins* [which] held that federal law forbids a state court to hold that a patent licensee is, by virtue of having been licensed, estopped to challenge the patent's validity. Our case involves a negotiated clause rather than a doctrine that in effect reads a no-contest clause into every licensing agreement. The doctrine is apt to have a broader effect. . . . Furthermore, the logic of *Lear* does not extend to copyright licenses. The opinion is narrowly written. It emphasizes

> the important public interest in permitting full and free competition in the use of ideas which are in reality a part of the public domain. Licensees may often be the only individuals with enough economic incentive to challenge the patentability of an inventor's discovery. If they are muzzled, the public may continually be required to pay tribute to would-be monopolists without need or justification.

A patent empowers its owner to prevent anyone else from making or using his invention; a copyright just empowers its owner to prevent others from copying the particular verbal or pictorial or aural pattern in which he chooses to express himself. The economic power conferred is much smaller. There is no need for a rule that would automatically invalidate every no-contest clause. If a particular clause is used to confer monopoly power beyond the small amount that the copyright laws authorize, the clause can be attacked under section 1 of the Sherman Act as a contract in restraint of trade. Rumbleseat does not argue that the clause here restrained trade in that sense. The fact that we can find no antitrust case — or for that matter any other reported case — that deals with a no-contest clause in a copyright license is evidence that these clauses are not such a source of significant restraints on freedom to compete as might warrant a per se rule of illegality.

A further point, already alluded to, is that the competitive interest in confining copyright and patent protection to valid copyrights and patents has to do with the originality, novelty, etc. of the work that is copyrighted or patented, rather than with the owner's identity. Only the last question is in issue here;

the validity of the Post's copyrights, not the copyrightability of the Rockwell dolls, is in issue. Once it is decided that a work is copyrightable, the decision has been made that the additional cost per copy to the public is warranted by the encouragement that copyright protection gives to the creation of new and valuable works; whether or not the ownership of the copyright is contestable by a licensee is then a detail irrelevant to the competitive policies that underlie *Lear*. We have made this distinction in other contexts.

This overstates the case a little, because Rumbleseat argues among other things that the Post failed to register its copyrights properly. If that is right, maybe the Rockwell illustrations have fallen into the public domain. It seems more likely, though, that what happened (or may have happened, for of course the arbitrators may have been correct in upholding the validity of the Post's copyrights — if that is what they did) is that the Post failed to perfect copyright in its derivative works — the photographs, printed in the magazine, of Rockwell's illustrations. The Rockwell family, which owns the copyrights on the original illustrations, could still enjoin Rumbleseat's infringement. The argument that the family's copyrights fell into the public domain presumably relies on the old doctrine of indivisibility — a disfavored doctrine, however and one rejected years ago for magazines.

So probably the effect of the copyrights on the price and output of porcelain dolls would be about the same whether or not Rumbleseat succeeded in knocking out the Post's copyrights. At least this is a strong possibility. Unfortunately, because Rumbleseat failed to make the record before the arbitrators part of the record in this court, we have only the haziest idea of what was and was not in issue before the arbitrators; but doubts engendered by Rumbleseat's failures must be resolved against Rumbleseat. At all events the basic originality and hence copyrightability of the Rockwell drawings on which the design of the infringing dolls is ultimately based seem not to be in issue.

So we have a narrow and a broad holding on no-contest clauses: they are valid in copyright licenses (broad); they are valid when no issue of copyrightability is presented (narrow). These, we emphasize, are both holdings, and therefore bind the district courts in this circuit. Of course a court of coequal or superior authority to this court might find one more persuasive than the other, and not being bound as a matter of authority to follow our decisions could decide to adopt just one. AFFIRMED.

NOTES

1. What is the difference in terms of the balance of policies between an implied estoppel and an express "no contest" clause? In a patent license, should that difference lead to a result different than that reached in *Lear*?

2. The Court's ruling in *Lear* dealt with implied estoppel, but the agreement in *Lear* did contain a term that required the licensee to continue paying royalties until such time as the patent was declared invalid. As discussed in *Troxel*, the court concluded that the licensee could not be forced to make payments from the time the patent initially issued, but in the case, the licensee had contested the patent from the outset and had made no payments under the license. Does this result in *Lear* suggest anything about "no contest" clauses in patent licenses?

3. Contractual "no contest" clauses are common. Another type of clause is also common. This provision binds the licensee to not assert infringement claims based on conduct under the licensed technology against the licensor or its other licensees based on a patent (or copyright) held by the licensee and not covered by the primary license. Does this contract term present the same issue presented by the no contest term?

IDAHO POTATO COMMISSION v. M & M PRODUCE FARM & SALES
335 F.3d 130 (2d Cir. 2003)

FEINBERG, CIRCUIT JUDGE.

Plaintiff Idaho Potato Commission ("IPC") appeals from a May 2002 Memorandum and Order ("May 2002 Order") of the United States District Court [vacating] a $41,962 jury award for the IPC in its certification mark[1] infringement suit under the Lanham Act [against] M & M Produce Farm and Sales, M & M Packaging, Inc., and Matthew and Mark Rogowski individually (collectively "M & M"). Defendant M & M cross-appeals from the court's August 1998 Memorandum and Order ("August 1998 Order") denying M & M summary judgment on its counterclaims and holding that M & M was barred from seeking cancellation of the IPC marks by a no-challenge provision in its licensing agreement with the IPC. M & M argues on appeal that the no-challenge provision should not be enforced because it violates the public policy embodied in the Lanham Act. . . .

The IPC is an agency created by Idaho statute to promote the sale of Idaho russet potatoes and to prevent the substitution of potatoes grown in other regions as Idaho potatoes. To further these goals, the IPC has registered a number of certification marks with the United States Patent and Trademark Office, two of which are relevant to this appeal: (1) the word "IDAHO" in a distinctive font; and (2) the phrase "GROWN IN IDAHO" written inside an outline of the boundaries of the state of Idaho (collectively "the IPC marks"). Each mark certifies that "goods so marked are grown in the State of Idaho."

The IPC controls its marks through an elaborate licensing system that seeks to ensure the quality and geographic authenticity of potatoes packed in containers bearing the IPC marks. This system requires everyone in the chain of distribution, from in-state growers to out-of-state repackers and resellers, to be licensed in order to use the IPC certification marks on their packaging. Licensed vendors are also prevented from selling Idaho potatoes to nonlicensed customers for repacking or reselling.

The standard licensing agreements provide licensees with the right to use the IPC marks, an important benefit because certified Idaho potatoes sell for

---

[1] [FN 1] "A certification mark is a special creature created for a purpose uniquely different from that of an ordinary trademark or service mark. It is a mark owned by one person and used by others in connection with their goods or services to certify quality, regional or other origin." 3 MCCARTHY ON TRADEMARKS AND UNFAIR COMPETITION § 19.91.

more than non-Idaho potatoes. In return, licensees agree, among other things, to use the IPC marks only on potatoes that are certified as grown in Idaho and that meet the IPC's other quality standards. Licensees also agree to maintain purchase and sale records so that the IPC can check periodically for compliance and prevent "counterfeiting" (putting non-Idaho potatoes in bags bearing the IPC marks). . . .

Because the jury's verdict against M & M was predicated on the IPC's ownership of valid certification marks, we first discuss M & M's cross-appeal challenging the district court's August 1998 ruling that M & M was not entitled to summary judgment and was estopped by the licensing agreement from attacking those marks. We will then turn to the IPC's appeal from the district court's vacatur of its damages award. . . .

[Discussion]

The facts relevant to the issue are not in dispute. M & M signed a licensing agreement with the IPC in which M & M recognized the validity of the IPC marks and promised not to attack the rights of the IPC in those marks during the term of the agreement or at any time thereafter. The basic question on the facts before us, therefore, is whether such a provision in a certification mark licensing agreement is enforceable against a licensee when the licensee no longer holds a license. This question has apparently not yet been squarely decided by any federal circuit court.

M & M contends that the no-challenge provision in its licensing agreement should not be enforced because it violates the public policy embodied in the Lanham Act. It argues that by requiring licensees to forever waive their statutory right to challenge the IPC's marks, the IPC effectively avoids enforcement of the Lanham Act. M & M relies principally on the Supreme Court's opinion in *Lear, Inc. v. Adkins,* which held that the contract doctrine of licensee estoppel was trumped by the federal policy embodied in the patent laws. M & M argues that *Lear* should apply to certification mark licenses as it does to patent licenses because the public interest in both is similar. Thus, M & M asks us to adopt the rule stated by the United States Patent and Trademark Office, Trademark Trial and Appeal Board that "there can be no licensee estoppel involving a certification mark." . . .

Courts applying the principles articulated in *Lear* to patent disputes have enforced no-challenge contract provisions only when the interests in doing so outweigh the public interest in discovering invalid patents. Thus, in *Flex-Foot,* [*Inc. v. CRP, Inc.,* 238 F.3d 1362, 1368 (Fed. Cir. 2001),] the United States Court of Appeals for the Federal Circuit recently enforced an estoppel provision in a settlement agreement only after determining that the public policy in favor of settlements outweighed the public interest in patents. The court stated that "the important policy of enforcing settlement agreements and res judicata must themselves be weighed against the federal patent laws' prescription of full and free competition in the use of ideas that are in reality a part of the public domain." The court concluded that when an accused patent infringer contractually agrees to voluntarily dismiss litigation challenging the rights of a patent holder after having "had an opportunity to conduct discovery on validity issues," the accused infringer is contractually estopped from raising any challenge in a subsequent proceeding.

Other courts, including this one, have weighed these interests to reach differing results, but each has recognized the applicability of the balancing test first articulated in *Lear. See, e.g., Warner-Jenkinson Co. v. Allied Chem. Corp.,* 567 F.2d 184, 187-88 (2d Cir.1977) (licensee could litigate the validity of patent even though licensing agreement was entered into as part of a settlement of earlier litigation); *Schlegel Mfg. Co. v. U.S.M. Corp.,* 525 F.2d 775, 781 (6th Cir.1975) (enforcing consent decree, which recited that plaintiff's patent was valid); *Kraly v. Nat'l Distillers & Chem. Corp.,* 502 F.2d 1366, 1369 (7th Cir.1974) (concluding that a licensee was not estopped from challenging the validity of a patent even where a consent decree incorporated an understanding that the patent would not be challenged); *Massillon-Cleveland-Akron Sign Co. v. Golden State Adver. Co.,* 444 F.2d 425, 427 (9th Cir.1971) (holding that covenant in settlement agreement whereby defendants agreed not to contest validity of patent was unenforceable because in direct conflict with strong federal policy).

The *Lear* balancing test has also been frequently applied to trademark licensing contracts. As the district court here correctly noted, courts in this context have generally precluded licensees from challenging the validity of a mark they have obtained the right to use. However, courts have done so only after considering the public interest in trademarks. For example, in *Beer Nuts, Inc. v. King Nut Co.,* the Sixth Circuit explicitly used the *Lear* balancing test in upholding a written agreement not to challenge the validity of a trademark. 477 F.2d 326, 329 (1973). The court distinguished the public policy of trademarks — guarding the public from being deceived into purchasing an unwanted product — from that of patents and held, "When the balancing test is employed in the instant situation, we conclude that the public interest in [trademarks] . . . is not so great that it should take precedence over the rule of the law of contracts that a person should be held to his undertakings." [S]ee also *MWS Wire Indus., Inc. v. California Fine Wire Co.,* 797 F.2d 799, 803 (9th Cir.1986) (relying on *Beer Nuts* and holding that "[t]o permit [defendant] to reopen the question of the validity of the trademark at this juncture would severely undercut the policy favoring the amicable resolution of trademark disputes without resort to the courts").

Even when courts have not expressly applied the *Lear* test, they have recognized that agreements related to intellectual property necessarily involve the public interest. . . .

The IPC maintains that the *Lear* balancing test is inapplicable because unlike the contract in *Lear,* which was silent concerning the rights of the licensee to challenge the patent, the contract signed by M & M specifically precluded M & M from challenging the IPC's marks. However, this distinction does not negate the applicability of the *Lear* balancing test to the contract in this case. *Lear* itself recognized that federal policy embodied in the law of intellectual property can trump even explicit contractual provisions. The licensor in *Lear* argued that based on the licensee's explicit contractual agreement to pay royalties until invalidity of the patent had been determined by a court, the licensee was required to pay royalties for the duration of the litigation even if the patent in question was eventually declared invalid. The *Lear* Court disagreed and refused to enforce the contract on the same basis that it refused to apply licensee estoppel: "The parties' contract, however, is no more controlling on this issue than is the State's doctrine of estoppel, which is also rooted in contract principles." *Id. Lear* makes clear that courts should weigh the federal policy embodied in the law of intellectual property against even explicit contractual provisions and render unenforceable those provisions that would undermine the public interest. Also, as discussed above, other courts have applied *Lear* to explicit contract provisions. Thus, the explicit contractual provision in the licensing agreement between the IPC and M & M is no barrier to application of the *Lear* balancing test.

We turn now to application of this balancing test to the current dispute. In doing so, we must identify the public interest in certification marks and the public injury that might result from enforcement of the estoppel provision in the contract between M & M and the IPC. The IPC argues, and the district court agreed, that the trademark cases enforcing no-challenge provisions noted above are controlling with regard to certification marks because "certification marks are generally treated the same as trademarks." Although we recognize that trademarks and certification marks are "generally treated the same," we conclude that the difference between the public interests in certification marks and trademarks compels a different result in this context.

In the trademark context, as already noted, "[a] dealer's good will is protected . . . in order that the purchasing public may not be enticed into buying A's product when it wants B's product." Thus, agreements that allow the continued use of confusingly similar trademarks injure the public, and the important issue in litigation over trademark contracts is the public confusion that might result from enforcing the contract. *See* 15 U.S.C. § 1052(d) (permitting refusal of registration if a mark "so resembles [another] mark . . . as to be likely, when used on or in connection with the goods of the applicant, to cause confusion, or to cause mistake, or to deceive").

Significantly, trademark owners are granted a monopoly over their marks and can choose to license the marks to others on whatever conditions they deem appropriate, so long as confusion does not result. The same is not true of certification marks. Certification mark licensing programs are "a form of limited compulsory licensing," 3 MCCARTHY ON TRADEMARKS AND UNFAIR COMPETITION § 19.96, and the certifier has a "duty . . . to certify the goods or services of any person who meets the standards and conditions which the mark certifies."

That the owner of a certification mark "cannot refuse to license the mark to anyone on any ground other than the standards it has set," 3 MCCARTHY at § 19.96, is an important distinction between the policies embodied in trademarks and certification marks. It is true that certification marks are designed to facilitate consumer expectations of a standardized product, much like trademarks are designed to ensure that a consumer is not confused by the marks on a product. *See, e.g., Institut Nat'l Des Appellations d'Origine v. Brown-Forman Corp.,* 47 U.S.P.Q.2d 1875, 1889-90 (T.T.A.B.1998) (holding that same likelihood of confusion test applied in the context of trademarks also applies to certification marks). But the certification mark regime protects a further public interest in free and open competition among producers and distributors of the certified product. It protects the market players from the influence of the certification mark owner, *see* 15 U.S.C. § 1064(5) (listing grounds for cancellation of a certification mark when the neutrality of the rights holder is compromised), and aims to ensure the broadest competition, and therefore the best price and quality, within the market for certified products. *See* 15 U.S.C. § 1064(5)(D) (permitting cancellation of any certification mark owned by a registrant who "discriminately refuses to certify or to continue to certify the goods or services of any person who maintains the standards or conditions which such mark certifies"). From our review of the cases, it appears to us that this interest is akin to the public interest in the "full and free use of ideas in the public domain" embodied in the patent laws.

We believe that the estoppel provision in the contract between M & M and the IPC injures this public interest in a number of ways. First, the provision places a non-quality-control related restriction on the sellers of the certified product and other licensees that benefits the mark owner in contravention of the mark owner's obligation not to interfere with a free market for products meeting the certification criteria. Second, as in *Lear,* parties that have entered into a licensee relationship with the IPC may often be the only individuals with enough economic incentive to challenge the IPC's licensing scheme, and thus the only individuals with enough incentive to force the IPC to conform to the law.

Finally, to decide the issue of public injury we must look to the public interest implicated by the merits of the licensee's challenges. M & M alleges, among other things, that: (1) the IPC is a corporate entity dominated by producers of the certified products and that such domination violates the provisions in 15 U.S.C. § 1064(5)(B); (2) the IPC uses the goodwill derived from the certification marks as a trademark in violation of § 1064(5)(C); (3) the IPC imposes certification standards other than those that the certification mark is registered to certify in violation of § 1064(5)(D); and (4) the IPC discriminately refuses to certify potatoes that meet the standards for certification, also in violation of § 1064(5)(D). All of these challenges implicate the public interest in maintaining a free market for the certified product unaffected by the possible competing economic interests of the certification mark owner.

We believe these public interests are more substantial and more likely to be harmed if M & M is not allowed to press its claims than the public interests and de minimis harm alleged in the trademark-related cases that upheld contractual no-challenge provisions. Also, this case lacks a strong countervailing public interest other than the general interest in enforcing written contracts (like the interest in settlements) that persuaded courts to enforce contractual no-challenge provisions in other agreements. We therefore conclude that the district court erred in finding M & M contractually estopped as a matter of law from challenging the IPC marks. We express no view as to whether on remand M & M will be able to prove its counterclaims for cancellation of the marks. We hold only that M & M is not estopped from making and attempting to prove such claims in the first instance. . . .

Conclusion

[We] vacate the district court's August 1998 Order holding M & M estopped as a matter of law from bringing its counterclaims for cancellation of the IPC marks and remand for consideration of those claims on the merits. . . .

PROBLEM 8.5

OSI is the owner and operator of the "Open Source Approved" certification trademark. "Open Source" is a type of licensing for software that has an ardent group of adherents both within and outside the OSI Foundation. OSI has approved Client's use of the mark subject to Client taking two steps that Client believes are not truly necessary to be an "Open Source" product. Client believes that it can challenge the validity of the "Open Source Approved" mark because it is generic (e.g., a term widely used and not unique to OSI). Can Client challenge the validity of the mark and, at the same time, use the mark while not complying with the OSI requirements? If it does so, does the licensor have any remedy? What result if the mark is held to be valid and enforceable?

PROBLEM 8.6

Acme grants a license covering its ball bearing technology to Thomas. In return, Thomas agrees to pay royalties and to refrain from asserting its own patents against Acme and any other Acme licensee with respect to manufacturing of ball bearings. Assume that there are no antitrust concerns here, is this agreement enforceable?

D. Licensor Obligations: Value of the Rights

WESTOWNE SHOES, INC. v. BROWN GROUP, INC.
104 F.3d 994 (7th Cir. 1997)

POSNER, CHIEF JUDGE.

In this diversity suit based on Wisconsin law, affiliated firms, now defunct, that owned retail shoe stores in Wisconsin and that we shall refer to collectively as "Westowne" fired a blunderbuss full of charges, mostly based on the common law of contracts but with trademark and antitrust allegations thrown in, against Westowne's former supplier, the Brown Shoe Company of antitrust fame. The district court granted summary judgment for Brown. . . .

Brown manufactures a popular line of women's dressy shoes under the name "Naturalizer." Beginning in the early 1970s, Brown sold Naturalizers to Westowne for resale. It also licensed Westowne to use the name "Naturalizer" as part of Westowne's trade dress; that is, Westowne was permitted to use the name on its store signs (Brown even furnished the signs) and thus represent the stores to the consuming public as being authorized Naturalizer dealers. Westowne and the other licensees were not forbidden to sell other brands, and Westowne supplemented Naturalizers with women's casual shoes made by the

San Antonio Shoe Company, but 80 to 90 percent of the shoes that it sold were Naturalizers.

In 1987 Brown instituted [its] curiously named "purity" program, the focus of Westowne's wrath. Under this program, any store that wanted to retain "Naturalizer" in its sign, that is, wanted to represent itself as an authorized Naturalizer dealer or Naturalizer specialty store, had to cease selling brands other than Naturalizer. Brown was willing to continue selling Naturalizers to stores that carried other brands, but it required them to delete the word "Naturalizer" from their store signs and gave them a lower priority in the filling of orders.

The problem with "going pure" was that the Naturalizer line was not complete. It had dressy shoes, but not casual ones. So along with or as part of the purity program — for all we know, it was a principal purpose of the program — Brown developed a line of women's casual shoes under the Naturalizer label. It told Westowne that these shoes would be "stitch-by-stitch knock-offs" — that is, perfect imitations — of the popular SAS shoes. According to testimony that we must accept as true for purposes of this appeal, though without vouching for its truth, Brown's attempt to develop SAS "knock-offs" was a flop. They were so bad that not only was Westowne, which wanted to remain an authorized Naturalizer dealer and therefore stopped buying from SAS and began buying the knock-offs instead, unable to sell them; they also degraded the Naturalizer mark, making it difficult for Westowne to sell even the good Naturalizers — the original, dressy line — at a profit. Compounding Westowne's problems, it found it increasingly difficult to obtain the good Naturalizers. Brown has an "in stock" program, under which it maintains a large inventory of shoes from which to restock its dealers, enabling them to minimize their own inventory expense. As part of what Westowne describes as Brown's effort to monopolize the shoe business, Brown was busy buying up retail outlets and allocating all available inventory to them, thus starving independent dealers like Westowne; and it also sold to its own outlets at a lower price. Eventually Westowne went under and, owing Brown a considerable sum for shoes delivered but not paid for, brought this suit.

Westowne argues that Brown committed a breach of contract by putting Westowne to the miserable choice of losing its Naturalizer dealership (that is, the right to represent its stores as Naturalizer dealers) or replacing the SAS shoes that it carried with inferior knock-offs. The only written contract was the licensing agreement, and it does not bear on this contract claim. Westowne's argument is that the course of dealing between the parties, not any written contract, gave Westowne a contractual entitlement to remain a Naturalizer dealer indefinitely and forbade Brown to impose unreasonable conditions on the retention of the dealership, such as requiring the dealer to carry a substandard product. Westowne points out that the Wisconsin Fair Dealership Law, creates such an entitlement. True; but this is not a suit under the dealership act; such a suit would be barred by the act's one-year statute of limitations. Westowne's argument that the act creates entitlements which can then be enforced by a suit under the common law of contracts, with its six-year statute of limitations, is a transparent evasion of the statute of limitations in the dealership act.

The absence of a written contract other than the irrelevant licensing agreement and the multitudinous sales contracts, also irrelevant, covering particular shipments of shoes to Westowne's stores is not critical to the common law contract claim, because Brown has not raised a statute of frauds defense. What is critical is the absence of terms. Westowne's principal testified that he had a contract with Brown, but he was unable to answer such questions as, When did the contract start? When or under what conditions does it terminate? Is the "purity" program a violation? Did Brown so far relinquish its rights over its trademark as to entitle Westowne to sell another manufacturer's shoes from a store that holds itself out to be a Naturalizer dealership? What consideration did Brown receive for this trademark-endangering concession? The common law of contracts does not empower a court to write the parties' contract for them, but that is what Westowne is asking us to do.

Westowne also argues, however, that by promising it perfect imitations of SAS shoes, Brown induced it to forgo its remedies under the Wisconsin Fair Dealership Law until the statute of limitations ran out. (Under that law, according to Westowne, Brown could not have forced Westowne to give up its Naturalizer dealership just because Westowne insisted on continuing to carry SAS shoes.) Brown should therefore be estopped to — to what? Westowne is not very clear about this, but the only answer can be — to plead the statute of limitations in a suit under the dealership law. A defendant who takes steps to prevent the plaintiff from suing within the statute of limitations is equitably estopped to plead it. . . . But this principle presupposes a suit to which the statute of limitations has been interposed as a defense, in this case a suit under the Wisconsin Fair Dealership Act. Westowne has not sued under that act. We do not think it is permitted to recycle the statutory claim that it failed to make as a common law claim of promissory estoppel in which damages are sought, much as in a suit for legal malpractice, for the loss of the statutory claim. That approach would require speculation about what Westowne's remedies under the dealership law might have been had it sued under that law. Unnecessary speculation: unlike a case of legal malpractice, where the suit the lawyer botched is gone forever, a plaintiff who claims that the defendant by promises or otherwise prevented him from bringing a timely suit can bring an untimely suit against that defendant on the identical claim on which the timely suit would have been based. To disguise a statutory claim as a claim for promissory estoppel in an unnecessary effort to beat a statute of limitations is a formula for confusion, and the district court is not required to tolerate it.

Westowne makes the alternative argument for promissory estoppel — an argument happily free from any dependence on the unpleaded dealership law — that it relied on the promise of the stitch-by-stitch knock-offs by "going pure," that is, by discontinuing its purchases of SAS shoes. Yet at the same time it argues that it had to go pure because it could not afford to give up the Naturalizer sign. This means that it would have gone pure even if Brown had not promised a perfect substitute. So the promise made no difference. The promise is also the basis for Westowne's claim of misrepresentation, and fails for the same reason. Fraud is not actionable without harm. If, as Westowne itself asserts, it would have gone pure to retain its dealership, regardless of any representation concerning the SAS knock-offs, those representations caused it no harm. No harm, no tort. . . .

Westowne has other arrows in its quiver. It claims that Brown violated the trademark license by degrading the Naturalizer trademark by affixing it to the unwearable, unsalable knock-offs. While a trademark licensee (at least if he has an exclusive license), as well as the trademark's owner, can sue to protect the trademark from infringement . . . , he cannot sue the trademark owner for "infringing" the trademark. . . . There is no basis in either the federal or the state law of unfair competition for such a claim. The owner can if he wants, unless contractually committed otherwise, abandon the trademark, dilute it, attach it to goods of inferior quality, attach it to completely different goods — can, in short, take whatever steps he wants to jeopardize or even completely destroy the trademark. When cases speak of the trademark owner's "duty to ensure the consistency of the trademarked good or service," [they] mean that it is a condition of the continued validity of the trademark, [or] a defense to a consumer's claim of having been fooled by the substitution of an inferior good, not that it is a ground for a licensee's being allowed to sue to force the trademark owner to take steps to assure the trademark's continued validity.

We think that Westowne more or less understands all this, and is making solely a contract claim — that the trademark license obligated Brown to keep the Naturalizer mark up to snuff. A licensor might so promise, but this licensor did not. Westowne is asking us to make such a promise an implied term of every trademark licensing agreement, and that would be absurd. It would give licensees comprehensive power over the licensor's business — in this case power to tell Brown what kind or quality of shoes it can manufacture and sell under the Naturalizer label. Few licensors would agree to that, and there is no evidence that Brown is one of them. The office of implied contractual terms is to save contracting parties costs of negotiations by interpolating terms that they are pretty sure to have agreed to had they thought about the matter, not terms that they would be almost sure to reject; for the interpolation of such terms would increase rather than decrease the costs of contracting as parties busied themselves contracting around the interpolated terms. We add that Westowne's trademark claim is inconsistent with its other claims, all of which are premised on the continued potency of the Naturalizer mark.

AFFIRMED.

NOTES

1. Do you agree that recognizing a rule that the licensor must act in good faith to maintain the value of the licensed intellectual property is more intrusive on its business operations than the intrusion on the licensee's business by imposing obligations on a licensee's exploitation of the licensed property?

2. The *Restatement,* the UCC, and UCITA all provide that a contract carries with it an implied obligation of "good faith" in its performance. What constitutes "good faith" is the issue, as is the question of how that obligation relates to the express terms of the contract. As a general principle, good faith obligations are subordinate to express terms — the idea of good faith cannot take away that which the contract expressly grants. On the other hand, the UCC has long provided that the contractual obligation of good faith cannot be disclaimed. The most that can be done is to provide standards against which the obligation is measured. UCC § 1-201 (1998 Official Text).

3. In *Western Electric Co. v. Pacent Reproducer Corporation*, 42 F.2d 116, 116 (2d Cir. 1930), *cert. denied*, 282 U.S. 873 (1930), dealing with a non-exclusive licensee, the court commented: "the patent owner may freely license

> others, or may tolerate infringers, and in either case no right of the patent licensee is violated. Practice of the invention by others may indeed cause him pecuniary losses, but it does him no legal injury. Compare the analogous situation were the author of a copyrighted play grants a license to produce it, reserving motion pictures rights. . . . Infringement of the patent can no more be a legal injury to a bare licensee than a trespass upon Blackacre could be an injury to one having a nonexclusive right of way across Blackacre." Do you agree?

PROBLEM 8.7

Gooch, a famous name in women's apparel has licensed over 1,000 companies to use the Gooch trademark in manufacturing and selling clothing. Gooch maintains strict quality control over all of the licensees. After operating in this way for years, the Gooch family decides to leave the business. It contacts Hart clothing, its chief competitor in several markets. Hart agrees to acquire the Gooch trademark, licenses, and other assets for a stated price that Gooch thinks is fair.

After the sale, Hart decides to destroy the value of the Gooch trade name. It does so by making licenses available to anyone that desires one and by not exercising any control over the quality of products produced under the name. Sacks, a retailer that has a large business selling Gooch products, sues Hart for breach of the license under which Sacks operates. What result?

PROBLEM 8.8

Techno Company has licensed software and know-how to several manufacturers for use in their assembly lines. While the software is copyrighted, much of its value lies in the secret methods that it uses to make the assembly lines more efficient. As a result, Techno requires each licensee to sign a non-disclosure agreement and to establish procedures to prevent disclosure to others.

Techno has internal management problems. Because of those problems, portions of the secret process are disclosed to the industry. Other companies design and implement competing systems. Smith, one of the Techno licensees, sues for breach of its license. What result?

UCC Article 2 contains statutory provisions relating to both a hold-harmless obligation and to how the obligation can be enforced. Section 2-312(c) provides for an automatically created hold-harmless obligation in cases where the licensee provides specifications to be followed by the licensor:

(c) Unless otherwise agreed a seller who is a merchant regularly dealing in goods of the kind warrants that the goods shall be delivered free of the rightful claim of any third person by way of infringement or the like but a buyer who furnishes specifications to the seller must hold the seller harmless against any such claim which arises out of compliance with the specifications.

UCC § 2-312 (1998 Official Text).

In addition, UCC § 2-607 contains the following provisions:

(e) Where the buyer is sued for breach of a warranty or other obligation for which his seller is answerable over

(1) he may give his seller written notice of the litigation. If the notice states that the seller may come in and defend and that if the seller does not do so he will be bound in any action against him by his buyer by any determination of fact common to the two litigations, then unless the seller after seasonable receipt of the notice does come in and defend he is so bound.

(2) if the claim is one for infringement or the like (Subsection (c) of Section 2-312) the original seller may demand in writing that his buyer turn over to him control of the litigation including settlement or else be barred from any remedy over and if he also agrees to bear all expense and to satisfy any adverse judgment, then unless the buyer after seasonable receipt of the demand does turn over control the buyer is so barred.

UCC § 2-607 (1998 Official Text).

III. OBLIGATIONS FOR QUALITY OF PERFORMANCE

Issues about the quality of performance due in a license are handled in various ways. In some cases, qualitative obligations are in covenants (promises) of best efforts, reasonable care, or the like. In other cases, the license is in the nature of a quitclaim in which neither party gives express assurances or promises about quality. In still other cases, quality issues are bound up in the language of warranty or in promises regarding the maintenance and upgrading of the licensed subject matter.

Each framework comes with its own characteristics and problems. Cutting across all of these, however, is a distinction grounded in the source of the obligation. That source can be in implied obligations or in expressly undertaken obligations. That distinction is constant in law, but the content and conditions for the obligations vary widely.

Article 2 distinguishes between express and implied warranties. Express warranties are promises, representations or the like that become part of the "basis of the bargain" of the parties. UCC § 2-313 (1998 Official Text). These are part of the overt bargain between the parties; they may be contained in the written agreement. In contrast, implied warranties arise by operation of law unless disclaimed. UCC §§ 2-314, 315 (1998 Official Text). The implied warranties are the warranty of merchantability and the warranty of fitness for a particular purpose. The first gives implied assurances that the subject matter has quality equivalent to ordinary goods of the type, while the second gives implicit assurance that the subject matter goods will fit the purposes of the buyer who relied on the seller's expertise to select the appropriate goods.

We will spend little time on Article 2 warranties because they are covered in other courses and have limited importance to licensing other than software and their indirect influence through UCITA which adopts an analogous, but tailored, set of warranties. Outside of the UCC and UCITA, including in most patent, copyright, trade secret, and trademark licensing, different structures and presumptions exist. Even in UCITA, a specially tailored set of rules is promulgated for informational content and for cases where services are an important facet of the licensing transaction.

A. Services and Issues About Quality

DATA PROCESSING SERVICES, INC. v. L.H. SMITH OIL CORP.
492 N.E.2d 314 (Ind. App. 1986)

CONOVER, JUDGE.

Defendant-Appellant Data Processing Services, Inc. (DPS), appeals an adverse breach of contract judgment in favor of plaintiff-appellee, L.H. Smith Oil Corporation (Smith). We affirm.

Facts

DPS is in the business of custom computer programming. Smith sells petroleum products. The business relationship between these parties occurred between 1979 and 1981. Smith and DPS entered into an oral agreement under which DPS was to develop computer software for Smith's IBM System-32 computer. Later, DPS was engaged to develop and implement a data processing system for Smith's new IBM System-34 computer. DPS was to develop an accounting system to meet Smith's specific needs.

In 1981, after having paid several billings submitted by DPS, Smith refused to pay DPS's billing of $7,166.25. DPS sued Smith in Marion Municipal Court (Municipal Court). DPS there alleged breach of contract and open account. Smith answered, then later filed a petition to amend its answer to assert a counterclaim. This petition was denied. Smith then sued DPS in Marion Superior Court (Superior Court), asserting substantially the same claims as those it would have asserted had the Municipal Court granted its petition to amend. [The] causes were ordered consolidated.

Following trial before the court without [jury], judgment was rendered in Smith's favor. [DPS] appeals. . . .

Discussion and Decision

[The] trial court found Smith contracted for the development and the delivery of a "program" by DPS. It determined the program was a specially manufactured good within the meaning of [UCC § 2-501(1)(a) and (b)]. [DPS] contends the court erred when it determined the contract was for a "good," subject to the provisions of Art. 2 of the UCC. DPS asserts it was supplying "services," not "goods." Further, DPS argues there was no evidence of what product it was to supply to Smith.

Defining "goods," I.C. 26-1-2-105(1) of the UCC reads in part

"Goods" means all things (including specially manufactured goods) which are movable at the time of identification to the contract for sale other than the money in which the price is to be paid, investment securities (Article 8) and things in action. . . .

Heretofore this court has not been called upon to determine whether a contract to provide computer programming is a contract for the sale and purchase of goods and thus subject to the provisions of Article 2 of the UCC, or one for the performance of services, and thus subject to common law principles. . . .

In this case, [the] facts found by the trial court do not support a conclusion DPS sold goods to Smith. Thus the transaction does not fall within Article 2 of the UCC. It was error to so conclude.

The transaction here is clear-cut. Unlike many of the cases reported in other jurisdictions, DPS sold no "hardware" to Smith. Instead, DPS was retained to design, develop and implement an electronic data processing system to meet Smith's specific needs. The very terminology used by the trial court and the parties here show services, not goods were that for which Smith contracted. DPS was *to act* with specific regard to Smith's need. Smith bargained for DPS's skill in developing a system to meet its specific needs. Although the end result was to be preserved by means of some physical manifestation such as magnetic tape, floppy or hard disks, etc., which would generate the recordkeeping computer functions DPS was to develop, it was DPS's knowledge, skill, and ability for which Smith bargained. The sale of computer hardware or generally-available standardized software was not here involved. The mere means by which DPS's skills and knowledge were to be transmitted to Smith's computers was incidental.

The situation here is more analogous to a client seeking a lawyer's advice or a patient seeking medical treatment for a particular ailment than it is to a customer buying seed corn, soap, or cam shafts. While a tangible end product, such as floppy disks, hard disks, punch cards or magnetic tape used as a storage medium for the program may be involved incidentally in this transaction, it is the skill and knowledge of the programmer which is being purchased in the main, not the devices by which this skill and knowledge is placed into the buyer's computer. The means of transmission is not the essence of the agreement. Thus, the provisions of the UCC, including I.C. 26-1-2-314 (implied warranty of merchantability) and I.C. 26-1-2-315 (implied warranty of fitness for a particular purpose), do not apply.

Although the trial court's conclusion the transaction was for goods to which Article 2 of the UCC applies is clearly erroneous, reversal is not necessary. The findings of fact are sufficient to support the judgment on common law principles.

Those who hold themselves out to the world as possessing skill and qualifications in their respective trades or professions impliedly represent they possess the skill and will exhibit the diligence ordinarily possessed by well informed members of the trade or profession. We hold these principles apply with equal force to those who contract to develop computer programming.

The trial court found: (a) DPS represented it had the necessary expertise and training to design and develop a system to meet the needs of Smith; (b) DPS lacked the requisite skills and expertise to do the work; (c) DPS knew it lacked the skill and expertise; (d) DPS should have known Smith was dependent upon DPS's knowledge and abilities; and (e) DPS should have foreseen Smith would incur losses if DPS did not perform as agreed. These findings demonstrate DPS breached its implied promise of having the reasonable skill and ability to do the job for which it contracted. . . .

AFFIRMED.

NOTES

1. A decision that a transaction falls outside the scope of Article 2 yields a framework of obligations that are far different from that set out in the UCC. The implied obligations of the person engaged in providing services ordinarily consists of no more than an obligation to perform according to ordinary standards. The test does not focus on the result achieved, but on the process — reasonable and workmanlike conduct.

2. In contexts where the focus is on creation of custom or prototype work product for a client, cases split on whether to focus on the tangible product delivered, treating the transaction as one for goods, or on the method and effort used to create it. Thus, consider *USM Corp. v. Arthur Little Systems,* 546 N.E.2d 888 (Mass. App. 1989), where the court held that a software development contract was a transaction in goods that was breached when the resulting software did not meet response time and other qualitative characteristics for an acceptable product. The project was described as involving the development of a "turnkey" software system. This tended to focus the expectations of the parties on successful completion of a product, rather than merely on time and effort. Further:

> ADLS warranted that "at the time of delivery the system will be free of defects in design." The "system" must refer to the computer system which is the subject of the contract. In its ordinary sense, the word "design" would include the choice of hardware and software to work in combination with each other to do a particular job, and the inability of those products, in combination, to perform the required tasks within a reasonable response time would constitute a defect. . . . Additionally, ADLS warranted that "at the time of delivery the system . . . will be in substantial accordance with the functional specifications produced in Tasks 1-3, Attachment B.

3. In services contracts, the vendor-licensor commits by contract only that it possesses the skill that it represents itself to have and that it will exercise that skill in a workmanlike and reasonably careful manner. The workmanlike effort warranty does not create strict liability. To prove breach of warranty, it is necessary to show actions that breach reasonable (workmanlike) care obligations. *See Restatement (Second) of Torts* § 299A: "one who undertakes to render services in the practice of a profession or trade is required to exercise the skill and knowledge normally possessed by members of that profession *or trade*. . . ." The comment suggests that the rule applies to professionals and to anyone who undertakes to provide services to another in a skilled trade. Why is this language in the *Restatement of Torts* and not in the *Restatement of Contracts*?

PROBLEM 8.9

Engineer Corp. agreed to develop and design a prototype waste management system for Client that Client could then use in its national construction and development work. The project will take several months. Engineer will deliver a prototype system and all engineering drawings and the like. The agreement provides that Client will own the copyright to all drawings, and that it will have co-ownership of any patentable material developed in the project. The agreement also gives Client a license to use several Engineer patents, to the extent they are used in the developed system. The agreement also calls for an acceptance test period in which the system as delivered must meet specified standards before Client will pay the final $10 million payment.

When it is completed, the system meets the standard, but does not function at a sufficiently efficient level for Client to use it in its business. Client refuses to make the final payment. What result?

PROBLEM 8.10

Compuwin is a provider of software for large computer systems. It provides its software for a single license fee covering a two year license term. The fees for its most popular software are $50,000. In addition, Compuwin provides maintenance services for $20,000 per year. The maintenance fee gives the licensee 1) the right to call and obtain telephone support from Compuwin, 2) the right to receive at no additional charge, all upgrades and enhancements created by Compuwin during the two year term of the agreement, and 3) to have access for a maximum of 100 hours to programmers from Compuware to work on correcting problems in the user's system. Time beyond those hours is charged at ordinary hourly rates. The upgrades and enhancements are typically new code that cures problems discovered among a number of licensees or that improve the speed or performance of the software.

Compuwin has been sued by a licensee for breach of warranty and breach of the maintenance contract. The allegations are that the software as delivered contained a flaw that caused the computer to crash at random times. Compuware, it is alleged, failed to fix this problem during the last two years.

What result?

B. Quality of Information Content

For patent licensing, the primary patent treatises suggest that there exists no implied warranty by the licensor that the licensed invention has commercial utility for the particular licensee. While the cases are few and relatively old, they most likely still govern unless the subject matter falls within Article 2 or 2A. Some thus conclude that there are no implied warranties in a license, but that is true only in the purest form of patent licensing. In reference to more blended types of licensing, consider the following language of the *Restatement (Second) of Torts* §:

> One who, in the cause of his business, profession or employment, or in any other transaction in which he has a pecuniary interest, supplies false information for the guidance of others in their business transactions, is subject to liability for pecuniary loss caused to them by their justifiable reliance on the information, if he fails to exercise reasonable care or competence in obtaining or communicating the information.

This is the doctrine of negligent misrepresentation and its subject matter is information transferred to others for use in business. Whether this doctrine creates a "warranty" or not is less important than that it states an obligation in a contractual relationship. Does it apply to a licensor who provides, along with a license of a patent, know how information relating to how to use the licensed patent?

ROSENSTEIN v. STANDARD & POOR'S CORP.
636 N.E.2d 665 (Ill. App. 1993)

JUSTICE GREIMAN:

Alan Rosenstein (plaintiff) seeks reversal of the trial court's order dismissing with prejudice his complaint alleging negligent misrepresentation by Standard & Poor's (S & P) in incorporating an erroneous closing price of a particular stock in the Standard & Poor 100 and Standard & Poor 500 Indexes that established the sale price of plaintiff's option contracts.

S & P and the Chicago Board Options Exchange (CBOE) entered into a licensing agreement whereby S & P was the official source for calculating and disseminating the closing values of the S & P Indexes for the purpose of trading securities options. The settlement value of these options is the closing value of the indexes reported by S & P to the Options Clearing Corporation (OCC) following the close of trading on the Friday before the expiration date of the options. The OCC settles traders' options automatically. Plaintiff held 241 option contracts with the CBOE that were settled on December 15, 1989, the value determined by the reported S & P Indexes, and sought to recover his "losses" and those of the putative class members holding option contracts.

We affirm the trial court because S & P's liability has been expressly exculpated by the terms of the license agreement between S & P and the CBOE, and incorporated into the rules of the CBOE, which regulate plaintiff's transactions.

In the licensing agreement, to which sales are subject, S & P agreed to correct "inaccuracies in the S & P indexes within the control of S & P which are discovered by S & P or brought to its attention." Plaintiff's complaint, however, does not allege this provision of the agreement.

The complaint does set out the exculpatory clause included in the agreement: "S & P shall obtain information for inclusion in or for use in the calculation of the S & P Indexes from sources which S & P considers reliable, but S & P does not guarantee the accuracy and/or the completeness of any of the S & P Indexes or any data included therein. S & P MAKES NO WARRANTY, EXPRESS OR IMPLIED, AS TO RESULTS TO BE OBTAINED BY ANY PERSON OR ANY ENTITY FROM THE USE OF THE S & P INDEXES OR ANY DATA INCLUDED THEREIN IN CONNECTION WITH THE TRADING OF THE CONTRACTS, OR FOR ANY OTHER USE. S & P MAKES NO EXPRESS OR IMPLIED WARRANTIES OF MERCHANTABILITY OR FITNESS FOR A PARTICULAR PURPOSE FOR USE WITH RESPECT TO THE S & P INDEXES OR ANY DATA INCLUDED THEREIN. CBOE Rules shall expressly include the disclaimer language contained in this Paragraph 12(c)."

On the last day of trading before the expiration of December options on Friday, December 15, 1989, at 3:12 p.m., the New York Stock Exchange (NYSE) reported an inaccurate closing price for Ford Motor Company stock, one of the stock prices used by S & P to calculate its indexes. At 3:15 p.m., the NYSE reported a corrected closing price for Ford stock.

Plaintiff's complaint alleges S & P contracted with Automated Data Processing (ADP), to compute the indexes based upon price information received from the NYSE and that ADP received timely notice of the inaccuracy from the NYSE but failed to correct it. Had the corrected price been used to calculate the indexes, plaintiff apparently would not have lost $3,225 upon settlement of his options contracts by the OCC, which relied upon the index values as reported by S & P. S & P corrected the values on Monday, December 18, 1989, but this was after plaintiff, and others holding 92,000 option contracts, had settled the contracts using the earlier-reported values.

Plaintiff's complaint alleged that S & P negligently misrepresented the closing values of the two indexes, causing plaintiff and the class to suffer harm upon settlement of options traded under a licensing agreement with S & P.

The trial court granted S & P's 2-615 motion to dismiss with prejudice on the grounds that plaintiff did not and could not state a cause of action for negligent misrepresentation because plaintiff did not and could not plead any duty owed by S & P to plaintiff and plaintiff took no action in reliance of information disseminated by S & P.

The first issue for consideration in any negligence case is whether the trial court properly determined if defendant owed a duty to plaintiff as a matter of law. [To] state a cause of action for negligent misrepresentation, plaintiff must plead and prove: (1) a false statement of material fact, (2) carelessness or negligence in ascertaining the truth of the statement by defendant, (3) an intention to induce the other party to act, (4) action by the other party in reliance on the truth of the statements, (5) damage to the other party resulting from such reliance, and (6) a duty owed by defendant to plaintiff to communicate accurate information.

Plaintiff argues that his cause of action is not for a breach of a guarantee of accuracy or a warranty of merchantability or fitness for a particular purpose, but rather for a breach of S & P's duty to use due care in calculating and disseminating index values which it knew were going to be used by the OCC for automatic settlement of options contracts. Plaintiff contends that S & P licensed the indexes knowing traders would rely on the values in the automatic settlement of their contracts and specifically warranted a prompt correction of any inaccuracies, thus creating a duty to plaintiff and his class. Plaintiff argues that the disclaimer does not address S & P's duty to use due care in calculating and disseminating closing index values.

S & P responds by denying that the obligation to provide information creates a duty to the plaintiff or other traders; that it is a publisher protected by the First Amendment; that S & P Indexes are merely the products of its editorial judgment rather than misrepresented facts; that plaintiff did not act in reliance upon S & P Index values reported by S & P; that plaintiff may not sue in tort for disappointed commercial expectations; and that plaintiff purchased S & P Index options to be determined by S & P and that he therefore received that for which he bargained. Finally, S & P also asserts that the license agreement which is the basis for its purported liability is limited by the exculpatory clause which is set out in the complaint.

[In] considering S & P's duty to plaintiff, we first examine Justice Cardozo's opinion in *Glanzer v. Shepard* (1922), 233 N.Y. 236, 135 N.E. 275. Plaintiff contracted to pay a third party according to the actual weight of the beans as determined by defendant bean weigher. The bean weigher had negligently misrepresented the actual weight of the beans and was held to owe a duty to plaintiff and reimburse him for losses based upon the incorrect weight.

Plaintiff claims, and we tend to agree, that compilation is merely a sophisticated version of bean weighing.

In 1969, our supreme court considered the policy decision in *Glanzer* and determined that one who negligently supplies inaccurate information to one who relies upon such information would be liable if use of the information was foreseeable, if defendant knew the information would be used and relied upon by persons other than those in privity with him, and if the potential liability was restricted to a comparatively small group. *Rozny v. Marnul* (1969), 43 Ill.2d 54, 250 N.E.2d 656 (surveyor liable to third persons for inaccuracies in survey).

Having established the tort of negligent misrepresentation, *Moorman Manufacturing Co. v. National Tank Co.* (1982), 91 Ill.2d 69, 61 Ill.Dec. 746, 435 N.E.2d 443, provided scope and focus for the pursuit of such litigation in Illinois. *Moorman* held that disappointed commercial expectations could be redressed only in an action sounding in contract rather than in tort.

The supreme court was anxious that parties not circumvent contractual remedies when seeking recovery for economic losses; however, the exceptions noted by *Moorman* were actions for fraudulent misrepresentations or negligent misrepresentation against one who is in the business of supplying information for the guidance of others in their business transactions.

The *Moorman* exception regarding negligent misrepresentation has become the cutting edge for cases in Illinois. The focus is whether one is in the business of supplying information for the guidance of others or whether the information that is supplied is merely ancillary to the sale or in connection with the sale of merchandise or other matter. *Black, Jackson & Simmons Insurance Brokerage, Inc. v. International Business Machines Corp.* (1982), 109 Ill. App.3d 132, 64 Ill.Dec. 730, 440 N.E.2d 282 (where IBM supplied information on data processing system that system would be satisfactory for plaintiff's needs, it was not in the business of supplying information for the guidance of others).

The facts of each case must be considered to determine whether the *Moorman* exception applies. For example, where a defendant bank investigated the credit of its customer, it was not found to be in the business of supplying information for the guidance of plaintiff, a third party creditor who purported to rely on the information. *Popp v. Dyslin* (1986), 149 Ill.App.3d 956, 962, 102 Ill.Dec. 938, 500 N.E.2d 1039.

Other cases which found that the Moorman exception did not apply: where information was supplied by one joint venturer to the other about a project in which they had invested; an insurance agent in the business of providing information to others where the information was supplied in connection with the sale of an insurance policy; where information was provided in connection with the sale of building materials. Similarly, information supplied by an architect is transformed into the building that he designs, but such information does not meet the Moorman test.

On the other hand, we contrast *DuQuoin State Bank v. Norris City State Bank* (1992), 230 Ill.App.3d 177, 172 Ill.Dec. 317, 595 N.E.2d 678, with *Popp*. In *DuQuoin*, defendant bank was in the business of supplying credit information about its customers to other financial institutions and could be held liable.

A similar rule finding liability may obtain with respect to a termite inspector who is required to provide a report (*Perschall v. Raney* (1985) 137 Ill. App.3d 978, 92 Ill.Dec. 431, 484 N.E.2d 1286); accountants whose purpose and intent in the accountant-client relationship is to benefit or influence a third party whose reliance is based upon these negligent representations (*Brumley v. Touche Ross & Co.* (1985) 139 Ill.App.3d 831, 93 Ill.Dec. 816, 487 N.E.2d 641); accountant who prepares financial forecasts used in offering statements, where the intent was to influence investors to purchase bonds (*Dalton v. Alston & Bird* (S.D.Ill.1990) 741 F.Supp. 1322).

Unaffected are pre-*Moorman* decisions which determined that defendants were in the business of supplying information for the business guidance of others, such as a realtor from whom plaintiff sought advice rather than brokerage services (*Duhl v. Nash Realty, Inc.* (1981) 102 Ill.App.3d 483, 57 Ill.Dec. 904, 429 N.E.2d 1267); and a stock broker in the business of supplying information to customers (*Penrod v. Merrill Lynch* (1979), 68 Ill.App.3d 75, 24 Ill.Dec. 464, 385 N.E.2d 376).

[The] entire transaction that we consider in the instant case is founded upon information provided by the defendant. Option traders are required by the license agreement, the terms of which are incorporated into the Exchange rules, to exclusively use that information to settle their option contracts. Although S & P may suggest that it is merely selling a product, information is the product and it is clearly for the guidance of others in commercial transactions, and, in fact, the determinative factor in those business transactions. While S & P Indexes have been considered salable products, we do not believe that it sheds its character as information used to guide the economic destinies of others.

Additionally, we have required that the plaintiff reasonably rely upon the information conveyed by the defendant. Moreover, courts have further required that the information supplier know that the recipient intends to rely upon the information.

Plaintiff alleges the requisite reliance when OCC, authorized to actually settle the option contracts, uses the information in its analysis of the sums due plaintiff and therefore fulfills this necessary element.

We are not unmindful of the implications of the First Amendment to the United States Constitution on the purveyors of information. Publishers of books or periodicals are protected by constitutional imperatives as well as the limitations on one not in privity with the defendant where the publication is widely disseminated and the class of potential plaintiffs is multitudinous.

We do not quarrel with that notion; however, in the case at bar, S & P has specifically contracted to provide information upon which, to a certainty, investments will be encouraged and determined solely on the basis of S & P Index values. Users of the information are not casual passersby, but rather individually employing S & P's information in their reliance on the price which their options will bring at market.

Cases involving accountants' or appraisers' liability have generally been limited by the scope of the appraisers' liability to a smaller or limited class of potential investors or parties relying on the accounting information or appraisal. However, in cases which are not restrained by *Moorman* limitations, a defendant's negligent performance of its undertaking should extend to that class of persons defendant could reasonably have foreseen would be damaged by its negligent performance.

Again, we distinguish those cases from the case at bar because of the nature of the information to be supplied by S & P as well as the purpose for which that information was admittedly to be used. . . .

Lastly, we turn to the exculpatory clause set out in the License Agreement between S & P and the CBOE which is incorporated into the CBOE Rules to which plaintiff's purchases and sales are subject. The exculpatory clause by its terms provides that S & P does not guarantee the accuracy or the completeness of any of S & P indexes or the data included in them. Nor are any warranties provided as to results from the use of any of the data in connection with the trading of contracts. This language seems to directly relate to the transactions upon which plaintiff's cause of action is predicated.

While such exculpatory clauses may not be favored and are strictly construed against the benefiting party, there is a broad public policy permitting competent parties to contractually limit their respective liability and to allocate business risks in accordance with their business judgment.

Our courts have been willing to enforce contractual clauses exempting a party from liability for its own negligence if it is clear from the contract that the parties' intent was to shift the risk of loss unless it would be against the settled public policy of our State to do so or there is something in the social relationship of the parties militating against recognition of such agreement.

Plaintiff relies on *Scott & Fetzer*, 112 Ill.2d 378, 98 Ill.Dec. 1, 493 N.E.2d 1022, which declined to give effect to an exculpatory clause between the owner of a warehouse and a fire alarm service in connection with the claims of tenants not in privity with the fire alarm service. In *Scott & Fetzer* the court determined that the exculpatory clause was applicable only to the premises which were serviced under the contract and that the agreement between owner and fire alarm company did not negate any duty to other tenants in the same building. In that case, the other tenants had no privity or relationship with the fire alarm company. On the other hand, in the case at bar, plaintiff has entered into the purchase and sale of S & P indexes on the options exchange and does so subject to the exculpatory provisions of the license agreement which were a part of the CBOE rules regulating plaintiff's option trading.

McClure makes it clear that our courts are reluctant to find any special or social relationship that would obviate the impact of an exculpatory clause. However, we note the thoughtful dissent at the appellate level in *McClure Engineering Associates, Inc. v. Reuben Donnelley* (1981) 101 Ill.App.3d 1109, 57 Ill.Dec. 471, 428 N.E.2d 1151, and even critics of *McClure* would not put the plaintiff here on the same footing as the plaintiff in that case.

In *McClure*, the supreme court gave effect to an exculpatory clause where defendant was the publisher of a telephone directory who failed to publish a listing for which a contract had been executed. The dissent at the appellate level noted that the publisher of the telephone directory was the equivalent of a protected monopoly service with no competing company and no competing telephone directory. Certainly, the plaintiff here is not in the same position. On the contrary, this plaintiff makes a conscious decision to invest his money in the trading of options subject to the exculpatory clause which is part of the CBOE Licensing Agreement and Rules.

Even where a semi-public nature is found to permeate the transaction between the parties, the exculpatory clause will be recognized. We believe that the trial court erred in determining that S & P did not owe a duty to plaintiff, that it had a special position as publisher of stock market indexes, that plaintiff did not rely on S & P representation, and that plaintiff was not a member of a limited class that might have been foreseeable to S & P.

However, we nonetheless affirm the trial court because we believe that there is no claim of disparity in the bargaining power between the respective parties and that the relationship between plaintiff and S & P was voluntarily entered into and not of such a semi-public character that limitations upon liability might be contrary to public policy.

We therefore give effect to the exculpatory clause contained in the license agreement between CBOE and S & P and affirm the trial court.

AFFIRMED.

NOTE

First Amendment considerations have an impact on the scope of implied obligations related to informational content. The force of the First Amendment concern is directly associated with the extent to which the information is made widely available; in narrower relationships, a client-licensee's reliance and the nature of the relationship make courts more willing to find some qualitative obligation.

Winter v. GP Putnam's Sons, 38 F.2d 1033 (9th Cir. 1991), held that a publisher of a book involving mushroom recipes owed no duty or contractual obligation to the user of the book even though a mistaken recipe caused serious personal injury to the users. The court said:

> The purposes served by products liability law also are focused on the tangible world and do not take into consideration the unique characteristics of ideas and expression. Under products liability law, strict liability is imposed on the theory that "[t]he costs of damaging events due to defectively dangerous products can best be borne by the enterprisers who make and sell these products." . . . Although there is always some appeal to the involuntary spreading of costs of injuries in any area, the costs in any comprehensive cost/benefit analysis would be quite different were strict liability concepts applied to words and ideas. We place a high priority on the unfettered exchange of ideas. We accept the risk that words and ideas have wings we cannot clip and which carry them we know not where. The threat of liability without fault (financial responsibility for our words and ideas in the absence of fault or a special undertaking or responsibility) could seriously inhibit those who wish to share thoughts and theories. As a New York court commented, with the specter of strict liability, "would any author wish to be exposed . . . for writing on a topic which might result in physical injury? e.g. How to cut trees; How to keep bees?" One might add: "Would anyone undertake to guide by ideas expressed in words either a discrete group, a nation, or humanity in general?" Strict liability principles even when applied to products are not without their costs. Innovation may be inhibited. We tolerate these losses. They are much less disturbing than the prospect that we might be deprived of the latest ideas and theories.

C. Licensee Quality Judgments

Implied obligations are less likely to be found in transactions involving rights in informational content in part because of the subjective nature that judgments about quality entail. One person's classic work is another person's trash. That variation shapes more than the treatment of implied obligations. It also affects how the relationships are structured to begin with. Contracts in entertainment and publishing industries often reserve discretion for the licensee (or assignee) as to whether a particular submission is acceptable and whether or not to market it. The discretion is designed to allow the licensee's subjective choices to control. Yet, even subjective choices can be subject to some standards.

CHODOS v. WEST PUBLISHING COMPANY, INC.
292 F.3d 992 (9th Cir. 2002)

REINHARDT, CIRCUIT JUDGE.

This case presents the question of whether a publisher retains the right to reject an author's manuscript written pursuant to a standard industry agreement, even though the manuscript is of the quality contemplated by both parties. In this case, attorney Rafael Chodos entered into a standard Author Agreement with the Bancroft-Whitney Publishing Company under which he agreed to write a treatise on the intriguing subject of the law of fiduciary duty. The agreement is widely used in the publishing industry for traditional literary works as well as for specialized volumes. Bancroft-Whitney thought that the treatise would be successful commercially and that it would result in substantial profits for both the author and the publisher. After Chodos had spent a number of years fulfilling his part of the bargain and had submitted a completed manuscript, Bancroft-Whitney's successor, the West Publishing Company, came to a contrary conclusion. It declined to publish the treatise, citing solely sales and marketing reasons. Like a good lawyer, Chodos responded by suing for damages, first for breach of contract, and then, after amending his complaint to drop that claim, in quantum meruit. The district court held that under the terms of the contract West's decision not to publish was within its discretion, and granted summary judgment in West's favor. Chodos appeals, and we reverse.

I. Background

Rafael Chodos is a California attorney whose specialty is the law of fiduciary duty. His practice consists primarily of matters involving fiduciary issues such as partnership disputes, corporate dissolutions, and joint ventures. . . . Beginning in approximately 1989, Chodos began developing the idea of writing a treatise on the law of fiduciary duty that included a traditional print component as well as an electronic component that incorporated search engines, linking capabilities, and electronic indexing. Chodos sought to draw on both his legal and technological expertise, and was motivated in part by the fact that there was, and continues to be, no systematic scholarly treatment of the law of fiduciary duty.

In early 1995, Chodos sent a detailed proposal, which included a tentative table of contents, to the Bancroft-Whitney Corporation. Bancroft was at the time a leading publisher of legal texts. William Farber, an Associate Publisher, promptly responded to Chodos's proposal, and informed him that the Bancroft editorial staff was enthusiastic about both the subject matter and the technological features of the proposed project. In July, 1995, Bancroft and Chodos entered into an Author Agreement, which both parties agree is a standard form contract used to govern the composition of a literary work for hire.

The Author Agreement provided for no payments to Chodos prior to publication, and a 15% share of the gross revenues from sales of the work. Farber informed Chodos that a typical successful title published by Bancroft grossed $1 million over a five-year period, although Chodos's work, of course, might be more or less successful than the average. Chodos sought publication of the work not only for the direct financial rewards, but also for the enhanced professional reputation he might receive from the publication of a treatise, which in turn might result in additional referrals to his practice and increased fees for him.

From July, 1995 through June, 1998, Chodos's principal professional activity was the writing of the treatise. He significantly limited the time spent on his law practice, and devoted several hours each morning as well as most weekends to the book project. Chodos estimates that he spent at least 3600 hours over the course of three years on writing the treatise and developing the accompanying electronic materials. He did so with the guidance of Bancroft staff. [As] Chodos completed each of the chapters, he submitted them to Bancroft on a CD-ROM; the seventh and final chapter was sent to the publisher in February, 1998. When finished, the book consisted of 1247 pages.

In mid-1996, Bancroft-Whitney was purchased by the West Publishing Group. . . . The Bancroft editors, now employed by West, continued to work with Chodos in preparing the work for publication. . . . [In] the summer of 1998 the West editors provided him with detailed notes and suggestions, to which he diligently responded. In November, 1998, West again sent Chodos a lengthy letter including substantive editorial suggestions related to the organization of the book. In early December, 1998, West sent Chodos yet another letter, this time apologizing for delays in publication, and assuring him that publication would take place in the first quarter of 1999. Burt Levy, who replaced Farber as Chodos's editor, informed Chodos that copy editors were preparing the manuscript for release in the early part of that year.

After receiving no communication from Levy in January, 1999, Chodos contacted West to check on the status of his treatise. On February 4, 1999, Chodos received a response from Nell Petri [informing] Chodos that West had decided not to publish the book because it did not "fit within [West's] current product mix" and because of concerns about its "market potential." West admits, however, that the manuscript was of "high quality" and that its decision was not due to any literary shortcomings in Chodos's work.

The decision not to publish the treatise on fiduciary duty was made by Carole Gamble, who joined West as Director of Product Development and Management . . . at about the same time that Chodos completed the manuscript. In late 1998, West developed new internal criteria to guide publication decisions. Applying these criteria, Gamble decided not to go forward with the publication of the treatise. She did not in fact read what Chodos had written, but instead reviewed a detailed outline of the treatise and the original proposal for it. Gamble did not prepare a business analysis prior to making her decision. After Chodos informed West that in his view the publisher had breached its contract, West did prepare an economic projection that concluded that the publication of Chodos's work would be an unprofitable venture. Thus, this legal action was born. . . .

II. Discussion

Chodos makes two alternative arguments: first, that the standard Author Agreement is an illusory contract, and second, that if a valid contract does exist, West breached it. Under either theory of liability, Chodos contends that he is entitled to recover in quantum meruit.

A. The Author Agreement Is Not Illusory.

In support of his first argument, Chodos correctly notes that in order for a contract to be enforceable under California law, it must impose binding obligations on each party. The California Supreme Court has held that "if one of the promises leaves a party free to perform or to withdraw from the agreement at his own unrestricted pleasure, the promise is deemed illusory and it provides no consideration." Chodos contends that because the contract required him to produce a work of publishable quality, but allowed West, in its discretion, to decide unilaterally whether or not to publish his work, the contract violates the doctrine of mutuality of obligation and is therefore illusory.

California law, like the law in most states, provides that a covenant of good faith and fair dealing is an implied term in every contract. Thus, a court will not find a contract to be illusory if the implied covenant of good faith and fair dealing can be read to impose an obligation on each party. The covenant of good faith "finds particular application in situations where one party is invested with a discretionary power affecting the rights of another."

It is correct that the agreement at issue imposes numerous obligations on the author but gives the publisher "the right in its discretion to terminate" the publishing relationship after receiving the manuscript and determining that it is unacceptable. However, we conclude that the contract is not illusory because West's duty to exercise its discretion is limited by its duty of good faith and fair dealing. More specifically, because the standard Author Agreement obligates the publisher to make a judgment as to the quality or literary merit of the author's work — to determine whether the work is "acceptable" or "unacceptable" — it must make that judgment in good faith, and cannot reject a manuscript for other, unrelated reasons. Thus, Chodos's first argument fails.

B. West Breached the Agreement.

Chodos's alternative argument — that a contract exists and it was breached — is more persuasive. West contends that the Author Agreement allowed it to decline to publish the manuscript after Chodos completed writing it for *any* good-faith reason, regardless of whether the reason was related to the quality or literary merit of Chodos's manuscript. However, West's right to terminate the agreement is a limited one defined in two related provisions of the agreement. The first, the "acceptance clause," establishes that West may decline to publish Chodos's manuscript if it finds the work to be "unacceptable" in form and content. The acceptance clause, paragraph eight of the agreement, provides that:

> After timely receipt of the Work or any portion of the Work prepared by Author, Publisher shall review it as to both form and content, and notify Author whether it is acceptable or unacceptable in form and content under the terms of this Agreement. In the event that Publisher determines that the Work or any portion of the Work is unacceptable, Publisher shall notify Author of Publisher's determination and Publisher may exercise its rights under paragraph 4.

The second relevant provision (referred to in the acceptance clause as West's "rights under paragraph 4") allows West to terminate the publishing agreement if the author does not cure a failure in performance after being given an opportunity to do so. This provision, numbered paragraph four of the contract and entitled "Author's Failure to Perform," states:

> [I]f Publisher determines that the Work or any portion of it is not acceptable to publisher as provided in paragraph 8 [the acceptance

clause] . . . [a]fter thirty (30) days following written notice to author if Author has not cured such failure in performance Publisher has the right in its discretion to terminate this Agreement.

The district court agreed with West that in determining whether a manuscript is satisfactory in form and content under the acceptance clause of the standard Author Agreement, the publisher may in good faith consider solely the likelihood of a book's commercial success and other similar economic factors. We unequivocally reject the view that the relevant provisions of the Author Agreement may be so construed in the absence of additional language or conditions.

The expansive reading of the acceptance clause suggested by West is inconsistent with the language of the two contract clauses. Under the agreement, the publisher may deem a manuscript unacceptable only if it is deficient in "form and content." Thus, had Chodos submitted a badly written, poorly researched, disorganized or substantially incomplete work to West, the publisher would have been well within its rights to find that submission unacceptable under the acceptance clause — as it would were it to reject any work that it believed in good faith lacked literary merit. A publisher bargains for a product of a certain quality and is entitled to reject a work that in its good faith judgment falls short of the bargained-for standard. Nothing in the contract, however, suggests that the ordinary meaning of the words "form and content" was not intended, and nowhere in the contract does it state that the publisher may terminate the agreement if it changes its management structure or its marketing strategy, or if it revises its business or economic forecasts, all matters unrelated to "form and content."

To the contrary, the fact that the contract required West to afford Chodos an opportunity to cure any deficient performance supports our straightforward reading of the acceptance clause as a provision that relates solely to the quality or literary merit of a submitted work. As noted above, if West determined that Chodos's submission was unacceptable, he was to be given a period of time to cure his failure in performance. The inclusion of this provision indicates that a deficiency in "form and content" is one that the author has some power to cure. Chodos has no power to "cure" West's view that the marketplace for books on fiduciary duty had changed; nor could he "cure" a change in West's overall marketing strategy and product mix; nor, indeed, could he be expected to do much about a general downturn in economic conditions. The text and structure of the contract thus demonstrate that West's stated reasons for terminating the agreement were not among those contemplated by the parties.

The uncontroverted evidence in this case is that Chodos worked diligently in cooperation with West — indeed, with West's encouragement — to produce a work that met the highest professional standard, and that he was successful in that venture. His performance was induced by an agreement that permitted rejection of the completed manuscript only for deficiencies in "form and content." Chodos thus labored to complete a work of high quality with the expectation that, if he did so, it would be published. He devoted thousands of hours of labor to the venture, and passed up substantial professional opportunities, only for West to decide that due to the vagaries of its internal reorganizations and changes in its business strategies or in the national economy or the market for legal treatises, his work, albeit admittedly of high quality, was for naught. It would be inequitable, if not unconscionable, for an author to be forced to bear this considerable burden solely because of his publisher's change in management, its poor planning, or its inadequate financial analyses at the time it entered into the contract, or even because of an unexpected change in the market-place. Moreover, to allow a publisher to escape its contractual obligations for these reasons would be directly contrary to both the language and the spirit of the standard Author Agreement.

West urges us to affirm the district court's ruling because, in its view, it is well-accepted that, regardless of the contract's failure to mention economic circumstances or market demands, publishers have broad discretion under the acceptance clause of the standard Author Agreement to reject manuscripts for any good faith commercial reason. For this proposition, the district court cited two cases from the Second Circuit involving that same clause. Although at least one of the cases contains dicta that would support the district court's decision, both are distinguishable factually and legally. Moreover, to the extent that either case suggests that a publisher bound by the standard Author Agreement may terminate the contract for *any* reason so long as it acts in good faith, we respectfully reject that view.

In *Doubleday & Co. v. Curtis,* 763 F.2d 495, 496 (2d Cir.1985), a publisher rejected a manuscript by the well-known actor but neophyte author, Tony Curtis, on the basis of its poor literary quality. There, as here, the publishing agreement allowed the publisher to reject a submission if it was not satisfactory as to "form and content." However, in *Doubleday,* in direct contrast to the circumstances here, it was agreed that the manuscript was *unsatisfactory* in form and content. In *Doubleday,* Curtis's claim was that the publisher had a good-faith obligation under the contract to re-write his admittedly unsatisfactory manuscript and to transform it into one of publishable quality. The Second Circuit held that a publisher's good faith obligation does not stretch that far; thus, the Second Circuit's essential holding in *Doubleday* has no bearing on the present case.

It is true that the Second Circuit appears to have stated its holding in *Doubleday* more broadly than the case before the court warranted. The court said:

> [W]e hold that a publisher may, in its discretion, terminate a standard publishing contract, provided that the termination is made in good faith, and that the failure of an author to submit a satisfactory manuscript was not caused by the publisher's bad faith.

Id. at 501. Still, read in context, the holding does not make it clear whether the court meant that a publisher may reject a manuscript for reasons wholly unrelated to its literary worth or that it may do so only if it determines in good faith that the submitted work is unsatisfactory on its literary merits. If the former is the Second Circuit's view of the law, we respectfully disagree.

The district court also relied on *Random House, Inc. v. Gold,* 464 F. Supp. 1306 (S.D.N.Y.1979). That case is more apposite than *Doubleday* in that the district court there held that a publisher may consider economic circumstances when evaluating a manuscript's "form and content" under the standard publishing agreement. Although we disagree with that holding for the reasons set forth above, and are certainly not bound by it, we note that even in *Random House* the court did not go so far as to state that economic considerations may be the *sole* reason for a publisher to decline to publish a manuscript that is in every other respect acceptable. In *Random House,* as in *Doubleday,* the submitted manuscript was not of publishable quality. In contrast to Chodos's work, the editor at Random House considered the manuscript at issue to be "shallow and badly designed."

In sum, we reject the district court's determination that West acted within the discretion afforded it by the Author Agreement when it decided not to publish Chodos's manuscript. Because West concedes that the manuscript was of high quality and that it declined to publish it solely for commercial reasons rather than because of any defect in its form and content, we hold as a matter of law that West breached its agreement with Chodos.[2]

C. Chodos May Pursue a Quantum Meruit Claim.

The district court ruled that if West breached the contract, Chodos could proceed in quantum meruit, but only if the damages were not determinable under the contract. [Accordingly,] we must consider the remaining issues relevant to Chodos's quantum meruit claim.

Under California law, a party who has been injured by a breach of contract may generally elect what remedy to seek. In a leading case on election of remedies, the California Supreme Court stated:

> It is well settled in this state that one who has been injured by a breach of contract has an election to pursue any of three remedies, to wit: He may treat the contract as rescinded and may recover upon a quantum meruit so far as he has performed; or he may keep the contract alive, for the benefit of both parties, being at all times ready and able to perform; or, third, he may treat the repudiation as putting an end to the contract for all purposes of performance, and sue for the profits he would have realized if he had not been prevented from performing.

Alder v. Drudis, 30 Cal.2d 372, 381-82, 182 P.2d 195 (1947).

In employment contracts and contracts for personal services, like the one before us, the first option, an action in quantum meruit, is generally limited to cases in which the breach occurs after partial performance and the party seek-

---

[2] [FN 7] West also suggests that it was justified in not publishing the manuscript because Chodos did not submit it in a timely manner. This argument is without merit. Although the Author Agreement provided that Chodos was to deliver a completed manuscript by March, 1996, Levy admitted that authors who also maintained professional practices "always" took longer to write books than was initially anticipated, and Gamble stated that although authors are "often" late, she had never decided not to publish a work because it was not timely. West editors mentioned a deadline of any kind to Chodos on only one occasion. In January, 1998, Levy left a telephone message stating that Chodos must finish the work by June of that same year. Chodos complied with this request. West editors worked cooperatively with Chodos throughout the writing and editing process as he submitted the chapters *in seriatim,* even though most of the chapters were submitted after the March, 1996 date specified in the contract, and Chodos made numerous changes to those chapters at West's request. West therefore cannot now argue that the manuscript was submitted in an untimely fashion.

ing a recovery does not thereafter complete performance. . . . Thus, if a plaintiff has fully performed a contract, damages for breach is often the only available remedy. The California Supreme Court has, however, recognized an exception to the general rule. In *Oliver,* the court stated:

> The remedy of restitution in money is not available to one who has fully performed his part of a contract, if the only part of the agreed exchange for such performance that has not been rendered by the defendant is a sum of money constituting a liquidated debt; *but full performance does not make restitution unavailable if any part of the consideration due from the defendant in return is something other than a liquidated debt.*

Id. at 306, 273 P.2d 15 (adopting *Restatement of Contracts* § 350).

Assuming that Chodos fully performed his end of the bargain by delivering a completed manuscript to West, then whether Chodos can recover on a quantum meruit claim turns on whether the 15% of the gross revenues provided for in the agreement constitutes a "liquidated debt." According to Black's Law Dictionary, "[a] debt is liquidated when it is certain what is due and how much is due. That which has been made certain as to amount due by agreement of parties or by operation of law." *Black's Law Dictionary* 931 (6th ed. 1990). The term "liquidated debt" is similar to the term "liquidated damages," which the California courts have defined as "an amount of compensation to be paid in the event of a breach of contract, the sum of which is fixed and certain by agreement. . . ." *Kelly v. McDonald,* 98 Cal. App. 121, 125, 276 P. 404 (1929), *overruled in part on other grounds, McCarthy v. Tally,* 46 Cal.2d 577, 297 P.2d 981 (1956).

Chodos's entitlement to 15% of the revenues from his book on fiduciary duty is not a liquidated debt under California law, as it was not a certain or readily ascertainable figure. The mere existence of a fixed percentage royalty in a contract does not render that royalty a "liquidated debt," if the revenues to which that percentage figure is to be applied cannot be calculated with reasonable certainty. Here, it is impossible to determine even now what those revenues would have been had West not frustrated the completion of the contract. Had West honored its contractual obligations and published the treatise, the revenues would have depended on any number of circumstances, including how West chose to market the book, and how it was received by readers and critics. Accordingly, under *Oliver,* Chodos is entitled to sue for restitution for the time and effort he reasonably invested in writing the manuscript. We express no opinion as to how restitution should be calculated in this case, nor do we intimate any suggestion as to the appropriate amount of such recovery. . . .

III. Conclusion

[We] REVERSE the district court's grant of summary judgment in West's favor, and REMAND the case to the district court with instructions to enter summary judgment as to liability in Chodos's favor, and for further proceedings consistent with this opinion. . . .

NOTES

1. How should the trial court compute damages on remand in this case? Should the publisher be required to compensate Chodos for the full value of the thousands of hours he spent in developing and refining the manuscript? If the publisher correctly estimated that the book would not have sold well, was the author guaranteed that the royalties from the sale of the book would result in full compensation for those hours? If not, is such a recovery over-compensation for the breach, placing the plaintiff in a better position than he would have been had the contract been fully performed? Should the author receive compensation for his cost of self-publishing the book?

2. As the court notes, there is other authority (which it attempts to distinguish), suggesting that the standard author's contract gives the publisher far greater and more unrestricted discretion in electing to publish or not than that suggested by the court in *Chodos*. Which is the better rule — should completion of a manuscript entitle an author to publication under the contract? Assume that you are counsel for the publisher, how would you redraft the agreement to accommodate your client's right to shift its marketing choices and the like, without risk of lawsuit?

3. The court in this case suggests that it is "bad faith" to decide not to publish for purely economic or commercial reasons in light of the terms of this particular agreement. Other decisions, however, indicate that it is not bad faith to act in your own self-interest. Which is the better view or is it more accurate to conclude that the result in *Chodos* turned as much on the wording of the contract as it did on the concept of bad faith? In *Chodos,* according to the court, were there any reasons other than poor quality of manuscript that the publisher could use in its discretion to deny publication? If the decision must be based on lack of quality of the manuscript, is that in fact a discretionary choice or is it one that can be measured by objective criteria?

4. In *Nance v. Random House, Inc.*, 212 F. Supp. 2d 268 (S.D.N.Y. 2002), the court held that it was not bad faith to reject a manuscript. As in *Chodos,* the author and editors had engaged in an ongoing dialogue to improve and complete the manuscript, but this dialogue also reflected dissatisfaction with the depth and quality of the manuscript. The author claimed the basis for rejection was the poor sales performance of his prior books and that this was bad faith, but according to the court, offered no evidence that this was the reason. Additionally, the court observed:

> The Contract provided that Nance's manuscripts had to be "complete and satisfactory to [the] Publisher," and further stated that the publishers could reject a manuscript if they found it "unacceptable for any reason." Courts have interpreted such clauses to grant publishers wide discretion to terminate publishing contracts, "provided that the termination is made in good faith, and that the failure of the author to submit a satisfactory manuscript was not caused by the publisher's bad faith." "Dishonesty" or "willful neglect" are evidence of bad faith. In sum, the requirement that a work be "complete and satisfactory to [the] Publisher" gives the publisher the right to reject the work as long as it acts in good faith.

Id. at 272

(citing *Doubleday & Co. v. Curtis,* 763 F.2d 495, 501 (2d Cir. 1985)).

PROBLEM 8.11

Script writer's contract with motion picture studio requires the writer to deliver a script for a motion picture involving aliens from Mars invading the earth. The writer will receive $10,000, plus one percent of net profits from any motion picture made based the script. The contract allows Studio to reject the script or to decide to not produce and distribute a motion picture based on it "in Studio's full and complete discretion." The license to use the script is stated as "exclusive to Studio for the full term of the copyright in the script." Studio pays the $10,000, but for six years, declines to use the script. Writer sues. What result?

IV. THIRD PARTY PRODUCT LIABILITY

In addition to questions about warranty or other obligations between the immediate parties to the contract, in some circumstances, questions can arise about the liability risk of a licensor in context of third-party tort claims. These claims can arise under negligence theory or under theories associated with strict products liability. The field of products liability is in flux, being affected by liability limiting statutes in various jurisdictions, by case law grappling with new types of products or commercial assets, and by the promulgation of a new *Restatement (Third) of Products Liability* in 1998. We will touch on only those issues associated with licensing.

SNYDER v. ISC ALLOYS, LTD.
772 F. Supp. 244 (W.D. Pa. 1991)

MEMORANDUM OPINION AND ORDER

Plaintiffs Jacque Snyder and Eloise Simon filed these separate wrongful death and survival actions in which they seek to recover damages from ISC Alloys, Ltd. ("ISC"). Plaintiffs allege several theories of liability in their complaint including negligence, strict products liability and breach of warranty. The cases are now before the Court on ISC's motion for summary judgment which requires the Court to address, inter alia, a question of first impression: Specifically, whether the package of designs, technical drawings and professional advice ISC sold decedents' employer constitute a product within the meaning of Section 402(A) of the *Second Restatement of Torts*. Because this Court concludes that the package of designs, technical drawings and information ISC supplied is not a product, ISC's motion for summary judgment is granted in part. There are, however, questions of material fact that cannot be resolved based on the record currently before the Court, and that preclude the Court from granting ISC's request for summary judgment on the theory of negligent design.

I. The Facts

Decedents John Simon and Harold Snyder both worked at St. Joe's Resources Company ("St. Joe") in Monaca, Pennsylvania. Both sustained fatal injuries in 1985 when they entered a zinc dust plant located at St. Joe.

St. Joe operated the zinc dust plant pursuant to an exclusive licensing arrangement with defendant ISC Alloys, Limited ("ISC"), a British corporation. ISC developed and held patents on a process for converting solid zinc metal into zinc dust. In July of 1976, ISC granted St. Joe an exclusive license to use its process to manufacture zinc dust in the United States. Pursuant to the licensing agreement, ISC agreed to provide St. Joe with both the technical information and services necessary to use ISC's patented process. The technical information consisted of drawings illustrating the major components of the physical plant and an operating manual. The services provided by ISC to St. Joe consisted of advice during the design and construction of the plant. ISC personnel also trained St. Joe's employees to operate the plant once it had been constructed.

St. Joe hired an independent contractor who built the plant in accordance with ISC's specifications. [St. Joe] operated the zinc plant until December 1979 when poor economic conditions caused the company to close it. St. Joe then reopened the plant in July 1981. On two separate occasions, St. Joe personnel visited the ISC zinc plant in Bloxwich, England, to observe the zinc dust process used there. ISC sent its own personnel to the St. Joe facility to train St. Joe's employees when the facility was first opened in March 1978, and again in July 1981 when the plant went back into operation. ISC did not, however, have a continuing role in the operation of St. Joe's zinc dust plant.

The zinc dust plant used ISC's electrothermal process to convert slabs of zinc into zinc dust. This is accomplished by first turning a slab of zinc into a zinc vapor which is then blown by fans into the condenser. There, the vapor is condensed into zinc dust. Because the zinc dust is explosive in nature, the oxygen content in the condenser unit is kept as low as possible to reduce the possibility that a zinc cloud might ignite. Consequently, during the process the condenser unit's atmosphere is composed primarily of carbon monoxide, thereby rendering that atmosphere potentially fatal to any human exposed to it. The condenser unit must undergo occasional maintenance. The ISC Operating Manual states that the condenser must be cooled and the air inside ventilated before workers can enter to service the unit.

On July 24, 1985, both Harold Snyder and John Simon died as a result of entering St. Joe's zinc dust plant condenser unit before it had been properly ventilated. . . .

II. Analysis

[The] primary issue raised by this motion for summary judgment, specifically, whether the plans ISC sold to St. Joe constitute a "product" within the meaning of section 402A, is a pure question of law. For the reasons set forth below, I will grant defendant ISC's motion for summary judgment on the 402A strict liability count, as well as on the breach of warranty count. I will also grant ISC's motion on the counts alleging that ISC was negligent in failing to adequately test the venting procedures and failing to provide adequate warnings regarding the hazardous conditions in the zinc dust condenser because the duty to implement proper safety procedures and provide warnings had, as a matter of law, passed to St. Joe at the time of the decedents' deaths. On this record, however, I must deny ISC's motion on the counts alleging that ISC was negligent in designing a defectively small access door. . . .

A. Strict Liability

Pennsylvania has adopted the doctrine of strict products liability as set forth in section 402A of the *Second Restatement of Torts*. Pursuant to this theory, a manufacturer who sells a product in a defective condition unreasonably dangerous to the user will be held liable for any injuries or damages that result even if the seller has used all possible care in the preparation and sale of the product. *Restatement (Second) of Torts,* § 402A(1), (2)(a). Since adopting section 402A, Pennsylvania Courts have taken an expansive, rather than restrictive, view of who may be held strictly liable for placing defective products in the stream of commerce. Indeed, Pennsylvania Courts have imposed strict products liability for a defective product on all sellers in the chain of distribution.

These cases have all addressed the issue of which defendants can be held liable for damage caused by a defective product. They do not, however, consider the definitional issue of what may be classified as a product pursuant to section 402A, and provide no guidance for resolving the question before this Court, which is whether a Pennsylvania Court would expand the applicability of section 402A strict liability to reach a defendant who sold designs and technical advice rather than a finished product. I must first predict, then, how the Supreme Court of Pennsylvania would resolve this novel question. . . .

ISC contends that the license, technical drawings and information it sold to St. Joe do not constitute a product within the meaning of section 402A. ISC contends that what it sold to St. Joe is more aptly characterized as professional services, and thus beyond the reach of section 402A. I have reviewed the applicable Pennsylvania case law as well as the language of the *Restatement* itself and conclude that despite Pennsylvania's expansive treatment of who can be held liable under section 402A, ISC cannot be held strictly liable for decedents' death because the services ISC rendered do not constitute a product.

[I] have not found any cases from the Pennsylvania Courts that set forth an analytical framework for determining what constitutes a product. However, in *Cox v. Shaffer*, 223 Pa. Super. 429, 302 A.2d 456 (1973), the Pennsylvania Superior Court, relying on the actual language of section 402A, concluded that "[a] silo constructed in place on the employer's land is not the sale of a product." The Superior Court held section 402A "inapplicable by its very clear language and [found] no need to resort to any extended reasoning to support [its] conclusion that a building so constructed on the site is not a product within the meaning of section 402A." Thus, despite the Pennsylvania courts' apparent willingness to expand some facets of 402A liability, *Cox* clearly signals that Pennsylvania courts will not favor a broad definition of the word "product."

However, although I believe *Cox* supports defendants' claim that it did not supply a "product" within the meaning of section 402A, I do not believe it is dispositive of the instant case. [I] see two limitations on the precedential value of *Cox*. First, [there] are significant factual distinctions between this case and *Cox*. Second, [the] laconic nature of the *Cox* opinion does not provide adequate guidance. In *Abdul-Warith* [*v. Arthur McKee & Co.*, 488 F. Supp. 306, 310 (E.D.Pa.) *aff'd*, 642 F.2d 440 (3d Cir.1980)], the district court suggested that the Superior Court's opinion in *Cox* might stem from the fact that the silo was part of the realty and hence, not a product. Although I agree that this factor might have had some significance, I do not believe the *Cox* opinion can be construed so narrowly, nor do I believe that *Cox* is devoid of precedential value. On the contrary, I find that *Cox* favors a literal construction of the word "product" in keeping with the ideas set forth in section 402A of the Restatement.

[I conclude] that ISC's technical drawings, services and information with respect to the zinc dust plant do not constitute a product. As set forth more fully below, I reach this conclusion for two reasons. First, these items are not within the traditional meaning of the word "product." Second, these items are more aptly categorized as services.

I focus first on the proper interpretation of the word "product." Section 402A does not provide a definition of the word "product"; however, comment (d) provides that the rule applies to "an automobile, a tire, an airplane, a grinding wheel, a water heater, a gas stove, a power tool, a riveting machine, a chair and an insecticide." *Restatement (Second) Torts* § 402A, comment (d) (1965). Although this list is hardly exhaustive, all of the examples in comment (d) have one trait in common: all are finished items with a tangible form. The allegedly defective item supplied by ISC was merely an idea, expressed and configured in language and symbols, and as such it clearly lacked the completeness and tangibility that characterized the "products" set forth in the list above. Given the literal approach espoused in *Cox* and the *Restatement*'s list of examples, I do not believe mere ideas, information, communications and drawings can be considered products within the meaning of Pennsylvania law.

Moreover, to find ISC strictly liable pursuant to section 402A, I must not only ignore the difficulty of manipulating the definition of the word "product" to encompass the information ISC sold, but I must also ignore the undeniable fact that what ISC actually sold constituted services. Services, in turn, have traditionally been beyond the purview of section 402A. *See LaRossa v. Scientific Design Co.*, 402 F.2d 937, 941-43 (3d Cir.1968).

According to the Third Circuit, the social policy which favors strict liability for the manufacturer of defective products simply does not favor holding service professionals strictly liable. Unlike mass produced goods, services are not marketed to a wide variety of the general public. Thus, parties injured by poor services are in a better position to locate the tortfeasor and identify the defect caused by the tortfeasor's negligence. Therefore, as a general rule, those who sell professional services are not liable in the absence of negligence or intentional misconduct.

Moreover, I cannot hold ISC strictly liable pursuant to section 402A in light of the fact that there is no allegation, nor evidence to support an allegation, that ISC mass marketed the zinc dust process technology. The evolution of mass marketing was a primary impetus in the creation of modern strict products liability. *See generally*, Prosser, *The Fall of the Citadel*, 50 MINN. L. REV. 791 (1966). The law of strict products liability has its roots in *Henningsen v. Bloomfield Motors*, 32 N.J. 358, 161 A.2d 69 (1960). In that case, the New Jersey Supreme Court held that "modern marketing conditions," whereby producers place goods in the stream of commerce and promote their purchase by the public, create an implied warranty that the product is safe for its intended use. The *Henningsen* Court held that such producers are in the best position to either control the danger of the products or distribute any losses equitably, should they occur. The Court therefore concluded that such manufacturers should be held strictly liable.

Professor Prosser noted that by mass marketing products, manufacturers represent that the products are safe for use, and by packaging and advertising, manufacturers reinforce that belief. Thus, the fact of mass marketing, or at least some marketing, is an essential element of a claim of strict products liability. Indeed, the *Restatement* incorporates this notion in section 402A itself. Section 402A(1) requires that that defendant be "one who sells products," and subsection (2) further specifies that "the seller must be engaged in the business of selling such a product. . . ." *See Restatement (Second) of Torts* § 402A(1)(a). Comment (c) to section 402A states that the justification behind strict liability stems from the fact that "by marketing his product for use and consumption, [the seller] has undertaken and assumed a special responsibility toward any member of the consuming public. . . ." The *Restatement* further notes that "public policy demands that the burden of accidental injuries caused by products intended for consumption be placed upon those who market them, and be treated as a cost of production." *Restatement (Second) Torts*, § 402A, comment c.

The *Restatement* also teaches that, for liability to attach, a seller must also market the product on a somewhat consistent basis. Although it is not necessary for the seller to be engaged solely in the business of selling the defective product, an occasional seller cannot be held liable under section 402A.

Lacking guidance from the Pennsylvania Supreme Court on the question before me, I must consider the policy reasons cited generally in support of strict liability. The Pennsylvania Supreme Court has adopted section 402A, and in attempting to predict what that Court would do if confronted with the issue now before me, I must give proper weight to the policy underlying strict liability as embraced by the *Restatement*. In doing so, I cannot ignore the fact that there is no allegation, much less proof, that ISC ever marketed its technology to any party other than St. Joe. I will therefore grant defendant's motion for summary judgment on the count sounding in strict liability.

Even assuming arguendo that information ISC sold to St. Joe constituted a product, I would still be compelled to dismiss the plaintiff's count alleging strict liability. Section 402A applies only where the product reaches "the user or consumer without substantial change in the condition in which it is sold." *Restatement (Second) Torts* § 402A(1)(b) (1965). Obviously, what ISC sold here — information — did not reach the decedents in substantially the same condition in which it was sold. That information did not cause them injury. On the contrary, the injury causing instrumentality, although derived from ISC's plans, had an existence completely separate and independent of ISC's plans. Thus, when ISC relinquished control over the item it sold — namely the plans — the thing that ultimately caused decedents' deaths did not yet exist. ISC did not even have a role in supervising the zinc plant's construction. Accordingly, it cannot be held liable pursuant to section 402A.

B. Breach of Warranty

I turn next to ISC's contention that it cannot be held liable for breach of warranty. ISC, relying on *Salvador v. Atlantic Steel Boiler Co.*, 457 Pa. 24, 319 A.2d 903 (1974), contends that "the same legal relationship with the product which makes the defendant strictly liable for its defects also creates a cause of action against the defendant for breach of warranty." Defendant therefore concludes that it cannot be held strictly liable under a breach of warranty theory "unless he had [sic] been the seller of a product." Although I agree with defendant's ultimate conclusion — that it must have sold a "product" to be held liable for breach of warranty — this conclusion does not follow from its previous statement, nor from the *Salvador* opinion.

In *Salvador*, the Pennsylvania Supreme Court abolished the requirement of horizontal privity as an element of a breach of warranty case. The Court reasoned that this requirement was obsolete in light of its adoption of strict products liability as embodied in section 402A of the *Restatement*. Thus, the *Salvador* Court did draw an analogy between strict products liability in tort and breach of warranty. However, the Supreme Court's analysis in *Salvador* discussed only the question of privity. It did not reach the further question of what types of injury causing instrumentalities can give rise to breach of warranty liability.

Despite this flaw in defendant's reasoning, I agree with ISC's ultimate conclusion that it cannot be held liable for breach of warranty because this theory of recovery is inapplicable to ideas, information and services. The concept of breach of warranty stems from Article 2 of the Uniform Commercial Code. Article 2, in turn, governs the sale of goods. I believe that the goods covered by the U.C.C. are synonymous with the products covered by section 402A. I have already decided that ISC sold services rather than products. I have thus already implicitly decided that ISC did not sell "goods" within the meaning of Article 2. Accordingly, plaintiff cannot recover under a breach of warranty theory.

C. Negligence

I turn finally to ISC's contention that it cannot be held liable for negligence in the deaths of John Simon and Harold Snyder. Plaintiffs' complaint alleges three different theories of negligence. First, plaintiffs allege that ISC failed to design a safe entry to the condenser. Next, the complaint alleges that ISC failed to adequately test the venting system. Finally, it is claimed that ISC failed to warn the ultimate users of the danger of the carbon monoxide in the condenser. ISC argues that it owed no duty of care to the decedents. . . .

To prevail on a tort claim sounding in negligence, the plaintiff must prove that the defendant owed the plaintiff a duty of care. "Duty, in any given situation, is predicated on the relationship existing between the parties at the relevant time . . . and necessarily requires some degree of knowledge." However, mere knowledge of a dangerous situation will not give rise to a duty to act or warn. Instead, the defendant's conduct must actually create the hazardous condition. Entering into a contractual arrangement may, however, be deemed to be conduct that creates a hazardous condition. "[A] party to a contract by the very nature of his contractual undertaking may place himself in such a position that the law will impose upon him a duty to perform his con-tractual undertaking in such manner that third persons — strangers to the contract — will not be injured thereby." Thus, as a general rule, "a company which manufactures and erects a structure owes a duty of care to people who must work in the vicinity of the structure." Inherent in this obligation, is the duty "to design the structure in such a way that it will not be rendered unsafe because of the foreseeable actions of a third party." With these principles in mind, I turn to the question of whether ISC owed any duty of care to the decedents.

I can summarily dismiss ISC's first contention that it did not owe decedents a duty of care because they were not parties to the contract. Obviously, ISC knew that St. Joe would hire laborers to operate the zinc dust plant and, there-fore, the law imposed a duty upon ISC to design a safe facility.

In its second set of arguments, ISC attempts to shift liability from itself to St. Joe. [For the reasons set forth below,] I agree that the duty to warn the employees about the lethal atmosphere in the condenser and the duty to implement proper safety procedures had shifted to St. Joe. I do not, however, accept ISC's further contention that either the passage of time, lack of control or contractual arrange-ments relieved ISC of its duty to design a safe entry to the condenser unit.

ISC suggests that the accident in which Harold Snyder and John Simon died was the result of inadequate supervision. ISC thus argues that because it was not involved in the daily operation of the unit, it cannot be held liable for any injury that resulted from St. Joe's poor supervision. To that end, ISC relies upon § 452(2) of the *Restatement (Second) of Torts*, which provides: "where because of the lapse of time or otherwise, the duty to prevent harm to another threatened by the actor's negligent conduct is found to have shifted from the actor to a third person, the failure of such person to prevent such harm is a superseding cause." After reviewing the record, I conclude that St. Joe's super-vision of the zinc dust plant was poor. I also agree that ISC had discharged its duty to warn end users about the potentially lethal atmosphere in the con-denser unit and that St. Joe's departure from ISC's recommended ventilation procedure prevents the plaintiffs from holding ISC liable for failing to ade-quately test its venting procedures.

ISC correctly relies on section 452(2) of the *Restatement* for the proposition that either the lapse of time or some other event may shift liability for the actor's negligence to a third party. In *Guztan v. Altair Airlines*, 766 F.2d 135, 140 (3d Cir.1985), the Third Circuit noted that the Pennsylvania Supreme Court, relying on comment (d) to section 452, has set forth the following factors as relevant in determining whether the duty of care has shifted: The degree of danger and the magnitude of the risk of harm, the character and position of the third person who is to take the responsibility, his knowledge of the danger and the likelihood that he will not exercise proper care, his relation-ship to the plaintiff or to the defendant, the lapse of time, and perhaps other considerations.

The degree of the danger and the magnitude of the risk of harm were obvi-ously great here. A function of the operation of the zinc dust plant was the creation of lethal atmospheric conditions within the condenser unit. However, the character and position of the third party weigh heavily against imposing liability against ISC. St. Joe was a sophisticated industrial manufacturer which knew of the danger posed by the condenser unit's atmosphere. Indeed, in the operating manual, ISC set forth specific safety guidelines which provided that no entry must be allowed until responsible laboratory staff have checked the condenser atmosphere and certified it as safe for entry. Oxygen content must be normal and the presence of carbon monoxide ruled out. ISC thus specifically warned St. Joe of the danger inherent in the zinc dust process.

Moreover, once warned of this danger, St. Joe was in the best position to both warn employees of the dangerous atmospheric condition and implement appropriate safety measures. . . . I also conclude that any liability arising from ISC's failure to test the venting procedures had shifted to St. Joe. ISC informed St. Joe that the condenser unit had to be ventilated before workers could safely enter to perform maintenance. . . . Finally, and perhaps most importantly, St. Joe actually implemented a ventilation procedure that was substantially different than the procedure recommended by ISC. St. Joe had apparently used, without incident, its own ventilation procedure for some time prior to the accident which killed Snyder and Simon. . . . Thus, any liability for failing to test the ventilation system had shifted to St. Joe at the time of the accident.

This shifting of liability theory cannot, however, be invoked to relieve ISC of liability with regard to plaintiffs' allegation that the actual design of the condenser unit was defective. Plaintiffs allege that ISC acted negligently by designing an entry door which did not easily allow laborers to gain access to the condenser while wearing breathing apparatus. This allegation of negligence is different in character than an allegation of negligence based on a failure to warn theory. ISC was solely responsible for the design of the unit. Its responsibility to design a safe unit did not end when St. Joe began to operate the unit. Although St. Joe may have been in the best position to provide warnings and implement appropriate safety procedures when it began to operate the plant, St. Joe was never in the best position to create a plant designed to function safely. To the contrary, St. Joe paid ISC to design a functional and safe facility. Given its reliance on ISC to provide the design, it is highly unlikely that St. Joe would have changed the design to accommodate workers wearing breathing tanks.

Moreover, St. Joe acted reasonably in not altering the design of the condenser unit door. Indeed, inasmuch as ISC's safety procedure provided "no entry may be made without a second person immediately outside to continuously watch the person inside . . .," ISC contemplated that a laborer entering the unit might encounter problems necessitating rescue. The most obvious hazard a laborer might encounter would be carbon monoxide poisoning. If in fact the atmosphere remained lethal at the time of entry, a second person standing by could not effectuate a rescue without breathing apparatus. Thus ISC's admonition to have a second person standing by is a tacit guaranty that a worker could pass through the entry door while wearing breathing apparatus. Under the circumstances, it was entirely reasonable for St. Joe to rely on ISC to provide a safe design.

ISC claims, however, that section 14 of the Licensing Agreement "specifically contemplated that St. Joe would choose to alter or amend the zinc dust process over time to suit its particular needs." Section 14 of the Licensing Agreement provides that if St. Joe made any improvements to the zinc dust process, that it would communicate those improvements to ISC. Section 14 thus obligates St. Joe to share any improvements. It does not, however, obligate St. Joes to make improvements, or to test the safety of the plant. Indeed, the improvements discussed in section 14 are commercial improvements, i.e., those that would make the plant more productive and efficient. Hence, ISC cannot argue that section 14 shifted the duty to provide a safe design to St. Joe.

In summary, plaintiffs may proceed on the theory that ISC was negligent in designing a defectively small entry door. Given the fact that St. Joe paid for ISC's expertise in providing the design, St. Joe was not obligated to improve the design. The mere passage of time is not sufficient to shift liability for any faulty design from ISC to St. Joe.

ISC's final liability shifting argument is rooted in the text of the Licensing Agreement itself. Defendant claims that Sections 8.6.2(c) & (d) excuse it from any liability. The Licensing Agreement does in fact purport to absolve ISC from any liability for injury to persons or property caused by circumstances over which ISC had no control. However, ISC in fact had control over the design of the condenser door. Thus, section 8.6.2(c) is inapposite to whether ISC can be liable for a negligently designed door.

Section 8.6.2(d) provides that ISC cannot be held liable for "any occurrence whatsoever" once ISC had performed, or been released from performing the principal or secondary guarantee. The guarantees, in turn, relate to certain productivity levels. ISC contends that it cannot be held liable for the deaths of Simon and Snyder because they had performed the principal and secondary guarantees at the time of the accident. This contention is without merit. Although parties may sometimes contractually alter traditional notions of liability via indemnity clauses, "under Pennsylvania law, indemnity is disallowed if the indemnitee is actively negligent." Thus, "the law is well settled that the intention to include within the scope of an independent contract, a loss due to the indemnitee's own negligence must be expressed in clear and unequivocal language."

[Active] negligence is "negligence occurring in connection with activities conducted on the premises, as for example, negligence in the operation of machinery," whereas passive negligence "denotes negligence which permits defects, obstacles or pitfalls to exist upon the premises." Although the Pennsylvania Supreme Court did not use these specific terms, I believe passive negligence relates to acts of omission whereas active negligence relates to acts of commission. . . . In the instant case, ISC created the dangerous situation by designing an entry which could not easily accommodate a laborer wearing breathing apparatus. It was thus actively negligent in failing to design a safe plant.

Section 8.6.2(d) does not expressly or unequivocally relieve ISC from liability for its own negligence. Instead, it purports to relieve ISC from liability once it has performed the principal and secondary guarantees. The breadth of section 8.6.2(d) may, at first blush, appear to relieve ISC of liability. However, the language lacks the kind of specificity necessary to clearly and unequivocally absolve ISC of liability for its own negligence. Therefore, the language of the Licensing Agreement was insufficient to shift liability for a negligently designed door to St. Joe. . . .

Therefore, ISC's motion for summary judgment on the count alleging negligent design must be denied. An appropriate order will be entered.

NOTES

1. The original *Restatement* language on strict liability was replaced in 1998 with a new *Restatement (Third) of Products Liability*. Section 19 of the new *Restatement* provides a definition of "product":

> For purposes of this Restatement:
>
> (a) A product is tangible personal property distributed commercially for use or consumption. Other items, such as real property and electricity, are products when the context of their distribution and use is sufficiently analogous to the distribution and use of tangible personal property that it is appropriate to apply the rules stated in this Restatement.
>
> (b) Services, even when provided commercially, are not products. . . .

Comment d to this section of the *Restatement* addresses the treatment of information under this concept:

> [Issues have been raised about] intangible personal property. . . . The first consists of information in media such as books, maps, and navigational charts. Plaintiffs allege that the information delivered was false and misleading, causing harm when actors relied on it. They seek to recover against publishers in strict liability in tort based on product defect, rather than on negligence or some form of misrepresentation. Although a tangible medium such as a book, itself clearly a product, delivers the information, the plaintiff's grievance in such cases is with the information, not with the tangible medium. Most courts, expressing concern that imposing strict liability for the dissemination of false and defective information would significantly impinge on free speech have, appropriately, refused to impose strict products liability in these cases. One area in which some courts have imposed strict products liability involves false information contained in maps and navigational charts. In that context the falsity of the factual information is unambiguous and more akin to a classic product defect. However, the better view is that false information in such documents constitutes a misrepresentation that the user may properly rely upon.

Restatement (Third) of Products Liability § 19, cmt. d.

PROBLEM 8.12

EZ Electronics operates an online service available to electricians. The service charges a monthly fee of $50.00. It has approximately 4,000 subscribers. One part of the service provides information on how to install various types of electronic systems in new and used homes. Jones accesses this portion of the service and uses the information there to install an "automated house" system, which automates all electrical appliances and systems into a single control system. The installation is done according to EZ's instructions, but is faulty. One night, the system malfunctions and causes a major fire in a client's home. The client is severely injured. The client sues EZ. What result? What result if the client obtains a $500,000 award against Jones, who then sues EZ?

KENNEDY v. GUESS, INC.
806 N.E.2d 776 (Ind. 2004)

SHEPARD, CHIEF JUSTICE.

We consider here for the first time certain strict liability provisions in the Indiana Product Liability Act that render some distributors liable as though they had manufactured the product. The case arises from motions for summary judgment the trial court granted for two corporate defendants involved in distribution of an allegedly defective designer umbrella. We conclude the defendants did not establish that they were entitled to judgment. On a second question of first impression, we hold that those who license their trademarks for use on products that cause injury may have negligence liability proportionate to their role in the product's design, manufacturing, and distribution.

Facts and Procedural History

Kaye Kennedy purchased a "Guess" watch at a Lazarus Department Store in Indianapolis on November 22, 1996. As a gift for purchasing the watch, she received a free umbrella also bearing the "Guess" logo. On May 22, 1998, Kaye's husband Richard took the umbrella to work, where a co-worker swung it from the handle. The umbrella's shaft separated from the handle and struck Richard in the nose and sinus, causing injury. [The] Kennedys' complaint sought damages against Guess, Inc., Callanen International, Inc. (formerly known as Watches CGI, Inc.), Interasia Bag Manufacturers, Ltd., and Interasian Resources, Ltd. The complaint asserted both negligence and strict liability.

Interasia Bag, a Hong Kong corporation, manufactured the umbrella. Interasian Resources, located in New York, is a domestic affiliate of Interasia Bag. Callanen, a Connecticut corporation, is licensed by Guess to market products bearing the Guess logo, including the watch and umbrella at issue. . . . Callanen and Guess moved for summary judgment, which the trial court granted. The Court of Appeals reversed. . . .

I. Strict Liability Claim

Indiana's Product Liability Act (the "Act") governs all actions brought by a user or consumer against a manufacturer or seller for the physical harm caused by a product. It provides in pertinent part that:

a person who sells, leases, or otherwise puts into the stream of commerce any product in a defective condition unreasonably dangerous to any user or consumer or to the user's or consumer's property is subject to liability for physical harm caused by that product to the user or consumer if:

> (1) that user or consumer is in the class of persons that the seller should reasonably foresee as being subject to the harm caused by the defective condition;
>
> (2) the seller is engaged in the business of selling the product; and
>
> (3) the product is expected to and does reach the user or consumer without substantial alteration in the condition in which the product is sold by the person sought to be held liable under this article.

Ind.Code § 34-20-2-1 (1999). Actions for strict liability in tort are restricted to *manufacturers* of defective products.

[The court held that neither Callanen nor Guess was a manufacturer. Callanen, but not Guess, however, might be treated as a manufacturer under an exception that allows for treating a "manufacturer's principal distributor or seller" as a manufacturer in some limited cases. As to Guess, the court stated: "Where Guess is concerned, the designated information shows that Guess is not a distributor or seller of *any* sort, principal or otherwise. Guess neither ordered nor received the umbrellas at issue. It was never in possession of any of the umbrellas nor did it manufacture, supply, distribute, assemble, design, or sell them. Rather, Guess simply licensed its name to Callanen for placement on various products. There is no issue of fact disputing Guess' contention that it is not a 'principal distributor or seller.' Summary judgment in favor of Guess on this issue was proper. . . ."]

II. § 400 Negligence Claim

[To] prevail in a negligence action, the claimant must establish: (1) a duty, (2) a breach of that duty, and (3) injury resulting from that breach. . . .

Citing *Dudley Sports Co. v. Schmitt,* 151 Ind.App. 217, 279 N.E.2d 266, 273 (1972), the Kennedys argue that Guess and/or Callanen owe them a duty because Guess and/or Callanen can be considered "apparent manufacturers" of the umbrella under § 400. Section 400 provides, "One who puts out as his own product a chattel manufactured by another is subject to the same liability as though he were its manufacturer."[3] *Restatement (Second) of Torts* § 400 (1965).

The court in *Dudley Sports* employed § 400 to hold a vendor liable for the negligence of the manufacturer where the vendor placed its name on the product and gave no indication of who was the actual manufacturer. The *Dudley* court reasoned:

> When a vendor puts his name exclusively on a product, in no way indicating that it is the product of another, the public is induced to

---

[3] [FN 4] Comment (a) to § 400 defines "one who puts out a chattel" as "anyone who supplies it to others for their own use or for the use of third persons, either by sale or lease or by gift of loan."

believe that the vendor was the manufacturer of the product. This belief causes the public to rely upon the skill of the vendor. When products are held out in this manner, the ultimate purchaser has no available means of ascertaining who is the true manufacturer. By this act of concealment, the vendor vouches for the product and assumes the manufacturer's responsibility as his own.

A similar conclusion was reached in *Lucas v. Dorsey Corp.*, 609 N.E.2d 1191 (Ind.Ct.App.1993). This case represents our first occasion to explore the liability of trademark licensors.

The Court of Appeals reversed summary judgment on this claim finding that "a question of fact remains as to whether Guess or Callanen or both exercised the requisite degree of involvement in the stream of commerce to be considered an apparent manufacturer." We think this does not hold true with respect to Callanen. . . .

Whether a "holding out" has occurred should be judged from the viewpoint of the purchasing public, examining whether the public has been induced to believe that the vendor was the actual manufacturer of the product. There is nothing to suggest that the Kennedys were induced to believe Callanen was the manufacturer of the umbrella in question. The only name on the umbrella was "Guess"; the name "Callanen" was nowhere to be found.

[The] Kennedys rely heavily on the fact that Callanen and Guess had a trademark licensing agreement which gave Callanen the right to distribute products bearing the Guess name. Such evidence does not suggest Callanen held itself out as the manufacturer. From the consumer's perspective, Callanen had nothing to do with the manufacture of the umbrella. There is no reference to Callanen that would lead a reasonable purchaser to believe that it was the manufacturer of the umbrella. . . . Callanen did not design, manufacture, assemble, or test the umbrella. Any involvement Callanen had with the umbrella occurred after it was designed and manufactured. While Callanen did purchase the umbrellas for distribution, it received the umbrellas already packaged for distribution from Interasia Bag. Generally, Callanen did not even open the packaging unless it was going to send less than ten umbrellas to a particular store.

Callanen presented sufficient evidence to demonstrate that it did not hold itself out as a manufacturer. . . . The trial court was correct to grant Callanen summary judgment on the negligence claim.

We reach a different conclusion as to whether *Guess* could be considered an "apparent manufacturer."

Some jurisdictions impose liability on trademark licensors without any additional involvement in the stream of commerce. Guess argues that merely licensing the use of its trademark is insufficient to hold it liable under § 400 and that something more should be required. Guess relies on Chief Justice Peters' observation for the Connecticut Supreme Court that although "a non-manufacturer may under certain circumstances be held liable in the same manner as a manufacturer or seller of a defective product . . . most cases impose liability [under section 400] only after finding that the licensor had a significant role in the chain of distribution." *Burkert v. Petrol Plus of Naugatuck, Inc.,* 216 Conn. 65, 579 A.2d 26, 33-34 (1990).

Justice Peters explained that in jurisdictions where "additional involvement" is required, various factors determine whether there is sufficient involvement in the stream of commerce such that an entity is an "apparent manufacturer." Some factors courts examine to make this determination are the licensor's right of control over the product design, the fees received for the use of the trademark, the prominence of the trademark, supply of components, participation in advertisement and the degree of economic benefit to be gained from the licensing agreement.

In the *Petrol Plus* case, General Motors had licensed the use of its trademarked Dextron II transmission fluid. The fluid was actually manufactured by other companies, subject to GM testing, and eventually sold to Burkert by Petrol Plus. The Connecticut court held that General Motors was not an entity that "put out" the product since "GM was in no way involved with the sale, lease, gift or loan of the defective automatic transmission fluid." This distinguished GM's role from that played by Armour & Co., which the Connecticut high court had earlier held to be an apparent manufacturer of a can of corned beef labeled "Armour Veribest Products" from "Armour and Company, Foreign Distributors." *Burkhardt v. Armour & Co.,* 115 Conn. 249, 161 A. 385 (1932). The can had been placed in American commerce by Armour & Co., an Illinois corporation, which had obtained it from an Argentine Company named "Frigoritico Armour de la Plata," which had purchased it from an Argentine packing corporation, and so on. *Id.* at 391.

Indiana's *Dudley Sports* decision bears some of the characteristics of Armour. Dudley Sports put its own name on a baseball pitching machine manufactured by someone else and acted as the exclusive distributor of the device.

The present case is more like *Petrol Plus.* Like General Motors, Guess exercised some control over the product itself (like approving placement of the logo) but did not play any role as seller, manufacturer or distributor.

It might well be plausible to assess whether a trademark licensor is, as the *Restatement* puts it, "subject to the same liability as though he were [the product] manufacturer," by pouring over the licensor's level of involvement in the manufacture or distribution of the product. On the other hand, such an approach creates a regime in which liability is binary (either the same as the manufacturer or altogether non-existent) based on the examination of commercial activity that is anything but.

As Chief Justice Peters pointed out in *Petrol Plus,* trademark licensors have a duty under the Lanham Act to take reasonable measures to detect and prevent misleading or deceptive uses of the trademark. They are thus likely to take some ongoing role in the products bearing their mark lest they risk loss of the right associated with ownership of it.

A common law product liability system that, when it encounters muscular supervision by a licensor, imposes liability identical to that of the manufacturer, however, pushes the trademark holder in the opposition direction. It encourages the licensor to play as minor a role as possible in overseeing the design and manufacturing of products bearing the mark in order to preserve the "Sergeant Schultz" defense.[4] This is hardly in the best interest of consumers.

Thus, we conclude that Indiana common law should treat trademark licensors as having responsibility for defective products placed in the stream of commerce bearing their marks, but only so much of the liability for those defects as their relative role in the larger scheme of design, advertising, manufacturing, and distribution warrants. Consumers rightly expect that products bearing logos like "Guess" have been subject to some oversight by those who put their name on the product, but those same consumers can well imagine that in modern commerce the products they buy may have actually been manufactured by someone else.

The process of sorting out comparative fault in such settings can well be left to juries. Summary judgment for Guess on the negligence claim was inappropriate.

Therefore, we affirm in part and reverse in part, as indicated above.

NOTES

1. Do you agree that the quality control requirements that a trademark licensor must impose conflict with the risk of liability under products liability law?

2. Section 400 has been replaced by Section 14 of the *Restatement (Third) of Products Liability*:

> One engaged in the business of selling or otherwise distributing products who sells or distributes as its own a product manufactured by another is subject to the same liability as though the seller or distributor were the product's manufacturer.

With respect to trademark licensors, the comments suggest:

> The rule stated in this Section does not, by its terms, apply to the owner of a trademark who licenses a manufacturer to place the licensor's trademark or logo on the manufacturer's product and distribute it as though manufactured by the licensor. In such a case, even if purchasers of the product might assume that the trademark owner was the manufacturer, the licensor does not "sell or distribute as its own a product manufactured by another." Thus, the manufacturer may be liable under §§ 1-4, but the licensor, who does not sell or

---

[4] [FN 5] In *Indiana Dept. of State Revenue v. Safayan*, 654 N.E.2d 270, 274 (Ind.1995), we explained the "Sergeant Schultz" defense: "The Sergeant Schultz defense refers, of course, to the refrain of the character by that name in the television comedy, Hogan's Heroes. Sergeant Schultz was assigned the unenviable task of guarding Colonel Hogan and his men in a German prisoner of war camp during World War II. Each week, despite the best efforts of the camp's commandant, Colonel Klink, the 'prisoners' would successfully conduct espionage operations from inside the prison. And each week, the lovable, if incompetent, sergeant would stumble upon some clue to Hogan's activities. Instead of pursuing these leads, however, Schultz would simply declare, 'I know n-o-t-h-i-n-g, n-o-t-h-i-n-g.' "

otherwise distribute products, is not liable under this Section of this Restatement.

Trademark licensors are liable for harm caused by defective products distributed under the licensor's trademark or logo when they participate substantially in the design, manufacture, or distribution of the licensee's products. In these circumstances they are treated as sellers of the products bearing their trademarks.

Illustrations:

. . . .

3. MD owns a popular, well-known logo for sports equipment. RS is a manufacturer of sports equipment. MD licenses RS to place MD's logo on RS's equipment, but plays no other role in RS's operations. MD is not subject to liability for harm caused by defective products manufactured and distributed by RS. RS is subject to liability as a manufacturer.

4. The same facts as Illustration 3 except that MD participates substantially in, and exerts control over, RS's operations. MD is subject to liability as a manufacturer for harm caused by defective products distributed by RS. RS is also subject to liability as a manufacturer.

Restatement (Third) of Products Liability § 14, cmt. d.

TORRES v. GOODYEAR TIRE & RUBBER COMPANY, INC.
786 P.2d 939 (Ariz. 1990)

FELDMAN, J.

In this case we are asked to consider the liability of a trademark licensor for injuries caused by defects in a product produced and distributed by its licensee. The question was certified to us by the United States Court of Appeals for the Ninth Circuit. . . . [The] answer to the question whether a trademark licensor is liable under Arizona law is: sometimes yes and sometimes no, depending on the facts. . . .

Facts of this Case

Fortunately, the facts seem relatively undisputed.

Both Andrew and Walter Torres were injured in an automobile accident allegedly caused by tread separation of a Goodyear tire on a 1977 Triumph automobile driven by Walter. The tire was original equipment on the Triumph, which had been manufactured in Great Britain and which had been purchased by Walter's wife, Debra. The tire was marked "Goodyear."

The tire was manufactured by Goodyear GB and designed by GITC. Specifications for the manufacture of the tire were issued by either Goodyear Luxembourg or Goodyear GB. . . . Through its stock ownership in the subsidiaries, Goodyear is able to elect directors to the boards of each subsidiary to ensure that they follow Goodyear's policies. Goodyear International's main office is located in the United States in the same building as Goodyear's executive offices. . . .

Goodyear's actual ability to control Goodyear GB's production of Goodyear tires is pervasive. Either directly, or indirectly through its international subsidiaries, Goodyear has the ability to design the product, provide specifications for its manufacture, and control the method of manufacture and actual production of the tire. Goodyear has reserved the right to control the quality of all tires manufactured by Goodyear GB. It sets warranty policy and honors valid warranty claims on all tires bearing the Goodyear trademark, even though, as in this case, they are actually manufactured by a subsidiary.

Goodyear's ability to control Goodyear GB is not confined to power asserted indirectly through common directors and officers. Goodyear and Goodyear GB have entered into a licensing contract that permits Goodyear GB to manufacture Goodyear tires. The licensing agreement provides that tires will be manufactured in accordance with formulas, specifications, and directions given by Goodyear, and produced from materials approved by Goodyear. Goodyear GB is also required to comply with Goodyear's instructions on labeling, marketing, packaging, and advertising the tires. . . .

Common Law Strict Liability

A. Product Law in Arizona

This state long ago adopted the *Restatement (Second) of Torts* (Restatement) §402 and recognized strict liability of manufacturers and sellers of defective products that were unreasonably dangerous and caused physical harm to the consumer or his property. . . . Both the Restatement and our cases have used the terms "manufacturer" and "seller" almost interchangeably in applying the doctrine. . . .

The underlying objective of the doctrine was to place the risk of loss on those in the chain of distribution of defective, unreasonably dangerous goods. The doctrine was considered a policy device to spread the risk from one to whom a defective product may be a catastrophe, to those who marketed the product, profit from its sale, and have the know how to remove its defects before placing it in the chain of distribution. Given the policy formulation underlying strict liability, the degree of control possessed by Goodyear in the case before us is a factor that militates in favor of applying strict liability to such licensors.

These policy considerations have impelled our courts to abjure technical definitions in defining the categories of enterprise to which the doctrine of strict liability should apply. Among those who are neither manufacturers nor sellers, but who were involved in the chain of production or distribution of the product and have been subjected to strict liability, are lessors of products, donors of products, and dealers in used goods.

[We] believe [that] in Arizona the application of strict liability does not hinge on the technical limitations of the term seller or manufacturer as used in Restatement §402A. . . . Arizona has not yet decided whether trademark licensors may be held strictly liable for defects in the licensed product, although the application of strict liability to trademark licensors has been intimated on at least two occasions. . . . If we ignore the label of trademark licensor and consider only the policy objectives underlying the adoption of strict liability as described in [*Tucson Industries, Inc. v.*] *Schwartz*, [108 Ariz. 464, 501 P.2d 936 (1972),] we must focus our analysis on the character of the injury-producing conduct rather than the technical limitations of the term seller. Using this approach, the facts of this case place Goodyear well within the class mentioned by Judge Jacobson of those "in the business of placing products in the stream of commerce," and subject to the doctrine of strict liability. . . .

In arguing that it should not be held strictly liable, Goodyear relies heavily on the separate corporate identities of each of its subsidiaries. It points out that the corporate forms were strictly maintained — as we have no doubt is the case — and that courts should not ignore corporate organization. We have no intention of doing so, but we do not believe it is good law to allow multinational firms the freedom to compartmentalize strict liability by choosing organizational forms. . . . This court must also acknowledge the realities of the marketplace when it decides cases. . . . The marketplace, as described by the facts of this case, indicates very clearly that we deal with a tire designed to be a Goodyear tire, produced, packaged, advertised, and sold as a Goodyear tire, and warranted by Goodyear. . . .

Nor have we been cited to any case that holds, under similar facts, that the doctrine of strict liability should not apply to a trademark licensor. Actually, many courts considering the issue have instead taken the view that strict liability should be applied. For example, in a case very similar to the present case, a plaintiff sought to impose strict liability on Uniroyal, Inc. for injuries caused by an allegedly defective tire manufactured and sold by Uniroyal's Belgian subsidiary, *Uniroyal Englebert Belgique, S.A. Connelly v. Uniroyal, Inc.*, 75 Ill.2d 393, 27 Ill.Dec. 343, 389 N.E.2d 155 (1979), *cert. denied and appeal dismissed*, 444 U.S. 1060 (1980). Noting that strict liability was intended "to place the loss caused by defective products on those who create the risk and reap the profit," the Illinois Supreme Court held as follows:

> A licensor is an integral part of the marketing enterprise, and its participation in the profits reaped by placing a defective product in the stream of commerce . . . presents the same public policy reasons for the applicability of strict liability which supported the imposition of such liability on wholesalers, retailers and lessors. The societal purposes underlying . . . the case adopting strict liability in Illinois mandate that the doctrine be applicable to one who for a consideration, authorizes the use of his trademark, particularly when, as here, the product bears no indication that it was manufactured by any other entity.

Goodyear argues that none of the cases cited stands for the proposition that a mere trademark licensor can be held strictly liable in tort. It points out that in each of the cases, the facts showed the licensor was "integrally involved in the overall producing and marketing enterprise [so] that strict liability will follow." Goodyear is correct, but its analysis of the cases does not help its cause. If ever a defendant was involved "in the direct chain of sale leading from manufacturer to consumer," it is Goodyear. . . .

It can be said that all those who participate in the process of making products available to users for profit or financial gain are subject to liability on a negligence theory. This would include endorsers, licensors of trademarks, and franchisers. . . . The more difficult inquiry relates to strict liability. . . . The states that have passed on the question have treated the franchiser as if he were the seller, at least in those cases where many members of the general public would believe that the franchiser was either the owner, seller or at least exercising substantial control over the franchisee's processes. The licensor of a patent is often in a somewhat different position. The licensor's contract is generally nothing more than a contract authorizing the use of an alleged patent, i.e., an invention. The product sold by the licensee is generally not sold under the trade name of the licensor of the patent. The general public is not in most instances relying on the licensor. This is not to say the licensor may not participate to such an extent in the construction and sale of products made pursuant to a patent to justify the imposition of strict liability. . . .

[If] we were to deal with "nothing but a mere licensor" — one who merely licenses a manufacturer to use a particular patent or trademark — it might well be inappropriate to impose strict liability. However, this is not an issue we need to decide today because the facts . . . show that Goodyear is anything but a mere licensor. . . . We conclude, therefore, as a common law matter, trademark licensors who significantly participate in the overall process by which the product reaches its consumers, and who have the right to control the incidents of manufacture or distribution, are subject to liability under the rules of Restatement § 402A . . . in Arizona. . . .

Chapter 9

LICENSE TERMS TO PRESERVE AND EXPAND PROPERTY

I. INTRODUCTION TO THE ISSUE

Some licensed subject matter requires ongoing action to maintain its value and, even, its existence as property. Most notably, these include trademarks and trade secret rights, two topics we discuss in this chapter.

More generally, a licensee's conduct can be important in establishing and maintaining the licensor's rights against third parties. One illustration occurs in Section 287(a) of the Patent Act, which provides the following limitation on the right to collect damages for patent infringement:

> Patentees and persons making, offering for sale, or selling within the United States any patented article for or under them . . . may give notice to the public that the same is patented, either by fixing thereon the word "patent" or the abbreviation "pat.," together with the number of the patent, or when, from the character of the article, this cannot be done, by fixing to it, or to the package wherein one or more of them is contained, a label containing a like notice. In the event of failure to mark, no damages shall be recovered by the patentee in any action for infringement, except on proof that the infringer was notified of the infringement and continued to infringe thereafter, in which event damages may be recovered only for infringement occurring after such notice. Filing of an action for infringement shall constitute such notice.

If a licensee is engaged in manufacture and distribution of a patented product, the "marking" rule illustrates a case where the licensor's potential claims against third parties are affected by the licensee's conduct and, ultimately, the terms of the license. Express contractual terms on this point are common; the cases do not impose marking obligations on a licensee as an implied term. *Tulip Computers Intern. B.V. v. Dell Computer Corp.*, 2003 U.S. Dist. LEXIS 5409 (D. Del. 2003) (failure to mark triggered defense; license did not require marking and licensor did not insist on it).

While patent marking can be important, even more significant potential effects are present in trademark and trade secret licensing, to which we now turn.

II. TRADEMARK QUALITY CONTROL

A trademark is a symbol, word or other mark that becomes associated with a product or service in such a way as to identify the source of that product or service and its quality. Trademark infringement claims are, ultimately, claims that another person's unauthorized used the same or a similar mark in a manner that creates the risk of confusion among the relevant, consuming public. In cases where the mark owner is the user, changes in quality or product are nothing more than the ordinary evolution of a mark. But what of the circumstance in which a mark has come to be associated with a particular quality of product or service from a particular source and is then licensed to a third party for its use? While one could argue that any transfer of rights to use the mark to a third party is inconsistent with the identifying functions of a mark, that proposition is not followed in modern law and would, in fact, disable the huge franchise operations on which much of modern commerce depends.

The relationship between the property right and the identification function of the mark has led courts to place limits on the use of trademarks in licensing — limits associated with the obligation of the licensor (mark owner) to maintain and exercise control over the use of the mark even in the hands of a licensee. One frequently cited case is the Second Circuit's decision in *Dawn Donut Co. v. Hart's Food Stores, Inc.*, 267 F.2d 358 (2d Cir. 1959):

> Without the requirement of control, the right of a trademark owner to license his mark separately from the business in connection with which it has been used would create the danger that products bearing the same trademark might be of diverse qualities. If the licensor is not compelled to take some reasonable steps to prevent misuses of his trademark in the hands of others the public will be deprived of its most effective protection against misleading uses of a trademark. The public is hardly in a position to uncover deceptive uses of a trademark before they occur and will be at best slow to detect them after they happen. Thus, unless the licensor exercises supervision and control over the operations of its licensees the risk that the public will be unwittingly deceived will be increased and this is precisely what the Act is in part designed to prevent. Clearly the only effective way to protect the public where a trademark is used by licensees is to place on the licensor the affirmative duty of policing in a reasonable manner the activities of his licensees.

267 F.2d at 367.

BARCAMERICA INTERNATIONAL USA TRUST v. TYFIELD IMPORTERS, INC.
289 F.3d 589 (9th Cir. 2002).

O'SCANNLZAIN, CIRCUIT JUDGE.

We must decide whether a company engaged in "naked licensing" of its trademark, thus resulting in abandonment of the mark and ultimately its cancellation.

This case involves a dispute over who may use the "Leonardo Da Vinci" trademark for wines.

A

Barcamerica International USA Trust ("Barcamerica") traces its rights in the Leonardo Da Vinci mark to a February 14, 1984 registration granted by the United States Patent and Trademark Office ("PTO"), on an application filed in 1982. On August 7, 1989, the PTO acknowledged the mark's "incontestability." *See* 15 U.S.C.

§1115(b). Barcamerica asserts that it has used the mark continuously since the early 1980s. In the district court, it produced invoices evidencing two sales per year for the years 1980 through 1993: one to a former employee and the other to a barter exchange company. Barcamerica further produced invoices evidencing between three and seven sales per year for the years 1994 through 1998. These include sales to the same former employee, two barter exchange companies, and various sales for "cash." The sales volume reflected in the invoices for the years 1980 through 1988 range from 160 to 410 cases of wine per year. Barcamerica also produced sales summaries for the years 1980 through 1996 which reflect significantly higher sales volumes; these summaries do not indicate, however, to whom the wine was sold.

In 1988, Barcamerica entered into a licensing agreement with Renaissance Vineyards ("Renaissance"). Under the agreement, Barcamerica granted Renaissance the nonexclusive right to use the "Da Vinci" mark for five years or 4,000 cases, "whichever comes first," in exchange for $2,500. The agreement contained no quality control provision. In 1989, Barcamerica and Renaissance entered into a second agreement in place of the 1988 agreement. The 1989 agreement granted Renaissance an exclusive license to use the "Da Vinci" mark in the United States for wine products or alcoholic beverages. The 1989 agreement was drafted by Barcamerica's counsel and, like the 1988 agreement, it did not contain a quality control provision.[1] In fact, the only evidence in the record of any efforts by Barcamerica to exercise "quality control" over Renaissance's wines comprised (1) Barcamerica principal George Gino Barca's testimony that he occasionally, informally tasted of the wine, and (2) Barca's testimony that he relied on the reputation of a "world-famous winemaker" employed by Renaissance at the time the agreements were signed. (That winemaker is now deceased, although the record does not indicate when he died.) Nonetheless, Barcamerica contends that Renaissance's use of the mark inures to Barcamerica's benefit.

B

Cantine Leonardo Da Vinci Soc. Coop. a.r.l. ("Cantine"), an entity of Italy, is a wine producer located in Vinci, Italy. Cantine has sold wine products bearing the "Leonardo Da Vinci" tradename since 1972; it selected this name and mark based on the name of its home city, Vinci. Cantine began selling its "Leonardo Da Vinci" wine to importers in the United States in 1979. Since 1996, however, Tyfield Importers, Inc. ("Tyfield") has been the exclusive United States importer and distributor of Cantine wine products bearing the "Leonardo Da Vinci" mark. During the first eighteen months after Tyfield became Cantine's exclusive importer, Cantine sold approximately 55,000 cases of wine products bearing the "Leonardo Da Vinci" mark to Tyfield. During this same period, Tyfield spent between $250,000 and $300,000 advertising and promoting Cantine's products, advertising in *USA Today,* and such specialty magazines as *The Wine Spectator, Wine and Spirits,* and *Southern Beverage Journal.*

---

[1] [FN2] In fact, the 1989 Agreement specifically states that Renaissance "shall be solely responsible for any and all claims or causes of action for negligence, breach of contract, breach of warranty, or products liability arising from the sale or distribution of Products using the Licensed Mark."

Cantine learned of Barcamerica's registration of the "Leonardo Da Vinci" mark in or about 1996, in the course of prosecuting its first trademark application in the United States. Cantine investigated Barcamerica's use of the mark and concluded that Barcamerica was no longer selling any wine products bearing the "Leonardo Da Vinci" mark and had long since abandoned the mark. As a result, in May 1997, Cantine commenced a proceeding in the PTO seeking cancellation of Barcamerica's registration for the mark based on abandonment. Barcamerica responded by filing the instant action on January 30, 1998, and thereafter moved to suspend the proceeding in the PTO. The PTO granted Barcamerica's motion and suspended the cancellation proceeding.

Although Barca has been aware of Cantine's use of the "Leonardo Da Vinci" mark since approximately 1993, Barcamerica initiated the instant action only after Tyfield and Cantine commenced the proceeding in the PTO. A month after Barcamerica filed the instant action, it moved for a preliminary injunction enjoining Tyfield and Cantine from any further use of the mark. The district court denied the motion, finding, among other things, that "there is a serious question as to whether [Barcamerica] will be able to demonstrate a bona fide use of the Leonardo Da Vinci mark in the ordinary course of trade and overcome [the] claim of abandonment."

Thereafter, Tyfield and Cantine moved for summary judgment on various grounds. The district court granted the motion, concluding that Barcamerica abandoned the mark through naked licensing. The court further found that, in any event, the suit was barred by laches because Barcamerica knew several years before filing suit that Tyfield and Cantine were using the mark in connection with the sale of wine. This timely appeal followed. . . .

III

[Barcamerica] first challenges the district court's conclusion that Barcamerica abandoned its trademark by engaging in naked licensing. It is well-established that "[a] trademark owner may grant a license and remain protected provided quality control of the goods and services sold under the trademark by the licensee is maintained." But "[u]ncontrolled or 'naked' licensing may result in the trademark ceasing to function as a symbol of quality and controlled source." MCCARTHY ON TRADEMARKS AND UNFAIR COMPETITION § 18:48, at 18-79 (4th ed.2001). Consequently, where the licensor fails to exercise adequate quality control over the licensee, "a court may find that the trademark owner has abandoned the trademark, in which case the owner would be estopped from asserting rights to the trademark." Such abandonment "is purely an 'involuntary' forfeiture of trademark rights," for it need not be shown that the trademark owner had any subjective intent to abandon the mark. MCCARTHY § 18:48, at 18-79. Accordingly, the proponent of a naked license theory "faces a stringent standard" of proof.

A

Judge Damrell's analysis of this issue in his memorandum opinion and order is correct and well-stated, and we adopt it as our own. As that court explained,

In 1988, [Barcamerica] entered into an agreement with Renaissance in which [Barcamerica] granted Renaissance the non-exclusive right to use the "Da Vinci" mark for five years or 4,000 cases, "whichever comes first." There is no quality control provision in that agreement. In 1989, [Barcamerica] and Renaissance entered into a second agreement in place of the 1998 agreement. The 1989 agreement grants Renaissance an exclusive license to use the "Da Vinci" mark in the United States for wine products or alcoholic beverages. The 1989 agreement was to "continue in effect in perpetuity," unless terminated in accordance with the provisions thereof. The 1989 agreement does not contain any controls or restrictions with respect to the quality of goods bearing the "Da Vinci" mark. Rather, the agreement provides that Renaissance is "solely responsible for any and all claims or causes of action for negligence, breach of contract, breach of warranty, or products liability arising from the sale or distribution of Products using the Licensed Mark" and that Renaissance shall defend and indemnify plaintiff against such claims.

The lack of an express contract right to inspect and supervise a licensee's operations is not conclusive evidence of lack of control. "[T]here need not be formal quality control where 'the particular circumstances of the licensing arrangement [indicate] that the public will not be deceived.'" Indeed, "[c]ourts have upheld licensing agreements where the licensor is familiar with and relies upon the licensee's own efforts to control quality."

Here, there is no evidence that [Barcamerica] is familiar with or relied upon Renaissance's efforts to control quality. Mr. Barca represents that Renaissance's use of the mark is "controlled by" plaintiff "with respect to the nature and quality of the wine sold under the license," and that "[t]he nature and quality of Renaissance wine sold under the trademark is good." [Barcamerica]'s sole evidence of any such control is Mr. Barca's own apparently random tastings and his reliance on Renaissance's reputation. According to Mr. Barca, the quality of Renaissance's wine is "good" and at the time plaintiff began licensing the mark to Renaissance, Renaissance's winemaker was Karl Werner, a "world famous" winemaker.

Mr. Barca's conclusory statements as to the existence of quality controls is insufficient to create a triable issue of fact on the issue of naked licensing. While Mr. Barca's tastings perhaps demonstrate a minimal effort to monitor quality, Mr. Barca fails to state when, how often, and under what circumstances he tastes the wine. Mr. Barca's reliance on the reputation of the winemaker is no longer justified as he is deceased. Mr. Barca has not provided any information concerning the successor winemaker(s). While Renaissance's attorney, Mr. Goldman, testified that Renaissance "strive[s] extremely hard to have the highest possible standards," he has no knowledge of the quality control procedures utilized by Renaissance with regard to testing wine. Moreover, according to Renaissance, Mr. Barca never "had any involvement whatsoever regarding the quality of the wine and maintaining it at any level."

[Barcamerica] has failed to demonstrate any knowledge of or reliance on the actual quality controls used by Renaissance, nor has it demonstrated any ongoing effort to monitor quality.

[Barcamerica] and Renaissance did not and do not have the type of close working relationship required to establish adequate quality control in the absence of a formal agreement. *See, e.g., Taco Cabana Int'l, Inc.,* 932 F.2d [1113] at 1121 [(5th Cir. 1991)] (licensor and licensee enjoyed close working relationship for eight years); *Transgo, [Inc. v. Ajac Transmission Parts Corp.,]* 768 F.2d [1001] at 1017-18 (9th Cir. 1985) (licensor manufactured 90% of components sold by licensee, licensor informed licensee that if he chose to use his own parts "[licensee] wanted to know about it," licensor had ten year association with licensee and was familiar with his ability and expertise); *Taffy Original Designs, Inc. v. Taffy's Inc.,* 161 U.S.P.Q. 707, 713 (N.D.Ill.1966) (licensor and licensee were sisters in business together for seventeen years, licensee's business was a continuation of the licensor's and licensee's prior business, licensor visited licensee's store from time to time and was satisfied with the quality of the merchandise offered); *Arner v. Sharper Image Corp.,* 39 U.S.P.Q.2d 1282 (C.D.Cal.1995) (licensor engaged in a close working relationship with licensee's employees and license agreement provided that license would terminate if certain employees ceased to be affiliated with licensee). No such familiarity or close working relationship ever existed between [Barcamerica] and Renaissance. Both the terms of the licensing agreements and the manner in which they were carried out show that [Barcamerica] engaged in naked licensing of the "Leonardo Da Vinci" mark. Accordingly, [Barcamerica] is estopped from asserting any rights in the mark.

Barcamerica, at 9-13.

B

On appeal, Barcamerica does not seriously contest any of the foregoing. Instead, it argues essentially that because Renaissance makes good wine, the public is not deceived by Renaissance's use of the "Da Vinci" mark, and thus, that the license was legally acceptable. This novel rationale, however, is faulty. Whether Renaissance's wine was objectively "good" or "bad" is simply irrelevant. What matters is that Barcamerica played no meaningful role in holding the wine to a standard of quality — good, bad, or otherwise. As McCarthy explains,

It is important to keep in mind that "quality control" does not necessarily mean that the licensed goods or services must be of "high" quality, but merely of equal quality, whether that quality is high, low or middle. *The point is that customers are entitled to assume that the nature and quality of goods and services sold under the mark at all licensed outlets will be consistent and predictable.*

McCarthy § 18:55, at 18-94. And "it is well established that where a trademark owner engages in naked licensing, without any control over the quality of goods produced by the licensee, such a practice is *inherently deceptive* and constitutes abandonment of any rights to the trademark by the licensor." *First Interstate Bancorp v. Stenquist,* 16 U.S.P.Q.2d 1704, 1706 (N.D. Cal.1990).

Certainly, "[I]t is difficult, if not impossible to define in the abstract exactly how much control and inspection is needed to satisfy the requirement of quality control over trademark licensees." McCARTHY, § 18:55, at 18-94. And we recognize that "[t]he standard of quality control and the degree of necessary inspection and policing by the licensor will vary with the wide range of licensing situations in use in the modern marketplace." But in this case we deal with a relatively simple product: wine. Wine, of course, is bottled by season. Thus, at the very least, one might have expected Barca to sample (or to have some designated wine connoisseur sample) on an annual basis, in some organized way, some adequate number of bottles of the Renaissance wines which were to bear Barcamerica's mark to ensure that they were of sufficient quality to be called "Da Vinci." But Barca did not make even this minimal effort.

C

We therefore agree with Judge Damrell, and hold that Barcamerica engaged in naked licensing of its "Leonardo Da Vinci" mark — and that by so doing, Barcamerica forfeited its rights in the mark. . . .

NOTES

1. The proposition that the licensor must exercise quality controls over a trademark licensee or risk losing its underlying rights invites the questions of "how much control" and how is adequacy measured. For example, should courts look to the actual quality of the products or services created as a measure? Can one, for example, visualize a court or jury engaging in taste-testing wine produced by the licensee in *Barcamerica*? Is that the appropriate focus? *See Kentucky Fried Chicken v. Diversified Packaging,* 549 F.2d 368, 387 (5th Cir. 1977), suggesting that, in that case, "retention of a trademark requires only minimal quality control, for in this context we do not sit to assess the quality of products sold on the open market. We must determine whether Kentucky Fried has abandoned quality control; the consuming public must be the judge of whether the quality control efforts have been ineffectual." Is quality or consistency the issue?

2. If a licensor contracts with a company that follows extremely high standards in its business, should the licensor be able to rely on those standards in lieu of its own control? If the answer is "no," as suggested by *Barcamerica*, what is the basis for requiring control? The Fifth Circuit in *Taco Cabana Int'l, Inc. v. Two Pesos, Inc.,* 932 F.2d 1113 (5th Cir. 1991), *aff'd on other gds,* 505 U.S. 763 (1992), commented:

> Where the license parties have engaged in a close working relationship, and may justifiably rely on each parties' intimacy with standards and procedures to ensure consistent quality, and no actual decline in quality standards is demonstrated, we would depart from the purpose of the law to find an abandonment simply for want of all the inspection

and control formalities. . . . The history of the Stehling brothers' relationship warrants this relaxation of formalities. Prior to the licensing agreement at issue, the Stehling brothers operated Taco Cabana together for approximately eight years. Taco Cabana and TaCasita do not use significantly different procedures or products, and the brothers may be expected to draw on their mutual experience to maintain the requisite quality consistency. They cannot protect their trade dress if they operate their separate restaurants in ignorance of each other's operations, but they need not maintain the careful policing appropriate to more formal license arrangements.

Professor McCarthy in his treatise, however, summarizes this and other cases as follows:

[M]erely looking to the past [positive] results of such "non-control" will not usually serve the goal of quality assurance. Merely because reliance on the licensee's own self-interest has not resulted in a variation of quality in the past does not necessarily mean that such a situation will continue forever. It is difficult to see how the licensor can fulfill its duty to take reasonable steps to control quality merely by totally leaving the matter to the discretion of the licensee.

1 McCARTHY, McCARTHY ON TRADEMARKS AND UNFAIR COMPETITION § 18.17[3] (3d ed. 1992).

3. Modern trademark licensing is not confined to licenses for products or services similar to the original. If the licensed use is very different and is not within the scope of the licensor's prior business activities under the mark, what is the risk of confusion? The *Restatement (Third) of Unfair Competition* states:

If a licensee uses the trademark of a beer or soft drink manufacturer on clothing or glassware, for example, prospective purchasers may be unlikely to assume that the owner of the trademark has more than perfunctory involvement in the production or quality of the licensee's goods even if the manner of use clearly indicates sponsorship by the trademark owner. On the other hand, if the licensee's use is on goods similar or identical to those produced by the trademark owner, purchasers may be likely to assume that the goods are actually manufactured by the owner of the mark.

Restatement (Third) of Unfair Competition § 33, cmt. c (1995).

4. McCARTHY ON TRADEMARKS AND UNFAIR COMPETITION § 18:55 (2002) comments: "Control that is satisfactory for the license of a children's television program character or a plush doll toy will probably be much less than the extensive regulation system needed for the license of a famous mark on a system of quick-service food restaurants. The standard of quality control and the degree of necessary inspection and policing by the licensor will vary with the wide range of licensing situations in use in the modern market-place." Do you agree that this should be true? What if the licensor itself did not closely police its own procedures?

5. What is the relationship between terms of the license and the presence (or absence) of adequate quality control? As pointed out by the Second Circuit in *Dawn Donut*:

The absence, however, of an express contract right to inspect and supervise a licensee's operations does not mean that the plaintiff's method of licensing failed to comply with the requirements of the Lanham Act. Plaintiff may in fact have exercised control in spite of the absence of any express grant by licensees of the right to inspect and supervise. The question, then, with respect to both plaintiff's contract and non-contract licensees, is whether the plaintiff in fact exercised sufficient control.

267 F.2d at 368. The Second Circuit in *General Motors Corp. v. Gibson Chemical & Oil Corp.*, 786 F.2d 105, 110 (2d Cir. 1986), commented:

The critical question in determining whether a licensing program is controlled sufficiently by the licensor to protect his mark is whether the licensees' operations are policed adequately to guarantee the quality of the products sold under the mark.

EXXON CORP. v. OXXFORD CLOTHES INC.
109 F.3d 1070 (5th Cir. 1997)

GARWOOD, J.

Defendants-appellants Oxxford Clothes, Inc., and Oxxford Clothes XX, Inc. (Oxxford), appeal the district court's judgment dismissing Oxxford's affirmative defense of naked licensing and Oxxford's state law dilution counterclaim in this trademark dispute with plaintiff-appellee Exxon Corporation (Exxon). We affirm.

Facts and Proceedings Below

Both the "Exxon" mark and the complementary stylized interlocking "XX" symbol have been used by Exxon since the early 1970s, both marks receiving federal registration in 1972. In 1949, Oxxford federally registered as a trademark the name "Oxxford," written in the romanized alphabet but not including any stylized or interlocking "XX" design.

For more than two decades Exxon has aggressively protected its mark from infringement and/or dilution by seeking out and negotiating with other companies using marks similar to its own. In lieu of conclusive litigation, many of these companies opted to enter "phase out" agreements with Exxon in which the other company agreed that after existing stores of stationary, advertising materials, and products bearing the offending mark were exhausted, use of that mark would be discontinued. These phase out periods afforded the potentially infringing or diluting companies time to develop and implement a new mark. The phase out agreements did not contain any quality control mechanisms ensuring the quality of goods or services offered under the offending mark during the phase out period.[2]

---

[2] [FN1] Phase out agreements orchestrated by Exxon during the 1970s did give Exxon quality control rights over the alleged infringer or diluter's products. Later phase out agreements, however, did not give Exxon such rights. It is these later agreements on which Oxxford's naked licensing defense is based. There are some fourteen of these later agreements. . . .

In 1993, Oxxford began using a trademark featuring an interlocking "XX" design virtually identical to that long previously registered by Exxon. Exxon filed suit against Oxxford in October of 1994, complaining that Oxxford's use of the interlocking "XX" design infringed its federally-registered trademark, diluted Exxon's mark, and otherwise constituted an unfair business practice. Exxon amended its complaint twice, ultimately dropping all but its Texas law dilution claim.

In response to Exxon's second amendment of its complaint, Oxxford filed an amended answer raising a bevy of affirmative defenses, prime among these being an assertion that Exxon's phase out agreements with other allegedly infringing and diluting companies constituted "naked licenses." The gist of Oxxford's argument was that these agreements, insofar as they authorized third parties to continue to use infringing or diluting marks with Exxon's knowledge and approval, were "licenses"; and, because these "licenses" contained no quality control provision, they were "naked licenses" which, under prevailing law, could lead to forfeiture of Exxon's rights in its licensed marks. . . .

Discussion

Oxxford appeals the district court's grant of summary judgment rejecting its affirmative defense of naked licensing and its tarnishment-dilution counterclaim. [In] reviewing the district court's judgment, we consider the record de novo.

We consider first Oxxford's claim that the district court erred in granting Exxon summary judgment on Oxxford's affirmative defense of naked licensing. A naked license is a trademark licensor's grant of permission to use its mark without attendant provisions to protect the quality of the goods or services provided under the licensed mark. A trademark owner's failure to exercise appropriate control and supervision over its licensees may result in an abandonment of trademark protection for the licensed mark. Because naked licensing is generally ultimately relevant only to establish an unintentional trademark abandonment which results in a loss of trademark rights against the world, the burden of proof faced by third parties attempting to show abandonment through naked licensing is stringent.

Oxxford's appeal raises two central questions in relation to its naked licensing defense: 1) were the phase out agreements between Exxon and the third parties "licenses," and 2) did these agreements result in an abandonment of Exxon's mark? We address these questions in turn.

"[A] license to use a mark . . . is a transfer of limited rights, less than the whole interest which might have been transferred." Even if the parties intend no formal licensing agreement, "[i]n some circumstances . . . the entire course of conduct between a . . . trademark owner and an accused infringer may create an implied license." The essential inquiry is whether, under cover of the agreement claimed to be a license, "the licensee is engaging in acts which would infringe the licensor's mark but for the permission granted in the license."

However, not all agreements authorizing use of a protected mark may be categorized as "licenses." As noted above, the essential inquiry is whether the right granted by the subject agreement permits an infringing use of the license. For example, some agreements which allow another party use of the subject mark constitute "consent-to-use" agreements and not licenses. Such a consensual agreement "[i]s not an attempt to transfer or license the use of a trademark . . . but fixes and defines the existing trademark of each . . . [so] that confusion and infringement may be prevented." *Waukesha Hygeia Mineral Springs Co. v. Hygeia Sparkling Distilled Water Co.*, 63 F. 438, 441 (7th Cir.1894). Thus, we will not find the existence of a trademark license when an authorization of trademark use is structured in such a way as to avoid misleading or confusing consumers as to the origin and/or nature of the respective parties' goods.

Determining whether or not a particular agreement risks the possibility of allowing an infringing use of the mark, i.e., a use that creates a likelihood of consumer confusion, is, like the entirety of Oxxford's abandonment claim, ordinarily a factual inquiry. As the Federal Circuit has put it, "One must look at all of the surrounding circumstances . . . to determine if the consent reflects the reality of no likelihood of confusion in the marketplace. . . . For example, the parties may prefer the simplicity of a consent to the encumbrances of a valid trademark license. However, if the goods of the parties are likely to be attributed to the same source because of the use of the same or a similar mark, a license (not merely a consent) is necessary to cure the conflict." *In re Mastic*, 829 F.2d [1114] at 1116-1117 [(Fed.Cir.1987)].

Accordingly, if the goods or services of the concerned third parties were not ones which it is likely the public would confuse with those offered by Exxon, the phase out agreements are not licenses but rather some other, perhaps innominate, genre of trademark agreement.

The district court did not make any determination regarding the likelihood of consumer confusion presented by Exxon's phase out agreements. Accordingly, we elect to assume, arguendo only, that these agreements constituted "licenses" in a technical sense. This does not give us pause, however, since the question whether the third-party phase out agreements are "licenses" is merely, given the current posture of this case, a prelude to the ultimate question presented by Oxxford's appeal, i.e., whether the summary judgment evidence adduced would be adequate to support a finding that Exxon's course of action resulted in abandonment of its trademarks.

The naked licensing defense has traditionally been used in the context of infringement claims brought by the trademark owner; and, this case began in such a mode.

Federal law statutorily limits the defenses which may be invoked against a claim brought under the Lanham Act by the owner of an incontestable mark, as Exxon is, to the eight categories of affirmative defenses set out in subsections (1)-(8) of 15 U.S.C. § 1115(b). Accordingly, we turn our attention to the Lanham Act, the font of federal trademark law, to ascertain the scope and limits of Oxxford's naked licensing defense.

Oxxford's naked licensing defense, which as we have noted has ultimate relevance only to "abandonment," is authorized by 15 U.S.C. § 1115(b)(2). 15 U.S.C. § 1127, the definitional section of the Lanham Act, defines "abandonment" as follows:

> A mark shall be deemed to be "abandoned" if either of the following occurs:
>
> (1) When its use has been discontinued with intent not to resume such use. Intent not to resume may be inferred from circumstances. Nonuse for 3 consecutive years shall be prima facie evidence of abandonment. "Use" of a mark means the bona fide use of such mark made in the ordinary course of trade, and not made merely to reserve a right in the mark.
>
> (2) When any course of conduct of the owner, including acts of omission as well as commission, causes the mark to become the generic name for the goods or services on or in connection with which it is used or otherwise to lose its significance as a mark. Purchaser motivation shall not be a test for determining abandonment under this paragraph.

The definition of "abandonment" set forth in subpart (2) (formerly subpart (b)) is the specific statutory explication of unintentional abandonment, including abandonment due to naked licensing.

The language of subsection 1127(2) reflects that to prove "abandonment" the alleged infringer must show that, due to acts or omissions of the trademark owner, the incontestable mark has lost "its significance as a mark." This statutory directive reflects the policy considerations which underlie the naked licensing defense: "[if] a trademark owner allows licensees to depart from his quality standards, the public will be misled, and the trademark will cease to have utility as an informational device . . . [a] trademark owner who allows this to occur loses his right to use the mark." Conversely, if a trademark has not ceased to function as an indicator of origin there is no reason to believe that the public will be misled; under these circumstances, neither the express declaration of Congress's intent in subsection 1127(2) nor the corollary policy considerations which underlie the doctrine of naked licensing warrant a finding that the trademark owner has forfeited his rights in the mark.

Oxxford, pointing to recent precedent in this Circuit indicating that naked licensing results in an "involuntary trademark abandonment," posits that when a defendant proves that the trademark owner has licensed its mark without any quality control provisions the courts should presume a loss of significance. We disagree. Abandonment due to naked licensing is "involuntary" because, unlike abandonment through non-use, referred to in subsection 1127(1), an intent to abandon the mark is expressly not required to prove abandonment under subsection 1127(2). In addition, a trademark owner's failure to pursue potential infringers does not in and of itself establish that the mark has lost its significance as an indicator of origin. Instead, such a dereliction on the part of the trademark owner is largely relevant only in regard to the "strength" of the mark; absent an ultimate showing of loss of trade significance, subsection 1127(2) (and the incorporated doctrine of naked licensing) is not available as a defense against an infringement suit brought by that trademark owner. We, like the district court, would find it wholly anomalous to presume a loss of trademark significance merely because Exxon, in the course of diligently protecting its mark, entered into agreements designed to preserve the distinctiveness and strength of that mark. We decline Oxxford's invitation to judicially manufacture a presumption of loss of trademark significance under the facts of this case given that had Exxon simply ignored the prior threats to its marks no such presumption would obtain.

With the applicable legal standard clarified, we turn to the record before us. Exxon, commensurate with its burden under Rule 56, directed the district court's attention to Oxxford's failure to meaningfully address what is an essential component of its third-party naked licensing defense, i.e., a loss of trademark significance in Exxon's mark(s). Even were we to construe Oxxford's pleadings to allege the unlikely proposition that Exxon's registered marks, due to these third-party phase out agreements, have lost their distinctiveness as indicators of origin, Oxxford has offered absolutely no evidence to substantiate such a claim. Accordingly, we affirm the district court's ruling because Oxxford has failed to adduce evidence sufficient to allow a reasonable factfinder to conclude that Exxon has abandoned its marks. . . .

AFFIRMED.

NOTES

1. What is the policy support for the quality control idea: 1) that in some cases the mark owner abandoned its rights, or 2) that the rights owner should not be allowed, by its own licensing, to allow conduct that carries a risk of confusion? Do the different policies lead to different results about what standards determine if sufficient control was exercised?

2. Suppose that an infringing use of a trademark was inferior to the original mark owner's uses. When the mark owner threatens to sue the infringer, the parties agree that the infringer will discontinue use, but the mark owner permits this to occur after the Christmas season, when the infringer has is largest sales volume. This results in many consumers purchasing inferior products under the mark. What is the justification for allowing the mark owner to accept, without penalty, this harmful use of its mark?

PROBLEM 9.1

Jane's Palace, a company well-known in Toledo, Ohio, operates a traditional "greasy spoon" hamburger format — at all of its fifteen locations, there is little attention to the cleanliness or quality of the location, and little attention to how the hamburgers are made, except that there must be huge amounts of grease used on the grill. Nevertheless, Jane's has become a cult favorite and her company name is a recognized trademark in Toledo.

Currently tired of the hamburger business, Jane opens a woman's clothing store in East Toledo. She sells her hamburger locations to Wendy Ham, a national chain noted for its careful attention to cleanliness. Wendy receives a ten-year license to use the trademark "Jane's Palace" at the locations it purchased. When Wendy begins to clean up the locations, Jane demands that it stop doing so since Jane must monitor quality to protect her trademark. What result? Would the result be different if Wendy begins to use less grease on the hamburgers?

PROBLEM 9.2

Tomas develops a logo for Tomas' consulting business. After using the logo for several years, Tomas quits the business, selling the assets and client list to Jones, and licensing use of the logo to Jones. Jones was a coworker with Thomas for several years and is trustworthy. The license gives Tomas the right to approve all publications containing the logo and all uses of it by Jones. Tomas, however, never contacts Jones over the first three years after the sale. Tomas asks whether it still retains the trademark. What is your answer and what, if any further information would you require?

III. DISCLOSURE AND COMPETITION CLAUSES

As with trademarks, the continued existence of a trade secret or otherwise confidential material of value to a licensor requires that steps be taken to control the use of the information by the licensee. The Uniform Trade Secret Act (UTSA) states:

> "Trade secret" means information, including a formula, pattern, compilation, program, device, method, technique or process, that:
>
> 1. Derives independent economic value, actual or potential, from not being generally known to, and not being readily ascertainable by proper means by other persons who can obtain economic value from its disclosure, and
>
> 2. Is the subject of efforts that are reasonable under the circumstance to maintain its secrecy.

UTSA § 1(3). For present purposes, the most significant aspect of that definition lies in the last clause — reasonable efforts to maintain secrecy. In a licensing transaction, of course, those efforts stem from the terms of the license and the character of performance pursuant to it. In addition to considering the following materials, you may also wish to review *Expansion Plus, Inc. v. Brown-Foreman Corp.*, 132 F.3d 1083 (5th Cir. 1998), and *Celeritas Technologies, Ltd. v. Rockwell International, Inc.*, 150 F.3d 1354 (Fed. Cir. 1998), reproduced in Chapter 2.

IDX SYSTEMS CORP. v. EPIC SYSTEMS CORP.
285 F.3d 581 (7th Cir. 2002)

EASTERBROOK, CIRCUIT JUDGE.

Both IDX Systems and Epic Systems make software for use in managing the financial side of a medical practice: billing, insurance reimbursement and other collections, and the like. During the 1980s IDX sold this software package to two medical groups that later merged into the University of Wisconsin Medical Foundation, which now comprises more than 1,000 physicians. The Foundation continued to use IDX software until December 2000, when it switched to software developed by Epic. IDX believes that Mitchell Quade and Michael Rosencrance, former employees of Epic who came to manage data processing at the Foundation, not only instigated this change but also used their new positions to transfer valuable information to Epic. According to IDX's complaint, over the course of a year Quade and Rosencrance personally, and with the aid of other Foundation employees, furnished Epic with details about how IDX's software works, enabling Epic to enhance its own package and ultimately take the Foundation's business — and to match up better against IDX in the competition for other customers.

IDX's complaint [charges] the Foundation, Quade, and Rosencrance with stealing IDX's trade secrets and breaking contractual promises of confidentiality; it charges Epic with tortiously inducing the other defendants to do these things. The district court dismissed the tort claims against Epic on the pleadings, observing that Wis. Stat. § 134.90(6)(a) overrides any theory that conflicts with the state's law of trade secrets. Later it pared all contract-based claims out of the case, ruling that the confidentiality agreements are invalid under Wisconsin law (which the parties agree governs) because they do not contain temporal and geographic limitations. Finally, the court granted summary judgment to the defendants on the trade-secret claim, after concluding that IDX had failed to identify with specificity the trade secrets that it accuses the defendants of misappropriating. . . . We shall start where the district court ended: with the trade-secret claim.

Trade secrets are a subset of all commercially valuable information. Wisconsin has followed the Uniform Trade Secrets Act in defining "trade secret." . . . Thus to show that particular information is a trade secret, a firm such as IDX must demonstrate that it is valuable, not known to others who might profit by its use, and has been handled by means reasonably designed to maintain secrecy. Like the district judge, we think that IDX failed to do this. It has been both too vague and too inclusive, effectively asserting that all information in or about its software is a trade secret. That's not plausible — and, more to the point, such a broad assertion does not match up to the statutory definition. Reluctance to be specific is understandable; the more precise the claim, the more a party does to tip off a business rival to where the real secrets lie and where the rival's own development efforts should be focused. Still, tools such as protective orders are available to make this process less risky, and unless the plaintiff engages in a serious effort to pin down the secrets a court cannot do its job.

According to IDX, "a 43-page description of the methods and processes underlying and the inter-relationships among various features making up IDX's software package" is specific enough. No, it isn't. These 43 pages describe the software; although the document was created for this litigation, it does not separate the trade secrets from the other information that goes into any software package. Which aspects are known to the trade, and which are not? That's vital under the statutory definition. Likewise, IDX's tender of the complete documentation for the software leaves mysterious exactly which pieces of information are the trade secrets. As we remarked in *Composite Marine Propellers, Inc. v. Van Der Woude,* 962 F.2d 1263, 1266 (7th Cir.1992), a plaintiff must do more than just identify a kind of technology and then invite the court to hunt through the details in search of items meeting the statutory definition. What is more, many of the items that appear in the 43-page description, such as the appearance of data-entry screens, are exceedingly hard to call trade secrets: things that any user or passer-by sees at a glance are "readily ascertainable by proper means." Perhaps screen displays could be copyrighted, but no copyright claim has been advanced, and a trade-secret claim based on readily observable material is a bust. *Minnesota Mining & Manufacturing Co. v. Pribyl,* 259 F.3d 587 (7th Cir.2001), on which IDX principally relies, did not involve such self-revealing information. Other details, such as the algorithms that the software uses to do real-time error checking (a vaunted feature of IDX's software), may be genuine trade secrets, but IDX has not tried to separate them from elements such as its input and output formats. Nor does it contend that the defendants decompiled the object code or otherwise obtained access to the algorithms that power the program; it alleges only that Foundation transferred to Epic those details that ordinary users of the software could observe without reverse engineering.

Because (as what we have already written illustrates) it is hard to prove that particular information qualifies as a trade secret, many producers of intellectual property negotiate with their customers for additional protection. This is a step that Wisconsin permits. *See ProCD, Inc. v. Zeidenberg,* 86 F.3d 1447 (7th Cir.1996) (Wisconsin law). Following § 7 of the Uniform Trade Secrets Act, Wis. Stat. § 134.90(6) provides:

> (a) Except as provided in par. (b), this section displaces conflicting tort law, restitutionary law and any other law of this state providing a civil remedy for misappropriation of a trade secret.

> (b) This section does not affect any of the following:

>> 1. Any contractual remedy, whether or not based upon misappropriation of a trade secret.

>> 2. Any civil remedy not based upon misappropriation of a trade secret.

>> 3. Any criminal remedy, whether or not based upon misappropriation of a trade secret.

IDX and the Foundation (through its predecessors in interest) agreed to the sort of contractual remedy preserved in § 134.90(6)(b)1. The Foundation promised not to allow the software and related materials "furnished by" IDX to be "examined . . . for the purpose of creating another system" and vowed in addition not to "use or disclose or divulge to others any data or information relating to" the system or "the technology, ideas, concepts, know-how, and techniques embodied therein." IDX has evidence (enough to survive summary judgment) that the Foundation, Quade, and Rosencrance broke these promises by describing IDX's system in detail to Epic and helping it duplicate those features that the Foundation liked. Nonetheless, the district judge held, the promises are unenforceable because they are unlimited in temporal and geographic scope, and thus unduly restrain trade.

In reaching this conclusion, the district court relied on decisions requiring restrictive covenants limiting competition between employers and their ex-employees to be reasonable, a limitation that in Wisconsin entails some restrictions on time and scope. Rules limiting the extent of no-compete clauses are based on the fact that they tie up human capital and, if widely adopted, may have the practical effect of preventing horizontal competition in economically significant markets. *See* Paul H. Rubin & Peter Shedd, *Human Capital and Covenants Not to Compete*, 10 J. LEGAL STUDIES 93 (1981). But neither rationale applies to contracts that restrict the use of particular information between businesses that have vertical (supplier-to-customer) rather than horizontal (competitor-to-competitor) relations. *See* Benjamin E. Hermalin & Michael L. Katz, *Judicial Modification of Contracts Between Sophisticated Parties: A More Complete View of Incomplete Contracts and Their Breach*, 9 J.L. ECON. & ORG. 230 (1993); Robert Unikel, *Bridging the Trade Secret Gap*, 29 LOYOLA U. CHI. L.J. 841 (1998). IDX did not contract for limitations on Epic's ability to compete; contracts between IDX and the Foundation are vertical in nature and protect intellectual property without affecting competition. They may compel rivals such as Epic to do more work to develop software independently, but this promotes rather than restricts competition. *Kewanee Oil Co. v. Bicron Corp.*, 416 U.S. 470 (1974), holds that trade-secret law is compatible with antitrust law; the same can be said for contracts protecting intellectual property that, though not demonstrably a trade secret, is commercially valuable. Rivals such as Epic, as non-parties to the vertical arrangements, remain entitled to discover and use the information independently and to compete vigorously. Nothing in the antitrust laws gives one producer a right to sponge off another's intellectual property, even when the producer of that knowledge has a market share much larger than IDX's.

The parties have not cited, and we have not found, any Wisconsin statute or decision subjecting non-disclosure agreements between suppliers and users of intellectual property to the rules that govern non-competition clauses between employers and employees. To the contrary, *Fullerton Lumber Co. v. Torborg*, 270 Wis. 133, 139, 70 N.W.2d 585, 588 (1955), tells us that Wisconsin allows "a much greater scope of restraint in contracts between vendor and vendee than between employer and employee." Section 134.90(6)(b)1 implies that contracts about intellectual property are valid, even when they exceed the domain of trade secrets. Restrictions on disclosure may make intellectual property more valuable to its producer, and thus promote both the creation of knowledge and competition against other firms in the same industry. No one doubts this with physical property: General Motors is entitled to control 100% of its own output of mufflers, without handing any of them over to Ford or Toyota or Volkswagen. Permitting a producer the full return on its investment in mufflers (or any other product) is essential to promote investment in productive assets and rivalry with other producers. Just so with knowledge, an increasingly vital input into production. Why should IDX or any other maker of intellectual property be placed under legal rules that effectively entitle its rivals to a chunk of that asset's value?

No Wisconsin decision of which we are aware requires temporal or geographic limits as a condition to the enforcement of a non-disclosure agreement for intellectual property. It is impossible to understand how a non-disclosure agreement *could* place "geographical" limits on the dissemination of intellectual property comparable to those restricting the locale where a salesman may try to drum up customers for a new employer. If the Foundation were forbidden to disclose the details to Epic in Wisconsin, but allowed to do so in Indiana, that would be the same thing as permitting disclosure everywhere (and thus nixing all contractual limits) — for Epic could sell worldwide any software derived from what it learned in Indiana. Knowledge does not respect borders. *ProCD*, a case that the district court did not mention, enforced as a matter of Wisconsin law a contract placing worldwide restrictions on the use of intellectual property embedded in software.

Temporal limitations could make more sense. Perhaps Wisconsin's courts would deem contracts such as those between IDX and the Foundation to cover only information that is not generally known. What would be the point of forbidding the Foundation to talk in public about features of IDX's system that had been the subject of a review in a trade publication? But it is too early in this litigation to decide whether Wisconsin would curb the unqualified scope of this contractual language — and, if some limits would be interpolated into the text, whether these would shelter the actual disclosures that the Foundation made to Epic. (The Foundation contends, for example, that it had customized IDX's software extensively and disclosed to Epic details about its own additions rather than any information "furnished by" IDX and of which Epic was unaware before the disclosures. It also contends that IDX cannot establish damages. But these and other factual arguments must be developed through discovery rather than decided at the complaint stage.) . . .

The judgment of the district court is affirmed to the extent it granted judgment to the defendants on IDX's trade-secret claims. The remainder of the judgment is reversed, and the case is remanded for further proceedings consistent with this opinion.

NOTES

1. As *IDX* indicates, there are many reasons why parties might agree to a non-disclosure term in a license. If a non-disclosure obligation is present in a transaction, we encounter practical and legal issues in the standards regulating use and disclosure and to what extent performance corresponds to contract terms.

2. Claims based on breach of contract of a nondisclosure term often blend into a trade-secret analysis without a separate contract analysis because of the language in the contract. A commonly used term precludes disclosure of a "trade secret," and the trade secret analysis thus becomes pivotal for the contract breach analysis. A clause that states: "licensee agrees that it will not disclose trade secrets of licensor provided under this agreement," creates no obligation unless a trade secret exists.

3. The *Restatement (Third) of Unfair Competition* surprisingly argues that nondisclosure clauses may be unfair restraints on competition if used to cover material that is not a trade secret. *Restatement (Third) of Unfair Competition* § 40. No case law supports this idea. There are many reasons why a contract should be enforced apart from a trade secret claim. Indeed, in commercial practice, the ability to contractually eliminate issues about whether particular information meets trade secrecy requirements can be an important reason for an explicit non-disclosure agreement. Apparently, the *Restatement* merely intends to signal that competition policies may limit contract terms in some cases. Otherwise, a trade secret claim and a contract claim are independent bases for action. *See Celeritas Technologies, Ltd. v. Rockwell Intern. Corp.*, 150 F.3d 1354 (Fed. Cir. 1998), *cert. denied*, 525 U.S. 1106 (1999).

4. In digital and some other industries, technology can be provided without allowing the licensee access to the content of the technology. As a result, some licenses preclude the licensee from reverse engineering the software to access the methodology in it. Such clauses have been enforced unless there are anti-competitive or misuse effects in the particular case. We return to this in Chapter 14. *See DSC Communications Corp. v. Pulse Communications, Inc.*, 170 F.3d 1354 (Fed. Cir. 1999); *Bowers v. Baystate Technologies, Inc.*, 320 F.3d 1317 (Fed. Cir. 2003), *cert. denied*, 123 S. Ct. 2588 (2003). *Compare Alcatel USA, Inc. v. DGI Technologies., Inc.*, 166 F.3d 772 (5th Cir. 1999), *rehearing and rehearing en banc denied by* 180 F.3d 267 (1999).

5. As *IDX* indicates, non-competition clauses present more serious issues than do non-disclosure clauses. There are case law and statutes cabining in enforceability of non-competition clauses in transactions involving employees, where there exists not only a concern about competition, but also a concern about the imbalance in bargaining position between ordinary employees and employers. These cases are often discussed in reference to trade secret law. They are at the periphery of our concern in this book because the mix of interests present in employee cases typically differs from that in a commercial license.

PROBLEM 9.3

Rockport has data from studies it conducted about the effect of a type of fuel in operating automobiles. The data are not covered by a patent, although some reports of it might be copyrighted. Blazer Oil desires to obtain the data. The parties agree to a license for Blazer for the data and its use in Blazer's business.

a. Assume the license was silent on Blazer's right to disclose information to others. After the data are delivered, an employee leaves Rockport and offers the data to anyone who wants it. Rockport sues the employee for trade secret misappropriation. The employee claims that the data are not secret. What result?

b. Assume that the events in (a) did not happen. You are asked to draft non-disclosure terms for the license that are acceptable to both parties. You are to focus on the following: 1) what if the data become public knowledge, 2) what if the data relates to projects Blazer already has underway or duplicates other data it already has, 3) what if Blazer's ordinary handling of trade secrets is less restrictive than Rockport's? Draft suggested terms.

EDEN HANNON & CO. v. SUMITOMO TRUST & BANKING CO.
914 F.2d 556 (4th Cir. 1990)

RUSSELL, CIRCUIT JUDGE:

Eden Hannon & Co. ("EHC") is an investment company located in Alexandria, Virginia, and Sumitomo Trust & Banking Co. is a New York subsidiary of a Japanese bank. This appeal involves the competition between EHC and Sumitomo to purchase an investment portfolio from Xerox Corporation. In the past, EHC has produced extensive economic models for the purpose of valuing Xerox lease portfolios, bidding on these portfolios, and selling the income rights to the portfolios to institutional investors. In the late summer of 1988, Sumitomo indicated interest in purchasing a portfolio through EHC. To that end, Sumitomo signed a "Nondisclosure and Noncircumvention" agreement with EHC, in order to protect the confidential information that EHC later shared with Sumitomo. In violation of that agreement, and after taking possession of EHC's confidential analyses, Sumitomo bid on the December 1988 Xerox portfolio, won the bid, and made a direct purchase of the portfolio. EHC had bid also on that portfolio, and its bid was ranked third by Xerox officials.

EHC subsequently filed this suit, stating four counts: misappropriation of trade secrets, breach of contract, breach of fiduciary duty, and breach of the duty of good faith and fair dealing. Sumitomo denied these allegations. [After] hearing all of the evidence, the judge found that Sumitomo's actions constituted a breach of contract, and found that a misappropriation of trade secrets had not been proven. [As] a remedy, the district judge enjoined Sumitomo from repeating its violation of the [agreements]. Both parties [appealed.]

I

The "portfolio" that Xerox sells is composed of the right to receive the stream of income from a group of copiers leased by Xerox, and to receive the residual value of the copiers when the leases expire or are terminated. This is known as the Xerox Partnership Asset Strategy ("PAS") Program. Four times a year, Xerox invites a limited number of investors to bid for a portfolio, which typically contains several hundred copiers leased by Xerox to various customers for terms usually ranging from one to three years. EHC has been a regular bidder and frequent winner in the past, winning ten quarterly bids in the first three-and-a-half years of the program. The bids submitted to Xerox are not just dollar figures; instead, a bid consists of several components, and each component addresses how an element of the projected revenue stream would be divided between Xerox and the successful bidder.

EHC does not bid with its own money in these sales. Instead, it arranges in advance for a bank or insurance company to provide the monetary investment, and in return that investor receives all of the revenue generated by the leases. . . .

Given that EHC's value is in its knowledge, it must guard that knowledge jealously. On the other hand, it must also disclose a great amount of its confidential analysis regarding a proposed bid on a portfolio in order to convince an institution to bid from $25 million to more than $60 million on a single portfolio. To that end, EHC requires any interested investor to sign a "Nondisclosure and Noncircumvention Agreement" (an "Agreement") before it can receive any of EHC's confidential information. This Agreement requires that the investor not disclose the information it receives from EHC to other parties. Most importantly, it also requires that the potential investor "not independently pursue lease transactions" with Xerox's PAS Program "for a period equal to the term of the Purchase Agreement." Since the copiers are usually leased for one to three years, we presume that this term would prevent an investor from independently pursuing a portfolio for approximately three years.

Sumitomo was a potential investor interested in the PAS portfolio. Immediately after EHC won the June 1988 portfolio bid, a Sumitomo officer, Ragheed Shanti, based in the United States, telephoned EHC to express interest. In order to evaluate the PAS program, Shanti attempted to obtain EHC's economic data on their winning June bid. EHC insisted that it could not disclose that information without an Agreement signed by a Sumitomo representative. Shanti tried to avoid signing an Agreement, and then attempted to water down the provision that would require Sumitomo not to "independently pursue" portfolio purchases. . . . EHC refused this substitution, and Shanti eventually signed the original Agreement on the part of Sumitomo. During these negotiations over the language of the Agreement, Sumitomo admitted to EHC that it was also considering financing a portfolio bid by a competitor of EHC, DPF Leasing Services, Inc. ("DPF"). EHC indicated that the Agreement would not prevent Sumitomo from financing a competitor's bid. However, EHC did not want to create a new competitor that would use EHC's information to bid directly against it. Thus, the understanding between EHC and Sumitomo was that Sumitomo could finance a competitor's bid, but it could not directly bid (*i.e.,* "independently pursue") on a portfolio during the "term of the Purchase Agreement."

Once the Agreement was signed, EHC disclosed a great amount of confidential bidding information to Sumitomo. . . . However, Sumitomo and EHC could not reach a deal on a bid for the next portfolio to be offered in December, 1988. [This] did not prevent Sumitomo from participating in the bidding for the December portfolio, however. In fact, Sumitomo bid directly on the portfolio, in clear violation of the Agreement with EHC. At trial and in this appeal, Sumitomo has claimed that it only invested in a portfolio that was won by a competitor of EHC. However, this proposition was rejected below, and we reject it also. In submitting its bid, Sumitomo worked through Gerry Sherman, who was a former employee of DPF, a competitor of EHC. Sherman had formed his own one-man company, Oasis, which would work on bids for Xerox PAS portfolios. Sherman had experience from his days at DPF in the economic modelling and bidding process for such portfolios. Sumitomo argues that Oasis won the December bid by carrying out the same functions as EHC would have carried out.

This is not true. To us, and to the district court, it is clear that Oasis was merely a stalking horse for Sumitomo, and that Sumitomo was the direct bidder for the December portfolio. . . . Unfortunately, it is unclear whether Sherman also provided the financial advice to Sumitomo that enabled it to make its bid. Sherman did work on the Xerox PAS Program when he was employed by EHC's competitor, DPF. Sumitomo has claimed that it gained all of its knowledge on how to value and bid for a Xerox portfolio from Sherman. While Sumitomo admits that it had possession of the confidential materials it got from EHC, it claims that did not use these materials *at all*. It states that after negotiations fell through with EHC on August 25, 1988, Shanti put these materials in a box and never looked at them again. In a close call, the district judge found that Sumitomo had not misappropriated EHC's trade secrets, and thus, the district judge must have found Sumitomo's story more credible on this point.

Since our disposition of this case does not depend on knowing whether Sumitomo actually used this information, we will not dwell on the point. However, we have our doubts about the correctness of this finding. . . .

II

[The] district judge was correct in holding that Sumitomo breached its Noncircumvention and Nondisclosure Agreement with EHC. Sumitomo argued in this appeal, as they did below, that they did not "independently pursue" or obtain an interest in the December portfolio, and that they only invested through another outfit (Oasis) performing the same function as EHC. We agree with the district judge that facts do not support this position, and that it "defies logic and common sense." Oasis was merely a stalking horse for Sumitomo's efforts to avoid its obligations under the Agreement. The district judge correctly granted an injunction to prevent another violation of that Agreement in the future. However, EHC was entitled to additional equitable relief — a constructive trust on Sumitomo's illegally gotten gains. This remedy does not depend on proof of actual damage to EHC; instead, it focuses on the wrongful conduct of the violator. In order to explain why this remedy is available, it is necessary to explain the role that the Agreement played in the parties' relationship.

The Supreme Court of Virginia has decided several cases involving agreements not to compete in the employment law arena, and those cases are substantially similar to the case at bar. In many employment contracts, there is language stating that upon termination of the employment relationship, the employee is restricted from competing with the employer within a certain amount of time and within a certain geographical area (for the purposes of this opinion, these are called "employment agreements"). The Virginia courts have held repeatedly that employment agreements are enforceable if they pass a three-part reasonableness test:

> (1) Is the restraint, from the standpoint of the employer, reasonable in the sense that it is no greater than is necessary to protect the employer in some legitimate business interest?

> (2) From the standpoint of the employee, is the restraint reasonable in the sense that it is not unduly harsh and oppressive in curtailing his legitimate efforts to earn a livelihood?

> (3) Is the restraint reasonable from the standpoint of sound public policy?

Paramount Termite Control Co. v. Rector, 238 Va. 171, 380 S.E.2d 922, 924 (1989) (citations omitted). The agreements that pass this test may be enforced in equity.

The Noncircumvention and Nondisclosure Agreement [is] nearly identical in purpose to an employment agreement. Most importantly, an employment agreement enables an employer to expose his employees to the firm's trade secrets. Similarly, a noncircumvention agreement enables potential joint venturers to share confidential information regarding a possible deal. In both instances, the idea is to share trade secrets so that business can be conducted without losing control over the secrets. Often, the value of a firm is its special knowledge, and this knowledge may not be an idea protectible by patent or copyright. If that firm cannot protect that knowledge from immediate dissemination to competitors, it may not be able to reap the benefits from the time and money invested in building that knowledge. If firms are not permitted to construct a reasonable legal mechanism to protect that knowledge, then the incentive to engage in the building of such knowledge will be greatly reduced. Free riders will capture this information at little or no cost and produce a product cheaper than the firm which created the knowledge, because it will not have to carry the costs of creating that knowledge in its pricing. Faced with this free rider problem, this information may not be created, and thus everybody loses. To counteract that problem, an employer can demand that employees sign an employment agreement as a condition of their contract, and thus protect the confidential information. This means that if an employer takes in an employee and exposes that employee to trade secrets, the employer does not have to allow the employee to go across the street and set up shop once that employee has mastered the information. Although it was not explained in this detail, Virginia has recognized this interest in protecting confidential information.

These employment agreements (or in the present case, a noncircumvention agreement) are often necessary because it can be very difficult to prove the theft of a trade secret by a former employee. Often, the purpose of an employment agreement can be to prevent the dissemination of trade secrets, yet a mere ban on using trade secrets after the termination of employment would be difficult to enforce. Judge Lord explained the problem well in *Greenberg v. Croydon Plastics Co.,* 378 F.Supp. 806, 814 (E.D.Pa.1974):

> Plaintiffs in trade secret cases, who must prove by a fair preponderance of the evidence disclosure to third parties and use of the trade secret by the third parties, are confronted with an extraordinarily difficult task. Misappropriation and misuse can rarely be proved by convincing direct evidence. In most cases plaintiffs must construct a web of perhaps ambiguous circumstantial evidence from which the trier of fact may draw inferences which convince him that it is more probable than not that what the plaintiffs allege happened did in fact take place. Against this often delicate construct of circumstantial evidence there frequently must be balanced defendants' witnesses who directly deny everything.

Actually, Judge Lord's description of the problem covers just the tip of the iceberg. There are several problems with trying to prevent former employees from illegally using the former employer's trade secrets, and these problems are caused by the status of the law regarding the misappropriation of trade secrets. First, as Judge Lord depicted so well, it is difficult to prove that the trade secret was actually used. Second, the former employee tends to get "one free bite" at the trade secret. Most courts will refuse to enjoin the disclosure or use of a trade secret until its illegal use is imminent or until it has already occurred. By that time, much of the damage may be done. Third, even if a clearly illegal use of the trade secret by a former employee can be shown, most courts will not enjoin that person from working for the competition on that basis. Instead, they will merely enjoin future disclosure of the trade secret. Yet, policing the former employee's compliance with that injunction will be difficult. Finally, even if the employee does not maliciously attempt to use his former employer's trade secrets in the new employer's workplace, avoiding this use can be difficult. It would be difficult for the employee to guard the trade secret of the former employer and be effective for the new employer.

In order to avoid these problems, many employers ask their employees to sign non-competition agreements. These agreements prevent an employee from working with the competition within a limited geographical range of the former employer and for a limited time. As seen above, Virginia courts will only enforce these agreements if they are reasonable. Yet, when they are valid, they make the guarding of a trade secret easier since they remove the opportunity for the former employee to pass on the trade secret to the competition, either malevolently or benevolently. This does not supplant the need for law protecting trade secrets. Non-competition agreements cannot prevent disclosure anywhere in the world and until the end of time, for they would be held unreasonable. Instead, a non-competition agreement will merely prevent the illegal use of a trade secret next door in the near future, where the use might do the most damage.

EHC's position regarding potential investors was the same as an employer-employee relationship in regard to the use of trade secrets. The thing that made EHC valuable was its expertise in valuing lease portfolios. EHC would "sell" its knowledge of the value of a particular PAS portfolio to investors for a percentage of the profit. It was necessary for EHC to share its confidential economic models and projections on the particular bid in order to attract investors. Yet, if it gave this information to an investor without restriction, that investor would merely make the bid directly and cut EHC out of the deal, after EHC's investment in expertise and research made the bid possible.

EHC could have merely prohibited its potential customers from using its information if that customer became a rival bidder. Indeed, this was the essence of Shanti's counterproposal regarding the language of the agreement, which was rejected by EHC. Such an arrangement would have become an unenforceable honor system. In the present case, Sumitomo has denied that it used the materials it received from EHC, and claimed that it gained its expertise primarily from Gerry Sherman. The trial judge ultimately ruled that there had not been a misappropriation of trade secrets, but his ruling was based on Sumitomo's denials and the citing of Sherman's experience in the area. The trial court did not definitively discover whether Sumitomo actually used these materials, and there was no way that it could have found out. For that reason, EHC chose to include in its agreement with potential investors the noncircumvention clause. Armed with that agreement, EHC could protect its information by merely showing that an investor was competing contrary to the agreement, without having to prove that it was actually using EHC's confidential information.

Virginia courts have also recognized that firms have a legitimate interest in protecting their customer contacts. In *Paramount,* the court found that a termite extermination company could legitimately restrict its employees from going to work for a rival company in any county of Virginia where employees had worked, for two years after the termination of their employment. The court found that these restrictions are permissible when they reasonably take into account the need of the employee to make a living, and if they do not impair the competitive nature of the industry in question. In so ruling, the Virginia court implicitly recognized the investment that a firm has in its customer lists. It can require a great deal of time and personal contact to build a solid base of clients. If your sales representatives are free to leave the firm and try to take these clients along at any minute, this investment can be undermined and thus discouraged. An employment agreement that restricts this activity for a reasonable length of time and within a reasonable geographical reach can protect this investment while not harming competition in an industry with many competitors.

EHC had such legitimate interests in this case. One reason why it had a noncircumvention clause was to prevent its disclosures from creating new competitors. The competition for the PAS portfolios was already keen. Xerox invited a limited number of businesses to bid for the portfolios, and there were many other businesses who wanted a chance to bid that were seeking invitations. EHC had a legitimate fear that it would let a new bidder through the door if it educated that investor and gave it contacts to Xerox. Thus a reasonable noncircumvention clause was constructed to place a reasonable limit on competition from a temporary ally.

Thus, EHC's noncircumvention agreement is merely a twist on employment noncompetition agreements that have been recognized by the Virginia courts. That being so, we will briefly discuss the application of Virginia's three-factor test for reasonableness to the case at bar. We have reworked the terms of the test so that it will address noncircumvention agreements.

> 1. Is the restraint on circumvention no broader than is necessary, from the standpoint of the trade secret holder, to protect the holder from the disclosure of its confidential information? Yes. The limitation provided by the noncircumvention clause did not prevent Sumitomo from doing many things. Sumitomo could still invest in a bid won by a competitor of EHC; it could use this information internally in order to put together its own bid for lease portfolios offered by companies other than Xerox; and Sumitomo could bid directly for PAS portfolios in approximately three or four years after the Agreement was signed. This was a narrowly drawn limitation.

> 2. From the standpoint of the party that received the confidential information, is the restraint reasonable in the sense that it is not

unduly harsh and oppressive in curtailing the legitimate efforts of that party to conduct its business? Yes. Most importantly, Sumitomo could still invest immediately in any winning bids, including EHC's competitors. Also, Sumitomo could bid directly on any other lease program other than Xerox's, and it could directly invest in Xerox's PAS Program after several years. Furthermore, presumably Sumitomo can make (and has made) money in its other banking activities.

3. Is the restraint reasonable from the standpoint of sound public policy? Yes. This factor overlaps the area covered by the first two factors to a great extent. Presumably, public policy seeks to protect the development of trade secrets without ruining competition or driving the receiver of confidential information out of business. As discussed above, this noncircumvention agreement satisfies those concerns. EHC's economic modeling process receives some protection, the bidding for Xerox PAS portfolios remains highly competitive, and Sumitomo will certainly remain a profitable bank.

NOTES

1. The agreement in *Eden Hannon* protected the value of the information. In contrast to the analysis in that case, however, consider the discussion of the court in *Lasercomb America, Inc. v. Reynolds*, 911 F.2d 970 (1990), *appeal after remand*, 961 F.2d 211 (4th Cir. 1992), which is reproduced in Chapter 1. *Lasercomb* held that a 99 year non-competition clause in a software license constituted copyright misuse because it used the leverage of the software copyright to essentially take the other party out of the competitive marketplace unfairly.

2. Non-competition agreements in licenses are agreements between two or more commercial entities to forego competition in a particular context. Such agreements, especially if they involve horizontal competitors with market power, may present antitrust concerns if they over-reach to apportion relevant markets in an unreasonable manner. *Compare In re Cardizem CD Antitrust Litigation*, 332 F.3d 896 (6th Cir. 2003) (agreement for generic manufacturer to remain out of marketplace until patent expired or was declared invalid was per se violation of antitrust law), *with Valley Drug Co. v. Geneva Pharmaceuticals, Inc.*, 344 F.3d 1294 (11th Cir. 2003) (patent allows some reasonable restrictions and, thus, similar agreement not per se invalid).

IV. RIGHTS IN LICENSEE DEVELOPMENTS

LIU v. PRICE WATERHOUSE LLP
302 F.3d 749 (7th Cir. 2002)

KANNE, CIRCUIT JUDGE.

A jury found against Xiaomei Yang and Xu Liu on various copyright-infringement, breach-of-contract, breach-of-fiduciary-duty, and conversion-of-property claims. Yang and Liu now appeal. . . . We affirm the judgment of the district court.

I. Background

Price Waterhouse's Tax and Technology Group developed and marketed a tax preparation software package, the Tax Management System ("TMS"). The TMS software was initially a DOS-based program. But in 1994, Price Waterhouse hired Patrick J. McNerthney to develop a Windows (R) version (8.0) of the TMS software. McNerthney created a subprogram called RevUp32, which interfaced with the Windows (R) TMS program to access files created with the DOS-based program. Price Waterhouse owned the copyrights pertaining to both the TMS software and the RevUp32 program until it sold most of its TMS business assets to CLR in December 1995.

In March 1995, Yang, an employee acting on behalf of Price Waterhouse, attempted to locate computer programmers in China who could increase the speed of the RevUp32 program in return for a fee and a commitment by Price Waterhouse to outsource future projects to China. Yang contacted several Chinese programmers and eventually selected the Sichuan Sky Company Limited (the "Sky Company") to do the work. Shortly thereafter, Yang became concerned that Price Waterhouse and the Sky Company might exclude her from future projects. To alleviate Yang's fears, Stephen Desmond, Price Waterhouse's partner in charge of the Tax Technology Group, prepared a letter dated May 22, 1995, stating that if Yang successfully met the objectives of the "China Project," Price Waterhouse would appoint her to lead future ventures in China.

Yang and Gerard Niles, Price Waterhouse's Chief Development Officer and Senior Vice President of the Tax Technology Group, subsequently worked out the details of the arrangement between Yang and Price Waterhouse and set forth their agreement in a written letter dated June 7, 1995. The letter, signed by Niles, stated in pertinent part:

> Price Waterhouse LLP agrees to pay $25,000 (twenty-five thousand dollars) for each 25% increase in TMS speed resulting from work on the RevUp. After the initial 25% improvement is achieved, payment will be made in $1,000 increments for each percentage increase. For example, if the speed is increased by 49%, Price Waterhouse will pay $49,000.00.

> . . . .

> Price Waterhouse will be given 30 days upon receipt of the object code to perform acceptance testing. If Price Waterhouse discovers problems, the consultants agree to resolve any and all issues on a timely basis. When issues are resolved, the consultants will give Price Waterhouse an additional 30 days upon receipt of the revised object code to perform acceptance testing. Upon successful completion of acceptance testing and verification of the speed increases, Price Waterhouse will pay the aforementioned amount. . . . The Tax Technology Group will supply the source code for the RevUp. . . . It is clearly understood that the source code is the sole property of Price Waterhouse and Price Waterhouse gives no authority, implied or otherwise, to distribute or copy this source code in any way. Upon completion of the project, ALL source code will be given back to Price Waterhouse.

If this project is successful, Price Waterhouse will consider the same consultants as strong candidates for future development projects.

Price Waterhouse then disclosed to Yang the source code to the RevUp32 program. In turn, Yang disclosed the RevUp32-program source code to the Sky Company programmers. Using the original source code to the RevUp32 program, the Sky Company programmers successfully increased the speed of the RevUp32 program by 264%.

Upon completion of this newer, faster RevUp32 program (the "China RevUp32 program"), Yang sent the object code to the "China RevUp32 program" to Price Waterhouse. Although Yang was willing to turn over the object code to the China RevUp32 program, she refused to turn over the new source code unless Price Waterhouse guaranteed her future work in China, in addition to paying her the $264,000 she was due under the June 7, 1995 letter agreement. Price Waterhouse, however, refused to make any further guarantees to Yang and refused to pay Yang the $264,000 until the source code for the China RevUp32 program was turned over to Price Waterhouse. Subsequently, the Sky Company programmers asserted an ownership interest in the copyrights pertaining to the China RevUp32 program. They then proceeded to assign their asserted copyrights to Liu, Yang's daughter. Yang then registered the China-RevUp32-program copyrights in Liu's name.

In December 1995, CLR purchased the TMS software business from Price Waterhouse and began selling the TMS software, which incorporated the China RevUp32 program. Price Waterhouse and CLR then contacted Patrick McNerthney, the programmer who had authored the original RevUp32 program, and asked him to attempt to increase the speed of his original RevUp32 program. Because McNerthney was familiar with the original program, he was able to enhance the RevUp32 program for CLR in several weeks. Then, starting in November 1996, CLR substituted McNerthney's faster RevUp32 program for the China RevUp32 program in their TMS software.

In April 1997, Liu filed a suit for copyright infringement against Price Waterhouse and CLR for allegedly infringing her copyrights in the China RevUp32 program by selling the TMS software, which incorporated the China RevUp32 program. Price Waterhouse and CLR denied infringement and filed a counterclaim against Liu for copyright infringement, alleging that Liu infringed their copyrights in the China RevUp32 program by filing a copyright registration in her name. . . . [At trial the] jury determined that Price Waterhouse and CLR validly owned the copyrights in both the original RevUp32 program and the China RevUp32 program. . . .

In their answers to a series of special interrogatories, the jury found specifically that in the June 7, 1995 letter agreement, the parties intended that the copyrights pertaining to the China RevUp32 program would become the property of Price Waterhouse upon completion of the project and that the project was in fact completed. Further, the jury found that Yang was a Price Waterhouse employee while she worked in China and that therefore she was obligated to use her best efforts to protect Price Waterhouse's copyright interests. Additionally, the jury determined that Yang had not used her best efforts to protect the China RevUp32 program while she was employed at Price Waterhouse. . . .

II. Analysis

[Yang] and Liu do not dispute that Price Waterhouse authorized Yang and the Sky Company programmers to produce a derivative work using the original RevUp32 program. Instead, Yang and Liu contend that contrary to the findings below, the intent of the parties is irrelevant to the question of who owns the copyrights in the derivative work. They assert that even if the parties *intended* that Price Waterhouse would own the copyrights in the derivative work, Price Waterhouse *by law* cannot own these copyrights because the derivative work's authors did not execute a written document assigning ownership of the derivative work to Price Waterhouse pursuant to 17 U.S.C. § 204(a). Section 204(a) provides that "[a] transfer of copyright ownership, other than by operation of law, is not valid unless an instrument of conveyance, or a note or memorandum of the transfer, is in writing and signed by the owner of the rights conveyed or such owner's duly authorized agent."

Yang and Liu's reasoning is flawed. Price Waterhouse, as the owner of the copyrights in the original RevUp32 program, possesses the exclusive right to prepare derivative works from this original program. *See* 17 U.S.C. § 106(2); *Stewart v. Abend,* 495 U.S. 207, 220 (1990). Because Price Warehouse possesses such an exclusive right, in order for the Sky Company programmers to have lawfully prepared a derivative work, the programmers needed authorization from Price Waterhouse to use its original program. The June 7, 1995 letter agreement authorized Yang to recruit the Sky Company programmers to use its original work to prepare a derivative work. Because the trial court found that the language of the June 7, 1995 agreement was ambiguous, it was appropriate to look at the intent of the parties to determine the scope of the Sky Company programmers' authorization. The June 7, 1995 letter agreement stated that "[u]pon completion of the project, ALL source code will be given back to Price Waterhouse." Viewing this language in a light most favorable to Price Waterhouse and CLR, the license agreement provided that Price Waterhouse, not the Sky Company programmers, would obtain copyright ownership of the China RevUp32 program.

Further, obtaining copyright protection in the derivative work was beyond the scope of the permissible uses authorized by the June 7, 1995 letter agreement. *See* 1 NIMMER ON COPYRIGHT § 3.06, at 3-34.26 at 26(1) (2002) ("[T]he right to claim copyright in a noninfringing derivative work arises by operation of law, not through authority from the copyright owner of the underlying work. *Nonetheless, if the pertinent agreement between the parties affirmatively bars the licensee from obtaining copyright protection even in a licensed derivative work, that contractual provision would appear to govern.*") (emphasis added); *see also Gracen v. Bradford Exch.,* 698 F.2d 300, 303 (7th Cir.1983) (stating that "[e]ven if [Gracen] was authorized to exhibit her derivative works, she may not have been authorized to copyright them").

Contrary to Yang and Liu's argument on appeal, because the Sky Company programmers never had any ownership interest in the copyrights in the derivative China RevUp32 program, 17 U.S.C. § 204(a) is inapplicable. As the district court explained:

While the Copyright Act makes authors of derivative works the pre-sumptive owners of copyright rights in their contribution, it also allows parties to adjust those rights by contract. Here, the jury found that the parties to the letter agreement did just that — agreed that Price Waterhouse would hold the copyright in the derivative work. Because of the ambiguity in the letter agreement, it was necessary and proper for the jury to consider 'the parties' ' intent in entering into the letter agreement in order to determine the respective rights of Price Waterhouse, Yang and the subsequent authors of the derivative work, even though those subsequent authors, the Sky Company Programmers, did not sign the letter agreement.

Because the jury found that, pursuant to the June 7, 1995 letter agreement, the parties intended that Price Waterhouse would own the copyrights in the derivative work, we find no error in the district court's denial of Yang and Liu's motion for judgment as a matter of law and no abuse of discretion in the district court's denial of Yang and Liu's motion for a new trial. . . .

III. Conclusion

For the foregoing reasons, we AFFIRM the district court.

NOTES

1. In *Liu*, who owns the copyright if the contract is silent and there is no proof of intent of the parties?

2. As the court in *Liu* emphasized, copyright law gives the copyright owner the exclusive right to prepare derivative works from its copyrighted work. A different circumstance exists under patent law, where the patent rights are defined by the patent claims. New technology belongs to its inventor, even though its use may be blocked by a patent owned by someone else. In that context, the effort of a licensor to obtain rights in the subsequent or new material is, in effect, a request for a license or other transfer back from the licensee. Thus, the type of clause involved is often described as a grant back clause. The next excerpt suggests the present status of the law regarding such clauses.

U.S. DEPARTMENT OF JUSTICE AND THE FEDERAL TRADE COMMISSION ANTITRUST GUIDELINES FOR THE LICENSING OF INTELLECTUAL PROPERTY (APRIL 6, 1995)

— A grantback is an arrangement under which a licensee agrees to extend to the licensor of intellectual property the right to use the licensee's improve-ments to the licensed technology. Grantbacks can have procompetitive effects, especially if they are nonexclusive. Such arrangements provide a means for the licensee and the licensor to share risks and reward the licensor for making pos-sible further innovation based on or informed by the licensed technology, and both promote innovation in the first place and promote the subsequent licens-ing of the results of the innovation. Grantbacks may adversely affect competition, however, if they substantially reduce the licensee's incentives to engage in research and development and thereby limit rivalry in innovation markets.

— A non-exclusive grantback allows the licensee to practice its technology and license it to others. Such a grantback provision may be necessary to ensure that the licensor is not prevented from effectively competing because it is denied access to improvements developed with the aid of its own technology. Compared with an exclusive grantback, a non-exclusive grantback, which leaves the licensee free to license improvements technology to others, is less likely to have anticompetitive effects.

— The Agencies will evaluate a grantback provision under the rule of reason, *see generally Transparent-Wrap Machine Corp. v. Stokes & Smith Co.*, 329 U.S. 637, 645-48 (1947) (grantback provision in technology license is not per se unlawful), considering its likely effects in light of the overall structure of the licensing arrangement and conditions in the relevant markets. An important factor in the Agencies' analysis of a grantback will be whether the licensor has market power in a relevant technology or innovation market. If the Agencies determine that a particular grantback provision is likely to reduce significantly licensees' incentives to invest in improving the licensed technology, the Agencies will consider the extent to which the grantback provision has offsetting procompetitive effects, such as (1) promoting dissemination of licensees' improvements to the licensed technology, (2) increasing the licensors' incentives to disseminate the licensed technology, or (3) otherwise increasing competition and output in a relevant technology or innovation market. *See* section 4.2. In addition, the Agencies will consider the extent to which grantback provisions in the relevant markets generally increase licensors' incentives to innovate in the first place.

Chapter 10

DURATION OF A LICENSE

I. BASIC STANDARDS

The duration of a license is controlled by the agreement and typically dealt with expressly. The contract terms typically address the question either of two ways. In many licenses, duration is defined by express terms referring to objectively discernable events (e.g., "one year from date," "June 1, unless renewed," "fifteen performances"). An alternative approach links the duration of the license to a discretionary act or decision by one or both parties (e.g., "terminate at will"). Each format has its own business characteristics and legal characteristics.

If the agreement does not expressly address the duration of the license, common law or other default rules apply. They sometimes create surprising results, as the following case indicates.

TICKETRON LIMITED PARTNERSHIP v. THE FLIP SIDE, INC.
1993 U.S. Dist. LEXIS 8294, Case No. 92 C 0911 (N.D. Ill. 1993)

WILLIAMS, DISTRICT JUDGE.

On January 28, 1991, Ticketron and Flip Side entered into a [Terms of Agreement (TOA)] whereby Flip Side was licensed as a Ticketron outlet to sell tickets to various musical or theatrical productions, concerts, sporting events, and other attractions, through Ticketron's computerized ticketing system. Like with all Ticketron's ticket agents, Ticketron provided Flip Side with all the necessary equipment to sell tickets available on the Ticketron system on a first-come first-serve basis.

The "gross ticket price," defined in the TOA as the price paid by patrons for a ticket, included a service charge for the use of the Ticketron System and the net ticket price. Under the TOA, Flip Side was authorized to deduct 25% from the service charge as its compensation. Flip Side was then to remit the rest of the revenue, consisting of Ticketron's share of the service charge, the net ticket price which belonged to Ticketron's clients, and Ticketron's clients' share of the Service Charge, to Ticketron.

In addition, Paragraph 16(b) of the TOA provided:

> TICKETRON may assign or transfer this Agreement, and any revenues or other benefits receivable by TICKETRON hereunder to TICKETRON's lender(s) or any other entity or person provided that no such assignment shall relieve TICKETRON of its obligations hereunder without Terminal Operator's prior consent, which consent shall not be unreasonably withheld or delayed. Notwithstanding the foregoing,

no consent shall be required where TICKETRON's successor-in-interest acquires all or substantially all of TICKETRON's business and assets, whether by purchase, merger, operation of law, or otherwise.

On March 12, 1991, Ticketron and its related entities entered into an asset purchase agreement with Ticketmaster Holdings Group, Ltd. ("Ticketmaster") by which Ticketmaster was to purchase virtually all of Ticketron's assets. On May 22, 1991, Ticketron turned off Flip Side's equipment, effectively shutting down Flip Side as a Chicago Ticketron outlet. Ticketmaster's purchase of Ticketron's assets closed on May 23, 1991.

As of May 22, 1991, Flip Side owed Ticketron $89,102.45 for tickets sold through the Ticketron system. . . . Rather than remitting this money to Ticketron as required under the TOA, Flip Side retained the $89,102.45 as partial compensation to off-set its lost profits resulting from Ticketron's shutting down Flip Side's ticketing equipment before the termination date of the TOA. In addition, while Ticketron shut down the computers at Flip Side's facilities, Ticketron has not removed this equipment as required under the TOA. Flip Side has stored Ticketron's equipment at its Palatine, Illinois headquarters since the spring or summer of 1991.

The Parties' Cross Motions for Summary Judgment

[In] its counterclaim, Flip Side asserts that Ticketron breached the TOA by shutting down Flip Side's ticketing equipment before the termination date of the TOA. Ticketron counters that the TOA was merely a license permitting Flip Side to operate Ticketron terminals. Ticketron claims that under Illinois law, it was entitled to revoke the license at any time.

A license "entitles one party to use property subject to the management and control of the other party." *Application of Rosewell v. City of Chicago,* 387 N.E.2d 866, 870 (Ill.App.1979). In this case, the TOA provided that "Ticketron hereby licenses and authorizes" Flip Side to operate Ticketron terminals. The TOA defined a terminal as "an electronic unit, linked to Ticketron's computer facilities, that is capable of displaying information concerning the availability of Tickets for Attractions, issuing Tickets thereof, and generating related reports and data." Under the TOA, Ticketron retained ownership of all terminal equipment, and was responsible for all repair and maintenance. Ticketron was also responsible under the TOA for the costs of all utilities, other than electrical utilities, consumed in operating the terminals, as well the installation, maintenance, and usage charges of a dedicated telephone line from Ticketron's central computer to each terminal.

The TOA also provided that Ticketron had the right to add or delete attractions at any time, and change ticket prices, times and dates of performances, and seating arrangements. In addition, the TOA did not guarantee Flip Side a certain number of available tickets. Tickets that were available to Flip Side were also available to other Ticketron outlets on a first-come-first-served basis.

Such evidence adequately demonstrates that the TOA was a license. As Illinois law requires, Flip Side was given a license to access Ticketron's computer facilities, while Ticketron maintained management and control over its equipment and its computerized ticketing system. Indeed, the only TOA provision which is not indicative of a license is Paragraph 16A because licenses generally are not assignable. While this is not the general rule for licenses, the parties were free and chose to change the nature of their license through their contractual agreement. Therefore, the fact that Ticketron allowed Flip Side to assign the TOA without its prior written consent did not render the license ineffective.

Having determined that the TOA was a license, the remaining question is whether this license was revocable. Under Illinois law, licenses are generally revocable at anytime at the will of the licensor. *Soderholm v. Chicago Nat. League Ball Club,* 587 N.E.2d 517, 520 (Ill.App.1992). Illinois courts have only restrained "the exercise of the legal right to revoke a license when the conduct of the licensor has been such that the assertion of the legal title would operate as a fraud upon the licensee."

In this case, no evidence has been presented which suggests that Ticketron's termination of Flip Side's access to its computer facilities operated as fraud against Flip Side. As previously discussed, Ticketron maintained ownership and control of the equipment and the computerized ticketing system, and offered no guarantees regarding ticket availability on its system. In addition, Flip Side was not required to expend money to prepare tickets and ticket envelopes. These items were provided free of charge by Ticketron. Flip Side was also not required to finance the marketing campaign for the ticket sales. Under the TOA, this was also Ticketron's obligation.

Furthermore, no evidence has been presented which suggests that the TOA granted Flip Side an irrevocable license. Indeed, while the TOA provided that it ran from January 14, 1991 through January 13, 1996, the TOA did not otherwise provide for its termination by either party. Ticketron argues that the TOA granted Flip Side a license that was revocable at will because it provided that (1) Ticketron could add or delete attractions at any time, and (2) Ticketron could sell all or substantially all of its business and assets without prior consent from Flip Side. While these provisions may have affected the parties' rights under the TOA, this court is not persuaded that these provisions adequately demonstrate that the TOA was revocable. At best, Paragraph 16(B) of the TOA did not require Ticketron to continue its obligations under the TOA if it sold substantially all its assets to a third party. While this provision lends strong support for Ticketron's actions in this case, Paragraph 16(B) does not specifically establish that the TOA was revocable at will.

Since the TOA is silent on this issue, this court finds that it has no alternative but to look to Illinois law to determine whether the TOA is revocable. As previously stated, Illinois law provides that licenses generally are revocable at will. Absent evidence from the TOA to the contrary, this court finds that the TOA was revocable at will as Ticketron suggests and Ticketron did not breach its contract with Flip Side by revoking the TOA. As stated above, the language of Paragraph 16(b) lends strong support to this determination because it did not require Ticketron to continue its obligations under the TOA if it sold substantially all of its assets to a third party, such as Ticketmaster in this instance. Therefore, Flip Side's request for summary judgment on this counterclaim is denied. . . .

NOTES

1. *Ticketron* was not an intellectual property license. The license involved access. To the extent that property rights are involved in this type of license, they involve the right to regulate access to an online or other information system. The legal basis lies in a combination of trespass, communications, and criminal laws. *See* RAYMOND T. NIMMER & HOLLY K. TOWLE, THE LAW OF COMMERCIAL ELECTRONIC TRANSACTIONS § 8.01 (2003, 2007).

2. Two issues. One deals with duration of an agreement when the agreement is silent and neither party acts to end it. The second deals with whether the license is revocable during that time without breach of the contract. Article 2 states:

> Where the contract provides for successive performances but is indefinite in duration, it is valid for a reasonable time but unless otherwise agreed may be terminated at any time by either party.

UCC § 2-309. This contemplates a judgment about the context ("reasonable time") coupled with a right of withdrawal "at will." A similar rule generally governs in common law. What is the justification for the rule? Of course, Article 2 does not apply to most licenses. What is the best rule outside of the scope of Article 2?

3. Dealing with a copyright license, the Ninth Circuit in *Rano v. Sipa Press, Inc.*, 987 F.2d 580 (9th Cir. 1993), held that the termination at will rule was preempted by Section 203 of the Copyright Act which provides that licenses are terminable at the will of the author during a five year period beginning at the end of thirty-five years from the date of the execution of the license unless they explicitly specify earlier termination. That decision has not attracted widespread following, as illustrated by our next case.

WALTHAL v. RUSK
172 F.3d 481 (7th Cir. 1999)

EVANS, CIRCUIT JUDGE.

Paul L. Walthal, Gibson J. Haynes, and Jeffrey S. Coffey are the Butthole Surfers. For the unenlightened, that's a musical group. In 1984 they entered into an agreement with Corey Rusk, who had formed a company which eventually became Touch and Go Distributions, Inc. and Touch and Go Records, Inc., both Illinois corporations. Under the agreement, Touch and Go was granted the nonexclusive right to manufacture and sell copies of the Butthole Surfers' musical performances in return for a 50 percent share of the net profits.

One would ordinarily think that an agreement of the type we just described would be in writing, for as Yogi Berra observed, "A oral contract isn't worth the paper it's written on." But, alas, the Butthole Surfers and Touch and Go never got around to writing up their deal. So what we have here is simply an oral licensing agreement between the parties that had no specified duration; it did not set out any circumstances giving rise to a right of termination. Under the agreement, until the dispute before us raised its head, the Butthole Surfers provided Touch and Go with six recorded performances and one video performance to manufacture and sell.

On December 4, 1995, the Butthole Surfers demanded that the agreed 50/50 split be changed to a more favorable (for them) 80/20 split and that the agreement terminate in 3 years. Touch and Go responded, in writing, that it considered the parties bound by the original agreement. On December 8 the Butthole Surfers sent a letter terminating the agreement effective immediately and demanding a return of inventory. Touch and Go, however, continued to copy and sell the performances — an action that fueled this suit claiming copyright infringement along with several pendent state-law claims.

The district court granted a summary judgment motion filed by the Butthole Surfers on the pivotal issue in the case — whether 17 U.S.C. § 203 prohibits the termination of the agreement. The court determined that the Butthole Surfers' termination of the licensing agreement was effective. [This] appeal followed.

Touch and Go presents two primary issues. The first is that the licensing agreement is irrevocable because consideration — the 50 percent share of the profits — was paid. This contention is without merit. The other issue . . . is that termination of the agreement was prohibited by § 203 of the Copyright Act. The argument here is that the statute prohibits the termination of a copyright license — including one of unspecified duration arising out of an oral agreement — prior to 35 years from the date the license was granted. It is to this issue we now turn.

Section 203 provides that "the exclusive or nonexclusive grant of a transfer or license of copyright or of any right under a copyright . . . is subject to termination" under certain conditions. As relevant here, subsection (3) provides:

> Termination of the grant may be effected at any time during a period of five years beginning at the end of thirty-five years from the date of execution of the grant.

The disagreement before us is simply whether the statute establishes 35 years as a minimum or maximum term of a grant. That is, is the statute an attempt to ensure that regardless of the terms of the agreement — say an agreement for the life of the copyright — between the copyright owner and the licensee, the agreement can, nevertheless, be terminated after 35 years, or whether no agreement can be terminated until 35 years have passed, or something in between those extremes.

Despite the fact that § 203 was enacted over 20 years ago as part of the Copyright Act of 1976, there is very limited case law on its interpretation. The only case from a court of appeals is from the Ninth Circuit, *Rano v. Sipa Press*, 987 F.2d 580 (1993). . . . [The] court said that the "application of [the] principle of California contract law [that indefinite term contracts can be terminated at will] would directly conflict with federal copyright law" so the state law, the court concluded, was preempted. The court then interpreted § 203 to mean that unless a license explicitly specifies an earlier termination date, it cannot be terminated prior to 35 years.

To put it mildly, this result is deplored by commentators. If the *Rano* decision were a Broadway show, bad reviews would have forced it to close after opening night. Nimmer, for instance, finds *Rano* a "remarkable result," a "wayward result," "stunning, both for its utter absence of support in law and for the breadth of its error." Nimmer says that the 35-year period in § 203 is a maximum period that a contract can be enforced, not a minimum as *Rano* holds. *See* 3 MELVILLE B. NIMMER & DAVID NIMMER, NIMMER ON COPYRIGHTS § 11.01 (1998). William T. Rintala says that the *Rano* court's ruling turns protection for authors into a "windfall for those acquiring rights for an indefinite term." William T. Rintala, *Copyright Update — Substantive Law*, 379 PLI/Pat at 271, 325-26 (Practicing Law Institute, Patents, Copyrights, Trademarks, and Literary Property Course Handbook Series, 1994). Yet another commentator calls *Rano* a "ridiculously incorrect interpretation of the statute. It takes a provision meant to protect the author and turns it into a straitjacket." Mark F. Radcliffe, *Copyright Ownership Issues*, 411 PLI/Pat at 243, 300 (Practicing Law Institute, Patents, Copyrights, Trademarks, and Literary Property Course Handbook Series, 1995).

We think it's time to take a fresh look at § 203, putting the statute in context, and because its plain meaning is not perfectly clear, we will cast a glance at its legislative history for whatever guidance it might disclose. The term of a copyright is the life of the author plus 50 years. 17 U.S.C. § 302(a). The ownership of a copyright vests in the author, who, of course, may transfer his rights as he sees fit. A "transfer of copyright ownership" is an "assignment, mortgage, exclusive license, or any other conveyance, alienation, or hypothecation of a copyright or of any of the exclusive rights comprised in a copyright, whether or not it is limited in time or place of effect, but not including a nonexclusive license." 17 U.S.C. § 101. Transfers of ownership must be in writing. Nonexclusive licenses are excluded from the definition of "transfer of copyright ownership." Therefore, nonexclusive licenses such as the one we are considering here may be granted orally, but they do not transfer ownership of the copyright.

The purpose of § 203 is to give authors and their heirs a second chance to market works even after a transfer of rights has been made. Often, it is not clear soon after the creation of a work how valuable it will prove to be. Congress intended to safeguard "authors against unremunerative transfers." The provision was needed "because of the unequal bargaining position of authors, resulting in part from the impossibility of determining a work's value until it has been exploited." H.R. Rep. No. 94-1476, at 124 (1976). Therefore, if an author had granted a license for the life of the copyright, or for some long period of time, he could nevertheless terminate the license after 35 years and look around for a better deal. The House and Senate reports both said:

> Nothing contained in this section or elsewhere in this legislation is intended to extend the duration of any license, transfer or assignment made for a period of less than thirty-five years. If, for example, an agreement provides an earlier termination date or lesser duration, or

> if it allows the author the right of canceling or terminating the agreement under certain circumstances, the duration is governed by the agreement. Likewise, nothing in this section or legislation is intended to change the existing state of the law of contracts concerning the circumstances in which an author may cancel or terminate a license, transfer, or assignment.

H.R. Rep. No. 94-1476, at 128; S. Rep. No. 94-473, at 111.

In this context it makes no sense that a 35-year period be considered a minimum under the statute. If the term of the license originally granted was less than 35 years, the statute simply does not compel that the license be effective for 35 years. And even the *Rano* court did not go so far. The Ninth Circuit said that §203 means that agreements are terminable only after 35 years "*unless they explicitly specify an earlier termination date.*" But the court nevertheless determined that if the agreement contained no termination date, it must continue for 35 years because §203 preempted state contract law providing for termination at will of contracts of unspecified length. By this reasoning, a contract for a specific term of less than 35 years does not conflict with the 35-year period but a contract which is terminable at will by operation of law does.

We disagree with any such conclusion. In general, state contract laws pertain to the transfer of interests under the Copyright Act. Section 203(b)(5) itself specifically provides that termination of a grant under the statute "in no way affects rights arising under any other Federal, State, or foreign laws." In our case it is undisputed that, unless it is preempted, Illinois law applies to the dispute and that under the law of Illinois a contract of unspecified length is terminable at will. And when a contract is silent as to its length, it is implicit that it can be terminated by either side. . . .

However, as the *Rano* court correctly points out, state contract law cannot provide the basis of a decision if that law conflicts with federal law. Under the principle of preemption, for instance, in light of the existence of §203, we could not use common law rules for the interpretation of contracts to require that a contract for the life of the copyright be enforced for that length of time. That interpretation would be in direct conflict with §203. In contrast, a contract which implicitly provides for termination, as this one does under Illinois law, presents no conflict with §203. This contract does not differ in any meaningful way from a contract which specifies a term of, for instance, 10 years, which would be terminable at the end of the 10-year period. And, in fact, in addition to allowing termination if the contract allows for a specific earlier termination date, Congress said that the statute also provides that a contract might allow the author the right to cancel or terminate the agreement "under certain circumstances," in which case the duration is "governed by the agreement." We conclude that allowing terminations under Illinois law does not conflict with §203, but rather is, in fact, in keeping with the intent of §203. Therefore, there is no issue of preemption.

Under Illinois law, this contract can be terminated, and it is undisputed that the Butthole Surfers' letter of December 8, 1995, did just that. That letter rendered the license agreement kaput.

Accordingly, the decision of the district court is AFFIRMED.

NOTES

1. Which was the better analysis, *Rano* or *Walthal*?

2. The Ninth Circuit has not retracted *Rano*, but in *Scholastic Entertainment, Inc. v. Fox Entertainment Group, Inc.*, 336 F.3d 982 (9th Cir. 2003), the court held that state law governed termination of a copyright license with an express termination date not in conflict with Section 203.

3. *Rano, Walthal,* and other cases hold that the common law uses a presumption of "termination at will." There is contrary authority. Indeed, Professor Goldstein comments that the "few courts to address the issue have generally held that, in the absence of language providing for a shorter or longer term, the duration of a copyright contract should be measured by the remaining term of copyright in the work." 1 PAUL GOLDSTEIN, COPYRIGHT § 4.6.3.3a (2d ed. 1999). *Accord* 3 DAVID NIMMER & MELVILLE NIMMER, NIMMER ON COPYRIGHT § 10.10[F] (1999) ("Where an assignment or license does not expressly prescribe the period or term of its duration, it will generally be construed (in the absence of evidence of a contrary intent) to be effective for the duration of the then existing copyright term of the work."). *See P.C. Films Corp. v. MGM/UA Home Video, Inc.*, 45 USPQ2d 1850 (2d Cir. 1998) ("where a contract is silent as to the duration of the grant of copyright rights, the contact is read to convey rights for the initial copyright period"), *cert. denied*, 119 S. Ct. 542 (1998).

A leading treatise suggests a similar conclusion for patent licenses: "A license not expressly limited in duration, continues till the patent expires, or the license is surrendered in pursuance of its own provision, or is terminated by a new agreement, or is forfeited by the licensee." 6 LIPSCOMB'S WALKER ON PATENTS § 20:30 (3d ed. 1987).

4. Which rule is appropriate — reasonable time subject to termination at will or length of the term of the licensed intellectual property right? Remember that these are default rules subject to the terms of the agreement.

5. UCITA provides that if "an agreement does not specify its duration, to the extent allowed by other law," the general rule is that "the agreement is enforceable for a time reasonable in light of the licensed subject matter and commercial circumstances but may be terminated as to future performances at will by either party during that time on giving seasonable notice to the other party." UCITA § 308(1) (2000 Official Text).

There are several exceptions to the general rule in UCITA. Thus, "the duration of the license is perpetual as to the contractual rights and contractual use restrictions if . . . the license is of a computer program that does not license source code but that transfers ownership of a copy or delivery of a copy for a contract fee, the total amount of which is fixed at or before the time of delivery of the copy." This reflects common commercial understanding in software transactions. Also, UCITA provides for a perpetual license (subject to cancellation for breach) if "the license expressly granted the right to incorporate or use the licensed information or informational rights with information or informational rights from other sources in a combined work for public distribution or public performance."

PROBLEM 10.1

Scorsee holds the copyright to the successful Broadway play — "My Life." It gives licenses to publicly perform the play to community and local theaters throughout the country for $40,000. Typically, in the industry, local theaters pay for a license each year in which they plan to perform the play. The standard form license is silent on duration. Denver Arts Theater purchases a license. It performs the play in that year. The next year, it performs the play again, without acquiring another license from Scorsee. Scorsee sues. Denver argues that it has a license for performances. What result?

PROBLEM 10.2

Under an informal arrangement, Brazil Up-Date obtains a license to "distribute copies of TV Globo's copyrighted programming in the United States." This arrangement was not in a written agreement, but was based on the course of dealings between the parties. After working for several years, TV Globo sends notice of termination and then sues when the licensee continues to distribute the program. What result?

PROBLEM 10.3

Software Publisher grants Major a license to use Software's data processing software in Major's business. The license is for $100,000 paid on execution of the agreement. The written license is silent on duration. Software delivers the program on a CD.

Three years into the license, Software sends Major a letter stating that it was exercising its right to terminate the license, effective three months from the date of the letter. It states that any continued use of the software after the termination date is a breach of the license.

What result?

II.   EXERCISE OF THE RIGHT TO TERMINATE

INTERGRAPH CORP. v. INTEL CORP.
195 F.3d 1346 (Fed. Cir. 1999)

[The trial court held that Intel's termination of a contract giving Intergraph advance access to Intel design developments created an unconscionable effect and was therefore prohibited under UCC Article 2. The appellate court reversed.]

Intel is a manufacturer of high performance computer microprocessors. The microprocessors are sold to producers of various computer-based devices, who adapt and integrate the microprocessors into products that are designed and sold for particular uses. These producers are called original equipment manufacturers, or OEMs. Intergraph Corporation is an OEM, and develops, makes, and sells computer workstations that are used in producing computer-aided graphics. From 1987 to 1993 Intergraph's workstations were based on a high performance microprocessor developed by the Fairchild division of National Semiconductor, embodying what is called the "Clipper" technology. Intergraph owns the Clipper technology and patents thereon. In 1993 Intergraph discontinued use of Clipper microprocessors in its workstations and switched to Intel microprocessors. In 1994 Intel designated Intergraph a "strategic customer" and provided Intergraph with various special benefits, including proprietary information and products, under non-disclosure agreements.

Starting in late 1996 Intergraph charged several Intel OEM customers with infringement of the Clipper patents based on their use of Intel microprocessors. The accused companies sought defense and indemnification from Intel. Negotiations ensued between Intel and Intergraph. Intel inquired about a license to the Clipper patents, but the proposed terms were rejected by Intergraph as inadequate. Intel then proposed certain patent cross-licenses, also rejected by Intergraph. Intel also proposed that the non-disclosure agreement relating to a new joint development project include a license to the Clipper patents; this too was rejected by Intergraph. As negotiations failed and threats continued the relationship deteriorated, and so did the technical assistance and other special benefits that Intel had been providing to Intergraph.

In November 1997 Intergraph sued Intel for infringement of the Clipper patents. Intergraph also charged Intel with other violations of law, including fraud, misappropriation of trade secrets, negligence, wantonness and willfulness, breach of contract, intentional interference with business relations, breach of express and implied warranties, and violation of the Alabama Trade Secrets Act. Intergraph demanded that Intel be enjoined from infringement of the Clipper patents, and the award of compensatory and punitive damages and trebled damages.

Intergraph moved to enjoin Intel pendente lite from cutting off or delaying provision of the special benefits that Intel had previously provided to Intergraph. Following Intel's opposition to this motion Intergraph amended its complaint to charge Intel with violation of the antitrust laws. After a hearing, the district court held that Intel was a monopolist and had violated sections 1 and 2 of the Sherman Act or was likely to be so shown, and issued a preliminary injunction that included the following provisions:

> a. Intel shall supply Intergraph with all Intel product information, including but not limited to technical, design, development, defect, specification, support, supply, future product, product release or sample data, whether existing in product data books, "yellow backs," Confidential Information Transmittal Records, email or other mediums . . . , whether it is on an advance basis for the development of motherboards, graphics subsystems or workstations utilizing Intel's existing, or future generation products (hereinafter "Product Development"), or current products as needed for support of such products. . . .

Intel appeals, arguing that no law requires it to give such special benefits, including its trade secrets, proprietary information, intellectual property, prerelease products, allocation of new products, and other preferences, to an entity that is suing it on charges of multiple wrongdoing and is demanding damages and the shutdown of its core business. Intel states that its commercial response to Intergraph's suit is not an antitrust violation. . . . Intergraph's response is that it can not survive in its highly competitive graphics workstation business without these services and benefits from Intel, and that the district court simply acted to preserve Intergraph's prior commercial position while the parties litigate unrelated patent issues. . . .

The Non-Disclosure Agreements

In 1994 Intel and Intergraph entered into the first of a series of non-disclosure agreements concerning the protection of Confidential Information as defined therein. The Agreements provide that "Neither party has any obligation to disclose Confidential Information to the other," that there is no "obligation to buy or sell products," that both parties may "cease giving Confidential Information to the other party without liability," and that either party can "terminate this Agreement at any time without cause upon notice to the other party" with return of the Confidential Information. Under these agreements Intel provided Intergraph with the trade secret and proprietary information and pre-release products here at issue.

The district court ruled that "Intel's retaliatory lawsuits and the threatened and actual termination of its non-disclosure agreements (NDAs) with Intergraph, under which Intel provided technical information to Intergraph, constitute unlawful restraints of trade." The court held that Intel could not terminate the agreements and the provision of Confidential Information thereunder, since there was no legitimate business justification for doing so. The court concluded that "Intel's enforcement of the at-will termination provisions through two retaliatory lawsuits and other threatened actions is unreasonably onerous and intended to restrain competition by Intergraph and others." However, onerous actions do not in themselves constitute antitrust violations. "[The Sherman] Act does not purport to afford remedies for all torts committed by or against persons engaged in interstate commerce." . . .

The district court also ruled that the at-will termination clause was "unconscionable" at the time the non-disclosure agreements were entered into, or at least would be unconscionable if Intel were now permitted to terminate the agreements and discontinue the disclosures they had enabled. The district court rejected the argument that unconscionability as a ground of contract illegality was intended for consumer protection, and held that "the principle applies with equal force in the commercial field." We observe, however, that the Alabama courts, like others, have emphasized that "[r]ecission of a contract for unconscionability is an extraordinary remedy usually reserved for the protection of the unsophisticated and the uneducated." Although Intergraph is a much smaller company than Intel, it is one of the Fortune 1000, and does not plead inadequate legal advice in its commercial dealings. The Alabama Code comments that "The principle is one of the prevention of oppression and unfair surprise and not of disturbance of allocation of risks because of superior bargaining power." Ala. Code Section 7-2-302 Comment (1) (1997). Applying this state law, the Alabama courts have recognized that "it is not the province of the court to make or remake a contract for the parties."

Trade secrets and other proprietary information and products including pre-release samples of chips are commercial property, and the terms of their disclosure and use are traditional matters of commercial contract. Intergraph does not state that it objected to the mutual at-will termination provision when the contract was entered. Indeed, the district court found that when Intergraph switched from the Clipper technology "Mr. Grove did not commit Intel to provide a perpetual supply of chips, pre-released chips, or confidential information [and] did not commit Intel to any continued or 'perpetual business relationship' with Intergraph."

In an agreement relating to confidential information, negotiated between commercial entities, it is not the judicial role to rewrite the contract and impose terms that these parties did not make. Such intrusion into the integrity of contracts requires more than changed relationships. No fraud or deception is here alleged. Even on the district court's view of the mutual termination clause as unconscionable, the remedy would be rescission or imposition of a termination notice period, not the Sherman Act remedy of enforced disclosure of trade secrets and proprietary information and provision of pre-released products, none of which is required to be disclosed under any agreement. Neither the conclusion that the termination of the agreements violated the Sherman Act, nor the content of the injunction, can be supported on the ground that the non-disclosure agreements contained a termination at-will provision.

Alternatively, the district court held that since the non-disclosure agreements lacked a termination date, the court could impose one. The court ruled that "reasonable notification would take effect at the conclusion of the Deschutes and Merced Programs continuing through 1999." This reformation, adding some twenty months to the date of the court's injunction Order, is not accompanied by an analysis of the original understanding of the parties or by evidence of objective termination parameters for similar agreements, and is without precedent. Although the weight of this aspect has been diluted by the passage of time and other events, this judicial revision of the parties' contract is without support.

Non-disclosure agreements were apparently also involved in connection with Intel's refusal to authorize help to Intergraph for removal of a "bug" or defect in a product, an event described by the district court as "requiring Intergraph to spend substantial time and resources to solve the problem and delaying Intergraph's product entry into the market." The withdrawal of technical service is not a violation of the antitrust laws. Even when the parties are in competition with each other "an act of pure malice by one business competitor against another does not, without more, state a claim under the federal antitrust laws."

The preliminary injunction can not be sustained. . . .

NOTES

1. *Intergraph* involved a variety of issues, including antitrust claims, all of which were resolved in favor of Intel. See Chapter 13.

2. Unconscionability doctrine originated in UCC Article 2 as a restriction on the ability of persons with undue advantage in a contract to unfairly and by surprise obtain oppressive terms harmful to the other party. The focus is ordinarily on the contracting process, not on performance. Section 2-309 is an exception. It provides:

> (c) Termination of a contract by one party except on the happening of an agreed event requires that reasonable notification be received by the other party and an agreement dispensing with notification is invalid if its operation would be unconscionable.

UCC § 3-309 (1998 Official Text). In a contract between companies that provides either party a right to terminate at will, when would the exercise of rights under that clause be unconscionable?

3. UCC § 1-208 provides:

> A term providing that one party or his successor in interest may accelerate payment or performance or require collateral or additional collateral "at will" or "when he deems himself insecure" or in words of similar import shall be construed to mean that he shall have power to do so only if he in good faith believes that the prospect of payment or performance is impaired. The burden of establishing lack of good faith is on the party against whom the power has been exercised.

If that rule applied in *Intel*, would the result change?

4. Why would parties desire a termination at will provision? Before you leap to the conclusion that it is entirely a matter of the licensor's economic leverage, consider the advantages a licensee receives.

5. Federal law and the law in many states regulates at will termination in franchise contracts. The rationale is that franchisees "need" protection against arbitrary termination where they have invested significant capital in the franchise. The assumption is often that the franchisor is a sophisticated company, while the franchisee is an unsophisticated individual. Many franchise laws preclude termination except for "cause."

PROBLEM 10.4

Your Client is involved in negotiation of a license of trade secrets. The license will require annual payments of $5,000 per year plus 3% royalties on any products produced using the licensed secrets. On the table is a clause providing that the license terminates whenever the information provided becomes publicly known through no fault of either party. As an alternative, the license could provide that it can be terminated at will by either party. Which would you prefer as Licensor? Which is preferable for Licensee?

III. EFFECT OF TERMINATION

UCC § 2-106(c) provides:

> On "termination" all obligations which are still executory on both sides are discharged but any right based on prior breach or performance survives.

"Termination" occurs when either party pursuant to a power created by the agreement or law puts an end to the contract otherwise than for its breach. UCITA adopts a similar rule, but spells out a number of obligations that survive termination unless the agreement otherwise provides. These include:

(a) Except as otherwise provided in subsection (b), on termination all obligations that are still executory on both sides are discharged.

(b) The following survive termination:

(1) a right based on previous breach or performance of the contract;

(2) an obligation of confidentiality, nondisclosure, or noncompetition to the extent enforceable under other law;

(3) a contractual use term applicable to any licensed copy or information received from the other party, or copies made of it, which are not returned or returnable to the other party;

(4) an obligation to deliver, or dispose of information, materials, documentation, copies, records, or the like to the other party, an obligation to destroy copies, or a right to obtain information from an escrow agent;

(5) a choice of law or forum;

(6) an obligation to arbitrate or otherwise resolve disputes by alternative dispute resolution procedures;

(7) a term limiting the time for commencing an action or for giving notice;

(8) an indemnity term . . . ;

(9) a limitation of remedy or modification or disclaimer of warranty;

(10) an obligation to provide an accounting and make any payment due under the accounting; and

(11) any term that the agreement provides will survive.

UCITA § 616 (2000 Official Text).

SHEPARD'S COMPANY v. THE THOMSON CORP.
1999 U.S. Dist. LEXIS 21051, Case No. C-3-99-318 (S.D. Ohio 1999)

RICE, DISTRICT JUDGE.

Shepard's/McGraw-Hill, Inc., the predecessor-in-interest to Plaintiff Shepard's Company ("Shepard's"), entered into two agreements with Defendant's predecessor-in-interest, West Publishing Company ("West"), whereby West obtained a license to use Shepard's citation service and trademarks. In both of those agreements, West acknowledged that Shepard's/McGraw-Hill owned those trademarks and that the use of them by West would cease upon the termination of the agreements. In April, 1996 Shepard's, through its predecessor-in-interest, [entered into] a letter agreement providing, *inter alia,* that either party intending not to renew the [agreements] would be required to give at least one year's notice of that intention. On June 25, 1998, Plaintiffs informed the Defendant that [they did not] intend to renew the 1988 and 1991 agreements. As a result, the Defendant's license to use Shepard's trademarks and citation service terminated as of July 2, 1999.

The Plaintiffs bring this litigation, claiming that, despite the fact that the 1988 and 1991 agreements have terminated and, therefore, Defendant no longer has a license to use Shepard's trademarks, the Defendant is continuing to use those trademarks in a manner which constitutes infringement in violation of [the Lanham Act].

1. The Continued Uses of Shepard's Trademarks by the Defendant

The first screen that one sees upon signing onto Westlaw contains various messages, highlights and announcements. The first such message provides:

> Shepard's is no longer available on Westlaw. West Group offers you KeyCite, a full citator service that meets all your citation research needs. Please call our KeyCite Reference Attorney Hotline at 1-800-207-9378 for research assistance or more information. To arrange training, please contact your CALR Coordinator or Designee.

After signing onto Westlaw and discovering an interesting decision, during the course of a search, one may wish to utilize a citator service to check the current viability of that decision or to ascertain how other courts have interpreted and dealt with it. To accomplish that, one could press the "SH" button on the toolbar. By placing the cursor on the "SH" button, before pressing that button, the word "Shepard's" appears in a box, indicating that use of said button will connect you with Shepard's. If one presses that button, a dialog box appears, giving the user four alternatives, to wit: "Insta-Cite," "Quick Cite," "Shepard's" and "Shepard's PreView." Next to each of those choices is a circle which is white in the middle. If one places her cursor in the middle of one of the circles and presses the left button on her mouse, a black dot appears in that circle, thus selecting which of the four services she wishes to access. Shepard's is the programed choice (the black dot appears in the circle next to Shepard's, when the dialog box is first seen); therefore, the user can access that service merely by pressing her return key. Upon accessing Shepard's, the user is greeted by the following message:

> Shepard's is no longer available on Westlaw. West Group offers you KeyCite, a full citator service that meets all your citation needs. Please call our KeyCite Reference Attorney Hotline at 1-800-207-9378 to get a Free KeyCite Password or to arrange free phone training.

. . . The underlined "KeyCite" (italicized on Defendant's screen) provides a direct link to that service; by placing her cursor on that word and pushing the left mouse button, the user can go directly to KeyCite. . . .

2. What the Plaintiffs Want . . .

On the first page of their motion, the Plaintiffs state that they want a Temporary Restraining Order to prohibit Defendant "from using, illegally and without authorization, Shepard's registered trademark SHEPARD'S on or in connection with West's on-line services, websites and software, other than West proprietary software currently installed on users' computers." On page 23, they elaborate on what they are seeking:

> For purposes of its temporary restraining order request, Shepard's is focusing strictly on (1) the continued uses of the SHEPARD'S marks within the on-line services, websites and software of West, which are immediately, effectively and economically subject to West's control (as opposed to infringing uses embedded in West proprietary software already installed on users' computers); and (2) the uses of entries at the West on-line services, websites and software that are directing customers to West's competing KeyCite citation services.

As an example of the second category, upon which the Plaintiffs are focusing, they cite the message that one sees upon accessing Shepard's by using the "SH" button. The Plaintiffs, however, state that they have no objection to the Defendant continuing to inform users that Shepard's is no longer available (although they want the Court to require the Defendant to state that Shepard's is the registered trademark of the Shepard's Company). Rather, the focus of their request is on the use of the trademark SHEPARD'S in connection with KeyCite, particularly when one attempts to access Shepard's, is told that KeyCite is available and is given the option of going directly to KeyCite with a link. Although the Plaintiffs have not expressly so stated, the Court concludes that they also object to the connective use of Shepard's and KeyCite on the initial screen, seen by the user upon signing onto Westlaw. . . .

What the Plaintiffs do not want is any type of Temporary Restraining Order, requiring West to alter the proprietary software that has been installed in users' computers.

3. Standards for Granting a Temporary Restraining Order . . .

Given that Temporary Restraining Orders are not normally appealable, there are very few cases which actually set forth the applicable standards for granting such relief. . . . [The] Court deems it appropriate to apply the familiar four-part test, applicable to motions for Preliminary Injunction, to determine whether to grant a Temporary Restraining Order. . . . Herein, a number of factors convinces this Court that, assuming the Plaintiffs are entitled to the requested relief, it is appropriate to grant a mandatory Temporary Restraining Order. . . .

4. Application of the four-part test

A. . . . Likelihood of Success on the Merits

With their motion, the Plaintiffs assert that the Defendant's continued use of the SHEPARD'S and other trademarks (i.e., SHEPARD'S PREVIEW) constitutes infringement in violation of §§ 32 and 43 of the Lanham Act, 15 U.S.C. §§ 1114 and 1125. Under those statutes, a person infringes upon another's trademark, when he uses it without consent in a manner which is likely to cause confusion. Although a District Court normally will apply an eight-part test to determine whether the plaintiff has established a likelihood of confusion, it is not necessary to apply that test in the instant case. In *U.S. Structures, Inc. v. J.P. Structures. Inc.,* 130 F.3d 1185, 1190 (6th Cir.1997), the Sixth Circuit held that the "continued, unauthorized use of an original trademark by one whose license has been terminated is sufficient to establish 'likelihood of confusion.'" Thus, the continued use of the SHEPARD'S and other trademarks by the Defendant, after its license had been terminated, in an effort to cause users of its services to utilize KeyCite when they have attempted to access a Shepard's service, is sufficient to establish likelihood of confusion.

However, not every use of another's trademark, even where there is a likelihood of confusion, constitutes infringement. Rather, under 15 U.S.C. §1115(b)(4), an alleged infringer has a defense even to an incontestable mark when "the use of the name, term, or device charged to be an infringement is a use, otherwise than as a mark, of the party's individual name in his own business, or of the individual name of anyone in privity with such party, or of a term or device which is descriptive of and used fairly and in good faith only to describe the goods or services of such party, or their geographic origin." This fair use defense is predicated upon the principle that no one should able to appropriate descriptive language by registering a trademark. In *Park 'N Fly, Inc. v. Dollar Park and Fly, Inc.,* 469 U.S. 189 (1985), the Supreme Court described §1115(b)(4) as allowing "the nontrademark use of descriptive terms used in an incontestable mark." *See also Cosmetically Sealed Industries, Inc. v. Chesebrough-Pond's USA Co.,* 125 F.3d 28, 30 (2nd Cir.1997) ("Fair use is a defense to liability under the Lanham Act even if a defendant's conduct would otherwise constitute infringement of another's trademark."). To prevail on the fair use defense, the defendant must establish that it has used the plaintiff's mark, in good faith, to describe its (defendant's) product and otherwise than as a trademark. *Sands, Taylor & Wood Co. v. Quaker Oats Co.,* 978 F.2d 947, 951 (7th Cir.1992). In *WCVB-TV v. Boston Athletic Ass'n,* 926 F.2d 42 (1st Cir.1991), then Chief Judge Breyer discussed the doctrine of fair use under trademark law, in a lawsuit in which it was alleged that a television station was infringing upon the trademark, "Boston Marathon," by televising the event and using that phrase to describe what it was televising:

> Third, and perhaps most importantly, the record provides us with an excellent reason for thinking that Channel 5's use of the words "Boston Marathon" would not confuse the typical Channel 5 viewer. That reason consists of the fact that those words do more than call attention to Channel 5's program; they also describe the event that Channel 5 will broadcast. Common sense suggests (consistent with the record here) that a viewer who sees those words flash upon the screen will believe simply that Channel 5 will show, or is showing, or has shown, the marathon, not that Channel 5 has some special approval from the BAA to do so. In technical trademark jargon, the use of words for descriptive purposes is called a "fair use," and the law usually permits it even if the words themselves also constitute a trademark. If, for example, a t-shirt maker placed the words "Pure Cotton" (instead of the words "Boston Marathon") on his t-shirts merely to describe the material

from which the shirts were made, not even a shirt maker who had a registered trademark called "Pure Cotton" could likely enjoin their sale.

Id. at 46.

With respect to the initial screen, the Defendant has not used the SHEPARD'S trademark in a trademark sense. Rather, Defendant merely informs the user that Shepard's is no longer available and that an alternative citator, KeyCite, *is* available. The use of Shepard's on that screen is analogous to comparative advertising (i.e., Coca Cola stating in an advertisement that Coke is better than Pepsi; although Pepsi's trademark is used, it does not constitute infringement). Indeed, in its letter brief, Defendant has cited a number of cases in which courts have stated that one party may use another's trademark in comparative advertising.

Defendant also uses the SHEPARD'S trademark, when a customer attempts to access that service either by pushing the "SH" button or clicking onto "Citator Services." Upon taking one of these actions, the user sees a message, telling him that Shepard's is no longer available, informing him about KeyCite and giving him the option of going directly to KeyCite by a link. Unlike the initial screen, that information is conveyed only after the user has attempted to access Shepard's. Using the SHEPARD'S trademark to direct the user to KeyCite does not constitute a fair use. Rather, it is analogous to cases in which courts have concluded that a defendant has infringed upon a plaintiff's trademark by using that trademark to direct customers to the defendant's product. For instance, in *Brookfield Communications, Inc. v. West Coast Entertainment Corp.,* 174 F.3d 1036 (9th Cir.1999), the Ninth Circuit held that the District Court had erroneously denied the plaintiff's requested Preliminary Injunction, preventing the defendant from using the plaintiff's trademark in a metatag of its web site (a metatag is a code which describes the contents of a web site), because using the plaintiff's trademark in that manner would have the effect of steering consumers who were using the Internet to that web site. The Ninth Circuit indicated that infringement would occur if the defendant were permitted to use the plaintiff's trademark to capture initial customer attention, even though the consumer did not purchase products from the defendant under the mistaken impression that he was purchasing the plaintiff's products. Herein, the Defendant is using the SHEPARD'S trademark to capture the consumers' attention and then directing them to its KeyCite service. There is no need for Plaintiffs to demonstrate that their customers were misled into using the Defendant's citator service.

Based upon the foregoing, the Court concludes that the Plaintiffs have established a strong or substantial likelihood of success on the merits of their claims under §§ 32 and 43 of the Lanham Act, with respect to the Defendant's use of the SHEPARD'S trademark, *in connection* with KeyCite and *after* a customer has attempted to access the Shepard's service. However, the Plaintiffs have failed to establish a likelihood of success on the merits, strong or otherwise, with respect to the use of the SHEPARD'S trademark, in connection with KeyCite, on the initial screen.

B. . . . Irreparable Harm if a Temporary Restraining Order Is Not Granted

Recently, the Sixth Circuit addressed irreparable harm in the context of trademark infringement, reiterating that "a court need only find that a defendant is liable for infringement or unfair competition for it to award injunctive relief." Therefore, it is not necessary for the Plaintiffs to present evidence that they will suffer irreparable harm, if the Defendant is not restrained from using the SHEPARD'S trademark, *in connection* with KeyCite and *after* a customer has attempted to access the Shepard's service, given that the Court has found that the Plaintiffs have established a strong or substantial likelihood of success on the merits of their claim that such use constitutes infringement. On the other hand, since the Court has concluded that the Plaintiffs have failed to establish a likelihood of success on the merits, strong or otherwise, with respect to the use of the SHEPARD'S trademark, in connection with KeyCite *on the initial screen,* it concludes that the Plaintiffs will not suffer irreparable injury if *that* activity is not restrained.

C. Whether the Issuance . . . Will Cause Substantial Harm to Others

With respect to the harm which the Defendant could suffer, the Court focuses exclusively upon the use of the SHEPARD'S trademark, *in connection* with KeyCite and *after* a customer has attempted to access the Shepard's service. Since the Court has concluded that the Plaintiffs have failed to demonstrate either a strong likelihood of success on the merits or irreparable injury, concerning the allegation that the use of the SHEPARD'S trademark, in connection with Key Cite on the initial screen, constitutes infringement, it will not restrain that activity, regardless of whether such restraint would cause the Defendant to suffer harm. In its letter brief, the Defendant asserts that it will be harmed, if restrained in the manner in which the Plaintiffs request. Although conceding that it could remove the allegedly infringing uses of the SHEPARD'S trademark from its computers in a relatively short period of time (less than five days) for a modest cost (less than $10,000), the Defendant contends that a restraining order will cause it great harm through the loss of customer goodwill. According to Defendant, customers pushing the "SH" button will not know what to do if they push that button and are merely told that Shepard's is no longer available. In addition, Defendant fears that it will have to hire 20 additional service representatives, for at least 60 days, to field the telephone calls from angry and frustrated customers who feel that they have been left in the lurch. The Defendant fears that it will cost $200,000 to hire the necessary representatives. The Court accepts that the Defendant will suffer some harm if the requested restraining order is granted. Nevertheless, given this Court's above conclusions, concerning Plaintiffs' strong likelihood of success on the merits and irreparable injury, balancing the harm the Defendant contends it will suffer against those factors causes the Court to conclude that the equities tip decidedly in favor of the Plaintiffs. A number of considerations support this conclusion. *First,* the Court will not restrain the Defendant from using the message on the initial screen, informing users that Shepard's is no longer available and that KeyCite is. Thus, every time a customer signs onto Westlaw, he or she will be told of the availability of Defendant's citator service, as a substitute for those of the Plaintiffs previously provided by the Defendant. Thus, Defendant ought not to need its covey of customer-soothing, additional representatives. While this will ameliorate any harm the Defendant will suffer if restrained, there is no way to lessen the Plaintiffs' harm, in the event that a Temporary Restraining Order is not granted. *Second,* as is explained below, the Court will not make its restraining order completely effective for a period of five days from date, to permit the Defendant time to remove the infringing uses of the SHEPARD'S trademark from its on-line services, websites and software, other than proprietary software current installed on users' computers. That additional period of time, when coupled with the almost two weeks during which the Defendant has continued to use that trademark in an infringing manner, will have afforded the Defendant more than two weeks, after its licenses were terminated, to have educated its customers about the availability of KeyCite as a substitute for Shepard's. *Third,* the Defendant has known, since November, 1998, that the Plaintiffs would not renew these licenses. Thus, the Defendant has had almost eight months to wean its customers from Shepard's to KeyCite. Indeed, according to the Defendant's letter brief, it has, since May 3, 1999, informed customers, pushing the "SH" button, that Shepard's would not be available after July 1, 1999, and that KeyCite was an alternative service.

D. Whether the Public Interest Will Be Served. . . .

The public interest favors competition, while, at the same time, supporting the enforcement of trademark laws in order to avoid confusion in the marketplace. Therefore, since the Plaintiffs have established a substantial likelihood of success on the merits on their contention that Defendant's continued use of the SHEPARD'S trademark, *in connection* with KeyCite and *after* a customer has attempted to access the Shepard's service, constitutes infringement, the public interest favors restraining that activity. On the other hand, since the Court has concluded that the Plaintiffs have failed to establish a likelihood of success on the merits, strong or otherwise, with respect to the use of the SHEPARD'S trademark, in connection with KeyCite on the initial screen, the public interest does not favor restraining that activity. . . .

In sum, the Court sustains in part and overrules in part the Plaintiffs' Motion for Temporary Restraining Order. . . .

NOTES

1. In *Xerox Corp. v. Hewlett-Packard Co.*, 63 F. Supp. 2d 1317 (D. Kan. 1999), the manufacturer of computer printers brought a contract action against the representative of a chip producer concerning a dispute over rights to chips used in the manufacture of printers after the chip manufacturer terminated the license agreement with the printer manufacturer. The court held that a printer manufacturer was entitled to a preliminary injunction prohibiting the representative from refusing to deliver 4000 chips that were already the subject of purchase orders. While termination appeared appropriate, the license provided that termination did not alter the right to distribute products already acquired. The court determined that this included those as to which a firm purchase order had been given and accepted.

2. In *SNA, Inc. v. Array*, 51 F. Supp. 2d 554, 559 (E.D. Pa. 1999), *j'mt aff'd*, 259 F.3d 717 (2001), Horizon had "a fiduciary responsibility not to duplicate or copy, or permit others to duplicate or copy any or all of the Seawind aircraft, part of the aircraft, accessories, options, drawings, instructions, printed matter or the like which shall all be designated as proper proprietary information." The court held: "Plaintiffs are entitled to have the molds returned to them. . . ."

PROBLEM 10.5

Carson gives a license to Pederson, under which Carson allows Pederson to use the Carson trademark on widgets manufactured and sold by Pederson. The contract provides for termination by either party "at will" on ninety days notice. Pederson manufactures 10,000 widgets per week under this agreement, selling each for $10, although some sales take four or five months.

On June 1, Carson sends Pederson notice that the agreement will terminate on September 15. When it receives the notice, Pederson has 15,000 Carson widgets in stock. On September 15, it has 18,000 widgets in stock. Without contacting Carson, Pederson sells the 18,000 widgets in the months following September 15.

Carson sues for breach of contract and trademark infringement. What result?

PROBLEM 10.6

Carson enters a copyright license with Pederson, under which Carson allows Pederson to copy, distribute and sell Carson's work in hardcover books. The contract provides for termination by either party "at will" on ninety days notice. Pederson creates 10,000 books per week, selling each for $40, although some sales take four or five months after the books are created.

On June 1, Carson sends Pederson notice that the agreement will terminate on September 15. When it receives the notice, Pederson has 15,000 books in stock. On September 15, it has 18,000 books. Without contacting Carson, Pederson sells the 18,000 books in the months following September 15.

Carson sues for breach of contract and infringement. What result?

IV.   FRANCHISE LICENSES AND TERMINATION

Most states and the federal government have enacted legislation to regulate franchise agreements. Some regulations impose disclosure rules, while others focus on the substance of the relationship, including when the franchisor may terminate or refuse to renew the franchise. A rationale for limiting the conditions under which the licensor (franchisor) can terminate the agreement is that the franchisee's investment requires protection against arbitrary termination. The following concerns a federal statute addressing these issues.

PDV MIDWEST REFINING, L.L.C. v. ARMADA OIL AND GAS CO.

305 F.3d 498 (6th Cir. 2002)

CLAY, CIRCUIT JUDGE.

Defendants Armada Oil & Gas Company, Inc. ("Armada"), Allie Berry, Ali K. Jawad, and Sam Haddas appeal the November 30, 2000 final judgment of the district court, after a bench trial, in favor of Plaintiffs, PDV Midwest Refining, L.L.C. ("PDV-MR") and CITGO Petroleum Corporation ("CITGO"), on Defendants' counterclaim against Plaintiffs for violations of the Petroleum Marketing Practices Act ("PMPA"), 15 U.S.C. § 2801, *et seq.* Specifically, Defendants contend that the district court erred in granting summary judgment in favor of Plaintiffs as to whether, under the PMPA, Plaintiffs' voluntary loss and/or sale of a trademark that Defendants had been granted a right to use constituted a valid reason for termination of the franchise relationship between Armada and a now defunct subsidiary of Plaintiffs' parent company. . . . For the reasons that follow, we AFFIRM the judgment of the district court.

BACKGROUND

[PDV-MR and CITGO] are subsidiaries of Petroleos de Venezuela, S.A. ("PDV"). In 1989, PDV and Unocal entered into a joint venture to form UNO-VEN. PDV and Unocal became 50 percent owners of UNO-VEN from 1989 until the two parent companies decided to restructure UNO-VEN in the late 1990s. Unocal brought marketing and a license to use the Union 76 trademark to the partnership, and PDV brought a fixed price crude oil supply agreement to the partnership. Pursuant to a trademark license agreement, UNO-VEN acquired the right to use the trademarks of its parent company Unocal.

In 1990, Armada entered into a contract with UNO-VEN to purchase Union 76 brand gasoline, which Armada then resold to independently owned gas stations. Armada became an UNO-VEN "jobber" which, as explained at trial, means essentially the same thing as marketer or distributor or franchisee. The agreement was renewed in 1995, and remained in effect throughout the relevant period of the UNO-VEN Armada relationship. The agreement . . . provided that UNO-VEN could terminate or non-renew its agreement with Armada for any reason permitted under the PMPA. . . .

On December 26, 1996, PDV and Unocal entered into a non-binding letter of intent ("LOI") regarding the restructuring of UNO-VEN. By its terms, the LOI was intended to provide a framework for continuing negotiations between the parties. It stated that the letter was "not intended to represent or constitute a binding agreement between, or commitment on the part of," either party, as "to the matters addressed" therein. . . .

During negotiations, PDV became aware that as part of its decision to exit the downstream segment of the industry, Unocal had sold its Union 76 trademark to another company, Tosco Corporation. . . . The restructuring of UNO-VEN was completed on April 11, 1997, pursuant to the Partnership Interest Retirement Agreement ("PIRA"). PDV acquired Unocal's 50 percent interest in

UNO-VEN. PDV-MR agreed to pay approximately $250 million to Unocal to acquire substantially all of UNO-VEN's marketing and refining assets. The PIRA provided that PDV-MR could designate a party to administer UNO-VEN's franchise agreements (such as the one UNO-VEN had with Defendant Armada). PDV-MR designated CITGO to oversee this administration. The April 11, 1997 agreement also entitled PDV-MR to use the Union 76 trademark for the 12-month period after the closing date of the transaction.

CITGO sent a letter to all UNO-VEN distributors, including Armada, dated April 18, 1997, which provided initial notice of the UNO-VEN/PDV-MR contract reached on April 11, 1997. That letter stated that after UNO-VEN's refining and marketing assets were transferred to PDV-MR, "there will be a twelve (12) month transition period during which CITGO has agreed to supply [Union 76] branded petroleum products to [Armada]." During this transition period, [Armada] will be able to continue to use the [Union 76] marks, and accept the Union 76 credit card. During this transition period, [Armada's] UNO-VEN agreements will continue in place. . . .

On April 30, 1997, UNO-VEN sent all Union 76-branded franchisees, including Armada, written notification of termination of the franchise relationship by certified mail, as required by the PMPA. . . .

DISCUSSION

. . . .

Congress enacted the PMPA in 1978 to create a uniform set of rules covering the grounds for termination and non-renewal of motor fuel marketing franchises, and "to protect 'franchisees from arbitrary or discriminatory termination or non-renewal of their franchises.'" Congress enacted the PMPA to allay three specific concerns: "[1] that franchisee independence may be undermined by the use of actual or threatened termination or nonrenewal to compel compliance with franchisor marketing policies; [2] that gross disparity of bargaining power may result in franchise agreements that amount to contracts of adhesion; and [3] that termination or nonrenewal may disrupt the reasonable expectations of the parties that the franchise relationship will be a continuing one." The "[m]ost important . . . thing the [PMPA] is intended to prevent is the appropriation of hard-earned good will that occurs when a franchisor arbitrarily takes over a business that the franchisee has turned into a successful going concern." Consistent with congressional intent, this Court "must grant the PMPA a liberal construction consistent with its overriding purpose to protect franchisees." To that end, "[t]he PMPA prohibits termination of any franchise agreement or non-renewal of any franchise relationship except on the basis of specifically enumerated grounds and upon compliance with certain notification requirements."

This Court has recognized, however, that in adopting the PMPA, Congress struck "an explicit statutory balance between the interest of franchisees in freedom from arbitrary and discriminatory franchise terminations and the interest of franchisors in freedom to transfer motor fuel marketing assets in response to changing marketing conditions." Thus, "although Congress . . . intended strong protection of the interest of franchisees[,] . . . in an age of increasing corporate competition, the major petroleum firms must retain the freedom to seek greater economic efficiency through corporate reorganizations, mergers and acquisitions." . . .

> With regard to the termination of franchises, § 2802(a) of the PMPA provides:

> Except as provided in subsection (b) of this section . . . , no franchisor engaged in the sale, consignment, or distribution of motor fuel in commerce may . . . (1) terminate any franchise . . . prior to the conclusion of the term, or the expiration date, stated in the franchise; or (2) fail to renew any franchise relationship. . . .

15 U.S.C. § 2802(a)(1)(2). Subsection (b) of § 2802 delineates some of the grounds for termination or non-renewal of a franchise relationship. That subsection states in pertinent part that a franchisor may terminate or fail to renew such a relationship if the following transpires:

> The occurrence of *an event which is relevant to the franchise relationship* and as a result of which termination of the franchise or nonrenewal of the franchise relationship is reasonable, if such event occurs during the period the franchise is in effect and the franchisor first acquired actual or constructive knowledge of such occurrence . . . (i) not more than 120 days prior to the date on which notification of termination or nonrenewal is given. . . .

15 U.S.C. § 2802(b)(2)(C)(i) (emphasis added).

Further, subsection 2802(c) lists 12 examples of events relevant to the franchise relationship that may form a proper basis for termination. That subsection provides in pertinent part:

> As used in subsection (b)(2)(C) of [§ 2802], "an event which is relevant to the franchise relationship and as a result of which termination of the franchise or nonrenewal of the franchise relationship is reasonable" includes events such as

> . . . .

> (6) loss of the franchisor's right to grant the right to use the trademark which is the subject of the franchise, unless such loss was due to trademark abuse, violation of Federal or State law, or other fault or negligence of the franchisor, which such abuse, violation, or other fault or negligence of the franchisor, is related to action taken in bad faith by the franchisor.

15 U.S.C. § 2802(c), (c)(6).

Although there are 12 specific grounds outlined under § 2802(c) upon which termination or non-renewal is proper, the statute itself makes clear that this list is not exclusive, but merely illustrative. Legislative history supports this view. Congress delegated to the courts the discretion to determine what events, other than those enumerated, constitute an event which is relevant to the franchise relationship as a result of which termination or non-renewal is reasonable.

Courts must carefully scrutinize the reasonableness of terminations whether or not the terminating event is specifically enumerated in § 2802(c). "[T]he grounds specified as justification for termination or nonrenewal of a franchise are intentionally broad enough to provide to franchisors the flexibility which may be needed to respond to changing market conditions . . . [but] not so broad as to deny franchisees meaningful protections from . . . discriminatory terminations. . . ."

A franchisor needs to provide only one valid reason for termination under the PMPA. Thus, notice of a legitimate ground for termination is not made ineffective by defective notice for additional grounds for termination. With that backdrop in mind, we turn to the various arguments raised in this appeal.

B. Whether Voluntary Loss of a Trademark May Justify Termination. . . .

Defendants first argue that the district court erred in granting summary judgment on the ground that Unocal's sale of its trademark constituted a "loss of the franchisor's right to grant the right to use the trademark," as defined in the PMPA.

In *Russo [v. Texaco, Inc.]*, 808 F.2d 221 [(2d Cir. 1986)], the Second Circuit squarely addressed this issue. In that case, the appellants claimed that Texaco, Inc. violated the PMPA when it terminated their franchises. Texaco decided to purchase certain assets of Getty Oil Company. Because of the size of the purchase, Texaco realized that it might face antitrust violations if it did not divest certain assets it had acquired. Therefore, Texaco agreed to sell to Power Test most of Getty's gasoline station assets and supply contracts, among other things, but Texaco was to have retained ownership of the "Getty" trademark. However, the Federal Trade Commission ("FTC") intervened in the Texaco Getty transaction, as the agency believed that "'[c]ontrol by Texaco of Getty's marketing operations is likely to reduce price competition in the gasoline and middle distillate marketing provided by Getty. . . .'" A final consent order required that Texaco divest in good faith its ownership of the Getty brand name and trademark. On March 4, 1985, Texaco informed Getty dealers (the appellants in that action) that their franchise relationships would be terminated pursuant to 15 U.S.C. § 2802(b)(2)(C) of the PMPA. Texaco asserted that the termination was based on the fact that it had lost the right to grant the use of the trademark that was the subject of the franchise. The appellants responded by arguing, among other things, that the word "loss" in § 2802(c)(6) "implies an involuntary loss of the right to grant the right to use a trademark and that Texaco's divestment of the 'Getty' trademark was voluntary." The Second Circuit rejected this argument. It found that "loss" as used in § 2802(c) intends to cover voluntary and involuntary situations. It looked to the PMPA's legislative history as well as to decisions from other circuits to reach its holding. . . .

Defendants urge this Court to reject the reasoning of *Russo* on several grounds, none of which we find persuasive. . . . After *Russo* was decided, the Eleventh Circuit also held that 15 U.S.C. § 2802(c)(4) "encompasses a franchisor's voluntary relinquishment of its lease." *Hutchens v. Eli Roberts Oil Co.*, 838 F.2d 1138, 1141 (11th Cir.1988). . . .

The Eleventh Circuit held that "in deciding whether the termination of a franchisor's underlying lease falls within section 2802(c)(4) the cause of the lease's termination is not determinative. Rather, we must be satisfied that the termination represents an arms length transaction. . . ." Thus, "[a]s long as the franchisor's decision to relinquish its lease is an arms length transaction in which it actually gives up control over the premises, it makes no difference whether the relinquishment is accomplished through *cancellation* of the lease or a decision not to renew it."

We believe that the district court did not err in finding that a loss of a trademark can be voluntary under the PMPA. [While] there is no text in the legislative history regarding whether "loss" of a trademark under § 2802(c)(6) may be voluntary as it pertains to a legitimate reason to terminate a franchise under § 2802(b)(2)(C), legislative history and the weight of judicial authority regarding "loss" of a lease under § 2802(c)(4) indicates that the loss under that provision may be voluntary or involuntary. Reading the word "loss" in the two subsections *in pari materia,* there is no reason why the same meaning should not be attributed to the word in both places. *United States v. Stauffer Chem. Co.,* 684 F.2d 1174, 1184 (6th Cir.1982) (holding that "[i]n interpreting the meaning of one provision of an act it is proper that all other provisions *in pari materia* also be considered"). In *Stauffer,* this Court reasoned that since the term "representative" appeared in two sections of the Clean Air Act that both dealt with inspections by the Environmental Protection Agency, and the meaning of the term was clear as to one of the sections, the term should be construed consistently in both sections. Such reasoning favors finding that the district court in the instant case did not err inasmuch as the word "loss" appears in § 2802(c) twice, and that section deals exclusively with events that are relevant to the franchise relationship and as a result of which termination or non-renewal of the franchise relationship is reasonable. Because the loss of a lease may be voluntary, so too may the loss of a trademark.

. . . Defendants further contend that whether voluntary or involuntary, the franchisor's right to grant the right to use a trademark cannot serve as a basis for the termination of a franchise where the loss of the trademark resulted from the fault or negligence and occurred as a result of bad faith on the part of the franchisor. Defendants contend that a fact question exists as to whether divestiture of the trademark rights in the present case was undertaken in good faith or merely taken to avoid the PMPA requirements. [Those] issues were not resolved until after trial.

C. Reasons Offered for Termination

. . . Plaintiffs argue that they provided Defendants with two valid reasons for their termination of the franchise, neither being withdrawal from the relevant market, and neither of which is pretext for what was really a withdrawal from the relevant market. Plaintiffs contend that their decision to end the franchise must stand or fall on at least one valid reason, and, more importantly, on the reasons for termination that they actually provided to Defendants.

[The] April 30 termination letter set forth two grounds for the termination: (1) that an event had occurred which is relevant to the franchise relationship and as a result of which termination of the franchise and non-renewal of the franchise relationship is reasonable, and (2) that UNO-VEN had lost the right to grant the use of the trademark which is the subject of the franchise. . . .

Pursuant to 15 U.S.C. § 2802(b)(2)(C), in order for notice of an event listed under § 2802(c) (such as notice regarding loss of a trademark) to be timely, the franchisor could not have acquired actual or constructive knowledge of the event that triggered the termination more than 120 days prior to the date on which notification of the termination was given. *Id.* Defendants contend that even if the loss of the trademark was the true reason for Armada's termination, it would not be a valid reason unless Unocal or UNO-VEN had actual or constructive knowledge of the loss of the trademark no more than 120 days before the official termination notice was issued on April 30, 1997. Defendants contend that Plaintiffs failed to meet their burden of showing that the Unocal sale of its trademark to Tosco occurred in March 1997, as the district court found. Defendants point out that Marty Sedlacek at his deposition stated that the trademark rights at issue were sold to Tosco months before the Letter of Intent was entered into on December 26, 1996. Further, Defendants point out that Thompson testified that PDV-MR's procuring the Union 76 logo was not discussed during any of the negotiations to which he was a party. However, Thompson never testified, as Defendants appear to contend, that Unocal had sold the Union 76 trademark or that he knew that Unocal had sold the trademark when the LOI was executed in December 1996. He testified that it was revealed at some point during the negotiation sessions that Unocal was in negotiations with Tosco to buy Unocal's West Coast refining marketing assets, and that PDV-MR found out about the sale sometime in March 1997.

The district court found as a matter of fact that on March 31, 1997, Unocal sold to Tosco the Union 76 trademarks along with all of Unocal's West Coast refining and marketing assets. . . . The district court found that termination was proper, pursuant to 15 U.S.C. § 2802(b)(2)(C), as a result of the UNO-VEN restructuring, and pursuant to § 2802(c)(6), as a result of the loss of the trademarks. The district court acknowledged that the reasons provided by Plaintiffs regarding the termination were related, but the court analyzed them separately.

As for the restructuring, the district court explained that under the PIRA, UNO-VEN's internal structure changed drastically. . . . The restructuring is not an *event* enumerated as a ground for termination under § 2802(c). Under this circuit's jurisprudence, even where the relevant event that occurs is enumerated under 15 U.S.C. § 2802(c), this Court must still "scrutinize the reasonableness of the termination." The district court scrutinized the reasonableness of the termination in the instant case to determine whether it was made in good faith and in the normal course of business. When considering whether a non-enumerated event constitutes a permissible basis for termination, courts generally determine whether one of the enumerated events is similar to an event actually listed under the Act. . . .

§ 2802(c)(6) explicitly states that loss of a trademark constitutes a permissible ground for termination. However, there are other sections under § 2802(c) that "involve situations where the occurrence of the event disables the franchisor from providing an essential element of the franchise [such as] 'loss of a franchisor's right to grant possession of the leased marketing premises through expiration of an underlying lease;' [or] 'condemnation . . . of the leased premises' . . . ." *Russo v. Texaco, Inc.,* 630 F.Supp. 682, 688 (E.D.N.Y.1986) (citations omitted). As the district court in *Russo* noted, these events suggest a sort of "involuntary loss of the right to franchise by the franchisor." *Id.* Whether the event that triggered the decision to terminate can be characterized as voluntary or involuntary, however, is not dispositive, as it is the reasonableness of the decision to terminate that is critical. § 2802(c); *Russo,* 630 F.Supp. at 688 ("Involuntariness is not . . . the *sine qua non* of reasonableness."). Further, as this Court has stated, although the PMPA's purpose is to regulate coercive relationships between franchisors and franchisees, and to protect franchisees from discriminatory and arbitrary practices, the PMPA struck a balance between those goals and "the interests of franchisors in freedom to transfer motor fuel marketing assets in response to changing marketing conditions." *May-Som [Gulf, Inc. v. Chevron U.S.A., Inc.*, 869 F.2d [917] at 921 [(6th Cir. 1989)]. This Court explained that the PMPA "constituted a diminution of the property rights of franchisors and thus should not be interpreted to reach beyond its original language and purpose." *Id.* (citing *Checkrite Petroleum, Inc. v. Amoco Oil Co.,* 678 F.2d 5, 8 (2d Cir.), *cert denied,* 459 U.S. 833 (1982)).

Further, this Court has noted that in balancing the competing interests of the PMPA "in an age of increasing corporate competition, the major petroleum firms must retain the freedom to seek greater economic efficiency through corporate reorganizations, mergers and acquisitions." This Court also explained:

> There is nothing in the language of the [PMPA] suggesting that a major national acquisition and large scale divestiture for bona fide business reasons was intended to be stymied by the right of individual franchisees to insist on a prior relationship on exactly its former terms. A permanent status quo in the relationships of major national oil corporations with each other was not mandated by Congress through the PMPA. In a rapidly changing economy fixed preservation of business relationships may spell financial death to the detriment of franchisees as well as franchisors.

In evaluating an economic business decision as it pertains to the PMPA, Congress cautioned against courts applying the business judgment rule, that is, whether a particular business decision was wise. Rather, courts should determine whether the business decision at issue was made in good faith, a subjective standard, and whether the determination was made in the normal course of business. "The good faith requirement looks to whether the franchisor's actions are designed to conceal selective discrimination against individual franchises, . . . but avoid[s] judicial scrutiny of the business judgment itself."

In the instant case, we agree with the district court that there is no evidence that the Unocal PDV transaction regarding UNO-VEN was conducted in anything other than good faith. The evidence showed that UNO-VEN had been an economic drain on PDV-MR because the partnership agreement contained a fixed margin provision whereby PDV had to supply UNO-VEN with crude oil at a price substantially below prevailing market prices. PDV had tried to buy out Unocal's share in UNO-VEN prior to 1996, but Unocal wanted too much money. Finally, in or around 1996, Unocal decided to exit the "downstream" segment of the oil industry, which involves the refining and marketing segment of the industry, and Unocal agreed to lower its asking price. PDV-MR paid approximately $250 million to purchase Unocal's share of UNO-VEN.

Further, as part of the restructuring, UNO-VEN's trademark license agreement was terminated. As part of Unocal's plan to exit the downstream segment of the business in an arms-length transaction, separate from the PDV Unocal deal, Unocal sold its rights to the Union 76 trademarks to Tosco. UNO-VEN's relinquishment of its trademark rights was an essential part of the overall transaction. *Cf. May-Som,* 869 F.2d at 921-22 (explaining that the PMPA does not require a large scale divestiture undertaken for *bona fide* business reasons to be stymied by the right of individual franchisees to insist on a prior franchise relationship on exactly its former terms). Defendants have failed to point to a shred of evidence that would establish that the sale of the trademark to Tosco and UNO-VEN's related loss of the trademark were undertaken in bad faith. *See Reyes v. Atlantic Richfield Co., ARCO,* 12 F.3d 1464, 1469-70 (9th Cir.1993) (explaining that once a franchisor shows that termination occurred for a valid reason under the PMPA, franchisee is entitled to present evidence to show that the termination was based on an illegitimate criterion). Likewise, other than speculation, Defendants have failed to show that Plaintiffs' restructuring was not conducted in good faith and for valid business reasons. *Id.* Therefore, we hold that the restructuring and loss of the trademarks constituted a valid and reasonable basis to terminate the franchise. *Cf. Russo,* 630 F.Supp. at 688 (holding that large scale divestiture of assets, including trademark rights, constituted a sufficient basis for termination of franchise under the PMPA). Inasmuch as only one valid reason is needed under the PMPA to terminate a franchise, Plaintiffs here, which have offered two, albeit related and intertwined, reasons for the termination, certainly have met their burden of showing that termination was proper.

D. Withdrawal from the Relevant Geographic Market

As explained earlier, Defendants also argue that the real reason Plaintiffs terminated their franchise relationship with Armada was because Plaintiffs intended to withdraw from the market and not, as Plaintiffs contend, as result of loss of the trademark and/or UNO-VEN restructuring. Defendants contend that they have produced evidence that the real reason for the termination was Unocal's decision to withdraw from the midwest market and that the specific notice requirements for such withdrawal were not met. Pursuant to 15 U.S.C. § 2802(b)(2)(E), termination is proper

> [i]n the case of any franchise entered into prior to June 19, 1978, and in the case of any franchise entered into or renewed on or after such date (the term of which is 3 years or longer, or with respect to which the franchisee was offered a term of 3 years or longer), a determination made by the franchisor in good faith and in the normal course of business to withdraw from the marketing of motor fuel through retail outlets in the relevant geographic market area in which the marketing premises are located, if (i) such determination — (I) was made after

the date such franchise was entered into or renewed, and (II) was based upon the occurrence of changes in relevant facts and circumstances after such date. . . .

Where the decision to terminate involves § 2802(b)(2)(E), a franchisor must meet the notice requirements set forth in § 2804(b)(2)(B), which means that they must "promptly provide a copy of such notification, together with a plan describing the schedule and conditions under which the franchisor will withdraw from the marketing of motor fuel through retail outlets in the relevant geographic area, to the Governor of each State which contains a portion of such area." . . .

Defendants also contend that the real reason for the alleged "withdrawal" was so that PDV-MR could allow CITGO to convert the UNO-VEN stations to CITGO stations. . . . However, even assuming Plaintiffs may have had other motives for extending the one-year period, that does not negate their legitimate reasons for terminating the franchise. In addition, one of the principal purposes of the Act is to prevent the appropriation of hard-earned good will that occurs when a franchisor arbitrarily takes over a business that the franchisee has turned into a successful going concern. Inasmuch as the stations that Plaintiffs took over were to be rebranded to other brands and CITGO did not intend to use the good will established with the Union 76 brand, Plaintiffs did not contravene the purposes of the PMPA in that regard. . . .

NOTES

1. Why is one party limited in its right to end a contractual relationship with the other? State laws vary widely in the degree to which they regulate the conditions under which non-renewal or termination can occur. The statutes often reflect a legislative mandate to protect the franchisee. *See, e.g.,* New Jersey Franchise Practices Act, N.J. Stat. § 56:10-5 (franchise may not be terminated, cancelled, or non-renewed "without good cause."); Ill. S.H. ch. 121½, ¶ 751 et seq. (prohibits arbitrary, bad faith or unconscionable conduct).

2. Franchisee protection laws also deal with other aspects of the relationship, including disclosure of the risks and conditions involved in the relationship.

CONSUMERS INTERNATIONAL, INC. v. SYSCO CORP.
951 P.2d 897 (Ariz. App. 1998)

Voss, Judge.

Plaintiff-Appellant Consumers International, Inc. (CI) appeals from the trial court's judgment in favor of Defendant-Appellee Sysco Corporation (Sysco) on CI's claim of wrongful termination of the parties' business relationship. . . . The sole issue on appeal is whether the implied covenant of good faith and fair dealing inherent in every contract requires that a termination-at-will clause in a distribution agreement be interpreted to require "good cause."

Because we conclude that the contract contained no such requirement, and that the trial court correctly entered summary judgment on this basis, we affirm.

Facts and Procedural History

The parties entered into a written "Master Distribution Agreement" on October 1, 1993. The agreement provided that Sysco would serve as supplier of at least eighty percent of the enumerated food service products that CI distributed to its retail customers. The products included both national brands and Sysco brands.

The agreement provided as follows regarding its duration:

9. Term

The term of this Agreement will begin on October 1, 1993, and terminate two years from that date. This Agreement may be terminated prior to such date.

> (a) By either party upon thirty (30) days written notice to the other party for failure of the other party to comply with any provision of this Agreement;

> (b) By SYSCO upon written notice to Customer if Customer's financial position deteriorates materially, determined by SYSCO in its sole judgment; and

> (c) By either party upon sixty (60) days prior written notice to the other party.

On December 13, 1993, Sysco sent the following termination letter to CI, indicating its sixty-day notice:

> This letter is to serve as notification to Consumers International that SYSCO Corporation, and its operating subsidiaries and divisions, is hereby terminating our Master Distribution Agreement with Consumers International.The Master Distribution Agreement will therefore terminate sixty days hence, being February 12, 1994.

In August 1995, CI brought this action against SYSCO, alleging, among other things, wrongful termination of the contract based on Sysco's breach of the implied covenant of good faith and fair dealing. CI contended that the agreement implicitly contained an "implied covenant that the right of termination would only be exercised in good faith." . . .

DISCUSSION

On appeal, CI contends that the implied covenant of good faith and fair dealing inherent in every contract mandates that early termination of a distribution agreement be restricted to reasons constituting "good cause." Because Sysco has not given any "good cause" reason for early termination of this contract, CI contends that summary judgment was inappropriate on its wrongful termination claim.

As a preliminary matter, we note that CI asserts that its relationship with Sysco is "akin" to that of a franchisee.[1] Much of the case law on which CI relies involves franchise relationships. We need not, however, determine whether this distribution agreement constituted a "franchise" to resolve this issue; even assuming, without deciding, that the business relationship at issue here was a franchise-type relationship, our conclusion would be the same.

CI contends that, because it is a small distributor and Sysco is a large supplier, the contractual relationship between them must be viewed as an unequal one, and that public policy therefore compels limiting enforcement of the broad termination clause to good cause. CI finds support for this argument in the common law of Arizona and other jurisdictions and in analogous Arizona statutory provisions relating to supplier/dealer relationships of oil companies and liquor suppliers.

We begin with the premise that, under general principles of contract law, absent statutory regulation, parties may freely contract for any lawful purposes, including franchise agreements for the distribution of products. Freedom to contract has long been considered a valuable right:

> [I]f there is one thing which more than another public policy requires it is that [people] of full age and competent understanding shall have the utmost liberty of contracting, and that their contracts when entered into freely and voluntarily shall be held sacred and shall be enforced by Courts of Justice. Therefore, you have this paramount public policy to consider — that you are not lightly to interfere with this freedom of contract.

Wood Motor Co. v. Nebel, 150 Tex. 86, 238 S.W.2d 181, 185 (1951).

This general rule has been modified by Arizona courts in some limited circumstances, however, when enforcement of contractual terms may be either unconscionable because of the unequal bargaining power of the parties, or contravene public policy.

The Arizona Legislature has also statutorily modified the freedom to contract in certain limited types of franchise relationships. Unlike many other states, however, our legislature has not statutorily regulated the termination of all franchise contracts.

We begin our analysis with an examination of the common law of other jurisdictions on the specific issue of franchise no-cause termination agreements, and then turn to existing general Arizona contract law to resolve this issue.

Other Jurisdictions

Many of the common law cases cited by CI in the area of "good-cause" termination developed in the 1970s during a shortage of oil supplies in the United

---

[1] [FN 2] The definition of "franchise" varies widely from state to state, and is not consistent throughout the case law cited by the parties. One important aspect that is consistent, however, is that a "franchise" is distinguished by "the distribution of goods or services under the trademark of the franchisor." See generally Erwin S. Barbre, J.D., Validity, Construction, and Effect of State Franchising Statute, 67 A.L.R.3d 1299, 1304 (1975 & Supp. Aug. 1997).

States. During that economic crisis, many courts began to limit the enforcement of contractual termination rights between large oil companies and their smaller retail dealers by construing distribution contracts to include an inherent requirement that the contract not be terminated except for "good cause." These courts based termination clause limitations on common law public policy concerns reflected in recent enactments of state legislation regulating either the petroleum industry specifically or franchise arrangements in general. For example, in [*Shell Oil Co. v.*] *Marinello,* [63 N.J. 402, 307 A.2d 598, 602 (N.J. 1973),] the court noted the New Jersey Legislature's recent enactment of the Franchise Practices Act, which "prohibits a franchisor from terminating, canceling or failing to renew a franchise without good cause which is defined as the failure by the franchisee to substantially comply with the requirements imposed on him by the franchise." Although the statute did not apply retroactively to the *Marinello* contract, the court found this legislative regulation to reflect the "public policy" of the state:

> [T]he Act reflects the legislative concern over long-standing abuses in the franchise relationship, particularly provisions giving the franchisor the right to terminate, cancel or fail to renew the franchise. To that extent the provisions of the Act merely put into statutory form the extant public policy of this State.

Thus, the court found void as against public policy a termination clause in a dealer agreement that gave Shell Oil Corporation the "absolute" right to terminate on ten days notice.

Similarly, other courts have concluded that when parties to a "chain-style" franchise agreement do not expressly provide for termination without cause, the contract is interpreted to include a "good cause" termination requirement. Courts have also refused to enforce unilateral termination provisions based on the supplier's sole judgment that the dealer has impaired the supplier's good will. Additionally, courts have found implicit in a franchise contract for a term of years the "reasonable expectation," under "principles of good faith and commercial reasonableness," that the supplier will not arbitrarily or summarily terminate the franchise agreement.

As more states enacted laws regulating these business relationships, including franchises, such distribution agreements were frequently interpreted to include a "good cause" requirement for termination, basically requiring some act of default or wrongdoing on the part of the franchisee to enable the franchisor to assert its termination power. *See generally* Timothy H. Fine, *Recent Developments in State Law Affecting Franchising,* 1980 ARIZ. ST. L.J. 547 (1980). However, some courts were careful to limit the application of the "good cause" termination requirement to situations containing the following factors: (1) the existence of a true franchise-type relationship, regardless of the name placed on it, because of the concern of the unequal bargaining powers of the parties in such a relationship, and (2) the non-existence of an explicit provision allowing termination without cause.

Not all jurisdictions followed this trend to imply a "good cause" termination requirement in a franchise contract. Some courts refused to equate "good cause" with "good faith," finding no breach of the covenant of good faith and fair dealing in a no-cause termination provided for by the explicit terms of the contract. *McDonald's Corp. v. Markim,* 209 Neb. 49, 306 N.W.2d 158, 163 (1981); *Witmer v. Exxon,* 394 A.2d at 1285; *Gianelli Distributing Co. v. Beck & Co.,* 172 Cal.App.3d 1020, 219 Cal.Rptr. 203, 209 (1985). In *Witmer,* for example, the court reasoned that the existence of a no-cause termination clause in a contract was relevant to determine the [*Atlantic Richfield v.*] *Razumic*[, 480 Pa. 366, 390 A.2d 736, 742 (Pa. 1978),] standards of good faith and commercial reasonableness to protect the "reasonable expectations" of the franchisee in maintaining his franchise:

> Where there is no explicit termination clause . . . , a franchisee indeed has a reasonable expectation that the relationship will not be terminated arbitrarily without cause. However, when the actions of the franchisor are within plain and explicit enabling clauses of the lease, we find it impossible to say that the reasonable expectations of the franchisee have been violated.

394 A.2d at 1285. Likewise, in *Gianelli,* the court concluded that the covenant of good faith and fair dealing did not require a good cause termination requirement be applied as a matter of law, for the following reasons:

> [C]ases carefully limit application of the covenant of good faith and fair dealing [to termination clauses] to situations in which there is a special relationship due to unequal bargaining power or a special element of reliance, whereas in an ordinary business contract where these special circumstances do not exist, we believe the covenant cannot be applied to specially protect one party by requiring cause for termination.

219 Cal.Rptr. at 209. See also Triangle Mining Co. v. Stauffer Chem. Co., 753 F.2d 734 (9th Cir.1985):

> [Courts] have implied a covenant of good faith in situations involving the termination of employment contracts, insurance contracts, and — sometimes — franchise or dealership arrangements. Where there exists no special element of reliance or unequal bargaining power, however, courts generally conclude that "[w]hen the right to terminate the contract is absolute under the clear wording of the agreement the motive of the party in terminating such an agreement is irrelevant to the question of whether the termination is effective."

Thus, the implied covenant of good faith and fair dealing "in and of itself" does not require "good cause" for termination of a franchise contract.

Other cases have refused to find franchise no-cause termination clauses either against public policy or unconscionable. A common thread in these cases is that an implied "good cause" requirement will not be imposed on a distribution agreement in situations where bargaining power exists for both parties, where the contract contains an explicit no-cause termination provision of which the parties were aware when entering the contract, or where no evidence of bad faith termination is otherwise established. As discussed below, all of those factors apply to the distribution agreement at issue in this case.

Arizona Common Law

Arizona has not adopted a franchise regulation act analogous to those relied on in the decisions of many other jurisdictions to reflect the public policy of the state. Rather, our legislature has seen fit to regulate termination of such business relationships only in the areas of petroleum and liquor distribution and automobile dealers and wreckers. We therefore need not engage in the "public policy" argument that other state courts have found compelling based on emerging legislation. We are also aware of the inherent dangers in declaring "public policy" in an area the legislature has not regulated. . . . We thus decline CI's invitation to find a "good cause" termination requirement in a franchise agreement as a matter of "public policy" based on the legislature's regulation in certain other industries. As the trial court aptly noted in this case, the legislature has regulated business relationships in the limited areas about which it was concerned; had it intended to include all franchise agreements within that statutory structure, it could have done so.

Instead, we look to Arizona common law as set forth in court decisions. In *Wagenseller* [*v. Scottsdale Memorial Hospital*, 147 Ariz. 370, 710 P.2d 1025 (1985)], our supreme court recognized a common law "public policy" exception to the termination at-will doctrine in an employment context, holding that an "at-will" employee may be fired for good cause or for no cause, "but not for bad cause — that which violates public policy." The court found Arizona's public policy "is articulated in our state's constitution and statutes, as embodiment of 'the public conscience of the people of this state,'" as well as in the decisions of our courts. The court limited the public policy exception to apply only in "at-will" situations, where the parties have not made any express agreement regarding the duration of the relationship.

The *Wagenseller* court rejected, however, the argument that the covenant of good faith and fair dealing that is implied in every contract prevents a "no cause" employment termination. Although "good faith" requires "that neither party do anything that will injure the rights of the other to receive the benefits of their agreement," it "does not create a duty for the employer to terminate the employee only for good cause," nor does it "protect the employee from a 'no-cause' termination."

We reject CI's argument on appeal that *Wagenseller* compels us to equate "good cause" with "good faith." The lack of a "good cause" for termination of the distribution agreement is not any evidence that Sysco wrongfully terminated the contract. . . . Based on *Wagenseller,* as well as the reasoning of the jurisdictions in other states, and absent any evidence of bad faith or violation of public policy in enforcing the termination clause, we conclude that Sysco was entitled to summary judgment in its favor on the wrongful termination claim.

CI also argues that summary judgment was inappropriate because a question of fact existed about CI's "reasonable expectation" that the termination clause would not be enforced except for a good cause, such as CI's "bankruptcy or some other unusual factor." CI contends that a reasonable juror could conclude that Sysco's representations induced this expectation, and that a limitation on the right to terminate thus became part of the contract. *See generally*

Darner Motor Sales, Inc. v. Universal Underwriters Ins. Co., 140 Ariz. 383, 682 P.2d 388 (1984).

In *Darner,* our supreme court held that an insurer could be estopped from enforcing a boilerplate exclusion of coverage that conflicted with the insured's reasonable expectation of coverage. The circumstances under which the expectation arose included the following:

1. The insured's expectation was induced by the words or conduct of the insurer or its agent.

2. The insurer or its agent included the limitation in the contract as a "boilerplate" provision, knowing or having reason to know that the insured would not have agreed to it had the insured known it was there.

3. The insured was unaware of the boilerplate exclusion.

4. The fact finder must find that the insured had no duty to read the policy.

Id. at 385-87. The *Darner* court adopted the "reasonable expectations" principle to "recognize the realities of the insurance business and the methods used in modern insurance practice," and to dispel the fictions that insureds actually "bargain" for the terms of their coverage, are aware of and understand the terms of their coverage, or have any power to eliminate boilerplate provisions in a standardized form.

We find this case distinguishable from both *Darner* and *Wagenseller* in many respects. First, this was a negotiated contract with CI represented by counsel. Second, it was entered into during a time when CI was also negotiating with another supplier; thus, CI did not have a complete lack of bargaining power. Third, the record is clear that it contained an explicit no-cause termination provision of which the parties were aware. . . . Fourth, the contract contains terms, of which CI admits it was aware, that would be inconsistent with what CI contends was its "reasonable expectation" that termination would not occur except for "good cause." The distribution agreement contains not only the "no cause" termination clause in paragraph 9(c), but it also contains a "good cause" termination clause in paragraph 9(a), which provides for termination by either party with thirty days notice for failure to comply with the agreement. For us to construe the "no cause" clause to mean nothing more than the "good cause" clause would render paragraph 9(c) superfluous. Furthermore, the agreement provides another "good cause" termination provision in paragraph 9(b), upon notice, for material deterioration of CI's financial position. This presumably is the termination clause that would be enforced in the event of CI's bankruptcy, not paragraph 9(c). Because of the inclusion of these two other distinct provisions for "good cause" termination, it would not be reasonable for CI to have "expectations" that paragraph 9(c) would only be enforced for circumstances limited to either its wrongdoing or its bankruptcy. Based on the explicit provisions in the agreement and CI's awareness and understanding of those provisions, therefore, *Darner* would not apply to create a fact issue of CI's reasonable expectations that would preclude summary judgment.

CONCLUSION

We conclude that, in the absence of a contrary contract provision or statutory regulation, a franchisor's enforcement of a "no-cause" termination clause need not be for "good cause." Bad faith cannot be evidenced in a distribution agreement simply from a "no cause" termination in accordance with the explicit terms of the contract. CI has failed to establish any "reasonable expectation" of an implied requirement of a "good cause" termination under the circumstances of this case. For the foregoing reason, the trial court properly entered summary judgment on the wrongful termination claim. AFFIRMED.

Chapter 11

ROYALTIES AND OTHER PAYMENT SYSTEMS

I. COMPENSATION AND ROYALTIES IN GENERAL

The compensation or pricing systems used in licensing employ a wide variety of formats. In many contexts, the licensor receives a single payment for a license. This is common in the software industry and in other contexts where the license is to an end user. In contrast, other license agreements, especially those in which the licensed information is to be used by the licensee for manufacturing, redistribution, or inclusion in other products, calculate the licensor's compensation in the form of a "royalty."

The term "royalty" is used in different ways in different industries and different agreements. Black's Law Dictionary, however, captures the most common meaning in licensing in the following definition:

> A payment made to an author or inventor for each copy of a work or article sold under a copyright or patent.

BLACK'S LAW DICTIONARY (8th ed. 2004) ("royalty").

As we shall see, cases sometimes broaden the idea of a "royalty" beyond this, but in general business parlance a reference to a "royalty" refers to payments that depend or vary on the productivity of use of licensed intellectual property. A royalty may be a fixed price per unit sold, a percentage of revenue/sales/income generated, or some other measure that suits the transaction. The rates or approach may vary over time as the licensee's utilization and success also changes.

However structured, a royalty allocates the risk of market or commercial failure and the advantages of market success of the licensed subject matter; it can also shape the economic incentives or disincentives that the licensee has in using the subject matter or other technology. Dealing with proper arrangement of these issues involves a number of business decisions. In general, compensation based on a royalty comprises three elements: 1) the base against which the royalty is computed, 2) the rate of royalty charged, and 3) the duration of the obligation. The following examples reflect different approaches that may be suitable (or not) depending on the commercial deal:

- "10% of the net profits from the public performance of the licensed motion picture during the term of this license"

- "10% of the gross profits from the public performance of the licensed motion picture during the term of this license"

- "$50.00 for every computer system sold that contains the licensed technology in operable form for use by the system purchaser"

- "$50.00 for each computer system sold whether or not the system contains an operable copy of the licensed technology"

- "3% of the sales price of widgets produced using the licensed technology"

- "3% of the net profits from all sales made by the licensee during the term of the license"

- "$50.00 for each copy of the licensed information authorized by the license, whether or not a copy is actually made or sold" (e.g., "$5 million for the right to make 100,000 copies of the software")

As a general principle, royalty arrangements involve pricing decisions left to the choice of the parties. Professor Dratler comments:

> Although the law places no general restriction on the magnitude of royalties, there are customary levels of royalty in many industries. These customary levels serve as a starting point (and sometimes an end point) for private bargaining, but of course they are subject to variation with business circumstances. . . .

JAY DRATLER, LICENSING OF INTELLECTUAL PROPERTY (1999).

Law generally leaves the details of the royalty to the market and the negotiations of the parties. But there are many contract interpretation issues: what did the parties mean when they provided for a royalty of "10% of net profits from the sale of copies"? In addition, there are case law themes that restrict the ability of parties to tailor a royalty arrangement to a particular context.

PROBLEM 11.1

A proposed license between Apex and IBC allows use of IBC's patented chemical coating process by Apex, a producer of electronic devices used in the engines of modern tractors. The royalty provision states: "Licensee shall pay to Licensor a royalty upon distribution of any Licensee product with which any of the products produced with the licensed technologies are bundled or incorporated (the 'Royalty-Bearing Product') equal to $2.50 per copy of Royalty-Bearing Product Distributed."

a. In reviewing this proposed license, what issues would you raise for consideration by the client (pick either Apex or IBC) that should be clarified? What clarification would you suggest?

b. Compare (a) to the following provision: "For each copy of a Licensee Product incorporating or distributed with the Covered Licensed Product or Licensed Technology that is Distributed [a defined term that will speak to distribution by the Licensee or others], Licensee shall pay to Licensor a royalty equal to five percent (5%) of the total amount invoiced by Licensee with respect to the Licensee Product, excluding taxes and delivery charges."

II. ROYALTY BASE ISSUES

There is an adage that states: "1% of something is better than 90% of nothing." As this shows, the base against which a royalty rate is computed shapes the economic return for the licensor and the obligation of the licensee. But there may be more involved in defining a royalty base than simply the money that is owed.

During the early 1990s, Microsoft Corporation used a variety of royalty formats in its agreements with licensees who integrated Microsoft software into the licensee's computer or other systems (often described as Original Equipment Manufacturers or OEM). Microsoft might be paid in any one of the following three ways:

- A per unit royalty for each computer sold (or produced) containing the Microsoft system

- A one time fee by the licensee for the right to repackage and distribute a stated number of copies of the software product

- A per unit fee charged for each computer sold regardless of whether it contains a copy of the Microsoft software

Assuming that each arrangement will produce roughly the same net return under the license to Microsoft, are there any reasons to favor one over the other? From the licensee (OEM) perspective, what are the different incentives or business considerations that might lead it to prefer one approach over another? As you think about these alternatives, you should be aware that in the early 1990s Microsoft entered into a consent decree under antitrust law under which it agreed to discontinue use of the third alternative in some cases. Can you see the reason for that result?

A.   Interpretation of the Royalty Base

ALLEN ARCHERY, INC. v. PRECISION SHOOTING EQUIPMENT, INC.
865 F.2d 896 (7th Cir. 1989)

WOOD, JR., CIRCUIT JUDGE.

This is a contract case arising out of a patent license granted by plaintiff-appellee Allen Archery, Inc. ("Allen") to defendant-appellant Precision Shooting Equipment ("Precision") and defendant Paul E. Shepley. The parties dispute the amount of royalties due Allen for the use by Precision of Allen's invention. . . .

I. FACTUAL BACKGROUND

On December 30, 1969, United States patent No. 3,486,495 entitled "Archery Bow with Draw Force Multiplying Attachments" was issued to Holless W. Allen. The patent was assigned to plaintiff-appellant Allen Archery, Inc. in 1973 and it expired in 1986. The patent relates to an archery bow known commonly to archers and the archery industry as the "compound bow."

The longbow or straight bow has been in existence for centuries and consists of a single piece of material with a single bowstring attached to the ends of the limbs. Another traditional bow, the recurve bow, is similar to the longbow, but its limbs curve forward at the tips where the bowstring is attached. The cross-bow is a weapon having a short bow known as a "prod." The prod is mounted crosswise at the end of a stock.

The compound bow system covered by Allen's patent employs rotatable pul-leys or cams and multiple-line lacing of the bowstring or cable to create com-pound leverage. The important advantage of the compound bow, as opposed to more conventional bows, is that the compound bow casts an arrow at greater speed with increased striking power while reducing the amount of force needed to draw the bow. . . . A compound bow comprises a handle section and a pair of limbs secured to the handle section. An eccentric wheel or cam is mounted on the end of each limb. A bowstring is trained around the wheels to present a central stretch and two end stretches. The central stretch includes a nocking point for receiving the nock or slotted tail of an arrow. The pulley wheels may be round or oval-shaped and are referred to as eccentrics since they are mounted off center in either case. *Id.*

The compound bow quickly became popular in archery circles. Within eight years of obtaining a patent, Allen had licensed virtually the entire archery industry. When the compound bow first appeared, all of the compound bows built under the licenses were modifications of the longbow or straight bow. Not until 1982 was a crossbow developed that used a compound bow prod.

. . . Pursuant to an agreement dated July 1, 1973, Shepley became a licensee under the patent. Precision . . . is a sublicensee under the patent pursuant to a sublicensing agreement with Shepley dated November 1, 1975. . . .

[The] disputes between Allen and Precision center on their differing inter-pretations of the licensing agreement. The agreement basically gives Precision a license to manufacture, use, and sell "bows embodying the inventions cov-ered" by the compound bow patent held by Allen. Precision had to pay royal-ties to Allen during the life of the agreement on each bow sold and on replacement parts. The royalty schedule provided that Precision pay a royalty of 5 1/2 percent of the net selling price on the first 31,000 bows sold during a one-year period and a 5 percent royalty on any other bows sold during that same one-year period. The agreement stipulates that:

> Licensor agrees that royalties are not to be paid on accessories such as stabilizers and sights and their mountings, bow quivers and fish reels, which are invoiced, billed or sold as separate items from the complete basic operable bow.

Although a number of issues were raised in the district court concerning the construction of the licensing agreement, only certain main points of dispute remain. Precision began manufacturing crossbows embodying the compound bow principle in 1982. Allen contends that the "complete basic operable bow" described in the licensing agreement includes both the stock and the prod of the crossbow. The Crossfire, Foxfire, and Spitfire crossbows, all manufactured and sold by Precision, utilize the compound principle. Precision argues that the "complete basic operable bow" is provided by the prod alone and that Allen is entitled to no royalties on the value of the stock. Precision notes that when a crossbow is shipped, the prod is not attached to the stock. Precision claims that the prod of the crossbow could be used as an operable bow. Precision values the prod alone at $75, an amount arrived at through a comparison with its regular bow line and also based on the manufacturing cost of the product.

The parties also dispute the definition of accessories that are exempted from the royalty obligation. Allen contends that the overdraw mechanism which is standard equipment on the Mach II model bow is not an accessory. An overdraw is a device that enables a bow to shoot a shorter-than-normal arrow. The overdraw uses a ledge mounted on the side of the bow handle to support the tip of the arrow. The tip of the arrow can then be supported behind the handle of the bow and does not need to project forward from the front of the bow as is usually the case. Precision claims that the overdraw is an accessory since the Mach II could be a "complete basic operable bow" without it. Allen also asserts that the special camouflage paint applied to some bows is part of the basic bow since it is invoiced and billed as part of the basic bow price. Precision states that the special paint is in reality sold separately and the royalty obligation does not apply. Precision also disputes the computation of royalties on sales made outside the United States. . . .

II. DISCUSSION

[The issues] revolve around the proper construction of the licensing agreement as it relates to crossbows and "accessories." *Richards v. Liquid Controls Corp.*, 26 Ill. App. 3d 111, 325 N.E.2d 775 (1975), sets out the method for construing contracts in Illinois:

> The primary objective is to give effect to the intention of the parties. This is to be determined solely from the language used in the executed agreement when there is not ambiguity, but a strict construction which reaches a different result from that intended by the parties should not be adopted. Previous agreements, negotiations and circumstances may be considered in finding the meaning of the words used and when there is an ambiguity, or when the language used is susceptible of more than one meaning, extrinsic evidence is admissible to show the meaning of the words used.

Precision asserts that the language of the licensing agreement is ambiguous and it disputes the meaning of such terms as "complete basic operable bow," "bows embodying the inventions covered by said patent," and "accessories . . . invoiced, billed, or sold as separate items." The district court found that the language used in the agreement was not ambiguous. The court stated that there was no evidence before it concerning prior negotiations or agreements that could be considered in determining the meaning of the terms.

Examining the issue of how crossbows fit under the term "complete basic operable bow," the district court found that Precision was obligated to pay royalties on the full sale price of any crossbow embodying the Allen compound bow invention. The court rejected Precision's contention that the prod and the stock could be separated for the purposes of computing royalties. Finding that the agreement was meant to cover all bows embodying the inventions, the court stated that the stock of a crossbow was an integral part of the bow, not a mere accessory. . . .

A review of the record indicates that the district court was correct in its determination that the entire sale price of a crossbow was subject to the royalty payment set forth in the licensing agreement. Precision, in paying royalties to Allen on its compound crossbow sales, had only paid royalties on the supposed value of the prod minus the stock. It unilaterally set this price at $75 per compound crossbow. Precision sold a large number of these compound crossbows, far more than its sales of conventional or noncompound crossbows. Each of these compound bows sold is marked with the Allen patent number.

It is strained logic to argue that because the prod can be separated from the stock, it can qualify as a "complete basic operable bow." In attempting to define those terms, we must find the "ordinary and usual connotation attributable to those words." While it may be possible for some people to fire an arrow from the prod minus the stock, it is clear that an ordinary user would not consider the prod on its own to be a complete bow. The owner's manual shipped with every crossbow clearly explains how the prod is to be mounted on the stock and drawn and shot only after it has been secured to the stock; nowhere is it suggested that the prod is operable as a separate unit. It is of no consequence that Precision did not manufacture crossbows at the time it obtained the license, since the agreement covers all bows embodying the patented principles, including those bows not yet designed or built. The district court's conclusion that royalties must be paid on the full sale price of the crossbows was correct.

The case of *Richards v. Liquid Controls Corp.,* 26 Ill. App. 3d 111, 325 N. E.2d 775 (1975), presents a very similar fact situation. Richards was an inventor who developed equipment to improve the control of fluids for industry. Richards assigned his patents to AMMCO Tools, which agreed to pay 5 percent of the net selling price of every Air Eliminator sold embodying the inventions acquired from Richards and 21/2 percent of other devices embodying those inventions. There was to be one payment on each complete device sold and no payments for repair or replacement parts. The dispute there, as here, centered on what constituted a complete device. The assignee argued that the royalty did not apply to any device attached to parts actually embodying the invention. In *Richards,* the court found that the term "complete device" meant the invention plus all other parts attached to it. The court refused to restrict royalty payments solely to the patented portion of the complete devices sold. Payments were due on the price of any complete device so long as the device contained or embodied one of the inventions.

Precision . . . argues that since the licensing agreement does not specifically detail how royalties should be apportioned for crossbows, overdraw mechanisms, and paint, the court should not include nonpatented elements in the determination of royalty obligations. Precision points to the case of *Velsicol Chemical Corp. v. Hooker Chemical Corp.,* 230 F. Supp. 998 (N.D. Ill. 1964), for the proposition that royalties should be computed in proportion to the use of the patented device. However, the Velsicol case involves a situation that in many ways is unique to the chemical industry. In Velsicol, the defendant's patented end product used the plaintiff's patented chlorendic as an ingredient.

Unlike the present case, Velsicol concerns products where both the component and the end product are patented by the respective parties. The proportionate use argument does not apply here where there is no issue of relative contribution between the parties. Precision also attempts to distinguish the Richards case by pointing out that it involved the assignment of a patent rather than the granting of a license, but this distinction does not change the Richards case's applicability to the present fact situation.

The lesson offered by the *Richards* case becomes more useful when we consider the question of whether the overdraw mechanism on the Mach II bow and the camouflage paint found on some bows qualify as accessories under the agreement. The district court found that they were not accessories within the meaning of the agreement and ordered that royalty payments be made on the full sale price of the bow including the overdraw and the camouflage paint. The district court emphasized the testimony of a Precision manager who stated that no accessories are attached to a bow when a bow is shipped. Working from that premise, the court determined that, since the overdraw mechanism and the camouflage paint were both attached to the bow when shipped, they could not be accessories.

While this proposition at first may seem to be an over-simplification, by looking closely at the licensing agreement, we conclude that the district court's finding that items attached to a bow cannot be accessories is correct. The licensing agreement provides that accessories will be excluded from royalty calculations if they are invoiced separately. Precision did not choose to invoice the paint jobs or the overdraw devices separately. It included them, as well as the crossbow stocks, in the invoice prices of the respective bows. This leads to the conclusion that they are part of the complete bow. Also, the agreement names items that it considers accessories, such as "stabilizers, sights, and their mountings, bow quivers, and fish reels." These items are all clearly separable from the "complete basic operable bow." Camouflage paint and overdraw mechanisms are not separable items and should not be considered as accessories. . . .

NOTES

1. The agreement in *Allen Archery,* as interpreted by the court, results in the licensor obtaining income from a royalty base that extends beyond the scope of the licensed patent. What is the business rationale for such arrangements? If a company holds a copyright on the virus screening software it licenses to the manufacturer of a computer system, would it be appropriate to charge royalties based on "all computer systems sold" or should the royalties be limited to "each copy of the software made and distributed as part of a computer system"? As we shall see, legal considerations may limit the use of an expanded royalty base in some cases, but expanded base arrangements are common in some industries.

2. Does an expanded royalty base necessarily mean a higher economic return to the licensor? To understand why it does not, ask yourself what fixed rate or percentage royalty would be appropriate in the two software illustrations set out in Note 1. Assuming the parties desired to make roughly the same business deal and viewed the royalty base as a matter of convenience, would the royalty rate be the same in each illustration?

PROBLEM 11.2

Tangle has a license to "manufacture and sell Post's patented cardboard folding machine." Paragraph 4 of the license provides that Tangle will pay a royalty of 3% of the retail sale price of all "machines covered by this license and any improvements thereon." During the negotiations, the parties discussed the fact that Tangle maintains a leading research center on machinery of this type and frequently achieves advances that often qualify for patents. Post, in contrast, is primarily a manufacturer and marketing company, although it does some research.

During the second year of the ten-year license, Post's engineers discover a modification of the machines that enables more efficient operations. Post begins to sell the modified machines as "Tangle-2," and this model quickly dominates the market. Tangle-2 machines sell retail for $100,000. Tangle-1 machines remain available for their original retail price of $60,000. Post sells 10,000 Tangle-2 machines during the year. It remits a royalty check of $12,000,000 to Tangle. Tangle sues, claiming that it is owed $30,000,000. What result?

PROBLEM 11.3

Pacific is licensed to manufacture and sell cable made with a particular metal composition and covered by a patent held by XC. Royalties are "$2 per running foot of all cable produced." Pacific uses two different manufacturing processes to produce cable with the same metal composition as the XC cable. One type, which is produced by a process different from that used by XC, also has slightly different levels of heat resistance. Pacific produces 100,000 running feet of each type of cable. How much does it owe to XC?

B.J. THOMAS v. GUSTO RECORDS, INC.
939 F.2d 395 (6th Cir. 1991)

MARTIN, JR., CIRCUIT JUDGE.

All the plaintiffs in this diversity action, except for Vernon McFadden who is the widower and personal representative of Addie Harris McFadden, have the unusual status of being successful popular musicians. They brought suit against Gusto Records, Inc. and G.M.L., Inc. in this Tennessee diversity action seeking royalties from the use of master recordings of their songs. Essentially, this is a breach of contract action. The case was tried without a jury and the district court awarded the plaintiffs a total of $843,209.89 plus prejudgment interest for failure to pay royalties due. Gusto and G.M.L. have appealed this judgment. The defendants do not dispute they are liable; they merely contend the amount owed is far less than the amount awarded by the district court. For the reasons which follow, we affirm.

. . . B.J. Thomas is most famous for his recording of the theme song for the movie "Butch Cassidy and the Sundance Kid" . . . . Among his accolades are eleven gold records, two platinum albums, and five Grammy awards. Shirley Owens Alston, Doris Coley Jackson, Beverly Lee and Addie Harris McFadden, [are] members of a singing group known as the Shirelles. . . . Among their accolades are twelve top ten hits, including two number ones. . . . Gene Pitney's most successful song . . . reached number two on the popular charts in 1962. Pitney was especially successful singing movie theme songs, "A Town Without Pity" and "(The Man Who Shot) Liberty Valance," and writing songs for other popular stars. . . .

As the district court aptly noted, record companies transferred the master recordings of the plaintiffs' songs through "mesne conveyances," until G.M.L. purchased them in the mid-1980's. G.M.L. owned the masters, while Gusto sold copies of them for the retail trade. . . . Gusto and G.M.L. concede that an owner of the master recordings incurs any royalty obligations that arise during its ownership. Defendants make this concession after having profited throughout most of the 1980's from sales and licensure of the plaintiffs' masters without much regard to this obligation. In fact, this stance of neglecting the plaintiffs' rights was consistent with most record companies who owned the plaintiffs' master recordings through much of the 1970's and throughout the 1980's.

The district court found . . . that Pitney should recover $187,762.44 plus interest, that Thomas should recover $177,299.77 plus interest, and that each member of the Shirelles should recover $119,537.07 plus interest. In reaching these amounts the district court accepted, with minor exceptions, the plaintiffs' expert's testimony on custom and usage in the music industry. Most importantly, the court accepted his testimony that, absent a contractual provision to the contrary, the musician receives half of the fees received from licensing the masters to unaffiliated third parties. The trial court's decision was also based in large part upon the unseemly record keeping practices of Gusto, which forever prevent an exact determination of royalties earned by the plaintiffs. Gusto and G.M.L. timely filed this appeal.

The defendants assert the trial court erred on numerous grounds. First, they argue that clear language in the contracts of B.J. Thomas and the Shirelles prevents the consideration of evidence concerning industry custom and practice in determining royalties from domestic licensing. Thomas and the Shirelles entered into contracts with Scepter Records, Inc. in 1968 and 1961, respectively. The provisions of the two contracts in question are identical, except as to the royalty rate, and provide the following:

> 4. For the rights herein granted and the service to be rendered by you we shall pay you as royalty a sum equal to [4% for the Shirelles] [5% for Thomas] of the net retail list price in the United States of America based on 90% of all double-faced records manufactured and sold by us and paid for, on both faces of which are embodied only the selections

recorded hereunder; and one-half of the respective amounts of such royalties of 90% of all records manufactured and sold by us and paid for on only one face of which are embodied only the selections recorded hereunder. In the case of phonograph records and other copies manufactured and sold in foreign countries by any subsidiary, affiliate, licensee or nominees to whom we have supplied a copy or duplicate of a master or matrix or tape of any such recordings, we will pay you one-half of the United States of America royalty rate out of all net license fees paid and received by us for phonograph records and other copies so manufactured and sold.

. . . .

8. All recordings and all records and reproductions made therefrom together with the performances embodied therein, shall be entirely our property, free of any claims whatsoever by you or any person deriving any rights or interest from you. Without limitation of the foregoing, we shall have the right to make phonograph records, tape recordings or other reproductions of the performances embodied in such recordings by any method now or hereafter known, and to sell and deal in the same under any trade mark or trade names or labels designated by us, or we may at our election refrain therefrom. . . .

Gusto and G.M.L. assert that paragraph four is unambiguous with regard to royalties from domestic licensing, arguing that the "obvious implication" of silence on the issue is that the parties agreed there would be no such royalties. We do not find that implication so obvious.

Both parties agree that New York law should be applied to resolve this issue. The resolution of any ambiguity in a written contract is to be determined by the court as a matter of law. Not only are these contracts silent on many issues, e.g. domestic licensing royalties, many of the provisions which the contracts do set forth are perfectly obscure. Paragraph eight of both contracts, for example, if read independently, could be interpreted as a provision in which Thomas and the Shirelles signed away any and all rights. Indeed, the defendants assert this is what the paragraph means with respect to royalties from domestic licensing. Without an integration clause or more evidence in the documents supporting this harsh interpretation, we cannot accept this reading of the contracts. Because of the ambiguities in these contracts, we believe the district court properly looked beyond the written contract to determine the true intentions of the parties.

New York cases have consistently held that custom may be used to clarify ambiguities or to "fill gaps" in an agreement. Gusto asserts these cases are inapposite because custom and practice cannot be used to contradict the express terms of the contracts. The problem with this argument is that the contracts in question are silent with respect to royalties from domestic licensing; there are no express terms in the contracts explaining the parties' intentions on this issue. Paragraph 4 sets forth the royalty rate on the record company's own sales and on *foreign* sales by "any subsidiary, affiliate, licensee or nominee[]. . . ." Paragraph 8 merely establishes the record company's title free of any claim to ownership by the artists. Because no provision in the contracts of B.J. Thomas or the Shirelles pertains to royalties from domestic licensing income which could be contradicted by incorporating into the contracts the custom in the music industry with respect to that issue, the district court properly accepted the fifty percent royalty rate as the rate intended by the parties.

Gusto and G.M.L. next argue that the district court incorrectly calculated the royalty rate for foreign license income. They assert that the royalty rate designated for foreign sales by "subsidiar[ies], affiliate[s], licensee[s], or nominees" set forth in paragraph four dictates a much lower rate than the fifty percent rate used by the district court. The clause in question provides a royalty rate based upon recordings manufactured and sold outside the United States "by any subsidiary, affiliate, licensee, or nominees to whom [the master's owner has] supplied a copy or duplicate of a master. . . ." The defendants rely upon the use of the term licensee, arguing that it should apply to all licensing arrangements the owner of the masters engages in.

These arguments fail for three reasons. First, as the record reflects, many licensing contracts include fixed fee payments to the owner of the masters. Attempting to compute an artist's royalty payment in such an instance with the formula set forth in paragraph four does not make sense. One of the three variables used in the formula is based upon the "retail list price" of the record sold, another is based upon the volume of records sold. Neither of these variables would be helpful in computing a royalty when the payment involved is a fixed fee for use of a master, unless the licensee is using the master recording to copy for the retail music record industry and the licensee gives the owner of the masters, the licensor, data on the volume of records sold. Reviewing this record, we believe such a combination would be unlikely except when the licensee has some business relationship with the owner of the masters. This takes us to our second point.

The contract and the term "licensee" can be reasonably interpreted, without creating any internal inconsistencies or illogical conclusions, when we view the clause in question in its entirety. The term "licensee" is found in the paragraph where the formula for royalties from retail sales is set forth. It is the third word in a series of four; we read "licensee" as being of a similar kind to the other words in the series: "subsidiary," "affiliate," and "nominee," the term "licensee" is used in paragraph four to describe an entity having some business relationship connecting it with the owner of the masters, not an independent entity acting for its own profit.

G.M.L. and Gusto provide just such an example of connected entities. Owned and operated by the same individual, G.M.L. owns the master recordings, while Gusto is in the business of manufacturing and marketing copies of those recordings. By reading paragraph four in its entirety, we see that it was designed to include the royalty rate for this type of relationship and that the parties did not set forth a royalty rate for the foreign licensing income at issue.

The final problem with the defendants' argument is the fact that the artists received royalties at a rate of fifty percent on foreign licensing income in the past. The prior construction of a contract by the parties before the contract became the subject of this controversy is a prominent factor in determining the meaning of the contract. That neither Gusto nor G.M.L. were parties to the contract at the time the fifty percent royalty rate payments were made is of little assistance to their argument. As Gusto and G.M.L. concede, their purchase of the master recordings created an obligation to pay the royalties to the artists on those masters. Looking to the construction of the ambiguous contracts by prior owners of the masters helps in determining the obligation. Together these three factors, the results from applying the royalty formula set forth to typical licensing payments; the entire structure of paragraph four; and the past construction of the contract, convince us that the district court properly accepted fifty percent as the royalty rate for the foreign license income at issue in the Thomas and Shirelles contracts. . . .

Gusto and G.M.L. also argue the district court erred in finding them liable for royalties incurred by the prior owners of the masters. . . . The determination of whether Gusto and G.M.L. are liable for royalties owed by the prior owner of the masters, Koala Records, is not determined by looking to the contracts between the plaintiffs and the original owners. Rather, we must look to the agreements between the defendants and Koala. The issue is: what did Koala sell to Gusto and G.M.L.? Did their sale of the master recordings include the transfer of royalty obligations incurred but not yet paid? [Tennessee law governs this issue.] We believe Tennessee would probably follow the general rule that a corporation purchasing the assets of another does not assume liabilities unless one of three exceptions is met: an express or implied assumption as to liability, consolidation, merger, or other similar connection between the two companies, or fraud in the transfer between the companies.

The objective facts set forth in the record support the conclusion that there was an assumption in this case that G.M.L. and Gusto would accept Koala's liability. Among other things, the defendants claimed the rights to royalties earned before the date of sale, March 6, 1984, and the right to charge expenses of prior owners against the plaintiffs' royalties. The implication of such broad rights is that Koala's sale included much more than the mere sale of the master recordings. Indeed, viewed in the light most favorable to the plaintiff, the defendants' own expert explicitly testified that Koala's sale and Gusto's purchase included Gusto's obligation to assume the payment of accrued but unpaid royalties. We do not believe the district court committed a clear error by finding Gusto and G.M.L. liable for royalties owed by the prior owner of the masters. . . .

AFFIRMED

NOTES

1. Black's Law Dictionary defines "mesne" as: "Occupying a middle position; intermediate or intervening, esp. in time of occurrence or performance (the mesne encumbrance has priority over the third mortgage, but is subordinate to the first mortgage). . . ." BLACK'S LAW DICTIONARY (2004).

2. *Gusto Records*, besides providing an insight into business practices in an industry, shows the importance of trade use and business practice in formulating the terms of a license. If the parties had wanted to exclude trade use evidence, would a simple "merger clause" excluding the existence of any representations or promises outside the written agreement suffice? If not, what would be necessary to avoid being bound by the business practice evidence that was crucial in this case?

B.   Legal Risks in Using an Expanded Base

ZENITH RADIO CORP. v. HAZELTINE RESEARCH, INC.
395 U.S. 100 (1969)

MR. JUSTICE WHITE.

Petitioner Zenith Radio Corporation (Zenith) is a Delaware Corporation which for many years has been successfully engaged in the business of manufacturing radio and television sets for sale in the United States and foreign countries. A necessary incident of Zenith's operations has been the acquisition of licenses to use patented devices in the radios and televisions it manufactures, and its transactions have included licensing agreements with respondent Hazeltine Research, Inc. (HRI), an Illinois corporation which owns and licenses domestic patents, principally in the radio and television fields. HRI is the wholly owned subsidiary of respondent Hazeltine Corporation (Hazeltine), a substantially larger and more diversified company that has among its assets numerous foreign patents — including the foreign counterparts of HRI's domestic patents — which it licenses for use in foreign countries.

Until 1959, Zenith had obtained the right to use all HRI domestic patents under HRI's so-called standard package license. In that year, however, with the expiration of Zenith's license imminent, Zenith declined to accept HRI's offer to renew, asserting that it no longer required a license from HRI. Negotiations proceeded to a stalemate, and in November 1959, HRI brought suit in the Northern District of Illinois, claiming that Zenith television sets infringed HRI's patents on a particular automatic control system. Zenith's answer alleged invalidity of the patent asserted and noninfringement, and further alleged that HRI's claim was unenforceable because of patent misuse as well as unclean hands through conspiracy with foreign patent pools. On May 22, 1963, more than three years after its answer had been filed, Zenith filed a counterclaim against HRI for treble damages and injunctive relief, alleging violations of the Sherman Act by misuse of HRI patents, including the one in suit, as well as by conspiracy among HRI, Hazeltine, and patent pools in Canada, England, and Australia. Zenith contended that these three patent pools had refused to license the patents placed within their exclusive licensing authority, including Hazeltine patents to Zenith and others seeking to export American-made radios and televisions into those foreign markets.

The District Court, sitting without a jury, ruled for Zenith in the infringement action. . . . On the counterclaim, the District Court ruled, first that HRI had misused its domestic patents by attempting to coerce Zenith's acceptance of a five-year package license, and by insisting on extracting royalties from unpatented products. Judgment was entered in Zenith's favor. . . . Second, HRI and Hazeltine were found to have conspired with the foreign patent pools to exclude Zenith from the Canadian, English, and Australian markets. Hazeltine had granted the pools the exclusive right to license Hazeltine patents in their respective countries and had shared in the pools' profits, knowing that each pool refused to license its patents for importation and that each enforced its ban on imports with threats of infringement suits. HRI, along with its coconspirator, Hazeltine, was therefore held to have conspired with the pools to restrain the trade or commerce of the United States, in violation of § 1 of the Sherman Act. . . .

On appeal by HRI and Hazeltine, the Court of Appeals set aside entirely the judgments for damages and injunctive relief entered against Hazeltine, ruling that the District Court lacked jurisdiction over that company and that the stipulation relied upon by the District Court was an insufficient basis for entering judgment against Hazeltine. With respect to Zenith's patent misuse claim, the Court of Appeals affirmed the treble-damage award against HRI, but modified in certain respects the District Court's injunction against further misuse. . . .

We granted certiorari. . . .

III. THE PATENT-MISUSE ISSUE

[The] only misuse issue we need consider at length is whether the Court of Appeals was correct in striking the last clause from Paragraph A of the injunction,[1] which enjoined HRI from

> A. Conditioning directly or indirectly the grant of a license to defendant-counterclaimant, Zenith Radio Corporation, or any of its subsidiaries, under any domestic patent upon the taking of a license under any other patent or upon the paying of royalties on the manufacture, use or sale of apparatus not covered by such patent.

This paragraph of the injunction was directed at HRI's policy of insisting upon acceptance of its standard five-year package license agreement, covering the 500-odd patents within its domestic licensing portfolio and reserving royalties of the licensee's total radio and television sales, irrespective of whether the licensed patents were actually used in the products manufactured.

In striking the last clause of Paragraph A the Court of Appeals, in effect, made two determinations. First, under its view of *Automatic Radio Mfg. Co. v. Hazeltine Research, Inc.*, 339 U.S. 827 (1950), conditioning the grant of a pat-

---

[1] [FN 2] The District Court's injunction also included a paragraph barring HRI from continuing to coerce acceptance of its package license through the mechanism of offering a much lower royalty rate for those licensees who take a license on the entire package of patents rather than a license on merely a few of them. Paragraph B enjoined HRI from "Conditioning directly or indirectly the grant of any license to defendant-counterclaimant, Zenith Radio Corporation, or any of its subsidiaries, under any domestic patent upon the payment of the same or greater royalty rate than the rate at which licenses have been granted or offered to others under a group of domestic patents which includes said patent." The Court of Appeals modified this paragraph in certain respects, but we do not disturb these modifications.

ent license upon payment of royalties on unpatented products was not misuse of the patent. Second, since such conduct did not constitute patent misuse, neither could it be violative of the antitrust laws within the meaning of § 16 of the Clayton Act, under which Zenith had sought and the District Court had granted the injunction. With respect to the first determination, we reverse the Court of Appeals. We hold that conditioning the grant of a patent license upon payment of royalties on products which do not use the teaching of the patent does amount to patent misuse.

The trial court's injunction does not purport to prevent the parties from serving their mutual convenience by basing royalties on the sale of all radios and television sets, irrespective of the use of HRI's inventions. The injunction reaches only situations where the patentee directly or indirectly "conditions" his license upon the payment of royalties on unpatented products — that is, where the patentee refuses to license on any other basis and leaves the licensee with the choice between a license so providing and no license at all. Also, the injunction takes effect only if the license is conditioned upon the payment of royalties "on" merchandise not covered by the patent — where the express provisions of the license or their necessary effect is to employ the patent monopoly to collect royalties, not for the use of the licensed invention, but for using, making, or selling an article not within the reach of the patent.

A patentee has the exclusive right to manufacture, use, and sell his invention. The heart of his legal monopoly is the right to invoke the State's power to prevent others from utilizing his discovery without his consent. The law also recognizes that he may assign to another his patent, in whole or in part, and may license others to practice his invention. But there are established limits which the patentee must not exceed in employing the leverage of his patent to control or limit the operations of the licensee. Among other restrictions upon him, he may not condition the right to use his patent on the licensee's agreement to purchase, use, or sell, or not to purchase, use, or sell, another article of commerce not within the scope of his patent monopoly. His right to set the price for a license does not extend so far, whatever privilege he has "to exact royalties as high as he can negotiate." And just as the patent's leverage may not be used to extract from the licensee a commitment to purchase, use, or sell other products according to the desires of the patentee, neither can that leverage be used to garner as royalties a percentage share of the licensee's receipts from sales of other products; in either case, the patentee seeks to extend the monopoly of his patent to derive a benefit not attributable to use of the patent's teachings.

In *Brulotte v. Thys Co.,* [379 U.S. 29, 33 (1964),] the patentee licensed the use of a patented machine, the license providing for the payment of a royalty for using the invention after, as well as before, the expiration date of the patent. Recognizing that the patentee could lawfully charge a royalty for practicing a patented invention prior to its expiration date and that the payment of this royalty could be postponed beyond that time, we noted that the post-expiration royalties were not for prior use but for current use, and were nothing less than an effort by the patentee to extend the term of his monopoly beyond that granted by law. *Brulotte* thus articulated in a particularized context the principle that a patentee may not use the power of his patent to levy a charge for making, using, or selling products not within the reach of the monopoly granted by the Government.

Automatic Radio is not to the contrary; it is not authority for the proposition that patentees have carte blanche authority to condition the grant of patent licenses upon the payment of royalties on unpatented articles. In that case, Automatic Radio acquired the privilege of using all present and future HRI patents by promising to pay a percentage royalty based on the selling price of its radio receivers, with a minimum royalty of $10,000 per year. HRI sued for the minimum royalty and other sums. Automatic Radio asserted patent misuse in that the agreement extracted royalties whether or not any of the patents were in any way used in Automatic Radio receivers. The District Court and the Court of Appeals approved the agreement as a convenient method designed by the parties to avoid determining whether each radio receiver embodied an HRI patent. The percentage royalty was deemed an acceptable alternative to a lump-sum payment for the privilege to use the patents. This Court affirmed.

Finding the tie-in cases such as *International Salt Co. v. United States*, 332 U.S. 392 (1947), . . . the Court considered reasonable the "payment of royalties according to an agreed percentage of the licensee's sales," since "[s]ound business judgment could indicate that such payment represents the most convenient method of fixing the business value of the privileges granted by the licensing agreement." It found nothing "inherent" in such a royalty provision which would extend the patent monopoly. Finally, the holding by the Court was stated to be that in licensing the use of patents "it is not per se a misuse of patents to measure the consideration by a percentage of the licensee's sales."

Nothing in the foregoing is inconsistent with the District Court's injunction against conditioning a license upon the payment of royalties on unpatented products or with the principle that patent leverage may not be employed to collect royalties for producing merchandise not employing the patented invention. The Court's opinion in *Automatic Radio* did not deal with the license negotiations which spawned the royalty formula at issue and did not indicate that HRI used its patent leverage to coerce a promise to pay royalties on radios not practicing the learning of the patent. No such inference follows from a mere license provision measuring royalties by the licensee's total sales even if, as things work out, only some or none of the merchandise employs the patented idea or process, or even if it was foreseeable that some undetermined portion would not contain the invention. It could easily be, as the Court indicated in *Automatic Radio*, that the licensee as well as the patentee would find it more convenient and efficient from several standpoints to base royalties on total sales than to face the burden of figuring royalties based on actual use. If convenience of the parties rather than patent power dictates the total-sales royalty provision, there is no misuse of the patents and no forbidden conditions attached to the license.

The Court also said in *Automatic Radio* that if the licensee bargains for the privilege of using the patent in all of his products and agrees to a lump sum or a percentage-of-total-sales royalty, he cannot escape payment on this basis by demonstrating that he is no longer using the invention disclosed by the patent. We neither disagree nor think such transactions are barred by the trial court's injunction. If the licensee negotiates for "the privilege to use any or all of the patents and developments as [he] desire[s] to use them," he cannot complain that he must pay royalties if he chooses to use none of them. He could not then charge that the patentee had refused to license except on the basis of a total-sales royalty.

But we do not read *Automatic Radio* to authorize the patentee to use the power of his patent to insist on a total-sales royalty and to override protestations of the licensee that some of his products are unsuited to the patent or that for some lines of his merchandise he has no need or desire to purchase the privileges of the patent. In such event, not only would royalties be collected on unpatented merchandise, but the obligation to pay for nonuse would clearly have its source in the leverage of the patent.

We also think patent misuse inheres in a patentee's insistence on a percentage-of-sales royalty, regardless of use, and his rejection of licensee proposals to pay only for actual use. Unquestionably, a licensee must pay if he uses the patent. Equally, however, he may insist upon paying only for use, and not on the basis of total sales, including products in which he may use a competing patent or in which no patented ideas are used at all. There is nothing in the right granted the patentee to keep others from using, selling, or manufacturing his invention which empowers him to insist on payment not only for use but also for producing products which do not employ his discoveries at all.

Of course, a licensee cannot expect to obtain a license, giving him the privilege of use and insurance against infringement suits, without at least footing the patentee's expenses in dealing with him. He cannot insist upon paying on use alone and perhaps, as things turn out, pay absolutely nothing because he finds he can produce without using the patent. If the risks of infringement are real and he would avoid them, he must anticipate some minimum charge for the license — enough to insure the patentee against loss in negotiating and administering his monopoly, even if in fact the patent is not used at all. But we discern no basis in the statutory monopoly granted the patentee for his using that monopoly to coerce an agreement to pay a percentage royalty on merchandise not employing the discovery which the claims of the patent define.

Although we have concluded that *Automatic Radio* does not foreclose the injunction entered by the District Court, it does not follow that the injunction was otherwise proper. Whether the trial court correctly determined that HRI was conditioning the grant of patent licenses upon the payment of royalties on unpatented products has not yet been determined by the Court of Appeals. And if there was such patent misuse, it does not necessarily follow that the misuse embodies the ingredients of a violation of either §1 or §2 of the Sherman Act, or that Zenith was threatened by a violation so as to entitle it to an injunction under §16 of the Clayton Act. Whether the findings and the evidence are sufficient to make out an actual or threatened violation of the antitrust laws so as to justify the injunction issued by the District Court has not been considered by the Court of Appeals, and we leave the matter to be dealt with by that court in the first instance.

Judgment of Court of Appeals affirmed in part and reversed in part, and case remanded.

MR. JUSTICE HARLAN, dissenting in part.

I concur in Parts I and II of the Court's opinion. However, I do not join Part III, in which the Court holds that a patent license provision which measures royalties by a percentage of the licensee's total sales is lawful if included for the "convenience" of both parties but unlawful if "insisted upon" by the patentee.

My first difficulty with this part of the opinion is that its test for validity of such royalty provisions is likely to prove exceedingly difficult to apply and consequently is apt to engender uncertainty in this area of business dealing, where certainty in the law is particularly desirable. In practice, it often will be very hard to tell whether a license provision was included at the instance of both parties or only at the will of the licensor. District courts will have the unenviable task of deciding whether the course of negotiations establishes "insistence" upon the suspect provision. Because of the uncertainty inherent in such determinations, parties to existing and future licenses will have little assurance that their agreements will be enforced. And it may be predicted that after today's decision the licensor will be careful to embellish the negotiations with an alternative proposal, making the court's unraveling of the situation that much more difficult.

Such considerations lead me to the view that any rule which causes the validity of percentage-of-sales royalty provisions to depend upon subsequent judicial examination of the parties' negotiations will disserve rather than further the interests of all concerned. Hence, I think that the Court has fallen short in failing to address itself to the question whether employment of such royalty provisions should invariably amount to patent misuse.

My second difficulty with this part of the Court's opinion is that in reality it overrules an aspect of a prior decision of this Court, *Automatic Radio Mfg. Co. v. Hazeltine Research, Inc.*, without offering more than a shadow of a reason in law or economics for departing from that earlier ruling. Despite the Court's efforts to distinguish Automatic Radio, it cannot be denied that the Court there sustained a Hazeltine patent license of precisely the same tenor as the one involved here, on the ground that "[t]his royalty provision does not create another monopoly; it creates no restraint of competition beyond the legitimate grant of the patent."

In finding significance for present purposes in some of the qualifying language in *Automatic Radio*, I believe that the Court today has misconstrued that opinion. A reading of the opinion as a whole satisfies me that the *Automatic Radio* Court did not consider it relevant whether Hazeltine Research had "insisted" upon inclusion of the disputed provision, and that in emphasizing that the royalty terms had no "inherent" tendency to extend the patent monopoly and were not a "per se" misuse of patents, the Court was simply endeavoring to distinguish prior decisions in which patent misuse was found when the patent monopoly had been employed to "create another monopoly or restraint of competition." Until now no subsequent decision has in any way impaired this aspect of *Automatic Radio*.

Since the Court's decision finds little if any support in the prior case law, one would expect from the Court an exposition of economic reasons for doing away with the *Automatic Radio* doctrine. However, the nearest thing to an economic rationale is the Court's declaration that:

just as the patent's leverage may not be used to extract from the
licensee a commitment to purchase, use, or sell other products according to the desires of the patentee, neither can that leverage be used to
garner as royalties a percentage share of the licensee's receipts from
sales of other products; in either case, the patentee seeks to extend the
monopoly of his patent to derive a benefit not attributable to use of the
patent's teachings.

. . . What the Court does not undertake to explain is how insistence upon a
percentage-of-sales royalty enables a patentee to obtain an economic "benefit
not attributable to use of the patent's teachings," thereby involving himself in
patent misuse. For it must be remembered that all the patentee has to license
is the right to use his patent. It is solely for that right that a percentage-of-sales
royalty is paid, and it is not apparent from the Court's opinion why this method
of determining the amount of the royalty should be any less permissible than
the other alternatives, whether or not it is "insisted" upon by the patentee.

One possible explanation for the Court's result, which seems especially
likely in view of the Court's exception for cases where the provision was
included for the "convenience" of both parties, is a desire to protect licensees
against overreaching. But the Court does not cite, and the parties have not
presented, any evidence that licensees as a class need such protection.
Moreover, the Court does not explain why a royalty based simply upon use
could not be equally overreaching.

Another possible justification for the Court's result might be that a royalty based
directly upon use of the patent will tend to spur the licensee to "invent around" the
patent or otherwise acquire a substitute which costs less, while a percentage-of-
sales royalty can have no such effect because of the licensee's knowledge that he
must pay the royalty regardless of actual patent use. No hint of such a rationale
appears in the Court's opinion. Moreover, under this theory a percentage-of-sales
royalty would be objectionable largely because of resulting damage to the rest of
the economy, through less efficient allocation of resources, rather than because of
possible harm to the licensee. Hence, the theory might not admit of the Court's
exception for provisions included for the "convenience" of both parties.

Because of its failure to explain the reasons for the result reached in Part
III, the Court's opinion is of little assistance in answering the question which
I consider to be the crux of this part of the case: whether percentage-of-sales
royalty provisions should be held without exception to constitute patent misuse. A recent economic analysis argues that such provisions may have two
undesirable consequences. First, as has already been noted, employment of
such provisions may tend to reduce the licensee's incentive to substitute other,
cheaper "inputs" for the patented item in producing an unpatented end-product. Failure of the licensee to substitute will, it is said, cause the price of the
end-product to be higher and its output lower than would be the case if substitution had occurred. Second, it is suggested that under certain conditions a
percentage-of-sales royalty arrangement may enable the patentee to garner
for himself elements of profit, above the norm for the industry or economy,
which are properly attributable not to the licensee's use of the patent but to

other factors which cause the licensee's situation to differ from one of "perfect competition," and that this cannot occur when royalties are based upon use.

If accepted, this economic analysis would indicate that percentage-of-sales royalties should be entirely outlawed. However, so far as I have been able to find, there has as yet been little discussion of these matters either by lawyers or by economists. And I find scant illumination on this score in the briefs and arguments of the parties in this case. The Court has pointed out both today and in *Automatic Radio* that percentage-of-sales royalties may be administratively advantageous for both patentee and licensee. In these circumstances, confronted, as I believe we are, with the choice of holding such royalty provisions either valid or invalid across the board, I would, as an individual member of the Court, adhere for the present to the rule of *Automatic Radio*.

NOTES

1. What is the difference between expanding a royalty base as a matter of "convenience" and expanding it in a manner that constitutes misuse? Was Justice Harlan correct in concluding that the distinction was unclear and could not easily be applied in the world of actual transactions?

2. A finding of patent or copyright misuse sets out a defense to an infringement claim. Misuse and antitrust rulings against licensing of intellectual property rights were common or at least commonly threatened during the 1960s and early 1970s, based in part on a belief that the intellectual property right in itself created excessive leverage, and in part that the risk of impropriety was high and should be curtailed by strict judicial (and agency) control. The intensity of these beliefs faded in the modern era. One manifestation of that is the Patent Misuse Reform Act of 1988, which added clauses (4) and (5) to Section 271(d) of the Patent Act. Section 271(d) provides:

> No patent owner otherwise entitled to relief for infringement or contributory infringement of a patent shall be denied relief or deemed guilty of misuse or illegal extension of the patent right by reason of his having done one or more of the following: (1) derived revenue from acts which if performed by another without his consent would constitute contributory infringement of the patent; (2) licensed or authorized another to perform acts which if performed without his consent would constitute contributory infringement of the patent; (3) sought to enforce his patent rights against infringement or contributory infringement; (4) refused to license or use any rights to the patent; or (5) conditioned the license of any rights to the patent or the sale of the patented product on the acquisition of a license to rights in another patent or purchase of a separate product, unless, in view of the circumstances, the patent owner has market power in the relevant market for the patent or patented product on which the license or sale is conditioned.

35 U.S.C. § 271(d). Clause (5) requires proof of market power as a basis for a particular misuse claim. In the absence of market power (e.g., the ability to control prices without risk of effective competition), what rationale exists for a ruling such as that in *Zenith*?

3. In an antitrust context in 2006, the Supreme Court in *Illinois Tool Works, Inc. v. Independent Ink, Inc.*, 126 S.Ct. 1281 (2006), held that a presumption of market power based on the mere existence of a patent has no support in economic theory or in commercial fact. The Court held that, while "some . . . arrangements are . . . unlawful, such as those that are the product of a true monopoly or a marketwide conspiracy, that conclusion must be supported by proof of power in the relevant market rather than by a mere presumption thereof."

4. With or without market power, what is the abuse that is present in a case of an expanded royalty base demanded by the licensor? Royalties are simply pricing mechanisms. Consider the following: Licensor will charge 10% royalty for a patent where the royalty base is limited to sales of Item #1 (the item using the patented technology), or 5% for a royalty base that includes Item #1 and Item #2, the latter of which does not use the licensed technology. If the sales income from both items is the same, what is the abuse risked by demanding a royalty base that includes both products? If Item #2 produces a larger sales and income value, is including it merely a matter of asking for a higher price?

5. If the licensor in note 4 has no market power because other, interchangeable alternatives exist, is an arrangement for a royalty based on activity not covered by its intellectual property right an abuse of that right?

PROBLEM 11.4

Sony holds patents in a technology that enables the conversion of signals involved in High Definition Television systems. The technology is involved in competition with technology patented by Micro Systems, a smaller company in Los Angeles. Sony and Micro commercialize their technology through one-year licenses with various television manufacturers. Sony currently holds about 70% of the market.

Sony changes its licensing practice. Previously, it charged a flat fee royalty for each television manufactured containing its technology. Its new licensing framework charges a flat fee for all televisions manufactured by the licensee, regardless of whether the television contains the Sony technology. Because of the Sony market share and the fact that the net income to Sony under the new arrangement remains the same (although they change the royalty rate), most licensees accept the new deal. Does the new licensing arrangement create a misuse or other problem?

III.   ROYALTY RATE ISSUES

Royalty obligations extend over time. Because of this, parties face a risk that changing economic and other conditions will alter the value of the bargain in a way that makes it desirable for either or both to adjust the base, the rate or other characteristics of the royalty. In many cases, no contract right to adjust is provided for in the license. In such cases, if adaptations are made to the changed circumstances, they require mutually agreed modifications of the contract. In other cases, however, adjustment procedures are set out in the license.

A. Agreed Modifications of the Rate

While commercial practice in most industries accepts modification of contract terms in long-term contracts, contract law raises questions about the right of parties to modify a contract. One obstacle comes from the common law concept that modifications that are not supported by adequate consideration are unenforceable. Enforceability is suspect unless each party receives or gives up something of legally cognizable value. In evaluating whether that occurred, the underlying premise is that each party is already obligated to perform according to the contractual terms and simply promising to perform is not consideration for the changed promise.

While the *Restatement (Second) of Contracts* advocates the enforceability of modifications made without consideration, it does so under a surprisingly restrictive standard. Section 89 states:

§ 89. Modification of Executory Contract

A promise modifying a duty under a contract not fully performed on either side is binding

(a) if the modification is fair and equitable in view of circumstances not anticipated by the parties when the contract was made; or

(b) to the extent provided by statute; or

(c) to the extent that justice requires enforcement in view of material change of position in reliance on the promise.

Comment:

. . . This Section relates primarily to adjustments in on-going transactions. Like offers and guaranties, such adjustments are ancillary to exchanges and have some of the same presumptive utility. Indeed, paragraph (a) deals with bargains which are without consideration only because of the rule that performance of a legal duty to the promisor is not consideration. . . . The limitation to a modification which is "fair and equitable" goes beyond absence of coercion and requires an objectively demonstrable reason for seeking a modification. The reason for modification must rest in circumstances not "anticipated" as part of the context in which the contract was made, but a frustrating event may be unanticipated for this purpose if it was not adequately covered, even though it was foreseen as a remote possibility. When such a reason is present, the relative financial strength of the parties, the formality with which the modification is made, the extent to which it is performed or relied on and other circumstances may be relevant to show or negate imposition or unfair surprise.

The same result called for by paragraph (a) is sometimes reached on the ground that the original contract was "rescinded" by mutual agreement and that new promises were then made which furnished consideration for each other. That theory is rejected here because it is fictitious when the "rescission" and new agreement are simultaneous, and because if logically carried out it might uphold unfair and inequitable modifications.

Restatement (Second) of Contracts § 89 (1981).

Article 2 provides that modifications are enforceable without consideration. U.C.C. § 2-209 (1998 Official Text). The comments to that section, however, refer to modifications made in "good faith," and at least some courts have demanded that the "agreement" to modify an existing contract be in "good faith." UCITA provides that no "consideration" is required to enforce a modification, but does not contain the Article 2 comment about "good faith", leaving the issue to courts in the event of a claim of over-reaching or other disputes.

PROBLEM 11.5

Licensee has been using Licensor's trademark for five years under a license that calls for a 7% gross sales price royalty for all goods sold bearing the trademark. The license has several more years to run. During the past year, however, Licensee has been losing market share. This is, in part, because the products it sells under the trademark carry higher production costs and, thus, higher prices than it's primary competitor. It proposes to licensor a change in the royalty rate to 3%, calculating that the change will make its prices more competitive. Licensor agrees to the change. Three months later, however, it contacts Licensee, stating that it has changed its mind and will reinstate the 7% rate effective the next month. Despite this notice, Licensee continues to send payment only for 3%, which Licensor refuses. Licensor sues. What result?

B.   Royalty Escalation Clauses

Where a license involves payments computed over an extended time, how should it deal with the reality that economic and other circumstances may change over that time? There are various approaches to this in commercial practice.

One approach is to give the licensor the right to alter rates as circumstances change.

Is a license that allows one party to increase or decrease the royalty rate at will or under a stated condition enforceable? Is such clause enforceable if it does not provide a maximum (or minimum), leaving that to the discretion of the party who has the power to make the change?

ARBITRON, INC. v. TRALYN BROADCASTING, INC.
400 F.3d 130 (2d Cir. 2006)

CALABRESI, CIRCUIT JUDGE.

This breach of contract dispute raises the question of whether, under New York law, two parties entering into a licensing agreement for radio ratings and data may authorize one party to adjust the price of that data unilaterally at some point in the future. Several issues of New York contract law are peripherally implicated in this case, and some of them are sufficiently important and unsettled that, under different circumstances, they might warrant certification to the New York Court of Appeals for resolution. But ultimately, we conclude that the contract before us delegated, with unmistakable clarity, price-setting authority to a single party, and that New York law does not invalidate such contracts. We therefore vacate the district court's order of summary judgment and remand for reconsideration.

I. BACKGROUND

Plaintiff-appellant Arbitron, Inc. ("Arbitron") . . . is a popular listener-demographics data provider for . . . radio stations. Arbitron licenses its copyrighted listener data to regional AM and FM stations, which then use the demographic profiles of station listeners to attract advertisers. In 1997, Arbitron entered into one such license . . . (the "License Agreement") with defendant Tralyn Broadcasting, Inc. ("Tralyn"). . . . The License Agreement permitted Tralyn's only radio station . . . to use Arbitron listening data reports. Over its five-year term, the License Agreement charged Tralyn a monthly rate of $1,729.57 for the use of Arbitron's listening data reports. . . .

[Another] clause of the agreement (the "escalation clause") provided that, were Tralyn or its successor to acquire additional radio stations in the same or adjacent regional markets, a new license fee would be charged. . . . Any new licensing fee would be set... at Arbitron's discretion. The clause provided:

> In the event that Arbitron consents to the assignment of this Agreement, Arbitron reserves the right to redetermine the rate to be charged to the assignee. . . . Station agrees that . . . if it is or was purchased or controlled by an entity owning or otherwise controlling other radio stations in this Market or an adjacent Market . . . Station . . . will report the change and the effective date thereof to Arbitron. . . . Station further agrees that Arbitron may redetermine its Gross Annual Rate for the Data, Reports and Services licensed hereunder, as well as any Supplementary Services, effective the first month following the date of the occurrence. Notwithstanding Station's failure to notify Arbitron . . . . Arbitron may redetermine the Station's Gross Annual Rate for all Data, Reports and Services, as well as any Supplementary Services, based on the foregoing, effective the first month following the date of the occurrence.

On October 31, 1999, Tralyn was purchased by JMD, Inc. ("JMD") . . . At the time JMD acquired Tralyn and WLNF-FM, JMD also controlled at least four other stations. . . . The purchase agreement . . . assigned to JMD the License Agreement . . . But in violation of Paragraph 11 . . . neither JMD nor Tralyn obtained Arbitron's prior written consent to the . . . assignment. Nor did they provide Arbitron with notice of a change in ownership. . . . Instead, from November 1999 until June 2002, JMD simply paid the original single-station monthly license fee to Arbitron. In return, Arbitron provided WLNF-FM with updated listening data. . . . .

In June 2000, Arbitron discovered . . . that JMD had purchased Tralyn . . . Arbitron thereupon notified JMD . . . that it was exercising its right to increase the monthly licensing fee under the escalation clause of the License Agreement. Arbitron determined JMD's new annual license fee by multiplying the single-station license fee ($1,779.57) by five ($8,897.85) to reflect the five JMD stations that could now share Arbitron's listener data. It then reduced that figure by 35% to reflect the typical volume discount for licenses covering five or more stations. . . . .

JMD never paid . . . [Arbitron] stopped sending JMD its listening data reports. . . .

Arbitron filed the instant suit against Tralyn and JMD on November 1, 2001.. . . .

On June 5, 2003, the district court . . . granted summary judgment . . . to JMD. The district court concluded that because "[n]either the escalation clause . . . nor any other section of the Agreement, contains any basis for determining the new rate to be paid Arbitron in the event changes in ownership occur," the License Agreement's escalation clause was unenforceably vague under New York law. The district court reasoned that . . . .

> [B]efore the power of law can be invoked to enforce a promise, it must be sufficiently certain and specific so that what was promised can be ascertained. Otherwise, a court, in intervening would be imposing its own conception of what the parties should or might have undertaken, rather than confining itself to the implementation of a bargain to which they have mutually committed themselves. Thus, definitiveness as to material matters is of the very essence of contract law. Impenetrable vagueness and uncertainty will not do.

Because the district court considered the escalation clause to be "impenetrabl[y] vague[ ]" for want of a missing term, it deemed that portion of the License Agreement unenforceable under New York law, and therefore awarded summary judgment to JMD. Arbitron now challenges the district court's decision.

II. DISCUSSION

[We reverse.]

The district court based its decision on three New York cases, each dealing with contracts for the sale or lease of real property. Upon review of these same cases, we conclude that the escalation clause is enforceable under the common law of New York . . . because the clause before us is not an "agreement to agree," under which future negations between the parties must occur, but is instead an acknowledgment that, if certain conditions arise in the future, *no* new agreement is required before Arbitron may set new license terms. . . .

The seminal New York precedent . . . *Joseph Martin, Jr., Delicatessen, Inc. v. Schumacher,* 417 N.E.2d 541 (1981). There, the Court of Appeals was faced with an agreement between a landlord and a tenant to lease a commercial space for five years at a monthly rate beginning at $500 and escalating over five years to $650, with the option to renew the lease for another five-year term at a rent to be determined by the parties. At the close of the lease's five-year term, the landlord sought to increase the rent from $650 to $900 monthly. Surprised, the tenant employed an assessor, who appraised the market value of the premises at no more than $550 per month. The tenant sued for specific performance, seeking a new five-year lease at the fair market rate of $550. In resolving the case, the *Delicatessen* majority recognized that the U.C.C. . . . counseled in favor of supplying missing price terms to save and enforce the agreement, and that the terms supplied by a court under the U.C.C. would correspond to a good's fair market value. Nevertheless, because the New York statute's terms made clear that leases or contracts for the sale of real property were not covered by the U.C.C., the Court of Appeals refused to enforce the agreement. It concluded that

> it is rightfully well settled in the common law of contracts in this State that a mere agreement to agree, in which a material term is left for future negotiations, is unenforceable. This is especially true of the amount to be paid for the sale or lease of real property. The rule applies all the more, and not the less, when, as here, the extraordinary remedy of specific performance is sought.

In a separate opinion, Judge Meyer concurred in the judgment and opined that the U.C.C.'s principles might now be part of the common-law fabric of New York commercial law. And for similar reasons, Judge Jasen dissented altogether.

[In] *Cobble Hill Nursing Home v. Henry & Warren Corp.,* 548 N.E.2d 203 (1989), the Court of Appeals again faced the question of unspecified price terms. The contract in *Cobble Hill* gave the plaintiff a purchase option for a nursing home, but did not provide a specific price for the property. The agreement instead permitted plaintiff to buy the property "at a price determined by the Department [of Health] in accordance with the Public Health Law and all applicable rules and regulations of the Department." When the plaintiff exercised that option and attempted to buy the nursing home at the price set by the Department of Health, defendants refused to honor the option, citing a perceived discrepancy between the property's fair market value and the Department of Health's assessment. Plaintiff filed suit for breach of contract, seeking specific performance at the price set by the Department. *Id.* Defendants claimed that the agreement was unenforceably vague because its four corners did not include a definite price term. *Id.* Evaluating these arguments, the Court of Appeals emphasized that "[f]ew principles are better settled in the law of contracts than the requirement of definiteness," and that under New York law "[i]f an agreement is not reasonably certain in its material terms, there can be no legally enforceable contract." But it also noted that

> a price term is not necessarily indefinite because the agreement fails to specify a dollar figure, or leaves fixing the amount for the future, or contains no computational formula. Where at the time of agreement the parties have manifested their intent to be bound, a price term may be sufficiently definite if the amount can be determined objectively without the need for new expressions by the parties; a method for reducing uncertainty to certainty might, for example, be found within the agreement or ascertained by reference to an extrinsic event, commercial practice or trade usage. A price so arrived at would have been the end product of agreement between the parties themselves.

Applying that reasoning to the option contract, the Court concluded that, because it was "apparent from the agreement that these parties reposed discretion in the Department to make the price determination, limited only by the requirement that it apply provisions that were suitable, pertinent and appropriate for the task at hand," and because "[t]he terms of agreement and the appropriate remedy can be readily determined, and it is plain that the parties intended this to be a complete and binding contract," there was "no legal justification for voiding this agreement."

Most recently, in *In Re Express Indus. & Terminal Corp.*, 715 N.E.2d 1050 (1999), the Court of Appeals refused to enforce a lease agreement whose material terms, including the price term, were simply left blank by the parties. A unanimous Court concluded that because the lease agreement's terms--including the date on which an option would expire, and the amount of rent reduction that would correspond to the exercise of that option--were represented by blank spaces, and because there was "no objective evidence that the parties [to the lease agreement] intended that [the lessor] be allowed to fill in these blanks with any reasonable terms [it] chose," the contract was not enforceable under New York law. But the Court also suggested that, in the face of sufficient evidence demonstrating that both parties intended to give one party the power to select "any reasonable terms [it] chose," a similar contract for the sale or lease of real property might be enforceable.

[We] conclude that the License Agreement's escalation clause is indeed enforceable under the common law of New York. The escalation clause, unlike the promise to set a future rent rate collectively in *Delicatessen*, does not require the parties to reach an "agreement" on price at some point in the future. That is, the escalation clause is not an "agreement to agree." Instead, like the contract in *Cobble Hill,* it is a mechanism for objectively setting material terms in the future without further negotiations between both parties. It does so, moreover, with "sufficient evidence that both parties intended that [pricing] arrangement." The escalation clause clearly and unambiguously states that, in the event that Tralyn or its successors acquired new radio stations in the same (or an adjacent) geographic market, "Arbitron may redetermine its Gross Annual Rate for the Data, Reports and Services licensed hereunder . . . effective the first of the month following [the acquisition]." The escalation clause further provides, in unambiguous language, that Arbitron may exercise this power to "redetermine" the license fee "[n]otwithstanding Station's failure to notify Arbitron" that an acquisition had occurred.

The intent of the parties is manifest in the language of the agreement. Both Arbitron and Tralyn explicitly agreed that Arbitron was authorized to adjust the license fee in the event that Tralyn or its successors began to operate additional stations. This fact makes the instant case very different from those disputes in which courts are faced with "no objective evidence" of a shared intent to permit one party to set prices in the future. And it in no way leads a court enforcing the contract to "impos[e] its own conception of what the parties should or might have undertaken." Accordingly, we conclude that the district court erred in holding the License Agreement's escalation clause "impenetrably vague" under New York law.

In reaching this conclusion, we note that . . . under New York's implementation of the Uniform Commercial Code, there is a strong presumption that agreements are enforceable even if their price terms are not definite. N.Y. U.C.C. § 2-305 provides that:

> (1) The parties *if they so intend* can conclude a contract for sale even though the price is not settled. In such a case the price is a reasonable price at the time for delivery if (a) nothing is said as to price; or (b) the price is left to be agreed by the parties and they fail to agree; or (c) the price is to be fixed in terms of some agreed market or other standard as set or recorded by a third person or agency and it is not so set or recorded.

> (2) A price to be fixed by the seller or by the buyer means a price for him to fix in good faith.

> . . .

Because we believe that the License Agreement's escalation clause is not inconsistent with New York law, we conclude that the district court erred in granting summary judgment to JMD. . . . On remand, the district court may wish to consider whether Arbitron has exercised its authority under the escalation clause in "good faith" within the meaning of N.Y. U.C.C. § 2-305 (which, as we have previously noted, may or may not apply to a "license" of this sort), or more generally, in a manner consistent with Arbitron's implied duty of fair dealing under New York law. We express no opinion on either question.

NOTES

1. What was the policy basis for the lower court's ruling? Is a contract that gives one party control over an important term truly a binding contract? How would you write a discretionary escalation (or reduction clause) in light of *Arbitron*?

2. Many rate escalation clauses refer to objective events, such as the passage of time, changes in a governmental index, or number of sales produced. The issues then, if any, typically focus on interpreting the meaning of the objective reference used by the parties. *See The Vermont Teddy Bear Co. v. Tyco Indus., Inc.*, 80 F. Supp. 2d 36 (N.D.N.Y. 2002) (Toy manufacturer denied summary judgment where fact issue existed as to whether license's annual royalty increase was contingent upon defendant's introduction of additional products).

3. Should a license clause that gives either party the right to unilaterally alter the royalty rate be enforceable?

PROBLEM 11.6

Epoch plans to open an online site relating to the listing and sale of coins. Vendors will pay $15 per listing to list their coins on Epoch's basic service, and an additional $10 per listing to list their coins on the "premium" service. Each listing is for two months. In order to maintain quality, Epoch will require that the vendor provide background information and agree before making any listings to a service agreement covering all of the vendor's listings. There will be at least 2 million vendors signed up with Epoch by the end of the first year, accounting for 9 million listings. Epoch expects to adjust its pricing as circumstances change. How should it approach that latter issue in its contracts? For example, its president has suggested simply stating in the agreement that "all prices are subject to change at any time by Epoch." Would that work?

C. "Most Favored" Licensee Clauses

Non-exclusive licensees do not have the power to preclude the licensor from licensing to others. This creates a risk that others will negotiate a better "price" for the technology, especially in long term licensing arrangements. The risk is potentially significant for a licensee that invests based on the rights covered by the license. As a result, many licenses contain terms that relate to the licensor's grant of additional licenses or that attempt to give the earlier licensee the benefits of more favorable arrangements that later licensees obtain. These clauses are typically described as a "most favored licensee" clause. They are among the most frequently litigated contract clauses in licensing.

WILLEMIJN HOUDSTERMAATSCHAPPIJ BV v. STANDARD MICROSYSTEMS CORP.
925 F. Supp. 193 (S.D.N.Y. 1996)

OWEN, S.J.

Willemijn Houdstermaatschappij, BV ("Willemijn") petitions this court to confirm an arbitration award which denied Standard Microsystems Corporation ("SMC") benefits under a most-favored-licensee clause contained in the parties' October 1, 1992 License Agreement. SMC's petition urges the court to vacate the award as manifestly unjust.

Willemijn is a holding company incorporated in the Netherlands whose primary business is the licensing of U.S. Patent Re. 31,852 ("the '852 patent"). The '852 patent, was issued in 1985 as a reissue of an earlier 1981 patent, describes a data communication system for transmitting information between a central master computer and several subordinated terminal units. SMC is a Delaware Corporation which manufactures, among other products, interfaces permitting the connection of computers and peripheral equipment to token ring data communications systems; SMC's token ring systems conform with the 802.5 and FDDI standard promulgated by the Institute of Electrical and Electronic Engineers.

In a license agreement effective as of October 1, 1992, Willemijn granted SMC a non-exclusive license to manufacture and distribute data communication systems within the scope of the '852 patent as well as certain other auxiliary products. Article 5.9 of the Agreement provided that

> [i]f Willemijn, after execution of this agreement by both parties, grants
> a license under the Licensed Patent containing provisions that require

payments at rates of royalty less than provided for in [the royalty provisions of the agreement], Willemijn shall promptly notify [SMC] of those royalty provisions. [SMC] shall then be entitled, upon written request . . . to substitute for [its royalty] provisions . . . the corresponding provisions of such other license but only if [SMC] also agrees to accept any other terms and conditions of such other license identified by Willemijn to [SMC].

The parties agreed to submit any claims arising under the agreement to arbitration.

Almost five years earlier, in 1988, Willemijn and another of its licensees, Proteon, Inc., had submitted to arbitration the question whether the '852 patent covered 802.5 and FDDI token ring systems manufactured by Proteon. The Proteon-Willemijn arbitration panel concluded on April 13, 1994 that the '852 patent did not cover Proteon's token ring data communication systems. . . . Proteon subsequently petitioned for a confirmation of the award in the Southern District of New York. However, before the court acted and in order to avoid further litigation, Willemijn and Proteon entered into an agreement effective May 3, 1994, pursuant to which Willemijn granted Proteon immunity from suit under the '852 patent. Accordingly, the court never acted on the petition. Willemijn at no time advised SMC of its dispute with Proteon, the arbitration demand, or the arbitration award.

On November 17, 1994, SMC demanded arbitration before the American Arbitration Association in accordance with the license agreement. SMC alleged that Willemijn had breached the agreement by granting Proteon a royalty-free license to manufacture products covered by the '852 patent without notifying SMC and offering it equally favorable terms. . . . On September 28 and 29, 1995, the three-member arbitration panel issued the following [decision]:

3. Was the Most Favored License (MFL) clause 5.9 in the License Agreement between the Parties brought into effect to the benefit of CLAIMANT by the granting of an immunity of suit under U.S. Patent Re. 31,852 in a Settlement Agreement, dated May 3, 1994, between RESPONDENT and one of its former Licensees, Proteon, Inc., and was the License Agreement breached when RESPONDENT did not notify CLAIMANT of the Settlement Agreement or offer CLAIMANT the terms provided therein? Decision: No, by Arbitrators Ronald Abramson and Louis H. Reens. Arbitrator Garold E. Bramblett finds that as of May 3, 1994, the date of the Settlement Agreement between Proteon and RESPONDENT, the Most Favored Licensee clause 5.9 entitled CLAIMANT to a zero percent royalty rate.

The purpose of a most-favored-licensee clause is "to protect [a licensee] from a competitive disadvantage resulting from more favorable terms granted to another licensee." In this case, Willemijn granted Proteon immunity from suit after Proteon, before three arbitrators, had successfully challenged the scope of Willemijn's patent under their license agreement. Having bargained for and received a most-favored-licensee clause, SMC was entitled to no less than a royalty-free license once Proteon was released from the obligation to pay royalties. To conclude otherwise would place SMC at a severe competitive disadvantage with respect to Proteon.

Two of the three arbitrators here, however, reached the conclusion that SMC was not entitled to the benefit of its bargain. Since the arbitrators have given no explanation for their decision, as is their right, I must confirm the award "if a ground for [their] decision can be inferred from the facts of the case."

Willemijn offers two possible explanations for the arbitrators' decision. First, that the 1994 Willemijn-Proteon agreement did not trigger SMC's most-favored-licensee clause. Willemijn concedes that its agreement with Proteon constitutes a license. Indeed, it is well established that a patent holder grants a license by agreeing "not to seek an injunction against infringement and not to sue for damages therefore." *Shatterproof Glass Corp. v. Libbey-Owens-Ford Co.*, 482 F.2d 317 (6th Cir. 1973); *see General Talking Pictures Corp. v. Western Electric Co.*, 304 U.S. 175 (1938) (acknowledging that the grant of a non-exclusive license amounts "to no more than a mere waiver of the right to sue" (internal quotation marks omitted)).

Willemijn nevertheless asserts that the 1994 Willemijn-Proteon agreement did not trigger SMC's most-favored-licensee clause because it did not contain any provisions "requir[ing]" the "payment" of "royalt[ies]." Willemijn's expert testified before the panel that SMC's most-favored-licensee clause was "very narrow" and evinced the parties' intent that only a subsequent license which "require[d] payment" at a lower "rate of royalty" would entitle SMC to seek substitution of its royalty provisions. Because the 1994 agreement only granted Proteon immunity from suit, it did not in any way reduce or alter Proteon's obligation to pay royalties, which remained operative (if unenforceable). In other words, if the 1994 agreement provided that Proteon was "required" to "pay" a "rate of royalty" of 0.0001% (or even a "rate" of zero percent, for that matter), SMC would be entitled to a substitution of terms; however, because the agreement merely waived Willemijn's right to demand payment of any royalties due, SMC is not entitled to substitution.

This argument is meritless. A licensor's grant of immunity from suit in settlement of a dispute under a prior license agreement is "the equivalent of a license" and may trigger another licensee's most-favored-licensee clause. By relinquishing the right to sue for royalties, Willemijn has granted Proteon a royalty-free license. To conclude otherwise would allow Willemijn to eviscerate the effect of SMC's most-favored-licensee clause by, for example, "requiring" a subsequent licensee to pay a higher royalty rate and then waiving the right to sue for all or part of that rate. The arbitrators could not have seriously considered Willemijn's argument that the parties intended this construction and the untenable outcomes it could generate. I note that Willemijn's expert offered no explanation why anyone would make such a distinction, let alone consent to it.

Second, Willemijn argues that SMC is not entitled to a substitution of royalty provisions because it cannot accept all the terms and conditions of the 1994 Willemijn-Proteon agreement as required by the most-favored-licensee clause. In exchange for immunity from suit, Proteon agreed to dismiss its petition to confirm an arbitration award releasing it from the obligation to pay further royalties to Willemijn under the '852 patent. SMC does not possess a similar arbitration award ripe for confirmation. Willemijn therefore presumes that SMC is unable to "agree to accept" this additional term.

Under Willemijn's proposed interpretation of the license agreement, it may freely evade its duty to offer comparable terms to SMC simply by making any more favorable arrangement extended to another licensee contingent upon a condition which is inapplicable to SMC. The Second Circuit rejected precisely this argument in [*H. v.*] *Novamont* [*Corp. NNA.*, 704 F.2d 48, 53 (2d Cir. 1983)].

There the licensor had granted a subsequent licensee a more beneficial royalty provision containing a condition inapplicable to a prior most-favored licensee. The court rejected the condition precedent and extended the more beneficial provision to the most-favored licensee, noting that "giving literal effect" to the condition "would be an evasion of the intention of the parties to the clause."

It is also irrelevant that the 1994 Willemijn-Proteon agreement merely implemented an arbitration award that already released Proteon from an obligation to make royalty payments. SMC bargained for the right not to be placed at a competitive disadvantage by Willemijn. The question whether Proteon could have continued manufacturing products without obtaining a license from Willemijn "is not germane to any purpose of the MFL clause." As the Second Circuit noted in Novamont,

> [i]t is likely to be generally true that a licensor's grant of more favorable terms is supported by a sound business reason, but the benefit of more favorable terms is exactly what the person whose license includes an MFL clause has bargained for and to which he is entitled.

SMC has agreed not to pursue any further claims, either before a panel of arbitrators or in court, regarding the validity of the '852 patent. It was therefore unquestionably entitled to enjoy the same royalty-free license extended to Proteon.

Since Willemijn's arguments before the panel fail and since I can conceive of no other basis for the arbitrators' decision, I conclude that the two arbitrators in the majority manifestly disregarded and failed to honor the "well-defined, explicit, and clearly applicable" terms of the parties' agreement, and that they disregarded as well the law that a party is entitled to the benefit of terms clearly stated and intended in such a contract. Were it not for what happened here, this fundamental principle of contract law would hardly need iteration.

> [W]here the terms of [a contract] are unambiguous, they must be given their plain and ordinary meaning, and a court must refrain from rewriting the agreement. Under such circumstances, the question is one of law, and summary judgment is proper. In the words of Judge Weinfeld: Contracts of insurance, like other contracts are to be construed to effectuate the parties' intent as expressed by the words the parties used, and if the terms of the contract are clear and unambiguous, the Court must enforce the plain, ordinary and common meaning of those terms.

An award given by arbitrators who ignore this principle may be vacated. . . . In the case before me, the two arbitrators did not merely err or misunderstand the law; they disregarded the fundamental tenet of contract law that the unambiguous terms of an agreement are to be honored. The disregard here was all the more manifest when, in this stark and compelling setting, it was cloaked by the majority of the arbitrators in the single word "no."

Accordingly, SMC's petition to vacate the arbitration award is granted and the award is vacated. . . .

STUDIENGESELLSCHAFT KOHLE M.B.H. v. HERCULES INC.
105 F.3d 629 (Fed. Cir. 1997)

MAYER, J.

In 1986, Studiengesellschaft Kohle m.b.H. (SGK) sued Hercules, Inc.; Himont U.S.A., Inc.; and Himont, Inc. (collectively "Hercules") for patent infringement. Hercules counterclaimed, alleging that SGK had breached the most favored licensee provision of their license agreement by failing to offer Hercules a license with the same terms it offered other licensees. But for the breach, Hercules argued, it would have been licensed under the patents at issue during the period in question, thereby insulating it from infringement. The district court agreed and entered judgment for Hercules. Because SGK has not established that the court made any clearly erroneous findings of fact or error of law, we affirm. . . .

Background

SGK is the licensing arm of the MaxPlanck Institute for Coal Research in Germany and the successor-in-interest to Professor Karl Ziegler, the Institute's former head, who died in 1973. . . . Hercules manufactured and sold plastics from the 1950s through 1983, when it sold its polypropylene business to Himont U.S.A., Inc.

In the early 1950s, SGK invented a catalyst that could be used to make plastics, such as polyethylene and polypropylene. In 1954, SGK and Hercules entered a "polyolefin contract" (the "1954 contract") granting Hercules a non-exclusive license under SGK's "Patent Applications and Patents Issued Thereon." Although the United States had not issued SGK any patents at that time, the contract contemplated that Hercules would be licensed under any SGK patent issued in the future in the plastics field. The contract included a most favored licensee provision, set forth in pertinent part:

> If a license shall hereafter be granted by [SGK] to any other licensee in the United States or Canada to practice the Process or to use and sell the products of the Process under [SGK's] inventions, Patent Applications or Patents or any of them, then [SGK] shall notify Hercules promptly of the terms of such other license and if so requested by Hercules, shall

make available to Hercules a copy of such other license and Hercules shall be entitled, upon demand if made three (3) months after receiving the aforementioned notice, to the benefit of any lower royalty rate or rates for its operations hereunder in the country or countries (US and Canada) in which such rates are effective, as of and after the date such more favorable rate or rates became effective under such other license but only for so long as and to the same extent and subject to the same conditions that such . . . lower royalty rate or rates shall be available to such other licensee; provided, however, that Hercules shall not be entitled to such more favorable rate or rates without accepting any less favorable terms that may have accompanied such more favorable rate or rates.

The contract also contained a termination clause, which granted SGK the right to terminate the agreement and the licenses upon sixty days written notice if Hercules failed to make royalty payments when due. However, Hercules had the right to cure its default by paying SGK "all sums then due under [the] Agreement," in which case the licenses would remain in full force and effect.

The contract would be construed under Delaware law.

The parties amended the contract [in 1972] . . . by granting Hercules "a fully paid-up" license through December 3, 1980, the date the '115 patent expired, under SGK's "U.S. Patent rights with respect to polypropylene . . . up to a limit of six hundred million pounds (600,000,000) per year sales." For sales exceeding that amount, Hercules was obligated to pay SGK royalties of one percent of its "Net Sales Price." As to SGK's patents expiring after December 3, 1980, Hercules possessed the right, upon request, to obtain "a license on terms no worse than the most favored other paying licensee of [SGK]." SGK concedes that this provision granted Hercules the "right to the most favored paying licensee's terms regardless of whether those terms had been granted before or after 1972." The amendment also provided that the terms and conditions of the 1954 contract remained in "full force and effect except as modified by, or inconsistent with, this amendment." SGK concedes that "the notice provision, indeed the whole [most-favored licensee] clause, 'survived the 1972 Agreement.'"

On November 14, 1978, SGK was issued U.S. Patent No. 4,125,698 ('698 patent) for the "Polymerization of Ethylenically Unsaturated Hydrocarbons." The parties agree that under the 1972 amendment Hercules was licensed under the '698 patent, without any additional payment, through December 3, 1980. It is also undisputed that this patent is covered by the 1954 agreement, as amended.

In March 1979, SGK sent Hercules a letter terminating the 1954 contract and the licenses granted under it "for failure to account and make royalty payments" when due. In accordance with the agreement, the letter stated that the termination would become effective in sixty days unless the "breach" had been corrected and the payments made. Hercules paid SGK $339,032 within the sixty-day period, which SGK accepted. Although SGK possessed the right to question any royalty statement made by Hercules, and to have a certified public accountant audit Hercules' books to verify or determine royalties paid or payable, it did not do so.

On May 1, 1980, more than seven months before the expiration of Hercules' "paid-up" license, SGK granted Amoco Chemicals Corporation (Amoco) a non-exclusive "paid-up" license to make, use, and sell products covered by SGK's polypropylene patents in the United States. In exchange, Amoco paid SGK $1.2 million. SGK does not dispute that the '698 patent is covered by this license or that it failed to apprise Hercules of the license at the time it was granted. Hercules first learned of Amoco's license in 1987, after SGK commenced this action. It demanded an equivalent license retroactive to December 3, 1980. SGK refused, contending that (1) Amoco was not a "paying licensee," as contemplated by the 1972 amendment; (2) Hercules' request was too late; and (3) Amoco's license was granted as part of a settlement agreement. . . .

On December 3, 1986, SGK filed suit in the United States District Court for the District of Delaware, charging Hercules with infringement of the '698 patent. Hercules counterclaimed, alleging that the 1954 license, as amended, required SGK to notify it of the Amoco agreement in 1980, the terms of which it was entitled to obtain via the most favored licensee provision of the 1954 contract, as amended. Hercules argued that it would have exercised its right to obtain a license on Amoco's terms had SGK not breached that provision. It claimed, therefore, that it was entitled to such license, retroactive to December 3, 1980, upon paying SGK $1.2 million. The court agreed and entered judgment for Hercules. This appeal followed.

Discussion

. . . SGK concedes that the notice provision was effective but argues that it was only obligated to provide Hercules with notice of any license with terms more favorable than Hercules' license. In 1972, Hercules obtained a "paid-up" license under SGK's patents through December 3, 1980. In 1978, the '698 patent issued. Hercules was licensed under that patent, without additional cost, by virtue of the 1972 license. Because Hercules obtained a "free" license under the '698 patent for the first 600 million pounds, no terms could be more favorable, according to SGK. So, it had no duty to apprise Hercules of the Amoco license.

SGK's interpretation does violence to the plain language of the 1954 contract. The notice clause did not condition SGK's obligation to inform Hercules of other licenses on whether such licenses were more favorable. It required SGK to notify Hercules promptly of the terms of a license granted "to any other licensee." Under SGK's construction, the power to determine whether another license was more favorable resided not with Hercules, but with SGK. That simply was not what the agreement provided. It is true that the 1954 contract granted Hercules the right, upon demand, to the benefit of any "more favorable rate or rates." However, that clause signified nothing more than the commercial reality that Hercules would opt only for a license whose terms it thought were more favorable than its own. It did not divest Hercules of the right to decide which terms were more favorable. Indeed, such a decision will not always be apparent when one considers the myriad combinations of royalty payments, lump-sum payments, and technology transfers a license can effect. Consequently, the court was correct that SGK's failure to provide notice constituted a breach of the license agreement.

SGK next says that it had no obligation to grant Hercules a license with terms equivalent to those in the Amoco license because Amoco was not a "paying licensee" within the meaning of the 1972 amendment. Again, we turn to the plain language of the license and interpret it anew. The 1972 amendment provided that for any of SGK's patents expiring after December 3, 1980, including the '698 patent, SGK would "grant Hercules, upon request, a license on terms no worse than the most favored other paying licensee of [SGK]." SGK contends that Amoco was not a "paying licensee" because it made just one lump-sum payment and no royalty payments; only licensees that make ongoing royalty payments are "paying licensee[s]."

In construing the term "paying licensee," we must give the words their ordinary meaning unless a contrary intent appears. The ordinary meaning of the term "paying licensee" is one who gives money for a license. *See Webster's II New Riverside University Dictionary* 863 (1984) (defining "pay" as "[t]o give money to in return for goods or services rendered"). SGK has not established that the parties intended that the term should mean something else. We see no distinction between one who makes an up-front, lump-sum payment and one who makes continuing royalty payments. Indeed, such a distinction would be doubly doubtful because a "paid-up" license presumably includes potential future royalty payments discounted to their net present value.

SGK also argues that the $1.2 million payment was in settlement of litigation; Amoco was not intended to be a "paying licensee." But the court found that Amoco paid SGK $1.2 million for a paid-up license for unlimited production under, inter alia, the '698 patent. SGK has not shown how this finding is clearly erroneous: Amoco was a "paying licensee."

Even were we to accept SGK's interpretation as reasonable, however, the provision would be ambiguous because Hercules' construction is also reasonable. Under such circumstances, and in the absence of any extrinsic evidence clearly establishing the parties' intent, we construe the term "paying licensee" against the drafter of the language — SGK — under the doctrine of contra proferentem. So, Hercules' interpretation would still prevail.

According to SGK, even if Hercules is entitled to terms equivalent to those in the Amoco license, it exercised its option too late to be effective. This argument fails because the only requirement in the 1954 contract or its amendments that limits the time in which Hercules must request a license is that it be within three months of receiving the required notice. Because SGK failed to notify Hercules of the Amoco license, that time limitation never began. The court found that Hercules first became aware of the Amoco license in 1987 through discovery in this case. Hercules demanded an equivalent license on or about March 16, 1987, so even if constructive notice could trigger the three-month limitation, Hercules met it.

SGK also contends that the court erred in concluding that Hercules was entitled to a license retroactive to December 3, 1980. It argues that for six years Hercules intentionally manufactured products covered by the '698 patent, which it thought was invalid, without a license. Only after this court ruled that the patent had not been proven invalid, did Hercules become interested in obtaining a license. It requested a license retroactive to the date its allegedly infringing activities began, thereby insulating itself from any infringement claim. SGK argues that "nothing in Hercules' option provides for such a right."

To be sure, neither we nor the parties can know with certainty whether Hercules would have exercised its right to a license on Amoco's terms in 1980, had it received the required notice. To that extent the prospect of absolving six years of alleged infringement via a retroactive license is troubling. But the uncertainty was caused by SGK's breach, the consequences of which it must bear. The 1954 contract expressly and unambiguously provides Hercules with the right to obtain the terms of another license "effective, as of and after the date such more favorable rate or rates became effective under such other license." The agreement must stand as written. Hercules is entitled to the terms of the Amoco license effective May 1980, when the Amoco license became effective.

Finally, the parties disagree on whether Hercules must pay interest on the $1.2 million license fee. Because the court has not addressed this issue, we remand.

Conclusion

Accordingly, the judgment of the United States District Court for the District of Delaware is affirmed, and the case is remanded.

NOTES

1. "Most favored" clauses often lead to disputes about whether the specific clause applies to cases where an infringement claim against a third party results in a judicial finding or a settlement leading to a payment for past use. If the issue is addressed in the agreement, how should a licensor deal with the effect of litigation settlements? Are the parties' interests at odds or consistent?

2. In *Wang Laboratories v. OKI Electric Industry Co.,* 15 F. Supp. 2d 166 (D. Mass. 1998), the court held that a "most favored licensee" provision that required Wang to notify and to grant equally beneficial terms to OKI should Wang provide another licensee with more favorable running royalty rates or a more favorable running royalty base did not cover a settlement agreement that required the defendant to make a lump sum payment that covered both past infringement and future use.

> Monies received as a settlement for past tortious use of patents are not the equivalent of royalties. . . . Since a settlement is not a royalty, imposing a penalty for past tortious uses that is more favorable than the royalty rate does not violate an MFL clause.

> Courts confronting this issue have been motivated in part by a desire to encourage settlements for patent infringement. Indeed, enabling patent owners to negotiate settlements independent of the MFL rate fosters resolution of patent infringement disputes without recourse to the

courts. Moreover, this policy safeguards the interests of MFLs. A non-exclusive license — like the one involved in the instant case and the relevant precedents — confers no standing on a licensee to protect the patent against other infringers. Each non-exclusive licensee therefore must rely on the patent holder to prevent competition, with no legal redress if the patent holder chooses not to act. Forcing a patent owner to resolve license infringements only at the risk of forfeiting a portion of the royalties paid by an MFL could actually create a disincentive to protect the MFL patent interest, giving rise to a situation in which infringers would compete unchecked against MFLs. In addition, there is authority to the effect that the concepts of both royalty and license are necessarily prospective, rendering a "retroactive royalty agreement" a legal nullity. The courts that have dealt with this issue have concluded that a license is a prospective grant of permission to use the patents.

Similarly, the court in *Studiengesellschaft Kohle m.b.H. v. Novamont Corp.*, 704 F.2d 48 (2d Cir. 1983), commented that truly parallel treatment of licensees and past infringers might require "that the licensor must insist upon an exaction from the later licensee for past infringement which is equivalent to the royalty terms governing the [MFL] during the same period, or must make a refund . . . [but that] MFL clauses do not seem to have been drawn so as to compel that degree of equivalency. . . ."

3. How should subsequent license terms be compared to the original? "Court decisions, not surprisingly, have not established even general criteria for determining the relative worth of different licenses." Brunsvold & Payne, *Five Important Clauses: A Practical Guide*, 2 TECH. LICENSING 367, 374 (1982). If you were drafting a clause, how would you recommend dealing with the "more beneficial" issue?

4. Are there policy reasons to restrain in law the expressed intent of the parties or is the law here simply a matter of settling on ordinary interpretations of particular and common contract terms? For example, if a license between Little Professor and Big Company provides that the non-exclusive license royalty will be adjusted downward to any fee or royalty given by Little Professor to anyone in a license or other settlement of litigation, including a pro rated payment for past infringements, should that be enforceable?

PROBLEM 11.7

Draft a "most favored licensee" clause for franchise agreements entered into by Big Burger with its several thousand franchisees. The licenses deal primarily with trademark rights and use of special procedures to make burgers. There are over 1,000 franchises and several hundred added per year. Big Burger is frequently involved in litigation about its trademark and with some of its franchisees.

PROBLEM 11.8

Small Company grants Big Company a license to use Small's patented process for an annual royalty of $100 for each item produced by use of the process. Over the initial years of the license, Big manufactures an average of 5,000 items per year using the patent. The license provides that "Big is entitled to substitute the terms of any more beneficial subsequent license of the Patent granted in the same field of use."

Three years into the deal, Small grants a single payment license to Major Company to use the patented process in Major's manufacturing in the same field of use as Big. The payment is $1 million. Major anticipates making about 1,000 items per year for the two years of the license.

a. Is Small required to give Big notice of this new license if the contract is silent on the issue?

b. Big sues to obtain the terms that Major obtained. What result? How would you redraft the agreement for Small to give it more flexibility in negotiating with future licensees?

IV. DURATION OF ROYALTY

BRULOTTE v. THYS CO.
379 U.S. 29 (1965)

MR. JUSTICE DOUGLAS.

Respondent, owner of various patents for hop-picking, sold a machine to each of the petitioners for a flat sum and issued a license for its use. Under that license there is payable a minimum royalty of $500 for each hop-picking season or $3.33 1/3 per 200 pounds of dried hops harvested by the machine, whichever is greater. The licenses by their terms may not be assigned nor may the machines be removed from Yakima County. The licenses issued to petitioners listed 12 patents relating to hop-picking machines; but only seven were incorporated into the machines sold to and licensed for use by petitioners. Of those seven all expired on or before 1957. But the licenses issued by respondent to them continued for terms beyond that date.

Petitioners refused to make royalty payments accruing both before and after the expiration of the patents. This suit followed. One defense was misuse of the patents through extension of the license agreements beyond the expiration date of the patents. The trial court rendered judgment for respondent and the Supreme Court of Washington affirmed. The case is here on a writ of certiorari.

We conclude that the judgment below must be reversed insofar as it allows royalties to be collected which accrued after the last of the patents incorporated into the machines had expired.

The Constitution by Art. I, § 8 authorizes Congress to secure "for limited times" to inventors "the exclusive right" to their discoveries. Congress exercised that power by 35 U.S.C. § 154 which provides in part as follows: "Every patent shall contain a short title of the invention and a grant to the patentee, his heirs or assigns, for the term of seventeen years, of the right to exclude others from making, using, or selling the invention throughout the United States, referring to the specification for the particulars thereof. . . ."

The right to make, the right to sell, and the right to use "may be granted or conferred separately by the patentee." But these rights become public property once the 17-year period expires. As stated by Chief Justice Stone, speaking for the Court in *Scott Paper Co. v. Marcalus Mfg. Co.*, 326 U.S. 249: ". . . any attempted reservation or continuation in the patentee or those claiming under him of the patent monopoly, after the patent expires, whatever the legal device employed, runs counter to the policy and purpose of the patent laws."

The Supreme Court of Washington held that in the present case the period during which royalties were required was only "a reasonable amount of time over which to spread the payments for the use of the patent." But there is intrinsic evidence that the agreements were not designed with that limited view. As we have seen, the purchase price in each case was a flat sum, the annual payments not being part of the purchase price but royalties for use of the machine during that year. The royalty payments due for the post-expiration period are by their terms for use during that period, and are not deferred payments for use during the pre-expiration period. Nor is the case like the hypothetical ones put to us where non-patented articles are marketed at prices based on use. The machines in issue here were patented articles and the royalties exacted were the same for the post-expiration period as they were for the period of the patent. That is peculiarly significant in this case in view of other provisions of the license agreements. The license agreements prevent assignment of the machines or their removal from Yakima County after, as well as before, the expiration of the patents.

Those restrictions are apt and pertinent to protection of the patent monopoly; and their applicability to the post-expiration period is a telltale sign that the licensor was using the licenses to project its monopoly beyond the patent period. They forcefully negate the suggestion that we have here a bare arrangement for a sale or a lease at an undetermined price based on use. The sale or lease of unpatented machines on long-term payments based on a deferred purchase price or on use would present wholly different considerations. Those arrangements seldom rise to the level of a federal question. But patents are in the federal domain; and "whatever the legal device employed" a projection of the patent monopoly after the patent expires is not enforceable. The present licenses draw no line between the term of the patent and the post-expiration period. The same provisions as respects both use and royalties are applicable to each. The contracts are, therefore, on their face a bald attempt to exact the same terms and conditions for the period after the patents have expired as they do for the monopoly period. We are, therefore, unable to conjecture what the bargaining position of the parties might have been and what resultant arrangement might have emerged had the provision for post-expiration royalties been divorced from the patent and nowise subject to its leverage.

IV.DURATION OF ROYALTY

In light of those considerations, we conclude that a patentee's use of a royalty agreement that projects beyond the expiration date of the patent is unlawful per se. If that device were available to patentees, the free market visualized for the post-expiration period would be subject to monopoly influences that have no proper place there.

Automatic Radio Co. v. Hazeltine, 339 U.S. 827, is not in point. While some of the patents under that license apparently had expired, the royalties claimed were not for a period when all of them had expired. That license covered several hundred patents and the royalty was based on the licensee's sales, even when no patents were used. The Court held that the computation of royalty payments by that formula was a convenient and reasonable device. We decline the invitation to extend it so as to project the patent monopoly beyond the 17-year period.

A patent empowers the owner to exact royalties as high as he can negotiate with the leverage of that monopoly. But to use that leverage to project those royalty payments beyond the life of the patent is analogous to an effort to enlarge the monopoly of the patent by tieing the sale or use of the patented article to the purchase or use of unpatented ones. The exaction of royalties for use of a machine after the patent has expired is an assertion of monopoly power in the post-expiration period when, as we have seen, the patent has entered the public domain. We share the views of the Court of Appeals in *Ar-Tik Systems, Inc. v. Dairy Queen, Inc.*, 3 Cir., 302 F.2d 496, 510, that after expiration of the last of the patents incorporated in the machines "the grant of patent monopoly was spent" and that an attempt to project it into another term by continuation of the licensing agreement is unenforceable.

REVERSED.

MR. JUSTICE HARLAN, dissenting.

The Court holds that the Thys Company unlawfully misused its patent monopoly by contracting with purchasers of its patented machines for royalty payments based on use beyond the patent term. I think that more discriminating analysis than the Court has seen fit to give this case produces a different result.

The patent laws prohibit post-expiration restrictions on the use of patented ideas; they have no bearing on use restrictions upon nonpatented, tangible machines. We have before us a mixed case involving the sale of a tangible machine which incorporates an intangible, patented idea. My effort in what follows is to separate out these two notions, to show that there is no substantial restriction on the use of the Thys idea, and to demonstrate that what slight restriction there may be is less objectionable than other post-expiration use restrictions which are clearly acceptable.

I

It surely cannot be questioned that Thys could have lawfully set a fixed price for its machine and extended credit terms beyond the patent period. It is equally unquestionable, I take it, that if Thys had had no patent or if its patent had expired, it could have sold its machines at a flexible, undetermined price based on use; for example, a phonograph record manufacturer could sell a recording of a song in the public domain to a juke-box owner for an undetermined consideration based on the number of times the record was played.

Conversely it should be equally clear that if Thys licensed another manufacturer to produce hop-picking machines incorporating any of the Thys patents, royalties could not be exacted beyond the patent term. Such royalties would restrict the manufacturer's exploitation of the idea after it falls into the public domain, and no such restriction should be valid. To give another example unconnected with a tangible machine, a song writer could charge a royalty every time his song — his idea — was sung for profit during the period of copyright. But once the song falls into the public domain each and every member of the public should be free to sing it.

In fact Thys sells both a machine and the use of an idea. The company should be free to restrict the use of its machine, as in the first two examples given above. It may not restrict the use of its patented idea once it has fallen into the public domain. Whether it has done so must be the point of inquiry.

Consider the situation as of the day the patent monopoly ends. Any manufacturer is completely free to produce Thys-type hop-pickers. The farmer who has previously purchased a Thys machine is free to buy and use any other kind of machine whether or not it incorporates the Thys idea, or make one himself if he is able. Of course, he is not entitled as against Thys to the free use of any Thys machine. The Court's opinion must therefore ultimately rest on the proposition that the purchasing farmer is restricted in using his particular machine, embodying as it does an application of the patented idea, by the fact that royalties are tied directly to use.

To test this proposition I again put a hypothetical. Assume that a Thys contract called for neither an initial flat-sum payment nor any annual minimum royalties; Thys' sole recompense for giving up ownership of its machine was a royalty payment extending beyond the patent term based on use, without any requirement either to use the machine or not to use a competitor's. A moment's thought reveals that, despite the clear restriction on use both before and after the expiration of the patent term, the arrangement would involve no misuse of patent leverage. Unless the Court's opinion rests on technicalities of contract draftsmanship and not on the economic substance of the transaction, the distinction between the hypothetical and the actual case lies only in the cumulative investment consisting of the initial and minimum payments independent of use, which the purchaser obligated himself to make to Thys. I fail to see why this distinguishing feature should be critical. If anything the investment will encourage the purchaser to use his machine in order to amortize the machine's fixed cost over as large a production base as possible. Yet the gravamen of the majority opinion is restriction, not encouragement, of use.

II

The essence of the majority opinion may lie in some notion that "patent leverage" being used by Thys to exact use payments extending beyond the patent term somehow allows Thys to extract more onerous payments from the farmers than would otherwise be obtainable. If this be the case, the Court must in some way distinguish long-term use payments from long-term installment payments of a flat-sum purchase price. For the danger which it seems to fear would appear to inhere equally in both, and as I read the Court's opinion, the latter type of arrangement is lawful despite the fact that failure to pay an installment under a conditional sales contract would permit the seller to recapture the machine, thus terminating — not merely restricting — the farmer's use of it. Furthermore, since the judgments against petitioners were based almost entirely on defaults in paying the $500 minimums and not on failures to pay for above minimum use, any such distinction of extended use payments and extended installments, even if accepted, would not justify eradicating all petitioners' obligations beyond the patent term, but only those based on use above the stated minimums; for the minimums by themselves, being payable whether or not a machine has been used, are precisely identical in substantive economic effect to flat installments.

In fact a distinction should not be accepted based on the assumption that Thys, which exploits its patents by selling its patented machines rather than licensing others to manufacture them, can use its patent leverage to exact more onerous payments from farmers by gearing price to use instead of charging a flat sum. Four possible situations must be considered. The purchasing farmer could overestimate, exactly estimate, underestimate, or have no firm estimate of his use requirements for a Thys machine. If he overestimates or exactly estimates, the farmer will be fully aware of what the machine will cost him in the long run, and it is unrealistic to suppose that in such circumstances he would be willing to pay more to have the machine on use than on straight terms. If the farmer underestimates, the thought may be that Thys will take advantage of him; but surely the farmer is in a better position than Thys or anyone else to estimate his own requirements and is hardly in need of the Court's protection in this respect. If the farmer has no fixed estimate of his use requirements he may have good business reasons entirely unconnected with "patent leverage" for wanting payments tied to use, and may indeed be willing to pay more in the long run to obtain such an arrangement. On final example should illustrate my point:

At the time when the Thys patent term still has a few years to run, a farmer who has been picking his hops by hand comes into the Thys retail outlet to inquire about the mechanical pickers. The salesman concludes his description of the advantages of the Thys machine with the price tag — $20,000. Value to the farmer depends completely on the use he will derive from the machine; he is willing to obligate himself on long credit terms to pay $10,000, but unless the machine can substantially outpick his old hand-picking methods, it is worth no more to him. He therefore offers to pay $2,000 down, $400 annually for 20 years, and an additional payment during the contract term for any production he can derive from the machine over and above the minimum amount he could pick by hand. Thys accepts, and by doing so, according to the majority, commits a per se misuse of its patent. I cannot believe that this is good law.

I would affirm.

NOTES

1. Ten years after *Brulotte*, the Court in *Aronson v. Quick Point Pencil Co.*, 440 U.S. 257 (1979), distinguished *Brulotte* and held that there was no preemption of a license requiring that a licensee continue to pay royalties with respect to sales of an item covered by a patent application even if a patent on the underlying technology failed to issue. The license was entered into while the patent application was pending and might be rejected. Yet, the license provided only for a reduction of royalty if no patent issued, not a complete removal of the royalty obligation. Distinguishing *Brulotte* on the grounds that the *Brulotte* doctrine was based on the putative "leverage" of a patent that allowed a patentee to exact post-expiration royalties, the Court said:

> Commercial agreements traditionally are the domain of state law. State law is not displaced merely because the contract relates to intellectual property which may or may not be patentable; the states are free to regulate the use of such intellectual property in any manner not inconsistent with federal law. In this as in other fields, the question of whether federal law pre-empts state law involves a consideration of whether that law "stands as an obstacle to the accomplishment and execution of the full purposes and objectives of Congress." If it does not, state law governs. . . . Enforcement of Quick Point's agreement . . . is not inconsistent with any of these aims. Permitting inventors to make enforceable agreements licensing the use of their inventions in return for royalties provides an additional incentive to invention.

2. Earlier, we mentioned the Patent Misuse Reform Act of 1988, 35 U.S.C. § 271(d). Would that Act have altered the result in *Brulotte*? Does *Brulotte* depend on actual of leverage based on the patent, a presumption that leverage exists, or a policy unrelated to the exercise of patent leverage? What distinguishes an invalid royalty extension from an installment payment that goes beyond the term of the patent?

3. *Brulotte* has been widely criticized. For example, Judge Posner commented: "The Supreme Court's majority opinion reasoned that by extracting a promise to continue paying royalties after expiration of the patent, the patentee extends the patent beyond the term fixed in the patent statute and therefore in violation of the law. That is not true. After the patent expires, anyone can make the patented process or product without being guilty of patent infringement. The patent can no longer be used to exclude anybody from such production. Expiration thus accomplishes what it is supposed to accomplish. For a licensee in accordance with a provision in the license agreement to go on paying royalties after the patent expires does not extend the duration of the patent either technically or practically, because, as this case demonstrates, if the licensee agrees to continue paying royalties after the patent expires the royalty rate will be lower. The duration of the patent fixes the limit of the patentee's power to extract royalties; it is a detail whether he extracts them at a higher rate over a shorter period of time or a lower rate over a longer period of time." *Scheiber v. Dolby Laboratories, Inc.*, 293 F.3d 1014 (7th Cir. 2002).

4. In an antitrust context in 2006, the Supreme Court in *Illinois Tool Works, Inc. v. Independent Ink, Inc.*, 126 S.Ct. 1281 (2006), held that a presumption of market power based solely on the existence of a patent has no support in economic theory or in commercial fact. The Court held that, while "some . . . arrangements are . . . unlawful, such as those that are the product of a true monopoly or a marketwide conspiracy, that conclusion must be supported by proof of power in the relevant market rather than by a mere presumption thereof." Does this undermine and, perhaps, invalidate the rule in *Bulotte*? If not, why?

PROBLEM 11.9

Dinner Corp. and Mason Enterprises agree on a license to Dinner of five patents owned by Mason, relating to the design and operation of food processing systems in a high volume restaurant. The patents are inter-related and must be used together to be effective. The patents expire at two-year intervals, beginning next year, with the last one expiring nine years from the date of the agreement. Dinner operates twenty restaurants. The parties agree that the value of using the package of technology is $500,000 per year per restaurant. It is not clear whether Dinner will open new restaurants or close some of the existing ones during the term of the contract. In the spirit of all entrepreneurs, Dinner would like to defer as much of this payment as long as possible.

a. Assuming that the license does not cover technology other than the five patents, how would you structure the term of the license and the royalty payment obligation?

b. How would your answer change if, along with the five patents, Mason will provide Dinner with know-how and some confidential information about how best to employ the technology?

V.   ASSIGNING ROYALTY OBLIGATIONS

BROADCAST MUSIC, INC. v. HIRSCH
104 F.3d 1163 (9th Cir. 1997)

SCHWARZER, SENIOR DISTRICT JUDGE.

The question we decide in this case is whether a federal tax lien takes priority over prior unrecorded assignments of the taxpayer's rights to receive royalty income from the performance of a copyrighted work.

Broadcast Music, Inc. ("BMI") licenses the public performance rights in copyrighted musical compositions. It collects and pays royalties arising from licensed public performances of copyrighted compositions. Ronald Miller is a songwriter to whom BMI paid royalties derived from his compositions. To satisfy debts Miller owed appellants Staenberg and Hirsch, he executed assignments to them in 1989 of future royalties and directed BMI to pay Staenberg and Hirsch directly. Before the debts were satisfied, however, the Internal Revenue Service ("IRS") assessed deficiencies against Miller, and in 1992, 1993 and 1994 the IRS recorded notices of tax liens against his royalty income. The IRS served BMI with notices of levy, whereupon BMI filed this interpleader action to resolve the conflicting claims to Miller's royalty income.

The district court granted the government's motion for summary judgment. . . . Staenberg and Hirsch appeal from the judgment. . . .

II.   APPLICATION OF THE COPYRIGHT ACT

Under the Act, "[a]s between two conflicting transfers, the one executed first prevails if it is recorded, in the manner required to give constructive notice under subsection (c). . . ." 17 U.S.C. §205(d). Staenberg and Hirsch's assignments were never recorded with the Copyright Office. The IRS tax liens, however, did not have to be recorded to be perfected. Thus, the first question is whether the assignments to Hirsch and to Staenberg were transfers subject to the recordation rules of the Act (i.e., whether they were a "transfer of copyright ownership or other document pertaining to a copyright," 17 U.S.C. §205(a)). If they were, the failure to record them prevents them from priming the later IRS liens.

The Act defines "transfer of copyright ownership" as "an assignment, mortgage, exclusive license, or any other conveyance, alienation, or hypothecation of a copyright or of any of the exclusive rights comprised in a copyright. . . ." 17 U.S.C. §101. The assignments on their face did not transfer any interest in a copyright or in any of the exclusive rights comprised in a copyright. Indeed, the government admits as much in its Statement of Genuine Issues in Opposition to Hirsch's Motion for Summary Judgment, where it states that "[t]he Hirsch Assignments are not assignments of copyrights or of interests in copyrights." Although the government made no such admission with respect to Staenberg, it otherwise makes no distinction between the interests of Staenberg and those of Hirsch. Thus, the Staenberg assignment must be treated in the same way as Hirsch's.

That Miller may have been a beneficial owner of copyrights, as the government argues, is irrelevant to determining whether a transfer occurred according to sections 101, 201(d), or 205(d) of the Act. Beneficial ownership arises by virtue of section 501(b) for the purpose of enabling an author or composer to protect his economic interest in a copyright that has been transferred. Beneficial ownership is a standing doctrine that does not determine the scope or substance of rights under a copyright. Regardless of whether beneficial ownership may somehow have passed to Staenberg and Hirsch, the assignments did not amount to "transfers of copyright ownership."

Nor are the assignments "other documents pertaining to a copyright" within the meaning of section 205(a), which defines the scope of potentially recordable documents under the Act. The Copyright Office's regulations define a document pertaining to a copyright as one that "has a direct or indirect relationship to the existence, scope, duration, or identification of a copyright, or to the ownership, division, allocation, licensing, transfer, or exercise of rights under a copyright." Assignments of interests in royalties have no relationship to the existence, scope, duration or identification of a copyright, nor to "rights under a copyright." For that reason, and in light of the preceding discussion, we see no basis for finding the assignments to be documents "pertaining to a copyright."

The government, citing *In re Peregrine Entertainment, Ltd.*, 116 B.R. 194 (C.D.Cal.1990), further contends that the Staenberg and Hirsch assignments are recordable because they are security interests in a copyright. We need not decide whether the priority rule under section 205(d) is coextensive with the recording provisions of section 205(a). It is sufficient that this case does not involve an assignment of a security interest — there is no evidence that Miller owned a copyright and had a security interest he could assign. Rather, this is a case of outright assignments of a right to receive royalties for the purpose of satisfying a debt. Thus, the rationale for recordation underlying the *Peregrine* case — to provide notice to prospective creditors or purchasers of the copyright who may rely to their detriment on the appearance of ownership of rights under a copyright — is inapposite. It is true, as the government points out, that the document executed by Miller purported to assign a security interest. But that document was the standard form prepared by BMI, which BMI required for all assignments, regardless of whether they conveyed a security interest. Hirsch, Staenberg, and BMI all insist that the document did not accurately reflect the transaction. The record supports their position and there is no evidence to the contrary. Under New York law, which the parties expressly incorporated in the assignments as determinative of their rights under it, the court looks to the substance of a contract rather than to its form. Even if the terms of the assignment document were inexact, "no particular words or phrases are required to effect an assignment." *Pro Cardiaco Pronto Socorro Cardiologica S.A. v. Trussell,* 863 F.Supp. 135, 138 (S.D.N.Y.1994). The government's brief describes the transaction accurately when it states that Miller "was simply arranging to pay a debt that he owed to [Staenberg and Hirsch] out of the royalties that BMI would be accruing on [his] behalf."

III. APPLICATION OF NEW YORK LAW

Having concluded that the provisions of the Act do not apply to determining priority among the competing claims, we turn to state law to determine "to what extent the taxpayer had 'property' or 'rights to property' to which [a] tax lien could attach." As noted, the assignment form specified that the rights of the parties under it shall be determined in accordance with New York law, and none of the parties to this action disputes the choice of law clause.

The IRS liens attach to "all property and rights to property, whether real or personal, belonging to [the taxpayer]." 26 U.S.C. § 6321. Thus, the question is whether, under New York law, the instruments executed by Miller in favor of Staenberg and Hirsch transferred all of his rights to the future royalties he purported to assign (i.e., whether Miller had anything left to which the liens could attach). The government contends that Miller's assignments were deficient, both because Miller retained control over the source of the monies and because the BMI assignment forms transferred only security interests.

Under New York law, "an assignment occurs only where the assignor retains no control over the funds, no authority to collect and no power to revoke." The government argues that an "agreement to pay a debt out of a designated fund 'does not operate as a legal or equitable assignment since the assignor retains control over the subject matter.'" *Miller v. Wells Fargo Bank Int'l Corp.,* 540 F.2d 548, 558 (2d Cir.1976) But the critical fact in *Miller* was that the assignor "retain[ed] control over the fund or [maintained] authority to collect or [had the] power to revoke." Here, in contrast, Miller did not control the royalty payments after executing the assignments, and in those assignments, he expressly "waive[d] [his] right to terminate [his] agreement with BMI until

[his] loan[s] . . . [were] repaid." The assignments thus constituted irrevocable instructions to pay the specified sums directly to Staenberg and to Hirsch as royalties came into BMI's hands. While Miller retained a residual interest in the excess royalty income over the amounts assigned, he had no control whatever over the amounts he had assigned. A valid assignment exists where, as here, a "document . . . designates that money be paid to a third party [i.e., Hirsch or Staenberg] . . . [and] the document directs the obligor [i.e., BMI] to pay the third party from those specific funds owing to the assignor [i.e., Miller]." *Pro Cardiaco Pronto Socorro Cardiologica S.A.,* 863 F.Supp. at 138.

The government argues that the assignments merely transferred security interests that were never perfected. But, as noted above, we must look to the substance, not the form of the transaction. Miller made complete assignments of the monies specified in the assignment documents, leaving him without a current vested interest.

SUMMARY AND CONCLUSION

Because the assignments to Hirsch and to Staenberg were not subject to the Act's recording rules, their failure to record them with the Copyright Office did not leave the assignments unperfected. Because those assignments were complete under New York law, they transferred Miller's interests to Hirsch and to Staenberg before the IRS tax liens could attach.

The judgment of the district court is REVERSED. . . .

NOTES

1. *Hirsch* bifurcates legal coverage. The effect of a transaction in establishing property interests in the underlying intellectual property is governed by property-rights law, while the effect of a transfer of the *contract* rights to payment is otherwise governed by other law. *See generally* RAYMOND T. NIMMER & JEFF DODD, MODERN LICENSING LAW ch. 16 (2004).

2. State law has changed since *Hirsch* with the adoption of Revised Article 9. With several enumerated exceptions, Article 9 applies to both security interests and sales of payment rights arising out of licensing agreements. The latter are described in Article 9 as "accounts." UCC § 9-102(a)(2) (2000 Official Draft). The exceptions are as follows:

- A sale of accounts as part of a sale of the business out of which they arose.
- An assignment of accounts for the purposes of collection only.
- An assignment to an assignee obligated to perform under the contract.
- An assignment of a single account to an assignee in full or partial satisfaction of a preexisting debt.

UCC § 9-109(d) (2000 Official Draft).

Chapter 12

REMEDIES ON BREACH OF A LICENSE

I. INTRODUCTION

This chapter deals with remedies in the event of a breach of a license. While license agreements fall within the general framework that pertains to contract breach claims in general, they also involve many unique issues in part because of their subject matter and in part because of the commercial context i n which the arise.

A primary source of that uniqueness lies in the interaction between contract and intellectual property law. The blend of these two areas of law, seen throughout this book, is especially important in reference to remedies. Breach of a license often brings into play a choice among remedies under contract or property law, or under both. In addition, some licenses are covered by the codified contract law of the UCC or UCITA, while many others arise under common law. While there are similarities between the codified rules and the common law, there are also important differences.

Another important difference lies in the contractual subject matter itself. For transactions in goods, a particular object (good) often defines the focus of the transaction. As a result, disposition or replacement of, or substitution for that item provides a convenient focus for remedies. In contrast, licensed subject matter is intangible and often readily reproducible. The reference point for remedies is seldom a particular item (e.g., copy). We will see this most explicitly in reference to damages issues and in the extent to which alternative or "substitute" transactions are considered as an appropriate gauge for the loss caused by a breach of contract.

Consider, for example, what damages are appropriate in the following:

> Jake Corp. agrees to build a serialtron machine for Bundy for $100,000. It completes construction, but for no valid reason, Bundy refuses to complete the deal. Jake is able to sell the machine to Scavenger for $90,000. Jake sues Bundy for Bundy's breach.

> Jake agrees to grant a non-exclusive license to Bundy to build and sell Jake's patented serialtron machine for $100,000. For no valid reason, Bundy repudiates the transaction, believing another technology is better. Jake gives a license on the same technology to Core Company for $120,000. It sues Bundy for damages for Bundy's breach.

II. BREACH, WAIVER AND OTHER EVENTS

A breach of contract occurs if a party fails to perform a contractual promise, exceeds a contractual limitation, or engages in conduct that gives the other party the right to treat the likelihood of breach in the future as sufficient to constitute a breach today (anticipatory repudiation). *Restatement (Second) of*

Contracts § 250 (1981). The definition of breach thus refers back to what obligations or limitations are established by the agreement. The *Restatement (First) of Contracts* states:

> A breach of contract is a non-performance of any contractual duty of immediate performance. A breach may be total or partial, and may take place by failure to perform acts promised, by prevention or hindrance, or by repudiation.

Restatement (First) of Contracts § 312. The *Restatement (Second) of Contracts* § 235 states: "When performance of a duty under a contract is due any non-performance is a breach." UCITA provides:

> Whether a party is in breach of contract is determined by the agreement or, in the absence of agreement, this [Act]. A breach occurs if a party without legal excuse fails to perform an obligation in a timely manner, repudiates a contract, or exceeds a contractual use term, or otherwise is not in compliance with an obligation placed on it by this [Act] or the agreement. . . . Whether a breach of a contractual use term is an infringement or a misappropriation is determined by applicable informational property rights law.

UCITA § 701(a) (2000 Official Text). *See also* UCC §§ 2A-508, 523 (1998 Official Text).

PROBLEM 12.1

JJG Corporation grants CIT a license to use JJG copyrighted software in the CIT office in Baton Rouge. After working with the software for several months, CIT makes an additional copy and begins to use the software in its Chicago office. JJG sues for breach of contract. What result?

The idea that breach of contract consists of a failure to do what was promised results in different outcomes depending on what one views as the promises involved. A narrow view of a license yields a narrow view of what constitutes breach. For example, is a licensor whose technology is not effective liable for breach in the absence of an express warranty? The answer lies in one's view about what are the implicit obligations undertaken in a license. Is a licensee that exceeds the limitations on use of a licensed subject matter in breach of the contract? In most cases, the answer is yes.

TOPPS CHEWING GUM, INC. v. IMPERIAL TOY CORP.
686 F. Supp. 402 (E.D.N.Y. 1988)

BARTELS, DISTRICT JUDGE.

This is a motion for summary judgment by plaintiff Topps Chewing Gum, Inc. limited to the issue of liability for alleged breach of a license and trademark agreement by the defendant Imperial Toy Corporation (hereinafter "Imperial"), and also a motion for dismissal of Imperial's four counterclaims. At the same time Imperial cross-moves for summary judgment with respect to its counterclaims for breach of contract and for breach of express warranty of title. . . .

Facts

The parties entered into a "best efforts" contract beginning May 12, 1986 and expiring December 31, 1987 which granted Imperial exclusive rights to manufacture, sell and/or distribute in the U.S. and Canada goods bearing Topps' trademark "GARBAGE PAIL KIDS" (hereinafter "GPK"). No mention was made in the contract of the place where these articles had to be manufactured or acquired except for a rider to the agreement which provided that "[m]anufacture or shipment from or to any country other than the United States or Canada . . ." required the prior written approval of Topps. Topps warranted that, "we own or control the specified proprietary subject matter . . . and have the right to grant license rights to use thereof in the Territory." Topps further promised to indemnify Imperial against "all claims, suits, damages and expenses, including legal fees, arising out of our breach of our representation hereunder." . . .

At the time the contract was entered into, a separate action was pending in the United States District Court for the Northern District of Georgia, entitled *Original Appalachian Artworks v. Topps Chewing Gum, Inc.* (hereinafter "the Georgia action") in which OAA, the copyright holders of the "Cabbage Patch Dolls," brought suit against the current plaintiff claiming infringement of its copyright through Topps' use of the GPK mark. In light of the pending OAA litigation, Imperial sought and obtained assurances from LMI, Topps' agent, that Topps would likely prevail in the Georgia action as soon as May 1986. Upon this point, Topps agreed to the following clauses: "You (Imperial) are fully aware of the *Original Appalachian Artwork, Inc. (OAA) v. Topps Chewing Gum, Inc.* lawsuit now pending in the U.S. District Court for the Northern District of Georgia. . . . In the event OAA is granted an injunction against Topps, all prepaid royalties shall be refunded . . . and this License shall cease."

On August 29, 1986, . . . the Georgia court ruled that OAA "is entitled to a preliminary injunction. Said injunction will issue upon application of the plaintiff. The plaintiff will be required to post a substantial bond. . . ." Because OAA never made the application or posted this bond, the preliminary injunction never issued. On February 2, 1988, Topps eventually settled the case by entering into a stipulation with OAA which, *inter alia,* granted Topps unqualified use of the GPK name through September 1, 1987 (in the U.S.) and February 1988 (abroad), and the Georgia action was dropped.

The defendant obtained at least some of its GPK articles from abroad for sale in the U.S. Upon learning of the Georgia decision, even though no bond had been filed, the U.S. Customs Service nevertheless began to deny entry of Imperial's GPK goods into the United States beginning in September 1986. The basis for this action was that the goods allegedly infringed upon OAA's rights in Cabbage Patch Dolls. Imperial now claims that because all such GPK articles were made outside the United States, it was effectively prevented from enjoying the benefits of its licensing arrangement with Topps and further contends that several of its customers, concerned about the effects of the Georgia decision and the customs seizures, cancelled orders for GPK articles. As a result, Imperial claims it was forced to sell what GPK products it had already imported at "distress" prices.

Imperial unsuccessfully sought Topps' cooperation in persuading the Customs Service to free the seized goods and allegedly expended $3665.00 in attorneys' fees unsuccessfully fighting the seizures. Imperial's customs counsel wrote several letters to the U.S. Customs Service. . . . At no time did Imperial inform Topps that it considered that the contract had "ceased" until it filed its answer and counterclaim in response to Topps' amended complaint.

On October 31, 1986, Imperial wrote to Topps, stating that "under normal circumstances, the first royalty payment would have been due" but because of the effects of the Georgia court decision and the seizures "we are not prepared to make any payments at this time. . . ." [Pursuant] to the terms of the contract, Topps gave Imperial ten days written notice that it would terminate the contract effective November 27, 1986 unless it received all past due royalty payments. Imperial failed to remit such payments and . . . Topps terminated the contract. To date, Imperial has made no payments other than the initial $25000 royalty advance, even though Topps claims that Imperial continued to sell the GPK articles at least through December 1986. Imperial sold $2,939,598.20 worth of licensed articles as of the end of September 1986, and it sold another $312,532.72 in licensed articles in the three following months. Topps then brought this suit, seeking, *inter alia,* royalties allegedly owed to it by Imperial, an injunction and an accounting. . . .

Discussion

[I. Alleged Misrepresentations]

Imperial alleges that the contract is invalid because of certain misrepresentations: (1) fraudulent representations made to induce Imperial to enter into the license agreement and (2) misrepresentations of ownership. Both of these . . . are predicated upon alleged statements made by Topps that the Georgia decision would be favorable. . . .

a. Fraudulent Inducement

Imperial claims that the contract is invalid because it was predicated upon the misrepresentation that the Georgia decision would be a favorable one, thereby fraudulently inducing Imperial to enter into the agreement. The contract itself belies that allegation. . . . Any representations made as to the probable outcome of the *OAA* litigation could only have involved statements which Imperial should obviously have known were ones of opinion only and which were based on facts stated in the *OAA* pleadings themselves, which were open for public inspection. Moreover, Imperial's own attorneys' opinion as to the probable outcome was available to it. An erroneous or misleading opinion as to the outcome of a litigation, standing alone, is an insufficient predicate for invoking these affirmative defenses. Such predictions are inherently uncertain given the hazardous nature of litigation and cannot be considered as the kind of misrepresentations that would make the contract voidable. . . .

b. Ownership

The question of whether Topps misrepresented its ownership of the GPK trademark and copyrights might be one of fact not subject to a summary judgment were it not clearly stated in the agreement between the parties that "[i]n the event OAA is granted an injunction against Topps, all prepaid royalties shall be refunded . . . and this License shall cease." This provision clearly indicates that Imperial was fully aware of any uncertainty of Topps' title and of the immediate remedy available if its title were defective. In other words, as a matter of law, there could be no reliance on the part of Imperial or any misrepresentation of ownership on the part of Topps in view of the express injunction provision of the contract. Such alleged misrepresentation of ownership was therefore made immaterial by the insertion of the injunction clause into the contract.

II. Breach of Warranty

The licensing agreement provided that Topps warrant and represent that it owned or controlled "the specified proprietary subject matter . . . and have the right to grant license rights to use thereof in the Territory [United States and Canada]." Topps has continuously maintained a registered trademark and copyright registrations for Garbage Pail Kids, and Imperial has never disputed this fact. It is well settled that a registered trademark is *prima facie* evidence of the validity of such right. Nevertheless, Imperial has described the decision of the *OAA* court and the actions of the Customs Service as a breach of warranty of title and the denial of Topps' ability to license any GPK rights to Imperial. No court, however, has held that Topps does not own or have a proprietary interest in the GPK trademark and copyright registrations. Aside from this contention of Imperial, the indicia of Topps' title to the trademark and copyright registrations are clear. Both parties contemplated that the issuance of an injunction would be evidence of a breach but such an injunction was never issued.

III. Injunction

There is no doubt that on August 2, 1986, the Georgia court did issue a "preliminary injunction" requiring the plaintiff to post a substantial bond. However, does the word "injunction" include a preliminary injunction that was never made effective? . . . The meaning of the word "injunction" is clear; it does not mean a preliminary injunction, particularly where no bond was ever posted. There is no need to resort to any outside evidence to determine either the meaning thereof or the parties' intent. To interpret the word injunction otherwise would torture the meaning of the word. . . .

In connection with the Georgia decision, it is necessary to refer to the action of the Customs Service, since, in fact, the Customs Service predicated the prohibition of importation of the Imperial goods upon the *OAA* decision. The Customs Service is not a legal entity whose decisions can affect the valid title to either the GPK copyright or trademark, nor can its actions be equated to an injunction. Indeed, Imperial has already acknowledged this in its communications with the Service. Moreover, the statements of Imperial's counsel to the Service to the effect that Topps had title and that there was no infringement of OAA's title, makes it now impossible for Imperial to claim that the Custom Service's bar was a breach of the agreement.[1]

---

[1] [FN7] Even if one were to assume that the Georgia decision placed a cloud on the right Imperial received to use the GPK copyright and trademark, thereby constituting a breach of warranty of title on the part of Topps, the actions and declarations of Imperial described in our discussion of waiver, *infra,* clearly indicate that it had waived its right to place Topps in breach.

IV. Substantial Frustration

The reaction of the Customs Service to the Georgia court decision which barred imports of the GPK might be considered as a substantial frustration of the contract, thereby excusing Imperial from its obligations thereunder. This theory, though not advanced by Imperial, could only be of advantage to Imperial if there was a written understanding or condition at the beginning of the contract or any time thereafter that Imperial was to obtain its products or materials solely from abroad. However, it is manifest that there was no such understanding or condition at any time and Imperial was free and entitled to obtain its products from domestic sources. Indeed, a rider to the contract specifically provided that Topps had veto power over "[m]anufacture or shipment (of GPK articles) from or to any country other than the United States or Canada. . . ." Therefore, it is difficult to see how the purpose of Imperial in entering into the agreement was substantially frustrated. The *Restatement of Contracts* § 265, Comments, lists the following factors that must be established to make out such a claim, thereby excusing performance on a contract: "First, . . . the [object] that is frustrated . . . must be so completely the basis of the contract that, as both parties understand, without it the transaction would make little sense. Second, . . . the frustration must be so severe that it is not fairly to be regarded as within the risks he assumed under the contract. Third, the non-occurrence of the frustrating event must have been a basic assumption on which the contract was made . . . so that it cannot be fulfilled without undue hardship."

In a word, the basis of the agreement was the right to use the GPK copyright and trademark in the United States and Canada. Each party assumed the risk of a binding injunction. The actions of the Customs Service based on the Georgia decision, even if they were legal, merely prevented the importation of GPK articles into the United States. Imperial at all times was fully capable of using domestic sources, either in the United States or in Canada, to produce these goods. Therefore, the only frustrating event which could have destroyed the value of the contract would have been a final and binding decision that Topps did not hold valid title to the GPK copyright and trademark, thereby preventing any use whatsoever by Topps of the GPK. As we have already noted, there was never any such binding court decision to that effect. Thus, the salient factors to establish substantial frustration as set forth above are absent.

V. Waiver

Since it is often not clear that a party has waived its legal right(s), the waiver issue frequently involves questions of fact, and cannot be decided on a summary judgment motion. Nevertheless, ". . . [o]ccasionally it is proved by the express declaration of the party, or by [its] undisputed acts or language so inconsistent with [its] purpose to stand upon [its] rights as to leave no opportunity for a reasonable inference to the contrary. Then the waiver is established as a matter of law." This is the situation in which Imperial finds itself.

Here, both parties have extensively briefed the question of whether Imperial waived and relinquished any right it may have had to terminate the agreement and to cease performing thereunder. Such discussion is immaterial since waiver is pertinent only if there were breaches of the agreement by Topps. Assuming there were such breaches, however, we conclude there was a waiver by Imperial. We believe the principle was well stated in *Specialities Development Corp. v. C-O-Two Fire Equipment Co.,* 207 F.2d 753 (3d Cir.1953), *cert. denied,* 347 U.S. 919 (1954), where the court said that:

> We do not find anything in this or any other New York case which we have located to throw doubt upon the general proposition that one against whom a material breach is committed must make up his mind what he is going to do about it, and that if he goes ahead without performance he is not excused from liability under the terms of the contract.

A party to a contract surrenders its right to claim that the contract was terminated by the other party's breach when it chooses nevertheless to perform the contract.

Imperial contends that it waived no claims for breach of contract but simply continued its performance in order to mitigate damages after the Georgia decision and the bar of the Customs Service. The undisputed facts nevertheless show that: (1) Imperial proclaimed to the Customs Service that, in effect, there had been no breach by Topps; (2) after the Georgia decision Imperial continued to enjoy the use of the right of the GPK license by selling over $300,000 worth of licensed articles; and (3) the excuse offered by Imperial that it was mitigating damages in selling after the Georgia decision was distinctly unauthorized by the provision of the agreement which stated that:

> On expiration or termination hereof, all royalties are immediately due and payable, and [Imperial] shall immediately stop manufacture, sale and distribution of all articles licensed and send [Topps] a complete inventory report and accounting with payment due within 30 days. . . .

This provision cannot now be ignored under the excuse of mitigation of damages.

Finally, in its letter of October 30, 1986, Imperial clearly demonstrated to Topps that it did not view the Georgia preliminary injunction decision as the type of injunction referred to in the contract. Rather, Imperial merely stated that "the outcome (of the *OAA* matter) is still in doubt," and that it was not prepared to pay royalties until the "problems" caused thereby would be resolved by the subsequent trial concerning the injunction. In other words, Imperial had made up its mind to go ahead with the agreement. . . .

Conclusion

For all of the foregoing reasons, summary judgment is granted in favor of Topps on the issue of liability on its first and second causes of action. Imperial's counterclaims are accordingly dismissed. . . .

NOTES

1. Assuming the licensee was acting in good faith in *Topps,* what should it have done when importation of the product was prevented by a federal agency in order to avoid breaching its contract?

2. *Topps* illustrates some of the defenses and options that can be presented in a situation where there are required ongoing performances, often by both parties. In the absence of contractual terms, neither common law nor the various codifications of contract law that might apply give clear answers that guide the conduct of the parties before the ultimate answer of a court. A licensee (or licensor) presented with an arguable breach by the other party faces several options each of which might have legal consequences that are difficult to predict when the actual events transpire. Waiver may result from continuing to perform as if there had been no breach. Breach by the originally aggrieved party may result if the party ceases to perform when the circumstances are later construed as not justifying that action. Election of remedies may also occur.

To provide a vehicle to reduce risk, Article 2 and UCITA provide for seeking "adequate assurances of performance" in cases where one party becomes reasonably insecure about the prospects of future performance by the other. The remedy requires reasonable grounds for insecurity and notice in a record to the other party of that fact. It allows the insecure party to suspend performance until adequate assurances are received from the other person and, if assurances are not received within a reasonable time not to exceed thirty days, the rule allows the party to treat the events as a repudiation of the contract. UCC § 2-609 (1998 Official Text); UCITA § 708 (2000 Official Text). This doctrine exists in common law in many, but not all states.

3. The Bankruptcy Court in *Record Club of America v. United Artists Records, Inc.,* 80 B.R. 271 (Bankr. S.D.N.Y. 1987), held that repudiation of the agreement by the licensor excused a licensee's failure to pay the minimum royalty. "Although a repudiation will not excuse performance when the non-repudiating party is unable to prove it is ready, willing, and able to perform, the willingness and ability to perform need not continue after the repudiation. All of UAR's assertions relate to Record Club's willingness, ability and preparedness to perform subsequent to UAR's repudiation. Therefore, these assertions are irrelevant to Record Club's damage claim."

4. The court in *ARP Films, Inc. v. Marvel Entertainment Group, Inc.,* 952 F.2d 643 (2d Cir. 1991), held that the licensee's withholding of payments and accounting reports from the licensor of a cartoon character copyright could not be treated as self-help designed to force the copyright owner to retract repudiation of the license, but was a material breach of contract. It commented:

> On the heels of Marvel's repudiation (the First Termination), ARP had two options: (1) it could have stopped performance and sued for total breach; or (2) it could have affirmed the contract by continuing to perform while suing in partial breach. In this case, ARP's decision to continue receiving benefits pursuant to the 1976 Agreement was tantamount to an election to affirm the contract. In view of this

affirmance, ARP's refusal to perform its end of the bargain, by making payments and providing reports, was impermissible. Further, the district court correctly concluded that the breach by plaintiffs in failing to make the payments and provide the reports required by the 1976 Agreement was material as a matter of law, thus authorizing Marvel to terminate the contract. Paragraph 8 of the 1976 Agreement explicitly singled out plaintiffs' obligation to provide "prompt accounting" for distributions as a term and condition of the agreement, the substantial breach of which authorized Marvel to terminate the license provided by the agreement. In addition, failure to tender payment is generally deemed a material breach of a contract. Finally, as the district court found, and the subsequent accounting confirmed, the amounts withheld from Marvel by plaintiffs were very substantial.

5. In *Medimmune, Inc. v. Genentech, Inc.*, 2007 WL 43797 (U.S. 2007), the Court held that a patent licensee has standing to challenge the validity of a licensed patent even though it continues to pay royalties under the license. The challenge was brought as a declaratory judgment action and the Court addressed the case in terms of Article III standing. It held that standing existed in that the continued payment of royalties was "coerced" by the threat of a patent infringement suit and attendant remedies. The Court did not address whether contract law doctrines might render this challenge ineffective because a challenging party cannot both accept the benefits of a contract and contest its validity, or whether a promise to not sue for invalidity would be enforceable.

KLIPSCH INC. v. WWR TECHNOLOGY INC.
127 F.3d 729 (8th Cir. 1997)

Bowman, J.

In 1992, Klipsch, WWR, and WWR's then-parent company entered into a series of agreements involving Klipsch's professional loudspeaker business. Besides an Asset Purchase Agreement, a Security Agreement, and a Manufacturing Agreement, the parties entered into a Non-Exclusive Patent and Trademark License, Non-Competition and Right of First Refusal Agreement [hereinafter License Agreement], which granted various Klipsch licenses to WWR. [Klipsch held a debenture issued in lieu of part of the purchase price in the transaction.] The License Agreement was revised by an August 5, 1994, Extension and Modification Agreement [hereinafter Extension Agreement] entered into by Klipsch, WWR, and WWR's current parent company, Concept Technologies Group, Inc. (Concept). The agreement effectively extended the maturity date of the original debenture and substituted Concept in the place of WWR's previous parent company in the original agreements. The agreement also provided, inter alia, that upon default or breach of the substitute debenture, "[t]he licenses shall automatically terminate, and all rights thereunder shall revert to Klipsch." The substitute debenture allowed Klipsch the option to require redemption at any time on or after June 30, 1995, provided prior written notice to Concept was given, and it stated that Klipsch shall receive periodic payments of interest from Concept. After Klipsch gave sufficient prior notice of redemption, Concept was unable to redeem the substitute debenture. Additionally, Concept failed to pay timely the July 1, 1995, interest payment.

In a July 5, 1995 correspondence, Klipsch informed Concept of two consequences of its failed redemption and late interest payment — Klipsch had a right to pursue its security interest in the collateral held by WWR, and the licenses granted to WWR had terminated and reverted to Klipsch. On July 24, 1995, Klipsch filed a complaint against WWR and Concept, in which Klipsch sought from WWR the assets that served as collateral pursuant to the Security Agreement and from Concept the remaining balance of principal and interest on the substitute debenture less any proceeds realized from disposition of the collateral. WWR paid the remaining balance on the substitute debenture on August 15, 1995, and after resolving issues of attorney fees and expenses, the District Court dismissed the case on November 6, 1995.

August 15, 1995, also marked the date that Klipsch filed its complaint in the present action, naming only WWR as a defendant and alleging trademark infringement pursuant to 15 U.S.C. Section 1114 (1994), patent infringement pursuant to 15 U.S.C. Section 1125(a) (1994), and unfair competition. . . . Klipsch's right to recover under these various theories grows from the failure of WWR or Concept to redeem the substitute debenture and their failure to make a timely interest payment, just as the right to recover did in the first action. . . . The District Court granted summary judgment in favor of WWR . . . on December 19, 1996. . . .

IV.

The District Court . . . granted summary judgment to WWR based on the affirmative defense of waiver. . . . The court found that Klipsch waived its right to enforce the automatic termination provision of the License Agreement by its prior acceptances of defective performance. Thus, despite the breach of the substitute debenture, the rights under the License Agreement remained with WWR, thereby rendering Klipsch's assertions in this action untenable.

Klipsch advances various arguments as to why the District Court erred in granting summary judgment to WWR based on the affirmative defense of waiver. First, Klipsch contends that the agreements' non-waiver clauses prevented it from waiving the right to enforce the termination provision. Second, even assuming the unenforceability of the non-waiver clauses, genuine issues of material fact existed as to whether Klipsch actually waived its right to terminate the License Agreement. Third, any waiver that may have been previously granted by Klipsch had been sufficiently revoked by the time WWR and Concept failed to redeem the substitute debenture. . . .

Non-waiver provisions exist in or are incorporated into each of the relevant agreements. As an example, the non-waiver provision in the License Agreement provides:

> The waiver by either party of any breach of this Agreement by the other party in a particular instance shall not operate as a waiver of

subsequent breaches of the same or different kind. The failure of either party to exercise any rights under this Agreement in a particular instance shall not operate as a waiver of such party's right to exercise the same or different rights in subsequent instances.

The District Court found that under Indiana law the existence of the non-waiver provisions does not prohibit WWR from asserting the defense of waiver. . . .

Klipsch relies upon the Indiana Supreme Court's decision in *Van Bibber v. Norris*, 419 N.E.2d 115 (Ind. 1981), to support its argument that the non-waiver provision in the License Agreement prevents WWR from asserting the defense of waiver. In *Van Bibber*, the parties entered into an installment sale security agreement, which provided for debtor's purchase of a mobile home from seller. During the course of the agreement, seller's bank accepted numerous late payments from debtor, without declaring a default. In the sixth year of the security agreement, however, after an untimely payment, the bank declared a default and repossessed the mobile home. The trial court found that the bank, through its pattern of accepting late payments, had waived its right to enforce strict compliance with the terms of the security agreement. The Indiana Supreme Court reversed, holding that the trial court improperly had ignored the security agreement's non-waiver clause, which prevented the acceptance of late payments from acting as a waiver of the bank's right to strictly enforce the terms of the agreement.

We hold that *Van Bibber* does prevent WWR from successfully asserting its waiver defense. The District Court noted that "[a] broad interpretation of *Van Bibber* would bar WWR's waiver argument," but found "that such a broad interpretation would be improper." The District Court reasoned that language in *Van Bibber* strongly indicated that the Indiana Commercial Code compelled that court's holding, and that Indiana cases decided since *Van Bibber* extend its holding only to cases involving non-waiver clauses in the mortgage context. We believe that the language in *Van Bibber* is sufficiently expansive to apply to this case. The late payments relied upon by WWR to support its waiver argument involved late payments on two notes and a previous debenture, both of which had been issued by WWR and its prior parent company as part of the original transaction involving the sale of Klipsch's professional loudspeaker business. Klipsch did not sell its professional loudspeaker business's assets to WWR in exchange for a one-time lump sum payment; instead payments were due on these various instruments at different times, similar to an installment contract. The specific purpose of the non-waiver clause as stated in *Van Bibber*, "avoiding the risk of waiver by notifying the debtor in a contract term that the secured party's acceptance of late payments cannot be relied on as treating the time provisions as modified or waived," seems equally germane to the present case. If the parties' License Agreement "is to be truly effective according to its terms, we must conclude that [Klipsch] did not waive its rights to demand strict compliance and to pursue its contract and statutory remedies." Additionally, rather than narrow the breadth of *Van Bibber*'s holding, we believe that subsequently decided Indiana cases expand the holding. While the District Court and WWR reference a string of cases applying *Van Bibber*'s holding to cases involving a mortgage, there is no authority that the holding is limited to the mortgage or other particular contexts.

Moreover, irrespective of the enforceability of the non-waiver clauses, WWR has not demonstrated a pattern of accepting late payments that would justify a determination of waiver of the License Agreement's automatic termination provision. As evidence of waiver, the District Court referred to several instances, spanning from April 1993 to January 1994, where Klipsch extended the maturity date on the two notes that had been issued as part of the original transaction involving the sale of Klipsch's assets. Moreover, the court noted that the Manufacturing Agreement had been extended twice, lastly as part of the August 5, 1994, Extension Agreement, which also effectively extended the maturity date of the original debenture by replacing that debenture with a substitute debenture with a later maturity date. There is no evidence that Klipsch ever waived any of its rights under the Extension Agreement or the substitute debenture. *See van de Leuv* [*v. Methodist Hosp.*], 642 N.E.2d [531] at 533 [(Ind. Ct. App. 1994)] ("Waiver is an intentional relinquishment of a known right involving both knowledge of the existence of the right and the intention to relinquish it."). The instances of defective performance accepted by Klipsch, the most recent of which was on August 5, 1994, did not constitute a waiver of Klipsch's right to invoke the License Agreement's automatic termination provision for a breach of the substitute debenture. Klipsch arguably may have waived the right to enforce the License Agreement's automatic termination provision for late payment on the notes or the original debenture, but it had never waived its right to enforce strict compliance with the terms of the substitute debenture. To the contrary, a month before Klipsch's failed redemption attempt, Klipsch sent Concept a notice indicating its intention to exercise its redemption option.

Summary judgment in favor of WWR on the grounds of waiver should be reversed, and summary judgment on the grounds of waiver should be entered in favor of Klipsch. . . . REVERSED

NOTES

1. *Klipsch* and *Topps* illustrate the uncertainty that can arise with respect to which party breached and which is the injured person in a relationship that involves ongoing performance by each party, and also the interaction between conduct in performing (or not performing) and remedial provisions of the written contract. In one respect, the interaction demonstrates the need to carefully draft terms of the written contract. In another respect, however, it demonstrates that there can be a gap between the terms of the writing and the behavior of the parties. This may result in the behavior setting the actual, operative terms, rather than the writing. This can happen under language of waiver, estoppel, or under modern concepts that course of performance evidence provides guidance on the meaning of the agreement.

2. Not all cases follow the approach in *Klipsch* to a "no waiver" clause. What is the argument against non-enforcement? In some cases, courts may desire to protect a particular, less advantaged participant in the contract. Beyond that, is there a principled reason why a waiver should be enforced even in the face of a contract clause? Consider the following language of UCC § 2-209:

(2) A signed agreement which excludes modification . . . except by a signed writing cannot be otherwise modified. . . .

. . . .

(4) Although an attempt at modification . . . does not satisfy the requirements of subsection (2) . . . it can operate as a waiver.

(5) A party who has made a waiver affecting an executory portion of the contract may retract the waiver by reasonable notification received by the other party that strict performance will be required of any term waived, unless the retraction would be unjust in view of a material change of position in reliance on the waiver.

UCC § 2-209 (1998 Official Text). Can one waive a "no waiver" clause?

III. MATERIALITY AND NON-MONETARY REMEDIES

While any breach of contract by one party entitles the other party to a remedy, the ability of the injured party to end the contract and pursue remedies related to that result depends on the type of breach involved. While the terms of the contract can alter this, the basic common law concept is that ending the contract requires that the breach be "material." The concept is expressed in the *Restatement (Second) of Contracts* in the following language:

> [It] is a condition of each party's remaining duties to render performance . . . under an exchange of promises that there be no uncured material failure by the other party to render any such performance due at an earlier time.

Restatement (Second) of Contracts § 237. The *Restatement* uses language of "conditions" that is not routinely used in modern case law but serves a mighty role in academics; the concept, however, is that the obligation to perform and, thus, the enforceable contract, can be ended based on an uncured, material breach. UCITA follows the same rule. UCITA § 601 (2000 Official Text). Article 2 and UCITA refer to ending executory obligations of a contract for breach as "cancellation." Common law courts are likely to refer to it as "termination" or "rescission."

The idea is that the breach must be important in order to justify ending the contract. UCC Article 2 refers to a breach that "substantially impairs" the value of an "installment contract" (essentially an agreement with ongoing performance obligations). UCC § 2-612 (1998 Official Text). In cases where the contract calls for a single delivery of goods, however, Article 2 requires a "conforming tender" (often mislabeled as "perfect tender"). UCC § 2-601 (buyer may reject if the "goods or the tender of delivery fail in any respect to conform to the contract."). But that tighter standard is cabined in by various other rules such as a right to cure, consideration of trade use, and the like, which make it unlikely that a minor flaw in delivered goods will justify ending the contract.

The *Restatement (Second) of Contracts* § 241 sets out factors to be considered in assessing materiality:

(a) the extent to which the injured party will be deprived of the benefit which he reasonably expected;

(b) the extent to which the injured party can be adequately compensated for the part of that benefit of which he will be deprived;

(c) the extent to which the party failing to perform or to offer to perform will suffer forfeiture;

(d) the likelihood that the party failing to perform or to offer to perform will cure his failure, taking account of all the circumstances including any reasonable assurances;

(e) the extent to which the behavior of the party failing to perform or to offer to perform comports with standards of good faith and fair dealing.

While some courts use these factors, language in many actual court decisions indicates that material breach requires a virtually total failure of the agreed consideration.

PROBLEM 12.2

Consider which of the following should be sufficient to cancel a license:

a. In a multi-year license to use patented technology in return for a stated royalty due on the first of each year, the licensee has not paid by January 30th.

b. In a software license, making two copies that exceed the number of copies it has been licensed to make. Does it matter how many copies were permitted under the license?

c. In a trade secret license, failing to obtain a confidentiality agreement from one of the licensee's contractors, which it was required to do under the license.

d. In a trademark license, a failure to follow quality procedures mandated by the license.

RANO v. SIPA PRESS, INC.
987 F.2d 580 (9th Cir. 1993)

BRUNETTI, CIRCUIT JUDGE:

This appeal from a dismissal for lack of personal jurisdiction and grant of summary judgment in a copyright infringement suit turns on issues of federal preemption of state law in the copyright field and the termination of copyright licenses. For the reasons stated below, we affirm in part, reverse in part, and remand.

Facts and Proceedings Below

The parties to this appeal include: Plaintiff-Appellant Kip Rano, a professional photographer and citizen of Great Britain . . . and Defendants-Appellees Sipa Press, a French corporation, Sipa Press, Inc., a Delaware subsidiary corporation, and Sipa, Inc., a New York subsidiary corporation (collectively Sipa), and Goskin Sipahioglu, President and one of three owners of Sipa Press. Sipa is a photograph distribution syndicate.

In France, on or before 1978, the parties entered into an oral copyright license agreement whereby Rano granted to Sipa a non-exclusive license of unspecified duration to reproduce, distribute, sell, and authorize others to reproduce, distribute, and sell his photographs. In return, Sipa agreed to store and develop the negatives and to pay fifty percent of the net royalties generated from its sales and distributions.

The relationship went smoothly for about eight years. Pursuant to agreement, Rano submitted several thousand of his photographs to Sipa, which Sipa distributed and paid royalties for. In March of 1986, however, Rano sent a letter to Sipahioglu informing him that he was changing agencies and that he would no longer be sending his negatives to Sipa. He gave as his reasons Sipa's failure to timely pay royalties, low sales, poor photography assignments, and unwillingness to reimburse certain expenses. Starting in July of 1986, Rano made several requests that Sipa return all of the negatives he had sent to them. Finally, on March 12, 1987, Rano informed Sipahioglu that he "did not authorize Sipa to sell any more of [his] photographs."

In July of 1989, Rano sued Sipa and Sipahioglu alleging that Sipa infringed his copyright by: (1) failing to credit him for a photograph of the Duchess of York, the former Sara Ferguson; (2) failing to pay certain royalties; (3) continuing to distribute some of his photographs after he demanded their return and after he had attempted to terminate their licensing agreement; (4) failing to return some of his photographs upon demand; and (5) placing defective copyright notices on slide mounts for his photographs. Rano also alleged state breach of contract, intentional interference with economic relationship, and malicious conversion claims. As a remedy for the copyright infringement claims, Rano sought an injunction against Sipa's further use of his photographs, the delivery of the photographs for impoundment, a declaratory judgment as to the rights to his photographs, compensatory and punitive damages, and costs of the suit and attorney's fees.

. . . After reviewing the affidavits and memoranda submitted by the parties and conducting a hearing, the district court granted Sipa's motion for summary judgment, holding that all but one of Rano's copyright infringement claims did not constitute copyright claims under the Copyright Act, but were merely breach of contract claims. The one claim that did allege copyright infringement — failure to affix a proper copyright notice — was, as a matter of law, meritless because the notice Sipa did provide was adequate to protect his copyright. . . .

Discussion

. . . .

IV. Allegations of Copyright Infringement.

Rano alleges infringement of two of the rights granted to him, as creator of the photographs, by the Copyright Act: the right to reproduce the copyrighted work in copies and the right to distribute copies of the work to the public by sale or other transfer of ownership. Rano concedes that, under normal circumstances, his licensing agreement with Sipa would provide Sipa with a valid defense against his copyright infringement claim. Rano argues, however, that although he and Sipa did at one time have a copyright agreement, he terminated the agreement with Sipa. He claims that the termination deprived Sipa of its right to use the negatives Rano already had sent to Sipa, and that Sipa's subsequent use of Rano's negatives constituted copyright infringement.

It is undisputed that the licensing agreement did not contain any provision, either express or implied, regarding its duration. Rano relies on two theories to prove that he properly terminated the agreement. First, Rano argues that California law provides for termination at will of a contract of unspecified duration. [The court held that this rule of law was preempted by federal copyright law.] Second, Rano argues that California law provides for the termination of a contract upon the material breach of the contract by the other party, and that Sipa's alleged actions constituted material breaches of the licensing agreement, permitting him to terminate the agreement. . . .

Rano argues that Sipa materially breached the licensing agreement and that the breach gave him the right to terminate the agreement. Although licensing agreements are not terminable at will, under federal and state law a material breach of a licensing agreement gives rise to a right of rescission which allows the nonbreaching party to terminate the agreement. After the agreement is terminated, any further distribution would constitute copyright infringement.

Here, it is clear that Rano attempted to rescind the agreement. The question is whether he had the right to rescind. A breach will justify rescission of a licensing agreement only when it is "of so material and substantial a nature that [it] affect[s] the very essence of the contract and serve[s] to defeat the object of the parties. . . . [The breach must constitute] a total failure in the performance of the contract."

Rano has not provided evidence sufficient to withstand summary judgment on this issue. Rano points to a number of acts that he contends constitutes a material breach, but only those acts preceding Rano's purported termination on March 12, 1987 are relevant. These acts include Sipa's alleged failure to pay royalties, failure to return negatives, and failure to credit for the Sara Ferguson photograph. The first two breaches claimed by Rano, upon which he relies most heavily, are not supported by the record. Sipa actually paid Rano 99.99% of the royalties due him up to approximately the time Rano sought to terminate the licensing agreement, excluding royalties due for photos published in the United States from 1985 to 1986. Of the latter, Sipa paid 86.85% of the royalties due. As to the second alleged breach, nothing in the letters evidencing the oral contract between the parties provided for a return of Rano's negatives on demand. Rano merely points to a letter from Sipa stating that the negatives would be filed at its offices and "could be returned if necessary, although [Sipa] would want to keep them for a while." Finally, Rano provides no evidence to support his claim that he was due credit for the photograph of Sara Ferguson. Sipa provided evidence that the photograph was taken by another journalist; the duty was on Rano to show there was a genuine issue as to this fact.

Even if we found Rano's allegations had merit, however, we could not conclude that Sipa materially breached the licensing agreement in light of the fact that the parties enjoyed a harmonious eight-year relationship (in which Rano received royalties and credit for his work). "After considerable performance, a slight breach which does not go 'to the root' of the contract will not justify termination." WITKIN, SUMMARY OF CALIFORNIA LAW § 795 (9th ed. 1987). . . .

Conclusion

We affirm the district court's grant of summary judgment in favor of Sipa on the issue of copyright infringement as to Rano's claims based on material breach. . . .

NOTES

1. Is the analysis in *Rano* consistent with the Restatement? If common law is what the court in *Rano* suggests, where did the *Restatement* find its rule? Under *Rano*, when can a party cancel a contract for non-payment or for late payment?

2. The ability to cancel a contract for breach has special significance in intellectual property licenses because, after the contract is terminated, continued use of the licensed subject matter may constitute infringement. In *Columbia Pictures Television v. Krypton Broadcasting of Birmingham*, 106 F.3d 284 (9th Cir. 1997), the court addressed whether termination of a license to broadcast various televisions shows for failure to timely pay required royalties was appropriate. Holding that termination was proper, the court commented:

> Feltner argues that a triable issue of fact exists as to whether the defendants' breach of the license agreements was sufficiently material to enable Columbia to terminate the agreements. In support of his argument, Feltner cites *Rano v. Sipa Press, Inc.* . . . and *Fantasy, Inc. v. Fogerty*, 984 F.2d 1524 (9th Cir.1993), . . . which held that the licensing agreement at issue was not rightfully terminated because the licensee's breach did not "go to the root of the matter," *Fantasy,* , or did not "constitute a total failure in the performance of the contract." *Rano.* However, both *Rano* and *Fantasy* dealt with licensing agreements that did not have an express contractual provision authorizing termination. In contrast, each of the license agreements in this case has an express provision authorizing Columbia to terminate the

agreement if the licensee "fails to make payments of the License Fee or any portion thereof when due." Because these agreements expressly consider the failure to timely pay royalties material, Columbia's termination of the agreements was proper. *See Fantasy,* 984 F.2d at 1529 (stating that "a bona fide dispute concerning royalty payments does not automatically constitute a material breach *unless the contract so provides*") (emphasis added).

3. Non-payment of royalties is the most frequently litigated setting in which the materiality of the breach is contested. In this regard, contrast the discussion in *Rano* with the comments of the Second Circuit in *ARP Films, Inc. v. Marvel Entertainment Group, Inc.,* 952 F.2d 643 (2d Cir. 1991), where it held that the licensee's withholding of payments and accounting reports from the licensor of a copyright was a material breach. It noted simply that: "[Failure] to tender payment is generally deemed a material breach of a contract. Finally, as the district court found, and the subsequent accounting confirmed, the amounts withheld from Marvel by plaintiffs were very substantial." Is this approach preferable to that suggested in *Rano*?

FOSSON v. PALACE (WATERLAND), LTD.
78 F.3d 1448 (9th Cir. 1996)

POOLE, CIRCUIT JUDGE:

Plaintiff/Appellant Mark Fosson is the composer and copyright holder of a song entitled "Picture of Your Daddy" ("the Composition"). Defendants/Appellees Palace (Waterland) Ltd., and The Good Film Co., Ltd. (collectively "the Producers") are producers of a motion picture entitled "Waterland," ("the Film") which was released in the United States theatrically in late 1992. Defendant/Appellee Film Finances Services, Ltd. partly financed the production of the Film.

Fosson's Composition was first recorded on an Atlantic Records release in early 1992. In March 1992, a representative of Atlantic Records contacted Fosson's manager, Kathleen Capper, and told her that the Producers would be willing to pay Fosson $1,250.00 to license his Composition for use in the Film's soundtrack. At that time, Capper indicated that Fosson would grant the license in return for prompt payment of the offered fee, and a "music cue sheet" to be provided to Broadcast Music, Inc. identifying Fosson as the composer and allowing him to collect public performance royalties once the Film was released.

In May 1992, the Producers contacted Capper directly. Peter Afterman, acting on behalf of the Producers, sent Capper an unsigned form contract ("the Synchronization License" or "Synch License") dated May 7, 1992. The Synch License — which contains both preprinted and typewritten provisions — grants the Producers the nonexclusive, irrevocable right to use the Composition in the Film. The Synch License also provides that if the Composition was used, the Producers would pay Fosson the agreed license fee of $1,250.00, and provide the music cue sheet upon his written request. Further, the Synch License contains a clause that provides that in the event of any breach by the

Producers, Fosson would be limited to his remedies at law, and would have no right to terminate or rescind the contract.[2]

Fosson read the entire Synch License and discussed it with Capper. Thereafter, both Fosson and Capper signed the agreement and Fosson returned it to Afterman. . . . Throughout the summer of 1992, Capper made several phone calls to Afterman regarding payment of the $1,250.00 license fee. . . . Afterman finally put Capper in touch with the Producers in the United Kingdom, who informed her that the production had gone into receivership and that all outstanding payables were being disbursed by Film Finances, Inc. Capper sent her first written request to Film Finances for payment of the license fee on October 10, 1992.

Receiving no immediate response, Capper sent a second letter on October 20 in which she stated that Film Finances was in breach of the Synch License, and that if payment was not made by October 29, the fee would increase to $10,000.00. Film Finances responded by fax that the person responsible for authorizing payment had been out of town for several weeks, but that he would contact Capper on October 26. By October 29, Capper still had not received payment. On that date, she sent another letter to Film Finances informing them that they could contact Fosson directly to discuss the licensing fee. In this final letter, Capper did not mention either the $1,250.00 or $10,000.00 license amount.

The Film was released theatrically in the United States on November 6, 1992. Fosson was listed in the Film's credits as the composer and copyright owner of the Composition. To this point, however, no license fee had been paid. Sometime after the release of the Film, Capper turned the matter over to her attorney, Leonard Korobkin. Korobkin wrote a letter to the Producers on November 30, 1992 in which he reaffirmed Fosson's grant of the Synch License in May, and advised them of their subsequent default. However, Korobkin characterized Capper's October 20, 1992 letter as withdrawing Fosson's "offer" to license the Composition for $1,250.00 and substituting a new offer for $10,000.00. Korobkin's letter also demanded that the higher amount be paid within ten (10) days. . . .

The $10,000.00 demand was never satisfied and, in May 1993, Fosson filed an action for copyright infringement in federal district court against the Producers, exhibitors and distributor of the Film, and Film Finances. . . . By order dated March 15, 1994, the district court granted summary judgment in favor of all defendants and denied Fosson's motion. This timely appeal followed. . . .

IV. Discussion

In its order of March 15, 1994, the district court found that the written Synch License was a valid contract. The court went on to find that even assuming the

---

[2] [FN2] The relevant portion of the paragraph reads: "11. *Remedies:* . . . In the event of any breach by Company of this Agreement, Licensor shall be limited to Licensor's remedy at law for damaged [sic], if any, and shall not have any right to terminate or rescind this Agreement or to in any way enjoin or restrain the production, distribution, advertisement, telecast, exhibition or other exploitation of the Picture."

Synch License was not valid, Fosson had granted the Producers an implied license to use the Composition in the Film. Either way, the court held, Fosson was precluded as a matter of law from bringing suit for copyright infringement. We address both findings in turn.

A. *Validity of the Written Synch License.*

Based on the undisputed evidence, the district court found that Fosson executed the Synch License and, therefore, authorized the Producers' use of the Composition in the Film. Although the court did not expressly find that the Synch License, on its face, was supported by valid consideration, it concluded that a valid contract was formed, and that Fosson was bound by its terms. . . .

Fosson's contention that the Synch License lacks consideration is based on the precise language of paragraph 7. The paragraph reads in pertinent part:

> If the Composition is used by Company in the Picture, in consideration of Licensor's execution of the agreement and grant of such license, Company shall pay Licensor [$1250], payable as follows: _____ [blank in original].

Fosson asserts that the language of the paragraph renders the promise illusory because the Producers were not obligated to use the Composition in the Film, nor did the contract specify when payment should be made. The latter proposition is not fatal because, under California law, where no time limit is specified for the performance of an act, a reasonable time is implied. Thus, the failure to specify a timeframe for payment of the license fee would not render the contract illusory.

The Defendants/Appellees counter that the Synch License should be interpreted as a unilateral contract by which the Producers agreed to pay Fosson $1,250.00 if the Composition was used. . . . However, the district court did not expressly interpret the Synch License to be a unilateral contract. Moreover, such a finding would be contrary to established principles of contract interpretation in California. *See Patty v. Berryman,* 95 Cal.App.2d 159, 212 P.2d 937, 942 (1949) ("If doubt [exists] as to whether the agreement was bilateral or unilateral, such doubt would have to be resolved by interpreting the agreement to be bilateral. . . . There is a presumption in favor of interpreting ambiguous agreements to be bilateral rather than unilateral."). Therefore, absent any evidence to rebut the presumption of a bilateral contract, we cannot conclude that a valid unilateral contract was formed.

In California, the doctrine of mutuality of obligation requires that the promises on each side of a contract must be binding obligations in order to be consideration for each other. WITKIN, SUMMARY OF CALIFORNIA LAW, CONTRACTS § 228 (9th ed. 1987). "In a bilateral contract, the promise of one party is consideration for that of another." WITKIN, at § 215. "[A]ny valid promise, whether absolute or conditional, is sufficient consideration for another promise." Moreover, the California Supreme Court has articulated two rules to guide the analysis of conditional promises.

First, "[i]n every contract there is an implied covenant of good faith and fair dealing that neither party will do anything which injures the right of the other to receive the benefits of the agreement." *Bleecher v. Conte,* 29 Cal.3d 345, 213 Cal.Rptr. 852, 698 P.2d 1154, 1156 (1981). "Second, if a contract is capable of two constructions, the court must choose that interpretation which will make the contract legally binding if it can be so construed without violating the intention of the parties."

The California Supreme Court decision in *Mattei* [*v. Hopper*], 330 P.2d 625 (Cal.1958), is instructive regarding our interpretation of the instant contract provision under the second rule. In *Mattei,* the court held that a contract for the sale of real estate was "neither illusory nor lacking in mutuality of obligation because the parties inserted a provision . . . making plaintiff's performance dependent on his satisfaction with the [commercial] leases to be obtained by him." In other words, although obtaining the leases was completely within the control of the plaintiff, the court found that "a contract arose, and plaintiff was given the power and privilege to terminate it in the event he did not obtain such leases."

Applying the principles of *Bleecher* and *Mattei,* we conclude that paragraph 7 of the Synch License constitutes a valid conditional promise. A reasonable construction of paragraph 7 would be that Fosson would be paid a fee of $1,250.00 in exchange for his grant of the license if, in fact, the Composition was used in the Film. Moreover, paragraph 7 can be read such that neither party would be bound to the terms of the Synch License if the Composition was not used. Similar to the contract provision at issue in *Mattei,* although use of the Composition was within the Producer's discretion and control, we hold that a valid contract arose by virtue of the obligations the Producers agreed to assume in the event the Composition was used. Further, the Producers were under an implied obligation to act fairly to protect Fosson's rights and benefits under the contract. . . .

Having determined that a license was granted by Fosson, the district court found as a matter of law that Fosson cannot recover for copyright infringement. . . . Our recent decision in *Rano v. Sipa Press, Inc.,* 987 F.2d 580 (9th Cir.1993), . . . recognized the rule applied in other circuits that once a non-breaching party to an express copyright license obtains and exercises a right of rescission by virtue of a material breach of the agreement, any further distribution of the copyrighted material would constitute infringement.

The *Rano* court began its analysis of the copyright infringement claim by analyzing whether Rano had a right to rescind the license and whether, in fact, he had attempted to exercise any such right. In *Rano,* this presented a largely factual inquiry based on the materiality of the defendant's alleged breaches. In this case, however, the analysis encompasses both a legal and factual inquiry, both of which must be resolved against Fosson.

First, Fosson admitted that he read and understood the Synch License provision in which he waived his right to rescind or terminate the agreement. Having determined the validity of the Synch License, we have previously noted that in California "[a] clear and unambiguous contractual provision providing for an exclusive remedy for breach will be enforced." Thus, Fosson had no right to rescind as a matter of law by virtue of his waiver.

Second, even assuming that the Producer's breach was material, Fosson stated in deposition that he did not consider Capper's October 20 letter to be a notice of rescission or termination, nor did Korobkin ever state that the license was rescinded. Therefore, according to the undisputed facts, Fosson never attempted to exercise any right of rescission. . . .

Accordingly, the district court's grant of summary judgment in favor of the defendants on this issue was proper.

NOTES

1. In *Fosson,* when was the contract formed? When was the payment due under the contract? If the entire fee was not paid when due, what is the justification for not allowing the licensor the right to terminate (cancel) the contract?

2. Contract terms such as that in *Fosson* are common in the motion picture industry and other industries where large investments are made on the assumption that a license will continue to be in force. They reflect the special investment and risk factors present in these industries. To understand the licensee's concern, consider what would have occurred if the licensor could terminate the contract for non-payment after the film was released? Recall that the exclusive rights of a copyright owner include the exclusive right to publicly perform the copyrighted work.

3. All relevant sources of contract law recognize the right of the parties to limit remedies and to establish an exclusive remedy. UCITA specifically refers to the right to contractually preclude the right to "cancel" the contract. UCITA § 803 provides:

(a) Except as otherwise provided in this section and in Section 804:

(1) an agreement may provide for remedies in addition to or in substitution for those provided in this [Act] and may limit or alter the measure of damages recoverable under this [Act] or a party's other remedies under this [Act], such as by precluding a party's right to cancel for breach of contract, limiting remedies to returning or delivering copies and repayment of the contract fee, or limiting remedies to repair or replacement of the nonconforming copies; and

(2) resort to a contractual remedy is optional unless the remedy is expressly agreed to be exclusive, in which case it is the sole remedy.

UCITA § 803(a) (2000 Official Text). Both UCITA and Article 2 provide that if an exclusive remedy fails of its "essential purpose," then the party may resort to other remedies as provided by law or agreement. UCC § 2-719(2) (1998 Official Text). Common law does not contain a similar provision, but if it had, would the remedy limitation in *Fosson* have been enforceable?

4. In *Micro Data Base Systems, Inc. v. Nellcor Puritan Bennett, Inc.,* 165 F.3d 1154 (7th Cir. 1999), Judge Easterbrook affirmed a lower court's refusal to issue an injunction against the termination of a license to distribute copyrighted software as part of a larger product. The licensee had argued that termination would cause irreparable harm because it would take up to one year to find replacement software suitable for its products. The court rejected this argument because it appeared that the licensee's chances of eventual success were low and, in any event, the damages if any from termination was quantifiable, meaning that the harm, if wrongfully caused, could be remedied. The court commented: "To obtain interlocutory relief . . . the applicant must show that the costs of false negatives (the costs of denying interlocutory relief, when the applicant ultimately prevails on the merits) exceed the costs of false positives (the costs of granting interim relief, when the applicant eventually loses on the merits). When irreparable injury is great, the costs of false negatives can exceed the costs of false positives even if the probability of success is low, provided the costs an injunction imposes on the adverse party also are low." "Indeed, we doubt that business losses from termination of a distribution license are irreparable. Only money is at issue. Courts routinely tote up and award as damages the loss inflicted by wrongful terminations of distributorships. Nellcor has not explained why the usual tools of damages calculation would fail to capture its injury, if MDBS has acted wrongfully."

PROBLEM 12.3

Browning holds a license to a patent owned by Whitney. The license is to use the patented technology for the entire term of the patent. It requires quarterly payment of royalties based on a percentage of Browning's manufacturing output from systems using the patent. There are no provisions for termination of the license. Browning has invested several million dollars in developing a manufacturing system around the patented technology. During two quarters in the second year of the license, Browning fails to make the required royalty payment. Whitney sends a notice terminating the license for breach. Browning ignores this notice and continues to use the technology. Whitney sues for infringement. What result?

IV. DISTINGUISHING CONTRACT AND PROPERTY REMEDIES

A breach of a license that involves subject matter covered by intellectual property rights may result in claims for intellectual property infringement in addition or in lieu of contract breach claims. The availability of intellectual property claims typically occurs in one of two contexts:

   • The defendant's conduct falls outside the scope of the license and, thus, is never protected by the license.

   • The defendant's conduct occurs after the protective shield of the license has disappeared either because the license term expired or because the license was terminated or cancelled for breach.

Where there has been both a breach and an infringement, there may be an election of remedy issue for the licensor. There is no per se bar against claiming damages and other relief under both theories, but the law precludes double recovery for the same harm and, as we shall see, some cases preclude incon- sistent relief — e.g., recovery that both affirms and denies the presence of a license with respect to the conduct in question. *MCA Television Ltd v. Public Interest Corp.*, 171 F.3d 1265 (11th Cir. 1999). While injunctive and similar relief is typically more readily available under intellectual property law, there is no single rule about which type of action produces greater or lesser recovery in damages.

The remedies under intellectual property law, however, may offer remedies other than damages. For example, infringement claims traditionally carry a presumption about availability of <u>preliminary</u> injunctive relief, impoundment of infringing articles and costs and attorneys' fees. On the injunctive relief issue, however, a Supreme Court decision about "permanent injunctions" that we discuss below may alter the equation.

UNITED STATES NAVAL INSTITUTE v. CHARTER COMMUNICATIONS, INC.
936 F.2d 692 (2d Cir. 1991)

KEARSE, CIRCUIT JUDGE:

This case returns to us following our remand in *United States Naval Institute v. Charter Communications, Inc.,* 875 F.2d 1044 (2d Cir.1989) ("*Naval I*"), to the United States District Court for the Southern District of New York . . . for the fashioning of relief in favor of plaintiff United States Naval Institute ("Naval") against defendant Charter Communications, Inc., and Berkley Publishing Group (collectively "Berkley"), for breach of an agreement with respect to the publication of the paperback edition of *The Hunt For Red October* ("*Red October*" or the "Book"). On remand, the district court awarded Naval $35,380.50 in damages, $7,760.12 as profits wrongfully received by Berkley, and $15,319.27 as prejudgment interest on the damages awarded, plus costs. . . .

I. Background

The events leading to this action . . . will be summarized here only briefly. Naval, as the assignee of the author's copyright in *Red October,* entered into a licensing agreement with Berkley in September 1984 (the "Agreement"), granting Berkley the exclusive license to publish a paperback edition of the Book "not sooner than October 1985." Berkley shipped its paperback edition to retail outlets early, placing those outlets in position to sell the paperback prior to October 1985. As a result, retail sales of the paperback began on September 15, 1985, and early sales were sufficiently substantial that the Book was near the top of paperback bestseller lists before the end of September 1985.

Naval commenced the present action when it learned of Berkley's plans for early shipment, and it unsuccessfully sought a preliminary injunction. After trial, the district judge dismissed the complaint. He ruled that Berkley had not breached the Agreement because it was entitled, in accordance with industry custom, to ship prior to the agreed publication date. On appeal, we reversed. Though we upheld the district court's finding that the Agreement did not prohibit the early shipments themselves, we concluded that if the "not sooner than October 1985" term of the Agreement had any meaning whatever, it meant at least that Berkley was not allowed to cause such voluminous paper-back retail sales prior to that date, and that Berkley had therefore breached the Agreement. Accordingly, we remanded for entry of a judgment awarding Naval appropriate relief.

On the remand, Naval asserted that it was entitled to recovery for copyright infringement. . . . Berkley, on the other hand, challenged Naval's right to any recovery at all, contending, *inter alia,* that Berkley could not be held liable for copyright infringement since the Agreement had made it the exclusive licensee of the paperback edition copyright as of September 14, 1984; it argued that Naval therefore had at most a claim for breach-of-contract but that Berkley could not be held liable on that basis because Naval had disavowed its pursuit of a contract claim. . . . In a Memorandum and Order dated July 17, 1990 ("July 17 Order"), the district judge rejected Berkley's claim that "its prema-ture publication of the paperback edition constituted only a contract violation and not an infringement of Naval's copyright." . . . He concluded that Naval was entitled to recover damages for copyright infringement, comprising actual damages suffered by Naval plus Berkley's profits "attributable to the infringe-ment," 17 U.S.C. §504(b). . . .

II. Discussion

[For the reasons below,] we conclude that Naval is not entitled to recover for copyright infringement or to be awarded attorney's fees. Naval is, however, entitled to recover for breach of contract, and we affirm the district court's award of actual damages and of prejudgment interest.

A. Naval's Claim of Copyright Infringement

Under the Copyright Act, "[a]ny of the exclusive rights comprised in a copy-right . . . may be transferred . . . and owned separately. The owner of any particular exclusive right is entitled, to the extent of that right, to all of the protection and remedies accorded to the copyright owner by this title." 17 U.S.C. §201(d)(2). An exclusive license granted by the copyright owner consti-tutes a transfer of ownership of the copyright rights conveyed in the license.

Copyright "[i]nfringement is the violation of an owner's copyright interest by a non-owner. . . . It is elementary that the lawful owner of a copyright is inca-pable of infringing a copyright interest that is owned by him." *Cortner v. Israel,* 732 F.2d 267, 271 (2d Cir.1984). Hence, an exclusive licensee of any of the rights comprised in the copyright, though it is capable of breaching the contractual obligations imposed on it by the license, cannot be liable for infringing the copyright rights conveyed to it. *See Fantastic Fakes, Inc. v. Pickwick International, Inc.,* 661 F.2d 479, 483-84 (5th Cir. Unit B 1981) ("mere breach of covenant may support a claim of damages for breach of con-tract but will not disturb the remaining rights and obligations under the license including the authority to use the copyrighted material"); *see also* 3 M. NIMMER & D. NIMMER, NIMMER ON COPYRIGHT, §12.02 at 12-29 (1990) ("Once the copyright owner grants an exclusive license of particular rights, only the exclusive licensee and not his grantor may sue for later occurring infringements of such rights. Indeed, the licensor may be liable to the exclusive licensee for copyright infringement if the licensor exercises rights which have theretofore been exclusively licensed.").

The Agreement between Naval and Berkley . . . granted Berkley, in ¶ 1, "the exclusive right to publish and reproduce, distribute and sell English-language paperback editions" of the Book in the United States and certain other areas. Paragraph 2 of the Agreement stated that "[t]he term of this license will begin on the date written above"; it stated that the term of the license would continue until at least five years after the date of Berkley's "first publication" of the Book. Paragraph 4 provided that Berkley was to publish the paperback edition "not sooner than October 1985."

These provisions contradict the district court's finding that Berkley's publication date "governed when the license would take effect." Paragraph 2 provided that the license took effect on "the date written above"; since September 14, 1984, was the only date mentioned in the Agreement prior to ¶ 3, the license term began on that date. Further, ¶ 2's distinct references to (a) "the date written above" to define the start of the license term, and (b) Berkley's "first publication" date to anchor the continuation of the license term reveal that the parties deliberately did not define the start of the term by Berkley's first publication date. Thus, according to the express provisions of the Agreement, Berkley became the owner of the right to publish the paperback edition of the book in September 1984 and remained the owner of that right for at least five years after its first publication of that edition in 1985. Its publication of that edition in 1985 therefore could not constitute copyright infringement.

In arguing the contrary, Naval relies principally on Kamakazi Music Corp. v. Robbins Music Corp., 684 F.2d 228 (2d Cir.1982); Gilliam v. American Broadcasting Companies, Inc., 538 F.2d 14 (2d Cir.1976); and The Robert Stigwood Group Limited v. Sperber, 457 F.2d 50 (2d Cir.1972). Its reliance is misplaced since in each of those cases the plaintiff, not the defendant, owned the pertinent copyright rights at the time of the infringements for which the plaintiff sued. In addition, Naval seeks to suggest that in Naval I this Court upheld its claim for copyright infringement. That suggestion is wishful thinking. Though we ruled that Berkley was liable for breaching the Agreement, we nowhere suggested that it had infringed the copyright.

In sum, though we ruled in *Naval I* that Berkley is liable to Naval for breach of the Agreement, Berkley is not liable for copyright infringement. It follows that the district court's award of relief under the Copyright Act must be set aside.

B. Contract Damages

Our ruling that Naval is not entitled to recover under the Copyright Act does not, as Berkley would have it, require the entry of judgment in favor of Berkley. Though Berkley argues that Naval had abandoned its contract claim for money damages prior to trial, we thereafter ruled in *Naval I* that Naval was entitled to recover for breach of contract. . . . As Naval has renounced any effort at rescission and has accepted Berkley's payments of substantial copyright royalties for paperback sales under the Agreement, plainly the relief to which Naval is entitled on its meritorious breach-of-contract claim is money damages.

The damages awarded by the district court on remand had two components: (1) Naval's lost profits resulting from Berkley's early publication of the paperback edition of the Book, and (2) Berkley's profits attributable to its assumed infringement. For the reasons discussed above, the latter component of the award cannot stand. The former component, however, may properly measure damages under a breach-of-contract theory.

Since the purpose of damages for breach of contract is to compensate the injured party for the loss caused by the breach, 5 CORBIN ON CONTRACTS § 1002, at 31 (1964), those damages are generally measured by the plaintiff's actual loss, *see, e.g., Restatement (Second) of Contracts* § 347 (1981). While on occasion the defendant's profits are used as the measure of damages, this generally occurs when those profits tend to define the plaintiff's loss, for an award of the defendant's profits where they greatly exceed the plaintiff's loss and there has been no tortious conduct on the part of the defendant would tend to be punitive, and punitive awards are not part of the law of contract damages. *See generally Restatement (Second) of Contracts* § 356 comment *a* ("The central objective behind the system of contract remedies is compensatory, not punitive."); *id.* comment *b* (agreement attempting to fix damages in amount vastly greater than what approximates actual loss would be unenforceable as imposing a penalty); *id.* § 355 (punitive damages not recoverable for breach of contract unless conduct constituting the breach is also a tort for which such damages are recoverable).

Here, the district court found that Berkley's alleged $724,300 profits did not define Naval's loss because many persons who bought the paperback in September 1985 would not have bought the book in hardcover but would merely have waited until the paperback edition became available. This finding is not clearly erroneous, and we turn to the question of whether the district court's finding that Naval suffered $35,380.50 in actual damages was proper.

In reaching the $35,380.50 figure, the court operated on the premise that, but for the breach by Berkley, Naval would have sold in September the same number of hardcover copies it sold in August. Berkley challenges that premise as speculative and argues that since Naval presented no evidence as to what its September 1985 sales would have been, Naval is entitled to recover no damages. It argues alternatively that the court should have computed damages on the premise that sales in the second half of September, in the absence of Berkley's premature release of the paperback edition, would have been made at the same rate as in the first half of September. Evaluating the district court's calculation of damages under the clearly erroneous standard of review, we reject Berkley's contentions.

The record showed that, though there was a declining trend of hardcover sales of the Book from March through August 1985, Naval continued to sell its hardcover copies through the end of 1985, averaging some 3,000 copies a month in the latter period. It plainly was not error for the district court to find that the preponderance of the evidence indicated that Berkley's early shipment of 1,400,000 copies of its paperback edition, some 40% of which went to retail outlets and led to the Book's rising close to the top of the paperback bestseller lists before the end of September 1985, caused Naval the loss of some hardcover sales prior to October 1985.

As to the quantification of that loss, we think it was within the prerogative of the court as finder of fact to look to Naval's August 1985 sales. Though there was no proof as to precisely what the unimpeded volume of hardcover sales would have been for the entire month of September, any such evidence would necessarily have been hypothetical. But it is not error to lay the normal uncertainty in such hypotheses at the door of the wrongdoer who altered the proper course of events, instead of at the door of the injured party. The court was not required to use as the starting point for its calculations Naval's actual sales in the first half of September, *i.e.,* those made prior to the first retail sale of the paperback edition. Berkley has not called to our attention any evidence in the record to indicate that the sales in a given month are normally spread evenly through that month. Indeed, it concedes that "[t]o a large degree, book sales depend on public whim and are notoriously unpredictable. . . ." Thus, nothing in the record foreclosed the possibility that, absent Berkley's breach, sales of hardcover copies in the latter part of September would have outpaced sales of those copies in the early part of the month. Though the court accurately described its selection of August 1985 sales as its benchmark as "generous[ ]," it was not improper, given the inherent uncertainty, to exercise generosity in favor of the injured party rather than in favor of the breaching party.

In all the circumstances, we cannot say that the district court's calculation of Naval's damages was clearly erroneous. . . .

For the foregoing reasons, we reverse so much of the judgment as granted Naval $7,760.12 as an award of Berkley's profits. In all other respects, the judgment is affirmed.

NOTES

1. Would the result in *Naval Institute* be the same if the contract were a non-exclusive license, leaving ownership of the copyright in the licensor? As the court alludes to, an exclusive license, by conveying ownership, may place the original author or inventor in a position from which it can be sued by its licensee for infringement of what was once its own intellectual property. See Chapter 4. Is there a contractual provision that the licensor in *Naval Institute* could have used that would allow it to sue under copyright law if the licensee engaged in the conduct that actually occurred in this case? Why was the court concerned about when the license became effective?

2. While contract damages are ordinarily directed toward protecting the injured party's expectation interest (putting the person economically in the position it would have had if there had been full performance), intellectual property rights damages reflect a different base and flow toward a different purpose. They are remedies for intrusion on a property interest and, thus, tend to measure the loss in value of that interest or the wrongful gains obtained by the party engaging in the intrusion. For example, Section 504 of the Copyright

Act provides for recovery of 1) the copyright owner's actual damages *and* any additional profits of the infringer attributable to the infringement, or 2) statutory damages in appropriate cases. Notice that, while contract damages often include recovery of the *plaintiff's* lost profit, the copyright statute refers to recovery of the *defendant's* profit. What explains the difference?

3. The Patent Act provides: "[The] court shall award the claimant damages adequate to compensate for the infringement, but in no event less than a reasonable royalty for the use made of the invention by the infringer, together with interest and costs as fixed by the court." 35 U.S.C. §284. In what way is this damage measure different from that under contract law? Does the answer depend on the terms of the license?

4. A person cannot receive a double recovery for the same injury. UCITA §801 (2000 Official Text). Double recovery issues can arise in claims against a licensee for breach and for infringement. Resolving the issue focuses on identifying the basis of a recovery of damages and whether the same basis applies to both awards. *Kepner-Tregoe, Inc. v. Vroom,* 186 F.3d 283 (2d Cir. 1999), illustrates the analysis. The court there held that a person who transferred a copyrighted executive management system, retaining only the right to use it in his own classes, did not have the right to use the system in a later software product. In effect, it used the material outside the scope of its license. Doing so was copyright infringement and breach of contract. The court awarded both infringement damages and contract breach damages, rejecting the argument that this was a double recovery. The statutory infringement damages stemmed from the author's willful acts of copyright infringement, while contractual damages represented the losses incurred for having to enforce its copyright rights stemming from author's breach of licensing agreement.

PROBLEM 12.4

Ben grants a license to Software Publisher to reproduce and distribute copies of Ben's word processing software. The agreement provides for payment of a 5% royalty on the gross price of all copies of the software sold or licensed to third parties. Software Publisher distributes 100,000 copies of the software, reaping a total gross income of $10,000,000. Its profit on these transactions is $7 million. Publisher fails to pay any royalty to Ben. Claiming breach of contract, Ben sues. What result? What result if the lawsuit is for copyright infringement based on the claim that distribution of the software was outside the scope of the license? How would the results change if Publisher's profit were only $100,000.

The difference between intellectual property and contract remedies heightens the importance of deciding whether breach allowed the licensor to cancel the license. It also leads to a distinction between the terms of a license that define the license scope (e.g., what conduct is covered by the license grant) and covenants (e.g., promises made by the licensee, but not conditioning the scope). We encountered this in the *Sun Microsystems* case in Chapter 5, but another visit to the issue is appropriate here.

GRAHAM v. JAMES
144 F.3d 229 (2d Cir. 1998)

JACOBS, CIRCUIT JUDGE.

Background

The facts, as found by the district court after a bench trial, are as follows: Graham, until recently doing business as Night Owl Computer Service, markets CD-ROM disks containing compilations of computer programs known as "Shareware," "Freeware," and "Public Domain software." "Shareware" are programs that are created and released to the public to sample, with the understanding that anyone using the software will register with the author and remit a fee. "Freeware" is software available for free use. "Public Domain software" is software unprotected by copyright. Each of Graham's CD-ROM disk releases contains 5,000 to 10,000 such programs.

Graham's first CD-ROM disk release, called PDSI-001, was unwieldy because it lacked a file-retrieval program. So before releasing his second CD-ROM product, Graham asked Jeffrey Anderson, a student, to compose a file-retrieval program. Anderson developed a program called NIGHT.EXE in the QuickBASIC programming language; that program was then incorporated into Graham's second CD-ROM disk release, PDSI-002. . . . Dissatisfied with Anderson's program, Graham purchased a license for FOLIO, a file-retrieval program with retrieval and decompression capabilities, that Graham used for his next two releases.

In March 1991, he contacted James, a self-taught computer programmer, part-time taxi driver, and computer equipment salesman, and explained to him in general terms what was needed. James agreed to create a file-retrieval program in exchange for a CD-ROM disk drive and credit on the final product. He then created a different QuickBASIC version of NIGHT.EXE, which was included on PDSI-004. . . . Using "Borland's C++" language (said to be a superior programming language), James then developed a new version of NIGHT. EXE, which we will call the "C version." The C version was included in PDSI-004-1, released on August 2, 1991. This was an entirely new program, and Graham's contribution was limited to communicating the general requirements of the program and collaborating on the organization of the files that the program retrieved.

In composing the C version, James built into it a notice attributing authorship and copyright to himself. In September 1991, Graham and James argued over the copyright notice, with Graham claiming the copyright under the work-for-hire doctrine. . . . At trial, the parties presented conflicting testimony regarding their compensation and licensing arrangement. . . . The district court found that "the parties had orally agreed that James would provide Graham with a file retrieval program written in Borland's C++" and "that Graham would pay James $1,000 for each version provided thereof and one dollar for each disk sold."

After the late-night telephone conversation, Graham removed James's copyright notice, repaired a "bug" in the program, and proceeded to release a new version of PDSI-004-1. In October 1991, Graham released PDSI-005. . . .

In September or October 1991, James sold the C version of NIGHT.EXE to another CD-ROM publisher. Graham sued and moved for a preliminary injunction, claiming ownership of the copyright in the C version under the work-for-hire doctrine and asserting that James had infringed Graham's copyright by selling the program. James counterclaimed, alleging that *he* owned the copyright and that Graham had infringed his copyright by installing the C version on his CD-ROM releases and removing James's copyright notice. James also asserted counterclaims for breach of the licensing agreement, unfair competition, defamation, and tortious interference with contractual relations. . . . After a bench trial . . . the district court found for James on his breach of contract and copyright infringement counterclaims. . . .

Discussion

Graham challenges the finding — on which rests the conclusion that the C version was not a work for hire — that James developed the C version as an independent contractor rather than as an employee. We agree with the district court's analysis and conclusion. [As a result, James held the copyright.] . . .

Under federal law, "nonexclusive licenses may . . . be granted orally, or may even be implied from conduct." 3 MELVILLE B. NIMMER & DAVID NIMMER, NIMMER ON COPYRIGHT § 10.03[A][7]. The district court found that Graham and James had entered into a licensing agreement under which Graham promised to pay James $1,000 for each CD-ROM release containing the C version and one dollar for each disk sold. Graham does not contest on appeal that he breached this agreement by failing to make the required payments, and therefore we affirm the district court's award of breach of contract damages.

However, the award of copyright damages in this case is problematic. A copyright owner who grants a nonexclusive license to use his copyrighted material waives his right to sue the licensee for copyright infringement. . . . Moreover, Graham's failure to credit James with the copyright on the C version did not itself amount to copyright infringement. According to Nimmer, "The generally prevailing view in this country under copyright law has been that an author who sells or licenses her work does not have an inherent right to be credited as author of the work. In line with that general rule, it has been held not to infringe an author's copyright for one who is licensed to reproduce the work to omit the author's name." 3 NIMMER on COPYRIGHT, supra, § 8D.03[A][1], at 8D-32. Thus, as James concedes, the district court could not have found that Graham infringed James's copyright unless the licensing agreement already had been rescinded; the problem is that the district court made no such finding. James endeavors to overcome that problem in four ways, but without success.

[James argues] that the license was voided when Graham breached its conditions by nonpayment of royalties and removal of James's copyright notice. This argument turns — and fails — on the distinction in contract between a condition and a covenant. Generally, "[i]f the [licensee's] improper conduct constitutes a breach of a covenant undertaken by the [licensee] . . . and if such covenant constitutes an enforcible contractual obligation, then the [licensor] will have a cause of action for breach of contract," not copyright infringement. 3 NIMMER ON COPYRIGHT, § 10.15[A], at 10-120. However, "[i]f the nature of a licensee's violation consists of a failure to satisfy a condition to the license . . ., it follows that the rights dependant upon satisfaction of such condition have not been effectively licensed, and therefore, any use by the licensee is without authority from the licensor and may therefore, constitute an infringement of copyright." A condition has been defined as "any fact or event which qualifies a duty to perform."

We think that the payment of royalties and the inclusion of a notice crediting James's authorship are to be considered covenants, not conditions. The construction of the licensing agreement is governed by New York law. Generally speaking, New York respects a presumption that terms of a contract are covenants rather than conditions. *See Grand Union Co. v. Cord Meyer Dev. Co.,* 761 F.2d 141, 147 (2d Cir.1985) ("In the absence of more compelling evidence that the parties intended to create a condition, the negotiation provision must be construed as a promise or covenant."). Graham and James orally agreed to the licensing agreement and did not clearly delineate its conditions and covenants. Further, it is important that James turned over the C version for use before any royalties were paid, and that the first version of PDSI-004-1 was published with the proper notice of authorship, because contract obligations that are to be performed after partial performance by the other party are not treated as conditions.

Guided by that analysis, together with New York's presumption favoring covenants over conditions and the district court's clear finding that a licensing agreement came into existence, we conclude that the notice and royalty obligations would likely be considered covenants, and cannot be relied upon by James as conditions.

Finally, James argues that even if the nonpayment of royalties and the removal of James's authorship credit amount to no more than breaches of covenants, these breaches terminated the license. A material breach of a covenant will allow the licensor to rescind the license and hold the licensee liable for infringement for uses of the work thereafter. Under New York law, rescission is permitted if the breach is "material and willful, or, if not willful, so substantial and fundamental as to strongly tend to defeat the object of the parties in making the contract." *Septembertide Publ'g, B.V. v. Stein and Day, Inc.,* 884 F.2d 675, 678 (2d Cir.1989).

Even assuming Graham materially breached the licensing agreement and that James was entitled to rescission, such rescission did not occur automatically without some affirmative steps on James's part. 22A N.Y. Jur.2d *Contracts* § 497 (1996) ("The failure of a party to perform his part of a contract does not *per se* rescind it. The other party must manifest his intention to rescind within a reasonable time."). Similarly, although James sometimes characterizes the licensing agreement as abandoned, abandonment of a contract can be accomplished only through mutual assent of the parties, as demonstrated by positive and unequivocal conduct inconsistent with an intent to be bound. New York law does not presume the rescission or abandonment of a contract and the party asserting rescission or abandonment has the burden of proving it.

We vacate the copyright infringement award because: (i) the record does not show that James was permitted to and did rescind the license or that Graham and James agreed to abandon the licensing agreement; (ii) the district court made no finding on this issue; and (iii) it does not appear that the district court recognized this defect in its decision. We remand for determinations as to whether Graham materially breached the licensing agreement and whether the agreement was actually rescinded or abandoned prior to the allegedly infringing acts, and for any further proceedings needed to make those determinations.

NOTES

1. The distinction between covenant and condition is relevant not only to the ultimate remedy, but also to the availability of preliminary injunctive relief. Intellectual property law claims traditionally have enjoyed a presumption that irreparable harm will occur in the absence of injunction, while contract claims do not. To refresh your memory on this, you might refer back to *Sun Microsystems, Inc. v. Microsoft Corp.*, 188 F.3d 1115 (9th Cir. 1999), in Chapter 5. The claim there was that Microsoft was violating compatibility requirements in its license with Sun. After the Court of Appeals highlighted the distinction between a covenant and a condition, the trial court concluded that the compatibility standard was a covenant, not a condition limiting scope of the license:

> the language and structure of the [license] suggest that the compatibility obligations are separate covenants and not conditions of, or restrictions on, the license grants. The license grants . . . allow Microsoft to distribute the Technology and Derivative Works of the Technology as part of a Product but say nothing about the license grants being subject to, conditional on, or limited by compliance with the compatibility obligations.

Sun Microsystems, Inc. v. Microsoft Corporation, 81 F. Supp. 2d 1026, 1032 (N.D. Cal. 2000).

PROBLEM 12.5

In the following examples, what is the scope of the license and what are covenants?

a. A technology license provides: "Licensee is granted the right to use the technology in the Southwest United States. Licensee promises to pay $100,000 per month for use of the technology."

b. A motion picture license provides: "Licensee is granted the right to publicly perform the Motion Picture during the month of June at the theater located at 1112 Hammond Street, Cleveland."

PROBLEM 12.6

Media 100 obtains a license to use MSI's CG Option 2.0 software. At the time of the agreement, Media 100 only manufactures systems for use in Apple Computers. The license provides:

> Subject to [Media 100] timely paying all amounts owing hereunder, upon payment of the $75,000 license fee stated in section 3.2 for the CG Option 2.0 license, then [Media 100] shall have a paid-up license to (1) modify the CG Option 2.0 source code; (2) generate executable code versions of CG Option 2.0; (3) distribute executable code versions of CG Option 2.0 when integrated with [Media 100]'s Media 100 hardware and software used for digital video editing, and such versions shall be licensed only for use on such hardware.

The royalties are 5% of gross sales of products involving CG Option 2.0 in original or modified form. During the term of the license, Media 100 begins to develop a product for Microsoft Windows systems. It modifies CG Option 2.0 to work in this system and begins to distribute the new product and distributes 100,000 of the new product. MSI sues for infringement. What result?

BASSETT v. MASHANTUCKET PEQUOT TRIBE
204 F.3d 343 (2d Cir. 2000)

LEVAL, CIRCUIT JUDGE:

Plaintiff Debra Bassett, doing business as Bassett Productions, appeals from the dismissal of her complaint against Defendants Mashantucket Pequot Tribe (the "Tribe"), Mashantucket Pequot Museum & Research Center (the "Museum"), Theresa Bell, and Jack Campisi. The complaint charged Defendants with copyright infringement, breach of contract, and various state-law torts. The United States District Court for the District of Connecticut dismissed the copyright claims against the Tribe and the Museum for lack of subject matter jurisdiction, dismissed the state-law claims against the Tribe pursuant to the doctrine of tribal immunity. . . . We affirm the dismissal of the copyright claims against the Tribe, although for different reasons. . . .

Background

According to the allegations of the complaint: Plaintiff Debra Bassett operates a business, Bassett Productions, that produces films and television programs. Defendant Mashantucket Pequot Tribe is a federally recognized Indian tribe with a reservation located within the geographical boundaries of the State of Connecticut. Defendant Mashantucket Pequot Museum is a Connecticut corporation located on the Pequot Reservation.

In October 1994, Bassett met with representatives of the Tribe to discuss the possibility of producing a film for the Museum about the Pequot War of 1636-38. In November, Defendant Theresa Bell, acting individually and as a representative of the Tribe, signed a "confidential disclosure agreement" in which she agreed that all information received from Bassett Productions was proprietary, and was to be returned to Bassett Productions at its request. In May 1995, Defendant Jack Campisi, communicating with Bassett on behalf of the Tribe, advised her that the Tribe intended to hire her to produce the film, contingent on the negotiation of a satisfactory contract and the Tribe's acceptance of a script for the film.

In August 1995, Bassett Productions entered into a letter agreement with the Tribe (the "Letter Agreement") for the development and production of a film about the 1636-38 Pequot War. The Letter Agreement identified Bassett Productions as the "Producer" and the Tribe as the "Owner," but did not define these terms. It stipulated that Bassett Productions would "hire and supervise the development and writing of a screenplay by Keith Merrill and George Burdeau," and that the Tribe would "compensate" Bassett Productions for development costs according to an agreed schedule. It also stipulated that "at such time" that the Tribe approved the final draft of the screenplay, Bassett Productions would have exclusive rights to produce the film for exhibition at the Pequot Museum.

Some time before October 30, 1995, Bassett had delivered to the Tribe a script that she herself had written based on a "script scenario" she had developed with assistance from her associate Allan Eckert. The script was prominently marked on its first page, "Copr. 1995 Bassett Entertainment Corporation."

On October 30, 1995, Bassett received a notice from the Tribe terminating the Letter Agreement. The notice asserted that Bassett had not "perform[ed] the contract as the parties anticipated." Following the termination of the Letter Agreement, the Tribe continued to pursue the development and production of a film on the 1636-38 Pequot War for exhibition at the Museum. In October 1996, filming was completed on a motion picture entitled, "The Witness." Bassett asserts the Tribe intends to screen the film at the Museum "in the near future" as part of "an interstate-driven tourist attraction." . . .

In September 1996, Bassett commenced this lawsuit in the United States District Court for the District of Connecticut. The complaint sought an injunction as well as other copyright remedies on the ground that the Tribe and the Museum used Bassett's copyrighted script without her consent or license in order to produce their own film; it further alleged that they breached the Letter Agreement, and that they committed various state-law torts resulting in injury to Bassett. . . . The district court granted Defendants' motion to dismiss the complaint, and Bassett appealed.

Discussion

28 U.S.C. § 1338(a) states that federal district courts "shall" have exclusive, original jurisdiction "of any civil action arising under any Act of Congress relating to . . . copyrights." It is well-established that not every complaint that refers to the Copyright Act "arises under" that law for purposes of Section 1338(a). *See, e.g., T.B. Harms Co. v. Eliscu,* 339 F.2d 823, 824 (2d Cir.1964) (Friendly, J.) (noting that this principle traces to "precedents going back for more than a century"). In particular, "the federal grant of a . . . copyright has not been thought to infuse with any national interest a dispute as to

ownership or contractual enforcement turning on the facts or on ordinary principles of contract law." Here, the district court, relying on our discussion in dictum in *Schoenberg v. Shapolsky Publishers, Inc.,* 971 F.2d 926, 932-33 (2d Cir.1992), dismissed the claims based on the conclusion that Bassett's "copyright infringement claims . . . do not 'arise under' federal copyright laws for purposes of 28 U.S.C. § 1338(a), but are merely incidental to [her] state law [contract] claims." Bassett contends that the court erred in dismissing her claims on the basis of *Schoenberg.* She argues that her copyright claims neither depend on nor result from claims for breach of contract. She further maintains that, because she sought a remedy expressly granted by the Copyright Act, her copyright claims do "arise under" the Act pursuant to the rule of *T.B. Harms.*

Whether a complaint asserting factually related copyright and contract claims "arises under" the federal copyright laws for the purposes of Section 1338(a) "poses among the knottiest procedural problems in copyright jurisprudence." 3 MELVILLE B. NIMMER & DAVID NIMMER, NIMMER ON COPYRIGHT § 12.01[A], at 12-4 (1999) ("NIMMER"). Such claims characteristically arise where the defendant held a license to exploit the plaintiff's copyright, but is alleged to have forfeited the license by breaching the terms of the licensing contract and thus to infringe in any further exploitation.

Prior to our landmark decision in *T.B. Harms,* several district courts in the Second Circuit resolved the issue of jurisdiction under Section 1338 for "hybrid" claims raising both copyright and contract issues by attempting to discern whether the copyright issues constituted the "essence" of the dispute, or whether instead the copyright issues were "incidental to" the contract dispute. That approach, however, left a class of plaintiffs who suffered copyright infringement bereft of copyright remedies. Plaintiffs whose federal lawsuits were dismissed for lack of subject matter jurisdiction on the ground that their copyright claims were "incidental to" their contract claims had no way either to obtain an adjudication of infringement or to obtain relief provided by the Copyright Act, because the Act confers exclusive jurisdiction over copyright claims on federal courts. . . .

In *T.B. Harms,* Judge Friendly recognized the complexity of the problem of defining when a case "arises under" the Copyright Act. In synthesizing Supreme Court cases that had considered the issue of federal jurisdiction in a variety of contexts, Judge Friendly established a test for this circuit that focused on whether and how a complaint implicates the Copyright Act. The plaintiff in *T.B. Harms* sought a declaratory judgment that he was the sole owner of renewal copyrights. At issue was whether one of the defendants had previously assigned his interest in the copyrights to the plaintiff's agent, or whether this defendant had retained his interest and had validly assigned it at a later date to a second defendant. No claim of infringement was asserted and no relief provided by the Copyright Act was sought. The district court dismissed the action for lack of subject matter jurisdiction on the ground that the "fundamental controversy" at issue concerned the execution of an assignment, not an alleged infringement of copyright. The court of appeals likewise found a lack of jurisdiction, but relied on quite different reasoning.

Judge Friendly began his analysis by examining Supreme Court precedent addressing the question when a federal court properly exercises jurisdiction under Section 1338, which creates jurisdiction in the federal courts in "any civil action arising under any Act of Congress relating to patents . . . [and] copyrights," among others. He identified two lines of authority as particularly important. First, in *American Well Works Co. v. Layne & Bowler Co.*, 241 U.S. 257, 260 (1916), Justice Holmes explained that a "suit arises under the law that creates the cause of action." According to Judge Friendly, Justice Holmes' interpretation of Section 1338 explained the exercise of federal jurisdiction "in a great many cases, notably copyright and patent infringement actions, both clearly authorized by the respective federal acts, and thus unquestionably within the scope of 28 U.S.C. § 1338." Judge Friendly observed that "in the many infringement suits that depend only on some point of fact and require no construction of federal law, no other explanation may exist." Second, Judge Friendly discussed *Smith v. Kansas City Title & Trust Co.*, 255 U.S. 180 (1921), in which the Supreme Court held that a claim created by state law might still "arise under" federal law "if the complaint discloses a need for determining the meaning or application of such a law."

Synthesizing the Supreme Court authorities, Judge Friendly concluded that a suit "arises under" the Copyright Act if:

> (1) "[T]he complaint is for a remedy expressly granted by the Act, e.g., a suit for infringement or for the statutory royalties for record repro-duction . . .;" or,

> (2) "[T]he complaint . . . asserts a claim requiring construction of the Act. . . ." *Id.* at 828.

As the suit in *T.B. Harms* did not fall within any of these enumerated categories, the court found that it did not "arise under" the copyright laws for purposes of Section 1338 and that jurisdiction was therefore lacking.

The *T.B. Harms* test differed significantly from the essence-of-the-dispute or merely-incidental test. The analysis under *T.B. Harms* turns on what is alleged on the face of the complaint, while the essence-of-the-dispute or merely-incidental test looks rather at what defense will be proffered. For example, if the complaint alleges copyright infringement or seeks an injunc-tion under the Copyright Act, under *T.B. Harms* the federal court has jurisdic-tion; under the other test, in contrast, the court must ascertain whether the defendant will defend only by reference to state law matters, such as a claim of contractual entitlement, or will raise defenses based on the Copyright Act.

The *T.B. Harms* test avoids problems that result from the essence-of-the-dispute test. By rejecting reliance on whether the copyright claim could be characterized as "incidental" and instead focusing the inquiry under Section 1338 on whether a plaintiff's complaint "[was] for a remedy expressly granted by the Act," *T.B. Harms* ensured that plaintiffs who sought copyright remedies that depended on a prior showing of contractual entitlement would not be left without the remedies promised by the Copyright Act. *T.B. Harms* also obvi-ated the need for courts to determine at the outset of litigation whether copy-right claims were incidental to contract claims — a difficult determination to make even after discovery and trial, and one that cannot be made reliably on the basis of the complaint alone.

Judge Friendly's solution to the problem posed by Section 1338 has been widely admired by the leading copyright scholars.[3] The *T.B. Harms* test has been adopted by all the circuits that have considered the question whether a suit arises under the Copyright Act for purposes of Section 1338, if the disputed issues include non-copyright matters.

Nearly thirty years after the *T.B. Harms* decision, a panel of this court in *Schoenberg* undertook in dictum to state the test for determining the existence of Section 1338 jurisdiction in cases alleging violations of the Copyright Act resulting from breach of contract. The plaintiff, an author, alleged that he had licensed the defendant, a publisher, to publish plaintiff's work. The license obligated the defendant to publish within six months of plaintiff's delivery of the manuscript, to promote and market the work, and to license foreign language editions. According to plaintiff's allegations, the publisher breached numerous obligations of the license. As a result of these failures, plaintiff claimed that the license was terminated and that defendant's further publication of the work constituted an infringement. Although the appeal related to a different issue, the opinion undertook to state "the appropriate test under the *T.B. Harms* paradigm, for determining whether a suit 'arises under' the Copyright Act when it alleges infringement stemming from a breach of contract."

The opinion acknowledged that [i]n *T.B. Harms,* Judge Friendly wrote that, "an action 'arises under' the Copyright Act if and only if the complaint is for a remedy expressly granted by the Act," and that "[b]ecause Schoenberg is seeking damages for the alleged infringement as well as an injunction against future infringements, his complaint on its face asserts a claim 'arising under' the Copyright Act." It observed, however, that notwithstanding the *T.B. Harms* formulation, some district courts had "looked beyond the complaint in

---

[3] [FN4] We recognize that the literature includes some criticism of *T.B. Harms,* but we believe it is easily answered. The primary criticism voiced is that the test has been applied by subsequent courts in a contradictory manner. . . . We do not disagree that subsequent opinions have not been uniform. Some courts, purporting to follow *T.B. Harms,* have cited it for the proposition it rejected — that federal courts must look beyond the face of the complaint to ascertain whether the "primary and controlling issue" or "essence" of the dispute is a matter of federal copyright law or state contract law. Nothing can be found in Judge Friendly's opinion to support the use of the "principal and controlling issue" test. Indeed, the opinion took pains to underscore that federal jurisdiction has been found proper "in the many infringement suits that depend only on some point of fact and require no construction of federal law." *T.B. Harms,* 339 F.2d at 826. . . . If *T.B. Harms* is to be faulted for the confusion found among subsequent opinions, it is not because of any fault in the test it stated, but rather because the test was explained in such terse, economical terms that it has been sometimes misunderstood and misapplied.

The other main criticism raised against the *T.B. Harms* standard is that by requiring federal courts to accept all cases in which the complaint seeks a remedy provided by the Copyright Act or raises a claim requiring interpretation of the Act, it might "open the floodgates," drowning federal courts in the "litigation of cases that are at heart contract disputes." We believe this criticism is greatly exaggerated. . . . Furthermore, there is a built-in check on plaintiffs who seek to use Section 1338 as a means of obtaining federal jurisdiction over a purely contractual dispute by inappropriate or bad-faith pleading of a copyright claim. This is the risk that, once the federal court dismisses the copyright claim, it may decide to refuse supplemental jurisdiction over the remaining state law claims.

order to determine whether the plaintiff was really concerned with the infringement of his copyright, or, alternatively, was, in fact, more interested in" free enjoyment of his property or other non-copyright issues. Other courts, it noted, had adopted the even "broader proposition that no claim arises under the Copyright Act whenever an infringement would necessarily result from the breach of a contract that licensed or assigned a copyright."

In undertaking to reconcile the varying approaches of those district court opinions (and perhaps concluding that the authority of *T.B. Harms* extended only to disputes over copyright ownership and not to hybrid copyright/contract claims), *Schoenberg* created a new, complex three-step test; the first step of the test was precisely that which *T.B. Harms* had rejected — whether the claim for copyright remedies is " 'merely incidental' " to a determination of contract rights. The opinion declared that in hybrid copyright and contract cases Section 1338 jurisdiction should be analyzed in the following manner:

> A district court must first ascertain whether the plaintiff's infringement claim is only "incidental" to the plaintiff's claim seeking a determination of ownership or contractual rights under the copyright. . . . If it is determined that the claim is not merely incidental, then a district court must next determine whether the complaint alleges a breach of a condition to, or a covenant of, the contract licensing or assigning the copyright. . . . [I]f a breach of a condition is alleged, then the district court has subject matter jurisdiction. . . . But if the complaint merely alleges a breach of a contractual covenant in the agreement that licenses or assigns the copyright, then the court must undertake a third step and analyze whether the breach is so material as to create a right of rescission in the grantor. If the breach would create a right of rescission, then the asserted claim arises under the Copyright Act.

Id. at 932-33 (citations omitted).

We believe for a number of reasons that the *Schoenberg* test is unworkable. At the outset, it overlooks that, because the Copyright Act gives federal courts *exclusive* jurisdiction to enforce its provisions, a plaintiff who is denied access to a federal forum on the theory that his copyright claims are incidental to a contract dispute is thereby absolutely denied the benefit of copyright remedies. Such a denial of copyright remedies undermines the Act's capacity to protect copyright interests. A plaintiff with meritorious copyright claims and entitlement to the special remedies provided by the Act is deprived of these remedies merely because the first hurdle of proving entitlement is a showing of a contractual right.

A second problem with the *Schoenberg* test is that it is vague. *Schoenberg* characterizes the first part of its test in two ways: whether "the 'essence' of the plaintiff's claim" is in contract or copyright, or whether the "infringement claim is only 'incidental' to the plaintiff's claim seeking determination of ownership or contractual rights under the copyright." The meaning of either of these phrases is difficult to discern. At one juncture, *Schoenberg* suggests that the focus of inquiry should be on the plaintiff's motivations ("whether the plaintiff was really concerned with the infringement of his copyright or, alternatively, was, in fact, more interested in whether he would be allowed to enjoy his property free from the contract claims of the defendant"). District courts applying the "only incidental" test, in turn, have construed it in various other ways.

The *Schoenberg* test suffers from other defects as well. Because the analysis under *Schoenberg* is based more on the defense than on the demands asserted in the complaint, the plaintiff's attorney can have no way of telling whether the action should be filed within the exclusive jurisdiction of the federal court or in state court. Furthermore, the complaint will not necessarily reveal whether its claim of infringement and prayer for copyright remedies is "incidental to" a contract dispute. Indeed, it might not mention the assertedly forfeited license at all. Instead, it might simply state that the defendant is infringing plaintiff's copyright and demand an injunction, leaving it to the defendant's answer to claim justification in the license (to which the plaintiff plans to reply that the defendant's license was terminated as a result of its breach). A court examining such a complaint would have no idea whether the "essence" of plaintiff's claim would turn out to be a matter of contract, much less whether plaintiff's "real[] concern[]" lay in the infringement, or whether plaintiff was "more interested" in peaceful "enjoy[ment of] his property."

Nor can the court necessarily rely on the defendant to bring the question of subject matter jurisdiction promptly to its attention. When a complaint raises copyright issues, the defendant, like the plaintiff, may think it desirable to have them adjudicated in federal court, rather than entrust them to a state court, which has no experience with the Copyright Act. The consequence may well be that the federal court will not discover the predominance of contract issues, and consequently its own supposed lack of jurisdiction under *Schoenberg,* until well into trial; indeed, the discovery may not be made until the party that lost at trial (perhaps even the plaintiff) argues on appeal, for the first time, that the copyright issues were incidental and that the court therefore lacked subject matter jurisdiction.

Furthermore, even if the complaint sets forth in full the allegations relating to the license, and the defendant promptly moves to dismiss, the *Schoenberg* test requires the court to make complex factual determinations relating to the merits at the outset of the litigation — before the court has any familiarity with the case. Ascertaining what are a plaintiff's principal motives in bringing suit, and what issues will loom largest in the case, may well require extensive hearings and fact finding. The need for such fact finding recurs at each stage of *Schoenberg*'s three-step formula. Thus, if a court finds that a copyright claim is not "merely incidental to" a contract claim (step one), it must still determine whether the contractual term alleged to have been breached was in the nature of a covenant or a condition (step two). And if it finds that the alleged breach was of a covenant, the court must next determine "whether the breach is so material as to create a right of rescission," failing which the case must be dismissed (step three). This third inquiry in particular, which entails an assessment of the importance of the particular covenant, as well as the seriousness of the breach, raises questions that are not appropriately, easily or reliably answered at the start of litigation. . . .

For the reasons discussed above, we conclude that, for claims of infringement arising from, or in the context of, an alleged contractual breach, this circuit's standard for determining jurisdiction under Section 1338 is furnished by *T.B. Harms,* and not by *Schoenberg.* When a complaint alleges a claim or seeks a remedy provided by the Copyright Act, federal jurisdiction is properly invoked.

Applying the *T.B. Harms* standard to this case leads us to conclude that Bassett's copyright claims "arise under" the Copyright Act for purposes of Section 1338. Unlike the complaint in *T.B. Harms,* the complaint in this case alleges that the defendants, without authority, used plaintiff's copyrighted script to produce a new film intended and advertised for imminent exhibition. The amended complaint alleged copyright infringement and sought "a remedy expressly granted by the Act," *T.B. Harms,* 339 F.2d at 828, specifically, an injunction against further infringement of Bassett's copyrighted script. Because the complaint alleges the defendants violated the Copyright Act and seeks the injunctive remedy provided by the Act, under the rule of *T.B. Harms,* the action falls within the jurisdictional grant of Section 1338. The district court's contrary holding was in error. . . .

Medimune

V. DAMAGES

Damages recovery in the event of a breach can proceed from either or both of two distinctly different conceptual bases: contract remedies and intellectual property infringement. As we have seen, these approaches to determining compensable damages proceed from different conceptual bases. In most cases, they co-exist, so long as courts avoid awarding a double recovery.

From the perspective of contract law, a breach of contract gives the injured party the right to remedies aimed primarily at the goal that the injured person should be put in as good of a position as if the contract had been performed. The *Restatement (Second) of Contracts* summarizes the case law in terms of three protected interests:

- *Expectation Interest:* "which is [the party's] interest in having the benefit of his bargain by being put in as good a position as he would have been in had the contract been performed"

- *Reliance Interest:* "which is [the party's] interest in being reimbursed for loss caused by reliance on the contract by being put in as good a position as he would have been in had the contract not been made"

- *Restitution Interest:* "which is [the party's] interest in having restored to him any benefit that he has conferred on the other party"

Restatement (Second) of Contracts § 344. The remedies are defined by the bargain and its performance or non-performance. Property rights claims are based on a different concept. They deal with compensation for harm to the property or loss in the value of that property.

UNIVERSAL GYM EQUIPMENT, INC. v. ERWA EXERCISE EQUIPMENT LTD.
827 F.2d 1542 (Fed. Cir. 1987)

FRIEDMAN, CIRCUIT JUDGE.

These are an appeal and a cross-appeal from a judgment of the United States District Court for the District of Maryland, in a suit charging patent infringement, breach of contract, and unfair competition. . . . We uphold the findings of noninfringement and breach of contract, but remand the case to the district court to reconsider and, if necessary, to recalculate the damages.

I

A. *Background.* Universal Gym Equipment, Inc. manufactures and sells exercise weight-lifting machines. It brought the present suit against Atlantic Health and Fitness Corporation (Atlantic), ERWA Exercise Equipment Limited (ERWA) and ERWA's wholly-owned subsidiary, Global Gym and Fitness Equipment Limited (Global), which also manufactures and sells exercise weight-lifting machinery.

Both Universal and Global make and sell "standard resistance" and "variable resistance" weight-lifting machines; in the latter, the amount of force the user is required to exert varies during the exercise cycle. Such variation apparently is desirable because it corresponds to the variations in available muscle strength during exercise, so that the muscles are continuously worked at a level of nearly maximum effort.

The complaint charged (1) that the three defendants had (a) infringed Universal's U.S. Patent Re. 31,170 (the '170 patent), and (b) engaged in unfair competition and misused trade secrets, and (2) that ERWA and Global (as ERWA's successor) had breached a 1972 contract between Universal and ERWA. The complaint sought damages, an injunction, and specific performance of the contractual provision allegedly violated. . . .

. . . .

C. *The Contract.* In 1972, Universal and ERWA entered into an agreement under which ERWA could manufacture, market, and sell Universal exercise machines in Canada under Universal trademarks, in return for paying royalties to Universal. The agreement obligated Universal to "provide [ERWA] with plans and specifications which [Universal] has found necessary to insure proper assembly and performance of Licensed Product," as well as to "make [Universal]' s engineer available to [ERWA] in Canada for the purpose of acquainting [ERWA] with said know-how." ERWA promised to keep the technical knowledge thus acquired confidential.

The agreement provided for termination, by either party without cause, upon 6 months' notice. Paragraph 18 of the agreement further provided that after termination ERWA

> shall not thereafter manufacture, use, sell, or distribute any products which include any of the features, designs, technical information, or said know-how of [Universal] and will not thereafter use Licensed

Trademarks or any other trademark or trade style in any way similar to any of those of [Universal].

Universal gave notice of termination on April 12, 1978, and the agreement terminated as of November 20, 1978.

In August 1978, ERWA's principals formed Global as a wholly-owned subsidiary of ERWA. On November 21, 1978, using ERWA's facilities and employees, Global began manufacturing and selling exercise equipment; ERWA became a holding company. . . .

II. Infringement

[The] district court ruled that Universal had not established infringement, either literal or under the doctrine of equivalents. Universal here challenges only the latter ruling. [We affirm the District Court ruling.]

III. Breach of Contract

A. ERWA and Global (collectively Global) contend the district court improperly upheld and applied paragraph 18 of the agreement in violation of *Sears, Roebuck & Co. v. Stiffel Co.,* 376 U.S. 225 (1964), and *Compco Corp. v. Day-Brite Lighting, Inc.,* 376 U.S. 234 (1964). According to Global, these cases state that "when a publicly available article is unprotected by a patent or copyright, state law (there Illinois and here California) may not forbid others from making that article." Global further contends: "To the same effect is *Kewanee Oil Co. v. Bicron Corp.,* 416 U.S. 470 (1974), and *Lear, Inc. v. Adkins,* 395 U.S. 653 (1969), both of which decisions recognized that ideas in general circulation are dedicated to the common good unless they are protected by a valid patent." In other words, Global contends that those cases establish that the patent law preempts the application of state law to provide relief for the breach of the contract provision involved in this case.

[The court held that these decisions do not preclude application of state law to provide a damages remedy for breach of the agreement. "The question . . . is not whether the patent law bars the state from granting relief under its unfair competition law against copying an unpatented article. The question is whether the patent law precludes the application of state law to validate and award damages for a licensee's breach of a contractual provision by which the licensee agreed that, after its license to manufacture the licensor's product had terminated, the licensee would not include the licensor's features and designs in the licensee's products. In our view the patent law does not preclude the application of state contract law to provide damages for breach of this agreement."]

IV. Damages

. . . The district court held that under California law, Universal was entitled to recover the profits it lost as a result of Global's breach of paragraph 18 — a standard that Global does not challenge. The court correctly undertook to determine (1) which of the sales that Global made after the agreement was terminated would have been made by Universal if Global had not violated that provision and (2) the profit Universal would have made on those sales.

Global contends that the court erred in basing its damage award upon the full profit Universal would have realized from the sales of its machines rather than limiting it to the portion of the profit attributable to the Universal "features and designs" that the particular Global machine incorporated. According to Global:

> During the liability trial, [Universal's sales manager] identified a number of parts he considered to be present in both the [Universal and Global machines]. These totaled 136 parts. [Global's witness] testified during the liability trial that the [Global] machine had a total of 1282 parts. The ratio of 136 parts to 1282 parts results in a percentage of 10.6%, counting each part that [Universal] identified as being present in both . . . machines.

Global argues that Universal therefore was entitled to only 10.6 percent of Global's profit.

The district court correctly rejected that contention. As the court pointed out:

> Paragraph 18(d) of the 1972 agreement prohibited the manufacture of [sic] sale of any *products* which included *any* of Universal's features and designs. The use of the word "products" indicates beyond any question that in fact entire machines were contemplated as being subject to the breach of contract provision; the fact that such features or designs might constitute only 10.6% of the total number of parts is simply irrelevant. The issue is whether the machines contain any of the features or designs in question.

Global argues that its liability should be limited to the sales of machines for which royalties would have been payable under the 1972 licensing agreement. We agree with the district court's reasoning in rejecting this argument:

> The contract itself does not limit the restriction to machines subject to royalty payments; to the contrary, it prohibited the manufacture or sale of *any* machines containing features and designs of Universal Gym. . . . It is the presence of the features and designs, not the payment of royalties, that determines whether the machine in question is subject to an award of damages.

Global next contends that the damage award cannot stand because Universal provided no direct evidence that Universal would have made any of the sales that Global made after the agreement was terminated. The record shows, however, that Universal's sales decreased when, after the termination, Global began selling standard resistance machines that incorporated Universal's features and designs. In these circumstances, and in the absence of any evidence by Global that there was some other convincing explanation for Universal's loss of sales, the district court reasonably inferred causation.

The district court's award of damages reflected the court's finding that, had it not been for Global's violation of paragraph 18, Universal would have made 42.1 percent of the sales that Global made of machines incorporating Universal's "features and designs." That finding was based upon the total share of United States sales of ordinary resistance exercising machines (excluding Global's share of the market), which the district court found Universal had. Global challenges these calculations as based upon an estimate or guess and relating only to one of the seven years for which damages were awarded.

The district court's determination was based upon a table submitted by Universal showing "the relative market share of several companies competing in the United States in the year 1984 and Universal's market share in the worldwide market." Because there was "no other basis upon which to calculate Universal's market share, the Court accepts the United States sales as the most appropriate means of calculation."

Mr. Klinge, Universal's vice president in charge of sales, testified that these market share figures were "based on an estimate by Frank Smith and is strictly an estimate. . . . These are all estimates based on just our knowledge that we picked up with our experience but no hard data to back them up. This is an industry where figures are not readily available." Global introduced no evidence of its own to contradict this evidence, or to show that the market shares for other years were different from 1984. In the circumstances, we cannot say the district court erred in accepting the only evidence before it dealing with the subject.

Global, however, argues that the district court's damage award was flawed because, in determining Universal's share of the market, the court failed to consider the market share of Nautilus Corporation, which it alleges was Universal's principal competitor. Universal responds that Nautilus' share properly was excluded since the damage award was based upon sales of standard resistance machines and Nautilus manufactured only variable resistance equipment. The difficulty with Universal's position is that it appears that in determining market shares, the district court used data that included both standard and variable resistance machines. . . . Since the district court did not explain the reason for its use of these figures, we cannot say whether or not they are correct. If the district court intended to limit its market share analysis to Global's sales of standard resistance machines and excluded Nautilus because the latter did not make such machines, the proper figures would have been those shown on the first table of DX 226.

If, on the other hand, the court intended its market share analysis to cover both standard and variable resistance machines, as its use of the combined table might suggest, then the court should have explained why (1) Nautilus' sales were excluded, and (2) Global's sales of variable resistance machines (which the court found to not breach paragraph 18) were subtracted along with the sales of standard resistance machines.

We therefore must vacate the damage award and remand for the district court to reconsider, and if necessary recalculate, the damages in accordance with this opinion. . . .

NOTES

1. Lost profit as a result of breach is a common measure of damages in contract litigation. Recovery of lost profits is subject to ordinary concepts that the

loss must be foreseeable and that the damages must be established with reasonable certainty and not be speculative, and that the contract not preclude
recovery of the profits. The *Restatement (Second) of Contracts* § 352 comments
that a

> party cannot recover damages for breach of a contract for loss beyond
> the amount that the evidence permits to be established with reason-
> able certainty. Courts have traditionally required greater certainty in
> the proof of damages for breach of a contract than in the proof of dam-
> ages for a tort. The requirement does not mean, however, that the
> injured party is barred from recovery unless he establishes the total
> amount of his loss. It merely excludes those elements of loss that can-
> not be proved with reasonable certainty.

Did the proof in *Universal Gym* meet this standard?

2. In transactions governed by Article 2, lost profits issues are typically litigated with respect to a buyer's claim for damages, where lost profits typically
fall within the standards applicable to "consequential damages." Article 2
defines "consequential damages" in the following terms:

> (b) Consequential damages resulting from the seller's breach include

> (1) any loss resulting from general or particular requirements and
> needs of which the seller at the time of contracting had reason to know
> and which could not reasonably be prevented by cover or otherwise;
> and

> (2) injury to person or property proximately resulting from any breach
> of warranty.

This rule is often assumed to correspond to the doctrine of *Hadley v. Baxendale,*
9 Exch. 341, 156 Eng. Rep. 145 (1854), which distinguished between general
damages (flowing in the ordinary course from the breach), and special damages
(resulting from particular circumstances of the injured party, but recoverable
only if the other party had reason to know that there was a risk of such losses).
Unlike that case, however, consequential damages include losses from both the
general and particular circumstances of the buyer. If either standard applied
in *Universal Gym,* would lost profits have been recoverable?

In general, common law does not use the concept of "consequential damages," but refers to "special" or "general" damages, reflecting a dichotomy set
out in *Hadley* that disallows recovery of damages based on special needs or
circumstances of the injured party unless the other party had reason to know
that those special circumstances existed.

3. Article 2 does not provide for consequential damages for the seller, but it
does contain a rule that allows for recovery of the seller's profits from the contemplated sale in circumstances that some have described as lost volume
sales. The relevant provision states:

> (a) Subject to Subsection (b) . . . the measure of damages for non-accep-
> tance or repudiation by the buyer is the difference between the market
> price at the time and place for tender and the unpaid contract price

together with any incidental damages . . . but less expenses saved in consequence of the buyer's breach.

(b) If the measure of damages provided in Subsection (a) is inadequate to put the seller in as good a position as performance would have done then the measure of damages is the profit (including reasonable over-head) which the seller would have made from full performance by the buyer, together with any incidental damages . . . due allowance for costs reasonably incurred and due credit for payments or proceeds of resale.

UCC § 2-708 (1998 Official Text). As recognized in UCITA, the lost volume concept has routine significance in reference to non-exclusive licenses since the licensor's supply of additional licenses is potentially infinite and the effect of a licensee's breach is to cause a loss of volume for many licensors.

The *Restatement* sets out the common law application of this concept:

> The injured party is limited to damages based on his actual loss caused by the breach. If he makes an especially favorable substitute transac-tion, so that he sustains a smaller loss than might have been expected, his damages are reduced by the loss avoided as a result of that trans-action. . . . If he arranges a substitute transaction that he would not have been expected to do [otherwise] his damages are similarly limited by the loss so avoided. . . . Recovery can be had only for loss that would not have occurred but for the breach. . . . Whether a subsequent trans-action is a substitute for the broken contract sometimes raises difficult questions of fact. If the injured party could and would have entered into the subsequent contract, even if the contract had not been broken, and could have had the benefit of both, he can be said to have "lost volume" and the subsequent transaction is not a substitute for the broken contract. The injured party's damages are then based on the net profit that he has lost as a result of the broken contract. Since entrepreneurs try to operate at optimum capacity, however, it is pos-sible that an additional transaction would not have been profitable and that the injured party would not have chosen to expand his busi-ness by undertaking it had there been no breach. It is sometimes assumed that he would have done so, but the question is one of fact to be resolved according to the circumstances of each case.

Restatement (Second) of Contracts § 347, cmts. e, f.

PROBLEM 12.7

Technology Company holds patents on several technologies used in farming. It makes that technology available to farmers nationally under a non-exclu-sive one-year license for a fee of $50,000. During the past two years, it has averaged 15,000 licenses nationally. Farmer Brown contracts for three licenses, one each for all three of the farms that Brown operates. Shortly after contracting for the licenses and before paying the fee, however, Brown discov-ers a company that offers a competing technology at lesser cost. It repudiates all three licenses. Technology sues for damages. What recovery should be allowed and why?

U.S. VALVES, INC. v. DRAY
212 F.3d 1368 (Fed. Cir. 2000)

RADER, CIRCUIT JUDGE.

Robert F. Dray, Sr. (Dray) exclusively licensed his patent to U.S. Valves, Inc. in 1991. After his business relationship with U.S. Valves deteriorated, Dray himself began manufacturing and selling valves with the patented technology. U.S. Valves sued Dray for breach of contract, claiming that Dray sold valves covered by the licensed patents. Dray counterclaimed, seeking an accounting and damages for unpaid royalties. The district court found that Dray had sold valves in violation of the agreement, issued a permanent injunction barring Dray from making any further sales, and awarded U.S. Valves damages of $241,351.17. Dray appeals the judgment. U.S. Valves appeals the amount of the damages award. Because the trial court correctly ascertained liability, but misapplied important principles of calculating damages, this court affirms-in-part, reverses-in-part, and remands. . . .

This court applies the law of the applicable state in evaluating damages for breach of contract, a state claim of action. In Illinois, the proper measure of damages in a breach of contract case is the amount that will place the nonbreaching party in as satisfactory a position as it would have been had the contract been fully performed. If lost profits are awarded as damages for breach of contract, the amount of those profits need be proven only with reasonable, not exact, certainty.

Dray admitted that he manufactured and sold infringing valves before the district court issued its preliminary injunction on June 5, 1997. . . .

The damages calculation in this case is particularly complex because Dray sold two types of valves. One type of valve sold by Dray was certainly a licensed product; the other valve — the sliding ring — may have been covered by the agreement. Rather than determine the total sales of licensed product, the district court merely used summary figures alleged to show Dray's shipments and invoices. This evidence does not show, however, the number of licensed products manufactured and sold by Dray. In the first place, the shipment summary lists a large number of different valve types, and it is not known how many came within the license agreement, and how many did not. The U.S. Valves manager who prepared the summary conceded that she could "no way . . . be certain of what was shipped." With only conflicting testimony to provide direction, the district court concluded that Dray had indeed sold licensed product both before and after the injunction date. The district court then calculated post-injunction damages by assuming that any valves Dray sold after the injunction with the same name and same price as those sold before that date were licensed product. This method neglects other sales within the agreement, including perhaps the sliding ring valves if they fall within the agreement, and is thus incorrect.

Indeed, the most important missing piece of the damages puzzle is a determination of the status of the sliding ring valves under the agreement. Dray asserts that he sold only products that did not come under the license agreement after June 5, 1997. To properly calculate the damages from the breach, the trial court must determine the truth of that assertion by determining whether valves produced by Dray after June 5, 1997 infringe the patents licensed to U.S. Valves. The license agreement covers "[a]ll future improvements, modifications or enhancements of the Licensed Product made by the Licensor." This broad language may encompass the sliding ring valve, but that determination requires a proper analysis. On remand, the trial court may proceed to determine whether the sliding ring valves fall within the terms of the license agreement. On the other hand, the trial court may also determine that U.S. Valves had an opportunity to supply an adequate record for computation of damages, but failed to carry its burden of proof.

If the district court elects to determine, according to the best available evidence, the number of products covered by the agreement sold by Dray, it may wish to reconsider the formula for calculating lost profits. On the inadequate record before it, the district court added the invoice amounts for all valves sold by Dray before the injunction to the amounts for valves the court counted after the injunction date. This estimation arrived at the figure of $242,085. From this figure, the district court deducted Dray's royalty to arrive at "compensatory damages" to U.S. Valves of $193,668. This calculation errs in manifold ways: it is too imprecise in the determination of how many of the valves Dray sold were really licensed product; it assumes that U.S. Valves would have sold valves at the same prices that Dray did (not, e.g., for more, to cover its license fees to Dray); and it cavalierly neglects the manufacturing cost of the valves. U.S. Valves, who may be responsible for the deficient record, tries to justify this last omission with the explanation that the marginal costs of manufactured valves are negligible compared to the fixed costs such as office overhead and equipment lease. Yet U.S. Valves' own testimony at trial was that only thirty percent of the cost of production in the industry is such overhead, while the average cost of valve production is sixty-five percent of sales. These figures suggest that the marginal cost of valve production may be about forty-six percent of sales. Any calculation of the profits that U.S. Valves may have lost due to sales of licensed product by Dray requires some such cost deduction from the figure used for gross sales of licensed product.

On remand, the district court may make findings to determine the number of valves sold that were also covered by the agreement and the profits attributable to those sales. As noted before, the district court may also determine that plaintiff failed in its burden to supply a record sufficient to calculate damages. . . .

U.S. Valves argues that the district court's damages remedy does not protect against future harm. Future harm, however, is speculative. Because the district court has enjoined Dray from producing licensed products, future harm should never occur. Moreover, the license agreement gives no basis to award damages for future sales. That agreement did not even mention future sales but instead set up an ongoing arrangement in which the parties would apportion future revenues from the continuing sale of licensed valves. The agreement was to last until "the expiration of the Patent or subsequent improvement patents" unless terminated by the licensor for specific cause or by the licensee if the licensed product proved to be unpatentable. At the time of the agreement, the '282 patent's issue date, and therefore its expiration date, were not known. Further, at the time of the agreement, the parties could not predict the issuance of continuation patents, which would extend the license agreement. Without any way to determine future profits, any award of damages for these future profits would be wholly speculative.

To introduce some degree of precision to its future-profits argument, at trial U.S. Valves presented expert testimony on lost future profits calculated with a computer forecasting model. The record before this court does not disclose whether the district court used this evidence, or whether the court "ensur[ed] that an expert's testimony both rests on a reliable foundation and is relevant to the task at hand." Without such assurance, and in the light of the impossibility of calculating at the time of the simulation the life of the license agreement, this testimony also appears conjectural.

Speculative or contingent profits, as opposed to those a plaintiff would certainly earn but for the default, are recoverable only when the record permits estimation of probable profits with reasonable certainty. Therefore, the district court correctly denied U.S. Valves' request for damages for future harm.

DUNKIN' DONUTS OF AMERICA, INC. v. MINERVA, INC.
956 F.2d 1566 (11th Cir. 1992)

HATCHETT, CIRCUIT JUDGE:

In this breach of contract case, we affirm the magistrate judge's grant of judgment n.o.v. reducing damages awarded to the franchisees, denial of judgment n.o.v. as to the franchisor's liability, and denial of the franchisees' motion for attorney's fees.

FACTS

In 1976, Katherine Apostoleres became the sole shareholder of Minerva, Inc., which owned the rights to a Dunkin' Donuts of America, Inc. (Dunkin') franchise in Brandon, Florida. In 1978, Apostoleres became the sole shareholder of Rosebud, Inc., which owned the rights to a Dunkin' franchise in Temple Terrace, Florida. Apostoleres and her family (the franchisees) operated both stores.

In early 1982, Dunkin' offered to all its franchisees the right to renew the term of the franchisee's existing franchise agreement for an additional ten years at a fixed cost of $5,000. In return, the franchise owner would be required to participate in a program to abide by advertising decisions favored by at least two-thirds of the local franchise owners in a given television market. Apostoleres refused to accept the offer because she did not want to be bound by the "two-thirds" clause.

In August, 1982, Dunkin' employees audited Apostoleres's Temple Terrace and Brandon stores including use of the "yield and usage" method which projects a store's gross sales by taking the weights of a small number of donuts and extrapolating how many donuts should have been produced based upon those weights. The franchisees' agreements with Dunkin' did not provide authority to conduct an audit based upon such methodology.

In late 1982, the audits revealed that reported sales generally agreed with the sales run through the cash registers, bank deposits, and tax returns for the audited period; however, the yield and usage analysis detected an apparent underreporting of gross sales at both stores. The franchisees denied any underreporting and asserted that the yield and usage analysis provided inherently unreliable results.

In September, 1985, Dunkin' again audited the franchisees' stores. The audit of the Temple Terrace store disclosed no underreporting. The audit of the Brandon store reflected an underreporting of gross sales based upon the yield and usage analysis. . . . In a June 17, 1986 letter, Dunkin' gave the franchisees notice of immediate termination of the franchises. Despite the notice of termination and the ensuing litigation, the franchisees have continued to operate profitably the two stores as Dunkin' franchises. . . .

Procedural History

In June, 1986, Dunkin' filed a two-count complaint alleging that the franchisees breached provisions of the franchise agreements. . . . On January 25, 1989, the parties jointly requested that the district court refer the case to a United States magistrate judge for all further proceedings, including trial, and the district court granted the motion. The . . . jury returned a verdict against Dunkin' on its breach of contract claim . . . and in favor of the franchisees on their breach of contract claim, awarding the franchisees $650,000. . . . On December 8, 1989, the magistrate judge granted Dunkin's motion for judgment notwithstanding the verdict as to damages and reduced the $650,000 award to [$2].

Discussion

[We agree that a reasonable jury could have found that Dunkin' breached its obligation of good faith and fair dealing.]

Upon a material breach by Dunkin' of the franchise agreements, it is undisputed that Apostoleres was entitled to recover compensatory or expectancy damages — an amount intended to put Apostoleres in the position she would have been had Dunkin' fully performed under the agreements. If appropriate, such damages include lost future profits. The parties also agree that assuming Dunkin' materially breached the franchise agreements, Apostoleres could suspend her performance under the franchise agreements and sue for total breach.

Apostoleres, however, did not suspend her performance. Nevertheless, Apostoleres argues that she preserved her claim for damages by filing the counterclaims. Specifically, Apostoleres contends that upon the jury's finding of material breach by Dunkin', she is entitled to sever her relationship with Dunkin' and recover damages which include lost future profits over the remaining term of the franchise agreements, though she acknowledges that she must first tender her interest in the franchises to Dunkin'. In response, Dunkin' argues that Apostoleres presented no evidence that Dunkin's breach damaged the franchisees, and that because Apostoleres continued to perform under the franchise agreements and refused to pay Dunkin' compensation for the alleged underreporting, Apostoleres failed to preserve her right to rescind the agreement. . . .

In *Cities Service Helex, Inc. v. United States,* 543 F.2d 1306, 1313, 211 Ct. Cl. 222 (1976), the court examined the effect of continued performance after a material breach of contract:

> A material breach does not automatically and *ipso facto* end a contract. It merely gives the injured party the right to end the agreement; the injured party can choose between canceling the contract and continuing it. If he decides to close the contract and so conducts himself, both parties are relieved of their further obligations and the injured party is entitled to damages to the end of the contract term (to put him in the position he would have occupied if the contract had been completed). If he elects instead to continue the contract, the obligations of both parties remain in force and the injured party may retain only a claim for damages for partial breach.

A fair reading of Apostoleres's counterclaim reveals no indication that Apostoleres brought her lawsuit on the theory that Dunkin' committed breach, and in response to such breach, she wished to stop performance and recover lost future profits. In fact, Apostoleres sought injunctive relief to prevent Dunkin' from "unlawfully terminating or attempting to terminate Counterclaimant's franchises." Concerning damages, Apostoleres's counterclaim states that her businesses "have been damaged and have or will suffer the complete destruction of their business and business reputation, including the loss of goodwill," and she therefore seeks compensatory damages. Apostoleres never pleaded relief seeking to terminate or rescind the franchise agreements. In response to a standard arbitration interrogatory asking "in detail the elements of damage for which the plaintiff contends they are entitled to recover," Apostoleres responded, "[c]ompensatory damages for lost business."

At the pretrial conference held eleven days before trial, it was unclear whether Apostoleres had based her theory of recovery on damages suffered to the stores' ongoing operations, or rather on damages that would occur should she choose to stop operating the donut stores. . . .

[In] *Northern Helex Co. v. United States,* 455 F.2d 546, 197 Ct.Cl. 118 (1972), the court held that an injured party may continue performance in certain circumstances and yet reserve its right to claim a material breach without the breaching party's assent. In that case, however, Northern Helex notified the government that it considered the government's failure to make payments a material breach which Northern Helex did not waive by the acceptance of payments or the continuation of performance. Apostoleres made no such reservation.

. . . In this case, contrary to her contention, Apostoleres need not have operated the donut stores to maintain financial stability. At any time, she was free to sell her interest in the franchises.

We conclude that Apostoleres is entitled to recover only for those lost profits or lost future profits related to her ongoing operation caused by Dunkin's breach. Because, in Apostoleres's counsel's own words, "this record is deplete of any evidence demonstrating that my clients were damaged in the interim from the time that they were audited or sought to be terminated and until today," the magistrate judge properly granted judgment n.o.v. as to damages. . . .

AFFIRMED.

CLARK, SENIOR CIRCUIT JUDGE, concurring in part and dissenting in part:

Although concurring in those parts of the opinion with respect to affirming the rulings against Dunkin' Donuts, I dissent with respect to the principal holding in this case because the majority misreads the record at a critical point and for that or some other reason fails to apply long-established legal principles governing a party's right to elect a particular remedy when two or more are available to him. . . .

Although its exact basis for decision is unclear, the majority seems to hold that Apostoleres had to reserve her right to seek damages for total breach while continuing performance. The record demonstrates that Apostoleres in fact made a sufficient reservation of rights in her counterclaim and during the course of the proceedings. . . .

The majority is wrong on more than its interpretation of the record. The majority seems to hold that Apostoleres made an election of remedies by continuing performance without an explicit reservation of rights. This holding imports an antiquated doctrine into the law of Massachusetts that has been specifically rejected by that state's courts. Massachusetts law is that, if no estoppel is created by the continued performance of a contract, no remedy has been elected, and damages for total breach of contract may be had.

A. The Election of Remedies Doctrine

The majority's approach to the election of remedies doctrine has been rejected by the courts of Massachusetts, as well as most other courts. These courts look only to whether an estoppel was created in determining whether an aggrieved party has elected a remedy. These courts have adopted the position of Professor Corbin, who has written,

> The view with respect to election of remedies that is now becoming the prevailing one and that ought to be accepted is that, where a party injured by a breach definitely manifests a choice of a remedy that is actually available to him, in the place of some other alternative remedy, such a manifestation will bar an action for the latter remedy, provided that the party against whom the remedy is asked made a substantial change of position in reliance on the manifestation of intention before notice of its retraction. *This makes the conclusiveness of an "election" depend upon the existence of facts sufficient to create an "estoppel."* Cases stating this view are now very numerous and hold either that the remedy asked was not barred because there was no basis for an estoppel, or that an election was conclusive only because such a basis had been proved. The mere bringing of a suit asking one

remedy rather than another practically never affords ground for an estoppel and is not sufficient reason to deny an application for an alternative remedy.

5A A. CORBIN[, CORBIN ON CONTRACTS] § 1220, at 461-65 [(1960)]. In short, if there has been no estoppel created, there has been no conclusive election of remedies.

In the relatively recent case of *Plunkett v. First Federal Savings & Loan Association,* 18 Mass.App.Ct. 294, 464 N.E.2d 1381 (1984), the Appeals Court of Massachusetts held that the plaintiffs' actions in pressing for continued performance of an agreement, and their failure to take action to set aside the agreement, did not create an election of remedies such that the plaintiffs could not later attempt to set aside the agreement. In so holding, the court looked only to the fact that no estoppel was created by the plaintiffs' attempts to seek continued performance of the agreement. The court noted, "The [plaintiffs] are not barred from seeking to enforce . . . their claim against [the defendant] by any principle that they have elected to follow an inconsistent remedy without a clear attempt to rescind or set aside the 1972 agreement." The court cited, *inter alia,* the above-quoted section of *Corbin on Contracts* in reaching its conclusion and remarked, "These authorities suggest that principles concerning election of remedies have been much modified in recent years." The *Plunkett* case is precisely on point here, as *Plunkett* essentially holds that continued performance after a breach of an agreement does not, without an estoppel, prevent a subsequent request for an inconsistent remedy. The majority therefore applies an incorrect analysis as a matter of state law.

I add that many other authorities support the approach to election of remedies taken by Massachusetts. The influential *Restatement (Second) of Contracts* states with regard to election of remedies,

> If a party has more than one remedy under the rules stated in this Chapter, his manifestation of a choice of one of them by bringing suit or otherwise is not a bar to another remedy unless the remedies are inconsistent and the other party materially changes his position in reliance on the manifestation.

[*Restatement (Second) of Contracts,* § 378, at 228 (1981); *see also id.* (comment a; "A change of position is 'material' within the meaning of this Section if it is such that in all the circumstances a shift in remedies would be unjust.").]

The Uniform Commercial Code is applicable by analogy to franchise agreements. U.C.C. § 2-703, comment 1. The official commentary notes that the U.C.C. "rejects any doctrine of election of remedy as a fundamental policy." Moreover, "Whether the pursuit of one remedy bars another depends entirely on the facts of the individual case." By analyzing election of remedies on a case-by-case basis, the U.C.C. essentially adopts the Corbin view that an estoppel must be created for an election to bar relief.

Indeed, the principal case relied upon by the majority found an estoppel prior to finding an election of remedies. The majority quotes language from the decision of the former Court of Claims in *Cities Service Helex, Inc. v. United States* to support its holding that Apostoleres' continued performance worked an election of remedies. Elsewhere in its opinion, the Court of Claims discussed three formulations of the doctrine. Under the strictest approach, "any act indicating an intent to continue the contract is an election." The intermediate formulation of the doctrine allows a plaintiff to continue performance, provided an explicit reservation of rights is made. The most lenient view of the doctrine finds an election of remedies only when an estoppel is created. The majority seems to have selected the intermediate formulation for application here. However, the *Cities Service Helex* court reached its conclusion only after finding an election of remedies under all existing formulations of the election doctrine, including the estoppel approach. Even by the measure of its own citations, the majority is out-of-step with the great weight of authority in its failure to determine whether an estoppel was created by the continued performance of the franchise agreements. In doing so, the majority fails to follow binding Massachusetts law.

B. Was an Estoppel Created?

Massachusetts courts have defined the three elements of estoppel as follows:

> (1) A representation or conduct amounting to a representation intended to induce a course of conduct on the part of the person to whom the representation is made.

> (2) An act or omission resulting from the representation, whether actual or by conduct, by the person to whom the representation is made.

> (3) Detriment to such person as a consequence of the act or omission.

Cellucci v. Sun Oil Co., 320 N.E.2d 919, 923 (1974), *aff'd,* 368 Mass. 811, 331 N.E.2d 813 (1975). [None of these elements is satisfied in this case.] . . .

III.

I must address the further question of whether Apostoleres was entitled to the full amount of the jury's award of damages. The magistrate judge reduced the damages to one dollar for each franchise. The magistrate judge articulated two reasons for this reduction: First, "Massachusetts courts addressing the issue of the proper remedy for breach of implied covenant of good faith and fair dealing in the at-will employment context have rejected any attempt to fashion relief based on compensation for future services." Second, the magistrate found no causal connection between Dunkin's actions and Apostoleres' claimed loss of the entire value of the business. However, the magistrate judge improperly analogized the franchise agreements to the at-will employment context, and she failed to recognize that . . . Apostoleres' claim sounded in anticipatory repudiation.

A. The At-Will Employment Analogy

The magistrate judge should not have relied upon caselaw concerning at-will employment agreements, because those agreements by definition run indefinitely. The franchise agreements here were for a specific term of years. In cases involving employment agreements for a definite term, the

Massachusetts courts allow recovery for wrongful termination to be based upon a calculation of the wages that would have been earned under the agreement.

[B. Anticipatory Repudiation]

Another basis for affording Apostoleres the benefit of the jury's award is that Dunkin' committed a breach of contract by anticipatory repudiation. Dunkin' wrongfully repudiated the franchise agreements, and Apostoleres accepted that repudiation. Because Apostoleres' continued performance did not work an estoppel, she was entitled to terminate the agreements and receive the lost future profits of the franchises.

The *Restatement (Second) of Contracts* states, "Where an obligor repudiates a duty before he has committed a breach by non-performance and before he has received all of the agreed exchange for it, his repudiation alone gives rise to a claim for damages for total breach." [*Restatement (Second) of Contracts* § 253(1) (1979).] The *Restatement* defines a claim for damages for total breach of contract as "one for damages based on all of the injured party's remaining rights to performance." I note that Massachusetts is the only state that refuses to recognize actions for anticipatory repudiation of contracts. There are a number of exceptions to this refusal. One exception is that "when an anticipatory repudiation is accompanied by an actual breach, an action may be brought for breach of the entire contract at once." In our case, Apostoleres claimed (and the jury found) that Dunkin' had committed an actual breach of the contract by wrongfully auditing Apostoleres' records prior to Dunkin's repudiation. Therefore, Apostoleres could maintain suit on an anticipatory repudiation in Massachusetts. A second exception arises from Massachusetts' adoption of the Uniform Commercial Code, which provides for actions for anticipatory repudiation. As to the sale of goods, and by analogy to the franchise contracts involved here, Massachusetts has accepted the doctrine of anticipatory repudiation. Finally, Massachusetts may recognize an exception "where the contract may fairly be interpreted as establishing between the parties a present relation of mutual obligations." Such a relationship was clearly formed through the parties' franchise agreements. In sum, Apostoleres' claim for anticipatory repudiation fits squarely into several exceptions to Massachusetts' anomalous refusal to allow such claims.

Dunkin's actions in sending the notices of termination and in filing this lawsuit amounted to "an unqualified refusal, or declaration of inability, substantially to perform according to the terms of [its] obligation." Apostoleres was accordingly entitled to treat their relationship as at an end. But Apostoleres did not have to treat Dunkin's notices of termination and lawsuit as a breach of contract. One court has written,

> It would seem on principle that the declaration of such intention [not to carry out the contract] is not in itself and unless acted upon by the promisee a breach of the contract. . . . [S]uch declaration only becomes a wrongful act if the promisee elects to treat it as such. If he does so elect, it becomes a breach of contract, and he can recover upon it as such.

[*Roehm v. Horst,* 178 U.S. 1, 13 (1900).]

Dunkin' could have withdrawn its notices of termination and lawsuit prior to Apostoleres' manifestation of intent to treat the franchise agreements as over. As Professor Williston discusses, "[U]nless the repudiation is withdrawn it operates as a 'continuing offer' of a breach which may be taken advantage of at any time." This court has held,

> All that is required to close the door to repentance is definite action indicating that the anticipatory breach has been accepted as final, and this requisite can be supplied either by the filing of a suit or firm declaration, as here, that unless within a fixed time the breach is repudiated, it will be accepted.

[*United States v. Seacoast Gas Co.*, 204 F.2d 709, 711 (5th Cir.), *cert. denied*, 346 U.S. 866 (1953).] As discussed in part I.A, Apostoleres' counterclaim should be construed as an acceptance of Dunkin's repudiation and termination of the franchise agreements. . . . Thereafter, . . . Dunkin' could not retract its repudiation of the parties' agreements. The jury's verdict sealed the matter, awarding Apostoleres the value of the businesses. Dunkin's change of position in agreeing to continue with the contracts following the jury's verdict was predictable but cannot erase its breach of contract by repudiation and Apostoleres' acceptance thereof.

Whether due to the inappropriateness of specific performance or Dunkin's anticipatory repudiation, Apostoleres was entitled to recover the full amount of the lost future profits of the franchises.

NOTE

In *MCA Television Ltd v. Public Interest Corp.*, 171 F.3d 1265 (11th Cir. 1999), the court held that a liquidated damages provision in a television program license was an invalid penalty. The clause allowed the licensor to recover the accelerated amount of all future license fees and to enforce copyright claims against any subsequent showings of the licensed programs after the license was cancelled. According to the court, the licensor was given the benefit of all of the income it anticipated from the license, but also to prevent use of the programs as if the license did not exist. The court explained its result as follows:

> In light of the Florida cases, this scheme cannot be read to reflect a good faith effort by the parties to liquidate their damages. MCA drafted the contract so that the whole contract price must be paid in the event of a breach, because the "industry custom of licensing films substantially in advance of scheduled telecast, ha[s] the effect of rendering films hereunder unmarketable in the area covered by the telecasting from the designated city during any period encompassed by th[e] Agreement." Presumably, the idea here is that if PIC breached after the viewing season had begun, there would be no one left in Tampa to purchase MCA's programming and that as a result MCA would be unable to resell the programming in that market to make up the contract price. Assuming that this claim is correct as a factual matter, payment of the full contract price in the event of a breach

would thus be the only way to protect MCA's expectation interest in the contract.

However, once MCA is guaranteed the full contract price in this way, its damages have been fully liquidated. That is, in the event of PIC's breach, the full contract price, and nothing more, is the measure of MCA's damages. Any further recovery on this contract would thus be by definition in excess of the amount of MCA's expectation interest in the contract. . . .

Any licensee in PIC's position understands that copyright violation is a serious matter. The whole point of entering into licensing contracts such as those at issue here is to secure the consent of the license holder to the use of its material, in order to allow licensees to air copyrighted material in the agreed-upon manner without incurring liability in copyright infringement for doing so. Although a licensee should be able to treat a duly purchased broadcast license as precisely that — a license to use the material in the manner agreed to without the fear of a copyright infringement action for doing so — MCA through the wording of its contracts retains the right to wield the threat of a lawsuit for copyright infringement — and thus the threat of double recovery — as a club to pressure PIC to perform. This is nothing if not a clause "held in terrorem over the promisor to deter him from breaking his promise" such as is prohibited by Florida law.

In *MCA*, if the liquidated damages clause was not present and, when the exclusive license was breached, there were no potential licensees for the region, what damages would be appropriate for the licensor? Given an award of those damages, would the licensee be entitled to continue to show the programs, even if it did not comply with the license?

PROBLEM 12.8

Enterprise owns a resort hotel in Alaska. The hotel is the only hotel in a 30 mile radius. Enterprise contacts Hyatt Industries, an international hotel and franchise company about obtaining a franchise to use the Hyatt name on the hotel. The franchise fee is $100,000 initially and $40,000 per month for a hotel the size of the Enterprise location. The five-year agreement provides that, in the event of material breach by licensee, Hyatt can terminate the license to use its name and recover the total fees then unpaid for the entire term of the license. It also provides that termination of the license does not prejudice Hyatt's rights under any other law.

After one year of operation, Hyatt discovers that Enterprise failed to conform to the quality provisions of the agreement. It notifies Enterprise that the license is terminated. It then sues for the $1,900,000 remaining on the license. It also seeks an injunction against continued use of the Hyatt name. What result?

Part III: SELECTED ISSUES IN LICENSING

Chapter 13

SELECTED ANTITRUST ISSUES

I. ANTITRUST AND LICENSING — A LEGACY

There was a time when licensing law seemed entirely caught up in antitrust doctrine and intellectual property misuse concerns. That time, which spanned several decades, ending in the mid to late 1970s, was characterized by judicial and governmental agency hostility to intellectual property and the commercialization of it. While much of that hostility has dissipated and, for some time has morphed into a supportive legal approach to licensing, important remnants of the earlier approach remain. In some venues we may be seeing advocacy for a return to a more restrictive approach to curb perceived abuse.

During that earlier time of hostility, the policy of the Department of Justice (DOJ) reflected the view that certain clauses in patent licenses tended to be per se unlawful under antitrust doctrine, property misuse doctrine, or both. Andewelt, *Department of Justice Antitrust Policy,* in 1 DOMESTIC AND FOREIGN TECHNOLOGY LICENSING LAW 401 (1982). These included the so-called "nine no no's":

- Requiring a licensee to purchase unpatented materials

- Requiring a licensee to assign back subsequent patents

- Restricting a purchaser of a patented product in its resale

- Restricting licensee's dealing in products and services outside the patent scope

- Agreeing to not grant additional licenses without the licensee's consent

- Licensing a group of patents only as a package

- Conditioning the license on royalties computed in a manner not related to licensee sales or use

- Restricting sale of products made with a patented process

- Specifying a minimum price for the licensee's sale of licensed products

See 5 Trade Reg. Rep. (CCH) 50, 146 (1972); Arnold, *An Overview of Antitrust and Misuse Law,* 1982 PLI TECHN. LICENSING 43, 151; RAYMOND T. NIMMER, THE LAW OF COMPUTER TECHNOLOGY §§ 7:10-7:12 (1997, 2004). A common thread in this list involves leveraging of the intellectual property to contractually control conduct or products outside the scope of the property right. Concern about such leveraging remains important in modern law, but how that concern is implemented has in most cases shifted. The shift was signaled by a number of court decisions that, among other things, eliminated *per se* liability for some practices and by the promulgation in 1995 by the Justice Department and the Federal Trade Commission (the "Agencies") of the "Antitrust Guidelines for Licensing of Intellectual Property."

ANTITRUST GUIDELINES FOR THE LICENSING OF INTELLECTUAL PROPERTY
U.S. Department of Justice and the Federal Trade Commission
April 6, 1995

1. Intellectual property protection and the antitrust laws

1.0 . . . The intellectual property laws and the antitrust laws share the common purpose of promoting innovation and enhancing consumer welfare. The intellectual property laws provide incentives for innovation and its dissemination and commercialization by establishing enforceable property rights for the creators of new and useful products, more efficient processes, and original works of expression. In the absence of intellectual property rights, imitators could more rapidly exploit the efforts of innovators and investors without compensation. Rapid imitation would reduce the commercial value of innovation and erode incentives to invest, ultimately to the detriment of consumers. The antitrust laws promote innovation and consumer welfare by prohibiting certain actions that may harm competition with respect to either existing or new ways of serving consumers.

2. General principles

2.0 These Guidelines embody three general principles:

• for the purpose of antitrust analysis, the Agencies regard intellectual property as being essentially comparable to any other form of property;

• the Agencies do not presume that intellectual property creates market power in the antitrust context; and

• the Agencies recognize that intellectual property licensing allows firms to combine complementary factors of production and is generally procompetitive.

2.1 Standard antitrust analysis applies to intellectual property

The Agencies apply the same general antitrust principles to conduct involving intellectual property that they apply to conduct involving any other form of tangible or intangible property. That is not to say that intellectual property is in all respects the same as any other form of property. Intellectual property has important characteristics, such as ease of misappropriation, that distinguish it from many other forms of property. These characteristics can be taken into account by standard antitrust analysis, however, and do not require the application of fundamentally different principles. . . .

Intellectual property law bestows on the owners of intellectual property certain rights to exclude others. These rights help the owners to profit from the use of their property. An intellectual property owner's rights to exclude are similar to the rights enjoyed by owners of other forms of private property. As with other forms of private property, certain types of conduct with respect to intellectual property may have anticompetitive effects against which the antitrust laws can and do protect. Intellectual property is thus neither particularly free from scrutiny under the antitrust laws, nor particularly suspect under them. . . .

2.2 Intellectual property and market power

Market power is the ability profitably to maintain prices above, or output below, competitive levels for a significant period of time. The Agencies will not presume that a patent, copyright, or trade secret necessarily confers market power upon its owner. . . .

2.3 Procompetitive benefits of licensing

Intellectual property typically is one component among many in a production process and derives value from its combination with complementary factors. [Licensing,] cross-licensing, or otherwise transferring intellectual property (hereinafter "licensing") can facilitate integration of the licensed property with complementary factors of production. This integration can lead to more efficient exploitation of the intellectual property, benefiting consumers through the reduction of costs and the introduction of new products. Such arrangements increase the value of intellectual property to consumers and to the developers of the technology. By potentially increasing the expected returns from intellectual property, licensing also can increase the incentive for its creation and thus promote greater investment in research and development.

Sometimes the use of one item of intellectual property requires access to another. An item of intellectual property "blocks" another when the second cannot be practiced without using the first. For example, an improvement on a patented machine can be blocked by the patent on the machine. Licensing may promote the coordinated development of technologies that are in a blocking relationship.

Field-of-use, territorial, and other limitations on intellectual property licenses may serve procompetitive ends by allowing the licensor to exploit its property as efficiently and effectively as possible. These various forms of exclusivity can be used to give a licensee an incentive to invest in the commercialization and distribution of products embodying the licensed intellectual property and to develop additional applications for the licensed property. The restrictions may do so, for example, by protecting the licensee against free-riding on the licensee's investments by other licensees or by the licensor. They may also increase the licensor's incentive to license, for example, by protecting the licensor from competition in the licensor's own technology in a market niche that it prefers to keep to itself. These benefits of licensing restrictions apply to patent, copyright, and trade secret licenses, and to know-how agreements.

EXAMPLE 1

Situation: [ComputerCo] develops a new, copyrighted software program for inventory management. The program has wide application in the health field. ComputerCo licenses the program in an arrangement that imposes both field of use and territorial limitations. Some of

ComputerCo's licenses permit use only in hospitals; others permit use only in group medical practices. ComputerCo charges different royalties for the different uses. All of ComputerCo's licenses permit use only in specified portions of the United States and in specified foreign countries. The licenses contain no provisions that would prevent or discourage licensees from developing, using, or selling any other program, or from competing in any other good or service other than in the use of the licensed program. None of the licensees are actual or likely potential competitors of ComputerCo in the sale of inventory management programs.

Discussion: The key competitive issue raised by the licensing arrangement is whether it harms competition among entities that would have been actual or likely potential competitors in the absence of the arrangement. Such harm could occur if, for example, the licenses anticompetitively foreclose access to competing technologies (in this case, most likely competing computer programs), prevent licensees from developing their own competing technologies (again, in this case, most likely computer programs), or facilitate market allocation or price-fixing for any product or service supplied by the licensees. If the license agreements contained such provisions, the Agency evaluating the arrangement would analyze its likely competitive effects. . . . In this hypothetical, there are no such provisions and thus the arrangement is merely a subdivision of the licensor's intellectual property among different fields of use and territories. The licensing arrangement does not appear likely to harm competition among entities that would have been actual or likely potential competitors if ComputerCo had chosen not to license the software program. The Agency therefore would be unlikely to object to this arrangement. [The] Agency's conclusion as to likely competitive effects could differ if, for example, the license barred licensees from using any other inventory management program.

3. Antitrust concerns and modes of analysis

3.1 Nature of the concerns

While intellectual property licensing arrangements are typically welfare-enhancing and procompetitive, antitrust concerns may nonetheless arise. For example, a licensing arrangement could include restraints that adversely affect competition in goods markets by dividing the markets among firms that would have competed using different technologies. An arrangement that effectively merges the research and development activities of two of only a few entities that could plausibly engage in research and development in the relevant field might harm competition for development of new goods and services. An acquisition of intellectual property may lessen competition in a relevant antitrust market. The Agencies will focus on the actual effects of an arrangement, not on its formal terms.

The Agencies will not require the owner of intellectual property to create competition in its own technology. However, antitrust concerns may arise when a licensing arrangement harms competition among entities that would have been actual or likely potential competitors in a relevant market in the absence of the license (entities in a "horizontal relationship"). A restraint in a licensing arrangement may harm such competition, for example, if it facilitates market division or price-fixing. In addition, license restrictions with respect to one market may harm such competition in another market by anticompetitively foreclosing access to, or significantly raising the price of, an important input, or by facilitating coordination to increase price or reduce output. When it appears that such competition may be adversely affected, the Agencies will follow the analysis set forth below. . . .

3.3 Horizontal and vertical relationships

As with other property transfers, antitrust analysis of intellectual property licensing arrangements examines whether the relationship among the parties to the arrangement is primarily horizontal or vertical in nature, or whether it has substantial aspects of both. A licensing arrangement has a vertical component when it affects activities that are in a complementary relationship, as is typically the case in a licensing arrangement. For example, the licensor's primary line of business may be in research and development, and the licensees, as manufacturers, may be buying the rights to use technology developed by the licensor. Alternatively, the licensor may be a component manufacturer owning intellectual property rights in a product that the licensee manufactures by combining the component with other inputs, or the licensor may manufacture the product, and the licensees may operate primarily in distribution and marketing.

In addition to this vertical component, the licensor and its licensees may also have a horizontal relationship. For analytical purposes, the Agencies ordinarily will treat a relationship between a licensor and its licensees, or between licensees, as horizontal when they would have been actual or likely potential competitors in a relevant market in the absence of the license.

The existence of a horizontal relationship between a licensor and its licensees does not, in itself, indicate that the arrangement is anticompetitive. Identification of such relationships is merely an aid in determining whether there may be anticompetitive effects arising from a licensing arrangement. Such a relationship need not give rise to an anticompetitive effect, nor does a purely vertical relationship assure that there are no anticompetitive effects.

The following examples illustrate different competitive relationships among a licensor and its licensees.

EXAMPLE 5

Situation: AgCo, a manufacturer of farm equipment, develops a new, patented emission control technology for its tractor engines and licenses it to FarmCo, another farm equipment manufacturer. AgCo's emission control technology is far superior to the technology currently owned and used by FarmCo, so much so that FarmCo's technology does not significantly constrain the prices that AgCo could charge for its technology. AgCo's emission control patent has a broad scope. It is likely that any improved emissions control technology that FarmCo could develop in the foreseeable future would infringe AgCo's patent.

Discussion: Because FarmCo's emission control technology does not significantly constrain AgCo's competitive conduct with respect to its emission control technology, AgCo's and FarmCo's emission control technologies are not close substitutes for each other. FarmCo is a consumer of AgCo's technology and is not an actual competitor of AgCo in the relevant market for superior emission control technology of the kind licensed by AgCo. Furthermore, FarmCo is not a likely potential competitor of AgCo in the relevant market because, even if FarmCo could develop an improved emission control technology, it is likely that it would infringe AgCo's patent. This means that the relationship between AgCo and FarmCo with regard to the supply and use of emissions control technology is vertical. Assuming that AgCo and FarmCo are actual or likely potential competitors in sales of farm equipment products, their relationship is horizontal in the relevant markets for farm equipment. . . .

3.4 Framework for evaluating licensing restraints

In the vast majority of cases, restraints in intellectual property licensing arrangements are evaluated under the rule of reason. The Agencies' general approach in analyzing a licensing restraint under the rule of reason is to inquire whether the restraint is likely to have anticompetitive effects and, if so, whether the restraint is reasonably necessary to achieve procompetitive benefits that outweigh those anticompetitive effects. *See Federal Trade Commission v. Indiana Federation of Dentists*, 476 U.S. 447 (1986); *NCAA v. Board of Regents of the University of Oklahoma*, 468 U.S. 85 (1984); *Broadcast Music, Inc. v. Columbia Broadcasting System, Inc.*, 441 U.S. 1 (1979); 7 Phillip E. Areeda, *Antitrust Law* § 1502 (1986). *See also* part 4.

In some cases, however, the courts conclude that a restraint's "nature and necessary effect are so plainly anticompetitive" that it should be treated as unlawful per se, without an elaborate inquiry into the restraint's likely competitive effect. *Federal Trade Commission v. Superior Court Trial Lawyers Association*, 493 U.S. 411, 433 (1990); *National Society of Professional Engineers v. United States*, 435 U.S. 679, 692 (1978). Among the restraints that have been held per se unlawful are naked price-fixing, output restraints, and market division among horizontal competitors, as well as certain group boycotts and resale price maintenance.

To determine whether a particular restraint in a licensing arrangement is given per se or rule of reason treatment, the Agencies will assess whether the restraint in question can be expected to contribute to an efficiency-enhancing integration of economic activity. In general, licensing arrangements promote such integration because they facilitate the combination of the licensor's intellectual property with complementary factors of production owned by the licensee. A restraint in a licensing arrangement may further such integration by, for example, aligning the incentives of the licensor and the licensees to promote the development and marketing of the licensed technology, or by substantially reducing transactions costs. If there is no efficiency-enhancing integration of economic activity and if the type of restraint is one that has been accorded per se treatment, the Agencies will challenge the restraint under the per se rule. Otherwise, the Agencies will apply a rule of reason analysis.

Application of the rule of reason generally requires a comprehensive inquiry into market conditions. However, that inquiry may be truncated in certain circumstances. If the Agencies conclude that a restraint has no likely anticompetitive effects, they will treat it as reasonable, without an elaborate analysis of market power or the justifications for the restraint. Similarly, if a restraint facially appears to be of a kind that would always or almost always tend to reduce output or increase prices, and the restraint is not reasonably related to efficiencies, the Agencies will likely challenge the restraint without an elaborate analysis of particular industry circumstances. . . .

4. General principles concerning the Agencies' evaluation of licensing arrangements under the rule of reason. . . .

4.1.2 Licensing arrangements involving exclusivity

A licensing arrangement may involve exclusivity in two distinct respects. First, the licensor may grant one or more *exclusive licenses*, which restrict the right of the licensor to license others and possibly also to use the technology itself. Generally, an exclusive license may raise antitrust concerns only if the licensees themselves, or the licensor and its licensees, are in a horizontal relationship. Examples of arrangements involving exclusive licensing that may give rise to antitrust concerns include cross-licensing by parties collectively possessing market power . . . , and acquisitions of intellectual property rights.

A non-exclusive license of intellectual property that does not contain any restraints on the competitive conduct of the licensor or the licensee generally does not present antitrust concerns even if the parties to the license are in a horizontal relationship, because the non-exclusive license normally does not diminish competition that would occur in its absence.

A second form of exclusivity, *exclusive dealing*, arises when a license prevents or restrains the licensee from licensing, selling, distributing, or using competing technologies. Exclusivity may be achieved by an explicit exclusive dealing term in the license or by other provisions such as compensation terms or other economic incentives. Such restraints may anticompetitively foreclose access to, or increase competitors' costs of obtaining, important inputs, or facilitate coordination to raise price or reduce output, but they also may have procompetitive effects. For example, a licensing arrangement that prevents the licensee from dealing in other technologies may encourage the licensee to develop and market the licensed technology or specialized applications of that technology. The Agencies will take into account such procompetitive effects in evaluating the reasonableness of the arrangement.

The antitrust principles that apply to a licensor's grant of various forms of exclusivity to and among its licensees are similar to those that apply to comparable vertical restraints outside the licensing context, such as exclusive territories and exclusive dealing. However, the fact that intellectual property may in some cases be misappropriated more easily than other forms of property may justify the use of some restrictions that might be anticompetitive in other contexts.

As noted earlier, the Agencies will focus on the actual practice and its effects, not on the formal terms of the arrangement. A license denominated as non-exclusive (either in the sense of exclusive licensing or in the sense of exclusive dealing) may nonetheless give rise to the same concerns posed by formal exclusivity. A non-exclusive license may have the effect of exclusive licensing if it is structured so that the licensor is unlikely to license others or to practice the technology itself. A license that does not explicitly require exclusive dealing may have the effect of exclusive dealing if it is structured to increase significantly a licensee's cost when it uses competing technologies. However, a licensing arrangement will not automatically raise these concerns merely because a party chooses to deal with a single licensee or licensor, or confines his activity to a single field of use or location, or because only a single licensee has chosen to take a license.

EXAMPLE 8

Situation: NewCo, the inventor and manufacturer of a new flat panel display technology, lacking the capability to bring a flat panel display product to market, grants BigCo an exclusive license to sell a product embodying NewCo's technology. BigCo does not currently sell, and is not developing (or likely to develop), a product that would compete with the product embodying the new technology and does not control rights to another display technology. Several firms offer competing displays, BigCo accounts for only a small proportion of the outlets for distribution of display products, and entry into the manufacture and distribution of display products is relatively easy. Demand for the new technology is uncertain and successful market penetration will require considerable promotional effort. The license contains an exclusive dealing restriction preventing BigCo from selling products that compete with the product embodying the licensed technology.

Discussion: This example illustrates both types of exclusivity in a licensing arrangement. The license is exclusive in that it restricts the right of the licensor to grant other licenses. In addition, the license has an exclusive dealing component in that it restricts the licensee from selling competing products.

The inventor of the display technology and its licensee are in a vertical relationship and are not actual or likely potential competitors in the manufacture or sale of display products or in the sale or development of technology. Hence, the grant of an exclusive license does not affect competition between the licensor and the licensee. The exclusive license may promote competition in the manufacturing and sale of display products by encouraging BigCo to develop and promote the new product in the face of uncertain demand by rewarding BigCo for its efforts if they lead to large sales. Although the license bars the licensee from selling competing products, this exclusive dealing aspect is unlikely in this example to harm competition by anticompetitively foreclosing access, raising competitors' costs of inputs, or facilitating anticompetitive pricing because the relevant product market is unconcentrated, the exclusive dealing restraint affects only a small proportion of the outlets for distribution of display products, and entry is easy. On these facts, the evaluating Agency would be unlikely to challenge the arrangement. . . .

4.2 Efficiencies and justifications

If the Agencies conclude, upon an evaluation of [market factors] that a restraint in a licensing arrangement is unlikely to have an anticompetitive effect, they will not challenge the restraint. If the Agencies conclude that the restraint has, or is likely to have, an anticompetitive effect, they will consider whether the restraint is reasonably necessary to achieve procompetitive efficiencies. If the restraint is reasonably necessary, the Agencies will balance the procompetitive efficiencies and the anticompetitive effects to determine the probable net effect on competition in each relevant market.

The Agencies' comparison of anticompetitive harms and procompetitive efficiencies is necessarily a qualitative one. The risk of anticompetitive effects in a particular case may be insignificant compared to the expected efficiencies, or vice versa. As the expected anticompetitive effects in a particular licensing arrangement increase, the Agencies will require evidence establishing a greater level of expected efficiencies.

The existence of practical and significantly less restrictive alternatives is relevant to a determination of whether a restraint is reasonably necessary. If it is clear that the parties could have achieved similar efficiencies by means that are significantly less restrictive, then the Agencies will not give weight to the parties' efficiency claim. In making this assessment, however, the Agencies will not engage in a search for a theoretically least restrictive alternative that is not realistic in the practical prospective business situation faced by the parties.

When a restraint has, or is likely to have, an anticompetitive effect, the duration of that restraint can be an important factor in determining whether it is reasonably necessary to achieve the putative procompetitive efficiency. The effective duration of a restraint may depend on a number of factors, including the option of the affected party to terminate the arrangement unilaterally and the presence of contract terms (e.g., unpaid balances on minimum purchase commitments) that encourage the licensee to renew a license arrangement. Consistent with their approach to less restrictive alternative analysis generally, the Agencies will not attempt to draw fine distinctions regarding duration; rather, their focus will be on situations in which the duration clearly exceeds the period needed to achieve the procompetitive efficiency.

The evaluation of procompetitive efficiencies, of the reasonable necessity of a restraint to achieve them, and of the duration of the restraint, may depend on the market context. A restraint that may be justified by the needs of a new entrant, for example, may not have a procompetitive efficiency justification in different market circumstances. . . .

II. STATUTORY FRAMEWORK

Antitrust law in the United States is nominally statutory law. The antitrust statutes, however, are so thin in phrasing that decades of case law and regulations give them their primary content. The primary federal statutes are the Sherman Act, the Clayton Act, and the Robinson-Patman Act.

The Sherman Act (15 U.S.C. §§ 1-7) is the most important for licensing. Sherman Act Section 1 states:

> Every contract, combination in the form of trust or otherwise, or conspiracy, in restraint of trade or commerce among the several States, or with foreign nations, is hereby declared to be illegal.

15 U.S.C. § 1. On this sparse language rests volumes of case law and trillions of dollars of economic impact. Section 1 deals with contracts, agreements, conspiracies, and combinations and does not cover unilateral conduct. But since Section 1 covers contracts, it applies to licenses.

Sherman Act Section 1 bans agreements in "restraint of trade or commerce." The Act does not define what such a restraint might be. To understand what is or is not a "restraint of trade," then, one must turn to hundreds of reported court decisions, the agency interpretations, and to the literature that is legion, especially in law and economics. Although the interpretation of "restraint or trade or commerce" has varied over the years, one common theme is that the statute prohibits only those practices that *unreasonably* restrain competition. Judicial recognition of this limit led to formulation of the so-called "rule of reason" analysis that dominates current antitrust law. Writing in 1918, the Supreme Court set out the general contours of the approach to Section 1:

> The true test of legality is whether the restraint imposed is such as merely regulates and perhaps thereby promotes competition or whether it is such as may suppress or even destroy competition. To determine that question the court must ordinarily consider the facts peculiar to the business to which the restraint is applied; its condition before and after the restraint was imposed; the nature of the restraint and its effect, actual or probable. The history of the restraint, the evil believed to exist, the reason for adopting the particular remedy, the purpose or end sought to be attained, are all relevant facts.

Board of Trade of City of Chicago v. United States, 246 U.S. 231, 238 (1918).

Sherman Act Section 2 states:

> Every person who shall monopolize, or attempt to monopolize, or combine or conspire with any other person or persons, to monopolize any part of the trade or commerce among the several States, or with foreign nations, shall be deemed guilty of a felony.

15 U.S.C. § 2. As with Section 1, violations of Section 2 may result in civil or criminal penalties; injured parties may receive three times their damages. Section 2 does not require joint action or an unlawful agreement, but the conduct in question must do more than restrain trade or commerce: Section 2 deals with monopolization. The Sherman Act does not define "monopolization,"

but merely *being* or becoming a monopoly does not in trigger liability. Monopoly status, acquired through ordinary competition, superior products, effort, hard competition or other ordinary business practices is not illegal under Section 2. On the other hand, seeking or attaining monopoly status by unfair or anti-competitive means may violate Section 2.

Section 2 cases focus on whether the defendant had sufficient market power to be treated as having, or as having attempted to achieve, monopoly status. The general concept of "market power" refers to the ability to raise prices or restrict output for a significant period of time, unaffected by the responsive actions of competitors or potential competitors. The *Antitrust Guidelines on Licensing* describes the concept as: "the ability profitably to maintain prices above, or output below, competitive levels for a significant period of time." UNITED STATES DEPARTMENT OF JUSTICE AND FEDERAL TRADE COMMISSION, ANTITRUST GUIDELINES IN LICENSING OF INTELLECTUAL PROPERTY § 2.2 (1995). For a monopolization or attempted monopolization claim to be proven, it is not sufficient merely that a firm holds some market power. It must be shown that, viewed in context, this power is sufficient to attain or seriously threaten to achieve the prohibited acts of wrongfully obtaining or attempting to obtain a monopoly position unlawfully.

The Clayton Act, enacted in 1914, augments the Sherman Act. The Clayton Act delineates specific prohibited acts. These are stated in terms that require analysis of the factual environment. Clayton Act rules include:

- Section 2: "It shall be unlawful for any person engaged in commerce, in the course of such commerce, either directly or indirectly, to discriminate in price between different purchasers of commodities of like grade and quality . . . where the effect of such discrimination may be substantially to lessen competition or tend to create a monopoly in any line of commerce, or to injure, destroy, or prevent competition with any person who either grants or knowingly receives the benefit of such discrimination, or with customers of either of them. . . ." 15 U.S.C. § 13.

- Section 3: "It shall be unlawful for any person engaged in commerce . . . to lease or make a sale or contract for sale of goods, wares, merchandise, machinery, supplies, or other commodities, whether patented or unpatented, for use, consumption, or resale . . . or fix a price charged therefore, or discount from, or rebate upon, such price, on the condition, agreement, or understanding that the lessee or purchaser thereof shall not use or deal in the goods, wares, merchandise, machinery, supplies, or other commodities of a competitor or competitors of the lessor or seller, where the effect of such lease, sale, or contract for sale or such condition, agreement, or understanding may be to substantially lessen competition or tend to create a monopoly in any line of commerce." 15 U.S.C. § 14.

- Section 7: "No person . . . shall acquire . . . the whole or any part of the stock . . . or any part of the assets of another person engaged also in commerce . . . where in any line of commerce or in any activity affecting commerce in any section of the country, the effect of such acquisition may be substantially to lessen competition, or to tend to create a monopoly." 15 U.S.C. § 18.

Clayton Act rules often overlap coverage of the Sherman Act.

The Robinson-Patman Act (15 USC § 13(a), et. seq.) proscribes price discrimination in sales of goods or services to competing commercial customers. Under this statute, purchasers who are in competition with each other should generally be charged the same price for the same product and given promotional support on a proportionately equal basis for items like advertising and product demonstrators. The Robinson-Patman Act does not apply to licenses of intellectual property as such — it applies to commodities, not intangibles.

III. TYING ARRANGEMENTS

Historically, the most significant issue in antitrust analysis of licensing lies in the question of whether the presence of an intellectual property right gives the holder of that right presumptive economic or market power for purposes of an antitrust analysis, or whether the presence of the right is merely one part of the mix that goes into the overall analysis of whether the antitrust defendant had sufficient power to engage in anticompetitive conduct.

The issue was most clearly demonstrated in reference to antitrust tying claims. A "tying arrangement" exists if a party conditions a license or sale of one product on the other party's acceptance of a license or purchase of another product. *See Northern Pacific Railway Co. v. United States*, 356 U.S. 1, 5-6 (1958) ("A tying arrangement is an agreement by a party to sell one product but only on the condition that the buyer also purchases a different (or tied) product, or at least agrees that he will not purchase that product from any other supplier."). Four elements are considered in evaluating the presence or absence of tying:

1. The existence of at least two distinct products or services

2. The sale of the tying product or service conditioned on the purchase of the tied product or service

3. The defendant has sufficient economic or market power over the tying product to restrain competition for another product

4. The amount of commerce involved is not insubstantial

Eastman Kodak Co. v. Image Technical Servs., Inc., 504 U.S. 451 (1992). Tying does not exist simply because one manufacturer offers two or more products as an integrated system or as a multi-product package. The element that transforms such practices into tying is compulsion or coercion based on a compelled linkage of two or more separate products and market power with respect to one of them.

The presence of an antitrust violation hinges on "the seller's exploitation of its control over the tying product to force the purchase of a tied product." *Jefferson Parish Hosp. Dist. No. 2 v. Hyde*, 466 U.S. 2, 12 (1984).

ILLINOIS TOOL WORKS INC. v. INDEPENDENT INK, INC.
547 U.S. 28 (2006)

Justice STEVENS. . . .

In *Jefferson Parish Hospital Dist. No. 2 v. Hyde,* 466 U.S. 2 (1984), we repeated the well-settled proposition that "if the Government has granted the seller a patent or similar monopoly over a product, it is fair to presume that the inability to buy the product elsewhere gives the seller market power." This presumption of market power, applicable in the antitrust context when a seller conditions its sale of a patented product (the "tying" product) on the purchase of a second product (the "tied" product), has its foundation in the judicially created patent misuse doctrine. In 1988, Congress substantially undermined that foundation, amending the Patent Act to eliminate the market power presumption in patent misuse cases. The question presented to us today is whether the presumption of market power in a patented product should survive as a matter of antitrust law despite its demise in patent law. We conclude that the mere fact that a tying product is patented does not support such a presumption.

I

Petitioners, Trident, Inc., and its parent, Illinois Tool Works Inc., manufacture and market printing systems that include three relevant components: (1) a patented piezoelectric impulse ink jet printhead; (2) a patented ink container, consisting of a bottle and valved cap, which attaches to the printhead; and (3) specially designed, but unpatented, ink. Petitioners sell their systems to original equipment manufacturers (OEMs) who are licensed to incorporate the printheads and containers into printers that are in turn sold to companies for use in printing barcodes on cartons and packaging materials. The OEMs agree that they will purchase their ink exclusively from petitioners, and that neither they nor their customers will refill the patented containers with ink of any kind.

Respondent, Independent Ink, Inc., has developed an ink with the same chemical composition as the ink sold by petitioners. . . . Independent filed suit against Trident seeking a judgment of noninfringement and invalidity of Trident's patents. [It] alleged that petitioners are engaged in illegal tying and monopolization in violation of §§ 1 and 2 of the Sherman Act.

[The] District Court granted petitioners' motion for summary judgment on the Sherman Act claims. It rejected respondent's submission that petitioners "necessarily have market power in the market for the tying product as a matter of law solely by virtue of the patent on their printhead system, thereby rendering [the] tying arrangements *per se* violations of the antitrust laws." . . . The parties settled their other claims, and respondent appealed.

After a careful review of the "long history of Supreme Court consideration of the legality of tying arrangements," the Court of Appeals for the Federal Circuit reversed the District Court's decision as to respondent's § 1 claim. [It] concluded that the "fundamental error" in petitioners' submission was its disregard of "the duty of a court of appeals to follow the precedents of the Supreme Court until the Court itself chooses to expressly overrule them." We granted certiorari to undertake a fresh examination of the history of both the judicial and legislative appraisals of tying arrangements. Our review is informed by extensive scholarly comment and a change in position by the administrative agencies charged with enforcement of the antitrust laws.

II

American courts first encountered tying arrangements in the course of patent infringement litigation. Such a case came before this Court in *Henry v. A.B. Dick Co.,* 224 U.S. 1 (1912), in which, as in the case we decide today, unpatented ink was the product that was "tied" to the use of a patented product through the use of a licensing agreement. Without commenting on the tying arrangement, the Court held that use of a competitor's ink in violation of a condition of the agreement-that the rotary mimeograph "'may be used only with the stencil, paper, ink and other supplies made by A.B. Dick Co.'"-constituted infringement of the patent on the machine. Chief Justice White dissented, explaining his disagreement with the Court's approval of a practice that he regarded as an "attempt to increase the scope of the monopoly granted by a patent . . . which tend[s] to increase monopoly and to burden the public in the exercise of their common rights Two years later, Congress endorsed Chief Justice White's disapproval of tying arrangements, enacting § 3 of the Clayton Act. See 38 Stat. 731 (applying to "patented or unpatented" products); see also *Motion Picture Patents Co. v. Universal Film Mfg. Co.,* 243 U.S. 502, 517-518, 37 S.Ct. 416, 61 L.Ed. 871 (1917) (explaining that, in light of § 3 of the Clayton Act, *A.B. Dick* "must be regarded as overruled"). And in this Court's subsequent cases reviewing the legality of tying arrangements we, too, embraced Chief Justice White's disapproval of those arrangements.

In the years since *A.B. Dick,* four different rules of law have supported challenges to tying arrangements. They have been condemned as improper extensions of the patent monopoly under the patent misuse doctrine, as unfair methods of competition under § 5 of the Federal Trade Commission Act, as contracts tending to create a monopoly under § 3 of the Clayton Act, and as contracts in restraint of trade under § 1 of the Sherman Act. In all of those instances, the justification for the challenge rested on either an assumption or a showing that the defendant's position of power in the market for the tying product was being used to restrain competition in the market for the tied product. As we explained in *Jefferson Parish,* 466 U.S., at 12, "[o]ur cases have concluded that the essential characteristic of an invalid tying arrangement lies in the seller's exploitation of its control over the tying product to force the buyer into the purchase of a tied product that the buyer either did not want at all, or might have preferred to purchase elsewhere on different terms."

Over the years, however, this Court's strong disapproval of tying arrangements has substantially diminished. Rather than relying on assumptions, in its more recent opinions the Court has required a showing of market power in the tying product. Our early opinions consistently assumed that "[t]ying arrangements serve hardly any purpose beyond the suppression of competition. In 1962, in *Loew's,* 371 U.S., at 47-48, the Court relied on this assumption despite evidence of significant competition in the market for the tying product. And as recently as 1969, Justice Black, writing for the majority, relied on the assumption as support for the proposition "that, at least when certain prerequisites are met, arrangements of this kind are illegal in and of themselves, and no specific showing of unreasonable competitive effect is required." *Fortner Enterprises, Inc. v. United States Steel Corp.,* 394 U.S. 495 *(Fortner I).* Explaining the Court's decision to allow the suit to proceed to trial, he stated that "decisions rejecting the need for proof of truly dominant power over the tying product have all been based on a recognition that because tying arrangements generally serve no legitimate business purpose that cannot be achieved in some less restrictive way, the presence of any appreciable restraint on competition provides a sufficient reason for invalidating the tie."

Reflecting a changing view of tying arrangements, four Justices dissented in *Fortner I,* arguing that the challenged "tie"-the extension of a $2 million line of credit on condition that the borrower purchase prefabricated houses from the defendant-might well have served a legitimate purpose. *Id.,* at 510, 89 S.Ct. 1252 (opinion of White, J.); *id.,* at 520, 89 S.Ct. 1252 (opinion of Fortas, J.). In his opinion, Justice White noted that promotional tie-ins may provide "uniquely advantageous deals" to purchasers. *Id.,* at 519, 89 S.Ct. 1252. And Justice Fortas concluded that the arrangement was best characterized as "a sale of a single product with the incidental provision of financing." *Id.,* at 522, 89 S.Ct. 1252.

The dissenters' view that tying arrangements may well be procompetitive ultimately prevailed; indeed, it did so in the very same lawsuit. After the Court remanded the suit in *Fortner I,* a bench trial resulted in judgment for the plaintiff, and the case eventually made its way back to this Court. Upon return, we unanimously held that the plaintiff's failure of proof on the issue of market power was fatal to its case-the plaintiff had proved "nothing more than a willingness to provide cheap financing in order to sell expensive houses." *United States Steel Corp. v. Fortner Enterprises, Inc.,* 429 U.S. 610 (1977) *(Fortner II).*

The assumption that "[t]ying arrangements serve hardly any purpose beyond the suppression of competition," rejected in *Fortner II,* has not been endorsed in any opinion since. Instead, it was again rejected just seven years later in *Jefferson Parish,* where, as in *Fortner II,* we unanimously reversed a Court of Appeals judgment holding that an alleged tying arrangement constituted a *per se* violation of § 1 of the Sherman Act. Like the product at issue in the *Fortner* cases, the tying product in *Jefferson Parish*-hospital services-was unpatented, and our holding again rested on the conclusion that the plaintiff had failed to prove sufficient power in the tying product market to restrain competition in the market for the tied product-services of anesthesiologists.

In rejecting the application of a *per se* rule that all tying arrangements constitute antitrust violations, we explained: "[W]e have condemned tying arrangements when the seller has some special ability-usually called 'market power'-to force a purchaser to do something that he would not do in a competitive market. . . . *Per se* condemnation-condemnation without inquiry into actual market conditions-is only appropriate if the existence of forcing is probable. Thus, application of the *per se* rule focuses on the probability of anticompetitive consequences. . . . For example, if the Government has granted the seller a patent or similar monopoly over a product, it is fair to presume that the inability to buy the product elsewhere gives the seller market power. Any effort to enlarge the scope of the patent monopoly by using the market power it confers to restrain competition in the market for a second product will undermine competition on the merits in that second market. Thus, the sale or lease of a patented item on condition that the buyer make all his purchases of a separate tied product from the patentee is unlawful."

Notably, nothing in our opinion suggested a rebuttable presumption of market power applicable to tying arrangements involving a patent on the tying good. Instead, it described the rule that a contract to sell a patented product on condition that the purchaser buy unpatented goods exclusively from the patentee is a *per se* violation of § 1 of the Sherman Act.

Justice O'Connor wrote separately in *Jefferson Parish,* concurring in the judgment on the ground that the case did not involve a true tying arrangement because, in her view, surgical services and anesthesia were not separate products. In her opinion, she questioned not only the propriety of treating any tying arrangement as a *per se* violation of the Sherman Act, but also the validity of the presumption that a patent always gives the patentee significant market power, observing that the presumption was actually a product of our patent misuse cases rather than our antitrust jurisprudence. It is that presumption, a vestige of the Court's historical distrust of tying arrangements, that we address squarely today.

III

Justice O'Connor was, of course, correct in her assertion that the presumption that a patent confers market power arose outside the antitrust context as part of the patent misuse doctrine. That doctrine had its origins in *Motion Picture Patents Co. v. Universal Film Mfg. Co.,* 243 U.S. 502 (1917), which found no support in the patent laws for the proposition that a patentee may "prescribe by notice attached to a patented machine the conditions of its use and the supplies which must be used in the operation of it, under pain of infringement of the patent," Although *Motion Picture Patents Co.* simply narrowed the scope of possible patent infringement claims, it formed the basis for the Court's subsequent decisions creating a patent misuse defense to infringement claims when a patentee uses its patent "as the effective means of restraining competition with its sale of an unpatented article."

Without any analysis of actual market conditions, these patent misuse decisions assumed that, by tying the purchase of unpatented goods to the sale of the patented good, the patentee was "restraining competition," or "secur[ing] a limited monopoly of an unpatented material". In other words, these decisions presumed "[t]he requisite economic power" over the tying product such that the patentee could "extend [its] economic control to unpatented products."

The presumption that a patent confers market power migrated from patent law to antitrust law in *International Salt Co. v. United States,* 332 U.S. 392 (1947). In that case, we affirmed a District Court decision holding that leases of patented machines requiring the lessees to use the defendant's unpatented salt products violated §1 of the Sherman Act and §3 of the Clayton Act as a matter of law. Although the Court's opinion does not discuss market power or the patent misuse doctrine, it assumes that "[t]he volume of business affected by these contracts cannot be said to be insignificant or insubstantial and the tendency of the arrangement to accomplishment of monopoly seems obvious."

The assumption that tying contracts "ten[d] . . . to accomplishment of monopoly" can be traced to the Government's brief in *International Salt,* which relied heavily on our earlier patent misuse decision in *Morton Salt.* The Government described *Morton Salt* as "present[ing] a factual situation almost identical with the instant case," and it asserted that "although the Court in that case did not find it necessary to decide whether the antitrust laws were violated, its language, its reasoning, and its citations indicate that the policy underlying the decision was the same as that of the Sherman Act." Building on its assertion that *International Salt* was logically indistinguishable from *Morton Salt,* the Government argued that this Court should place tying arrangements involving patented products in the category of *per se* violations of the Sherman Act. United States Brief 26-33.

Our opinion in *International Salt* clearly shows that we accepted the Government's invitation to import the presumption of market power in a patented product into our antitrust jurisprudence. While we cited *Morton Salt* only for the narrower proposition that the defendant's patents did not confer any right to restrain competition in unpatented salt or afford the defendant any immunity from the antitrust laws, given the fact that the defendant was selling its unpatented salt at competitive prices, the rule adopted in *International Salt* necessarily accepted the Government's submission that the earlier patent misuse cases supported the broader proposition "that this type of restraint is unlawful on its face under the Sherman Act". . . .

IV

Although the patent misuse doctrine and our antitrust jurisprudence became intertwined in *International Salt,* subsequent events initiated their untwining. This process has ultimately led to today's reexamination of the presumption of *per se* illegality of a tying arrangement involving a patented product, the first case since 1947 in which we have granted review to consider the presumption's continuing validity.

Three years before we decided *International Salt,* this Court had expanded the scope of the patent misuse doctrine to include not only supplies or materials used by a patented device, but also tying arrangements involving a combination patent and "unpatented material or [a] device [that] is itself an integral part of the structure embodying the patent." In reaching this conclusion, the Court explained that it could see "no difference in principle" between cases involving elements essential to the inventive character of the patent and elements peripheral to it; both, in the Court's view, were attempts to "expan[d] the patent beyond the legitimate scope of its monopoly."

Shortly thereafter, Congress codified the patent laws for the first time. At least partly in response to our *Mercoid* decision, Congress included a provision in its codification that excluded some conduct, such as a tying arrangement involving the sale of a patented product tied to an "essential" or "nonstaple" product that has no use except as part of the patented product or method, from the scope of the patent misuse doctrine. § 271(d). Thus, at the same time that our antitrust jurisprudence continued to rely on the assumption that "tying arrangements generally serve no legitimate business purpose," Congress began chipping away at the assumption in the patent misuse context from whence it came.

It is Congress' most recent narrowing of the patent misuse defense, however, that is directly relevant to this case. Four years after our decision in *Jefferson Parish* repeated the patent-equals-market-power presumption, Congress amended the Patent Code to eliminate that presumption in the patent misuse context. The relevant provision reads:

> "(d) No patent owner otherwise entitled to relief for infringement or contributory infringement of a patent shall be denied relief or deemed guilty of misuse or illegal extension of the patent right by reason of his having done one or more of the following: . . . (5) conditioned the license of any rights to the patent or the sale of the patented product on the acquisition of a license to rights in another patent or purchase of a separate product, *unless, in view of the circumstances, the patent owner has market power in the relevant market for the patent or patented product on which the license or sale is conditioned.*" 35 U.S.C. § 271(d)(5) (emphasis added).

The italicized clause makes it clear that Congress did not intend the mere existence of a patent to constitute the requisite "market power." Indeed, fairly read, it provides that without proof that Trident had market power in the relevant market, its conduct at issue in this case was neither "misuse" nor an "illegal extension of the patent right."

While the 1988 amendment does not expressly refer to the antitrust laws, it certainly invites a reappraisal of the *per se* rule announced in *International Salt*. A rule denying a patentee the right to enjoin an infringer is significantly less severe than a rule that makes the conduct at issue a federal crime punishable by up to 10 years in prison. It would be absurd to assume that Congress intended to provide that the use of a patent that merited punishment as a felony would not constitute "misuse." Moreover, given the fact that the patent misuse doctrine provided the basis for the market power presumption, it would be anomalous to preserve the presumption in antitrust after Congress has eliminated its foundation.

After considering the congressional judgment reflected in the 1988 amendment, we conclude that tying arrangements involving patented products should be evaluated under the standards applied in cases like *Fortner II* and *Jefferson Parish* rather than under the *per se* rule applied in *Morton Salt* and *Loew's*. While some such arrangements are still unlawful, such as those that are the product of a true monopoly or a marketwide conspiracy, that conclusion must be supported by proof of power in the relevant market rather than by a mere presumption thereof.[1]

V

Rather than arguing that we should retain the rule of *per se* illegality, respondent contends that we should endorse a rebuttable presumption that patentees possess market power when they condition the purchase of the patented product on an agreement to buy unpatented goods exclusively from the patentee. Respondent recognizes that a large number of valid patents have little, if any, commercial significance, but submits that those that are used to impose tying arrangements on unwilling purchasers likely do exert significant market power. Hence, in respondent's view, the presumption would have no impact on patents of only slight value and would be justified, subject to being rebutted by evidence offered by the patentee, in cases in which the patent has sufficient value to enable the patentee to insist on acceptance of the tie. . . .

The opinion that imported the "patent equals market power" presumption into our antitrust jurisprudence, however, provides no support for respondent's proposed alternative. In *International Salt,* it was the existence of the patent on the tying product, rather than the use of a requirements tie, that led the Court to presume market power. 332 U.S., at 395, 68 S.Ct. 12 ("The appellant's patents confer a limited monopoly of the invention they reward"). Moreover, the requirements tie in that case did not involve any price discrimination between large volume and small volume purchasers or evidence of noncompetitive pricing. Instead, the leases at issue provided that if any competitor offered salt, the tied product, at a lower price, "the lessee should be free to buy in the open market, unless appellant would furnish the salt at an equal price."

As we have already noted, the vast majority of academic literature recognizes that a patent does not necessarily confer market power. See n. 4, *supra.* Similarly, while price discrimination may provide evidence of market power, particularly if buttressed by evidence that the patentee has charged an above-market price for the tied package. We are not persuaded that the combination of these two factors should give rise to a presumption of market power when neither is sufficient to do so standing alone. Rather, the lesson to be learned from *International Salt* and the academic commentary is the same: Many tying arrangements, even those involving patents and requirements ties, are fully consistent with a free, competitive market. For this reason, we reject both respondent's proposed rebuttable presumption and their narrower alternative.

It is no doubt the virtual consensus among economists that has persuaded the enforcement agencies to reject the position that the Government took

---

[1] FN4. Our imposition of this requirement accords with the vast majority of academic literature on the subject. See, e.g., 10 Areeda ¶ 1737a ("[T]here is no economic basis for inferring any amount of market power from the mere fact that the defendant holds a valid patent"); Burchfiel, Patent Misuse and Antitrust Reform: "Blessed be the Tie?" 4 Harv. J.L. & Tech. 1, 57, and n. 340 (noting that the market power presumption has been extensively criticized and citing sources); 1 H. Hovenkamp, M. Janis, & M. Lemley, IP and Antitrust § 4.2a (2005 Supp.) ("[C]overage of one's product with an intellectual property right does not confer a monopoly"); W. Landes & R. Posner, The Economic Structure of Intellectual Property Law 374 (2003) (hereinafter Landes & Posner).

when it supported the *per se* rule that the Court adopted in the 1940's. See *supra,* at 1288. In antitrust guidelines issued jointly by the Department of Justice and the Federal Trade Commission in 1995, the enforcement agencies stated that in the exercise of their prosecutorial discretion they "will not presume that a patent, copyright, or trade secret necessarily confers market power upon its owner." U.S. Dept. of Justice and FTC, Antitrust Guidelines for the Licensing of Intellectual Property § 2.2 (Apr. 6, 1995). While that choice is not binding on the Court, it would be unusual for the Judiciary to replace the normal rule of lenity that is applied in criminal cases with a rule of severity for a special category of antitrust cases.

Congress, the antitrust enforcement agencies, and most economists have all reached the conclusion that a patent does not necessarily confer market power upon the patentee. Today, we reach the same conclusion, and therefore hold that, in all cases involving a tying arrangement, the plaintiff must prove that the defendant has market power in the tying product. . . .

It is so ordered.

Justice ALITO took no part in the consideration or decision of this case.

DIGIDYNE CORP. v. DATA GENERAL CORP.
734 F.2d 1336 (9th Cir. 1984)

BROWNING, CHIEF JUDGE:

The issue presented for review is whether Data General's refusal to license its NOVA operating system software except to purchasers of its NOVA central processing units (CPUs) is an unlawful tying arrangement under section 1 of the Sherman Act . . . and section 3 of the Clayton Act. We conclude that it is.

I.

Defendant Data General manufactures a computer system known as NOVA. The system consists of a NOVA CPU designed to perform a particular "instruction set" or group of tasks, and a copyrighted NOVA operating system called RDOS containing the basic commands for operation of the system. Not all operating systems work with all CPUs. Plaintiffs produce emulator NOVA CPUs designed to perform the NOVA instruction set and thus to make use of defendant's RDOS.

Data General refuses to license its RDOS to anyone who does not also purchase its NOVA CPU. Plaintiffs allege that this constitutes an unlawful tying arrangement; the defendant's RDOS being the tying product, the NOVA instruction set CPU being the tied product.

Plaintiffs filed a number of actions alleging violations of section 1 of the Sherman Act and section 3 of the Clayton Act. The actions were consolidated. The issues of liability and damages were segregated for trial. This appeal is from a judgment on liability. . . . Trial, limited to the issue of defendant's economic power, resulted in a jury verdict for plaintiffs. Defendant's motion for judgment n.o.v. or for a new trial was granted. Plaintiffs appealed.

II.

A tying arrangement is illegal if it is shown to restrain competition unreasonably or is illegal *per se,* without such a showing, if certain prerequisites are met. *Fortner Enterprises v. U.S. Steel Corp.,* 394 U.S. 495, 498-500 (1969) *(Fortner I).* The prerequisites of *per se* illegality are: (1) separate products, the purchase of one (tying product) being conditioned on purchase of the other (tied product); (2) sufficient economic power with respect to the tying product to restrain competition appreciably in the tied product; and (3) an effect upon a substantial amount of commerce in the tied product. These prerequisites were satisfied in this case. We therefore do not consider whether competition was in fact unreasonably restrained.

The district court properly granted summary judgment on the first and third of the required elements of a *per se* violation, holding that on the undisputed facts the NOVA instruction set CPU and defendant's RDOS are separate products and the volume of commerce in NOVA instruction set CPUs tied to the purchase of defendant's RDOS is substantial.

We adopt the district court's reasoning on these issues. . . . The undisputed facts summarized in the district court's opinion establish that a demand existed for NOVA instruction set CPUs separate from defendant's RDOS, and that each element of the NOVA computer system could have been provided separately and selected separately by customers if defendant had not compelled purchasers to take both. The remaining element necessary to establish a *per se* violation — defendant's possession of sufficient economic power with respect to the tying product, defendant's RDOS — was tried to a jury and resolved in plaintiffs' favor. The district court erred in setting aside this verdict or, alternatively, ordering a new trial.

III.

One of the purposes of a *per se* rule is to avoid an "incredibly complicated and prolonged economic investigation . . . to determine at large whether a particular restraint has been unreasonable." Although not requiring as extensive an inquiry as would be necessary to determine whether the tie-in violated the general standard of reasonableness, the district court held that plaintiffs "could not recover on the alleged tie-ins unless they identified and proved the relevant market for the tying and tied products." The trial that followed "focused upon the definition of the relevant markets" for the two products, which the Court characterized as the "critical issue," and consumed forty-five days.

The district court recognized that detailed market analysis was not required in a *per se* tying case prior to *United States Steel Corp. v. Fortner Enterprises, Inc.,* 429 U.S. 610 (1977) *(Fortner II),* but read that opinion as rejecting this approach in favor of a requirement of "some degree of market analysis even in a per se case." The court relied particularly upon language in *Fortner II,* which states the question to be:

> whether the seller has the power, within the market for the tying product, to raise prices or to require purchasers to accept burdensome terms that could not be exacted in a completely competitive market. In

short, the question is whether the seller has some advantage not shared by his competitors in the market for the tying product.

429 U.S. at 620.

From the district court's analysis of the asserted deficiencies in plaintiffs' proof, it appears the court read this statement as requiring proof of power to fix the price of the tying product in the whole of the relevant market as defined by the inquiry described in *United States v. E.I. du Pont de Nemours & Co.,* 351 U.S. 377 (1956), a monopolization case. In this the district court erred. Possession by the seller of such monopoly power is sufficient to establish *per se* illegality, but it is not required.

As the Supreme Court said in *United States v. Loew's, Inc.,* 371 U.S. 38, 45 (1962):

> Market dominance — some power to control price and to exclude competition — is by no means the only test of whether the seller has the requisite economic power. Even absent a showing of market dominance, the crucial economic power may be inferred from the tying product's desirability to consumers or from uniqueness in its attributes.

This position was re-affirmed in the *Fortner* cases. In *Fortner I*:

> The standard of "sufficient economic power" does not, as the District Court held, require that the defendant have a monopoly or even a dominant position throughout the market for the tying product. Our tie-in cases have made unmistakably clear that the economic power over the tying product can be sufficient even though the power falls far short of dominance and *even though the power exists only with respect to some of the buyers in the market.* . . . [T]he presence of any appreciable restraint on competition provides a sufficient reason for invalidating the tie. Such appreciable restraint results *whenever the seller can exert some power over some of the buyers in the market, even if his power is not complete over them and over all other buyers in the market.* . . . [D]espite the freedom of some or many buyers from the seller's power, other buyers — whether few or many, whether scattered throughout the market or part of some group within the market — can be forced to accept the higher price because of their stronger preferences for the product, and the seller could therefore choose instead to force them to accept a tying arrangement that would prevent free competition for their patronage in the market for the tied product. Accordingly, the proper focus of concern is whether the seller has the power to raise prices, or impose other burdensome terms such as a tie-in, *with respect to any appreciable number of buyers within the market.*

394 U.S. at 502-04 (emphasis added). . . .

Nor is a restraint on competition that is substantial in terms of the entire market for the tied product required. "If only a single purchaser were 'forced' with respect to the purchase of a tied item, the resultant impact on competition would not be sufficient to warrant the concern of antitrust law." Beyond that, however, it need only appear that "a substantial volume of commerce is foreclosed," *id.*, which the court earlier defined as "substantial enough in terms of dollar-volume so as not to be merely *de minimis.*" *Fortner I* at 501. . . .

IV.

There was abundant evidence that defendant's RDOS was distinctive and particularly desirable to a substantial number of buyers, and could not be readily produced by other sellers. There was also substantial evidence that defendant's insistence upon licensing its RDOS only to purchasers of defendant's NOVA instruction set CPU, led buyers to purchase defendant's NOVA CPUs who would not have bought them or would have bought them elsewhere absent the tying requirement.

Although expressing some doubt as to the sufficiency of the evidence, the district court assumed defendant's RDOS was superior to competing operating systems and was viewed as uniquely desirable by buyers. We do not share the court's hesitancy about the adequacy of the proof of the strong preference of many customers for RDOS. It was a most popular product. Experts, customers, and even competitors testified to its many advantages over competitive products. Defendant's own officials expressed the same opinion in pre-litigation documents.

Defendant's RDOS has copyright protection. Defendant also claimed the production of RDOS required use of defendant's trade secrets. The RDOS copyright established both the distinctiveness of RDOS and a legal bar to its reproduction by competitors. "The requisite economic power is presumed when the tying product is patented or copyrighted." *United States v. Loew's, Inc.,* 371 U.S. at 45. The copyright confers upon defendant "some advantages not shared by his competitors in the market for the tying product." *Fortner II,* 429 U.S. at 620. "[T]he copyright monopolies in *United States v. Paramount Pictures, Inc.,* 334 U.S. 131 and *United States v. Loew's Inc.,* 371 U.S. 38 . . . represented tying products that the Court regarded as sufficiently unique to give rise to a presumption of economic power." 429 U.S. at 619. . . .

There is abundant evidence, including testimony of defendant's own executives, customers, and plaintiffs' expert witnesses, that defendant's RDOS could not be reproduced without infringing defendant's copyright and utilizing defendant's trade secrets. Defendant vigorously pursued those who assertedly violated defendant's proprietary rights. Additionally, there was evidence that creating and testing a compatible system would require millions of dollars and years of effort. One of defendant's officers testified that the passage of the time required to reproduce RDOS would render the completed software obsolete.

The power to coerce that RDOS gave the defendant was enhanced by the fact that many of defendant's customers were "locked in" to the use of RDOS. Briefly, defendant sells RDOS and NOVA CPUs primarily to original equipment manufacturers (OEMs) who combine them with application software (a set of instructions that allows the system to accomplish a particular task) to create a complete computer system for resale. Application system software for particular uses is developed by OEMs at substantial expense. Once developed, application software for a particular use may be used by an OEM in producing any number of computer systems for that use for resale to different customers.

However, application software is designed to function only with a particular operating system. OEMs who construct their application software to function with defendant's RDOS therefore must purchase an RDOS for each computer system they assemble using that application software. Because of the tying condition, they also must purchase one of defendant's NOVA instruction set CPUs for each such computer system they sell.

An OEM can free itself from this "lock in" only by abandoning its application software compatible with defendant's RDOS, in which it has a substantial investment, or converting the software so that it may be used with another operating system. There was abundant testimony that conversion was not economically feasible. The defendant argues that "lock-in" is irrelevant in determining its market power because OEMs are aware of the tie when they select an operating system for the computer system they are assembling. At that point, defendant argues, the OEM has made no investment in application software and, as a result, chooses freely among competing systems. This characterization of the market is not accurate. As the evidence in this case establishes, the initial choice is not free of forcing. Defendant's operating system has been shown to be unique as a matter of law and distinctively attractive as a matter of fact. Defendant's initial leverage is magnified by the lock-in. By 1979, 93 percent of defendant's NOVA CPU sales were made to locked-in customers. These buyers were not only forced to buy defendant's CPUs initially to acquire the operating system they found most attractive, they were thereafter forced to buy defendant's CPUs for their subsequent needs in order to acquire the only operating system they could economically use. Not even a decision by CPU manufacturers to broaden their base and compete in the operating system market would have alleviated the problem, for the locked-in customers were not free to choose among competing operating systems. RDOS was the only operating system that would allow them to realize the benefit of their investment in application software, an investment that in some cases totaled millions of dollars.

[The] power arising from the special attraction of RDOS, coupled with the copyright protection, the trade secret barrier, and the lock-in, was evidenced by defendant's minimum equipment configuration (MEC) program. To obtain defendant's RDOS all licensees were required to purchase not only defendant's CPU but also a set quantity of other peripheral hardware, or pay a program license charge. Defendant's national accounts manager accurately referred to the charge as a "penalty." Customers testified they were forced to buy peripherals from defendant they otherwise would not have purchased. . . . The tie-in of RDOS to defendant's NOVA instruction set CPU was an equally conscious exercise of economic power in one market to gain an advantage in others. As one of defendant's managers wrote in an intra-company memorandum, "[p]rotection from knock-off products still lies in software licensing restrictions."

The district court properly rejected defendant's argument, vigorously renewed in this court, "that it must bundle its software together with its CPUs in order to recover its substantial investment in software research and development," and that "it would be unfair to permit emulator-CPU manufacturers to reap the benefits of [defendant's] software [research and development] when they sell their competing CPUs for use with [defendant's] software." . . . As the district court said, "Recovery of investment costs has been explicitly excluded from the narrowly-construed exceptions to the *per se* rule against tie-ins." Defendant "has not shown, nor has it raised a genuine issue of fact with respect to its ability to show at trial, that it is any less capable than was Jerrold Electronics [*United States v. Jerrold Electronics Corp.*, 187 F.Supp. 545 (E.D.Pa.1960), *aff'd per curiam*, 365 U.S. 567 (1961),] of adopting the less restrictive alternative of restructured prices in order to recoup its investment costs and maintain its incentive for further innovation." . . .

V.

Most, although not all, of the trial court's reasons for setting aside the verdict are traceable to the court's view that the legality of a tying arrangement must be tested by the seller's economic power throughout the market for the tying product, and by the relative substantiality of the restraint on competition in the tied product market considered as a whole.

As we have said, the trial court assumed customers regarded RDOS as "uniquely desirable and that it in fact possesses various features which render it superior to other software," but concluded that plaintiffs had failed to prove that defendant's "competitors were prevented from developing functionally equivalent software." Conceding that the copyright on RDOS and the trade secrets involved in its creation precluded development by defendant's competitors of "compatible" software, the court held plaintiffs had failed to prove the effect of defendant's copyright and secrets on the development of software "comparable" to RDOS.

The court erroneously imposed the burden of proof on plaintiffs. The RDOS copyright created a presumption of economic power sufficient to render the tying arrangement illegal *per se*. [Editors note] Independent Ink reversed this view.] . . .

As the authorities cited earlier establish, the focus of the prohibition against tying arrangements is quite different. The concern is not with the restraint on competition in the tying product but on competition in the market for the tied product. What is required is not monopoly power in the tying product market, but only sufficient power to enable the seller to restrict competition in the tied product. If a seller's product is distinctive, not available from other sources, and sufficiently attractive to some buyers to enable the seller by tying arrangements to foreclose a part of the market for a tied product, the adverse impact on competition in the tied product is not diminished by the fact that other sellers may be selling products similar to the tying product. . . .

The law was succinctly summarized in *Carpa, Inc. v. Ward Foods, Inc.*, 536 F.2d 39, 48 (5th Cir.1976), a trademark tying case, in a manner particularly pertinent here:

> What is required is a factual assessment of the tying product's uniqueness and desirability, not its market power in the sense of a Section 2 Sherman Act violation. Uniqueness, of course, presupposes that com-

petitors are in some way foreclosed from offering the distinctive prod-uct. *Fortner* points out . . . that such barriers may be legal, as in the cases of patented or copyrighted products. Trademarks surely may be included in the list of such legal restraints, and, as with copyrighted material, *the mere presence of competing substitutes is insufficient to destroy the legal, and more importantly the economic, distinctiveness of the trademark.*

. . . . The question is not whether other operating systems with which RDOS competed were as good as RDOS or better in the eyes of some buyers, but rather whether RDOS, available only from defendant, was sufficiently attrac-tive to some customers to enable defendant to require those who wished to obtain it also to buy from defendant NOVA instruction set CPUs they might otherwise have purchased from others. As we have seen, evidence of the defendant's possession of such power was ample. Clearly the availability of "comparable" or "functionally equivalent" operating systems would not have freed "locked-in" OEMs of the pressure, imposed by their investment in appli-cation software "compatible" only with RDOS, that compelled them to accede to defendant's condition that they purchase defendant's NOVA CPU in order to obtain RDOS. . . .

WILL v. COMPREHENSIVE ACCOUNTING CORP.
776 F.2d 665 (7th Cir. 1985)

EASTERBROOK, CIRCUIT JUDGE.

Franchising spread from hamburgers to the preparation of tax returns and then to the provision of regular accounting services. The Comprehensive Accounting Corporation authorizes accountants to provide service in Comprehensive's name. The franchisees agree to live up to Comprehensive's standards and to supply reports to clients in Comprehensive's style and bear-ing its trademark. This appears to be useful to clients — perhaps because of the standardized method of doing business, perhaps because of Comprehensive's policing of its franchisees. Comprehensive is profitable, and so are the franchi-sees. The business of a franchisee apparently may be sold for more than two times annual gross revenues, while businesses of accountants in solo practice usually fetch much less.

Comprehensive's services to its franchisees include data processing. The accountants send data from clients' businesses to Comprehensive, which returns reports generated by its large computer. The contract between Comprehensive and its franchisees permits the franchisees to have data pro-cessed elsewhere, provided "the Comprehensive E.D.P. [electronic data pro-cessing] is not competitive for like services of the same quality, with the same turnabout time." In recent years small computers have become less expensive, and independent firms have written programs for these small computers that enable them to generate accounting reports and otherwise manage clients' data. Comprehensive's franchisees became interested in these smaller com-puters, which potentially could cut their costs of computation below the prices offered by Comprehensive.

Comprehensive did not take this gracefully. It had a large computer in place; the cost of this was sunk, so payments from franchisees for computation were mostly profit. Comprehensive's revenues from data processing reached $3.5 million yearly; these revenues were the firm's principal source of profit. The franchisees' savings from buying their own small computers would translate into losses for Comprehensive. It therefore insisted that franchisees use only small computers that would produce reports that looked *exactly* like those Comprehensive produced itself. Comprehensive says that it insisted on duplication in order to protect the reputation of its service mark and maintains that it was entitled by contract to be finicky; the franchisees say that Comprehensive was just postponing the inevitable, in .breach of contract.

Duplication was hard. The commercially available programs were not designed to ape Comprehensive's reports, and the output of Comprehensive's printer also looked different from the output of the low-price printers some franchisees wanted to use. Comprehensive promised to find and approve a small computer system that would meet its quality standards. It settled on a system that would be restricted to franchisees with 200 or more clients; most had fewer. Even the approval of this system moved slowly, with several changes of configuration that led some franchisees to conclude that Comprehensive would never be satisfied. In 1982 it announced that it would approve a system with programs Comprehensive had designed itself; it apparently planned to charge enough for these to make up for lost revenues from its larger computer.

Several franchisees decided to strike out on their own. Comprehensive threatened them with termination when it found out about this, so some franchisees installed small computers without informing Comprehensive. Comprehensive terminated five franchises in August 1981, sued three of them for substantial sums, and tried to persuade their clients to migrate to other accountants. As other franchisees began to use different systems, Comprehensive terminated them too.

Ten of the terminated franchisees and two others brought this suit against Comprehensive. . . . They maintained that Comprehensive broke its contract by insisting that they purchase computation from Comprehensive. . . . The franchisees also argued that Comprehensive had violated § 1 of the Sherman Act, 15 U.S.C. § 1, by "tying" data processing (the tied product) to the franchise (the tying product).

The district court conducted a jury trial. The jury returned a general verdict for the defendants on the antitrust theory. Six plaintiffs prevailed on the contract theory and six lost. . . .

I

Section 1 of the Sherman Act prohibits any "contract, combination . . . , or conspiracy, in restraint of trade. . . ." The plaintiffs therefore needed to prove some cooperative undertaking. Establishing the necessary combination in a tying case requires exceeding subtlety, because the substantive theory of tying law depends on coercion to take two products as a package. The joint sale of two products is a "tie" only if the seller exploits its control of the tying product "to force the buyer into the purchase of a tied product that the buyer either did not want at all, or might have preferred to purchase elsewhere on different terms." *Jefferson Parish Hospital District No. 2 v. Hyde,* 466 U.S. 2 (1984). A tie within the meaning of antitrust depends on showing that the buyer did *not* want to take both products from the same vendor. "[T]here is nothing inherently anticompetitive about packaged sales. Only if [buyers] are forced to purchase [the tied] services as a result of the [seller's] market power would the arrangement have anticompetitive consequences." If the buyer wants both products together — as, for example, the buyer of an automobile wants both chassis and engine together, even though they could be sold separately — there is no forcing, and so there is no tie-in.

As a linguistic matter, proof that the buyer took both products in a package against his will negates the existence of a "contract, combination, or conspiracy." The plaintiffs' position here is complicated by their contract, which they insist establishes that they did not agree to buy their computing services from Comprehensive. Tying is not cooperation among competitors, the focus of § 1, it is aggressive conduct akin to monopolization under § 2 of the Sherman Act. Tying usually is challenged under § 3 of the Clayton Act, 15 U.S.C. § 14, which addresses the practice explicitly. Joint action becomes an issue only when the plaintiff tries to take advantage of *per se* rules under § 1.

Perma Life Mufflers, Inc. v. International Parts Corp., 392 U.S. 134, 88 S.Ct. 1981, 20 L.Ed.2d 982 (1968), overruled in part on other grounds by *Copperweld Corp. v. Independence Tube Corp.,* 467 U.S. 752 (1984), provides plaintiffs with an escape hatch. The Court stated that a franchisee "can clearly charge a combination between [the franchisor] and himself, as of the day he unwillingly complied with the restrictive franchise agreements, . . . or between [the franchisor] and other franchise dealers, whose acquiescence in [the] firmly enforced restraints was induced by 'the communicated danger of termination' . . ." 392 U.S. at 142, 88 S.Ct. at 1986. Although the franchise contract in *Perma Life* established the tie-in of which the franchisees complained, the essential principle — that "unwilling compliance" satisfies the joint action requirement of § 1 — applies to our case too. . . .

II

The court told the jury that in order to find a violation of the antitrust laws, it had to find six elements: (1) that data processing and the franchise are separate products;[2] (2) that the products were tied; (3) that there was an agreement; (4) that Comprehensive had market power; (5) that the plaintiffs suffered direct injury; and (6) that the damages were reasonably ascertainable. The court also instructed the jury that Comprehensive was entitled to

---

[2] [FN] No mean feat because "franchises" (the tying product here) are just names and methods of doing business, not "products" and some courts have held that as a matter of law there cannot be a tie-in between a name and a product, *see Krehl v. Baskin-Robbins Ice Cream Co.,* 664 F.2d 1348 (9th Cir.1982); *Principe v. McDonald's Corp.,* 631 F.2d 303 (4th Cir.1980), *cert. denied,* 451 U.S. 970, 101 S.Ct. 2047, 68 L.Ed.2d 349 (1981); *Jack Walters* [*& Sons Corp. v. Morton Building, Inc.,*] *supra,* 737 F.2d [698] at 704-05 [(7th Cir. 19840)] (reserving the question). A tie involves products that may be sold in separate markets. But a method of doing business (the franchise) is not sold separately from the ingredients that go into the method of business. A franchiser and its franchisees are part of a business organization not altogether different from vertical integration. *See* G. Frank Mathewson & Ralph A. Winter, *The Economics of Franchise Contracts,* 28 J.L. & Econ. 503 (1985). We need not consider the implications of this approach, however.

use a tie-in if that was the "least restrictive means" of upholding its standards under its trademark. *See* Benjamin Klein & Lester F. Saft, *The Law and Economics of Franchise Tying Contracts*, 28 J.L. & ECON. 345 (1985) (discussing the rationale of this defense). Plaintiffs challenge several of these instructions, most vigorously those concerning the justification of protecting the trademark. . . .

We need not sift through the . . . instructions, however, because plaintiffs' case has a fatal weakness. They did not establish market power. They failed as a matter of law. This failure makes every other element of the anti-trust case irrelevant.

The purpose of the rule against certain tying arrangements is to stop the extension of market power from one product to another. The idea is that a firm with a monopoly of one product may refuse to deal except on terms that will lead to a monopoly of another. It also may be possible to use tying arrangements to extract a higher profit through price discrimination.[3] Both the extension of power and the practice of price discrimination are impossible unless the seller has substantial market power. This means power over price, the ability to induce buyers to pay more money by cutting back the supply of goods available for purchase. The best way to show power over price is to establish directly that the price of the tied package is higher than the price of components sold in competitive markets.

The early tying cases involved patented products, and the Supreme Court assumed that the patents conferred market power. . . .

United States Steel Corp. v. Fortner Enterprises, Inc., 429 U.S. 610 (1977) (*Fortner II*), considered "uniqueness," the other traditional way to establish market power in tying cases. U.S. Steel offered nonrecourse, low-interest, 100% credit to those who bought its prefabricated houses; you could not get the loan without taking the house. The Court treated this as unique. No one else offered a similar package. Yet it held that as a matter of law factual uniqueness was not enough; in order to establish market power by showing a unique package, the plaintiff must prove that "the seller has some advantage not shared by his competitors in the market for the tying product." In other words, the plaintiff must show a barrier to entry that prevents competition. If rivals may design and offer a similar package for a similar cost, there is no barrier, and without a barrier there is no market power: "Without any evidence that the [seller] had some cost advantage over its competitors — or could offer a form of financing that was significantly differentiated from that which other lenders could offer if they so elected — the unique character of its financing does not support the conclusion [of] market power." . . .

---

[3] [FN2] There has been a debate among both judges and scholars concerning the effects of tying arrangements. The close division on the rationale in *Hyde* was attributable in part to this. On the scholarly debate, compare PHILLIP AREEDA & DONALD F. TURNER, V ANTITRUST LAW ¶¶ 1129c, 1134b (1980); ROBERT H. BORK, THE ANTITRUST PARADOX 140-44, 372-75 (1978); and ROGER D. BLAIR & DAVID L. KASERMAN, ANTITRUST ECONOMICS 381-405 (1985), with Louis Kaplow, *Extension of Monopoly Power Through Leverage*, 85 COLUM. L. REV. 515 (1985). *See also* S.J. Liebowitz, *Tie-in Sales and Price Discrimination*, 21 ECONOMIC INQUIRY 387 (1983). Many scholars, and at least four Justices, would analyze tying arrangements under the Rule of Reason or permit them outright even when the seller has substantial market power. We need not join the debate, given the conclusions discussed below.

Plaintiffs did not claim, let alone offer evidence to show, that the price they paid for the franchise-computation package is higher than the price for those two products purchased in separate markets. The evidence — which shows that franchisees' businesses were worth more as a result of being members of the Comprehensive system — tends to show that the package Comprehensive furnished on the whole was beneficial, not priced at a monopoly level. They therefore failed to show market power directly. *Kypta v. McDonald's Corp.,* 671 F.2d 1282 (11th Cir.), *cert. denied,* 459 U.S. 857 (1982), holds that unless the plaintiff shows that the package price was elevated the suit must be dismissed without further ado. That is a sound position, for unless the package price exceeds the competitive price of its components, we have a replay of *Fortner II.* There U.S. Steel used "cheap financing in order to sell expensive houses"; here, for all the evidence shows, Comprehensive licensed its trademark cheaply in order to sell expensive computation.

To the extent plaintiffs may use market share or uniqueness as proxies for power over price, they failed on both counts. There is no evidence about Comprehensive's market share. The whole Comprehensive system is a pygmy among the large, national firms. There are also thousands of smaller firms. Many businesses produce accounting services internally, and these in-house services also are part of the market because they are substitutes for what the plaintiffs do.

Plaintiffs' principal argument was uniqueness. All they proved, however, is that Comprehensive's franchising system is unusual; there are few similar systems, and Comprehensive may be the most successful franchisor of accountants. *Spartan* holds that such a showing is inadequate. Plaintiffs did not show or try to show that Comprehensive has a cost advantage over rivals and potential rivals, that there is a barrier to entry into the business of franchising. They did not show or try to show that rivals could not produce a similar package for a similar cost; without such a showing, they must lose.[4]

The Supreme Court emphasized in *Hyde* and again in *National Collegiate Athletic Ass'n* that tying may have competitive benefits. Sometimes the sale of the package is just a way to compete. Some accounting firms have offices throughout the nation and offer comprehensive services; a package franchising system may be a way to compete with the larger firms while retaining the advantages of independent ownership. Just about every conceivable method of

---

[4] [FN4] To the extent *Digidyne Corp. v. Data General Corp.,* 734 F.2d 1336 (9th Cir.1984), . . . holds that a plaintiff may prevail, without establishing power over price in the relevant market, by showing that rivals cannot produce *exactly* the same package, it conflicts with *Spartan, Kypta,* and several other cases, including *Jack Walters* in our circuit. *E.g., Systemized of New England, Inc. v. SCM, Inc.,* 732 F.2d 1030 (1st Cir.1984) (no market power as a matter of law in a unique system); *Domed Stadium Hotel, Inc., v. Holiday Inns, Inc.,* 732 F.2d 480 (5th Cir.1984) (no market power as a matter of law in a factually unique reservation system that occupied more than 20% of its market). Sellers may strive to differentiate their products from others in order to compete for the custom of patrons with slightly different needs or tastes. It would be perverse to turn this ordinary attribute of the competitive struggle into a source of illegality. No one may copy Comprehensive's trademark or its copyrighted materials precisely, but rivals may create similar items for similar costs. Only when there is a barrier to entry — when rivals' cost of creating similar items is higher than the full costs of the original creator — may differences in the design of the package be treated as proof of market power. *Spartan, Kypta,* and the other cases we have cited are in line with *Fortner II* and *Hyde;* we follow them rather than *Data General.*

organizing service is used in this business — national partnerships with blanket coverage, independent one-man offices, smaller partnerships, franchised systems, and in-house production. Each, including methods that revolve around tied packages, may be beneficial to some customers. In a competitive market the customers will pick the arrangements that work best for them. Antitrust law is based on the premise that when markets are competitive, the process of sellers' rivalry and buyers' choice produces the best results. Unless courts insist on a showing of market power, they run the risk of deleting one of the existing options and so reducing rather than enhancing the vigor of competition and the welfare of consumers.

Comprehensive had no market power. For that matter, it is not to be believed that Comprehensive wanted to monopolize (or posed a threat of monopolizing) computation services, the tied product. Competition in the computation business is exceptionally vigorous; plaintiffs' contract case depended on establishing that this vigorous competition made it cheaper to secure computation from vendors other than Comprehensive. Even if Comprehensive had some power, then, plaintiffs still must lose. "One of the threshold criteria the plaintiff must satisfy . . . is that there is a substantial danger that the tying seller will acquire market power in the tied product market." This case therefore did not need to go to the jury. . . . AFFIRMED.

NOTES

1. The Department of Justice *Antitrust Guidelines* of 1995 state that : "the Agencies do not presume that intellectual property creates market power in the antitrust context." The *Guidelines* further state:

> Market power is the ability profitably to maintain prices above, or output below, competitive levels for a significant period of time. The Agencies will not presume that a patent, copyright, or trade secret necessarily confers market power upon its owner. Although the intellectual property right confers the power to exclude with respect to the *specific* product, process, or work in question, there will often be sufficient actual or potential close substitutes for such product, process, or work to prevent the exercise of market power. If a patent or other form of intellectual property does confer market power, that market power does not by itself offend the antitrust laws. As with any other tangible or intangible asset that enables its owner to obtain significant supracompetitive profits, market power (or even a monopoly) that is solely "a consequence of a superior product, business acumen, or historic accident" does not violate the antitrust laws. Nor does such market power impose on the intellectual property owner an obligation to license the use of that property to others. As in other antitrust contexts, however, market power could be illegally acquired or maintained, or, even if lawfully acquired and maintained, would be relevant to the ability of an intellectual property owner to harm competition through unreasonable conduct in connection with such property.

U.S. Department of Justice and the Federal Trade Commission, ANTITRUST GUIDELINES FOR THE LICENSING OF INTELLECTUAL PROPERTY § 2.2 (1995).

A factor in determining whether a property right creates market power lies in one's definition of the applicable market. Defining a market in terms of the specific right itself (e.g., "the market for Patent Number 5555555") guaranties that the patent owner holds market power because of its control of the patent. In contrast, a market definition that covers a broader range (e.g., "the market for desk top computers") diminishes the potential impact of the property right. Indeed, many patents, trademarks, and copyrights have no market presence at all — they are market failures, albeit creative ones. *See A.I. Root Co. v. Computer/Dynamics, Inc.,* 806 F.2d 673 (6th Cir. 1986).

2. Tying requires the presence of two products or services. In *United States v. Microsoft Corp.,* 253 F.3d 34 (D.C. Cir. 2001), *cert. denied,* 534 U.S. 952 (2001), although the court sustained several monopolization claims against Microsoft based on its efforts to block out competition to its operating system monopoly from certain other software, the court held that a rule of reason, rather than per se liability, applied to a Sherman Act § 1 claim that Microsoft was unlawfully tying its operating system and its internet exploring program by bundling them together contractually and technologically. The court concluded that there was insufficient experience with or evidence about bundling this type of software to determine whether or not there were procompetitive reasons for it in some cases. Microsoft claimed that the bundled programs were a single product. The court commented:

> The *Jefferson Parish* Court resolved the matter [of a single product] in two steps. First, it clarified that "the answer to the question whether one or two products are involved" does not turn "on the functional relation between them." In other words, the mere fact that two items are complements, that "one is useless without the other," does not make them a single "product" for purposes of tying law. Second, reasoning that the "definitional question [whether two distinguishable products are involved] depends on whether the arrangement may have the type of competitive consequences addressed by the rule [against tying]," the Court decreed that "no tying arrangement can exist unless there is a sufficient *demand* for the purchase of [one] separate from [the other] to identify a distinct product market in which it is *efficient* to offer [them separately]." . . . The consumer demand test is a rough proxy for whether a tying arrangement may, on balance, be welfare-enhancing, and unsuited to per se condemnation. In the abstract, of course, there is always direct separate demand for products: assuming choice is available at zero cost, consumers will prefer it to no choice. Only when the efficiencies from bundling are dominated by the benefits to choice for enough consumers, however, will we actually observe consumers making independent purchases. In other words, perceptible separate demand is inversely proportional to net efficiencies. On the supply side, firms without market power will bundle two goods only when the cost savings from joint sale outweigh the value consumers place on separate choice. So bundling by all competitive firms implies strong net efficiencies. If a court finds either that there is no noticeable separate demand for the tied product or, there being no convincing direct evidence of separate demand, that the entire "competitive fringe"

engages in the same behavior as the defendant, then the tying and tied products should be declared one product and per se liability should be rejected.

United States v. Microsoft Corp., 253 F.3d at 72-74.

PROBLEM 13.1

SDS holds a patent for certain genetically engineered seeds. It distributes the seeds for use by purchasers, but requires that the purchasers also acquire SDS fertilizer and agree that the seeds will be used only with that fertilizer. There are five competitors in the market for seeds of the type covered by the SDS patent. SDS market share for seeds of the type is 30%, but of course it is the only source for the specific, patented seeds. A purchaser of seeds sues SDS for antitrust violations. What result?

IV. PACKAGE LICENSING AND POOLING

MCA TELEVISION LTD. v. PUBLIC INTEREST CORP.
171 F.3d 1265 (11th Cir. 1999)

BARKETT, J.

Public Interest Corporation ("PIC") appeals from a $1.8 million judgment entered in favor of MCA Television ("MCA") following a non-jury trial on MCA's breach of contract and copyright infringement claims. The district court found that PIC breached its licensing contracts with MCA, and violated MCA's copyright of several television shows by airing them after MCA revoked its broadcast licenses following PIC's breach of contract. In addition, MCA appeals the district court's ruling in favor of PIC's antitrust claim. PIC had alleged that MCA's conditioning of its licensing to PIC of several first-run television shows for barter on the willingness of PIC to license a further first-run series called Harry and the Hendersons for cash as well as barter constituted an illegal tying arrangement in violation of the Sherman Act. The district court agreed, but found that PIC failed to prove "antitrust injury" and thus merited no damages on its antitrust claim. We affirm in part and reverse in part.

Facts

At the time of the events giving rise to this action, PIC was a Florida corporation that owned and operated television station WTMV-TV in Lakeland, Florida. MCA owns and licenses syndicated television programs. In 1990, the parties entered into a licensing contract with respect to several first-run television shows. With respect to all but one of these shows, MCA exchanged the licenses on a "barter" basis for advertising time on WTMV. However, MCA conditioned this exchange on PIC's agreeing to license the remaining show, Harry and the Hendersons ("Harry"), for cash as well as for barter. PIC agreed to this arrangement, although it would not have chosen to license Harry if it did not have to do so in order to secure the licenses for the other shows. Both parties signed an interim contract reflecting these arrangements. In the following years, the parties entered into new contracts licensing four other MCA shows to PIC.

The contracts under which the parties operated contained the following language:

> When signed by [PIC] and MCA, this document shall constitute a valid and binding Agreement and shall be deemed to include the standard terms and conditions known as "Additional Provisions" which are contained in MCA's standard series syndication Licensing Agreement. Copies of the "Additional Provisions" are available on request and will be fully set forth in a long-form contract.

Each Licensing Agreement, under the heading "Additional Provisions of the Agreement," established a payment schedule and stated that any late payment constituted a default which gave MCA the right to terminate the license. . . . From the beginning, PIC's payments were consistently two to nine months behind schedule. This pattern of late payment continued for over two years without objection by MCA.

For two and a half years following the original contracts, PIC broadcast Harry, paying MCA with three minutes of advertising time per episode pursuant to the barter provisions of the contract. In September of 1993, before payments for the cash portion of the Harry contract were scheduled to begin, PIC informed MCA that it did not believe it was obligated under that portion of the contract. In April 1994, MCA demanded payment from PIC for Harry, as well as for the four other programs PIC had subsequently purchased. . . . In May of 1994, MCA gave PIC written notice of the termination of its broadcast rights. PIC requested an extension, which MCA granted through June 1, 1994. Negotiations continued through that date, but eventually fell apart. In a letter dated June 29, 1994, MCA suspended PIC's broadcast rights for all of its shows, and stated that "[a]ny telecasts of MCA programming by WTMV-TV on or after June 1, 1994, will be deemed unauthorized and shall constitute an infringement of MCA's copyrights in and to those programs." PIC nonetheless continued broadcasting MCA's programs, with the exception of Harry.

On July 1, 1994, MCA filed suit against PIC alleging copyright infringement and breach of contract. It also sought and obtained a preliminary injunction to prevent PIC from further broadcasts of its television shows. PIC filed a counterclaim, contending that MCA's actions were themselves in breach of contract and violated federal antitrust law, and continued its broadcasts of MCA programming until just before the district court enjoined it from so doing.

After a bench trial, the district court found that PIC had breached its licensing contracts with MCA prior to June 1, 1994, and that PIC's 106 broadcasts of MCA programs after that date constituted willful copyright infringement. . . . As for PIC's antitrust counterclaim, the district court found that the licensing contract for Harry was an illegal tying contract in violation of the Sherman Act and was therefore not enforceable. However, it concluded that PIC had failed to prove "antitrust injury" and that PIC was therefore entitled to no damages for MCA's antitrust violation.

Discussion

On its cross-appeal, MCA challenges the district court's finding that an agree-ment conditioning the licensing of several of MCA's shows for barter on PIC's willingness to license episodes of Harry and the Hendersons for cash as well as barter constituted an illegal tying arrangement in violation of Section 1 of the Sherman Act. *See* 15 U.S.C. Section 1. In reaching its conclusion, the district court relied on *United States v. Loew's, Inc.*, 371 U.S. 38 (1962). In that case, the Supreme Court held in the television licensing context that "block booking" arrangements — in which a copyright holder "license[s], or offer[s] for license, one feature or group of features on condition that the exhibitor will also license another feature or group of features released by the distributors," *United States v. Paramount Pictures, Inc.*, 334 U.S. 131, 156 (1948) — are per se illegal under the Sherman Act. *See Loew's*, 371 U.S. at 50 (applying *Paramount*'s per se pro-hibition on block booking to the licensing of films for television).

MCA argues that the district court erred in applying the per se standard established in *Loew's* for illegal block booking arrangements. According to MCA, in the recent case of *State Oil Co. v. Khan*, 118 S. Ct. 275 (1997), the Supreme Court, "for all intents and purposes, rejected the per se approach used by the District Court" and "made clear that the correct standard to be applied [when assessing the legality of tying arrangements] is the 'rule of rea-son' standard."

This assertion misstates the holding in *State Oil*. In that case, the Supreme Court addressed itself to a specific type of contractual arrangement known as "vertical maximum price fixing." In the prior case of *Albrecht v. Herald Co.*, 390 U.S. 145 (1968), the Court had held that vertical maximum price fixing constituted a per se violation of the Sherman Act. In *State Oil*, the Court over-ruled *Albrecht*, holding instead that the appropriate standard for evaluating the legality of vertical maximum price fixing is the rule of reason. *State Oil*, 118 S. Ct. at 285; *see id.* (reasoning that "rule-of-reason analysis will effec-tively identify those situations in which vertical maximum price fixing amounts to anticompetitive conduct").

Although the Court in *State Oil* noted its "reluctance to adopt per se rules," and likened vertical maximum price fixing to "the majority of commercial arrangements subject to the antitrust laws" that are "evaluated under the rule of reason," we find nothing in that case to support MCA's claim that *State Oil* stands for a rejection of the per se standard in any context other than that of vertical maximum price fixing. In fact, in *State Oil*, the Court reaffirmed that some forms of restraint on trade "have such predictable and pernicious anticom-petitive effect, and such limited potential for procompetitive benefit, that they are deemed unlawful per se." As the Court went on to explain, "[p]er se treat-ment is appropriate '[o]nce experience with a particular kind of restraint enables the Court to predict with confidence that the rule of reason will condemn it.'"

The contract between MCA and PIC for the licensing of Harry and the Hendersons matches precisely one of the specific contractual forms — "block booking" — for which the Supreme Court has deemed the per se standard appropriate. In *Paramount Pictures*, the Supreme Court defined "block book-ing" contracts as those in which a copyright holder "license[s], or offer[s] for license, one feature or group of features on condition that the exhibitor will also license another feature or group of features released by the distributors." The Harry contract plainly fits this description. And not once, but twice, the Supreme Court has clearly stated that such "block booking" contracts are among those economic arrangements that will always be "condemn[ed]" under the rule of reason and will therefore always merit a finding of per se illegality. *See Paramount Pictures*, 334 U.S. at 159 ("[W]e hold to be illegal [] a refusal to license one or more copyrights unless another copyright is accepted."); *Loew's*, 371 U.S. at 50 ("Appellants' block booked contracts [for television programs] are covered by the flat holding in *Paramount Pictures*.").

We are not persuaded by MCA's efforts to distinguish this case from the block booking condemned in *Paramount* and *Loew's*. In *Loew's*, the Supreme Court explained that this specific form of "tying arrangement" is illegal per se because the licensor by virtue of its copyright is presumed to have "economic leverage sufficient to induce his customers to take the tied product along with the tying item." MCA argues that because PIC desired its programming, not for its "uniqueness" but because PIC had no money and MCA was offering the licenses for barter, it was irrelevant to the inquiry that the programs were uniquely MCA's by virtue of copyright.

However, as the precedent makes clear, the licensee's reasons for wanting to license some of the licensor's programs and not others are irrelevant. The point is rather that each licensed program should stand on its own merits. "Where a high quality film greatly desired is licensed only if an inferior one is taken, the latter borrows quality from the former and strengthens its monopoly by drawing on the other. . . . Each [thus] stands not on its own footing but in whole or in part on the appeal which another film may have."

To determine whether the terms of the contract for Harry reflect coercive use of MCA's copyright, we must therefore look, not to the reason PIC found appealing the programs it wanted, but to the fact that it found unappealing the program it didn't. The district court found that PIC did not wish to license Harry for cash. Conditioning the licensing of the shows PIC did wish to license on its cash purchase of Harry thus allowed Harry to best the competition for the slot it eventually filled on PIC's roster entirely apart from its intrinsic appeal to PIC's programmers. This is precisely the sort of anticompetitive effect the per se rule of *Paramount* and *Loew's* intended to protect against, and unless and until the Supreme Court explicitly overrules these cases, we must adhere to the rule they establish. We therefore affirm the district court's conclusion that the Harry agreement was per se illegal under the Sherman Act.

V

Under Section 4 of the Clayton Act, "any person who shall be injured in his business or property by reason of anything forbidden in the antitrust laws" may recover "threefold the damages by him sustained, and the cost of suit, including a reasonable attorney's fee." 15 U.S.C. Section 15(a). To recover under this provision, the injured party must demonstrate not only an antitrust violation, but also "antitrust injury," that is, "injury of the type the antitrust laws were intended to prevent and that flows from that which makes the defendants' acts unlawful."

In *Loew's*, the Supreme Court explained that tying arrangements "are an object of antitrust concern for two reasons — they may force buyers into giving up the purchase of substitutes for the tied product, and they may destroy the free access of competing suppliers of the tied product to the consuming market." To be entitled to damages under the Clayton Act, PIC is therefore required to show that, as a consequence of its licensing of Harry, PIC suffered tangible financial harm for precisely these reasons — that PIC was unable to solicit, or be solicited for, more desirable programming to fill the slot allocated to Harry.

The district court found that no such showing was made. It therefore found no antitrust injury, and awarded no damages or attorney's fees to PIC on its antitrust claim. In reaching this conclusion, the district court treated separately the contractual provisions under which PIC licensed Harry for barter, and those under which PIC licensed Harry for cash.

With respect to the barter portions, PIC argued at trial that subsequent ratings revealed the fair market value of Harry to be $50 per episode, and that because PIC paid MCA three minutes of advertising per show, valued at $100 per minute, MCA therefore overcharged PIC by $250 per episode. The district court found PIC's assertion that its advertising time was worth $100 per minute to be unsubstantiated by the evidence, and also that PIC made no showing that it had other advertisers willing to pay "$100 per minute had the time not been taken by MCA." The district court also found that PIC was "desperate for programming" and that "no other syndicators would contract for programming on a barter basis with [PIC]." The district court therefore concluded that PIC proved no tangible harm as to the barter provisions of the Harry contract.

The district court reached the same conclusion as to the cash provisions of the contract. The district court reasoned that, because it had made the determination not to enforce that portion of the agreement, PIC will not have paid "any money in connection with the cash basis portion" and therefore will have "sustained no damages thereunder."

We agree that on the basis of the district court's unchallenged factual findings, PIC is foreclosed from arguing under the barter portion of the contract that it was prevented to its detriment from seeking other programming to fill the slot it gave to Harry. PIC was "desperate for programming," and testified that given the choice it would have taken Harry for barter because it would have "filled up airtime and didn't cost the station any money." By its own admission, therefore, PIC welcomed the barter portion of the contract and cannot now claim that it suffered antitrust injury thereby.

We do not, however, agree with the district court's disposition as to the cash portion of the contract. The district court reasoned that because PIC did not pay any portion of the amount owing on the contract, it was somehow not harmed thereby. This reasoning, however, fails to recognize that if PIC suffered antitrust injury of the sort the proscription on block booking was intended to prevent, it will have been as a result of opportunities lost at the time of contracting. As we noted above, tying arrangements "are an object of antitrust concern for two reasons — they may force buyers into giving up the purchase of substitutes for the tied product, and they may destroy the free access of competing suppliers of the tied product to the consuming market."

Any antitrust injury caused by the illegal contract for Harry would thus have begun to accrue at the moment PIC agreed to the contract, which is the very moment PIC's options for seeking alternative programming for the slot allotted to Harry, with the funds now earmarked for Harry, was foreclosed. This foreclosure is precisely the anti-competitive effect the proscription on block booking is intended to prevent. If PIC can prove that it suffered tangible financial harm as a result, it is entitled to treble damages.

Because the district court treated the contract as a nullity, it did not address the question whether PIC could successfully prove that it had suffered tangible financial harm as a result of the agreement's anticompetitive effects. We therefore reverse the district court's finding of no antitrust injury as it bears on the cash portion of the Harry contract, and remand this case to the district court for a determination on this question.

. . . REVERSED in part, and REMANDED.

NOTES

1. In *Paramount*, the Supreme Court commented, "The sole interest of the United States and the primary object in conferring the [copyright] monopoly lie in the general benefits derived by the public from the labors of authors. It is said that reward to the author or artist serves to induce release to the public of the products of his creative genius. But the reward does not serve its public purpose if it is not related to the quality of the copyright. Where a high quality film greatly desired is licensed only if an inferior one is taken, the latter borrows quality from the former and strengthens its monopoly by drawing on the other. The practice tends to equalize rather than differentiate the reward for the individual copyrights. Even where all the films included in the package are of equal quality, the requirements that all be taken if one is desired increases the market for some. Each stands not on its own footing but in whole or in part on the appeal which another film may have. [T]he result is to add to the monopoly of the copyright in violation of the principle of the patent cases involving tying clauses." *Paramount*, 334 U.S. at 158.

2. Does package licensing present issues different from those in an alleged tying? Is it essential, under *MCA*, to determine if the licensor has market power, or is such power presumed from the existence of the intellectual property rights? Is *MCA* valid authority given the Court's decision in *Independent Ink*?

ANTITRUST GUIDELINES FOR THE LICENSING OF INTELLECTUAL PROPERTY
U.S. Department of Justice and the Federal Trade Commission
April 6, 1995

5.5 Cross-licensing and pooling arrangements

Cross-licensing and pooling arrangements are agreements of two or more owners of different items of intellectual property to license one another or third parties. These arrangements may provide procompetitive benefits by integrating complementary technologies, reducing transaction costs, clearing blocking positions, and avoiding costly infringement litigation. By promoting the dissemination of technology, cross-licensing and pooling arrangements are often procompetitive.

Cross-licensing and pooling arrangements can have anticompetitive effects in certain circumstances. For example, collective price or output restraints in pooling arrangements, such as the joint marketing of pooled intellectual property rights with collective price setting or coordinated output restrictions, may be deemed unlawful if they do not contribute to an efficiency-enhancing integration of economic activity among the participants. *Compare NCAA*, 468 U.S. at 114 (output restriction on college football broadcasting held unlawful because it was not reasonably related to any purported justification), *with Broadcast Music*, 441 U.S. at 23 (blanket license for music copyrights found not per se illegal because the cooperative price was necessary to the creation of a new product). When cross-licensing or pooling arrangements are mechanisms to accomplish naked price fixing or market division, they are subject to challenge under the per se rule. *See United States v. New Wrinkle, Inc.*, 342 U.S. 371 (1952) (price fixing).

Settlements involving the cross-licensing of intellectual property rights can be an efficient means to avoid litigation and, in general, courts favor such settlements. When such cross-licensing involves horizontal competitors, however, the Agencies will consider whether the effect of the settlement is to diminish competition among entities that would have been actual or likely potential competitors in a relevant market in the absence of the cross-license. In the absence of offsetting efficiencies, such settlements may be challenged as unlawful restraints of trade. *Cf. United States v. Singer Manufacturing Co.*, 374 U.S. 174 (1963) (cross-license agreement was part of broader combination to exclude competitors).

Pooling arrangements generally need not be open to all who would like to join. However, exclusion from cross-licensing and pooling arrangements among parties that collectively possess market power may, under some circumstances, harm competition. *Cf. Northwest Wholesale Stationers, Inc. v. Pacific Stationery & Printing Co.*, 472 U.S. 284 (1985) (exclusion of a competitor from a purchasing cooperative not per se unlawful absent a showing of market power). In general, exclusion from a pooling or cross-licensing arrangement among competing technologies is unlikely to have anticompetitive effects unless (1) excluded firms cannot effectively compete in the relevant market for the good incorporating the licensed technologies and (2) the pool participants collectively possess market power in the relevant market. If these circumstances exist, the Agencies will evaluate whether the arrangement's limitations on participation are reasonably related to the efficient development and exploitation of the pooled technologies and will assess the net effect of those limitations in the relevant market.

Another possible anticompetitive effect of pooling arrangements may occur if the arrangement deters or discourages participants from engaging in research and development, thus retarding innovation. For example, a pooling arrangement that requires members to grant licenses to each other for current and future technology at minimal cost may reduce the incentives of its members to engage in research and development because members of the pool have to share their successful research and development and each of the members can free ride on the accomplishments of other pool members. *See generally United States v. Mfrs. Aircraft Ass'n, Inc.*, 1976-1 Trade Cas. (CCH) ¶ 60,810 (S.D.N.Y. 1975); *United States v. Automobile Mfrs. Ass'n*, 307 F. Supp. 617 (C.D. Cal. 1969), *appeal dismissed sub nom. City of New York v. United States*, 397 U.S. 248 (1970), *modified sub nom. United States v. Motor Vehicle Mfrs. Ass'n*, 1982-83 Trade Cas. (CCH) ¶ 65,088 (C.D. Cal. 1982). However, such an arrangement can have procompetitive benefits, for example, by exploiting economies of scale and integrating complementary capabilities of the pool members (including the clearing of blocking positions), and is likely to cause competitive problems only when the arrangement includes a large fraction of the potential research and development in an innovation market.

PROBLEM 13.2

Two leading manufacturers of a consumer electronic product hold patents that cover circuit designs for the product. The manufacturers assign several of their patents to a separate corporation wholly owned by the two firms. That corporation licenses the right to use the circuit designs to other consumer product manufacturers and establishes the license royalty rate. The manufacturers, however, assign to the corporation only patents that are blocking. None of the patents assigned to the corporation can be used without infringing a patent owned by the other firm. Does this arrangement violate antitrust law?

V.   REFUSALS TO LICENSE

IMAGE TECHNICAL
SERVICES INC. v. EASTMAN KODAK CO.
125 F.3d 1195 (9th Cir. 1997)

BEEZER, J.

Plaintiffs-Appellees Image Technical Services, and ten other independent service organizations ("ISOs") that service Kodak photocopiers and micrographic equipment sued the Eastman Kodak Co. ("Kodak") for violations of the Sherman Act. The ISOs alleged that Kodak used its monopoly in the market for Kodak photocopier and micrographic parts to create a second monopoly in the equipment service markets. A jury verdict awarded treble damages totaling $71.8 million. . . . [We] affirm in part, reverse in part and remand with instructions to amend the injunction.

I

Kodak manufactures, sells and services high volume photocopiers and micrographic (or microfilm) equipment. Competition in these markets is strong. . . . Despite comparable products in these markets, Kodak's equipment is distinctive. Although Kodak equipment may perform similar functions to that of its competitors, Kodak's parts are not interchangeable with parts used in other manufacturers' equipment.

Kodak sells and installs replacement parts for its equipment. Kodak competes with ISOs in these markets. Kodak has ready access to all parts necessary for repair services because it manufactures many of the parts used in its equipment and purchases the remaining necessary parts from independent original-equipment manufacturers. In the service market, Kodak repairs at least 80% of the machines it manufactures. ISOs began servicing Kodak equipment in the early 1980's, and have provided cheaper and better service at times, according to some customers. ISOs obtain parts for repair service from a variety of sources, including, at one time, Kodak.

As ISOs grew more competitive, Kodak began restricting access to its photocopier and micrographic parts. In 1985, Kodak stopped selling copier parts to ISOs, and in 1986, Kodak halted sales of micrographic parts to ISOs. Additionally, Kodak secured agreements from their contracted original-equipment manufacturers not to sell parts to ISOs. These parts restrictions limited the ISOs' ability to compete in the service market for Kodak machines. . . .

Kodak offers annual or multi-year service contracts to its customers. Service providers generally contract with equipment owners through multi-year service contracts. ISOs claim that they were unable to provide similar contracts because they lack a reliable supply of parts. Some ISOs contend that the parts shortage forced them out of business.

In 1987, the ISOs filed this action against Kodak, seeking damages and injunctive relief for violations of the Sherman Act. The ISOs claimed that Kodak both: (1) unlawfully tied the sale of service for Kodak machines with the sale of parts in violation of Section 1 of the Sherman Act, and (2) monopolized or attempted to monopolize the sale of service for Kodak machines in violation of Section 2 of the Sherman Act.

Kodak moved for summary judgment prior to discovery. The district court . . . granted summary judgment in Kodak's favor. We reversed. Kodak appealed to the Supreme Court, which affirmed the denial of summary judgment. . . . *Eastman Kodak Co. v. Image Technical Serv., Inc.,* 504 U.S. 451 (1992). After remand, the case proceeded to trial. . . . Before closing arguments, the ISOs withdrew their Section 1 tying and conspiracy claims. The remaining Section 2 attempted monopolization and monopolization claims were submitted to the jury. A unanimous verdict awarded damages to the ISO's totaling $71.8 million after trebling. . . .

II

Section 2 of the Sherman Act prohibits monopolies, attempts to form monopolies, as well as combinations and conspiracies to do so. . . . To prevail on a Section 2 attempt claim, the ISOs were required to establish: "(1) a specific intent to control prices or destroy competition; (2) predatory or anticompetitive conduct directed at accomplishing that purpose; (3) a dangerous probability of achieving 'monopoly power'; and (4) causal antitrust injury." The requirements of a Section 2 monopolization claim are similar, differing primarily in the requisite intent and the necessary level of monopoly power. To prevail on a Section 2 monopoly claim the ISOs were required to prove that Kodak: (1) possessed monopoly power in the relevant market and (2) willfully acquired or maintained that power. Section 2 plaintiffs must also establish antitrust injury. . . .

Monopoly power is "the power to control prices or exclude competition." . . . We hold that there is sufficient proof of market power by circumstantial evidence. . . .

III

Our conclusion that the ISOs have shown that Kodak has both attained monopoly power and exercised exclusionary conduct does not end our inquiry. Kodak's conduct may not be actionable if supported by a legitimate business justification. When a legitimate business justification supports a monopolist's exclusionary conduct, that conduct does not violate Section 2 of the Sherman Act. A plaintiff may rebut an asserted business justification by demonstrating either that the justification does not legitimately promote competition or that the justification is pretextual. . . .

B. Intellectual Property Rights

Kodak . . . attacks the district court's business justifications instructions for their failure to properly detail Kodak's intellectual property rights. . . .

1.

Kodak's challenge raises unresolved questions concerning the relationship between federal antitrust, copyright and patent laws. . . .

Antitrust law seeks to promote and protect a competitive marketplace for the benefit of the public. The Sherman Act, the relevant antitrust law here, prohibits efforts both to restrain trade by combination or conspiracy and the acquisition or maintenance of a monopoly by exclusionary conduct.

Patent law seeks to protect inventions, while inducing their introduction into the market for public benefit. Patent laws "reward the inventor with the power to exclude others from making, using or selling [a patented] invention throughout the United States." Meanwhile, the public benefits both from the faster introduction of inventions, and the resulting increase in market competition. Legally, a patent amounts to a permissible monopoly over the protected work. Patent laws "are in pari materia with the antitrust laws and modify them pro tanto (as far as the patent laws go)." *Simpson v. Union Oil Co.*, 377 U.S. 13, 24 (1964).

Federal copyright law "secure[s] a fair return for an author's creative labor" in the short run, while ultimately seeking "to stimulate artistic creativity for the general public good." The Copyright Act grants to the copyright owner the exclusive right to distribute the protected work. 17 U.S.C. § 106. This right encompasses the right to "refrain from vending or licensing," as the owner may "content [itself] with simply exercising the right to exclude others from using [its] property."

Clearly the antitrust, copyright and patent laws both overlap and, in certain situations, seem to conflict. This is not a new revelation. We have previously noted the "obvious tension" between the patent and antitrust laws: "[o]ne body of law creates and protects monopoly power while the other seeks to proscribe it." Similarly, tension exists between the antitrust and copyright laws.

Two principles have emerged regarding the interplay between these laws: (1) neither patent nor copyright holders are immune from antitrust liability, and (2) patent and copyright holders may refuse to sell or license protected work. . . .

2.

Next we lay out the problem presented here. The Supreme Court touched on this question in *Kodak*, i.e., the effect to be given a monopolist's unilateral refusal to sell or license a patented or copyrighted product in the context of a Section 2 monopoly leveraging claim. In footnote 29, [the] Supreme Court in *Kodak* . . . stated that a monopolist who acquires a dominant position in one market through patents and copyrights may violate Section 2 if the monopolist exploits that dominant position to enhance a monopoly in another market. Although footnote 29 appears in the Court's discussion of the Section 1 tying claim, the Section 2 discussion frequently refers back to the Section 1 discussion, and the Court's statement that "exploit[ing] [a] dominant position in one market to expand [the] empire into the next" is broad enough to cover monopoly leveraging under Section 2. By responding in this fashion, the Court in *Kodak* supposed that intellectual property rights do not confer an absolute immunity from antitrust claims.

The *Kodak* Court, however, did not specifically address the question of antitrust liability based upon a unilateral refusal to deal in a patented or copyrighted product. Kodak and its *amicus* correctly indicate that the right of exclusive dealing is reserved from antitrust liability. We find no reported case in which a court has imposed antitrust liability for a unilateral refusal to sell or license a patent or copyright. Courts do not generally view a monopolist's unilateral refusal to license a patent as "exclusionary conduct." This basic right of exclusion does have limits. For example, a patent offers no protection if it was unlawfully acquired. Nor does the right of exclusion protect an attempt to extend a lawful monopoly beyond the grant of a patent. Section 2 of the Sherman Act condemns exclusionary conduct that extends natural monopolies into separate markets. Much depends, therefore, on the definition of the patent grant and the relevant market.

The relevant market for determining the patent or copyright grant is determined under patent or copyright law. The relevant markets for antitrust purposes are determined by examining economic conditions. We recently noted the distinction between copyright market definition and antitrust market definition in *Triad Systems Corp. v. Southeastern Express Co.*, 64 F.3d 1330 (9th Cir. 1995). There, the plaintiff, Southeastern, argued that the copyright of the defendant, Triad, did not "extend to the service market" for Triad computers. We disagreed stating:

Triad invented, developed, and marketed its software to enable its customers and its own technicians to service Triad computers. Southeastern is getting a free ride when it uses that software to perform precisely the same service. Triad is entitled to licensing fees from Southeastern and other ISOs. . . .

Rather than merely requiring Southeastern to pay for future use, the district court enjoined Southeastern from servicing the computers that had licensed software. We never reached Southeastern's antitrust counterclaims, as they had not yet been tried. Neither did we refer to antitrust principles in defining the reach of Triad's copyright.

Parts and service here have been proven separate markets in the antitrust context, but this does not resolve the question whether the service market falls "reasonably within the patent [or copyright] grant" for the purpose of determining the extent of the exclusive rights conveyed. *Mallinckrodt, Inc. v. Medipart, Inc.*, 976 F.2d 700, 708-09 (Fed. Cir. 1992). These are separate questions, which may result in contrary answers. At the border of intellectual property monopolies and antitrust markets lies a field of dissonance yet to be harmonized by statute or the Supreme Court.

When an owner of intellectual property takes concerted action in violation of Section 1, this dissonance does not threaten his core right of exclusion. Contrary to the ISOs' arguments, there is an important difference between Section 1 tying and Section 2 monopoly leveraging: the limiting principles of Section 1 restrain those claims from making the impact on intellectual property rights threatened by Section 2 monopoly leveraging claims. Where, as here, the claim involves a failure to act that is at the heart of the property right, liability depends largely on market definition and lacks the limiting principles of Section 1. Under Section 2, "behavior that might otherwise not be of concern to the antitrust laws — or that might even be viewed as procompetitive — can take on exclusionary connotations when practiced by a monopolist." *Kodak*, 504 U.S. at 488 (Scalia, J. dissenting). Harmonizing antitrust monopoly theory with the monopolies granted by intellectual property law requires that some weight be given to the intellectual property rights of the monopolist.

The effect of claims based upon unilateral conduct on the value of intellectual property rights is a cause for serious concern. Unilateral conduct is the most common conduct in the economy. After Kodak, unilateral conduct by a manufacturer in its own aftermarkets may give rise to liability and, in one brand markets, monopoly power created by patents and copyrights will frequently be found. Under current law the defense of monopolization claims will rest largely on the legitimacy of the asserted business justifications, as evidenced by the jury instructions approved in *Aspen Skiing* [*Co. v. Aspen Highlands Skiing Corp.*, 472 U.S. 585 (1985)].

Without bounds, claims based on unilateral conduct will proliferate. The history of this case demonstrates that such claims rest on highly disputed factual questions regarding market definition. Particularly where treble damages are possible, such claims will detract from the advantages lawfully granted to the holders of patents or copyrights by subjecting them to the cost and risk of lawsuits based upon the effect, on an arguably separate market, of their refusal to sell or license. The cost of such suits will reduce a patent holder's "incentive . . . to risk the often enormous costs in terms of time, research, and development." *Kewanee Oil Co. v. Bicron Corp.*, 416 U.S. 470, 480 (1974). Such an effect on patent and copyright holders is contrary to the fundamental and complementary purposes of both the intellectual property and antitrust laws, which aim to "encourag[e] innovation, industry and competition."

3.

. . . Under the fact-based approaches of *Aspen Skiing* and *Kodak*, some measure must guarantee that the jury account for the procompetitive effects and statutory rights extended by the intellectual property laws. To assure such consideration, we adopt a modified version of the rebuttable presumption created by the First Circuit in *Data General*, and hold that "while exclusionary conduct can include a monopolist's unilateral refusal to license a [patent or] copyright," or to sell its patented or copyrighted work, a monopolist's "desire to exclude others from its [protected] work is a presumptively valid business justification for any immediate harm to consumers."

This presumption does not "rest on formalistic distinctions" which "are generally disfavored in antitrust laws"; rather it is based on "actual market realities." This presumption harmonizes the goals of the relevant statutes and takes into account the long term effects of regulation on these purposes. The presumption should act to focus the factfinder on the primary interest of both intellectual property and antitrust laws: public interest.

Given this presumption, the district court's failure to give any weight to Kodak's intellectual property rights in the jury instructions constitutes an abuse of discretion. This error was, however, harmless. The ISOs maintain that Kodak argued protection of intellectual property as a business justification to the jury, which rejected this justification as pretextual. An error in instructing the jury in a civil case does not require reversal if it is more probable than not harmless. . . .

Given the interplay of the antitrust and intellectual property laws discussed above, Kodak's contention that its refusal to sell its parts to ISOs was based on its reluctance to sell its patented or copyrighted parts was a presumptively legitimate business justification. Kodak may assert that its desire to profit from its intellectual property rights justifies its conduct, and the jury should presume that this justification is legitimately procompetitive.

Nonetheless, this presumption is rebuttable. . . .

Kodak defends its intellectual property rights "justification" against claims of pretext. Kodak argues that its subjective motivation is irrelevant. Kodak also contends, that a desire to best the competition does not prove pretext, nor does hostility to competitors. Kodak's argument and its accompanying authority stands for nothing more than the proposition that a desire to compete does not demonstrate pretext.

Evidence regarding the state of mind of Kodak employees may show pretext, when such evidence suggests that the proffered business justification played no part in the decision to act. Kodak's parts manager testified that patents "did not cross [his] mind" at the time Kodak began the parts policy. Further, no distinction was made by Kodak between "proprietary" parts covered by tooling or engineering clauses and patented or copyrighted products. In denying Kodak's motion for a new trial, the district court commented that Kodak was not actually motivated by protecting its intellectual property rights. Kodak argues that the district court should have allowed the jury to reach this conclusion.

Kodak photocopy and micrographics equipment requires thousands of parts, of which only 65 were patented. Unlike the other cases involving refusals to license patents, this case concerns a blanket refusal that included protected and unprotected products. From this evidence, it is more probable than not that the jury would have found Kodak's presumptively valid business justification rebutted on the grounds of pretext.

Kodak argues that the existence of some patented and copyrighted products undermines ISOs "all parts" theory. To the contrary, as discussed above, the "all parts" market reflects the "commercial realities" of the marketplace and the lack of identifiable separate markets for individual parts. The fact that Kodak did not differentiate between patented and nonpatented parts lends further support to the existence of these commercial realities. The jury accepted the "all parts" theory and found a scheme to monopolize the service market through Kodak's conduct. We hold that the district court's failure to instruct on Kodak's intellectual property rights was harmless. . . .

IN RE INDEPENDENT SERVICE ORGANIZATIONS ANTITRUST LITIGATION
203 F.3d 1322 (Fed. Cir. 2000)

CSU, L.L.C. appeals the judgment of the United States District Court for the District of Kansas, dismissing on summary judgment CSU's claims that Xerox's refusal to sell patented parts and copyrighted manuals and to license copyrighted software violates the antitrust laws. Because we agree with the district court that CSU has not raised a genuine issue as to any material fact and that Xerox is entitled to judgment as a matter of law, we affirm.

Background

Xerox manufactures, sells, and services high-volume copiers. Beginning in 1984, it established a policy of not selling parts unique to its series 10 copiers to independent service organizations ("ISOs"), including CSU, unless they were also end-users of the copiers. In 1987, the policy was expanded to include all new products as well as existing series 9 copiers. Enforcement of this policy was tightened in 1989, and Xerox cut off CSU's direct purchase of restricted parts. Xerox also implemented an "on-site end-user verification" procedure to confirm that the parts ordered by certain ISOs or their customers were actually for their end-user use. Initially this procedure applied to only the six most successful ISOs, which included CSU.

To maintain its existing business of servicing Xerox equipment, CSU used parts cannibalized from used Xerox equipment, parts obtained from other ISOs, and parts purchased through a limited number of its customers. For approximately one year, CSU also obtained parts from Rank Xerox, a majority-owned European affiliate of Xerox, until Xerox forced Rank Xerox to stop selling parts to CSU and other ISOs. In 1994, Xerox settled an antitrust lawsuit with a class of ISOs by which it agreed to suspend its restrictive parts policy for six and one-half years and to license its diagnostic software for four and one-half years. CSU opted out of that settlement and filed this suit alleging that Xerox violated the Sherman Act by setting the prices on its patented parts much higher for ISOs than for end-users to force ISOs to raise their prices. This would eliminate ISOs in general and CSU in particular as competitors in the relevant service markets for high speed copiers and printers. . . .

The district court granted summary judgment to Xerox dismissing CSU's antitrust claims and holding that if a patent or copyright is lawfully acquired, the patent or copyright holder's unilateral refusal to sell or license its patented invention or copyrighted expression is not unlawful exclusionary conduct under the antitrust laws, even if the refusal to deal impacts competition in more than one market. The court also held, in both the patent and copyright contexts, that the right holder's intent in refusing to deal and any other alleged exclusionary acts committed by the right holder are irrelevant to antitrust law. This appeal followed.

Discussion

The issue is whether the district court erred in granting Xerox's motion for summary judgment on CSU's antitrust claims. . . .

A.

Intellectual property rights do not confer a privilege to violate the antitrust laws. "But it is also correct that the antitrust laws do not negate the patentee's right to exclude others from patent property." "The commercial advantage gained by new technology and its statutory protection by patent do not convert the possessor thereof into a prohibited monopolist." "The patent right must be 'coupled with violations of Section 2,' and the elements of violation of 15 U.S.C. Section 2 must be met." "Determination of whether the patentee meets the Sherman Act elements of monopolization or attempt to monopolize is governed by the rules of application of the antitrust laws to market participants, with due consideration to the exclusivity that inheres in the patent grant."

A patent alone does not demonstrate market power. The United States Department of Justice and Federal Trade Commission have issued guidance that, even where it exists, such "market power does not 'impose on the intellectual property owner an obligation to license the use of that property to others.'" *United States Department of Justice and Federal Trade Comm'n Antitrust Guidelines for the Licensing of Intellectual Property* 4 (1995). There is "no reported case in which a court has imposed antitrust liability for a unilateral refusal to sell or license a patent. . . ." The patentee's right to exclude is further supported by section 271(d) of the Patent Act which states, in pertinent part, that "[n]o patent owner otherwise entitled to relief . . . shall be denied relief or deemed guilty of misuse or illegal extension of the patent right by reason of his having . . . (4) refused to license or use any rights to the patent. . . ." 35 U.S.C. Section 271(d) (1999).

The patentee's right to exclude, however, is not without limit. As we recently observed in *Glass Equipment Development Inc. v. Besten, Inc.*, [174 F.3d 1337, 50 U.S.P.Q.2D (BNA) 1300 (Fed. Cir. 1999),] a patent owner who brings suit to enforce the statutory right to exclude others from making, using, or selling the claimed invention is exempt from the antitrust laws, even though such a suit may have an anticompetitive effect, unless the infringement defendant proves one of two conditions. First, he may prove that the asserted patent was obtained through knowing and willful fraud [*Walker Process Equipment, Inc. v. Food Machinery & Chemical Corp.*, 382 U.S. 172 (1965)]. . . . Or he may demonstrate that the infringement suit was a mere sham to cover what is actually no more than an attempt to interfere directly with the business relationships of a competitor. Here, CSU makes no claim that Xerox obtained its patents through fraud in the Patent and Trademark Office. . . . CSU has alleged that Xerox misused its patents but has not claimed that Xerox's patent infringement counterclaims were shams.

To support its argument that Xerox illegally sought to leverage its presumably legitimate dominance in the equipment and parts market into dominance in the service market, CSU relies on a footnote in *Eastman Kodak Co. v. Image Technical Services, Inc.*, 504 U.S. 451, 480 n.29 (1992), that "[t]he Court has held many times that power gained through some natural and legal advantage such as a patent, . . . can give rise to liability if 'a seller exploits his dominant position in one market to expand his empire into the next.'" Notably, *Kodak* was a tying case when it came before the Supreme Court, and no patents had been asserted in defense of the antitrust claims against Kodak. Conversely, there are no claims in this case of illegally tying the sale of Xerox's patented parts to unpatented products. Therefore, the issue was not resolved by the *Kodak* language cited by CSU. Properly viewed within the framework of a tying case, the footnote can be interpreted as restating the undisputed premise that the patent holder cannot use his statutory right to refuse to sell patented parts to gain a monopoly in a market beyond the scope of the patent.

The cited language from *Kodak* does nothing to limit the right of the patentee to refuse to sell or license in markets within the scope of the statutory patent grant. In fact, we have expressly held that, absent exceptional circumstances, a patent may confer the right to exclude competition altogether in more than one antitrust market.

CSU further relies on the Ninth Circuit's holding on remand in *Image Technical Services* that "'while exclusionary conduct can include a monopolist's unilateral refusal to license a [patent] or to sell its patented . . . work, a monopolist's 'desire to exclude others from its [protected] work is a presumptively valid business justification for any immediate harm to consumers.'" By that case, the Ninth Circuit adopted a rebuttable presumption that the exercise of the statutory right to exclude provides a valid business justification for consumer harm, but then excused as harmless the district court's error in failing to give any instruction on the effect of intellectual property rights on the application of the antitrust laws. It concluded that the jury must have rejected the presumptively valid business justification as pretextual. This logic requires an evaluation of the patentee's subjective motivation for refusing to sell or license its patented products for pretext. We decline to follow *Image Technical Services*.

We have held that "if a [patent infringement] suit is not objectively baseless, an antitrust defendant's subjective motivation is immaterial." We see no more reason to inquire into the subjective motivation of Xerox in refusing to sell or license its patented works than we found in evaluating the subjective motivation of a patentee in bringing suit to enforce that same right. In the absence of any indication of illegal tying, fraud in the Patent and Trademark Office, or sham litigation, the patent holder may enforce the statutory right to exclude others from making, using, or selling the claimed invention free from liability under the antitrust laws. We therefore will not inquire into his subjective motivation for exerting his statutory rights, even though his refusal to sell or license his patented invention may have an anticompetitive effect, so long as that anticompetitive effect is not illegally extended beyond the statutory patent grant. It is the infringement defendant and not the patentee that bears the burden to show that one of these exceptional situations exists and, in the absence of such proof, we will not inquire into the patentee's motivations for asserting his statutory right to exclude. Even in cases where the infringement defendant has met this burden, which CSU has not, he must then also prove the elements of the Sherman Act violation.

We answer the threshold question of whether Xerox's refusal to sell its patented parts exceeds the scope of the patent grant in the negative. Therefore, our inquiry is at an end. Xerox was under no obligation to sell or license its patented parts and did not violate the antitrust laws by refusing to do so. . . .

Perhaps the most extensive analysis of the effect of a unilateral refusal to license copyrighted expression was conducted by the First Circuit in *Data General Corp. v. Gruman Systems Support Corp.*, 36 F.3d 1147 (1st Cir. 1994). There, the court noted that the limited copyright monopoly is based on Congress' empirical assumption that the right to "exclude others from using their works creates a system of incentives that promotes consumer welfare in the long term by encouraging investment in the creation of desirable artistic and functional works of expression. . . . We cannot require antitrust defendants to prove and reprove the merits of this legislative assumption in every case where a refusal to license a copyrighted work comes under attack." *Id.* at 1186-87. The court went on to establish as a legal standard that "while exclusionary conduct can include a monopolist's unilateral refusal to license a copyright, an author's desire to exclude others from use of its copyrighted work is a presumptively valid business justification for any immediate harm to consumers." The burden to overcome this presumption was firmly placed on the antitrust plaintiff. The court gave no weight to evidence showing knowledge that developing a proprietary position would help to maintain a monopoly in the service market in the face of contrary evidence of the defendant's desire to develop state-of-the-art diagnostic software to enhance its service and consumer benefit.

As discussed above, the Ninth Circuit adopted a modified version of this *Data General* standard. Both courts agreed that the presumption could be rebutted by evidence that "the monopolist acquired the protection of the intellectual property laws in an unlawful manner." The Ninth Circuit, however, extended the possible means of rebutting the presumption to include evidence that the defense and exploitation of the copyright grant was merely a pretextual business justification to mask anticompetitive conduct. The hazards of this approach are evident in both the path taken and the outcome reached. The jury in that case was instructed to examine each proffered business justification for pretext, and no weight was given to the intellectual property rights in the instructions. This permitted the jury to second guess the subjective motivation of the copyright holder in asserting its statutory rights to exclude under the copyright laws without properly weighing the presumption of legitimacy in asserting its rights under the copyright laws. While concluding that the failure to weigh the intellectual property rights was an abuse of discretion, the Ninth Circuit nevertheless held the error harmless because it thought the jury must have rejected the presumptive validity of asserting the copyrights as pretextual. This is in reality a significant departure from the First Circuit's central premise that rebutting the presumption would be an uphill battle and would only be appropriate in those rare cases in which imposing antitrust liability is unlikely to frustrate the objectives of the Copyright Act.

We believe the First Circuit's approach is more consistent with both the antitrust and the copyright laws and is the standard that would most likely be followed by the Tenth Circuit in considering the effect of Xerox's unilateral right to refuse to license or sell copyrighted manuals and diagnostic software on liability under the antitrust laws. We therefore reject CSU's invitation to examine Xerox's subjective motivation in asserting its right to exclude under the copyright laws for pretext, in the absence of any evidence that the copyrights were obtained by unlawful means or were used to gain monopoly power beyond the statutory copyright granted by Congress. In the absence of such definitive rebuttal evidence, Xerox's refusal to sell or license its copyrighted works was squarely within the rights granted by Congress to the copyright holder and did not constitute a violation of the antitrust laws.

NOTES

1. Should refusal to license an intellectual property right or to sell an item covered by such rights be treated differently than a refusal to sell or lease other tangible property? A core principle of property law is that the owner can choose to offer the property to others or not. Its decision in this regard is protected in law unless, in context, anticompetitive impacts cognizable under antitrust law are the result.

2. Which of the two approaches is appropriate? What is a "pretextual" claim of protecting an intellectual property right? If, as the owner of a patent or copyright, I choose to not allow competitors in a market in which I participate to use my intellectual property against me, is that business decision properly grounded on property law or pretextual?

PROBLEM 13.3

Regis Systems holds 60% of the market for plastic screws used in airplane construction. The remaining portion is split among three competitors. Five of the varieties of plastic screws that Regis sells are covered by patents. It asks two questions:

a. Can it refuse to license its patents or sell its patented screws to its competitors? If it does so, the most likely result is that its market share for all plastic screws will increase to 90% over the next year because the Regis patented designs have become industry standards.

b. Regis is about to open a new division in which it will manufacture and sell certain major parts for aircraft. These parts use plastic screws. Currently, the part market is comprised of ten competitors with equal market shares. Regis has never sold these parts before, but does license or sell its patented screws to participants in the market. May it discontinue selling or licensing the screws when it begins its own manufacturing?

VI. ESSENTIAL FACILITIES AND DUTY TO LICENSE

INTERGRAPH CORP. v. INTEL CORP.
195 F.3d 1346 (Fed. Cir. 1999)

Newman, J.

Intel Corporation appeals the grant of a preliminary injunction by the United States District Court for the Northern District of Alabama. We vacate the injunction.

Intel is a manufacturer of high performance computer microprocessors. The microprocessors are sold to producers of various computer-based devices, who adapt and integrate the microprocessors into products that are designed and sold for particular uses. These producers are called original equipment manufacturers, or OEMs. Intergraph Corporation is an OEM, and develops, makes, and sells computer workstations that are used in producing computer-aided graphics. From 1987 to 1993 Intergraph's workstations were based on a high performance microprocessor developed by the Fairchild division of National Semiconductor, embodying what is called the "Clipper" technology. Intergraph owns the Clipper technology and patents thereon. In 1993 Intergraph discontinued use of Clipper microprocessors in its workstations and switched to Intel microprocessors. In 1994 Intel designated Intergraph a "strategic customer" and provided Intergraph with various special benefits, including proprietary information and products, under non-disclosure agreements.

Starting in late 1996 Intergraph charged several Intel OEM customers with infringement of the Clipper patents based on their use of Intel microprocessors. The accused companies sought defense and indemnification from Intel. Negotiations ensued between Intel and Intergraph. Intel inquired about a license to the Clipper patents, but the proposed terms were rejected by Intergraph as inadequate. Intel then proposed certain patent cross-licenses, also rejected by Intergraph. Intel also proposed that the non-disclosure agreement relating to a new joint development project include a license to the Clipper patents; this too was rejected by Intergraph. As negotiations failed and threats continued the relationship deteriorated, and so did the technical assistance and other special benefits that Intel had been providing to Intergraph.

In November 1997 Intergraph sued Intel for infringement of the Clipper patents. . . . Intergraph moved to enjoin Intel pendente lite from cutting off or delaying provision of the special benefits that Intel had previously provided to Intergraph. Following Intel's opposition to this motion Intergraph amended its complaint to charge Intel with violation of the antitrust laws. After a hearing, the district court held that Intel was a monopolist and had violated sections 1 and 2 of the Sherman Act or was likely to be so shown, and issued a preliminary injunction that [in effect required Intel to continue supply its product information the Intergraph and set aside an allocation of a supply of processors and the like (described collectively as "Chips") for Intergraph].

Intel appeals, arguing that no law requires it to give such special benefits, including its trade secrets, proprietary information, intellectual property, prerelease products, allocation of new products, and other preferences, to an entity that is suing it on charges of multiple wrongdoing and is demanding damages and the shutdown of its core business. Intel states that its commercial response to Intergraph's suit is not an antitrust violation, and that this "garden-variety patent dispute" does not warrant the antitrust remedy here imposed. . . . Intergraph's response is that it can not survive in its highly competitive graphics workstation business without these services and benefits from Intel, and that the district court simply acted to preserve Intergraph's prior commercial position while the parties litigate unrelated patent issues. . . .

We conclude that the antitrust rulings of the district court are incorrect in law or are devoid of sufficient factual support to present a substantial likelihood of establishing an antitrust law violation with respect to the issues presented. We also conclude that the district court's alternate contract-based ground for the injunction is unsupported on the facts presented.

Intel as "Monopolist"

The district court ruled that Intergraph is likely to succeed in showing that Intel is a "monopolist," whereby Intel's withdrawal of the benefits it had previously accorded to Intergraph and other actions were deemed to violate sections 1 and 2 of the Sherman Act. The court relied on several legal theories, viz.: (1) the essential facility theory and the corollary theory of refusal to deal, (2) leveraging and tying, (3) coercive reciprocity, (4) conspiracy and other acts in restraint of trade, (5) improper use of intellectual property, and (6) retaliatory enforcement of the non-disclosure agreements.

The court alternatively ruled that Intergraph is likely to succeed on its contract claims, including the claim that the mutual at-will termination provision of the non-disclosure agreements is unconscionable. . . .

Intel states that unlawful monopolization was not shown, as a matter of law, because Intergraph and Intel are not competitors. Unlawful monopolization requires both the existence of monopoly power and anticompetitive conduct. *See* 3 PHILLIP E. AREEDA & HERBERT HOVENKAMP, ANTITRUST LAW, Para. 650a, at 66 (1996) ("Unlawful monopolization under Section 2 of the Sherman Act requires both power and 'exclusionary' or anticompetitive conduct before any kind of relief is appropriate."). Monopoly power is generally defined as the power to control prices or exclude competition in a relevant market; anticompetitive conduct is generally defined as conduct whose purpose is to acquire or preserve the power to control prices or exclude competition. . . . The prohibited conduct must be directed toward competitors and must be intended to injure competition. . . . Such conduct must affect the relevant product market, that is, the "area of effective competition" between the defendant and plaintiff. . . .

The antitrust law has consistently recognized that a producer's advantageous or dominant market position based on superiority of a commercial product and ensuing market demand is not the illegal use of monopoly power prohibited by the Sherman Act. In *Aspen Skiing Co. v. Aspen Highlands Skiing Corp.*, 472 U.S. 585, 596 n.19 (1985), the Court explained that "[t]he offense of monopoly under Section 2 of the Sherman Act has two elements: (1) the possession of monopoly power in the relevant market and (2) the willful acquisition or maintenance of that power as distinguished from growth or development as a consequence of a superior product, business acumen, or historic accident." Product superiority and the ensuing market position, flowing from a company's research, talents, commercial efforts, and financial commitments, do not convert the successful enterprise into an illegal monopolist under the Sherman Act.

Intel does not dispute the high market share achieved by its high performance microprocessors. However, that is not a violation of law. Intel stresses that it is not in competition with Intergraph in any relevant market; that its relationship with Intergraph is that of supplier and customer, not competitor. Although the district court found that Intel and Intergraph compete or will compete in the future in the "graphics subsystems" market, Intel points out, and Intergraph does not dispute, that neither firm possesses monopoly power in this market. Intel stresses that violation of the Sherman Act requires the use of monopoly power to exclude competition or maintain prices, none of which is here alleged.

Although the district court recognized that Intel's market power derives from the technological superiority of its products, the court found a prima facie case of market power based on Intel's market share of high performance microprocessors, and concluded that Intel had willfully acquired and maintained monopoly power in the high-end microprocessor market, although the record did not show an effect on competition in any market in which Intergraph competes with Intel. . . .

Intel's market power in the microprocessor market is irrelevant to the issues of this case, all of which relate to the effect of Intel's actions on Intergraph's position in its own markets. . . .

The conduct complained of is Intel's withdrawal or reduction of technical assistance and special benefits, particularly pre-release access to Intel's new products, in reaction to Intergraph's suit for patent infringement. However, the Sherman Act does not convert all harsh commercial actions into antitrust violations. Unilateral conduct that may adversely affect another's business situation, but is not intended to monopolize that business, does not violate the Sherman Act. Although Intergraph stresses the adverse effect on its business of Intel's proposed withdrawal of these special benefits, the record contains no analysis of the effect of such action on competition among manufacturers of graphics subsystems or high-end workstations. "The antitrust laws were enacted for 'the protection of competition, not competitors,'" *Brunswick Corp. v. Pueblo Bowl-O-Mat, Inc.*, 429 U.S. 477, 488 (1977). . . .

The district court found that Intel possessed monopoly power in two "relevant markets": (1) the market for high-end microprocessors, and (2) the submarket of Intel microprocessors. Neither one is a market in which Intergraph and Intel are in competition with each other. Intergraph states that it competes in the microprocessor market by virtue of its Clipper patents. However, the patent grant is a legal right to exclude, not a commercial product in a competitive market. Intergraph abandoned the production of Clipper microprocessors in 1993, and states no intention to return to it. Firms do not compete in the same market unless, because of the reasonable interchangeability of their products, they have the actual or potential ability to take significant business away from each other. . . .

Intel's conduct with respect to Intergraph does not constitute the offense of monopolization or the threat thereof in any market relevant to competition with Intergraph. The Sherman Act is a law in the public, not private, interest. . . .

The "Essential Facility" Theory

The "essential facility" theory of Sherman Act violation stems from *United States v. Terminal RR Ass'n*, 224 U.S. 383 (1912), wherein a group of railroads formed an association that controlled the railroad terminals, bridges, and switching yards serving the City of St. Louis. The Court held that this association was formed for an anticompetitive purpose, that the railroad terminals, bridges, and yards were facilities essential to competing railroads, and that section 1 of the Sherman Act was violated.

The district court found that "the Advance Chips Samples and advance design and technical information are essential products and information necessary for Intergraph to compete in its markets." Reasoning that "[t]he antitrust laws impose on firms controlling an essential facility the obligation to make the facility available on non-discriminatory terms," the court held that Intel's action in withdrawing these benefits violated the Sherman Act. . . . Intergraph argues that the essential facility theory provides it with the entitlement, in view of its dependence on Intel microprocessors, to Intel's technical assistance and other special customer benefits, because Intergraph needs those benefits in order to compete in its workstation market. However, precedent is quite clear that the essential facility theory does not depart from the need for a competitive relationship in order to incur Sherman Act liability and remedy. . . .

Although the viability and scope of the essential facility theory has occasioned much scholarly commentary, no court has taken it beyond the situation of competition with the controller of the facility, whether the competition is in the field of the facility itself or in a vertically related market that is controlled by the facility. That is, there must be a market in which plaintiff and defendant compete, such that a monopolist extends its monopoly to the downstream market by refusing access to the facility it controls. Absent such a relevant market and competitive relationship, the essential facility theory does not support a Sherman Act violation.

Ignoring this weight of jurisprudence, Intergraph argues that violation of the Sherman Act under the essential facility theory does not depend on whether Intel and Intergraph are competitors in any market. That is incorrect. As we have discussed, the presence of a competitive relationship is fundamental to invoking the Sherman Act to force access to the property of another. Other than as a remedy for illegal acts, the antitrust laws do not compel a company to do business with anyone — customer, supplier, or competitor. The notion that withholding of technical information and samples of pre-release chips violates the Sherman Act, based on essential facility jurisprudence, is an unwarranted extension of precedent and can not be supported on the premises presented. The district court erred in holding that Intel's superior microprocessor product and Intergraph's dependency thereon converted Intel's special customer benefits into an "essential facility" under the Sherman Act. The court's ruling of antitrust violation can not be sustained on this ground.

Intergraph also phrases Intel's action in withholding access to its proprietary information, pre-release chip samples, and technical services as a "refusal to deal," and thus illegal whether or not the criteria are met of an "essential facility." However, it is well established that "[i]n the absence of any purpose to create or maintain a monopoly, the [Sherman] act does not restrict the long recognized right of a trader or manufacturer engaged in an entirely private business, freely to exercise his own independent discretion as to parties with whom he will deal." *United States v. Colgate & Co.*, 250 U.S. 300, 307 (1919). Intel states that it continued to sell its products to Intergraph, that it did not refuse to deal with Intergraph as with any regular customer, and that the antitrust laws do not require it to give preferred treatment to a customer that is suing it. . . . Although we have observed a few rulings wherein a court has, for example, barred the termination of a distributor during litigation, no case has held that the divulgation of proprietary information and the provision of special or privileged treatment to a legal adversary can be compelled on a "refusal to deal" antitrust premise. . . .

Conclusion

Despite the district court's sensitive concern for Intergraph's well-being while it conducts its patent suit against Intel, there must be an adverse effect on competition in order to bring an antitrust remedy to bear. The remedy of compulsory disclosure of proprietary information and provision of pre-production chips and other commercial and intellectual property is a dramatic remedy for antitrust illegality, and requires violation of antitrust law or the likelihood that such violation would be established. In the proceedings whose record is before us, Intergraph has not shown a substantial likelihood of success in establishing that Intel violated the antitrust laws in its actions with respect to Intergraph, or that Intel agreed by contract to provide the benefits contained in the injunction. The preliminary injunction is vacated.

NOTES

1. One of the many claims against Intel was "monopoly leveraging." The Federal Circuit rejected that claim. Later, in a different case, the Supreme Court in a footnote undermined the cases that had supported the monopoly leveraging theory. In *Verizon Commun., Inc. v. Trinko*, 124 S. Ct. 872 (2004), the Court rejected a variety of claims against Verizon that were based on its allegedly poor response to the needs of competitors in the telecommunications market where it was the incumbent local exchange carrier. On the leveraging issue, the Court commented: "The Court of Appeals also thought that respondent's complaint might state a claim under a 'monopoly leveraging' theory. . . . We disagree. To the extent the Court of Appeals dispensed with a requirement that there be a 'dangerous probability of success' in monopolizing a second market, it erred. In any event, leveraging presupposes anticompetitive conduct, which in this case could only be the refusal-to-deal claim we have rejected." *Id.* at 883 n.4.

2. *Trinko* also involved an "essential facilities" argument. The Court commented:

> We conclude that Verizon's alleged insufficient assistance in the provision of service to rivals is not a recognized antitrust claim under this Court's existing refusal-to-deal precedents. This conclusion would be unchanged even if we considered to be established law the "essential facilities" doctrine crafted by some lower courts, under which the Court of Appeals concluded respondent's allegations might state a claim. *See generally* Areeda, *Essential Facilities: An Epithet in Need of Limiting Principles*, 58 ANTITRUST L.J. 841 (1989). We have never recognized such a doctrine, and we find no need either to recognize it or to repudiate it here. It suffices for present purposes to note that the indispensable requirement for invoking the doctrine is the unavailability of access to the "essential facilities"; where access exists, the doctrine serves no purpose. Thus, it is said that "essential facility claims should . . . be denied where a state or federal agency has effective power to compel sharing and to regulate its scope and terms." P. AREEDA & H. HOVENKAMP, ANTITRUST LAW 150, ¶ 773e (2003 Supp.). . . . To the extent respondent's "essential facilities" argument is distinct from its general § 2 argument, we reject it.

VII. ANTITRUST INJURY

The mere fact that a competitor has engaged in sharp and effective competitive behavior does not state an antitrust claim. Antitrust law protects "competition," not competitors. The difference is important. To be actionable, harm to a particular company must reflect the defendant's anti-competitive behavior, not simply its success in the marketplace. The following case illustrates the difference.

ADDAMAX CORP. v. OPEN SOFTWARE FOUNDATION, INC.
152 F.3d 48 (1st Cir. 1998)

BOUDIN, CIRCUIT JUDGE.

Addamax Corporation brought a federal antitrust suit against Open Software Foundation ("OSF"), Hewlett-Packard Company and Digital Equipment Corporation. After a bench trial limited to the issues of causation and damages, the district court found that antitrust violations, even if they were assumed to have occurred, were not a material cause of Addamax's failure in the line of business at issue. Addamax now appeals and we affirm.

We begin with a statement of those background facts that are more or less undisputed. Addamax was created by Dr. Peter A. Alsberg in 1986 and, in 1987, began to focus on developing security software for Unix operating systems. Unix is a very popular operating system for larger computers, and security software is a component that can be used with the operating system to restrict outside access to sensitive information and to restrict a particular user to information consistent with that user's security classification.

During this period, the National Computer Security Center, a division of the federal government's National Security Agency, rated security software, giving ratings (ranging from the most to the least secure) of A, B-3, B-2, B-1, C-2, C-1 and D. Addamax decided to produce B-1 software for Unix operating systems, a level of security demanded primarily by government users. During the years 1988-89, Addamax did develop B-1 security software for at least two different versions of Unix.

While Addamax was trying to produce its security software, a different struggle was developing between AT&T — the inventor of Unix — and a number of major computer manufacturers. Although originally Unix had been freely licensed by AT&T, it appears that in the late 1980s AT&T began restricting its licenses in the face of various software modifications being introduced by individual licensees; and at the same time, AT&T began to develop a close working relationship with Sun Microsystems, a major microprocessor manufacturer. Other hardware manufacturers professed to fear that AT&T was trying to establish a single dominant version of Unix, intending to exclude the proprietary Unix variations from the market.

Accordingly, in May 1988, a number of important computer manufacturers — including defendants Hewlett-Packard and Digital Equipment Corp. — formed the Open Software Foundation as a non-profit joint research and development venture. . . . At least one of OSF's professed objectives was to develop an alternative Unix operating system, denominated OSF-1, as a competitor to the Unix system being developed jointly by AT&T and Sun Microsystems.

In 1989, while OSF-1 was still being developed, OSF decided that it should include security software at the B-1 level. At that time, only three companies — AT&T, Addamax and SecureWare, Inc. — were producing security software for the Unix system. On November 1, 1989, OSF sent a "request for technology" to Addamax and SecureWare, soliciting bids for a B-1 security component for the new OSF-1 system. Bids were submitted on November 27, 1989, and OSF selected SecureWare on December 22, 1989. There is some indication that the Addamax security software was more sophisticated — one witness agreed that the contrast was between a Cadillac and a Chevette — but the Addamax price may also have appeared more substantial.[5] In any event, OSF-1 itself was never a very successful product.

Addamax continued to sell its own B-1 software for some period after losing the bid. Nothing prevented OSF "sponsors" (the founding members of OSF) or "members" (a great many other companies) from using Addamax security software for their own programs; and OSF sponsors and members were not the only potential buyers of Addamax's program. However, by 1991, Addamax began to phase out its B-1 security software, turning away new buyers so that it could devote its resources to the development of a new security software product, in which it appears that the company was successful.

In April 1991, Addamax filed a complaint in the district court against OSF, Hewlett-Packard and Digital, alleging various violations of federal and state antitrust law. As later amended, the complaint charged the defendants, together with other companies associated with OSF, with horizontal price fixing, boycott, and otherwise unlawful joint venture behavior in violation of the Sherman and the Clayton Acts. A central theme, although not the only one, was that the defendants had conspired to force down the price for security software below the free-market level and otherwise to limit or impair the ability of Addamax to compete as a supplier of security software. . . .

[The] parties entered into a stipulation that the damage phase of the case would be tried first, on a jury waived basis, to determine "whether the defendants' conduct was a material cause of injury in fact to the plaintiff and, if so, the amount of damages." The stipulation further provided:

> Solely for purposes of this stipulation, the Court will assume that the defendants' conduct as alleged in the Amended Complaint and described in the non-damages portions of the expert reports of Drs. Comanor and Howe occurred and violates the federal and state law accounts. However, the Court will not assume, but will hear and take evidence on, whether there was injury in fact to the plaintiff as a result of that conduct and, if so, the amount of damages, which is the subject of this phase of the trial.

Trial was conducted over 12 days. . . . In May 1997, the district court issued a decision concluding that the defendants' conduct was "not a material cause" of Addamax's losses. The court found that the B-1 software market was a highly

---

[5] [FN3] SecureWare sought a single up-front payment of $3 million. Addamax requested an up-front payment of half this amount with royalties on OSF-1 systems sold before 1992. If one were optimistic about OSF-1 prospects, Addamax's bid could have appeared higher, although not in retrospect.

risky business, that Addamax's belatedly-offered product was "too expensive and too complex, and . . . actually exceeded B-1 requirements." The court said that Addamax faced severe competition from AT&T in the B-1 market and that SecureWare's product was "a cheaper and simpler" one. Accordingly, the court held on the merits that Addamax was not entitled to any damages.

Addamax has now appealed. . . .

As we explained in an earlier case, per se rules under section 1 of the Sherman Act have left only a couple of "serious candidates" for per se treatment: these include price or output fixing agreements (horizontal market division agreements are of essentially the same character) and "*certain* group boycotts or concerted refusals to deal." *U.S. Healthcare, Inc. v. Healthsource, Inc.,* 986 F.2d 589, 593 (1st Cir.1993). Since those words were written, the categories have been narrowed even further by the Supreme Court's decision to overrule *Albrecht v. The Herald Co.,* 390 U.S. 145 (1968), and thereby to exclude from per se treatment vertical maximum resale price fixing agreements. *State Oil Co. v. Khan,* 522 U.S. 3 (1997).

Where a plaintiff proves conduct that falls within a per se category, nothing more is needed for liability; the defendants' power, illicit purpose and anticompetitive effect are all said to be irrelevant. But courts have been very careful to confine per se treatment to conduct of the type that is almost always actually or potentially anticompetitive and has no redeeming benefits (*e.g.,* reduced costs, increased competition) worthy of being weighed against the negative effects. Per se offenses remain very important — they include horizontal price fixing — but only for conduct that fits squarely within the "ever narrowing per se niche."

Joint venture enterprises like OFC, unless they amount to complete shams, are rarely susceptible to per se treatment. Where the venture is producing a new product — here, the OFC-1 software package — there is patently a potential for a productive contribution to the economy, and conduct that is strictly ancillary to this productive effort (*e.g.,* the joint venture's decision as to the price at which it will purchase inputs) is evaluated under the rule of reason. This is so even if we accept, pursuant to the stipulation, the *arguendo* premise that OSF and those connected with it represented a large portion of the market for purchasing B-1 security software and represented a large portion of some kind of output market for integrated Unix software programs.

Addamax points to fragments of evidence that, assuming a full context were established, might or might not suggest that OSF was an aggressive response to the AT&T-Sun venture and that Hewlett-Packard had a secret agenda to favor SecureWare over Addamax (for reasons that are never made quite clear), regardless of whether Addamax offered a superior product. None of the evidence pointed to by Addamax suggests that OSF-1 was other than a legitimate, if ultimately unsuccessful, product; and there is nothing to suggest that the ancillary decisions — what inputs to purchase, at what price, and from whom — were not legitimately related to this effort. In this context, flinging around terms like "cartel" and "boycott" do not convert a rule of reason claim into a per se one.

On the other hand, neither is a joint venture "per se" legal. Any joint venture, especially one that involves competitors, tends to be susceptible to attack under section 1's rule of reason — on the theory that the operations of the joint venture represent collaboration of the separate entities that own or control it. How far this theory can be pressed in the case of a truly integrated enterprise, whose "owners" were no more than stockholders, is a matter we need not pursue; we will assume here that the OSF joint venture, or some aspect of it, could be condemned under section 1 if the balance of harms and benefits tipped in favor of harms; questions of power and motive are primarily clues to such effects.

At this point, Addamax's most straightforward claim would be that OSF's concentration of purchasing power in the supposed "market" for acquiring B-1 security software was so great that it imposed a significant risk of forcing prices below competitive levels, and that those risks outweighed any benefit from the venture or, more plausibly, that the venture could achieve those benefits in a less restrictive fashion, *i.e.,* without creating a substantial threat of monopsony pricing. Whether or not this theory could be proved, we are here assuming liability *arguendo.* The question remains whether Addamax established — either as a matter of law or based on the evidence — some causal connection between this assumed violation by defendants and Addamax's failure in the B-1 security software business.

Addamax first argues that the stipulation required the district court to find that the assumed violation was a material cause of injury to Addamax. Addamax's reading is contrary both to the explicit language of the stipulation and to its evident purpose. The stipulation said that the first phase of the bench trial was to determine "whether" defendants' conduct was "a material cause of injury in fact" to Addamax (and, if so, the amount of damages), assuming *arguendo* that a violation of law had occurred. Pointedly, the stipulation went on to emphasize that although the existence of a violation was to be assumed, the court "will not assume, but will hear and take evidence on," the question whether there was "injury in fact to the plaintiff as a result of" the attributed conduct.

Certainly both Addamax's complaint and its experts *asserted* that the alleged conduct has caused injury, but this was not part of the facts to be assumed *arguendo.* The stipulation did not assume the truth of the complaint, but only that defendants had engaged in the "conduct" alleged in the complaint. Under the stipulation, the reports of Addamax's experts were assumed to be true only in describing the conduct and not its consequences; that is made clear by the reference in the stipulation to assuming the truth of the "non damages portions of the expert reports."

Addamax's more interesting argument is its claim that the case law, and the economic theory that underlies it, require a conclusion that the conduct assumed *arguendo* to comprise a violation must have caused injury to Addamax. The broadest version of this proposition is Addamax's claim that under the rule of reason, conduct is condemned only because it has an anticompetitive effect. Therefore, Addamax argues, there must have been some injury to it, and the only question that remains is to calculate the amount of damages.

A more specific version of the argument, also advanced, is that in this very case the complaint's straightforward charge is that the defendants engaged in an agreement that had the effect of reducing price for B-1 security systems and since Addamax was a provider of B-1 security programs, it necessarily was injured by a reduction in price. An alternative version is Addamax's claim that the joint venturers were engaged in suppressing demand for their own output — Unix programs like OSF-1 embodying B-1 software — and this in turn reduced the demand, and presumably therefore price, volume or both, for suppliers of the input.

It is technically an overstatement to say that actual anticompetitive impact is a requirement of liability in a rule-of-reason case. True, as a practical matter, most courts would be unlikely to condemn an otherwise legitimate joint venture absent some showing of anticompetitive effect. But in principle, a sufficiently high *risk* of an anticompetitive effect, coupled with marginal benefits (or none at all that could not be achieved through an easily available less restrictive alternative) might justify condemnation under the rule of reason.

But all this is beside the point. Even if we assume that the OSF purchasing consortium was capable of exercising monopsony power directly or through coordination of its sponsor/members' actions, it does not follow that Addamax was a victim or that the alleged below-market price offered by the consortium materially affected Addamax. The only formal purchase by OSF involving Addamax was based on the November 1989 request for technology, in which SecureWare was the successful supplier. If below market price was paid, SecureWare, and not Addamax, was directly injured.

To be sure, Addamax claims that its sales opportunities were indirectly curtailed. While the OSF sponsors and members were free to purchase B-1 security programs from anyone they wanted on an individual basis, Addamax claims that winning the OSF-1 sale would have amounted to a valuable OSF endorsement, spurring other sales. But it is hard to see this loss as a consequence of monopsony pricing. In all events, Addamax's claim of secondary injury reduces itself to an issue of fact — not an issue that can be taken as resolved by stipulation or case law.

As a preface to its factual claims, Addamax asserts that the district court's decision recognizes a "defense" of mismanagement. A plaintiff's mismanagement is not a bar to recovery where an antitrust violation is a material cause of injury. But mismanagement is certainly relevant to the factual question whether the antitrust violation had such an effect or whether the plaintiff is entirely the cause of its own failure.

We turn then to the question whether the district court erred in its factual determination that Addamax's inability to succeed in its efforts to sell its B-1 security program for Unix more widely was materially caused by the defendants' conduct. On this issue, Addamax bore the burden of proof at trial. On appeal, the district court's findings and ultimate conclusion of fact are entitled to stand unless found to be clearly erroneous.

Addamax is mistaken in its suggestion that the district court misunderstood the legal standard for causation: quite unlike *Haverhill Gazette Co. v. Union Leader Corp.*, 333 F.2d 798 (1st Cir.1964), the district judge properly asked whether the defendants' assumed conduct had been a substantial or material cause of the losses claimed by Addamax. Although we there cautioned against an unduly rigid view of causation in computing damages once injury had been established, nothing in the opinion relieved the plaintiff from making the statutory showing (fully satisfied in *Haverhill*) that the violation had caused at least some injury to the plaintiff's business or property.

Here, the district court was presented with two competing versions of reality. Addamax's witnesses took the view that Addamax developed a superior B-1 product and its failure to succeed resulted from defendants' machinations which forced down the price of the product to sub-competitive levels and suppressed output for Unix software incorporating B-1 security programs. In some places, Addamax describes itself as the target, and elsewhere as the accidental victim, of a larger conspiracy directed against AT&T.

The defense version, which the district court adopted, was derived from defense depositions, cross-examination of the plaintiffs' experts and numerous documents. In this view, Addamax engaged in risky entry into a market dominated by AT&T, an established supplier of B-1 security software for Unix; the Addamax system was oversophisticated, expensive, arrived late, and never received the important certification from NSA's National Computer Security Center. And, in a market characterized by ever-changing demands, AT&T's promised development of a follow-on B-2 system made the market for B-1 security software for Unix inherently risky and in some measure transitional. There is nothing inherently implausible about either version; everything depends on the evidence.

In fairness to Addamax, the factual analysis in its brief represents exactly the kind of detailed critique of the evidence that fairly presents the question whether the district judge's findings are adequately supported by the record. Addamax identifies specific findings with which it disagrees, cites to record evidence it thinks was misconstrued, furnishes citations to the record for propositions it advances, points to counterveiling evidence that it says the district judge ignored and misinterpreted. In this respect, the brief deserves to be taken seriously, and we have done so.

But while in a few instances the district court may have misinterpreted an exhibit or ignored some fact that softens or qualifies the inference it draws, Addamax's own critique is filled with one-sided versions of events and refusals to confront evidence in support of the district court's findings. What emerges from our own review of the record is that the district court had evidence to support each of its key findings: that the business was a risky one; that Addamax entered late, with a high-priced, overbuilt and uncertified product; that AT&T and SecureWare, in different ways, posed major problems for Addamax; that many of Addamax's problems, including losses of customers, had begun before the OSF selection of SecureWare; and that changes in market conditions proved to be adverse to Addamax. . . . The district court did not commit "clear error" in finding the facts in favor of defendants. . . .

AFFIRMED.

Chapter 14

LIMITING DOCTRINES DERIVED FROM PROPERTY LAW

I. NATURE OF THE ISSUE

At various places in this book, we have encountered cases in which courts were asked to limit or invalidate licensing arrangements, or impose sanctions based on those arrangements, based on policies purportedly fundamental to intellectual property law, especially federal patent and copyright law.

As we have seen, the importance of these limiting concepts has varied over time. Their bite in limiting commercial use of informational assets was strongest in the era of judicial and federal agency hostility to intellectual property and its commercialization — the late 1950s through the mid 1970s. As that hostility changed to acceptance and then to support, the role of property law limitations on licensing practice diminished, but it never ended entirely. This may be because, at some level, there are indeed core values that may restrain use of contract, property and other legal devices to control information and technology in an open society. The problem has been to distinguish core principles from transitory political positions.

The hostility to licensing around the 1960s resulted in courts articulating rules many of which, today, seem archaic and misplaced. Indeed, as discussed in Chapter 13, in 2007 in *Independent Ink*, the Supreme Court explicitly rejected a core theory from that period as applied to antitrust law — the presumption that the mere presence of a patent gives the patent owner market power. Many other themes have given way to a more open market principle. Today, however, we are still seeing a contest between advocates of rights expansion and advocates of rights restriction. Each lays claim to fundamental principles, but which one's will be dominant in the immediate future remains to be seen.

This chapter takes a closer look at themes of restriction that may emanate from the property rights themselves and the subject matter with which they deal. We place those doctrines and the theories that limit them in their current context, but the student should also keep in mind the dynamic tension that these doctrines evidence. We are dealing with a liquid, flowing mass, rather than a set of fixed, immutable rules.

II. POLICY PREEMPTION AND CONTRACT CHOICE

The idea of preemption is simple: in some cases, federal law precludes enforcement of state law rules applicable to a particular issue. There are three types of preemption:

> 1. *Express preemption:* Federal law expressly provides for preemption.

2. *Field preemption:* Federal law entirely and exclusively occupies a field.

3. *Conflict preemption:* State law is inconsistent with and impedes the achievement of federal policy in federal statute or regulation.

See Saridakis v. United Airlines, 166 F.3d 1272, 1276 (9th Cir. 1999); *Hunter Douglas, Inc. v. Harmonic Design, Inc*, 153 F.3d 1318 (Fed. Cir. 1998).

Federal patent law has no express statutory preemption rule. In contrast, Copyright Act Section 301 states:

> [All] legal and equitable rights that are equivalent to any of the exclusive rights within the general scope of copyright . . . in works of authorship that are fixed in a tangible medium of expression and come within the subject matter of copyright . . . are governed exclusively by [the Copyright Act]. [But nothing] in this title annuls or limits any rights or remedies under the . . . law . . . of any state with respect to . . . activities violating legal or equitable rights that are not equivalent to any of the exclusive rights within the general scope of copyright.

Review *ProCD v. Zeidenberg* in Chapter 1.

LEAR, INC. v. ADKINS
395 U.S. 653 (1969)

Mr. Justice Harlan:

In January of 1953, John Adkins, an inventor and mechanical engineer, was hired by Lear Incorporated for the purpose of solving a vexing problem the company had encountered in its efforts to develop a gyroscope which would meet the increasingly demanding requirements of the aviation industry. The gyroscope is an essential component of the navigational system in all aircraft, enabling the pilot to learn the direction and altitude of his airplane. With the development of the faster airplanes of the 1950's, more accurate gyroscopes were needed, and the gyro industry consequently was casting about for new techniques which would satisfy this need in an economical fashion. Shortly after Adkins was hired, he developed a method of construction at the company's California facilities which improved gyroscope accuracy at a low cost. Lear almost immediately incorporated Adkins' improvements into its production process to its substantial advantage.

The question that remains unsettled in this case, after eight years of litigation in the California courts, is whether Adkins will receive compensation for Lear's use of those improvements which the inventor has subsequently patented. At every stage of this lawsuit, Lear has sought to prove that, despite the grant of a patent by the Patent Office, none of Adkins' improvements were sufficiently novel to warrant the award of a monopoly under the standards delineated in the governing federal statutes. Moreover, the company has sought to prove that Adkins obtained his patent by means of a fraud on the Patent Office. In response, the inventor has argued that since Lear had entered into a licensing agreement with Adkins, it was obliged to pay the agreed royalties regardless of the validity of the underlying patent.

The Supreme Court of California unanimously vindicated the inventor's position. While the court recognized that generally a manufacturer is free to challenge the validity of an inventor's patent, it held that "one of the oldest doctrines in the field of patent law establishes that so long as a licensee is operating under a license agreement, he is estopped to deny the validity of his licensor's patent in a suit for royalties. The theory underlying this doctrine is that a licensee should not be permitted to enjoy the benefit afforded by the agreement while simultaneously urging that the patent which forms the basis of the agreement is void."

Almost 20 years ago, in its last consideration of the doctrine, this Court also invoked an estoppel to deny a licensee the right to prove that his licensor was demanding royalties for the use of an idea which was in reality a part of the public domain. *Automatic Radio Manufacturing Co. v. Hazeltine Research, Inc.*, 339 U.S. 827 (1950). We granted certiorari in the present case to reconsider the validity of the *Hazeltine* rule in the light of our recent decisions emphasizing the strong federal policy favoring free competition in ideas which do not merit patent protection.

I

At the very beginning of the parties' relationship, Lear and Adkins entered into a rudimentary one-page agreement which provided that although "[a]ll new ideas, discoveries, inventions etc. related [to] vertical gyros become the property of Mr. John S. Adkins," the inventor promised to grant Lear a license as to all ideas he might develop "on a mutually satisfactory royalty basis." As soon as Adkins' labors yielded tangible results it quickly became apparent to the inventor that further steps should be taken to place his rights to his ideas on a firmer basis. On February 4, 1954, Adkins filed an application with the Patent Office in an effort to gain federal protection for his improvements. At about the same time, he entered into a lengthy period of negotiations with Lear in an effort to conclude a licensing agreement which would clearly establish the amount of royalties that would be paid.

These negotiations finally bore fruit on September 15, 1955, when the parties approved a complex 17-page contract which carefully delineated the conditions upon which Lear promised to pay royalties for Adkins' improvements. The parties agreed that "if the United States Patent Office refuses to issue a patent on the substantial claims [contained in Adkins' original patent application] or if such a patent so issued is subsequently held invalid then in any of such events Lear at its option shall have the right forthwith to terminate the specific license so affected or to terminate this entire Agreement. . . ."

As the contractual language indicates, Adkins had not obtained a final Patent Office decision as to the patentability of his invention at the time the licensing agreement was concluded. Indeed, he was not to receive a patent until January 5, 1960. This long delay has its source in the special character of Patent Office procedures. The regulations do not require the Office to make a final judgment on an invention's patentability on the basis of the inventor's original application. While it sometimes happens that a patent is granted at this early stage, it is far more common for the Office to find that although certain of the applicant's claims may be patentable, certain others have been fully anticipated by the earlier developments in the art. In such a situation, the Patent Office does not attempt to separate the wheat from the chaff on its own initiative. Instead, it rejects the application, giving the inventor the right to make an amendment which narrows his claim to cover only those aspects of the invention which are truly novel. It often happens however, that even after an application is amended, the Patent Office finds that some of the remaining claims are unpatentable. When this occurs, the agency again issues a rejection which is subject to further amendment. And so the process of rejection and amendment continues until the Patent Office Examiner either grants a patent or concludes that none of the inventor's claims could possibly be patentable, at which time a final rejection is entered on the Office's records. Thus, when Adkins made his original application in 1954, it took the average inventor more than three years before he obtained a final administrative decision on the patentability of his ideas, with the Patent Office acting on the average application from two to four times.

The progress of Adkins' effort to obtain a patent followed the typical pattern. In his initial application, the inventor made the ambitious claim that his entire method of constructing gyroscopes was sufficiently novel to merit protection. The Patent Office, however, rejected this initial claim, as well as two subsequent amendments, which progressively narrowed the scope of the invention sought to be protected. Finally, Adkins narrowed his claim drastically to assert only that the design of the apparatus used to achieve gyroscope accuracy was novel. In response, the Office issued its 1960 patent, granting a 17-year monopoly on this more modest claim.

During the long period in which Adkins was attempting to convince the Patent Office of the novelty of his ideas, however, Lear had become convinced that Adkins would never receive a patent on his invention and that it should not continue to pay substantial royalties on ideas which had not contributed substantially to the development of the art of gyroscopy. In 1957, after Adkins' patent application had been rejected twice, Lear announced that it had searched the Patent Office's files and had found a patent which it believed had fully anticipated Adkins' discovery. As a result, the company stated that it would no longer pay royalties on the large number of gyroscopes it was producing at its plant in Grand Rapids, Michigan (the Michigan gyros). Payments were continued on the smaller number of gyros produced at the company's California plant for two more years until they too were terminated on April 8, 1959 (the California gyros).

As soon as Adkins obtained his patent in 1960, he brought this lawsuit in the California Superior Court. He argued to a jury that both the Michigan and the California gyros incorporated his patented apparatus and that Lear's failure to pay royalties on these gyros was a breach both of the 1955 contract and of Lear's quasi-contractual obligations. Although Lear sought to raise patent invalidity as a defense, the trial judge directed a verdict of $16,351.93 for Adkins on the California gyros, holding that Lear was estopped by its licensing agreement from questioning the inventor's patent. The trial judge took a different approach when it came to considering the Michigan gyros. Noting that the Company claimed that it had developed its Michigan designs independently of Adkins' ideas, the court instructed the jury to award the inventor recovery only if it was satisfied that Adkins' invention was novel, within the meaning of the federal patent laws. When the jury returned a verdict for Adkins of $888,122.56 on the Michigan gyros, the trial judge granted Lear's motion for judgment notwithstanding the verdict, finding that Adkins' invention had been completely anticipated by the prior art.

Once again both sides appealed, this time to the California Supreme Court, which took yet another approach to the problem presented. The court rejected the Court of Appeals' conclusion that the 1955 license gave Lear the right to terminate its royalty obligations in 1959. Since the 1955 agreement was still in effect, the court concluded, relying on the language we have already quoted, that the doctrine of estoppel barred Lear from questioning the propriety of the Patent Office's grant. The court's adherence to estoppel, however, was not without qualification. After noting Lear's claim that it had developed its Michigan gyros independently, the court tested this contention by considering "whether what is being built by Lear [in Michigan] springs *entirely*" (emphasis supplied) from the prior art. Applying this test, it found that Lear had in fact "utilized the apparatus patented by Adkins throughout the period in question," reinstating the jury's $888,000 verdict on this branch of the case.

II

Since the California Supreme Court's construction of the 1955 licensing agreement is solely a matter of state law, the only issue open to us is raised by the court's reliance upon the doctrine of estoppel to bar Lear from proving that Adkins' ideas were dedicated to the common welfare by federal law. In considering the propriety of the State Court's decision, we are well aware that we are not writing upon a clean slate. The doctrine of estoppel has been considered by this Court in a line of cases reaching back into the middle of the 19th century. Before deciding what the role of estoppel should be in the present case and in the future, it is, then, desirable to consider the role it has played in the past.

A

While the roots of the doctrine have often been celebrated in tradition, we have found only one 19th century case in this Court that invoked estoppel in a considered manner. And that case was decided before the Sherman Act made it clear that the grant of monopoly power to a patent owner constituted a limited exception to the general federal policy favoring free competition. *Kinsman v. Parkhurst*, 18 How. 289 (1855). Curiously a second decision often cited as supporting the estoppel doctrine points clearly in the opposite direction. *St. Paul Plow Works v. Starling*, 140 U.S. 184 (1891), did not even question the right of the lower courts to admit the licensee's evidence showing that the patented device was not novel. A unanimous Court merely held that, where there was conflicting evidence as to an invention's novelty, it would not reverse the decision of the lower court upholding the patent's validity.

In the very next year, this Court found the doctrine of patent estoppel so inequitable that it refused to grant an injunction to enforce a licensee's promise never to contest the validity of the underlying patent. "It is as important to the public that competition should not be repressed by worthless patents, as that the patentee of a really valuable invention should be protected in his monopoly. . . ." *Pope Manufacturing Co. v. Gormully*, 144 U.S. 224, 234 (1892).

Although this Court invoked an estoppel in 1905 without citing or considering *Pope*'s powerful argument, the doctrine was not to be applied again in this Court until it was revived in *Automatic Radio Manufacturing Co. v. Hazeltine Research, Inc., supra*, which declared, without prolonged analysis, that licensee estoppel was "the general rule." In so holding, the majority ignored the teachings of a series of decisions this Court had rendered during the 45 years since [*United States v.*] *Harvey* [*Steel Co.*, 196 U.S. 310 (1905),] had been decided. During this period, each time a patentee sought to rely upon his estoppel privilege before this Court, the majority created a new exception to permit judicial scrutiny into the validity of the Patent Office's grant. Long before *Hazeltine* was decided, the estoppel doctrine had been so eroded that it could no longer be considered the "general rule," but was only to be invoked in an ever-narrowing set of circumstances.

B

The estoppel rule was first stringently limited in a situation in which the patentee's equities were far more compelling than those presented in the typical licensing arrangement. *Westinghouse Electric & Manufacturing Co. v. Formica Insulation Co.*, 266 U.S. 342 (1924), framed a rule to govern the recurring problem which arises when the original patent owner, after assigning his patent to another for a substantial sum, claims that the patent is worthless because it contains no new ideas. The courts of appeals had traditionally refused to permit such a defense to an infringement action on the ground that it was improper both "to sell and keep the same thing." Nevertheless, *Formica* imposed a limitation upon estoppel which was radically inconsistent with the premises upon which the "general rule" is based. The Court held that while an assignor may not directly attack the validity of a patent by reference to the prior state of the art, he could introduce such evidence to narrow the claims made in the patent. "The distinction seems nice one but seems to be workable." Workable or not, the result proved to be an anomaly: if a patent had some novelty *Formica* permitted the old owner to defend an infringement action by showing that the invention's novel aspects did not extend to include the old owner's products; on the other hand, if a patent had no novelty at all, the old owner could not defend successfully since he would be obliged to launch the direct attack on the patent that *Formica* seemed to forbid. The incongruity of this position compelled at least one court of appeals to carry the logic of the *Formica* exception to its logical conclusion. In 1940 the Seventh Circuit held that a licensee could introduce evidence of the prior art to show that the licensor's claims were not novel at all and thus successfully defend an action for royalties.

In *Scott Paper Co. v. Marcalus Manufacturing Co.*, 326 U.S. 249 (1945), this Court adopted a position similar to the Seventh Circuit's, undermining the basis of patent estoppel even more than *Formica* had done. In *Scott*, the original patent owner had attempted to defend an infringement suit brought by his assignee by proving that his product was a copy of an expired patent. The Court refused to permit the assignee to invoke an estoppel, finding that the policy of the patent laws would be frustrated if a manufacturer was required to pay for the use of information which, under the patent statutes, was the property of all. Chief Justice Stone, for the Court, did not go beyond the precise question presented by a manufacturer who asserted that he was simply copying an expired patent. Nevertheless it was impossible to limit the *Scott* doctrine to such a narrow compass. If patent policy forbids estoppel when the old owner attempts to show that he did no more than copy an expired patent, why should not the old owner be also permitted to show that the invention lacked novelty because it could be found in a technical journal or because it was obvious to one knowledgeable in the art? As Justice Frankfurter's dissent indicated, there were no satisfactory answers to these questions. The *Scott* exception had undermined the very basis of the "general rule."

C

At about the time *Scott* was decided, this Court developed yet another doctrine which was profoundly antithetic to the principles underlying estoppel. In *Sola Electric Co. v. Jefferson Electric Co.*, 317 U.S. 173 (1942), the majority refused to permit a licensor to enforce the license's price-fixing provisions without permitting the licensee to contest the validity of the underlying patent. Since the price-fixing clause was per se illegal but for the existence of a valid patent, this narrow exception could be countenanced without compromising the general estoppel principle. But the *Sola* Court went further: it held that since the patentee had sought to enforce the price-fixing clause, the licensee could also avoid paying royalties if he could show that the patent was invalid. Five years later, the "anti-trust exception" was given an even more extensive scope in the *Katzinger* and *MacGregor* cases [*Edward Katzinger Co. v. Chicago Metallic Manufacturing Co.*, 329 U.S. 394 (1947); *MacGregor v. Westinghouse Electric & Manufacturing Co.*, 329 U.S. 402 (1947)]. Here, licensors were not permitted to invoke an estoppel despite the fact that they sought only to collect their royalties. The mere existence of a price-fixing clause in the license was held to be enough to bring the validity of the patent into question. Thus in the large number of cases in which licensing agreements contained restrictions that were arguably illegal under the anti-trust laws, the doctrine of estoppel was a dead letter. Justice Frankfurter, in dissent, went even further, concluding that *Katzinger* and *MacGregor* had done all but repudiate the estoppel rule: "If a doctrine that was vital law for more than ninety years will be found to have now been deprived of life, we ought at least to give it decent public burial."

D

Lower courts, both state and federal, have also hedged the impact of estoppel by creating exceptions which have indicated recognition of the broader policies pointing to a contrary approach. . . .

III

The uncertain status of licensee estoppel in the case law is a product of judicial efforts to accommodate the competing demands of the common law of contracts and the federal law of patents. On the one hand, the law of contracts forbids a purchaser to repudiate his promises simply because he later becomes dissatisfied with the bargain he has made. On the other hand, federal law requires that all ideas in general circulation be dedicated to the common good unless they are protected by a valid patent. *Sears, Roebuck v. Stiffel Co.*, [376 U.S. 225 (1964)]; *Compco Corp. v. Day-Brite Lighting Inc.*, [376 U.S. 234 (1964)]. When faced with this basic conflict in policy, both this Court and courts throughout the land have naturally sought to develop an intermediate position which somehow would remain responsive to the radically different concerns of the two different worlds of contract and patent. The result has been a failure. Rather than creative compromise, there has been a chaos of conflicting case law, proceeding on inconsistent premises. Before renewing the search for an elusive middle ground, we must reconsider on their own merits the arguments which may properly be advanced on both sides of the estoppel question.

A

It will simplify matters greatly if we first consider the most typical situation in which patent licenses are negotiated. In contrast to the present case, most manufacturers obtain a license after a patent has issued. Since the Patent Office makes an inventor's ideas public when it issues its grant of a limited monopoly, a potential licensee has access to the inventor's ideas even if he does not enter into an agreement with the patent owner. Consequently, a manufacturer gains only two benefits if he chooses to enter a licensing agreement after the patent has issued. First, by accepting a license and paying royalties for a time, the licensee may have avoided the necessity of defending an expensive infringement action during the period when he may be least able to afford one. Second, the existence of an unchallenged patent may deter others from attempting to compete with the licensee.

Under ordinary contract principles the mere fact that some benefit is received is enough to require the enforcement of the contract, regardless of the validity of the underlying patent. Nevertheless, if one tests this result by the standard of good-faith commercial dealing, it seems far from satisfactory. For the simple contract approach entirely ignores the position of the licensor who is seeking to invoke the court's assistance on his behalf. Consider, for example, the equities of the licensor who has obtained his patent through a fraud on the Patent Office. It is difficult to perceive why good faith requires that courts should permit him to recover royalties despite his licensee's attempts to show that the patent is invalid.

Even in the more typical cases, not involving conscious wrongdoing, the licensor's equities are far from compelling. A patent, in the last analysis, simply represents a legal conclusion reached by the Patent Office. Moreover, the legal conclusion is predicated on factors as to which reasonable men can differ widely. Yet the Patent Office is often obliged to reach its decision in an ex parte proceeding, without the aid of the arguments which could be advanced by parties interested in proving patent invalidity. Consequently, it does not seem to us to be unfair to require a patentee to defend the Patent Office's judgment when his licensee places the question in issue, especially since the licensor's case is buttressed by the presumption of validity which attaches to his patent. Thus, although licensee estoppel may be consistent with the letter of contractual doctrine, we cannot say that it is compelled by the spirit of contract law, which seeks to balance the claims of promisor and promisee in accord with the requirements of good faith.

Surely the equities of the licensor do not weigh very heavily when they are balanced against the important public interest in permitting full and free competition in the use of ideas which are in reality a part of the public domain. Licensees may often be the only individuals with enough economic incentive to challenge the patentability of an inventor's discovery. If they are muzzled, the public may continually be required to pay tribute to would-be monopolists without need or justification. We think it plain that the technical requirements of contract doctrine must give way before the demands of the public interest in the typical situation involving the negotiation of a license after a patent has issued.

We are satisfied that *Automatic Radio Co. v. Hazeltine Research, Inc.*, itself the product of a clouded history, should no longer be regarded as sound law in respect of its "estoppel" holding, and that holding is now overruled.

B

The case before us, however, presents a far more complicated estoppel problem than the one which arises in the most common licensing context. The problem arises out of the fact that Lear obtained its license in 1955, more than four years before Adkins received his 1960 patent. Indeed, from the very outset of the relationship, Lear obtained special access to Adkins' ideas in return for its promise to pay satisfactory compensation.

Thus, during the lengthy period in which Adkins was attempting to obtain a patent, Lear gained an important benefit not generally obtained by the typical licensee. For until a patent issues, a potential licensee may not learn his licensor's ideas simply by requesting the information from the Patent Office. During the time the inventor is seeking patent protection, the governing federal statute requires the Patent Office to hold an inventor's patent application in confidence. If a potential licensee hopes to use the ideas contained in a secret patent application, he must deal with the inventor himself, unless the inventor chooses to publicize his ideas to the world at large. By promising to pay Adkins royalties from the very outset of their relationship, Lear gained immediate access to ideas which it may well not have learned until the Patent Office published the details of Adkins' invention in 1960. At the core of this case, then, is the difficult question whether federal patent policy bars a State from enforcing a contract regulating access to an unpatented secret idea.

Adkins takes an extreme position on this question. The inventor does not merely argue that since Lear obtained privileged access to his ideas before 1960, the company should be required to pay royalties accruing before 1960 regardless of the validity of the patent which ultimately issued. He also argues that since Lear obtained special benefits before 1960, it should also pay royalties during the entire patent period (1960-1977), without regard to the validity of the Patent Office's grant. We cannot accept so broad an argument.

Adkins' position would permit inventors to negotiate all important licenses during the lengthy period while their applications were still pending at the Patent Office, thereby disabling entirely all those who have the strongest incentive in showing that a patent is worthless. While the equities supporting Adkins' position are somewhat more appealing than those supporting the typical licensor, we cannot say that there is enough of a difference to justify such a substantial impairment of overriding federal policy.

Nor can we accept a second argument which may be advanced to support Adkins' claim to at least a portion of his post-patent royalties, regardless of the validity of the Patent Office grant. The terms of the 1955 agreement provide that royalties are to be paid until such time as "the patent is held invalid," and the fact remains that the question of patent validity has not been finally determined in this case. Thus, it may be suggested that although Lear must be allowed to raise the question of patent validity in the present lawsuit, it must also be required to comply with its contract and continue to pay royalties until its claim is finally vindicated in the courts.

The parties' contract, however, is no more controlling on this issue than is the State's doctrine of estoppel, which is also rooted in contract principles. The decisive question is whether overriding federal policies would be significantly frustrated if licensees could be required to continue to pay royalties during the time they are challenging patent validity in the courts.

It seems to us that such a requirement would be inconsistent with the aims of federal patent policy. Enforcing this contractual provision would give the licensor an additional economic incentive to devise every conceivable dilatory tactic in an effort to postpone the day of final judicial reckoning. We can perceive no reason to encourage dilatory court tactics in this way. Moreover, the cost of prosecuting slow-moving trial proceedings and defending an inevitable appeal might well deter many licensees from attempting to prove patent invalidity in the courts. The deterrence effect would be particularly severe in the many scientific fields in which invention is proceeding at a rapid rate. In these areas, a patent may well become obsolete long before its 17-year term has expired. If a licensee has reason to believe that he will replace a patented idea with a new one in the near future, he will have little incentive to initiate lengthy court proceedings, unless he is freed from liability at least from the time he refuses to pay the contractual royalties. Lastly, enforcing this contractual provision would undermine the strong federal policy favoring the full and free use of ideas in the public domain. For all these reasons, we hold that Lear must be permitted to avoid the payment of all royalties accruing after Adkins' 1960 patent issued if Lear can prove patent invalidity.

C

Adkins' claim to contractual royalties accruing before the 1960 patent issued is, however, a much more difficult one, since it squarely raises the question whether, and to what extent, the States may protect the owners of unpatented inventions who are willing to disclose their ideas to manufacturers only upon payment of royalties. [We] have concluded, after much consideration, that even though an important question of federal law underlines this phase of the controversy, we should not now attempt to define in even a limited way the extent, if any, to which the States may properly act to enforce the contractual rights of inventors of unpatented secret ideas. Given the difficulty and importance of this task, it should be undertaken only after the state courts have, after fully focused inquiry, determined the extent to which they will respect the contractual rights of such inventors in the future. Indeed, on remand, the California courts may well reconcile the competing demands of patent and contract law in a way which would not warrant further review in this Court.

The judgment of the Supreme Court of California is vacated and the case is remanded to that court for further proceedings not inconsistent with this opinion.

NOTES

1. Although *Lear* has never been overruled, its reasoning has not been expansively applied. For a discussion of subsequent case law, see Chapter 8.

2. The basic premise in *Lear* is that a federal policy exists that favors invalidation of patents granted by the Patent Office. Why should such policy exist?

3. Among the cases on which *Lear* relied were the 1964 decisions in *Sears, Roebuck & Co. v. Stiffel,* 376 U.S. 225 (1964), and *Compco Corp. v. Day-Brite Lighting, Inc.,* 376 U.S. 234 (1964). In those cases, the Supreme Court used patent policy conflict preemption to invalidate state-law judgments of unfair competition based on allegations that the defendants copied mechanical devices, the patents as to which had been previously invalidated. The Court held that state law could not enforce a purported right to bar copying where federal patent rules left the copied article unprotected, stating that: "[to] forbid copying [under state law] would interfere with the federal policy . . . of allowing free access to copy whatever the federal patent and copyright laws leave in the public domain." *Sears* and *Compco* adopted a negative policy conflict analysis based on supposed public-domain policies contained in patent law. The five years encompassing *Sears, Compco* and *Lear* were the high water mark of federal policy preemption associated with intellectual property and state law.

The defendants in *Sears* and *Compco* did not breach a license, confidential, or any other relationship with the plaintiff. Some of the language used in the Court's opinions, however, seemed to raise questions about whether federal preemption might also apply to such relationships. Ten years later the Court decided *Kewanee Oil Co. v. Bicron Corp.,* 416 U.S. 470 (1974). *Kewanee* dealt with trade secret misappropriation of a crystal structure that was within the subject matter of patent law, but probably not patentable. The trade secret owner had not sought patent protection. The trial court granted an injunction against former employees based on trade secret concepts involving a breach of a confidential relationship. The Supreme Court affirmed that ruling. The Court commented that in the absence of express preemption, conflict preemption occurs only if state law "erects an 'obstacle to the accomplishment' of the objectives of Congress." Trade secrecy law deals with the maintenance of standards of commercial ethics and encouraging invention. These objectives differ from, but do not conflict with federal patent law policy.

ARONSON v. QUICK POINT PENCIL CO.
440 U.S. 257 (1979)

MR. CHIEF JUSTICE BURGER delivered the opinion of the Court.

We granted certiorari to consider whether federal patent law pre-empts state contract law so as to preclude enforcement of a contract to pay royalties to a patent applicant, on sales of articles embodying the putative invention, for so long as the contracting party sells them, if a patent is not granted.

(1)

In October 1955 the petitioner, Mrs. Jane Aronson, filed an application, Serial No. 542677, for a patent on a new form of keyholder. Although ingenious, the design was so simple that it readily could be copied unless it was protected by patent. In June 1956, while the patent application was pending, Mrs. Aronson negotiated a contract with the respondent, Quick Point Pencil Co., for the manufacture and sale of the keyholder.

The contract was embodied in two documents. In the first, a letter from Quick Point to Mrs. Aronson, Quick Point agreed to pay Mrs. Aronson a royalty of 5% of the selling price in return for "the exclusive right to make and sell keyholders of the type shown in your application, Serial No. 542677." The letter further provided that the parties would consult one another concerning the steps to be taken "[i]n the event of any infringement."

The contract did not require Quick Point to manufacture the keyholder. Mrs. Aronson received a $750 advance on royalties and was entitled to rescind the exclusive license if Quick Point did not sell a million keyholders by the end of 1957. Quick Point retained the right to cancel the agreement whenever "the volume of sales does not meet our expectations." The duration of the agreement was not otherwise prescribed.

A contemporaneous document provided that if Mrs. Aronson's patent application was "not allowed within five (5) years, Quick Point Pencil Co. [would pay] two and one half percent (2 1/2%) of sales [so] long as you [Quick Point] continue to sell same."

In June 1961, when Mrs. Aronson had failed to obtain a patent on the keyholder within the five years specified in the agreement, Quick Point asserted its contractual right to reduce royalty payments to 2 1/2% of sales. In September of that year the Board of Patent Appeals issued a final rejection of the application on the ground that the keyholder was not patentable, and Mrs. Aronson did not appeal. Quick Point continued to pay reduced royalties to her for 14 years thereafter.

The market was more receptive to the keyholder's novelty and utility than the Patent Office. By September 1975 Quick Point had made sales in excess of $7 million and paid Mrs. Aronson royalties totaling $203,963.84; sales were continuing to rise. However, while Quick Point was able to pre-empt the market in the earlier years and was long the only manufacturer of the Aronson keyholder, copies began to appear in the late 1960's. Quick Point's competitors, of course, were not required to pay royalties for their use of the design. Quick Point's share of the Aronson keyholder market has declined during the past decade.

(2)

In November 1975 Quick Point commenced an action in the United States District Court for a declaratory judgment, pursuant to 28 U.S.C. § 2201, that the royalty agreement was unenforceable. Quick Point asserted that state law which might otherwise make the contract enforceable was preempted by federal patent law. This is the only issue presented to us for decision.

(3)

On this record it is clear that the parties contracted with full awareness of both the pendency of a patent application and the possibility that a patent might not issue. The clause de-escalating the royalty by half in the event no patent issued within five years makes that crystal clear. Quick Point apparently placed a significant value on exploiting the basic novelty of the device, even if no patent issued; its success demonstrates that this judgment was well founded. Assuming, *arguendo,* that the initial letter and the commitment to pay a 5% royalty was subject to federal patent law, the provision relating to the 2 1/2% royalty was explicitly independent of federal law. The cases and principles relied on by the Court of Appeals and Quick Point do not bear on a contract that does not rely on a patent, particularly where, as here, the contracting parties agreed expressly as to alternative obligations if no patent should issue.

Commercial agreements traditionally are the domain of state law. State law is not displaced merely because the contract relates to intellectual property which may or may not be patentable; the states are free to regulate the use of such intellectual property in any manner not inconsistent with federal law. *Kewanee Oil Co. v. Bicron Corp.,* 416 U.S. 470, 479 (1974); *see Goldstein v. California,* 412 U.S. 546 (1973). In this as in other fields, the question of whether federal law pre-empts state law "involves a consideration of whether that law 'stands as an obstacle to the accomplishment and execution of the full purposes and objectives of Congress.'" If it does not, state law governs.

In *Kewanee Oil Co.,* we reviewed the purposes of the federal patent system. First, patent law seeks to foster and reward invention; second, it promotes disclosure of inventions, to stimulate further innovation and to permit the public to practice the invention once the patent expires; third, the stringent requirements for patent protection seek to assure that ideas in the public domain remain there for the free use of the public.

Enforcement of Quick Point's agreement with Mrs. Aronson is not inconsistent with any of these aims. Permitting inventors to make enforceable agreements licensing the use of their inventions in return for royalties provides an additional incentive to invention. Similarly, encouraging Mrs. Aronson to make arrangements for the manufacture of her keyholder furthers the federal policy of disclosure of inventions; these simple devices display the novel idea which they embody wherever they are seen.

Quick Point argues that enforcement of such contracts conflicts with the federal policy against withdrawing ideas from the public domain and discourages recourse to the federal patent system by allowing states to extend "perpetual protection to articles too lacking in novelty to merit any patent at all under federal constitutional standards," *Sears, Roebuck & Co. v. Stiffel Co.,* 376 U.S. 225, 232 (1964).

We find no merit in this contention. Enforcement of the agreement does not withdraw any idea from the public domain. The design for the keyholder was not in the public domain before Quick Point obtained its license to manufacture it. In negotiating the agreement, Mrs. Aronson disclosed the design in confidence. Had Quick Point tried to exploit the design in breach of that confidence, it would have risked legal liability. It is equally clear that the design entered the public domain as a result of the manufacture and sale of the keyholders under the contract.

Requiring Quick Point to bear the burden of royalties for the use of the design is no more inconsistent with federal patent law than any of the other costs involved in being the first to introduce a new product to the market, such as outlays for research and development, and marketing and promotional expenses. For reasons which Quick Point's experience with the Aronson keyholder demonstrate, innovative entrepreneurs have usually found such costs to be well worth paying.

Finally, enforcement of this agreement does not discourage anyone from seeking a patent. Mrs. Aronson attempted to obtain a patent for over five years. It is quite true that had she succeeded, she would have received a 5% royalty only on keyholders sold during the 17-year life of the patent. Offsetting the limited terms of royalty payments, she would have received twice as much per dollar of Quick Point's sales, and both she and Quick Point could have licensed any others who produced the same keyholder. Which course would have produced the greater yield to the contracting parties is a matter of speculation; the parties resolved the uncertainties by their bargain.

(4)

No decision of this Court relating to patents justifies relieving Quick Point of its contract obligations. We have held that a state may not forbid the copying of an idea in the public domain which does not meet the requirements for federal patent protection. *Compco Corp. v. Day-Brite Lighting, Inc.,* 376 U.S. 234 (1964); *Sears, Roebuck & Co. v. Stiffel Co., supra.* Enforcement of Quick Point's agreement, however, does not prevent anyone from copying the keyholder. It merely requires Quick Point to pay the consideration which it promised in return for the use of a novel device which enabled it to pre-empt the market.

In *Lear, Inc. v. Adkins,* 395 U.S. 653 (1969), we held that a person licensed to use a patent may challenge the validity of the patent, and that a licensee who establishes that the patent is invalid need not pay the royalties accrued under the licensing agreement subsequent to the issuance of the patent. Both holdings relied on the desirability of encouraging licensees to challenge the validity of patents, to further the strong federal policy that only inventions which meet the rigorous requirements of patentability shall be withdrawn from the public domain. Accordingly, neither the holding nor the rationale of *Lear* controls when no patent has issued, and no ideas have been withdrawn from public use.

Enforcement of the royalty agreement here is also consistent with . . . *Brulotte v. Thys Co.,* 379 U.S. 29 (1964). There, we held that the obligation to pay royalties in return for the use of a patented device may not extend beyond the life of the patent. The principle underlying that holding was simply that the monopoly granted *under a patent* cannot lawfully be used to "negotiate with the leverage of that monopoly." The Court emphasized that to "use that leverage to project those royalty payments beyond the life of the patent is analogous to an effort to enlarge the monopoly of the patent." *Id.* at 33. Here the reduced royalty which is challenged, far from being negotiated "with the leverage" of a patent, rested on the contingency that no patent would issue within five years.

No doubt a pending patent application gives the applicant some additional bargaining power for purposes of negotiating a royalty agreement. The pending application allows the inventor to hold out the hope of an exclusive right to exploit the idea, as well as the threat that the other party will be prevented from using the idea for 17 years. However, the amount of leverage arising from a patent application depends on how likely the parties consider it to be that a valid patent will issue. Here, where no patent ever issued, the record is entirely clear that the parties assigned a substantial likelihood to that contingency, since they specifically provided for a reduced royalty in the event no patent issued within five years.

This case does not require us to draw the line between what constitutes abuse of a pending application and what does not. It is clear that whatever role the pending application played in the negotiation of the 5% royalty, it played no part in the contract to pay the 2 1/2% royalty indefinitely.

Our holding in *Kewanee Oil Co.* puts to rest the contention that federal law pre-empts and renders unenforceable the contract made by these parties. There we held that state law forbidding the misappropriation of trade secrets was not pre-empted by federal patent law. We observed:

> Certainly the patent policy of encouraging invention is not disturbed by the existence of another form of incentive to invention. In this respect the two systems [patent and trade secret law] are not and never would be in conflict.

Enforcement of this royalty agreement is even less offensive to federal patent policies than state law protecting trade secrets. The most commonly accepted definition of trade secrets is restricted to confidential information which is not disclosed in the normal process of exploitation. *See Restatement of Torts* § 757,

Comment *b*, p. 5 (1939). Accordingly, the exploitation of trade secrets under state law may not satisfy the federal policy in favor of disclosure, whereas disclosure is inescapable in exploiting a device like the Aronson keyholder.

Enforcement of these contractual obligations, freely undertaken in arm's-length negotiation and with no fixed reliance on a patent or a probable patent grant, will

> encourage invention in areas where patent law does not reach, and will prompt the independent innovator to proceed with the discovery and exploitation of his invention. Competition is fostered and the public is not deprived of the use of valuable, if not quite patentable, invention.

The device which is the subject of this contract ceased to have any secrecy as soon as it was first marketed, yet when the contract was negotiated the inventiveness and novelty were sufficiently apparent to induce an experienced novelty manufacturer to agree to pay for the opportunity to be first in the market. Federal patent law is not a barrier to such a contract. REVERSED.

NOTES

1. Are *Lear, Kewanee*, and *Aronson* consistent?

2. The Supreme Court returned to these issues in a non-contractual setting in *Bonito Boats, Inc. v. Thunder Craft Boats, Inc.*, 489 U.S. 141 (1989). The Court there invalidated a state law that barred all persons from duplicating vessel hulls or component parts by means of any "direct molding process" from vessels or parts distributed to the public. The Florida statute did not require any contract or other relationship between the parties — it was a property rights statute. The state attempted to create rights for the hull design that were good "against the world." The Court held that the Florida statute created *property* protections for designers good against all other persons in a manner left free from property rights control under patent law and that this created a conflict with federal policy. As the Court stated, "The Florida law [improperly] prohibits the entire public from engaging in a form of reverse engineering of a product in the public domain." Subsequently, Congress enacted similar protections as a matter of federal law.

III. PATENT MISUSE

MORTON SALT CO. v. G.S. SUPPIGER CO.
314 U.S. 488 (1942)

MR. CHIEF JUSTICE STONE delivered the opinion of the Court.

Respondent brought this suit in the district court for an injunction and an accounting for infringement of its Patent No. 2,060,645 . . . on a machine for depositing salt tablets, a device said to be useful in the canning industry for adding predetermined amounts of salt in tablet form to the contents of the cans.

Upon petitioner's motion, [the] trial court, without passing on the issues of validity and infringement, granted summary judgment dismissing the complaint. It took the ground that respondent was making use of the patent to restrain the sale of salt tablets in competition with its own sale of unpatented tablets, by requiring licensees to use with the patented machines only tablets sold by respondent. The Court of Appeals for the Seventh Circuit reversed. . . .

Both respondent's wholly owned subsidiary and the petitioner manufacture and sell salt tablets used and useful in the canning trade. The tablets have a particular configuration rendering them capable of convenient use in respondent's patented machines. Petitioner makes and leases to canners unpatented salt deposition machines, charged to infringe respondent's patent. For reasons we indicate later, nothing turns on the fact that petitioner also competes with respondent in the sale of the tablets, and we may assume for purposes of this case that petitioner is doing no more than making and leasing the alleged infringing machines. The principal business of respondent's subsidiary, from which its profits are derived, is the sale of salt tablets. In connection with this business, and as an adjunct to it, respondent leases its patented machines to commercial canners, some two hundred in all, under licenses to use the machines upon condition and with the agreement of the licensees that only the subsidiary's salt tablets be used with the leased machines.

It thus appears that respondent is making use of its patent monopoly to restrain competition in the marketing of unpatented articles, salt tablets, for use with the patented machines, and is aiding in the creation of a limited monopoly in the tablets not within that granted by the patent. A patent operates to create and grant to the patentee an exclusive right to make, use and vend the particular device described and claimed in the patent. But a patent affords no immunity for a monopoly not within the grant and the use of it to suppress competition in the sale of an unpatented article may deprive the patentee of the aid of a court of equity to restrain an alleged infringement by one who is a competitor. It is the established rule that a patentee who has granted a license on condition that the patented invention be used by the licensee only with unpatented materials furnished by the licensor, may not restrain as a contributory infringer one who sells to the licensee like materials for like use. . . .

The grant to the inventor of the special privilege of a patent monopoly carries out a public policy adopted by the Constitution and laws of the United States, "to promote the Progress of Science and useful Arts, by securing for limited Times to . . . Inventors the exclusive Right" to their "new and useful" inventions. But the public policy which includes inventions within the granted monopoly excludes from it all that is not embraced in the invention. It equally forbids the use of the patent to secure an exclusive right or limited monopoly not granted by the Patent Office and which it is contrary to public policy to grant.

It is a principle of general application that courts, and especially courts of equity, may appropriately withhold their aid where the plaintiff is using the right asserted contrary to the public interest. Respondent argues that this doctrine is limited in its application to those cases where the patentee seeks to restrain contributory infringement by the sale to licensees of competing unpatented articles, while here respondent seeks to restrain petitioner from a direct infringement, the manufacture and sale of the salt tablet depositor. It is said that the equitable maxim that a party seeking the aid of a court of equity must come into court with clean hands applies only to the plaintiff's wrongful conduct in the particular act or transaction which raises the equity, enforcement of which is sought; that where, as here, the patentee seeks to restrain the manufacture or use of the patented device, his conduct in using the patent to restrict competition in the sale of salt tablets does not foreclose him from seeking relief limited to an injunction against the manufacture and sale of the infringing machine alone.

Undoubtedly equity does not demand that its suitors shall have led blameless lives; but additional considerations must be taken into account where maintenance of the suit concerns the public interest as well as the private interests of suitors. Where the patent is used as a means of restraining competition with the patentee's sale of an unpatented product, the successful prosecution of an infringement suit even against one who is not a competitor in such sale is a powerful aid to the maintenance of the attempted monopoly of the unpatented article, and is thus a contributing factor in thwarting the public policy underlying the grant of the patent. Maintenance and enlargement of the attempted monopoly of the unpatented article are dependent to some extent upon persuading the public of the validity of the patent, which the infringement suit is intended to establish. Equity may rightly withhold its assistance from such a use of the patent by declining to entertain a suit for infringement, and should do so at least until it is made to appear that the improper practice has been abandoned and that the consequences of the misuse of the patent have been dissipated.

The reasons for barring the prosecution of such a suit against one who is not a competitor with the patentee in the sale of the unpatented product are fundamentally the same as those which preclude an infringement suit against a licensee who has violated a condition of the license by using with the licensed machine a competing unpatented article, or against a vendee of a patented or copyrighted article for violation of a condition for the maintenance of resale prices. It is the adverse effect upon the public interest of a successful infringement suit in conjunction with the patentee's course of conduct which disqualifies him to maintain the suit, regardless of whether the particular defendant has suffered from the misuse of the patent. Similarly equity will deny relief for infringement of a trademark where the plaintiff is misrepresenting to the public the nature of his product either by the trademark itself or by his label. The patentee, like these other holders of an exclusive privilege granted in the furtherance of a public policy, may not claim protection of his grant by the courts where it is being used to subvert that policy.

It is unnecessary to decide whether respondent has violated the Clayton Act, for we conclude that in any event the maintenance of the present suit to restrain petitioner's manufacture or sale of the alleged infringing machines is contrary to public policy and that the district court rightly dismissed the complaint for want of equity. REVERSED.

USM CORP. v. SPS TECHNOLOGIES, INC.
694 F.2d 505 (7th Cir. 1982)

POSNER, CIRCUIT JUDGE.

SPS, a manufacturer of industrial fasteners, owned a patent, issued in 1963, on a patch-type self-locking industrial fastener. In 1969 it sued USM, a competing manufacturer of fasteners, for infringement. After a trial on the issue whether USM had a valid license under the patent by virtue of a grant-back clause in a licensing agreement between the parties, the district court held that USM did not have a valid license. The parties then settled the case by entry of a consent judgment in which USM acknowledged that the patent was valid and had been infringed. As part of the settlement SPS granted USM a license which allowed USM to continue using the patent but required it to pay royalties to SPS.

In 1974, three years after SPS's suit had been settled, USM brought the present suit, seeking to invalidate SPS's patent and get back the royalties it had paid since the settlement. . . . USM's suit not only challenges the validity of the patent but also alleges that certain terms that first appeared in the license agreement entered into at the termination of the first suit constitute patent misuse. As these terms could not have been challenged in the first suit, USM's challenge to them cannot be barred by res judicata. The district court granted summary judgment for SPS. . . . USM's appeal brings this ruling up to us along with the rulings on fraud and res judicata. . . .

The . . . issue is whether SPS committed patent misuse by including a differential royalty schedule in the license agreement entered into as part of the settlement of the earlier suit. The agreement requires USM to remit to SPS 25 percent of any royalties it obtains by sublicensing SPS's patent, except that if USM should happen to sublicense any of four companies that SPS had previously licensed directly USM must remit 75 percent of the royalties obtained from the sublicensee(s).

The doctrine of patent misuse has been described as an equitable concept designed to prevent a patent owner from using the patent in a manner contrary to public policy. *Morton Salt Co. v. G.S. Suppiger Co.*, 314 U.S. 488 (1942). This is too vague a formulation to be useful; taken seriously it would put all patent rights at hazard; and in application the doctrine has largely been confined to a handful of specific practices by which the patentee seemed to be trying to "extend" his patent grant beyond its statutory limits. An early example was fixing the price at which the purchaser of the patented item could resell it. The courts reasoned (in rather a circular fashion, one must admit) that once the patent owner had given up title to the patented item his patent rights were at an end, and any further restriction on the purchaser would extend the patent beyond its statutory bounds. Similar thinking lies behind the most common application of the doctrine, which is to prevent the patent owner from requiring his licensees to buy an unpatented staple item used with the patented device — for example, ink with a mimeograph machine. *See generally Dawson Chem. Co. v. Rohm & Haas Co.,* 448 U.S. 176, 188-93 (1980).

Both examples — resale price maintenance and tying — suggest an overlap between misuse and antitrust principles. But although resale price maintenance by patentees was condemned as misuse shortly after *Dr. Miles Medical Co. v. John D. Park & Sons Co.,* 220 U.S. 373 (1911), held that the Sherman Act forbade resale price maintenance in nonpatent cases, and patent tie-ins were condemned as misuse shortly after the enactment of the tying provision (section 3) of the Clayton Act, in both instances the condemnation of the patentee's conduct was based on the doctrine of patent misuse rather than on antitrust law. More recently the doctrine has been used to forbid the patentee to require his licensees to pay royalties beyond the expiration of the patent, *Brulotte v. Thys Co.,* 379 U.S. 29 (1964), or to measure royalties by the sales of unpatented end products containing the patented item, or to require licensees not to make any items competing with the patented item.

As an original matter one might question whether any of these practices really "extends" the patent. The patentee who insists on limiting the freedom of his purchaser or licensee — whether to price, to use complementary inputs of the purchaser's choice, or to make competing items — will have to compensate the purchaser for the restriction by charging a lower price for the use of the patent. If, for example, the patent owner requires the licensee to agree to continue paying royalties after the patent expires, he will not be able to get him to agree to pay as big a royalty before the patent expires.

In all of these cases the patentee's total income may be higher — why else would he impose the restriction? But there is nothing wrong with trying to make as much money as you can from a patent. True, a tie-in can be a method of price discrimination. It enables the patent owner to vary the amount he charges for the use of the patent by the intensity of each user's demand for the patent (e.g., the mimeograph), as measured by the user's consumption of the tied product (e.g., the ink). But since, as we shall see, there is no principle that patent owners may not engage in price discrimination, it is unclear why one form of discrimination, the tie-in, alone is forbidden.

But whether decided rightly or wrongly these are all cases where the license purports to enlarge the licensee's obligations beyond the limits of the patent grant. There is nothing of that sort here. But we must also consider whether the patent-misuse doctrine goes beyond these specific practices and constitutes a general code of patent licensing distinct from antitrust law.

The doctrine arose before there was any significant body of federal antitrust law, and reached maturity long before that law (a product very largely of free interpretation of unclear statutory language) attained its present broad scope. Since the antitrust laws as currently interpreted reach every practice that could impair competition substantially, it is not easy to define a separate role for a doctrine also designed to prevent an anticompetitive practice — the abuse of a patent monopoly. One possibility is that the doctrine of patent misuse, unlike antitrust law, condemns any patent licensing practice that is even trivially anticompetitive, at least if it has no socially beneficial effects. This might seem to explain cases such as *Duplan Corp. v. Deering Milliken, Inc.,*

444 F.Supp. 648, 697 (D.S.C.1977), *aff'd in relevant part*, 594 F.2d 979 (4th Cir.1979), which held that a patent tie-in agreement is misuse per se unless the patentee shows that he had some nonmonopolistic reason for the tie-in, such as protection of goodwill. To prove a tie-in prima facie unlawful under the antitrust laws all you have to show is that the defendant has some economic power in the market for the tying product, *United States Steel Corp. v. Fortner Enterprises, Inc.,* 429 U.S. 610 (1977), and *Duplan* eliminates this requirement in misuse cases. But if a patentee has no market power (and, of course, not every patent confers market power), he cannot use a tie-in to practice price discrimination, which presupposes market power. Much less can he lever his way into a dominant position in the market for the tied product. The logical presumption in such a case is that the tie-in promotes efficiency — and there is no lack of hypotheses as to how it might do that. *See* BORK, THE ANTITRUST PARADOX 375-81 (1978). It is hard to understand why in these circumstances, where if any presumption is warranted it is that the tie-in promotes efficiency rather than reduces competition, the burden of proof on the issue of misuse should be shifted to the patentee.

But probably cases like *Duplan* — which was, like *Motion Picture Patents Co.* [*v. Universal Film Mfg. Co.*, 243 U.S. 502, 517-18, 61 L. Ed. 871, 37 S. Ct. 416 (1917)], a tie-in case — are best understood simply as applications of the patent-misuse doctrine within its conventional, rather stereotyped boundaries. Outside those boundaries there is increasing convergence of patent-misuse analysis with standard antitrust analysis. One still finds plenty of statements in judicial opinions that less evidence of anticompetitive effect is required in a misuse case than in an antitrust case. But apart from the conventional applications of the doctrine we have found no cases where standards different from those of antitrust law were actually applied to yield different results. . . .

If misuse claims are not tested by conventional antitrust principles, by what principles shall they be tested? Our law is not rich in alternative concepts of monopolistic abuse; and it is rather late in the day to try to develop one without in the process subjecting the rights of patent holders to debilitating uncertainty.

We come at last to the particulars of USM's charge of patent misuse, which the district court dismissed on summary judgment and which for the reasons just explained we think must be evaluated under antitrust principles. The basic charge is simply that SPS has set a discriminatory royalty schedule. But no general principle of antitrust law forbids charging different prices to different customers, what is often but loosely called "price discrimination." (The technical economic definition of price discrimination is disparity of price-cost ratios rather than of prices alone.) It is not illegal per se, even under section 2(a) of the Clayton Act as amended by the Robinson-Patman Act, 15 U.S.C. § 13(a). It might in a particular case be condemned as an attempt to monopolize or as an act of monopolization under section 2 of the Sherman Act, 15 U. S.C. § 2, or as a violation of the Rule of Reason under section 1 of that Act, but USM has made no effort to prove the elements of any of these offenses.

Specifically, there is no antitrust prohibition against a patent owner's using price discrimination to maximize his income from the patent. . . .

USM has made no offer to prove that competition in the manufacture or sale of the products made by SPS's licensees and sublicensees (corresponding to the shrimp peelers) would be greater but for the royalty differential; and it is unlikely that it would be. The main differential is in the amount of royalties retained by USM rather than in the amount paid by the sublicensees. True, there potentially is some differential in that amount. While the usual royalty rate is 4 percent, of which USM retains 3 percent and SPS gets 1 percent, if USM sublicenses the four companies already licensed by SPS and those companies do not drop their SPS licenses, the royalty rate rises to 5 percent, with USM retaining 1 percent and SPS getting the other 4 percent. But a one percent cost difference is too small to give rise to an inference of significant competitive effect.

Conceivably the much larger difference between the amount of royalties retained by USM and the amount retained by SPS could affect competition not among the sublicensees but between these two firms. USM presented evidence that its technology embodying SPS's patent was superior to SPS's own technology and that SPS had imposed the royalty retention differential because it knew that without it USM would outcompete SPS to license the four companies. Even if this were true, it would not get USM very far in making out an antitrust case; as the district court pointed out, the essence of the patent grant is to allow the patentee to exclude competition in the use of the patented invention or, within broad limits not apparently exceeded here, to license competitors only on such terms as he sees fit. In any event, USM made no effort to present evidence of actual or probable anticompetitive effect in a relevant market, as is required in every Rule of Reason antitrust case in the Seventh Circuit. There is no argument that the royalty differential is unlawful per se. Patent licensing agreements between competitors are sometimes struck down under antitrust law, of course, but only upon proof of an anticompetitive effect beyond that implicit in the grant of the patent. *See* Priest, *Cartels and Patent License Arrangements,* 20 J. LAW & ECON. 309 (1977).

Moreover, the licensing agreement entitles the four companies licensed directly by SPS to obtain a sublicense from USM on the same terms as USM's other sublicensees. If USM's technology really were better than SPS's — enough better at any rate to make it worth their while to pay an additional one percent royalty to be able to use it — the four companies would have taken up their right to get sublicenses from USM. That USM would have been worse off if they had done so than it would have been had it negotiated a different licensing agreement with SPS in settlement of the earlier litigation is not in itself a basis for finding a violation of the antitrust laws. Those laws are solicitous not of the individual firm but of the competitive process. When, four years into the case [USM] had presented no evidence of actual or probable anticompetitive effect, the dismissal of its misuse claim on a motion for summary judgment was proper

The fact that the four direct licensees of SPS had the right at little or no additional cost to demand sublicenses from USM casts doubt, moreover, on USM's explanation of why SPS imposed the royalty retention differential. An alternative explanation is supplied in a deposition submitted by SPS in support of its motion for summary judgment, though not referred to by the district court. The deposition suggests that the royalty retention differential was an effort to overcome a "free rider" problem. SPS rather than USM had licensed the four companies in question and wanted a fair return on its efforts in doing so. There are costs to lining up licensees, as USM itself has emphasized in contending that 1 percent is too little to compensate it for sublicensing SPS's four direct licensees. Otherwise SPS would not allow USM to keep 75 percent of the royalties on sublicenses obtained by USM. That is compensation for USM's efforts in arranging for the use of the patent. It is overcompensation if the efforts are SPS's, as apparently was the case with the four companies in question; if, in other words, USM wants to reap where SPS has sown. In these circumstances the royalty differential would not even be "discriminatory" in any interesting sense. And antitrust law increasingly is tolerant of contractual arrangements that reduce free-rider problems and thereby increase competition (here, competition to line up patent users).

Admittedly there is irony in our recitation of the reasons that the challenged features of the licensing agreement may actually be procompetitive and in any event are not anticompetitive, when the district court found, in findings that we have not reviewed, that the patent was procured by fraud and was therefore invalid. If the patent really is invalid, and well it may be, the licensing agreement may be altogether more sinister than our discussion implies; USM and SPS are, after all, competitors. But unless we are to overrule [*American Equipment Corp. v.*] *Wikomi* [*Mfg. Co.*, 630 F.2d 544 (7th Cir. 1980),] which we have no mind to do, we must approach the misuse issue on the assumption that the patent is valid, for the defense of res judicata prevents USM from showing the contrary. Of course nothing we say in this opinion is intended to prejudge any other challenge that may be brought against SPS's patent; and, in any event, the patent has now expired, and can no longer restrain trade.

To sum up, we vacate the order of the district court holding SPS's patent invalid and granting USM other relief, and otherwise we affirm the orders appealed from, with costs in this court to SPS.

NOTES

1. *Mallinckrodt, Inc. v. Medipart, Inc.*, 976 F.2d 700 (Fed. Cir. 1992), dealt with a case in which the district court held that a "single use only" notice on a product can not be enforced by suit for patent infringement. The court said:

> The district court did not decide whether the form of the "single use only" notice was legally sufficient to constitute a license or condition of sale from Mallinckrodt to the hospitals. . . . Instead, the district court held that no restriction whatsoever could be imposed under the patent law, whether or not the restriction was enforceable under some other law, and whether or not this was a first sale to a purchaser with notice.

The court concluded that this "ruling is incorrect, for if Mallinckrodt's restriction was a valid condition of the sale, then . . . it was not excluded from enforcement under the patent law."

> The enforceability of restrictions on the use of patented goods derives from the patent grant, which is in classical terms of property: the right

to exclude. . . . The district court's ruling that Mallinckrodt's restriction on reuse was unenforceable was an application of the doctrine of patent misuse, although the court declined to use that designation. The concept of patent misuse arose to restrain practices that did not in themselves violate any law, but that drew anticompetitive strength from the patent right, and thus were deemed to be contrary to public policy. The policy purpose was to prevent a patentee from using the patent to obtain market benefit beyond that which inheres in the statutory patent right. [The] cases established that price-fixing and tying restrictions accompanying the sale of patented goods were *per se* illegal. These cases did not hold, and it did not follow, that all restrictions accompanying the sale of patented goods were deemed illegal. . . . Restrictions on use are judged in terms of their relation to the patentee's right to exclude from all or part of the patent grant. . . . The appropriate criterion is whether Mallinckrodt's restriction is reasonably within the patent grant, or whether the patentee has ventured beyond the patent grant and into behavior having an anticompetitive effect not justifiable under the rule of reason. Should the restriction be found to be reasonably within the patent grant, *i.e.,* that it relates to subject matter within the scope of the patent claims, that ends the inquiry. However, should such inquiry lead to the conclusion that there are anticompetitive effects extending beyond the patentee's statutory right to exclude, these effects do not automatically impeach the restriction. Anticompetitive effects that are not *per se* violations of law are reviewed in accordance with the rule of reason.

2. The Patent Misuse Reform Act of 1988 added clauses (4) and (5) to Section 271(d) of the Patent Act. Section 271(d) provides:

No patent owner otherwise entitled to relief for infringement or contributory infringement of a patent shall be denied relief or deemed guilty of misuse or illegal extension of the patent right by reason of his having done one or more of the following: (1) derived revenue from acts which if performed by another without his consent would constitute contributory infringement of the patent; (2) licensed or authorized another to perform acts which if performed without his consent would constitute contributory infringement of the patent; (3) sought to enforce his patent rights against infringement or contributory infringement; (4) refused to license or use any rights to the patent; or (5) conditioned the license of any rights to the patent or the sale of the patented product on the acquisition of a license to rights in another patent or purchase of a separate product, unless, in view of the circumstances, the patent owner has market power in the relevant market for the patent or patented product on which the license or sale is conditioned.

35 U.S.C. § 271(d). Clause (5) requires proof of market power as a basis for a particular type of misuse claim.

3. In *Illinois Tool Works, Inc v. Independent Ink, Inc.,* 547 U.S. 28 (2006) the Court rejected a presumption of market power from the presence of a patent in an antitrust tying case, implicitly rejecting a core element of the analysis in *Morton Salt:* "After considering the congressional judgment reflected in the

1988 amendment, we conclude that tying arrangements involving patented products should be evaluated under the standards applied in cases like *Fortner II* and *Jefferson Parish* rather than under the *per se* rule applied in *Morton Salt* and *Loew's*. While some such arrangements are still unlawful, such as those that are the product of a true monopoly or a marketwide conspiracy, that conclusion must be supported by proof of power in the relevant market rather than by a mere presumption thereof."

IV. COPYRIGHT MISUSE

Review the *Lasercomb* case from Chapter 1.

VIDEO PIPELINE, INC. v. BUENA VISTA HOME ENTERTAINMENT, INC.
342 F.3d 191 (3d Cir. 2003)

AMBRO, CIRCUIT JUDGE.

In this copyright case we review the District Court's entry of a preliminary injunction against Video Pipeline, Inc.'s online display of "clip previews." A "clip preview," as we use the term, is an approximately two-minute segment of a movie, copied without authorization from the film's copyright holder, and used in the same way as an authorized movie "trailer." We reserve the term "trailer" for previews created by the copyright holder of a particular movie (or under the copyright holder's authority).

Video Pipeline challenges the injunction on the ground that its internet use of the clip previews is . . . fair use . . . and, alternatively, that appellees Buena Vista Home Entertainment, Inc. and Miramax Film Corp. may not receive the benefits of copyright protection because they have engaged in copyright misuse. We reject both arguments. . . .

Background

Video Pipeline compiles movie trailers onto videotape for home video retailers to display in their stores. To obtain the right to distribute the trailers used in the compilations, Video Pipeline enters into agreements with various entertainment companies. It entered into such an agreement, the Master Clip License Agreement ("License Agreement"), with Disney in 1988, and Disney thereafter provided Video Pipeline with over 500 trailers for its movies.

In 1997, Video Pipeline took its business to the web, where it operates VideoPipeline.net and VideoDetective.com. The company maintains a database accessible from VideoPipeline.net, which contains movie trailers Video Pipeline has received throughout the years. Video Pipeline's internet clients — retail web sites selling home videos — use VideoPipeline.net to display trailers to site visitors. The site visitors access trailers by clicking on a button labeled "preview" for a particular motion picture. The requested trailer is then "streamed" for the visitor to view (because it is streamed the trailer cannot be downloaded to or stored on the visitor's computer). The operators of the web sites from which the trailers are accessed — Video Pipeline's internet clients — pay a fee to have the trailers streamed based on the number of megabytes shown to site visitors. Video Pipeline has agreements to stream trailers with approximately 25 online retailers, including Yahoo!, Amazon, and Best Buy.

As noted, Video Pipeline also operates VideoDetective.com. On this web site, visitors can search for movies by title, actor, scene, genre, *etc.* When a search is entered, the site returns a list of movies and information about them, and allows the user to stream trailers from VideoPipeline.net. In addition to displaying trailers, VideoDetective.com includes a "Shop Now" button to link the user to a web site selling the requested video. Visitors to VideoDetective.com can also win prizes by playing "Can You Name that Movie?" after viewing a trailer on the site.

Video Pipeline included in its online database trailers it received under the License Agreement from Disney. Because the License Agreement did not permit this use, Disney requested that Video Pipeline remove the trailers from the database. It complied with that request. On October 24, 2000, however, Video Pipeline filed a complaint in the District Court for the District of New Jersey seeking a declaratory judgment that its online use of the trailers did not violate federal copyright law. Disney shortly thereafter terminated the License Agreement.

Video Pipeline decided to replace some of the trailers it had removed at Disney's request from its database. In order to do so, it copied approximately two minutes from each of at least 62 Disney movies to create its own clip previews of the movies. . . .

Video Pipeline stores the clip previews in its database and displays them on the internet in the same way it had displayed the Disney trailers. In content, however, the clip previews differ from the trailers. Each clip preview opens with a display of the Miramax or Disney trademark and the title of the movie, then shows one or two scenes from the first half of the movie, and closes with the title again. Disney's trailers, in contrast, are designed to entice sales from a target market by using techniques such as voice-over, narration, editing, and additional music. Video Pipeline's clip previews use none of these marketing techniques.

Disney also makes its trailers available online. It displays them on its own web sites in order to attract and to keep users there (a concept called "stickiness") and then takes advantage of the users' presence to advertise and sell other products. Disney has also entered into agreements to link its trailers with other businesses, and, for example, has such a link with the Apple Computer home page.

Video Pipeline amended its complaint to seek a declaratory judgment allowing it to use the clip previews. Disney filed a counterclaim alleging copyright infringement. . . .

Discussion

Three of the four statutory factors indicate that Video Pipeline's internet display of the clip previews will not qualify as a fair use. . . . The District Court therefore correctly held that Video Pipeline has failed to show that it will likely prevail on its fair use defense. . . .

B. Copyright Misuse

Video Pipeline further contends that Disney has misused its copyright and, as a result, should not receive the protection of copyright law. Video Pipeline points to certain licensing agreements that Disney has entered into with three companies and sought to enter into with a number of other companies operating web sites. Each of these licensing agreements provides that Disney, the licensor, will deliver trailers by way of hyperlinks for display on the licensee's web site. The Agreements further state:

> The Website in which the Trailers are used may not be derogatory to or critical of the entertainment industry or of [Disney] (and its officers, directors, agents, employees, affiliates, divisions and subsidiaries) or of any motion picture produced or distributed by [Disney] . . . [or] of the materials from which the Trailers were taken or of any person involved with the production of the Underlying Works. Any breach of this paragraph will render this license null and void and Licensee will be liable to all parties concerned for defamation and copyright infringement, as well as breach of contract. . . .

As Video Pipeline sees it, such licensing agreements seek to use copyright law to suppress criticism and, in so doing, misuse those laws, triggering the copyright misuse doctrine.

Neither the Supreme Court nor this Court has affirmatively recognized the copyright misuse doctrine. There is, however, a well-established patent misuse doctrine, and . . . other courts of appeals have extended the doctrine to the copyright context.

The misuse doctrine extends from the equitable principle that courts "may appropriately withhold their aid where the plaintiff is using the right asserted contrary to the public interest." *Morton Salt,* 314 U.S. at 492. Misuse is not cause to invalidate the copyright or patent, but instead "precludes its enforcement during the period of misuse." To defend on misuse grounds, the alleged infringer need not be subject to the purported misuse. *Morton Salt,* 314 U.S. at 494 ("It is the adverse effect upon the public interest of a successful infringement suit in conjunction with the patentee's course of conduct which disqualifies him to maintain the suit, regardless of whether the particular defendant has suffered from the misuse of the patent."); *Lasercomb,* 911 F.2d at 979 ("[T]he fact that appellants here were not parties to one of Lasercomb's standard license agreements is inapposite to their copyright misuse defense. The question is whether Lasercomb is using its copyright in a manner contrary to public policy, which question we have answered in the affirmative.").

Misuse often exists where the patent or copyright holder has engaged in some form of anti-competitive behavior. More on point, however, is the underlying policy rationale for the misuse doctrine set out in the Constitution's Copyright and Patent Clause: "to promote the Progress of Science and useful Arts." Const. Art. I, § 8, cl. 8. The "ultimate aim" of copyright law is "to stimulate artistic creativity for the general public good." Put simply, our Constitution emphasizes the purpose and value of copyrights and patents. Harm caused by their misuse undermines their usefulness.

Anti-competitive licensing agreements may conflict with the purpose behind a copyright's protection by depriving the public of the would-be competitor's creativity. The fair use doctrine and the refusal to copyright facts and ideas also address applications of copyright protection that would otherwise conflict with a copyright's constitutional goal. But it is possible that a copyright holder could leverage its copyright to restrain the creative expression of another without engaging in anti-competitive behavior or implicating the fair use and idea/expression doctrines. . . .

The licensing agreements in this case do seek to restrict expression by licensing the Disney trailers for use on the internet only so long as the web sites on which the trailers will appear do not derogate Disney, the entertainment industry, etc. But we nonetheless cannot conclude on this record that the agreements are likely to interfere with creative expression to such a degree that they affect in any significant way the policy interest in increasing the public store of creative activity. The licensing agreements do not, for instance, interfere with the licensee's opportunity to express such criticism on other web sites or elsewhere. There is no evidence that the public will find it any more difficult to obtain criticism of Disney and its interests, or even that the public is considerably less likely to come across this criticism, if it is not displayed on the same site as the trailers. Moreover, if a critic wishes to comment on Disney's works, the fair use doctrine may be implicated regardless of the existence of the licensing agreements. Finally, copyright law, and the misuse doctrine in particular, should not be interpreted to require Disney, if it licenses its trailers for display on any web sites but its own, to do so willy-nilly regardless of the content displayed with its copyrighted works. Indeed such an application of the misuse doctrine would likely decrease the public's access to Disney's works because it might as a result refuse to license at all online display of its works.

Thus, while we extend the patent misuse doctrine to copyright, and recognize that it might operate beyond its traditional anti-competition context, we hold it inapplicable here. On this record Disney's licensing agreements do not interfere significantly with copyright policy (while holding to the contrary might, in fact, do so). The District Court therefore correctly held that Video Pipeline will not likely succeed on its copyright misuse defense. . . .

We . . . Affirm. . . .

V. REVERSE ENGINEERING CLAUSES — AN ILLUSTRATION

ALCATEL USA v. DGI TECHNOLOGIES, INC.
166 F.3d 772 (5th Cir. 1999)

Wiener, Circuit Judge:

The complex intellectual property action that we hear on appeal today involves a multifaceted dispute between two competitors in the telecommunications equipment manufacturing industry. [Alcatel USA], Inc. (formerly DSC Communications Corporation ("DSC")) filed suit against [DGI Technologies], Inc. ("DGI"), alleging that DGI infringed DSC's copyrights, misappropriated its trade secrets, and engaged in unfair competition by misappropriating its time, labor, skill and money. DGI, in turn, asserted that DSC violated § 2 of the Sherman Act, interfered with DGI's prospective business relations, and also engaged in unfair competition. After a lengthy trial, the district court entered a set-off judgment in favor of DSC and an order enjoining DGI from selling the infringing products.

[We] affirm the district court's grant of a judgment as a matter of law ("JML") in favor of DSC, dismissing DGI's antitrust claim. We also affirm the jury's determination that damages are due to DSC on its claim of misappropriation of trade secrets, and the district court's injunction against DGI, based in part on this claim. Because DSC misused its copyrights, however, we reverse the portions of the injunction tailored by the district court as relief from DGI's copyright infringement. . . .

I

Facts and Proceedings

DSC designs, manufactures, and sells equipment ("switches") comprising telephone switching systems. Its customers are long-distance telephone service providers, such as MCI and Sprint. A telephone switch routes long distance telephone calls to their destinations. DSC switches are controlled by its copyrighted operating system software. DSC regularly implements new features in its switches by upgrading its software, a process that costs DSC millions of dollars.

DSC does not sell its operating system software — as it does the switches — but instead licenses its use pursuant to a licensing agreement. The licensing agreement provides that (1) the operating system software remains the property of DSC; (2) the customer has the right to use the software only to operate its switch; (3) the customer is prohibited from copying the software or disclosing it to third parties; and (4) the customers are authorized to use the software only in conjunction with DSC-manufactured equipment.

The record evidence shows that DSC's customers, like other long distance providers, frequently need to expand the call-handling capacity of their switches. One way to expand the call-handling capacity of DSC switches is to add groups of "cards" to the switch. Prior to 1989, DSC was the only manufacturer of expansion cards for its own switches. In 1989, DGI was founded to design and sell such cards for use with DSC switches.

DGI contends that it developed its cards by analyzing DSC's unpatented products and then duplicating their functionality — a process referred to as "reverse engineering." [DGI] further insists that, from its inception, DSC repeatedly attempted to thwart DGI's entry into the market. [DSC], on the other hand, asserts that DGI did not engage in legitimate reverse engineering, but rather misappropriated DSC's intellectual property by wrongfully obtaining schematics and manuals provided only to DSC customers on the express condition that there be no disclosure to third parties. DSC also notes that each manual contained a plainly visible copyright notice.

In any event, between 1992 and 1994, DGI developed and introduced four DSC-compatible cards — the Digital Trunk Interface ("DTI"), the Bus Terminator ("BT"), the Digital Tone Detector ("DTD"), and the Pulse Code Modulation Interface ("PCMI"). None of these initial DGI cards were microprocessor cards, however. A microprocessor card contains firmware, which is software embedded in a memory chip on the card. When installed in a switch, a microprocessor card controls the "boot up" — that is, it downloads DSC's copyrighted operating system software into its random access memory ("RAM"). A DTI, DTD, or BT card alone cannot expand the capacity of a switch; a customer must install a group of cards together with a microprocessor card to achieve expansion. For this reason, DGI obtained DSC microprocessor cards — then known as MP-2s — in the used market to sell along with three DGI cards. This enabled DGI to offer a customer a complete expansion card complement, which it did.

In 1995, as a result of a new dialing plan implemented by the Federal Communications Commission ("FCC") and customer demands for new features, DSC revised and expanded its operating system software. These changes required DSC customers to upgrade to a new microprocessor card — the MP-8. As few MP-8 cards were available on the used market, DGI was no longer able to offer a complete card complement. [This] motivated DGI to develop its own microprocessor card — the DMP-2800.

To develop a microprocessor card, DGI [needed] to understand DSC's firmware. For this purpose, DGI purchased an MP-8 card and, using a "burner" to remove the DSC firmware from a memory chip, obtained the machine-readable object code. DGI engineers then used a process called "disassembly" to convert the firmware into human-readable form. In this way, DGI was able to write its own firmware — which it claims is not substantially similar to DSC's firmware — for its DMP-2800 microprocessor card. DSC asserts that DGI violated the copyright on its firmware when it copied DSC's firmware several times in this process.

Second, the DGI microprocessor card had to accept a download from the switch of the DSC operating system. To obtain the software needed for this function, several DGI engineers took an MP-8 card to NTS Communications ("NTS"), a DSC switch owner/software licensee and DGI customer. There, Ernie Carrasco, an NTS employee who also consulted for DGI, placed the MP-8 card into an NTS switch and copied the operating system to a laptop computer. DGI engineers then took the laptop back to DGI. DSC maintains that DGI never told NTS that it was copying and removing DSC's copyrighted software, only that it was "testing" MP-8 cards.

DGI engineers returned to NTS several times to test MP-8 cards containing versions of DGI's firmware. To avoid having to perform all this testing at NTS, DGI modified an MP-8 card to include a device called a "punch" card or "snooper" card, which monitored the firmware during the operating system download. Using this snooper card, DGI was able to understand which parts of the DSC firmware were accessed during the "boot" of the operating system.

DSC maintains that DGI used this snooper card to copy the messages contained in DSC's copyrighted operating system software. It insists that, but for DGI's "theft" of DSC's operating system, it would have been extremely expensive and time-consuming for DGI to develop its own microprocessor card.

DGI counters that the copy was used only to discern the size of the operating system download to the MP-8 card, as it was investigating the possibility of upgrading the older MP-2 card. DGI insists that, as the content of the software was irrelevant in determining its size, it never even disassembled the operating system software from unreadable machine language.

DSC filed suit in 1994. . . . DGI counterclaimed. . . . After a three week trial, the jury returned a mixed verdict, finding that DSC violated the Sherman Act, interfered with DGI's contractual relations, and engaged in unfair competition, and that DGI infringed certain DSC copyrights, engaged in unfair competition by misappropriating DSC's time, labor, skill, and money, and misappropriated DSC's trade secrets. The jury also determined that both parties had "unclean hands."

II

A. DGI's Antitrust Claim

The jury found DSC liable under § 2 of the Sherman Act for monopolization of the expansion and enhancement market for DSC-manufactured switches and awarded DGI $750,000 in lost profits and $1.5 million in future lost profits on that claim. The district court overturned this verdict, however, holding that (1) there was insufficient evidence to establish that expansion cards are the relevant market for antitrust purposes, and (2) DGI's damage model was hopelessly flawed. . . .

The offense of monopoly under § 2 of the Sherman Act has two elements: (1) the possession of monopoly power in the relevant market and (2) the willful acquisition or maintenance of that power as distinguished from growth or development as a consequence of a superior product, business acumen, or historic accident. Thus, to prove a monopolization claim, the plaintiff must first establish the relevant product market. DGI disputes the district court's conclusion that it failed to prove that the "capacity enhancement and expansion products" market for DSC-manufactured switches is the relevant market for antitrust purposes.

As DGI stresses, in determining the relevant product market, "the reality of the marketplace must serve as the lodestar." . . . We agree with the district court's determination that DGI's characterization of the expansion products market as the relevant market is at odds with market realities. The record shows that the prices for two-thirds of all of DSC's cards are set at the time a telephone company purchases a switch, either because the customer purchases the one frame that the switch must have to operate, or through a future or life-cycle pricing scheme negotiated at the time of purchase. DGI's model excludes all these cards from its relevant market, not an insignificant flaw in the model.

Furthermore, DGI's proposed market does not acknowledge that the purchase of a new frame with cards is only one of several ways a telephone company can expand its call-handling capacity. For instance, a company can purchase a new switch from DSC or from another switch manufacturer, purchase a used switch from DSC or a broker, or trade for or lease capacity in another company's network. In addition, as many of DSC's customers, such as MCI, are dual-sourced — that is, they own switches built by more than one manufacturer — they can purchase a new frame for one of their non-DSC switches. All of these capacity handling options are also omitted from DGI's relevant market.

We are convinced that DGI . . . is "trying to define the market as narrowly as possible (in order to make it look as if [defendant] had market power)." Because (1) DGI did not present legally sufficient evidence that DSC's customers faced significant information and switching costs, and (2) DGI's proffered relevant market does not comport with market realities, its aftermarket monopoly claim fails as a matter of law. As such, the district court did not err in granting DSC's motion for a JML dismissing DGI's antitrust claim. . . .

2. Copyright Infringement

[DGI] insists that, even assuming that it committed acts of copyright infringement, the "copyright misuse" doctrine precludes injunctive relief based on that infringement. This doctrine — which has its historical roots in the unclean hands defense — "bars a culpable plaintiff from prevailing on an action for the infringement of the misused copyright." It "forbids the use of the [copyright] to secure an exclusive right or limited monopoly not granted by the [Copyright] Office and which it is contrary to public policy to grant." The copyright misuse defense is analogous to the patent misuse defense, which was originally recognized by the Supreme Court in *Morton Salt Co. v. G.S. Suppiger*. The Fourth Circuit was the first to extend the rationale behind patent misuse to copyrights. . . .

We recognized the copyright misuse defense in [a prior appeal by the parties to this court, *DSC I*]. We noted that "DSC seems to be attempting to use its copyright to obtain a patent-like monopoly over unpatented microprocessor cards." Speculating that DGI might prevail on a copyright misuse defense, we refused to expand the preliminary injunction issued by the district court.

Not surprisingly, DGI argues, based on *DSC I*, that on remand the district court abused its discretion when it ignored the jury's finding that DSC misused its operating system copyright and entered the permanent injunction. DGI reasons that, as DSC's software is licensed to customers to be used only in conjunction with DSC-manufactured hardware, DSC indirectly seeks to obtain patent-like protection of its hardware — its microprocessor card — through the enforcement of its software copyright. DSC responds that its actions do not constitute misuse, inasmuch as its licensing agreement does not prohibit the independent development of compatible operating system software. As DSC points out, it was this "attempt[] to suppress any attempt by the licensee to independently implement" competing software that the court condemned in *Lasercomb*.

We agree with the [jury's] finding that DSC's licensing agreement for its operating system constitutes misuse. The district court instructed the jury, in pertinent part: "[I]f DSC has used its copyrights to indirectly gain commercial control over products DSC does not have copyrighted, then copyright misuse may be present. . . ."

[The] public policy which includes original works within the granted monopoly excludes from it all that is not embraced in the original expression. It equally forbids the use of the copyright to secure an exclusive right or limited monopoly not granted by the Copyright Office and which is contrary to public policy to grant. A reasonable juror could conclude, based on the licensing agreement, that "DSC has used its copyrights to indirectly gain commercial control over products DSC does not have copyrighted," namely, its microprocessor cards. The facts on which we based our misuse prediction in *DSC I* have not changed substantially. As we reasoned then: Any competing microprocessor card developed for use on DSC phone switches must be compatible with DSC's copyrighted operating system software. In order to ensure that its card is compatible, a competitor such as DGI must test the card on a DSC phone switch. Such a test necessarily involves making a copy of DSC's copyrighted operating system, which copy is downloaded into the card's memory when the card is booted up. If DSC is allowed to prevent such copying, then it can prevent anyone from developing a competing microprocessor card, even though it has not patented the card. Under these facts, DSC's assertion that its licensing agreement does not prohibit the independent development of compatible software is simply irrelevant. Despite the presence of some evidence — the testimony of a DSC executive — that DGI could have developed its own software, there was also evidence that it was not technically feasible to use a non-DSC operating system because the switch has a "common control" scheme in which each microprocessor card in a network of such cards runs the same operating system. Hence, without the freedom to test its cards in conjunction with DSC's software, DGI was effectively prevented from developing its product, thereby securing for DSC a limited monopoly over its uncopyrighted microprocessor cards. Furthermore, the jury instructions never mentioned that misuse could only be present if DSC's agreement prohibited the independent development of software. Consequently, we conclude that the district court abused its discretion in awarding injunctive relief based on DGI's infringing acts.

We reach this conclusion despite the jury's finding that DGI acted with unclean hands in its acquisition and use of DSC's copyrighted software, firmware, and manuals. DSC insists that, based on this finding, DGI is barred from invoking an equitable defense, and DSC is entitled to injunctive relief notwithstanding its alleged copyright misuse. We reject this contention. . . .

Conclusion

For the foregoing reasons, we affirm the district court's grant of a JML in favor of DSC, dismissing DGI's antitrust claim. [Because] DSC misused its copyrights, however, we reverse the portions of the injunction tailored by the district court as relief from DGI's copyright infringement. . . .

BOWERS v. BAYSTATE TECHNOLOGIES, INC.
320 F.3d 1317 (Fed. Cir. 2003)

RADER, CIRCUIT JUDGE.

Following trial in the United States District Court for the District of Massachusetts, the jury returned a verdict for Harold L. Bowers on his patent infringement, copyright infringement, and breach of contract claims, while rejecting Baystate Technologies, Inc.'s claim for patent invalidity. The jury awarded Mr. Bowers separate damages on each of his claims. The district court, however, omitted the copyright damages as duplicative of the contract damages. . . .

I

Harold L. Bowers (Bowers) created a template to improve computer aided design (CAD) software, such as the CADKEY tool of Cadkey, Inc. Mr. Bowers filed a patent application for his template on February 27, 1989. On June 12, 1990, United States Patent No. 4,933,514 ('514 patent) issued from that application. . . .

Mr. Bowers commercialized the '514 patent template as Cadjet for use with CADKEY. . . .

Baystate contends that the Copyright Act preempts the prohibition of reverse engineering embodied in Mr. Bowers' shrink-wrap license agreements. Swayed by this argument, the district court considered Mr. Bowers' contract and copyright claims coextensive. The district court instructed the jury that "reverse engineering violates the license agreement only if Baystate's product that resulted from reverse engineering infringes Bowers' copyright because it copies protectable expression." Mr. Bowers lodged a timely objection to this instruction. This court holds that, under First Circuit law, the Copyright Act does not preempt or narrow the scope of Mr. Bowers' contract claim.

Courts respect freedom of contract and do not lightly set aside freely-entered agreements. Nevertheless, at times, federal regulation may preempt private contract. The Copyright Act provides that "all legal or equitable rights that are equivalent to any of the exclusive rights within the general scope of copyright . . . are governed exclusively by this title." 17 U.S.C. § 301(a) (2000). The First Circuit does not interpret this language to require preemption as long as "a state cause of action requires an extra element, beyond mere copying, preparation of derivative works, performance, distribution or display." *Data Gen. Corp. v. Grumman Sys. Support Corp.*, 36 F.3d 1147, 1164 (1st Cir.1994) (quoting *Gates Rubber Co. v. Bando Chem. Indus.*, 9 F.3d 823, 847, 28 USPQ2d 1503, 1520 (10th Cir.1993)); *see also Computer Assoc. Int'l, Inc. v. Altai, Inc.*, 982 F.2d 693, 716 (2d Cir.1992) ("But if an 'extra element' is 'required instead of or in addition to the acts of reproduction, performance, distribution or display, in order to constitute a state-created cause of action, then the right does not lie "within the general scope of copyright," and there is no preemption.' "). Nevertheless, "[n]ot every 'extra element' of a state law claim will establish a qualitative variance between the rights protected by federal copyright law and those protected by state law."

In *Data General,* Data General alleged that Grumman misappropriated its trade secret software. Grumman obtained that software from Data General's customers and former employees who were bound by confidentiality agreements to refrain from disclosing the software. In defense, Grumman argued that the Copyright Act preempted Data General's trade secret claim. The First Circuit held that the Copyright Act did not preempt the state law trade secret claim. Beyond mere copying, that state law claim required proof of a trade secret and breach of a duty of confidentiality. These additional elements of proof, according to the First Circuit, made the trade secret claim qualitatively different from a copyright claim. *Id.* In contrast, the First Circuit noted that claims might be preempted whose extra elements are illusory, being "mere label[s] attached to the same odious business conduct." For example, the First Circuit observed that "a state law misappropriation claim will not escape preemption . . . simply because a plaintiff must prove that copying was not only unauthorized but also commercially immoral."

The First Circuit has not addressed expressly whether the Copyright Act preempts a state law contract claim that restrains copying. This court perceives, however, that *Data General*'s rationale would lead to a judgment that the Copyright Act does not preempt the state contract action in this case. Indeed, most courts to examine this issue have found that the Copyright Act does not preempt contractual constraints on copyrighted articles. *See, e.g., ProCD, Inc. v. Zeidenberg,* 86 F.3d 1447, 39 USPQ2d 1161 (7th Cir.1996) (holding that a shrink-wrap license was not preempted by federal copyright law). . . .

In *ProCD,* for example, the court found that the mutual assent and consideration required by a contract claim render that claim qualitatively different from copyright infringement. Consistent with *Data General*'s reliance on a contract element, the court in *ProCD* reasoned: "A copyright is a right against the world. Contracts, by contrast, generally affect only their parties; strangers may do as they please, so contracts do not create 'exclusive rights.'" Indeed, the Supreme Court recently noted "[i]t goes without saying that a contract cannot bind a nonparty." *EEOC v. Waffle House, Inc.,* 534 U.S. 279 (2002). This court believes that the First Circuit would follow the reasoning of *ProCD* and the majority of other courts to consider this issue. This court, therefore, holds that the Copyright Act does not preempt Mr. Bowers' contract claims.

In making this determination, this court has left untouched the conclusions reached in *Atari Games v. Nintendo* regarding reverse engineering as a statutory fair use exception to copyright infringement. *Atari Games Corp. v. Nintendo of America, Inc.,* 975 F.2d 832 (Fed.Cir.1992). In *Atari,* this court stated that, with respect to 17 U.S.C. § 107 (fair use section of the Copyright Act), "[t]he legislative history of section 107 suggests that courts should adapt the fair use exception to accommodate new technological innovations." *Atari,* 975 F.2d at 843. This court noted "[a] prohibition on all copying whatsoever would stifle the free flow of ideas without serving any legitimate interest of the copyright holder." Therefore, this court held "reverse engineering object code to discern the unprotectable ideas in a computer program is a fair use." *Id.* Application of the First Circuit's view distinguishing a state law contract claim having additional elements of proof from a copyright claim does not alter the findings of *Atari.* Likewise, this claim distinction does not conflict with the expressly defined circumstances in which reverse engineering is not copyright infringement under 17 U.S.C. § 1201(f) (section of the Digital Millennium Copyright Act) and 17 U.S.C. § 906 (section directed to mask works).

Moreover, while the Fifth Circuit has held a state law prohibiting all copying of a computer program is preempted by the federal Copyright Act, *Vault*

Corp. v. Quaid Software, Ltd., 847 F.2d 255 (5th Cir.1988), no evidence suggests the First Circuit would extend this concept to include private contractual agreements supported by mutual assent and consideration. The First Circuit recognizes contractual waiver of affirmative defenses and statutory rights. . . . Thus, case law indicates the First Circuit would find that private parties are free to contractually forego the limited ability to reverse engineer a software product under the exemptions of the Copyright Act. Of course, a party bound by such a contract may elect to efficiently breach the agreement in order to ascertain ideas in a computer program unprotected by copyright law. Under such circumstances, the breaching party must weigh the benefits of breach against the arguably de minimus damages arising from merely discerning non-protected code.

This court now considers the scope of Mr. Bowers' contract protection. [Contract] terms receive "the sense and meaning of the words which the parties have used; and if clear and free from ambiguity the words are to be taken and understood in their natural, usual and ordinary sense."

In this case, the contract unambiguously prohibits "reverse engineering." That term means ordinarily "to study or analyze (a device, as a microchip for computers) in order to learn details of design, construction, and operation, perhaps to produce a copy or an improved version." *Random House Unabridged Dictionary* (1993); *see also The Free On-Line Dictionary of Computing* (2001), at http://wombat.doc (last visited Jul. 17, 2002). Thus, the contract in this case broadly prohibits any "reverse engineering" of the subject matter covered by the shrink-wrap agreement.

The record amply supports the jury's finding of a breach of that agreement. . . .

As discussed above, the district court erred in instructing the jury that copyright law limited the scope of Mr. Bowers' contract protection. Notwithstanding that error, this court may affirm the jury's breach of contract verdict if substantial record evidence would permit a reasonable jury to find in favor of Mr. Bowers based on a correct understanding of the law. The shrink-wrap agreements in this case are far broader than the protection afforded by copyright law. Even setting aside copyright violations, the record supports a finding of breach of the agreement between the parties. In view of the breadth of Mr. Bowers' contracts, this court perceives that substantial evidence supports the jury's breach of contract verdict relating to both the DOS and Windows versions of Draft-Pak. . . .

Baystate does not contest the contract damages amount on appeal. Thus, this court sustains the district court's award of contract damages. Mr. Bowers, however, argues that the district court abused its discretion by dropping copyright damages from the combined damage award. To the contrary, this court perceives no abuse of discretion.

The shrink-wrap license agreement prohibited, *inter alia,* all reverse engineering of Mr. Bowers' software, protection encompassing but more extensive than copyright protection, which prohibits only certain copying. Mr. Bowers' copyright and contract claims both rest on Baystate's copying of Mr. Bowers' software. Following the district court's instructions, the jury considered and awarded damages on each separately. This was entirely appropriate. The law is clear that the jury may award separate damages for each claim, "leaving it to the judge to make appropriate adjustments to avoid double recovery." In this case, the breach of contract damages arose from the same copying and included the same lost sales that form the basis for the copyright damages. The district court, therefore, did not abuse its discretion by omitting from the final damage award the duplicative copyright damages. Because this court affirms the district court's omission of the copyright damages, this court need not reach the merits of Mr. Bowers' copyright infringement claim. . . .

DYK, CIRCUIT JUDGE, concurring in part and dissenting in part.

[Based] on the petition for rehearing and the opposition, I have concluded that our original decision on the preemption issue, reaffirmed in today's revision of the majority opinion, was not correct. . . . The majority's approach permits state law to eviscerate an important federal copyright policy reflected in the fair use defense, and the majority's logic threatens other federal copyright policies as well. I respectfully dissent.

I

Congress has made the Copyright Act the exclusive means for protecting copyright. . . . The test for preemption by copyright law, like the test for patent law preemption, should be whether the state law "substantially impedes the public use of the otherwise unprotected" material. *Bonito Boats, Inc. v. Thunder Craft Boats, Inc.,* 489 U.S. 141, 157, 167 (1989) (state law at issue was preempted because it "substantially restrict[ed] the public's ability to exploit ideas that the patent system mandates shall be free for all to use."); *Sears, Roebuck & Co. v. Stiffel Co.,* 376 U.S. 225, 231-32 (1964). In the copyright area, the First Circuit has adopted an "equivalent in substance" test to determine whether a state law is preempted by the Copyright Act. *Data Gen. Corp. v. Grumman Sys. Support Corp.,* 36 F.3d 1147, 1164-65 (1st Cir.1994). That test seeks to determine whether the state cause of action contains an additional element not present in the copyright right, such as scienter. If the state cause of action contains such an extra element, it is not preempted by the Copyright Act. However, "such an action is equivalent in substance to a copyright infringement claim [and thus preempted by the Copyright Act] where the additional element merely concerns *the extent to which* authors and their licensees can prohibit unauthorized copying by third parties." *Id.* at 1165 (emphasis in original).

II

The fair use defense is an important limitation on copyright. . . . We correctly held in *Atari Games Corp. v. Nintendo of America, Inc.,* 975 F.2d 832, 843 (Fed.Cir.1992), that reverse engineering constitutes a fair use under the Copyright Act. The Ninth and Eleventh Circuits have also ruled that reverse engineering constitutes fair use. No other federal court of appeals has disagreed.

We emphasized in *Atari* that an author cannot achieve protection for an idea simply by embodying it in a computer program. "An author cannot acquire patent-like protection by putting an idea, process, or method of operation in an unintelligible format and asserting copyright infringement against those who try to understand that idea, process, or method of operation." Thus, the fair use defense for reverse engineering is necessary so that copyright protection does not "extend to any idea, procedure, process, system, method of operation, concept, principle, or discovery, regardless of the form in which it is described, explained, illustrated, or embodied in such work," as proscribed by the Copyright Act.

III

A state is not free to eliminate the fair use defense. Enforcement of a total ban on reverse engineering would conflict with the Copyright Act itself by protecting otherwise unprotectable material. If state law provided that a copyright holder could bar fair use of the copyrighted material by placing a black dot on each copy of the work offered for sale, there would be no question but that the state law would be preempted. A state law that allowed a copyright holder to simply label its products so as to eliminate a fair use defense would "substantially impede" the public's right to fair use and allow the copyright holder, through state law, to protect material that the Congress has determined must be free to all under the Copyright Act.

I nonetheless agree with the majority opinion that a state can permit parties to contract away a fair use defense or to agree not to engage in uses of copyrighted material that are permitted by the copyright law, if the contract is freely negotiated. A freely negotiated agreement represents the "extra element" that prevents preemption of a state law claim that would otherwise be identical to the infringement claim barred by the fair use defense of reverse engineering.

However, state law giving effect to shrinkwrap licenses is no different in substance from a hypothetical black dot law. Like any other contract of adhesion, the only choice offered to the purchaser is to avoid making the purchase in the first place. State law thus gives the copyright holder the ability to eliminate the fair use defense in each and every instance at its option. . . .

IV

There is, moreover, no logical stopping point to the majority's reasoning. The *amici* rightly question whether under our original opinion the first sale doctrine and a host of other limitations on copyright protection might be eliminated by shrinkwrap licenses in just this fashion. *See* Brief for Electric Frontier Foundation et al. as *Amici Curiae* 10. If by printing a few words on the outside of its product a party can eliminate the fair use defense, then it can also, by the same means, restrict a purchaser from asserting the "first sale" defense, embodied in 17 U.S.C. § 109(a), or any other of the protections Congress has afforded the public in the Copyright Act. That means that, under the majority's reasoning, state law could extensively undermine the protections of the Copyright Act.

V

The Fifth Circuit's decision in *Vault* directly supports preemption of the shrinkwrap limitation. The majority states that *Vault* held that "a state law prohibiting all copying of a computer program is preempted by the federal

Copyright Act" and then states that "no evidence suggests the First Circuit would extend this concept to include private contractual agreements supported by mutual assent and consideration." But, in fact, the Fifth Circuit held that the specific provision of state law that authorized contracts prohibiting reverse engineering, decompilation, or disassembly of computer programs was preempted by federal law because it conflicted with a portion of the Copyright Act and because it "touche[d] upon an area' of federal copyright law." From a preemption standpoint, there is no distinction between a state law that explicitly validates a contract that restricts reverse engineering (*Vault*) and general common law that permits such a restriction (as here). . . .

I do not read *ProCD, Inc. v. Zeidenberg,* 86 F.3d 1447 (7th Cir.1996), the only other court of appeals shrinkwrap case, as being to the contrary, even though it contains broad language stating that "a simple two-party contract is not 'equivalent to any of the exclusive rights within the general scope of copyright.' " In *ProCD,* the Seventh Circuit validated a shrinkwrap license that restricted the use of a CD-ROM to non-commercial purposes, which the defendant had violated by charging users a fee to access the CD-ROM over the Internet. The court held that the restriction to non-commercial use of the program was not equivalent to any rights protected by the Copyright Act. Rather, the "contract reflect[ed] private ordering, essential to efficient functioning of markets." The court saw the licensor as legitimately seeking to distinguish between personal and commercial use. "ProCD offers software and data for two prices: one for personal use, a higher price for commercial use," the court said. The defendant "wants to use the data without paying the seller's price." The court also emphasized that the license "would not withdraw any information from the public domain" because all of the information on the CD-ROM was publicly available.

The case before us is different from *ProCD*. The Copyright Act does not confer a right to pay the same amount for commercial and personal use. It does, however, confer a right to fair use, 17 U.S.C. § 107, which we have held encompasses reverse engineering.

ProCD and the other contract cases are also careful not to create a blanket rule that all contracts will escape preemption. The court in that case emphasized that "we think it prudent to refrain from adopting a rule that anything with the label 'contract' is necessarily outside the preemption clause." It also noted with approval another court's "recogni[tion of] the possibility that some applications of the law of contract could interfere with the attainment of national objectives and therefore come within the domain" of the Copyright Act. *Id.* The Eighth Circuit too cautioned in *National Car Rental* [*Sys., Inc. v. Computer Assocs. Int'l, Inc.*, 991 F.2d 426, 26 USPQ2d 1370 (8th Cir. 1993),] that a contractual restriction could impermissibly "protect rights equivalent to the exclusive copyright rights."

I conclude that *Vault* states the correct rule; that state law authorizing shrinkwrap licenses that prohibit reverse engineering is preempted; and that the First Circuit would so hold because the extra element here "merely concerns *the extent to which* authors and their licensees can prohibit unauthorized copying by third parties." I respectfully dissent.

NOTES

1. In fact, in *Vault,* the lower court had held that there was no contract. Thus, without the validating statute, there would be no obligation because no contract was ever created. Unlike *Baystate, Zeidenberg,* and other contract law preemption decisions, then, *Vault* did not involve preemption of a contract claim, but preemption of a state statute that created rights not dependent on contract.

2. *Zeidenberg* allowed a shrinkwrap contractual restriction on the use of factual data. The Copyright Act provides that copyright can create no rights in factual information. This express provision, it might be thought, is even more persuasive than the general, balancing test that arises under the fair use defense. Why, then, does Jude Dyk argue that *Zeidenberg* was a distinguishable case? If a person agrees to not do something, should its choice to breach that agreement bear on whether its conduct is "fair use"?

3. The Second Circuit in *Register.com v. Verio, Inc.,* 356 F.3d 393 (2d Cir. 2004), enforced a standard form, online contract that limited use of factual data downloaded from an online site. Is that different from the context in *Baystate?*

4. To create an enforceable contract under general contract law, must a licensor or other provider be willing to and in fact bargain for its terms? If not, does the concept in Judge Dyk's opinion regarding negotiated and other contracts set out a defensible position on preemption?

Chapter 15

LICENSES AND BANKRUPTCY ISSUES

I. CONTEXT OF BANKRUPTCY

A federal bankruptcy proceeding filed by either party places the license relationship into contact with a law whose fundamental principles differ from ordinary law. Bankruptcy law focuses on adjusting the relationship between a debtor's assets and the obligations of the debtor. It does so in reference to the reality that in an ordinary bankruptcy the debtor is insolvent. The two definitions of insolvency are:

- Insolvency consists of the sum of the debtor's assets being less than the sum of the debtors existing obligations (debts)

- Insolvency consists of the inability to pay the obligations as they become due

Bankruptcy law provides for two general types of proceedings: liquidation and reorganization. The most common bankruptcy is a liquidation, also described as a "Chapter 7 proceeding" because special rules for this type of bankruptcy are in the 700 series of the Bankruptcy Code (e.g., Chapter 7). In a Chapter 7 liquidation the debtor's assets are collected and sold, and the money obtained from the sale distributed to creditors on a pro rata basis for unsecured creditors of equal type. The mere filing of bankruptcy transfers the assets of the debtor to the bankruptcy estate and shifts how the assets are handled, from a focus on handling the debtor's property for its benefit, to handling nonexempt property to optimize financial return to unsecured creditors. 11 U.S.C. § 541. The assets are collected and sold by a trustee, subject to judicial supervision. Actions by creditors to collect against or seize assets of the estate are automatically stayed by operation of the Bankruptcy Code, unless or until the Bankruptcy Court grants relief from the stay. 11 U.S.C. § 362.

A bankruptcy liquidation of a business ends the company. Although the corporate shell may remain, it is emptied of assets. In contrast, if the debtor is an individual, the liquidation does not include assets exempt under federal or state law. In addition, a bankruptcy liquidation involving an individual as debtor typically results in "discharge" of the debtor's debts. A discharge is, in essence, an injunction against subsequent efforts by creditors to collect their claims from the debtor. 11 U.S.C. §§ 523, 524. Assets that are non-exempt are sold and their value is distributed pursuant to bankruptcy law which, with exceptions for certain debts, mandates payment of secured claims followed by pro rata distribution to unsecured creditors.

In contrast to liquidation, bankruptcy law also provides procedures in which the debtor does not relinquish all its assets, but can restructure its financial position by modifying debts and assets and paying the modified obligations over time. The most significant reorganization procedure for licensing is business reorganization under Chapter 11 of the Bankruptcy Code. A Chapter 11

proceeding is complex. As in liquidations, the mere filing of bankruptcy transfers the debtor's assets into a bankruptcy estate. 11 U.S.C. § 541. The automatic stay against creditors claiming or seizing assets channels virtually all
disputes into the Bankruptcy Court. 11 U.S.C. § 362. The basic procedure
typically involves the debtor's business management continuing to operate the
company in order to capture for creditors and other claimants the value of an
ongoing business. While many Chapter 11 proceedings result in a sale of the
business assets, the proceeding allows the debtor and the creditors to adjust
the business in order to optimize value pursuant to a "reorganization plan"
that they develop.

In an ordinary Chapter 11, the debtor becomes a "debtor-in-possession" with
trustee-like obligations to creditors. The concept is that the existing business
managers are better able to operate and optimize a business than an independent trustee. The focus is to develop and obtain approval of a plan of reorganization that remakes the debtor into a viable business by restructuring debts,
ownership, and other aspects of the pre-bankruptcy debtor.

PROBLEM 15.1

Company owes $1 million. It has operated a gun store for several years,
owning the building and the personal property (guns and targets) in its possession. The value of these items, if sold today, is $200,000. Company's income,
after expenses and paying employees, is enough monthly to pay the principle
and interest on its $100,000 real estate mortgage. There is $50,000 per month
left over, which covers all payments to current suppliers of bullets, targets and
other essentials, but leaves nothing for other creditors, including the trademark owner that has licensed use of its name to Company. The payment on
that license would be $10,000 per month. As an operating business, Company
is valued at $600,000.

a. What result if Company files for liquidation?

b. What result if it chooses a Chapter 11 proceeding and all claimants will
agree to a new structure that does not cause each a major loss of value?

II. EFFECTS OF THE FILING

Without more, filing a bankruptcy petition causes an immediate transfer by
law of all the debtor's "property" into the bankruptcy estate. That transfer has
immediate impact on persons dealing with the debtor. It changes with whom
one must deal and what rules apply. The description of "property" in bankruptcy law is broad because the goal is to reap as much value for creditors as
possible. 11 U.S.C. § 541(a) provides in relevant part that:

> The commencement of a case . . . creates an estate. Such estate is com-
> prised of all the following property, wherever located and by whomever
> held: . . . all legal or equitable interests of the debtor in property as of the
> commencement of the case [and various designated types of property
> acquired after commencement of the case].

This covers various assets, including intellectual property rights, as well as contractual rights. While there are various exclusions from this coverage, the important point for our purposes is that it does not typically extend to interests that have been transferred or terminated prior to the filing, unless the bankruptcy estate is subsequently able to recover the property.

Timing also matters, because the bankruptcy filing places an immediate, automatic stay on most efforts to collect from, enforce rights against, or take or use property of the estate. 11 U.S.C. § 362 provides in relevant part:

> (a) Except as provided in subsection (b) of this section, a petition filed under [this title] operates as a stay, applicable to all entities, of —
>
> > (1) the commencement or continuation, including the issuance or employment of process, of a judicial, administrative, or other action or proceeding against the debtor that was or could have been commenced before the commencement of the case under this title, or to recover a claim against the debtor that arose before the commencement of the case under this title;
> >
> > (2) the enforcement, against the debtor or against property of the estate, of a judgment obtained before the commencement of the case under this title;
> >
> > (3) any act to obtain possession of property of the estate or of property from the estate or to exercise control over property of the estate;
> >
> > (4) any act to create, perfect, or enforce any lien against property of the estate;
> >
> > . . . .
> >
> > (6) any act to collect, assess, or recover a claim against the debtor that arose before the commencement of the case under this title; . . . .

The stay shifts the focus of subsequent activities related to a license to the bankruptcy estate and the Bankruptcy Court. It precludes some otherwise permissible acts unless the actor obtains prior court approval for them because the conduct involved would, if effective, remove property from the bankruptcy estate. Section 362 also provides for criteria under which a party may seek relief from the stay — from the Bankruptcy Court.

PROBLEM 15.2

Which of the following would be permitted under the automatic stay created by the filing of Debtor's bankruptcy on June 1?

a. A notice from licensor to Debtor that terminates a copyright license held by Debtor when the notice is delivered on May 30.

b. A filing on June 10 of an action in state court to recover previously delivered materials and obtain an injunction against Debtor who has been a franchise owner of the Licensor's trade name.

c. Filing a lawsuit for copyright infringement on May 30.

UNITED STATES v. INSLAW, INC.
932 F.2d 1467 (D.C. Cir. 1991)

WILLIAM, CIRCUIT JUDGE:

Section 362(a) of the Bankruptcy Code imposes an automatic stay of "any act to obtain possession of property of the estate . . . or to exercise control over property of the estate" [after bankruptcy is filed]. 11 U.S.C. § 362(a)(3) (1988). Inslaw, Inc., after filing for reorganization under Chapter 11 of the Bankruptcy Code, invoked § 362(a) to secure bankruptcy court adjudication of . . . its prolonged dispute with the Department of Justice over the Department's right to use a case-tracking software system that Inslaw had provided under contract. Inslaw claimed that the Department had violated the stay provision by continuing, and expanding, its use of the software [PROMIS] in its U.S. Attorneys' offices [after the bankruptcy filing]. The bankruptcy court found a willful violation and the district court affirmed on appeal. [We reverse.]

II

[Inslaw's] major allegation concerns the Department's use of enhanced PROMIS after the filing of the bankruptcy petition. The bankruptcy court concluded first that the privately-funded enhancements to PROMIS were proprietary trade secrets owned by Inslaw, and then that the Department's continued use of these enhancements, and in particular its post-petition installation of enhanced PROMIS in 23 U.S. Attorneys' offices (in addition to the 22 where Inslaw had made installations), were a "willful exercise of control over the property of the estate."

The automatic stay protects "property of the estate." This estate is created by the filing of a petition and comprises property of the debtor "wherever located and by whomever held," including (among other things) "all legal or equitable interests of the debtor in property as of the commencement of the case." 11 U.S.C. § 541(a)(1) (1988). It is undisputed that this encompasses causes of action that belong to the debtor, as well as the debtor's intellectual property, such as interests in patents, trademarks and copyrights. The estate also includes property recoverable under the Code's "turnover" provisions, which allow the trustee to recover property that "was merely out of the possession of the debtor, yet remained 'property of the debtor.'"

In its brief Inslaw refers rather vaguely to its interest in the enhanced PROMIS software as the "property of the estate" over which the Department supposedly exercised control. But for meaningful analysis, Inslaw's interests must be examined separately. One set of interests consists of (1) the computer tapes containing copies of the source and object codes that Inslaw sent to the Department on April 20, 1983 and (2) the copies of enhanced PROMIS that Inslaw installed on Department hardware between August 1983 and January 1984. As to these, Inslaw held no possessory interest when it filed for bankruptcy on February 7, 1985. Nor can it claim a possessory interest over them through the Code's turnover provisions, [because] as Inslaw freely admits, the Department held possession of the copies under a claim of ownership (its view of the contract . . .) and claimed the right to use enhanced PROMIS without further payment. [A] debtor cannot use the turnover provisions to liquidate contract disputes or otherwise demand assets whose title is in dispute. Indeed, Inslaw never sought possession of the copies under the turnover provisions.

The bankruptcy court instead identified the relevant property as Inslaw's intangible trade secret rights in the PROMIS enhancements. It then found that the Department's continuing use of these intangible enhancements was an "exercise of control" over property of the estate.

If the bankruptcy court's idea of the scope of "exercise of control" were correct, the sweep of § 362(a) would be extraordinary — with a concomitant expansion of the jurisdiction of the bankruptcy court. Whenever a party against whom the bankrupt holds a cause of action (or other intangible property right) acted in accord with his view of the dispute rather than that of the debtor-in-possession or bankruptcy trustee, he would risk a determination by a bankruptcy court that he had "exercised control" over intangible rights (property) of the estate.

[Such] assertions of bankruptcy court jurisdiction raise severe constitutional problems. . . . Even apart from constitutional concerns, Inslaw's view of § 362(a) would take it well beyond Congress's purpose. The object of the automatic stay provision is essentially to solve a collective action problem — to make sure that creditors do not destroy the bankrupt estate in their scramble for relief. Fulfillment of that purpose cannot require that every party who acts in resistance to the debtor's view of its rights violates § 362(a) if found in error by the bankruptcy court. Thus, someone defending a suit brought by the debtor does *not* risk violation of § 362(a)(3) by filing a motion to dismiss the suit, though his resistance may burden rights asserted by the bankrupt. Nor does the filing of a lis pendens violate the stay (at least where it does not create a lien), even though it alerts prospective buyers to a hazard and may thereby diminish the value of estate property. And the commencement and continuation of a cause of action against the debtor that arises post-petition, and so is not stayed by § 362(a)(1), does not violate § 362(a)(3). Since willful violations of the stay expose the offending party to liability for compensatory damages, costs, attorney's fees, and, in some circumstances, punitive damages, *see* 11 U.S.C. § 362(h) (1988), it is difficult to believe that Congress intended a violation whenever someone already in possession of property mistakenly refuses to capitulate to a bankrupt's assertion of rights in that property.

[Our] understanding of § 362(a) does not expose bankrupts to any troubling hazard. Here, for example, Inslaw retains whatever intangible property rights it had in enhanced PROMIS at the time of filing. If the Department has violated the [contract,] Inslaw as debtor-in-possession has all the access to court enjoyed by any victim of a contract breach by the United States government. If [the alleged modification of the contract] was induced by fraud, [then] Inslaw has its contract remedies or perhaps a suit for conversion. Assuming that its privately-funded enhancements to PROMIS qualify as proprietary trade secrets, [it] may be able to sue the government under the Trade Secrets Act or even under the Administrative Procedure Act for improper disclosures of its trade secrets by government officials.

[Because] the Department has taken no actions since the filing of the bankruptcy petition that violate the automatic stay, the bankruptcy court must, as both a statutory and constitutional matter, defer to adjudication of these matters by other forums. . . . *So ordered.*

NOTE

If a licensee of a trade secret threatens to wrongfully disclose that trade secret after the filing of bankruptcy by the licensor, what recourse does the licensor's bankruptcy estate have?

COMPUTER COMMUNICATIONS, INC. v. CODEX CORP.
824 F.2d 725 (9th Cir. 1987)

Tang, Circuit Judge:

Codex Corporation (Codex) appeals a judgment of the district court affirming the bankruptcy court's determination that Codex violated the Bankruptcy Code's automatic stay provision, 11 U.S.C. § 362 (1982), and breached its contract with Computer Communications, Inc. (CCI). Codex unilaterally terminated its contract to purchase computer equipment from CCI after CCI filed a petition for reorganization under [Chapter 11].

11 U.S.C. § 362 provides that the filing of a bankruptcy petition automatically stays "any act to obtain possession of property of the estate. . . ." 11 U.S.C. § 362(a)(3). The courts below held that the automatic stay prohibited Codex from unilaterally terminating the Agreement. We agree. Even if Codex had a valid reason for terminating the Agreement, it still was required to petition the court for relief from the automatic stay under § 362(d).

An examination of the legislative history and overall statutory scheme supports our conclusion. According to the legislative history, the purpose of the automatic stay is to give the debtor a breathing spell from creditors, to stop all collection efforts, and to permit the debtor to attempt repayment or reorganization. Congress intended the scope of the stay to be broad. "All proceedings are stayed, including arbitration, license revocation, administrative, and judicial proceedings. Proceeding in this sense encompasses civil actions as well, and all proceedings even if they are not before governmental tribunals."

11 U.S.C. § 541 (1982) defines property of the estate. It neither explicitly includes or excludes contract rights. The definition includes "all legal or equitable interests of the debtor in property as of the commencement of the case." The legislative history states that the scope for this paragraph is broad. "It includes all kinds of property, including tangible or intangible property [and] causes of action. . . ." H.R.Rep. No. 595 at 367. This court has held that insurance contracts are embraced in the statutory definition of "property."

The automatic stay does not permanently prohibit a party from retrieving property from the possession of the bankrupt estate. Section 362(d) provides that upon notice and hearing, the court shall grant relief from the stay. Congress intended the relief proceeding to be a summary one in which the only issues will be the "lack of adequate protection, the debtor's equity in the property, and the necessity of the property to an effective reorganization of the debtor, or the existence of other cause for relief from the stay."

Codex argues that the trial court erred because the contract was not property of the estate. It asserts that 11 U.S.C. § 365 (1982), pertaining to executory contracts and unexpired leases, sanctioned its termination of the contract.

Section 365 provides that a trustee may assume or reject any executory contract or unexpired lease of the debtor. The contract, argues Codex, never became property of the estate because the trustee did not and could not assume it. An executory contract is one in which performance remains due to some extent on both sides. Section 365(e) generally prohibits exercise of bankruptcy termination clauses in such contracts:

> Notwithstanding a provision in an executory contract or unexpired lease, or in applicable law, an executory contract or unexpired lease of the debtor may not be terminated or modified . . . at any time after the commencement of the case solely because of a provision in such contract or lease that is conditioned on . . . the commencement of a case under this title. . . .

Subparagraph (2), however, creates an exception where "applicable law excuses a party, other than the debtor, to such contract or lease from accepting performance from or rendering performance to the trustee or an assignee of such contract or lease. . . ." 11 U.S.C. § 365(e)(2)(A)(i). Codex argues that Massachusetts law excused it from accepting performance from an assignee for three reasons: 1) the Agreement was a personal service contract; 2) even if it was not a personal service contract, it was a contract based on "a relation of personal confidence"; and 3) assignment of the contract would have revealed Codex's trade secrets.

The bankruptcy court held that § 365(e)(2) did not permit Codex to terminate the contract unilaterally finding that the Amended Agreement was not a contract for personal services. Likewise, the district court concluded that the contract was almost entirely for the sale of goods. We need not reach that question, however, because we hold that even if § 365(e)(2) allowed Codex to terminate the contract, § 362 automatically stayed termination.

Codex argues that, since executory contracts do not automatically vest in the bankrupt estate, but must be assumed by the executor, they are not automatically stayed. Codex cites COLLIER ON BANKRUPTCY, which states "[p]resumably the automatic stay of section 362, which prohibits a creditor from terminating or accelerating after the petition, will not apply to these special kinds of contracts or leases." 2 COLLIER ON BANKRUPTCY ¶ 365.06[1] (15th ed. 1987). Codex also cites several cases that follow the COLLIER analysis.

We find this argument unavailing. The version of 11 U.S.C. § 541 in effect at the time plainly stated that a contract comes within the definition of "property of the estate" despite non-assignability or the existence of a bankruptcy default clause.

> [A]n interest of the debtor becomes property of the estate . . . notwithstanding any provision —
>
>> (A) that restricts or conditions transfer of such interest by the debtor; or
>
>> (B) that is conditioned on the insolvency or financial condition of the debtor, or the commencement of a case under this title, or the appointment of or the taking possession by a trustee . . . and that affects or gives an option to effect a forfeiture, modification, or termination of the debtor's interest in property.

11 U.S.C. §541(c)(1). Codex argues that even if §541(c)(1) overrides the contract, it does not override Massachusettes law. We read the introductory phrase, "notwithstanding any provision," broadly to include not only contract provisions but also any provision of non-bankruptcy law. We note that Congress recently clarified the statute and it now states "notwithstanding any provision in an agreement, transfer instrument, *or applicable nonbankruptcy law. . . .*" 11 U.S.C. §541(c)(1). . . .

The legislative history emphasizes that the stay is intended to be broad in scope. Congress designed it to protect debtors and creditors from piecemeal dismemberment of the debtor's estate. The automatic stay statute itself provides a summary procedure for obtaining relief from the stay. All parties benefit from the fair and orderly process contemplated by the automatic stay and judicial relief procedure. Judicial toleration of an alternative procedure of self-help and post hoc justification would defeat the purpose of the automatic stay. Accordingly, we affirm the bankruptcy and district courts on the ground that Codex violated the automatic stay by unilaterally terminating the contract and do not reach the question of whether this contract is non-assignable under Massachusetts law. . . . AFFIRMED.

NOTE

The fact that a contractual right becomes part of the estate does not necessarily mean that the debtor's estate can reap value from that contract. But before we reach that issue, consider the impact of Section 541 on one of the most common provisions of real estate leases and intellectual property licenses — a clause that provides that the contract automatically terminates if a party to it files bankruptcy.

PROBLEM 15.3

TX is a licensor of its name, confidential processes, and copyrights for running hair style studios for professional men. It has several hundred licensees, each of which must renew in order to keep their licenses. TX desires to structure its licenses for the next round of renewals so that it can simply close down any licensee that may or does file bankruptcy. Would a contract term that terminates the license in the event the licensee becomes insolvent suffice? What about a term that ends the license if a bankruptcy is filed? What of a term that allows termination whenever the licensor sends written notice of it? Other suggestions? *See* 11 U.S.C. §§ 541, 365.

III. EXECUTORY CONTRACTS

Among the interests that pass to the estate are the contract rights that existed at the time of filing. These contracts are included in the estate whether or not the contract has been fully performed. As to contract rights that are "executory," the Bankruptcy Code gives the trustee in bankruptcy or the debtor in possession the right to assume or reject the contract.

The term "executory contract" ordinarily means that substantial performance remains on both sides of the agreement such that breach by either party would be material and excuse performance by the other party. Section 365 generally gives the debtor the right to assume or reject executory contracts, subject to various procedural and substantive conditions.

- "Rejection" constitutes a breach of the contract and a refusal to continue performing promises under the contract. The other contracting party is left with a damages claim against the estate.

- "Assume" implies a decision to take on the contract obligations under the license. Where the contract is in breach, in order to assume it, the debtor or its estate must cure or provide adequate assurance that it will cure the defaults. If a contract has been properly assumed, it may be retained by the debtor and performed, or assigned, subject to court approval.

The purpose of creating these rights is to enable the debtor in possession in bankruptcy or the trustee to achieve maximum value from the assets of the estate, which may require assuming beneficial contracts and rejecting burdensome contracts. While court approval is required, the standard for assumption or rejection is generally at the business judgment of the debtor or the trustee as long as the proposed action complies with statutory standards regarding cure of defaults and the like. *See In re Richmond Metal Finishers, Inc.*, 756 F.2d 1043 (4th Cir. 1985).

IN RE CLAREMONT ACQUISITION CORPORATION, INC.
113 F.3d 1029 (9th Cir. 1997)

MERHIGE, SENIOR DISTRICT JUDGE:

Facts and Procedural History

Debtors operated Cadillac, Pontiac/GMC Truck, Ford, Isuzu and Hyundai dealerships at the Claremont Auto Center in Claremont, California. On or about November 7, 1994, Debtors ceased operating their automobile dealerships. On November 20, 1994, Debtors commenced a Chapter 11 bankruptcy proceeding. On March 31, 1995, the bankruptcy court approved Worthington as the purchaser of the Debtors' assets, including the dealer franchises. Applying California Vehicle Code § 11713.3(e), which prohibits transfer of an automobile franchise agreement without the consent of the manufacturer whose consent may not be unreasonably withheld, the bankruptcy court required the consent of GM prior to ordering the assignment of the franchise agreements to Worthington. GM refused to consent to the assignment, prompting Debtors to seek an order compelling the assignment. After hearing argument, the bankruptcy court entered an order finding that GM had unreasonably withheld consent within the meaning of Cal.Veh.Code § 11713.3(e). The bankruptcy court therefore ordered GM to accept the assignment of Debtors' GM Dealer and Service Agreements (the "GM Dealer Agreements") from the Debtors to Worthington. The bankruptcy court also ruled that pursuant to § 365(b)(2)(D) of the Bankruptcy Code (the "Code"), Debtors were not required to cure any nonmonetary defaults in order to assume and assign their contracts to Worthington.

GM appealed the order compelling assignment of the GM Dealer Agreements. The district court found that the bankruptcy court had misapplied Cal.Veh. Code § 11713.3(e) and reversed the bankruptcy court's order as it applied to GM. The district court affirmed, however, the bankruptcy court's interpretation of § 365(b)(2)(D). Worthington and Debtors now appeal the district court's decision with respect to the application of § 11713.3(e) to the assignment. GM has filed a cross-appeal challenging the district court's interpretation of § 365(b)(2)(D). . . .

Discussion

Section 365(b)(2) of the Code provides:

> Paragraph (1) of this subsection [imposing the requirement of curing defaults prior to assumption and assignment] does not apply to a default that is a breach of a provision relating to —
>
> . . . .
>
> (D) the satisfaction of any penalty rate or provision relating to a default arising from any failure by the debtor to perform nonmonetary obligations under the executory contract or unexpired lease.

11 U.S.C. § 365(b)(2)(D). Both GM and Worthington argue that the language of subsection (D) is unambiguous, but are at opposite poles as to its meaning. Worthington asserts that under subsection (D), it is not required to cure nonmonetary defaults. GM, on the other hand, reads subsection (D) as stating that, in curing defaults concerning nonmonetary obligations, the Debtor does not have to cure any *penalties* arising from a nonmonetary default.

The bankruptcy court adopted Worthington's construction of subsection (D). Accordingly, the court held that Worthington's failure to operate the dealerships was a breach of a "provision relating to a default arising from [a] failure of the debtor to perform [a] nonmonetary obligation," which, according to subsection (D), was a default that did not have to be cured before assumption and assignment. We review the bankruptcy court's construction of the statute *de novo.*

The difference between the parties' interpretations of § 365(b)(2)(D) centers on the effect of the word "or" in subsection (D). Worthington argues that the word "or" operates to create two distinct and independent exceptions to the cure requirements of paragraph (1). Worthington apparently reasons that the clause preceding the word "or" excepts "satisfaction of any *penalty* rate" from the cure requirements, and that the clause following "or" is a catch-all provision excepting from cure *any* "nonmonetary obligations."

GM disagrees with this interpretation of the statute. GM argues that the word "penalty" in subsection (D) modifies *both* "rate" and "provision." Because the provision of the GM Dealer Agreement at issue in this case is not a penalty provision, *i.e.,* a liquidated damage provision, GM contends that the subsection (D) exception does not apply and the GM Dealer Agreements may not be assigned.

We find the construction offered by GM to be the more reasonable interpretation of the statute. A proper reading of subsection (D) requires that the adjective "penalty" modify *both* the words "rate" and "provision," not just the word "rate." Furthermore, like the word "penalty," the word "satisfaction" must also define both "rate" and "provision." Stated differently, subsection (D) provides an exception from cure for satisfaction of "penalty rates" and "penalty provisions." When construed in this manner, the clause following the word "or" is not a catch-all exception to paragraph (1), but instead an exception concerning those provisions of a contract which impose a penalty for a debtor's failure to perform a nonmonetary obligation.

The proper construction of § 365(b)(2)(D) is readily apparent upon consideration of how the statute would read if the word "or" connected two distinct exceptions, as Worthington suggests. If this were the case, one should be able to delete the first clause, and the statute would still make sense. . . . This construction of the section is both grammatically incorrect and nonsensical. The more logical construction of subsection (D) would have the words "satisfaction" and "penalty" relate to both "rate" and "provision." . . . Unlike Worthington's construction, this construction is grammatically correct.

GM's interpretation of § 365(b)(2)(D) is further supported by consideration of the general structure of § 365 which suggests that Congress intended subsection (D) to address a single issue: the payment of penalties. In each instance that Congress added a separate or independent exception to § 365(b)(1), it created a separate subclause in § 365(b)(2). The bankruptcy court's interpretation, however, requires a deviation from that general construction principle, as it results in a single subclause containing two completely different and unrelated exceptions. Furthermore, if subsection (D) is a catch-all provision, as Worthington contends, then subsections (A) through (C) of § 365(b)(2) would be superfluous, as they would be encompassed by subsection (D). Conversely, applying the terms "satisfaction" and "penalty" to both clauses in subsection (D) unifies the single provision. The first clause addresses penalty rates which are commonly imposed where a debtor's breach was monetary in nature. The second clause addresses the payment of penalties under liquidated damage provisions where the debtor's breach was nonmonetary in nature.

[Under] the interpretation we adopt today, the § 365(b)(2)(D) exception does not apply to Debtors' default. Debtors' failure to operate the franchises for seven consecutive days is not a default of a contractual provision relating to the satisfaction of a penalty rate or the payment of a penalty. Accordingly, Debtors' obligation to cure their default is not excused. Because Debtors are unable to now cure their default, the GM Dealer Agreements may not be assumed and assigned. . . .

NOTE

Why should bankruptcy law provide the debtor with any right to cure a default in an executory contract? If prior to bankruptcy, the default led to cancellation of the license, would the cure provisions nevertheless apply?

LUBRIZOL ENTERPRISES, INC. v. RICHMOND METAL FINISHERS, INC.
756 F.2d 1043 (4th Cir. 1985)

PHILLIPS, CIRCUIT JUDGE:

The question is whether Richmond Metal Finishers (RMF), a bankrupt debtor in possession, should have been allowed to reject as executory a technology licensing agreement with Lubrizol Enterprises (Lubrizol) as licensee. The bankruptcy court approved rejection pursuant to 11 U.S.C. § 365(a); but the district court reversed on the basis that within contemplation of § 365(a), the contract was not executory and, alternatively, that rejection could not reasonably be expected substantially to benefit the bankrupt debtor. We reverse and remand for entry of judgment in conformity with that entered by the bankruptcy court.

I

In July of 1982, RMF entered into the contract with Lubrizol that granted Lubrizol a nonexclusive license to utilize a metal coating process technology owned by RMF. RMF owed the following duties to Lubrizol under the agreement: (1) to notify Lubrizol of any patent infringement suit and to defend in such suit; (2) to notify Lubrizol of any other use or licensing of the process, and to reduce royalty payments if a lower royalty rate agreement was reached with another licensee; and (3) to indemnify Lubrizol for losses arising out of any misrepresentation or breach of warranty by RMF. Lubrizol owed RMF reciprocal duties of accounting for and paying royalties for use of the process and of cancelling certain existing indebtedness. The contract provided that Lubrizol would defer use of the process until May 1, 1983, and in fact, Lubrizol has never used the RMF technology.

RMF filed a petition for bankruptcy pursuant to Chapter 11 of the Bankruptcy Code on August 16, 1983. As part of its plan to emerge from bankruptcy, RMF sought, pursuant to § 365(a), to reject the contract with Lubrizol in order to facilitate sale or licensing of the technology unhindered by restrictive provisions in the Lubrizol agreement. On RMF's motion for approval of the rejection, the bankruptcy court properly interpreted § 365 as requiring it to undertake a two-step inquiry to determine the propriety of rejection: first, whether the contract is executory; next, if so, whether its rejection would be advantageous to the bankrupt. Making that inquiry, the bankruptcy court determined that both tests were satisfied and approved the rejection. But, as indicated, the district court then reversed that determination on the basis that neither test was satisfied and disallowed the rejection. This appeal followed.

II

We conclude initially that, as the bankruptcy court ruled, the technology licensing agreement in this case was an executory contract, within contemplation of 11 U.S.C. § 365(a). Under that provision a contract is executory if performance is due to some extent on both sides. This court has recently adopted Professor Countryman's more specific test for determining whether a contract is "executory" in the required sense. By that test, a contract is executory if the " 'obligations of both the bankrupt and the other party to the contract are so far unperformed that the failure of either to complete the performance would constitute a material breach excusing the performance of the other.'" This issue is one of law that may be freely reviewed by successive courts.

Applying that test here, we conclude that the licensing agreement was at the critical time executory. RMF owed Lubrizol the continuing duties of notifying Lubrizol of further licensing of the process and of reducing Lubrizol's royalty rate to meet any more favorable rates granted to subsequent licensees. By their terms, RMF's obligations to give notice and to restrict its right to license its process at royalty rates it desired without lowering Lubrizol's royalty rate extended over the life of the agreement, and remained unperformed. Moreover, RMF owed Lubrizol additional contingent duties of notifying it of suits, defending suits and indemnifying it for certain losses.

The unperformed, continuing core obligations of notice and forbearance in licensing made the contract executory as to RMF. In *Fenix Cattle Co. v. Silver (In re Select-A-Seat Corp.)*, 625 F.2d 290, 292 (9th Cir.1980), the court found that an obligation of a debtor to refrain from selling software packages under an exclusive licensing agreement made a contract executory as to the debtor notwithstanding the continuing obligation was only one of forbearance. Although the license to Lubrizol was not exclusive, RMF owed the same type of unperformed continuing duty of forbearance arising out of the most favored licensee clause running in favor of Lubrizol. Breach of that duty would clearly constitute a material breach of the agreement.

Moreover, the contract was further executory as to RMF because of the contingent duties that RMF owed of giving notice of and defending infringement suits and of indemnifying Lubrizol for certain losses arising out of the use of the technology. Contingency of an obligation does not prevent its being executory under § 365. *See In re Smith Jones, Inc.*, 26 B.R. 289, 292 (Bankr.D.Minn.1982) (warranty obligations executory as to promisor); *In re O.P.M. Leasing Services, Inc.*, 23 B.R. 104, 117 (Bankr.S.D.N.Y.1982) (obligation to defend infringement suits makes contract executory as to promisor). Until the time has expired during which an event triggering a contingent duty may occur, the contingent obligation represents a continuing duty to stand ready to perform if the contingency occurs. A breach of that duty once it was triggered by the contingency (or presumably, by anticipatory repudiation) would have been material.

Because a contract is not executory within the meaning of § 365(a) unless it is executory as to both parties, it is also necessary to determine whether the licensing agreement was executory as to Lubrizol. We conclude that it was.

Lubrizol owed RMF the unperformed and continuing duty of accounting for and paying royalties for the life of the agreement. It is true that a contract is not executory as to a party simply because the party is obligated to make payments of money to the other party. Therefore, if Lubrizol had owed RMF nothing more than a duty to make fixed payments or cancel specified indebtedness under the agreement, the agreement would not be executory as to Lubrizol. However, the promise to account for and pay royalties required that Lubrizol deliver written quarterly sales reports and keep books of account subject to inspection by an independent Certified Public Accountant. This promise goes beyond a mere debt, or promise to pay money, and was at the critical time executory. Additionally, subject to certain exceptions, Lubrizol was obligated to keep all license technology in confidence for a number of years.

Since the licensing agreement is executory as to each party, it is executory within the meaning of § 365(a), and the district court erred as a matter of law in reaching a contrary conclusion.

III

There remains the question whether rejection of the executory contract would be advantageous to the bankrupt. Courts addressing that question must start with the proposition that the bankrupt's decision upon it is to be accorded the deference mandated by the sound business judgment rule as generally applied by courts to discretionary actions or decisions of corporate directors.

As generally formulated and applied in corporate litigation the rule is that courts should defer to — should not interfere with — decisions of corporate directors upon matters entrusted to their business judgment except upon a finding of bad faith or gross abuse of their "business discretion." Transposed to the bankruptcy context, the rule as applied to a bankrupt's decision to reject an executory contract because of perceived business advantage requires that the decision be accepted by courts unless it is shown that the bankrupt's decision was one taken in bad faith or in gross abuse of the bankrupt's retained business discretion.

In bankruptcy litigation the issue is of course first presented for judicial determination when a debtor, having decided that rejection will be beneficial within contemplation of § 365(a), moves for approval of the rejection. The issue thereby presented for first instance judicial determination by the bankruptcy court is whether the decision of the debtor that rejection will be advantageous is so manifestly unreasonable that it could not be based on sound business judgment, but only on bad faith, or whim or caprice. That issue is one of fact to be decided as such by the bankruptcy court by the normal processes of fact adjudication. And the resulting fact determination by the bankruptcy court is perforce then reviewable up the line under the clearly erroneous standard.

Here, the bankruptcy judge had before him evidence not rebutted by Lubrizol that the metal coating process subject to the licensing agreement is RMF's principal asset and that sale or licensing of the technology represented the primary potential source of funds by which RMF might emerge from bankruptcy. The testimony of RMF's president, also factually uncontested by Lubrizol, indicated that sale or further licensing of the technology would be facilitated by stripping Lubrizol of its rights in the process and that, correspondingly, continued obligation to Lubrizol under the agreement would hinder RMF's capability to sell or license the technology on more advantageous terms to other potential licensees. On the basis of this evidence the bankruptcy court determined that the debtor's decision to reject was based upon sound business judgment and approved it.

On appeal the district court simply found to the contrary that the debtor's decision to reject did not represent a sound business judgment. . . . We conclude that in both of these respects the district court's factual findings, at odds with those of the bankruptcy court, were clearly erroneous and cannot stand. . . .

REVERSED AND REMANDED

NOTES

1. The court in *Otto Preminger Films, Ltd. v. Quintex Entertainment, Ltd.*, 950 F.2d 1492 (9th Cir. 1991), held that a contract involving an obligation to colorize certain motion pictures and conveying to the colorizing company a right to distribute the movies was an executory contract. The unperformed obligations required the licensor to: (1) refrain from selling the rights to the movies to third parties; (2) indemnify and defend the licensee; and (3) exercise creative control over the colorization and marketing of the pictures. The licensee was contractually obligated to give an accounting and to pay royalties for sales of the pictures. Colorization had not been completed at the time of bankruptcy.

Compare two decisions involving book contracts in which the publisher received distribution rights in return for obligations to account for and pay royalties. Neither was an executory contract. *In re Learning Publications, Inc.*, 94 B.R. 763, 765 (Bankr. M.D. Fla. 1988); *In re Stein & Day, Inc.*, 81 BR 263, 267 (Bankr. S.D.N.Y. 1988). In both cases, the authors had completed their portion of the contract by submitting the completed book manuscript.

2. In *Fenix Cattle Co. v. Silver*, 625 F.2d 290 (9th Cir. 1980), the court held that an exclusive software license was executory because the licensee had an ongoing obligation to account for sales and to pay royalties, while the licensor had a continuing obligation to not license the software to third parties and to not sue to enforce an infringement claim against the licensee for its conduct under the license.

PROBLEM 15.4

ADBY, a mass market software publisher whose primary products are software that enables users to draw graphic designs, files bankruptcy on March 10. At that time, it has 10,000 licenses with end users. All of these were created by enforceable shrinkwrap agreements and based on payment by the licensee of a one-time fee. The licenses were perpetual in length and required that the licensee not use the software for commercial purposes. Another 50 licenses existed between ADBY and distributors. These agreements allowed the licensees to make and distribute copies of the software in machines of their manufacture. The agreements were for five years. In the bankruptcy, the issue is whether all or any of these agreements are executory contracts. What is your advice?

IN RE PIONEER FORD SALES, INC.
729 F.2d 27 (1st Cir. 1984)

BREYER, CIRCUIT JUDGE.

The Ford Motor Company appeals a federal district court decision allowing a bankrupt Ford dealer (Pioneer Ford Sales, Inc.) to assign its Ford franchise over Ford's objection to a Toyota dealer (Toyota Village, Inc.). The district court decided the case on the basis of a record developed in the bankruptcy court. The bankruptcy court had approved the transfer, which ran from Pioneer to Fleet National Bank (Pioneer's principal secured creditor) and then to Toyota Village. Fleet sought authorization for the assignment because Toyota Village will pay $10,000 for the franchise and buy all parts and accessories in Pioneer's inventory at fair market value (about $75,000); if the franchise is not assigned, Ford will buy only some of the parts for between $45,000 and $55,000. Thus, the assignment will increase the value of the estate. Fleet is the appellee here.

The issue that the case raises is the proper application of 11 U.S.C. § 365(c)(1)(A), an exception to a more general provision, 11 U.S.C. § 365(f)(1), that allows a trustee in bankruptcy (or a debtor in possession) to assign many of the debtor's executory contracts even if the contract itself says that it forbids assignment. The exception at issue reads as follows:

> (c) The trustee [or debtor in possession] may not assume or assign an executory contract . . . of the debtor, whether or not such contract . . . prohibits assignment if —
>
>> (1)(A) applicable law excuses [the other party to the contract] from accepting performance from . . . an assignee . . . whether or not [the] . . . contract . . . prohibits . . . assignment.

The words "applicable law" in this section mean "applicable non-bankruptcy law." Evidently, the theory of this section is to prevent the trustee from assigning (over objection) contracts of the sort that contract law ordinarily makes nonassignable, *i.e.* contracts that cannot be assigned when the contract itself is silent about assignment. At the same time, by using the words in (1)(A) "whether *or not* the contract prohibits assignment," the section prevents parties from using contractual language to prevent the trustee from assigning contracts that (when the contract is silent) contract law typically makes assignable. Thus, we must look to see whether relevant nonbankruptcy law would allow Ford to veto the assignment of its basic franchise contract "whether or not" that basic franchise contract itself specifically "prohibits assignment."

The nonbankruptcy law to which both sides point us is contained in Rhode Island's "Regulation of Business Practices Among Motor Vehicle Manufacturers, Distributors and Dealers" Act, R.I.Gen.Laws § 31-5.1-4(C)(7). It states that

> [N]o dealer . . . shall have the right to . . . assign the franchise . . . without the consent of the manufacturer, except that such consent shall not be unreasonably withheld.

The statute by its terms, allows a manufacturer to veto an assignment where the veto is reasonable but not otherwise. The statute's language also indicates that it applies "whether or not" the franchise contract itself restricts assignment. Thus, the basic question that the case presents is whether Ford's veto was reasonable in terms of the Rhode Island law.

Neither the district court nor the bankruptcy court specifically addressed this question. Their failure apparently arose out of their belief that 11 U.S.C. § 365(c)(1)(A) refers only to traditional personal service contracts. But in our view they were mistaken. The language of the section does not limit its effect to personal service contracts. It refers *generally* to contracts that are not assignable under nonbankruptcy law. State laws typically make contracts for personal services nonassignable (where the contract itself is silent); but they make other sorts of contracts nonassignable as well. The legislative history of § 365(c) says nothing about "personal services." To the contrary, it speaks of letters of credit, personal loans, and leases — instances in which assigning a contract may place the other party at a significant disadvantage. The history thereby suggests that (c)(1)(A) has a broader reach.

The source of the "personal services" limitation apparently is a bankruptcy court case, *In re Taylor Manufacturing, Inc.*, 6 B.R. 370 (N.D. Ga. 1980), which other bankruptcy courts have followed. The *Taylor* court wrote that (c)(1)(A) should be interpreted narrowly, in part because it believed that (c)(1)(A) conflicted with another section, (f)(1), which states in relevant part:

> Except as provided in subsection (c) . . ., notwithstanding a provision . . . in applicable law that prohibits . . . the assignment of [an executory] contract . . . the trustee may assign [it]. . . .

As a matter of logic, however, we see no conflict, for (c)(1)(A) refers to state laws that prohibit assignment "whether or not" the contract is silent, while (f)(1) contains no such limitation. Apparently (f)(1) includes state laws that prohibit assignment only when the contract is *not* silent about assignment; that is to say, state laws that enforce contract provisions prohibiting assignment. *See* 1 NORTON, BANKRUPTCY LAW AND PRACTICE § 23.14. These state laws are to be ignored. The section specifically excepts (c)(1)(A)'s state laws that forbid assignment even when the contract *is* silent; they are to be heeded. . . .

Although the district court did not explicitly decide whether Ford's veto was reasonable, it decided a closely related question. Under other provisions of § 365 a bankruptcy court cannot authorize assignment of an executory contract if 1) the debtor is in default, unless 2) there is "adequate assurance of future performance." § 365(b)(1)(C). Pioneer is in default, but the bankruptcy and district courts found "adequate assurance." For the sake of argument, we shall assume that this finding is equivalent to a finding that Ford's veto of the assignment was unreasonable. And, we shall apply a "clearly erroneous" standard in reviewing the factual element in this lower court finding. On these assumptions, favorable to Fleet, we nonetheless must reverse the district court, for, in our view, any finding of unreasonableness, based on this record, is clearly erroneous.

Our review of the record reveals the following critical facts. First, in accordance with its ordinary business practice and dealer guidelines incorporated into the franchise agreement, Ford would have required Toyota Village, as a dealer, to have a working capital of at least $172,000, of which no more than half could be debt. Toyota Village, however, had a working capital at the end of 1981 of $37,610; and its net worth was $31,747. . . .

Second, at a time when Japanese cars have sold well throughout the United States, Toyota Village has consistently lost money. . . .

At the same time, the record contains no significant evidence tending to refute the natural inference arising from these facts. The bankruptcy court mentioned five factors that it said showed that Toyota Village gave "adequate assurance" that it could do the job.

    1) Toyota Village was an established dealership.

2) Toyota Village was "located within 500 yards of the present Ford dealership."

3) Toyota Village had a proven track record for selling cars.

4) Toyota Village was willing and able to pay $15,000 that Pioneer still owed Ford.

5) The owner and sole stockholder of Toyota Village testified that he was willing and able to fulfill the franchise agreement.

The first of these factors (dealer experience), while favoring Toyota Village, is weak, given the record of continuous dealership losses. The second (location) proves little, considering that Pioneer went bankrupt at the very spot. The third (track record) cuts against Toyota Village, not in its favor, for its track record is one of financial loss. The fourth (willingness to pay a $15,000 debt that Pioneer owed Ford) is relevant, but it shows, at most, that Toyota Village *believed* it could make a success of the franchise. The fifth (ability to act as franchisee) is supported by no more than a simple statement by the owner of Toyota Village that he could do the job.

We do not see how the few positive features about Toyota Village that the record reveals can overcome the problem of a history of losses and failure to meet Ford's capital requirements. In these circumstances, Ford would seem perfectly reasonable in withholding its consent to the transfer. Thus, Rhode Island law would make the franchise unassignable. . . .

One might still argue that under Rhode Island law the only "reasonable" course of action for Ford is to allow the transfer and then simply terminate Toyota Village if it fails to perform adequately. This suggestion, however, overlooks the legal difficulties that Ford would have in proving cause for termination under the Rhode Island "Regulation of Business Practices Among Motor Vehicle Manufacturers, Distributors and Dealers" Act. R.I.Gen.Laws § 31-5.1-4(D)(2). The very purpose of the statute — protecting dealer reliance — suggests that it ought to be more difficult for a manufacturer to terminate a dealer who has invested in a franchise than to oppose the grant of a franchise to one who has not. In any event, the law does not suggest a manufacturer is "unreasonable" in objecting to a transfer unless he would have "good cause" to terminate the transferee. And, to equate the two standards would tend to make the "unreasonable" provision superfluous. Thus, we conclude that the Rhode Island law would make the franchise unassignable on the facts here revealed. Therefore, neither the bankruptcy court nor the district court had the power to authorize the transfer. . . .

For these reasons, the judgment of the district court is *Reversed.*

NOTES

1. As discussed in Chapter 6, numerous courts have held that a licensee's interest in a non-exclusive copyright or patent license is not transferable without the consent of the licensor. The rule of nonassignability as a matter of federal policy was confirmed by the Ninth Circuit Court of Appeals in *Everex*

Systems, Inc. v. Cadtrax Corp. (In re CFLC, Inc.), 89 F.3d 673 (9th Cir. 1996). The rule, in effect, excludes a bankrupt licensee's interest in a non-exclusive license from Section 365. In *Everex*, the court held that a non-exclusive patent license was an executory contract for bankruptcy purposes, but could not be assumed or assigned because, as a matter of federal law, a nonexclusive license was not assignable without the consent of the licensor. The license was a onetime payment, royalty-free, worldwide license to use certain computer graphics technology. The contract specified that it was nontransferable and that it was to be construed according to California law. The attempt to assume and assign the license came in the context of a sale of substantially all of the debtor's assets. Nevertheless, federal law prevented assignment. While the court recognized that in patent licensing, state law generally controls on contract issues, with respect to assignability, federal law controls and establishes that a license is not assignable. This court refused to ignore this case law and, indeed, affirmatively accepted the policy premise, which it stated as follows:

> The fundamental policy of the patent system is to encourage the creation and disclosure of new, useful, and non-obvious advances in technology and design by granting the inventor the reward of the exclusive right to practice the invention for a period of years. Allowing free assignability — or, more accurately, allowing states to allow free assignability — of non-exclusive patent licenses would undermine the reward that encourages invention because a party seeking to use the patented invention could either seek a license from the patent holder or seek an assignment of an existing patent license from a licensee. In essence, every licensee would become a potential competitor with the licensor-patent holder in the market for licenses under the patents.

2. Section 541 of the Bankruptcy Code provides that a contract becomes property of the estate "notwithstanding any provision in an agreement, transfer instrument, or applicable nonbankruptcy law . . . that restricts or conditions transfer of such interest by the debtor." 11 U.S.C. §541(c). Section 365, however, provides:

> (c) The trustee may not assume or assign any executory contract or unexpired lease of the debtor, whether or not such contract or lease prohibits or restricts assignment of rights or delegation of duties, if —
>
>> (1)(A) applicable law excuses a party, other than the debtor, to such contract or lease from accepting performance from or rendering performance to an entity other than the debtor or the debtor in possession, whether or not such contract or lease prohibits or restricts assignment of rights or delegation of duties; and
>>
>> (B) such party does not consent to such assumption or assignment. . . .

How can these provisions be reconciled?

3. In *Institut Pasteur v. Cambridge Biotech Corp.*, 104 F.3d 489 (1st Cir. 1997), the court refused to apply the *Everex* theory of non-assignability as applied to a case where a reorganization in bankruptcy resulted in the creation of a nominally new entity as the original licensee, but the difference was based on pro forma, rather than an actual change in the licensee. The court commented:

> These contentions are foreclosed by our decision in *Summit Inv. & Dev. Corp. v. Leroux (In re Leroux)*, 69 F.3d 608 (1st Cir. 1995). . . . As in the present case, in *Leroux* we were urged to interpret subsections 365(c) and (e) as mandating a "hypothetical test." Under such an approach, the chapter 11 debtor would lose its option to *assume* the contract, even though it never intended to assign the contract to another entity, if either the particular executory contract or the applicable nonbankruptcy law purported to terminate the contract automatically upon the filing of the chapter 11 petition or to preclude its assignment to an entity not a party to the contract. We rejected the proposed hypothetical test in *Leroux*, holding instead that subsections 365(c) and (e) contemplate a case-by-case inquiry into whether the nondebtor party (*viz.*, Pasteur) *actually* was being "forced to accept performance under its executory contract from someone other than the debtor party with whom it originally contracted." Where the particular transaction envisions that the debtor-in-possession would assume and continue to perform under an executory contract, the bankruptcy court cannot simply presume as a matter of law that the debtor-in-possession is a legal entity *materially* distinct from the prepetition debtor with whom the nondebtor party (*viz.*, Pasteur) contracted. Rather, "sensitive to the rights of the nondebtor party (*viz.*, Pasteur)," the bankruptcy court must focus on the performance actually to be rendered by the debtor-in-possession with a view to ensuring that the nondebtor party (*viz.*, Pasteur) will receive "the full benefit of [its] bargain."

4. Under Section 365, a bankrupt licensor can reject an executory contract. The right to reject does not hinge on there being a default. Rejection reflects a decision by the bankrupt to not perform, but to breach the agreement. Any claim for damages that the non-breaching licensee may have is treated as a pre-petition, general claim against the estate.

If a licensor in bankruptcy (or its trustee) rejects a license, can the licensee continue to use the licensed subject matter? Under one analysis, rejection of the license is a rejection of the promise to not sue for infringing acts and, therefore, excludes any right to use without a threat of infringement liability. Section 365(n) of the Bankruptcy Code ameliorates the result for licensees of "intellectual property."

> (n)(1) If the trustee rejects an executory contract under which the debtor is a licensor of a right to intellectual property, the licensee under such contract may elect —
>
> (A) to treat such contract as terminated by such rejection if such rejection by the trustee amounts to such a breach as would entitle the licensee to treat such contract as terminated by virtue of its own terms, applicable nonbankruptcy law, or an agreement made by the licensee with another entity; or
>
> (B) to retain its rights (including a right to enforce any exclusivity

provision of such contract, but excluding any other right under applicable nonbankruptcy law to specific performance of such contract) under such contract and under any agreement supplementary to such contract, to such intellectual property (including any embodiment of such intellectual property to the extent protected by applicable nonbankruptcy law), as such rights existed immediately before the case commenced, for —

(i) the duration of such contract; and

(ii) any period for which such contract may be extended by the licensee as of right under applicable nonbankruptcy law.

(2) If the licensee elects to retain its rights, as described in paragraph (1)(B) of this subsection, under such contract —

(A) the trustee shall allow the licensee to exercise such rights;

(B) the licensee shall make all royalty payments due under such contract for the duration of such contract and for any period described in paragraph (1)(B) of this subsection for which the licensee extends such contract; and

(C) the licensee shall be deemed to waive —

(i) any right of setoff it may have with respect to such contract under this title or applicable nonbankruptcy law; and

(ii) any claim allowable under section 503(b) of this title arising from the performance of such contract.

(3) If the licensee elects to retain its rights, as described in paragraph (1)(B) of this subsection, then on the written request of the licensee the trustee shall —

(A) to the extent provided in such contract, or any agreement supplementary to such contract, provide to the licensee any intellectual property (including such embodiment) held by the trustee; and

(B) not interfere with the rights of the licensee as provided in such contract, or any agreement supplementary to such contract, to such intellectual property (including such embodiment) including any right to obtain such intellectual property (or such embodiment) from another entity. . . .

"Intellectual property" includes trade secret, copyright, patent, and confidential material "to the extent protected under applicable nonbankruptcy law." 11 U.S.C. § 101(50). It does not cover trademarks or licenses of access to online sites. Likewise, it does not cover licenses of data that are not protected under the listed intellectual property laws.

IN RE PRIZE FRIZE, INC.
32 F.3d 426 (9th Cir. 1994)

NOONAN, CIRCUIT JUDGE:

This case, of first impression in any circuit, turns on whether license fees, paid by a licensee for the use of technology, patents, and proprietary rights, are "royalties" within the meaning of 11 U.S.C. § 365(n)(2)(B) and, as such, must continue to be paid after the licensor in bankruptcy has exercised its statutory right to reject the contract.

Facts

The debtor, Prize Frize, Inc., is the owner and licensor of all technology, patents, proprietary rights and related rights used in the manufacture and sale of a french fry vending machine. On March 6, 1991, the debtor entered into a License Agreement granting an exclusive license to utilize the proprietary rights and to manufacture, use and sell the vending machine. In consideration for the license to use the proprietary information and related rights, the licensee agreed to pay the debtor a $1,250,000 license fee — $300,000 to be paid within ten days of execution of the agreement with the balance due in $50,000 monthly payments. The licensee also agreed to pay royalty payments based on a percentage of franchise fees, of net marketing revenues and of any sales of the machines or certain related products. The license agreement also provided that if there was a failure of design and/or components of the machines to the extent that they were not fit for their intended use and were withdrawn from service, then the licensee's obligations would be suspended for a period of 180 days, during which time the debtor was entitled to cure any defect. Encino Business Management, Inc. (EBM) is the successor licensee under this license.

The debtor filed its Chapter 11 petition on March 12, 1991. In September of 1991, EBM, which had become the licensee, stopped making the $50,000 per month license fee payments and has made no payments since. EBM contends that there is a design defect in the machines which caused the machines to be withdrawn from service and which allowed the suspension of its obligation to pay the debtor.

The debtor subsequently filed a motion to reject the license agreement with EBM and to compel EBM to elect whether it wished to retain its rights under section 365(n)(1). EBM did not file a written response to the motion. At the hearing, EBM's counsel indicated that he did not oppose rejection. He disputed, however, that EBM should be required to immediately pay $350,000 in past due license fee payments, contending that the obligation to make such payments was suspended because of the purported design defect.

The bankruptcy court entered an order indicating that the debtor might reject the agreement, that EBM might elect whether to retain its rights under the agreement pursuant to section 365(n)(1) and that if EBM elected to retain its rights under the agreement it must do the following: (1) make all license fee payments presently due in the amount of $350,000 within seven days of its election; (2) pay the $400,000 balance of the license fee in monthly installments of $50,000; and (3) waive any and all rights of setoff with respect to the contract and applicable non-bankruptcy law and any claim under section 503(b) arising from performance under the agreement. The court's order also stated that assuming, *arguendo,* that EBM's payment obligations were properly suspended, the 180-day suspension period had ended and the September to March monthly payments were now due.

EBM appealed. . . .

Analysis

No evidence has been presented by EBM of design defect, and so we do not consider this basis for EBM's appeal but proceed to its principal contention.

Section 365 of the Bankruptcy Code is an intricate statutory scheme governing the treatment by the trustee in bankruptcy or the debtor-in-possession of the executory contracts of the debtor. There is no dispute that the license agreement between EBM and the debtor was executory, i.e. there were obligations on both sides which to some extent were unperformed. Consequently, the debtor had the right to reject the contract. However, section 365(n)(1) qualifies this right when the debtor is "a licensor of a right to intellectual property." There is no dispute that the debtor is such a licensor. Consequently, EBM as "the licensee under such contract" could make an election. § 365(n)(1). EBM could either treat the contract as terminated as provided by (n)(1)(A), or EBM could retain its rights to the intellectual property for the duration of the contract and any period for which the contract might be extended by the licensee as of right under applicable nonbankruptcy law.

EBM elected to retain its rights. It was then obligated to "make all royalty payments due under such contract." By the terms of the statute EBM was also "deemed to waive any right of setoff it may have with respect to such contract under this title or applicable nonbankruptcy law."

Section 365(n) has struck a fair balance between the interests of the bankrupt and the interests of a licensee of the bankrupt's intellectual property. The bankrupt cannot terminate and strip the licensee of rights the licensee had bargained for. The licensee cannot retain the use of those rights without paying for them. It is essential to the balance struck that the payments due for the use of the intellectual property should be analyzed as "royalties," required by the statute itself to be met by the licensee who is enjoying the benefit of the bankrupt's patents, proprietary property, and technology. [The] legislative history buttresses this commonsense interpretation of "royalties" in the statute.

EBM's principal argument is that the licensing agreement itself makes a distinction between what the agreement calls "license fees" and what the agreement calls "royalty payments." The "royalty payments" in the agreement are percentages payable on the retail sales price of each machine sold by EBM; the "license fees" in the agreement are the sums here in dispute which were to be paid for the license to manufacture and sell the vending machine. EBM's argument is not frivolous. Nonetheless the parties by their choice of names cannot alter the underlying reality nor change the balance that the Bankruptcy Code has struck. Despite the nomenclature used in the agreement, the license fees to be paid by EBM are royalties in the sense of section 365(n). Section 365(n) speaks repeatedly of "licensor" and "licensee" with the clear implication that payments by licensee to licensor for the use of intellectual property are, indifferently, "licensing fees" or "royalties," and, as royalties, must be paid by the licensee who elects to keep its license after the licensor's bankruptcy. The same indifference to nomenclature in referring to a licensee's lump sum or percentage-of-sales payments as royalties is apparent in patent cases.

EBM's fallback position on appeal is that the debtor has been freed by its rejection of the contract from the obligations assumed by the debtor under Article V ("Representations, Warranties and Covenants by PFI") of the agreement. These obligations included the debtor's agreement to hold EBM harmless from any claim arising out of events preceding the agreement, to defend any infringement suit relating to technology or design included in the machine, and to prosecute at its own expense any infringers of the rights granted by the agreement. The debtor also represented that the design of the Stand-Alone Machine was free from material defects. These obligations raise the question whether it is proper to consider all of the license fees as royalties or whether some portion of the fees should be allocated to payment for the obligations assumed by the debtor. Neither the bankruptcy court nor the BAP addressed this possibility. They did not because EBM did not present this question to them. It is consequently too late to raise it here. EBM still has its unsecured claim for breach of the entire license agreement that § 365(g) accords it. As its appeal was non-frivolous, no attorney's fees are awarded.

As what the licensing agreement denominates "license fees" must be regarded as "royalty payments" for purposes of § 365(n)(1)(B), the judgment [is] AFFIRMED.

IV. ASSET SALES AND LICENSED ASSETS

A bankruptcy proceeding often involves a sale of all or part of the debtor's assets. The Bankruptcy Code allows various procedures for sale of assets. For example, the trustee (or debtor in possession) has authority to continue to operate a bankrupt business and, as a result, to sell assets in the ordinary course of that business. 11 U.S.C. § 363. The terms of the sale, of course, control the interests transferred. Thus, in *Freeland v. HPA Asset, Ltd.*, 2002 U.S. App. LEXIS 7846 (Fed. Cir. 2002), the court held that a sale of all patents owned or used by the debtor company did not include a patent that, at the time, was allegedly owned by an affiliate of the debtor.

The Bankruptcy Code also allows sales of assets with court approval other than in the ordinary course of business. In many cases, the sale occurs at auction, but the Code also authorizes other types of sales. A bankruptcy sale can be made subject to designated interests or "free and clear" of all interests. 11 U.S.C. § 363. Since the sale procedure entails confirmation or approval by the bankruptcy court, such terms are often of a more binding and absolute nature than are ordinary sale terms grounded merely in contract law.

LICENSING BY PAOLO, INC. v. SINATRA (IN RE GUCCI)
126 F.3d 380 (2d Cir. 1997)

CARDAMONE, CIRCUIT JUDGE:

This appeal represents the final chapter in the long history of Paolo Gucci's battle with appellees Guccio Gucci, S.p.A. and Gucci America, Inc. (collectively referred to as Guccio Gucci or the Gucci companies) over the use of the Gucci family name to market consumer goods — a battle that continues after Paolo Gucci's death. It began when Paolo Gucci, who was the chief designer in the family's business in Italy, left Guccio Gucci to design and market products under his own name. In 1994 he filed for Chapter 11 bankruptcy and 20 months later, he died. The bankruptcy estate's primary asset was the Paolo Gucci name, which was sold in a bankruptcy court auction pursuant to 11 U.S.C. § 363(b). During the course of the proceedings, Guccio Gucci, as well as Paolo Gucci creditors and licensees, bid for the rights associated with the Paolo Gucci name and designs. Guccio Gucci's offer of $3.65 million was determined to be the highest and best bid, and the U.S. Bankruptcy Court for the Southern District of New York (Gallet, B.J.) authorized the sale of Paolo Gucci's assets to Guccio Gucci. On appeal to the district court (Griesa, C.J.), the order authorizing the sale was affirmed.

Although appellants moved in the district court for a stay of the order authorizing the sale, they were unsuccessful in obtaining either that relief or obtaining a timely stay by this Court of the district court order. Thus, appellants in taking this appeal were in the same procedural posture as a person who shuts the barn door after the horse has been stolen. It is too late. After the sale of the bankrupt estate had been consummated, and without a stay in place, the creditors and licensees appealed. Their appeal, not surprisingly, was held to be moot. One issue does remain viable, however — the purchaser's good faith.

Appellants, Licensing by Paolo, Inc. (Licensing), Paolo Gucci Design Studio, Ltd. (Design Studio), Trackwise Sales Corporation (Trackwise) and Orologi Paolo, Inc. (Orologi), seek reversal of the sale on the ground that Guccio Gucci is not a good faith purchaser. They contend that its ongoing litigation against the Paolo Gucci marks worldwide, and particularly in South Korea during the pendency of the automatic stay, were intended to devalue the estate's assets. They assert, in addition, that Guccio Gucci acted in bad faith by using the sale to purchase assets that it knew were not part of the bankruptcy estate and by colluding with the bankruptcy trustee to effect the purchase. We conclude that although the Gucci companies' conduct was fiercely competitive, it does not constitute bad faith within the meaning of the Bankruptcy Code's § 363(m) sufficient to set aside the sale order. Hence, we affirm. . . .

Analysis

Section 363 of the Bankruptcy Code authorizes the use, sale or lease of property of the estate in the course of a corporate reorganization under Chapter 11. A sale of a substantial part of a Chapter 11 estate other than in the ordinary course of business may be conducted if a good business reason exists to support it. Purchasers of these assets are protected from a reversal of the sale on appeal so long as they acted in good faith. 11 U.S.C. § 363(m).

Section 363(m) maximizes the purchase price of assets because without this assurance of finality, purchasers could demand a large discount for investing in a property that is laden with the risk of endless litigation as to who has rights to estate property. Because appellants were denied a stay pending appeal of the sale order and the sale itself has been consummated, the only

question before us is whether the buyer, Guccio Gucci, is a good faith purchaser under § 363(m). . . .

In its approval of the sale of the estate's assets, the bankruptcy court found
that Guccio Gucci was a good-faith purchaser within the meaning of § 363(m).
Bankruptcy courts routinely make a finding of good faith at the time of the
§ 363 sale approval. Although we have not squarely faced this issue, some
courts read the Bankruptcy Code to require such a finding. *Compare Abbotts,*
788 F.2d at 149-50 (good-faith finding is required), *with Onouli-Kona Land Co.
v. Estate of Richards (In re Onouli-Kona Land Co.),* 846 F.2d 1170, 1174 & n.
1 (9th Cir. 1988) (bankruptcy court may, but is not required to, make finding
of good-faith purchaser); *see also New York Life Ins. Co. v. Revco D.S., Inc. (In
re Revco D.S., Inc.),* 901 F.2d 1359, 1366 (6th Cir. 1990) (explicit finding
required for § 364(e)). Moreover, practitioners counsel parties involved in a
§ 363 sale to condition their offer to purchase on the bankruptcy court's including in its order approving the sale a specific finding of the purchaser's good
faith. *See, e.g.,* David A. Warfield, *Bankruptcy Bazaar: Purchasing Assets out
of Bankruptcy Court,* 51 J. Mo. B. 283, 286 (1995); Alesia Ranney-Marinelli,
Asset Sales in a Chapter 11 Bankruptcy Case, 738 PLI/Comm. 89, 126 n. 26
(PLI Commercial Law and Practice Course Handbook Series, No. A4-4498,
1996) (same). Guccio Gucci conditioned its bid in this fashion and the bankruptcy court made an express finding that it had acted in good faith. . . .

Although the Bankruptcy Code does not define the meaning of "good-faith
purchaser," most courts have adopted a traditional equitable definition: "one
who purchases the assets for value, in good faith and without notice of adverse
claims." We need not address the "for value" claim directly. Generally speaking, a purchaser who pays 75 percent of the appraised value of the assets has
tendered value, *Abbotts,* but where the purchaser is found to have acted in
good faith the auction price suffices to demonstrate that the purchaser paid
"value" for the assets. As a consequence, because none of the parties point to
anything in the record that indicates the appraised value of the assets sold,
the crux of this appeal is Guccio Gucci's good faith.

Good faith of a purchaser is shown by the integrity of his conduct during the
course of the sale proceedings; where there is a lack of such integrity, a good
faith finding may not be made. A purchaser's good faith is lost by "fraud, collusion between the purchaser and other bidders or the trustee, or an attempt
to take grossly unfair advantage of other bidders."

Collectively, appellants' arguments that Guccio Gucci was not a good-faith
purchaser is less a claim of fraud, collusion or unfair advantage in the bidding
process and more an attack on its general business practices. The appropriate
scope of inquiry regarding a purchaser's good faith is not nearly so broad. As
just defined, the good-faith analysis is focused on the purchaser's conduct in
the course of the bankruptcy proceedings. This includes the purchaser's
actions in preparation for and during the sale itself. That is, the good-faith
requirement prohibits fraudulent, collusive actions specifically intended to
affect the sale price or control the outcome of the sale.

Our understanding of the scope of the good-faith inquiry is informed by the
reasoning of the Third Circuit in *Abbotts.* There, unsuccessful bidders alleged

that the purchaser ADC, in exchange for a lucrative employment offer to Abbotts' principal officer, manipulated the timing of Abbotts' bankruptcy filing so that the bankruptcy court had no choice but to accept an interim agreement between ADC and Abbotts, the terms of which were designed to preclude any truly competitive bidding for debtor Abbotts' assets at the subsequent auction. The court recognized that, if these allegations were true, "the situation was ripe for collusion and interested dealing" between the purchaser and the debtor, which could preclude a finding of good faith. Although the conduct in question was alleged to have begun before the bankruptcy proceedings were initiated, the relevant inquiry still remained whether that conduct was intended to control the sale price or take unfair advantage of prospective bidders. . . .

As proof of Guccio Gucci's bad faith appellants point to the following: (a) its worldwide litigation challenging the use of the Paolo Gucci marks, which effectively devalued those trademarks as assets; (b) its efforts to gain control of assets beyond the scope of the bankruptcy estate; (c) its alleged collusion with the Trustee; and (d) its purchase of the estate's assets with the intent to destroy them in violation of public policy. We consider each of these points in turn.

A. *Litigation and Administrative Proceedings*

The purchaser's bad faith is first evidenced, appellants maintain, by the litigation it conducted to devalue the Paolo Gucci assets, its violation of the automatic stay during its pursuit of the litigation and administrative proceedings in Korea, and its harassment of Korean department stores that were Trackwise's sublicensees. Appellants further declare that because Guccio Gucci's perceived value of owning the trademarks did not depend upon their future marketability, its actions were designed to enable it to step in and buy the trademarks for a price less than that for which they would have otherwise sold.

We do not think the record shows that Guccio Gucci's litigation and alleged harassment campaign was specifically directed at controlling the sale price or taking unfair advantage of the bidders. Instead, the record indicates that, at least from the time Paolo Gucci began his own business, Guccio Gucci had adopted an aggressive litigation strategy to protect its own trademarks from infringement. This ongoing pattern of litigation undermines the argument that the Gucci companies instituted trademark prosecutions with the intent to control the sale price of the bankrupt estate's assets. Rather, it is a continuation of their established business strategy. Further, this conduct was widely known to all bidders, none of whom complained about its effect on their ability to bid at the time when their bids were submitted. . . .

Similarly, Guccio Gucci's alleged violations of the automatic stay provision do not undermine the good-faith determination. The Bankruptcy Code's automatic stay provision enjoins, *inter alia,* "the commencement or continuation, including the issuance or employment of process, of a judicial, administrative, or other action or proceeding against the debtor that was or could have been commenced before the commencement [of the bankruptcy]" and "any act to obtain possession of property of the estate or of property from the estate or to exercise control over property of the estate." 11 U.S.C. §§ 362(a)(1) & (a)(3). We have ruled that an action taken against a nondebtor which would inevitably have an adverse impact upon the property of the estate must be barred by the automatic stay provision. . . .

Appellants urge us to adopt a *per se* rule that a party's violation of the automatic stay renders it incapable of being a good faith purchaser under § 363(m). We decline that invitation for two reasons. First, we have already held that the actions themselves, which are described as violations of the stay, did not undermine Guccio Gucci's status as a good faith purchaser within the meaning of § 363(m) because they were *not* aimed at influencing the price of the sale. Moreover, even if the actions did violate § 362(a), the automatic stay provision includes its own effective policing measures. A willful violator of the stay may be held in contempt and is liable for compensatory and punitive damages. § 362(h).

B. Use . . . to Gain Control of Assets . . .

Design Studio maintains Guccio Gucci also acted in bad faith by conditioning its offer on the inclusion of property in the bankruptcy estate which it knew properly belonged to Design Studio. Design Studio's position is based on an agreement it made with Paolo Gucci after his bankruptcy filing under which he conferred a license on Design Studio to market all designs created after the filing of his bankruptcy petition. In its October 9, 1996 decision the bankruptcy court held that any post-petition designs created by Paolo Gucci are to be marketed under the Paolo name and trademark and are property of the estate. The October 15, 1996 order approving the sale of assets to Guccio Gucci listed post-petition designs as included in the sale.

We emphasize that whether the post-petition designs were part of the estate and whether the bankruptcy court erroneously authorized the sale of property outside the scope of that estate are questions that are now moot. Section 363(m) limits appellate review of a consummated sale whenever the sale is authorized under § 363(b) — regardless of the merits of legal arguments raised against it. Because the sale was not stayed, § 363(m) permits us to only consider the issue of good faith. Thus, we are unable to reach or decide the question of the ownership of post-petition designs.

In addition, the record does not indicate that Guccio Gucci's conduct constituted bad faith. In the context of this case's complicated facts and issues of first impression, there was at least a colorable claim that the bankruptcy estate owned the post-petition designs created to bear Paolo Gucci's name and trademark because they were so inexorably tied to the existing licensing business that it would be impossible to separate the two. The Trustee expressed his view that the estate owned the designs, and the representatives of decedent Paolo Gucci's estate did not assert any ownership interests in them. Moreover, Orologi, a competing bidder whom Design Studio does not allege colluded with Guccio Gucci, requested the same condition in its bid. Finally, although Guccio Gucci included the post-petition designs condition in its offer, its request was publicly made and no evidence of deceit or fraud was shown. Hence, the imposition of the subject sale condition did not constitute bad faith. . . .

D. Public Policy Considerations

There is no question that some consequences of this sale are unsettling. As a result of it, several businesses that have made substantial investments to develop a market for Paolo Gucci goods will suffer. However, contrary to arguments made by appellants, Guccio Gucci's intent to terminate trademark licenses and destroy the trademarks themselves did not constitute bad faith within the meaning of §363(m), nor does it violate public policy.

Any apparent inequities in this case are as much an indictment of bankruptcy law generally as they are of the Gucci companies' intended use of the assets, *see* Stuart M. Riback, *The Interface of Trademarks and Bankruptcy,* J. Proprietary Rts., June 1994, at 2, 3-6; David M. Jenkins, *Licenses, Trademarks, and Bankruptcy, Oh My!: Trademark Licensing and the Perils of Licensor Bankruptcy,* 25 J. Marshall L.Rev. 143, 155-59 (1991); Richard Lieb, *The Interrelationship of Trademark Law and Bankruptcy Law,* 64 Am. Bankr.L.J. 1, 35-38 (1990).

Yet neither inequities or use of the estate's assets is relevant to our limited review of Guccio Gucci's conduct in preparation for and during the course of the sale proceeding. The Bankruptcy Code allows the trustee, subject to court approval, to reject or terminate executory contracts. 11 U.S.C. §365(a). This provision was perceived as having a chilling effect on intellectual property licensing because it authorized the stripping of an innocent licensee's rights — rights which are central to the licensee's ongoing business. In response, Congress enacted §365(n) to give these licensees the option to retain certain rights despite the trustee's rejection of the license. However, the Act's protection is limited to the Bankruptcy Code's definition of "intellectual property" — which does not include trademarks. Consequently, it may be seen that Congress specifically excluded trademark licensees from this protection accorded other intellectual property licensees.

While equitable concerns noted above may allow reversal of a bankruptcy order to reject a specific license in a specific instance, the limited question before us is whether Guccio Gucci purchased the assets in good faith. We conclude that Guccio Gucci's intended use of the assets purchased is not relevant to the good faith inquiry, and therefore we agree with the bankruptcy court's determination that Guccio Gucci is a good faith purchaser within the meaning of §363(m). . . .

Chapter 16

SELECTED ISSUES IN SOFTWARE TRANSACTIONS

I. INTRODUCTION

Digital information industries drive a substantial part of the modern information economy. They also shape many of the issues that arise in modern licensing law. We have seen issues associated with digital transactions throughout this book.

This chapter expands on that earlier coverage with respect to software transactions. In this chapter and the next, we address digital transactions in two broad categories — software transactions and online contracts.

II. CONTRACT FORMATION

The enforceability of shrink-wrap and similar licenses had been disputed for a number of years. Modern case law, however, routinely enforces such contracts when the terms are presented in a proper manner to obtain assent. The earliest decisive cases are *ProCD, Inc. v. Zeidenberg*, 86 F.3d 1447 (7th Cir. 1996), reproduced in Chapter 1, *M.A. Mortenson Co., Inc. v. Timberline Software Corp.*, 970 P.2d 803 (Wash. 2000), reproduced in Chapter 2, and *Hill vs. Gateway 2000 Inc.*, 105 F.3d 1147 (7th Cir. 1997).

The basic theme holds that providers of information can determine on what basis they distribute their products; markets and that choices made by individual purchasers determine whether the preferences of the information provider can survive in the real world marketplace. As that premise is implemented, in law, it depends on the transferee's agreement to the terms. Agreement does not mean that the transferee must be given a choice to obtain the information with or without the proposed terms, but that the transferee have notice of the terms, a chance to read them, and the opportunity to reject the transaction if the terms are not acceptable. In cases where the terms do not appear for acceptance until after an initial agreement is made, UCITA and the cases require that the transferee have some reason to believe that the later presentation of terms was anticipated at the time of the initial contact between the parties. UCITA § 208 (2000 Official Text).

The terms must be contractual — e.g., they must become contractual obligations or limitations. Although it did not deal with software, the Federal Circuit's comments in *Jazz Photo Corp. v. International Trade Commission*, 264 F.3d 1094 (Fed. Cir. 2001), *cert. denied*, 536 U.S. 950 (2002), are relevant. The court there was dealing with a patented camera distributed for a single use only. In this case, the label and statements on the container for the product merely indicated that the single use camera would not be returned after the film was processed. The court said:

> These packing instructions are not in the form of a contractual agreement by the purchaser to limit reuse of the camera. There is no showing of a "meeting of the minds" whereby the purchaser, and those obtaining the purchaser's discarded camera may be deemed to have breached a contract or violated a license limited to a single use of a camera.

The statements were instructions warning of about a future event, not conditions of the sale. Since they were not contractual in nature, there was an unconditional sale of the cameras. That unconditional sale exhausted the patent as to each camera.

UCITA's summary of the requirements for creating contract terms is modeled on the *Restatement*; modern case law corresponds to it:

- A person adopts the terms of a record if the person manifests assent to it. UCITA § 208; *Restatement (Second) of Contracts* § 211.

- A person manifests assent to a record if the person, acting with knowledge of, or after having an opportunity to review the record or term or a copy of it:

    (1) authenticates the record or term with intent to adopt or accept it; or

    (2) intentionally engages in conduct or makes statements with reason to know that the other party or its electronic agent may infer from the conduct or statement that the person assents to the record or term. UCITA § 112(a) (2000 Official Text); *Restatement (Second) of Contracts* § 19.

- A person has an opportunity to review a record only if it is made available in a manner that ought to call it to the attention of a reasonable person and permit review. If a record or term is available for review only after a person becomes obligated to pay or begins its performance, the person has an opportunity to review only if it has a right to a return if it rejects the record. UCITA § 112(e) (2000 Official Text).

PROBLEM 16.1

Consider whether or not the following creates a contract: A licensor embeds code in a program file that must be specifically accessed to be read and is not referred to in other respects. The code is a license that when displayed states: "this software is transferred subject to the following license: 1) the software may be reproduced for personal, non-commercial use; 2) commercial use is prohibited; 3) software provided as is with no warranties." Licensee acquires a copy of the software for $400.00 from a retail store. Should the format be changed in order to establish a contract?

PROBLEM 16.2

Transferee acquires network software from CA Software. When the software package is installed, the first screen displays a license and states that the licensee indicates assent to the terms by clicking on the "I agree" button. If licensee does not assent, the software cannot be installed. There is no provision for the licensee to obtain a refund of the amount it has already paid to CA if it refuses the license. Does this procedure create a contract if the licensee assents? Does it create a contract if the licensee declines?

III. ELECTRONIC RESTRICTIONS ON USE

Digital technology makes it possible to use electronic (automated) controls to augment agreed restrictions on use. Much of the literature about such restrictions is associated with copyright law issues and focuses on federal law that provides for legal sanctions against persons who circumvent or distribute technology to circumvent such use. That issue is important and the politics associated with it are controversial. But that is not the primary focus here. Rather, we are concerned with how digital or other technological controls interact with contractual use restrictions established between two contracting parties.

Let's assume a simple transaction:

> Digital Content Publisher licenses Distributor to make and distribute commercially up to 50,000 copies of Publisher's digital product. Publisher delivers a master copy of the product to Distributor. The master copy contains technology that allows 50,000 copies, but erases the content after 50,000 copies are made.

This restriction on use of the digital product corresponds to and ensures compliance with the contractual terms. The Distributor did not contract for the right to make 51,000 copies and the technology limits the use of the master copy accordingly.

The coordination between contract and technology restriction here seems fairly straightforward, but does it present any issues about which law should be concerned? For example, if the 50,001st copy was especially important and the licensee forgot about the contractual limitations, should it have a right to make an additional copy? Are there consumer illustrations in which enforcing a contract according to its terms is "unfair"? One red herring that we should avoid here is the breach of contract problem — what if the technology allows 45,000 copies, but the contract calls for 50,000? UCITA states simply that this is a breach of contract if it prevents the licensee from making the 45,001 copy.

A. Contract and DMCA

The terms of the agreement between the parties sets the legal basis for a licensor to use restrictions that cabin-in the licensee's performance in a manner consistent with the contract, subject to ordinary restrictions on contract terms such as unconscionability, misuse and the like. In addition, the anticircumvention rules of the Digital Millennium Copyright Act (DMCA) may play a role. In relevant part, 17 U.S.C. § 1201 provides:

(a) Violations regarding circumvention of technological measures. —

(1)

(A) No person shall circumvent a technological measure that effectively controls access to a work protected under this title. . . .

(B) The prohibition contained in subparagraph (A) shall not apply to persons who are users of a copyrighted work which is in a particular class of works, if such persons are, or are likely to be in the succeeding 3-year period, adversely affected by virtue of such prohibition in their ability to make noninfringing uses of that particular class of works under this title, as determined under subparagraph (C).

(C) During the 2-year period described in subparagraph (A), and during each succeeding 3-year period, the Librarian of Congress, upon the recommendation of the Register of Copyrights, . . . shall make the determination in a rulemaking proceeding for purposes of subparagraph (B) of whether persons who are users of a copyrighted work are, or are likely to be in the succeeding 3-year period, adversely affected by the prohibition under subparagraph (A) in their ability to make noninfringing uses under this title of a particular class of copyrighted works. . . .

(2) No person shall manufacture, import, offer to the public, provide, or otherwise traffic in any technology, product, service, device, component, or part thereof, that —

(A) is primarily designed or produced for the purpose of circumventing a technological measure that effectively controls access to a work protected under this title;

(B) has only limited commercially significant purpose or use other than to circumvent a technological measure that effectively controls access to a work protected under this title; or

(C) is marketed by that person or another acting in concert with that person with that person's knowledge for use in circumventing a technological measure that effectively controls access to a work protected under this title.

(3) As used in this subsection —

(A) to "circumvent a technological measure" means to descramble a scrambled work, to decrypt an encrypted work, or otherwise to avoid, bypass, remove, deactivate, or impair a technological measure, without the authority of the copyright owner; and

(B) a technological measure "effectively controls access to a work" if the measure, in the ordinary course of its operation, requires the application of information, or a process or a treatment, with the authority of the copyright owner, to gain access to the work.

(b) Additional violations. —

(1) No person shall manufacture, import, offer to the public, provide, or otherwise traffic in any technology, product, service, device, component, or part thereof, that —

(A) is primarily designed or produced for the purpose of circumventing protection afforded by a technological measure that effectively protects a right of a copyright owner under this title in a work or a portion thereof;

(B) has only limited commercially significant purpose or use other than to circumvent protection afforded by a technological measure that effectively protects a right of a copyright owner under this title in a work or a portion thereof; or

(C) is marketed by that person or another acting in concert with that person with that person's knowledge for use in circumventing protection afforded by a technological measure that effectively protects a right of a copyright owner under this title in a work or a portion thereof.

(2) As used in this subsection —

(A) to "circumvent protection afforded by a technological measure" means avoiding, bypassing, removing, deactivating, or otherwise impairing a technological measure; and

(B) a technological measure "effectively protects a right of a copyright owner under this title" if the measure, in the ordinary course of its operation, prevents, restricts, or otherwise limits the exercise of a right of a copyright owner under this title.

DMCA deals both with actual circumvention of a technological measure and with marketing devices intended to be used to circumvent the technological measures. It provides various "safe harbor" or exemption provisions with respect to designated types of circumvention or "marketing."

DAVIDSON & ASSOC. v. JUNG
422 F3d 630 (8th Cir. 2005)

SMITH, CIRCUIT JUDGE.

Davidson & Associates, Inc. d/b/a Blizzard Entertainment ("Blizzard") and Vivendi Universal Games, Inc. ("Vivendi"), owner of copyrights in computer game software and online gaming service software sued Ross Combs ("Combs"), Rob Crittenden ("Crittenden"), Jim Jung ("Jung"), and Internet Gateway, Inc. ("Internet Gateway") (collectively referred to as "Appellants"), for breach of contract, circumvention of copyright protection system, and trafficking in circumvention technology. Both parties moved for summary judgment. The district court granted summary judgment in favor of Blizzard and Vivendi . . . We affirm.

I. Background

A. Factual Background

Blizzard, a California corporation and subsidiary of Vivendi, creates and sells software games for personal computers. This appeal concerns the particular Blizzard games "StarCraft," "StarCraft: Brood War," "WarCraft II: Battle.net Edition," "Diablo," and "Diablo II: Lord of Destruction." Combs and Crittenden are computer programmers, Jung is a systems administrator, and Internet Gateway is an Internet service provider based in St. Peters, Missouri. Jung is also the president, co-owner, and day-to-day operator of Internet Gateway.

In January 1997, Blizzard officially launched "Battle.net," a 24-hour online-gaming service available exclusively to purchasers of its computer games. The Battle.net service has nearly 12 million active users who spend more that 2.1 million hours online per day. Blizzard holds valid copyright registrations covering Battle.net and each of its computer games at issue in this litigation. Battle.net is a free service that allows owners of Blizzard games to play each other on their personal computers via the Internet. Battle.net mode allows users to create and join multi-player games that can be accessed across the Internet, to chat with other potential players, to record wins and losses and save advancements in an individual password-protected game account, and to participate with others in tournament play featuring elimination rounds. Players can set up private "chat channels" and private games on Battle.net to allow players to determine with whom they wish to interact online. These Battle.net mode features are only accessible from within the games.

Like most computer software, Blizzard's games can be easily copied and distributed over the Internet. Blizzard has taken steps to avoid piracy by designing Battle.net to restrict access and use of the Battle.net mode feature of the game. Each time a user logs onto Battle.net, a Battle.net server examines the user's version of the game software. If a Blizzard game does not have the latest software upgrades and fixes, the Battle.net service updates the customer's game before allowing the game to play in Battle.net mode.

With the exception of "Diablo," each authorized version of a Blizzard game comes with a "CD Key." A CD Key is a unique sequence of alphanumeric characters printed on a sticker attached to the case in which the CD-ROM was packaged. To log on to Battle.net and access Battle.net mode, the game initiates an authentication sequence or "secret handshake" between the game and the Battle.net server. In order to play the Blizzard game contained on a

CD-ROM, a user must first install the game onto a computer and agree to the terms of the End User License Agreement ("EULA") and Terms of Use ("TOU"), both of which prohibit reverse engineering. At the end of both the EULA and TOU, Blizzard includes a button with the text, "I Agree" in it, which the user must select in order to proceed with the installation. Users are also required to enter a name and the CD Key during installation of Battle.net and Blizzard games.[1]

The outside packaging of all Blizzard games, except for Diablo, contains a statement that use of the game is subject to the EULA and that use of Battle.net is subject to the terms of the TOU. The terms of neither the EULA nor the TOU appear on the outside packaging. If the user does not agree to these terms, the game may be returned for a full refund of the purchase price within thirty (30) days of the original purchase. Combs, Crittenden, and Jung installed Blizzard games and agreed to the terms of the EULA. Crittenden and Jung logged onto Battle.net and agreed to the TOU.

The users of Battle.net have occasionally experienced difficulties with the service. To address their frustrations with Battle.net, a group of non-profit volunteer game hobbyists, programmers, and other individuals formed a group called the "bnetd project." The bnetd project developed a program called the "bnetd.org server" that emulates the Battle.net service and permits users to play online without use of Battle.net. The bnetd project is a volunteer effort and the project has always offered the bnetd program for free to anyone. Combs, Crittenden, and Jung were lead developers for the bnetd project.

The bnetd project was organized and managed over the Internet through a website, www.bnetd.org, that was made available to the public through equipment provided by Internet Gateway. The bnetd.org emulator provides a server that allows gamers unable or unwilling to connect to Battle.net to experience the multi-player features of Blizzard's games. The bnetd.org emulator also provides matchmaking services for users of Blizzard games who want to play those games in a multi-player environment without using Battle.net. Bnetd.org attempted to mirror all of the user-visible features of Battle.net, including online discussion forums and information about the bnetd project, as well as access to the program's computer code for others to copy and modify.

---

[1] FN 4 The EULA contains the following language:
YOU SHOULD CAREFULLY READ THE FOLLOWING END USER LICENSE AGREEMENT BEFORE INSTALLING THIS SOFTWARE PROGRAM. BY INSTALLING, COPYING, OR OTHER WISE USING THE SOFTWARE PROGRAM YOU AGREE TO BE BOUND BY THE TERMS OF THIS AGREEMENT. IF YOU DO NOT AGREE TO THE TERMS OF THIS AGREEMENT, PROMPTLY RETURN THE UNUSED SOFTWARE PROGRAM TO THE PLACE OF PURCHASE OR CONTACT BLIZZARD ENTERTAINMENT CUSTOMER SERVICE . . . FOR A FULL REFUND OF THE PURCHASE PRICE WITHIN THIRTY DAYS OF THE ORIGINAL PURCHASE. This software program (the "Program"), any printed materials, any on-line or electronic documentation, and any and all copies and derivative works of such software program and materials are the copyrighted work of Blizzard Entertainment.
* * *
Subject to that Grant of Licence hereinabove, you may not, in whole or in part, copy, photocopy, reproduce, translate, *reverse engineer,* derive source code, modify, disassemble, decompile, create derivative works based on the Program, or remove any proprietary notices or labels on the Program without the prior consent, in writing, of Blizzard.

To serve as a functional alternative to Battle.net, bnetd.org had to be compatible with Blizzard's software. In particular, compatibility required that bnetd.org speak the same protocol language that the Battle.net speaks. By speaking the same protocol language, the bnetd programs would be interoperable with Blizzard games. Once game play starts, a user perceives no difference between Battle.net and the bnetd.org.

By necessity, Appellants used reverse engineering to learn Blizzard's protocol language and to ensure that bnetd.org worked with Blizzard games. Combs used reverse engineering to develop the bnetd.org server, including a program called "tcpdump" to log communications between Blizzard games and the Battle.net server. Crittenden used reverse engineering to develop the bnetd. org server, including using a program called "Nextray." Crittenden also used a program called "ripper" to take Blizzard client files that were compiled together in one file and break them into their component parts. Crittenden used the ripper program to determine how Blizzard games displayed ad banners so that bnetd.org could display ad banners to users in the format that Blizzard uses on the Battle.net service. Combs tried to disassemble a Blizzard game to figure out how to implement a feature that allowed bnetd.org to protect the password that a user enters when creating an account in Battle.net mode. Crittenden made an unauthorized copy of a Blizzard game in order to test the interoperability of the bnetd.org server with multiple games.

Blizzard designed its games to connect only to Battle.net servers. To enable a Blizzard game to connect to a bnetd.org server instead of a Battle.net server, bnetd had to modify the computer file that contained the Internet address of the Battle.net servers. As part of the bnetd project, Combs participated in the development of a utility program called "BNS" to allow Blizzard games to connect to bnetd.org servers more easily. Through the BNS program, the game sends the bnetd.org server information about its CD Key. An individual can thus play one of the Blizzard games at issue over the Internet via bnetd.org rather than Battle.net. According to Blizzard, the EULAs and TOUs prohibit this activity.

Bnetd.org has important operational differences from Battle.net. When bnetd.org receives the CD Key information, unlike Battle.net, it does not determine whether the CD Key is valid or currently in use by another player. The bnetd.org server computer code always sends the game an "okay" reply regardless of whether the CD Key is valid or currently in use by another player. The bnetd .org emulator always allows the Blizzard games to access Battle.net mode features even if the user does not have a valid or unique CD Key. Blizzard did not disclose the methods it used to generate CD Keys or to confirm the validity of CD Keys.

Combs, Crittenden, and Jung used Blizzard games to log into bnetd .org. Crittenden was aware that unauthorized versions of Blizzard games were played on bnetd.org. Jung knew that the bnetd.org emulator did not require that Blizzard games provide valid CD Keys. Combs suspected that the bnetd. org emulator would not know the difference between a real game and a pirated game. Combs and Crittenden either sent portions of the bnetd software to Jung to place on the www.bnetd.org website for download or put the software on the website themselves. Combs made the bnetd software available on his website located at www.cs.nmsu.edu/~~rcombs/sc/. Also distributed was the BNS utility program which allowed Blizzard games to connect to bnetd.org. The source code was made available as an "open source" application, meaning that others were free to copy the source code and distribute it with or without modifications. Because the bnetd.org source code was freely available, others developed additional Battle.net emulators based on the bnetd.org source code. Binary versions of the bnetd.org were distributed which made it more convenient for users to set up and access the emulator program. Internet Gateway has donated space on its computers for use by the bnetd project. Internet Gateway also hosted a bnetd.org server that anyone on the Internet could access and use to play Blizzard games in Battle.net mode.

B. Procedural Background

Blizzard and Vivendi brought suit in the United States District Court for the Eastern District of Missouri. The second amended complaint alleged copyright infringement in violation of 17 U.S.C. § 501; circumvention of copyright protection systems and trafficking in circumvention technology in violation of 17 U.S.C. § 1201(a); federal trademark infringement in violation of 15 U.S.C. § 1114(1); federal false designation of origin in violation of 15 U.S.C. § 1125(c); common law trademark infringement and unfair competition claims; and breach of the EULA and TOU. Appellants counterclaimed, requesting declaratory relief . . . The district court entered a consent decree [which] resolved all claims except for the claims of circumvention of copyright protection systems and trafficking in circumvention technology under 17 U.S.C. § 1201(a), breach of the EULA and TOU, and the counterclaims for declaratory relief for non-circumvention and unenforceability of the EULA and TOU.

Both sides motioned for summary judgment. The district court granted summary judgment in favor of Blizzard and Vivendi. . . . Appellants brought this appeal, disputing violations of the DMCA, and now argue that the state breach-of-contract claims were preempted by federal copyright law.

II. Discussion

A. Preemption

. . . . This case concerns conflict preemption. Conflict preemption applies when there is no express preemption but (1) it is impossible to comply with both the state and federal law or when (2) the state law stands as an obstacle to the accomplishment and execution of the full purposes and objectives of Congress. Appellants, relying upon *Vault v. Quaid Software Ltd.,* 847 F.2d 255, 268-70 (5th Cir.1988), argue that the federal Copyright Act preempts Blizzard's state law breach-of-contract claims. We disagree.

In *Vault,* plaintiffs challenged the Louisiana Software License Enforcement Act, which permitted a software producer to impose contractual terms upon software purchasers provided that the terms were set forth in a license agreement comporting with the statute. "Enforceable terms [under the Louisiana statute] include the prohibition of: (1) any copying of the program for any purpose; and (2) modifying and/or adapting the program in any way, including adaptation by reverse engineering, decompilation or disassembly." The Louisiana statute defined reverse engineering, decompiling or disassembling as "any process by which computer software is converted from one form to another form which is more readily understandable to human beings, including without limitation any decoding or decrypting of any computer program which has been encoded or encrypted in any manner." The Fifth Circuit held that the Louisiana statute conflicted with the rights of computer program owners under the Copyright Act, specifically 17 U.S.C. § 117, which permits a computer program owner to make an adaptation of a program provided that the adaption is either created as an essential step in the utilization of the computer program in conjunction with a machine or is for archival purpose only.

Unlike in *Vault,* the state law at issue here neither conflicts with the interoperability exception under 17 U.S.C. § 1201(f) nor restricts rights given under federal law. Appellants contractually accepted restrictions on their ability to reverse engineer by their agreement to the terms of the TOU and EULA. "[P]rivate parties are free to contractually forego the limited ability to reverse engineer a software product under the exemptions of the Copyright Act[,]"and "a state can permit parties to contract away a fair use defense or to agree not to engage in uses of copyrighted material that are permitted by the copyright law if the contract is freely negotiated." While *Bowers* and *Nat'l Car Rental* were express preemption cases rather than conflict preemption, their reasoning applies here with equal force. By signing the TOUs and EULAs, Appellants expressly relinquished their rights to reverse engineer. Summary judgment on this issue was properly granted in favor of Blizzard and Vivendi.

B. DMCA Claims and Interoperability Exception

Congress enacted the DMCA in 1998 to implement the World Intellectual Property Organization Copyright Treaty ("WIPO Treaty"). WIPO requires contracting nations to "provide adequate legal protection and effective legal remedies against the circumvention of effective technological measures that are used by authors in connection with the exercise of their rights under this Treaty or the Berne Convention and that restrict acts, in respect of their works, which are not authorized by the authors concerned or permitted by law." The DMCA contains three provisions targeted at the circumvention of technological protections.

The first is § 1201(a)(1), the anti-circumvention provision. This provision prohibits a person from "circumvent[ing] a technological measure that effectively controls access to a work protected under [Title 17, governing copyright]." . . . Section 1201(a)(1) differs from the second and third provisions in that it targets the use of a circumvention technology, not the trafficking in such a technology.

The second and third provisions are §§ 1201(a)(2) and 1201(b)(1), the "anti-trafficking provisions." These sections are similar, except that § 1201(a)(2) covers those who traffic in technology that can circumvent "a technological measure *that effectively controls access* to a work protected under" Title 17, whereas § 1201(b)(1) covers those who traffic in technology that can circumvent "protection afforded by a technological measure *that effectively protects a right of a copyright owner* under" Title 17. 17 U.S.C. §§ 1201(a)(2) & (b)(1). In other words, although both sections prohibit trafficking in a

circumvention technology, the focus of § 1201(a)(2) is circumvention of technologies designed to *prevent access* to a work, and the focus of § 1201(b)(1) is
circumvention of technologies designed to *permit access* to a work but *prevent
copying* of the work or some other act that infringes a copyright.

The district court determined that Appellants's reverse engineering violated
§ 1201(a)(1) as well as § 1201(a)(2). We agree.

1. Anti-Circumvention Violation

Section 1201(a)(1) provides that "[n]o person shall circumvent a technological measure that effectively controls access to a work protected under this
title." The term "circumvent a technological measure" "means to descramble a
scrambled work, to decrypt an encrypted work, or otherwise to avoid, bypass,
remove, deactivate, or impair a technological measure, without the authority
of the copyright owner." 17 U.S.C. § 1201(3)(A). "Effectively controls access to
a work" means that the measure, in the ordinary course of its operation,
requires the application of information, or a process or a treatment, with the
authority of the copyright owner, to gain access to the work. 17 U.S.C.
§ 1201(3)(B).

Blizzard games, through Battle.net, employed a technological measure, a
software "secret handshake" (CD key), to control access to its copyrighted
games. The bnetd.org emulator developed by Appellants allowed the Blizzard
game to access Battle.net mode features without a valid or unique CD key. As
a result, unauthorized copies of the Blizzard games were played on bnetd.org
servers. After Appellants distributed the bnetd program, others developed
additional Battle.net emulators based on the bnetd source code. Appellants's
distribution of binary versions of the bnetd program facilitated set up and
access to the emulator program.

Relying on *Lexmark Int'l, Inc. v. Static Control Components, Inc.*, 387 F.3d
522 (6th Cir.2004), Appellants argue that Battle.net mode is a strictly functional
process that lacks creative expression, and thus DMCA protections do not apply.
Lexmark Int'l, Inc., concerned two computer programs: the first was known as
the "Toner Loading Program" and the second was known as the "Printer Engine
Program." *Id.* at 528. DMCA anti-circumvention claims were brought after
Lexmark's authentication sequence contained in its printer cartridges were
allegedly circumvented. The district court in that case held that Lexmark's
authentication sequence effectively controlled access to the programs because it
controlled the consumers' ability to make use of those programs. *Id.* at 546. The
Sixth Circuit reversed, holding that it was not Lexmark's authentication
sequence that controlled access to the programs, but the purchase of a Lexmark
printer that allowed access to the program. "No security device, in other words,
protects access to the . . . program and no security device accordingly must be
circumvented to obtain access to that program code."

Here, Battle.net's control measure was not freely available. Appellants
could not have obtained a copy of Battle.net or made use of the literal elements
of Battle.net mode without acts of reverse engineering, which allowed for a
circumvention of Battle.net and Battle.net mode. Unlike in *Lexmark Int'l, Inc.*,
Battle.net mode codes were not accessible by simply purchasing a Blizzard

game or logging onto Battle.net., nor could data from the program be translated into readable source code after which copies were freely available without some type of circumvention. Appellants misread *Lexmark Int'l, Inc.* and we are unpersuaded that summary judgment on the anti-circumvention violations was improperly granted in favor of Blizzard and Vivendi.

2. Anti-trafficking Violations

Section 1201(a)(2) provides that:

No person shall manufacture, import, offer to the public, provide, or otherwise traffic in any technology, product, service, device, component, or part thereof, that . . . is primarily designed or produced for the purpose of circumventing a technological measure that effectively controls access to a work protected under this title; . . . has only limited commercially significant purpose or use other than to circumvent a technological measure that effectively controls access to a work protected under this title; *or* . . . is marketed by that person or another acting in concert with that person with that person's knowledge for use in circumventing a technological measure that effectively controls access to a work protected under this title.

17 U.S.C. § 1201(a)(2). The bnetd.org emulator had limited commercial purpose because its sole purpose was to avoid the limitations of Battle.net. There is no genuine issue of material fact that Appellants designed and developed the bnetd.org server and emulator for the purpose of circumventing Blizzard's technological measures controlling access to Battle.net and the Blizzard games. Summary judgment was properly granted in favor of Blizzard and Vivendi on the anti-trafficking violations.

3. Interoperability Exception

The DMCA contains several exceptions, including one for individuals using circumvention technology "for the sole purpose" of trying to achieve "interoperability" of computer programs through reverse engineering. *See* 17 U.S.C. § 1201(f). Subsection (f)(4) defines interoperability as "the ability of computer programs to exchange information, and such programs mutually to use the information which has been exchanged." 17 U.S.C. § 1201(f)(4). Appellants argue that the interoperability exception applies to any alleged infringement of Blizzard games and Battle.net. To successfully prove the interoperability defense under § 1201(f), Appellants must show: (1) they lawfully obtained the right to use a copy of a computer program; (2) the information gathered as a result of the reverse engineering was not previously readily available to the person engaging in the circumvention; (3) the sole purpose of the reverse engineering was to identify and analyze those elements of the program that were necessary to achieve interoperability of an independently created computer program with other programs; and (4) the alleged circumvention did not constitute infringement.

Appellants' circumvention in this case constitutes infringement. As detailed earlier, Blizzard's secret handshake between Blizzard games and Battle.net effectively controlled access to Battle.net mode within its games. The purpose of the bnetd.org project was to provide matchmaking services for users of Blizzard games who wanted to play in a multi-player environment without using Battle.net. The bnetd.org emulator enabled users of Blizzard games to access Battle.net mode features without a valid or unique CD key to enter Battle.net. The bnetd.org emulator did not determine whether the CD key was valid or currently in use by another player. As a result, unauthorized copies of the Blizzard games were freely played on bnetd.org servers. Appellants failed to establish a genuine issue of material fact as to the applicability of the interoperability exception. The district court properly granted summary judgment in favor of Blizzard and Vivendi on the interoperability exception.

Summary judgment in favor of Blizzard and Vivendi is affirmed.

NOTES

1. In *Pearl Investment v. Standard I/O*, 257 F. Supp. 2d 326 (D. Me. 2003), the court held that the plaintiff's virtual private network (VPN) was protected by DMCA. The VPN was the electronic equivalent to a locked door. The issue of whether the technological measure effectively controlled access to a protected copyrighted work was analyzed solely with reference to how the measure worked in the ordinary course of its operation. The fact that the programmer had alternative means of access to the software by virtue of having written the software and maintained a backup file was irrelevant under DMCA.

2. Section 1201 contains several exemptions from liability. These include:

(c) Other rights, etc., not affected. —

(1) Nothing in this section shall affect rights, remedies, limitations, or defenses to copyright infringement, including fair use, under this title.

. . . .

(d) Exemption for nonprofit libraries, archives, and educational institutions. —

(1) A nonprofit library, archives, or educational institution which gains access to a commercially exploited copyrighted work solely in order to make a good faith determination of whether to acquire a copy of that work for the sole purpose of engaging in conduct permitted under this title shall not be in violation of subsection (a)(1)(A) [subject to various listed limitations].

. . . .

(f) Reverse engineering. —

(1) Notwithstanding the provisions of subsection (a)(1)(A), a person who has lawfully obtained the right to use a copy of a computer program may circumvent a technological measure that effectively controls access to a particular portion of that program for the sole purpose of identifying and analyzing those elements of the program that are necessary to achieve interoperability of an independently created computer program with other programs, and that have not

previously been readily available to the person engaging in the circumvention, to the extent any such acts of identification and analysis do not constitute infringement under this title.

(2) Notwithstanding the provisions of subsections (a)(2) and (b), a person may develop and employ technological means to circumvent a technological measure, or to circumvent protection afforded by a technological measure, in order to enable the identification and analysis under paragraph (1), or for the purpose of enabling interoperability of an independently created computer program with other programs, if such means are necessary to achieve such interoperability, to the extent that doing so does not constitute infringement under this title.

(3) The information acquired through the acts permitted under paragraph (1), and the means permitted under paragraph (2), may be made available to others if the person referred to in paragraph (1) or (2), as the case may be, provides such information or means solely for the purpose of enabling interoperability of an independently created computer program with other programs, and to the extent that doing so does not constitute infringement under this title or violate applicable law other than this section.

(4) For purposes of this subsection, the term "interoperability" means the ability of computer programs to exchange information, and of such programs mutually to use the information which has been exchanged.

(g) Encryption research. —

(1) Definitions. — For purposes of this subsection —

(A) the term "encryption research" means activities necessary to identify and analyze flaws and vulnerabilities of encryption technologies applied to copyrighted works, if these activities are conducted to advance the state of knowledge in the field of encryption technology or to assist in the development of encryption products; and

(B) the term "encryption technology" means the scrambling and descrambling of information using mathematical formulas or algorithms.

(2) Permissible acts of encryption research. — Notwithstanding the provisions of subsection (a)(1)(A), it is not a violation of that subsection for a person to circumvent a technological measure as applied to a copy, phonorecord, performance, or display of a published work in the course of an act of good faith encryption research if —

(A) the person lawfully obtained the encrypted copy, phonorecord, performance, or display of the published work;

(B) such act is necessary to conduct such encryption research;

(C) the person made a good faith effort to obtain authorization before the circumvention; and

(D) such act does not constitute infringement under this title or a violation of applicable law other than this section, including section 1030 of title 18 and those provisions of title 18 amended by the Computer Fraud and Abuse Act of 1986.

(3) Factors in determining exemption. — In determining whether a person qualifies for the exemption under paragraph (2), the factors to be considered shall include —

(A) whether the information derived from the encryption research was disseminated, and if so, whether it was disseminated in a manner reasonably calculated to advance the state of knowledge or development of encryption technology, versus whether it was disseminated in a manner that facilitates infringement under this title or a violation of applicable law other than this section [17 U.S.C.A. § 1 et seq.], including a violation of privacy or breach of security;

(B) whether the person is engaged in a legitimate course of study, is employed, or is appropriately trained or experienced, in the field of encryption technology; and

(C) whether the person provides the copyright owner of the work to which the technological measure is applied with notice of the findings and documentation of the research, and the time when such notice is provided.
. . .

CHAMBERLAIN GROUP, INC. v. SKYLINK TECHNOLOGIES, INC.
381 F.3d 1178 (Fed. Cir. 2004)

GAJARSA, CIRCUIT JUDGE.

The Chamberlain Group, Inc. ("Chamberlain") appeals the November 13, 2003 summary judgment of the United States District Court for the Northern District of Illinois in favor of Skylink Technologies, Inc. ("Skylink"), finding that Skylink is not violating the anti-trafficking provisions of the Digital Millennium Copyright Act ("DMCA"). . . . Chamberlain's claims . . . that the District Court incorrectly construed the DMCA as placing a burden upon Chamberlain to prove that the circumvention of its technological measures enabled *unauthorized* access to its copyrighted software. But Skylink's accused device enables only uses that copyright law explicitly authorizes, and is therefore presumptively legal. Chamberlain has neither proved nor alleged a connection between Skylink's accused circumvention device and the protections that the copyright laws afford Chamberlain capable of overcoming that presumption. [We affirm] summary judgment in favor of Skylink.

Background

[The technology] at issue involves Garage Door Openers (GDOs). A GDO typically consists of a hand-held portable transmitter and a garage door opening device mounted in a homeowner's garage. The opening device, in turn, includes both a receiver with associated signal processing software and a motor to open or close the garage door. In order to open or close the garage door, a user must activate the transmitter, which sends a radio frequency (RF) signal to the receiver located on the opening device. Once the opener receives a recognized signal, the signal processing software directs the motor to open or close the garage door.

When a homeowner purchases a GDO system, the manufacturer provides both an opener and a transmitter. Homeowners who desire replacement or spare transmitters can purchase them in the aftermarket. Aftermarket consumers have long been able to purchase "universal transmitters" that they can program to interoperate with their GDO system regardless of make or model. . . . Chamberlain places no explicit restrictions on the types of transmitter that the homeowner may use with its system at the time of purchase. Chamberlain's customers therefore assume that they enjoy all of the rights associated with the use of their GDOs and any software embedded therein that the copyright laws and other laws of commerce provide.

This dispute involves Chamberlain's Securityk line of GDOs and Skylink's Model 39 universal transmitter. Chamberlain's Securityk GDOs incorporate a copyrighted "rolling code" computer program that constantly changes the transmitter signal needed to open the garage door. Skylink's Model 39 transmitter, which does not incorporate rolling code, nevertheless allows users to operate Securityk openers. Chamberlain alleges that Skylink's transmitter renders the Securityk insecure by allowing unauthorized users to circumvent the security inherent in rolling codes. Of greater legal significance, however, Chamberlain contends that because of this property of the Model 39, Skylink is in violation of the anti-trafficking clause of the DMCA's anticircumvention provisions, specifically § 1201(a)(2).

The code in a standard (i.e., non-rolling code) GDO transmitter is unique but fixed. . . . A user wishing to set up a new transmitter for use with her Securityk GDO must switch the opener to "program mode" and send a signal from the transmitter to the opener. The opener stores both the fixed and rolling components of the transmitted signal. When the user switches the opener back to "operate mode," the system is set and the user may operate the opener with the newly programmed transmitter. . . . Skylink began marketing and selling universal transmitters in 1992. . . . Although Chamberlain concedes that the Model 39 transmitter is capable of operating many different GDOs, it nevertheless asserts that Skylink markets the Model 39 transmitter for use in circumventing its copyrighted rolling code computer program. Chamberlain supports this allegation by pointing to the Model 39's setting that operates *only* Chamberlain's rolling code GDOs. . . .

Chamberlain *has not* alleged either that Skylink infringed its copyright or that Skylink is liable for contributory copyright infringement. What Chamberlain *has* alleged is that because its opener and transmitter both incorporate computer programs "protected by copyright" and because rolling codes are a "technological measure" that "controls access" to those programs, Skylink is prima facie liable for violating § 1201(a)(2). In the District Court's words, "Chamberlain claims that the rolling code computer program has a protective measure that protects itself. Thus, only one computer program is at work here, but it has two functions: (1) to verify the rolling code; and (2) once the rolling code is verified, to activate the GDO motor, by sending instructions to a microprocessor in the GDO."

. . . Chamberlain sued Skylink under 17 U.S.C. § 1201(a)(2), a statutory provision that neither the Seventh Circuit nor any previous District Court in the Seventh Circuit had ever considered. To date, in fact, only the Second Circuit has construed § 1201(a)(2), and that construction focused on First Amendment issues rather than on an application of the statute to case-specific facts. *See Universal City Studios v. Corley,* 273 F.3d 429 (2d Cir.2001) ("*Corley*"). . . . Skylink submitted several defenses, arguing that: (1) the Model 39 transmitter serves a variety of functions that are unrelated to circumvention; (2) Chamberlain has failed to demonstrate that its GDOs contain a computer program protected by copyright; (3) consumers use the Model 39 transmitter to activate the Securityk GDOs with Chamberlain's consent; (4) Skylink has not violated the DMCA because it falls within a safe harbor provision per § 1201(f); and (5) Chamberlain's rolling code computer program does not protect a copyrighted computer program, but instead protects an uncopyrightable process. Though the District Court commented on all of these arguments, it based its rulings entirely on Skylink's third argument concerning authorization and consent. [The] District Court concluded that because Chamberlain never restricted its customers' use of competing transmitters with its Securityk line, those customers had implicit authorization to use Skylink's Model 39. Because of that implicit authorization, Chamberlain could not possibly meet its burden of proving that Skylink trafficked in a device designed to circumvent a technological measure to gain unauthorized access to Chamberlain's copyrighted computer programs. . . .

D. The Statute and Liability under the DMCA

The essence of the DMCA's anticircumvention provisions is that §§ 1201(a), (b) establish causes of action for liability. They do not establish a new property right. The DMCA's text indicates that circumvention is not infringement, 17 U.S.C. § 1201(c)(1) ("Nothing in this section shall affect rights, remedies, limitations, or defenses to copyright infringement, including fair use, under this title."), and the statute's structure makes the point even clearer. This distinction between property and liability is critical. Whereas copyrights, like patents, are property, liability protection from unauthorized circumvention merely creates a new cause of action under which a defendant may be liable. The distinction between property and liability goes straight to the issue of authorization, the issue upon which the District Court both denied Chamberlain's and granted Skylink's motion for summary judgment.

A plaintiff alleging copyright infringement need prove *only* "(1) ownership of a valid copyright, and (2) copying of constituent elements of the work that are original." "[T]he existence of a license, exclusive or nonexclusive, creates an affirmative defense to a claim of copyright infringement." In other words, under Seventh Circuit copyright law, a plaintiff only needs to show that the defendant has used her property; the burden of proving that the use was authorized falls squarely on the defendant. The DMCA, however, *defines* circumvention as an activity undertaken "without the authority of the copyright owner." 17 U.S.C. § 1201(a)(3)(A). The plain language of the statute therefore requires a plaintiff alleging circumvention (or trafficking) to prove that the defendant's access was unauthorized — a significant burden where, as here, the copyright laws authorize consumers to use the copy of Chamberlain's software embedded in the GDOs that they purchased. The premise underlying this initial assignment of burden is that the copyright laws authorize members of the public to access a work, but not to copy it. The law therefore places the burden of proof on the party attempting to establish that the circumstances of its case deviate from these normal expectations; defendants must prove authorized copying and plaintiffs must prove unauthorized access.

The distinction between property and liability also addresses an important policy issue that Chamberlain puts into stark focus. According to Chamberlain, the 1998 enactment of the DMCA "renders the pre-DMCA history in the GDO industry irrelevant. By prohibiting the trafficking and use of circumvention technology, the DMCA fundamentally altered the legal landscape. . . ." Chamberlain reiterated and strengthened this assertion at oral argument, claiming that the DMCA overrode all pre-existing consumer expectations about the legitimate uses of products containing copyrighted embedded software. Chamberlain contends that Congress empowered manufacturers to prohibit consumers from using embedded software products in conjunction with competing products when it passed § 1201(a)(1). According to Chamberlain, *all* such uses of products containing copyrighted software to which a technological measure controlled access are now per se illegal under the DMCA unless the manufacturer provided consumers with *explicit* authorization. Chamberlain's interpretation of the DMCA would therefore grant manufacturers broad exemptions from both the antitrust laws and the doctrine of copyright misuse.

Such an exemption, however, is only plausible if the anticircumvention provisions established a new property right capable of conflicting with the copyright owner's other legal responsibilities — which as we have already explained, they do not. The anticircumvention provisions convey no additional property rights in and of themselves; they simply provide property owners with new ways to secure their property. Like all property owners taking legitimate steps to protect their property, however, copyright owners relying on the anticircumvention provisions remain bound by all other relevant bodies of law. Contrary to Chamberlain's assertion, the DMCA emphatically *did not* "fundamentally alter" the legal landscape governing the reasonable expectations of consumers or competitors; *did not* "fundamentally alter" the ways that courts analyze industry practices; and *did not* render the pre-DMCA history of the GDO industry irrelevant.

What the DMCA did was introduce new grounds for liability in the context of the unauthorized access of copyrighted material. The statute's plain language requires plaintiffs to prove that those circumventing their technological measures controlling access did so "without the authority of the copyright owner." Our inquiry ends with that clear language. We note, however, that the statute's structure, legislative history, and context within the Copyright Act all support our construction. They also help to explain why Chamberlain's warranty conditions and website postings cannot render users of Skylink's Model 39 "unauthorized" users for the purposes of establishing trafficking liability under the DMCA.

E. Statutory Structure and Legislative History

[The Second Circuit,] as a precursor to its constitutional analysis, summarized the statute's history and structure:

> The DMCA was enacted in 1998 to implement the World Intellectual Property Organization Copyright Treaty (WIPO Treaty), which requires contracting parties to provide adequate legal protection and effective legal remedies against the circumvention of effective technological measures that are used by authors in connection with the exercise of their rights under this Treaty or the Berne Convention and that restrict acts, in respect of their works, which are not authorized by the authors concerned or permitted by law. Even before the treaty, Congress had been devoting attention to the problems faced by copyright enforcement in the digital age. Hearings on the topic have spanned several years. . . . This legislative effort resulted in the DMCA.

> The Act contains three provisions targeted at the circumvention of technological protections. The first is subsection 1201(a)(1)(A), the anticircumvention provision. This provision prohibits a person from circumvent[ing] a technological measure that effectively controls access to a work protected under [Title 17, governing copyright]. . . .

> The second and third provisions are subsections 1201(a)(2) and 1201(b)(1), the anti-trafficking provisions. . . . Subsection 1201(a)(1) differs from both of these anti-trafficking subsections in that it targets the use of a circumvention technology, not the trafficking in such a technology.

> The DMCA contains exceptions. . . .

Corley, 273 F.3d at 440-41.

Here, as in *Corley,* the primary statutory clause at issue is § 1201(a)(2) of the DMCA, though other subsections of § 1201 are also implicated. Unlike the Second Circuit in *Corley,* which provided only enough of the statutory construction to address constitutional challenges, however, we must construe the full boundaries of anticircumvention and anti-trafficking liability under the DMCA. We must determine the Congressional intent embodied in the statute's language, and then enforce the correctly construed statute to the facts at hand.

Because the DMCA is a complex statute creating several new causes of action, each subject to numerous exceptions, we must also ensure that our construction makes sense given the statute's entirety. We must therefore consider briefly the relationship among the liabilities created under §§ 1201(a)(1), (a)(2), and (b). Statutory structure and legislative history both make it clear that § 1201 applies only to circumventions reasonably related to protected rights. Defendants who traffic in devices that circumvent access controls in ways that facilitate infringement may be subject to liability under § 1201(a)(2). Defendants who use such devices may be subject to liability under § 1201(a)(1) whether they infringe or not. Because all defendants who traffic in devices that circumvent rights controls necessarily facilitate infringement, they may be subject to liability under § 1201(b). Defendants who use such devices may be subject to liability for copyright infringement. And finally, defendants whose circumvention devices do not facilitate infringement are not subject to § 1201 liability.

The key to understanding this relationship lies in § 1201(b), which prohibits trafficking in devices that circumvent technological measures tailored narrowly to protect an individual right of the copyright owner while nevertheless allowing access to the protected work. Though § 1201(b) parallels the anti-trafficking ban of § 1201(a)(2), there is no narrowly tailored ban on direct circumvention to parallel § 1201(a)(1). This omission was intentional. . . .

> The prohibition in 1201(a)(1) [was] necessary because prior to [the DMCA], the conduct of circumvention was never before made unlawful. The device limitation in 1201(a)(2) enforces this new prohibition in conduct. The copyright law has long forbidden copyright infringements, so no new prohibition was necessary. The device limitation in 1201(b) enforces the longstanding prohibitions on infringements.

S.Rep. No. 105-90 at 12 (1998).

Prior to the DMCA, a copyright owner would have had no cause of action against anyone who circumvented any sort of technological control, but did not infringe. The DMCA rebalanced these interests to favor the copyright owner; the DMCA created circumvention liability for "digital trespass" under § 1201(a)(1). It also created trafficking liability under § 1201(a)(2) for facilitating such circumvention and under § 1201(b) for facilitating infringement (both subject to the numerous limitations and exceptions outlined throughout the DMCA).

The importance of "rebalancing" interests in light of recent technological advances is manifest in the DMCA's legislative history. Though the Supreme Court has recognized that interim industrial developments may erode the "persuasive effect of legislative history," Congressional intent evident in relatively recent legislation like the DMCA may provide useful context in interpreting the statutory language. Though "we do not resort to legislative history to cloud a statutory text that is clear," we nevertheless recognize that "words are inexact tools at best, and hence it is essential that we place the words of a statute in their proper context by resort to the legislative history."

The most significant and consistent theme running through the entire leg-islative history of the anticircumvention and anti-trafficking provisions of the DMCA, §§ 1201(a)(1), (2), is that Congress attempted to balance competing interests, and "endeavored to specify, with as much clarity as possible, how the right against anti-circumvention would be qualified to maintain balance between the interests of content creators and information users." H.R.Rep. No. 105-551, at 26 (1998). The Report of the House Commerce Committee con-cluded that § 1201 "fully respects and extends into the digital environment the bedrock principle of 'balance' in American intellectual property law for the benefit of both copyright owners and users."

The crux of the present dispute over statutory construction therefore stems from a dispute over the precise balance between copyright owners and users that Congress captured in the DMCA's language.

> Defendants argue . . . that the DMCA should not be construed to reach their conduct [or product] . . . because the DMCA, so applied, could prevent those who wish to gain access to technologically protected copyrighted works in order to make . . . non-infringing use of them from doing so. . . . Technological access control measures have the capacity to prevent fair uses of copyrighted works as well as foul. Hence, there is a potential tension between the use of such access con-trol measures and fair use, [as well as the much broader range of explicitly noninfringing use]. . . . As the DMCA made its way through the legislative process, Congress was preoccupied with precisely this issue. Proponents of strong restrictions on circumvention of access control measures argued that they were essential if copyright holders were to make their works available in digital form because digital works otherwise could be pirated too easily. Opponents contended that strong anticircumvention measures would extend the copyright monopoly inappropriately and prevent many fair uses of copyrighted material. Congress struck a balance. . . .

[*Universal City Studios, Inc. v.*] *Reimerdes,* 111 F.Supp.2d [294] at 304 [(S. D.N.Y. 2000)] (citations omitted). We must understand that balance to resolve this dispute.

F. Access and Protection

Congress crafted the new anticircumvention and anti-trafficking provisions here at issue to help bring copyright law into the information age. Advances in digital technology over the past few decades have stripped copyright owners of much of the technological and economic protection to which they had grown accustomed. Whereas large-scale copying and distribution of copyrighted material used to be difficult and expensive, it is now easy and inexpensive. The *Reimerdes* court correctly noted both the economic impact of these advances and their consequent potential impact on innovation. Congress therefore crafted legislation restricting some, but not all, technological measures designed either to access a work protected by copyright, § 1201(a), or to infringe a right of a copyright owner, § 1201(b).

Though as noted, circumvention *is not* a new form of infringement but rather a new violation prohibiting actions or products that facilitate infringement, it is significant that virtually every clause of § 1201 that mentions "access" links "access" to "protection." The import of that linkage may be less than obvious. Perhaps the best way to appreciate the necessity of this linkage — and the disposition of this case — is to consider three interrelated questions inherent in the DMCA's structure: What does § 1201(a)(2) prohibit above and beyond the prohibitions of § 1201(b)? What is the relationship between the sorts of "access" prohibited under § 1201(a) and the rights "protected" under the Copyright Act? and What is the relationship between anti-circumvention liability under § 1201(a)(1) and anti-trafficking liability under § 1201(a)(2)? The relationships among the new liabilities that these three provisions, §§ 1201(a)(1), (a)(2), (b), create circumscribe the DMCA's scope — and therefore allow us to determine whether or not Chamberlain's claim falls within its purview. And the key to disentangling these relationships lies in understanding the linkage between access and protection.

Chamberlain urges us to read the DMCA as if Congress simply created a new protection for copyrighted works without any reference at all either to the protections that copyright owners already possess or to the rights that the Copyright Act grants to the public. Chamberlain has not alleged that Skylink's Model 39 infringes its copyrights, nor has it alleged that the Model 39 contributes to third-party infringement of its copyrights. Chamberlain's allegation is considerably more straightforward: The only way for the Model 39 to interoperate with a Securityk GDO is by "accessing" copyrighted software. Skylink has therefore committed a per se violation of the DMCA. Chamberlain urges us to conclude that no necessary connection exists between access and *copyrights*. Congress could not have intended such a broad reading of the DMCA. *Accord Corley,* 273 F.3d at 435 (explaining that Congress passed the DMCA's anti-trafficking provisions to help copyright owners protect their works *from piracy* behind a digital wall).

Chamberlain derives its strongest claimed support for its proposed construction from the trial court's opinion in *Reimerdes,* a case involving the same statutory provision. Though Chamberlain is correct in considering some of the *Reimerdes* language supportive, it is the differences between the cases, rather than their similarities, that is most instructive in demonstrating precisely what the DMCA permits and what it prohibits.

The facts here differ greatly from those in *Reimerdes*. There, a group of movie studios sought an injunction under the DMCA to prohibit illegal copying of digital versatile discs (DVDs). The plaintiffs presented evidence that each motion picture DVD includes a content scrambling system (CSS) that permits the film to be played, but not copied, using DVD players that incorporate the plaintiffs' licensed decryption technology. *Id.* The defendant provided a link on his website that allowed an individual to download DeCSS, a program that allows the user to circumvent the CSS protective system and to view *or to copy* a motion picture from a DVD, whether or not the user has a DVD player with the licensed technology. The defendant proudly trumpeted his actions as "electronic civil disobedience." The court found that the defendant had violated 17 U.S.C. § 1201(a)(2)(A) because DeCSS had only one purpose: to decrypt CSS.

Chamberlain's proposed construction of the DMCA ignores the significant differences between defendants whose accused products enable copying and those, like Skylink, whose accused products enable only legitimate uses of copyrighted software. Chamberlain's repeated reliance on language targeted at defendants trumpeting their "electronic civil disobedience," *id.* at 303, 312, apparently led it to misconstrue significant portions of the DMCA. Many of Chamberlain's assertions in its brief to this court conflate the property right of copyright with the liability that the anticircumvention provisions impose.

Chamberlain relies upon the DMCA's prohibition of "fair uses . . . as well as foul," to argue that the enactment of the DMCA eliminated all existing consumer expectations about the public's rights to use purchased products because those products might include technological measures controlling access to a copyrighted work. But Chamberlain appears to have overlooked the obvious. The possibility that § 1201 might prohibit some otherwise noninfringing public uses of copyrighted material, arises simply because the Congressional decision to create liability and consequent damages for making, using, or selling a "key" that essentially enables a *trespass* upon intellectual property need not be identical in scope to the liabilities and compensable damages for *infringing* that property; it is, instead, a rebalancing of interests that "attempt[s] to deal with special problems created by the so-called digital revolution." [*In re*] *Aimster* [*Copyright Litigation*], 334 F.3d [643] at 655 [(7th Cir. 2003)].

Though *Reimerdes* is not the only case that Chamberlain cites for support, none of its other citations are any more helpful to its cause. In three other cases, *Lexmark International, Inc. v. Static Control Components, Inc.,* 253 F.Supp.2d 943, 969 (E.D. Ky. 2003), *Sony Computer Entertainment America, Inc. v. Gamemasters,* 87 F.Supp.2d 976 (N.D.Cal.1999), and *RealNetworks,* 2000 U.S. Dist. LEXIS 1889, the trial courts did grant preliminary injunctions under the DMCA using language supportive of Chamberlain's proposed construction. None of these cases, however, is on point. In *Lexmark,* 253 F. Supp.2d at 971, the trial court ruled that the defendant's conduct constituted copyright infringement. In *Sony,* 87 F.Supp.2d 987, the plaintiff's allegations included both trademark and copyright infringement, and the defendant conceded that its product made "temporary modifications" to the plaintiff's copyrighted computer program. In *RealNetworks,* the defendant's product allegedly disabled RealNetworks' "copy switch," RealNetworks' technological measure designed to let the owner of copyrighted material being streamed over RealNetworks' media player either enable or disable copying upon streaming. The court stated explicitly that the avoidance of the copy switch appeared to have little commercial value other than circumvention and the consequent infringement that it enabled. In short, the access alleged in all three cases was intertwined with a protected right. None of these cases can support a construction as broad as the one that Chamberlain urges us to adopt, even as persuasive authority.

Furthermore, though the severance of access from protection appears plausible taken out of context, it would also introduce a number of irreconcilable problems in statutory construction. The seeming plausibility arises because the statute's structure could be seen to suggest that § 1201(b) strengthens a copyright owner's abilities to protect its recognized *rights,* while § 1201(a) strengthens a copyright owner's abilities to protect *access* to its work without regard to the legitimacy (or illegitimacy) of the actions that the accused access enables. Such an interpretation is consistent with the Second Circuit's description: "[T]he focus of subsection 1201(a)(2) is circumvention of technologies designed to *prevent access* to a work, and the focus of subsection 1201(b)(1) is circumvention of technologies designed to *permit access* to a work but *prevent copying* of the work or some other act that infringes a copyright." *Corley,* 273 F.3d at 440-41 (emphasis in original).

It is unlikely, however, that the Second Circuit meant to imply anything as drastic as wresting the concept of "access" from its context within the Copyright Act, as Chamberlain would now have us do. Were § 1201(a) to allow copyright owners to use technological measures to block *all* access to their copyrighted works, it would effectively create two distinct copyright regimes. In the first regime, the owners of a typical work protected by copyright would possess only the rights enumerated in 17 U.S.C. § 106, subject to the additions, exceptions, and limitations outlined throughout the rest of the Copyright Act — notably but not solely the fair use provisions of § 107.[2] Owners who feel that technology has put those rights at risk, and who incorporate technological measures to protect those rights from technological encroachment, gain the additional ability to hold traffickers in circumvention devices liable under § 1201(b) for putting their rights back at risk by enabling circumventors who use these devices to infringe.

Under the second regime that Chamberlain's proposed construction implies, the owners of a work protected by *both* copyright *and* a technological measure that effectively controls access to that work per § 1201(a) would possess *unlimited* rights to hold circumventors liable under § 1201(a) *merely for accessing that work,* even if that access enabled *only* rights that the Copyright Act grants to the public. This second implied regime would be problematic for a number of reasons. First, as the Supreme Court recently explained, "Congress' exercise of its Copyright Clause authority must be rational." In determining whether a particular aspect of the Copyright Act "is a rational exercise of the legislative authority conferred by the Copyright Clause . . . we defer substantially to Congress. It is Congress that has been assigned the task of defining the scope of the limited monopoly that should be granted to authors . . . *in order to give the public appropriate access* to their work product." Chamberlain's proposed construction of § 1201(a) implies that in enacting the DMCA, Congress attempted to "give the public appropriate access" to copyrighted works by allowing copyright owners to deny all access to the public. Even under the substantial deference due Congress, such a redefinition borders on the irrational.

That apparent irrationality, however, is not the most significant problem that this second regime implies. Such a regime would be hard to reconcile with the DMCA's statutory prescription that "[n]othing in this section shall affect

---

2 [FN 14] We do not reach the relationship between § 107 fair use and violations of § 1201. The District Court in *Reimerdes* rejected the DeCSS defendants' argument that fair use was a *necessary* defense to § 1201(a), *Reimerdes,* 111 F.Supp.2d at 317; because *any* access enables some fair uses, any act of circumvention would embody its own defense. We leave open the question as to when § 107 might serve as an affirmative defense to a prima facie violation of § 1201. For the moment, we note only that though the traditional fair use doctrine of § 107 remains unchanged as a defense to copyright infringement under § 1201(c)(1), circumvention is not infringement.

rights, remedies, limitations, or defenses to copyright infringement, including fair use, under this title." 17 U.S.C. § 1201(c)(1). A provision that prohibited access without regard to the rest of the Copyright Act would clearly affect rights and limitations, if not remedies and defenses. Justice Souter has remarked that "[n]o canon of statutory construction familiar to me specifically addresses the situation in which two simultaneously enacted provisions of the same statute flatly contradict one another. We are, of course, bound to avoid such a dilemma if we can, by glimpsing some uncontradicted meaning for each provision." Chamberlain's proposed construction of § 1201(a) would flatly contradict § 1201(c)(1) — a simultaneously enacted provision of the same statute. We are therefore bound, if we can, to obtain an alternative construction that leads to no such contradiction.

Chamberlain's proposed severance of "access" from "protection" in § 1201(a) creates numerous other problems. Beyond suggesting that Congress enacted *by implication* a new, highly protective alternative regime for copyrighted works; contradicting other provisions of the same statute including § 1201(c)(1); and ignoring the explicit immunization of interoperability from anticircumvention liability under § 1201(f); the broad policy implications of considering "access" in a vacuum devoid of "protection" are both absurd and disastrous. Under Chamberlain's proposed construction, explicated at oral argument, disabling a burglar alarm to gain "access" to a home containing copyrighted books, music, art, and periodicals would violate the DMCA; anyone who did so would unquestionably have "circumvent[ed] a technological measure that effectively controls access to a work protected under [the Copyright Act]." § 1201(a)(1). The appropriate deterrents to this type of behavior lie in tort law and criminal law, *not* in copyright law. Yet, were we to read the statute's "plain language" as Chamberlain urges, disabling a burglar alarm would be a per se violation of the DMCA.

In a similar vein, Chamberlain's proposed construction would allow any manufacturer of any product to add a single copyrighted sentence or software fragment to its product, wrap the copyrighted material in a trivial "encryption" scheme, and thereby gain the right to restrict consumers' rights to use its products in conjunction with competing products. In other words, Chamberlain's construction of the DMCA would allow virtually any company to attempt to leverage its sales into aftermarket monopolies — a practice that both the antitrust laws, and the doctrine of copyright misuse, normally prohibit.

Even were we to assume arguendo that the DMCA's anticircumvention provisions created a new property right, Chamberlain's attempt to infer such an exemption from copyright misuse and antitrust liability would *still* be wrong. We have noted numerous times that as a matter of Federal Circuit law, "[i]ntellectual property rights do not confer a privilege to violate the antitrust laws. But it is also correct that the antitrust laws do not negate [a] patentee's right to exclude others from patent property." *CSU, L.L.C. v. Xerox Corp.,* 203 F.3d 1322, 1325 (Fed.Cir.2000) (citations omitted). In what we previously termed "the most extensive analysis of the effect of a unilateral refusal to license copyrighted expression," *id.,* among our sister Circuits, the First Circuit explained that: "[T]he Copyright Act does not explicitly purport to limit the scope of the Sherman Act. . . . [W]e must harmonize the two [Acts] as best we can." *Data Gen. Corp. v. Grumman Sys. Support Corp.,* 36 F.3d 1147,

1186-87 (1st Cir.1994). Our previous consideration of *Data General* led us to conclude that it was "consistent with both the antitrust and the copyright laws and
is the standard that would most likely be followed by the Tenth Circuit." . . .

Finally, the requisite "authorization," on which the District Court granted
Skylink summary judgment, points to yet another inconsistency in
Chamberlain's proposed construction. The notion of authorization is central to
understanding § 1201(a). Underlying Chamberlain's argument on appeal that
it has not granted such authorization lies the necessary assumption that
Chamberlain is entitled to prohibit legitimate purchasers of its embedded software from "accessing" the software by using it. Such an entitlement, however,
would go far beyond the idea that the DMCA allows copyright owner to prohibit "fair uses . . . as well as foul." Chamberlain's proposed construction would
allow copyright owners to prohibit *exclusively fair* uses even in the absence of
any feared foul use. It would therefore allow any copyright owner, through a
combination of contractual terms and technological measures, to repeal the
fair use doctrine with respect to an individual copyrighted work — or even
selected copies of that copyrighted work. Again, this implication contradicts
§ 1201(c)(1) directly. Copyright law itself authorizes the public to make certain
uses of copyrighted materials. Consumers who purchase a product containing
a copy of embedded software have the inherent legal right to use that copy of
the software. What the law authorizes, Chamberlain cannot revoke.[3]

Chamberlain's proposed severance of "access" from "protection" is entirely
inconsistent with the context defined by the total statutory structure of the
Copyright Act, other simultaneously enacted provisions of the DMCA, and
clear Congressional intent. It "would lead to a result so bizarre that Congress
could not have intended it." The statutory structure and the legislative history
both make it clear that the DMCA granted copyright holders additional legal
protections, but neither rescinded the basic bargain granting the public noninfringing and fair uses of copyrighted materials, § 1201(c), nor prohibited
various beneficial uses of circumvention technology, such as those exempted
under §§ 1201(d), (f), (g), (j).

We therefore reject Chamberlain's proposed construction in its entirety. We
conclude that 17 U.S.C. § 1201 prohibits only forms of access that bear a reasonable relationship to the protections that the Copyright Act otherwise
affords copyright owners. While such a rule of reason may create some uncertainty and consume some judicial resources, it is the only meaningful reading
of the statute. Congress attempted to balance the legitimate interests of copyright owners with those of consumers of copyrighted products. The courts
must adhere to the language that Congress enacted to determine how it
attempted to achieve that balance.

As we have seen, Congress chose to create new causes of action for circumvention and for trafficking in circumvention devices. Congress did not choose
to create new property rights. That is the choice that we have identified. "It is

---

[3] [FN 17] It is not clear whether a consumer who circumvents a technological measure controlling access to a copyrighted work in a manner that enables uses permitted under the Copyright
Act but prohibited by contract can be subject to liability under the DMCA. Because Chamberlain
did not attempt to limit its customers' use of its product by contract, however, we do not reach this
issue.

not for us to resolve the issues of public policy implicated by the choice we have identified. Those issues are for Congress." *Corley,* 273 F.3d at 458. Were we to interpret Congress's words in a way that eliminated all balance and granted copyright owners carte blanche authority to preclude all use, Congressional intent would remain unrealized.

Congress chose words consistent with its stated intent to balance two sets of concerns pushing in opposite directions. The statute lays out broad categories of liability and broad exemptions from liability. It also instructs the courts explicitly *not* to construe the anticircumvention provisions in ways that would effectively repeal longstanding principles of copyright law. The courts must decide where the balance between the rights of copyright owners and those of the broad public tilts subject to a fact-specific rule of reason. Here, Chamberlain can point to no protected property right that Skylink imperils. The DMCA cannot allow Chamberlain to retract the most fundamental right that the Copyright Act grants consumers: the right to use the copy of Chamberlain's embedded software that they purchased.

G. Chamberlain's DMCA Claim

The proper construction of § 1201(a)(2) therefore makes it clear that Chamberlain cannot prevail. A plaintiff alleging a violation of § 1201(a)(2) must prove: (1) ownership of a valid *copyright* on a work, (2) effectively controlled by a *technological measure,* which has been circumvented, (3) that third parties can now *access* (4) *without authorization,* in a manner that (5) infringes or facilitates infringing a right *protected* by the Copyright Act, because of a product that (6) the defendant either (i) *designed or produced* primarily for circumvention; (ii) made available despite only *limited commercial significance* other than circumvention; or (iii) *marketed* for use in circumvention of the controlling technological measure. A plaintiff incapable of establishing any one of elements (1) through (5) will have failed to prove a prima facie case. A plaintiff capable of proving elements (1) through (5) need prove only one of (6)(i), (ii), or (iii) to shift the burden back to the defendant. At that point, the various affirmative defenses enumerated throughout § 1201 become relevant.

The District Court analyzed Chamberlain's allegations in precisely the appropriate manner — a narrow focus on Skylink's behavior, intent, and product within the broader context of longstanding expectations throughout the industry. . . . Chamberlain met the first element, copyright ownership, and for the purposes of its summary judgment motions accepted Chamberlain's evidence of the second element, technological access control. The District Court granted Skylink's motion for summary judgment because Chamberlain failed to meet its burden on the fourth element, the lack of authorization. Chamberlain emphatically contests this conclusion on appeal, though mostly by reiterating arguments that the District Court correctly rejected.

Chamberlain, however, has failed to show not only the requisite lack of authorization, but also the necessary fifth element of its claim, the critical nexus between access and protection. Chamberlain neither alleged copyright infringement *nor explained how the access provided by the Model 39 transmitter facilitates the infringement of any right that the Copyright Act protects.* There can therefore be no reasonable relationship between the access that homeowners gain to Chamberlain's copyrighted software when using Skylink's Model 39 transmitter and the protections that the Copyright Act grants to Chamberlain. The Copyright Act authorized Chamberlain's customers to use the copy of Chamberlain's copyrighted software embedded in the GDOs that they purchased. Chamberlain's customers are therefore immune from § 1201(a)(1) circumvention liability. In the absence of allegations of either copyright infringement or § 1201(a)(1) circumvention, Skylink cannot be liable for § 1201(a)(2) trafficking. The District Court's grant of summary judgment in Skylink's favor was correct. Chamberlain failed to allege a claim under 17 U.S.C. § 1201. . . .

We therefore affirm . . . summary judgment in favor of Skylink.

NOTES

1. Under the court's interpretation, what is the function of 1201(b), which deals with technology devices that protect intellectual property rights? Is it not true that the court's discussion eliminates any reason for that second provision?

2. Does a user of the defendant's device breach its contract with the garage system provider? Was the software licensed to the end user or a copy sold?

3. The court emphasizes that the DMCA did not create a property right. Other than as a matter of arcane jurisprudence, why is that issue important for the court's decision? Actually, the owner of a place does have a right to control access to it and, for most people, that is a property right.

4. *Corely,* the Second Circuit decision, held that an injunction against distribution of circumvention code on the Internet did not violate the First Amendment. It addressed an issue alluded to in *Skylink*, but not resolved — the treatment of limitations on fair use. The argument of the defendant was that there should be a right to copy (or modify) works *in digital form* regardless of the terms under which the copies were distributed. *Corely* rejected that argument, as have Congress and the U.S. Copyright Office:

> We know of no authority for the proposition that fair use, as protected by the Copyright Act, much less the Constitution, guarantees copying by the optimum method or in the identical format of the original. . . . DMCA does not impose even an arguable limitation on the opportunity to make a variety of traditional fair uses of DVD movies, such as commenting on their content, quoting excerpts from their screenplays, and even recording portions of the video images and sounds on film or tape by pointing a camera . . . at a monitor as it displays the DVD movie. The fact that the resulting copy will not be as perfect or as manipulable as a digital copy obtained by having direct access to the DVD movie in its digital form, provides no basis for a claim of unconstitutional limitation of fair use. . . . Fair use has never been held to be a guarantee of access to copyrighted material in order to copy it by the fair user's preferred technique or in the format of the original.

Technology may limit access to digital copies and preclude copying or modification in digital form, but this does not preclude other uses or means of excerpting or commenting. Fair use is not a right to take material in digital form merely because that is convenient.

5. The comments of the California Supreme Court in *DVD Copy Control Ass'n, Inc. v. Bunner,* 75 P.3d 1 (Cal. 2003), are relevant. That court upheld an injunction against Internet posting of DeCSS decryption code. The defendant had argued that his disclosure of the code was part of a debate on issues of public interest. Rejecting this argument, the court observed:

> [The] content of the trade secrets neither involves a matter of public concern nor implicates the core purpose of the First Amendment. [Plaintiff's] trade secrets in the CSS technology . . . convey *only* technical information about the method used by specific private entities to protect their intellectual property. Bunner posted these secrets . . . on the Internet so Linux users could enjoy and use DVD's and so others could improve the functional capabilities of DeCSS. He did not post them to comment on any public issue or to participate in any public debate. . . . Thus, these trade secrets . . . address matters of purely private concern and not matters of public importance. . . . Disclosure of this highly technical information adds nothing to the public debate over the use of encryption software or the DVD industry's efforts to limit unauthorized copying of movies on DVDs. And the injunction does not hamper Bunner's ability to "discuss and debate" these issues. . . .

PROBLEM 16.3

Software Co. is planning to distribute video games in media useable for three uses. The games will cost $50.00. If more than three uses are desired, the purchaser must log on to Software's site and purchase a code allowing additional uses. Is it preferable for Software to use a license or should it rely solely on technological means?

PROBLEM 16.4

Professor is engaged in computer security research. Professor discovers a means of circumventing the most popular encryption system used by commercial companies to protect access to their software. Professor plans to present the findings at a conference. At the same time, Hacker discovered a flaw in the second most popular encryption system. Hacker plans to post this on its website in order to destroy the evil empire of copyright owners. Does DMCA prevent either of these activities?

STORAGE TECHNOLOGY CORP. v. CUSTOM HARDWARE ENGINEERING & CONSULTING, INC.,
-- F.3d ---, 2005 WL 2030281 (Fed. Cir. 2005)

BRYSON, CIRCUIT JUDGE.

Storage Technology Corporation ("StorageTek") manufactures automated tape cartridge libraries that can store massive amounts of computer data. The cartridge libraries consist of Library Storage Modules, or "silos," that contain numerous tape cartridges, tape drives for reading the cartridges, and a robot arm for moving the cartridges. Connected to each silo is a Library Control Unit that controls the robotic mechanisms in the silo and monitors their progress. The individual silos and Control Units are connected via a local area network to a Library Management Unit, which is a computer that can direct and control several silos. To access data from the library, a user sends a request for the data to the Management Unit. The Management Unit then transmits commands to the appropriate Control Unit to find and read the tape cartridge containing the requested data. The Control Unit then sends the data over the network back to the Management Unit.

A central element of this case concerns what occurs when the entire tape library is first turned on. Upon startup, the Management Unit loads executable code, called the "9330 code," from its hard drive into its random access memory ("RAM"). When the Control Unit is powered up, the Management Unit sends other code, called the "9311 code," across the network to the Control Unit, where it is loaded into the Control Unit's memory. Both processes happen automatically, without any action by the library user.

StorageTek's claims in this case stem from the fact that the 9330 and 9311 computer code is copyrighted. StorageTek describes both the 9330 and 9311 code as consisting of two intertwined, but distinct, groups: functional code and maintenance code. While StorageTek never specifies which portions of its copyrighted code fall into each group, it states that the functional code consists of the portions of the computer program that cause the Management Unit and Control Unit to run, while the maintenance code consists of the portions of the program that diagnose malfunctions and maintain the performance of the Management Unit and Control Unit. When StorageTek sells its tape libraries to customers, the company does not sell the software that runs the library. Rather, it only licenses the programs to its customers. The license covers only the functional code portions of the software, and it specifically excludes the maintenance code. However, StorageTek provides the entire code to the customer. Both the functional and maintenance code are automatically loaded into the RAM of the Control Unit and Management Unit upon startup, and copying the entire code is necessary to activate and run the library.

Custom Hardware Engineering & Consulting, Inc., ("CHE") is an independent business that repairs data libraries manufactured by StorageTek. In order to diagnose problems with the libraries, CHE intercepts and interprets error messages produced by the maintenance code. The error messages are known as fault symptom codes. The fault symptom codes are generated by the Control Unit and are transmitted to the Management Unit over the network within a package of information, called an Event Message. To ensure that the Control Unit is configured to send the fault symptom codes, CHE needs to override a password protection scheme, called GetKey, which was written by StorageTek to disallow certain unauthorized reconfigurations of the maintenance code on the Control Unit. CHE has used two devices to circumvent GetKey. The original device, called a Library Event Manager ("LEM"), was connected to the network between the Control Unit and the Management Unit. The LEM worked by trying different passwords to "crack" GetKey. The LEM then allowed CHE to force the Control Unit to send fault symptom codes over the network after rebooting the Management Unit and Control Unit. CHE has ceased using the LEM in favor of a different device, the Enhanced Library Event Manager ("ELEM"). The ELEM also is attached to the network between the Control Unit and Management Unit. Rather than "cracking" the GetKey password, the ELEM mimics a signal from the Management Unit to the Control Unit upon rebooting the Control Unit, which causes the maintenance code on the Control Unit to be configured to send the fault symptom codes. CHE then intercepts the Event Messages and interprets the fault symptom codes. Based on the information in those error codes, CHE is able to diagnose and repair the data libraries.

StorageTek brought an action in the United States District Court for the District of Massachusetts against CHE and its president, David York. StorageTek alleged that CHE committed copyright infringement when CHE rebooted and reconfigured its customers' Control Units and Management Units. Additionally, StorageTek alleged that CHE violated the anticircumvention provision of the Digital Millennium Copyright Act ("DMCA") when CHE circumvented the GetKey protection system to force the customer's Control Unit to transmit error codes. . . .

Upon bringing suit, StorageTek asked the district court to issue a preliminary injunction against CHE. After a hearing on the motion, the district court agreed that StorageTek had shown a substantial likelihood of success on the copyright [and] DMCA [claims].

I

CHE does not deny that the copyrighted maintenance code is copied into the Control Unit's or Management Unit's RAM when the company reboots its customers' systems. *See MAI Sys. Corp. v. Peak Computer, Inc.,* 991 F.2d 511, 518-19 (9th Cir.1993). Nor does CHE dispute that the duplication of the maintenance code is outside the explicit grant of StorageTek's software license to its customers. Absent a defense, CHE's actions would constitute copyright infringement. CHE maintains, however, that its replication of the maintenance code is permissible based on a variety of defenses. Specifically, CHE argues that the copying is protected by sections 117(a) and 117(c) of the Copyright Act, 17 U.S.C. §§ 117(a), 117(c), and the doctrine of fair use. CHE also claims that it is implicitly authorized to copy the maintenance code and that StorageTek's copyright on the code is invalid.

A

CHE first asserts that section 117(c) of the Copyright Act shields it from liability for copyright infringement. Section 117(c) has not previously been construed by the First Circuit or any court of appeals, and we therefore treat the issue as one of first impression. Section 117(c) provides that

> it is not an infringement for the owner or lessee of a machine to make or authorize the making of a copy of a computer program if such copy is made solely by virtue of activation of a machine that lawfully contains an authorized copy of the computer program, for purpose only of maintenance or repair of that machine, if—

(1) such new copy is used in no other manner and is destroyed immediately after the maintenance or repair is completed; and

(2) with respect to any computer program or part thereof that is not necessary for the machine to be activated, such program or part thereof is not
accessed or used other than to make such new copy by virtue of the activation
of the machine.

CHE's position is that its actions are protected by section 117(c) because the
owners of the tape libraries authorize CHE to turn on the Control Units and
Management Units to maintain and repair the tape libraries, and the duplication of the software into RAM is necessary for the machine to function. CHE
also argues that its activities fall directly within Congress's purpose in enacting section 117(c), which was to "ensure that independent service organizations do not inadvertently become liable for copyright infringement merely
because they have turned on a machine in order to service its hardware components." . . .

The requirement in section 117(c)(1) that the new copy of the computer program be destroyed after maintenance or repair is completed can be achieved
in most cases by turning off the machine, which erases the copy from RAM. In
this case, the evidence showed that CHE reboots the storage libraries at the
conclusion of its maintenance contract with the owners of the storage libraries,
thus destroying the copy of the computer program in RAM. However, the district court determined that the destruction of the copy at that point does not
satisfy the requirements of section 117(c)(1) because CHE "fails to destroy the
copies they make immediately after completion of repairs." In other words, the
district court looked to whether CHE rebooted the machines each time it
repaired a particular malfunction in the silo. The flaw in the court's analysis
is that it focuses on the term "repair" in the statute, while ignoring the term
"maintenance."

Section 117(d) defines "repair" as "the restoring of the machine to the state
of working in accordance with its original specifications. . . ." 17 U.S.C.
§ 117(d)(2). It defines "maintenance" as "the servicing of the machine in order
to make it work in accordance with its original specifications. . . ." 17 U.S.C.
§ 117(d)(1). Those two definitions make clear that Congress contemplated two
distinct activities. The term "repair" denotes fixing a broken machine that is
no longer "working in accordance with its original specifications." That term
would apply whenever there is a discrete problem with the machine, e.g.,
when there are "worn or defective components such as memory chips, circuit
boards, and hard drives" that need to be replaced. S.Rep. No. 105-190, at 58
(1998). Once the machine is "restored" to its original working condition, the
new copy of the program would have to be destroyed immediately in order for
section 117(c) to apply. In contrast, the term "maintenance" has a much
broader temporal connotation. The Senate Report on section 117 characterized
"maintenance" as including "checking the proper functioning of [ ] components." Id. Thus, maintenance, or "servicing," was meant to encompass monitoring systems for problems, not simply fixing a single, isolated malfunction.

This interpretation of the term "maintenance" comports with the general
policy underlying the enactment of section 117(c). That policy was "to ensure

that independent service organizations do not inadvertently become liable for copyright infringement merely because they have turned on a machine in order to service its hardware components." Congress thus sought to protect the class of companies that fix and maintain computer systems, as opposed to those that would make other commercial use of copyrighted material. The point of requiring that copies be "destroyed immediately after the maintenance or repair is completed" was not to create artificial restraints on companies engaged in legitimate repair and maintenance activities, but to prevent persons from invoking the protection of section 117 and then later using the copied material for a prohibited purpose. It would run counter to that objective to construe section 117(c) narrowly to apply only to companies that performed repair in discrete, temporally isolated stages, rather than to construe the statute to apply to repair and maintenance services generally, so long as the companies' only reason for copying the software at issue was to fix and maintain the machines on which the software was running.

In its analysis of section 117(c), the district court gave considerable weight to the testimony of StorageTek's expert, Christian Hicks. The court noted that Mr. Hicks testified that a copy of the copyrighted software program remains in the Management and Control Units' RAM on an ongoing basis as the system operates with the LEM or ELEM attached. Because that description did not comport with the notion of "repair," the court held section 117(c) inapplicable. In describing CHE's process, however, Mr. Hicks noted that "the LEM and ELEM stay in place at the facilities so that when problems occur," CHE can detect and fix the malfunction. That is the same as saying that while the LEM and ELEM are attached, CHE "checks the proper functioning" of the storage library and ensures that the machine "works in accordance with its original specifications." Accordingly, CHE's actions fall within the definition of maintenance in section 117. Moreover, when CHE's maintenance contract is over, CHE stops its maintenance and immediately reboots the storage library, thereby destroying the copy of the copyrighted program. CHE's actions therefore appear to comply with the requirement of section 117(c)(1). While CHE may actively check to ensure that the silo is free from errors over an extended period of time, the protection of section 117 does not cease simply by virtue of the passage of time. Rather, it ceases only when that maintenance ends.

In the alternative, StorageTek contends that CHE cannot avail itself of section 117(c) because the statute requires that "with respect to any computer program or part thereof that is not necessary for the machine to be activated, such program or part thereof is not accessed or used. . . ." According to StorageTek, the maintenance code is "not necessary for the machine to be activated," and CHE's access to and use of the maintenance code to generate the Event Message signal therefore makes CHE liable for infringement. That assertion turns on the meaning of "maintenance code." StorageTek's license agreement states that the maintenance code is software "which detects, records, displays and/or analyzes malfunctions in [the] Equipment." Because those processes are distinct from "activating the machine," StorageTek argues that duplication of the maintenance code is not covered by section 117(c).

Unfortunately, determining whether a particular piece of software is "necessary for the machine to be activated" is not as simple as it might appear. On the one hand, not all code that resides in a machine's RAM after the completion of the startup routine qualifies as "necessary for the machine to be activated," even though that code is put into RAM as part of the activation process. If that were so, the requirement of section 117(c)(2) would effectively be read out of the statute, since under that interpretation there would be no program that was copied by virtue of activation but could not otherwise be accessed or used. At the same time, the code "necessary for the machine to be activated" cannot be the minimal amount of code that, when loaded into RAM, causes the machine to produce any response. For instance, the programs and drivers that allow the monitor on a personal computer to function do not fall outside the protection of section 117(c) simply because the computer itself can be activated and can function without a monitor attached. If section 117(c) were read that restrictively, accessing copyrighted software that controlled the monitor would put parties at risk of infringement, which would thwart Congress's desire to ensure "that an independent service provider may turn on a client's computer machine in order to service its hardware components." S.Rep. No. 105-190, at 57.

In enacting section 117(c), Congress gave some indication of what it considered to be "necessary for the machine to be activated." Specifically, the House Report on section 117(c) noted that software is necessary for the machine to be activated if it "need[s] to be so loaded in order for the machine to be turned on." H.R.Rep. No. 105-551, pt. 1, at 28. As examples of software that need not be loaded in order for the machine to function, the Report listed programs marketed as separate products that load into RAM along with the operating system or software that the owner of the machine has independently configured the computer to load during initialization. *Id.* Therefore, separate "freestanding programs" that load into RAM upon startup clearly may not be accessed under section 117(c)(2).

Congress's clearest indication of what it considered to be "necessary for the machine to be activated," however, is found not in section 117(c), but in section 117(d). As we have noted, section 117(d) defines repair and maintenance in terms of allowing the system to work "in accordance with its original specifications and any changes to those specifications authorized for that machine." Thus, the service provider must be able to cause the machine to boot up in order to determine if it "works in accordance with its original specifications." Accessing software programs, such as freestanding diagnosis and utility programs, that are not needed to boot up the computer and make that determination, goes too far because access to those programs is not strictly necessary to verify that the computer is "working in accordance with its original specifications."

In some instances, it may be difficult to determine whether particular software is necessary to make the computer function and to ascertain whether the computer is working properly. In this case, however, both parties agree that the maintenance code is so entangled with the functional code that the entire code must be loaded into RAM for the machine to function at all. That is, loading the maintenance code into RAM is necessary for the Management or Control Unit "to be turned on." Contrary to the dissent's position, the fact that the maintenance code has other functions, such as diagnosing malfunctions in the equipment, is irrelevant. Moreover, the possibility that StorageTek could have written the maintenance code as a separate, "freestanding" program that would not have been needed to start the machine does not affect the statutory analysis of the system that StorageTek in fact created. Finally, although the maintenance code can be reconfigured to perform fewer functions, as the dissent points out, what StorageTek can do with the maintenance code after the system boots up is irrelevant. As the statutory text and legislative history make clear, the phrase "necessary for the machine to be activated" refers to the portion of code that must be copied in order for the machine "to be turned on." In this case, copying the maintenance code into RAM is indispensable for the machine to be turned on or activated; its functionality (or lack thereof) after bootup is moot.

Finally, StorageTek contends that section 117(c) does not apply to CHE's conduct because CHE does not reboot the machine and make a copy of the copyrighted code "for purpose only of maintenance or repair." Specifically, StorageTek maintains that CHE reboots the machine in order to circumvent GetKey and gain access to the fault symptom codes. That argument is unconvincing because CHE's entire purpose in obtaining the fault symptom codes is to diagnose and repair the silos. StorageTek's argument that CHE's activity is not "for purpose only of maintenance or repair" is akin to suggesting that it would be impermissible to activate a keyboard on a personal computer for the purpose of maintenance or repair because the real purpose of activating the keyboard would be to allow the user to type. That line of reasoning, if accepted, would quickly destroy the protection that section 117(c) affords. If CHE had rebooted the storage library and loaded its own proprietary code to detect and diagnose errors in the silo, that activity would surely be considered "repair and maintenance." Merely because CHE uses StorageTek's proprietary maintenance code to do the same thing does not cause CHE's activities to no longer be "for the purpose only of maintenance or repair of that machine." In sum, we conclude that CHE is likely to prevail on the merits of its argument that section 117(c) protects its act of copying of StorageTek's maintenance code into RAM.

B

CHE argues in the alternative that even if the section 117(c) defense is unavailable, CHE is not liable for copyright infringement because it enjoys the benefits of its customers' licenses to copy StorageTek's 9330 and 9311 code in order to activate their machines. StorageTek's license agreement with its customers allows the customers to copy StorageTek's software into RAM "for the sole purpose of enabling the specific unit of Equipment for which the Internal Code was provided to perform its data storage and retrieval or other operating functions." Therefore, the customers do not commit infringement merely by activating their Management and Control Units and consequently copying StorageTek's software into RAM. As an agent of those storage library owners, CHE also does not commit copyright infringement simply by turning on the owners' machines. *See Hogan Sys., Inc. v. Cybersource Int'l, Inc.,* 1997 WL 311526, at *4 (N.D.Tex. June 2, 1997), *aff'd,* 158 F.3d 319 (5th Cir.1998) (although the license at issue did "not specifically authorize a third-party consultant to use, copy, or modify Umbrella software," the court found that while the defendants "are engaged in consulting services on behalf of Norwest, Defendants' activities are 'sheltered under' Norwest's license rights").

StorageTek argues that CHE's use of the maintenance code must constitute infringement because the license agreement specifically excludes the use of the maintenance code. Because CHE's customers are not allowed to access the maintenance code, StorageTek asserts that when CHE does so, it must be infringing StorageTek's copyright. There are two flaws in that line of reasoning. First, CHE's customers are given the right to copy the maintenance code into the RAM of their machines. The license specifically authorizes the customers to use the code to "enabl[e] the specific unit of Equipment." The parties are in agreement that both the maintenance code and functional code portions of the 9330 or 9331 code must be loaded into RAM in order to activate the Control and Management Units. In order to activate the Control and Maintenance Units, the maintenance code must be copied. The license thus authorizes the copying of that code.

Second, StorageTek's argument conflates a claim based on copyright infringement and an action based on breach of contract. To succeed in a copyright action, "the copying must be beyond the scope of a license possessed by the defendant," and the source of the copyright owner's complaint must be grounded in a right protected by the Copyright Act, such as unlawful reproduction or distribution. *See* 17 U.S.C. § 106. In contrast, the rights granted by contract can be much broader. As an example, consider a license in which the copyright owner grants a person the right to make one and only one copy of a book with the caveat that the licensee may not read the last ten pages. Obviously, a licensee who made a hundred copies of the book would be liable for copyright infringement because the copying would violate the Copyright Act's prohibition on reproduction and would exceed the scope of the license. Alternatively, if the licensee made a single copy of the book, but read the last ten pages, the only cause of action would be for breach of contract, because reading a work does not violate any right protected by copyright law. Likewise, in this case, the copying of the maintenance code is permitted by the license. The use of the code may violate the license agreement, but it is not forbidden by copyright law and cannot give rise to an action for copyright infringement.

Although there is language in some cases that can be read to suggest that copyright protection extends to all conduct that would violate the user's license, the decisions in those cases are not that broad. For example, in *S.O.S., Inc. v. Payday, Inc.*, the Ninth Circuit stated that a "licensee infringes the owner's copyright if its use exceeds the scope of its license." 886 F.2d 1081, 1087 (9th Cir.1989). In that case, however, it was clear that the "use" the copyright owner was complaining about was the defendant's "copying and modification of the software." *Id.* at 1085. Similarly in *John G. Danielson, Inc. v. Winchester-Conant Props., Inc.*, 322 F.3d 26, 41 (1st Cir.2003), the First Circuit noted that "[u]ses of the copyrighted work that stay within the scope of a nonexclusive license are immunized from infringement suits." Not only did the court not state that "uses" that fall outside the scope of the license would necessarily constitute a copyright violation, but the allegedly unlawful "use" in that case was the copying of architectural plans. *Id.* at 32; *see Data*

Gen. Corp. v. Grumman Sys. Support Corp., 36 F.3d 1147, 1167 (1st Cir.1994). In light of their facts, those cases thus stand for the entirely unremarkable principle that "uses" that violate a license agreement constitute copyright infringement only when those uses would infringe in the absence of any license agreement at all.

StorageTek maintains that regardless of the scope of its licenses vis-a-vis the equipment owners, the licenses do not extend rights to third parties. In particular, StorageTek points to the language of its standard license agreement, which states that the equipment owner may not "sublicense, assign, lease or permit another person to use Internal Code (except as provided . . . below)." The company argues that this provision forbids CHE from copying StorageTek's code into RAM by starting up the Control and Management Units. That argument, however, ignores the rest of the license agreement. The prohibition on third-party use of the code is modified by a later provision stating that equipment owners "may transfer possession of Internal Code only with the transfer of the Equipment on which its use is authorized." Additionally, the license grants the customer the use of the code for "the sole purpose of enabling the specific unit of Equipment for which the Internal Code was provided. . . ." The clear implication of those sections is that the license is tied to the piece of equipment on which the software resides. Thus, the authorized use is tied to a particular machine, rather than a particular person. In fact, one version of StorageTek's license agreement expressly contemplates third-party use of the equipment, noting that "misuse of the Equipment or negligence by Customer or a third party" is not included within the maintenance provision of the license. Thus, the prohibition against assigning or permitting another to use the code is clearly a restriction on giving a third party a copy of the code that is divorced from the machine "on which its use is authorized." In this case, CHE is merely turning on the machine on which the use of the code is authorized. *See Green Book Int'l Corp. v. Inunity Corp.,* 2 F.Supp.2d 112, 116 n. 1 (D.Mass.1998) (multiple individuals may use computer under a license, "which limits use to 'only one single-user computer,' without any additional restriction on the identity of the person who, from time to time, physically sat at and operated such computer"). Because the whole purpose of the license is to allow the tape library owners to activate their machines without being liable for copyright infringement, such activity by the licensee and its agents is implicitly authorized by the license agreement unless the agreement explicitly prohibits third parties from powering up the machines.

Other cases involving software license agreements support that reading of StorageTek's agreement, albeit indirectly. For example, in *MAI Systems,* the Ninth Circuit held that a third party was not authorized to copy licensed software into RAM by activating a computer. However, the court held that the license did not cover such copying because the license prohibited third parties from copying the software. 991 F.2d at 517. The license in *MAI Systems* was so restrictive that only three employees of the licensee were allowed to use and copy portions of the software. *Id.* at 517 n. 3. It was only because the license contained such severe, explicit restrictions that the court held that third parties were prohibited from copying the software by activating the machine. The court in *MAI Systems* would not have had to rest its decision on those restrictive license terms if third parties were disallowed from copying the software even in the absence of such restrictive language in the license. *See also SMC Promotions, Inc. v. SMC Promotions,* 355 F.Supp.2d 1127, 1132 (C.D.Cal.2005) (forbidding third-party copying by relying on the explicit language of the license, which stated that licensees "may not delegate or authorize any other person to do so, whether on [the licensees'] behalf or otherwise").

StorageTek, of course, could have drafted the license agreement to explicitly disallow copying by third parties through activation of the equipment owners' machines. In the absence of such language, however, CHE's copying appears to be protected as long as CHE is acting as an agent of the equipment owners. . . .

II

The DMCA claim is based on CHE's circumvention of the GetKey protocol. Specifically, StorageTek maintains that the use of the ELEM and LEM devices violates section 1201(a)(1) of title 17 of the United States Code, which prohibits any person from "circumvent[ing] a technological measure that effectively controls access to a work protected under this title." While the First Circuit has not addressed the scope of the DMCA's prohibition under section 1201(a), this court has confronted the issue in *Chamberlain Group, Inc. v. Skylink Technologies, Inc.,* 381 F.3d 1178 (Fed.Cir.2004).

In *Chamberlain* we held that . . . section 1201 "prohibits only forms of access that bear a reasonable relationship to the protections that the Copyright Act otherwise affords copyright owners." *Id.* at 1202. A copyright owner alleging a violation of section 1201(a) consequently must prove that the circumvention of the technological measure either "infringes or facilitates infringing a right protected by the Copyright Act."

In this case, the LEM and ELEM devices allow CHE to bypass GetKey and gain access to the maintenance code. Furthermore, the manner in which the ELEM and LEM function requires that the Control or Management Units be rebooted, causing the protected software to be copied into RAM. Nonetheless, simply because the ELEM or LEM allows access to the copyrighted work concurrently with the copying does not mean that the ELEM or LEM "facilitates" copyright infringement. Consequently, the district court erred by failing to consider whether or not such facilitation occurred.

We held above that it is unlikely StorageTek will succeed on the merits of its copyright claim. To the extent that CHE's activities do not constitute copyright infringement or facilitate copyright infringement, StorageTek is foreclosed from maintaining an action under the DMCA. That result follows because the DMCA must be read in the context of the Copyright Act, which balances the rights of the copyright owner against the public's interest in having appropriate access to the work. Therefore, courts generally have found a violation of the DMCA only when the alleged access was intertwined with a right protected by the Copyright Act. To the extent that StorageTek's rights under copyright law are not at risk, the DMCA does not create a new source of liability.

Even if StorageTek were able to prove that the automatic copying of the software into RAM constituted copyright infringement, however, it would still have to show that the LEM or ELEM facilitated that infringement. If such a nexus were not required, the careful balance that Congress sought to achieve between the "interests of content creators and information users" would be upset.

The problem in this case is that the copying of the software into RAM when the Control or Management Units are rebooted takes place regardless of whether the LEM or ELEM is used. Hence, there is no nexus between any possible infringement and the use of the circumvention devices. Rather, CHE's circumvention of GetKey only allows CHE to use portions of the copyrighted software that StorageTek wishes to restrict technologically. The activation of the maintenance code may violate StorageTek's contractual rights vis-a-vis its customers, but those rights are not the rights protected by copyright law. There is simply not a sufficient nexus between the rights protected by copyright law and the circumvention of the GetKey system.

A court must look at the threat that the unauthorized circumvention potentially poses in each case to determine if there is a connection between the circumvention and a right protected by the Copyright Act. In this case, the threat from CHE's circumvention of GetKey is distinct from the dangers that StorageTek's copyright protects against.

In sum, the district court failed to consider whether the circumvention of the GetKey system either infringes or facilitates infringing a right protected by the Copyright Act. We conclude that it is unlikely that StorageTek will prevail on its claim under section 1201(a) in this case because the ELEM and LEM devices are not reasonably related to any violation of the rights created by the Copyright Act.

VACATED and REMANDED.

B. Remedy for Breach

Electronic restrictions can also be used to enforce remedies for breach, rather than merely prevent breach. This use of electronic control presents concerns because, unlike agreed limitations, technology that allows closing down software for breach may be misused to provide excessive leverage against the licensee.

Two state laws provide a basis for use of electronic devices without judicial authorization. Self-help "repossession" is authorized in U.C.C. Article 9 (secured financing) and Article 2A (leases). A lessor or secured party can, without going to court, repossess or render the property unusable. UCC §§ 2A-525 (1998 Official Text), 9-609 (2000 Official Text). The only limits are that there has been a default (breach) and that the act of repossessing or rendering unusable not involve breach of the peace. Neither statute otherwise restricts the use of remote electronic access to activate an electronic restriction. UCITA, on the other hand, places strict procedural and substantive restrictions on this option and, in its 2002 Official Text, bans electronic self-help. Which is the better rule?

PROBLEM 16.5

Client is a small company that develops custom software and often works with large company clients. On numerous occasions, it has been unable to obtain timely payment from a client who argues that the software is not fully effective, even though it has no true basis for this claim. Client is considering the use of electronic codes to disable the software as a method of combating this problem. What do you advise?

AMERICAN COMPUTER TRUST
LEASING v. JACK FARRELL
763 F. Supp. 1473 (D. Minn. 1991)

DOTY, DISTRICT JUDGE.

Plaintiff American Computer Trust Leasing ("ACTL") brought suit against defendants Boerboom International, Inc. and Jack Farrell Implement Co. (collectively referred to as the defendants) to collect payments for computer hardware leased from ACTL. Boerboom and Farrell each claim that their obligation should be excused because the hardware did not work properly. The defendants also bring various counterclaims [including] software deactivation claims alleging that their computer software was wrongfully deactivated. . . .

Farrell and Boerboom are presently Case agricultural equipment dealers and were IH dealers before the January 1985 sale of IH's farm equipment business to Case. Before 1983, IH furnished computer services directly to all of its farm implement dealers in exchange for a monthly fee. IH decided to outsource the dealer computer services because of the severe financial strain it experienced during the early 1980s as a result of the downturn in the U.S. farm economy. . . . IH decided to endorse only one vendor, ADP, and ADP and IH entered into a contract on May 16, 1983. The contract required ADP to develop a communications software package called the Dealer Communications Systems ("DCS") which would enable IH and its dealers to communicate with each other through a dealers communications network ("DCN") and also permit dealers to communicate amongst themselves. . . .

Both the contracts between IH and ADP and between IH and its dealers expressly provide that vendors other than ADP could provide computer services to the dealers. . . . IH had a considerable investment in its computerized dealer communication network. . . .

Defendant Boerboom had served as an IH dealer since at least 1980. Boerboom agreed to purchase an ADP system on October 9, 1984. . . . Shortly thereafter, on November 6, 1984, Boerboom entered into an equipment lease for an ADP Series 2000 Model 2020 computer system. IH received a $500 royalty payment as a result of Boerboom's purchase. . . .

Defendant Farrell had been an IH dealer since 1962. Farrell also attended the roll-out meeting sponsored by IH and ADP on October 9, 1984. On January 31, 1985, IH sold its agricultural equipment business to Case. . . . On May 9, 1985, approximately three months after becoming a Case dealer, Farrell signed an ADP software license agreement and an ADP equipment purchase agreement. In August 1985, the purchase agreement was modified when Farrell signed an agreement to lease rather than buy the equipment. In that contract, Farrell leased a Series 2000 Model 2015 computer system. . . .

The relationship between the defendants, and ADP and ACTL is governed by three contracts: the purchase and maintenance agreement and the software license agreement with ADP, and the equipment lease agreement with ACTL. Under the purchase and maintenance agreement and the software license agreement, Boerboom and Farrell each agreed to purchase computer hardware from ADP, to pay ADP a monthly fee for maintenance and support of the computer hardware and to license several software applications from ADP. Both Boerboom and Farrell decided to exercise their options to lease their computer hardware from ACTL. . . . Boerboom and Farrell both entered into an equipment lease agreement with ACTL which provided for a seven-year term of monthly lease payments to ACTL. Neither IH nor Case is a party to the contracts between the defendants and ADP and ACTL.

After acquiring the IH assets, Case extended offers to both Farrell and Boerboom to become agricultural equipment dealers for Case. Farrell and Boerboom accepted their respective offers. . . .

. . . Boerboom and Farrell defaulted on their obligations to ACTL under the equipment lease agreements and ACTL seeks judgment against them. . . .

Discussion

[ADP seeks] summary judgment on all of defendants' counterclaims except for the breach of express warranty claims. [It claims that ADP] had a legal right to deactivate Farrell's software for nonpayment. . . .

In Count VIII, Farrell seeks damages pursuant to Minn.Stat. §548.05 for trespass, claiming trespass occurred when ADP wrongfully entered Farrell's computer system and also appropriated and destroyed Farrell's accounting and inventory records. The Minnesota statute provides for damages for trespass as follows:

> Whoever shall carry away, use or destroy any wood, timber, lumber, hay, grass, or other personal property of another person, without lawful authority, shall be liable to the owner thereof for treble the amount of damages assessed therefore in the action to recover such damages.

Minn.Stat. §548.05. Minnesota courts hold that property must be "produced by and grown upon land" to come within the terms of this statute. *Mondt v. Sexter Realty Co.,* 293 N.W.2d 376, 377 (Minn.1980). The *Mondt* court further held that home furnishings, toys and clothing do not constitute such personal property. *Id.* Moreover, the term "or other personal property" has been confined to property similar to property previously enumerated in the statute, limiting trespass to things which are the product of the soil. The alleged deactivation is not the taking of the type of property governed by this statute and thus ADP's motion for summary judgment on that claim is granted.

In Count IX, Farrell claims that ADP/ACTL and/or Harvester/Case made "wrongful entry into Farrell's property and by use of direct force appropriated and destroyed its accounting and/or inventory and/or accounting records." Farrell contends that those actions obstructed its free use of its property and thus constitutes statutory nuisance in violation of Minn.Stat. § 561.01. The Minnesota nuisance statute provides that:

> Anything which is injurious to health, or indecent or offensive to the senses, or an obstruction to the free use of property, so as to interfere with the comfortable enjoyment of life or property, is a nuisance.

Minn.Stat. § 561.01. Private nuisance has been defined as:

> an interference with the use and enjoyment of land. The ownership or rightful possession of land necessarily involves the right not only to unimpaired condition of the property itself, but also to some reasonable comfort and convenience in its occupation.

W. Keeton, D. Dobbs, R. Keeton & D. Owen, *Prosser and Keeton on the Law of Torts* § 87, at 619 (5th ed. 1984). There can be no nuisance if a party cannot show an injury stemming from an interest in land. The alleged deactivation, even if it occurred as defendants contend, is not the type of injury which courts have found to violate the nuisance statute because the use of a computer system is not the type of property protected by the statute. Based on the foregoing, ADP's motion for summary judgment on the statutory nuisance claim is granted. . . .

Boerboom and Farrell also seek recovery from ADP and the other third-party defendants on the theory that ADP and/or IH wrongfully gained access to defendants' computer systems and misappropriated their property. In Count X, Farrell alleges a violation of 18 U.S.C. § 2511, which outlaws the interception and disclosure of wire or oral communications. This statute bars activities such as wiretapping and eavesdropping through the use of electronic surveillance. It does not outlaw the authorized use of computer data and thus has no applicability to the present case because both defendants allowed ADP access to their computer systems pursuant to their contracts with ADP. Steven Farrell and Stephen Boerboom both acknowledged that they were aware that ADP and/or IH could access to their computer systems. Because they allowed such access, they cannot claim that any alleged access was unlawful. Moreover, even if the statute applied to the present case, defendants proffer no evidence that their wire communications were actually intercepted or disclosed. They merely allege that ADP somehow got into their computer systems and used this access to snoop for unspecified purposes. The only evidence to support this allegation is that the indicator lights on the computer systems would sometimes be illuminated.

The defendants also seek relief for an alleged violation of 18 U.S.C. §§ 2701-10. This statute, the Electronic Communications Privacy Act, bars unlawful access to stored communications. The statute, however, is not directed to the type of harm alleged by the defendants. As noted above, the defendants consented to ADP's access and cannot now claim that such access was unauthorized. . . .

Based on the foregoing, ADP's motion for summary judgment on defendants' claims concerning the misappropriation of their wire communication is granted.

NOTES

1. As suggested in *Farrell*, an important element in the few cases on this issue is whether the licensee expressly or implicitly consented to the inclusion of the disabling device in the software. In *Texas Preventive Imaging v. Eisenberg*, 1996 U.S. Dist. LEXIS 19990, SA CV 96-71 AHS (EEx) (C.D. Cal. 1996), the court held that a claim was properly stated for a private remedy under the federal Computer Fraud and Abuse Act, 18 U.S.C. § 1030 (CFAA). After the software was installed, Defendants apparently sent plaintiffs "update disks" periodically to update the system. One "update" floppy computer disk, unknown to plaintiff, contained disabling codes — "time bombs" which render a software program inoperable at a pre-set time and date. The court concluded that the CFAA applied, although the damaging code was not sent electronically. It quoted the legislative history of a 1994 amendment to the Act as follows:

> The new subsection of the CFAA created by this bill places the focus on harmful intent and resultant harm, rather than on the technical concept of computer access. . . . The computer abuse amendments make it a felony intentionally to cause harm to a computer or the information stored in it by transmitting a computer program or code — including destructive computer viruses — without the knowledge and authorization of the person responsible for the computer attacked. This is broader than existing law, which prohibits intentionally accessing a federal interest computer without authorization, if that causes damage.

The court further commented: "During debates on the 1994 amendment, software manufacturers objected to the possibility that their practice of inserting 'disabling codes' in software programs would be criminalized because disabling codes can be used as a legitimate security measure. On this issue, Senator Leahy stated that the new language would not criminalize the use of disabling codes 'when their use is pursuant to a lawful licensing agreement that specifies the conditions for reentry or software disablement.'"

2. UCITA, Section 816 (2000 Official Text) provides:

(a) In this section, "electronic self-help" means the use of electronic means to exercise a licensor's rights under Section 815(b).

(b) On cancellation of a license, electronic self-help is not permitted, except as provided in this section. Electronic self-help is prohibited in mass-market transactions.

(c) [To be an enforceable agreement] to permit electronic self-help, the licensee [must have] separately [manifested] assent to a term authorizing use of electronic self-help. The term must:

(1) provide for notice of exercise as provided in subsection (d);

(2) state the name of the person designated by the licensee to which notice of exercise must be given and the manner in which notice must be given and place to which notice must be sent to that person; and

(3) provide a simple procedure for the licensee to change the designated person or place.

(d) Before resorting to electronic self-help authorized by a term of the license, the licensor shall give notice in a record to the person designated by the licensee stating:

(1) that the licensor intends to resort to electronic self-help as a remedy on or after 15 days following receipt by the licensee of the notice;

(2) the nature of the claimed breach that entitles the licensor to resort to self-help; and

(3) the name, title, and address, including direct telephone number, facsimile number, or e-mail address, to which the licensee may communicate concerning the claimed breach. . . .

(f) Even if the licensor complies with subsections (c) and (d), electronic self-help may not be used if the licensor has reason to know that its use will result in substantial injury or harm to the public health or safety or grave harm to the public interest substantially affecting third persons not involved in the dispute. . . .

IV. OWNERSHIP AND SOFTWARE DEVELOPMENT

PROBLEM 16.6

Client is a company that provides custom software development services for various commercial entities. What provisions should its contracts contain regarding ownership of the product it creates? From the perspective of the customer, what provisions are appropriate?

AYMES v. BONELLI
980 F.2d 857 (2d Cir. 1992)

In May 1980, Aymes was hired by Jonathan Bonelli, the president and chief executive officer of Island, to work as a computer programmer. Island operated a chain of retail stores selling swimming pools and related supplies. Aymes, who received a graduate degree from Cornell University's School of Engineering in 1981, worked with Island's computer systems from 1980 to 1982.

During that period, Aymes created a series of programs called "CSALIB" under the general direction of Bonelli, who was not a professional computer programmer. CSALIB was used by Island to maintain records of cash receipts, physical inventory, sales figures, purchase orders, merchandise transfers, and price changes. There was no written agreement between Bonelli and Aymes assigning ownership or copyright of CSALIB. Aymes does contend, however, that Bonelli made him an oral promise that CSALIB would only be used at one computer in one Island office.

Aymes did most of his programming at the Island office, where he had access to Island's computer hardware. He generally worked alone, without assistants or co-workers, and enjoyed considerable autonomy in creating CSALIB. This autonomy was restricted only by Bonelli who directed and instructed Aymes on what he wanted from the program. Bonelli was not, however, sufficiently skilled to write the program himself.

Although Aymes worked semi-regular hours, he was not always paid by the hour and on occasion presented his bills to Bonelli as invoices. At times, Aymes would be paid by the project and given bonuses for finishing the project on time. It is undisputed that Aymes never received any health or other insurance benefits from Island. It is similarly undisputed that Island never paid an employer's percentage of Aymes's payroll taxes and never withheld any of his salary for federal or state taxes. In fact, Aymes was given an Internal Revenue Service 1099 Non-Employee Compensation form instead of the standard employee W-2 form.

Aymes left Island in September 1982 when Bonelli unilaterally decided to cut Aymes's hours. . . . On March 12, 1985, Aymes registered CSALIB in his own name with the United States Copyright Office. On March 21, 1985, Aymes filed a complaint against Bonelli and Island in the United States District Court for the Southern District of New York, alleging copyright infringement under the Copyright Act of 1976 and various state claims.

. . . The district court further held that Aymes had no copyright over CSALIB because the program was a "work made for hire," which meant that the authorship belonged to Island under 17 U.S.C. § 201(b) (1988). Accordingly, the court dismissed Aymes's copyright infringement claim.

Discussion

Under the Copyright Act of 1976, copyright ownership "vests initially in the author or authors of the work." Although the author is generally the party who actually creates the copyrightable work, the Act provides:

> In the case of a work made for hire, the employer or other person for whom the work was prepared is considered the author for purposes of this title, and, unless the parties have expressly agreed otherwise in a written instrument signed by them, owns all of the rights comprised in the copyright.

Id. § 201(b). The Act defines a work made for hire as: "(1) a work prepared by an employee within the scope of his or her employment; or (2) a work specially ordered or commissioned for use . . . if the parties expressly agree in a written instrument signed by them that the work shall be considered a work made for hire."

It is undisputed that Aymes and Bonelli never signed a written agreement assigning ownership rights in CSALIB. We must therefore consider whether the program was a work prepared by Aymes as an employee within the scope of his employment. If so, CSALIB qualifies as a "work made for hire" whose copyright belongs to Island as Aymes's employer.

The Copyright Act does not define the terms "employee" or "employment," and, consequently, the application of these terms is left to the courts. In *Reid,* the Supreme Court addressed the question of when an individual is an employee under the work for hire doctrine. Relying extensively on the legislative history of the Copyright Act, the Court concluded that to "determine whether a work is for hire under the Act, a court first should ascertain, using principles of the general common law of agency, whether the work was prepared by an employee or an independent contractor." The Court then set forth the factors to be used in making this determination:

> In determining whether a hired party is an employee under the general common law of agency, we consider the hiring party's right to control the manner and means by which the product is accomplished. Among the other factors relevant to this inquiry are the skill required, the source of the instrumentalities and tools, the location of the work; the duration of the relationship between the parties, whether the hiring party has the right to assign additional projects to the hired party; the extent of the hired party's discretion over when and how long to work; the method of payment; the hired party's role in hiring and paying assistants; whether the work is part of the regular business of the hiring party; whether the hiring party is in business; the provision of employee benefits, and the tax treatment of the hired party.

109 S. Ct. at 2178-79. The Court noted that no single factor is determinative.

I. Application of the *Reid* Test

[We] begin our analysis by noting that the *Reid* test can be easily misapplied, since it consists merely of a list of possible considerations that may or may not be relevant in a given case. *Reid* established that no one factor was dispositive, but gave no direction concerning how the factors were to be weighed. It does not necessarily follow that because no one factor is dispositive all factors are equally important, or indeed that all factors will have relevance in every case. The factors should not merely be tallied but should be weighed according to their significance in the case.

For example, the factors relating to the authority to hire assistants will not normally be relevant if the very nature of the work requires the hired party to work alone. In such a case, that factor should be accorded no weight in applying the *Reid* test. Having the authority to hire assistants, however, might have great probative value where the individual claiming to be an independent contractor does exercise authority to enlist assistants without prior approval of the party that hired him. In the latter case, this show of authority would be highly indicative that the hired party was acting as an independent contractor.

Some factors, therefore, will often have little or no significance in determining whether a party is an independent contractor or an employee. In contrast, there are some factors that will be significant in virtually every situation. These include: (1) the hiring party's right to control the manner and means of creation; (2) the skill required; (3) the provision of employee benefits; (4) the tax treatment of the hired party; and (5) whether the hiring party has the right to assign additional projects to the hired party. These factors will almost always be relevant and should be given more weight in the analysis, because they will usually be highly probative of the true nature of the employment relationship.

Although the *Reid* test has not yet received widespread application, other courts that have interpreted the test have in effect adopted this weighted approach by only addressing those factors found to be significant in the individual case. *See, e.g., Marco v. Accent Publishing Co.,* 969 F.2d 1547 (3d Cir.1992) (holding that photographer was an independent contractor while ignoring some factors and noting that some were "indeterminate" and should not be considered); *MacLean Assocs., Inc. v. Wm. M. Mercer-Meidinger-Hansen, Inc.,* 952 F.2d 769 (3d Cir.1991) (in appeal from a directed verdict for hiring party, holding that a computer programmer could be an independent contractor without addressing several of the *Reid* factors); *M.G.B. Homes, Inc. v. Ameron Homes, Inc.,* 903 F.2d 1486 (11th Cir.1990) (finding that a drafting service operated as an independent contractor to a builder based on only eight factors, ignoring others); *Johannsen v. Brown,* 797 F.Supp. 835 (D.Or.1992) (finding that artist/printer is a graphic designer based on several factors, ignoring others); *Kunycia v. Melville Realty Co.,* 755 F.Supp. 566 (S.D.N.Y.1990) (finding an architect to be an independent contractor on the basis of only four factors, ignoring others); *Kelstall-Whitney v. Mahar,* No. 89 Civ. 4684, 1990 U.S. Dist. LEXIS 6186 (E.D.Pa. May 23, 1990) (finding that computer programmer was independent contractor based on only a few factors, ignoring others).

In contrast, in the instant case the district court gave each factor equal weight and simply counted the number of factors for each side in determining that Aymes was an employee. In so doing, the district court over-emphasized indeterminate and thus irrelevant factors having little or no bearing on Aymes's case. Because we find that the *Reid* test was not intended to be applied in a mechanistic fashion, we review each of the factors and consider their relative importance in this case. We begin by addressing those factors bearing most significantly in our analysis.

a. The Right to Control

The district court did not specifically address whether Aymes or Island Swimming had the right to control the manner of CSALIB's creation. Even without a specific finding, it is clear from the record that Bonelli and Island had the right to control the manner in which CSALIB was created. Aymes disputed Bonelli's purported skill at programming, but even without such knowledge Bonelli was capable of directing Aymes on CSALIB's necessary function. Aymes was not working entirely alone. He received significant input from Bonelli in programming CSALIB, and worked under programming limitations placed by Bonelli. Consequently, this factor weighs heavily in favor of finding that Aymes was an employee.

b. The Level of Skill

The district court found that although Aymes's ability as a programmer required skills "beyond the capacity of a layman, it required no peculiar expertise or creative genius." We disagree. Aymes's work required far more than merely transcribing Bonelli's instructions. Rather, his programming demanded that he use skills developed while a graduate student at Cornell and through his experience working at a family run company. Other courts that have addressed the level of skill necessary to indicate that a party is an independent contractor have held architects, photographers, graphic artists, drafters, and indeed computer programmers to be highly-skilled independent contractors.

We therefore conclude that the district court erred in relying on Aymes's relative youth and inexperience as a professional computer programmer. Rather, the court should have examined the skill necessary to perform the work. In this case, Aymes was clearly a skilled craftsman. Consequently, this factor weighs heavily in his favor.

c./d. The Employee Benefits and Tax Treatment

The district court found that Aymes received no employee benefits from Island, but disregarded this factor as merely being an indication that Aymes was an employee who worked "off the books." It is undisputed that Aymes was not provided with health, unemployment, or life insurance benefits. Similarly, it is uncontested that Island did not pay a share of Aymes's social security taxes and did not withhold federal or state income taxes.

The failure of Island to extend Aymes any employment benefits or to pay any of his payroll taxes is highly indicative that Aymes was considered an outside independent contractor by Island. Indeed, these two factors constitute virtual admissions of Aymes's status by Bonelli himself. Moreover, they also point out a basic inequity in Aymes's treatment. Island benefited from treating Aymes like an independent contractor when it came to providing benefits and paying a percentage of his payroll taxes. Island should not in one context be able to claim that Aymes was an independent contractor and ten years later deny him that status to avoid a copyright infringement suit.

These two factors are given even greater weight because they are undisputed in this case. During the ten years in which this case has been litigated, all the other issues have been hotly contested. But for purposes of benefits and taxes, Island definitely and unequivocally chose not to treat Aymes as an employee. Island deliberately chose to deny Aymes two basic attributes of employment it presumably extended to its workforce. This undisputed choice is completely inconsistent with their defense.

The importance of these two factors is underscored by the fact that every case since *Reid* that has applied the test has found the hired party to be an independent contractor where the hiring party failed to extend benefits or pay social security taxes.

e. The Right to Assign Other Projects

The district court found that Bonelli had the right to and did assign Aymes other projects in addition to the creation of CSALIB. This is fairly strong evidence that Aymes was an employee, since independent contractors are typically hired only for particular projects. However, this factor carries less weight than those evaluated above, because the delegation of additional projects to Aymes is not inconsistent with the idea that he was Island's independent trouble shooter who might be asked to intervene as computer problems arose. Accordingly, this factor weighs fairly strongly but not conclusively for Island.

f. Remaining Factors

The remaining factors are relatively insignificant or negligible in weight because they are either indeterminate or inapplicable to these facts. It is important to address them each individually, however, to show why they are relatively insignificant. Although none carries much weight, they are addressed in order of their relative importance in this determination.

"The method of payment" is a fairly important factor, but it is indeterminate in this case because there is evidence to support both sides. The district court found that Aymes was sometimes paid hourly wages and at other times was paid a flat fee for completing a specific task. The court recognized that this factor "might lend some support to the idea that he was not an employee," since the lump sum payments indicate that Aymes was contracted for individual assignments. The payment of regular wages, however, indicate that Aymes was an employee. We therefore agree with the district court that this factor is indeterminate.

"Whether the work is Island's regular business" is a factor that weighs in favor of Aymes's contention that he was an independent contractor. The district court found that this factor weighed in Island's balance because "it was part of their regular business activity to modify programs for their computers." The district court misinterpreted the category, and its finding is, therefore, erroneous. The purpose of this factor is to determine whether the hired party is performing tasks that directly relate to the objective of the hiring party's business. For example, work done by a computer programmer employed by a computer software firm would be done in the firm's regular business. Because Island Swimming is involved in the business of selling swimming pools, however, Aymes's programming was not done in the company's regular business.

We find, however, that this factor will generally be of little use in evaluating a claim that a work was made for hire. This factor carries very little weight, because pool companies do not survive by merely hiring pool designers and salespeople. For example, most companies hire numerous support personnel such as managers, accountants, secretaries, custodians, and computer programmers. That Aymes did not work in Island's regular business is not strongly indicative of whether he was an independent contractor, even if it does weigh in his favor.

"Whether Island is in business" is a factor that will always have very little weight in this analysis. Island was in the pool business, but this indicates nothing about whether Aymes was an employee in that business. This factor will generally be of little help in this analysis, and it weighs negligibly in favor of Island in this case.

"The discretion over when and how long to work" is indeterminate since the district court found that Aymes had some degree of flexibility in his hours but that Island clearly had control over the project. The district court ruled that "this factor is fairly evenly balanced between the parties." We agree.

"The duration of the relationship" is a similarly inconclusive factor. The district court found that the relationship between the parties extended over a long period of time, which indicates that Aymes was an employee. Although Aymes worked two years for Island, he did occasional work for others at the same time. Moreover, there were undisputed gaps in his employment, which suggests that he was not a full-time employee. The district court's finding is not clearly erroneous, but given the particular facts of this case this factor has only slight weight in Island's favor.

"The location of the work" was not specifically addressed by the district court. It is clear from the record, however, that Aymes did most of his programming at Island's offices, even if he did do some work at home. However, since Aymes was required to work in Island's offices in order to have access to its computer hardware, this factor should be accorded negligible weight.

Similarly, "the source of the equipment" carries little weight in the analysis. All the equipment Aymes used was located at Island's office. Again, however, the programming by necessity had to be performed on Island's machines.

"The authority to hire assistants" is also virtually meaningless in a situation where the hired party does not need assistants.

A review of this analysis shows that the significant factors supporting Island's contention that Aymes was an employee include Island's right to control the means of CSALIB's creation and Island's right to assign other projects. The significant factors supporting Aymes's argument that he was an independent contractor include: the level of skill needed to create CSALIB; the decision of Island not to offer him benefits; and his payment of his own social security taxes. The other factors were either indeterminate, because they were evenly balanced between the parties, or of marginal significance, because they were inapplicable to these facts.

Examining the factors for each side in terms of their importance, we conclude that the only major factor strongly supporting Island is that it directed the creation of the program. Island did reserve the right to assign Aymes other projects, which is a major factor, but under these facts this was not necessarily inconsistent with an independent contractor relationship. Supporting Aymes's argument that he was an independent contractor, however, are several important factors — his skill, and the tax and benefit factors — that outweigh the elements supporting Island. The other factors outlined in *Reid* are either indeterminate or of negligible importance, and cannot outweigh the significance we attach to Island's choice to treat Aymes as an independent contractor when it was to Island's financial benefit. Now that this treatment is no longer to Island's benefit, the company must still adhere to the choice it made.

On balance, application of the *Reid* test requires that we find Aymes to be an independent contractor when he was creating CSALIB for Island. Consequently, we hold that CSALIB is not a work for hire. Aymes therefore owns the copyright as author of the program.

II. Issues on Remand

Having concluded that Aymes owns the copyright to CSALIB, we would ordinarily next consider the merits of Aymes's infringement claims. There is evidence in the record that Island is no longer using any part of Aymes's ten year old program. However, we cannot determine whether Island is infringing Aymes's copyright since the district court did not decide this issue.

We note, though, that the district court has already ruled that Aymes "cannot realistically dispute the fact that he sold defendants the computer program . . . and that defendants are, therefore, rightful owners of the program." The court went on to reason that Island had a clear right to use the program that it had purchased from Aymes. The court noted that the issue left unresolved was whether Island had made unlicensed derivatives of the program for other external corporations. However, three years later the district court found that Island never made an agreement with Aymes to limit Island's ability to use CSALIB on multiple machines. Although these findings make it unlikely that Aymes will prevail on his infringement claim, we remand to the district court for its determination. . . .

An additional issue on remand arises from Island's argument that Bonelli is a "joint owner" of the copyright to CSALIB under 17 U.S.C. §201(a) (1988) because of his contribution to its creation. Although CSALIB was not a work for hire, it might still possibly be considered a joint work due to Bonelli's involvement in its development. Because there were no specific findings of fact on this issue, we similarly remand the issue for the district court's determination.

Conclusion

Based on the foregoing, the judgment of the district court is reversed, and the case remanded for further proceedings not inconsistent with this opinion.

NOTES

1. *Bonelli* reserved the issue of whether the software might be considered to be a "joint work." "The authors of a joint work are coowners of copyright in the work." 17 U.S.C. §201(a). The Copyright Act defines "joint work" as "a work prepared by two or more authors with the intention that their contributions be merged into inseparable or interdependent parts of a unitary whole." 17 U.S.C. §101. In addition to requiring that the requisite intention be present, each author must have contributed to the expression in the work. Under these conditions, what would have to be proven in *Bonelli* to establish a joint work?

2. If an independent contractor does not create a work for hire and there is no transfer of ownership to the client, what rights does the client receive? For example, if a contractor creates an inventory control program for a client, can the client later modify that program to meet changing inventory needs? Can the client make additional copies of the software?

IXL, INC. v. ADOUTLET.COM, INC.
2001 U.S. Dist. LEXIS 3784, No. 01 C 0763 (N.D. Ill. 2001)

SCHENKIER, UNITED STATES MAGISTRATE JUDGE.

At its core, this case presents a basic contract dispute between iXL, Inc. ("iXL") and AdOutlet.Com, Inc. ("AdOutlet"). In its amended complaint, iXL claims that it entered into a contract with AdOutlet to provide consulting and web design services for a fee; that iXL provided the services; that iXL billed AdOutlet $2,913,708.00 for the work and expenses associated with those services; but that AdOutlet has paid only $1,195,505.00 of the billed amount, leaving a substantial shortfall that iXL now seeks to collect under theories of breach of contract, accounts stated, open book account, and quantum meruit. AdOutlet denies that it owes iXL anything beyond what AdOutlet already has paid; indeed, AdOutlet complains it has paid too much, and has asserted a breach of contract counterclaim seeking recovery of an unspecified amount for "significant costs and expenses" that AdOutlet allegedly has incurred because AdOutlet had to correct short-comings in iXL's performance.

Because the services for which the parties contracted involve copyright and other intellectual property, both the amended complaint and the counterclaim seek to expand this case into far more than a mere contract dispute. iXL claims that AdOutlet is using computer source code property that iXL created, but for which AdOutlet has not paid, and that AdOutlet thus has committed misappropriation, conversion and unauthorized use of intellectual property in violation of common law, and copyright infringement in violation of 17 U.S.C. § 101, *et. seq.* . . . It is this intellectual property side of the case that brings the matter before the Court at this time. iXL has moved for a preliminary injunction, seeking to bar AdOutlet from using the computer code and intellectual property allegedly supplied by iXL on AdOutlet's web site. . . .

[The] Court concludes that iXL has failed to make an adequate showing of likelihood of success or irreparable harm to support a preliminary injunction. Therefore, the Court respectfully recommends that the motion for preliminary injunction be denied. . . .

I.

. . . .

B. The Contracts Between the Parties.

On March 22, 2000, iXL and AdOutlet entered into a Master Service Agreement ("the Agreement"), pursuant to which iXL agreed to provide AdOutlet with consulting and web design services on an hourly fee and expense basis. As a substantial part of those services, iXL was to create computer "source code" to assist in the operation of AdOutlet's web site. . . .

The Agreement contemplated that the specific tasks that iXL would perform, and the price for those tasks, would be set forth in separate Statements of Work ("S.O.W."), which would incorporate the terms of the Agreement. . . .

Under the Agreement, iXL possessed the authority to "determine the method, details, and means of performing the services to be performed hereunder, subject to the standards set forth in the Statement of Work and the approval of Client, which shall not be unreasonably withheld." iXL warranted that it would perform services for AdOutlet "in material conformity to the specifications set forth in a Statement of Work contemplated hereunder in a professional and workmanlike manner." At the same time, the Agreement contained a disclaimer by iXL, stating that it did not warrant that its services would be "error free," or that AdOutlet would be able to obtain certain results due to the services provided by iXL, or that iXL was providing any warranty of merchantability, title, or fitness for a particular purpose.

The Agreement specified that for the services provided under the Agreement, AdOutlet "shall pay to iXL the fees in the amount and manner set forth in the Statement of Work," as well as expenses. The Agreement stated that fees and expenses would be billed monthly, and that amounts billed by iXL "will be due and payable within thirty (30) days after the due date of an invoice therefore from iXL." The Agreement provided for imposition of late charges of one and one-half percent per month. The Agreement also set forth the remedies that iXL could pursue in the event of nonpayment by AdOutlet. If AdOutlet failed to pay for sixty days after the date of the invoice, the Agreement authorized iXL's "suspension of the performance of the services." The Agreement further provided that if iXL pursued legal action to recover on unpaid invoices, AdOutlet would be liable to pay "in addition to any amount past due, plus interest accrued thereon, all reasonable expenses incurred by iXL in enforcing this Agreement, including, but not limited to, all expenses of any legal proceeding related thereto and all reasonable attorneys' fees incurred in connection therewith."

The Agreement provided for various circumstances under which the Agreement could be terminated. For example, the Agreement provided that upon a default of payment by AdOutlet, which had not been cured within thirty days, iXL could terminate the Agreement upon written notice. The Agreement further provided for termination upon other material defaults of duties and obligations under the Agreement (other than payment obligations), if there was a failure to substantially cure or commence a cure of the default within thirty days of receiving written notice. Termination for any of these foregoing reasons required notice, specifying the date of termination. The Agreement stated that upon termination of the Agreement for any of the specified reasons, AdOutlet "shall be obligated to pay iXL for all services rendered pursuant to any outstanding Statements of Work through the effective date of such termination". . . .

The Agreement also makes clear that iXL and AdOutlet did not intend to become "partners, joint venture's, representatives or agents of each other." . . .

2. Statements of Work.

Pursuant to the Agreement, the parties entered into six separate Statements of Work. . . . The Statements of Work defined the "Services" that iXL would perform as those set forth in the Statement of Work, and "Works" as "all deliverables developed or prepared by iXL in the performance of Services hereunder." The Statements of Work contemplated that in performing Services and Works for AdOutlet, iXL would use certain "Pre-Existing Works" that already had been developed by iXL; that iXL also would use certain "Client Materials" obtained from AdOutlet, such as information and ideas; and that iXL would create certain new material for AdOutlet. Paragraph 3 of the consulting terms and conditions set forth the ownership rights in these three different categories of materials. Because it is central to the present motion, we set forth below that provision in its entirety:

> 3. *"Work for Hire."* Client shall retain all title to Client Materials, including all copies thereof and all rights to patents, copyrights, trademarks, trade secrets and other intellectual property rights inherent in such Client Materials. iXL shall not, by virtue of this Statement or otherwise, acquire any proprietary rights whatsoever in the Client Materials, which shall be the sole and exclusive property of Client. *With the exception of Pre-Existing Works, the Services provided by iXL and the Works shall constitute "work made for hire" for Client . . . and Client shall be considered the author and shall be the copyright owner of the Works. If and to the extent that the foregoing provisions do not operate to vest fully and effectively in Client such rights, iXL hereby grants and assigns to Client all rights which may not have so vested, (except for rights in the Pre-Existing Works). . . .*

AdOutlet does not dispute that iXL actually worked the hours for which it billed AdOutlet. As the chart makes clear, and as the parties do not dispute, iXL has billed AdOutlet $2,913,708.00 for hours expended and expenses incurred in performing work pursuant to the Statements of Work and the Agreement; setting aside expenses, the total amount billed for the hourly component ($2,853,767.00) exceeded the cost estimate by $329,142.00. . . . The chart also reveals another fact that the parties do not dispute: that is, that AdOutlet has paid far less than the amount billed. AdOutlet has paid $1,195,505.00, leaving a balance billed but unpaid of $1,718,203.00. . . .

D. Disputes Between the Parties Concerning the Source Code.

During the summer of 2000, iXL sent portions of the source code to AdOutlet by e-mail. On or about October 1, 2000, iXL delivered to AdOutlet two compact discs containing the source code iXL created for the web site. As it was delivered to AdOutlet, the source code provided by iXL bore a legend stating that AdOutlet owns the copyright.

The payment disputes between the parties reflect the ongoing disagreements between the parties during iXL's performance of work of AdOutlet. . . . AdOutlet claims that despite receiving specific and detailed instructions from iXL, the source code prepared by iXL was fraught with defects, which over a period of several months iXL had difficulty in correcting and that, as a result, AdOutlet personnel had to fix. AdOutlet claims that the vast majority of the source code used for the AdOutlet web site thus was developed by AdOutlet, and not iXL.

While iXL does not directly dispute that it encountered some difficulties in supplying code and other information that met AdOutlet's requirements, iXL contends that iXL ultimately provided satisfactory code and other information — which iXL contends AdOutlet is using without paying for it. . . .

Despite its criticisms about the quality of the code iXL supplied, AdOutlet admits that it has not exercised its option under paragraph 2.3 of the terms and conditions to the Statements of Work to reject the source code, to return it to iXL, and to terminate the Agreement. Rather, AdOutlet has installed the source code and continues to use it on its web site. . . .

II.

"The purpose of a preliminary injunction is merely to preserve the relative positions of the parties until a trial on the merits can be held." . . . In this case, we believe that the motion for preliminary injunction may be resolved by focusing solely on the threshold elements, as plaintiff at this point has made out at best only a weak case for likelihood of success on the merits of the copyright claim and has failed to establish irreparable harm.

A. Likelihood of Success in the Merits.

iXL has established a reasonable likelihood of establishing that the source code at issue is copyrightable. . . .

The difficulty that iXL confronts is in establishing a likelihood of success on the proposition that iXL, rather than AdOutlet, is the owner of a copyright in the source code. On this point, iXL runs headlong into the language of the Agreement that iXL itself drafted. The Statements of Work specifically state that the Works and Services provided by iXL (which include the source code) are works made for hire for AdOutlet, and that AdOutlet "shall be considered the author and shall be the copyright owner of the works." This language plainly constitutes an express agreement that the source code is work made for hire, as required by 17 U.S.C. § 101. Under 17 U.S.C. § 201(b), the "person for whom the work was prepared [here, AdOutlet] is considered the author for purposes of this title, and, unless the parties have expressly agreed otherwise in a written instrument signed by them, owns all of the rights comprised in the copyright."

iXL contends that taken together, the Agreement and the Statements of Work show that the parties have "expressly agreed otherwise," by making full payment of the invoices a condition precedent to AdOutlet's ownership of the source code. In order for iXL to demonstrate likelihood of succeeding on this point, iXL must show both (1) that it is likely to succeed on its claim that AdOutlet breached the contract by nonpayment, and (2) that such a breach deprives iXL of ownership of the source code.

iXL has shown some likelihood of success on this first point. Under Illinois law (which governs under the choice of law provision in the Agreement), iXL must establish the following elements to prove a breach of contract claim: (1) the existence of a valid and enforceable contract; (2) performance by iXL; (3) breach by AdOutlet; and (4) resulting injury to iXL. There is nothing here to suggest that the Agreement and the Statements of Work, signed by both parties, are not valid and enforceable. Nor is there any dispute that iXL has billed AdOutlet for some $2.9 million of time and expense that iXL actually incurred in providing services to AdOutlet, that AdOutlet has not paid nearly that full amount, and that as a result iXL has suffered injury — iXL admittedly has received some $1.7 million less than it billed AdOutlet. While AdOutlet asserts that iXL failed to perform adequately under the Agreement and that AdOutlet's failure to pay the full amount is thus not a breach, there is evidence that could establish AdOutlet has accepted iXL's work. The evidence shows that AdOutlet has not returned the source code submitted by iXL, and has not exercised the procedure set forth in the contract for termination upon iXL's failure to timely correct non-conforming works: AdOutlet has not returned the source code and sought a refund. To the contrary, the evidence shows that AdOutlet is using the source code developed by iXL on the web site, and that the source code developed by iXL is a critical component to the operation of AdOutlet's web site. At oral argument, counsel for AdOutlet acknowledged that the question of whether there was adequate performance by iXL involves disputed facts that would have to be resolved by the jury at trial. Given these circumstances, the Court finds that iXL has established some likelihood of success on its claim of breach of contract.

However, iXL has not established a likelihood of success on the proposition that a breach of contract results in AdOutlet being deprived of ownership of the source code. The Statements of Work provide that the Services provided by iXL are "works made for hire" for AdOutlet. The Copyright Act provides that the person for whom the work was prepared is considered the author and owns the rights comprised in the copyright "unless the parties have expressly agreed otherwise in a written instrument signed by them." The Agreement and the Statements of Work contain no express agreement that AdOutlet will be considered the author of the source code and the owner of its copyright only after full payment of the invoices. Nor do these agreements state that AdOutlet is barred from using the source code in its web site if AdOutlet has failed to pay the full invoice amount. Indeed, when iXL delivered the CD Roms containing the source code on or about October 1, 2000 — by which time AdOutlet already was nearly $900,000 in arrears in payment for more than 60 days — iXL nonetheless affixed to the code a legend identifying AdOutlet as the holder of the copyright.

In the absence of an express agreement, iXL attempts to cobble together an implied condition that AdOutlet cannot own (or use) the source code until it has made full payment of the invoice price to iXL. iXL points to two provisions in particular, neither of which bears the weight that iXL seeks to place on it.

First, iXL points to paragraph 2.2 of the terms and conditions of the Statements of Work, which state that AdOutlet "shall perform the tasks set forth in the Statement as a condition to iXL's obligations to perform hereunder." iXL claims that this language establishes that full payment by AdOutlet is a condition precedent to AdOutlet being deemed the author and copyright holder of the source code. iXL certainly could have made full payment by AdOutlet a condition precedent. *See, e.g., MXL Industries, Inc. v. Mulder,* 252 Ill.App.3d, 18, 25, 191 Ill.Dec. 124, 623 N.E.2d 369 (2d Dist.1993) ("a condition precedent . . . is to be performed by one party to an existing contract before the other party is obligated to perform"). But it is hard to read paragraph 2.2 as doing so. The word "tasks" is not defined in the Agreement or in the Statements of Work. The Court finds it plausible that paragraph 2.2 is to be read in conjunction with paragraph 2.4, which provides that iXL's obligation to meet contractual deadlines is contingent upon AdOutlet complying "in a timely manner, with all reasonable requests of iXL." But to construe "task" to mean "full payment" by AdOutlet, as iXL argues, would make no sense. Read that way, under paragraph 2.2 iXL would have absolutely no "obligations to perform" until AdOutlet first had paid the full contract price — which is clearly not what the parties intended, as measured both by the wording of the contract and the actual course of performance by the parties.

Second, iXL relies on paragraph 3 of the terms and conditions, and in particular, the sixth sentence of that paragraph, which states as follows:

> If any of the Works except the Pre-Existing Works do not qualify for treatment as a "work for hire" or if iXL retains any interest in any components of the works for any other reason, iXL hereby grants, assigns and transfers to Client ownership of all United States and international copyrights and all other intellectual property rights in the Works, subject to certain rights of iXL described herein, and all the rights of use in respect thereof which are intended to be conferred hereunder and under the Statement, free and clear of any and all claims for royalties or other compensation except as stated in this Statement.

iXL correctly notes that the grant of right set forth in this sentence states that it is being made free and clear of any and all claims for royalties or other compensation *except as stated in this Statement.* But the Court does not believe that sentence makes payment a precondition to vesting of authorship and copyright ownership in AdOutlet, whether viewing the sentence in isolation or in the context of the entire paragraph.

Read in isolation, the Court believes that this sentence does not make the vesting of authorship and ownership contingent on payment, but rather, indicates that in transferring those rights, iXL did so free and clear of any claims for royalty or other compensation, but without waiver of iXL's right to payment as set forth in the Statements of Work. Put another way, this sentence does not make payment by AdOutlet a precondition to authorship and ownership rights in a source code vesting in AdOutlet; rather, the sentence makes clear that the vesting of those rights in AdOutlet does not extinguish iXL's right to payment for services.

Moreover, viewed in the context of the entire paragraph, it is hard to see as a practical matter when this sentence would come into operation. The third sentence of paragraph 3 states that as to the materials that shall constitute works made for hire (including the source code), AdOutlet "shall be considered the author and shall be the copyright owner of the works." That sentence has no ambiguity or qualification, and expresses no contingency in the vesting of authorship and ownership. The very next sentence, moreover, provides that "[i]f and to the extent that the foregoing provisions do not operate to vest fully and effectively in [AdOutlet] such rights iXL hereby grants and assigns to [AdOutlet] all rights which may not have so vested [ ] (except for rights in the Pre-Existing Works)." That sentence appears to account for the possibility that despite the parties' agreement, the Services or Works rendered by iXL might not qualify for copyright protection, in which case that sentence would vest ownership of any non-copyright material in AdOutlet — again, with that grant being unqualified and unconditional. In light of those two broad grants of ownership in AdOutlet, which cover the Works and Services both in the event they are copyrightable and in the event that they are not, it is hard to envision when the sixth sentence in paragraph 3.3 on which iXL relies would ever come into play. To the extent that there is any ambiguity about it, that uncertainty cuts against iXL, which drafted the contracts. Thus, we do not believe that paragraph 3.3 contains the kind of express statement required by 17 U.S.C. § 201(b) to limit or qualify AdOutlet's rights of ownership.

iXL also argues that in the absence of a clear contractual provision, the Court should imply payment by AdOutlet as a condition precedent to vesting of authorship and ownership of the source code by AdOutlet. While each side has cited authority to support its respective position that full payment is an implied condition precedent to vesting of authorship and ownership in AdOutlet, the Court does not find any of those authorities persuasive here. AdOutlet's authorities do not deal with the situation of a failure to pay by the client, as is alleged to be the case here. And iXL's authorities all deal with the scenario not present here: where the plaintiffs did not seek contract damages, but instead sought rescission of the contract and return of the intellectual property. In this case, iXL does not want the copyright material back, because it was created for AdOutlet's particular specifications and thus is useless by iXL (except perhaps for leverage in resolving this payment dispute).

In any event, we agree with the observation the court in *Royal v. Leading Edge Products, Inc.,* 833 F.2d 1, 3 (1st Cir.1987), that there is "scant reason" to imply any condition concerning ownership of a copyright when an "unambiguous compact occupies the field." In *Royal,* the defendant had entered into a royalty agreement with plaintiff, one of its employees. Plaintiff was thereafter terminated, and defendant ceased paying royalties. In rejecting the plaintiff's assertion that the copyright reverted to him as a result of the alleged failure to pay royalties, the court noted that the royalty agreement explicitly addressed the consequences that would flow from termination of employment, and that "[r]eversion of the copyright is not among those consequences." 833 F.2d at 3. The court reasoned that "[w]here, as here, the contract is clear, courts must be loath to presume added promises out of thin air," and that "[t]he express terms of [plaintiff's] bargain with the company leave no room for unstated conditions to creep into the deal."

In this case, iXL drafted the Agreement and the Statements of Work, and negotiated it at arms length with AdOutlet. iXL had every opportunity, and presumably every incentive, to provide in the Agreement and the Statements of Work for adequate safeguards to insure payment — including a provision that conditioned AdOutlet's right of ownership in use of the copyright information upon payment of the full invoice price. Now that the contract has gone sour, iXL asks the Court to step in and provide it with a remedy (and with leverage) that iXL did not bargain for. The Court does not believe that iXL has shown some likelihood of succeeding in that effort.

Conclusion

For the foregoing reasons, the Court respectfully recommends that iXL's motion for preliminary injunction be denied. . . .

V.   WARRANTY AND MAINTENANCE

Software licenses involve an interaction of several issues associated with warranty and warranty-like obligations. The first involves the question of what law applies: sale or lease of goods on the one hand, or common law on the other. As we have seen, software transactions are the only area of licensing in which any appreciable number of courts apply UCC Article 2, but there have been legislative and other developments suggesting a reconsideration of that principle. See our discussion in Chapter 1. Even after a determination is made about what law is applicable, however, there is a significant, unique interaction between warranty disclaimers, limited express warranties, and maintenance agreements in software licensing.

The following case suggests one dimension of the issue of what law applies and why that matters.

MICRO-MANAGERS, INC. v. GREGORY
434 N.W.2d 97 (Wisc. App. 1988)

DYKMAN, JUDGE.

Stanley Gregory d/b/a Consulting Engineers appeals from a judgment requiring him to pay Micro-Managers, Inc., (MMI) $24,503.68. MMI had sued Gregory for breach of contract after Gregory refused to pay for a computer program he had contracted for and had thereafter sold to a third party. The issues are: (1) whether the contract was a transaction for goods, and thus subject to the Uniform Commercial Code (U.C.C.); (2) whether there was an implied warranty from MMI to Gregory; (3) whether MMI substantially performed the contract; and (4) whether the trial court abused its discretion in denying Gregory's motion to amend his counterclaim. We conclude that: (1) the contract was mainly for services, and that therefore the U.C.C. does not apply; (2) there was no implied warranty; (3) MMI substantially performed the contract; and (4) the trial court did not abuse its discretion by denying Gregory's motion to amend his counterclaim. Therefore we affirm.

Facts

In the fall of 1982, Oilgear, an industrial manufacturing company in Milwaukee, contracted with Gregory to develop a new programmable controller to replace equipment which Oilgear was using. Gregory contacted Rex Peterson, general manager of MMI, who indicated MMI was interested in designing and developing the software required for the controller. Gregory's technical coordinator, Terry Coleman, met with his counterpart at MMI, Mike Christie, to find out whether MMI had the personnel and expertise to design and develop the required software in accordance with Oilgear's specifications.

After MMI had prepared certain cost estimates, Gregory told MMI to go ahead with the design and development of the controller software. MMI began work on the project on October 7, 1982.

On October 22, 1982, MMI drafted a letter incorporating what it believed to be the working arrangements between the parties. The letter provided that "all MMI time will be billed by MMI at a rate of $40/hour for software, $50/hour for engineering, and $75/hour for supervision. . . . Direct expenses will be billed as charged MMI." The letter also provided that MMI was to receive a fifteen percent incentive bonus if it completed the project on an accelerated schedule. The letter further provided that Gregory must give MMI a two-week project termination notice for termination to be effective. The letter ended: "If the terms of this letter meet with your understanding, please sign and return a copy to me no later than October 25, 1982."

On October 25, 1982, Coleman signed the letter, acknowledging receipt of the letter and confirming that the items in the letter had been discussed and agreed upon. During the next two months, the parties agreed to a number of amendments to the agreement. Gregory confirmed all of these changes with Oilgear. In January of 1983, Coleman and MMI agreed that the software was to be completed and ready for final testing by February 1, 1983 for MMI to earn the bonus.

On February 1, the parties from MMI (Sally Peterson, president of MMI, and Mike Christie) were not available. Gregory took the software from MMI but complained that it had not been completed to his satisfaction. However, Gregory did not permit MMI to correct any of the alleged defects in the software, and never communicated any specific objections to MMI regarding the software until legal action began.

Pursuant to the parties' stipulation, the trial court ordered the trial bifurcated because of the complexity of the issues. This was because many of Gregory's counterclaims against MMI would apply only if the parties' contract were one mainly for goods, and thus subject to U.C.C. strictures. In the first phase, the issue would be whether the contract was governed by the U.C.C., i.e., whether the contract was mainly for services or mainly for goods. . . . After the first phase, the trial court concluded that the October 22 letter was the contract, that it was mainly for services rather than goods, and that therefore the U.C.C. did not apply. . . .

Contract for Goods or Services?

Although at trial Gregory contested MMI's claim that the October 22, 1982 letter was the parties' contract, he does not argue on appeal that the trial court's conclusion is erroneous. The interpretation of an unambiguous contract presents a question of law which we review de novo. It is undisputed that this was a mixed contract, i.e., a contract for both goods and services. The issue is whether the mixed contract was predominantly for goods or for services.

> The test for inclusion or exclusion [within the U.C.C.] is not whether [contracts] are mixed, but, granting that they are mixed, whether their predominant factor, their thrust, their purpose, reasonably stated, is the rendition of service, with goods incidentally involved (e.g., contract

with artist for painting) or is a transaction of sale, with labor incidentally involved (e.g., installation of a water heater in a bathroom).

Gregory cites many cases which he alleges support construing the contract
as one primarily for goods. Nevertheless, we conclude that *Data Processing
v. L. H. Smith Oil Corp.*, 492 N.E.2d 314 (Ind.App.), *aff'd on rehearing*, 493
N.E.2d 1272 (Ind.App.1986) is on point and more compelling. In that case,
as here, the parties contracted for custom computer programming. The trial
court had reasoned that the contract was for the development and delivery of
a "program," which it concluded was a specially manufactured good covered
by U.C.C. warranty provisions. The appellate court phrased the issue as
"whether a contract to provide computer programming is a contract for the
sale and purchase of goods and thus subject to the provisions of article 2 of
the UCC, or one for the performance of services, and thus subject to common
law principles." The court noted that "DPS was *to act* with specific regard to
Smith's need. Smith bargained for DPS's skill in developing a system to meet
its specific needs." The court concluded the contract was for services, and not
subject to U.C.C. warranty provisions. The court held that the "mere means by
which DPS's skills and knowledge were to be transmitted to Smith's computers
was incidental."

In the present case, the contract provided that all MMI charges to Gregory
would be on the basis of time, at stated rates, and materials. Under *Bonebrake*
[*v. Cox*, 499 F.2d 951 (8th Cir. 1974)], we must determine whether the contract's predominant factor, thrust and purpose is the rendition of a service or
the transaction of a sale. As we did in *Van Sistine* [*v. Tollard*, 95 Wis. 2d 678,
684, 291 N.W.2d 636, 639 (Ct. App. 1980)], we may look to evidence of billing
to determine this issue. On January 18, 1983, Terry Coleman, an agent for
Gregory, wrote the following in a letter to Sally Peterson, president of MMI: "3.
The projected total, excluding bonus, is therefore approximately $59,828, of
which $55,968 is labor." In addition, we may look to the language of the con-
tract to determine whether it is more in accord with services instead of sales.
The contract speaks in terms of "man-days," "development," "time," "design,"
etc. These words connote the rendition of services and not a sales transaction.

Based on this evidence, we conclude that this was primarily a service contract. The method by which MMI transmitted that service was merely incidental. Therefore the transaction is not subject to the provisions of the U.C.C.

Warranties

[The] issue of express warranty is not before us, and we address only the
issues of whether there was an implied warranty in fact or law.

> A "warranty" is an assurance by one party to a contract of the exis-
> tence of a fact upon which the other party may rely. It is intended to
> relieve the promisee of any duty to ascertain the fact for himself, and
> amounts to a promise to indemnify the promisee for any loss if the fact
> warranted proves untrue.

The trial court held there was no implied warranty in fact. We uphold a trial
court's fact findings if, upon a review of the record, they are not clearly errone-

ous. The party relying upon a breach of warranty has the burden of proof to show the warranty. The trier of fact determines the weight of evidence and the credibility of witnesses.

The trial court concluded that the evidence did not support a finding that an implied warranty existed. Peterson testified that MMI's policy was to give clients what they expected, but that results were never guaranteed. She also testified that she told Gregory that the software project was of an experimental nature. The trial court believed Peterson, and found there was no implied warranty in fact. We affirm that finding because it is not clearly erroneous.

The next issue is whether there is an implied warranty in law. This is a legal question which we review de novo. In *Hoven v. Kelble,* 79 Wis.2d 444, 461-63, 256 N.W.2d 379, 388 (1977), the supreme court addressed this issue:

> A number of decisions in other jurisdictions have allowed recovery on the basis of strict liability (or the closely related doctrine of implied warranty) where the injury was due to a defective product supplied or used in the course of rendering a service to plaintiff. Several cases have allowed recovery on the basis of strict liability or implied warranty where "defective services" have been rendered, but these services have been of a relatively routine or simple nature. Where "professional" services are in issue the cases uniformly require that negligence be shown.

"If the activity of [the defendant] pursuant to its contract . . . be viewed as the rendering of professional services, then no matter how the basis of liability is described it amounts to no more than a claim of negligence in failing to perform these services with due care." *La Rossa v. Scientific Design Company,* 402 F.2d 937, 943 (3rd Cir.1968) (upholding trial court's dismissal of claim of breach of implied warranty). Gregory has not cited any case law holding that we should now recognize the existence of an implied warranty as a matter of law where professional services are rendered. Therefore we affirm the trial court on this issue. . . .

Substantial Performance

Gregory claims the issue of substantial performance still has to be tried. In its complaint, MMI claimed it had "performed for the defendants all the services requested by the defendants." In his answer, Gregory alleged that "the software developed by the Plaintiff did not substantially meet or conform with the specifications mutually agreed upon . . . in violation of the agreement between the parties," and that therefore "the consideration for the agreement between the parties totally failed." The trial court concluded that substantial performance had been tried in the first phase of the trial.

The test for substantial performance is whether the performance meets the essential purpose of the contract. The trial court concluded that MMI had promised to use its expertise and skill in designing and developing software, and that Gregory had promised to pay MMI for this service. Because the trial court found that MMI did use its expertise and skill, the court held that Gregory had received what he had bargained for. The trial court ruled against Gregory on the issue of failure of consideration, i.e., that MMI did not perform what it promised, by finding that MMI did perform its promise to use its skill and expertise. This finding subsumes the finding that MMI substantially performed its contract since it provided Gregory what he bargained for. No new trial was needed, since the issue had been disposed of.

Gregory alleges that the trial court's conclusion that the issue of substantial performance need not be tried was based solely on its findings that Gregory had accepted the software without complaint and received the benefit of it. Gregory claims that the scheduling order reserved the issue of acceptance and benefit for phase two of the trial, and that Gregory offered little if any evidence on these issues in phase one.

We need not address this claim of error. Even if the trial court's reasoning is erroneous, we may still affirm if the result is correct. Gregory claims that the software was virtually useless and that Gregory received no benefit from it. However, this argument goes to the quality of the work product, and not to whether MMI used its expertise and skill to develop it. Such an inquiry would be relevant if this were a contract for goods under the U.C.C., but since it is not, no such inquiry is required. Gregory does not contest the trial court's finding that MMI "used its skill and expertise in good faith and integrity to design and develop the software" and that MMI "exercised the degree of diligence and skill" which Gregory contracted for. Since MMI provided what it promised, it substantially complied with the contract. Whether Gregory accepted the end product or whether he received any benefit from the end product does not alter the fact of MMI's substantial performance of the contract. . . . AFFIRMED

NOTES

1. Cases involving software development contracts split on whether Article 2 or common law applies. As *Gregory* suggests, the difference is significant with respect to warranties. What should be examined in a development contract to determine if it is a services or a goods transaction? Contractual language? Payment criteria? When the contract is completed? More importantly, is it correct to focus on the comparison between goods and services, while ignoring the third category of "information" or "intellectual property" rights?

2. UCITA applies to computer program transactions whether or not the transaction would otherwise be considered services or goods. UCITA warranties establish a warranty of merchantability for the functional aspects of all programs distributed by merchants, and shape other implied warranties based on practical aspects of the actual transaction.

U.C.C. § 2-314 (1998 Official Text) reads, in pertinent part, as follows:

> Unless excluded or modified (Section 2-316), a warranty that the goods shall be merchantable is implied in a contract for their sale if the seller is a merchant with respect to goods of that kind. . . . Goods to be merchantable must be at least such as . . . are fit for ordinary purposes for which such goods are used. . . .

UCITA § 403 (2000 Official Text) provides:

(a) Unless the warranty is disclaimed or modified, a licensor that is a merchant with respect to computer programs of the kind warrants: (1) to its end user licensee that the computer program is fit for the ordinary purposes for which such computer programs are used. . . .

Does the commitment to providing a computer program of ordinary quality suggest that the program have no flaws? There is respectable theory that complex computer programs cannot be created without at least some flaws or bugs in them. See discussion in Lorin Brennan, *Why Article 2 Cannot Apply to Software Transactions*, 38 DUQUESNE L. REV. 459, 495-98 (2000) (discussing inability to guarantee "perfect" programs due to inherent limitations on computability). The Official Comments to UCITA observe:

> Merchantability does not require a perfect program, but that the subject matter be generally within the average standards applicable in commerce for programs having the particular type of use. The presence of some defects may be consistent with merchantability standards. Uniform Commercial Code § 2-314 (1998 Official Text) explains the concept in terms of "fair average," i.e., goods that center around the middle of a belt of quality — some may be better and some may be worse, but they cannot all be better and need not all be worse. That approach applies here. While perfection is an aspiration, it is not a requirement of an implied warranty for goods, computer programs or any other property. Indeed, a perfect program may not be possible at all.

> In the late 1990's, a popular operating system program for small computers used by both consumers and commercial licensees contained over ten million lines of code or instructions. In a computer, these instructions interact with each other and with code and operations of other programs. This contrasted with a commercial jet airliner that contained approximately six million parts, many of which involved no interactive function. Of course, the market price of the airliner and the program are materially different. Typical consumer goods contain fewer than one hundred parts and a typical book has fewer than one hundred fifty thousand words. Most computer programs not only have many lines of code, but must utilize and interact with code in third-party programs, further multiplying the possible interactions. It is often literally impossible or commercially unreasonable to guarantee that software of any complexity contains no errors that might cause unexpected behavior or intermittent malfunctions, so-called "bugs." The presence of such minor errors is fully within common expectation. The question for merchantability is not whether errors exist but whether the program still comes within the middle belt of quality in the applicable trade or industry, i.e., whether it is reasonably fit for the ordinary purposes for which such programs are used in accordance with average levels of quality and reasonable standards of program capability. A great deal of theoretical and practical work is currently focused on techniques to reduce the time and cost needed to determine program "correctness." Professional standards also exist for software quality evaluation. Commercially reasonable use of existing testing

techniques can be one benchmark of whether a computer program is merchantable in law. As industry standards evolve, what constitutes a merchantable program will evolve along with those standards.

UCITA §403, cmt. 3 (2000 Official Text). Query: *should* implied warranty law admit that information products may be imperfect, or should it require perfection?

The most common express contractual treatment of warranties in the software industry was borrowed from the hard goods industry — the agreement disclaims all implied warranties but provides that the software is delivered free of defects "of materials and workmanship" for ninety (or some other set number) of days. What does this mean in a software transaction where both parties understand that bugs may exist in the software code? What does it mean when the agreement states, as part of the express warranty, that the software provider will "replace, repair or refund the price of" any product that does not meet the no defect warranty? Under ordinary interpretation rules, in this context, the reference to no defects does not imply the impossible — perfect software. Does the express warranty cover bad programming?

The issue is compounded by the fact that many software companies offer maintenance contracts to licensees. "Maintenance" here is not the same as "maintenance" of a refrigerator — it does not deal with worn out parts. One article comments:

> Most software maintenance is done by the software vendor rather than an independent third-party company. The reasons for this are fairly obvious. First, most software is distributed in object code form only, thereby making it difficult for a third party to obtain adequate understanding of the software to maintain it. Second, if the third party attempts to modify the software, such modifications may be challenged as copyright infringement of the vendor's sole right to create derivative works.

> When the end-user buys software, he typically has two concerns which he seeks to address in a maintenance agreement with the software vendor. These are for the software vendor to correct errors that will surface over time (e.g., bugs) and for the software vendor to keep the software updated in order to be current. The software maintenance agreement is usually negotiated at the same time as the software license agreement. . . . There is no general understanding in the industry on the meaning of the terms "updates," "upgrades," and "enhancements" [in reference to such agreements]. These terms should be defined in the agreement to prevent disputes as to what is included and not included under them. If the term "enhancement" is not defined in the contract, then it [may] be interpreted as referring "only to improvements made to the product . . . itself, not to products that . . . could be used and marketed quite independently from" the version of the software product purchased by the end-user. . . .

Celia F. Rankin, *Computer Service and Maintenance Agreements*, 6 J. PROPRIETARY RTS. 2.

PROBLEM 16.7

Computer Associates (CA) distributes a variety of software in commercial end user markets. Its typical program contains 10 million lines of code and ordinarily includes up to 300 "bugs" that are known to affect performance in a minor way. This is typical of most programs. There may also be undiscovered bugs. CA licenses the programs for three-year license terms for fees that average $25,000 per year. CA also offers "maintenance" contracts for $5,000 per year under which it will give advice on problems encountered by licensees and will give the licensee any updates it releases to the program during the term of the contract. It asks how best to coordinate its warranty coverage on the license with its obligations under the maintenance contract. The license disclaims all implied warranties and gives an express warranty that the software will be free of "defects in material and workmanship" for ninety days after delivery. How do you respond?

MICROSOFT v. MANNING
914 S.W.2d 602 (Tex. App. 1995)

CORNELIUS, JUSTICE.

This is an appeal of the trial court's order granting class certification to a suit by appellees against Microsoft Corporation for breach of express and implied warranty, unjust enrichment, and violations of the Magnuson-Moss Warranty-Federal Trade Commission Improvement Act. . . . Microsoft contends that the district court abused its discretion in certifying the [class].

Microsoft Corporation [supplies] software for personal computers. At issue is its software MS-DOS 6.0, or Microsoft Disk Operating System. The disk operating system helps the user control the computer's basic functions, such as retrieving information stored in the computer's memory, writing and reading information stored on hard or floppy disks, and receiving typed characters from the keyboard.

Computer information is stored primarily on the hard drive. Users can increase their storage space by upgrading their equipment and buying newer, larger hard disks. In the late 1980s, software companies introduced disk compression software, which compresses the data on a hard disk, thereby increasing a computer's storage capacity by installing relatively inexpensive software instead of more expensive hardware.

MS-DOS 6.0 . . . contained disk compression software. Microsoft bought the rights to Vertisoft's compression program called DoubleDisk. The appellees argue that Microsoft used the compression feature, calling it DoubleSpace, with MS-DOS 6.0 without adequate testing. The compression software was faulty, they argue, and after Microsoft released it, customers started complaining that the compression software could in some cases destroy their data. . . . Appellees allege that, in order to correct the defect and provide new "data protection technology," Microsoft released an update, called MS-DOS 6.2. A reviewer's guide that Microsoft published in August 1993 stated, "We hope this new technology will not only provide extra protection for customers' data, but also increase customer's comfort in dealing with disk compression."

Appellees Mark Manning, Steve Collins, and Dana Schnitzer filed suit against Microsoft on December 6, 1993. . . . The appellees contend that Microsoft released MS-DOS 6.2 to correct the problems associated with MS-DOS 6.0 and DoubleSpace that caused loss of data. Microsoft sold MS-DOS 6.2 retail for $9.95. The appellees argue that the company should have corrected the problems with MS-DOS 6.0 without charge. They allege that some 10.5 million computer users acquired MS-DOS 6.0 and were damaged when they received a defective product that would cost $9.95 to remedy. The appellees do not seek consequential damages, i.e., damages for lost data. They seek as damages only the $9.95 upgrade fee they would have to pay to get MS-DOS 6.2, which corrected the defect in MS-DOS 6.0.

Microsoft argues that relatively few people, about three in 1,000, lost data after using MS-DOS 6.0. It alleges that most users lost no data and thus sustained no damage. The district court . . . finding that the appellees had met the requirements of Rule 42(a) and (b)(4), certified as a class "all persons and entities in the United States of America who have purchased or licensed MS-DOS 6.0 with DoubleSpace ("MS-DOS 6.0") sold separately and not pre-installed in any computer hardware and sold pre-installed in a computer's hardware." The certified causes of action are claims for economic damages, excluding consequential damages such as those resulting from alleged data loss. . . .

I.

Microsoft argues that the district court abused its discretion in certifying the class because the claims are founded on an unrecognized liability theory tailored to exclude the essential elements of individual causation and damages. It argues that the appellees, by excluding consequential damages and seeking only the upgrade price as damages, seek to certify a class of plaintiffs who have suffered no damages because they have lost no data. Without a common actual damage, Microsoft says, the appellees' case shatters into countless individual questions of law and fact not suitable for class action treatment.

One or more class members may sue as representative parties on behalf of all only if (1) the class is so numerous that joinder is impracticable, (2) the class has common questions of law or fact, (3) the representatives' claims are typical of the class claims, and (4) the representatives will fairly and adequately protect the class interests. Parties may maintain a class action if they and the action meet the stated requirements and the court finds that questions of law or fact common to the class members predominate over questions affecting individuals only, and that a class action is superior to other available methods for the fair and efficient adjudication of the controversy. . . . It is not necessary for the plaintiffs to prove a prima facie case of liability to be entitled to certification. The probability of the plaintiffs' success on the merits of their claims is an improper standard by which to measure class certification. . . .

Microsoft contends that, by including in the class individuals whose only injury was purchasing the software, the trial court relied on a novel and improper theory of liability. It argues that appellees have structured their class to eliminate two essential elements of their claims, causation and damages. Without this improper theory, it alleges, the class members would be only those individuals who actually lost data. Microsoft argues that including all purchasers as class members will lead to a proliferation of individual fact questions, such as whether individual class members lost data, whether the product caused the data loss, and what actual damages the user suffered.

Microsoft contends that other courts have rejected the theory that a defect that does not manifest itself by causing consequential damages nevertheless damages the individual who purchases the defective product. It relies mainly on the case of *Feinstein v. Firestone Tire and Rubber Co.*, 535 F.Supp. 595, 603 (S.D.N.Y.1982), where the court said that the theory that an unmanifested defect "'ipso facto caused economic loss' and breach of implied warranty is simply not the law."

In *Feinstein v. Firestone Tire and Rubber Co., supra,* the court found that where a purported automobile tire defect never manifested itself, the tires performed as expected and so did not breach the implied warranty under U. C.C. § 2-314(2)(c) (1989). The court noted that most of the tires sold to putative class members, by performing as they were supposed to for as long as they were supposed to, lived up to that "minimum level of quality" . . . .

Barbarin v. General Motors Corp., No. 84-0888 (D.C.D. Sept. 22, 1993), dealt with GM's X-cars, which the plaintiffs alleged had faulty brakes. The plaintiffs sued under the Magnuson-Moss Warranty Act, which provides that a consumer who is damaged by the failure of a supplier or warrantor to comply with any obligation under a written warranty or implied warranty may bring suit for damages. As a condition precedent to class actions, the Act requires that the warrantor be given reasonable opportunity to cure the deficiency. GM argued that its brake-related recalls cured the deficiency. The plaintiffs argued that they suffered economic damages on purchase because the value of the car received was less than the value of the car promised and that the cure was irrelevant except as an offset to damages. The court, relying in part on *Feinstein v. Firestone Tire and Rubber Co., supra,* stated that most cars with the brakes at issue never failed and that it would not certify as a class those purchasers whose brakes did not fail.

In *Yost v. General Motors Corp.,* [651 F. Supp. 656 (D.N.J. 1986),] the plaintiff alleged that water, oil, and coolant tended to mix in the crankcase of cars and that the leak was likely to cause irreparable engine damage. The court said that the plaintiff had not alleged damages, but only that "the potential leak is 'likely' to cause damage and 'may' create potential safety hazards." . . .

Microsoft also cites *American Suzuki Motor Corp. v. Superior Court of Los Angeles County,* 37 Cal.App.4th 1291, 44 Cal.Rptr.2d 526 (Cal.Ct.App. Sept. 21, 1995). There, in an implied warranty case involving Suzuki Samurai rollovers, the court found that most of the cars did not roll over because of high centers of gravity and so were fit for the "ordinary purpose" for which they were used.

The appellees rely on cases in which courts have certified classes including members who purchased defective products whose defects never manifested themselves. *See, e.g., Martin v. Amana Refrigeration, Inc.,* 435 N.W.2d 364

(Iowa 1989) (class members included those who purchased allegedly defective furnace and water heater units where units did not fail); *In re Cadillac V8-6-4 Class Action,* 93 N.J. 412, 461 A.2d 736 (1983) (court certified class whose members included all owners of engines at issue regardless of whether engines manifested problems); *Delgozzo v. Kenny,* 266 N.J.Super. 169, 628 A.2d 1080 (Ct.App.Div.1993) (appellate court ordered trial court to certify as a class New Jersey *purchasers* of furnaces and boilers with a "common design defect"). They argue that the cases relied on by Microsoft show, at most, a split of authority.

In both *Feinstein v. Firestone Tire and Rubber Co.* and *Barbarin v. General Motors Corp.,* which relied in part on the former, the defendant companies offered a remedy by recalls. Microsoft offered no such remedy. *Feinstein v. Firestone Tire and Rubber Co.* and *American Suzuki Motor Corp. v. Superior Court of Los Angeles County,* also were implied warranty cases in which the courts found that the particular products were fit for their ordinary purposes.

Software, however, is not like tires or cars. Tires and cars have a distinctly limited usable life. At the end of the product's life, the product and whatever defect it may have had pass away. If a defect does not manifest itself in that time span, the buyer has gotten what he bargained for. Software's useful life, however, is indefinite. Even though the defect is not manifest today, perhaps because the user is not using the data compression feature, it may manifest itself tomorrow. The only way for an MS-DOS 6.0 buyer to avoid the possibility of injury is to pay for the upgrade, never use the data compression feature, or use another operating system. The buyer never gets what he bargained for, i.e., an operating system with an effective data compression feature.

If we view the case as a breach of warranty case on a grand scale, the liability theory does not seem novel or improper. Away from the class action context, the measure of breach-of-warranty damages is the difference between the market value of property as warranted and the market value of property as delivered. In the absence of proof of market value as warranted, the price agreed on by the parties to the sale of personal property may be taken as the market value of that for which the parties contracted.

Microsoft expressly warranted that MS-DOS 6.0 would "perform substantially in accordance with the accompanying Product Manual(s) for a period of 90 days from the date of receipt," or Microsoft would replace or repair the software. Because of a defect in the software, which we almost must presume at this stage, MS-DOS 6.0 could not perform in accordance with the manual, and purchasers had to pay about $10.00 to correct the problem. The purchasers thought they were getting software that would be repaired without charge and in the end had to pay about $10.00 for repairs. Thus, MS-DOS 6.0 was worth about $10.00 less than the original purchase price. The appellees can mount similar arguments for their implied-warranty actions in that the software was not fit for the ordinary purpose for which software is used. Even if we accept Microsoft's arguments that few MS-DOS 6.0 users actually lost data, we have no way of knowing how many users were dissuaded from using DoubleSpace because of the risk of data loss and the well-publicized reports of the perceived defect. These purchasers may have paid for a data compression feature that they were afraid to use.

We believe that, if appellees prove that an individual defect exists in all original MS-DOS 6.0 software, it is not necessary for the purchasers to actually suffer a loss of data as a result of that defect for them to suffer damage. They have received less than they bargained for when they acquired the product. . . .

[We] do not believe that a purchaser who buys software that cannot perform as promised must nevertheless use the software and lose data before he can claim economic damage. We conclude that the trial court did not abuse its discretion by certifying a class whose members include those whose mere purchase of a defective product constitutes the purported injury.

NOTES

1. Several years after *Manning,* in *Compaq Computer Corp. v. LaPray,* 135 S.W.3d 657 (Tex. 2004), the Texas Supreme Court reversed the certification of a class based on a claim against Compaq that defects in floppy disk controller software breached the warranty of compliance with the user manual, even though the defect did not manifest itself for a particular user. The court cited the fact that, while UCC Article 2 applied, Article 2 was not uniform and could not support a national class with multiple different state laws applying.

2. Should a software "bug" that seldom affects performance be a breach of an express warranty that the product is free from defects in materials or workmanship under normal use during the ninety day warranty period? What are "defects" in "materials" and "workmanship"?

3. Many software publishers make contracts available to their licensees, typically described as software maintenance agreements, under which the publisher will for a fee provide the licensee with certain upgrades as they may be made generally available for the software and with services to correct software problems that affect the performance of the software for the licensee. Unlike with hard goods, maintenance in this sense does not entail repairing manufacturing defects or problems that result from extended use of the software. Ordinarily, defects repaired under a maintenance agreement will have been in the software as delivered. How should such contracts be coordinated with warranty disclaimers and express warranties?

VI. OPEN SOURCE SOFTWARE

A polarizing point in the software industry is in the competition between so-called "proprietary software" on one side, and "open source" and "free software" on the other. Popularly, the difference between the two camps lies in the extent to which each relies on intellectual property rights to create and control products. Some claim that companies that use or develop proprietary software depend on intellectual property rights, while those in the open world reject property-based controls. But open software often relies on copyright and contract, while proprietary software, on the other hand, often includes public domain code and ideas, and frequently makes software available on more flexible terms than licenses used by the open source or free software community.

See generally Robert W. Gomulkiewicz, *De-Bugging Open Source Software Licensing*, 64 U. PITT. L. REV. 75 (2002); David McGowan, *Legal Implications of Open-Source Software*, 2001 U. ILL. L. REV. 241; Greg Vetter, *The Collaborative Integrity of Open Source Software*, 20 UTAH L. REV. 563 (2004).

The difference between the two lies in the license, rather than software code, and in a commitment in the "free software" and "open source" (FSOS) communities to allowing software developed by one party to be modified and contributed to by another. There are hundreds of different licenses. FSOS software, however, tends to have several recurrent provisions that include:

- Source code made available to the licensee

- Licensee allowed to modify the software

- Licensee allowed to freely redistribute the software

- Licensee allowed to use the software as desired

- All warranties disclaimed upstream

The goal is to support a process of community or shared development and evolution of software. This is expected to enable higher quality software more quickly and to participate in a form of free speech community around the software environment.

Currently, the FSOS community is comprised of at least two separate camps. The one, described by participants and by its founder, Richard Stallman, as the "free software" movement, is aggressively normative in philosophy and proactive in perspective. Its leading organization is the Free Software Foundation (FSF), which was founded by Stallman in the 1980s. FSF was set up in part as a funding source for the so-called GNU project, a project to develop a variation of the Unix operating system that could be shared freely among developers.

The FSF theme emphasizes distribution of software in a manner that enables redistribution of the software by third parties and the making available of source code (to enable modification). The "free software" model incorporates so-called "copyleft" concepts that limit the ability of the subsequent parties to place proprietary restrictions over the free software when it is made available to others. The Preamble to the GPL comments: "To protect your rights, we need to make restrictions that forbid anyone to deny you these rights or ask you to surrender your rights."

The second camp is the "open source" community. Its primary organization is the Open Source Initiative (OSI), which manages a certification trademark. This branch of the community focuses primarily on making source code available. The principles adopted by the group go further, however, as indicated in the so-called "Open Source Definition," which provides guidance for the approval under the certification trademark. In general, "open source" themes emanating from OSI are less normative in content and more accepting of commercial, intellectual property development.

The website for the leading "free software" product (GNU/Linux) describes the two groups in the following terms:

The Free Software movement and the Open Source movement are like two political parties within our community. Radical groups are known for factionalism: organizations split because of disagreements on details of strategy, and then hate each other. They agree on the basic principles, and disagree only on practical recommendations; but they consider each other enemies, and fight each other tooth and nail.

For the Free Software movement and the Open Source movement, it is just the opposite on every point. We disagree on the basic principles, but agree on most practical recommendations. We work together on many specific projects. In the Free Software movement, we don't think of the Open Source movement as an enemy. The enemy is proprietary software. But we do want people in our community to know that we are not the same as them! So please mention the Free Software movement when you talk about the work we have done, and the software we have developed — such as the GNU/Linux operating system.

gnu.org/philosophy/free-software-for-freedom.html. The reference to "proprietary software" as the enemy conveys some of the flavor of the "free software" community. Its leading advocates view their movement as one that mounts social change. *See* Greg Vetter, *The Collaborative Integrity of Open Source Software*, 20 UTAH L. REV. 563 (2004). An evangelical attitude permeates the free software community. For example, another part of the GNU.org site contains the following discussion comparing "open source" and "free software":

The main argument for the term "open source software" is that "free software" makes some people uneasy. That's true: talking about freedom, about ethical issues, about responsibilities as well as convenience, is asking people to think about things they might rather ignore. This can trigger discomfort, and some people may reject the idea for that. . . . Years ago, free software developers noticed this discomfort reaction, and some started exploring an approach for avoiding it. They figured that by keeping quiet about ethics and freedom, and talking only about the immediate practical benefits . . . they might be able to "sell" the software more effectively to certain users, especially business. . . . This approach has proved effective, in its own terms. Today many people are switching to free software for purely practical reasons. That is good, as far as it goes, but that isn't all we need to do! . . . A certain amount of the "keep quiet" approach to business can be useful for the community, but we must have plenty of freedom talk too. . . . Most people involved with free software say little about freedom — usually because they seek to be "more acceptable to business." . . . Some GNU/Linux operating system distributions add proprietary packages to the basic free system, and they invite users to consider this an advantage, rather than a step backwards from freedom. We are failing to keep up with the influx of free software users, failing to teach people about freedom and our community as fast as they enter it. . . . To stop using the word "free" now would be a mistake; we need more, not less, talk about freedom. . . . We have to say, "It's free software and it gives you freedom!" — more and louder than ever before.

www.gnu.org/philosophy/free-software-for-freedom.html. What the movements have in common, however, is a focus on enabling "community" development of software products by emphasizing a need to make available source code and an absence of restrictions on modification. This entails a belief that it is a more effective method of developing quality software than the proprietary approach.

The "free software" movement had two significant events in its origination. In the mid-1980s, the Free Software Foundation (FSF) was set up by a group led by Stallman in part as a funding source for the GNU project. FSF released the first version of the GPL (GNU Public License) in 1989. Version 2 — the current version — was released in 1991. It is the single most widely used license in the FSOS community. That is true in part because of its association with the Linux operating system created initially by Linus Torvalds in the early 1990s. Linux source code was made available by Torvalds with the thought that other programmers would modify and enhance the kernal and make their modifications and enhancements available for public use so that others could build upon the modified or enhanced work.

How is "free software" free? Stallman described the term "free" in his "GNU Manifesto":

> The intention was that nobody would have to pay for "permission" to use the GNU system. But the words don't make this clear, and people often interpret them as saying that copies of GNU should always be distributed at little or no charge. That was never the intent. . . . Subsequently I have learned to distinguish carefully between "free" in the sense of freedom and "free" in the sense of price. Free software is software that users have the freedom to distribute and change. . . . The important thing is that everyone who has a copy has the freedom to cooperate with others in using it.[4]

The leading "free software" site (GNU.org) contains the following "free software" definition, which has significance in a process of informal certification aimed at preserving the purity of the movement:

> Free software is a matter of the users' freedom to run, copy, distribute, study, change and improve the software. More precisely, it refers to four kinds of freedom, for the users of the software:
>
> The freedom to run the program, for any purpose (freedom 0).
>
> The freedom to study how the program works, and adapt it to your needs (freedom 1). Access to the source code is a precondition for this.
>
> The freedom to redistribute copies so you can help your neighbor (freedom 2).
>
> The freedom to improve the program, and release your improvements to the public, so that the whole community benefits (freedom 3). Access to the source code is a precondition for this.

---

[4] [FN 1] <www.gnu.org/gnu/manifesto.html> at note 1.

> A program is free software if users have <u>all</u> of these freedoms. . . . In order for these freedoms to be real, they must be irrevocable as long as you do nothing wrong; if the developer of the software has the power to revoke the license, without your doing anything to give cause, the software is not free.

These premises define the core of a "free software" license.

The "free software" movement, however, also has a preference for license provisions described as "copyleft" and are present in the GNU General Public License (GPL). The concept is as follows:

> Copylefted software is free software whose distribution terms do not let redistributors add any additional restrictions when they redistribute or modify the software. This means that every copy of the software, even if it has been modified, must be free software. In the GNU Project, we copyleft almost all the software we write, because our goal is to give *every* user the freedoms implied by the term "free software." . . . Copyleft is a general concept; to actually copyleft a program, you need to use a specific set of distribution terms. There are many possible ways to write copyleft distribution terms, so in principle there can be many copyleft free software licenses. However, in actual practice nearly all copylefted software uses the [GNU GPL].[5]

This attribute of a free software license places restrictions on the redistribution of the software. This seeming deviation from the principle of "free software" is allegedly justified by its goal — to prevent a subsequent party from placing restrictions on the redistribution of the software that are inconsistent with the FSF principles.

The Open Source Initiative (OSI) was developed to make some of the premises of the FSOS community more acceptable to commercial entities. OSI states its perspective:

The basic idea behind open source is very simple: When programmers can read, redistribute, and modify the source code for a piece of software, the software evolves. People improve it, people adapt it, people fix bugs. And this can happen at a speed that, if one is used to the slow pace of conventional software development, seems astonishing. We in the open source community have learned that this rapid evolutionary process produces better software than the traditional closed model, in which only a very few programmers can see the source and everybody else must blindly use an opaque block of bits. Open Source Initiative exists to make this case to the commercial world.[6]

OSI's framework document is the Open Source Definition. The Open Source Definition states ten criteria for a license to qualify as "open source":[7]

> 1. Free Redistribution. The license may not restrict any party from selling or giving away the software as a component of an aggregate software distribution containing programs from several different

[5] [FN 2] What is copyleft?, www.gnu.org/gnu.html
[6] [FN 3] http://www.opensource.org/
[7] [FN 4] http://www.opensource.org/osd.html

sources. The license may not require a royalty or other fee for such sale.

2. Source Code. The program must include source code, and must allow distribution in source code as well as compiled form. Where some form of a product is not distributed with source code, there must be a well-publicized means of obtaining the source code for no more than a reasonable reproduction cost — preferably, downloading via the Internet without charge. . . .

3. Derived Works. The license must allow modifications and derived works, and must allow them to be distributed under the same terms as the license of the original software.

4. Integrity of the Author's Source Code. The license may restrict source-code from being distributed in modified form *only* if the license allows the distribution of "patch files" with the source code for the purpose of modifying the program at build time. The license must explicitly permit distribution of software built from modified source code. The license may require derived works to carry a different name or version number from the original software.

5. No Discrimination Against Persons or Groups. The license must not discriminate against any person or group of persons.

6. No Discrimination Against Fields of Endeavor. The license must not restrict anyone from making use of the program in a specific field of endeavor. For example, it may not restrict the program from being used in a business, or from being used for genetic research.

7. Distribution of License. The rights attached to the program must apply to all to whom the program is redistributed without the need for execution of an additional license by those parties.

8. License Must Not Be Specific to a Product. The rights attached to the program must not depend on the program's being part of a particular software distribution. If the program is extracted from that distribution and used or distributed within the terms of the program's license, all parties to whom the program is redistributed should have the same rights as those that are granted in conjunction with the original software distribution.

9. License Must Not Contaminate Other Software. The license must not place restrictions on other software that is distributed along with the licensed software. For example, the license must not insist that all other programs distributed on the same medium must be open-source software.

10. License Must Be Technology-Neutral. No provision of the license may be predicated on any individual technology or style of interface.

The reality is that there is a proliferation of licenses and license frameworks and that new products and FSOS entities enter the field frequently, often using licenses tailored to their particular interpretation of the principles of the community. What follows are three of the most important FSOS licenses.

THE BSD LICENSE

Copyright (c) <YEAR>, <OWNER>

All rights reserved.

Redistribution and use in source and binary forms, with or without modification, are permitted provided that the following conditions are met:

Redistributions of source code must retain the above copyright notice, this list of conditions and the following disclaimer.

Redistributions in binary form must reproduce the above copyright notice, this list of conditions and the following disclaimer in the documentation and/or other materials provided with the distribution.

Neither the name of the <ORGANIZATION> nor the names of its contributors may be used to endorse or promote products derived from this software without specific prior written permission.

THIS SOFTWARE IS PROVIDED BY THE COPYRIGHT HOLDERS AND CONTRIBUTORS "AS IS" AND ANY EXPRESS OR IMPLIED WARRANTIES, INCLUDING, BUT NOT LIMITED TO, THE IMPLIED WARRANTIES OF MERCHANTABILITY AND FITNESS FOR A PARTICULAR PURPOSE ARE DISCLAIMED. IN NO EVENT SHALL THE COPYRIGHT OWNER OR CONTRIBUTORS BE LIABLE FOR ANY DIRECT, INDIRECT, INCIDENTAL, SPECIAL, EXEMPLARY, OR CONSEQUENTIAL DAMAGES (INCLUDING, BUT NOT LIMITED TO, PROCUREMENT OF SUBSTITUTE GOODS OR SERVICES; LOSS OF USE, DATA, OR PROFITS; OR BUSINESS INTERRUPTION) HOWEVER CAUSED AND ON ANY THEORY OF LIABILITY, WHETHER IN CONTRACT, STRICT LIABILITY, OR TORT (INCLUDING NEGLIGENCE OR OTHERWISE) ARISING IN ANY WAY OUT OF THE USE OF THIS SOFTWARE, EVEN IF ADVISED OF THE POSSIBILITY OF SUCH DAMAGE.

NOTES

1. The BSD license was originated at the University of California. As with all of the leading FSOS licenses, it accommodates use by any person that elects to use it.

2. The most striking characteristic of the BSD license is its simplicity and breadth. The rights to use, modify, and redistribute are broadly granted. Under this license, authorized modifications may be copyrightable works of the licensee, who has no contractual limitations on what terms it uses in distributing its own code.

3. Another feature of the BSD framework concerns the legal basis under which the license and disclaimer might be enforceable. Does the BSD contemplate a contractual license? If not, what assurance does a transferee have that it obtained enforceable rights? Can the license be withdrawn? Notice that we are not asking whether BSD *is* a contract. That depends on how it is used by the parties, does it not?

PROBLEM 16.8

Tracer Corporation obtains software from AAA Software. It pays $50.00 for a copy of the software and agrees to a one year maintenance agreement with AAA. The software contains the BSD license, identifying AAA as the author of the code. There is no step in the process at which Tracer is asked to agree to the license. Consider the following:

a. Tracer incorporates the code into its product and begins distributing it. Tracer, however, has become embroiled in an argument with AAA, which threatens to withdraw the license. What are Tracer's rights?

b. Before incorporating the code into its product, Tracer makes significant modifications of it. When Tracer distributes the revised software, it requires the transferee to agree to license terms that preclude disclosure of the code and that prohibit further modification of the code. AAA sues for infringement of its code. What result? Can AAA withdraw the license?

GNU GENERAL PUBLIC LICENSE
Version 2, June 1991[8]

Copyright © 1991, 1999 Free Software Foundation, Inc. . . . Everyone is permitted to copy and distribute verbatim copies of this license document, but changing it is not allowed.

Preamble

The licenses for most software are designed to take away your freedom to share and change it. By contrast, the GNU General Public License is intended to guarantee your freedom to share and change free software — to make sure the software is free for all its users. This General Public License applies to most of the Free Software Foundation's software and to any other program whose authors commit to using it. (Some other Free Software Foundation software is covered by the GNU Library General Public License instead.) You can apply it to your programs, too.

When we speak of free software, we are referring to freedom, not price. Our General Public Licenses are designed to make sure that you have the freedom to distribute copies of free software (and charge for this service if you wish), that you receive source code or can get it if you want it, that you can change

---

[8] Author's note: as this is being written, a new version 3 of the GPL is being debated. It is not included here since its final form is not known and since many existing licenses rely on and will continue to rely on the earlier version reprinted here.

the software or use pieces of it in new free programs; and that you know you can do these things.

To protect your rights, we need to make restrictions that forbid anyone to deny you these rights or to ask you to surrender the rights. These restrictions translate to certain responsibilities for you if you distribute copies of the software, or if you modify it.

For example, if you distribute copies of such a program, whether gratis or for a fee, you must give the recipients all the rights that you have. You must make sure that they, too, receive or can get the source code. And you must show them these terms so they know their rights.

We protect your rights with two steps: (1) copyright the software, and (2) offer you this license which gives you legal permission to copy, distribute and/or modify the software.

Also, for each author's protection and ours, we want to make certain that everyone understands that there is no warranty for this free software. If the software is modified by someone else and passed on, we want its recipients to know that what they have is not the original, so that any problems introduced by others will not reflect on the original authors' reputations.

Finally, any free program is threatened constantly by software patents. We wish to avoid the danger that redistributors of a free program will individually obtain patent licenses, in effect making the program proprietary. To prevent this, we have made it clear that any patent must be licensed for everyone's free use or not licensed at all.

The precise terms and conditions for copying, distribution and modification follow.

TERMS AND CONDITIONS FOR COPYING, DISTRIBUTION AND MODIFICATION

0. This License applies to any program or other work which contains a notice placed by the copyright holder saying it may be distributed under the terms of this General Public License. The "Program", below, refers to any such program or work, and a "work based on the Program" means either the Program or any derivative work under copyright law: that is to say, a work containing the Program or a portion of it, either verbatim or with modifications and/or translated into another language. (Hereinafter, translation is included without limitation in the term "modification".) Each licensee is addressed as "you".

Activities other than copying, distribution and modification are not covered by this License; they are outside its scope. The act of running the Program is not restricted, and the output from the Program is covered only if its contents constitute a work based on the Program (independent of having been made by running the Program). Whether that is true depends on what the Program does.

1. You may copy and distribute verbatim copies of the Program's source code as you receive it, in any medium, provided that you conspicuously and appropriately publish on each copy an appropriate copyright notice and disclaimer

of warranty; keep intact all the notices that refer to this License and to the absence of any warranty; and give any other recipients of the Program a copy of this License along with the Program.

You may charge a fee for the physical act of transferring a copy, and you may at your option offer warranty protection in exchange for a fee.

2. You may modify your copy or copies of the Program or any portion of it, thus forming a work based on the Program, and copy and distribute such modifications or work under the terms of Section 1 above, provided that you also meet all of these conditions:

> a) You must cause the modified files to carry prominent notices stating that you changed the files and the date of any change.

> b) You must cause any work that you distribute or publish, that in whole or in part contains or is derived from the Program or any part thereof, to be licensed as a whole at no charge to all third parties under the terms of this License.

> c) If the modified program normally reads commands interactively when run, you must cause it, when started running for such interactive use in the most ordinary way, to print or display an announcement including an appropriate copyright notice and a notice that there is no warranty (or else, saying that you provide a warranty) and that users may redistribute the program under these conditions, and telling the user how to view a copy of this License. (Exception: if the Program itself is interactive but does not normally print such an announcement, your work based on the Program is not required to print an announcement.)

These requirements apply to the modified work as a whole. If identifiable sections of that work are not derived from the Program, and can be reasonably considered independent and separate works in themselves, then this License, and its terms, do not apply to those sections when you distribute them as separate works. But when you distribute the same sections as part of a whole which is a work based on the Program, the distribution of the whole must be on the terms of this License, whose permissions for other licensees extend to the entire whole, and thus to each and every part regardless of who wrote it.

Thus, it is not the intent of this section to claim rights or contest your rights to work written entirely by you; rather, the intent is to exercise the right to control the distribution of derivative or collective works based on the Program.

In addition, mere aggregation of another work not based on the Program with the Program (or with a work based on the Program) on a volume of a storage or distribution medium does not bring the other work under the scope of this License.

3. You may copy and distribute the Program (or a work based on it, under Section 2) in object code or executable form under the terms of Sections 1 and 2 above provided that you also do one of the following:

a) Accompany it with the complete corresponding machine-readable source code, which must be distributed under the terms of Sections 1 and 2 above on a medium customarily used for software interchange; or,

b) Accompany it with a written offer, valid for at least three years, to give any third party, for a charge no more than your cost of physically performing source distribution, a complete machine-readable copy of the corresponding source code, to be distributed under the terms of Sections 1 and 2 above on a medium customarily used for software interchange; or,

c) Accompany it with the information you received as to the offer to distribute corresponding source code. (This alternative is allowed only for noncommercial distribution and only if you received the program in object code or executable form with such an offer, in accord with Subsection b above.)

The source code for a work means the preferred form of the work for making modifications to it. For an executable work, complete source code means all the source code for all modules it contains, plus any associated interface definition files, plus the scripts used to control compilation and installation of the executable. However, as a special exception, the source code distributed need not include anything that is normally distributed (in either source or binary form) with the major components (compiler, kernel, and so on) of the operating system on which the executable runs, unless that component itself accompanies the executable.

If distribution of executable or object code is made by offering access to copy from a designated place, then offering equivalent access to copy the source code from the same place counts as distribution of the source code, even though third parties are not compelled to copy the source along with the object code.

4. You may not copy, modify, sublicense, or distribute the Program except as expressly provided under this License. Any attempt otherwise to copy, modify, sublicense or distribute the Program is void, and will automatically terminate your rights under this License. However, parties who have received copies, or rights, from you under this License will not have their licenses terminated so long as such parties remain in full compliance.

5. You are not required to accept this License, since you have not signed it. However, nothing else grants you permission to modify or distribute the Program or its derivative works. These actions are prohibited by law if you do not accept this License. Therefore, by modifying or distributing the Program (or any work based on the Program), you indicate your acceptance of this License to do so, and all its terms and conditions for copying, distributing or modifying the Program or works based on it.

6. Each time you redistribute the Program (or any work based on the Program), the recipient automatically receives a license from the original licensor to copy, distribute or modify the Program subject to these terms and conditions. You may not impose any further restrictions on the recipients'

exercise of the rights granted herein. You are not responsible for enforcing compliance by third parties to this License.

7. If, as a consequence of a court judgment or allegation of patent infringement or for any other reason (not limited to patent issues), conditions are imposed on you (whether by court order, agreement or otherwise) that contradict the conditions of this License, they do not excuse you from the conditions of this License. If you cannot distribute so as to satisfy simultaneously your obligations under this License and any other pertinent obligations, then as a consequence you may not distribute the Program at all. For example, if a patent license would not permit royalty-free redistribution of the Program by all those who receive copies directly or indirectly through you, then the only way you could satisfy both it and this License would be to refrain entirely from distribution of the Program.

If any portion of this section is held invalid or unenforceable under any particular circumstance, the balance of the section is intended to apply and the section as a whole is intended to apply in other circumstances.

It is not the purpose of this section to induce you to infringe any patents or other property right claims or to contest validity of any such claims; this section has the sole purpose of protecting the integrity of the free software distribution system, which is implemented by public license practices. Many people have made generous contributions to the wide range of software distributed through that system in reliance on consistent application of that system; it is up to the author/donor to decide if he or she is willing to distribute software through any other system and a licensee cannot impose that choice.

This section is intended to make thoroughly clear what is believed to be a consequence of the rest of this License.

8. If the distribution and/or use of the Program is restricted in certain countries either by patents or by copyrighted interfaces, the original copyright holder who places the Program under this License may add an explicit geographical distribution limitation excluding those countries, so that distribution is permitted only in or among countries not thus excluded. In such case, this License incorporates the limitation as if written in the body of this License.

9. The Free Software Foundation may publish revised and/or new versions of the General Public License from time to time. Such new versions will be similar in spirit to the present version, but may differ in detail to address new problems or concerns.

Each version is given a distinguishing version number. If the Program specifies a version number of this License which applies to it and "any later version", you have the option of following the terms and conditions either of that version or of any later version published by the Free Software Foundation. If the Program does not specify a version number of this License, you may choose any version ever published by the Free Software Foundation.

10. If you wish to incorporate parts of the Program into other free programs whose distribution conditions are different, write to the author to ask for permission. For software which is copyrighted by the Free Software Foundation,

write to the Free Software Foundation; we sometimes make exceptions for this. Our decision will be guided by the two goals of preserving the free status of all derivatives of our free software and of promoting the sharing and reuse of software generally.

NO WARRANTY

11. BECAUSE THE PROGRAM IS LICENSED FREE OF CHARGE, THERE IS NO WARRANTY FOR THE PROGRAM, TO THE EXTENT PERMITTED BY APPLICABLE LAW. EXCEPT WHEN OTHERWISE STATED IN WRITING THE COPYRIGHT HOLDERS AND/OR OTHER PARTIES PROVIDE THE PROGRAM "AS IS" WITHOUT WARRANTY OF ANY KIND, EITHER EXPRESSED OR IMPLIED, INCLUDING, BUT NOT LIMITED TO, THE IMPLIED WARRANTIES OF MERCHANTABILITY AND FITNESS FOR A PARTICULAR PURPOSE. THE ENTIRE RISK AS TO THE QUALITY AND PERFORMANCE OF THE PROGRAM IS WITH YOU. SHOULD THE PROGRAM PROVE DEFECTIVE, YOU ASSUME THE COST OF ALL NECESSARY SERVICING, REPAIR OR CORRECTION.

12. IN NO EVENT UNLESS REQUIRED BY APPLICABLE LAW OR AGREED TO IN WRITING WILL ANY COPYRIGHT HOLDER, OR ANY OTHER PARTY WHO MAY MODIFY AND/OR REDISTRIBUTE THE PROGRAM AS PERMITTED ABOVE, BE LIABLE TO YOU FOR DAMAGES, INCLUDING ANY GENERAL, SPECIAL, INCIDENTAL OR CONSEQUENTIAL DAMAGES ARISING OUT OF THE USE OR INABILITY TO USE THE PROGRAM (INCLUDING BUT NOT LIMITED TO LOSS OF DATA OR DATA BEING RENDERED INACCURATE OR LOSSES SUSTAINED BY YOU OR THIRD PARTIES OR A FAILURE OF THE PROGRAM TO OPERATE WITH ANY OTHER PROGRAMS), EVEN IF SUCH HOLDER OR OTHER PARTY HAS BEEN ADVISED OF THE POSSIBILITY OF SUCH DAMAGES.

NOTES

1. The GPL is the most often used FSOS license because of its association with the fee software movement and with the Linux operating system. It contains aggressive "copyleft" provisions — e.g., carrying forward of the terms of the GPL applicable to code that was not originally under GPL. Subsection 2(b) is an illustration: "You must cause any work that you distribute or publish, that in whole or in part contains or is derived from the Program or any part thereof, to be licensed as a whole at no charge to all third parties under the terms of this License." The GPL excludes coverage of mere aggregations of programs, but a risk is explicit for companies that use GPL code integrated with otherwise proprietary code. Does GPL require taking the other code "free"? What is the rationale for causing the license terms to extend out to other code? If a company merely links its software to code covered under GPL, is there a risk that it must comply with GPL when it distributes the combination?

2. Does GPL contemplate a contractual relationship? In considering this, review subsections 5 and 6. Can you describe what relationships are being

created there? Members of the FSOS community disagree on whether GPL contemplates a contract. The most vocal of those who argue that it does *not* is Eben Moglin, General Counsel of FSF. He has been quoted as saying:

> The word "license" has, and has had for hundreds of years, a specific technical meaning in the law of property. A license is a unilateral permission to use someone else's property. The traditional example given in the first-year law school Property course is an invitation to come to dinner at my house. If, when you cross my threshold, I sue you for trespass, you plead my "license," that is, my unilateral permission to enter on and use my property.
>
> A contract, on the other hand, is an exchange of obligations, either of promises for promises or of promises of future performance for present performance or payment. The idea that "licenses" to use patents or copyrights must be contracts is an artifact of twentieth-century practice, in which licensors offered an exchange of promises with users: "We will give you a copy of our copyrighted work," in essence, "if you pay us and promise to enter into certain obligations concerning the work." With respect to software, those obligations by users include promises not to decompile or reverse-engineer the software, and not to transfer the software.

Pamela Jones, *The GPL is a License, not a Contract*, http://lwn.net/articles/61292. *See* Eben Moglen, *Questioning SCO: A Hard Look at Nebulous Claims*, www. osdl.org/docs/eben_moglen_position_paper.pdf. Why is the issue important?

3. The status of a non-contractual notice under copyright or patent law is at best uncertain. For example, the Supreme Court decision in *Bobbs-Merril Company v. Straus*, 210 U.S. 339 (1908), which set out the first sale doctrine, held that non-contractual terms purporting to limit the rights of a purchaser of a copy were ineffective. A similar result was reached more recently in a patent case when the Federal Circuit held that mention of a single use restriction in the packaging of a camera did not become part of the contract and, thus, did not prevent an unconditional sale exhausting the patent. *Jazz Photo Corp. v. International Trade Commission*, 264 F.3d 1094 (Fed. Cir. 2001), *cert. denied*, 536 U.S. 950 (2002). On the other hand, even a buyer at a first sale does not obtain the right to make and distribute multiple copies.

4. Notice the treatment of patent infringement claims in subsection 7. How FSOS licenses can be adjusted to cope with patent rights is a significant issue. The GPL treatment is, at best, an incomplete treatment of a difficult topic.

PROBLEM 16.9

Client is contemplating use of two open source software elements as part of its overall software system. The overall system contains important code that Client considered to be a trade secret. One of the "open source" elements is governed by the GNU license while the other is governed by the BSD license. Determine what risks exist if it does so and how best to deal with those risks.

OPEN SOFTWARE LICENSE
v. 2.0

This Open Software License (the "License") applies to any original work of authorship (the "Original Work") whose owner (the "Licensor") has placed the following notice immediately following the copyright notice for the Original Work:

Licensed under the Open Software License version 2.0

1) **Grant of Copyright License.** Licensor hereby grants You a worldwide, royalty-free, non-exclusive, perpetual, sublicenseable license to do the following:

    a) to reproduce the Original Work in copies;

    b) to prepare derivative works ("Derivative Works") based upon the Original Work;

    c) to distribute copies of the Original Work and Derivative Works to the public, with the proviso that copies of Original Work or Derivative Works that You distribute shall be licensed under the Open Software License;

    d) to perform the Original Work publicly; and

    e) to display the Original Work publicly.

2) **Grant of Patent License.** Licensor hereby grants You a world-wide, royalty-free, non-exclusive, perpetual, sublicenseable license, under patent claims owned or controlled by the Licensor that are embodied in the Original Work as furnished by the Licensor, to make, use, sell and offer for sale the Original Work and Derivative Works.

3) **Grant of Source Code License.** The term "Source Code" means the preferred form of the Original Work for making modifications to it and all available documentation describing how to modify the Original Work. Licensor hereby agrees to provide a machine-readable copy of the Source Code of the Original Work along with each copy of the Original Work that Licensor distributes. Licensor reserves the right to satisfy this obligation by placing a machine-readable copy of the Source Code in an information repository reasonably calculated to permit inexpensive and convenient access by You for as long as Licensor continues to distribute the Original Work, and by publishing the address of that information repository in a notice immediately following the copyright notice that applies to the Original Work.

4) **Exclusions From License Grant.** Neither the names of Licensor, nor the names of any contributors to the Original Work, nor any of their trademarks or service marks, may be used to endorse or promote products derived from this Original Work without express prior written permission of the Licensor. Nothing in this License shall be deemed to grant any rights to trademarks, copyrights, patents, trade secrets or any other intellectual property of Licensor except as expressly stated herein. No patent license is granted to make, use, sell or offer to sell embodiments of any patent claims other than

the licensed claims defined in Section 2. No right is granted to the trademarks of Licensor even if such marks are included in the Original Work. Nothing in this License shall be interpreted to prohibit Licensor from licensing under different terms from this License any Original Work that Licensor otherwise would have a right to license.

5) **External Deployment.** The term "External Deployment" means the use or distribution of the Original Work or Derivative Works in any way such that the Original Work or Derivative Works may be used by anyone other than You, whether the Original Work or Derivative Works are distributed to those persons or made available as an application intended for use over a computer network. As an express condition for the grants of license hereunder, You agree that any External Deployment by You of a Derivative Work shall be deemed a distribution and shall be licensed to all under the terms of this License, as prescribed in section 1(c) herein.

6) **Attribution Rights.** You must retain, in the Source Code of any Derivative Works that You create, all copyright, patent or trademark notices from the Source Code of the Original Work, as well as any notices of licensing and any descriptive text identified therein as an "Attribution Notice." You must cause the Source Code for any Derivative Works that You create to carry a prominent Attribution Notice reasonably calculated to inform recipients that You have modified the Original Work.

7) **Warranty of Provenance and Disclaimer of Warranty.** Licensor warrants that the copyright in and to the Original Work and the patent rights granted herein by Licensor are owned by the Licensor or are sublicensed to You under the terms of this License with the permission of the contributor(s) of those copyrights and patent rights. Except as expressly stated in the immediately proceeding sentence, the Original Work is provided under this License on an "AS IS" BASIS and WITHOUT WARRANTY, either express or implied, including, without limitation, the warranties of NON-INFRINGEMENT, MERCHANTABILITY or FITNESS FOR A PARTICULAR PURPOSE. THE ENTIRE RISK AS TO THE QUALITY OF THE ORIGINAL WORK IS WITH YOU. This DISCLAIMER OF WARRANTY constitutes an essential part of this License. No license to Original Work is granted hereunder except under this disclaimer.

8) **Limitation of Liability.** Under no circumstances and under no legal theory, whether in tort (including negligence), contract, or otherwise, shall the Licensor be liable to any person for any direct, indirect, special, incidental, or consequential damages of any character arising as a result of this License or the use of the Original Work including, without limitation, damages for loss of goodwill, work stoppage, computer failure or malfunction, or any and all other commercial damages or losses. This limitation of liability shall not apply to liability for death or personal injury resulting from Licensor's negligence to the extent applicable law prohibits such limitation. Some jurisdictions do not allow the exclusion or limitation of incidental or consequential damages, so this exclusion and limitation may not apply to You.

9) **Acceptance and Termination.** If You distribute copies of the Original Work or a Derivative Work, You must make a reasonable effort under the

circumstances to obtain the express assent of recipients to the terms of this License. Nothing else but this License (or another written agreement between Licensor and You) grants You permission to create Derivative Works based upon the Original Work or to exercise any of the rights granted in Section 1 herein, and any attempt to do so except under the terms of this License (or another written agreement between Licensor and You) is expressly prohibited by U.S. copyright law, the equivalent laws of other countries, and by international treaty. Therefore, by exercising any of the rights granted to You in Section 1 herein, You indicate Your acceptance of this License and all of its terms and conditions. This License shall terminate immediately and you may no longer exercise any of the rights granted to You by this License upon Your failure to honor the proviso in Section 1(c) herein.

10) **Termination for Patent Action.** This License shall terminate automatically and You may no longer exercise any of the rights granted to You by this License as of the date You commence an action, including a cross-claim or counterclaim, for patent infringement (i) against Licensor with respect to a patent applicable to software or (ii) against any entity with respect to a patent applicable to the Original Work (but excluding combinations of the Original Work with other software or hardware).

11) **Jurisdiction, Venue and Governing Law.** Any action or suit relating to this License may be brought only in the courts of a jurisdiction wherein the Licensor resides or in which Licensor conducts its primary business, and under the laws of that jurisdiction excluding its conflict-of-law provisions. The application of the United Nations Convention on Contracts for the International Sale of Goods is expressly excluded. Any use of the Original Work outside the scope of this License or after its termination shall be subject to the requirements and penalties of the U.S. Copyright Act, 17 U.S.C. 101 et seq., the equivalent laws of other countries, and international treaty. This section shall survive the termination of this License.

12) **Attorneys Fees.** In any action to enforce the terms of this License or seeking damages relating thereto, the prevailing party shall be entitled to recover its costs and expenses, including, without limitation, reasonable attorneys' fees and costs incurred in connection with such action, including any appeal of such action. This section shall survive the termination of this License.

13) **Miscellaneous.** This License represents the complete agreement concerning the subject matter hereof. If any provision of this License is held to be unenforceable, such provision shall be reformed only to the extent necessary to make it enforceable.

14) **Definition of "You" in This License.** "You" throughout this License, whether in upper or lower case, means an individual or a legal entity exercising rights under, and complying with all of the terms of, this License. For legal entities, "You" includes any entity that controls, is controlled by, or is under common control with you. For purposes of this definition, "control" means (i) the power, direct or indirect, to cause the direction or management of such

entity, whether by contract or otherwise, or (ii) ownership of fifty percent (50%) or more of the outstanding shares, or (iii) beneficial ownership of such entity.

15) **Right to Use.** You may use the Original Work in all ways not otherwise restricted or conditioned by this License or by law, and Licensor promises not to interfere with or be responsible for such uses by You.

NOTES

1. The Open Software License (OSL) was written by Lawrence Rosen, General Counsel of OSI. It is a carefully articulated license template. Does OSL contemplate a contract?

2. OSL deals with patent claim issues in paragraph 2 and paragraph 10. In 2004, version 2.1 of OSL was proposed. The primary change was a revision of clause 10. The new wording reads:

> 10. Termination for Patent Action. This License shall terminate automatically and You may no longer exercise any of the rights granted to You by this License as of the date You commence an action, including a cross-claim or counterclaim, against Licensor or any licensee alleging that the Original Work infringes a patent. This termination provision shall not apply for an action alleging patent infringement by combinations of the Original Work with other software or hardware.

To understand the change, consider the scope of the original language regarding patent infringement suits. Are the conditions for termination limited to lawsuits related to the open source software?

PROBLEM 16.10

Tracer Corporation obtains software from AAA Software. It pays $50.00 for a copy of the software and agrees to a one year maintenance agreement with AAA. The software contains the OSL license, identifying AAA as the author of the code. Consider the following:

a. Tracer incorporates the code into its primary product and begins distributing it. Tracer, however, has become embroiled in an argument with AAA, which threatens to withdraw the license. What are Tracer's rights?

b. Before incorporating the code into its product, Tracer makes significant modifications of it. When Tracer distributes the revised software, it requires a transferee to agree to license terms that preclude disclosure of the code and prohibit further modification of the code. AAA sues for infringement. What result? Can AAA withdraw the license?

Chapter 17

SELECTED ISSUES IN ONLINE LICENSING

I. NATURE OF THE RELATIONSHIP

This chapter deals with online transactions involving information assets and systems. The importance of the topic, of course, comes from the advent of the Internet as a major venue for transactions. We have seen some online issues elsewhere in this book, but we focus here on several issues we have not previously considered.

While digital information can be obtained online under a number of different relationships, these can be grouped into three categories:

- Transactions in which information is available without contractual terms, subject only to intellectual property law restrictions on its use and further dissemination.

- Transactions in which contractual terms are set out with respect to specific information (or products) acquired from an online source (*see, e.g., Specht v. Netscape Communications Corporation,* 306 F.3d 17 (2d Cir. 2002), discussed in Chapter 2).

- Transactions in which contractual terms are set out with respect to access to the online site, which terms may also carry over to information or other products obtained from the site (*see, e.g., Register.com, Inc. v. Verio, Inc.,* 356 F.3d 393 (2d Cir. 2004)).

We are concerned in this chapter primarily with the second and third relationships, and especially the third. This latter type of transaction involves an "access contract" in which, while there may be a license of intellectual property, the predominant feature lies in a license to "access" or "use" the online site and materials in it. This is a license in a classical sense — a conditional permission to use the property of the licensor. *See* RAYMOND T. NIMMER & HOLLY K. TOWLE, THE LAW OF ELECTRONIC COMMERCIAL TRANSACTIONS ch. 10 (2007).

Access contracts often deal with issues very different from those in intellectual property ordinary licensing. For example:

- The contract defines the range of permissible behavior at the site *and* a licensor's right to exclude information or conduct from the site.

- The contract often deals with issues of data privacy, because persons who access a site may leave behind traces of their use.

- The contract often deals with what uses the licensee can make of information after it is obtained from the site.

A distinction may exist between the terms of access (or terms of use) and terms involved in any purchase (license or otherwise) of material available from the site. For example, in *Evans v. Matlock*, 2002 Tenn. App. LEXIS 906, No. M2001-02631-COA-R9-CV (Tenn. Ct. App. 2002), the issue was whether an arbitration clause in the e-Bay user agreement (access contract) applied to a dispute arising between the buyer and seller in an auction that occurred on the e-Bay system. The court held that the arbitration provision did not apply to the sale:

> While arbitration, as contrasted to litigation, is the favored method of resolving disputes, consent of the parties to arbitrate is required, and arbitration agreements rest upon the same legal footing as other contracts. Parties cannot be forced to arbitrate claims that they did not agree to arbitrate. We agree with the trial court that the arbitration clause is applicable only to controversies between e-Bay and the user and not to controversies between users. The Agreement provides that e-Bay is only a venue, and that "we are not involved in the actual transaction between buyers and sellers" and "cannot ensure that a buyer or seller will actually complete a transaction." The Arbitration Clause provides that arbitration shall be conducted in San Jose, California, and "either *you or e-Bay* may seek any interim or preliminary relief from a court of competent jurisdiction in San Jose, California . . . pending the completion of arbitration." [We] believe the Agreement is plain and unambiguous, and enforceable according to its terms.

Many access contracts involve an ongoing relationship between the licensee and the licensor with respect to the site or services. This presents at least two issues. First, under what circumstances and with what regularity must access be available? Second, as commercial and regulatory circumstances change, how can the relationship be adjusted to reflect the changes? The answers are complicated by the fact that the technology allows for thousands, if not millions of contractual relationships, handled on an automated, rather than individualized basis.

MATHIAS v. AMERICA ONLINE, INC.
2002 Ohio 814; 2002 Ohio App. LEXIS 876 (Ohio App. 2002)

PATTON, J.

Appellants, a group of eleven individual plaintiffs, appeal the trial court's decision to grant defendant, America Online, Inc.'s ("AOL") motion for summary judgment. [We affirm.]

In December 1996, appellants all subscribed to AOL. At the time, each of the appellants had been paying a monthly fee to AOL for access to the Internet and other services. The monthly fee was calculated at a rate of $9.95 per month for five hours of use, with an additional $2.95 for each additional hour. During December, AOL launched a new rate program which offered all existing and new subscribers a flat monthly rate of $19.95 for unlimited hourly use. In a December 1996 announcement, AOL presented the new monthly flat rate and stated that if subscribers accepted the offer "you can stay online as long as you want." The announcement also noted that "we do expect the sudden increase in use . . . to create some temporary 'traffic congestion.'"

AOL posted a second notice about its new flat rate offer. In the posting, dated December 2, 1996, AOL stated, in part,

GEARING UP FOR GROWTH

When we made the decision to switch to unlimited pricing, we knew demand would skyrocket. Rolling out the new pricing in December would create even higher usage, we realized, because December and January are normally among our busiest months. But we knew that many of you had been waiting patiently for a long time for a flat rate, and we didn't want you to have to wait any longer, so we made the decision to launch the unlimited pricing as soon as we could, which meant rolling it out this month. . . .

Although we have been making tremendous strides in ramping up our system capacity, *we do expect some bumps in the road over the next couple months, as we race to keep up with the demand. As a result, there is a good chance that you will experience problems from time to time, especially during our peak evening hours.* . . . We will certainly try to keep these *"traffic congestion"* problems to a minimum. . . .

We expect most of the *traffic congestion* to occur in our "prime time," which typically runs from about 8 p.m. until Midnight. That's when we experience the greatest demand, as more of our members are typically online. So, when possible, *I encourage you to sign on to AOL during other times of the day when the service is not as busy.* (Emphasis added).

Persons interested in taking advantage of the flat-rate offer were told "you must agree to AOL's Terms of Service (TOS) and Rules of the Road (ROR) which detail the terms of your AOL membership. You agree to read the TOS and the ROR which you can do now by clicking the Read Now button below." It is undisputed that each of the appellants clicked the button to read the TOS and that the entire document was posted for viewing.

The TOS contains ten separate paragraphs detailing all of the applicable terms of AOL's service agreement. In relevant part, the TOS provides:

3. . . . AOL Inc. reserves the right to change its fees and billing methods at any time effective thirty (30) days after an online posting in the billing area of the AOL Service (Keyword: Billing). If any such change is unacceptable to you, you may terminate your Membership as provided in Section 9 below. Your continued use of AOL following the effective date shall be deemed acceptance of such change.

. . . .

7. NO WARRANTY. MEMBER EXPRESSLY AGREES THAT USE OF AOL, AOL SOFTWARE, AOL'S EMAIL SERVICES AND IS AT MEMBERS SOLE RISK. AOL, AOLS EMAIL SERVICES AND AOL SOFTWARE ARE PROVIDED ON AN "AS IS," "AS AVAILABLE" BASIS WITHOUT WARRANTIES OF ANY KIND, EITHER EXPRESS OR IMPLIED, UNLESS SUCH WARRANTIES ARE LEGALLY

INCAPABLE OF EXCLUSION. AOL INC.'S ENTIRE LIABILITY AND YOUR EXCLUSIVE REMEDY WITH RESPECT TO USE OF AOL AND AOL SOFTWARE SHALL BE THE REPLACEMENT OF ANY DISKETTE FOUND TO BE DEFECTIVE. AOL INC.'S LIABILITY TO YOU FOR BREACH OF THIS AGREEMENT IS LIMITED SOLELY TO THE AMOUNT PAID BY YOU TO ACCESS AND USE AOL. BECAUSE SOME STATES DO NOT ALLOW THE EXCLUSION OR LIMITATION OF LIABILITY FOR CONSEQUENTIAL OR INCIDENTAL DAMAGES, IN SUCH STATES AOL INC.'S LIABILITY IS LIMITED TO THE EXTENT PERMITTED BY LAW.

. . . .

9. Termination. Either Member or AOL Inc. may terminate membership at any time. Members only right and sole remedy with respect to any dissatisfaction with any (i) TOS term, or policy or practice of AOL in operating AOL, (ii) Content available through AOL or change therein, or (iii) amount or type of fees or billing methods, or change therein, is to terminate Membership by delivering notice to AOL Inc.

At some unspecified time after they accepted the $19.95 rate, appellants began experiencing access problems. The record, however, is devoid of specific evidence indicating who experienced what type of problems, how often the problems occurred, or how long they continued. Generally, appellants claim that the most typical problems included busy signals when trying to log-on or being knocked off the system after they had gained access.

On November 25, 1998, appellants filed a complaint against the company. [The] record supports the fact that after each of the appellants accepted the flat rate of $19.95, they continued to use and pay for AOL on a monthly basis. AOL moved for summary judgment and asked for the case to be dismissed because appellants received exactly what AOL agreed to provide in the TOS. The trial court agreed and granted AOL summary judgment. . . . [We affirm.]

If a contract is clear and unambiguous, then its interpretation is a matter of law and there is no issue of fact to be determined. In the case at bar, the TOS includes key terms that appellants, not AOL, ignored. The TOS is clear, on its face, that AOL "reserve[d] the right to change its fees" and that if any such change was unacceptable to members they could terminate their membership "at any time." Moreover, the contract is unambiguous that "continued use of AOL following the effective date [of any change] shall be deemed acceptance of such change." The TOS is also straightforward that no warranty accompanies the service contract and that members accept services at their "sole risk" and on an "'AS IS,' 'AS AVAILABLE' BASIS." The TOS further provides an express limitation of AOL's potential liability to members where it states, in pertinent part:

AOL INC.'S ENTIRE LIABILITY AND YOUR EXCLUSIVE REMEDY WITH RESPECT TO USE OF AOL AND AOL SOFTWARE SHALL BE THE REPLACEMENT OF ANY DISKETTE FOUND TO BE DEFECTIVE. AOL INC.'S LIABILITY TO YOU FOR BREACH OF THIS AGREEMENT IS LIMITED SOLELY TO THE AMOUNT PAID BY YOU TO ACCESS AND USE AOL.

The TOS is unambiguous as to the mutual obligations between the parties. The uncontroverted evidence proves that it is appellants who failed to avail themselves of their available remedies, not that AOL denied them anything. Appellants continued to use and pay for AOL services. AOL cannot be held to have breached the TOS because, immediately upon accepting the new $19.95 monthly rate, members acknowledged that services would be provided on an availability basis.

Appellants not only signed on at their own risk but continued to use AOL's services on that same basis. Appellants admit that the gravamen of their complaint with AOL is the fact that they were inconvenienced by busy signals when trying to log-on or that they were bumped off the system once connected.

Beyond inconvenience, however, appellants fail to specify what damages they suffered. The record shows that appellants remained members even after they began experiencing problems. Appellants' conduct shows that they assented to all of the terms set forth in the TOS. As a matter of law, AOL was entitled to summary judgment because appellants received the full benefit of their bargain under the TOS. Accordingly, appellants are estopped from claiming any breach of contract by AOL or that they suffered damages.

Next, appellants argue that the trial court erred in granting summary judgment on their claims for fraud, negligent misrepresentation and violation of the Consumer Sales Practices Act. . . . In the case at bar, appellants allege that AOL made two false claims before and after they signed on to the TOS; it "offered a service it knew it could not provide" and it was making continual "attempts to fix" access difficulties. Other than these two claims, appellants present only generalized comments about AOL's purported dissemination of false information. . . . We turn now to the two specific representations appellants allege were false when made by AOL.

Appellants contend that AOL's use of the phrase "unlimited use" is interchangeable with the phrase "unrestricted access" and that AOL did not provide what it offered and knew it could not do so at any time. Neither the record nor any reasonable understanding of the phrase "unlimited use," however, support such a claim. This is especially true in light of the express warnings about access availability AOL provided before and after appellants accepted the offer. AOL never said members would have instant, unfettered, and uninterrupted access to its online services. We cannot ignore the uncontroverted fact that, in response to appellees' motions for summary judgment, appellants produced nothing to challenge the evidence of their own knowledge about AOL's definition of "unlimited use," that is, as member usage increased, so would access difficulty increase. AOL never equated "unlimited use" with "unrestricted access" and appellants have offered no evidence to show otherwise.

The record shows that, during the entire time AOL offered its new pricing package, it never stated that members' access would be completely without difficulty. The evidence shows that on several occasions, especially in the two documents we find most crucial,[1] AOL warned that it anticipated increased usage and, therefore, an increase in access problems. AOL's repeated access

---

[1] [FN 4] The December 2, 1996 posting and the TOS.

warnings were available to members, including appellants, before and after they "clicked the button" to activate the new flat-rate offer.

Further, after accepting the flat rate offer, appellants continued to use and pay for services from AOL, thus contradicting any credible claim that AOL's attempts to address the very difficulties it had warned members about were not accomplished. Because there is no evidence indicating otherwise, we must conclude that, by their conduct, appellants continually assented to the manner in which AOL provided services to them. Appellants' actions extinguish any reasonable claim for damages by them.

We find, therefore, that appellants have not presented sufficient evidence to meet any one, let alone all, of the elements necessary to satisfy a prima facie case for fraud, negligent misrepresentation or a violation of the Consumer Sales Practices Act by AOL either before or after they accepted, continued to use and pay for services from AOL. . . . The judgment of the trial court is affirmed.

NOTES

1. *Mathias* recognizes the right contractually to establish procedures for changes in the terms of an ongoing relationship. The ability to change terms can be important, especially given the rapidly changing legal and economic environment in which online services operate. But it may also create issues about assent and notice for users of the system. Arguably, standards of good faith and prohibitions against deceptive trade practices may require some notice of changed terms. In an online environment, how should notice of a change be given? Is posting on an accessible web page sufficient?

2. Traditional common law required consideration for an enforceable modification of a contract. Consideration could not be a promise to continue doing what a party was already obligated to do. What is the consideration for agreed changes in circumstances like that in *Mathias*? In *Boomer v. AT&T Corp.*, 309 F.3d 404, 415 (7th Cir. 2002), the court dealt a change in a telephone service contract to add an arbitration clause. It commented:

> Boomer further challenges the existence of a contract by arguing that there was no consideration for the CSA. . . . This argument is misplaced — in exchange for his agreement to arbitrate, AT&T agreed to provide continued telephone services. It is true that when there is an existing contractual obligation, a promise to continue performing that legal obligation lacks consideration. But AT&T had no legal obligation to continue providing Boomer with telephone services. Therefore, Boomer received something of legal value — continued service — In exchange for his promise to arbitrate.

UCC Article 2 rejects the common law rule and allows modifications contract to be enforceable without new consideration, although the comments and a few cases suggest that the modifications must be in good faith. UCC § 2-209 (1998 Official Text).

3. Was the change in *Mathias* a modification requiring agreement? Consider UCC § 2-311, which contemplates a procedure under which later specification of terms can be reserved to one party and made part of the contract without a need for a new agreement (modification):

> An agreement . . . which is otherwise sufficiently definite . . . to be a contract is not made invalid by the fact that it leaves particulars of performance to be specified by one of the parties. Any such specification must be made in good faith and within limits set by commercial reasonableness.

UCC § 2-311(a) (1998 Official Text). *See also* UCITA § 305 (2000 Official Text). Is this an appropriate framework for online services?

4. How should the licensor's obligation in an ongoing access contract be measured? UCITA § 611 suggests:

> (a) If an access contract provides for access over a period of time, the following rules apply:

>> (1) The licensee's rights of access are to the information as modified and made commercially available by the licensor from time to time during that period.

>> (2) A change in the content of the information is a breach of contract only if the change conflicts with an express term of the agreement.

>> (3) Unless it is subject to a contractual use term, information obtained by the licensee is free of any use restriction other than a restriction resulting from the informational rights of another person or other law.

>> (4) Access must be available:

>>> (A) at times and in a manner conforming to the express terms of the agreement; and

>>> (B) to the extent not expressly stated in the agreement, at times and in a manner reasonable for the particular type of contract in light of the ordinary standards of the business, trade, or industry.

PROBLEM 17.1

Client operates an online site that provides a forum for fantasy sports leagues for a fee. Draft terms for the contract that allow Client to adjust terms as the need arises, but that do not take undue advantage of users of the site.

II. ACCESS AND INFORMATION PLACED ON A SITE

The following language is from an online site operated by the Walt Disney Company as the site existed in 2002:

> By uploading materials to any Forum or submitting any materials to us, you automatically grant (or warrant that the owner of such materials expressly granted) us a perpetual, royalty-free, irrevocable, nonexclusive right and license to use, reproduce, modify, adapt,

publish, translate, publicly perform and display, create derivative works from and distribute such materials or incorporate such materials into any form, medium, or technology now known or later developed throughout the universe. In addition, you warrant that all so-called "moral rights" in those materials have been waived. . . .

[Our] long-standing company policy does not allow us to accept or consider creative ideas, suggestions, or materials other than those that we have specifically requested. We hope you will understand that it is the intent of this policy to avoid the possibility of future misunderstandings when projects developed by our professional staff might seem to others to be similar to their own creative work. Please do not send us any unsolicited original creative materials such as stories or ideas, screenplays, or original artwork. . . .

If, at our request, you send certain specific submissions (e.g., postings to chat boards, or contests) or, despite our request, you send us creative suggestions, ideas, notes, drawings, concepts, or other information (collectively, the "Submissions"), the Submissions shall be deemed, and shall remain, our property. [We] shall exclusively own all now-known or hereafter existing rights to the Submissions of every kind and nature throughout the universe and shall be entitled to unrestricted use of the Submissions for any purpose whatsoever, commercial or otherwise, without compensation to the provider of the Submissions.[2]

Terms of service or use should reflect issues important to the parties. What concerns do these contractual terms address for Disney? Although the foregoing language comes from one particular site, language such as this is common in the online world. It points to the fact that online licensing often involves an interactive exchange of information, rather than simply making information or rights available to the licensee.

A. Access, Contract Terms, and Trespass

Online licenses contractually permit a licensee to enter and use an online system owned or controlled by the licensor. The property law basis for this relationship comes from a number of different bodies of law, but many concern the simple right to control one's own property

eBAY v. BIDDER'S EDGE
100 F. Supp. 2d 1058 (N.D. Cal. 2000)

WHYTE, DISTRICT JUDGE.

I. BACKGROUND

eBay is an Internet-based, person-to-person trading site. eBay offers sellers the ability to list items for sale and prospective buyers the ability to search those listings and bid on items. The seller can set the terms and conditions of

[2] Walt Disney Internet Group (WDIG) Terms of Service, (http://disney.go.com/legal/conditions_of_use.html) (visited 9/21/02).

the auction. The item is sold to the highest bidder. The transaction is consummated directly between the buyer and seller without eBay's involvement. A potential purchaser looking for a particular item can access the eBay site and perform a key word search for relevant auctions and bidding status. eBay has also created category listings that identify items in over 2500 categories, such as antiques, computers, and dolls. Users may browse these category listing pages to identify items of interest.

Users of the eBay site must register and agree to the eBay User Agreement. Users agree to the seven page User Agreement by clicking on an "I Accept" button located at the end of the User Agreement. The current version of the User Agreement prohibits the use of "any robot, spider, other automatic device, or manual process to monitor or copy our web pages or the content contained herein without our prior expressed written permission." It is not clear that the version of the User Agreement in effect at the time BE began searching the eBay site prohibited such activity, or that BE ever agreed to comply with the User Agreement.

eBay currently has over 7 million registered users. Over 400,000 new items are added to the site every day. Every minute, 600 bids are placed on almost 3 million items. Users currently perform, on average, 10 million searches per day on eBay's database. Bidding for and sales of items are continuously ongoing in millions of separate auctions.

A software robot is a computer program which operates across the Internet to perform searching, copying and retrieving functions on the web sites of others. A software robot is capable of executing thousands of instructions per minute, far in excess of what a human can accomplish. Robots consume the processing and storage resources of a system, making that portion of the system's capacity unavailable to the system owner or other users. Consumption of sufficient system resources will slow the processing of the overall system and can overload the system such that it will malfunction or "crash." . . .

The eBay site employs "robot exclusion headers." A robot exclusion header is a message, sent to computers programmed to detect and respond to such headers, that eBay does not permit unauthorized robotic activity. Programmers who wish to comply with the Robot Exclusion Standard design their robots to read a particular data file, "robots.txt," and to comply with the control directives it contains.

To enable computers to communicate with each other over the Internet, each is assigned a unique Internet Protocol ("IP") address. . . . Once eBay identifies an IP address believed to be involved in robotic activity, an investigation into the identity, origin and owner of the IP address may be made in order to determine if the activity is legitimate or authorized. If an investigation reveals unauthorized robotic activity, eBay may attempt to ignore ("block") any further requests from that IP address. Attempts to block requests from particular IP addresses are not always successful. . . .

BE . . . does not host auctions. BE is an auction aggregation site designed to offer on-line auction buyers the ability to search for items across numerous on-line auctions without having to search each host site individually. As of March 2000, the BE web site contained information on more than five million items being auctioned on more than one hundred auction sites. BE also provides its users with additional auction-related services and information. The information available on the BE site is contained in a database of information that BE compiles through access to various auction sites such as eBay. . . . It is important to include information regarding eBay auctions on the BE site because eBay is by far the biggest consumer to consumer on-line auction site.

On June 16, 1997, over a year before the BE web site debuted, Peter Leeds wrote an email in response to an email from Kimbo Mundy, co-founder of BE. Mundy's email said, "I think the magazines may be overrating sites' ability to block. The early agent experiments, like Arthur Anderson's *BargainFinder* were careful to check the robots.txt file on every site and desist if asked." (*Id.*). Mundy wrote back: "I believe well-behaved robots are still expected to check the robots.txt file. . . . Our other concern was also legal. It is one thing for customers to use a tool to check a site and quite another for a single commercial enterprise to do so on a repeated basis and then to distribute that information for profit."

In early 1998, eBay gave BE permission to include information regarding eBay-hosted auctions for Beanie Babies and Furbies in the BE database. . . . On April 24, 1999, eBay verbally approved BE crawling the eBay web site for a period of 90 days. The parties contemplated that during this period they would reach a formal licensing agreement. They were unable to do so. It appears that the primary dispute was over the method BE uses to search the eBay database. . . .

Approximately 69% of the auction items contained in the BE database are from auctions hosted on eBay. . . . The parties agree that BE accessed the eBay site approximate 100,000 times a day. eBay alleges that BE activity constituted up to 1.53% of the number of requests received by eBay, and up to 1.10% of the total data transferred by eBay during certain periods in October and November of 1999. BE alleges that BE activity constituted no more than 1.11% of the requests received by eBay, and no more than 0.70% of the data transferred by eBay. . . . eBay now moves for preliminary injunctive relief preventing BE from accessing the eBay computer system. . . .

ANALYSIS

A. Balance of Harm

eBay asserts that it will suffer four types of irreparable harm if preliminary injunctive relief is not granted: (1) lost capacity of its computer systems resulting from to BE's use of automated agents; (2) damage to eBay's reputation and goodwill caused by BE's misleading postings; (3) dilution of the eBay mark; and (4) BE's unjust enrichment. The harm eBay alleges it will suffer can be divided into two categories. The first type of harm is harm that eBay alleges it will suffer as a result of BE's automated query programs burdening eBay's computer system ("system harm"). The second type of harm is harm that eBay alleges it will suffer as a result of BE's misrepresentations regarding the information that BE obtains through the use of these automated query programs ("reputational harm").

eBay does not seek an injunction that is tailored to independently address the manner in which BE uses the information it obtains from eBay. Even without accessing eBay's computer systems by robot, BE could inflict reputational harm by misrepresenting the contents of eBay's auction database or by misusing eBay's trademark. . . . Since eBay does not move independently or alternatively for injunctive relief tailored toward the alleged reputational harm, the court does not include the alleged reputational harm in the balance of harm analysis. . . .

. . . eBay alleges both economic loss from BE's current activities and potential harm resulting from the total crawling of BE and others. In alleging economic harm, eBay's argument is that eBay has expended considerable time, effort and money to create its computer system, and that BE should have to pay for the portion of eBay's system BE uses. eBay attributes a pro rata portion of the costs of maintaining its entire system to the BE activity. However, eBay does not indicate that these expenses are incrementally incurred because of BE's activities, nor that any particular service disruption can be attributed to BE's activities. eBay provides no support for the proposition that the pro rata costs of obtaining an item represent the appropriate measure of damages for unauthorized use. In contrast, California law appears settled that the appropriate measure of damages is the actual harm inflicted by the conduct:

> Where the conduct complained of does not amount to a substantial interference with possession or the right thereto, but consists of intermeddling with or use of or damages to the personal property, the owner has a cause of action for trespass or case, and may recover only the actual damages suffered by reason of the impairment of the property or the loss of its use.

Zaslow v. Kroenert, 29 Cal.2d 541, 551, 176 P.2d 1 (1946). Moreover, even if BE is inflicting incremental maintenance costs on eBay, potentially calculable monetary damages are not generally a proper foundation for a preliminary injunction. . . .

eBay's allegations of harm are based, in part, on the argument that BE's activities should be thought of as equivalent to sending in an army of 100,000 robots a day to check the prices in a competitor's store. This analogy, while graphic, appears inappropriate. Although an admittedly formalistic distinction, unauthorized robot intruders into a "brick and mortar" store would be committing a trespass to real property. There does not appear to be any doubt that the appropriate remedy for an ongoing trespass to business premises would be a preliminary injunction. More importantly, for the analogy to be accurate, the robots would have to make up less than two out of every one-hundred customers in the store, the robots would not interfere with the customers' shopping experience, nor would the robots even be seen by the customers. Under such circumstances, there is a legitimate claim that the robots would not pose any threat of irreparable harm. However, eBay's right to injunctive relief is also based upon a much stronger argument.

If BE's activity is allowed to continue unchecked, it would encourage other auction aggregators to engage in similar recursive searching of the eBay system such that eBay would suffer irreparable harm from reduced system performance, system unavailability, or data losses. BE does not appear to seriously contest that reduced system performance, system unavailability or data loss would inflict irreparable harm on eBay consisting of lost profits and lost customer goodwill. Harm resulting from lost profits and lost customer goodwill is irreparable because it is neither easily calculable, nor easily compensable and is therefore an appropriate basis for injunctive relief. Where, as here, the denial of preliminary injunctive relief would encourage an increase in the complained of activity, and such an increase would present a strong likelihood of irreparable harm, the plaintiff has at least established a possibility of irreparable harm.

In the patent infringement context, the Federal Circuit has held that a preliminary injunction may be based, at least in part, on the harm that would occur if a preliminary injunction were denied and infringers were thereby encouraged to infringe a patent during the course of the litigation. In the absence of preliminary injunctive relief, "infringers could become compulsory licensees for as long as the litigation lasts." The Federal Circuit's reasoning is persuasive. "The very nature of the patent right is the right to exclude others. . . . We hold that where validity and continuing infringement have been clearly established, as in this case, immediate irreparable harm is presumed. To hold otherwise would be contrary to the public policy underlying the patent laws." Similarly fundamental to the concept of ownership of personal property is the right to exclude others. If preliminary injunctive relief against an ongoing trespass to chattels were unavailable, a trespasser could take a compulsory license to use another's personal property for as long as the trespasser could perpetuate the litigation.

BE correctly observes that there is a dearth of authority supporting a preliminary injunction based on an ongoing trespass to chattels. In contrast, it is black letter law in California that an injunction is an appropriate remedy for a continuing trespass to real property. If eBay were a brick and mortar auction house with limited seating capacity, eBay would appear to be entitled to reserve those seats for potential bidders, to refuse entrance to individuals (or robots) with no intention of bidding on any of the items, and to seek preliminary injunctive relief against non-customer trespassers eBay was physically unable to exclude. The analytic difficulty is that a wrongdoer can commit an ongoing trespass of a computer system that is more akin to the traditional notion of a trespass to real property, than the traditional notion of a trespass to chattels, because even though it is ongoing, it will probably never amount to a conversion. The court concludes that under the circumstances present here, BE's ongoing violation of eBay's fundamental property right to exclude others from its computer system potentially causes sufficient irreparable harm to support a preliminary injunction.

BE argues that even if eBay is entitled to a presumption of irreparable harm, the presumption may be rebutted. The presumption may be rebutted by evidence that a party has engaged in a pattern of granting licenses to engage in the complained of activity such that it may be reasonable to expect that invasion of the right can be recompensed with a royalty rather than with an injunction, or by evidence that a party has unduly delayed in bringing suit, thereby negating the idea of irreparability. BE alleges that eBay has both engaged in a pattern of licensing aggregators to crawl its site as well as delayed in seeking relief. For the reasons set forth below, the court finds that neither eBay's limited licensing activities nor its delay in seeking injunctive relief while it attempted to resolve the matter without judicial intervention are sufficient to rebut the possibility of irreparable harm.

If eBay's irreparable harm claim were premised solely on the potential harm caused by BE's current crawling activities, evidence that eBay had licensed others to crawl the eBay site would suggest that BE's activity would not result in irreparable harm to eBay. However, the gravamen of the alleged irreparable harm is that if BE is allowed to continue to crawl the eBay site, it may encourage frequent and unregulated crawling to the point that eBay's system will be irreparably harmed. There is no evidence that eBay has indiscriminately licensed all comers. Rather, it appears that eBay has carefully chosen to permit crawling by a limited number of aggregation sites that agree to abide by the terms of eBay's licensing agreement. "The existence of such a [limited] license, unlike a general license offered to all comers, does not demonstrate a decision to relinquish all control over the distribution of the product in exchange for a readily computable fee." eBay's licensing activities appear directed toward limiting the amount and nature of crawling activity on the eBay site. Such licensing does not support the inference that carte blanche crawling of the eBay site would pose no threat of irreparable harm. . . .

BE argues that even if eBay will be irreparably harmed if a preliminary injunction is not granted, BE will suffer greater irreparable harm if an injunction is granted. According to BE, lack of access to eBay's database will result in a two-thirds decrease in the items listed on BE, and an one-eighth reduction in the value of BE, from $80 million to $70 million. Although the potential harm to BE does not appear insignificant, BE does not appear to have suffered any irreparable harm during the period it voluntarily ceased crawling the eBay site. Barring BE from automatically querying eBay's site does not prevent BE from maintaining an aggregation site including information from eBay's site. Any potential economic harm is appropriately addressed through the posting of an adequate bond. . . .

B. Likelihood of Success

1. Trespass

Trespass to chattels "lies where an intentional interference with the possession of personal property has proximately cause injury." *Thrifty-Tel v. Bezenek,* 46 Cal.App.4th 1559, 1566, 54 Cal.Rptr.2d 468 (1996). Trespass to chattels "although seldom employed as a tort theory in California" was recently applied to cover the unauthorized use of long distance telephone lines. Specifically, the court noted "the electronic signals generated by the [defendants'] activities were sufficiently tangible to support a trespass cause of action." Thus, it appears likely that the electronic signals sent by BE to retrieve information from eBay's computer system are also sufficiently tangible to support a trespass cause of action.

In order to prevail on a claim for trespass based on accessing a computer system, the plaintiff must establish: (1) defendant intentionally and without authorization interfered with plaintiff's possessory interest in the computer system; and (2) defendant's unauthorized use proximately resulted in damage to plaintiff. Here, eBay has presented evidence sufficient to establish a strong likelihood of proving both prongs and ultimately prevailing on the merits of its trespass claim.

a. BE's Unauthorized Interference

eBay argues that BE's use was unauthorized and intentional. eBay is correct. BE does not dispute that it employed an automated computer program to connect with and search eBay's electronic database. BE admits that, because other auction aggregators were including eBay's auctions in their listing, it continued to "crawl" eBay's web site even after eBay demanded BE terminate such activity.

BE argues that it cannot trespass eBay's web site because the site is publicly accessible. BE's argument is unconvincing. eBay's servers are private property, conditional access to which eBay grants the public. eBay does not generally permit the type of automated access made by BE. In fact, eBay explicitly notifies automated visitors that their access is not permitted. "In general, California does recognize a trespass claim where the defendant exceeds the scope of the consent."

Even if BE's web crawlers were authorized to make individual queries of eBay's system, BE's web crawlers exceeded the scope of any such consent when they began acting like robots by making repeated queries. *See City of Amsterdam v. Daniel Goldreyer, Ltd.*, 882 F.Supp. 1273, 1281 (E.D.N.Y.1995) ("One who uses a chattel with the consent of another is subject to liability in trespass for any harm to the chattel which is caused by or occurs in the course of any use exceeding the consent, even though such use is not a conversion."). Moreover, eBay repeatedly and explicitly notified BE that its use of eBay's computer system was unauthorized. The entire reason BE directed its queries through proxy servers was to evade eBay's attempts to stop this unauthorized access. The court concludes that BE's activity is sufficiently outside of the scope of the use permitted by eBay that it is unauthorized for the purposes of establishing a trespass. *See Civic Western Corp. v. Zila Industries, Inc.*, 66 Cal.App.3d 1, 17, 135 Cal. Rptr. 915 (1977) ("It seems clear, however, that a trespass may occur if the party, entering pursuant to a limited consent, . . . proceeds to exceed those limits . . .") (discussing trespass to real property).

eBay argues that BE interfered with eBay's possessory interest in its computer system. Although eBay appears unlikely to be able to show a substantial interference at this time, such a showing is not required. Conduct that does not amount to a substantial interference with possession, but which consists of intermeddling with or use of another's personal property, is sufficient to establish a cause of action for trespass to chattel. Although the court admits some uncertainty as to the precise level of possessory interference required to constitute an intermeddling, there does not appear to be any dispute that eBay can show that BE's conduct amounts to use of eBay's computer systems. Accordingly, eBay has made a strong showing that it is likely to prevail on the merits of its assertion that BE's use of eBay's computer system was an unauthorized and intentional interference with eBay's possessory interest.

b. Damage to eBay's Computer System

A trespasser is liable when the trespass diminishes the condition, quality or value of personal property. The quality or value of personal property may be "diminished even though it is not physically damaged by defendant's conduct." The Restatement offers the following explanation for the harm requirement:

> The interest of a possessor of a chattel in its inviolability, unlike the similar interest of a possessor of land, is not given legal protection by an action for nominal damages for harmless intermeddlings with the chattel. In order that an actor who interferes with another's chattel may be liable, his conduct must affect some other and more important interest of the possessor. Therefore, one who intentionally intermeddles with another's chattel is subject to liability only if his intermeddling is harmful to the possessor's materially valuable interest in the physical condition, quality, or value of the chattel, or if the possessor is deprived of the use of the chattel for a substantial time, or some other legally protected interest of the possessor is affected. . . . Sufficient legal protection of the possessor's interest in the mere inviolability of his chattel is afforded by his privilege to use reasonable force to protect his possession against even harmless interference.

Restatement (Second) of Torts § 218 cmt. e (1977).

eBay is likely to be able to demonstrate that BE's activities have diminished the quality or value of eBay's computer systems. BE's activities consume at least a portion of plaintiff's bandwidth and server capacity. Although there is some dispute as to the percentage of queries on eBay's site for which BE is responsible, BE admits that it sends some 80,000 to 100,000 requests to plaintiff's computer systems per day. Although eBay does not claim that this consumption has led to any physical damage to eBay's computer system, nor does eBay provide any evidence to support the claim that it may have lost revenues or customers based on this use, eBay's claim is that BE's use is appropriating eBay's personal property by using valuable bandwidth and capacity, and necessarily compromising eBay's ability to use that capacity for its own purposes.

BE argues that its searches represent a negligible load on plaintiff's computer systems, and do not rise to the level of impairment to the condition or value of eBay's computer system required to constitute a trespass. However, it is undisputed that eBay's server and its capacity are personal property, and that BE's searches use a portion of this property. Even if, as BE argues, its searches use only a small amount of eBay's computer system capacity, BE has nonetheless deprived eBay of the ability to use that portion of its personal property for its own purposes. The law recognizes no such right to use another's personal property. Accordingly, BE's actions appear to have caused injury to eBay and appear likely to continue to cause injury to eBay. If the court were to hold otherwise, it would likely encourage other auction aggregators to crawl the eBay site, potentially to the point of denying effective access to eBay's customers. If preliminary injunctive relief were denied, and other aggregators began to crawl the eBay site, there appears to be little doubt that the load on eBay's computer system would qualify as a substantial impairment of condition or value. California law does not require eBay to wait for such a disaster before applying to this court for relief. The court concludes that eBay has made a strong showing that it is likely to prevail on the merits of its trespass claim, and that there is at least a possibility that it will suffer irreparable harm if preliminary injunctive relief is not granted. eBay is therefore entitled to preliminary injunctive relief.

2. Copyright Preemption

BE argues that the trespass claim, along with eBay's other state law causes of action, "is similar to eBay's originally filed but now dismissed copyright infringement claim, and each is based on eBay's assertion that Bidder's Edge copies eBay's auction listings, a right within federal copyright law." BE is factually incorrect to the extent it argues that the trespass claim arises out of what BE does with the information it gathers by accessing eBay's computer system, rather than the mere fact that BE accesses and uses that system without authorization.

A state law cause of action is preempted by the Copyright Act if, (1) the rights asserted under state law are "equivalent" to those protected by the Copyright Act, and (2) the work involved falls within the "subject matter" of the Copyright Act as set forth in 17 U.S.C. §§ 102 and 103. . . . "In order not to be equivalent, the right under state law must have an extra element that changes the nature of the action so that it is qualitatively different from a copyright infringement claim." Here, eBay asserts a right not to have BE use its computer systems without authorization. The right to exclude others from using physical personal property is not equivalent to any rights protected by copyright and therefore constitutes an extra element that makes trespass qualitatively different from a copyright infringement claim. *But see Ticketmaster Corp. v. Tickets.Com, Inc.,* No. CV-99-7654, 2000 U.S. Dist. LEXIS 4553; 54 U.S.P.Q.2D 1344 (C.D. Cal. Mar. 27, 2000) (dismissing trespass claim based on unauthorized Internet information aggregation as preempted by copyright law). . . .

IV. ORDER

Bidder's Edge, its officers, agents, servants, employees, attorneys and those in active concert or participation with them who receive actual notice of this order by personal service or otherwise, are hereby enjoined pending the trial of this matter, from using any automated query program, robot, web crawler or other similar device, without written authorization, to access eBay's computer systems or networks, for the purpose of copying any part of eBay's auction database. . . . Nothing in this order precludes BE from utilizing information obtained from eBay's site other than by automated query program, robot, web crawler or similar device. . . .

NOTES

1. If Bidder's Edge had agreed to a contract with eBay, would the court still have had to examine whether or not automated access was a trespass? What is the function of a contract in this environment?

2. e-Bay is not password-protected as to access. Any user can come onto the site without registering. On the other hand, a visitor cannot bid on an auction without registering and agreeing to the e-Bay contract. Why does the site operate in this manner? If, instead, e-Bay were password protected, would the case against Bidder's Edge have been any different?

3. As *eBay* mentions, *Ticketmaster Corp. v. Tickets.Com, Inc.*, No. CV-99-7654, 2000 U.S. Dist. LEXIS 4553; 54 U.S.P.Q.2D 1344 (C.D. Cal. Mar. 27, 2000), held that a claim based on automated copying of factual data about tickets for entertainment and other events was preempted by copyright law. The court also held that Tickets.com, the defendant, was not bound by the Ticketmaster online terms and that access to what the court viewed as an unrestricted site could not be trespass. In a later proceeding, Ticketmaster had restructured its online assent procedure and the court held that Tickets.com breached the contract by automated retrieval and use of data from the Ticketmaster site, but that there still was no trespass because there was no proof of harm or threatened harm to the site. *Ticketmaster v. Tickets.com*, 2003 U.S. Dist. Lexis 6483 (C.D. Cal. 2003). The court said:

> The trespass to chattels issue requires adapting the ancient common law action to the modern age. . . . At the time of the preliminary injunction motion, only the *eBay* case was before the court. Since then, there have been a number of district court cases discussing the chattel theory (some published and some not). These cases tend to support the proposition that mere invasion or use of a portion of the web site by a spider is a trespass (leading at least to nominal damages), and that there need not be an independent showing of direct harm either to the chattel (unlikely in the case of a spider) or tangible interference with the use of the computer being invaded. However, scholars and practitioners alike have criticized the extension of the trespass to chattels doctrine to the internet context, noting that this doctrinal expansion threatens basic internet functions (*i.e.*, search engines) and exposes the flaws inherent in applying doctrines based on real and tangible property to cyberspace. . . . Pending appellate guidance, this court comes down on the side of requiring some tangible interference with the use or operation of the computer being invaded by the spider. *Restatement (Second) of Torts* § 219 requires a showing that "the chattel is impaired as to its condition, quality, or value." Therefore, unless there is actual dispossession of the chattel for a substantial time (not present here), the elements of the tort have not been made out. Since the spider does not cause physical injury to the chattel, there must be some evidence that the use or utility of the computer (or computer network) being "spiderized" is adversely affected by the use of the spider. No such evidence is presented here. This court respectfully disagrees with other district courts' finding that mere use of a spider to enter a publicly available web site to gather information, without more, is sufficient to fulfill the harm requirement for trespass to chattels.

Compare Oyster Software, Inc. v. Forms Processing, Inc., No. C-00-0724 JCS, 2001 U.S. Dist. LEXIS 22520 (N.D. Cal. 2001) (trespass claim sustained without proof of damage). *See* Laura Quilter, *Cyberlaw: The Continuing Expansion of*

Cyberspace Trespass to Chattels, 17 BERKELEY TECH. L.J. 421 (2002); Clifton Merrell, *Trespass to Chattels in the Age of the Internet,* 80 WASH. U. L.Q. 675 (2002).

Later, the Second Circuit court of appeals in *Register.com, Inc. v. Verio, Inc.,* 356 F.3d 393 (2d Cir. 2004), criticized the *Ticketmaster* contract law analysis and seemed to reject the trespass theory. The court stated:

> Verio also attacks the grant of the preliminary injunction against its accessing Register's computers by automated software programs performing multiple successive queries. This prong of the injunction was premised on Register's claim of trespass to chattels. Verio contends the ruling was in error because Register failed to establish that Verio's conduct resulted in harm to Register's servers and because Verio's robot access to the WHOIS database through Register was "not unauthorized." We believe the district court's findings were within the range of its permissible discretion. . . . The district court found that Verio's use of search robots, consisting of software programs performing multiple automated successive queries, consumed a significant portion of the capacity of Register's computer systems. While Verio's robots alone would not incapacitate Register's systems, the court found that if Verio were permitted to continue to access Register's computers through such robots, it was "highly probable" that other Internet service providers would devise similar programs to access Register's data, and that the system would be overtaxed and would crash. We cannot say these findings were unreasonable.

4. The tort of trespass requires tortious behavior related to the personal property, rather than to other interests of the plaintiff. This was the holding of the California Supreme Court in *Intel Corp. v. Hamidi,* 30 Cal. Rptr. 4th 1342, 71 P.3d 296 (Cal. 2003). *Hamidi* did not involve commercial trespass, but an effort by Intel to ward off e-mails sent by a disgruntled former employee to current Intel employees. The complaint was that the content of the e-mails disrupted employee time and morale, not that the e-mails had any effect on the Intel computer system or the data in it. Indeed, unlike the hundreds of thousands of recurrent contacts in eBay, there were far fewer e-mails here (actually, from the perspective of harm to system, a negligible number). The court accepted the theory of trespass to chattel involving computer access. But in a sharply divided opinion, the majority held that the Intel allegations did not state a claim of trespass. Some actual or threatened harm to the *asset* must be shown according to some of the judges.

PROBLEM 17.2

Client's online site contains valuable data. For several years, it relied on its right to exclude any third party from accessing the site as the basis for enforcing terms of service for the site. The terms of service include 1) a charge per minute of use, 2) a condition that any disputes about the quality of the information will be subject to binding arbitration, and 3) a provision that the user not use the data it obtains in a commercial use competitive with client's current uses. Should Client change its terms or practices?

PROBLEM 17.3

Client's online site provides information about the availability of antiquarian law books and the prices at which they are offered. It profits from this commercial site based on advertising revenue and does not require users of the site to agree to any contractual terms. ABB Books is a data aggregator that deals in information about antiquarian books, art and other collectibles. ABB acquires data from various sites, including Client's site, by the use of automated data robotic collectors that electronically visit all relevant sites thirty times per day, and additional times whenever a user of the ABB site requests relevant information. This practice diverts numerous customers from Client's site, losing advertising revenue. What should Client do to reduce the loss?

EF CULTURAL TRAVEL BV v. ZEFER CORP.
318 F.3d 58 (1st Cir. 2003)

BOUDIN, CHIEF JUDGE.

Defendant Zefer Corporation ("Zefer") seeks review of a preliminary injunction prohibiting it from using a "scraper tool" to collect pricing information from the website of plaintiff EF Cultural Travel BV ("EF"). This court earlier upheld the injunction against co-defendant Explorica, Inc. ("Explorica"). *EF Cultural Travel BV v. Explorica, Inc.,* 274 F.3d 577 (1st Cir.2001) ("*EF I*"). . . .

EF and Explorica are competitors in the student travel business. Explorica was started in the spring of 2000 by several former EF employees who aimed to compete in part by copying EF's prices from EF's website and setting Explorica's own prices slightly lower. EF's website permits a visitor to the site to search its tour database and view the prices for tours meeting specified criteria such as gateway (*e.g.,* departure) cities, destination cities, and tour duration. In June 2000, Explorica hired Zefer, which provides computer-related expertise, to build a scraper tool that could "scrape" the prices from EF's website and download them into an Excel spreadsheet.

A scraper, also called a "robot" or "bot," is nothing more than a computer program that accesses information contained in a succession of webpages stored on the accessed computer. . . . The scraper program used in this case was not designed to copy all of the information on the accessed pages (*e.g.,* the descriptions of the tours), but rather only the price for each tour through each possible gateway city.

Zefer built a scraper tool that scraped two years of pricing data from EF's website. After receiving the pricing data from Zefer, Explorica set its own prices for the public, undercutting EF's prices an average of five percent. EF discovered Explorica's use of the scraper tool during discovery in an unrelated state-court action. . . . EF then sued Zefer, Explorica, and several of Explorica's employees in federal court. Pertinently, EF sought a preliminary injunction on the ground that the copying violated the federal Copyright Act . . . and various provisions of the Computer Fraud and Abuse Act ("CFAA"). The district court refused to grant EF summary judgment on its copyright claim, but it did issue a preliminary injunction against all defendants based on one provision of the

CFAA, ruling that the use of the scraper tool went beyond the "reasonable expectations" of ordinary users. The preliminary injunction states *inter alia*:

> Explorica, Inc., its officers, agents, servants, employees, successors and assigns, all persons acting in concert or participation with Explorica, Inc., and/or acting on its behalf or direction are preliminarily enjoined to . . . refrain . . . from the use of a "scraper" program, or any other similar computer tool, to access any data useable or necessary for the compilation of prices on or from the website of plaintiff EF Cultural Travel and its related entities, and/or the EF Tour Database.

The defendants appealed. . . . [The] question presented is whether the preliminary injunction is proper as to Zefer. We conclude that it is proper even as to Zefer, which signed no confidentiality agreement, but on relatively narrow grounds. . . .

EF argues at the outset that our decision in *EF I* is decisive as to Zefer. But the ground we adopted there in upholding the injunction as to the other defendants was that they had apparently used confidential information to facilitate the obtaining of the EF data. Explorica was created by former EF employees, some of whom were subject to confidentiality agreements. Zefer's position in that respect is quite different than that of Explorica or former EF employees. It signed no such agreement, and its prior knowledge as to the agreement is an open question.

EF suggests that Zefer must have known that information provided to it by Explorica had been improperly obtained. This is possible but not certain, and there are no express district court findings on this issue; indeed, given the district court's much broader basis for its injunction, it had no reason to make any detailed findings as to the role of the confidentiality agreement. What can be gleaned from the record as to Zefer's knowledge certainly does not permit us to make on appeal the finding urged by EF.

What appears to have happened is that Philip Gormley, Explorica's Chief Information Officer . . . e-mailed Zefer a description of how EF's website was structured and identified the information that Explorica wanted to have copied; this may have facilitated Zefer's development of the scraper tool, but there is no indication that the structural information was unavailable from perusal of the website or that Zefer would have known that it was information subject to a confidentiality agreement.

EF also claims that Gormley e-mailed Zefer the "codes" identifying in computer shorthand the names of EF's gateway and destination cities. These codes were used to direct the scraper tool to the specific pages on EF's website that contained EF's pricing information. But, again, it appears that the codes could be extracted more slowly by examining EF's webpages manually, so it is far from clear that Zefer would have had to know that they were confidential. The only information that Zefer received that was described as confidential (passwords for tour-leader access) apparently had no role in the scraper project.

EF's alternative ground for affirmance is the rationale adopted by the district court for the preliminary injunction. That court relied on its "reasonable expectations" test as a gloss on the CFAA and then applied it to the facts of this case. Although we bypassed the issue in *EF I*, the district court's rationale would embrace Zefer as readily as Explorica itself. But the gloss presents a pure question of law to be reviewed *de novo* and, on this issue, we differ with the district court.

The CFAA provision relied upon by the district court states:

> Whoever . . . knowingly and with intent to defraud, accesses a protected computer without authorization, or exceeds authorized access, and by means of such conduct furthers the intended fraud and obtains anything of value, unless the object of the fraud and the thing obtained consists only of the use of the computer and the value of such use is not more than $5,000 in any 1-year period . . . shall be punished as provided in subsection (c) of this section.

18 U.S.C. § 1030(a)(4). The statute defines "exceeds authorized access" as "to access a computer with authorization and to use such access to obtain or alter information in the computer that the accesser is not entitled so to obtain or alter." The CFAA furnishes a civil remedy for individuals who suffer damages or loss as a result of a violation of the above section.

At the outset, one might think that EF could have difficulty in showing an intent to defraud. But Zefer did not brief the issue. . . . In addition, there may be an argument that the fraud requirement should not pertain to injunctive relief. Accordingly, we bypass these matters and assume that the fraud requirement has been satisfied or is not an obstacle to the injunction.

The issue, then, is whether use of the scraper "exceed[ed] authorized access." A lack of authorization could be established by an explicit statement on the website restricting access. (Whether public policy might in turn limit certain restrictions is a separate issue.) Many webpages contain lengthy limiting conditions, including limitations on the use of scrapers. However, at the time of Zefer's use of the scraper, EF had no such explicit prohibition in place, although it may well use one now.

The district court thought that a lack of authorization could also be inferred from the circumstances, using "reasonable expectations" as the test; and it said that three such circumstances comprised such a warning in this case: the copyright notice on EF's homepage with a link directing users to contact the company with questions; EF's provision to Zefer of confidential information obtained in breach of the employee confidentiality agreements; and the fact that the website was configured to allow ordinary visitors to the site to view only one page at a time.

We agree with the district court that lack of authorization may be implicit, rather than explicit. After all, password protection itself normally limits authorization by implication (and technology), even without express terms. But we think that in general a reasonable expectations test is not the proper gloss on subsection (a)(4) and we reject it. However useful a reasonable expectations test might be in other contexts where there may be a common understanding underpinning the notion, its use in this context is neither prescribed by the statute nor prudentially sound.

Our basis for this view is not, as some have urged, that there is a "presumption" of open access to Internet information. The CFAA, after all, is primarily a statute imposing limits on access and enhancing control by information providers. Instead, we think that the public website provider can easily spell out explicitly what is forbidden and, consonantly, that nothing justifies putting users at the mercy of a highly imprecise, litigation-spawning standard like "reasonable expectations." If EF wants to ban scrapers, let it say so on the webpage or a link clearly marked as containing restrictions.

This case itself illustrates the flaws in the "reasonable expectations" standard. Why should the copyright symbol, which arguably does not protect the substantive information anyway, or the provision of page-by-page access for that matter, be taken to suggest that downloading information at higher speed is forbidden? EF could easily include — indeed, by now probably has included — a sentence on its home page or in its terms of use stating that "no scrapers may be used," giving fair warning and avoiding time-consuming litigation about its private, albeit "reasonable," intentions.

Needless to say, Zefer can have been in no doubt that EF would dislike the use of the scraper to construct a database for Explorica to undercut EF's prices; but EF would equally have disliked the compilation of such a database manually without the use of a scraper tool. EF did not purport to exclude competitors from looking at its website and any such limitation would raise serious public policy concerns.

Although we conclude that the district court's rationale does not support an independent preliminary injunction against Zefer, there is no apparent reason to vacate the present injunction "as against Zefer." Despite being a party to the case, Zefer is not named in the ordering language of the injunction; it is merely precluded, like anyone else with notice, from acting in concert with, on behalf of, or at the direction of Explorica to use the scraper to access EF's information.

Under the applicable rules and case law, an injunction properly issued against a named party means that anyone else with notice is precluded from acting to assist the enjoined party from violating the decree or from doing so on behalf of that party. There is no reason why Zefer should be freer than any other third party who was never in this litigation to assist EF to violate the injunction against it or to do so on EF's behalf or at its direction. As we read the injunction, that is all that is forbidden.

It may still be of practical importance to Zefer to have clarified the limited basis on which we uphold the injunction. And nothing we have said would prevent EF, if it matters in continued litigation, from seeking to show that Zefer did use confidential information, aware that it was being supplied in violation of agreements made by former EF employees. It is also of some use for future litigation among other litigants in this circuit to indicate that, with rare exceptions, public website providers ought to say just what non-password protected access they purport to forbid.

Lastly, Zefer has alleged that the First Amendment would be offended if the statute were construed to forbid generally the use of scrapers to collect otherwise available information where there was no intent to defraud or harm the target website. Here, the preliminary injunction is premised on EF's misuse of confidential information and Zefer thus far is constrained only in helping a tentatively-identified wrongdoer in exploiting that confidential information. None of Zefer's arguments address this narrowed constraint or suggest to us that it is constitutionally doubtful.

The preliminary injunction is *affirmed.* . . .

NOTES

1. Should the standard for notice in a claim based on a criminal statute be the same as that for a claim based on the tort of trespass? Does the standard in either case require a contract? If not, what type of notice is sufficient?

2. Both the criminal law access rule and the idea of trespass treat a computer system as a protected asset. Are these causes of action inconsistent with claims that might arise under copyright law? Is or should there be a concept of fair use in laws that control online access?

PROBLEM 17.4

Client is developing an online site to sell women's sports clothing. It desires to regulate access to the site by competitors who might use automated or other methods to determine and undercut Client's pricing or to create aggregated sites at which customers can comparison shop without going to Client's location. It asks for advice on what steps to take to give it the opportunity to control such access. What do you advise?

B. Misuse of the Online System

The following is from an online contract once used by a consumer advocacy group:

You shall not upload to, or distribute to, or otherwise publish through the Forums any Communication which

    (i) is for commercial purposes or otherwise advertises or solicits for the sale of goods or services;

    (ii) is obscene, indecent, pornographic, profane, sexually explicit, or abusive;

    . . . .

    (iv) slanders, libels, defames, disparages, or otherwise violates the legal rights of any third party;

    (vi) infringes or violates the intellectual property rights, contract rights, or any other rights of any third party;

    (viii) contains software viruses or any other malicious code designed to interrupt, destroy or limit the functionality of any computer software or hardware or telecommunications equipment.[3]

---

[3] [FN 2] www.consumerreports.org/main/commerce/agreement.jsp? (visited 9/20/02).

JESSUP-MORGAN v. AMERICA ONLINE, INC.
20 F. Supp. 2d 1105 (E.D. Mich. 1998)

FEIKENS, DISTRICT JUDGE.

In June, 1995 Phillip Morgan filed a suit for divorce from Barbara Smith-Morgan (now Barbara Smith). The court granted the divorce in May 1996. Within weeks of the divorce judgment, Terry Jessup (Jessup) . . . married Phillip Morgan.

Jessup and Phillip Morgan began a relationship some time prior to January 1996, while Phillip Morgan and Barbara Smith were still married. On January 11, 1996 Jessup . . . used her AOL account to post publicly on the Internet a message meant to harass and injure Barbara Smith. Jessup posted the message under the "screen name" (*i.e.,* alias) of "Barbeeedol." . . . The listed telephone number was the phone number of Barbara Smith's parents' home, with whom Barbara Smith and her two young children were residing pending resolution of the divorce suit. Jessup posted the message in an Internet Usenet newsgroup entitled "alt. amazon-women.admirers," a public electronic bulletin board containing messages accessible to, and read by, a potential 40 million persons worldwide.

As intended by Jessup, posting this message resulted in persons Barbara Smith did not know calling her parents' home to request sexual liaisons with "Barbara." This gravely disturbed and distressed Barbara Smith and her parents. . . . Barbara Smith enlisted the aid of her brother. . . . He used a computer "search engine" to locate the posting of the offensive message on the Internet. . . . On January 12, 1996 Kenton Smith sent an e-mail message to AOL describing the posting and the calls to his parents' home. He asked AOL for information as to the identity of the person who posted the message. AOL reviewed Kenton Smith's complaint and the "Barbeeedol" message, and determined that the posting originated from Jessup's AOL account, which constituted an egregious breach of the AOL Member Agreement signed by Jessup. AOL, therefore, terminated its contract with Jessup on February 2, 1996, and closed her AOL account. AOL's records list the grounds for this termination as "excessive USENET abuse." The same day, AOL sent Kenton Smith two messages. The first message explained that, for confidentiality reasons, AOL could not disclose information about actions it took against other AOL members. The second message explained that as a matter of AOL policy, information identifying the AOL member who posted the offensive message could only be released in response to a subpoena.

On February 16, 1996 Barbara Smith's divorce attorney, Kathleen M. Dilger, served AOL with a civil subpoena for information which would identify the AOL member who authored the injurious message. On February 23, 1996, in compliance with the subpoena, AOL sent to Dilger a two-page summary containing basic identity information on the AOL account from which the "Barbeeedol" message originated. The summary revealed that Jessup was the holder of the account.

Terry Jessup-Morgan now brings suit against AOL, claiming that AOL's compliance with the subpoena was unlawful, tortious, and a breach of contract. . . . She requests various damages in excess of $47 million. . . .

III. AOL MEMBER AGREEMENT

To obtain her AOL service, Jessup executed a Member Agreement (Agreement) with AOL. The Agreement is governed by the AOL Terms of Service (TOS) and the AOL Rules of the Road (ROR). The TOS provides for AOL or Member termination of their contract at any time. The TOS provides that it is governed by the laws of the Commonwealth of Virginia, and by executing the Agreement Jessup and AOL agreed to submit to these laws. The ROR provides that:

> AOL Inc. does not disclose to private persons or companies information that identifies a Member's AOL screen name(s) with Member's actual name or other identity information, *unless required to do so by law or legal process served on AOL Inc. AOL Inc. reserves the right to make exceptions to this policy* of non-disclosure in exceptional circumstances (such as a suicide threat, or instances of suspected fraud) on a case by case basis and *at AOL's sole discretion.*

Rules of the Road, § 2.B(iv) (emphasis added).

By executing the Agreement, Jessup agreed to use her AOL account only for lawful purposes. The ROR specifically prohibits using AOL services to:

> (1) harass, threaten, embarrass, or cause distress, unwanted attention or discomfort upon another Member or user of AOL or other person or entity,

> (2) post or transmit sexually explicit images or other content which is deemed by AOL Inc. to be offensive,

> (3) transmit any unlawful, harmful, threatening, abusive, harassing, defamatory, vulgar, obscene, hateful, ethnically or otherwise objectionable Content,

> . . . .

> (5) impersonate any person . . . or communicate under a false name or a name that you are not entitled or authorized to use,

> . . . .

> (10) intentionally or unintentionally violate any applicable local, state, national or international law, including but not limited to any regulations having the force of law.

IV. DISCUSSION

Jessup breached her contract with AOL, particularly section 2.C(a), by posting the message which invited third persons to seek sexual liaisons with Barbara Smith. Jessup's breach of the Agreement prior to any alleged breach of the same contract by AOL bars her claim against AOL for breach of contract and implied and express warranties. Under Virginia law, when the initial breach is substantial, the party who breaches a contract first is barred from maintaining an action against another contracting party for its subsequent breach of, or failure to perform under, the contract. Here, Jessup's impersonation of Barbara Smith, and her posting of the message to harass and cause distress to Barbara, is certainly a substantial and material breach of the Agreement.

AOL did not breach the Agreement. According to the terms of the Agreement, AOL, at its discretion, could terminate a Member's account because the Member committed the acts Jessup did. AOL did so in this instance. In providing identifying information to Barbara Smith's lawyer pursuant to a civil subpoena, AOL complied with applicable law. The Agreement clearly provides for this compliance with proper legal process.

Jessup committed an egregious and intentionally harmful (to a third party) breach of the contract, and AOL acted responsibly in terminating her account and in providing information identifying her as the account holder that posted the harassing message on the Internet. Jessup provides no evidence that AOL breached any implied or express warranties. AOL is thus entitled to summary judgment on Jessup's breach of contract and implied and express warranties claim. . . .

AOL motions are hereby GRANTED.

NOTES

1. Are there limits on what the terms of an online system that regulate use can impose? Concepts of good faith and unconscionability play a role, but how? Should a conservative political site be allowed to terminate access and remove postings that are anti-conservative?

2. Many agreements allow termination if the subscriber uses the system to engage in spam. *See Monsterhut, Inc. v. Paetec Commun., Inc.*, 741 N.Y.S.2d 820 (N.Y.A.D. 2002) (Internet service provider could terminate service agreement in response to subscriber's sending of unsolicited, mass, commercial e-mail (spamming) in breach of the agreement.); *Hotmail Corp. v. Van$ Money Pie, Inc.*, 47 U.S.P.Q.2d 1020 (N.D. Cal. 1998).

3. Federal law entered the picture in 2004 with the Controlling the Assault of Non-Solicited Pornography and Marketing Act of 2003, P.L. 108-187 (2003) ("CANSPAM"). The federal law rests on these policies: (1) there is a substantial government interest in regulation of commercial electronic mail on a nationwide basis; (2) senders of commercial electronic mail should not mislead recipients as to the source or content of such mail; and (3) recipients of commercial electronic mail have a right to decline to receive additional commercial electronic mail from the same source. The federal act is broadly preemptive of state "spam" laws but does not preempt state laws on false or deceptive content, trespass, contract or tort. Nor does the statute affect terms of service of Internet service providers.

III. LIABILITY FOR THIRD-PARTY CONTENT

What is the obligation of an online provider for information that derives from third parties, but is provided to customers through the online site? That issue entails two very different questions. Both relate to the First Amendment and the related policy of how our law should treat conduits that make information and ideas available to others.

A. Incorrect Information: CDA § 230

47 U.S.C. § 230 provides in relevant part:

(c) Protection . . .

> (1) Treatment of publisher or speaker. No provider or user of an interactive computer service shall be treated as the publisher or speaker of any information provided by another information content provider.

> (2) Civil liability. No provider or user of an interactive computer service shall be held liable on account of —

> (A) any action voluntarily taken in good faith to restrict access to or availability of material that the provider or user considers to be obscene, lewd, lascivious, filthy, excessively violent, harassing, or otherwise objectionable, whether or not such material is constitutionally protected; or

> (B) any action taken to enable or make available to information content providers or others the technical means to restrict access to material described in paragraph (1).

> . . . .

(e) Effect on other laws

> (3) . . . Nothing in this section shall be construed to prevent any State from enforcing any State law that is consistent with this section. No cause of action may be brought and no liability may be imposed under any State or local law that is inconsistent with this section.

The immediate motivation for enacting Section 230 was to overrule a state court decision that seemed to create the risk of defamation liability for online providers who made efforts to screen or control content on their systems. The statute has had far broader implications.

GENTRY v. eBAY, INC.
99 Cal. App. 4th 816 (2002)

O'ROURKE, J.

Lars Gentry, Henry Camp, Mike Hyder, James Conboy, William Pommerening, and Michael Osacky (appellants) appeal a judgment of dismissal entered after the trial court sustained eBay, Inc.'s (eBay) demurrer to appellants' second amended complaint without leave to amend. In that pleading, appellants alleged eBay violated California's "Autographed Sports Memorabilia" statute by failing to furnish a certificate of authenticity to persons who purchased autographed sports-related collectibles through its Web site. Appellants also alleged eBay was negligent and engaged in unfair business practices under the unfair competition law (UCL) based on its failure to supply such certificates as well as its acts in distributing false certificates, permitting other false representations to be placed on its Web site, and making its own false or misleading representations. . . . We conclude appellants cannot state a cause of action against eBay under Civil Code section 1739.7 because their allegations reveal eBay did not sell or offer to sell the collectibles at issue. Additionally, we conclude imposition of Civil Code section 1739.7 liability on eBay in this particular case, as well as liability for negligence and violation of the UCL, is inconsistent with section 230 because appellants' causes of action ultimately hold eBay responsible for misinformation or misrepresentations originating with other defendants or third parties. . . .

Factual and Procedural Background

eBay promotes itself as the world's largest on-line marketplace for the sale of goods and services among its registered users. It operates an Internet-based service in which it enables member sellers to offer items for sale to member buyers in what eBay characterizes as either auction-style or fixed price formats. To better enable users to place items for sale on its site, eBay provides descriptions to its users under various product categories and subcategories. For sports items, eBay's Web site has a sports product category with the following subcategories: "Sports: Autographs"; "Sports: Memorabilia"; "Sports: Sporting Goods" and "Sports: Trading Cards." eBay's "Sports: Autographs" subcategory is further organized into sub-subcategories to differentiate autographed sports collectibles by particular leagues.

In September 1995, various individuals embarked on a plan to sell faked autographed sports memorabilia to consumers. Specifically, [the Marino defendants] purchased sporting goods items and photographs from retail stores, forged signatures of professional athletes upon them, and employed Wayne Bray and Donald Frangipani to produce false certificates of authenticity for the items. The Marino defendants then sold most of the forged items to Stanley Fitzgerald and Phil Scheinman, larger dealers who mostly used eBay auctions to eventually sell the forged items to consumers. Stanley Fitzgerald did business as "Stan The Man Memorabilia" and "Stan's Sports Memorabilia." Phil Scheinman did business as "Smokey's Sportscard, Inc."

Appellants are individuals who purchased forged autographed sports items including baseballs, photographs and autographed pieces of paper or "cuts," from Fitzgerald, Scheinman or the Marino defendants through eBay. . . .

Discussion

Civil Code section 1739.7, in title 1.1A, Autographed Sports Memorabilia, regulates the sale of autographed sports items, broadly termed "collectibles." The statute generally forbids dealers of collectibles from representing an item as a collectible "if it was not autographed by the sports personality in his or her own hand." It also places various obligations on such dealers. Specifically, subdivision (b) of the statute requires dealers to provide certificates of authenticity of a prescribed form and content. It provides in part: "Whenever a dealer, in selling or offering to sell to a consumer a collectible in or from this state, provides a description of that collectible as being autographed, the dealer shall furnish a certificate of authenticity to the consumer at the time of sale. The certificate of authenticity shall be in writing, shall be signed by the dealer or his or her authorized agent, and shall specify the date of sale." . . .

Appellants contend they stated a cause of action against eBay under Civil Code section 1739.7 by alleging eBay is an auctioneer that engages in the sale or offer for sale of autographed collectibles in or from this state, provides descriptions of collectibles as being autographed, yet has never furnished the requisite certificates of authenticity under the statute. . . .

[eBay is not within the statute.] [We] additionally hold, under the facts presented, placing liability upon eBay for failing to provide a warranty under Civil Code section 1739.7 would be inconsistent with and hence preempted by section 230, which was incorporated by Congress into the final version of the Communications Decency Act.

The operative provision of section 230 states:

> [n]o provider or user of an interactive computer service shall be treated as the publisher or speaker of any information provided by another information content provider. (47 U.S.C. § 230(c)(1).)

The statute further provides:

> (e) Effect on other laws . . .
>
> > (3) Nothing in this section shall be construed to prevent any State from enforcing any State law that is consistent with this section. No cause of action may be brought and no liability may be imposed under any State or local law that is inconsistent with this section.

In *Zeran v. America Online, Inc.* (4th Cir. 1997) 129 F.3d 327 (*Zeran*), the court held section 230, by its "plain language," created a federal immunity to any cause of action that would make interactive service providers liable for information originating with a third party user of the service. "Specifically, § 230 precludes courts from entertaining claims that would place a computer service provider in a publisher's role. Thus, lawsuits seeking to hold a service provider liable for its exercise of a publisher's traditional editorial functions — such as deciding whether to publish, withdraw, postpone or alter content — are barred." Reiterating Congress's findings and policy statements in section 230(a), (b), the court observed: "Congress recognized the threat that tort-based lawsuits pose to freedom of speech in the new and burgeoning Internet medium. The imposition of tort liability on service providers for the communications of others represented, for Congress, simply another form of intrusive government regulation of speech. Section 230 was enacted, in part, to maintain the robust nature of Internet communication and, accordingly, to keep government interference in the medium to a minimum. . . . None of this means, of course, that the original culpable party who posts defamatory messages would escape accountability. While Congress acted to keep government regulation of the Internet to a minimum, it also found it to be the policy of the United States 'to ensure vigorous enforcement of Federal criminal laws to deter and punish trafficking in obscenity, stalking, and harassment by means of computer.' Congress made a policy choice, however, not to deter harmful online speech through the separate route of imposing tort liability on companies that serve as intermediaries for other parties' potentially injurious messages."

Other courts have applied *Zeran*'s reasoning to bar not only defamation claims, but other tort causes of action asserted against interactive service providers. (*See, e.g., Kathleen R. v. City of Livermore* (2001) 87 Cal.App.4th 684, 692 [104 Cal.Rptr.2d 772] [Court of Appeal affirmed judgment of dismissal in city's favor holding a city was immune under § 230 from liability under state causes of action for misuse of public funds, nuisance and premises liability for library's acts in providing computers allowing access to pornography]; *Doe v. America Online, Inc.* (Fla. 2001) 783 So.2d 1010, 1013-1017 [following *Zeran* in concluding § 230 directly preempted Florida law in a negligence action based upon America Online, Inc.'s (AOL) distribution of information depicting child pornography; the court rejected the argument that allegations AOL knew or should have known about the distribution of such materials created liability distinct from that of any publisher]; *Schneider v. Amazon.com, Inc.* (2001) 108 Wash. App. 454 [31 P.3d 37] [Internet book vendor was immune from tort (negligent misrepresentation, interference with business expectancy) and contractual liability arising from allegedly false statements about the plaintiff and his business made by third parties in the book review section]). . . .

Section 230(c)(1) thus immunizes providers of interactive computer services (service providers) and their users from causes of action asserted by persons alleging harm caused by content provided by a third party. This form of immunity requires (1) the defendant be a provider or user of an interactive computer service; (2) the cause of action treat the defendant as a publisher or speaker of information; and (3) the information at issue be provided by another information content provider.

Appellants concede for purposes of this appeal that eBay is an interactive computer service providetr.[4] And appellants do not expressly challenge the application of section 230 to liability based on content placed on eBay's Web site by eBay's users or other third parties. Rather, they contend section 230 does not apply because they seek to enforce eBay's independent duty under the statute to furnish a warranty as the "'provider' of descriptions," not as a publisher. We disagree.

The substance of appellants' allegations reveal they ultimately seek to hold eBay responsible for conduct falling within the reach of section 230, namely,

---

[4] [FN 7] The statute defines the term "Interactive computer service" as "any information service, system, or access software provider that provides or enables computer access by multiple users to a computer server, including specifically a service or system that provides access to the Internet and such systems operated or services offered by libraries or educational institutions." (§ 230(f)(2).) The term "Information content provider" is defined as "any person or entity that is responsible, in whole or in part, for the creation or development of information provided through the Internet or any other interactive computer service." (§ 230(f)(3).) Even if appellants had not conceded the issue, the allegations of the second amended complaint indicate eBay's Web site enables users to conduct sales transactions, as well as provide information (feedback) about other users of the service. In this way, eBay provides an information service that enables access by multiple users to a computer server and brings it within the broad definition of an interactive computer service provider. (*Cf. Schneider v. Amazon.com, Inc., supra*, 31 P.3d at p. 40 & fn. 13 [noting Amazon. com's Web site permitted visitors to comment about authors and their work and thus provided an information service that necessarily enabled access by multiple users to a service].).

eBay's dissemination of representations made by the individual defendants, or the posting of compilations of information generated by those defendants and other third parties. Under section 230, eBay cannot be "treated as the publisher or speaker" of content supplied by other information content providers. (§ 230(c)(1).) If by imposing liability under Civil Code section 1739.7 we ultimately hold eBay responsible for content originating from other parties, we would be treating it as the publisher, viz., the original communicator, contrary to Congress's expressed intent under section 230(c)(1) and (e)(3).

In connection with appellants' argument relating to the sufficiency of their Civil Code section 1739.7 cause of action, appellants point out they alleged eBay provided its own descriptions of collectibles through its lists of product categories, but also assert, to the extent the individual defendants created the ultimate descriptions of their faked collectibles, eBay provided those descriptions within the meaning of the statute by making them available to the users of its Web site. In opposition to eBay's demurrer, they argued: "It does not matter under [Civil Code section] 1739.7 who 'creates' the original specific description of the memorabilia, because the obligation to furnish a warranty arises when a dealer 'provides' the description in offering or selling the item and the description characterizes the item as being autographed. . . . Therefore, although the specific description of an item originates with the seller, eBay, by making the description available over its auction website . . . , then 'provides' the description to its consumers."

While the fact eBay does not create the description may be of no significance to liability under Civil Code section 1739.7 as appellants maintain, it is highly significant for purposes of assessing the application of section 230. Appellants do not dispute the fact, judicially noticed by the trial court, that it was dealers Fitzgerald and Scheinman, not eBay, who chose their own category description for the item offered for sale. Thus, for purposes of applying section 230 immunity, we consider it was the individual defendants who falsely identified the product as authentically autographed in order to place their items on eBay for sale. On the basis of appellants' allegations, holding eBay responsible for providing a warranty under Civil Code section 1739.7 when it merely made the individual defendant's false product descriptions available to other users on its Web site, or provided the Web site on which the individual defendants designated their collectibles as autographed, puts eBay in the shoes of the individual defendants, making it responsible for their publications or statements. We therefore conclude enforcement of appellants' Civil Code section 1739.7 cause of action is inconsistent with section 230 because it would "stand as an obstacle to the accomplishment and execution of the full purposes and objectives of Congress."

III. *Negligence Cause of Action*

Apart from the cause of action under Civil Code section 1739.9, which we have held is barred, appellants' negligence cause of action is based on allegations that eBay itself misrepresented the safety of purchasing items from the individual defendants and knew or should have known the individual defendants were conducting unlawful practices but failed to ensure they comply with the law. In an attempt to plead around section 230 with respect to these causes of action, appellants generally allege eBay was an information content provider in that it was responsible for the creation of information, or development of information, for the online auction it provided through the Internet; that eBay did not act as an Internet service provider; and the information at issue (descriptions of collectibles as autographed) did not concern the publication of obscene or similarly objectionable materials.

These conclusory and argumentative allegations are followed by more specific averments. Appellants more specifically described the information purportedly developed by eBay for its "safety program," identifying it as consisting of a color-coded star symbol, a Power Sellers endorsement, and a Feedback Forum. Appellants alleged: "eBay encourages its users to rely upon its 'Feedback Forum' prior to engaging in a sales transaction. The Feedback Forum purportedly *allows dealers and consumers* to rate a sales transaction with a compliment (a 'Positive Feedback'), a criticism (a 'Negative Feedback'), or other comments (a 'Neutral Feedback'). eBay has advertised that, 'A positive eBay rating is worth its weight in gold.' A dealer or consumer who achieves a designated level of Positive Feedback is awarded a star symbol display next to the user name, which is color coded to indicate the amount of Positive Feedback received by the user. . . . In addition to the Feedback Forum, eBay designed a 'Power Sellers' endorsement, which purportedly is an award given to select eBay dealers based on the volume of sales and Positive Feedback ratings. . . . In reality, however, eBay's 'safety' programs have contributed to enormous damage to autographed sports memorabilia consumers. For example, the Feedback Forum allows anyone to rate a dealer, even if there has never been a sales transaction between the parties. Thus, Fitzgerald and Scheinman have at least hundreds of Positive Feedback ratings which are unrelated to any sales transactions. *Most, if not all, of these Positive Feedback ratings are self-generated or provided by other co-conspiring dealers.*"

None of these allegations place eBay outside the immunity for service providers. As eBay points out, the allegations reveal that eBay's Feedback Forum is comprised of negative or positive information provided by third party consumers and dealers. Likewise, the star symbol and "Power Sellers" designation is simply a representation of the amount of such positive information received by other users of eBay's Web site. Appellants' negligence claim is based on the assertion that the information is false or misleading because it has been manipulated *by the individual defendants or other co-conspiring parties.* Based on these allegations, enforcing appellants' negligence claim would place liability on eBay for simply compiling false and/or misleading content created by the individual defendants and other coconspirators. We do not see such activities transforming eBay into an information content provider with respect to the representations targeted by appellants as it did not create or develop the underlying misinformation. (*E.g., Ben Ezra, Weinstein, & Co. v. America Online, Inc., supra*, 206 F.3d 980, 985-986 [AOL's communication of errors in stock information provided by other entities, and deletion of stock symbols and other alteration of information from its data base to correct such errors was not "creation or development" of information under § 230's definition of an information content provider].) We are constrained from enforcing such liability under California law because it would treat eBay as the publisher or speaker of the individual defendants' materials, and thereby conflict with section 230.

We reach the same conclusion with regard to appellants' general assertion that eBay knew or should have known about the individual defendant's illegal or fraudulent conduct but failed to take steps to ensure they complied with the law. This claim seeks to hold eBay responsible for having notice of illegal activities conducted by others on its Web site, and for electing not to take action against those third parties, including by withdrawing or somehow altering the content placed by them. This is the classic kind of claim that *Zeran* found to be preempted by section 230, as one that seeks to hold eBay liable for its exercise of a publisher's traditional editorial functions. Such claims have been uniformly rejected by the courts that have considered them. . . .

Finally, taking as true the fact eBay makes the statement on its Web site that a positive eBay rating is "worth its weight in gold," such an assertion cannot support a cause of action for negligent misrepresentation regardless of federal statutory immunity because it amounts to a general statement of opinion, not a positive assertion of fact. An essential element of a cause of action for negligent misrepresentation is that the defendant must have made a misrepresentation as to a past or existing material fact. "The law is quite clear that expressions of opinion are not generally treated as representations of fact, and thus are not grounds for a misrepresentation cause of action. Representations of value are opinions." (*Neu-Visions Sports, Inc. v. Soren/McAdam/Bartells* (2000) 86 Cal.App.4th 303, 308 [103 Cal.Rptr.2d 159], citing BAJI No. 12.32, 5 WITKIN, SUMMARY OF CAL. LAW (9th ed. 1988) *Torts,* §678, pp. 779-780; and *Rest. 2d Torts,* §538A ["[a] representation is one of opinion if it expresses only (a) the belief of the maker, without certainty, as to the existence of a fact; or (b) his judgment as to quality, value, authenticity, or other matters of judgment"].) Although the line of demarcation between expressions of fact and opinion can be unclear at times, this is not such a case. This kind of vague, highly subjective statement as to the significance of a positive rating is not the sort of statement that a consumer would interpret as factual or upon which he or she could reasonably rely. . . .

The judgment is affirmed.

CARAFANO v. METROSPLASH
339 F.3d 1119 (9th Cir. 2003)

THOMAS, CIRCUIT JUDGE.

This is a case involving a cruel and sadistic identity theft. In this appeal, we consider to what extent a computer match making service may be legally responsible for false content in a dating profile provided by someone posing as another person. [We] conclude that the service is statutorily immune pursuant to 47 U.S.C. §230(c)(1).

I

Matchmaker.com is a commercial Internet dating service. For a fee, members of Matchmaker post anonymous profiles and may then view profiles of other members in their area, contacting them via electronic mail sent through the Matchmaker server. A typical profile contains one or more pictures of the subject, descriptive information such as age, appearance and interests, and answers to a variety of questions designed to evoke the subject's personality and reason for joining the service.

Members are required to complete a detailed questionnaire containing both multiple-choice and essay questions. In the initial portion of the questionnaire, members select answers to more than fifty questions from menus providing between four and nineteen options. Some of the potential multiple choice answers are innocuous; some are sexually suggestive. In the subsequent essay section, participants answer up to eighteen additional questions, including "anything that the questionnaire didn't cover." Matchmaker policies prohibit members from posting last names, addresses, phone numbers or e-mail addresses within a profile. Matchmaker reviews photos for impropriety before posting them but does not review the profiles themselves, relying instead upon participants to adhere to the service guidelines.

On October 23, 1999, an unknown person using a computer in Berlin posted a "trial" personal profile of Christianne Carafano in the Los Angeles section of Matchmaker. . . . The posting was without the knowledge, consent or permission of Carafano. . . .

Carafano is a popular actress. Under the stage name of Chase Masterson, Carafano has appeared in numerous films and television shows. . . . Pictures of the actress are widely available on the Internet, and the false Matchmaker profile "Chase529" contained several of these pictures. Along with fairly innocuous responses to questions about interests and appearance, the person posting the profile selected "Playboy/Playgirl" for "main source of current events" and "looking for a one-night stand" for "why did you call." In addition, the open-ended essay responses indicated that "Chase529" was looking for a "hard and dominant" man with "a strong sexual appetite" and that she "liked sort of being controlled by a man, in and out of bed." The profile text did not include a last name for "Chase" or indicate Carafano's real name, but it listed two of her movies (and, as mentioned, included pictures of the actress).

In response to a question about the "part of the LA area" in which she lived, the profile provided Carafano's home address. The profile included a contact e-mail address . . . which, when contacted, produced an automatic e-mail reply stating, "You think you are the right one? Proof it!!" [sic], and providing Carafano's home address and telephone number.

Unaware of the improper posting, Carafano soon began to receive messages responding to the profile. Although she was traveling at the time, she checked her voicemail on October 31 and heard two sexually explicit messages. When she returned to her home on November 4, she found a highly threatening and sexually explicit fax that also threatened her son. . . . As a result of the profile, she also received numerous phone calls, voicemail messages, written correspondence, and e-mail from fans through her professional e-mail account. . . . Carafano felt unsafe in her home, and she and her son stayed in hotels or away from Los Angeles for several months. . . .

Carafano filed a complaint in California state court against Matchmaker and its corporate successors, alleging invasion of privacy, misappropriation of the right of publicity, defamation, and negligence. . . .

II

The dispositive question in this appeal is whether Carafano's claims are barred by 47 U.S.C. §230(c)(1). . . . Through this provision, Congress granted most Internet services immunity from liability for publishing false or defamatory material so long as the information was provided by another party. As a result, Internet publishers are treated differently from corresponding publishers in print, television and radio.

Congress enacted this provision as part of the Communications Decency Act of 1996 for two basic policy reasons: to promote the free exchange of information and ideas over the Internet and to encourage voluntary monitoring for offensive or obscene material. Congress incorporated these ideas into the text of §230 itself, expressly noting that "interactive computer services have flourished, to the benefit of all Americans, with a minimum of government regulation," and that "[i]ncreasingly Americans are relying on interactive media for a variety of political, educational, cultural, and entertainment services." Congress declared it the "policy of the United States" to "promote the continued development of the Internet and other interactive computer services," "to preserve the vibrant and competitive free market that presently exists for the Internet and other interactive computer services," and to "remove disincentives for the development and utilization of blocking and filtering technologies."

In light of these concerns, reviewing courts have treated §230(c) immunity as quite robust, adopting a relatively expansive definition of "interactive computer service" and a relatively restrictive definition of "information content provider." Under the statutory scheme, an "interactive computer service" qualifies for immunity so long as it does not also function as an "information content provider" for the portion of the statement or publication at issue.

We recently considered whether §230(c) provided immunity to the operator of an electronic newsletter who selected and published an allegedly defamatory e-mail over the Internet. We held that the online newsletter qualified as an "interactive computer service" under the statutory definition and that the selection for publication and editing of an e-mail did not constitute partial "creation or development" of that information within the definition of "information content provider." Although the case was ultimately remanded for determination of whether the original author intended to "provide" his e-mail for publication, *id.* at 1035, the *Batzel* [*v. Smith*, 333 F.3d 1018 (9th Cir. 2003),] decision joined the consensus developing across other courts of appeals that §230(c) provides broad immunity for publishing content provided primarily by third parties.

> Congress made a policy choice . . . not to deter harmful online speech through the separate route of imposing tort liability on companies that serve as intermediaries for other parties' potentially injurious messages. Congress' purpose in providing the §230 immunity was thus evident. Interactive computer services have millions of users. The amount of information communicated via interactive computer services is therefore staggering. The specter of tort liability in an area of such prolific speech would have an obvious chilling effect. It would be impossible for service providers to screen each of their millions of

> postings for possible problems. Faced with potential liability for each
> message republished by their services, interactive computer service
> providers might choose to severely restrict the number and type of
> messages posted. Congress considered the weight of the speech inter-
> ests implicated and chose to immunize service providers to avoid any
> such restrictive effect.

Zeran, 129 F.3d at 330-31. Under § 230(c), therefore, so long as a third party
willingly provides the essential published content, the interactive service
provider receives full immunity regardless of the specific editing or selection
process.

The fact that some of the content was formulated in response to Matchmaker's
questionnaire does not alter this conclusion. Doubtless, the questionnaire
facilitated the expression of information by individual users. However, the
selection of the content was left exclusively to the user. The actual profile
"information" consisted of the particular options chosen and the additional
essay answers provided. Matchmaker was not responsible, even in part, for
associating certain multiple choice responses with a set of physical characteristics, a group of essay answers, and a photograph. Matchmaker cannot be
considered an "information content provider" under the statute because no
profile has any content until a user actively creates it.

As such, Matchmaker's role is similar to that of the customer rating system
at issue in *Gentry v. eBay, Inc.,* 99 Cal.App.4th 816, 121 Cal.Rptr.2d 703
(2002). . . . That Matchmaker classifies user characteristics into discrete categories and collects responses to specific essay questions does not transform
Matchmaker into a "developer" of the "underlying misinformation."

We also note that, as with eBay, Matchmaker's decision to structure the
information provided by users allows the company to offer additional features,
such as "matching" profiles with similar characteristics or highly structured
searches based on combinations of multiple choice questions. Without standardized, easily encoded answers, Matchmaker might not be able to offer these
services and certainly not to the same degree. Arguably, this promotes the
expressed Congressional policy "to promote the continued development of the
Internet and other interactive computer services."

Carafano responds that Matchmaker contributes much more structure and
content than eBay by asking 62 detailed questions and providing a menu of
"pre-prepared responses." However, this is a distinction of degree rather than
of kind, and Matchmaker still lacks responsibility for the "underlying misinformation."

Further, even assuming Matchmaker could be considered an information
content provider, the statute precludes treatment as a publisher or speaker for
"*any* information provided by *another* information content provider." 47 U.S.C.
§ 230(c)(1) (emphasis added). The statute would still bar Carafano's claims
unless Matchmaker created or developed the particular information at issue.
As the *Gentry* court noted,

> [T]he fact appellants allege eBay is an information content provider is
> irrelevant if eBay did not itself create or develop the content for which

appellants seek to hold it liable. It is not inconsistent for eBay to be an interactive service provider and also an information content provider; the categories are not mutually exclusive. The critical issue is whether eBay acted as an information content provider with respect to the information that appellants claim is false or misleading.

In this case, critical information about Carafano's home address, movie credits, and the e-mail address that revealed her phone number were transmitted unaltered to profile viewers. Similarly, the profile directly reproduced the most sexually suggestive comments in the essay section, none of which bore more than a tenuous relationship to the actual questions asked. Thus Matchmaker did not play a significant role in creating, developing or "transforming" the relevant information.

Thus, despite the serious and utterly deplorable consequences that occurred in this case, we conclude that Congress intended that service providers such as Matchmaker be afforded immunity from suit. Thus, we affirm the judgment of the district court, albeit on other grounds.

AFFIRMED.

NOTES

1. The distinction between service providers and content providers is central to Section 230 immunity. The *Carafano* court adopts a broad concept of "interactive computer service." *Compare* Patel, *Immunizing Internet Service Providers From Third-Party Internet Defamation Claims: How Far Should Courts Go?*, 55 VAND. L. REV. 647 (2002); Freiwald, *Comparative Institutional Analysis in Cyberspace: The Case of Intermediary Liability for Defamation*, 14 HARV. J.L. & TECH. 569 (2001).

2. Immunity for conduits for third party information is not limited to the online context. In *Winter v. GP Putnam's Sons*, 38 F.2d 1033 (9th Cir. 1991), for example, the court held that a publisher of a book involving mushroom recipes owed no obligation to the user of the book even though a mistaken recipe caused serious personal injury. The court said:

> The purposes served by products liability law also are focused on the tangible world and do not take into consideration the unique characteristics of ideas and expression. Under products liability law, strict liability is imposed on the theory that "[t]he costs of damaging events due to defectively dangerous products can best be borne by the enterprisers who make and sell these products." . . . Although there is always some appeal to the involuntary spreading of costs of injuries in any area, the costs in any comprehensive cost/benefit analysis would be quite different were strict liability concepts applied to words and ideas. We place a high priority on the unfettered exchange of ideas. We accept the risk that words and ideas have wings we cannot clip and which carry them we know not where. The threat of liability without fault (financial responsibility for our words and ideas in the absence of fault or a special undertaking or responsibility) could seriously inhibit

those who wish to share thoughts and theories. As a New York court commented, with the specter of strict liability, "[w]ould any author wish to be exposed . . . for writing on a topic which might result in physical injury? e.g. How to cut trees; How to keep bees?" One might add: "Would anyone undertake to guide by ideas expressed in words either a discrete group, a nation, or humanity in general?" Strict liability principles even when applied to products are not without their costs. Innovation may be inhibited. We tolerate these losses. They are much less disturbing than the prospect that we might be deprived of the latest ideas and theories.

3. In *Remsburg v. Docusearch, Inc.*, 816 A.2d 1001 (N.H. 2003), the court took a different approach to a related issue. After her daughter was fatally shot at her workplace, the victim's mother, as administrator of her daughter's estate, brought an action against an Internet-based investigation service and related defendants who sold her daughter's work address to the killer. The recitation of information purchased, however, indicates that the seller would not have known that the information would be misused and, indeed, one cannot imagine that the harm could have been prevented contractually (e.g., "You promise not to use the information to commit a serious felony"). The court acknowledged the general rule that one citizen does not have a duty to protect another from criminal attacks — this is because of the "fundamental unfairness of holding private citizens responsible for the unanticipated criminal acts of third parties." But it noted several exceptions to the general rule, including special circumstances, which can exist when "there is 'an especial temptation and opportunity for criminal misconduct brought about by the defendant.'"

> Thus, if a private investigator or information broker's (hereinafter "investigator" collectively) disclosure of information to a client creates a foreseeable risk of criminal misconduct against the third person whose information was disclosed, the investigator owes a duty to exercise reasonable care not to subject the third person to an unreasonable risk of harm. In determining whether the risk of criminal misconduct is foreseeable to an investigator, we examine two risks of information disclosure implicated by this case: stalking and identity theft. . . . The threats posed by stalking and identity theft lead us to conclude that the risk of criminal misconduct is sufficiently foreseeable so that an investigator has a duty to exercise reasonable care in disclosing a third person's personal information to a client. And we so hold. This is especially true when, as in this case, the investigator does not know the client or the client's purpose in seeking the information.

PROBLEM 17.5

Client operates a custom microprocessor company. During the past three months, Client has encountered difficulty in obtaining interim financing that it needs to set up custom jobs. It discovered that the source of the difficulty is a financial analysis of Client's business published in an online service that is available by subscription to banks and other lenders. The service, which publishes numerous such reports, made an error in its analysis of Client, leading to a negative report. When client did some investigation, it learned that the service obtains information from third party sources and, in addition to reproducing them, makes an evaluation of a company based on this data. The error, it turns out, came from one such source.

You are convinced that Client can state an effective claim under state law for negligence and for defamation against the service. Does Section 230 prevent the claim from being successful?

B. LIABILITY FOR THIRD-PARTY INFRINGEMENT: DMCA §512

Another form of potential liability for third-party content online deals with copyright infringement. Online systems are, in effect, giant copying machines, and reconciliation of the interests of copyright owners on the one hand with the interests of online users of providers on the other has been difficult. We leave questions of copyright infringement, direct and indirect, to another course. Our primary concern relates to contractual issues and, on that question, the Copyright Act provides explicit guidance in 17 U.S.C. §512.

ELLISON v. ROBERTSON
357 F.3d 1072 (9th Cir. 2004)

PREGERSON, CIRCUIT JUDGE:

Ellison appeals the district court's summary judgment dismissal of his copyright infringement action against America Online, Inc. (AOL). The copyright infringement action arose when, without Ellison's authorization, Stephen Robertson posted copies of some of Ellison's copyrighted short stories on a peer-to-peer file-sharing network, the USENET. Because AOL provides its subscribers access to the USENET news-group at issue, Ellison brought claims for vicarious and contributory copyright infringement against AOL. AOL moved for summary judgment. It asserted defenses to Ellison's infringement claims and alternatively argued that it qualified for one of the four safe harbor limitations of liability under Title II of the Digital Millennium Copyright Act (DMCA). The district court concluded that AOL was not liable for vicarious infringement. Although the court found there to be triable issues of material fact concerning Ellison's contributory infringement claim, it nonetheless granted summary judgment because it held that AOL qualified for the DMCA safe harbor limitation of liability under 17 U.S.C. §512(a).

We hold that the district court erred in granting AOL's motion for summary judgment. . . .

The Law of Copyright Infringement and the DMCA

Ellison alleges that AOL infringed his copyrighted works. As a threshold question, a plaintiff who claims copyright infringement must show: (1) ownership of a valid copyright; and (2) that the defendant violated the copyright owner's exclusive rights under the Copyright Act. We recognize three doctrines of copyright liability: direct copyright infringement, contributory copyright infringement, and vicarious copyright infringement. To prove a claim of direct copyright infringement, a plaintiff must show that he owns the copyright and that the defendant himself violated one or more of the plaintiff's exclusive rights under the Copyright Act. *A & M Records v. Napster, Inc.*, 239 F.3d 1004 (9th Cir. 2001) (*Napster II*). "One who, with knowledge of the infringing activity, induces, causes or materially contributes to the infringing conduct *of another* may be liable as a 'contributory' [copyright] infringer." We have interpreted the knowledge requirement for contributory copyright infringement to include both those with *actual knowledge* and those who *have reason to know* of direct infringement. A defendant is vicariously liable for copyright infringement if he enjoys a direct financial benefit from *another's* infringing activity and "has the right and ability to supervise" the infringing activity.

Congress enacted the DMCA in 1998 . . . Title II of the DMCA, the Online Copyright Infringement Liability Limitation Act (OCILLA). OCILLA endeavors to facilitate cooperation among Internet service providers and copyright owners "to detect and deal with copyright infringements that take place in the digital networked environment." Congress hoped to provide "greater certainty to service providers concerning their legal exposure for infringements that may occur in the course of their activities."

But "[r]ather than embarking on a wholesale clarification of" the various doctrines of copyright liability, Congress opted "to leave current law in its evolving state and, instead, to create a series of 'safe harbors,' for certain common activities of service providers." Under OCILLA's four safe harbors, service providers may limit their liability for claims of copyright infringement. 17 U.S.C. § 512(a-d). These safe harbors provide protection from liability for: (1) transitory digital network communications; (2) system caching; (3) information residing on systems or networks at the direction of users; and (4) information location tools. Far short of adopting enhanced or wholly new standards to evaluate claims of copyright infringement against online service providers, Congress provided that OCILLA's "limitations of liability apply if the provider is found to be liable *under existing principles of law*."

We thus agree with the district court that "[t]he DMCA did not simply rewrite copyright law for the on-line world." Congress would have done so if it so desired. Claims against service providers for direct, contributory, or vicarious copyright infringement, therefore, are generally evaluated just as they would be in the non-online world.

III. Ellison's Claims Against AOL
A. Contributory Copyright Infringement

Ellison alleged in his complaint that AOL was contributorily liable for copyright infringement. To substantiate his claim, he must show that AOL knew or had reason to know of the infringing activity taking place on its USENET servers and that AOL materially contributed to the infringing activity.

1. Knowledge

We first consider whether AOL knew or had reason to know of the infringing activity. The district court found that AOL did not have actual knowledge of the infringement before Ellison filed his copyright infringement action, but concluded that "a reasonable trier of fact could certainly find that AOL had reason to know that infringing copies of Ellison's works were stored on their Usenet servers." We agree.

AOL changed its contact e-mail address from "copyright@aol.com" to "aolcopyright@aol.com" in the fall of 1999, but waited until April 2000 to register the change with the U.S. Copyright Office. Moreover, AOL failed to configure the old e-mail address so that it would either forward messages to the new address or return new messages to their senders. In the meantime, complaints such as Ellison's went unheeded, and complainants were not notified that their messages had not been delivered. Furthermore, there is evidence in the record suggesting that a phone call from AOL subscriber John J. Miller to AOL should have put AOL on notice of the infringing activity on the particular USENET group at issue in this case, "alt.binaries.e-book." Miller contacted AOL to report the existence of unauthorized copies of works by various authors. Because there is evidence indicating that AOL changed its e-mail address in an unreasonable manner and that AOL should have been on notice of infringing activity we conclude that a reasonable trier of fact could find that AOL had reason to know of potentially infringing activity occurring within its USENET network.

2. Material Contribution

The second element a plaintiff must prove to succeed on a claim of contributory copyright infringement is that the defendant materially contributed to another's infringement. The district court found that Ellison demonstrated a triable issue regarding whether AOL materially contributed to the copyright infringement:

> The Court agrees with the findings of the court in *Netcom* [*Religious Tech. Ctr. v. Netcom On-Line Communication Servs., Inc.*, 923 F. Supp. 1231 (N.D. Cal. 1995),] that "[p]roviding a service that allows for the automatic distribution of all Usenet postings, infringing and noninfringing" can constitute a material contribution when the [Internet service provider] knows or should know of infringing activity on its system "yet continues to aid in the accomplishment of . . . [the direct infringer's] purpose of publicly distributing the postings."

In *Netcom,* the copyright holders of certain works of L. Ron Hubbard sued the operator of a news-group and a large Internet service provider, Netcom, for copyright infringement. The *Netcom* court held that the fact that the USENET service allowed Netcom's subscribers access to copyrighted works was sufficient to raise a triable issue regarding material contribution. We conclude that this reasoning applies to Ellison's claim of contributory copyright infringement. Because a reasonable trier of fact could conclude that AOL materially contributed to the copyright infringement by storing infringing copies of Ellison's works on its USENET groups and providing the groups' users with access to those copies, we agree with the district court's finding that this constituted a triable issue.

B. Vicarious Copyright Infringement

Ellison alleges that AOL is vicariously liable for copyright infringement. Thus, Ellison must show that AOL derived a direct financial benefit from the infringement and had the right and ability to supervise the infringing activity.

"Financial benefit exists where the availability of infringing material 'acts as a "draw" for customers.'" In *Napster II,* we found that Napster increased its userbase by providing its customers with access to pirated copies of protected works and that "[a]mple evidence support[ed] the district court's finding that Napster's future revenue [was] directly dependent upon increases in userbase." But in this case, the district court sought to distinguish *Napster II.* The district court emphasized that virtually all of Napster's "draw" of customers resulted from Napster's providing access to infringing material. Because AOL's USENET group access constituted a relatively insignificant draw when cast against AOL's vast array of products and services, the district court reasoned, AOL did not receive a direct financial benefit from the infringing activity.

The district court interprets *Fonovisa [Inc. v. Cherry Auction, Inc.,* 76 F.3d 259 (9th Cir. 1996),] and "direct financial benefit" to require a "substantial" proportion of a defendant's income to be directly linked to infringing activities for the purpose of vicarious liability analysis. We disagree with the addition of this quantification requirement. We concluded in *Fonovisa* that "the sale of pirated recordings at the Cherry Auction swap meet is a 'draw' for customers," which we held sufficient to state the financial benefit element of the claim for vicarious liability. *Fonovisa,* 76 F.3d at 263-64. There is no requirement that the draw be "substantial."

AOL offers access to USENET groups as part of its service for a reason: it helps to encourage overall subscription to its services. Here, AOL's future revenue is directly dependent upon increases in its userbase. Certainly, the fact that AOL provides its subscribers access to certain USENET groups constitutes a small "draw" in proportion to its overall profits, but AOL's status as a behemoth online service provider, by itself, does not insulate it categorically from vicarious liability. Regardless of what *fraction* of AOL's earnings are considered a direct result of providing its subscribers access to the USENET groups that contained infringing material — indeed, almost any aspect of AOL's services would appear *relatively* minuscule because of its sheer size — they would be earnings nonetheless. The essential aspect of the "direct financial benefit" inquiry is whether there is a causal relationship between the infringing activity and any financial benefit a defendant reaps, regardless of *how substantial* the benefit is in proportion to a defendant's overall profits.

Given this framework, the question before us is whether there is a triable issue of a material fact regarding whether AOL received a direct financial benefit from the copyright infringement. Ellison proffers the following evidence to support his contention that AOL received a direct financial benefit from the infringement: (1) an AOL securities filing that reflects the central importance of attracting and retaining subscribers for its business and revenue generation and (2) evidence indicating that many subscribers inquired about AOL blocking access to the USENET group at issue. This evidence is hardly compelling. We note that there is no evidence that indicates that AOL customers either subscribed because of the available infringing material or canceled subscriptions because it was no longer available. While a causal relationship might exist between AOL's profits from subscriptions and the infringing activity taking place on its USENET servers, Ellison has not offered enough evidence for a reasonable juror so to conclude.

We recognize, of course, that there is usually substantial overlap between aspects of goods or services that customers value and aspects of goods or services that ultimately draw the customers. There are, however, cases in which customers value a service that does not "act as a draw." Accordingly, Congress cautions courts that "receiving a one-time set-up fee and flat periodic payments for service . . . [ordinarily] would not constitute receiving a 'financial benefit directly attributable to the infringing activity.'" But "where the value of the service lies in providing access to infringing material," courts might find such "one-time set-up and flat periodic" fees to constitute a direct financial benefit. Thus, the central question of the "direct financial benefit" inquiry in this case is whether the infringing activity constitutes a draw for subscribers, not just an added benefit.

The record lacks evidence that AOL attracted or retained subscriptions because of the infringement or lost subscriptions because of AOL's eventual obstruction of the infringement. Accordingly, no jury could reasonably conclude that AOL received a direct financial benefit from providing access to the infringing material. Therefore, Ellison's claim of vicarious copyright infringement fails.

IV. AOL and the Safe Harbors from Liability Under the DMCA

To be eligible for any of the four safe harbor limitations of liability, a service provider must meet the conditions for eligibility set forth in OCILLA. The safe harbor limitations of liability only apply to a service provider that:

> (A) has adopted and reasonably implemented, and informs subscribers and account holders of the service provider's system or network of, a policy that provides for the termination in appropriate circumstances of subscribers and account holders of the service provider's system or network who are repeat infringers; and

> (B) accommodates and does not interfere with standard technical measures.

If a service provider does not meet these threshold requirements, it is not entitled to invoke OCILLA's safe harbor limitations on liability.

We hold that the district court erred in concluding on summary judgment that AOL satisfied the requirements of § 512(i). There is at least a triable issue of material fact regarding AOL's eligibility for the safe harbor limitations of liability in this case. Section 512(i)(1)(A) requires service providers to: (1) adopt a policy that provides for the termination of service access for repeat copyright infringers in appropriate circumstances; (2) implement that policy in a reasonable manner; and (3) inform its subscribers of the policy. It is difficult to conclude as a matter of law, as the district court did, that AOL had "reasonably implemented" a policy against repeat infringers. There is ample evidence in the record that suggests that AOL did not have an effective notification procedure in place at the time the alleged infringing activities were taking place. Although AOL did notify the Copyright Office of its correct e-mail address before Ellison's attorney attempted to contact AOL and did post its correct e-mail address on the AOL website with a brief summary of its policy as to repeat infringers, AOL also: (1) changed the e-mail address to which infringement notifications were supposed to have been sent; and (2) failed to provide for forwarding of messages sent to the old address or notification that the e-mail address was inactive. AOL should have closed the old e-mail account or forwarded the e-mails sent to the old account to the new one. Instead, AOL allowed notices of potential copyright infringement to fall into a vacuum and to go unheeded; that fact is sufficient for a reasonable jury to conclude that AOL had not reasonably implemented its policy against repeat infringers.

. . . .

Conclusion

We conclude that the district court correctly identified triable issues of fact with respect to Ellison's claim against AOL for contributory copyright infringement. We also agree with the district court that Ellison's claim for vicarious copyright infringement fails; Ellison did not offer sufficient evidence that AOL received a direct financial benefit from the infringement to survive summary judgment. Further, because we conclude that the district court failed to discern triable issues of fact concerning AOL's threshold eligibility under the DMCA's safe harbor limitations of liability, we reverse the district court's judgment on this matter. . . .

ALS SCAN, INC. v. REMARQ COMMUNITIES, INC.
239 F.3d 619 (4th Cir. 2001)

NIEMEYER, CIRCUIT JUDGE:

We are presented with an issue of first impression — whether an Internet service provider enjoys a safe harbor from copyright infringement liability as provided by Title II of the Digital Millennium Copyright Act ("DMCA") when it is put on notice of infringement activity on its system by an imperfect notice. Because we conclude that the service provider was provided with a notice of infringing activity that *substantially* complied with the Act, it may not rely on a claim of defective notice to maintain the immunity defense provided by the safe harbor. Accordingly, we reverse the ruling of the district court that found the notice fatally defective, and affirm its remaining rulings.

I

ALS Scan, Inc. . . . is engaged in the business of creating and marketing "adult" photographs. It displays these pictures on the Internet to paying subscribers and also sells them through the media of CD ROMs and videotapes. ALS Scan is holder of the copyrights for all of these photographs.

RemarQ Communities, Inc. . . . is an online Internet service provider that provides access to its subscribing members. It has approximately 24,000 subscribers to its newsgroup base and provides access to over 30,000 newsgroups which cover thousands of subjects. These newsgroups, organized by topic, enable subscribers to participate in discussions on virtually any topic, such as fine arts, politics, religion, social issues, sports, and entertainment. For example,

RemarQ provides access to a newsgroup entitled "Baltimore Orioles," in which users share observations or materials about the Orioles. It claims that users post over one million articles a day in these newsgroups, which RemarQ removes after about 8-10 days to accommodate its limited server capacity. In providing access to newsgroups, RemarQ does not monitor, regulate, or censor the content of articles posted in the newsgroup by subscribing members. It does, however, have the ability to filter information contained in the newsgroups and to screen its members from logging onto certain newsgroups, such as those containing pornographic material.

Two of the newsgroups to which RemarQ provides its subscribers access contain ALS Scan's name in the titles. These newsgroups — "alt.als" and "alt.binaries.pictures.erotica.als" — contain hundreds of postings that infringe ALS Scan's copyrights. These postings are placed in these newsgroups by RemarQ's subscribers.

Upon discovering that RemarQ databases contained material that infringed ALS Scan's copyrights, ALS Scan sent a letter, dated August 2, 1999, to RemarQ, stating:

> Both of these newsgroups ["alt.als" and "alt.binaries.pictures.erotica.als"] were created for the sole purpose of violating our Federally filed Copyrights and Tradename. These newsgroups contain virtually all Federally Copyrighted images. . . . Your servers provide access to these illegally posted images and enable the illegal transmission of these images across state lines.
>
> This is a cease and desist letter. You are hereby ordered to cease carrying these newsgroups within twenty-four (24) hours upon receipt of this correspondence. . . .
>
> America Online, Erol's, Mindspring, and others have all complied with our cease and desist order and no longer carry these newsgroups. . . .
>
> Our ALS Scan models can be identified at. . . . Our copyright information can be reviewed at. . . .

RemarQ responded by refusing to comply with ALS Scan's demand but advising ALS Scan that RemarQ would eliminate individual infringing items from these newsgroups if ALS Scan identified them "with sufficient specificity." ALS Scan answered that RemarQ had included over 10,000 copyrighted images belonging to ALS Scan in its newsgroups over the period of several months and that

> [t]hese newsgroups have apparently been created by individuals for the express sole purpose of illegally posting, transferring and disseminating photographs that have been copyrighted by my client through both its websites and its CD-ROMs. The newsgroups, on their face from reviewing messages posted thereon, serve no other purpose.

When correspondence between the parties progressed no further to resolution of the dispute, ALS Scan commenced this action, alleging violations of the Copyright Act and Title II of the DMCA, as well as unfair competition. In its complaint, ALS Scan alleged that RemarQ possessed actual knowledge that the newsgroups contained infringing material but had "steadfastly refused to remove or block access to the material." ALS Scan also alleged that RemarQ was put on notice by ALS Scan of the infringing material contained in its database. In addition to injunctive relief, ALS Scan demanded actual and statutory damages, as well as attorneys fees. It attached to its complaint affidavits establishing the essential elements of its claims.

In response, RemarQ filed a motion to dismiss the complaint or, in the alternative, for summary judgment, and also attached affidavits, stating that RemarQ was prepared to remove articles posted in its newsgroups if the allegedly infringing articles were specifically identified. It contended that because it is a provider of access to news-groups, ALS Scan's failure to comply with the DMCA notice requirements provided it with a defense to ALS Scan's copyright infringement claim.

The district court ruled . . . (1) that RemarQ could not be held liable for *direct* copyright infringement merely because it provided access to a newsgroup containing infringing material; and (2) that RemarQ could not be held liable for *contributory* infringement because ALS Scan failed to comply with the notice requirements set forth in the DMCA, 17 U.S.C. § 512(c)(3)(A). This appeal followed.

II

ALS Scan contends first that the district court erred in dismissing its *direct* copyright infringement claim. . . . In rejecting ALS Scan's direct infringement claim, the district court relied on the decision in *Religious Technology Center v. Netcom On-Line Communication Services, Inc.,* 907 F.Supp. 1361, 1368-73 (N. D.Cal.1995), which concluded that when an Internet provider serves, without human intervention, as a passive conduit for copyrighted material, it is not liable as a direct infringer. The *Netcom* court reasoned that "it does not make sense to adopt a rule that could lead to liability of countless parties whose role in the infringement is nothing more than setting up and operating a system that is necessary for the functioning of the Internet." That court observed that it would not be workable to hold "the entire Internet liable for activities that cannot reasonably be deterred." ALS Scan argues, however, that the better reasoned position, contrary to that held in *Netcom,* is presented in *Playboy Enterprises, Inc. v. Frena,* 839 F.Supp. 1552, 1555-59 (M.D.Fla.1993), which held a computer bulletin board service provider liable for the copyright infringement when it failed to prevent the placement of plaintiff's copyrighted photographs in its system, despite any proof that the provider had any knowledge of the infringing activities.

Although we find the *Netcom* court reasoning more persuasive, the ultimate conclusion on this point is controlled by Congress' codification of the *Netcom* principles in Title II of the DMCA. As the House Report for that Act states,

> The bill distinguishes between direct infringement and secondary liability, treating each separately. This structure is consistent with evolving case law, and appropriate in light of the different legal bases for and policies behind the different forms of liability. As to direct infringement, liability is ruled out for passive, automatic acts engaged in through a technological process initiated by another. Thus the bill essentially

codifies the result in the leading and most thoughtful judicial decision to date: *Religious Technology Center v. Netcom On-Line Communication Services, Inc.* In doing so, it overrules these aspects of *Playboy Enterprises, Inc. v. Frena,* 839 F.Supp. 1552 (M.D.Fla.1993), insofar as that case suggests that such acts by service providers could constitute direct infringement, and provides certainty that *Netcom* and its progeny, so far only a few district court cases, will be the law of the land.

Accordingly, we address only ALS Scan's claims brought under the DMCA itself.

III

For its principal argument, ALS Scan contends that it substantially complied with the notification requirements of the DMCA and thereby denied RemarQ the "safe harbor" from copyright infringement liability granted by that Act. *See* 17 U.S.C. §512(c)(3)(A). It asserts that because its notification was sufficient to put RemarQ on notice of its infringement activities, RemarQ lost its service-provider immunity from infringement liability. It argues that the district court's application of the DMCA was overly strict and that Congress did not intend to permit Internet providers to avoid copyright infringement liability "merely because a cease and desist notice failed to technically comply with the DMCA." . . .

Title II of the DMCA, designated the "Online Copyright Infringement Limitation Act" defines limitations of liability for copyright infringement to which Internet service providers might otherwise be exposed. The Act defines a service provider broadly to include any provider of "online services or network access, or the operator of facilities therefore," including any entity providing "digital online communications, between or among points specified by user, of material of the user's choosing, without modification to the content of the material as sent or received." 17 U.S.C. §512(k). Neither party to this case suggests that RemarQ is not an Internet service provider for purposes of the Act.

The liability-limiting provision applicable here, 17 U.S.C. §512(c), gives Internet service providers a safe harbor from liability for "infringement of copyright by reason of the storage at the direction of a user of material that resides on a system or network controlled or operated by or for the service provider" as long as the service provider can show that: (1) it has neither actual knowledge that its system contains infringing materials nor an awareness of facts or circumstances from which infringement is apparent, or it has expeditiously removed or disabled access to infringing material upon obtaining actual knowledge of infringement; (2) it receives no financial benefit directly attributable to infringing activity; *and* (3) it responded expeditiously to remove or disable access to material claimed to be infringing after receiving from the copyright holder a notification conforming with requirements of §512(c)(3). Thus, to qualify for this safe harbor protection, the Internet service provider must demonstrate that it has met all three of the safe harbor requirements, and a showing under the first prong — the lack of actual or constructive knowledge — is prior to and separate from the showings that must be made under the second and third prongs.

In this case, the district court evaluated the adequacy [of the notice] given to RemarQ under the third prong only. . . . In evaluating the third prong, requiring RemarQ to remove materials following "notification," the district court concluded that ALS Scan's notice was defective in failing to comply strictly with two of the six requirements of a notification — (1) that ALS Scan's notice include "a list of [infringing] works" contained on the RemarQ site and (2) that the notice identify the infringing works in sufficient detail to enable RemarQ to locate and disable them.

In support of the district court's conclusion, RemarQ points to the fact that ALS Scan never provided it with a "representative list" of the infringing photographs, as required by § 512(c)(3)(A)(ii), nor did it identify those photographs with sufficient detail to enable RemarQ to locate and disable them, as required by § 512(c)(3)(A)(iii). RemarQ buttresses its contention with the observation that not all materials at the offending sites contained material to which ALS Scan held the copyrights. RemarQ's affidavit states in this regard:

> Some, but not all, of the pictures users have posted on these sites appear to be ALS Scan pictures. It also appears that users have posted other non-ALS Scan's erotic images on these newsgroups. The articles in these newsgroups also contain text messages, many of which discuss the adult images posted on the newsgroups.

ALS Scan responds that the two sites in question — "alt.als" and "alt.binaries.pictures.erotica.als" — were created solely for the purpose of publishing and exchanging ALS Scan's copyrighted images. It points out that the address of the newsgroup is defined by ALS Scan's name. As one of its affidavits states:

> [RemarQ's] subscribers going onto the two offending newsgroups for the purpose of violating [ALS Scan's] copyrights, are actually aware of the copyrighted status of [ALS Scan's] material because (1) each newsgroup has "als" as part of its title, and (2) each photograph belonging to [ALS Scan] has [ALS Scan's] name and/or the copyright symbol next to it.

> Each of these two newsgroups was created by unknown persons for the illegal purpose of trading the copyrighted pictures of [ALS Scan] to one another without the need for paying to either (1) become members of [ALS Scan's] web site(s) or (2) purchasing the CD ROMs produced by [ALS Scan].

ALS Scan presses the contention that these two sites serve no other purpose than to distribute ALS Scan's copyrighted materials and therefore, by directing RemarQ to these sites, it has directed RemarQ to a representative list of infringing materials.

The DMCA was enacted both to preserve copyright enforcement on the Internet and to provide immunity to service providers from copyright infringement liability for "passive," "automatic" actions in which a service provider's system engages through a technological process initiated by another without the knowledge of the service provider. This immunity, however, is not presumptive, but granted only to "innocent" service providers who can prove they do not have actual or constructive knowledge of the infringement, as defined under any of the three prongs of 17 U.S.C. §512(c)(1). The DMCA's protection of an innocent service provider disappears at the moment the service provider loses its innocence, i.e., at the moment it becomes aware that a third party is using its system to infringe. At that point, the Act shifts responsibility to the service provider to disable the infringing matter, "preserv[ing] the strong incentives for service providers and copyright owners to cooperate to detect and deal with copyright infringements that take place in the digital networked environment." In the spirit of achieving a balance between the responsibilities of the service provider and the copyright owner, the DMCA requires that a copyright owner put the service provider on notice in a detailed manner but allows notice by means that comport with the prescribed format only "substantially," rather than perfectly. The Act states: "To be effective under this subsection, a notification of claimed infringement must be a written communication provided to the designated agent of a service provider that includes *substantially* the following. . . ." 17 U.S.C. §512(c)(3)(A) (emphasis added). In addition to substantial compliance, the notification requirements are relaxed to the extent that, with respect to multiple works, not all must be identified — only a "representative" list. And with respect to location information, the copyright holder must provide information that is "*reasonably* sufficient" to permit the service provider to "locate" this material. This subsection specifying the requirements of a notification does not seek to burden copyright holders with the responsibility of identifying every infringing work — or even most of them — when multiple copyrights are involved. Instead, the requirements are written so as to reduce the burden of holders of multiple copyrights who face extensive infringement of their works. Thus, when a letter provides notice equivalent to a list of representative works that can be easily identified by the service provider, the notice substantially complies with the notification requirements.

In this case, ALS Scan provided RemarQ with information that (1) identified two sites created for the sole purpose of publishing ALS Scan's copyrighted works, (2) asserted that virtually all the images at the two sites were its copyrighted material, and (3) referred RemarQ to two web addresses where RemarQ could find pictures of ALS Scan's models and obtain ALS Scan's copyright information. In addition, it noted that material at the site could be identified as ALS Scan's material because the material included ALS Scan's "name and/or copyright symbol next to it." We believe that with this information, ALS Scan substantially complied with the notification requirement of providing a representative list of infringing material as well as information reasonably sufficient to enable RemarQ to locate the infringing material. To the extent that ALS Scan's claims about infringing materials prove to be false, RemarQ has remedies for any injury it suffers as a result of removing or disabling non-infringing material.

Accordingly, we reverse the district court's ruling granting summary judgment in favor of RemarQ on the basis of ALS Scan's non-compliance with the notification provisions of 17 U.S.C. §512(c)(3)(A)(ii) and (iii). Because our ruling only removes the safe harbor defense, we remand for further proceedings on ALS Scan's copyright infringement claims and any other affirmative defenses that RemarQ may have. . . .

HENDRICKSON v. AMAZON.COM
298 F. Supp. 2d 914 (C.D. Cal. 2003)

HATTER, DISTRICT JUDGE.

Robert Hendrickson ("Hendrickson") owns the copyright to the movie *Manson,* which he has not released, or authorized to be released, in a digital video disc ("DVD") format. Thus, all copies of *Manson* sold in a DVD format infringe upon Hendrickson's copyright. On January 28, 2002, Hendrickson sent a letter to Amazon.com, Inc. ("Amazon"), notifying it that all copies of *Manson* on DVD infringe his copyright. On October 21, 2002, Hendrickson noticed that a *Manson* DVD was recently posted for sale by Demetrious Papaioannou ("Papaioannou") on Amazon's website. Two days later, Hendrickson purchased a copy of the DVD from Papaioannou, using Amazon's website credit services to facilitate the transaction.

Hendrickson, then, filed this action against Amazon and Papaioannou. . . . Amazon moved for summary judgment, asserting that it is not liable for direct copyright infringement, and that it is protected against vicarious infringement by the safe harbor provision of the Digital Millennium Copyright Act ("DMCA"). . . .

Because Amazon qualifies as an ISP under the DMCA, it is entitled to the safe harbor affirmative defense against a claim of vicarious copyright infringement if it establishes the following three elements:

A. It does not have actual knowledge that the material . . . on the system or network is infringing;

. . . .

(ii) in the absence of such actual knowledge, is not aware of facts or circumstances from which infringing activity is apparent; or

(iii) upon obtaining such knowledge or awareness, acts expeditiously to remove, or disable access to, the material;

B. It does not receive a financial benefit directly attributable to the infringing activity, in a case in which the service provider has the right, and ability to control such activity; and

C. Upon notification of claimed infringement . . . [it] responds expeditiously to remove, or disable access to, the material. . . .

17 U.S.C. § 512(c).

Hendrickson's January 28, 2002, letter to Amazon notified Amazon that all *Manson* DVDs were unauthorized by the copyright owner and that any sales of such DVDs conducted via the Amazon website would be infringing activity in violation of his exclusive right to distribute. . . . Amazon asserts that the letter neither substantially complied with the identification requirements of the DMCA, nor was it consistent with the intent of the DMCA, which is to facilitate robust development of the internet. The DMCA places the burden on the copyright owner to monitor the internet for potentially infringing sales. "[A] service provider need not monitor its service or affirmatively seek facts indicating infringing activity. . . ." To allow a plaintiff to shift its burden to the service provider would be contrary to the balance crafted by Congress. . . .

This Court previously granted summary judgment in favor of Hendrickson, in a previous action, by deciding that his January, 2002, letter substantially complied with the DMCA requirements as to eight named defendants. . . . However, because the DMCA is relatively new, the question as to how long an adequate notice should remain viable is still unanswered. "[T]he Committee [did] not intend [to] suggest that a provider must . . . monitor its service. . . ." H.R. at 61. The Committee, also, implied that both the copyright owner and the ISP should cooperate with each other to detect and deal with copyright infringement that takes place in the digital networked environment. Thus, it was not the intention of Congress that a copyright owner could write one blanket notice to all service providers alerting them of infringing material, thus, relieving him of any further responsibility and, thereby, placing the onus forever on the ISP. However, it is, also, against the spirit of the DMCA if the entire responsibility lies with the copyright owner to forever police websites in search of possible infringers.

In evaluating the balance crafted by Congress, courts traditionally employ a strong presumption that the plain language of a statute expresses congressional intent. The Ninth Circuit has consistently refused to defer to interpretations that conflict with plain statutory language. "If the term at issue has a settled meaning, we must infer that the legislature meant to incorporate the established meaning unless the statute dictates otherwise." The actual language of the DMCA is present tense. The service provider must have knowledge that the actual material "is infringing." Alternatively, it must be aware that infringing activity "is apparent." "The term activity is intended to mean activity *using* the material *on the system* or network. The Committee intends such activity to refer to wrongful activity that *is occurring on the site*. . . ." H.R. at 53 (emphasis added). Because the language of the statute is present tense, it clearly indicates that Congress intended for the notice to make the service provider aware of the infringing activity that is occurring at the time it receives the notice.

In interpreting a similar section of the DMCA, Congress states "[O]n line editors and catalogers would not be required to make discriminating judgments about *potential* copyright infringements." H.R. at 58. Although, the interpretation is referring to the reason for requiring the copyright owner to offer adequate notice, this interpretation must be read in conjunction with the plain language of the statute in addition to the intent of Congress that service providers not have to monitor their websites indefinitely.

Moreover, the purpose behind the notice is to provide the ISP with adequate information to find and examine the allegedly infringing material expeditiously. H.R. at 55. If the infringing material *is on* the website *at the time* the ISP receives the notice, then the information, that all *Manson* DVD's are infringing, can be adequate to find the infringing material expeditiously. However, if at the time the notice is received, the infringing material is not posted, the notice does not enable the service provider to locate infringing material that is not there, let alone do it expeditiously.

Recognizing that Congress tried to craft a balance between the responsibilities of the copyright owner and the ISP, there is a limit to the viability of an otherwise adequate notice. Hendrickson's January, 2002, letter, claiming all *Manson* DVDs violate his copyright, although adequate for the listings then on Amazon, cannot be deemed adequate notice for subsequent listings and sales, especially, as here, when the infringing item was posted for sale nine months after the date of the notice. . . .

To satisfy the second prong of the test, Amazon must show that it "does not receive a financial benefit directly attributable to the infringing activity, in a case in which the service provider has the right and ability to control such activity." Amazon does receive a financial benefit from its third party sellers, so its only defense is to prove that it does not have the right and ability to control such activity. Here, the infringing activity is the sale of the unauthorized work, not the posting of the listing. There is no evidence to suggest that Amazon had the ability to know that an infringing sale by a third party seller would occur. Amazon's evidence established that it never possessed the DVD, and never had the opportunity to inspect the item. Amazon merely provided the forum for an independent third party seller to list and sell his merchandise. Amazon was not actively involved in the listing, bidding, sale or delivery of the DVD. The fact that Amazon generated automatic email responses when the DVD was listed and again when it was sold, does not mean that Amazon was actively involved in the sale. Once a third party seller decides to list an item, the responsibility is on the seller to consummate the sale. While Amazon does provide transaction processing for credit card purchases, that additional service does not give Amazon control over the sale. In sum, Amazon's evidence shows that it did not have control of the sale of the DVD.

As discussed above, Amazon could not respond to the notice of claimed infringement and remove, or disable access to, the material since the notice was no longer viable. Thus, the third prong of the save harbor provision is not applicable.

Thus, Amazon has proven that it qualifies for the safe harbor affirmative defense of the DMCA. . . .

NOTES

1. If all copies of a work are infringing, what notification must an online system receive in order to be required to act?

2. Judge Posner, in *In re Aimster Copyright Litigation*, 334 F.3d 643 (7th Cir. 2003), affirmed a preliminary injunction against an online service that facilitated infringing transfers of copyrighted works between users of the system, suggesting that an affirmative duty to prevent infringement could arise without specific knowledge of specific infringements, but only under a balancing analysis. The court said:

> What is true is that when a supplier is offering a product or service that has noninfringing as well as infringing uses, some estimate of the respective magnitudes of these uses is necessary for a finding of con-

tributory infringement. . . . But the balancing of costs and benefits is necessary only in a case in which substantial noninfringing uses, present or prospective, are demonstrated. . . . Aimster has failed to produce any evidence that its service has ever been used for a noninfringing use, let alone evidence concerning the frequency of such uses. . . . We have to assume for purposes of deciding this appeal that no such evidence exists; its absence, in combination with the evidence presented by the recording industry, justified the district judge in concluding that the industry would be likely to prevail in a full trial on the issue of contributory infringement. . . . If the *only* effect of a service challenged as contributory infringement is to enable copyrights to be infringed, the magnitude of the resulting loss, even whether there is a net loss, becomes irrelevant to liability. Even when there are noninfringing uses of an Internet file-sharing service, moreover, if the infringing uses are substantial then to avoid liability as a contributory infringer the provider of the service must show that it would have been disproportionately costly for him to eliminate or at least reduce substantially the infringing uses.

In *Aimster*, the system included an encryption system that blocked even the service-provider from knowing what files were being transferred. The resulting lack of knowledge about specific incidents of infringement, however, did not and should not shield the service provider.

PROBLEM 17.6

You are counsel to an online auction company. Customers of this company are free to post items for sale at auction and others bid on the items. The agreements with all customers make it clear that the customers, rather than the online service, are the sellers and buyers. The online service plans to charge 4% of the sale price as a fee for operating the system, and a small set price for all listings. It expects that some of the listed items may be infringing materials.

a. Does the service qualify for the safe harbor protections?

b. Assuming that the system can qualify for Section 512 protection, draft appropriate policy provisions to be included in the user's contracts.

METRO-GOLDWYN-MAYER STUDIOS, INC. v. GROKSTER, LTD.
125 S.Ct. 2764 (2005)

Justice SOUTER delivered the opinion of the Court.

The question is under what circumstances the distributor of a product capable of both lawful and unlawful use is liable for acts of copyright infringement by third parties using the product. We hold that one who distributes a device with the object of promoting its use to infringe copyright, as shown by clear expression or other affirmative steps taken to foster infringement, is liable for the resulting acts of infringement by third parties.

I

A

Respondents, Grokster, Ltd., and StreamCast Networks, Inc., defendants in the trial court, distribute free software products that allow computer users to share electronic files through peer-to-peer networks, so called because users' computers communicate directly with each other, not through central servers. The advantage of peer-to-peer networks over information networks of other types shows up in their substantial and growing popularity. Because they need no central computer server to mediate the exchange of information or files among users, the high-bandwidth communications capacity for a server may be dispensed with, and the need for costly server storage space is eliminated. . . . . Given these benefits in security, cost, and efficiency, peer-to-peer networks are employed to store and distribute electronic files by universities, government agencies, corporations, and libraries, among others.

Other users of peer-to-peer networks include individual recipients of Grokster's and StreamCast's software, and although the networks that they enjoy through using the software can be used to share any type of digital file, they have prominently employed those networks in sharing copyrighted music and video files without authorization. A group of copyright holders (MGM for short, but including motion picture studios, recording companies, songwriters, and music publishers) sued Grokster and StreamCast for their users' copyright infringements, alleging that they knowingly and intentionally distributed their software to enable users to reproduce and distribute the copyrighted works in violation of the Copyright Act. MGM sought damages and an injunction.

Discovery . . . revealed the way the software worked, the business aims of each defendant company, and the predilections of the users. Grokster's eponymous software employs what is known as FastTrack technology, a protocol developed by others and licensed to Grokster. StreamCast distributes a very similar product except that its software, called Morpheus, relies on what is known as Gnutella technology. A user who downloads and installs either software possesses the protocol to send requests for files directly to the computers of others using software compatible with FastTrack or Gnutella. On the FastTrack network opened by the Grokster software, the user's request goes to a computer given an indexing capacity by the software and designated a supernode, or to some other computer with comparable power and capacity to collect temporary indexes of the files available on the computers of users connected to it. The supernode (or indexing computer) searches its own index and may communicate the search request to other supernodes. If the file is found, the supernode discloses its location to the computer requesting it, and the requesting user can download the file directly from the computer located. The copied file is placed in a designated sharing folder on the requesting user's computer, where it is available for other users to download in turn, along with any other file in that folder.

In the Gnutella network made available by Morpheus, the process is mostly the same, except that in some versions of the Gnutella protocol there are no supernodes. In these versions, peer computers using the protocol communicate directly with each other. . . .

Although Grokster and StreamCast do not therefore know when particular files are copied, a few searches using their software would show what is available on the networks the software reaches. MGM commissioned a statistician to conduct a systematic search, and his study showed that nearly 90% of the files available for download on the FastTrack system were copyrighted works. . . .

Grokster and StreamCast concede the infringement in most downloads, and it is uncontested that they are aware that users employ their software primarily to download copyrighted files, even if the decentralized FastTrack and Gnutella networks fail to reveal which files are being copied, and when. From time to time, moreover, the companies have learned about their users' infringement directly, as from users who have sent e-mail to each company with questions about playing copyrighted movies they had downloaded, to whom the companies have responded with guidance.

Grokster and StreamCast are not, however, merely passive recipients of information about infringing use. The record is replete with evidence that from the moment Grokster and StreamCast began to distribute their free software, each one clearly voiced the objective that recipients use it to download copyrighted works, and each took active steps to encourage infringement.

After the notorious file-sharing service, Napster, was sued by copyright holders for facilitation of copyright infringement, *A & M Records, Inc. v. Napster, Inc.,* 114 F.Supp.2d 896 (N.D.Cal.2000), aff'd in part, rev'd in part, 239 F.3d 1004 (C.A.9 2001), StreamCast gave away a software program of a kind known as OpenNap, designed as compatible with the Napster program and open to Napster users for downloading files from other Napster and OpenNap users' computers. Evidence indicates that "[i]t was always [StreamCast's] intent to use [its OpenNap network] to be able to capture email addresses of [its] initial target market so that [it] could promote [its] StreamCast Morpheus interface to them," App. 861; indeed, the OpenNap program was engineered "'to leverage Napster's 50 million user base.'"

StreamCast monitored both the number of users downloading its OpenNap program and the number of music files they downloaded. It also used the resulting OpenNap network to distribute copies of the Morpheus software and to encourage users to adopt it. Internal company documents indicate that StreamCast hoped to attract large numbers of former Napster users if that company was shut down by court order or otherwise, and that StreamCast planned to be the next Napster. A kit developed by StreamCast to be delivered to advertisers, for example, contained press articles about StreamCast's potential to capture former Napster users, and it introduced itself to some potential advertisers as a company "which is similar to what Napster was." It broadcast banner advertisements to users of other Napster-compatible software, urging them to adopt its OpenNap. An internal e-mail from a company executive stated: "'We have put this network in place so that when Napster pulls the plug on their free service . . . or if the Court orders them shut down prior to that . . . we will be positioned to capture the flood of their 32 million users that will be actively looking for an alternative.'"

Thus, StreamCast developed promotional materials to market its service as the best Napster alternative. One proposed advertisement read: "Napster Inc.

has announced that it will soon begin charging you a fee. That's if the courts don't order it shut down first. What will you do to get around it?" *Id.,* at 897. Another proposed ad touted StreamCast's software as the "# 1 alternative to Napster" and asked "[w]hen the lights went off at Napster . . . where did the users go?" *Id.,* at 836 (ellipsis in original). StreamCast even planned to flaunt the illegal uses of its software; when it launched the OpenNap network, the chief technology officer of the company averred that "[t]he goal is to get in trouble with the law and get sued. It's the best way to get in the new[s]."

The evidence that Grokster sought to capture the market of former Napster users is sparser but revealing, for Grokster launched its own OpenNap system called Swaptor and inserted digital codes into its Web site so that computer users using Web search engines to look for "Napster" or "[f]ree filesharing" would be directed to the Grokster Web site, where they could download the Grokster software. And Grokster's name is an apparent derivative of Napster.

StreamCast's executives monitored the number of songs by certain commercial artists available on their networks, and an internal communication indicates they aimed to have a larger number of copyrighted songs available on their networks than other file-sharing networks. . . . The point, of course, would be to attract users of a mind to infringe, just as it would be with their promotional materials developed showing copyrighted songs as examples of the kinds of files available through Morpheus. Morpheus in fact allowed users to search specifically for "Top 40" songs, which were inevitably copyrighted. Similarly, Grokster sent users a newsletter promoting its ability to provide particular, popular copyrighted materials.

In addition to this evidence of express promotion, marketing, and intent to promote further, the business models employed by Grokster and StreamCast confirm that their principal object was use of their software to download copyrighted works. Grokster and StreamCast receive no revenue from users, who obtain the software itself for nothing. Instead, both companies generate income by selling advertising space, and they stream the advertising to Grokster and Morpheus users while they are employing the programs. As the number of users of each program increases, advertising opportunities become worth more. Cf. App. 539, 804. While there is doubtless some demand for free Shakespeare, the evidence shows that substantive volume is a function of free access to copyrighted work. Users seeking Top 40 songs, for example, or the latest release by Modest Mouse, are certain to be far more numerous than those seeking a free Decameron, and Grokster and StreamCast translated that demand into dollars.

Finally, there is no evidence that either company made an effort to filter copyrighted material from users' downloads or otherwise impede the sharing of copyrighted files. . . .

B

After discovery, the parties on each side of the case cross-moved for summary judgment. The District Court limited its consideration to the asserted liability of Grokster and StreamCast for distributing the current versions of their software, leaving aside whether either was liable "for damages arising from *past* versions of their software, or from other past activities." The District Court held that those who used the Grokster and Morpheus software to download copyrighted media files directly infringed MGM's copyrights, a conclusion not contested on appeal, but the court nonetheless granted summary judgment in favor of Grokster and StreamCast as to any liability arising from distribution of the then current versions of their software. Distributing that software gave rise to no liability in the court's view, because its use did not provide the distributors with actual knowledge of specific acts of infringement.

The Court of Appeals affirmed. . . .

II

A

MGM and many of the *amici* fault the Court of Appeals's holding for upsetting a sound balance between the respective values of supporting creative pursuits through copyright protection and promoting innovation in new communication technologies by limiting the incidence of liability for copyright infringement. The more artistic protection is favored, the more technological innovation may be discouraged; the administration of copyright law is an exercise in managing the trade-off.

The tension between the two values is the subject of this case, with its claim that digital distribution of copyrighted material threatens copyright holders as never before, because every copy is identical to the original, copying is easy, and many people (especially the young) use file-sharing software to download copyrighted works. This very breadth of the software's use may well draw the public directly into the debate over copyright policy, Peters, Brace Memorial Lecture: Copyright Enters the Public Domain, 51 J. Copyright Soc. 701, 705-717 (2004) (address by Register of Copyrights), and the indications are that the ease of copying songs or movies using software like Grokster's and Napster's is fostering disdain for copyright protection, Wu, When Code Isn't Law, 89 Va. L.Rev. 679, 724-726 (2003). As the case has been presented to us, these fears are said to be offset by the different concern that imposing liability, not only on infringers but on distributors of software based on its potential for unlawful use, could limit further development of beneficial technologies. See, *e.g.,* Lemley & Reese, Reducing Digital Copyright Infringement Without Restricting Innovation, 56 Stan. L.Rev. 1345, 1386-1390 (2004).

The argument for imposing indirect liability in this case is, however, a powerful one, given the number of infringing downloads that occur every day using StreamCast's and Grokster's software. When a widely shared service or product is used to commit infringement, it may be impossible to enforce rights in the protected work effectively against all direct infringers, the only practical alternative being to go against the distributor of the copying device for secondary liability on a theory of contributory or vicarious infringement. See *In re Aimster Copyright Litigation,* 334 F.3d 643, 645-646 (C.A.7 2003).

One infringes contributorily by intentionally inducing or encouraging direct infringement, and infringes vicariously by profiting from direct infringement while declining to exercise a right to stop or limit it. Although "[t]he Copyright Act does not expressly render anyone liable for infringement committed by another," these doctrines of secondary liability emerged from common law principles and are well established in the law.

B

Despite the currency of these principles of secondary liability, this Court has dealt with secondary copyright infringement in only one recent case, and because MGM has tailored its principal claim to our opinion there, a look at our earlier holding is in order. In *Sony Corp. v. Universal City Studios,* this Court addressed a claim that secondary liability for infringement can arise from the very distribution of a commercial product. There, the product, novel at the time, was what we know today as the videocassette recorder or VCR. Copyright holders sued Sony as the manufacturer, claiming it was contributorily liable for infringement that occurred when VCR owners taped copyrighted programs because it supplied the means used to infringe, and it had constructive knowledge that infringement would occur. At the trial on the merits, the evidence showed that the principal use of the VCR was for "'time-shifting,'" or taping a program for later viewing at a more convenient time, which the Court found to be a fair, not an infringing, use. There was no evidence that Sony had expressed an object of bringing about taping in violation of copyright or had taken active steps to increase its profits from unlawful taping. Although Sony's advertisements urged consumers to buy the VCR to "'record favorite shows'" or "'build a library'" of recorded programs, neither of these uses was necessarily infringing.

On those facts, with no evidence of stated or indicated intent to promote infringing uses, the only conceivable basis for imposing liability was on a theory of contributory infringement arising from its sale of VCRs to consumers with knowledge that some would use them to infringe. But because the VCR was "capable of commercially significant noninfringing uses," we held the manufacturer could not be faulted solely on the basis of its distribution.

This analysis reflected patent law's traditional staple article of commerce doctrine, now codified, that distribution of a component of a patented device will not violate the patent if it is suitable for use in other ways. 35 U.S.C. § 271(c). The doctrine was devised to identify instances in which it may be presumed from distribution of an article in commerce that the distributor intended the article to be used to infringe another's patent, and so may justly be held liable for that infringement. "One who makes and sells articles which are only adapted to be used in a patented combination will be presumed to intend the natural consequences of his acts; he will be presumed to intend that they shall be used in the combination of the patent."

In sum, where an article is "good for nothing else" but infringement, there is no legitimate public interest in its unlicensed availability, and there is no injustice in presuming or imputing an intent to infringe. Conversely, the doctrine absolves the equivocal conduct of selling an item with substantial lawful as well as unlawful uses, and limits liability to instances of more acute fault than the mere understanding that some of one's products will be misused. It leaves breathing room for innovation and a vigorous commerce.

The parties and many of the *amici* in this case think the key to resolving it is the *Sony* rule and, in particular, what it means for a product to be "capable of commercially significant noninfringing uses." *Sony Corp. v. Universal City Studios, supra,* at 442, 104 S.Ct. 774. MGM advances the argument that granting summary judgment to Grokster and StreamCast as to their current activities gave too much weight to the value of innovative technology, and too little to the copyrights infringed by users of their software, given that 90% of works available on one of the networks was shown to be copyrighted. Assuming the remaining 10% to be its noninfringing use, MGM says this should not qualify as "substantial," and the Court should quantify Sony to the extent of holding that a product used "principally" for infringement does not qualify. As mentioned before, Grokster and StreamCast reply by citing evidence that their software can be used to reproduce public domain works, and they point to copyright holders who actually encourage copying. Even if infringement is the principal practice with their software today, they argue, the noninfringing uses are significant and will grow.

We agree with MGM that the Court of Appeals misapplied *Sony,* which it read as limiting secondary liability quite beyond the circumstances to which the case applied. *Sony* barred secondary liability based on presuming or imputing intent to cause infringement solely from the design or distribution of a product capable of substantial lawful use, which the distributor knows is in fact used for infringement. The Ninth Circuit has read *Sony's* limitation to mean that whenever a product is capable of substantial lawful use, the producer can never be held contributorily liable for third parties' infringing use of it; it read the rule as being this broad, even when an actual purpose to cause infringing use is shown by evidence independent of design and distribution of the product, unless the distributors had "specific knowledge of infringement at a time at which they contributed to the infringement, and failed to act upon that information." Because the Circuit found the StreamCast and Grokster software capable of substantial lawful use, it concluded on the basis of its reading of *Sony* that neither company could be held liable, since there was no showing that their software, being without any central server, afforded them knowledge of specific unlawful uses.

This view of *Sony,* however, was error, converting the case from one about liability resting on imputed intent to one about liability on any theory. Because *Sony* did not displace other theories of secondary liability, and because we find below that it was error to grant summary judgment to the companies on MGM's inducement claim, we do not revisit *Sony* further, as MGM requests, to add a more quantified description of the point of balance between protection and commerce when liability rests solely on distribution with knowledge that unlawful use will occur. It is enough to note that the Ninth Circuit's judgment rested on an erroneous understanding of *Sony* and to leave further consideration of the *Sony* rule for a day when that may be required.

C

Sony's rule limits imputing culpable intent as a matter of law from the characteristics or uses of a distributed product. But nothing in *Sony* requires courts to ignore evidence of intent if there is such evidence, and the case was never meant to foreclose rules of fault-based liability derived from the common law. *Sony Corp. v. Universal City Studios,* 464 U.S., at 439, 104 S.Ct. 774 ("If vicarious liability is to be imposed on Sony in this case, it must rest on the fact that it has sold equipment with constructive knowledge" of the potential for infringement). Thus, where evidence goes beyond a product's characteristics or the knowledge that it may be put to infringing uses, and shows statements or actions directed to promoting infringement, *Sony's* staple-article rule will not preclude liability.

The classic case of direct evidence of unlawful purpose occurs when one induces commission of infringement by another, or "entic[es] or persuad[es] another" to infringe, Black's Law Dictionary 790 (8th ed.2004), as by advertising. Thus at common law a copyright or patent defendant who "not only expected but invoked [infringing use] by advertisement" was liable for infringement "on principles recognized in every part of the law." *Kalem Co. v. Harper Brothers,* 222 U.S., at 62-63, 32 S.Ct. 20 (copyright infringement). See also *Henry v. A.B. Dick Co.,* 224 U.S., at 48-49, 32 S.Ct. 364 (contributory liability for patent infringement may be found where a good's "most conspicuous use is one which will co-operate in an infringement when sale to such user is invoked by advertisement" of the infringing use); *Thomson-Houston Electric Co. v. Kelsey Electric R. Specialty Co.,* 75 F. 1005, 1007- 1008 (C.A.2 1896) (relying on advertisements and displays to find defendant's "willingness . . . to aid other persons in any attempts which they may be disposed to make towards [patent] infringement"); *Rumford Chemical Works v. Hecker,* 20 F.Cas. 1342, 1346 (No. 12,133) (C.C.D.N.J.1876) (demonstrations of infringing activity along with "avowals of the [infringing] purpose and use for which it was made" supported liability for patent infringement).

The rule on inducement of infringement as developed in the early cases is no different today. Evidence of "active steps . . . taken to encourage direct infringement," such as advertising an infringing use or instructing how to engage in an infringing use, show an affirmative intent that the product be used to infringe, and a showing that infringement was encouraged overcomes the law's reluctance to find liability when a defendant merely sells a commercial product suitable for some lawful use, see, *e.g., Water Technologies Corp. v. Calco, Ltd.,* 850 F.2d 660, 668 (C.A.Fed.1988) (liability for inducement where one "actively and knowingly aid [s] and abet[s] another's direct infringement" (emphasis omitted)); *Fromberg, Inc. v. Thornhill,* 315 F.2d 407, 412-413 (C.A.5 1963) (demonstrations by sales staff of infringing uses supported liability for inducement); *Haworth Inc. v. Herman Miller Inc.,* 37 U.S.P.Q.2d 1080, 1090, 1994 WL 875931 (W.D.Mich.1994) (evidence that defendant "demonstrate[d] and recommend[ed] infringing configurations" of its product could support inducement liability); *Sims v. Mack Trucks, Inc.,* 459 F.Supp. 1198, 1215 (E.D.Pa.1978) (finding inducement where the use "depicted by the defendant in its promotional film and brochures infringes the . . . patent"), overruled on other grounds, 608 F.2d 87 (C.A.3 1979). Cf. W. Keeton, D. Dobbs, R. Keeton, & D. Owen, Prosser and Keeton on Law of Torts 37 (5th ed. 1984) ("There is a definite tendency to impose greater responsibility upon a defendant whose conduct was intended to do harm, or was morally wrong").

For the same reasons that *Sony* took the staple-article doctrine of patent law as a model for its copyright safe-harbor rule, the inducement rule, too, is a sensible one for copyright. We adopt it here, holding that one who distributes a device with the object of promoting its use to infringe copyright, as shown by clear expression or other affirmative steps taken to foster infringement, is liable for the resulting acts of infringement by third parties. We are, of course, mindful of the need to keep from trenching on regular commerce or discouraging the development of technologies with lawful and unlawful potential. Accordingly, just as *Sony* did not find intentional inducement despite the knowledge of the VCR manufacturer that its device could be used to infringe, 464 U.S., at 439, n. 19, 104 S.Ct. 774, mere knowledge of infringing potential or of actual infringing uses would not be enough here to subject a distributor to liability. Nor would ordinary acts incident to product distribution, such as offering customers technical support or product updates, support liability in themselves. The inducement rule, instead, premises liability on purposeful, culpable expression and conduct, and thus does nothing to compromise legitimate commerce or discourage innovation having a lawful promise.

III

A

The only apparent question about treating MGM's evidence as sufficient to withstand summary judgment under the theory of inducement goes to the need on MGM's part to adduce evidence that StreamCast and Grokster communicated an inducing message to their software users. The classic instance of inducement is by advertisement or solicitation that broadcasts a message designed to stimulate others to commit violations. MGM claims that such a message is shown here. It is undisputed that StreamCast beamed onto the computer screens of users of Napster-compatible programs ads urging the adoption of its OpenNap program, which was designed, as its name implied, to invite the custom of patrons of Napster, then under attack in the courts for facilitating massive infringement. Those who accepted StreamCast's OpenNap program were offered software to perform the same services, which a factfinder could conclude would readily have been understood in the Napster market as the ability to download copyrighted music files. Grokster distributed an electronic newsletter containing links to articles promoting its software's ability to access popular copyrighted music. And anyone whose Napster or free file-sharing searches turned up a link to Grokster would have understood Grokster to be offering the same file-sharing ability as Napster, and to the same people who probably used Napster for infringing downloads; that would also have been the understanding of anyone offered Grokster's suggestively named Swaptor software, its version of OpenNap. And both companies communicated a clear message by responding affirmatively to requests for help in locating and playing copyrighted materials.

In StreamCast's case, of course, the evidence just described was supplemented by other unequivocal indications of unlawful purpose in the internal communications and advertising designs aimed at Napster users ("When the lights went off at Napster . . . where did the users go?" App. 836 (ellipsis in original)). Whether the messages were communicated is not to the point on this record. The function of the message in the theory of inducement is to prove by a defendant's own statements that his unlawful purpose disqualifies him from claiming protection (and incidentally to point to actual violators likely to be found among those who hear or read the message). See *supra*, at 2779-2780. Proving that a message was sent out, then, is the preeminent but not exclusive way of showing that active steps were taken with the purpose of bringing about infringing acts, and of showing that infringing acts took place by using the device distributed. Here, the summary judgment record is replete with other evidence that Grokster and StreamCast, unlike the manufacturer and distributor in *Sony,* acted with a purpose to cause copyright violations by use of software suitable for illegal use. See *supra,* at 2772-2774.

Three features of this evidence of intent are particularly notable. First, each company showed itself to be aiming to satisfy a known source of demand for copyright infringement, the market comprising former Napster users. StreamCast's internal documents made constant reference to Napster, it initially distributed its Morpheus software through an OpenNap program compatible with Napster, it advertised its OpenNap program to Napster users, and its Morpheus software functions as Napster did except that it could be used to distribute more kinds of files, including copyrighted movies and software programs. Grokster's name is apparently derived from Napster, it too initially offered an OpenNap program, its software's function is likewise comparable to Napster's, and it attempted to divert queries for Napster onto its own Web site. Grokster and StreamCast's efforts to supply services to former Napster users, deprived of a mechanism to copy and distribute what were overwhelmingly infringing files, indicate a principal, if not exclusive, intent on the part of each to bring about infringement.

Second, this evidence of unlawful objective is given added significance by MGM's showing that neither company attempted to develop filtering tools or other mechanisms to diminish the infringing activity using their software. While the Ninth Circuit treated the defendants' failure to develop such tools as irrelevant because they lacked an independent duty to monitor their users' activity, we think this evidence underscores Grokster's and StreamCast's intentional facilitation of their users' infringement.

Third, there is a further complement to the direct evidence of unlawful objective. It is useful to recall that StreamCast and Grokster make money by selling advertising space, by directing ads to the screens of computers employing their software. As the record shows, the more the software is used, the more ads are sent out and the greater the advertising revenue becomes. Since the extent of the software's use determines the gain to the distributors, the commercial sense of their enterprise turns on high-volume use, which the record shows is infringing. This evidence alone would not justify an inference of unlawful intent, but viewed in the context of the entire record its import is clear. The unlawful objective is unmistakable.

B

In addition to intent to bring about infringement and distribution of a device suitable for infringing use, the inducement theory of course requires evidence of actual infringement by recipients of the device, the software in this case. As the account of the facts indicates, there is evidence of infringement on a gigantic scale, and there is no serious issue of the adequacy of MGM's showing on this point in order to survive the companies' summary judgment requests. Although an exact calculation of infringing use, as a basis for a claim of damages, is subject to dispute, there is no question that the summary judgment evidence is at least adequate to entitle MGM to go forward with claims for damages and equitable relief.

* * *

In sum, this case is significantly different from *Sony* and reliance on that case to rule in favor of StreamCast and Grokster was error. *Sony* dealt with a claim of liability based solely on distributing a product with alternative lawful and unlawful uses, with knowledge that some users would follow the unlawful course. The case struck a balance between the interests of protection and innovation by holding that the product's capability of substantial lawful employment should bar the imputation of fault and consequent secondary liability for the unlawful acts of others.

MGM's evidence in this case most obviously addresses a different basis of liability for distributing a product open to alternative uses. Here, evidence of the distributors' words and deeds going beyond distribution as such shows a purpose to cause and profit from third-party acts of copyright infringement. If liability for inducing infringement is ultimately found, it will not be on the basis of presuming or imputing fault, but from inferring a patently illegal objective from statements and actions showing what that objective was.

There is substantial evidence in MGM's favor on all elements of inducement, and summary judgment in favor of Grokster and StreamCast was error. On remand, reconsideration of MGM's motion for summary judgment will be in order.

The judgment of the Court of Appeals is vacated, and the case is remanded for further proceedings consistent with this opinion.

It is so ordered.

IV. CUSTOMER DATA — PRIVACY AND SECURITY ISSUES

Online digital systems obtain information from their licensees as a by-product of doing business. Especially when the licensees include private individuals, this means that the licensing structure is placed squarely within the modern turmoil that is occurring with reference to questions about privacy and data security. These questions have inevitably spilled over into transactional issues about the use of privacy and security policies in online systems.

A. Transactional Data and Privacy Policies

DWYER v. AMERICAN EXPRESS
652 N.E.2d 1351 (Ill. App. 1995)

JUSTICE BUCKLEY:

Plaintiffs, American Express cardholders, appeal the circuit court's dismissal of their claims for invasion of privacy and consumer fraud against defendants, American Express Company . . . for their practice of renting information regarding cardholder spending habits.

On May 13, 1992, the New York Attorney General released a press statement describing an agreement it had entered into with defendants. The following day, newspapers reported defendants' actions which gave rise to this agreement. According to the news articles, defendants categorize and rank their cardholders into six tiers based on spending habits and then rent this information to participating merchants as part of a targeted joint-marketing and sales program. For example, a cardholder may be characterized as "Rodeo Drive Chic" or "Value Oriented." In order to characterize its cardholders, defendants analyze where they shop and how much they spend, and also consider behavioral characteristics and spending histories. Defendants then offer to create a list of cardholders who would most likely shop in a particular store and rent that list to the merchant.

Defendants also offer to create lists which target cardholders who purchase specific types of items, such as fine jewelry. The merchants using the defendants' service can also target shoppers in categories such as mail-order apparel buyers, home-improvement shoppers, electronics shoppers, luxury lodgers, card members with children, skiers, frequent business travelers, resort users, Asian/European travelers, luxury European car owners, or recent movers. Finally, defendants offer joint-marketing ventures to merchants who generate substantial sales through the American Express card. Defendants mail special promotions devised by the merchants to its cardholders and share the profits generated by these advertisements.

On May 14, 1992, Patrick E. Dwyer filed a class action against defendants. His complaint alleges that defendants intruded into their cardholders' seclusion, commercially appropriated their cardholders' personal spending habits, and violated the Illinois consumer fraud statute and consumer fraud statutes in other jurisdictions. . . .

Plaintiffs have alleged that defendants' practices constitute an invasion of their privacy and violate the Illinois Consumer Fraud and Deceptive Business Practices Act (Act or Consumer Fraud Act) (Ill.Rev.Stat.1991, ch. 121 1/2 , par. 261 *et seq.* (now 815 ILCS 505/1 *et seq.* (1992))). For the reasons discussed below, we find that plaintiffs have not stated a cause of action under either of these theories.

Invasion of Privacy

There are four branches of the privacy invasion tort identified by the *Restatement (Second) of Torts*. These are: (1) an unreasonable intrusion upon the seclusion of another; (2) an appropriation of another's name or likeness; (3) a public disclosure of private facts; and (4) publicity which reasonably places another in a false light before the public. *Restatement (Second) of Torts* §§ 652B, 652C, 652D, 652E (1977); *W. Keeton, Prosser & Keeton on Torts* § 117, at 849-69 (5th ed. 1984). Plaintiffs' complaint includes claims under the first and second branches.

As a preliminary matter, we note that a cause of action for intrusion into seclusion has never been recognized explicitly by the Illinois Supreme Court. In *Lovgren v. Citizens First National Bank* (1989), 126 Ill.2d 411, 128 Ill.Dec. 542, 534 N.E.2d 987, the supreme court discussed this tort as enunciated by the Restatement and Prosser, but stated that its discussion did not imply a recognition of the action by the court. The court concluded that the defendants' alleged actions in that case did not constitute an unreasonable intrusion into the seclusion of another and declined to address the conflict among the appellate court districts as to whether the cause of action should be recognized in this State. The third district [however] recognized the intrusion tort in *Melvin v. Burling* (1986), 919, 490 N.E.2d 1011. . . . In *Melvin,* the court set out four elements which must be alleged in order to state a cause of action: (1) an unauthorized intrusion or prying into the plaintiff's seclusion; (2) an intrusion which is offensive or objectionable to a reasonable man; (3) the matter upon which the intrusion occurs is private; and (4) the intrusion causes anguish and suffering. Since the third district set out the four elements in *Melvin,* this district has applied these elements without directly addressing the issue of whether the cause of action exists in this State. . . .

Plaintiffs' allegations fail to satisfy the first element, an unauthorized intrusion or prying into the plaintiffs' seclusion. The alleged wrongful actions involve the defendants' practice of renting lists that they have compiled from information contained in their own records. By using the American Express card, a cardholder is voluntarily, and necessarily, giving information to defendants that, if analyzed, will reveal a cardholder's spending habits and shopping preferences. We cannot hold that a defendant has committed an unauthorized intrusion by compiling the information voluntarily given to it and then renting its compilation.

Plaintiffs claim that because defendants rented lists based on this compiled information, this case involves the disclosure of private financial information and most closely resembles cases involving intrusion into private financial dealings, such as bank account transactions. Plaintiffs cite several cases in which courts have recognized the right to privacy surrounding financial transactions. . . . However, we find that this case more closely resembles the sale of magazine subscription lists, which was at issue in *Shibley v. Time, Inc.* (1975), 45 Ohio App.2d 69, 341 N.E.2d 337. In *Shibley,* the plaintiffs claimed that the defendant's practice of selling and renting magazine subscription lists without the subscribers' prior consent "constitut[ed] an invasion of privacy because it amount[ed] to a sale of individual 'personality profiles,' which subjects the subscribers to solicitations from direct mail advertisers." The plaintiffs also claimed that the lists amounted to a tortious appropriation of their names and "personality profiles." The trial court dismissed the plaintiffs' complaint and the Court of Appeals of Ohio affirmed.

The *Shibley* court found that an Ohio statute, which permitted the sale of names and addresses of registrants of motor vehicles, indicated that the defendant's activity was not an invasion of privacy. The court considered a Federal district court case from New York, *Lamont v. Commissioner of Motor Vehicles* (S.D.N.Y.1967), 269 F.Supp. 880, *aff'd* (2d Cir.1967) 386 F.2d 449, *cert. denied* (1968), 391 U.S. 915, 88 S.Ct. 1811, 20 L.Ed.2d 654, to be insightful. In *Lamont,* the plaintiff claimed an invasion of privacy arising from the State's sale of its list of names and addresses of registered motor-vehicle owners to mail-order advertisers. The *Lamont* court held that however "noxious" advertising by mail might be, the burden was acceptable as far as the

Constitution is concerned. The *Shibley* court followed the reasoning in *Lamont* and held:

> The right to privacy does not extend to the mailbox and therefore it is constitutionally permissible to sell subscription lists to direct mail advertisers. It necessarily follows that the practice complained of here does not constitute an invasion of privacy even if appellants' unsupported assertion that this amounts to the sale of "personality profiles" is taken as true because these profiles are only used to determine what type of advertisement is to be sent.

Defendants rent names and addresses after they create a list of cardholders who have certain shopping tendencies; they are not disclosing financial information about particular cardholders. These lists are being used solely for the purpose of determining what type of advertising should be sent to whom. . . . Thus, we hold that the alleged actions here do not constitute an unreasonable intrusion into the seclusion of another. . . .

Considering plaintiffs' appropriation claim, the elements of the tort are: an appropriation, without consent, of one's name or likeness for another's use or benefit. *Restatement (Second) of Torts* § 652C (1977). This branch of the privacy doctrine is designed to protect a person from having his name or image used for commercial purposes without consent. According to the Restatement, the purpose of this tort is to protect the "interest of the individual in the exclusive use of his own identity, in so far as it is represented by his name or likeness." Illustrations of this tort provided by the Restatement include the publication of a person's photograph without consent in an advertisement; operating a corporation named after a prominent public figure without the person's consent; impersonating a man to obtain information regarding the affairs of the man's wife; and filing a lawsuit in the name of another without the other's consent. *Restatement (Second) of Torts* § 652C, Comment *b* (1965).

Plaintiffs claim that defendants appropriate information about cardholders' personalities, including their names and perceived lifestyles, without their consent. Defendants argue that their practice does not adversely affect the interest of a cardholder in the "exclusive use of his own identity," using the language of the Restatement. Defendants also argue that the cardholders' names lack value and that the lists that defendants create are valuable because "they identify a useful aggregate of potential customers to whom offers may be sent."

[We] again follow the reasoning in *Shibley* and find that plaintiffs have not stated a claim for tortious appropriation because they have failed to allege the first element. Undeniably, each cardholder's name is valuable to defendants. The more names included on a list, the more that list will be worth. However, a single, random cardholder's name has little or no intrinsic value to defendants (or a merchant). Rather, an individual name has value only when it is associated with one of defendants' lists. Defendants create value by categorizing and aggregating these names. Furthermore, defendants' practices do not deprive any of the cardholders of any value their individual names may possess.

Consumer Fraud Act

Plaintiffs' complaint also includes a claim under the Illinois Consumer Fraud Act. To establish a deceptive practice claim, a plaintiff must allege and prove (1) the misrepresentation or concealment of a material fact, (2) an intent by defendant that plaintiff rely on the misrepresentation or concealment, and (3) the deception occurred in the course of conduct involving a trade or commerce. . . .

According to the plaintiffs, defendants conducted a survey which showed that 80% of Americans do not think companies should release personal information to other companies. Plaintiffs have alleged that defendants did disclose that it would use information provided in the credit card application, but this disclosure did not inform the cardholders that information about their card usage would be used. It is highly possible that some customers would have refrained from using the American Express Card if they had known that defendants were analyzing their spending habits. Therefore, plaintiffs have sufficiently alleged that the undisclosed practices of defendants are material and deceptive.

As to the second element, the Act only requires defendants' intent that plaintiffs rely on the deceptive practice. Actual reliance is not required. . . . Defendants had a strong incentive to keep their practice a secret because disclosure would have resulted in fewer cardholders using their card. Thus, plaintiffs have sufficiently alleged that defendants intended for plaintiffs to rely on the nondisclosure of their practice.

The third element is not at issue in this case. However, defendants argue that plaintiffs have failed to allege facts that might establish that they suffered any damages. . . . Defendants contend, and we agree, that the only damage plaintiffs could have suffered was a surfeit of unwanted mail. We reject plaintiffs' assertion that the damages in this case arise from the disclosure of personal financial matters. Defendants only disclose which of their cardholders might be interested in purchasing items from a particular merchant based on card usage. Defendants' practice does not amount to a disclosure of personal financial matters. Plaintiffs have failed to allege how they were damaged by defendants' practice of selecting cardholders for mailings likely to be of interest to them. . . .

[We] affirm the order of the circuit court of Cook County.

Dwyer sets out the traditional United States approach to handling transactional data: other than in relationships that are presumptively confidential, data disclosed to or created jointly with another person can be freely used by that person. Of course, that presumption can be altered by contract. In the online world, virtually all sites have privacy policies, which may or may not become part of the contractual relationship. Even more generally, however, the presumption relied on in *Dwyer* has been under attack in this country and elsewhere through a variety of legislative and other actions giving individuals in some cases some control over the use of transactional data. The result is that virtually all online licenses deal with "privacy" issues. For many, the source of this came from the European Union "Data Protection" Directive.

EUROPEAN DATA PROTECTION DIRECTIVE

Article 2

Definitions

For the purposes of this Directive:

(a) "personal data" shall mean any information relating to an identified or identifiable natural person ("data subject"); an identifiable person is one who can identified, directly or indirectly, in particular by reference to an identification number or to one or more factors specific to his physical, physiological, mental, economic, cultural or social identity;

(b) "processing of personal data" ("processing") shall mean any operation or set of operations which is performed upon personal data, whether or not by automatic means such as collection, recording, organization, storage, adaptation or alteration, retrieval, consultation, use, disclosure by transmission, dissemination or otherwise making available, alignment or combination, blocking, erasure or destruction;

. . . .

(h) "the data subject's consent" shall mean any freely given specific and informed indication of his wishes by which the data subject signifies his agreement to personal data relating to him being processed.

Article 3

Scope

1. This Directive shall apply to the processing of personal data wholly or partly by automatic means, and to the processing otherwise than by automatic means of personal data which form part of a filing system or are intended to form part of a filing system.

. . . .

Article 7

Member States shall provide that personal data may be processed only if:

(a) the data subject has given his consent unambiguously; or

(b) processing is necessary for the performance of a contract to which the data subject is party or in order to take steps at the request of the data subject prior to entering into a contract; or

(c) processing is necessary for compliance with a legal obligation to which the controller is subject; or

(d) processing is necessary in order to protect the vital interest of the data subject; or

(e) processing is necessary for the performance of a task carried out in the public interest or in the exercise of official authority vested in the controller or in a third party to whom the data are disclosed; or

(f) processing is necessary for the purposes of the legitimate interests pursued by the controller or by the third party or parties to whom the data are disclosed, except where such interests are overridden by the interests or fundamental rights and freedoms of the data subject which require protection under Article 1(1).

. . . .

Article 10

Information in cases of collection of data from the data subject

Member States shall provide that the controller or his representative must provide a data subject from whom data relating to himself are collected with at least the following information, except where he already knows:

(a) the identity of the controller and of his representative, if any,

(b) the purposes of the processing for which the data are intended,

(c) any further information such as

— the recipients or categories of recipients of the data;

— whether replies to the questions are obligatory or voluntary, as well as the possible consequences of the failure to reply;

— the existence of the right of access to and the right to rectify the data concerning him insofar as they are necessary, having regard to the specific circumstances in which the data are collected, to guarantee fair processing in respect of the data subject.

. . . .

Article 17

Security of processing

1. Member States shall provide that the controller must implement appropriate technical and organizational measures to protect personal data against accidental or unlawful destruction or accidental loss and against unauthorized alteration, disclosure or access, in particular where the processing involves the transmission of data over a network, and against all other unlawful forms of processing. Having regard to the state of the art and the costs of their implementation, such measures shall ensure a level of security appropriate to the risks represented by the processing and the nature of the data to be protected.

2. The Member States shall provide that the controller must, where processing is carried out on his behalf, choose a processor who provides sufficient guarantees in respect of the technical security measures and organizational measures governing the processing to be carried out and must ensure compliance with those measures. . . .

NOTE

The EU Directive has had a significant impact on U.S. practices, in part because it seems to capture an increasing sensitivity to the control and use of personal data and in part because the Directive precludes transfer of personal data to countries that do not have adequate data protections. To respond to the argument that U.S. law does not, a set of "safe harbor" principles has been promulgated with the understanding that a voluntary choice by a company to adhere to the principles creates a presumption of compliance with EU standards. The principles in relevant part state:

> **NOTICE:** An organization must inform individuals about the purposes for which it collects and uses information about them, how to contact the organization with any inquiries or complaints, the types of third parties to which it discloses the information, and the choices and means the organization offers individuals for limiting its use and disclosure. This notice must be provided in clear and conspicuous language when individuals are first asked to provide personal information to the organization or as soon thereafter as is practicable, but in any event before the organization uses such information for a purpose other than that for which it was originally collected or processed by the transferring organization or discloses it for the first time to a third party.

> **CHOICE:** An organization must offer individuals the opportunity to choose (opt out) whether their personal information is (a) to be disclosed to a third party or (b) to be used for a purpose that is incompatible with the purpose(s) for which it was originally collected or subsequently authorized by the individual. . . . For sensitive information (i.e. personal information specifying medical or health conditions, racial or ethnic origin, political opinions, religious or philosophical beliefs, trade union membership or information specifying the sex life of the individual), they must be given affirmative or explicit (opt in) choice. . . .

> **ONWARD TRANSFER:** To disclose information to a third party, organizations must apply the Notice and Choice Principles. . . .

> **SECURITY:** Organizations creating, maintaining, using or disseminating personal information must take reasonable precautions to protect it from loss, misuse and unauthorized access, disclosure, alteration and destruction.

> **DATA INTEGRITY:** Consistent with the Principles, personal information must be relevant for the purposes for which it is to be used. An organization may not process personal information in a way that is incompatible with the purposes for which it has been collected or subsequently authorized by the individual. To the extent necessary for those purposes, an organization should take reasonable steps to ensure that data is reliable for its intended use, accurate, complete, and current.

> **ACCESS:** Individuals must have access to personal information about them that an organization holds and be able to correct, amend, or delete that information where it is inaccurate, except where the burden or expense of providing access would be disproportionate to the risks to the individual's privacy in the case in question, or where the rights of persons other than the individual would be violated.

ENFORCEMENT: Effective privacy protection must include mechanisms for assuring compliance with the Principles. . . .

CALIFORNIA PRIVACY POSTING ACT
Effective July 2004

§ 22575. (a) An operator of a commercial Web site or online service that collects personally identifiable information through the Internet about individual consumers residing in California who use or visit its commercial Web site or online service shall conspicuously post its privacy policy on its Web site, or in the case of an operator of an online service, make that policy available in accordance with paragraph (5) of subdivision (b) of Section [22577]. An operator shall be in violation of this subdivision only if the operator fails to post its policy within 30 days after being notified of noncompliance.

(b) The privacy policy required by subdivision (a) shall do all of the following:

(1) Identify the categories of personally identifiable information that the operator collects through the Web site or online service about individual consumers who use or visit its commercial Web site or online service and the categories of third-party persons or entities with whom the operator may share that personally identifiable information.

(2) If the operator maintains a process for an individual consumer who uses or visits its commercial Web site or online service to review and request changes to any of his or her personally identifiable information that is collected through the Web site or online service, provide a description of that process.

(3) Describe the process by which the operator notifies consumers who use or visit its commercial Web site or online service of material changes to the operator's privacy policy for that Web site or online service.

(4) Identify its effective date.

§ 22576. An operator of a commercial Web site or online service that collects personally identifiable information through the Web site or online service from individual consumers who use or visit the commercial Web site or online service and who reside in California shall be in violation of this section if the operator fails to comply with the provisions of Section 22575 or with the provisions of its posted privacy policy in either of the following ways:

(a) Knowingly and willfully.

(b) Negligently and materially.

§ 22577. For the purposes of this chapter, the following definitions apply:

(a) The term "personally identifiable information" means individually identifiable information about an individual consumer collected online by the operator from that individual and maintained by the operator in an accessible form, including any of the following:

(1) A first and last name.

(2) A home or other physical address, including street name and name of a city or town.

(3) An e-mail address.

(4) A telephone number.

(5) A social security number.

(6) Any other identifier that permits the physical or online contacting of a specific individual.

(7) Information concerning a user that the Web site or online service collects online from the user and maintains in personally identifiable form in combination with an identifier described in this subdivision.

(b) The term "conspicuously post" with respect to a privacy policy shall include posting the privacy policy through any of the following:

(1) A Web page on which the actual privacy policy is posted if the Web page is the homepage or first significant page after entering the Web site.

(2) An icon that hyperlinks to a Web page on which the actual privacy policy is posted, if the icon is located on the homepage or the first significant page after entering the Web site, and if the icon contains the word "privacy." The icon shall also use a color that contrasts with the background color of the Web page or is otherwise distinguishable.

(3) A text link that hyperlinks to a Web page on which the actual privacy policy is posted, if the text link is located on the homepage or first significant page after entering the Web site, and if the text link does one of the following:

(A) Includes the word "privacy."

(B) Is written in capital letters equal to or greater in size than the surrounding text.

(C) Is written in larger type than the surrounding text, or in contrasting type, font, or color to the surrounding text of the same size, or set off from the surrounding text of the same size by symbols or other marks that call attention to the language.

(4) Any other functional hyperlink that is so displayed that a reasonable person would notice it.

(5) IN THE CASE OF AN ONLINE SERVICE, ANY OTHER REASONABLY ACCESSIBLE MEANS OF MAKING THE PRIVACY POLICY AVAILABLE FOR CONSUMERS OF THE ONLINE SERVICE.

(c) The term "operator" means any person or entity that owns a Web site located on the Internet or an online service that collects and maintains personally identifiable information from a consumer residing in California who uses or visits the Web site or online service if the Web site or online service is operated for commercial purposes. It does not include any third party that operates, hosts, or manages, but does not own, a Web site or online service on the owner's behalf or by processing information on behalf of the owner.

(d) The term "consumer" means any individual who seeks or acquires, by purchase or lease, any goods, services, money, or credit for personal, family, or household purposes.

NOTES

1. It remains to be seen whether the California legislation survives preemption arguments under the Interstate Commerce Clause of the Constitution. The statute was the first general-purpose legislation requiring adoption of "privacy policies" in a digital environment.

2. The Federal Trade Commission (FTC) has been active in using its regulatory authority to prevent unfair and deceptive practices as a means to monitor online privacy policies and the extent of compliance with them. In *In the Matter of Eli Lilly and Co.*, No. 012 3214 (settled Jan. 18, 2002), the FTC settled a claim against Eli Lilly. On June 27, 2001 subscribers to Lilly's "Medimessenger" service, a website-based reminder service for Prozac users, were accidentally included in a mass e-mail announcing termination of the service. By addressing the notice to all subscribers' e-mail addresses, Eli Lilly revealed the identities of the subscribers. The FTC filed a complaint alleging that the publication of e-mail addresses disclosed personal information in violation of Eli Lilly's privacy policies and therefore was a violation of §5(a) of the FTC Act. In essence, the representations made in Eli Lilly's own privacy policies were alleged to be false and misleading, based on their subsequent violation, and therefore "unfair or deceptive acts or practices in or affecting commerce" in violation of §5(a). Eli Lilly entered into a consent order. For a period of 20 years Eli Lilly voluntarily agreed not to:

> misrepresent in any manner, expressly or by implication, the extent to which it maintains and protects the privacy or confidentiality of any personally identifiable information collected from or about consumers, in connection with the advertising, marketing, offering for sale or sale, in or affecting commerce, of any pharmaceutical, medical or other health-related product or service by respondent's Lilly USA division or through any corporation, subsidiary, division, or other entity.

Eli Lilly also agreed to develop a security program to protect personally identifiable information, conduct annual written reviews of the program, and agree to various reporting requirements regarding any future changes in Eli Lilly policies.

IN RE NORTHWEST AIRLINES PRIVACY LITIGATION
No. 04-126 (PAM/JSM) 2004 U.S. Dist. LEXIS 10580 (D. Minn. 2004)

MAGNUSON, J.

This matter is before the Court on a Motion to Dismiss filed by Defendants Northwest Airlines Corporation and Northwest Airlines, Inc. (collectively, "Northwest"). Seven putative class actions have been consolidated into a master case, and the Motion to Dismiss applies to the Amended Consolidated Class Action Complaint filed in the consolidated matter. . . . For the reasons that follow, the Court finds that Plaintiffs have failed to state any claims on which relief can be granted, and the Court therefore dismisses all of the individual Complaints.

BACKGROUND

Plaintiffs are customers of Defendant Northwest Airlines, Inc. ("Northwest"). After September 11, 2001, the National Aeronautical and Space Administration ("NASA") requested that Northwest provide NASA with certain passenger information in order to assist NASA in studying ways to increase airline security. Northwest supplied NASA with passenger name records ("PNRs"), which are electronic records of passenger information. PNRs contain information such as a passenger's name, flight number, credit card data, hotel reservation, car rental, and any traveling companions.

Plaintiffs contend that Northwest's actions constitute violations of the Electronic Communications Privacy Act ("ECPA"), 18 U.S.C. § 2701 et seq., the Fair Credit Reporting Act ("FCRA"), 15 U.S.C. § 1681, and Minnesota's Deceptive Trade Practices Act ("DTPA"), Minn.Stat. § 325D.44, and also constitute invasion of privacy, trespass to property, negligent misrepresentation, breach of contract, and breach of express warranties. The basis for most of Plaintiffs' claims is that Northwest's website contained a privacy policy that stated that Northwest would not share customers' information except as necessary to make customers' travel arrangements. Plaintiffs contend that Northwest's provision of PNRs to NASA violated Northwest's privacy policy, giving rise to the legal claims noted above. . . .

DISCUSSION

. . . .

B. The Electronic Communications Privacy Act

The ECPA prohibits a person or entity from

(1) intentionally access[ing] without authorization a facility through which an electronic communication service is provided; or

(2) intentionally exceeds an authorization to access that facility;

and thereby obtains, alters, or prevents authorized access to a wire or electronic communication while it is in electronic storage in such system shall be punished. . . .

18 U.S.C. § 2701(a). Plaintiffs argue that Northwest's access to its own electronic communications service is limited by its privacy policy, and that

Northwest's provision of PNRs to NASA violated that policy and thus constituted unauthorized access to the "facility through which an electronic communication service is provided" within the meaning of this section. Plaintiffs also allege that Northwest violated § 2702 of the ECPA, which states that "a person or entity providing an electronic communications service to the public shall not knowingly divulge to any person or entity the contents of a communication while in electronic storage by that service." 18 U.S.C. § 2702(a)(1).

Northwest argues first that it cannot violate § 2702 because it is not a "person or entity providing an electronic communications service to the public." . . . Whether Northwest is a provider of electronic communications service is a legal question, not a factual issue.

Defining electronic communications service to include online merchants or service providers like Northwest stretches the ECPA too far. Northwest is not an internet service provider. In fact, Northwest purchases its electronic communications service from a third party, Worldspan. Under these circumstances, Northwest is simply not an electronic communications service provider, and therefore cannot violate § 2702. *See, e.g., Crowley v. CyberSource Corp.,* 166 F.Supp.2d 1263 (N.D.Cal.2001) (finding online retailer not electronic communications service provider because retailer purchased electronic communications service from provider and did not independently provide such service to public).

Similarly, Northwest's conduct . . . does not constitute a violation of § 2701. Plaintiffs' claim is that Northwest improperly disclosed the information in PNRs to NASA. Section 2701 does not prohibit improper disclosure of information. Rather, this section prohibits improper access to an electronic communications service provider or the information contained on that service provider. There is no dispute that Northwest obtained Plaintiffs' personal information properly, in the ordinary course of business. Plaintiffs' complaint is not with how Northwest obtained the information, but with how Northwest subsequently used the information. Because § 2701 does not speak to the use of the information, it does not apply and Plaintiffs' claims under § 2701 fail as a matter of law. . . .

2. Remaining Claims

Finally, Northwest argues that Plaintiffs' remaining claims fail to state a claim on which relief can be granted. These claims are: trespass to property, intrusion upon seclusion, breach of contract, and breach of express warranties.

a. Trespass

To state a claim for trespass to property, Plaintiffs must demonstrate that they owned or possessed property, that Northwest wrongfully took that property, and that Plaintiffs were damaged by the wrongful taking. *H. Christiansen & Sons, Inc. v. City of Duluth,* 225 Minn. 475, 31 N.W.2d 270, 274 (Minn.1948). Plaintiffs contend that the information contained in the PNRs was Plaintiffs' property and that, by providing that information to NASA, Northwest wrongfully took that property.

As a matter of law, the PNRs were not Plaintiffs' property. Plaintiffs voluntarily provided some information that was included in the PNRs. It may be that the information Plaintiffs provided to Northwest was Plaintiffs' property. However, when that information was compiled and combined with other information to form a PNR, the PNR itself became Northwest's property. Northwest cannot wrongfully take its own property. Thus, Plaintiffs' claim for trespass fails.

b. Intrusion Upon Seclusion

Intrusion upon seclusion exists when someone "intentionally intrudes, physically or otherwise, upon the solitude or seclusion of another or his private affairs or concerns . . . if the intrusion would be highly offensive to a reasonable person." *Lake v. Wal-Mart Stores, Inc.*, 582 N.W.2d 231, 233 (Minn.1998) (quoting *Restatement (Second) of Torts* § 625B). Thus, to make out a claim for intrusion upon seclusion, Plaintiffs must show that the alleged intrusion would be highly offensive to a reasonable person. The Court may properly preliminarily determine whether the alleged intrusion is sufficiently offensive to state a claim for intrusion upon seclusion. When making this determination, the Court should consider the "degree of intrusion, the context, conduct and circumstances surrounding the intrusion as well as the intruder's motives and objectives, the setting into which he intrudes, and the expectations of those whose privacy is invaded."

In this instance, Plaintiffs voluntarily provided their personal information to Northwest. Moreover, although Northwest had a privacy policy for information included on the website, Plaintiffs do not contend that they actually read the privacy policy prior to providing Northwest with their personal information. Thus, Plaintiffs' expectation of privacy was low. Further, the disclosure here was not to the public at large, but rather was to a government agency in the wake of a terrorist attack that called into question the security of the nation's transportation system. Northwest's motives in disclosing the information cannot be questioned. Taking into account all of the factors listed above, the Court finds as a matter of law that the disclosure of Plaintiffs' personal information would not be highly offensive to a reasonable person and that Plaintiffs have failed to state a claim for intrusion upon seclusion.

c. Breach of Contract and Express Warranty

Northwest contends that the privacy policy on Northwest's website does not, as a matter of law, constitute a unilateral contract, the breach of which entitles Plaintiffs to damages. Northwest also argues that, even if the privacy policy constituted a contract or express warranty, Plaintiffs' contract and warranty claims fail because Plaintiffs have failed to plead any contract damages.

Whether a person's statements constitute a unilateral contract is a question of law for the Court to determine. Plaintiffs rely on the following statement from Northwest's website as the basis for their contract and warranty claims:

> When you reserve or purchase travel services through Northwest Airlines nwa.com Reservations, we provide only the relevant information required by the car rental agency, hotel, or other involved third party to ensure the successful fulfillment of your travel arrangements.

Plaintiffs do not allege that they actually read this privacy statement prior to providing Northwest with their personal information, although they do generally allege that they "relied to their detriment" on this policy.

The usual rule in contract cases is that "general statements of policy are not contractual." In the employment context, the Minnesota Supreme Court has found that statements in an employee handbook as specific as "[a] person is not dismissed without cause, and it is customary to give a warning and an opportunity to 'make good' before final dismissal" did not create an employment contract that altered the presumed at-will employment relationship. *Cederstrand v. Lutheran Bhd.*, 263 Minn. 520, 117 N.W.2d 213, 215-16 (Minn.1962). The court characterized the statement as a "general polic[y], not an offer of contractual character."

The privacy statement on Northwest's website did not constitute a unilateral contract. The language used vests discretion in Northwest to determine when the information is "relevant" and which "third parties" might need that information. Moreover, absent an allegation that Plaintiffs actually read the privacy policy, not merely the general allegation that Plaintiffs "relied on" the policy, Plaintiffs have failed to allege an essential element of a contract claim: that the alleged "offer" was accepted by Plaintiffs. Plaintiffs' contract and warranty claims fail as a matter of law.

Even if the privacy policy was sufficiently definite and Plaintiffs had alleged that they read the policy before giving their information to Northwest, it is likely that Plaintiffs' contract and warranty claims would fail as a matter of law. Defendants point out that Plaintiffs have failed to allege any contractual damages arising out of the alleged breach. As Defendants note, the damages Plaintiffs claim are damages arising out of the torts alleged in the Amended Complaint, not damages arising out of the alleged contract. Damages are an essential element of a breach of contract claim, and the failure to allege damages would be fatal to Plaintiffs' contract claims.

PROBLEM 17.7

Client operates a website at which consumers acquire a variety of products, from electronics to ordinary books. In the course of its sales, Client collects personal information about customers (e.g., name, address, credit card number, telephone, etc.). It also runs a purchasing club, allowing customers to register for free membership and receive various types of advertising and discounts. The registration form obtains additional personal information such as marital status, level of education, profession, etc. Client plans to sell or license this information to others for marketing. Also, it uses the information for its own internal purposes and for selling advertising space on its site. It wants you to draft a privacy policy for its use. Please respond.

B.   Security and Cookies

BODAH v. LAKEVILLE MOTOR EXPRESS, INC.
663 N.W.2d 550 (Minn. 2003)

ANDERSON, JUSTICE.

In this case, the court of appeals reversed the district court's order dismissing, on the pleadings, the complaint of respondents Sandra Bodah, Wayne Senne, John Tonsager, and Mark Urick (respondents). On review, we consider an issue of first impression: whether allegations . . . that appellant Lakeville Motor Express, Inc.'s (LME) dissemination by facsimile of 204 employee names and social security numbers to 16 related or associated terminal managers in six states . . . constitute the requisite "publicity" under Minnesota law to support a claim for publication of private facts, an invasion of privacy tort. We adopt the definition of "publicity" from the *Restatement (Second) of Torts* § 652D cmt. a (1977) and hold that the complaint does not allege the requisite "publicity" to support a claim for publication of private facts. . . .

LME, a trucking company based in Minnesota, transports shipments throughout the upper Midwest, including Minnesota, Illinois, Iowa, North Dakota, South Dakota, and Wisconsin. In distributing freight, LME utilizes trucking terminals that are either owned by LME or its agents or are owned by independent trucking companies. On January 4, 2001, LME Safety Director William Lowell Frame (Frame) sent a facsimile transmission to the terminal managers of 16 freight terminals. The cover sheet was addressed to "Terminal Managers," not to named individuals, and stated that the purpose of the fax was to allow LME to "keep computer records for terminal accidents-injuries etc." The cover sheet requested that the terminal managers "[p]lease review [the] list for your terminals[;] add or delete accordingly." Attached to the cover sheet was a five-page list of the names and social security numbers of 204 LME employees.

Shortly after LME disseminated the list, head Union Steward John Tonsager confronted Frame and LME President Peter Martin (Martin) about the dissemination of sensitive employee information and expressed his concern about identity theft. On May 1, 2001, Martin sent a letter to LME employees notifying them of the January 4 transmission. In the letter, Martin apologized for LME's mistake in sending the list to the other terminals and reported that the terminal managers were instructed to destroy or return the list immediately. Martin indicated that his instructions had been followed and that, as far as he knew, the terminal managers had not shared the information with anyone.

On or about September 6, 2001, respondents filed a class action lawsuit on behalf of themselves and all class members alleging that LME's dissemination of their social security numbers to the 16 terminal managers constituted an invasion of their right to privacy.

LME moved for dismissal of this action under Minn. R. Civ. P. 12.02(e) for failure to state a claim upon which relief may be granted. The district court determined that the dissemination did not constitute "publicity" under a claim for publication of private facts and granted LME's motion to dismiss. The court of appeals reversed and remanded, holding that "[a]n actionable situation requires a level of publication that unreasonably exposes the appellant to significant risk of loss under all the circumstances," and concluding that the appropriate consideration includes the nature of the private fact and the harm to which the plaintiff is exposed as a result of the dissemination as well as the breadth of disclosure. . . .

In *Lake v. Wal-Mart Stores, Inc.,* [582 N.W.2d 231 (Minn. 1998),] this court adopted three separate causes of action which are generally referred to as the tort of invasion of privacy: intrusion of seclusion, appropriation of a name or likeness of another, and publication of private facts. The rationale behind recognizing the tort of invasion of privacy is that "[t]he right to privacy is an integral part of our humanity; one has a public persona, exposed and active, and a private persona, guarded and preserved. The heart of our liberty is choosing which parts of our lives shall become public and which parts we shall hold close." According to *Lake,* to state a claim for publication of private facts, a plaintiff must demonstrate that one "'gives publicity to a matter concerning the private life of another . . . if the matter publicized is of a kind that (a) would be highly offensive to a reasonable person, and (b) is not of legitimate concern to the public.'" The *Lake* court did not define "publicity."

Under the Restatement, "'[p]ublicity' . . . means that the matter is made public, by communicating it to the public at large, or to so many persons that the matter must be regarded as substantially certain to become one of public knowledge." The Restatement distinguishes "publicity" for purposes of invasion of privacy from "publication" for defamation:

> "Publicity," as it is used in this Section, differs from "publication," as that term is used in §577 in connection with liability for defamation. "Publication," in that sense, is a word of art, which includes any communication by the defendant to a third person. . . . The difference is not one of the means of communication, which may be oral, written or by any other means. It is one of a communication that reaches, or is sure to reach, the public. Thus it is not an invasion of the right of privacy, within the rule stated in this Section, to communicate a fact concerning the plaintiff's private life to a single person or even to a small group of persons. On the other hand, any publication in a newspaper or a magazine, even of small circulation, or in a handbill distributed to a large number of persons, or any broadcast over the radio, or statement made in an address to a large audience, is sufficient to give publicity within the meaning of the term as it is used in this Section. The distinction, in other words, is one between private and public communication.

Id. . . . LME maintains that the dissemination by fax of a list of 204 employee names and social security numbers to 16 associated or related terminal managers in six states and the allegation that the private information is being shared or is accessible in general does not constitute "publicity" to support an invasion of privacy claim. Specifically, because the complaint does not allege that the dissemination of the numbers was to the public at large or that the disclosure involved so many people that the numbers were substantially certain to become public knowledge, as required by the Restatement, it fails to allege the requisite "publicity." Respondents contend that their complaint alleges sufficient "publicity" to defeat LME's Rule 12.02(e) motion. . . .

At the outset, we choose not to embrace the court of appeals' approach to defining "publicity." The court of appeals' hybrid approach uses the Restatement's breadth of disclosure analysis but adds as an additional factor "the nature of private data and the damage." . . . We think this definition emasculates the distinction between public and private by suggesting that "publicity" can be established by "either widespread dissemination *or improper use.*" Furthermore, by looking to the nature of the private data as part of the "publicity" element, the court blurs the distinction between the "publicity" element and the other elements of the tort of publication of private facts which require that the private data "not [be] of legitimate concern to the public" and that the publicity be "highly offensive." Finally, a lack of reasonableness is neither an element of the invasion of privacy tort of publication of private facts nor part of the publicity analysis. As such, the court of appeals' determination that "[a]n actionable situation requires a level of publication that unreasonably exposes the appellant to significant risk of loss under all the circumstances" inappropriately emphasizes the reasonableness of the defendant's actions.[5] . . .

We decide, instead, to adopt the Restatement definition of "publicity." We conclude, therefore, that "publicity" means that "the matter is made public, by communicating it to the public at large, or to so many persons that the matter must be regarded as substantially certain to become one of public knowledge." *Restatement (Second) of Torts* § 652D cmt. a. In doing so, we have considered whether there are legitimate or compelling reasons of public policy that justify imposing liability for egregious but limited disclosures of private information. We conclude, nevertheless, that the Restatement's publicity requirement best addresses the invasion of privacy cause of action — absent dissemination to the public at large the claimant's "private persona" has not been violated.

Furthermore, we think the Restatement definition appropriately limits the publication of private facts cause of action. Though much has been written on the subject, we reflect on the concerns of Samuel Warren and Justice Louis Brandeis — "the evil of the invasion of privacy by the newspapers" and "whether our law will recognize and protect the right to privacy in this and in other respects" — and Warren's and Brandeis' recognition of limitations to this right. Samuel D. Warren & Louis D. Brandeis, *The Right to Privacy,* 4 HARV. L.REV. 193, 195, 196, 214-19 (1890). These concerns provided the foundation for all four invasion of privacy torts but resonate particularly with the tort of publication of private facts. William L. Prosser, *Privacy,* 48 CAL. L.REV. 383, 383-89 (1960) (tracing the evolution of the four invasion of privacy torts). As Warren and Brandeis noted more than 100 years ago:

> The design of the law must be to protect those persons with whose affairs the community has no legitimate concern, from being dragged into an undesirable and undesired publicity and to protect all persons,

---

[5] [FN 5] Indeed, if an unauthorized transmission of private data actually resulted in pecuniary loss due to identity theft, a plaintiff may be able to bring a negligence action. . . . Likewise, a plaintiff may have a cause of action for negligent infliction of emotional distress if, because private information was shared, the plaintiff suffered severe emotional distress with accompanying physical manifestations. . . .

> whatsoever their position or station, from having matters which they
> may properly prefer to keep private, made public against their will.

Warren & Brandeis, *supra,* at 214-15. We understand the tort of publication
of private facts to focus on a very narrow gap in tort law — to provide a
remedy for the truthful but damaging dissemination of private facts, which
is nonactionable under defamation rules. The Restatement's definition of
"publicity," which requires a broad reach, constrains the tort of publication of
private facts.

We turn now to the application of the Restatement's publicity requirement
to the instant facts. We conclude that respondents' claim that LME disseminated 204 employees' social security numbers to 16 terminal managers in six
states does not constitute publication to the public or to so large a number of
persons that the matter must be regarded as substantially certain to become
public. . . .

We likewise conclude that respondents' allegation that the information "is
still being shared or is accessible in general" fails to aver "publicity." A similar
case, *Beverly v. Reinert,* 239 Ill.App.3d 91, 179 Ill.Dec. 789, 606 N.E.2d 621
(1992), supports our conclusion. In *Beverly,* the defendant, who filed a third-
party complaint for invasion of privacy, alleged that private matters were
disseminated by fax and reached members of the public, including: secretaries
in two lawyers' offices, the plaintiff's brother, unknown individuals in the
school district office or in the plaintiff's brother's insurance office and in the
office of one of the lawyers. He also alleged that the faxes had been "intercepted by persons whose personal computers were equipped to enable them to
receive such transmissions." The court affirmed dismissal of the claim:

> The defendant did not sufficiently allege the *public* disclosure of pri-
> vate facts. We need not plunge into a discussion of the comparative
> reliability of mail and fax communications. In this regard, the defen-
> dant has alleged no more than the *possibility* that unknown individu-
> als might have accidentally received or perhaps eavesdropped upon
> the otherwise private and confidential communications between the
> plaintiff's attorney and the defendant's attorney. Such possible inter-
> ception by nobody in particular [does not constitute] disclosure to the
> public (as the Restatement requires).

Id. at 626.

In this case, respondents make a general allegation that the social security
numbers have "not been redacted or erased and [are] still being shared or [are]
accessible in general." Yet attached to the complaint is the May 1, 2001 letter,
written by LME's president, indicating that the faxed list of social security
numbers has been returned or destroyed and not shared with anyone. Thus,
the allegation that the social security numbers are still being shared or are
generally accessible is mere speculation. We hold that the court of appeals
erred in reversing the dismissal of the complaint because the facts, as alleged,
do not support the conclusion that there is "publicity" to withstand a Rule
12.02(e) motion.

REVERSED.

NOTE

In *FTC v. Guess.com* (consent order available at http://www.ftc.gov/os/2003/06/guessagree.htm), Guess sold clothing and accessories online at guess.com. According to the FTC complaint, Guess' Web site has been vulnerable to commonly known attacks such as "Structured Query Language (SQL) injection attacks" and other web-based attacks. Guess' online statements, however, assured consumers that their personal information would be secure and protected. The company's claims included "This site has security measures in place to protect the loss, misuse, and alteration of information under our control" and "All of your personal information, including your credit card information and sign-in password, are stored in an unreadable, encrypted format at all times." In fact, according to the FTC, the personal information was not stored in an unreadable, encrypted format at all times and Guess' security measures failed to protect against SQL and other commonly known attacks. In settlement of a proceeding alleging deceptive practices, Guess agreed to various obligations, including following:

I. IT IS ORDERED that Respondents . . . shall not misrepresent in any manner, expressly or by implication, the extent to which Respondents maintain and protect the security, confidentiality, or integrity of any personal information collected from or about consumers.

II. IT IS FURTHER ORDERED that Respondents . . . shall establish and maintain a comprehensive information security program in writing that is reasonably designed to protect the security, confidentiality, and integrity of personal information collected from or about consumers. Such program shall contain administrative, technical, and physical safeguards appropriate to Respondents' size and complexity, the nature and scope of Respondents' activities, and the sensitivity of the personal information collected from or about consumers, including:

A. the designation of an employee or employees to coordinate and be accountable for the information security program.

B. the identification of material internal and external risks to the security, confidentiality, and integrity of personal information that could result in the unauthorized disclosure, misuse, loss, alteration, destruction, or other compromise of such information, and assessment of the sufficiency of any safeguards in place to control these risks. At a minimum, this risk assessment should include consideration of risks in each area of relevant operation, including, but not limited to: (1) employee training and management; (2) information systems, including network and software design, information processing, storage, transmission, and disposal; and (3) prevention, detection, and response to attacks, intrusions, or other systems failures.

C. the design and implementation of reasonable safeguards to ontrol the risks identified through risk assessment, and regular testing or monitoring of the effectiveness of the safeguards' key controls, systems, and procedures.

D. the evaluation and adjustment of Respondents' information security program in light of the results of the testing and monitoring required by subparagraph C, any material changes to Respondents' operations or business arrangements, or any other circumstances that Respondents know or have reason to know may have a material impact on the effectiveness of their information security program.

III. IT IS FURTHER ORDERED that Respondents obtain an assessment and report from a qualified, objective, independent third-party professional, using procedures and standards generally accepted in the profession, within one (1) year after service of the order, and biannually thereafter, that. . . .

VIII. This order will terminate twenty (20) years from the date of its issuance

CALIFORNIA SECURITY BREACH NOTICE ACT

SEC. 2. Section 1798.29 is added to the Civil Code, to read:

1798.29. . . .

(d) For purposes of this section, "breach of the security of the system" means unauthorized acquisition of computerized data that compromises the security, confidentiality, or integrity of personal information maintained by the agency. Good faith acquisition of personal information by an employee or agent of the agency for the purposes of the agency is not a breach of the security of the system, provided that the personal information is not used or subject to further unauthorized disclosure.

(e) For purposes of this section, "personal information" means an individual's first name or first initial and last name in combination with any one or more of the following data elements, when either the name or the data elements are not encrypted:

(1) Social security number.

(2) Driver's license number or California Identification Card number.

(3) Account number, credit or debit card number, in combination with any required security code, access code, or password that would permit access to an individual's financial account.

(f) For purposes of this section, "personal information" does not include publicly available information that is lawfully made available to the general public from federal, state, or local government records.

§ 1798.82. (a) Any person or business that conducts business in California, and that owns or licenses computerized data that includes personal information, shall disclose any breach of the security of the system following discovery or notification of the breach in the security of the data to any resident of California whose unencrypted personal information was, or is reasonably believed to have been, acquired by an unauthorized person. The disclosure shall be made in the most expedient time possible and without unreasonable delay, consistent with the legitimate needs of law enforcement, as provided in subdivision (c), or any measures necessary to determine the scope of the breach and restore the reasonable integrity of the data system.

(b) Any person or business that maintains computerized data that includes personal information that the person or business does not own shall notify the owner or licensee of the information of any breach of the security of the data immediately following discovery, if the personal information was, or is reasonably believed to have been, acquired by an unauthorized person.

(c) The notification required by this section may be delayed if a law enforcement agency determines that the notification will impede a criminal investigation. The notification required by this section shall be made after the law enforcement agency determines that it will not compromise the investigation.

(d) For purposes of this section, "breach of the security of the system" means unauthorized acquisition of computerized data that compromises the security, confidentiality, or integrity of personal information maintained by the person or business. Good faith acquisition of personal information by an employee or agent of the person or business for the purposes of the person or business is not a breach of the security of the system, provided that the personal information is not used or subject to further unauthorized disclosure.

(e) For purposes of this section, "personal information" means an individual's first name or first initial and last name in combination with any one or more of the following data elements, when either the name or the data elements are not encrypted:

(1) Social security number.

(2) Driver's license number or California Identification Card number.

(3) Account number, credit or debit card number, in combination with any required security code, access code, or password that would permit access to an individual's financial account.

(f) For purposes of this section, "personal information" does not include publicly available information that is lawfully made available to the general public from federal, state, or local government records.

(g) For purposes of this section, "notice" may be provided by one of the following methods:

(1) Written notice.

(2) Electronic notice, if the notice provided is consistent

with the provisions regarding electronic records and signatures set forth in Section 7001 of Title 15 of the United States Code.

(3) Substitute notice, if the person or business demonstrates that the cost of providing notice would exceed two hundred fifty thousand dollars ($250,000), or that the affected class of subject persons to be notified exceeds 500,000, or the person or business does not have sufficient contact information. Substitute notice shall consist of all of the following:

(A) E-mail notice when the person or business has an e-mail address for the subject persons.

(B) Conspicuous posting of the notice on the Web site page of the person or business, if the person or business maintains one.

(C) Notification to major statewide media.

(h) Notwithstanding subdivision (g), a person or business that maintains its own notification procedures as part of an information security policy for the treatment of personal information and is otherwise consistent with the timing requirements of this part, shall be deemed to be in compliance with the notification requirements of this section if the person or business notifies subject persons in accordance with its policies in the event of a breach of security of the system.

Table of Statutes

(References are to pages or page and note numbers)

Table of Cases

(Principal cases are in all caps; references are to pages)

E

S

T

U

INDEX

A

ACCESS CONTRACTS
Generally . . . 807
Changes in terms . . . 808
UCITA provisions . . . 833

ANTITRUST GUIDELINES
Generally . . . 608
Cross-licensing and pooling arrangements . . . 637
Grantbacks . . . 458
Market power . . . 609; 637

ANTITRUST ISSUES
Antitrust injury . . . 662
"Essential facility" theory . . . 657
"Monopoly leveraging" . . . 662
"Nine no no's" of patent licensing . . . 607
Package licensing and pooling . . . 637
Refusals to license . . . 646
Software transactions . . . 626; 638
Tying arrangements
    Generally . . . 618
    Franchises . . . 633
    Market power . . . 618; 637
    Software transactions . . . 626; 638

ANTITRUST STATUTES
Clayton Act . . . 618
Robinson-Patman Act . . . 618
Sherman Act . . . 616

APPLICABLE LAW
Assignment of rights . . . 246
Federal intellectual property law . . . 17
Implied licenses . . . 312
Software development warranties . . . 797
State contract law . . . 32

ASSIGNMENT OF RIGHTS
Generally . . . 245
Bona fide purchase, unauthorized transfers . . . 293
"Consent to transfer" clauses . . . 266
Exclusive licenses, distinguished . . . 141
Licenses, compared . . . 3
Non-assignment clauses
    "Consent to transfer" clauses . . . 266
    Mergers and acquisitions . . . 255
    Restatement (Second) of Contracts . . . 260
    UCITA provisions . . . 261
Patent rights . . . 246
Restatement (Second) of Contracts . . . 245
Royalty obligations . . . 543
UCC Article 2 . . . 246
UCITA provisions . . . 246

B

BAD FAITH (*See* GOOD FAITH)

BANKRUPTCY ISSUES
Asset sales and licensed assets . . . 732
Automatic stays . . . 711
Executory contracts . . . 716
Filing for bankruptcy
    Generally . . . 709
    Effect of filing . . . 710
Liquidation proceeding . . . 709
Reorganization proceeding . . . 709

BANKRUPTCY TRUSTEES
Assignment of patent rights . . . 246
Executory contracts . . . 716

BONA FIDE PURCHASE, UNAUTHORIZED TRANSFERS
Generally . . . 293

BREACH OF CONTRACT
Generally . . . 547
Damages (*See* DAMAGES)
Materiality . . . 559
Non-disclosure agreements . . . 62; 442
Remedies (*See* REMEDIES)
Restatement of Contracts . . . 547
Waiver of claims . . . 552

BREACH OF LICENSE
Contract breaches (*See* BREACH OF CONTRACT)
Remedies (*See* REMEDIES)

BSD LICENSE
Open source software . . . 813

C

CALIFORNIA PRIVACY POSTING ACT
Generally . . . 897

CALIFORNIA SECURITY BREACH NOTICE ACT
Generally . . . 909

CANCELLATION OF LICENSE (*See* TERMINATION OF LICENSE)

CHOICE OF LAW
Assignment of rights . . . 246
Federal intellectual property law . . . 17
Implied licenses . . . 312
Software development warranties . . . 797
State contract law . . . 32

CLAYTON ACT
Generally . . . 618